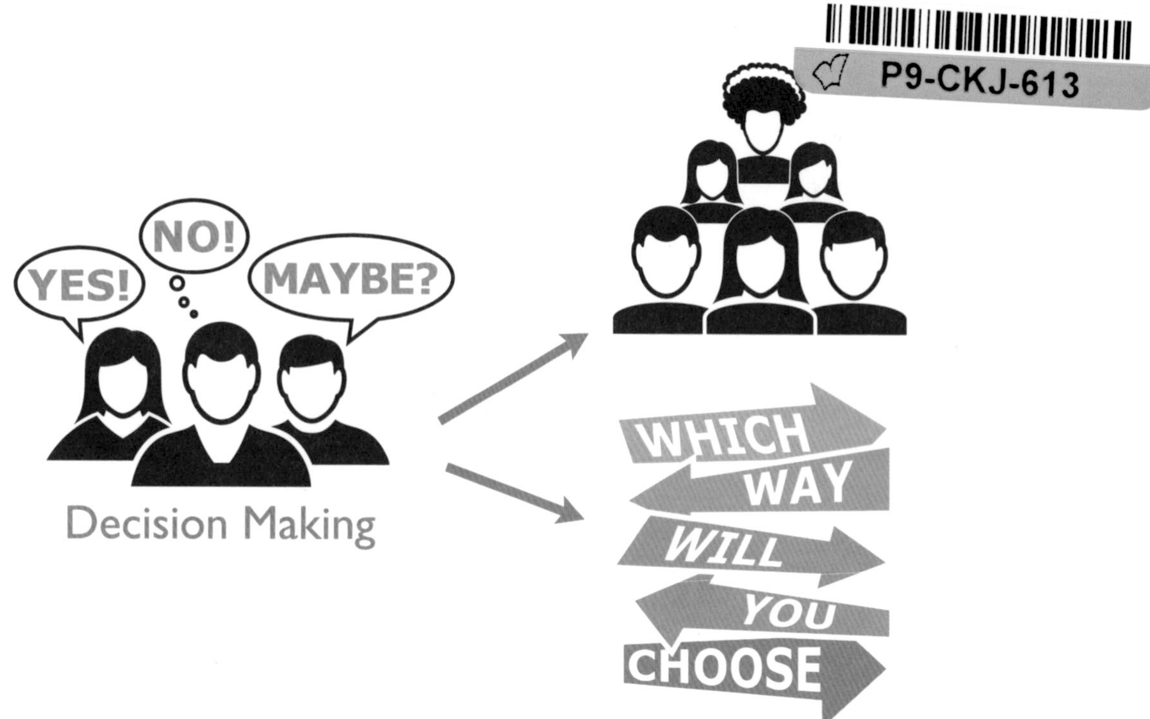

- **Decision making simulations** – place your students in the role of a key decision-maker where they are asked to make a series of decisions. The simulation will change and branch based on the decisions students make, providing a variation of scenario paths. Upon completion of each simulation, students receive a grade, as well as a detailed report of the choices they made during the simulation and the associated consequences of those decisions.

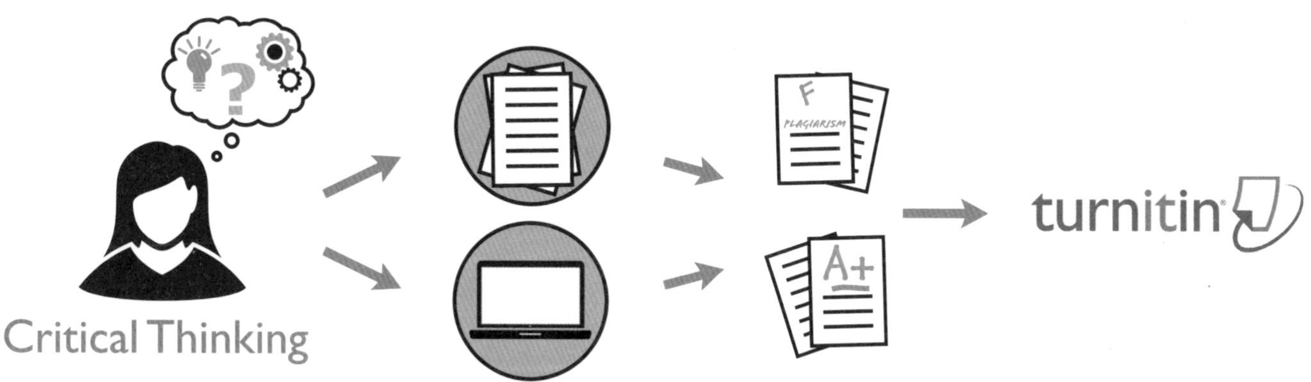

- **Writing Space** – better writers make great learners—who perform better in their courses. Providing a single location to develop and assess concept mastery and critical thinking, the Writing Space offers automatic graded, assisted graded and create your own writing assignments; allowing you to exchange personalized feedback with students quickly and easily.

  Writing Space can also check students' work for improper citation or plagiarism by comparing it against the world's most accurate text comparison database available from **Turnitin**.

Marketing

An Introduction Twelfth Edition

GARY ARMSTRONG
University of North Carolina

PHILIP KOTLER
Northwestern University

PEARSON

Boston Columbus Indianapolis New York San Francisco Upper Saddle River
Amsterdam Cape Town Dubai London Madrid Milan Munich Paris Montréal Toronto
Delhi Mexico City São Paulo Sydney Hong Kong Seoul Singapore Taipei Tokyo

Editor in Chief: Stephanie Wall
Acquisitions Editor: Mark Gaffney
Program Manager Team Lead: Ashley Santora
Program Manager: Jennifer M. Collins
Editorial Assistant: Daniel Petrino
Director of Marketing: Maggie Moylan
Executive Marketing Manager: Anne Fahlgren
Project Management Lead: Judy Leale
Senior Project Manager: Jacqueline A. Martin
Procurement Specialist: Nancy Maneri
Creative Director: Blair Brown
Senior Art Director: Janet Slowik
Interior and Cover Designer: Karen Quigley
VP, Director of Digital Strategy & Assessment: Paul Gentile
Digital Editor: Brian Surette
Digital Development Manager: Robin Lazrus
Digital Project Manager: Alana Coles
MyLab Product Manager: Joan Waxman
Digital Production Project Manager: Lisa Rinaldi
Full-Service Project Management: Roxanne Klaas, S4Carlisle Publishing Services
Composition: S4Carlisle Publishing Services
Printer/Binder: R.R. Donnelley/Menasha
Cover Printer: Lehigh-Phoenix Color/Hagerstown
Text Font: 10/12 Times LT Std

Library of Congress Cataloging-in-Publication Data
Armstrong, Gary (Gary M.)
Marketing : an introduction/Gary Armstrong, University of North Carolina,
Philip Kotler, Northwestern University.—Twelfth edition.
pages cm.
ISBN: 978-0-13-345127-6
1. Marketing. I. Kotler, Philip. II. Title.
HF5415.K625 2015
658.8—dc23 2013033986

3 4 5 6 7 8 9 10 V003 19 18 17 16 15 14

ISBN-13: 978-0-13-345127-6
ISBN-10: 0-13-345127-5

To Kathy, Betty, KC, Keri, Mandy, Matt,
Delaney, Molly, Macy, and Ben; Nancy, Melissa, and Jessica

About the Authors

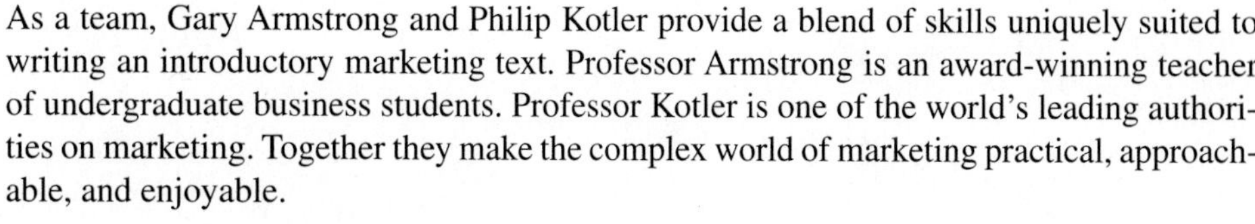

As a team, Gary Armstrong and Philip Kotler provide a blend of skills uniquely suited to writing an introductory marketing text. Professor Armstrong is an award-winning teacher of undergraduate business students. Professor Kotler is one of the world's leading authorities on marketing. Together they make the complex world of marketing practical, approachable, and enjoyable.

GARY ARMSTRONG is Crist W. Blackwell Distinguished Professor Emeritus of Undergraduate Education in the Kenan-Flagler Business School at the University of North Carolina at Chapel Hill. He holds an undergraduate degree and a master's degree in business from Wayne State University in Detroit, and he received his Ph.D. in marketing from Northwestern University. Dr. Armstrong has contributed numerous articles to leading business journals. As a consultant and researcher, he has worked with many companies on marketing research, sales management, and marketing strategy.

But Professor Armstrong's first love has always been teaching. His long-held Blackwell Distinguished Professorship is the only permanent endowed professorship for distinguished undergraduate teaching at the University of North Carolina at Chapel Hill. He has been very active in the teaching and administration of Kenan-Flagler's undergraduate program. His administrative posts have included Chair of Marketing, Associate Director of the Undergraduate Business Program, Director of the Business Honors Program, and many others. Through the years, he has worked closely with business student groups and has received several campus-wide and Business School teaching awards. He is the only repeat recipient of the school's highly regarded *Award for Excellence in Undergraduate Teaching,* which he received three times. Most recently, Professor Armstrong received the UNC Board of Governors Award for Excellence in Teaching, the highest teaching honor bestowed by the 16-campus University of North Carolina system.

PHILIP KOTLER is S. C. Johnson & Son Distinguished Professor of International Marketing at the Kellogg School of Management, Northwestern University. He received his master's degree at the University of Chicago and his Ph.D. at M.I.T., both in economics. Dr. Kotler is author of *Marketing Management* (Pearson Prentice Hall), now in its 14th edition and the world's most widely used marketing textbook in graduate schools of business worldwide. He has authored dozens of other successful books and has written more than 100 articles in leading journals. He is the only three-time winner of the coveted Alpha Kappa Psi award for the best annual article in the *Journal of Marketing*.

Professor Kotler was named the first recipient of four major awards: the *Distinguished Marketing Educator of the Year Award* and the *William L. Wilkie "Marketing for a Better World" Award,* both given by the American Marketing Association; the *Philip Kotler Award for Excellence in Health Care Marketing* presented by the Academy for Health Care Services Marketing; and the *Sheth Foundation Medal for Exceptional Contribution to Marketing Scholarship and Practice*. His numerous other major honors include the Sales and Marketing Executives International *Marketing Educator of the Year Award;* the European Association of Marketing Consultants and Trainers *Marketing Excellence Award;* the *Charles Coolidge Parlin Marketing Research Award;* and the *Paul D. Converse Award,* given by the American Marketing Association to honor "outstanding contributions to science in marketing." A recent Forbes survey ranks Professor Kotler in the top 10 of the world's most influential business thinkers. And in a recent *Financial Times* poll of 1,000 senior executives across the world, Professor Kotler was ranked as the fourth "most influential business writer/guru" of the twenty-first century.

Dr. Kotler has served as chairman of the College on Marketing of the Institute of Management Sciences, a director of the American Marketing Association, and a trustee of the Marketing Science Institute. He has consulted with many major U.S. and international companies in the areas of marketing strategy and planning, marketing organization, and international marketing. He has traveled and lectured extensively throughout Europe, Asia, and South America, advising companies and governments about global marketing practices and opportunities.

Brief Contents

Contents

Preface

The Twelfth Edition of ***Marketing: An Introduction***

On the Road to Learning Marketing!

Top marketers all share a common goal: putting consumers at the heart of marketing. Today's marketing is all about creating customer value and engagement in a fast-changing, increasingly digital and social marketplace.

Marketing starts with understanding consumer needs and wants, deciding which target markets the organization can serve best, and developing a compelling value proposition by which the organization can attract, keep, and grow targeted consumers. Then, more than just making a sale, today's marketers want to engage customers and build deep customer relationships that make their brands a meaningful part of consumers' conversations and lives. In this digital age, to go along with their tried-and-true traditional marketing methods, marketers have access to a dazzling set of new customer relationship–building tools—from the Internet, smartphones, and tablets to online, mobile, and social media—for engaging customers anytime, anyplace to shape brand conversations, experiences, and community. If marketers do these things well, they will reap the rewards in terms of market share, profits, and customer equity. In the 12th edition of *Marketing: An Introduction,* you'll learn how *customer value* and *customer engagement* drive every good marketing strategy.

Marketing: An Introduction makes the road to learning and teaching marketing more productive and enjoyable than ever. The 12th edition's streamlined approach strikes an effective balance between depth of coverage and ease of learning. Unlike more abbreviated texts, it provides complete and timely coverage of all the latest marketing thinking and practice. Unlike longer, more complex texts, its moderate length makes it easy to digest in a given semester or quarter.

Marketing: An Introduction's approachable organization, style, and design are well suited to beginning marketing students. The 12th edition's learning design—with integrative *Road to Marketing* features at the start and end of each chapter plus insightful author comments throughout—helps students to learn, link, and apply important concepts. Its simple organization and writing style present even the most advanced topics in an approachable, exciting way. The 12th edition brings marketing to life with deep and relevant examples and illustrations throughout. And when combined with MyMarketingLab, our online homework and personalized study tool, *Marketing: An Introduction* ensures that students will come to class well prepared and leave class with a richer understanding of basic marketing concepts, strategies, and practices. So fasten your seat belt and let's get rolling down the road to learning marketing!

What's New in the 12th Edition?

We've thoroughly revised the 12th edition of *Marketing: An Introduction* to reflect the major trends and forces impacting marketing in this digital age of customer value, engagement, and relationships. Here are just some of the changes you'll find in this edition:

- More than any other developments, sweeping new **online**, **social media**, **mobile**, **and other digital technologies** are now affecting how marketers, brands, and customers engage each other. The 12th edition features new and revised discussions and examples of the explosive impact of exciting *new digital marketing technologies* shaping marketing strategy and practice—from online, mobile, and social media engagement technologies discussed in Chapters 1, 5, 11, 12, and 14; to "online listening" and Webnology research tools in Chapter 4, online influence and brand communities in Chapter 5, and location-based marketing in Chapter 7; to the use of social media in business-to-business marketing and sales in Chapters 6 and 13; to consumer Web, social media, and mobile marketing, as well as other new communications technologies, in Chapters 1, 5, 12, 14, and throughout.

A new Chapter 1 section, *The Digital Age: Online, Mobile, and Social Media Marketing,* introduces the exciting new developments in digital and social media marketing. A completely revised Chapter 14, *Direct, Online, Social Media, and Mobile Marketing,* digs deeply into digital marketing tools such as Web sites, social media, mobile ads and apps, online video, e-mail, blogs, and other digital platforms that engage consumers anywhere, anytime via their computers, smartphones, tablets, Internet-ready TVs, and other digital devices. The 12th edition is packed with new stories and examples illustrating how companies employ digital technology to gain competitive advantage—from traditional marketing all-stars such as Nike, P&G, Southwest, and McDonald's to new-age digital competitors such as Google, Amazon.com, Apple, Netflix, Pinterest, and Facebook.

- The 12th edition features completely new and revised coverage of the emerging trend toward **customer engagement marketing**—building direct and continuous customer involvement in shaping brands, brand conversations, brand experiences, and brand community. The burgeoning Internet and social media have created better-informed, more-connected, and more-empowered consumers. Thus, today's marketers must now *engage* consumers rather than interrupting them. Marketers are augmenting their mass-media marketing efforts with a rich mix of online, mobile, and social media marketing that promotes deep consumer involvement and a sense of customer community surrounding their brands. Today's new engagement-building tools include everything from Web sites, blogs, in-person events, and video sharing to online communities and social media such as Facebook, YouTube, Pinterest, Twitter, and a company's own social networking sites.

  In all, today's more engaged consumers are giving as much as they get in the form of two-way brand relationships. The 12th edition contains substantial new material on **customer engagement** and related developments such as **consumer empowerment**, **crowdsourcing**, **customer co-creation**, and **consumer-generated marketing**. A new Chapter 1 section—*Engaging Customers*—introduces customer engagement marketing. This and other related customer engagement topics are presented in Chapter 1 (new sections: *Customer Engagement and Today's Digital and Social Media* and *Consumer-Generated Marketing*); Chapter 4 (qualitative approaches to gaining deeper customer insights); Chapter 5 (managing online influence and customer community through digital and social media marketing); Chapter 8 (crowdsourcing and customer-driven new product development); Chapter 12 (the new, more engaging marketing communications model); and Chapter 14 (direct digital, online, social media, and mobile marketing).
- The 12th edition continues to build on and extend the innovative **customer value framework** from previous editions. The customer value model presented in the first chapter is fully integrated throughout the remainder of the book. No other marketing text presents such a clear and compelling customer value approach.
- The 12th edition provides revised and expanded coverage of developments in the fast-changing area of **integrated marketing communications**. It tells how marketers are blending the new digital and social media tools—everything from Internet and mobile marketing to blogs, viral videos, and social media—with traditional media to create more targeted, personal, and engaging customer relationships. Marketers are no longer simply creating integrated promotion programs; they are practicing *marketing content management* in paid, owned, earned, and shared media. No other text provides more current or encompassing coverage of these exciting developments.
- Revised coverage in the 12th edition shows how companies and consumers continue to deal with **marketing in an uncertain economy** in the lingering aftermath of the Great Recession. Starting with a section in Chapter 1 and continuing with revised discussions in Chapters 3, 9, and elsewhere throughout the text, the 12th edition shows how now,

even as the economy recovers, marketers must focus on creating customer value and sharpening their value propositions in this era of more sensible consumption.

- New material throughout the 12th edition highlights the increasing importance of **sustainable marketing**. The discussion begins in Chapter 1 and ends in Chapter 16, which pulls marketing concepts together under a sustainable marketing framework. In between, frequent discussions and examples show how sustainable marketing calls for socially and environmentally responsible actions that meet both the immediate and the future needs of customers, companies, and society as a whole.
- The 12th edition provides new discussions and examples of the growth in **global marketing.** As the world becomes a smaller, more competitive place, marketers face new global marketing challenges and opportunities, especially in fast-growing emerging markets such as China, India, Brazil, Africa, and others. You'll find much new coverage of global marketing throughout the text, starting in Chapter 1 and discussed fully in Chapter 15.
- The 12th edition continues its emphasis on **measuring and managing return on marketing**, including many new end-of-chapter financial and quantitative marketing exercises that let students apply analytical thinking to relevant concepts in each chapter and link chapter concepts to the text's innovative and comprehensive Appendix 3, *Marketing by the Numbers.*
- The 12th edition continues to improve on its **innovative learning design**. The text's active and integrative "Road to Learning Marketing" presentation includes learning enhancements such as annotated chapter-opening stories, a chapter-opening objective outline, and explanatory author comments on major chapter figures. The chapter-opening "Chapter Road Map" layout helps to preview and position the chapter and its key concepts. "Speed Bump" concept checks highlight and reinforce important chapter concepts. Figures annotated with author comments help students to simplify and organize chapter material. End-of-chapter features help to summarize important chapter concepts and highlight important themes, such as digital and social media marketing, ethics, and financial marketing analysis. This innovative learning design facilitates student understanding and enhances learning.
- The 12th edition provides 16 new end-of-chapter company cases by which students can apply what they learn to actual company situations. Additionally, all of the chapter-opening stories and Marketing at Work highlights in the 12th edition are either new or revised for currency.

The Marketing Journey: Five Major Customer Value and Engagement Themes

The 12th edition of *Marketing: An Introduction* builds on five major customer value and engagement themes:

1. ***Creating value for customers in order to capture value from customers in return.*** Today's marketers must be good at *creating customer value, engaging customers,* and *managing customer relationships*. Outstanding marketing companies understand the marketplace and customer needs, design value-creating marketing strategies, develop integrated marketing programs that engage customers and deliver value and satisfaction, and build strong customer relationships and brand community. In return, they capture value from customers in the form of sales, profits, and customer equity.

   This innovative *customer value framework* is introduced at the start of Chapter 1 in a five-step marketing process model, which details how marketing *creates* customer value and engagement and *captures* value in return. The framework is carefully explained in the first two chapters and then integrated throughout the remainder of the text.
2. ***Customer engagement and today's digital and social media.*** New digital and social media have taken today's marketing by storm, dramatically changing how companies and brands engage consumers and how consumers connect and influence each other's brand behaviors. The 12th edition introduces and thoroughly explores the contemporary concept of *customer engagement marketing* and the exciting new digital and social media

technologies that help brands to engage customers more deeply and interactively. It starts with two major new Chapter 1 sections: *Customer Engagement and Today's Digital and Social Media* and *The Digital Age: Online, Mobile, and Social Media.* A completely revised Chapter 14, *Direct, Online, Social Media, and Mobile Marketing* summarizes the latest developments in digital engagement and relationship-building tools. Everywhere in between, you'll find revised and expanded coverage of the exploding use of digital and social tools to create customer engagement and build brand community.

3. ***Building and managing strong brands to create brand equity.*** Well-positioned brands with strong brand equity provide the basis upon which to build profitable customer relationships. Today's marketers must position their brands powerfully and manage them well to create valued customer brand experiences. The 12th edition provides a deep focus on brands, anchored by the Chapter 7 section *Branding Strategy: Building Strong Brands.*
4. ***Measuring and managing return on marketing.*** Especially in uneven economic times, marketing managers must ensure that their marketing dollars are being well spent. In the past, many marketers spent freely on big, expensive marketing programs, often without thinking carefully about the financial returns on their spending. But all that has changed rapidly. "Marketing accountability"—measuring and managing marketing return on investment—has now become an important part of strategic marketing decision making. This emphasis on marketing accountability is addressed in Chapter 2; Appendix 3, *Marketing by the Numbers;* and throughout the 12th edition.
5. ***Sustainable marketing around the globe.*** As new technologies make the world an increasingly smaller and more fragile place, marketers must be good at marketing their brands globally and in sustainable ways. New material throughout the 12th edition emphasizes the concepts of *global marketing* and *sustainable marketing*—meeting the present needs of consumers and businesses while also preserving or enhancing the ability of future generations to meet their needs. The 12th edition integrates global marketing and sustainability topics throughout the text. It then provides focused coverage on each topic in Chapters 15 and 16, respectively.

Real Travel Experiences: Marketing at Work

Marketing: An Introduction, 12th edition, guides new marketing students down the intriguing, discovery-laden road to learning marketing in an applied and practical way. The text takes a practical marketing-management approach, providing countless in-depth, real-life examples and stories that engage students with basic marketing concepts and bring the marketing journey to life. Every chapter contains a *First Stop* opening story plus *Marketing at Work* highlight features that reveal the drama of modern marketing. Students learn how:

- Amazon.com's deep-down passion for creating customer value and relationships has made it the world's leading digital retailer.
- Nike's outstanding success results from more than just making and selling good sports gear. It's based on a customer-focused strategy through which Nike creates brand engagement and close brand community with and among its customers.
- Sony's dizzying fall from market leadership provides a cautionary tale of what can happen when a company—even a dominant marketing leader—fails to adapt to its changing environment.
- Chipotle's sustainability mission isn't an add-on, created just to position the company as "socially responsible"—doing good is ingrained in everything the company does.
- At T-shirt and apparel maker Life is good, engagement and social media are about building meaningful customer engagement, measured by the depth of consumer commenting and community that surround the brand.
- Giant social network Facebook promises to become one of the world's most powerful and profitable digital marketers—but it's just getting started.
- Southwest's new-age direct and social media marketing capability for building up-close-and-personal interactions with customers makes the passenger-centered company the envy of its industry.

- Innovator Samsung has transformed itself by creating a seemingly endless flow of inspired new products that feature stunning design, innovative technology, life-enriching features, and a big dose of "Wow!"
- Low-fare airline Ryanair appears to have found a radical new pricing solution, one that customers are sure to love: Make flying free!
- The explosion of the Internet, social media, mobile devices, and other technologies has some marketers asking: "Who needs face-to-face selling anymore?"
- For Coca-Cola, marketing in Africa is like "sticking its hand into a bees' nest to get some honey."
- Under its "Conscious Consumption" mission, outdoor apparel and gear maker Patagonia takes sustainability to new extremes by telling consumers to buy *less*.

Beyond such features, each chapter is packed with countless real, engaging, and timely examples that reinforce key concepts. No other text brings marketing to life like the 12th edition of *Marketing: An Introduction*.

Marketing Journey Travel Aids

A wealth of chapter-opening, within-chapter, and end-of-chapter learning devices helps students to engage with marketing by learning, linking, and applying major concepts:

- ***Chapter openers.*** The active and integrative chapter-opening spread in each chapter features an *Objective Outline* that outlines chapter contents and learning objectives, a brief *Road Map—Previewing the Concepts* section that introduces chapter concepts, and a *First Stop* opening vignette—an engaging, deeply developed, illustrated, and annotated marketing story that introduces the chapter material and sparks student interest.
- ***Author comments and figure annotations.*** Throughout the chapter, author comments ease and enhance student learning by introducing and explaining major chapter sections and figures.
- ***Marketing at Work highlights.*** Each chapter contains two highlight features that provide an in-depth look at the real marketing practices of large and small companies.
- ***Speed Bumps.*** Concept checks within each chapter check student learning and help them apply key concepts.
- ***End of chapter: Reviewing the concepts.*** Sections at the end of each chapter summarize key chapter concepts and provide questions, exercises, and cases by which students can review and apply what they've learned. The *Chapter Review and Key Terms* section reviews major chapter concepts and links them to chapter objectives. It also provides a helpful listing of chapter key terms by order of appearance with page numbers that facilitate easy reference.
- ***Discussion Questions and Critical Thinking Exercises.*** These sections at the end of each chapter help students to keep track of and apply what they've learned in the chapter.
- ***Minicases and Applications.*** Brief *Online, Mobile, and Social Media Marketing; Marketing Ethics,* and *Marketing by the Numbers* sections at the end of each chapter provide short applications cases that facilitate discussion of current issues and company situations in areas such as digital and social media marketing, ethics, and financial marketing analysis. A *Video Case* section contains short vignettes with Discussion Questions to be used with a set of four- to seven-minute videos that accompanies the 12th edition. An end-of-chapter *Company Cases* section identifies which of the all-new company cases found in Appendix 1 are best for use with each chapter.

Additional marketing travel aids include:

- ***Company Cases.*** Appendix 1 contains 16 all-new company cases that help students to apply major marketing concepts to real company and brand situations.
- ***Marketing Plan.*** Appendix 2 contains a sample marketing plan that helps students to apply important marketing planning concepts.

- *Marketing by the Numbers.* An innovative Appendix 3 provides students with a comprehensive introduction to the marketing financial analysis that helps to guide, assess, and support marketing decisions.
- *Careers in Marketing.* Appendix 4 describes marketing career paths and guides students in finding marketing jobs and careers. This appendix is only available through MyMarketingLab.

More than ever before, the 12th edition of *Marketing: An Introduction* provides an effective and enjoyable total package for engaging students and moving them down the road to learning marketing!

A Total Teaching and Learning System

A successful marketing course requires more than an engaging, well-written book. Today's classroom requires a dedicated teacher and a fully integrated learning system. A total package of teaching and learning supplements extends this edition's emphasis on effective teaching and learning. The following aids support the 12th edition of *Marketing: An Introduction.*

Instructor's Manual

The Instructor's Manual plays a central role in organizing the teaching and learning package for the 12th edition. This manual has been designed so the instructor can plan lectures, discussions, online learning activities, and written assignments in a coordinated and efficient manner.

All 16 chapters of the text have been carefully reviewed in order to develop the most logical and helpful manual for you, the instructor. Primary features of the Instructor's Manual (IM) are as follows:

- ***Previewing the Concepts***. This brings the important chapter objectives into focus. These objectives are also listed at the beginning of each chapter of the IM.
- ***Just the Basics* and *Great Ideas.*** There are two sections to each chapter in the IM. The first section, **Just the Basics,** provides several sections that summarize the textbook chapter and end-of-chapter material, starting with the **Chapter Overview**. The second section of every IM chapter, **Great Ideas**, provides additional student projects and other material that will help you present the material and manage your time effectively.
- ***Annotated Chapter Notes/Outline.*** This section is the core of the Instructor's Manual. It contains a thorough yet concise outline of the entire chapter, including major and minor headings, and is specifically tied to key phrases and definitions. The instructor will also notice additional information throughout the outline, indicating where key material appears in the chapter and offering suggestions for the proper use of various teaching aids. These additional notations cover such important chapter content as: **Key Terms; Figures and Tables; Linking the Concepts, Chapter Objectives;** and the end-of-chapter material, including **Discussion Questions, Critical Thinking Exercises, Marketing by the Numbers,** and **Marketing Ethics**.
- ***Barriers to Effective Learning.*** This section, which begins the **Great Ideas** portion of the manual, has been developed to aid the instructor in understanding which of the concepts or activities contained in the textbook chapters may be difficult learning assignments for the average student. By reviewing this section, the instructor may be able to direct preparation toward those topics that are perceived as being more difficult. In addition, this section provides suggestions for dealing with difficult learning concepts.
- ***Student Projects.*** Three to five additional projects are listed for effective student learning. These can be done individually or in groups, and can be done in class or as homework assignments. These projects could also provide a rich source of extra-credit projects, if desired.
- ***Classroom Exercise/Homework Assignment.*** This is an additional assignment to help relate the textbook material to real-world situations. As the majority of these projects

depend on access to the Internet, they can be assigned as homework when there is no network connection in the classroom.

- ***Classroom Management Strategies.*** This section provides a timetable for individual chapter lectures. The timetables are based on a 60-minute class; you will need to increase or decrease the amount of time for each section of the chapter to account for shorter or longer class periods. The timetable provided normally has from four to six sections (time segments are suggested) that give guidance to the instructor on what topics to cover, how to coordinate these topics with text features (i.e., *figures, tables, Marketing at Work,* and other material, as appropriate), and in-class discussion suggestions.
- ***Company Case Teaching Notes.*** This section of the Instructor's Manual offers a synopsis, teaching objectives, answers to discussion questions, and suggestions on how to teach the case. It also indicates additional chapters in which the case can be used.
- ***Video Case Teaching Notes.*** The last section in the Instructor's Manual contains teaching notes to accompany the video cases found on the DVD accompanying the textbook and on MyMarketingLab, consisting of an Executive Summary, Questions, and Teaching Ideas for each case. Please contact your Pearson sales representative for access to the DVD containing the video segments noted.
- ***Professors on the Go.*** Designed with the busy professor in mind, this section serves to emphasize key material in the manual, so where an instructor who is short on time can take a quick look to find key concepts, activities, and exercises for the upcoming lecture.
- ***Appendixes.*** There are also four appendixes that support the main IM content and are concise, easy-to-use references: the *Company Cases* appendix, the *Marketing Plan* appendix, the *Marketing by the Numbers* appendix, and the Careers in Marketing appendix.

Additionally, the Annotated Instructor's Notes serve as a quick reference for the entire supplements package. Suggestions for using materials from the Instructor's Manual, PowerPoint slides, Test Item File, Video Library, and online material are offered for each section within every chapter. Visit www.pearsonhighered.com/armstrong to access these Annotated Instructor's Notes.

Test Item File

This Test Item File contains 1,600 questions, including multiple-choice, true/false, and essay questions. Each question is followed by the correct answer, the learning objective it ties to, the AACSB category, the question type (concept, application, critical thinking, or synthesis), the course learning outcome, and the difficulty rating.

TestGen

Pearson Education's test-generating software is available from www.pearsonhighered.com/irc. The software is PC/MAC compatible and preloaded with all of the Test Item File questions. You can manually or randomly view test questions and drag and drop to create a test. You can add or modify test-bank questions as needed.

Learning Management Systems

Our TestGen files are converted for use in Blackboard, WebCT, Moodle, Angel, D2L, and Respondus. These conversions can be found on the Instructor's Resource Center. Respondus can be downloaded from www.respondus.com.

Blackboard/WebCT

Blackboard and WebCT Course Cartridges are available for download from www.pearsonhighered.com/irc. These standard course cartridges contain the Instructor's Manual, and TestGen, and Instructor PowerPoint slides.

Instructor's Resource Center (IRC)

Register. Redeem. Login.

The Web site www.pearsonhighered.com is where instructors can access a variety of print, media, and presentation resources available with this text in downloadable, digital format. For this text, resources are also available for course management platforms such as Blackboard and WebCT, and Course Compass.

It gets better. Once you register, you will not have additional forms to fill out or multiple usernames or passwords to remember to access new titles and/or editions. As a registered faculty member, you can log in directly to download resource files and receive immediate access and instructions for installing course management content to your campus server.

Need help? Our dedicated technical support team is ready to assist instructors with questions about the media supplements that accompany this text. Visit http://247pearsoned.custhelp.com/ for answers to frequently asked questions and toll-free user support phone numbers. All instructor resources are in one place. It's your choice. They are available via a password-protected site at www.pearsonhighered.com/armstrong. Resources include the following:

- ***Instructor's Manual.*** Download the entire Instructor's Manual as a .zip file.
- ***Test Item File.*** Download the entire Test Item File as a .zip file.
- ***TestGen for PC/Mac.*** Download this easy-to-use software; it's preloaded with the 12th edition test questions and a user's manual.
- ***Image Library.*** Access many of the images, ads, illustrations, and features in the text, which are ideal for customizing your PowerPoint presentations.
- ***Instructor PowerPoint.*** This presentation includes basic outlines and key points from each chapter.
- ***Online Courses.*** Resources are available for course management platforms such as Blackboard and WebCT, including Test Bank conversions, PowerPoint presentations, and more.

Video Library

Videos illustrating the most important subject topics are available in two formats:

DVD—available for in-classroom use by instructors, includes videos mapped to Pearson textbooks.

MyMarketingLab—available for instructors and students, provides around-the-clock instant access to videos and corresponding assessment and simulations for Pearson textbooks. Contact your local Pearson representative to request access to either format.

More Valuable Resources

CourseSmart

CourseSmart eTextbooks were developed for students looking to save on required or recommended textbooks. Students simply select their eText by title or author and purchase immediate access to the content for the duration of the course using any major credit card. With a CourseSmart eText, students can search for specific keywords or page numbers, take notes online, print out reading assignments that incorporate lecture notes, and bookmark important passages for later review. For more information or to purchase a CourseSmart eTextbook, visit www.coursesmart.com.

Acknowledgments

No book is the work only of its authors. We greatly appreciate the valuable contributions of several people who helped make this new edition possible. As always, we owe very special thanks to Keri Jean Miksza for her dedicated and valuable help in *all* phases of the project, and to her husband Pete and little daughters Lucy and Mary for all the support they provide Keri during this often-hectic project.

We owe substantial thanks to Andy Norman of Drake University, for his valuable revision advice and skillful contributions in developing chapter vignettes and highlights, company and video cases, and the Marketing Plan appendix. We also thank Laurie Babin of the University of Louisiana at Monroe for her dedicated efforts in preparing end-of-chapter materials and keeping our Marketing by the Numbers appendix fresh. Additional thanks also go to Tony Henthorne for his work on the instructor's manual and Ansrsource for their work on the Test Bank and PowerPoint presentations.

Many reviewers at other colleges and universities provided valuable comments and suggestions for this and previous editions. We are indebted to all the reviewers and colleagues for their thoughtful input. Some of the current reviewers include:

TWELFTH EDITION REVIEWERS

Pari S. Bhagat, Ph.D., *Indiana University of Pennsylvania*
Sylvia Clark, *St. John's University*
Linda Jane Coleman, *Salem State University*
Mary Conran, *Temple University*
Lawrence K. Duke, *Drexel University*
Barbara S. Faries, MBA, *Mission College*
John Gaskins, *Longwood University*
David Koehler, *University of Illinois at Chicago*
Michelle Kunz, *Morehead State University*
Susan Mann, *University of Northwestern Ohio*
Thomas E. Marshall, M.B.E., *Owens Community College*
Nora Martin, *University of South Carolina*
Erika Matulich, *University of Tampa*
John T. Nolan, *SUNY, Buffalo State*
Nikolai Ostapenko, *University of the District of Columbia*
Bill Rice, *California State University*
David Robinson, *University of California, Berkeley*
Lisa Simon, *Cal Poly, San Luis Obispo*
Keith Starcher, *Indiana Wesleyan University*
Rhonda Tenenbaum, *Queens College*
Deborah Utter, *Boston University*
Tom Voigt, *Judson University*

ELEVENTH EDITION REVIEWERS

Sylvia Clark, *St. John's University*
Linda Coleman, *Salem State University*
Mary Conran, *Temple University*
Datha Damron-Martinez, *Truman State University*
Karen Halpern, *South Puget Sound Community College*
Jan Hardesty, *University of Arizona*
Erika Matulich, *University of Tampa*
Marc Newman, *Hocking College*
Keith Starcher, *Indiana Wesleyan University*
Thomas Voigt, *Judson University*

TENTH EDITION REVIEWERS

George Bercovitz, *York College*
Sylvia Clark, *St. John's University*
Datha Damron-Martinez, *Truman State University*
Ivan Filby, *Greenville College*
John Gaskins, *Longwood University*
Karen Halpern, *South Puget Sound Community College*
Jan Hardesty, *University of Arizona*
Hella-Ilona Johnson, *Olympic College*
Marc Newman, *Hocking College*
Vic Piscatello, *University of Arizona*
William M. Ryan, *University of Connecticut*
Elliot Schreiber, *Drexel University*
Rhonda Tenenbaum, *Queens College*
John Talbott, *Indiana University*
Robert Simon, *University of Nebraska, Lincoln*
Tom Voigt, *Judson University*
Terry Wilson, *East Stroudsburg University*

In addition, we thank all the reviewers of previous editions.

We also owe a great deal to the people at Pearson who helped develop this book. Marketing Editor Mark Gaffney provided insights and support during the revision. Program Manager Meeta Pendharkar provided valuable assistance in managing the many facets of this complex revision project. Senior Art Director Janet Slowik developed the 12th edition's exciting design, and Senior Project Manager Jacqueline Martin helped guide the book through the complex production process. We'd also like to thank Stephanie Wall, Anne Fahlgren, and Judy Leale. We are proud to be associated with the fine professionals at Pearson Education. We also owe a mighty debt of gratitude to Project Editor Roxanne Klaas and the fine team at S4Carlisle Publishing Services.

Finally, we owe many thanks to our families for all of their support and encouragement—Kathy, Betty, Mandy, Matt, KC, Keri, Delaney, Molly, Macy, and Ben from the Armstrong clan and Nancy, Amy, Melissa, and Jessica from the Kotler family. To them, we dedicate this book.

Gary Armstrong
Philip Kotler

Marketing

An Introduction

Twelfth Edition

PART 1: DEFINING MARKETING AND THE MARKETING PROCESS (CHAPTERS 1–2)
PART 2: UNDERSTANDING THE MARKETPLACE AND CUSTOMER VALUE (CHAPTERS 3–5)
PART 3: DESIGNING A CUSTOMER VALUE–DRIVEN STRATEGY AND MIX (CHAPTERS 6–14)
PART 4: EXTENDING MARKETING (CHAPTERS 15–16)

1 Marketing
Creating and Capturing Customer Value

CHAPTER ROAD MAP

Objective Outline

- OBJECTIVE 1 **Define marketing and outline the steps in the marketing process.** What Is Marketing? 4–6
- OBJECTIVE 2 **Explain the importance of understanding the marketplace and customers and identify the five core marketplace concepts.** Understanding the Marketplace and Customer Needs 6–8
- OBJECTIVE 3 **Identify the key elements of a customer-driven marketing strategy and discuss the marketing management orientations that guide marketing strategy.** Designing a Customer-Driven Marketing Strategy 9–12; Preparing an Integrated Marketing Plan and Program? 12–13
- OBJECTIVE 4 **Discuss customer relationship management and identify strategies for creating value *for* customers and capturing value *from* customers in return.** Building Customer Relationships 13–21; Capturing Value from Customers 21–24
- OBJECTIVE 5 **Describe the major trends and forces that are changing the marketing landscape in this age of relationships.** The Changing Marketing Landscape 24–29

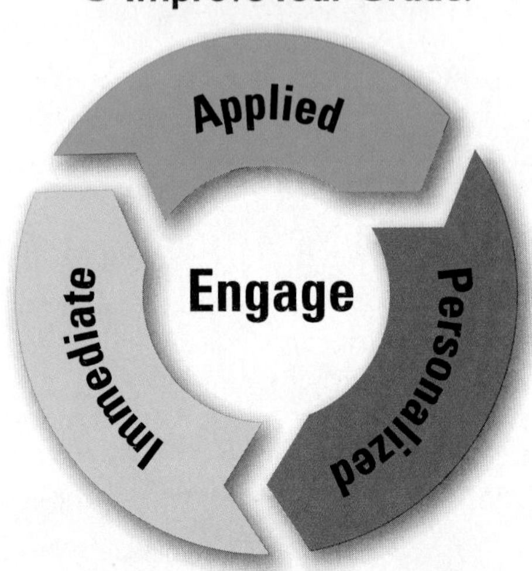

Previewing the Concepts

This chapter introduces you to the basic concepts of marketing. We start with the question: What is marketing? Simply put, marketing is managing profitable customer relationships. The aim of marketing is to create value for customers in order to capture value from customers in return. Next we discuss the five steps in the marketing process—from understanding customer needs, to designing customer-driven marketing strategies and integrated marketing programs, to building customer relationships and capturing value for the firm. Finally, we discuss the major trends and forces affecting marketing in this new age of digital, mobile, and social media. Understanding these basic concepts and forming your own ideas about what they really mean to you will provide a solid foundation for all that follows.

Let's start with a good story about marketing in action at Amazon.com, by far the world's leading online and digital marketer. The secret to Amazon's success? It's really no secret at all. Amazon is flat-out customer obsessed. It has a deep-down passion for creating customer value and relationships. In return, customers reward Amazon with their buying dollars and loyalty. You'll see this theme of creating customer value in order to capture value in return repeated throughout this chapter and the remainder of the text.

---

*Over 10 million students improved their results using the Pearson MyLabs. Visit **mymktlab.com** for simulations, tutorials, and end-of-chapter problems.

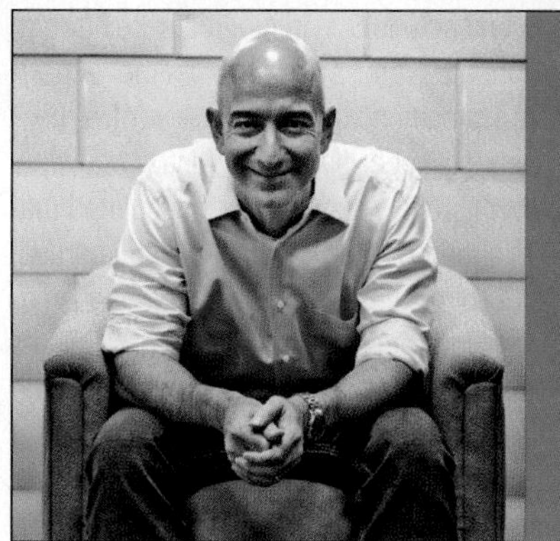

"We see our customers as invited guests to a party, and we are the hosts. It's our job every day to make every important aspect of the customer experience a little better." – Jeff Bezos

» Amazon.com does much more than just sell goods online. It creates satisfying online customer experiences. "The thing that drives everything is creating genuine value for customers," says Amazon founder and CEO Bezos, shown here.

Contour by Getty Images.

First Stop

Amazon.com: Obsessed with Creating Customer Value and Relationships

When you think of shopping online, chances are good that you think first of Amazon. The online pioneer first opened its virtual doors in 1995, selling books out of founder Jeff Bezos's garage in suburban Seattle. Amazon still sells books—lots and lots of books. But it now sells just about everything else as well, from music, electronics, tools, housewares, apparel, and groceries to fashions, loose diamonds, and Maine lobsters.

From the start, Amazon has grown explosively. Its annual sales have rocketed from a modest $150 million in 1997 to more than $61 billion today. During the past five years, despite a shaky economy, Amazon's revenues have grown by an amazing 35 percent annually. This past holiday season, Amazon.com sold more than 26.5 million items to its 188 million active customers worldwide—that's 306 items per second. Analysts predict that by 2015, Amazon will become the youngest company in history to hit $100 billion in revenues (it took Walmart 34 years). That would make it the nation's second-largest retailer, trailing only Walmart.

What has made Amazon such an amazing success story? Founder and CEO Bezos puts it in three simple words: "Obsess over customers." To its core, the company is relentlessly customer driven. "The thing that drives everything is creating genuine value for customers," says Bezos. Amazon believes that if it does what's good for customers, profits will follow. So the company starts with the customer and works backward. Rather than asking what it can do with its current capabilities, Amazon first asks: Who are our customers? What do they need? Then, it develops whatever capabilities are required to meet those customer needs.

Amazon.com's deep-down passion for creating customer value and relationships has made it the world's leading online retailer. Amazon has become the model for companies that are obsessively and successfully focused on delivering customer value.

At Amazon, every decision is made with an eye toward improving the Amazon.com customer experience. In fact, at many Amazon meetings, the most influential figure in the room is "the empty chair"—literally an empty chair at the table that represents the all-important customer. At times, the empty chair isn't empty, but is occupied by a "Customer Experience Bar Raiser," an employee who is specially trained to represent customers' interests. To give the empty chair a loud, clear voice, Amazon relentlessly tracks performance against nearly 400 measurable customer-related goals.

Amazon's obsession with serving the needs of its customers drives the company to take risks and innovate in ways that other companies don't. For example, when it noted that its book-buying customers needed better access to e-books and other digital content, Amazon developed the Kindle e-reader, its first-ever original product. The Kindle took more than four years and a whole new set of skills to develop. But Amazon's start-with-the-customer thinking paid off handsomely. The Kindle is now the company's number-one selling product, and Amazon.com now sells more e-books than hardcovers and paperbacks combined. What's more, the company's new Kindle Fire tablet now leads the market for low-priced tablet computers. Thus, what started as an effort to improve the customer experience now gives Amazon a powerful presence in the burgeoning world of digital and social media. Not only does the Kindle allow access to e-books, music, videos, and apps sold by Amazon, it makes interacting with the online giant easier than ever. Customers use their Kindles to shop Amazon.com and interact with the company on its blogs and social media pages.

Perhaps more important than *what* Amazon sells is *how* it sells. Amazon wants to deliver a special experience to every customer. Most Amazon.com regulars feel a surprisingly strong relationship with the company, especially given the almost complete lack of actual human interaction. Amazon obsesses over making each customer's experience uniquely personal. For example, the Amazon.com site greets customers with their very own personalized home pages, and its "Recommendations for You" feature offers personalized product recommendations. Amazon was the first company to sift through each customer's past purchases and the purchasing patterns of customers with similar profiles to come up with personalized site content. Amazon wants to personalize the shopping experience for each individual customer. If it has 188 million customers, it reasons, it should have 188 million stores.

Visitors to Amazon.com receive a unique blend of benefits: huge selection, good value, low prices, and convenience. But it's the "discovery" factor that makes the buying experience really special. Once on the Amazon.com site, you're compelled to stay for a while—looking, learning, and discovering. Amazon.com has become a kind of online community in which customers can browse for products, research purchase alternatives, share opinions and reviews with other visitors, and chat online with authors and experts. In this way, Amazon does much more than just sell goods online. It creates direct, personalized customer relationships and satisfying online experiences. Year after year, Amazon places at or near the top of almost every customer satisfaction ranking, regardless of industry.

Based on its powerful growth, many analysts have speculated that Amazon.com will become the Walmart of the Web. In fact, some argue, it already is. Although Walmart's total sales of $469 billion dwarf Amazon's $61 billion in sales, Amazon's Internet sales are more than 15 times greater than Walmart's. So it's Walmart that's chasing Amazon on the Web. Put another way, Walmart wants to become the Amazon.com of the Web, not the other way around. However, despite its mammoth proportions, to catch Amazon online, Walmart will have to match the superb Amazon customer experience, and that won't be easy.

Whatever the eventual outcome, Amazon has become the poster child for companies that are obsessively and successfully focused on delivering customer value. Jeff Bezos has known from the very start that if Amazon creates superior value for customers, it will earn their business and loyalty, and success will follow in terms of company profits and returns. As Bezos puts it, "When things get complicated, we simplify them by asking, 'What's best for the customer?' We believe that if we do that, things will work out in the long term."[1]

Today's successful companies have one thing in common: Like Amazon, they are strongly customer focused and heavily committed to marketing. These companies share a passion for understanding and satisfying customer needs in well-defined target markets. They motivate everyone in the organization to help build lasting customer relationships based on creating value.

Customer relationships and value are especially important today. Facing dramatic technological advances and deep economic, social, and environmental challenges, today's customers are relating digitally with companies and each other, spending more carefully, and reassessing their relationships with brands. The new digital, mobile, and social media developments have revolutionized how consumers shop and interact, in turn calling for new marketing strategies and tactics. In these fast-changing times, it's now more important than ever to build strong customer relationships based on real and enduring customer value.

We'll discuss the exciting new challenges facing both customers and marketers later in the chapter. But first, let's introduce the basics of marketing.

Author Comment
Pause here and think about how you'd answer this question before studying marketing. Then see how your answer changes as you read the chapter.

What Is Marketing?

Marketing, more than any other business function, deals with customers. Although we will soon explore more-detailed definitions of marketing, perhaps the simplest definition is this one: *Marketing is managing profitable customer relationships.* The twofold goal of marketing is to attract new customers by promising superior value and to keep and grow current customers by delivering satisfaction.

For example, McDonald's fulfills its "i'm lovin' it" motto by being "our customers' favorite place and way to eat" the world over, giving it nearly as much market share as its nearest four competitors combined. Walmart has become the world's largest retailer—and the world's second-largest company—by delivering on its promise, "Save Money. Live Better." Facebook has attracted more than a billion active Web and mobile users worldwide by helping them to "connect and share" with the people in their lives."[2]

Sound marketing is critical to the success of every organization. Large for-profit firms, such as Google, Target, Procter & Gamble, Toyota, and Microsoft, use marketing. But so do not-for-profit organizations, such as colleges, hospitals, museums, symphony orchestras, and even churches.

» **Marketing is all around you, in good-old traditional forms and in a host of new forms, from Web sites and mobile phone apps to videos and online social media.**
Justin Lewis.

You already know a lot about marketing—it's all around you. Marketing comes to you in the good-old traditional forms: You see it in the abundance of products at your nearby shopping mall and the ads that fill your TV screen, spice up your magazines, or stuff your mailbox. But in recent years, marketers have assembled a host of new marketing approaches, everything from imaginative Web sites and mobile phone apps to blogs, online videos, and social media. These new approaches do more than just blast out messages to the masses. They reach you directly, personally, and interactively. » Today's marketers want to become a part of your life and enrich your experiences with their brands—to help you *live* their brands.

At home, at school, where you work, and where you play, you see marketing in almost everything you do. Yet, there is much more to marketing than meets the consumer's casual eye. Behind it all is a massive network of people and activities competing for your attention and purchases. This book will give you a complete introduction to the basic concepts and practices of today's marketing. In this chapter, we begin by defining marketing and the marketing process.

Marketing Defined

What *is* marketing? Many people think of marketing as only selling and advertising. We are bombarded every day with TV commercials, catalogs, spiels from salespeople, and online pitches. However, selling and advertising are only the tip of the marketing iceberg.

Today, marketing must be understood not in the old sense of making a sale—"telling and selling"—but in the new sense of *satisfying customer needs.* If the marketer engages consumers effectively, understands their needs, develops products that provide superior customer value, and prices, distributes, and promotes them well, these products will sell easily. In fact, according to management guru Peter Drucker, "The aim of marketing is to make selling unnecessary."[3] Selling and advertising are only part of a larger *marketing mix*—a set of marketing tools that work together to satisfy customer needs and build customer relationships.

Marketing
The process by which companies create value for customers and build strong customer relationships in order to capture value from customers in return.

Broadly defined, marketing is a social and managerial process by which individuals and organizations obtain what they need and want through creating and exchanging value with others. In a narrower business context, marketing involves building profitable, value-laden exchange relationships with customers. Hence, we define **marketing** as the process by which companies create value for customers and build strong customer relationships in order to capture value from customers in return.[4]

The Marketing Process

This important figure shows marketing in a nutshell. By creating value *for* customers, marketers capture value *from* customers in return. This five-step process forms the marketing framework for the rest of the chapter and the remainder of the text.

» **Figure 1.1** presents a simple, five-step model of the marketing process for creating and capturing customer value. In the first four steps, companies work to understand consumers, create customer value, and build strong customer relationships. In the final step, companies reap the rewards of creating superior customer value. By creating value *for* consumers, they in turn capture value *from* consumers in the form of sales, profits, and long-term customer equity.

» **Figure 1.1** The Marketing Process: Creating and Capturing Customer Value

In this chapter and the next, we will examine the steps of this simple model of marketing. In this chapter, we review each step but focus more on the customer relationship steps—understanding customers, building customer relationships, and capturing value from customers. In Chapter 2, we look more deeply into the second and third steps—designing value-creating marketing strategies and constructing marketing programs.

Author Comment
Marketing is all about creating value for customers. So, as the first step in the marketing process, the company must fully understand consumers and the marketplace in which it operates.

Understanding the Marketplace and Customer Needs

As a first step, marketers need to understand customer needs and wants and the marketplace in which they operate. We examine five core customer and marketplace concepts: (1) *needs, wants, and demands*; (2) *market offerings (products, services, and experiences)*; (3) *value and satisfaction*; (4) *exchanges and relationships*; and (5) *markets*.

Customer Needs, Wants, and Demands

Needs
States of felt deprivation.

Wants
The form human needs take as they are shaped by culture and individual personality.

Demands
Human wants that are backed by buying power.

The most basic concept underlying marketing is that of human needs. Human **needs** are states of felt deprivation. They include basic *physical* needs for food, clothing, warmth, and safety; *social* needs for belonging and affection; and *individual* needs for knowledge and self-expression. Marketers did not create these needs; they are a basic part of the human makeup.

Wants are the form human needs take as they are shaped by culture and individual personality. An American *needs* food but *wants* a Big Mac, french fries, and a soft drink. A person in Papua, New Guinea, *needs* food but *wants* taro, rice, yams, and pork. Wants are shaped by one's society and are described in terms of objects that will satisfy those needs. When backed by buying power, wants become **demands**. Given their wants and resources, people demand products and services with benefits that add up to the most value and satisfaction.

Outstanding marketing companies go to great lengths to learn about and understand their customers' needs, wants, and demands. They conduct consumer research, analyze mountains of customer data, and observe customers as they shop and interact, offline and online. People at all levels of the company—including top management—stay close to customers. For example, Kroger chairman and CEO David Dillon regularly dons blue jeans and roams the aisles of local Kroger supermarkets, blending in with and talking to other shoppers. Similarly, Walmart president and CEO Michael Duke and his entire executive team make regular store and in-home visits with customers to get to know them and understand their needs. Top McDonald's marketers hold frequent Twitter chats, connecting directly with McDonald's Twitter followers, both fans and critics, to learn their thoughts about topics ranging from nutrition and sustainability to products and brand promotions.[5]

Market Offerings—Products, Services, and Experiences

Market offerings
Some combination of products, services, information, or experiences offered to a market to satisfy a need or want.

Consumers' needs and wants are fulfilled through **market offerings**—some combination of products, services, information, or experiences offered to a market to satisfy a need or a want. Market offerings are not limited to physical *products*. They also include *services*—activities or benefits offered for sale that are essentially intangible and do not result in the ownership of anything. Examples include banking, airline, hotel, retailing, and home repair services.

More broadly, market offerings also include other entities, such as *persons*, *places*, *organizations*, *information*, and *ideas*. For example, the "Pure Michigan" campaign markets the state of Michigan as a tourism destination that "lets unspoiled nature and authentic character revive your spirits." The Ad Council and the National Highway Traffic Safety Administration created a "Stop the Texts. Stop the Wrecks." campaign that markets the idea of eliminating texting while driving. The campaign points out that a texting driver is 23 times more likely to get into a crash that a non-texting driver. And the "Let's Move" public service campaign, jointly sponsored by the U.S. Department of Agriculture and the U.S. Department of Health and Human Services, markets the idea of reducing childhood obesity by urging kids and their families to make healthier food choices and increase their physical activity. One ad promotes "Family Fun Friday: Dance. Play. Go for a walk in the park. Make every Friday the day you and your family get moving."[6]

Marketing myopia
The mistake of paying more attention to the specific products a company offers than to the benefits and experiences produced by these products.

Many sellers make the mistake of paying more attention to the specific products they offer than to the benefits and experiences produced by these products. These sellers suffer from **marketing myopia**. They are so taken with their products that they focus only on existing wants and lose sight of underlying customer needs.[7] They forget that a product is only a tool to solve a consumer problem. A manufacturer of quarter-inch drill bits may think that the customer needs a drill bit. But what the customer *really* needs is a quarter-inch hole. These sellers will have trouble if a new product comes along that serves the customer's need better or less expensively. The customer will have the same *need* but will *want* the new product.

Smart marketers look beyond the attributes of the products and services they sell. By orchestrating several services and products, they create *brand experiences* for consumers. For example, you don't just visit Walt Disney World Resort; you immerse yourself and your family in a world of wonder, a world where dreams come true and things still work the way they should. You're "in the heart of the magic!" says Disney.

Similarly, >> Angry Birds is much more than just a mobile game app. To more than 200 million fans in 116 countries, it's a deeply involving experience. As one observers puts it: "Angry Birds land is a state of mind—a digital immersion in addictively cheerful destruction, a refuge from the boredom of subway commutes and doctors' waiting rooms, where the fine art of sling-shotting tiny brightly hued birds at wooden fortresses to vanquish pigs taking shelter inside makes eminent sense and is immensely satisfying." The game's creator, Rovio Entertainment, plans to expand the Angry Birds experience through everything from animated short videos (called *Angry Birds Toons*) and 3-D animated movies to a growing list of licensed toys, apparel, yard art, and even Angry Birds–branded playgrounds and activity parks.[8]

>> Marketing experiences: More than just a mobile game app, Angry Birds is "a digital immersion in addictively cheerful destruction." Creator Rovio plans to expand the Angry Birds experience through animated videos, licensed products, and even Angry birds–branded playgrounds and activity parks.

Archivo CEET GDA Photo Service/Newscom.

Customer Value and Satisfaction

Consumers usually face a broad array of products and services that might satisfy a given need. How do they choose among these many market offerings? Customers form expectations about the value and satisfaction that various market offerings will deliver and buy accordingly. Satisfied customers buy again and tell others about their good experiences. Dissatisfied customers often switch to competitors and disparage the product to others.

Marketers must be careful to set the right level of expectations. If they set expectations too low, they may satisfy those who buy but fail to attract enough buyers. If they set expectations too high, buyers will be disappointed. Customer value and customer satisfaction are key building blocks for developing and managing customer relationships. We will revisit these core concepts later in the chapter.

Exchanges and Relationships

Exchange
The act of obtaining a desired object from someone by offering something in return.

Marketing occurs when people decide to satisfy their needs and wants through exchange relationships. **Exchange** is the act of obtaining a desired object from someone by offering something in return. In the broadest sense, the marketer tries to bring about a response to some market offering. The response may be more than simply buying or trading products and services. A political candidate, for instance, wants votes; a church wants membership; an orchestra wants an audience; and a social action group wants idea acceptance.

Marketing consists of actions taken to create, maintain, and grow desirable exchange *relationships* with target audiences involving a product, service, idea, or other object. Companies want to build strong relationships by consistently delivering superior customer value. We will expand on the important concept of managing customer relationships later in the chapter.

Markets

Market
The set of all actual and potential buyers of a product or service.

The concepts of exchange and relationships lead to the concept of a market. A **market** is the set of actual and potential buyers of a product or service. These buyers share a particular need or want that can be satisfied through exchange relationships.

Marketing means managing markets to bring about profitable customer relationships. However, creating these relationships takes work. Sellers must search for buyers, identify their needs, design good market offerings, set prices for them, promote them, and store and deliver them. Activities such as consumer research, product development, communication, distribution, pricing, and service are core marketing activities.

Although we normally think of marketing as being carried out by sellers, buyers also carry out marketing. Consumers market when they search for products, interact with companies to obtain information, and make their purchases. In fact, today's digital technologies, from Web sites and smartphone apps to the explosion of the social media, have empowered consumers and made marketing a truly two-way affair. Thus, in addition to customer relationship management, today's marketers must also deal effectively with *customer-managed relationships*. Marketers are no longer asking only "How can we influence our customers?" but also "How can our customers influence us?" and even "How can our customers influence each other?"

>> Figure 1.2 shows the main elements in a marketing system. Marketing involves serving a market of final consumers in the face of competitors. The company and competitors research the market and interact with consumers to understand their needs. Then they create and send their market offerings and messages to consumers, either directly or through marketing intermediaries. Each party in the system is affected by major environmental forces (demographic, economic, natural, technological, political, and social/cultural).

Each party in the system adds value for the next level. The arrows represent relationships that must be developed and managed. Thus, a company's success at building profitable relationships depends not only on its own actions but also on how well the entire system serves the needs of final consumers. Walmart cannot fulfill its promise of low prices unless its suppliers provide merchandise at low costs. And Ford cannot deliver a high-quality car-ownership experience unless its dealers provide outstanding sales and service.

>> Figure 1.2 A Modern Marketing System

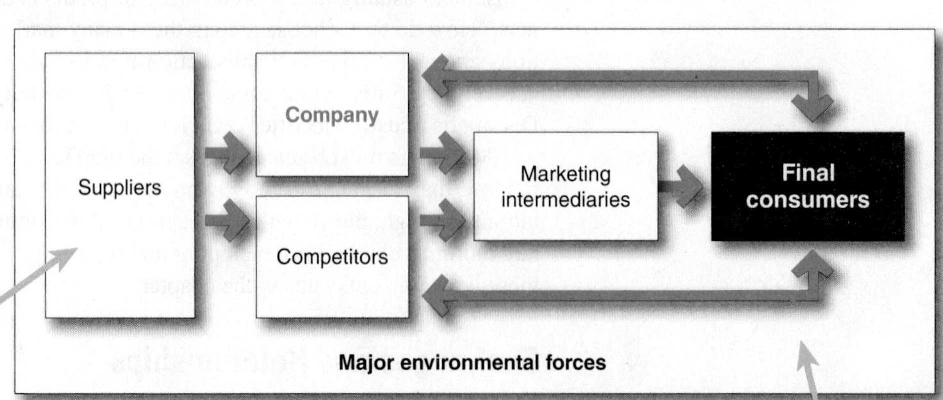
Suppliers
Company
Competitors
Marketing intermediaries
Final consumers
Major environmental forces
Each party in the system adds value. Walmart cannot fulfill its promise of low prices unless its suppliers provide low costs. Ford cannot deliver a high-quality car-ownership experience unless its dealers provide outstanding service.
Arrows represent relationships that must be developed and managed to create customer value and profitable customer relationships.

Author Comment
Once a company fully understands its consumers and the marketplace, it must decide which customers it will serve and how it will bring them value.

Designing a Customer-Driven Marketing Strategy

Once it fully understands consumers and the marketplace, marketing management can design a customer-driven marketing strategy. We define **marketing management** as the art and science of choosing target markets and building profitable relationships with them. The marketing manager's aim is to find, attract, keep, and grow target customers by creating, delivering, and communicating superior customer value.

Marketing management
The art and science of choosing target markets and building profitable relationships with them.

To design a winning marketing strategy, the marketing manager must answer two important questions: *What customers will we serve (what's our target market)?* and *How can we serve these customers best (what's our value proposition)?* We will discuss these marketing strategy concepts briefly here and then look at them in more detail in Chapters 2 and 6.

Selecting Customers to Serve

The company must first decide *whom* it will serve. It does this by dividing the market into segments of customers (*market segmentation*) and selecting which segments it will go after (*target marketing*). Some people think of marketing management as finding as many customers as possible and increasing demand. But marketing managers know that they cannot serve all customers in every way. By trying to serve all customers, they may not serve any customers well. Instead, the company wants to select only customers that it can serve well and profitably. For example, Nordstrom profitably targets affluent professionals; Dollar General profitably targets families with more modest means.

Ultimately, marketing managers must decide which customers they want to target and on the level, timing, and nature of their demand. Simply put, marketing management is *customer management* and *demand management.*

Choosing a Value Proposition

The company must also decide how it will serve targeted customers—how it will *differentiate and position* itself in the marketplace. A brand's *value proposition* is the set of benefits or values it promises to deliver to consumers to satisfy their needs. Facebook helps you "connect and share with the people in your life," whereas YouTube "provides a place for people to connect, inform, and inspire others across the globe." BMW promises "the ultimate driving machine," whereas the diminutive Smart car suggests that you "Open your mind to the car that challenges the status quo." New Balance's Minimus shoes are "like barefoot only better"; and with Vibram FiveFingers shoes, "You are the technology."

Such value propositions differentiate one brand from another. They answer the customer's question, "Why should I buy your brand rather than a competitor's?" Companies must design strong value propositions that give them the greatest advantage in their target markets. » For example, Vibram FiveFingers shoes promise the best of two worlds—running with shoes and without. "You get all the health and performance benefits of barefoot running combined with a Vibram sole that protects you from elements and obstacles in your path." With Vibram FiveFingers shoes, "The more it looks like a foot, the more it acts like a foot."

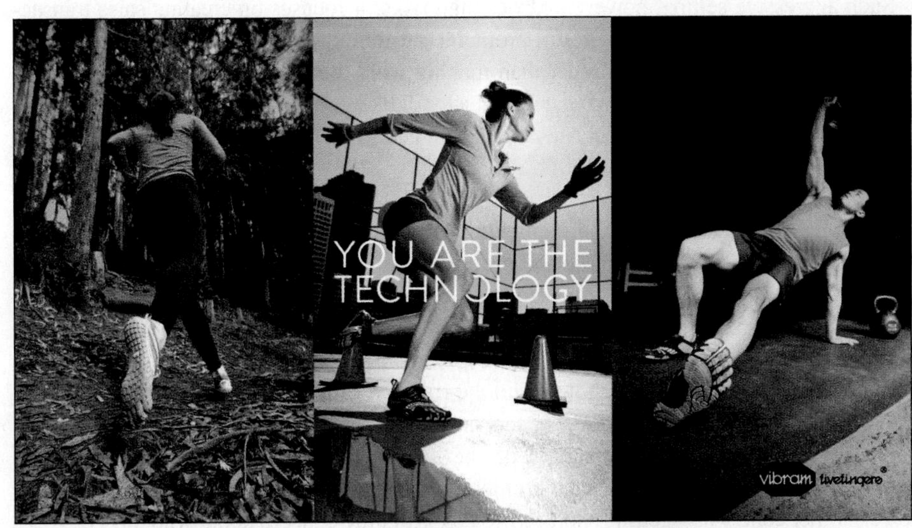

» **Value propositions: With Vibram FiveFingers shoes, "You are the technology."**
Vibram USA, Inc.

Marketing Management Orientations

Marketing management wants to design strategies that will build profitable relationships with target consumers. But what *philosophy* should guide these marketing strategies? What weight should be given to the interests of customers, the organization, and society? Very often, these interests conflict.

There are five alternative concepts under which organizations design and carry out their marketing strategies: the *production*, *product*, *selling*, *marketing*, and *societal marketing concepts*.

The Production Concept

Production concept
The idea that consumers will favor products that are available and highly affordable; therefore, the organization should focus on improving production and distribution efficiency.

The **production concept** holds that consumers will favor products that are available and highly affordable. Therefore, management should focus on improving production and distribution efficiency. This concept is one of the oldest orientations that guides sellers.

The production concept is still a useful philosophy in some situations. For example, both personal computer maker Lenovo and home appliance maker Haier dominate the highly competitive, price-sensitive Chinese market through low labor costs, high production efficiency, and mass distribution. However, although useful in some situations, the production concept can lead to marketing myopia. Companies adopting this orientation run a major risk of focusing too narrowly on their own operations and losing sight of the real objective—satisfying customer needs and building customer relationships.

The Product Concept

Product concept
The idea that consumers will favor products that offer the most quality, performance, and features; therefore, the organization should devote its energy to making continuous product improvements.

The **product concept** holds that consumers will favor products that offer the most in quality, performance, and innovative features. Under this concept, marketing strategy focuses on making continuous product improvements.

Product quality and improvement are important parts of most marketing strategies. However, focusing *only* on the company's products can also lead to marketing myopia. For example, some manufacturers believe that if they can "build a better mousetrap, the world will beat a path to their doors." But they are often rudely shocked. Buyers may be looking for a better solution to a mouse problem but not necessarily for a better mousetrap. The better solution might be a chemical spray, an exterminating service, a housecat, or something else that suits their needs even better than a mousetrap. Furthermore, a better mousetrap will not sell unless the manufacturer designs, packages, and prices it attractively; places it in convenient distribution channels; brings it to the attention of people who need it; and convinces buyers that it is a better product.

The Selling Concept

Selling concept
The idea that consumers will not buy enough of the firm's products unless the firm undertakes a large-scale selling and promotion effort.

Many companies follow the **selling concept**, which holds that consumers will not buy enough of the firm's products unless it undertakes a large-scale selling and promotion effort. The selling concept is typically practiced with unsought goods—those that buyers do not normally think of buying, such as insurance or blood donations. These industries must be good at tracking down prospects and selling them on a product's benefits.

Such aggressive selling, however, carries high risks. It focuses on creating sales transactions rather than on building long-term, profitable customer relationships. The aim often is to sell what the company makes rather than making what the market wants. It assumes that customers who are coaxed into buying the product will like it. Or, if they don't like it, they will possibly forget their disappointment and buy it again later. These are usually poor assumptions.

The Marketing Concept

Marketing concept
A philosophy in which achieving organizational goals depends on knowing the needs and wants of target markets and delivering the desired satisfactions better than competitors do.

The **marketing concept** holds that achieving organizational goals depends on knowing the needs and wants of target markets and delivering the desired satisfactions better than competitors do. Under the marketing concept, customer focus and value are the *paths* to sales and profits. Instead of a product-centered *make-and-sell* philosophy, the marketing concept is a customer-centered *sense-and-respond* philosophy. The job is not to find the right customers for your product but to find the right products for your customers.

>> **Figure 1.3** contrasts the selling concept and the marketing concept. The selling concept takes an *inside-out* perspective. It starts with the factory, focuses on the company's existing products, and calls for heavy selling and promotion to obtain profitable sales. It focuses primarily on customer conquest—getting short-term sales with little concern about who buys or why.

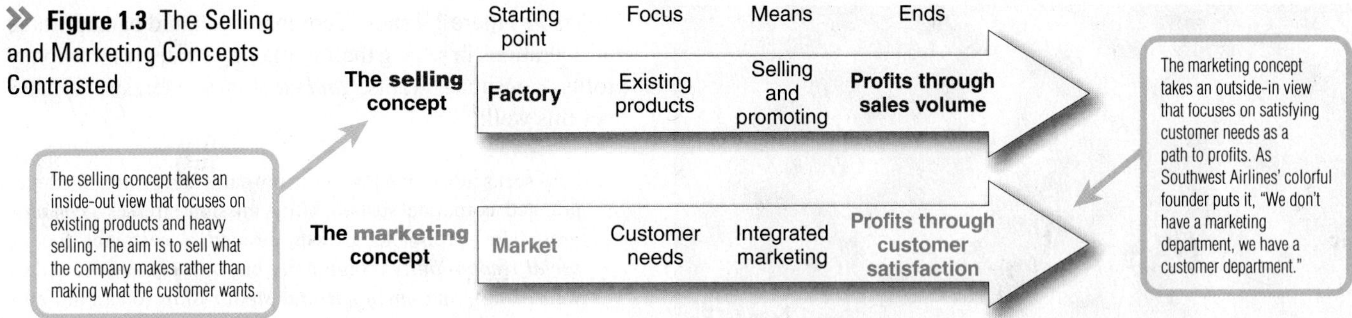
Starting point
Focus
Means
Ends
The selling concept
Factory
Existing products
Selling and promoting
Profits through sales volume
The marketing concept
Market
Customer needs
Integrated marketing
Profits through customer satisfaction
The selling concept takes an inside-out view that focuses on existing products and heavy selling. The aim is to sell what the company makes rather than making what the customer wants.
The marketing concept takes an outside-in view that focuses on satisfying customer needs as a path to profits. As Southwest Airlines' colorful founder puts it, "We don't have a marketing department, we have a customer department."

» **Figure 1.3** The Selling and Marketing Concepts Contrasted

In contrast, the marketing concept takes an *outside-in* perspective. As Herb Kelleher, the colorful founder of Southwest Airlines, once put it, "We don't have a marketing department; we have a customer department." The marketing concept starts with a well-defined market, focuses on customer needs, and integrates all the marketing activities that affect customers. In turn, it yields profits by creating relationships with the right customers based on customer value and satisfaction.

Implementing the marketing concept often means more than simply responding to customers' stated desires and obvious needs. *Customer-driven* companies research customers deeply to learn about their desires, gather new product ideas, and test product improvements. Such customer-driven marketing usually works well when a clear need exists and when customers know what they want.

In many cases, however, customers *don't* know what they want or even what is possible. As Henry Ford once remarked, "If I'd asked people what they wanted, they would have said faster horses."[9] For example, even 20 years ago, how many consumers would have thought to ask for now-commonplace products such as tablet computers, smartphones, digital cameras, 24-hour online buying, and GPS systems in their cars? Such situations call for *customer-driving* marketing—understanding customer needs even better than customers themselves do and creating products and services that meet both existing and latent needs, now and in the future. As an executive at 3M put it, "Our goal is to lead customers where they want to go before *they* know where they want to go."

The Societal Marketing Concept

Societal marketing concept
The idea that a company's marketing decisions should consider consumers' wants, the company's requirements, consumers' long-run interests, and society's long-run interests.

The **societal marketing concept** questions whether the pure marketing concept overlooks possible conflicts between consumer *short-run wants* and consumer *long-run welfare.* Is a firm that satisfies the immediate needs and wants of target markets always doing what's best for its consumers in the long run? The societal marketing concept holds that marketing strategy should deliver value to customers in a way that maintains or improves both the consumer's *and society's* well-being. It calls for *sustainable marketing*, socially and environmentally responsible marketing that meets the present needs of consumers and businesses while also preserving or enhancing the ability of future generations to meet their needs.

Even more broadly, many leading business and marketing thinkers are now preaching the concept of *shared value,* which recognizes that societal needs, not just economic needs, define markets.[10] The concept of shared value focuses on creating economic value in a way that also creates value for society. A growing number of companies known for their hard-nosed approaches to business—such as GE, Google, IBM, Intel, Johnson & Johnson, Nestlé, Unilever, and Walmart—are rethinking the interactions between society and corporate performance. They are concerned not just with short-term economic gains, but with the well-being of their customers, the depletion of natural resources vital to their businesses, the viability of key suppliers, and the economic well-being of the communities in which they produce and sell. One prominent marketer calls this *Marketing 3.0.* "Marketing 3.0 organizations are values-driven," he says. "I'm not talking about being value-driven. I'm talking about 'values' plural, where values amount to caring about the state of the world."[11]

United As One
Making A Difference

The societal marketing concept: According to UPS, social responsibility "isn't just good for the planet. It's good for business."

Cheryl Gerber/AP Photo.

As **Figure 1.4** shows, companies should balance three considerations in setting their marketing strategies: company profits, consumer wants, *and* society's interests. UPS does this well:[12]

> UPS seeks more than just short-run sales and profits. Its three-pronged corporate sustainability mission stresses *economic prosperity* (profitable growth through a customer focus), *social responsibility* (community engagement and individual well-being), and *environmental stewardship* (operating efficiently and protecting the environment). Whether it involves greening up its operations or urging employees to volunteer time in their communities, UPS proactively seeks opportunities to act responsibly. For example, UPS employees donate 1.6 million volunteer hours each year to efforts such as United Way's Live United campaign to improve the education, income, and health of the nation's communities. UPS knows that doing what's right benefits both consumers and the company. By operating efficiently and acting responsibly, it can "meet the needs of the enterprise . . . while protecting and enhancing the human and natural resources that will be needed in the future." Social responsibility "isn't just good for the planet," says the company. "It's good for business."

Author Comment

The customer-driven marketing strategy discussed in the previous section outlines which customers the company will serve (the target market) and how it will serve them (positioning and the value proposition). Now, the company develops marketing plans and programs—a marketing mix—that will actually deliver the intended customer value.

Preparing an Integrated Marketing Plan and Program

The company's marketing strategy outlines which customers it will serve and how it will create value for these customers. Next, the marketer develops an integrated marketing program that will actually deliver the intended value to target customers. The marketing program builds customer relationships by transforming the marketing strategy into action. It consists of the firm's *marketing mix*, the set of marketing tools the firm uses to implement its marketing strategy.

The major marketing mix tools are classified into four broad groups, called the *four Ps* of marketing: product, price, place, and promotion. To deliver on its value proposition, the firm must first create a need-satisfying market offering (product). It must then decide how much it will charge for the offering (price) and how it will make the offering available to target consumers (place). Finally, it must communicate with target customers about the offering and persuade them of its merits (promotion). The firm must blend each marketing mix tool into a comprehensive integrated marketing program that communicates and delivers the intended value to chosen customers. We will explore marketing programs and the marketing mix in much more detail in later chapters.

Figure 1.4 Three Considerations Underlying the Societal Marketing Concept

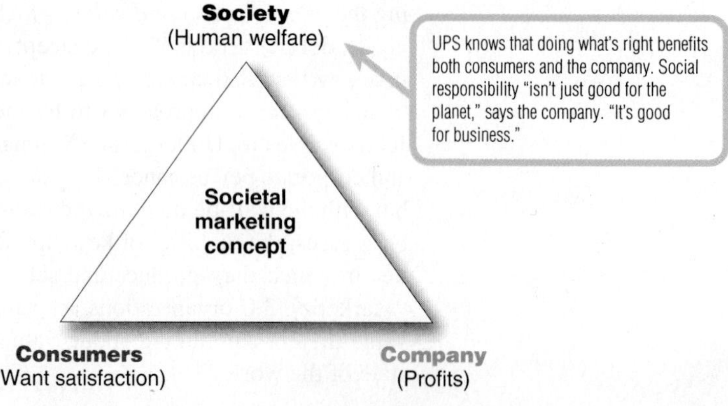
Society
(Human welfare)
Societal marketing concept
Consumers
(Want satisfaction)
Company
(Profits)
UPS knows that doing what's right benefits both consumers and the company. Social responsibility "isn't just good for the planet," says the company. "It's good for business."

SPEED BUMP LINKING THE CONCEPTS

Stop here for a moment and stretch your mind. What have you learned so far about marketing? For the moment, set aside the more formal definitions we've examined and try to develop your own understanding of marketing.

- In *your own words*, what *is* marketing? Write down *your* definition. Does your definition include such key concepts as customer value and relationships?
- What does marketing *mean* to you? How does it affect your daily life?
- What brand of athletic shoes did you purchase last? Describe your relationship with Nike, Adidas, Reebok, Puma, Converse, New Balance, or whatever brand of shoes you purchased.

Author Comment
Doing a good job with the first three steps in the marketing process sets the stage for step four, building and managing customer relationships.

Building Customer Relationships

The first three steps in the marketing process—understanding the marketplace and customer needs, designing a customer-driven marketing strategy, and constructing a marketing program—all lead up to the fourth and most important step: building and managing profitable customer relationships. We first discuss the basics of customer relationship management. Then, we examine how companies go about engaging customers on a deeper level in this age of digital and social marketing.

Customer Relationship Management

Customer relationship management
The overall process of building and maintaining profitable customer relationships by delivering superior customer value and satisfaction.

Customer relationship management is perhaps the most important concept of modern marketing. In the broadest sense, **customer relationship management** is the overall process of building and maintaining profitable customer relationships by delivering superior customer value and satisfaction. It deals with all aspects of acquiring, keeping, and growing customers.

Relationship Building Blocks: Customer Value and Satisfaction

The key to building lasting customer relationships is to create superior customer value and satisfaction. Satisfied customers are more likely to be loyal customers and give the company a larger share of their business.

Customer-perceived value
The customer's evaluation of the difference between all the benefits and all the costs of a marketing offer relative to those of competing offers.

Customer Value. Attracting and retaining customers can be a difficult task. Customers often face a bewildering array of products and services from which to choose. A customer buys from the firm that offers the highest **customer-perceived value**—the customer's evaluation of the difference between all the benefits and all the costs of a market offering relative to those of competing offers. Importantly, customers often do not judge values and costs "accurately" or "objectively." They act on *perceived* value.

To some consumers, value might mean sensible products at affordable prices. To other consumers, however, value might mean paying more to get more. For example, a top-of-the-line Weber Summit E-670 barbecue grill carries a suggested retail price of $2,600, more than five times the price of competitor Char-Broil's best grill. According to Weber, the stainless steel Summit grill "embraces true grilling luxury with the highest quality materials, exclusive features, and stunning looks." However, Weber's marketing also suggests that the grill is a real value, even at the premium price. For the money, you get practical features such as all-stainless-steel construction, spacious cooking and work areas, lighted control knobs, a tuck-away motorized rotisserie system, and an LED tank scale that lets you know how much propane you have left in the tank. Is the Weber Summit grill worth the premium price compared to less expensive grills? To many consumers, the answer is no. But to the target segment of affluent, hard-core grillers, the answer is yes.[13]

Customer satisfaction
The extent to which a product's perceived performance matches a buyer's expectations.

Customer Satisfaction. **Customer satisfaction** depends on the product's perceived performance relative to a buyer's expectations. If the product's performance falls short of expectations, the customer is dissatisfied. If performance matches expectations, the customer is satisfied. If performance exceeds expectations, the customer is highly satisfied or delighted.

Outstanding marketing companies go out of their way to keep important customers satisfied. Most studies show that higher levels of customer satisfaction lead to greater customer loyalty, which in turn results in better company performance. Smart companies aim to delight customers by promising only what they can deliver and then delivering more than they promise. Delighted customers not only make repeat purchases but also become willing marketing partners and "customer evangelists" who spread the word about their good experiences to others.

For companies interested in delighting customers, exceptional value and service become part of the overall company culture. For example, year after year, JetBlue ranks at or near the top of the airline industry in terms of customer satisfaction. » The company's slogan—"JetBlue: YOU ABOVE ALL"—tells customers that they are at the heart of the company's strategy and culture:[14]

> JetBlue has an evangelistic zeal for creating first-rate, customer-satisfying experiences. At JetBlue, customer care starts with basic amenities that exceed customer expectations, especially for a low-cost carrier—leather coach seats with extra leg room, free premium snacks, free satellite TV. But it's the *human* touch that really makes JetBlue special. JetBlue employees not only *know* the company's core values—safety, integrity, caring, passion, and fun—they *live* them. Those heart-felt values result in outstanding customer experiences, making JetBlue customers the most satisfied and enthusiastic of any in the airline industry.
>
> In fact, JetBlue often lets its customers do the talking. For example, its "Experience JetBlue" Web site and *Blue Tales* blog feature real first-person testimonials from devoted fans. And in a former advertising campaign, called "Sincerely, JetBlue," actual customers gave voice to specific service heroics by dedicated JetBlue employees. For example, customer Brian related how a JetBlue flight attendant dashed from the plane just before takeoff to retrieve a brand-new iPod he'd left in a rental car. And the Steins from Darien, Connecticut, told how they arrived late at night for a family vacation in Florida with their three very tired small children only to learn that their hotel wouldn't take them in. "Out of nowhere we heard a voice from behind us, go ahead, take my room," the Steins recalled. "A superhero in a JetBlue pilot's uniform, who sacrificed his room graciously, saved our night. And we slept like babies. Thank you, JetBlue." So, JetBlue really means it when it tells customers, YOU ABOVE ALL. It "gets us back to our DNA, our original mission, bringing humanity back to air travel," says JetBlue's senior VP of marketing.

» Creating customer satisfaction: JetBlue creates first-rate, customer-satisfying experiences. Its slogan—JetBlue: YOU ABOVE ALL—tells customers that they are at the very heart of JetBlue's strategy and culture.

JetBlue Airways.

Other companies that have become legendary for their service heroics include Zappos.com, The Ritz-Carlton Hotel Company, Amazon.com, and Nordstrom department stores (see Marketing at Work 1.1). However, a company doesn't need to have over-the-top service to create customer delight. For example, no-frills grocery chain Aldi has highly satisfied customers, even though they have to bag their own groceries and can't use credits cards. Aldi's everyday very low pricing on good-quality products delights customers and keeps them coming back. Thus, customer satisfaction comes not just from service heroics, but from how well a company delivers on its basic value proposition and helps customers solve their buying problems.

Although a customer-centered firm seeks to deliver high customer satisfaction relative to competitors, it does not

MARKETING AT WORK 1.1

Nordstrom: Taking Care of Customers No Matter What It Takes

Nordstrom is legendary for outstanding customer service. The upscale department store chain thrives on stories about its service heroics, such as employees dropping off orders at customers' homes or warming up their cars on a cold day while customers spend a little more time shopping. Then there's the one about the Nordstrom employee who split pairs of shoes in order to fit a man with different sized feet, or the sales clerk who ironed a new shirt for a customer who needed it for a meeting that afternoon. In another case, a man reportedly walked into Nordstrom to return a set of tires that he insisted he'd bought there. Nordstrom doesn't sell tires. But without hesitation, even though his receipt clearly indicated a different store, the Nordstrom clerk refunded the man's money out of her own pocket. Later, on her lunch hour, she took the tires and receipt to the store where they'd been purchased and got her money back.

Whether factual or fictional, such stories are rooted in actual customer experiences at Nordstrom. It seems that almost everyone who shops regularly at Nordstrom has their own favorite story to tell. As one journalist noted after seeing the chain near the top of yet another Customer Service Hall of Fame list, "It almost gets old: Nordstrom and its legendarily good customer service." But such stories never get old at Nordstrom.

Superb customer service is deeply rooted in the 100-year-old Nordstrom's DNA, as summarized in its staunchly held mantra: Take care of customers no matter what it takes. Although many companies pay homage to similar pronouncements hidden away in their mission statements, Nordstrom really means it—and really makes it happen. Consider these customer-delight-inducing stories:

- One man tells a story about his wife, a loyal Nordstrom customer, who died with $1,000 owing on her Nordstrom account. Not only did Nordstrom settle the account, it also sent flowers to the funeral.
- A woman had been shopping with her daughter at San Diego's ritzy Horton Plaza. After browsing in Nordstrom for a while and believing nobody was around, she said with an exhausted sigh, as if thinking out loud to herself, "I could sure use a Dr. Pepper." Sure enough, within only a few short minutes, a Nordstrom employee appeared out of nowhere with an ice-cold can of Dr. Pepper.
- One late November, a woman buying a sweater as a Christmas present for her husband found just the one she wanted at Nordstrom, but not in the right color or size. No worries, said the Nordstrom manager. He'd find her one in plenty of time for the holidays. A week before Christmas, just as the woman was beginning to worry, the manager called ahead and delivered the sweater to her home, already beautifully gift wrapped. That's amazing enough, but here's the back story: The manager hadn't been able to find the right sweater after all. But while discussing the problem with his wife, he learned that she'd already bought that very sweater for *him* for Christmas, and that it was already wrapped and under their tree. The manager and his wife quickly agreed to pass his sweater along to the customer.

How does Nordstrom consistently exceed customer expectations? For starters, it hires people who truly enjoy serving other people. Then, it trains them thoroughly on the intricacies of providing customer care and turns them loose. Nordstrom trusts its employees to make the right judgments without bogging them down with procedures and policies. The famous Nordstrom employee "handbook" consists of a single card containing only 75 words, among them: "Rule #1: Use best judgment in all situations. There will be no additional rules." As a result, at Nordstrom, customer service doesn't come across as sales clerks reciting rehearsed scripts. Rather, it's about Nordstrom people genuinely connecting with and serving customers.

To motivate its employees even more, Nordstrom collects and recycles stories of customer service heroics. Every Nordstrom register supplies pens and paper with which customers can share their good experiences. Every morning, in the main lobby of each store, managers share some of the best customer stories from the previous day and reward the employees involved for their good deeds. In turn, the feel-good stories inspire everyone in the store to continue the cycle of pampering customers and making them feel special.

Founded in 1901 by Swedish immigrant John W. Nordstrom, the company is now run by the fourth generation of Nordstroms—brothers Blake, Pete, and Erik and second-cousin

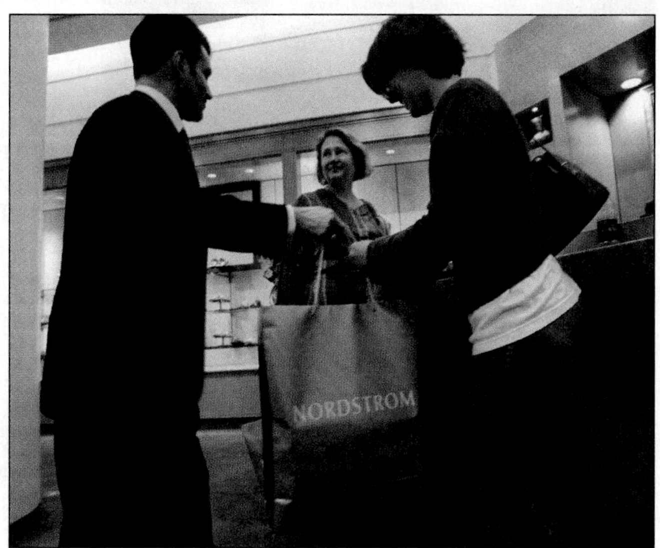

>> Delighting customers: Customer service is deeply rooted in Nordstrom's DNA, as summarized in its staunchly held mission: Take care of customers no matter what it takes.

Associated Press.

Jamie Nordstrom—in a way that would make their great-great-grandfather proud. This team of young executives is giving Nordstrom's ageless philosophy a dose of modern technology. For example, they recently restructured the chain's entire purchasing and inventory management system, making it easier for front-line employees to quickly find and obtain items that customers want. When the system went live, sales immediately surged. But more important, customer service improved dramatically. As Jamie Nordstrom puts it, "You are saying 'yes' to a customer more often."

Creating customer delight has been good for Nordstrom's bottom line over the years. Last year alone, even in the still-recovering post-recession retailing economy, Nordstrom's sales grew almost 12 percent to a record $12.1 billion. And while rival department stores have grown little or not at all, Nordstrom continued to gain market share with three straight years of growth.

As Erik Nordstrom shared these and other good tidings with shareholders at the most recent Nordstrom annual meeting, he also shared yet another story of customer delight. He told of a woman in North Carolina who recently lost the diamond from her wedding ring while trying on clothes at a Nordstrom store. A store security worker saw her crawling on the sales floor under the racks and joined the search. When they came up empty, the security employee enlisted the help of two building-services workers, who vacuumed the area and then opened the vacuum cleaner bags and painstakingly searched the contents, where they recovered the sparkling gem.

After showing a video clip featuring the delighted shopper, to thunderous applause, Erik Nordstrom introduced the three employees to the shareholders. Extending his hand to the three, Nordstrom proclaimed that when it comes to taking care of customers no matter what it takes, "this raises the bar."

Sources: Amy Martinez, "Tale of Lost Diamond Adds Glitter to Nordstrom's Customer Service," *Seattle Times,* May 11, 2011; Cotten Timberlake, "How Nordstrom Bests Its Retail Rivals," *Bloomberg Businessweek,* August 11, 2011, www.businessweek.com/magazine/how-nordstrom-bests-its-retail-rivals-08112011.html; "Legends of Unbelievable Nordstrom Service," *Toddand.com,* February 18, 2007, http://toddand.com/2007/02/18/legends-of-unbelievable-nordstrom-service/; Karen Aho, "The 2012 Customer Service Hall of Fame," *MSNMoney,* http://money.msn.com/investing/2012-customer-service-hall-of-fame-1; Christian Conte, "Nordstrom Customer Service Tales Not Just Legend," *Business Journal,* September 7, 2012, www.bizjournals.com/jacksonville/blog/retail_radar/2012/09/nordstrom-tales-of-legendary-customer.html?page=all; and http://shop.nordstrom.com/c/company-history, accessed November 2013.

attempt to *maximize* customer satisfaction. A company can always increase customer satisfaction by lowering its prices or increasing its services. But this may result in lower profits. Thus, the purpose of marketing is to generate customer value profitably. This requires a very delicate balance: The marketer must continue to generate more customer value and satisfaction but not "give away the house."

Customer Relationship Levels and Tools

Companies can build customer relationships at many levels, depending on the nature of the target market. At one extreme, a company with many low-margin customers may seek to develop *basic relationships* with them. For example, Procter & Gamble's Tide detergent does not phone or call on all of its consumers to get to know them personally. Instead, Tide creates relationships through brand-building advertising, Web sites, and social media presence. At the other extreme, in markets with few customers and high margins, sellers want to create *full partnerships* with key customers. For example, P&G sales representatives work closely with the Walmart, Kroger, and other large retailers that sell Tide. In between these two extremes, other levels of customer relationships are appropriate.

Relationship marketing tools: The MyPanera loyalty rewards program not only lets Panera track individual customer purchases, it also lets the company build unique relationships with each MyPanera member.

Courtesy of Gary Armstrong.

Beyond offering consistently high value and satisfaction, marketers can use specific marketing tools to develop stronger bonds with customers. For example, many companies offer *frequency marketing programs* that reward customers who buy frequently or in large amounts. Airlines offer frequent-flyer programs, hotels give room upgrades to frequent guests, and supermarkets give patronage discounts to "very important customers." These days almost every brand has a loyalty rewards program. For example, fast-casual restaurant Panera has a MyPanera loyalty program that surprises frequent customers with things like complimentary bakery-café items, exclusive tastings and demonstrations, and invitations to special events. Almost half of all Panera purchases are logged on MyPanera cards. The program not only lets Panera track individual customer purchases, it also lets the company build unique relationships with each MyPanera member.[15]

Other companies sponsor *club marketing programs* that offer members special benefits and create member communities. For example, Apple encourages customers to form local Apple user groups. More than 800 registered Apple user groups worldwide offer monthly meetings, a newsletter, advice on technical issues, training classes, product discounts, and a forum for swapping ideas and stories with like-minded Apple fans. Similarly, buy one of those Weber grills and you can join the Weber Nation—"the site for real people who love their Weber grills." Membership gets you exclusive access to online grilling classes, an interactive recipe box, grilling tips and 24/7 telephone support, audio and video podcasts, straight-talk forums for interacting with other grilling fanatics, and even a chance to star in a Weber TV commercial. "Become a spatula-carrying member today," says Weber.[16]

Engaging Customers

Significant changes are occurring in the nature of customer brand relationships. Today's digital technologies—the Internet and the surge in online, mobile, and social media—have profoundly changed the ways that people on the planet relate to one another. In turn, these events have had a huge impact on how companies and brands connect with customers, and how customers connect with and influence each other's brand behaviors.

Customer Engagement and Today's Digital and Social Media

The digital age has spawned a dazzling set of new customer relationship–building tools, from Web sites, online ads and videos, mobile ads and apps, and blogs to online communities and the major social media, such as Twitter, Facebook, YouTube, Instagram, and Pinterest.

Yesterday's companies focused mostly on mass marketing to broad segments of customers at arm's length. By contrast, today's companies are using online, mobile, and social media to refine their targeting and to engage customers more deeply and interactively. The *old marketing* involved marketing brands *to* consumers. The *new marketing* is **customer-engagement marketing**—fostering direct and continuous customer involvement in shaping brand conversations, brand experiences, and brand community. Customer-engagement marketing goes beyond just selling a brand to consumers. Its goal is to make the brand a meaningful part of consumers' conversations and lives.

Customer-engagement marketing
Making the brand a meaningful part of consumers' conversations and lives by fostering direct and continuous customer involvement in shaping brand conversations, experiences, and community.

The burgeoning Internet and social media have given a huge boost to customer-engagement marketing. Today's consumers are better informed, more connected, and more empowered than ever before. Newly empowered consumers have more information about brands, and they have a wealth of digital platforms for airing and sharing their brand views with others. Thus, marketers are now embracing not only customer relationship management, but also *customer-managed relationships,* in which customers connect with companies and with each other to help forge their own brand experiences.

Greater consumer empowerment means that companies can no longer rely on marketing by *intrusion*. Instead, they must practice marketing by *attraction*—creating market offerings and messages that engage consumers rather than interrupt them. Hence, most marketers now augment their mass-media marketing efforts with a rich mix of online, mobile, and social media marketing that promotes brand–consumer engagement and conversation.

For example, companies post their latest ads and videos on social media sites, hoping they'll go viral. They maintain an extensive presence on Twitter, YouTube, Facebook, Google+, Pinterest, and other social media to create brand buzz. They launch their own blogs, mobile apps, online microsites, and consumer-generated review systems, all with the aim of engaging customers on a more personal, interactive level.

Take Twitter, for example. Organizations ranging from Dell, JetBlue, and Dunkin' Donuts to the Chicago Bulls, NASCAR, and the Los Angeles Fire Department have created Twitter pages and promotions. They use "tweets" to start conversations with and between Twitter's more than 500 million registered users, address customer service issues, research customer reactions, and drive traffic to relevant articles, Web and mobile marketing sites, contests, videos, and other brand activities.

Similarly, almost every company has something going on Facebook these days. Starbucks has more than 34 million Facebook "fans"; Coca-Cola has more than 61 million. And every major marketer has a YouTube channel where the brand and its fans post current ads and other entertaining or informative videos. Artful use of the social media can get consumers involved with and talking about a brand.

Customer engagement and social media: Hertz's "Share It Up" social media campaign gave larger discounts to customers who shared Hertz coupons with social network friends. At least 45 percent of users who saw the coupons ended up sharing them.

Hertz System, Inc.

Rental car company Hertz uses a broad range of digital and social media to engage its customers and boost sales:[17]

> A recent Hertz study found that consumers who engage in social conversations about the brand are 30 percent more likely to make a purchase than those who don't. And customers who engage in Hertz-related social activity in early stages of the rental process are four times more likely to visit Hertz's Web site. So, Hertz now incorporates social media in almost all of its marketing, such as Twitter hashtags, links to major social media, and sharing features. For example, Hertz's Twitter feed is a 140-character customer-service line that tends to each problem and question posted by members. On the brand's Facebook and Google+ pages, Hertz posts specials, such as waiving the young driver fee for car rentals during the spring break season. On its "Traveling at the Speed of Hertz" YouTube channel, Hertz posts its latest commercials as well as videos about new features such as its Express-Rent Interactive Kiosks. More than just creating conversations, Hertz also uses the social media to help build sales. Last year, the brand ran a "Share It Up" campaign on Facebook using social coupons to increase visibility. Users who shared the coupons with friends on Facebook and other social networks earned larger discounts based on how often they shared the coupon with friends. At least 45 percent of users who saw the coupon ended up sharing it.

The key to engagement marketing is to find ways to enter consumers' conversations with engaging and relevant brand messages. Simply posting a humorous video, creating a social media page, or hosting a blog isn't enough. Successful engagement marketing means making relevant and genuine contributions to consumers' lives and conversations. According to David Oksman, chief marketer for T-shirt and apparel maker Life is good, engagement and the social media are "about deep meaningful relationships that go beyond the product you are selling. The real depth of engagement is in the commenting and community that go on [around the brand]" (see Marketing at Work 1.2).[18]

Consumer-Generated Marketing?

Consumer-generated marketing
Brand exchanges created by consumers themselves—both invited and uninvited—by which consumers are playing an increasing role in shaping their own brand experiences and those of other consumers.

A growing form of customer-engagement marketing is **consumer-generated marketing**, by which consumers themselves are playing a bigger role in shaping their own brand experiences and those of others. This might happen through uninvited consumer-to-consumer exchanges in blogs, video-sharing sites, social media, and other digital forums. But increasingly, companies themselves are inviting consumers to play a more active role in shaping products and brand content.

Some companies ask consumers for new product and service ideas. For example, at its My Starbucks Idea site, Starbucks collects ideas from customers on new products, store changes, and just about anything else that might make their Starbucks experience better. "You know better than anyone else what you want from Starbucks," says the company at the Web site. "So tell us. What's your Starbucks idea? Revolutionary or simple—we want to hear it." The site invites customer to share their ideas, vote on and discuss the ideas of others, and see which ideas Starbucks has implemented.[19]

Other companies are inviting customers to play an active role in shaping ads. For example, for the past seven years, PepsiCo's Doritos brand has held a "Crash the Super Bowl" contest in which it invites 30-second ads from consumers and runs the best ones during the game. The consumer-generated ads have been a huge success. Last year, from more than 3,500 entries, Doritos aired two fan-produced ads during the Super Bowl. Past campaigns have produced numerous top-place finishers in the *USA Today* Ad Meter rankings, earning their creators $1 million in cash prizes from PepsiCo's Frito-Lay division. Both of last year's ads finished in the top six, and the contest was again deemed a huge success. For the first time, Doritos moved the campaign from the brand's Web site to Facebook. Thanks to Facebook's viral capabilities, the five finalist Doritos ads captured more than 100 million views. In addition, the number of Doritos Facebook fans pushed past the 4 million mark during the campaign. According to Frito-Lay's

MARKETING AT WORK 1.2

Life is good: Engaging Customers and Spreading Optimism

Building customer engagement may sound simple at first. But meaningful engagement involves much more than just tacking a buzzword onto a mission statement or setting up social media pages. The fibers of true customer engagement are woven deeply into the company and brand culture.

For starters, a brand must have a story to tell—an authentic, engagement-worthy sense of purpose that goes beyond the product. Then, rather than force-feeding the brand to customers, the company must engage them on their own terms, letting them help shape and share their own brand experiences. Finally, weaving the brand into customers' lives requires going where customers congregate. Increasingly, that means meeting up with customers in the digital world with online and social media.

All of these customer-engagement essentials seem to come naturally to T-shirt and apparel maker Life is good. The brand was founded with a deeply felt sense of purpose: spreading the power of optimism. "Optimism is where everything begins for us," says David Oksman, head of marketing at Life is good. "Optimism is not a strategy. It's ingrained in who we are."

In fact, Life is good doesn't even consider itself a clothing company. Instead, it's a lifestyle brand that spreads the power of optimism. As Oksman puts it, "Many companies might say, 'We have a great T-shirt, it's good quality, and it's got a fun saying on it.' That's not how we think. For us, it's rallying people around the belief [in] the power of optimism . . . everything spirals out from there." The company backs its optimism philosophy with good deeds. For example, it donates 10 percent of its net profits each year to the Life is good Foundation to help kids in need.

It all started with founders Bert and John Jacobs selling T-shirts out of an old van at colleges and street fairs. After five years, with little to show for their efforts and on the verge of closing up shop, the brothers gathered friends at their apartment to get feedback on a new set of designs. The friends overwhelmingly chose Jake—the now-familiar beret-wearing, happy-go-lucky stick figure—and the slogan, "Life is good." Jake has now become a pop-culture icon. And the company's apparel has become a canvas for the optimistic Life is good message.

Life is good's infectious philosophy is a powerfully engaging one that people want to embrace and pass along to others. As Oksman explains, "The brand is about helping people to open up, create relationships, and connect with other people. We think engagement . . . spreading optimism . . . is what we do."

Such fundamental Life is good concepts—connecting, sharing, spreading optimism—don't lend themselves well to traditional apparel marketing that pushes products and messages out to the masses. Instead, the Jacobs brothers understood that nurturing the Life is good brand would require letting customers interact with and share the brand on their own terms. For example, every year the brand holds a Life is good Festival that draws tens of thousands of fans with family-friendly activities and an all-star entertainment lineup.

More recently, as all things digital have exploded onto the marketing scene, online and social media have become a perfect fit for sharing the Life is good mission with customers. Today, the company fosters a community of Optimists with more than 1.7 million Facebook fans, 172,000 Twitter followers, 34 Pinterest boards, and an active YouTube channel. Life is good Radio provides a 24/7 playlist, because—as the site tells us—"Good tunes and good vibes go hand in hand."

But the strongest platform for engaging customers is the brand's own Web site, Lifeisgood.com. For example, the site's "Good Vibes" section gives brand fans a "breath of fresh share." One of the most active customer-engagement sites found anywhere online, Good Vibes is home to a thriving community of optimists. It's a place where fans can share photos, videos, and stories showing the brand's role in their trials, triumphs, and optimism. The postings illustrate the depth of engagement and inspiration the Life is good brand engenders. Here are just a few examples from the hundreds, even thousands, of user-generated postings you'll find at the Lifeisgood.com Good Vibes section:

- *Jake and Jackie.* A photo of a couple's forearms, one featuring a colorful tattoo of Jake, the other a tattoo of his female counterpart Jackie, each with the Life is good tagline. "Here are pictures of our tattoos," says the couple. "Life is truly good!"

>> Engaging customers: Life is good starts with a deeply felt, engagement-worthy sense of purpose: spreading the power of optimism. Then, "the real depth of engagement is in the commenting and community that go on around the brand."

The Life is good Company.

- *Love Is in the Air.* A couple holding up a Life is good banner, proclaiming "We used this pic [to spread] news of our engagement!!"
- *Thanks from Sebeta!* A picture of two young boys with the caption, "A couple of the blind students at the Sebeta School for the Blind in Sebeta, Ethiopia, rocking in their new Life is good shirts!"
- *Snow Shoeing the Winter Away.* A picture posted by a registered nurse from northeast Washington of herself in a wintery forest. "At age 54 I learned to downhill ski," she says, "and this year, at age 59, I put on my first pair of snowshoes. As an RN for 40 years, I have seen way too many lives end early. So to honor those [whose] years were short, I am living my life to the fullest and it is good!"
- *All the Way Full.* A photo of a family of four on the beach accompanied by this story: "Throughout my Grace's treatment for a malignant brain tumor, we looked for silver linings. A friend gave me one of your shirts—HALF FULL—and it entered heavy rotation in my wardrobe. Grace loves the softness of the shirt, which was particularly nice against chemo-sore skin. Though only five at the time of her diagnosis, Grace understood fully the meaning of the shirt, and declared, "But Mommy, you're not HALF FULL, you're ALL THE WAY FULL!" And so ALL THE WAY FULL is how we're getting through cancer. This June, Grace will be two years beyond the end of treatment. We wanted to make sure you knew the significance your positivity has played in our lives."

These kinds of interactions from brand lovers are customer engagement at its best. In the end, the brand belongs to those who use and share it. Says Oksman, "We don't solicit [the stories] at all. Ultimately, we don't own optimism, our community does. So we want to create tools to let our consumers engage." True engagement is "about deep meaningful relationships that go beyond the product you are selling. The real depth of engagement is in the commenting and community that go on [around the brand]."

Today, Life is good products are sold at more than 3,500 retailers nationwide, including six company-owned stores and the Lifeisgood.com Web site. The privately owned company's revenues are estimated at well over $100 million per year. But the brand's impact on its customers' lives goes well beyond its sales revenues. If optimism sells, so does customer engagement. For both the brand and its customers, Life is good.

Sources: Based on information from Gordon Wyner, "Getting Engaged," *Marketing Management*, Fall 2012, pp. 4–9; Bob Garfield and Doug Levy, "The Dawn of the Relationship Era," *Advertising Age*, January 2, 2012, pp. 1, 8–11; David Aponovich, "Powered by People, Fueled by Optimism," *Fast Company*, July 18, 2012, www.fastcompany.com/1842834/life-good-powered-people-fueled-optimism; "Bert and John Jacobs Deliver Commencement Address at 94th Annual Bentley University Ceremony," *Wall Street Journal*, March 18, 2012, http://online.wsj.com/article/PR-CO-20130318-909680.html?mod=crnews; and www.lifeisgood.com and www.lifeisgood.com/good-vibes/, accessed November 2013.

VP of marketing, "People like to talk about the videos, and [Facebook] reaches their circle of friends." The real value of such engagement lies in the fact that consumers are seeking out and sharing the brand messages rather than being unwilling recipients.[20]

Despite the successes, however, harnessing consumer-generated content can be a time-consuming and costly process, and companies may find it difficult to glean even a little gold from all the garbage. » For example, when Heinz invited consumers to submit homemade ads for its ketchup on its YouTube page, it ended up sifting through more than 8,000 entries, of which it posted nearly 4,000. Some of the amateur ads were very good—entertaining and potentially effective. Most, however, were so-so at best, and others were downright dreadful. In one ad, a contestant chugged ketchup straight from the bottle. In another, the would-be filmmaker brushed his teeth, washed his hair, and shaved his face with Heinz's product.[21]

» Harnessing consumer-generated marketing: When H.J. Heinz invited consumers to submit homemade ads for its ketchup brand on YouTube, it received more than 8,000 entries—some very good but most only so-so or even downright dreadful.

AJ Mast/The New York Times/Redux Pictures.

As consumers become more connected and empowered, and as the boom in digital and social media technologies continues, consumer brand engagement—whether invited by marketers or not—will be an increasingly important marketing force. Through a profusion of consumer-generated videos, shared reviews, blogs, apps, and Web sites, consumers are playing a growing role in shaping their own and other consumers' brand experiences. Engaged consumers are now having a say in everything from product design, usage, and packaging to brand messaging, pricing, and distribution. Brands must embrace this new consumer empowerment and master the new digital and social media relationship tools or risk being left behind.

Partner Relationship Management

When it comes to creating customer value and building strong customer relationships, today's marketers know that they can't go it alone. They must work closely with a variety of marketing partners. In addition to being good at *customer relationship management,* marketers must also be good at **partner relationship management**—working closely with others inside and outside the company to jointly bring more value to customers.

Partner relationship management
Working closely with partners in other company departments and outside the company to jointly bring greater value to customers.

Traditionally, marketers have been charged with understanding customers and representing customer needs to different company departments. However, in today's more connected world, every functional area in the organization can interact with customers. The new thinking is that—no matter what your job is in a company—you must understand marketing and be customer focused. Rather than letting each department go its own way, firms must link all departments in the cause of creating customer value.

Marketers must also partner with suppliers, channel partners, and others outside the company. Marketing channels consist of distributors, retailers, and others who connect the company to its buyers. The *supply chain* describes a longer channel, stretching from raw materials to components to final products that are carried to final buyers. Through *supply chain management*, companies today are strengthening their connections with partners all along the supply chain. They know that their fortunes rest on more than just how well they perform. Success at delivering customer value rests on how well their entire supply chain performs against competitors' supply chains.

Author Comment
Look back at Figure 1.1. In the first four steps of the marketing process, the company creates value *for* target customers and builds strong relationships with them. If it does that well, it can capture value *from* customers in return, in the form of loyal customers who buy and continue to buy the company's brands.

Capturing Value from Customers

The first four steps in the marketing process outlined in Figure 1.1 involve building customer relationships by creating and delivering superior customer value. The final step involves capturing value in return in the form of sales, market share, and profits. By creating superior customer value, the firm creates highly satisfied customers who stay loyal and buy more. This, in turn, means greater long-run returns for the firm. Here, we discuss the outcomes of creating customer value: customer loyalty and retention, share of market and share of customer, and customer equity.

Creating Customer Loyalty and Retention

Good customer relationship management creates customer satisfaction. In turn, satisfied customers remain loyal and talk favorably to others about the company and its products. Studies show big differences in the loyalty of customers who are less satisfied, somewhat satisfied, and completely satisfied. Even a slight drop from complete satisfaction can create an enormous drop in loyalty. Thus, the aim of customer relationship management is to create not only customer satisfaction but also customer delight.

Keeping customers loyal makes good economic sense. Loyal customers spend more and stay around longer. Research also shows that it's five times cheaper to keep an old customer than acquire a new one. Conversely, customer defections can be costly. Losing a customer means losing more than a single sale. It means losing the entire stream of purchases that the customer would make over a lifetime of patronage. For example, here is a classic illustration of **customer lifetime value**:[22]

Customer lifetime value
The value of the entire stream of purchases a customer makes over a lifetime of patronage.

> Stew Leonard, who operates a highly profitable four-store supermarket in Connecticut and New York, once said that he sees $50,000 flying out of his store every time he sees a sulking customer. Why? Because his average customer spends about $100 a week, shops 50 weeks a year, and remains in the area for about 10 years. If this customer has an unhappy experience and switches to another supermarket, Stew Leonard's has lost $50,000 in lifetime revenue. The loss can be much greater if the disappointed customer shares the bad experience with other customers and causes them to defect.
>
> To keep customers coming back, Stew Leonard's has created what the *New York Times* has dubbed the "Disneyland of Dairy Stores," complete with costumed characters, scheduled entertainment, a petting zoo, and animatronics throughout the store. From its humble beginnings as a small dairy store in 1969, Stew Leonard's has grown at an amazing pace. It's built 29 additions onto the

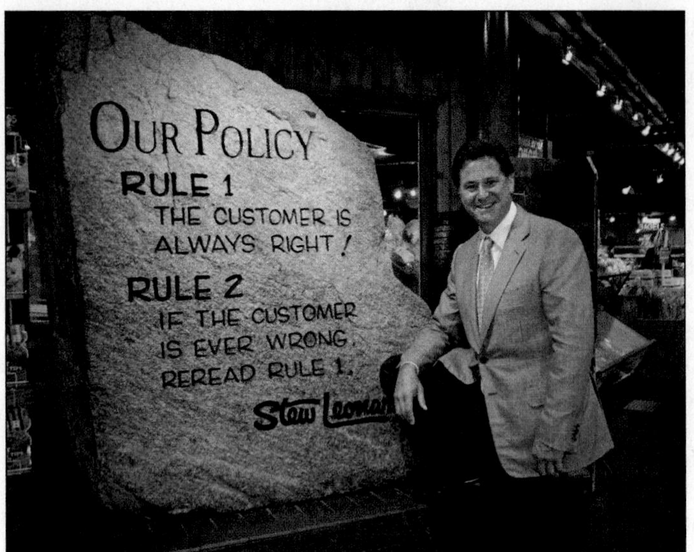

Customer lifetime value: To keep customers coming back, Stew Leonard's has created the "Disneyland of dairy stores." Rule #1—The customer is always right. Rule #2—If the customer is ever wrong, reread Rule #1.

Courtesy of Stew Leonard's.

original store, which now serves more than 300,000 customers each week. This legion of loyal shoppers is largely a result of the store's passionate approach to customer service. "Rule #1: The customer is always right. Rule #2: If the customer is ever wrong, reread rule #1."

Stew Leonard is not alone in assessing customer lifetime value. Lexus, for example, estimates that a single satisfied and loyal customer is worth more than $600,000 in lifetime sales. And the estimated lifetime value of a young mobile phone consumer is $26,000.[23] In fact, a company can lose money on a specific transaction but still benefit greatly from a long-term relationship. This means that companies must aim high in building customer relationships. Customer delight creates an emotional relationship with a brand, not just a rational preference. And that relationship keeps customers coming back.

Growing Share of Customer

Beyond simply retaining good customers to capture customer lifetime value, good customer relationship management can help marketers increase their **share of customer**—the share they get of the customer's purchasing in their product categories. Thus, banks want to increase "share of wallet." Supermarkets and restaurants want to get more "share of stomach." Car companies want to increase "share of garage," and airlines want greater "share of travel."

Share of customer
The portion of the customer's purchasing that a company gets in its product categories.

To increase share of customer, firms can offer greater variety to current customers. Or they can create programs to cross-sell and up-sell to market more products and services to existing customers. For example, Amazon.com is highly skilled at leveraging relationships with its 188 million customers to increase its share of each customer's spending budget:[24]

> Once they log onto Amazon.com, customers often buy more than they intend. And Amazon does all it can to help make that happen. The online giant continues to broaden its merchandise assortment, creating an ideal spot for one-stop shopping. And based on each customer's purchase and search history, the company recommends related products that might be of interest. This recommendation system influences up to 30 percent of all sales. Amazon's ingenious Amazon Prime two-day shipping program has also helped boost its share of customers' wallets. For an annual fee of $79, Prime members receive delivery of all their purchases within two days, whether it's a single paperback book or a 60-inch HDTV. According to one analyst, the ingenious Amazon Prime program "converts casual shoppers, who gorge on the gratification of having purchases reliably appear two days after the order, into Amazon addicts." As a result, after signing up for Prime, shoppers more than triple their annual Amazon.com purchases. A Prime member is about eight times more valuable to Amazon than a non-Prime member.

Building Customer Equity

We can now see the importance of not only acquiring customers but also keeping and growing them. The value of a company comes from the value of its current and future customers. Customer relationship management takes a long-term view. Companies want not only to create profitable customers but also "own" them for life, earn a greater share of their purchases, and capture their customer lifetime value.

What Is Customer Equity?

Customer equity
The total combined customer lifetime values of all of the company's customers.

The ultimate aim of customer relationship management is to produce high *customer equity*.[25] **Customer equity** is the total combined customer lifetime values of all of the company's current and potential customers. As such, it's a measure of the future value of the company's customer base. Clearly, the more loyal the firm's profitable customers, the higher its customer equity. Customer equity may be a better measure of a firm's performance than current sales or market share. Whereas sales and market share reflect the past, customer equity suggests the future. Consider Cadillac:[26]

Managing customer equity: To increase customer lifetime value, Cadillac is trying to make the Caddy cool again with edgier, high-performance designs that target a younger generation of consumers.

© Transtock/Corbis.

In the 1970s and 1980s, Cadillac had some of the most loyal customers in the industry. To an entire generation of car buyers, the name *Cadillac* defined "The Standard of the World." Cadillac's share of the luxury car market reached a whopping 51 percent in 1976, and based on market share and sales, the brand's future looked rosy. However, measures of customer equity would have painted a bleaker picture. Cadillac customers were getting older (average age 60) and average customer lifetime value was falling. Many Cadillac buyers were on their last cars. Thus, although Cadillac's market share was good, its customer equity was not.

Compare this with BMW. Its more youthful and vigorous image didn't win BMW the early market share war. However, it did win BMW younger customers (average age about 40) with higher customer lifetime values. The result: In the years that followed, BMW's market share and profits soared while Cadillac's fortunes eroded badly. BMW overtook Cadillac in the 1980s. In recent years, Cadillac has struggled to make the Caddy cool again with edgier, high-performance designs that target a younger generation of consumers. The brand now positions itself as "The New Standard of the World" with marketing pitches based on "power, performance, and design." However, for the past decade, Cadillac's share of the luxury car market has stagnated. The moral: Marketers should care not just about current sales and market share. Customer lifetime value and customer equity are the name of the game.

Building the Right Relationships with the Right Customers

Companies should manage customer equity carefully. They should view customers as assets that need to be managed and maximized. But not all customers, not even all loyal customers, are good investments. Surprisingly, some loyal customers can be unprofitable, and some disloyal customers can be profitable. Which customers should the company acquire and retain?

The company can classify customers according to their potential profitability and manage its relationships with them accordingly. **Figure 1.5** classifies customers into one of four relationship groups, according to their profitability and projected loyalty.[27] Each group requires a different relationship management strategy. *Strangers* show low potential profitability and little projected loyalty. There is little fit between the company's offerings and their needs. The relationship management strategy for these customers is simple: Don't invest anything in them.

Butterflies are potentially profitable but not loyal. There is a good fit between the company's offerings and their needs. However, like real butterflies, we can enjoy them for only a short while and then they're gone. An example is stock market investors who trade shares often and in large amounts but who enjoy hunting out the best deals without building a regular relationship with any single brokerage company. Efforts to convert butterflies into loyal customers are rarely successful. Instead, the company should enjoy the butterflies for the moment. It should create satisfying and profitable transactions with them, capturing as much of their business as possible in the short time during which they buy from the company. Then, it should cease investing in them until the next time around.

True friends are both profitable and loyal. There is a strong fit between their needs and the company's offerings. The firm wants to make continuous relationship investments to delight these customers and nurture, retain, and grow them. It wants to turn true friends into *true believers*, who come back regularly and tell others about their good experiences with the company.

Barnacles are highly loyal but not very profitable. There is a limited fit between their needs and the company's offerings. An example is smaller bank customers who bank regularly but do not generate enough returns to cover the costs of maintaining their accounts. Like barnacles on the hull of a ship, they create drag. Barnacles are perhaps the most problematic customers. The company might be able to improve their profitability by selling them more, raising their fees, or reducing service to them. However, if they cannot be made profitable, they should be "fired."

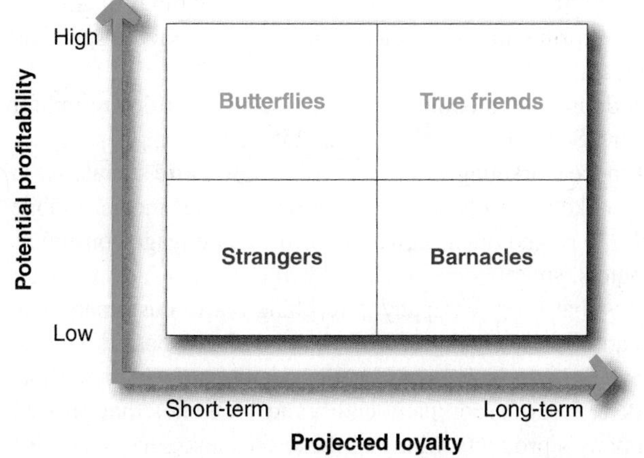

Figure 1.5 Customer Relationship Groups

The point here is an important one: Different types of customers require different relationship management strategies. The goal is to build the *right relationships* with the *right customers.*

SPEED BUMP LINKING THE CONCEPTS

We've covered a lot of ground. Again, pause for a moment and develop *your own* thoughts about marketing.

- In *your own words,* what *is* marketing and what does it seek to accomplish?
- How well does Nordstrom manage its relationships with customers? What customer relationship management strategy does it use? What relationship management strategy does Walmart use?
- Think of a company for which you are a "true friend." What strategy does this company use to manage its relationship with you?

Author Comment
Marketing doesn't take place in a vacuum. Now that we've discussed the five steps in the marketing process, let's look at how the ever-changing marketplace affects both consumers and the marketers who serve them. We'll look more deeply into these and other marketing environment factors in Chapter 3.

The Changing Marketing Landscape

Every day, dramatic changes are occurring in the marketplace. Richard Love of HP observed, "The pace of change is so rapid that the ability to change has now become a competitive advantage." Yogi Berra, the legendary New York Yankees catcher and manager, summed it up more simply when he said, "The future ain't what it used to be." As the marketplace changes, so must those who serve it.

In this section, we examine the major trends and forces that are changing the marketing landscape and challenging marketing strategy. We look at five major developments: the digital age, the changing economic environment, the growth of not-for-profit marketing, rapid globalization, and the call for more ethics and social responsibility.

The Digital Age: Online, Mobile, and Social Media Marketing

The explosive growth in digital technology has fundamentally changed the way we live—how we communicate, share information, access entertainment, and shop. By 2016, an estimated 3 billion people—more than 40 percent of the world's population—will be online. A majority of them will be using smartphones and other mobile devices to access the Web. Nearly half of all American adults now own smartphones; 50 percent of those adults use their smartphones to access social media sites. These numbers will only grow as digital technology rockets into the future.[28]

Most consumers are totally smitten with all things digital. For example, according to one study, more than half of Americans keep their mobile phone next to them when they sleep—they say it's the first thing they touch when they get up in the morning and the last thing they touch at night. Favorite online and mobile destinations include the profusion of Web sites and social media that have sprung up. Americans who use social media spend an average of 3.2 hours per day doing so.[29]

Digital and social media marketing
Using digital marketing tools such as Web sites, social media, mobile apps and ads, online video, e-mail, and blogs that engage consumers anywhere, at any time, via their digital devices.

The consumer love affair with digital and mobile technology makes it fertile ground for marketers trying to engage customers. So it's no surprise that the Internet and rapid advances in digital and social media have taken the marketing world by storm. **Digital and social media marketing** involves using digital marketing tools such as Web sites, social media, mobile ads and apps, online video, e-mail, blogs, and other digital platforms that engage consumers anywhere, anytime via their computers, smartphones, tablets, Internet-ready TVs, and other digital devices. These days, it seems that every company is reaching out to customers with multiple Web sites, newsy Tweets and Facebook pages, viral ads and videos posted on YouTube, rich-media e-mails, and mobile apps that solve consumer problems and help them shop.

At the most basic level, marketers set up company and brand Web sites that provide information and promote the company's products. Many of these sites also serve as online brand communities, where customers can congregate and exchange brand-related interests and information. For example, Mountain Dew's "This Is How We Dew" Web site serves as a lifestyle hub where the brand's super-passionate fans can check out the latest Mountain Dew ads and videos, vote on new flavors, follow the adventures of Mountain Dew's amateur skateboarding team, "chase the taste" with NASCAR driver Dale Earnhardt, Jr., or just check out the Mountain Dew product lineup.[30]

Beyond brand Web sites, most companies are also integrating social and mobile media into their marketing mixes.

Social Media Marketing

It's hard to find a brand Web site, or even a traditional media ad, that doesn't feature links to the brand's Facebook, Twitter, Google+, YouTube, Pinterest, Instagram, or other social media sites. The social media provide exciting opportunities to extend customer engagement and get people talking about a brand. » Nearly 90 percent of all U.S. companies now use social media as part of their marketing mixes. By various estimates, social media spending accounts for about 10 percent of marketing budgets and will rise to an estimated nearly 20 percent within the next five years.[31]

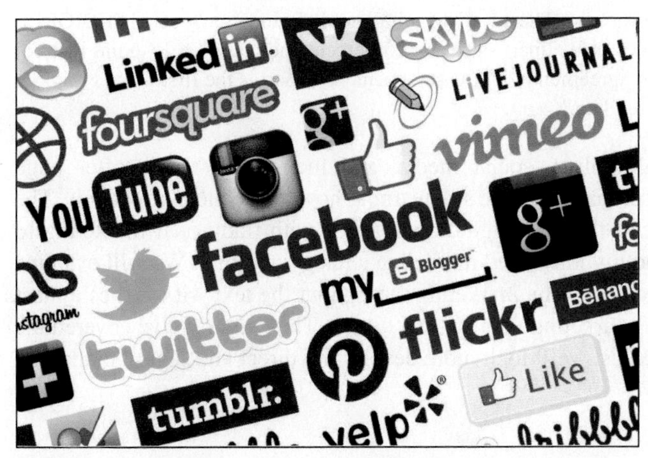

» **Social media marketing: 90 percent of all U.S. companies now use social media. It's hard to find a brand that doesn't feature Facebook, Twitter, Google+, Pinterest, Instagram, YouTube, and other social media sites.**

© Anatolii Babii/Alamy.

Some social media are huge—Facebook has more than 1 billion members; Twitter has more than 500 million registered users. Reddit, the online social news community, has nearly 63 million unique visitors a month from 174 countries. But more focused social media sites are also thriving, such as CafeMom, an online community of 10 million moms who exchange advice, entertainment, and commiseration at the community's online, Facebook, Twitter, Pinterest, YouTube, Google+, and mobile sites. Online social networks provide a digital home where people can connect and share important information and moments in their lives.

Using the social media might involve something as simple as a contest or promotion to garner Facebook Likes, Tweets, or YouTube postings. For example, when Boylan Bottling Company ran Facebook promotions giving free bottles of its Shirley Temple soda to consumers who shared the promotion with others, Facebook chatter about the brand jumped to five times normal. But more than just "Likes," "tweets," or video posts, the goal of most social media campaigns is *social sharing,* getting people to talk with others and pass along their positive brand experiences. As Boylan Bottling's CEO puts it: "We've done some advertising to get Facebook likes, . . . but we've found that Facebook is a better place to percolate a frenzy around our brand."[32]

Method, maker of eco-friendly household cleaning and personal care products, relies *exclusively* on social media to promote its products and engage customers. Its quirky, zero-dollar global brand campaign—Clean Happy—is built entirely around 90-second brand videos posted on YouTube, Facebook, Twitter, and Method's blogger network. "We are the people against dirty," the videos proclaim. "Join us and clean happy." The social media work well for smaller brands like Method, which has an engaging eco-based story to tell. "The brands we compete against thrive in a 30-second spot world, . . . but we can't afford to go there yet," says Method's cofounder Eric Ryan. However, "brands [like ours] that have stories to tell have an advantage [in social media]."[33]

Mobile Marketing

Mobile marketing is perhaps that fastest-growing digital marketing platform. Twenty-nine percent of smartphone owners use their phones for shopping-related activities—browsing product information through apps or the mobile Web, making in-store price comparisons, reading online product reviews, finding and redeeming coupons, and more.[34] Smartphones are ever-present, always on, finely targeted, and highly personal. This makes them ideal for engaging customers anytime, anywhere as they move through the buying process. For example, Starbucks customers can use their mobile devices for everything from finding the nearest Starbucks and learning about new products to placing and paying for orders.

Marketers use mobile channels to stimulate immediate buying, make shopping easier, enrich the brand experience, or all of these. For example, P&G recently used mobile marketing to boost sampling through vending machines—called Freebies—that it placed in

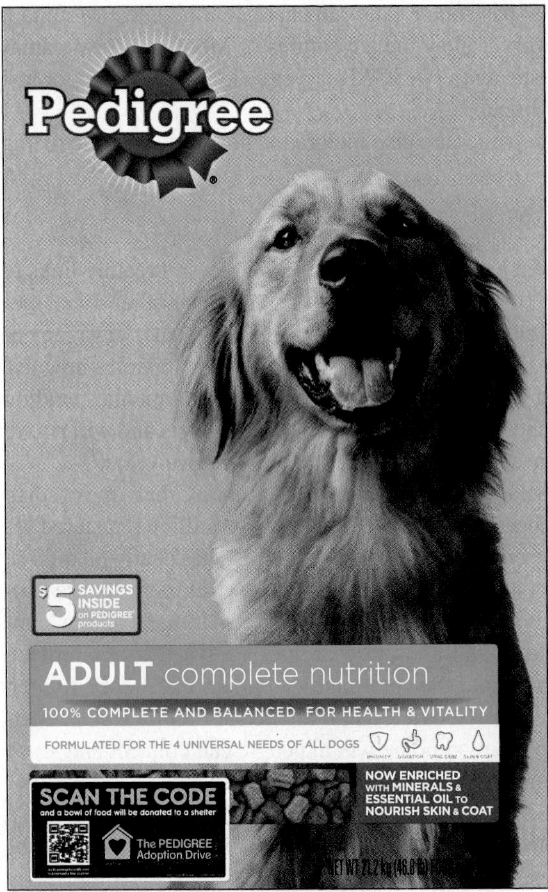

Mobile marketing: PEDIGREE and Walmart ran a mobile campaign to promote the retailer as a place to shop for pet food while also improving the brand's sales. Customers used their phones to scan QR codes in ads (here at lower left) or on packages in stores.

Walmart stores. To get a sample of, say, Tide Pods, customers first used their mobile phones in the store to check into the Tide Pods Facebook site, where they received product information and marketing.

Walmart and PEDIGREE joined forces to run a mobile-based "Pets Love Walmart" campaign to promote the retailer as a place to shop for pet food while also improving the brand's sales:[35]

> Prior to the "Pets Love Walmart" campaign, of the 90 million pet owners who shop weekly at Walmart, fewer than 60 percent were buying pet food from the retailer. That left plenty of opportunity to capture more sales. When shoppers used their phones in stores to scan QR codes on PEDIGREE pet food packages, a "bowl of food" was donated directly to a pet shelter. The code also sent shoppers to a mobile Web site within Walmart.com, where they found promotional offers, information about pet care and Walmart's in-store pet education events, and a link to make additional charitable donations to local pet shelters. The award-winning mobile campaign boosted PEDIGREE brand sales in Walmart stores by 25 percent and caused a 15-point jump in customer agreement with the statement "Walmart is the first place I think of for pet supplies."

Although online, social media, and mobile marketing offer huge potential, most marketers are still learning how to use them effectively. The key is to blend the new digital approaches with traditional marketing to create a smoothly integrated marketing strategy and mix. We will examine digital and social media marketing throughout the text—it touches almost every area of marketing strategy and tactics. Then, after we've covered the marketing basics, we'll look more deeply into direct and digital marketing in Chapter 14.

The Changing Economic Environment

The Great Recession of 2008 to 2009 and its aftermath hit American consumers hard. After two decades of overspending, new economic realities forced consumers to bring their consumption back in line with their incomes and rethink their buying priorities.

In today's post-recession era, consumer incomes and spending are again on the rise. However, even as the economy has strengthened, rather than reverting to their old free-spending ways, Americans are now showing an enthusiasm for frugality not seen in decades. Sensible consumption has made a comeback, and it appears to be here to stay. The new consumer spending values emphasize simpler living and more value for the dollar. Despite their rebounding means, consumers continue to buy less, clip more coupons, swipe their credit cards less, and put more in the bank.

Many consumers are reconsidering their very definition of the good life. "People are finding happiness in old-fashioned virtues—thrift, savings, do-it-yourself projects, self-improvement, hard work, faith, and community," says one consumer behavior expert. "We are moving from mindless to mindful consumption." The new, more frugal spending values don't mean that people have resigned themselves to lives of deprivation. As the economy has improved, consumers are indulging in luxuries and bigger-ticket purchases again, just more sensibly. "Luxury is [again] on the 'to-do' list," says the expert, "but people are taking a more mindful approach to where, how, and on what they spend."[36]

In response, companies in all industries—from discounters such as Target to luxury brands such as Lexus and De Beers diamonds—have realigned their marketing strategies with the new economic realities. More than ever, marketers are emphasizing the *value* in their value propositions. They are focusing on value-for-the-money, practicality, and durability in their product offerings and marketing pitches.

Even as the economy strengthens, Americans are now showing an enthusiasm for frugality not seen in decades. More sensible spending might be here to stay.

For example, for years discount retailer Target focused increasingly on the "Expect More" side of its "Expect More. Pay Less." value proposition. Its carefully cultivated "upscale-discounter" image successfully differentiated it from Walmart's more hard-nosed "lowest-price" position. But when the economy soured, many consumers worried that Target's trendier assortments and hip marketing also meant higher prices. So Target has shifted its balance more toward the "Pay Less" half of the slogan, making certain that its prices are in line with Walmart's and that customers know it. Although still trendy, Target's marketing now emphasizes more practical price and savings appeals.[37]

At the other extreme, even diamond marketer De Beers has adjusted its value proposition to these more sensible times. One De Beers ad, headlined "Here's to Less," makes that next diamond purchase seem—what else—downright practical. Although a diamond purchase might be spendy up front, the ad points out, it's something you'll never have to replace or throw away. As the old James Bond thriller suggests, a diamond is forever.

In adjusting to the new economy, companies may be tempted to cut their marketing budgets and slash prices in an effort to coax more frugal customers into opening their wallets. However, although cutting costs and offering selected discounts can be important marketing tactics, smart marketers understand that making cuts in the wrong places can damage long-term brand images and customer relationships. The challenge is to balance the brand's value proposition with the current times while also enhancing its long-term equity. Thus, rather than slashing prices in uncertain economic times, many marketers hold the line on prices and instead explain why their brands were worth it.

The Growth of Not-for-Profit Marketing

In recent years, marketing has also become a major part of the strategies of many not-for-profit organizations, such as colleges, hospitals, museums, zoos, symphony orchestras, and even churches. The nation's not-for-profits face stiff competition for support and membership. Sound marketing can help them attract membership, funds, and support.

For example, not-for-profit St. Jude Children's Research Hospital has a special mission: "Finding cures. Saving children." Named the most-trusted charity in the nation by Harris Interactive, St. Jude serves some 5,700 patients each year and is the nation's top children's cancer hospital. What's even more special is that St. Jude does not deny any child treatment for financial reasons—families never have to pay for treatment not covered by insurance. So how does St. Jude support its $1.7 million daily operating budget? By raising funds through powerhouse marketing:[38]

> This past winter, you saw something about St. Jude Children's Hospital about anywhere you looked—in public service announcements (PSAs), on the Discovery Channel's "American Chopper," on the lapel pins of Fox Sports announcers, in Facebook new feeds, and at the checkout counters of major retailers ranging from Target and Williams-Sonoma to pizza peddler Domino's. None of this happened by chance. Rather, it resulted from high-powered marketing. St. Jude targets a broad range of consumers using a mix of event marketing, celebrity star power, and corporate partnerships. Fundraising efforts include everything from PSAs and a sophisticated Internet and social media presence to Trike-a-thons, Math-a-thons, an Up 'Til Dawn student challenge, and a Dream Home Giveaway. More than 50 corporate sponsors—including Target, Domino's, Williams-Sonoma, Regal Cinemas, and Expedia—participate in St. Jude's annual Thanks and Giving campaign, » which asks consumers to "give thanks for the healthy kids in your life, and give to those who are not." The companies donate a portion of their sales or ask customers to donate at the sales counter. Through its broad outreach, St. Jude raises hundreds of millions of dollars each year—nearly $700 million last year alone.

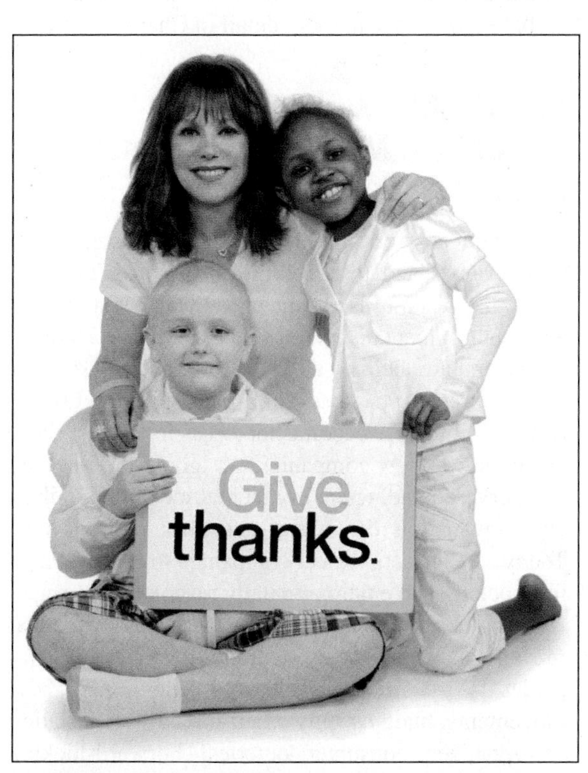

» Not-for-profit marketing: St. Jude's annual Thanks and Giving campaign asks consumers to "give thanks for the healthy kids in your life, and give to those who are not."

PR Newswire/Associated Press.

Government agencies have also shown an increased interest in marketing. For example, the U.S. military has a marketing plan to attract recruits to its different services, and various government agencies are now designing social marketing campaigns to encourage energy conservation and concern for the environment or discourage smoking, illegal drug use, and obesity. Even the once-stodgy U.S. Postal Service has developed innovative marketing to sell commemorative stamps, promote its Priority Mail services, and lift its image as a contemporary and competitive organization. In all, the U.S. government is the nation's 56th largest advertiser, with an annual advertising budget of more than $738 million.[39]

Rapid Globalization

As they are redefining their customer relationships, marketers are also taking a fresh look at the ways in which they relate with the broader world around them. Today, almost every company, large or small, is touched in some way by global competition. A neighborhood florist buys its flowers from Mexican nurseries, and a large U.S. electronics manufacturer competes in its home markets with giant Korean rivals. A fledgling Internet retailer finds itself receiving orders from all over the world at the same time that an American consumer goods producer introduces new products into emerging markets abroad.

American firms have been challenged at home by the skillful marketing of European and Asian multinationals. Companies such as Toyota, Nestlé, and Samsung have often outperformed their U.S. competitors in American markets. Similarly, U.S. companies in a wide range of industries have developed truly global operations, making and selling their products worldwide. Quintessentially American McDonald's now serves 69 million customers daily in more than 34,000 local restaurants in 119 countries worldwide—71 percent of its corporate revenues come from outside the United States. Similarly, Nike markets in 190 countries, with non-U.S. sales accounting for 58 percent of its worldwide sales.[40] Today, companies are not just selling more of their locally produced goods in international markets; they are also sourcing more supplies and components abroad and developing new products for specific markets around the world.

Thus, managers in countries around the world are increasingly taking a global, not just local, view of the company's industry, competitors, and opportunities. They are asking: What is global marketing? How does it differ from domestic marketing? How do global competitors and forces affect our business? To what extent should we "go global"? We will discuss the global marketplace in more detail in Chapter 15.

Sustainable marketing: Patagonia believes in "using business to inspire solutions to the environmental crisis." It backs these words by pledging at least 1 percent of its sales or 10 percent of its profits, whichever is greater, to the protection of the natural environment.

Patagonia, Inc.

Sustainable Marketing—The Call for More Environmental and Social Responsibility

Marketers are reexamining their relationships with social values and responsibilities and with the very Earth that sustains us. As the worldwide consumerism and environmentalism movements mature, today's marketers are being called on to develop *sustainable marketing* practices. Corporate ethics and social responsibility have become hot topics for almost every business. And few companies can ignore the renewed and very demanding environmental movement. Every company action can affect customer relationships. Today's customers expect companies to deliver value in a socially and environmentally responsible way.

The social responsibility and environmental movements will place even stricter demands on companies in the future. Some companies resist these movements, budging only when forced by legislation or organized consumer outcries. Forward-looking companies, however, readily accept their responsibilities to the world around them. They view sustainable marketing as an opportunity to do well by doing good.

They seek ways to profit by serving immediate needs and the best long-run interests of their customers and communities.

Some companies, such as Patagonia, Ben & Jerry's, Timberland, Method, and others, practice *caring capitalism*, setting themselves apart by being civic minded and responsible. They build social responsibility and action into their company value and mission statements. »For example, when it comes to environmental responsibility, outdoor gear marketer Patagonia is "committed to the core." "Those of us who work here share a strong commitment to protecting undomesticated lands and waters," says the company's Web site. "We believe in using business to inspire solutions to the environmental crisis." Patagonia backs these words with actions. Each year it pledges at least 1 percent of its sales or 10 percent of its profits, whichever is greater, to the protection of the natural environment.[41] We will revisit the topic of sustainable marketing in greater detail in Chapter 16.

Author Comment
Remember Figure 1.1 outlining the marketing process? Now, based on everything we've discussed in this chapter, we'll expand that figure to provide a roadmap for learning marketing throughout the remainder of the text.

So, What Is Marketing?: Pulling It All Together

At the start of this chapter, Figure 1.1 presented a simple model of the marketing process. Now that we've discussed all the steps in the process, »**Figure 1.6** presents an expanded model that will help you pull it all together. What is marketing? Simply put, marketing is the process of building profitable customer relationships by creating value for customers and capturing value in return.

This expanded version of Figure 1.1 at the beginning of the chapter provides a good road map for the rest of the text. The underlying concept of the entire text is that marketing creates value for customers in order to capture value from customers in return.

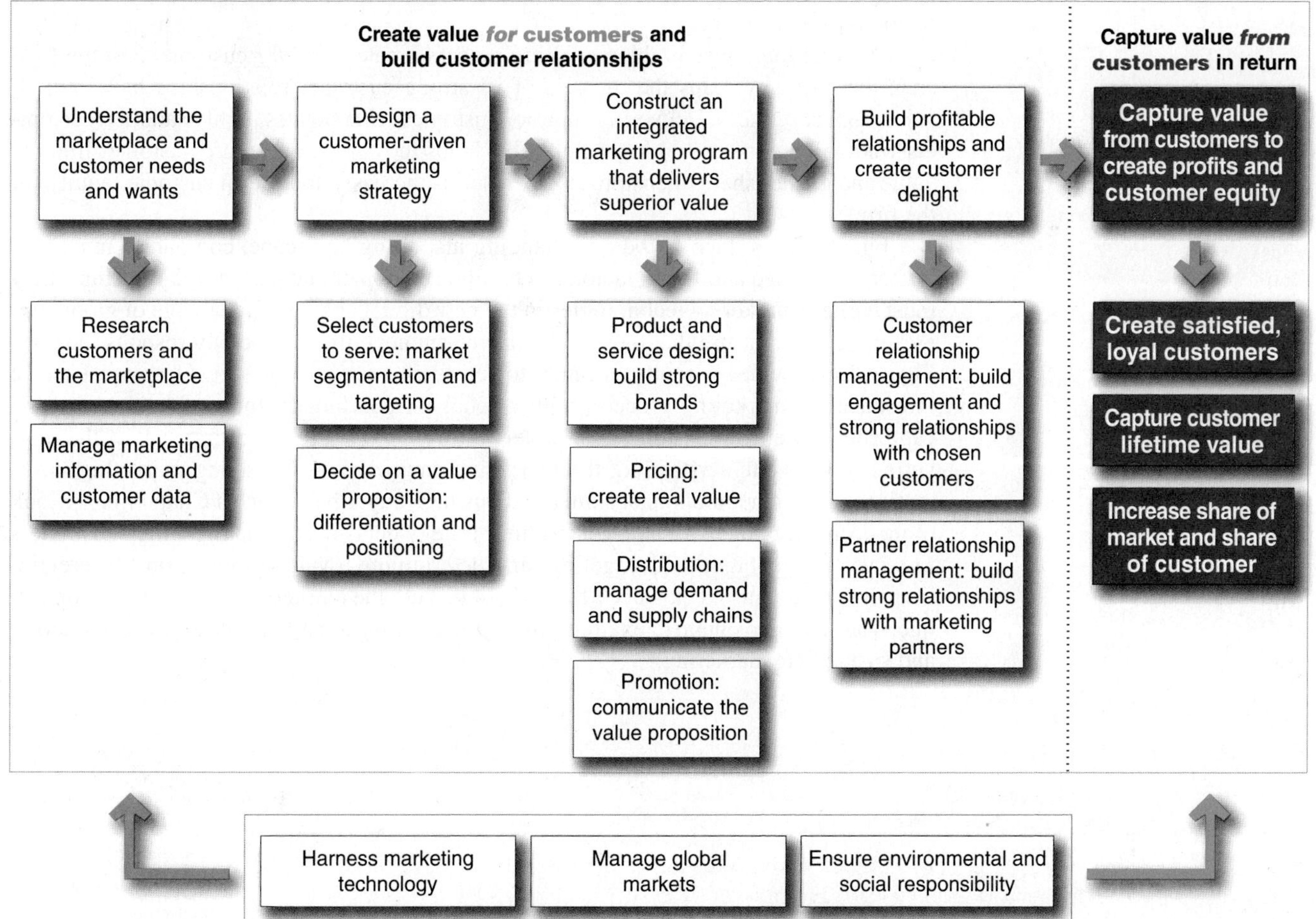

» **Figure 1.6** An Expanded Model of the Marketing Process

The first four steps of the marketing process focus on creating value for customers. The company first gains a full understanding of the marketplace by researching customer needs and managing marketing information. It then designs a customer-driven marketing strategy based on the answers to two simple questions. The first question is "What consumers will we serve?" (market segmentation and targeting). Good marketing companies know that they cannot serve all customers in every way. Instead, they need to focus their resources on the customers they can serve best and most profitably. The second marketing strategy question is "How can we best serve targeted customers?" (differentiation and positioning). Here, the marketer outlines a value proposition that spells out what values the company will deliver to win target customers.

With its marketing strategy chosen, the company now constructs an integrated marketing program—consisting of a blend of the four marketing mix elements, the four Ps—that transforms the marketing strategy into real value for customers. The company develops product offers and creates strong brand identities for them. It prices these offers to create real customer value and distributes the offers to make them available to target consumers. Finally, the company designs promotion programs that communicate the value proposition to target customers and persuade them to act on the market offering.

Perhaps the most important step in the marketing process involves building value-laden, profitable relationships with target customers. Throughout the process, marketers practice customer relationship management to create customer satisfaction and delight. They engage customers in the process of creating brand conversations, experiences, and community. In creating customer value and relationships, however, the company cannot go it alone. It must work closely with marketing partners both inside the company and throughout its marketing system. Thus, beyond practicing good customer relationship management and customer-engagement marketing, firms must also practice good partner relationship management.

The first four steps in the marketing process create value *for* customers. In the final step, the company reaps the rewards of its strong customer relationships by capturing value *from* customers. Delivering superior customer value creates highly satisfied customers who will buy more and buy again. This helps the company capture customer lifetime value and greater share of customer. The result is increased long-term customer equity for the firm.

Finally, in the face of today's changing marketing landscape, companies must take into account three additional factors. In building customer and partner relationships, they must harness marketing technologies in the new digital age, take advantage of global opportunities, and ensure that they act in an environmentally and socially responsible way. Figure 1.6 provides a good road map to future chapters of this text. Chapters 1 and 2 introduce the marketing process, with a focus on building customer relationships and capturing value from customers. Chapters 3 through 5 address the first step of the marketing process—understanding the marketing environment, managing marketing information, and understanding consumer and business buyer behavior. In Chapter 6, we look more deeply into the two major marketing strategy decisions: selecting which customers to serve (segmentation and targeting) and determining a value proposition (differentiation and positioning). Chapters 7 through 14 discuss the marketing mix variables, one by one. The final two chapters examine special marketing considerations: global marketing and sustainable marketing.

MyMarketingLab

Go to **mymktlab.com** to complete the problems marked with this icon .

END OF CHAPTER | REVIEWING THE CONCEPTS

CHAPTER REVIEW AND KEY TERMS

Objectives Review

Today's successful companies—whether large or small, for-profit or not-for-profit, domestic or global—share a strong customer focus and a heavy commitment to marketing. The goal of marketing is to build and manage profitable customer relationships.

OBJECTIVE 1 Define marketing and outline the steps in the marketing process. (pp 4–6)

Marketing is the process by which companies create value for customers and build strong customer relationships in order to capture value from customers in return. The marketing process involves five steps. The first four steps create value *for* customers. First, marketers need to understand the marketplace and customer needs and wants. Next, marketers design a customer-driven marketing strategy with the goal of getting, keeping, and growing target customers. In the third step, marketers construct a marketing program that actually delivers superior value. All of these steps form the basis for the fourth step, building profitable customer relationships and creating customer delight. In the final step, the company reaps the rewards of strong customer relationships by capturing value *from* customers.

OBJECTIVE 2 Explain the importance of understanding the marketplace and customers and identify the five core marketplace concepts. (pp 6–8)

Outstanding marketing companies go to great lengths to learn about and understand their customers' *needs*, *wants*, and *demands*. This understanding helps them to design want-satisfying market offerings and build value-laden customer relationships by which they can capture *customer lifetime value* and greater *share of customer*. The result is increased long-term *customer equity* for the firm.

The core marketplace concepts are needs, wants, and demands; market offerings (products, services, and experiences); value and satisfaction; exchange and relationships; and markets. Wants are the form taken by human needs when shaped by culture and individual personality. When backed by buying power, wants become demands. Companies address needs by putting forth a value proposition, a set of benefits that they promise to consumers to satisfy their needs. The value proposition is fulfilled through a market offering, which delivers customer value and satisfaction, resulting in long-term exchange relationships with customers.

OBJECTIVE 3 Identify the key elements of a customer-driven marketing strategy and discuss the marketing management orientations that guide marketing strategy. (pp 9–13)

To design a winning marketing strategy, the company must first decide whom it will serve. It does this by dividing the market into segments of customers (*market segmentation*) and selecting which segments it will cultivate (*target marketing*). Next, the company must decide *how* it will serve targeted customers (how it will *differentiate and position* itself in the marketplace).

Marketing management can adopt one of five competing market orientations. The *production concept* holds that management's task is to improve production efficiency and bring down prices. The *product concept* holds that consumers favor products that offer the most in quality, performance, and innovative features; thus, little promotional effort is required. The *selling concept* holds that consumers will not buy enough of an organization's products unless it undertakes a large-scale selling and promotion effort. The *marketing concept* holds that achieving organizational goals depends on determining the needs and wants of target markets and delivering the desired satisfactions more effectively and efficiently than competitors do. The *societal marketing concept* holds that generating customer satisfaction *and* long-run societal well-being through sustainable marketing strategies is key to both achieving the company's goals and fulfilling its responsibilities.

OBJECTIVE 4 Discuss customer relationship management and identify strategies for creating value *for* customers and capturing value *from* customers in return. (pp 13–24)

Broadly defined, *customer relationship management* is the process of building and maintaining profitable customer relationships by delivering superior customer value and satisfaction. *Customer-engagement marketing* aims to make a brand a meaningful part of consumers' conversations and lives through direct and continuous customer involvement in shaping brand conversations, experiences, and community. The aim of customer relationship management and customer engagement is to produce high *customer equity,* the total combined customer lifetime values of all of the company's customers. The key to building lasting relationships is the creation of superior *customer value* and *satisfaction.*

Companies want to not only acquire profitable customers but also build relationships that will keep them and grow "share of customer." Different types of customers require different customer relationship management strategies. The marketer's aim is to build the *right relationships* with the *right customers.* In return for creating value *for* targeted customers, the company captures value *from* customers in the form of profits and customer equity.

In building customer relationships, good marketers realize that they cannot go it alone. They must work closely with marketing partners inside and outside the company. In addition to being good at customer relationship management, they must also be good at *partner relationship management.*

OBJECTIVE 5 Describe the major trends and forces that are changing the marketing landscape in this age of relationships. (pp 24–29)

Dramatic changes are occurring in the marketing arena. The digital age has created exciting new ways to learn about and relate to individual customers. As a result, advances in digital and social media have taken the marketing world by storm. Online, social media, and mobile marketing offer exciting new opportunities to target customers more selectively and engage them more deeply. Although the new digital and social media offer huge potential, most marketers are still learning how to use them effectively. The key is to blend the new digital approaches with traditional marketing to create a smoothly integrated marketing strategy and mix.

The Great Recession hit American consumers hard, causing them to rethink their buying priorities and bring their consumption back in line with their incomes. Even as the post-recession economy has strengthened, Americans are now showing an enthusiasm for frugality not seen in decades. Sensible consumption has made a comeback, and it appears to be here to stay. More than ever, marketers must now emphasize the *value* in their value propositions. The challenge is to balance a brand's value proposition with current times while also enhancing its long-term equity.

In recent years, marketing has become a major part of the strategies for many not-for-profit organizations, such as colleges, hospitals, museums, zoos, symphony orchestras, and even churches. Also, in an increasingly smaller world, many marketers are now connected *globally* with their customers and marketing partners. Today, almost every company, large or small, is touched in some way by global competition. Finally, today's marketers are also reexamining their ethical and societal responsibilities. Marketers are being called on to take greater responsibility for the social and environmental impacts of their actions.

Pulling it all together, as discussed throughout the chapter, the major new developments in marketing can be summed up in a single concept: *creating and capturing customer value*. Today, marketers of all kinds are taking advantage of new opportunities for building value-laden relationships with their customers, their marketing partners, and the world around them.

Key Terms

Objective 1
Marketing (p 5)

Objective 2
Needs (p 6)
Wants (p 6)
Demands (p 6)
Market offerings (p 6)
Marketing myopia (p 7)
Exchange (p 7)
Market (p 8)

Objective 3
Marketing management (p 9)
Production concept (p 10)
Product concept (p 10)
Selling concept (p 10)
Marketing concept (p 10)
Societal marketing concept (p 11)

Objective 4
Customer relationship management (p 13)
Customer-perceived value (p 13)
Customer satisfaction (p 14)
Customer-engagement marketing (p 17)
Consumer-generated marketing (p 18)
Partner relationship management (p 21)
Customer lifetime value (p 21)
Share of customer (p 22)
Customer equity (p 22)

Objective 5
Digital and social media marketing (p 24)

DISCUSSION AND CRITICAL THINKING

Discussion Questions

1-1. Define *marketing* and outline the steps in the marketing process. (AACSB: Written and Oral Communication)

1-2. What is marketing myopia, and how can it be avoided? (AACSB: Written and Oral Communication; Reflective Thinking)

1-3. What is customer-engagement marketing, and how is it related to the surge in digital and social media technologies? (AACSB: Written and Oral Communication; Reflective Thinking)

1-4. What is consumer-generated marketing? Describe examples of both invited and uninvited consumer exchanges. (AACSB: Written and Oral Communication; Reflective Thinking)

1-5. Discuss trends impacting marketing and the implications of these trends on how marketers deliver value to customers. (AACSB: Written and Oral Communication)

Critical Thinking Exercises

1-6. Select a publically traded company and research how much was spent on marketing activities in the most recent year of available data. What percentage of sales does marketing expenditures represent for the company? Have these expenditures increased or decreased over the past five years? Write a brief report of your findings. (AACSB: Written and Oral Communication; Analytic Thinking)

1-7. Go to the Web site of a company, organization, or specific brand that has a link to Facebook, Google+, YouTube, Twitter, and/or Pinterest. Click on the links and describe how that company is using social media to market its products. Evaluate its effectiveness in creating customer engagement. (AACSB: Written and Oral Communication; Information Technology; Reflective Thinking)

1-8. Search the Internet for salary information regarding jobs in marketing from a Web site such as www.simplyhired.com/a/salary/search/q-marketing or a similar site. What is the national average salary for five different jobs in marketing? How do the averages compare in different areas of the country? Write a brief report on your findings. (AACSB: Written and Oral Communication; Information Technology; Reflective Thinking)

MINICASES AND APPLICATIONS

Online, Mobile, and Social Media Marketing Xbox One

Eight years after the launch of its wildly successful Xbox 360, Microsoft finally announced its new Xbox One to be released at the end of 2013. The company is hoping the new console will turn around its 71 percent plunge in profits in 2012. The Xbox One touts a blue-ray video player, voice-activated on-demand movies and TV, Skype calling, and social media integration. Smart-TV features will customize menus for each player and tailor content for individual users. Xbox Live's 48 million members will be able to interact on social media during special televised events such as the Olympics, Super Bowl, Oscars, and other special programming. Games will have greater artificial intelligence, enabling players to feel like the virtual athletes are making decisions on their own. Sports data such as daily performance and injury updates will feed into online games, such as *Madden NFL*, mirroring their real-world counterparts. Players will be able to augment live televised games with fantasy football stats that can be shared with friends via Skype and Microsoft's Smart-Glass apps. One thing the Xbox One won't be able to do is play old games. Competitor Sony plans to come out with its PlayStation 4 that will have touch-sensors in its controller and allow players to play any game—current or old—instantly over the Internet. Both companies are banking on more digital and social media applications to save them from the fate competitor Nintendo faced with its failed Wii U console introduced in 2012.

1-9. Debate whether these new features in game consoles are enough to survive against the growth of smartphone and tablet apps that offer free or inexpensive games. (AACSB: Written and Oral Communication; Reflective Thinking)

1-10. Brainstorm three new game console features incorporating digital, mobile, or social media technology to encourage consumer interaction and engagement with gaming. (AACSB: Written and Oral Communication; Reflective Thinking)

Marketing Ethics Goodbye Big Gulp?

With two-thirds of adults and one-third of school-aged children in the United States overweight or obese, the mayor of New York City, Michael Bloomberg, took action against the soft drink industry. Mayor Bloomberg banned big sugary drinks such as 7-Eleven's mammoth 32-ounce "Big Gulp." The ban put a 16-ounce cap on fountain and bottled drinks sold at restaurants, theaters, and sporting events. Although the ban applied to drinks having more than 25 calories per 8-ounces, it did not apply to 100 percent juice or milk-based beverages. Establishments serving fountain drinks feared a significant revenue drop because these drinks are often marked up at 10 to 15 times their cost. Many consumers opposed the ban because they perceived it as further encroachment of the "nanny state." Even though this ban did not go into effect because a judge ruled that Mayor Bloomberg did not have jurisdiction to impose such a ban, he has already banned smoking in public parks and trans fats in restaurant foods, as well as requiring chain restaurants to include calorie information on menus. New York is not the only city taking action. The San Francisco city council passed the Healthy Food Incentive Ordinance, banning toys inside children's meals that do not meet strict nutritional standards. This leads many to ask, "What's next?"

1-11. Should marketers embrace the societal marketing concept with respect to foods or products that could be harmful to consumers? Discuss an example of a company embracing the societal marketing concept with respect to the obesity epidemic. (AACSB: Written and Oral Communication; Ethical Understanding and Reasoning)

Marketing by the Numbers Consumers Rule!

Consumer consumption makes up a large portion of the U.S. gross domestic product (GDP). The American Customer Satisfaction Index (ACSI) is an economic barometer of consumers' satisfaction with goods and services across many sectors of the economy. The company that produces the index interviews nearly 80,000 Americans annually to create a national, sector, industry, and company satisfaction index. The ACSI benchmarks 10 economic sectors, 43 industries, and hundreds of companies and federal and local government sectors. Although the sales and profit data are historical, the ACSI is considered a leading economic indicator of macroeconomic growth. Marketers use this index to measure the pulse of the consumer. Research has shown it to be a predictor of GDP and personal consumption expenditure (PCE) growth, and even stock market performance.

1-12. Visit www.theacsi.org/ and learn about the American Customer Satisfaction Index (ASCI). Write a report explaining the index and compare indices for five different industries along with the national average. Are there differences in customer satisfaction among industries? Explain why or why not. (AACSB: Written and Oral Communication; Information Technology; Reflective Thinking)

1-13. The Customer Satisfaction Index (CSI) is measured similarly in other countries. Find another country's CSI and compare results to the American Customer Satisfaction Index (ACSI). Are U.S. consumers more or less satisfied than consumers in the other country? Are trends in the national score similar? (AACSB: Written and Oral Communication; Information Technology; Reflective Thinking)

Video Case Zappos

These days, online retailers are a dime a dozen, and many don't make a lasting impact. Yet, in only a short time, Zappos has become a billion dollar e-tailer and an important part of the Amazon.com empire. How did Zappos hit the dot-com jackpot? By providing its customers with some of the best service available anywhere. Zappos showers its customers with such perks as free shipping both ways, surprise upgrades to overnight service, a 365-day return policy, and a call center that is always open. Customers are also delighted by employees who are empowered to spontaneously hand out rewards based on unique needs.

With such attention to customer service, it's no surprise that Zappos has an almost cult-like following of repeat customers. However, remaining committed to the philosophy that the customer is always right can be challenging. This video highlights some of the dilemmas that can arise from a highly customer-centric strategy. Zappos also demonstrates the ultimate rewards they receive from keeping that commitment.

After viewing the video featuring Zappos, answer the following questions:

1-14. How would you describe Zappos' market offering?

1-15. What is Zappos' value proposition? How does it relate to its market offering?

1-16. How does Zappos build long-term customer relationships?

Company Cases 1 In-N-Out / 9 JCPenney / 14 Pinterest

See Appendix 1 for cases appropriate for this chapter. **Case 1, In-N-Out Burger: Customer Value the Old-Fashioned Way.** In-N-Out Burger provides value to customers by giving them exactly what they want, and never changing a thing. **Case 9, JCPenney: The Struggle to Find Optimum Price.** JCPenney tried to fix a pricing problem with a new strategy, only to create a new pricing problem. **Case 14, Pinterest: Revolutionizing the Web—Again.** Pinterest has revolutionized Web design, and is influencing consumer purchase decisions in the process.

MyMarketingLab

Go to **mymktlab.com** for Auto-graded writing questions as well as the following Assisted-graded writing questions:

1-17. When implementing customer relationship management, why might a business desire fewer customers over more customers? Shouldn't the focus of marketing be to acquire as many customers as possible? (AACSB: Written and Oral Communication; Reflective Thinking)

1-18. Is it fair to single out specific products for restrictions such as New York City's proposed size cap on soft drinks? Discuss this argument from all sides of this issue: government, soft drink marketers, and consumers. (AACSB: Written and Oral Communication; Reflective Thinking)

1-19. Mymktlab Only—comprehensive writing assignment for this chapter.

2 Company and Marketing Strategy

Partnering to Build Customer Value and Relationships

CHAPTER ROAD MAP

Objective Outline

- OBJECTIVE 1 **Explain company-wide strategic planning and its four steps.** Company-Wide Strategic Planning: Defining Marketing's Role 38–42
- OBJECTIVE 2 **Discuss how to design business portfolios and develop growth strategies.** Designing the Business Portfolio 42–46
- OBJECTIVE 3 **Explain marketing's role in strategic planning and how marketing works with its partners to create and deliver customer value.** Planning Marketing: Partnering to Build Customer Relationships 46–48
- OBJECTIVE 4 **Describe the elements of a customer-driven marketing strategy and mix and the forces that influence it.** Marketing Strategy and the Marketing Mix 48–54
- OBJECTIVE 5 **List the marketing management functions, including the elements of a marketing plan, and discuss the importance of measuring and managing return on marketing investment.** Managing the Marketing Effort 54–58; Measuring and Managing Return on Marketing Investment 58–59

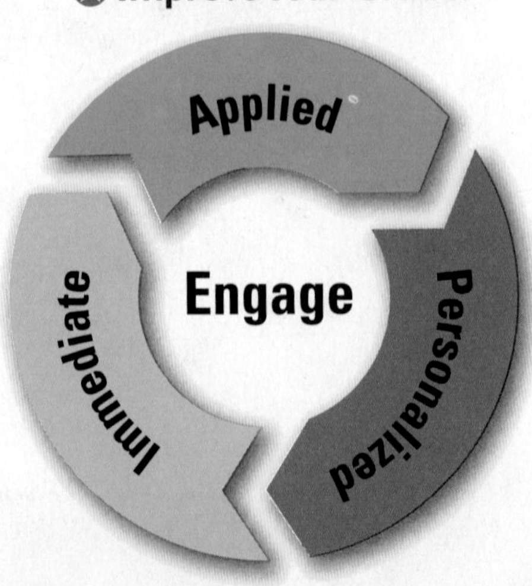

Previewing the Concepts

In the first chapter, we explored the marketing process by which companies create value for consumers to capture value from them in return. In this chapter, we dig deeper into steps two and three of that process: designing customer-driven marketing strategies and constructing marketing programs. First, we look at the organization's overall strategic planning, which guides marketing strategy and planning. Next, we discuss how, guided by the strategic plan, marketers partner closely with others inside and outside the firm to create value for customers. We then examine marketing strategy and planning—how marketers choose target markets, position their market offerings, develop a marketing mix, and manage their marketing programs. Finally, we look at the important step of measuring and managing return on marketing investment (marketing ROI).

First, let's look at Nike, a good company and a good marketing strategy story. During the past several decades, Nike has built the Nike swoosh into one of the world's best-known brand symbols. Nike's outstanding success results from much more than just making and selling good sports gear. It's based on a customer-focused marketing strategy through which Nike creates valued brand engagement and a close brand community with and among its customers.

*Over 10 million students improved their results using the Pearson MyLabs. Visit **mymktlab.com** for simulations, tutorials, and end-of-chapter problems.

» **Nike has mastered social networking, both online and off, creating deep engagement and community among customers. Its Nike+ and FuelBand apps and technologies have made Nike a part of the daily fitness routines of millions of customers around the world.**

Stefano Dal Pozzolo/Contrasto/Redux.

First Stop

Nike's Customer-Driven Marketing: Building Brand Engagement and Community

The Nike "swoosh"—it's everywhere! Just for fun, try counting the swooshes whenever you pick up the sports pages or watch a basketball game or tune into a televised soccer match. Over the past nearly 50 years, through innovative marketing, Nike has built the ever-present swoosh into one of the best-known brand symbols on the planet.

Early on, a brash, young Nike revolutionized sports marketing. To build image and market share, the brand lavishly outspent competitors on big-name endorsements, splashy promotional events, and big-budget, in-your-face "Just Do It" ads. Whereas competitors stressed technical performance, Nike built customer relationships. Beyond shoes, apparel, and equipment, Nike marketed a way of life, a genuine passion for sports, a "just-do-it" attitude. Customers didn't just wear their Nikes, they *experienced* them. As the company stated on its Web page, "Nike has always known the truth—it's not so much the shoes but where they take you."

Nike powered its way through the early years, aggressively adding products in a dozen new sports, including baseball, golf, skateboarding, wall climbing, bicycling, and hiking. It seemed that things just couldn't be going any better. In the late 1990s, however, Nike stumbled and its sales slipped. As the company grew larger, its creative juices seemed to run a bit dry and buyers seeking a new look switched to competing brands. Looking back, Nike's biggest obstacle may have been its own incredible success. As sales grew, the swoosh may have become too common to be cool. Instead of being *anti*establishment, Nike *was* the establishment, and its hip, once-hot relationship with customers cooled. Nike needed to rekindle the brand's meaning to consumers.

Nike's outstanding success results from much more than just making good sports gear. The iconic company's strategy is to build engagement and a sense of community with and between the Nike brand and its customers.

To turn things around, Nike returned to its roots: new product innovation and a focus on customer relationships. But it set out to forge a new kind of brand–customer connection—a deeper, more personal, more engaging one. This time around, rather than simply outspending competitors on big media ads and celebrity endorsers that talk *at* customers, Nike shifted toward cutting-edge digital and social media marketing tools that interact *with* customers to build brand connections and community. According to one industry analyst, "the legendary brand blew up its single-slogan approach and drafted a whole new playbook for the digital era."

Nike still invests heavily in traditional advertising. But its spending on TV and print media has dropped by a whopping 30 percent in only three years, even as its global marketing budget has increased steadily. Traditional media now account for only about 20 percent of the brand's $1 billion U.S. promotion budget. Instead, Nike spends the lion's share of its marketing budget on nontraditional media. Using community-oriented, digital-based social networking tools, Nike is now building communities of customers who talk not just with the company about the brand, but with each other as well.

Nike has mastered social networking, both online and off. Whether customers come to know Nike through ads, in-person events at Niketown stores, a local Nike running club, or at one of the company's profusion of community Web and social media sites, more and more people are bonding closely with the Nike brand.

Nike has raced ahead of its industry in the use of today's new social networking tools. In a recent ranking of 42 sportswear companies, digital consultancy L2 crowned Nike "top genius" in "digital IQ" for its innovative use of online, mobile, and social media. L2 also placed Nike first in creating brand "tribes"—large groups of highly engaged users—with the help of social media platforms such as Facebook, Twitter, Instagram, and Pinterest. For example, the main Nike Facebook page has more than 12.6 million Likes. The Nike Basketball page adds another 5 million, NIKEiD 2 million more, and Nike Running another 1.4 million. More than just numbers, Nike's social media presence engages customers at a high level and gets them talking with each other about the brand.

Nike excels at cross-media campaigns that integrate the new media with traditional tools to build brand community. For example, Nike's "Find Your Greatness" campaign for the 2012 Olympics launched two days before the opening ceremonies—not with splashy media ads but with a video posted on YouTube, Nike Web sites, and other digital platforms. The compelling video featured people getting in touch with their inner athlete. Then, on opening day, Nike followed up with big-budget TV ads in 25 countries based on the video. But rather than just running the ads in isolation, the campaign urged customers to share their feelings about the "Find Your Greatness" message via Twitter and other digital media using a "#findgreatness" hashtag. Within a month, the video had been viewed more than 5 million times on Nike's YouTube channel alone.

Nike has also built brand community through groundbreaking mobile apps and technologies. For example, its Nike+ apps have helped Nike become a part of the daily fitness routines of millions of customers around the world. The Nike+ FuelBand, for instance, is an ergonomic work of art. Worn on the wrist, FuelBand converts just about every imaginable physical movement into NikeFuel, Nike's own universal activity metric. According to a recent Nike video called "Counts," whether your activity is running, jumping, baseball, skating, dancing, stacking sports cups, or chasing chickens, it counts for Nike Fuel points. "Life is a sport," the video concludes. "Make it count." Everyday athletes can use NikeFuel to track their personal performance, then share and compare it across sports and geographic locations with others in the global Nike community. The Nike+ FuelBand mobile app lets users watch their progress, get extra motivation on the go, and stay connected with friends.

Nike+ has engaged a huge global brand community. The tickers on nikeplus.com update continuously with numbers in the billions: 35,566,409,830 steps taken, 50,841,842,647 calories burned, and 14,364,639,579 NikeFuel points earned. The site also tracks personal achievements earned and daily goals hit by individuals in the Nike+ community. To date, the millions of Nike+ users worldwide have logged 844,265,265 miles. That's 33,740 trips around the world or 1,759 journeys to the moon and back.

Thus, Nike has built a new kinship and sense of community with and between the brand and its customers. Nike's marketing strategy is no longer only about big-budget ads at arm's length and aloof celebrity endorsers. Instead, the brand is connecting directly with customers, whether it's through local running clubs, a performance-tracking wristband, a 30-story billboard that posts fan headlines from Twitter, or videos that debut on YouTube rather primetime TV. More than just something to buy, the Nike brand has once again become a part of customers' lives and times.

As a result, Nike remains the world's largest sports apparel company, an impressive 25 percent larger than closest rival adidas. During the past seven years, even as the faltering economy left most sports apparel and footwear competitors gasping for breath, Nike's global sales and income sprinted ahead nearly 60 percent.

As in sports competition, the strongest and best-prepared brand has the best chance of winning. With deep brand–customer relationships comes powerful competitive advantage. And Nike is once again very close to its customers. Notes Nike CEO Mark Parker, "Connecting used to be, 'Here's some product, and here's some advertising. We hope you like it.' Connecting today is a dialogue."[1]

Author Comment
Company-wide strategic planning guides marketing strategy and planning. Like marketing strategy, the company's broader strategy must also be customer focused.

Company-Wide Strategic Planning: Defining Marketing's Role

Strategic planning
The process of developing and maintaining a strategic fit between the organization's goals and capabilities and its changing marketing opportunities.

Each company must find the game plan for long-run survival and growth that makes the most sense given its specific situation, opportunities, objectives, and resources. This is the focus of **strategic planning**—the process of developing and maintaining a strategic fit between the organization's goals and capabilities and its changing marketing opportunities.

Strategic planning sets the stage for the rest of planning in the firm. Companies usually prepare annual plans, long-range plans, and strategic plans. The annual and long-range plans deal with the company's current businesses and how to keep them going. In contrast, the strategic plan involves adapting the firm to take advantage of opportunities in its constantly changing environment.

At the corporate level, the company starts the strategic planning process by defining its overall purpose and mission (see **» Figure 2.1**). This mission is then turned into detailed supporting objectives that guide the entire company. Next, headquarters decides what portfolio of businesses and products is best for the company and how much support to give each one. In turn, each business and product develops detailed marketing and other departmental plans that support the company-wide plan. Thus, marketing planning occurs at the business-unit, product, and market levels. It supports company strategic planning with more detailed plans for specific marketing opportunities.

>> Figure 2.1 Steps in Strategic Planning

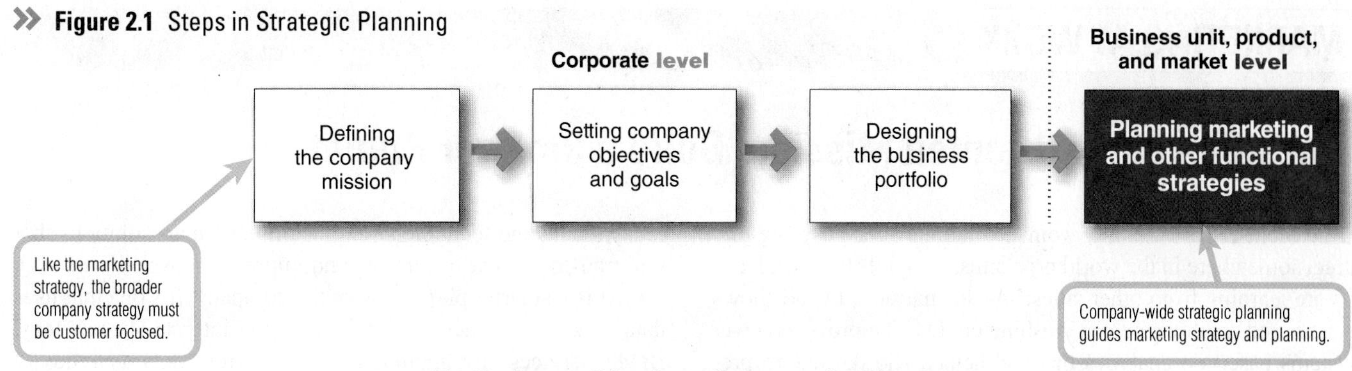

Defining a Market-Oriented Mission

An organization exists to accomplish something, and this purpose should be clearly stated. Forging a sound mission begins with the following questions: What *is* our business? Who is the customer? What do consumers value? What *should* our business be? These simple-sounding questions are among the most difficult the company will ever have to answer. Successful companies continuously raise these questions and answer them carefully and completely.

Mission statement
A statement of the organization's purpose—what it wants to accomplish in the larger environment.

Many organizations develop formal mission statements that answer these questions. A **mission statement** is a statement of the organization's purpose—what it wants to accomplish in the larger environment. A clear mission statement acts as an "invisible hand" that guides people in the organization.

Some companies define their missions myopically in product or technology terms ("We make and sell furniture" or "We are a chemical-processing firm"). But mission statements should be *market oriented* and defined in terms of satisfying basic customer needs. Products and technologies eventually become outdated, but basic market needs may last forever. For example, IBM doesn't define itself as just a computer hardware and software company. It wants to provide data and information technology solutions that help customers "build a smarter planet" (see Marketing at Work 2.1). Likewise, social scrapbooking site Pinterest doesn't define itself as just an online place to post pictures. Its mission is to give people a social media platform for collecting, organizing, and sharing things they love. And Chipotle's mission isn't to sell burritos. Instead, the restaurant promises "Food with Integrity," highlighting its commitment to the immediate and long-term welfare of customers and the environment. To back its mission, Chipotle's serves only the very best natural, sustainable, local ingredients. **>> Table 2.1** provides several other examples of product-oriented versus market-oriented business definitions.[2]

>> Table 2.1 Product- versus Market-Oriented Business Definitions

Company	Product-Oriented Definition	Market-Oriented Definition
Facebook	We are an online social network.	We connect people around the world and help them share important moments in their lives.
Hulu	We are an online video service.	We help people enjoy their favorite video content anytime, anywhere.
Home Depot	We sell tools and home repair and improvement items.	We empower consumers to achieve the homes of their dreams.
NASA	We explore outer space.	We reach for new heights and reveal the unknown so that what we do and learn will benefit all humankind.
Revlon	We make cosmetics.	We sell lifestyle and self-expression; success and status; memories, hopes, and dreams.
Ritz-Carlton Hotels & Resorts	We rent rooms.	We create the Ritz-Carlton experience—a memorable stay that far exceeds guests' already high expectations.
Walmart	We run discount stores.	We deliver low prices every day and give ordinary folks the chance to buy the same things as rich people. "Save Money. Live Better."

MARKETING AT WORK 2.1

IBM's Customer-Oriented Mission: Build a Smarter Planet

In a recent IBM TV ad, a woman standing on a busy big-city street somewhere in the world proclaims, "All over the world, cities are learning from other cities." As she narrates, the ad shows how shared solutions helped Washington, D.C., improve its sewer systems based on analytics that had helped Rio de Janeiro prepare for flooding emergencies and helped Singapore make traffic flow more efficiently. What connects these seemingly separate activities in cities around the world? The woman explains: "With two thousand projects underway, IBM is helping to make cities smarter. I'm an IBMer. Let's build a smarter planet, city by city."

That's IBM today—a full-service supplier of digital-age data technologies and services. But not that many years ago, IBM was known mostly for peddling mainframe computers, PCs, and other basic computer system components. Back then, if you'd asked top managers at "Big Blue" what their mission was, they might well have answered, "to sell computer hardware and software." IBM had dominated the computer market for decades, achieving astounding success. By the early 1990s, however, a heavily product-focused IBM had lost sight of its customers' needs. Sales and profits tumbled and IBM was rapidly becoming a big blue dinosaur.

Since those sadly blue days, however, IBM has undergone a remarkable transformation. The turnaround started with top IBM managers meeting face to face with important customers—what they called "bear-hugging customers"—to learn about their problems and priorities. The managers learned that in this connected digital age, companies face a perplexing array of data and information technologies. Today's customers don't need just computers and software. Instead, they need total solutions to ever-more-bewildering data and information problems. Such solutions often involve a complex, integrated mix of hardware, software, services, and advice across collaborative online, mobile, and social networks.

This realization led to a fundamental redefinition of IBM's business. Now, if you ask IBM managers to define the mission, they'll tell you, "we deliver *smart solutions* to customers' data and information technology problems." Under this new customer-solutions mission, IBM began shifting emphasis away from computer hardware. Instead, it added a full slate of integrated IT, software, and business consulting services. Customers can still buy mainframes computers from IBM, but they are more likely to buy services, systems, and advice. The transformed IBM now works arm in arm with customers on everything from assessing, planning, designing, and implementing their data analytics and IT systems to actually running the systems for them.

IBM's customer-focused mission is summed up by the company's five-year-old marketing and positioning campaign: "Let's Build a Smarter Planet." The campaign markets IBM as a company that helps customers turn today's data and technology explosion into smart solutions that will transform their businesses and improve the world's data IQ. "What is a smarter planet?" asks the company. It's one that uses data in an "instrumented, intelligent, and interconnected" way. IBM's services now include everything from data analytics to mobile, social business, and cloud-computing technologies.

IBM smart solutions span an incredible breadth of industries and processes—from commerce and digital communications to health care, education, and sustainability. For example, one Smarter Planet ad tells how IBM is helping to "track food from farm to fork" in an effort to reduce the 25 percent of the world's food currently lost to spoilage. At the other extreme, ads tell how IBM analytics helped New York City's NYPD cut crime by 35 percent and New York State save $889 million by catching tax dodgers.

Here are just a few more examples showing how IBM has applied its "Smarter Planet" mission to finding solutions across its diverse customer base.

- IBM's MobileFirst group helped Air Canada design, implement, and manage a self-service customer check-in and travel information system that lets customers travel smarter and Air Canada keep smarter track of how these services are used and valued. The system—a blend of sophisticated IBM hardware, software, and services—lets customers conveniently access a broad array of check-in and information services through Web, kiosk, and mobile devices. It then provides Air Canada with the analytics needed to improve the design, costs, and customer value of the system.
- IBM's SmartCloud group helped Russell's Convenience—a 25-store Western-U.S. convenience store chain—set up a system by which employees can collaborate across stores and with suppliers to improve service to customers. Before working with IBM, Russell's management relied on scattered phone calls, e-mail, and travel to keep track of planning and day-to-day

>> **IBM's customer-focused mission is summed up by the company's marketing and positioning campaign: "Let's Build a Smarter Planet."**

business issues, and many tasks fell through the cracks. Now, using IBM's SmartCloud Engage services, employees and selected suppliers have instant access to cloud-based social networking and collaboration tools. Instead of searching through e-mails or making multiple phone calls, employees can now interact systematically online in real time. "IBM is helping our [stores] to operate as one business—one that is connected, informed, and cohesive," says the company's president.

- Vestas Wind Systems, the world's largest wind energy company, needed to find good wind turbine locations that would optimize energy output and maximize return on investment. IBM's Smart Analytics groups found the solution in its BigInsights software and "Firestorm" supercomputer (capable of 150 trillion calculations per second). The IBM system pinpoints the best turbine placements by analyzing massive amounts of data, such as weather reports, tidal phases, geospatial and sensor data, satellite images, deforestation maps, and weather modeling research. Such analysis used to take weeks. But thanks to IBM's smart solution, it can now be done in less than one hour. Once a turbine is operational, Vestas engineers use the analytics system to predict its performance, analyze how each blade reacts to weather changes, and determine the best times to schedule maintenance.

Thus, IBM doesn't just sell computers anymore. Under its broader, customer-oriented mission, today's IBM provides cutting-edge data analytics and solutions-based services that make customers and the world better and smarter. In fact, more than 90 percent of IBM's profits now come from software, services, financing, and business-consulting solutions.

Whether it's smarter business operations, smarter city management, smarter healthcare, or smarter anything else, what's smart for IBM's customers is also smart for IBM. In the five years since the start of the "Building a Smarter Planet" campaign, IBM's stock price has spurted from around $70 per share to more than $200. By defining itself in terms of the customer needs it solves rather that the products it sells, IBM has transformed itself from a big blue dinosaur to the blue horizons of tomorrow's smarter planet.

Sources: Based on information and examples from Ashlee Vance, "IBM on a Mission to Save the Planet," *Bloomberg Businessweek*, March 5, 2012, pp. 51–52; Natalie Zmuda, "How Purpose Affects the Bottom Line," *Advertising Age*, October 8, 2012, http://adage.com/article/print/237597/; "Vestas Wind Systems Turns to IBM Big Data Analytics for Smarter Wind Energy," October 24, 2011, www-03.ibm.com/press/us/en/pressrelease/35737.wss; "Russell's Convenience Chooses IBM for Cloud Collaboration," *CSPnet.com*, August16,2011, www.cspnet.com/news/technology/articles/russells-convenience-chooses-ibm-cloud-collaboration; "Air Canada: On a Never-Ending Push to Make Life Simpler for the Customer," www.ibm.com/smarterplanet/us/en/leadership/aircanada/assets/pdf/AirCanada_Paper.pdf, accessed May 2013; "IBM Smarter Cities: The Future City Is a Smarter City," www.youtube.com/watch?v=vm8iDpfWpjw, accessed October 2013; and "What Is a Smarter Planet?" www.ibm.com/smarterplanet/us/en/overview/ideas/index.html?re=sph, accessed October 2013.

Customer-focused mission: The fast-growing Buffalo Wild Wings chain's mission is to provide a total eating and social environment that "fuels the sports fan experience." As a result, it creates in-store and online experiences that promote brand fan engagement.

Mission statements should be meaningful and specific yet motivating. Too often, mission statements are written for public relations purposes and lack specific, workable guidelines. Instead, they should emphasize the company's strengths and tell forcefully how it intends to win in the marketplace. For example, Google's mission isn't to be the world's best search engine. It's to give people a window into the world's information, wherever it might be found.[3]

Finally, a company's mission should not be stated as making more sales or profits; profits are only a reward for creating value for customers. Instead, the mission should focus on customers and the customer experience the company seeks to create. Thus, the fast-growing Buffalo Wild Wings restaurant chain's mission isn't just to sell the most wings at a profit:[4]

> Customers do, in fact, come to Buffalo Wild Wings to eat wings and drink beer, but also to watch sports, trash talk, cheer on their sports teams, and meet old friends and make new ones—that is, a total eating and social experience. "We realize that we're not just in the business of selling wings," says the company. "We're something much bigger. We're in the business of fueling the sports fan experience." True to that broader mission, Buffalo Wild Wings creates in-store and online promotions that inspire camaraderie. "It's about giving them tools to not just be spectators but advocates of the brand," says the chain. For example, the brand's very active Web site draws 1.4 million visitors per month and its Facebook page has more than 10 million fans. Pursuing

a customer-focused mission has paid big dividends for Buffalo Wild Wings. The wing joint's sales have quadrupled in the past eight years and the company brags that it's the number one brand in its industry for fan engagement.

Setting Company Objectives and Goals

The company needs to turn its mission into detailed supporting objectives for each level of management. Each manager should have objectives and be responsible for reaching them. For example, most Americans know H. J. Heinz for its ketchup—it sells more than 650 billion bottles of ketchup each year. But Heinz owns a breadth of other food products under a variety of brands, ranging from Heinz and Ore-Ida to Classico. Heinz ties this diverse product portfolio together under this mission: "As the trusted leader in nutrition and wellness, Heinz—the original Pure Food Company—is dedicated to the sustainable health of people, the planet, and our company."

This broad mission leads to a hierarchy of objectives, including business objectives and marketing objectives. >> Heinz's overall objective is to build profitable customer relationships by developing foods "superior in quality, taste, nutrition, and convenience" that embrace its nutrition and wellness mission. It does this by investing heavily in research. However, research is expensive and must be funded through improved profit, so improving profits becomes another major objective for Heinz. Profits can be improved by increasing sales or reducing costs. Sales can be increased by improving the company's share of domestic and international markets. These goals then become the company's current marketing objectives.

Marketing strategies and programs must be developed to support these marketing objectives. To increase its market share, Heinz might broaden its product lines, increase product availability and promotion in existing markets, and expand into new markets. For example, Heinz recently added "Grillers" potatoes ready for outdoor grilling to its Ore-Ida product line to keep demand for its potatoes strong during the summer season. And it purchased an 80 percent stake in Quero, a Brazilian brand of tomato-based sauces, ketchup, condiments, and vegetables. Quero is expected to double Heinz's sales in Latin America this year and to serve as a platform to market Heinz in Brazil.[5]

These are Heinz's broad marketing strategies. Each broad marketing strategy must then be defined in greater detail. For example, increasing the product's promotion may require more advertising and public relations efforts; if so, both requirements will need to be spelled out. In this way, the firm's mission is translated into a set of objectives for the current period.

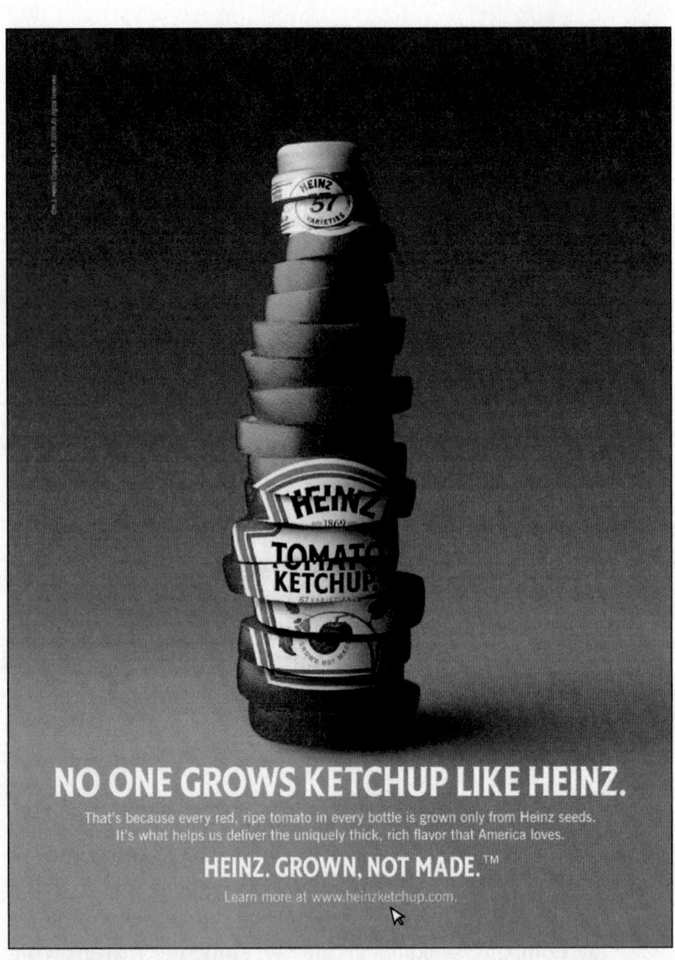

>> **Heinz's overall objective is to build profitable customer relationships by developing foods "superior in quality, taste, nutrition, and convenience" that embrace its nutrition and wellness mission.**

Designing the Business Portfolio

Business portfolio
The collection of businesses and products that make up the company.

Guided by the company's mission statement and objectives, management now must plan its business portfolio—the collection of businesses and products that make up the company. The best **business portfolio** is the one that best fits the company's strengths and weaknesses to opportunities in the environment.

Most large companies have complex portfolios of businesses and brands. Strategic and marketing planning for such business portfolios can be a daunting but critical

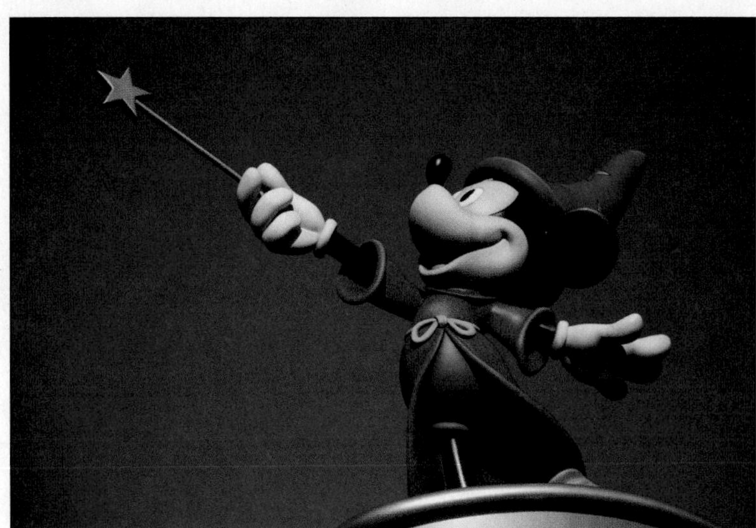

Managing the business portfolio: Most people think of Disney as theme parks and wholesome family entertainment, but over the past two decades, it's become a sprawling collection of media and entertainment businesses that requires big doses of the famed "Disney magic" to manage.

Martin Beddall/Alamy.

task. For example, ESPN's portfolio consists of more than 50 business entities, ranging from multiple ESPN cable channels to ESPN Radio, ESPN.com, *ESPN The Magazine*, and even ESPN Zone sports-themed restaurants. In turn, ESPN is just one unit in the even broader, more complex portfolio of its parent company, The Walt Disney Company. The Disney portfolio includes its many Disney theme parks and resorts; Disney studio entertainment (movie, television, and theatrical production companies such as Walt Disney Pictures, Pixar, Touchstone Pictures, Pixar Animation, and Marvel Studios); Disney consumer products (from apparel and toys to interactive games); and a sizable collection of broadcast, cable, radio, and Internet media businesses (including ESPN and the ABC Television Network). Managing this vast business portfolio profitably requires more than a little of Disney's famed magic.

Business portfolio planning involves two steps. First, the company must analyze its *current* business portfolio and determine which businesses should receive more, less, or no investment. Second, it must shape the *future* portfolio by developing strategies for growth and downsizing.

Analyzing the Current Business Portfolio

Portfolio analysis
The process by which management evaluates the products and businesses that make up the company.

The major activity in strategic planning is business **portfolio analysis**, whereby management evaluates the products and businesses that make up the company. The company will want to put strong resources into its more profitable businesses and phase down or drop its weaker ones.

Management's first step is to identify the key businesses that make up the company, called *strategic business units* (SBUs). An SBU can be a company division, a product line within a division, or sometimes a single product or brand. The company next assesses the attractiveness of its various SBUs and decides how much support each deserves. When designing a business portfolio, it's a good idea to add and support products and businesses that fit closely with the firm's core philosophy and competencies.

The purpose of strategic planning is to find ways in which the company can best use its strengths to take advantage of attractive opportunities in the environment. For this reason, most standard portfolio analysis methods evaluate SBUs on two important dimensions: the attractiveness of the SBU's market or industry and the strength of the SBU's position in that market or industry. The best-known portfolio-planning method was developed by the Boston Consulting Group, a leading management consulting firm.[6]

Growth-share matrix
A portfolio-planning method that evaluates a company's SBUs in terms of market growth rate and relative market share.

The Boston Consulting Group Approach. Using the now-classic Boston Consulting Group (BCG) approach, a company classifies all its SBUs according to the **growth-share matrix**, as shown in **Figure 2.2**. On the vertical axis, *market growth rate* provides a measure of market attractiveness. On the horizontal axis, *relative market share* serves as a measure of company strength in the market. The growth-share matrix defines four types of SBUs:

1. ***Stars.*** Stars are high-growth, high-share businesses or products. They often need heavy investments to finance their rapid growth. Eventually their growth will slow down, and they will turn into cash cows.
2. ***Cash cows.*** Cash cows are low-growth, high-share businesses or products. These established and successful SBUs need less investment to hold their market share. Thus, they produce a lot of the cash that the company uses to pay its bills and support other SBUs that need investment.
3. ***Question marks.*** Question marks are low-share business units in high-growth markets. They require a lot of cash to hold their share, let alone increase it.

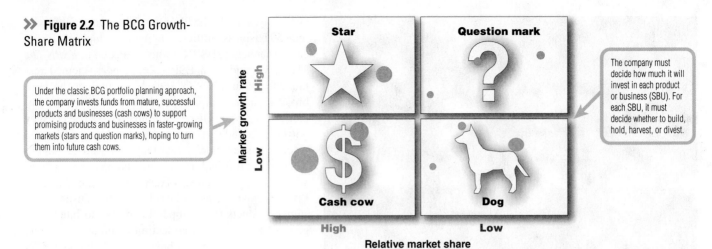

Figure 2.2 The BCG Growth-Share Matrix

Under the classic BCG portfolio planning approach, the company invests funds from mature, successful products and businesses (cash cows) to support promising products and businesses in faster-growing markets (stars and question marks), hoping to turn them into future cash cows.

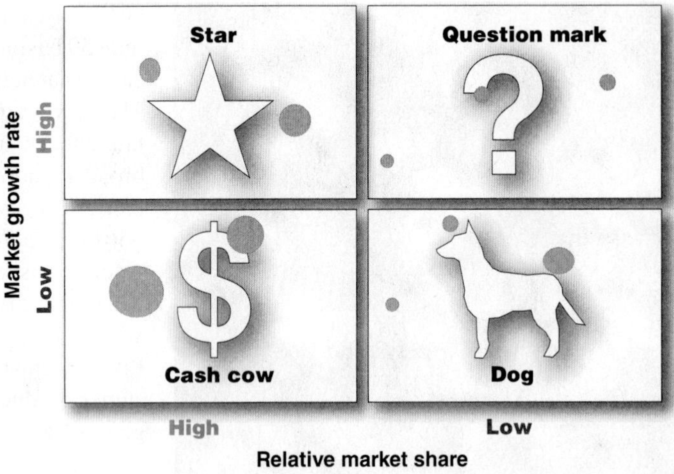

The company must decide how much it will invest in each product or business (SBU). For each SBU, it must decide whether to build, hold, harvest, or divest.

Management has to think hard about which question marks it should try to build into stars and which should be phased out.

4. ***Dogs.*** Dogs are low-growth, low-share businesses and products. They may generate enough cash to maintain themselves but do not promise to be large sources of cash.

The 10 circles in the growth-share matrix represent the company's 10 current SBUs. The company has two stars, two cash cows, three question marks, and three dogs. The areas of the circles are proportional to the SBU's dollar sales. This company is in fair shape, although not in good shape. It wants to invest in the more promising question marks to make them stars and maintain the stars so that they will become cash cows as their markets mature. Fortunately, it has two good-sized cash cows. Income from these cash cows will help finance the company's question marks, stars, and dogs. The company should take some decisive action concerning its dogs and its question marks.

Once it has classified its SBUs, the company must determine what role each will play in the future. It can pursue one of four strategies for each SBU. It can invest more in the business unit to *build* its share. Or it can invest just enough to *hold* the SBU's share at the current level. It can *harvest* the SBU, milking its short-term cash flow regardless of the long-term effect. Finally, it can *divest* the SBU by selling it or phasing it out and using the resources elsewhere.

As time passes, SBUs change their positions in the growth-share matrix. Many SBUs start out as question marks and move into the star category if they succeed. They later become cash cows as market growth falls, and then finally die off or turn into dogs toward the end of the life cycle. The company needs to add new products and units continuously so that some of them will become stars and, eventually, cash cows that will help finance other SBUs.

Problems with Matrix Approaches. The BCG and other formal methods revolutionized strategic planning. However, such centralized approaches have limitations: They can be difficult, time consuming, and costly to implement. Management may find it difficult to define SBUs and measure market share and growth. In addition, these approaches focus on classifying *current* businesses but provide little advice for *future* planning.

Because of such problems, many companies have dropped formal matrix methods in favor of more customized approaches that better suit their specific situations. Moreover, unlike former strategic planning efforts that rested mostly in the hands of senior managers at company headquarters, today's strategic planning has been decentralized. Increasingly, companies are placing responsibility for strategic planning in the hands of cross-functional teams of divisional managers who are close to their markets.

For example, think again about The Walt Disney Company. Most people think of Disney as theme parks and wholesome family entertainment. But in the mid-1980s, Disney set up a powerful, centralized strategic planning group to guide its direction and growth.

>> Figure 2.3 The Product/Market Expansion Grid

	Existing products	**New products**
Existing markets	Market penetration	Product development
New markets	Market development	Diversification

Companies can grow by developing new markets for existing products. For example, Starbucks is expanding rapidly in China, which by 2015 will be its second-largest market, behind only the United States.

Through diversification, companies can grow by starting or buying businesses outside their current product/markets. For example, Starbucks is entering the "health and wellness" market with stores called Evolution By Starbucks.

Over the next two decades, the strategic planning group turned The Walt Disney Company into a huge and diverse collection of media and entertainment businesses. The sprawling company grew to include everything from theme resorts and film studios (Walt Disney Pictures, Touchstone Pictures, Pixar, and others) to media networks (ABC Television plus ESPN, Disney Channel, parts of A&E and the History Channel, and a half dozen others) to consumer products and a cruise line.

The newly transformed company proved hard to manage and performed unevenly. To improve performance, Disney disbanded the centralized strategic planning unit, decentralizing its functions to Disney division managers. As a result, Disney retains its position at the head of the world's media conglomerates. And even through the recently weak economy, Disney's sound strategic management of its broad mix of businesses has helped it fare better than rival media companies.[7]

Developing Strategies for Growth and Downsizing

Product/market expansion grid
A portfolio-planning tool for identifying company growth opportunities through market penetration, market development, product development, or diversification.

Market penetration
Company growth by increasing sales of current products to current market segments without changing the product.

Beyond evaluating current businesses, designing the business portfolio involves finding businesses and products the company should consider in the future. Companies need growth if they are to compete more effectively, satisfy their stakeholders, and attract top talent. At the same time, a firm must be careful not to make growth itself an objective. The company's objective must be to manage "profitable growth."

Marketing has the main responsibility for achieving profitable growth for the company. Marketing needs to identify, evaluate, and select market opportunities and establish strategies for capturing them. One useful device for identifying growth opportunities is the **product/market expansion grid**, shown in **>> Figure 2.3**.[8] We apply it here to Starbucks:[9]

> In only three decades, Starbucks has grown at an astonishing pace, from a small Seattle coffee shop to a nearly $13.3 billion powerhouse with more than 18,000 retail stores in 62 countries. In the United States alone, Starbucks serves more than 70 million espresso-dependent customers each week. Starbucks gives customers what it calls a "third place"—away from home and away from work. Growth is the engine that keeps Starbucks perking. However, in recent years, the company's remarkable success has drawn a full litter of copycats, ranging from direct competitors such as Caribou Coffee to fast-food merchants such as McDonald's McCafe. Almost every eatery, it seems, now serves its own special premium brew. >> To maintain its incredible growth in an increasingly overcaffeinated marketplace, Starbucks must brew up an ambitious, multipronged growth strategy.

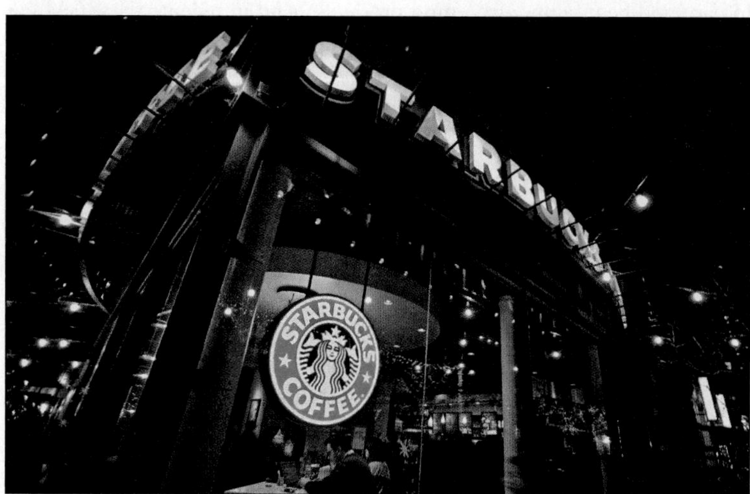

>> Strategies for growth: To maintain its incredible growth, Starbucks has brewed up an ambitious, multipronged growth strategy.

Bloomberg via Getty Images.

First, Starbucks' management might consider whether the company can achieve deeper **market penetration**—making more sales to current customers without changing its original products. It might add new stores in current market areas to make it easier for customers to visit. In fact, Starbucks plans to add 3,000 new stores over the next five years. Improvements in advertising, prices, service, menu selection, or store design might encourage customers to stop by more often, stay longer, or buy more during each visit. For example, Starbucks is remodeling many of its stores to give them more of a neighborhood feel—with earth tones, wood counters, and handwritten menu boards. And to boost business beyond the breakfast rush, which still constitutes the bulk of the company's revenue, the chain has added an evening menu in some markets featuring wine, beer, and tapas such as "Warmed Rosemary and Brown Sugar Cashews" and "Bacon Wrapped Dates with Balsamic Glaze."

Market development
Company growth by identifying and developing new market segments for current company products.

Second, Starbucks might consider possibilities for **market development**—identifying and developing new markets for its current products. For instance, managers could review new demographic markets. Perhaps new groups—such as seniors—could be encouraged to visit Starbucks coffee shops for the first time or to buy more from them. Managers could also review new geographic markets. Starbucks is now expanding swiftly in non-U.S. markets, especially Asia. The company recently opened its 1,000th store in Japan, expects to have 1,500 stores in China by 2015, and plans to more than double its number of stores in South Korea to 700 by 2016.

Product development
Company growth by offering modified or new products to current market segments.

Third, Starbucks could consider **product development**—offering modified or new products to current markets. For example, to capture a piece of the $2 billion single-serve market, Starbucks developed Via instant coffee, and sells its coffees and Tazo teas in K-Cup packs that fit Keurig at-home brewers. Starbucks recently introduced a lighter-roast coffee called Blonde, developed to meet the tastes of the 40 percent of U.S. coffee drinkers who prefer lighter, milder roasts. Starbucks is also forging ahead into new product categories. For instance, it recently entered the $8 billion energy drink market with Starbucks Refreshers, a beverage that combines fruit juice and green coffee extract.

Diversification
Company growth through starting up or acquiring businesses outside the company's current products and markets.

Finally, Starbucks might consider **diversification**—starting up or buying businesses beyond its current products and markets. For example, the company recently acquired Evolution Fresh, a boutique provider of super-premium fresh-squeezed juices. Starbucks intends to use Evolution as its entry into the "health and wellness" category, including standalone stores called Evolution By Starbucks.

Companies must not only develop strategies for growing their business portfolios but also strategies for *downsizing* them. There are many reasons that a firm might want to abandon products or markets. The firm may have grown too fast or entered areas where it lacks experience. The market environment might change, making some products or markets less profitable. For example, in difficult economic times, many firms prune out weaker, less-profitable products and markets to focus their more limited resources on the strongest ones. Finally, some products or business units simply age and die.

When a firm finds brands or businesses that are unprofitable or that no longer fit its overall strategy, it must carefully prune, harvest, or divest them. For example, P&G just recently sold off the last of its food brands, Pringles, to Kellogg, allowing the company to focus on household care and beauty and grooming products. And in recent years, GM has pruned several underperforming brands from its portfolio, including Oldsmobile, Pontiac, Saturn, Hummer, and Saab. Weak businesses usually require a disproportionate amount of management attention. Managers should focus on promising growth opportunities, not fritter away energy trying to salvage fading ones.

Author Comment
Marketing can't go it alone in creating customer value. Marketing must work closely with other departments to form an effective internal company value chain and with other companies in the marketing system to create an external value delivery network that jointly serves customers.

Planning Marketing: Partnering to Build Customer Relationships

The company's strategic plan establishes what kinds of businesses the company will operate and its objectives for each. Then, within each business unit, more detailed planning takes place. The major functional departments in each unit—marketing, finance, accounting, purchasing, operations, information systems, human resources, and others—must work together to accomplish strategic objectives.

Marketing plays a key role in the company's strategic planning in several ways. First, marketing provides a guiding *philosophy*—the marketing concept—that suggests the company strategy should revolve around creating customer value and building profitable relationships with important consumer groups. Second, marketing provides *inputs* to strategic planners by helping to identify attractive market opportunities and assessing the firm's potential to take advantage of them. Finally, within individual business units, marketing designs *strategies* for reaching the unit's objectives. Once the unit's objectives are set, marketing's task is to help carry them out profitably.

Customer value is the key ingredient in the marketer's formula for success. However, as noted in Chapter 1, although marketing plays a leading role, it alone cannot produce superior value for customers. It can be only a partner in attracting, keeping, and growing customers. In addition to *customer relationship management*, marketers must also practice *partner relationship management*. They must work closely with partners in other company departments to form an effective internal *value chain* that serves customers. Moreover, they must partner effectively with other companies in the marketing system to form a competitively superior external *value delivery network*. We now take a closer look at the concepts of a company value chain and a value delivery network.

Partnering with Other Company Departments

Value chain
The series of internal departments that carry out value-creating activities to design, produce, market, deliver, and support a firm's products.

Each company department can be thought of as a link in the company's internal **value chain.**[10] That is, each department carries out value-creating activities to design, produce, market, deliver, and support the firm's products. The firm's success depends not only on how well each department performs its work but also on how well the various departments coordinate their activities.

For example, Walmart's goal is to create customer value and satisfaction by providing shoppers with the products they want at the lowest possible prices. Marketers at Walmart play an important role. They learn what customers need and stock the stores' shelves with the desired products at unbeatable low prices. They prepare advertising and merchandising programs and assist shoppers with customer service. Through these and other activities, Walmart's marketers help deliver value to customers.

The value chain: Walmart's ability to help you "Save oney. Live Better." by offering the right products at lower ices depends on the contributions of people in all of the mpany's departments.

digitallife/Alamy.

However, the marketing department needs help from the company's other departments. »Walmart's ability to help you "Save Money. Live Better." depends on the purchasing department's skill in developing the needed suppliers and buying from them at low cost. Walmart's information technology (IT) department must provide fast and accurate information about which products are selling in each store. And its operations people must provide effective, low-cost merchandise handling.

A company's value chain is only as strong as its weakest link. Success depends on how well each department performs its work of adding customer value and on how the company coordinates the activities of various departments. At Walmart, if purchasing can't obtain the lowest prices from suppliers, or if operations can't distribute merchandise at the lowest costs, then marketing can't deliver on its promise of unbeatable low prices.

Ideally, then, a company's different functions should work in harmony to produce value for consumers. But, in practice, interdepartmental relations are full of conflicts and misunderstandings. The marketing department takes the consumer's point of view. But when marketing tries to improve customer satisfaction, it can cause other departments to do a poorer job *in their terms*. Marketing department actions can increase purchasing costs, disrupt production schedules, increase inventories, and create budget headaches. Thus, other departments may resist the marketing department's efforts.

Yet marketers must find ways to get all departments to "think consumer" and develop a smoothly functioning value chain. One marketing expert puts it this way: "True market orientation . . . means that the entire company obsesses over creating value for the customer and views itself as a bundle of processes that profitably define, create, communicate, and deliver value to its target customers. . . . Everyone must do marketing regardless of function or department." Says another, "Engaging customers today requires commitment from the entire company. We're all marketers now."[11] Thus, whether you're an accountant, an operations manager, a financial analyst, an IT specialist, or a human resources manager, you need to understand marketing and your role in creating customer value.

Partnering with Others in the Marketing System

In its quest to create customer value, the firm needs to look beyond its own internal value chain and into the value chains of its suppliers, distributors, and, ultimately, its customers. Consider McDonald's. People do not swarm to McDonald's only because they love the chain's hamburgers. Consumers flock to the McDonald's *system*, not only to its food products. Throughout the world, McDonald's finely tuned value delivery system delivers a high standard of QSCV—quality, service, cleanliness, and value. McDonald's is effective only to the extent that it successfully partners with its franchisees, suppliers, and others to jointly create "our customers' favorite place and way to eat."

Value delivery network
The network made up of the company, its suppliers, its distributors, and, ultimately, its customers who partner with each other to improve the performance of the entire system.

More companies today are partnering with other members of the supply chain—suppliers, distributors, and, ultimately, customers—to improve the performance of the customer **value delivery network**. Competition no longer takes place only between individual competitors. Rather, it takes place between the entire value delivery networks created by these competitors. Thus, Toyota's performance against Ford depends on the quality of Toyota's overall value delivery network versus Ford's. Even if Toyota makes the best cars, it might lose in the marketplace if Ford's dealer network provides more customer-satisfying sales and service.

SPEED BUMP LINKING THE CONCEPTS

Pause here for a moment to apply what you've read in the first part of this chapter.

- Why are we talking about company-wide strategic planning in a marketing text? What *does* strategic planning have to do with marketing?
- What are Nike's strategy and mission? What role does marketing play in helping Nike to accomplish its strategy and mission?
- What roles do other Nike departments play, and how can the company's marketers partner with these departments to maximize overall customer value? What roles do Nike's suppliers and resellers play?

Author Comment
Now that we've set the context in terms of company-wide strategy, it's time to discuss customer-driven marketing strategies and programs.

Marketing Strategy and the Marketing Mix

The strategic plan defines the company's overall mission and objectives. Marketing's role is shown in >> **Figure 2.4**, which summarizes the major activities involved in managing a customer-driven marketing strategy and the marketing mix.

Marketing strategy
The marketing logic by which the company hopes to create customer value and achieve profitable customer relationships.

Consumers are in the center. The goal is to create value for customers and build profitable customer relationships. Next comes **marketing strategy**—the marketing logic by which the company hopes to create this customer value and achieve these profitable relationships. The company decides which customers it will serve (segmentation and targeting) and how (differentiation and positioning). It identifies the total market and then divides it into smaller segments, selects the most promising segments, and focuses on serving and satisfying the customers in these segments.

Guided by marketing strategy, the company designs an integrated *marketing mix* made up of factors under its control—product, price, place, and promotion (the four Ps). To find the best marketing strategy and mix, the company engages in marketing analysis, planning, implementation, and control. Through these activities, the company watches and adapts to the actors and forces in the marketing environment. We will now look briefly at each activity. In later chapters, we will discuss each one in more depth.

Figure 2.4 Managing Marketing Strategies and the Marketing Mix

Marketing intermediaries
Competitors
Marketing analysis
Marketing planning
Product
Segmentation
Targeting
Customer value and relationships
Place
Price
Positioning
Differentiation
Promotion
Marketing control
Marketing implementation
Suppliers
Publics
At its core, marketing is all about creating customer value and profitable customer relationships.
Marketing strategy involves two key questions: Which customers will we serve (segmentation and targeting)? and How will we create value for them (differentiation and positioning)? Then, the company designs a marketing program—the four Ps—that delivers the intended value to targeted consumers.

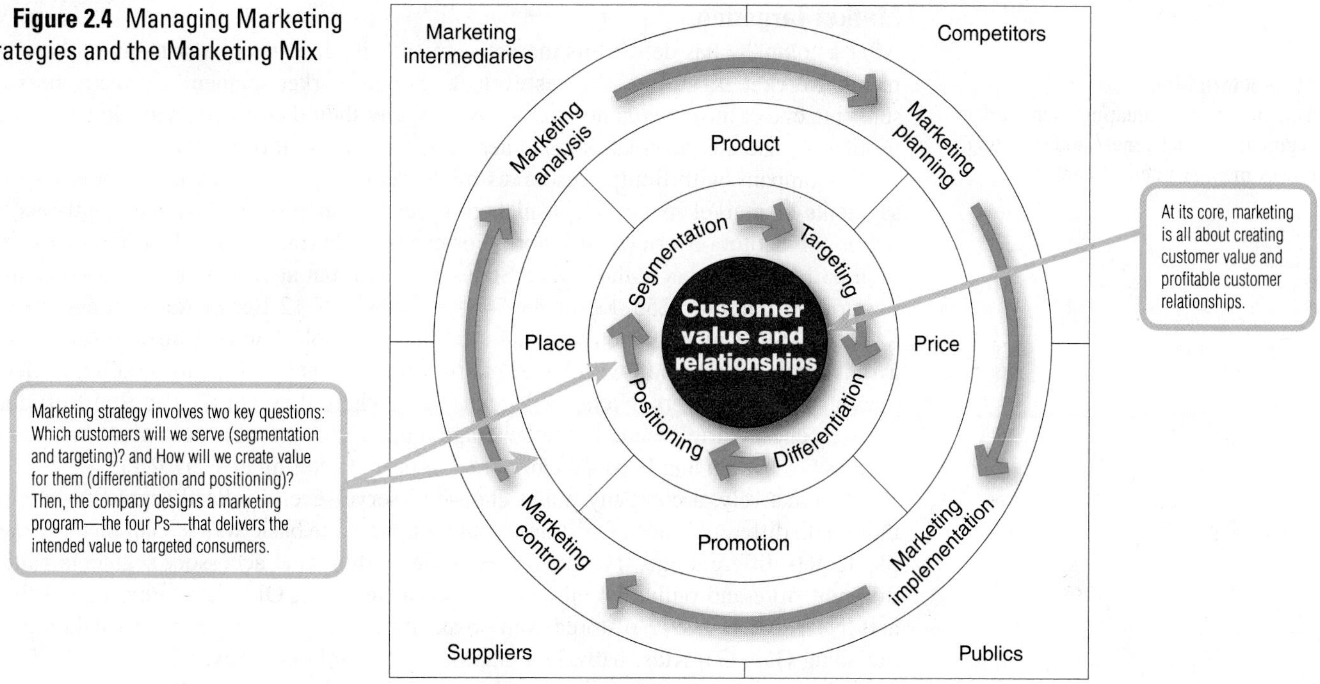

Customer-Driven Marketing Strategy

To succeed in today's competitive marketplace, companies must be customer centered. They must win customers from competitors and then keep and grow them by delivering greater value. But before it can satisfy customers, a company must first understand customer needs and wants. Thus, sound marketing requires careful customer analysis.

Companies know that they cannot profitably serve all consumers in a given market—at least not all consumers in the same way. There are too many different kinds of consumers with too many different kinds of needs. Most companies are in a position to serve some segments better than others. Thus, each company must divide up the total market, choose the best segments, and design strategies for profitably serving chosen segments. This process involves *market segmentation*, *market targeting*, *differentiation*, and *positioning*.

Market Segmentation

The market consists of many types of customers, products, and needs. The marketer must determine which segments offer the best opportunities. Consumers can be grouped and served in various ways based on geographic, demographic, psychographic, and behavioral factors. The process of dividing a market into distinct groups of buyers who have different needs, characteristics, or behaviors, and who might require separate products or marketing programs, is called **market segmentation**.

Market segmentation
Dividing a market into distinct groups of buyers who have different needs, characteristics, or behaviors, and who might require separate products or marketing programs.

Every market has segments, but not all ways of segmenting a market are equally useful. For example, Tylenol would gain little by distinguishing between low-income and high-income pain-relief users if both respond the same way to marketing efforts. A **market segment** consists of consumers who respond in a similar way to a given set of marketing efforts. In the car market, for example, consumers who want the biggest, most comfortable car regardless of price make up one market segment. Consumers who care mainly about price and operating economy make up another segment. It would be difficult to make one car model that was the first choice of consumers in both segments. Companies are wise to focus their efforts on meeting the distinct needs of individual market segments.

Market segment
A group of consumers who respond in a similar way to a given set of marketing efforts.

Market Targeting

Market targeting
The process of evaluating each market segment's attractiveness and selecting one or more segments to enter.

After a company has defined its market segments, it can enter one or many of these segments. **Market targeting** involves evaluating each market segment's attractiveness and selecting one or more segments to enter. A company should target segments in which it can profitably generate the greatest customer value and sustain it over time.

A company with limited resources might decide to serve only one or a few special segments or market niches. Such nichers specialize in serving customer segments that major competitors overlook or ignore. For example, Ferrari sells only 1,500 of its very-high-performance cars in the United States each year but at very high prices—such as its Ferrari 458 Italia at $255,000 or the 740-horsepower F-12 Berlinetta at an eye-opening $400,000. Most nichers aren't quite so exotic. Profitable low-cost airline Allegiant Air avoids direct competition with larger major airline rivals by targeting smaller, neglected markets and new flyers. Nicher Allegiant "goes where they ain't." And Red Bull dominates its energy drink niche in the beverage industry so well that even giant competitors such as Coca-Cola and PepsiCo can't crack it (see Marketing at Work 2.2).

Alternatively, a company might choose to serve several related segments—perhaps those with different kinds of customers but with the same basic wants. Gap Inc., for example, targets different age, income, and lifestyle clothing and accessory segments with six different store and online brands: Gap, Banana Republic, Old Navy, Piperlime, Athleta, and INTERMIX. The Gap store brand breaks its segment down into even smaller niches, including Gap, GapKids, babyGap, GapMaternity, and GapBody.[12] Or a large company (for example, car companies like Honda and Ford) might decide to offer a complete range of products to serve all market segments.

Positioning
Arranging for a product to occupy a clear, distinctive, and desirable place relative to competing products in the minds of target consumers.

Most companies enter a new market by serving a single segment; if this proves successful, they add more segments. For example, Nike started with innovative running shoes for serious runners. Large companies eventually seek full market coverage. Nike now makes and sells a broad range of sports products for just about anyone and everyone, with the goal of "helping athletes at every level of ability reach their potential."[13] It designs different products to meet the special needs of each segment it serves.

Positioning: The 100-year-old Del Monte brand positions itself as "Bursting with Life: Made in America. Picked and packed at the peak of ripeness. Same essential ingredients as fresh."

Del Monte Corporation.

Market Differentiation and Positioning

After a company has decided which market segments to enter, it must determine how to differentiate its market offering for each targeted segment and what positions it wants to occupy in those segments. A product's *position* is the place it occupies relative to competitors' products in consumers' minds. Marketers want to develop unique market positions for their products. If a product is perceived to be exactly like others on the market, consumers would have no reason to buy it.

Positioning is arranging for a product to occupy a clear, distinctive, and desirable place relative to competing products in the minds of target consumers. Marketers plan positions that distinguish their products from competing brands and give them the greatest advantage in their target markets.

Audi promises "Truth in Engineering"; Subaru is "Confidence in Motion." Coke is all about "open happiness"; Pepsi says "live for now." Del Monte is "Bursting with Life"; Cascadian Farm products are "Certified Organic. Guaranteed Delicious." At Panera you can "Live Consciously. Eat Deliciously." At Wendy's, "Quality Is Our Recipe." Such deceptively simple statements form the backbone of a product's marketing strategy. For example, the iconic 100 year old Del Monte brand designed its entire integrated marketing campaign—from television and print ads to its online, mobile, and social media content—around the "Bursting with Life" positioning. More than just words, the campaign slogan positions Del Monte's canned fruits and vegetables as quality ingredients that contribute to a healthy lifestyle. They are "grown in America, picked and packed at the peak of ripeness, [and contain the] same essential nutrients as fresh."

MARKETING AT WORK 2.2

Red Bull: This Nicher "Gives You Wings"

There's no question: Coca-Cola and PepsiCo dominate the global beverage industry. Each boasts leading brands in almost every category, from carbonated soft drinks to enhanced juice drinks to bottled waters. Last year, Coca-Cola sold more than $48 billion worth of beverages worldwide; PepsiCo was a solid runner-up at $32 billion. Both companies spend hundreds of millions of dollars annually on sophisticated marketing and advertising programs, and few competitors can match their distribution prowess. So how does a small company breaking into the beverage business compete with such global powerhouses? The best answer: It doesn't—at least not directly. Instead, it finds a unique market niche and runs where the big dogs don't.

That's what Red Bull does. When Red Bull first introduced its energy drink more than 25 years ago, few imagined that it would become the $5 billion-dollar-a-year success that it is today. Red Bull has succeeded by avoiding head-to-head battles with giants like Coca-Cola and Pepsi. Instead, it found a new beverage niche—energy drinks—that the market leaders had overlooked. Then, it energized this niche with a unique product, brand personality, and marketing approach.

Back in 1987, energy drinks simply didn't exist. If you wanted a quick pick-me-up, about the only options were caffeinated soft drinks or a good old cup of coffee. But Red Bull founder Dietrich Mateschitz saw an unfilled customer need. He formulated a new beverage containing a hefty dose of caffeine, along with little-known ingredients such as taurine and glucuronolactone. It tasted terrible. But it packed the right punch, producing unique physical-energy and mental-clarity benefits. To make the new beverage even more distinctive, Mateschitz gave it a unique name—Red Bull, packaged it in a slim 8.3-ounce blue-and-silver can with a distinct red-and-yellow logo, and tagged it with a $2-per-can price. With that unlikely combination, a whole new energy drink category was born, with Red Bull as its only player.

The unique Red Bull product demanded equally unique brand positioning and personality, a declaration that this was no ordinary beverage. Red Bull's early marketing didn't disappoint. The brand's first and still only slogan—"Red Bull Gives You Wings"—communicated the product's energy-inducing benefits. More important, it tapped into the forces that moved the brand's narrow target niche—customers seeking to live life in the adrenalin-stoked fast lane.

To reinforce the "Gives You Wings" brand promise, and in line with the new brand's meager early finances, Red Bull shunned the big-budget mass-media advertising common in the beverage industry at the time. Instead, it relied on grassroots, high-octane sports and event marketing. It sponsored extreme sports events and athletes who were overlooked by big beverage competitors but were spiking in popularity with Red Bull's target customers, events such as snowboarding and freestyle motocross, and athletes like Shawn White and Travis Pastrana.

In the years since, Red Bull has turned event marketing into a science. Today, the brand holds hundreds of events each year in dozens of sports around the world. Each event features off-the-grid experiences designed to bring the high-octane world of Red Bull to its narrow but impassioned community of enthusiasts. Red Bull owns Formula 1 car racing teams and soccer clubs. Its name is plastered all over events such as the Red Bull Crashed Ice World Championship, the Red Bull Cliff Diving World Series, and the annual Red Bull Rampage free ride mountain bike competition. But it's not just about the events. It's about creating tactile engagements where people can feel, touch, taste, and live the brand face to face rather than simply reading about or watching it. Red Bull doesn't just sponsor an event—it *is* the event. The brand experience is often as much of the story as the event itself.

Just one example of Red Bull's niche marketing genius is the Red Bull Stratos project, in which extreme skydiver Felix Baumgartner jumped from a helium balloon 128,000 feet (more than 24 miles) above the earth, breaking the sound barrier and numerous other records in the process. The jump also set records for consumer brand engagement. Baumgartner diving into space fit perfectly with Red Bull's "Gives You Wings" brand message. And both Baumgartner's capsule and his space-age jumpsuit were emblazoned with the Red Bull name and logo. More than 8 million people watched the event live on 40 TV stations and 130 digital channels. For months before and after the event, you couldn't see or hear anything about Baumgartner without thinking about Red Bull.

Red Bull's niche marketing engages customers in a way that big-budget traditional marketing by competitors like Coca-Cola or Pepsi can't. According to one sports marketing executive, "When you're in the Super Bowl, you're one of 70 ads or so. When you go around the NASCAR track, you're one of

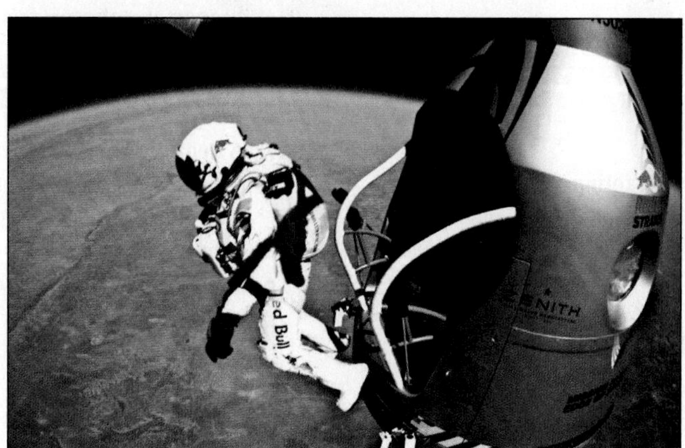

» Niche marketing: Red Bull uses grassroots, high-octane event marketing to engage and energize its focused customer core, building an impassioned brand community that even resourceful competitors such as Coca-Cola and PepsiCo can't crack.

Red Bull Stratos/ZUMA Press/Newscom.

44 teams. This is about owning something that will leave an impression." For example, within 40 minutes of posting photos of Baumgartner's jump, Red Bull's Facebook page gained almost 216,000 Likes, 10,000 comments, and over 29,000 shares. On Twitter, literally half of the worldwide trending topics were related to Red Bull Stratos. And by one estimate, 90 million people worldwide followed the campaign on social media, creating 60 million trusted brand impressions. You just can't buy that kind of consumer engagement in traditional media. "Red Bull Stratos was a priceless brand experience," concludes one social marketing analyst. "No company has ever triggered brand advocacy at this scale."

More than just a niche beverage company, Red Bull today has become a close-knit brand community that engages customers with both products and absorbing brand content. Beyond its products, Red Bull produces a steady stream of event and social media content that engages and entertains brand fans in relevant ways. During the last few years, for example, Red Bull's Media House unit has filmed movies, signed a deal with NBC for a show called *Red Bull Signature Series*, developed reality-TV ideas with big-name producers, become one of YouTube's biggest partners in publishing original content, and loaded its own Web and mobile sites with unique content features. "Whenever we [have done] any event, or signed an athlete or executed a project, everything has been put on film or photographed. Stories have been told," says the head of the Red Bull Media House unit. "It's part of the DNA of the brand."

Thus, Red Bull can't compete directly across the board with the Coca-Colas and PepsiCos of the beverage industry—it doesn't even try. Then again, given the depth of consumer engagement and loyalty that Red Bull engenders in its own small corner of the beverage world, Coke and Pepsi have found it even more difficult to compete with Red Bull in the energy drink niche. Red Bull still owns 44 percent of the energy drink category it created, with other independents Monster and Rockstar holding strong second- and third-place positions. By contrast, despite hefty investments, Coca-Cola and PepsiCo have yet to put much of a dent in the category. Coca-Cola's NOS and Full Throttle brands capture only about a 5 percent combined market share; Pepsi's Amp and Kickstart brands have suffered the same dismal fate.

That's what niche marketing is all about—a well-defined brand engaging a focused customer community with meaningful brand relationships that even large and resourceful competitors can't crack. Through smart niching, Red Bull has given its customers—and itself—new wings and a whole new shot of energy.

Sources: Travis Hoium, "Coke and Pepsi Up against a Young Monster—and Losing," *Daily Finance*, March 26, 2013, www.dailyfinance.com/on/coke-pepsi-monster-beverage-energy-drinks/; Janean Chun, "Bull Stratos May Change Future of Marketing," *Huffington Post*, October 15, 2012, www.huffingtonpost.com/2012/10/15/red-bull-stratos-marketing_n_1966852.html; Brian Kotlyar, "7 Social Campaign Insights from Red Bull Stratos," *DG Blog*, October 23, 2012, http://dachisgroup.com/2012/10/7-social-campaign-insights-from-redbull-stratos//; Teressa Iezzi, "Red Bull Media House," *Fast Company*, March, 2013, www.fastcompany.com/most-innovative-companies/2012/red-bull-media-house; and www.redbull.com/us/en, accessed October 2013.

In positioning its brand, a company first identifies possible customer value differences that provide competitive advantages on which to build the position. A company can offer greater customer value by either charging lower prices than competitors or offering more benefits to justify higher prices. But if the company *promises* greater value, it must then *deliver* that greater value. Thus, effective positioning begins with **differentiation**—actually *differentiating* the company's market offering so that it gives consumers more value. Once the company has chosen a desired position, it must take strong steps to deliver and communicate that position to target consumers. The company's entire marketing program should support the chosen positioning strategy.

Differentiation
Actually differentiating the market offering to create superior customer value.

Developing an Integrated Marketing Mix

After determining its overall marketing strategy, the company is ready to begin planning the details of the **marketing mix**, one of the major concepts in modern marketing. The marketing mix is the set of tactical marketing tools that the firm blends to produce the response it wants in the target market. The marketing mix consists of everything the firm can do to influence the demand for its product. The many possibilities can be collected into four groups of variables—the four Ps. >> **Figure 2.5** shows the marketing tools under each P.

Marketing mix
The set of tactical marketing tools—product, price, place, and promotion—that the firm blends to produce the response it wants in the target market.

- ***Product*** means the goods-and-services combination the company offers to the target market. Thus, a Ford Escape consists of nuts and bolts, spark plugs, pistons, headlights, and thousands of other parts. Ford offers several Escape models and dozens of optional features. The car comes fully serviced and with a comprehensive warranty that is as much a part of the product as the tailpipe.
- ***Price*** is the amount of money customers must pay to obtain the product. For example, Ford calculates suggested retail prices that its dealers might charge for

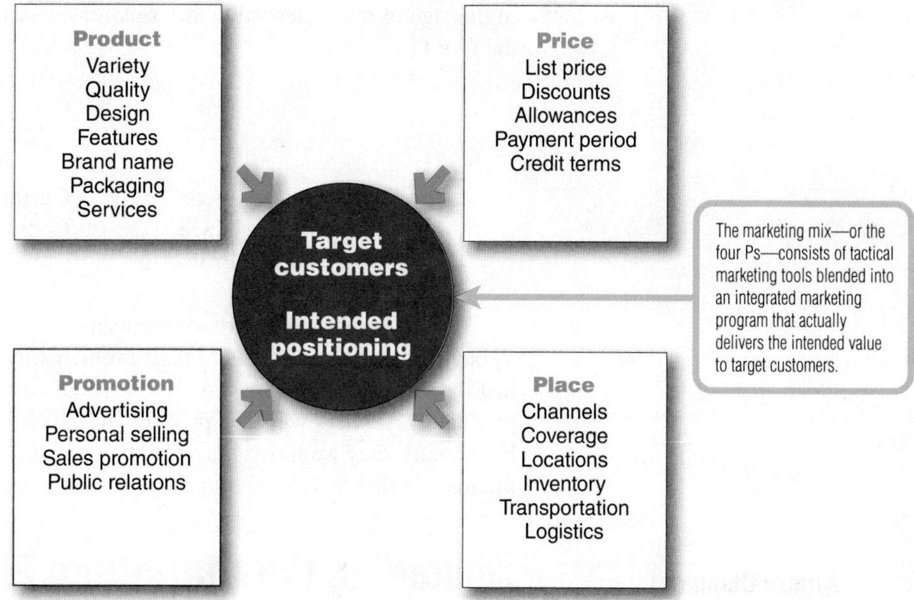

»» Figure 2.5 The Four Ps of the Marketing Mix

each Escape. But Ford dealers rarely charge the full sticker price. Instead, they negotiate the price with each customer, offering discounts, trade-in allowances, and credit terms. These actions adjust prices for the current competitive and economic situations and bring them into line with the buyer's perception of the car's value.

- ***Place*** includes company activities that make the product available to target consumers. Ford partners with a large body of independently owned dealerships that sell the company's many different models. Ford selects its dealers carefully and strongly supports them. The dealers keep an inventory of Ford automobiles, demonstrate them to potential buyers, negotiate prices, close sales, and service the cars after the sale.
- ***Promotion*** refers to activities that communicate the merits of the product and persuade target customers to buy it. Ford spends more than $2.1 billion each year on U.S. advertising to tell consumers about the company and its many products.[14] Dealership salespeople assist potential buyers and persuade them that Ford is the best car for them. Ford and its dealers offer special promotions—sales, cash rebates, and low financing rates—as added purchase incentives. And the Ford's Facebook, Twitter, YouTube, and other social media platforms engage consumers with the brand and other brand fans.

An effective marketing program blends the marketing mix elements into an integrated marketing program designed to achieve the company's marketing objectives by delivering value to consumers. The marketing mix constitutes the company's tactical tool kit for establishing strong positioning in target markets.

Some critics think that the four Ps may omit or underemphasize certain important activities. For example, they ask, "Where are services? Just because they don't start with a *P* doesn't justify omitting them." The answer is that services, such as banking, airline, and retailing services, are products too. We might call them *service products*. "Where is packaging?" the critics might ask. Marketers would answer that they include packaging as one of many product decisions. All said, as Figure 2.5 suggests, many marketing activities that might appear to be left out of the marketing mix are included under one of the four Ps. The issue is not whether there should be 4, 6, or 10 Ps so much as what framework is most helpful in designing integrated marketing programs.

There is another concern, however, that is valid. It holds that the four Ps concept takes the seller's view of the market, not the buyer's view. From the buyer's viewpoint, in this age of customer value and relationships, the four Ps might be better described as the four Cs:[15]

4Ps	4Cs
Product	Customer solution
Price	Customer cost
Place	Convenience
Promotion	Communication

Thus, whereas marketers see themselves as selling products, customers see themselves as buying value or solutions to their problems. And customers are interested in more than just the price; they are interested in the total costs of obtaining, using, and disposing of a product. Customers want the product and service to be as conveniently available as possible. Finally, they want two-way communication. Marketers would do well to think through the four Cs first and then build the four Ps on that platform.

Author Comment
So far we've focused on the *marketing* in marketing management. Now, let's turn to the *management*.

Managing the Marketing Effort

In addition to being good at the *marketing* in marketing management, companies also need to pay attention to the *management*. Managing the marketing process requires the four marketing management functions shown in **Figure 2.6**—*analysis, planning, implementation,* and *control*. The company first develops company-wide strategic plans and then translates them into marketing and other plans for each division, product, and brand. Through implementation, the company turns the plans into actions. Control consists of measuring and evaluating the results of marketing activities and taking corrective action where needed. Finally, marketing analysis provides the information and evaluations needed for all the other marketing activities.

Marketing Analysis

SWOT analysis
An overall evaluation of the company's strengths (S), weaknesses (W), opportunities (O), and threats (T).

Managing the marketing function begins with a complete analysis of the company's situation. The marketer should conduct a **SWOT analysis** (pronounced "swat" analysis), by which it evaluates the company's overall strengths (S), weaknesses (W), opportunities (O), and threats (T) (see **Figure 2.7**). Strengths include internal capabilities, resources, and positive situational factors that may help the company serve its customers and achieve its

Figure 2.6 Managing Marketing: Analysis, Planning, Implementation, and Control

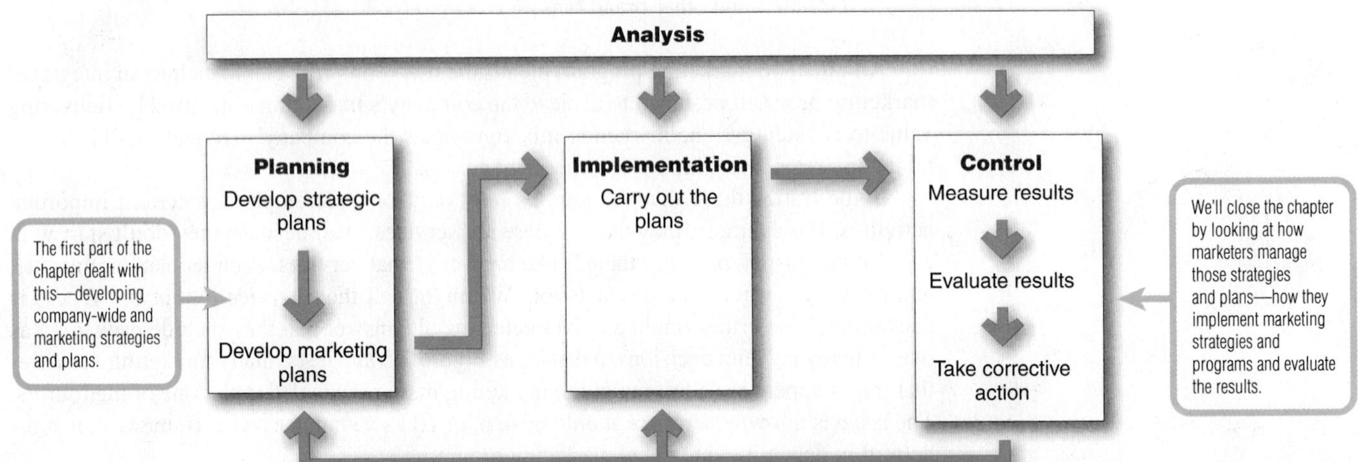

»» Figure 2.7 SWOT Analysis: Strengths (S), Weaknesses (W), Opportunities (O), and Threats (T)

objectives. Weaknesses include internal limitations and negative situational factors that may interfere with the company's performance. Opportunities are favorable factors or trends in the external environment that the company may be able to exploit to its advantage. And threats are unfavorable external factors or trends that may present challenges to performance.

Strengths
Internal capabilities that may help a company reach its objectives
Weaknesses
Internal limitations that may interfere with a company's ability to achieve its objectives
Opportunities
External factors that the company may be able to exploit to its advantage
Threats
Current and emerging external factors that may challenge the company's performance
Internal
External
Positive
Negative
The goal of SWOT analysis is to match the company's strengths to attractive opportunities in the environment, while eliminating or overcoming the weaknesses and minimizing the threats.
Hang on to this figure! SWOT analysis (pronounced "swat" analysis) is a widely used tool for conducting a situation analysis. You'll find yourself using it a lot in the future, especially when analyzing business cases.

The company should analyze its markets and marketing environment to find attractive opportunities and identify environmental threats. It should analyze company strengths and weaknesses as well as current and possible marketing actions to determine which opportunities it can best pursue. The goal is to match the company's strengths to attractive opportunities in the environment, while simultaneously eliminating or overcoming the weaknesses and minimizing the threats. Marketing analysis provides inputs to each of the other marketing management functions. We discuss marketing analysis more fully in Chapter 3.

Marketing Planning

Through strategic planning, the company decides what it wants to do with each business unit. Marketing planning involves choosing marketing strategies that will help the company attain its overall strategic objectives. A detailed marketing plan is needed for each business, product, or brand. What does a marketing plan look like? Our discussion focuses on product or brand marketing plans.

»» Table 2.2 outlines the major sections of a typical product or brand marketing plan. (See Appendix 2 for a sample marketing plan.) The plan begins with an executive summary that quickly reviews major assessments, goals, and recommendations. The main section of the plan presents a detailed SWOT analysis of the current marketing situation as well as potential threats and opportunities. The plan next states major objectives for the brand and outlines the specifics of a marketing strategy for achieving them.

A *marketing strategy* consists of specific strategies for target markets, positioning, the marketing mix, and marketing expenditure levels. It outlines how the company intends to create value for target customers in order to capture value in return. In this section, the planner explains how each strategy responds to the threats, opportunities, and critical issues spelled out earlier in the plan. Additional sections of the marketing plan lay out an action program for implementing the marketing strategy along with the details of a supporting *marketing budget*. The last section outlines the controls that will be used to monitor progress, measure return on marketing investment, and take corrective action.

Marketing Implementation

Marketing implementation
Turning marketing strategies and plans into marketing actions to accomplish strategic marketing objectives.

Planning good strategies is only a start toward successful marketing. A brilliant marketing strategy counts for little if the company fails to implement it properly. **Marketing implementation** is the process that turns marketing *plans* into marketing *actions* to accomplish

» Table 2.2 Contents of a Marketing Plan

Section	Purpose
Executive summary	Presents a brief summary of the main goals and recommendations of the plan for management review, helping top management find the plan's major points quickly.
Current marketing situation	Describes the target market and the company's position in it, including information about the market, product performance, competition, and distribution. This section includes the following: • A *market description* that defines the market and major segments and then reviews customer needs and factors in the marketing environment that may affect customer purchasing. • A *product review* that shows sales, prices, and gross margins of the major products in the product line. • A review of *competition* that identifies major competitors and assesses their market positions and strategies for product quality, pricing, distribution, and promotion. • A review of *distribution* that evaluates recent sales trends and other developments in major distribution channels.
Threats and opportunities analysis	Assesses major threats and opportunities that the product might face, helping management to anticipate important positive or negative developments that might have an impact on the firm and its strategies.
Objectives and issues	States the marketing objectives that the company would like to attain during the plan's term and discusses key issues that will affect their attainment.
Marketing strategy	Outlines the broad marketing logic by which the business unit hopes to create customer value and relationships and the specifics of target markets, positioning, and marketing expenditure levels. How will the company create value for customers in order to capture value from customers in return? This section also outlines specific strategies for each marketing mix element and explains how each responds to the threats, opportunities, and critical issues spelled out earlier in the plan.
Action programs	Spells out how marketing strategies will be turned into specific action programs that answer the following questions: *What* will be done? *When* will it be done? *Who* will do it? *How* much will it cost?
Budgets	Details a supporting marketing budget that is essentially a projected profit-and-loss statement. It shows expected revenues and expected costs of production, distribution, and marketing. The difference is the projected profit. The budget becomes the basis for materials buying, production scheduling, personnel planning, and marketing operations.
Controls	Outlines the controls that will be used to monitor progress, allow management to review implementation results, and spot products that are not meeting their goals. It includes measures of return on marketing investment.

strategic marketing objectives. Whereas marketing planning addresses the *what* and *why* of marketing activities, implementation addresses the *who*, *where*, *when*, and *how*.

Many managers think that "doing things right" (implementation) is as important as, or even more important than, "doing the right things" (strategy). The fact is that both are critical to success, and companies can gain competitive advantages through effective implementation. One firm can have essentially the same strategy as another, yet win in the marketplace through faster or better execution. Still, implementation is difficult—it is often easier to think up good marketing strategies than it is to carry them out.

In an increasingly connected world, people at all levels of the marketing system must work together to implement marketing strategies and plans. » At Michelin, for example, marketing implementation for the company's original equipment, replacement, industrial, and commercial tires requires day-to-day decisions and actions by thousands of people both inside and outside the organization. Marketing managers make decisions about target segments, branding, product development, pricing, promotion, and distribution. They talk with engineering about product designs, with manufacturing about production and

THE RIGHT
TIRE CHANGES
EVERYTHING
Michelin makes some of the most fuel efficient,* longest lasting tires. Plus they offer more security with their incredible stopping power. See how the right tire changes everything at **michelinman.com/righttire.**
*Based on comparative rolling resistance testing. Copyright ©2009 Michelin North America, Inc. All rights reserved. The Michelin Man is a registered trademark owned by Michelin North America, Inc.
MICHELIN
a better way forward

Marketing implementation: At Michelin, marketing implementation requires that thousands of people inside and outside the company work together to convince customers that "The right tire changes everything."

Michelin North America.

inventory levels, and with finance about funding and cash flows. They also connect with outside people, such as advertising agencies to plan ad campaigns and the news media to obtain publicity support. The sales force works closely with automobile manufacturers and supports independent Michelin dealers and large retailers like Walmart in their efforts to convince buyers of all types and sizes of tires that "The right tire changes everything."

Marketing Department Organization

The company must design a marketing organization that can carry out marketing strategies and plans. If the company is very small, one person might do all the research, selling, advertising, customer service, and other marketing work. As the company expands, however, a marketing department emerges to plan and carry out marketing activities. In large companies, this department contains many specialists—product and market managers, sales managers and salespeople, market researchers, and advertising experts, among others.

To head up such large marketing organizations, many companies have now created a *chief marketing officer* (or CMO) position. This person heads up the company's entire marketing operation and represents marketing on the company's top management team. The CMO position puts marketing on equal footing with other "C-level" executives, such as the chief operating officer (COO) and the chief financial officer (CFO). As a member of top management, the CMO's role is to champion the customer's cause—to be the "chief customer officer."[16]

Modern marketing departments can be arranged in several ways. The most common form of marketing organization is the *functional organization*. Under this organization, different marketing activities are headed by a functional specialist—a sales manager, an advertising manager, a marketing research manager, a customer service manager, or a new product manager. A company that sells across the country or internationally often uses a *geographic organization*. Its sales and marketing people are assigned to specific countries, regions, and districts. Geographic organization allows salespeople to settle into a territory, get to know their customers, and work with a minimum of travel time and cost. Companies with many very different products or brands often create a *product management organization*. Using this approach, a product manager develops and implements a complete strategy and marketing program for a specific product or brand.

For companies that sell one product line to many different types of markets and customers who have different needs and preferences, a *market* or *customer management organization* might be best. A market management organization is similar to the product management organization. Market managers are responsible for developing marketing strategies and plans for their specific markets or customers. This system's main advantage is that the company is organized around the needs of specific customer segments. Many companies develop special organizations to manage their relationships with large customers. For example, companies such as P&G and Stanley Black & Decker have created large teams, or even whole divisions, to serve large customers, such as Walmart, Target, Safeway, or Home Depot.

Large companies that produce many different products flowing into many different geographic and customer markets usually employ some *combination* of the functional, geographic, product, and market organization forms.

Marketing organization has become an increasingly important issue in recent years. More and more, companies are shifting their brand management focus toward *customer management*—moving away from managing only product or brand profitability and

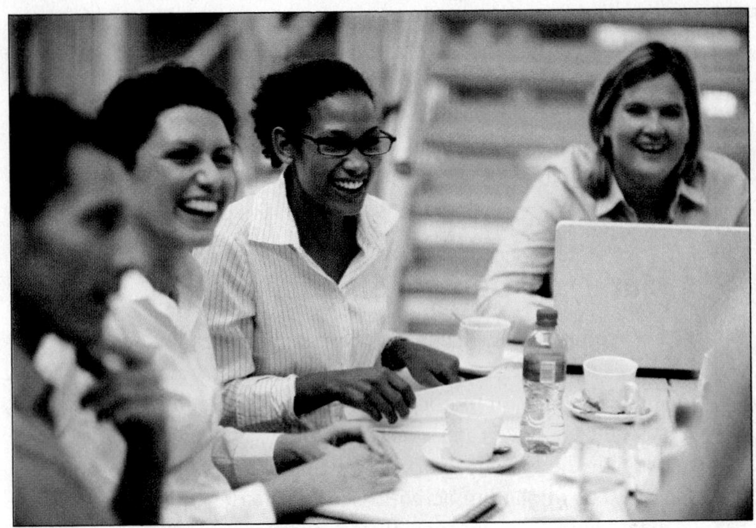

Marketers must continually plan their analysis, implementation, and control activities.

© Yuri Arcurs/Shutterstock.

toward managing customer profitability and customer equity. They think of themselves not as managing portfolios of brands but as managing portfolios of customers. And rather than managing the fortunes of a brand, they see themselves as managing customer–brand engagement, experiences, and relationships.

Marketing Control

Because many surprises occur during the implementation of marketing plans, marketers must practice constant **marketing control**—evaluating the results of marketing strategies and plans and taking corrective action to ensure that the objectives are attained. Marketing control involves four steps. Management first sets specific marketing goals. It then measures its performance in the marketplace and evaluates the causes of any differences between expected and actual performance. Finally, management takes corrective action to close the gaps between goals and performance. This may require changing the action programs or even changing the goals.

Marketing control
Measuring and evaluating the results of marketing strategies and plans and taking corrective action to ensure that the objectives are achieved.

Operating control involves checking ongoing performance against the annual plan and taking corrective action when necessary. Its purpose is to ensure that the company achieves the sales, profits, and other goals set out in its annual plan. It also involves determining the profitability of different products, territories, markets, and channels. *Strategic control* involves looking at whether the company's basic strategies are well matched to its opportunities. Marketing strategies and programs can quickly become outdated, and each company should periodically reassess its overall approach to the marketplace.

Author Comment
Measuring marketing return on investment has become a major emphasis. But it can be difficult. For example, a Super Bowl ad reaches more than 100 million consumers but may cost $4 million for 30 seconds of airtime. How do you measure the return on such an investment in terms of sales, profits, and building customer engagement and relationships? We'll look at this question again in Chapter 12.

Measuring and Managing Return on Marketing Investment

Marketing managers must ensure that their marketing dollars are being well spent. In the past, many marketers spent freely on big, expensive marketing programs and flashy advertising campaigns, often without thinking carefully about the financial returns on their spending. Their goal was often a general one—to "build brands and consumer preference." They believed that marketing produces intangible creative outcomes, which do not lend themselves readily to measures of productivity or return.

In today's leaner economic times, however, all that has changed. The free-spending days have been replaced by a new era of marketing measurement and accountability. More than ever, today's marketers are being held accountable for linking their strategies and tactics to measurable marketing performance outcomes. One important marketing performance measure is **marketing return on investment** (or **marketing ROI**). *Marketing ROI* is the net return from a marketing investment divided by the costs of the marketing investment. It measures the profits generated by investments in marketing activities.

Marketing return on investment (or marketing ROI)
The net return from a marketing investment divided by the costs of the marketing investment.

In one recent survey, 64 percent of senior marketers rated accountability as a top 3 concern, well ahead of the 50 percent rating the hot topic of integrated marketing communications as a top concern. However, another survey found that only 45 percent of organizations were satisfied with their measurement of marketing ROI. A startling 57 percent of CMOs don't take ROI measures into account when setting their marketing budgets, and an even-more startling 28 percent said they base their marketing budgets on "gut instinct." Clearly, marketers must think more strategically about the marketing performance returns of their marketing spending.[17]

Marketing ROI can be difficult to measure. In measuring financial ROI, both the *R* and the *I* are uniformly measured in dollars. For example, when buying a piece of equipment, the productivity gains resulting from the purchase are fairly straightforward. As of yet, however, there is no consistent definition of marketing ROI. For instance, returns such as advertising and brand-building impact aren't easily put into dollar returns.

A company can assess marketing ROI in terms of standard marketing performance measures, such as brand awareness, sales, or market share. Many companies are assembling such measures into *marketing dashboards*—meaningful sets of marketing performance measures in a single display used to monitor strategic marketing performance. Just as automobile dashboards present drivers with details on how their cars are performing, the marketing dashboard gives marketers the detailed measures they need to assess and adjust their marketing strategies. For example, VF Corporation uses a marketing dashboard to track the performance of its more than 30 lifestyle apparel brands—including Wrangler, Lee, The North Face, Vans, Nautica, 7 For All Mankind, Timberland, and others. VF's marketing dashboard tracks brand equity and trends, share of voice, market share, online sentiment, and marketing ROI in key markets worldwide, not only for VF brands but also for competing brands.[18]

Increasingly, however, beyond standard performance measures, marketers are using customer-centered measures of marketing impact, such as customer acquisition, customer engagement, customer retention, customer lifetime value, and customer equity. These measures capture not only current marketing performance but also future performance resulting from stronger customer relationships. >> **Figure 2.8** views marketing expenditures as investments that produce returns in the form of more profitable customer relationships.[19] Marketing investments result in improved customer value, engagement, and satisfaction, which in turn increases customer attraction and retention. This increases individual customer lifetime values and the firm's overall customer equity. Increased customer equity, in relation to the cost of the marketing investments, determines return on marketing investment.

Regardless of how it's defined or measured, the marketing ROI concept is here to stay. In good times or bad, marketers will be increasingly accountable for the performance outcomes of their activities. As one marketer puts it, marketers "have got to know how to count."[20]

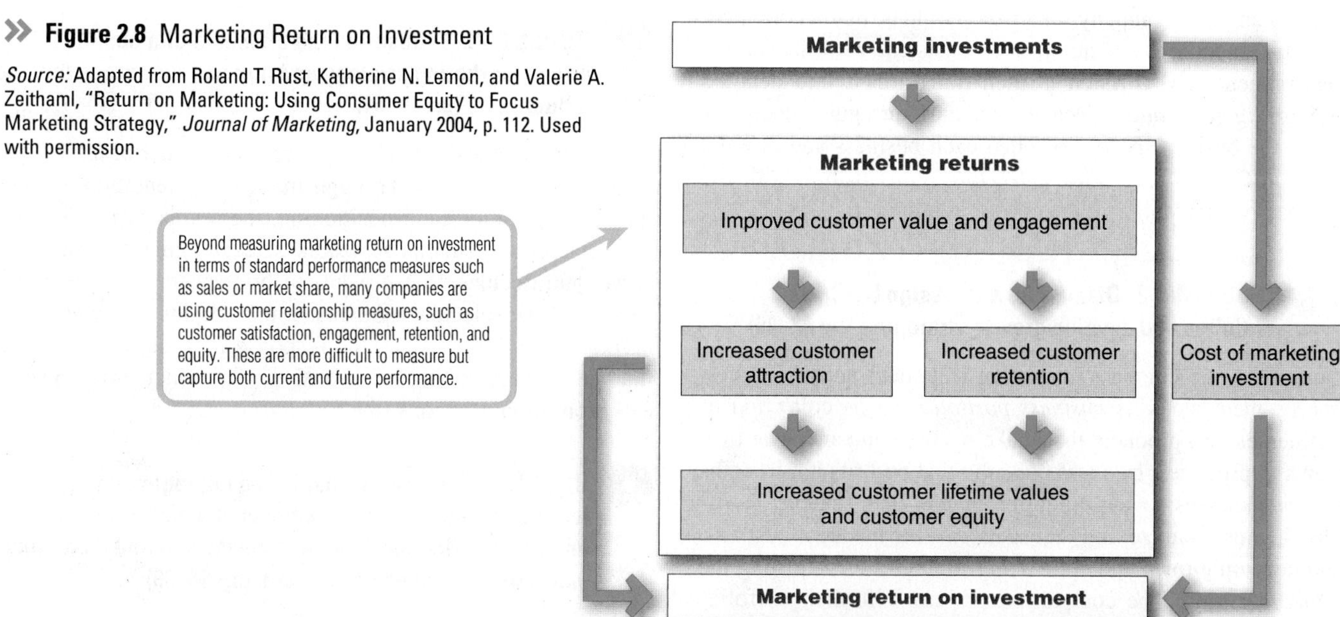
Marketing investments
Marketing returns
Improved customer value and engagement
Increased customer attraction
Increased customer retention
Cost of marketing investment
Increased customer lifetime values and customer equity
Marketing return on investment
Beyond measuring marketing return on investment in terms of standard performance measures such as sales or market share, many companies are using customer relationship measures, such as customer satisfaction, engagement, retention, and equity. These are more difficult to measure but capture both current and future performance.

>> **Figure 2.8** Marketing Return on Investment

Source: Adapted from Roland T. Rust, Katherine N. Lemon, and Valerie A. Zeithaml, "Return on Marketing: Using Consumer Equity to Focus Marketing Strategy," *Journal of Marketing*, January 2004, p. 112. Used with permission.

MyMarketingLab

Go to **mymktlab.com** to complete the problems marked with this icon .

END OF CHAPTER REVIEWING THE CONCEPTS

CHAPTER REVIEW AND KEY TERMS

Objectives Review

In Chapter 1, we defined marketing and outlined the steps in the marketing process. In this chapter, we examined company-wide strategic planning and marketing's role in the organization. Then we looked more deeply into marketing strategy and the marketing mix and reviewed the major marketing management functions. So you've now had a pretty good overview of the fundamentals of modern marketing.

OBJECTIVE 1 Explain company-wide strategic planning and its four steps. (pp 38–42)

Strategic planning sets the stage for the rest of the company's planning. Marketing contributes to strategic planning, and the overall plan defines marketing's role in the company.

Strategic planning involves developing a strategy for long-run survival and growth. It consists of four steps: (1) defining the company's mission, (2) setting objectives and goals, (3) designing a business portfolio, and (4) developing functional plans. The company's *mission* should be market oriented, realistic, specific, motivating, and consistent with the market environment. The mission is then transformed into detailed *supporting goals and objectives*, which in turn guide decisions about the business portfolio. Then each business and product unit must develop *detailed marketing plans* in line with the companywide plan.

OBJECTIVE 2 Discuss how to design business portfolios and develop growth strategies. (pp 42–46)

Guided by the company's mission statement and objectives, management plans its *business portfolio*, or the collection of businesses and products that make up the company. The firm wants to produce a business portfolio that best fits its strengths and weaknesses to opportunities in the environment. To do this, it must analyze and adjust its *current* business portfolio and develop *growth* and *downsizing* strategies for adjusting the *future* portfolio. The company might use a formal portfolio-planning method. But many companies are now designing more-customized portfolio-planning approaches that better suit their unique situations.

OBJECTIVE 3 Explain marketing's role in strategic planning and how marketing works with its partners to create and deliver customer value. (pp 46–48)

Under the strategic plan, the major functional departments—marketing, finance, accounting, purchasing, operations, information systems, human resources, and others—must work together to accomplish strategic objectives. Marketing plays a key role in the company's strategic planning by providing a *marketing concept philosophy* and *inputs* regarding attractive market opportunities. Within individual business units, marketing designs *strategies* for reaching the unit's objectives and helps to carry them out profitably.

Marketers alone cannot produce superior value for customers. Marketers must practice *partner relationship management*, working closely with partners in other departments to form an effective *value chain* that serves the customer. And they must also partner effectively with other companies in the marketing system to form a competitively superior *value delivery network*.

OBJECTIVE 4 Describe the elements of a customer-driven marketing strategy and mix and the forces that influence it. (pp 48–54)

Customer value and relationships are at the center of marketing strategy and programs. Through market segmentation, targeting, differentiation, and positioning, the company divides the total market into smaller segments, selects segments it can best serve, and decides how it wants to bring value to target consumers in the selected segments. It then designs an *integrated marketing mix* to produce the response it wants in the target market. The marketing mix consists of product, price, place, and promotion decisions (the four Ps).

OBJECTIVE 5 List the marketing management functions, including the elements of a marketing plan, and discuss the importance of measuring and managing marketing return on investment. (pp 54–59)

To find the best strategy and mix and to put them into action, the company engages in marketing analysis, planning, implementation, and control. The main components of a *marketing plan* are the executive summary, the current marketing situation, threats and opportunities, objectives and issues, marketing strategies, action programs, budgets, and controls. Planning good strategies is often easier than carrying them out. To be successful, companies must also be effective at *implementation*—turning marketing strategies into marketing actions.

Marketing departments can be organized in one way or a combination of ways: *functional marketing organization*, *geographic organization*, *product management organization*, or *market management organization*. In this age of customer relationships, more and more companies are now changing their organizational focus from product or territory management to customer relationship management. Marketing organizations carry out *marketing control*, both operating control and strategic control.

More than ever, marketing accountability is the top marketing concern. Marketing managers must ensure that their marketing dollars are being well spent. In a tighter economy, today's marketers face growing pressures to show that they are adding value in line with their costs. In response, marketers are developing better measures of *marketing return on investment*. Increasingly, they are using customer-centered measures of marketing impact as a key input into their strategic decision making.

Key Terms

Objective 1
Strategic planning (p 38)
Mission statement (p 39)

Objective 2
Business portfolio (p 42)
Portfolio analysis (p 43)
Growth-share matrix (p 43)
Product/market expansion grid (p 45)
Market penetration (p 45)
Market development (p 46)
Product development (p 46)
Diversification (p 46)

Objective 3
Value chain (p 47)
Value delivery network (p 48)

Objective 4
Marketing strategy (p 48)
Market segmentation (p 49)
Market segment (p 49)
Market targeting (p 50)
Positioning (p 50)
Differentiation (p 52)
Marketing mix (p 52)

Objective 5
SWOT analysis (p 54)
Marketing implementation (p 55)
Marketing control (p 58)
Marketing return on investment (marketing ROI) (p 58)

DISCUSSION AND CRITICAL THINKING

Discussion Questions

2-1. Define *strategic planning* and briefly describe the four steps that lead managers and the firm through the strategic planning process. Discuss the role marketing plays in this process. (AACSB: Written and Oral Communication)

2-2. What is a SWOT analysis? How is this analysis useful in developing and implementing marketing strategies? (AACSB: Written and Oral Communication)

2-3. Explain the roles of market segmentation, market targeting, differentiation, and positioning in implementing an effective marketing strategy. (AACSB: Written and Oral Communication)

2-4. Define each of the four Ps. What insights might a firm gain by considering the four Cs rather than the four Ps? (AACSB: Written and Oral Communication; Reflective Thinking)

2-5. How are marketing departments organized? Which organization is best? (AACSB: Written and Oral Communication, Reflective Thinking)

2-6. Discuss the four marketing management functions. (AACSB: Written and Oral Communication)

Critical Thinking Exercises

2-7. In a small group, research a company and construct a growth-share matrix of the company's products, brands, or strategic business units. Recommend a strategy for each unit in the matrix. (AACSB: Written and Oral Communication; Reflective Thinking)

2-8. Find the mission statements of two for-profit and two not-for-profit organizations. Evaluate these mission statements with respect to their market orientations. (AACSB: Written and Oral Communication; Reflective Thinking)

MINI CASES AND APPLICATIONS

Online, Mobile, and Social Media Marketing The PC-osaurus

In 2011, Hewlett-Packard CEO Leo Apothekar made the strategic decision to exit the personal computer (PC) business, but he got fired and incoming CEO Meg Wittman reversed that decision. However, sales of PCs have plummeted since the introduction of post-PC devices such as tablets, e-readers, and smartphones. In the first quarter of 2013 alone, total PC shipments fell almost 14 percent, and no one felt that more than leading PC-maker HP. The company's PC sales fell 23.7 percent that quarter. Now, PC-makers are dropping prices—some more than 50 percent—on laptops and some are offering touchscreens to compete with tablets and mobile devices in an attempt to gain back market share. HP's former CEO wanted to shift strategic focus more toward offering software to business markets. Maybe he had read the future correctly and was on the right strategic path. With the game-changing introduction of tablets, mobile technology, and social media, the future is not what it used to be.

2-9. Explain which product/market expansion grid strategy PC-makers are currently pursuing to deal with the threat of post-PC devices. Is this a smart strategy? (AACSB: Written and Oral Communication; Reflective Thinking)

Marketing Ethics Digital Dark Side

More than half of the world's population lives under autocratic regimes, limiting access to the Internet. But that is changing, opening new market opportunities for companies specializing in digital monitoring technologies. Everything an oppressive regime needs to build a digital police state is commercially available and is being implemented. For example, filtering devices manufactured by Blue Coat Systems, a Silicon Valley–based company, are used in Syria to suppress civil unrest. Although Blue Coat Systems acknowledges this, it claims it did not sell the product to the Syrian government. North Korea, China, Libya, and other oppressive states demand data mining software and surveillance cameras as well as cutting-edge technologies that collect, store, and analyze biometric information. As social media proliferate in these countries, off-the-self facial recognition software and cloud computing can identify people in a matter of seconds, enabling these states to quash dissent. Although the United States may have sanctions against U.S.-based companies selling products to these governments, others may not, resulting in those countries' products as well as U.S.-based products getting into the hands of oppressive regimes.

2-10. In most cases, it is not illegal to sell such products to governments, oppressive or otherwise. But is it moral? Should companies be allowed to pursue a market development strategy wherever they find demand? (AACSB: Written and Oral Communication; Ethical Understanding and Reasoning)

2-11. Research the Blue Coat Systems incident and write a report of your findings. Did the company illegally sell surveillance products to Syria? Which element of the marketing mix is most related to this issue? (AACSB: Written and Oral Communication; Reflective Thinking)

Marketing by the Numbers Walmart vs. Target

In the period ending January, 2013, Walmart reported profits of almost \$17 billion on sales of just under \$470 billion. For that same period, Target posted a profit of almost \$3 billion on sales of \$73 billion. So Walmart is a better marketer, right? Sales and profits provide information to compare the profitability of these two competitors, but between these numbers is information regarding the efficiency of marketing efforts in creating those sales and profits. Appendix 3, Marketing by the Numbers, discusses other marketing profitability measures beyond the return on marketing investment (marketing ROI) measure described in this chapter. Review Appendix 3 to answer the questions using the following information from Walmart's and Target's incomes statements (all numbers are in thousands):

	Walmart	Target
Sales	\$469,162,000	\$73,301,000
Gross Profit	\$116,674,000	\$22,733,000
Marketing Expenses	\$ 66,654,750	\$11,415,000
Net Income (Profit)	\$ 16,999,000	\$ 2,999,000

2-12. Calculate profit margin, net marketing contribution, marketing return on sales (or marketing ROS), and marketing return on investment (or marketing ROI) for both companies. Which company is performing better? (AACSB: Written and Oral Communication; Information Technology; Analytical Thinking)

2-13. Go to Yahoo! Finance (http://finance.yahoo.com/) and find the income statements for two other competing companies. Perform the same analysis for these companies that you performed in the previous question. Which company is doing better overall and with respect to marketing? For marketing expenses, use 75 percent of the company's reported "Selling General and Administrative" expenses, as not all of the expenses in that category are marketing expenses. (AACSB: Written and Oral Communication; Analytical Thinking; Reflective Thinking)

Video Case OXO

You might know OXO for its well-designed, ergonomic kitchen gadgets. But OXO's expertise at creating handheld tools that look great and work well has promoted the company to expand into products for bathrooms, garages, offices, babies' rooms, and even medicine cabinets. In the past, this award-winning manufacturer has managed to move its products into almost every home in the United States by relying on a consistent, sometimes nontraditional marketing strategy.

However, in a highly competitive and turbulent market, OXO has focused on evaluating and modifying its marketing strategy in order to grow the brand. This video demonstrates how OXO is using strategic planning to ensure that its marketing strategy results in the best marketing mix for the best and most profitable customers.

After viewing the video featuring OXO, answer the following questions:

2-14. What is OXO's mission?

2-15. What are some of the market conditions that have led OXO to reevaluate its marketing strategy?

2-16. How has OXO modified its marketing mix? Are these changes in line with its mission?

Company Cases 2 Dyson America / 1 In-N-Out Burger / 3 Xerox

See Appendix 1 for cases appropriate for this chapter. **Case 2, Dyson: Solving Customer Problems in Ways They Never Imagined.** Dyson focuses on ho-hum product lines that haven't changed in decades, infusing them with technology that solves consumers' long-accepted problems. **Case 1, In-N-Out Burger: Customer Value the Old-Fashioned Way.** In-N-Out Burger provides value to customers by giving them exactly what they want, and never changing a thing. **Case 3, Xerox: Adapting to the Turbulent Marketing Environment.** When the marketing environment changed and photocopying began to decline, Xerox created a new strategy that would allow it to succeed.

MyMarketingLab

Go to **mymktlab.com** for Auto-graded writing questions as well as the following Assisted-graded writing questions:

2-17. Marketers are increasingly held accountable for demonstrating marketing success. Research the various marketing metrics, in addition to those described in the chapter and Appendix 3, used by marketers to measure marketing performance. Write a brief report of your findings. (AACSB: Written and Oral Communication; Reflective Thinking)

2-18. Discuss how companies such as HP and other PC-makers can adapt to and capitalize on new online, mobile, or social media technologies. (AACSB: Written and Oral Communication; Reflective Thinking)

2-19. Mymktlab Only—comprehensive writing assignment for this chapter.

PART 1: DEFINING MARKETING AND THE MARKETING PROCESS (CHAPTERS 1–2)
PART 2: UNDERSTANDING THE MARKETPLACE AND CUSTOMER VALUE (CHAPTERS 3–5)
PART 3: DESIGNING A CUSTOMER VALUE–DRIVEN STRATEGY AND MIX (CHAPTERS 6–14)
PART 4: EXTENDING MARKETING (CHAPTERS 15–16)

3 Analyzing the Marketing Environment

CHAPTER ROAD MAP

Objective Outline

OBJECTIVE 1 **Describe the environmental forces that affect the company's ability to serve its customers.** The Microenvironment 67–70; The Macroenvironment 70–72

OBJECTIVE 2 **Explain how changes in the demographic and economic environments affect marketing decisions.** The Demographic Environment 72–79; The Economic Environment 79–81

OBJECTIVE 3 **Identify the major trends in the firm's natural and technological environments.** The Natural Environment 81–82; The Technological Environment 82–83

OBJECTIVE 4 **Explain the key changes in the political and cultural environments.** The Political and Social Environment 84–87; The Cultural Environment 87–90

OBJECTIVE 5 **Discuss how companies can react to the marketing environment.** Responding to the Marketing Environment 90–92

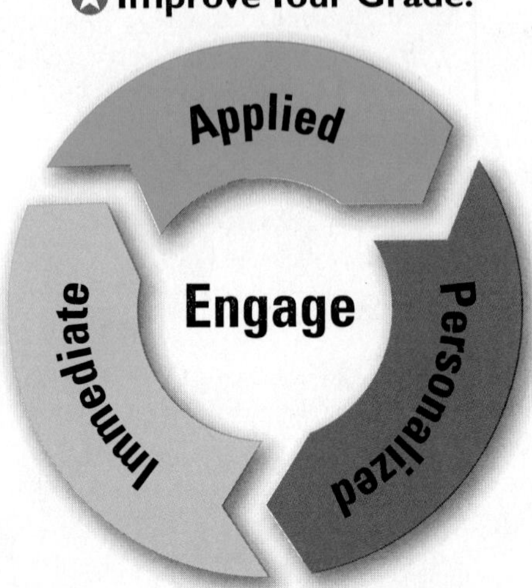

Previewing the Concepts

So far, you've learned about the basic concepts of marketing and the steps in the marketing process for engaging and building profitable relationships with targeted consumers. Next, we'll begin digging deeper into the first step of the marketing process—understanding the marketplace and customer needs and wants. In this chapter, you'll see that marketing operates in a complex and changing environment. Other actors in this environment—suppliers, intermediaries, customers, competitors, publics, and others—may work with or against the company. Major environmental forces—demographic, economic, natural, technological, political, and cultural—shape marketing opportunities, pose threats, and affect the company's ability to build customer relationships. To develop effective marketing strategies, a company must first understand the environment in which marketing operates.

To start, let's look at Microsoft, the technology giant that dominated the computer software world throughout the 1990s and much of the 2000s. With the recent decline in standalone personal computers and the surge in digitally connected devices—everything from smartphones and tablets to Internet-connected

*Over 10 million students improved their results using the Pearson MyLabs. Visit **mymktlab.com** for simulations, tutorials, and end-of-chapter problems.

» **In the fast-changing digital marketing environment, mighty Microsoft is making fresh moves to reestablish itself as a brand that consumers can't live without in the post-PC world.**

Getty Images.

TVs—mighty Microsoft has struggled a bit recently to find its place in a fast-changing digital marketing environment. Now, however, the tech giant is making fresh moves to reestablish itself as a relevant brand that consumers can't live without in the post-PC world.

First Stop

Microsoft: Adapting to the Fast-Changing Digital Marketing Environment

Just a dozen years ago, talking high tech meant talking about the almighty personal computer. Intel provided the PC microprocessors, and manufacturers such as Dell and HP built and marketed the machines. But it was Microsoft that really drove the PC industry—it made the operating systems that made most PCs go. As the dominant software developer, Microsoft put its Windows operating system and Office productivity suite on almost every computer sold.

The huge success of Windows drove Microsoft's revenues, profits, and stock price to dizzying heights. By the start of 2000, the total value of Microsoft's stock had hit a record $618.9 billion, making it the most valuable company in history. In those heady days, no company was more relevant than Microsoft.

But moving into the new millennium, the high-tech marketing environment took a turn. PC sales growth flattened as the world fell in love with a rush of alluring new digital devices and technologies. It started with iPods and smartphones, and evolved rapidly into a full complement of digital devices—from e-readers, tablets, and sleek new laptops to Internet-connected TVs and game consoles. These devices are connected and mobile, not stationary standalones like the PC. They link users to an ever-on, head-spinning new world of information, entertainment, and socialization options. And, for the most part, these new devices don't use the old Microsoft products. Increasingly, even the trusty old PC has become a digital-connection device—a gateway to the Web, social media, and cloud computing. And these days, much of that can be done without once-indispensable Microsoft software.

Microsoft is undergoing a dramatic transformation to better align itself with the new digital world order in the post-PC era. More than just making the software that makes PCs run, Microsoft wants to be a full digital devices and services company that connects people to communication, productivity, entertainment, and one another.

In this new digitally connected world, Microsoft found itself lagging behind more-glamorous competitors such as Google, Apple, Samsung, and even Amazon and Facebook, which seemed to provide all things digital—the smart devices, the connecting technologies, and even the digital destinations. Over the past decade, although still financially strong and still the world's dominant PC software provider with 1.3 billion Windows users around the world, Microsoft has lost some of its luster. In the year 2000—due largely to the collapse of the stock market technology bubble—Microsoft's value plummeted by 60 percent. And whereas other tech stocks recovered, Microsoft's share price and profits have languished at 2000's levels for the past dozen years or more.

But recently, Microsoft has begun a dramatic transformation in its vision and direction to better align itself with the new digital world order. Today, rather than just creating the software that makes PCs run, Microsoft wants to be a full-line digital devices and services company that delivers "delightful, seamless technology experiences" that connect people to communication, productivity, entertainment, and one another. Its mission is to help people and businesses realize their full professional and personal potential.

To make this mission a reality, over the past few years, Microsoft has unleashed a flurry of new, improved, or acquired digital products and services. Over one short span, it introduced a new version of Windows that serves not just computers but also tablets and smartphones; a next-generation Xbox console; a music and movie service to rival iTunes and Google Play; an upgraded version of Skype (acquired in 2011); a SkyDrive cloud storage solution; and even an innovative new tablet—the Microsoft Surface—that will give it a firmer footing in digital devices. Also rumored to be in the works is an Xbox TV device for TV streaming. And the company recently acquired Yammer, a Web-services provider and hip maker of business social networking tools—a sort of Facebook for businesses. In its boldest expansion move yet, Microsoft recently paid more than $7 billion dollars to acquire Nokia's smartphone business.

More important than the individual new devices, software, and services is the way that they all work together to deliver a full digital experience. It all starts with Windows 8, a dramatic digital-age metamorphosis from previous Windows versions. Windows 8 employs large, colorful, interactive tiles and touchscreen navigation, making it feel lively and interactive. It works seamlessly across desktops and laptops, tablets, phones, and even Xbox, providing the cloud-based connectivity that today's users crave.

Using Windows 8 software and apps with Windows-based devices and cloud computing services, you can select a movie from a tablet, start playing it on the TV, and finish watching it on your phone, pausing to call or text a friend using Skype. What you do on one Windows device is automatically updated on other devices. Playlists created or songs and TV programs purchased from a mobile device will be waiting for you on your home PC. And Windows 8 is a social creature; for example, it updates contacts automatically with tweets and photos from friends.

The latest version of Office has also been transformed for the connected age. Using touchscreen interfaces, you can use an Office app and share files across PCs, Windows tablets, Windows phones, and even Macs via the SkyDrive cloud. Or you can tap into a continuously updated, online-only version of Office from almost any device. In fact, Microsoft views Office as a service, not software. It plans to sell the service by subscription: $100 per year will get you Office, 20 gigabytes of SkyDrive storage, and 60 minutes of free Skype calls per month. "It embraces the notion of social," says Microsoft CEO Steve Ballmer. "You stay connected and share information with the people you care about."

Perhaps Microsoft's biggest about-face is the development of its own hardware devices. In the past, the company has relied on partners like Dell, HP, and Nokia to develop the PCs, tablets, and phones that run its software. But to gain better control in today's superheated digital and mobile markets, Microsoft is now doing its own hardware development. For starters, it developed the cutting-edge Surface tablet. The Surface not only employs the Windows 8 interface and connectivity, it sports a nifty kickstand and thin detachable keyboard that also serves as a cover, making the Surface a unique combination of tablet and mini-laptop. The Surface, plus Xbox and the Nokia smartphone acquisition, will give Microsoft better control of access to three important new digital screens beyond the PC—tablets, TVs, and phones.

Thus, Microsoft's sweeping transformation is well under way. The company is putting a whopping $1.5 billion of marketing support behind its revamped mission and all its new software, hardware, and services. Still, Microsoft has a long way to go. Although Windows 8, the Surface tablet, and other initiatives appear off to a decent start, many tentative customers are playing wait-and-see. Many still see Microsoft as mostly a PC software company. It will take a sustained effort to change both customer and company thinking. Some skeptics think that Microsoft may still be to too tightly wedded to the olds ways. "Just having the Windows name still around captures the problems of this company," says one technology forecaster. "In their heads, they know the personal computer revolution is over and that they have to move on, but in their hearts they can't do it. If Microsoft is around in 100 years, they will try and sell us a Windows teleporter."

But Microsoft seems to be making all the right moves to stay with or ahead of the times. Microsoft's sales have trended upward over the past few years, and the company is confident that it's now on the right track. "It truly is a new era at Microsoft—an era of incredible opportunity for us . . . and for the people and businesses using our products to reach their full potential," says CEO Balmer. "Although we still have a lot of hard work ahead, our products are generating excitement. And when I pause to reflect on how far we've come over the past few years and how much further we'll go in the next [few], I couldn't be more excited and optimistic."[1]

Marketing environment
The actors and forces outside marketing that affect marketing management's ability to build and maintain successful relationships with target customers.

A company's **marketing environment** consists of the actors and forces outside marketing that affect marketing management's ability to build and maintain successful relationships with target customers. Like Microsoft, companies constantly watch and adapt to the changing environment—or, in many cases, lead those changes.

More than any other group in the company, marketers must be environmental trend trackers and opportunity seekers. Although every manager in an organization should watch the outside environment, marketers have two special aptitudes. They have disciplined methods—marketing research and marketing intelligence—for collecting information about the marketing environment. They also spend more time in customer and competitor environments. By carefully studying the environment, marketers can adapt their strategies to meet new marketplace challenges and opportunities.

The marketing environment consists of a *microenvironment* and a *macroenvironment*. The **microenvironment** consists of the actors close to the company that affect its ability to serve its customers—the company, suppliers, marketing intermediaries, customer markets, competitors, and publics. The **macroenvironment** consists of the larger societal forces that affect the microenvironment—demographic, economic, natural, technological, political, and cultural forces. We look first at the company's microenvironment.

Author Comment
The microenvironment includes all the actors close to the company that affect, positively or negatively, its ability to create value for and relationships with customers.

The Microenvironment

Marketing management's job is to build relationships with customers by creating customer value and satisfaction. However, marketing managers cannot do this alone. » **Figure 3.1** shows the major actors in the marketer's microenvironment. Marketing success requires building relationships with other company departments, suppliers, marketing intermediaries, competitors, various publics, and customers, which combine to make up the company's value delivery network.

Microenvironment
The actors close to the company that affect its ability to serve its customers—the company, suppliers, marketing intermediaries, customer markets, competitors, and publics.

Macroenvironment
The larger societal forces that affect the microenvironment—demographic, economic, natural, technological, political, and cultural forces.

The Company

In designing marketing plans, marketing management takes other company groups into account—groups such as top management, finance, research and development (R&D), purchasing, operations, and accounting. All of these interrelated groups form the internal environment. Top management sets the company's mission, objectives, broad strategies, and policies. Marketing managers make decisions within these broader strategies and plans. Then, as we discussed in Chapter 2, marketing managers must work closely with other company departments. With marketing taking the lead, all departments—from manufacturing and finance to legal and human resources—share the responsibility for understanding customer needs and creating customer value.

Suppliers

Suppliers form an important link in the company's overall customer value delivery network. They provide the resources needed by the company to produce its goods and services. Supplier problems can seriously affect marketing. Marketing managers must watch supply availability and costs. Supply shortages or delays, labor strikes, natural disasters, and other events can cost sales in the short run and damage customer satisfaction in the long run. Rising supply costs may force price increases that can harm the company's sales volume.

Most marketers today treat their suppliers as partners in creating and delivering customer value. For example, giant Swedish furniture retailer IKEA doesn't just buy from its

» **Figure 3.1** Actors in the Microenvironment

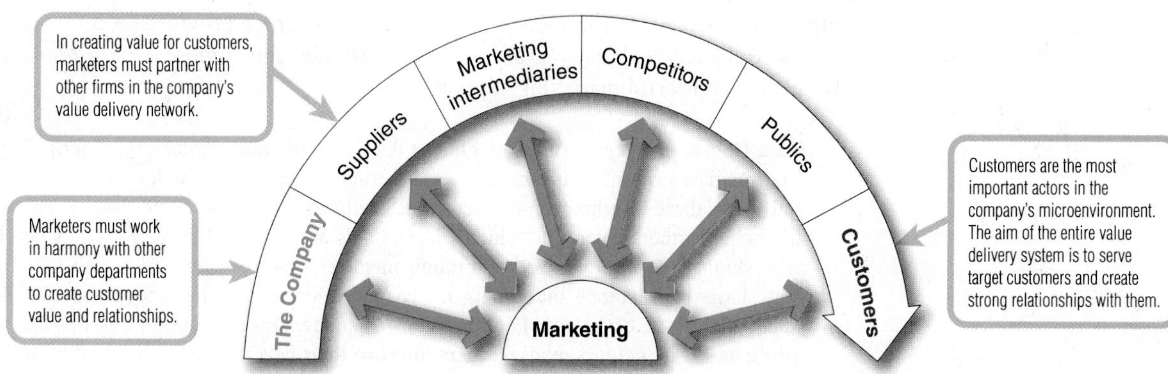
In creating value for customers, marketers must partner with other firms in the company's value delivery network.
Marketers must work in harmony with other company departments to create customer value and relationships.
Customers are the most important actors in the company's microenvironment. The aim of the entire value delivery system is to serve target customers and create strong relationships with them.
The Company
Suppliers
Marketing intermediaries
Competitors
Publics
Customers
Marketing

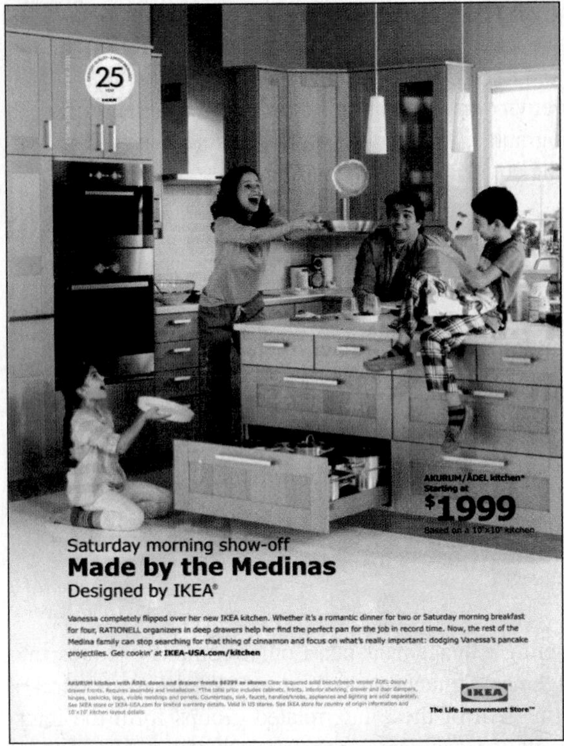

25
AKURUM/ÄDEL kitchen*
Starting at
$1999
Based on a 10'x10' kitchen
Saturday morning show-off
Made by the Medinas
Designed by IKEA®
Vanessa completely flipped over her new IKEA kitchen. Whether it's a romantic dinner for two or Saturday morning breakfast for four, RATIONELL organizers in deep drawers help her find the perfect pan for the job in record time. Now, the rest of the Medina family can stop searching for that thing of cinnamon and focus on what's really important: dodging Vanessa's pancake projectiles. Get cookin' at IKEA-USA.com/kitchen
IKEA
The Life Improvement Store™

Giant Swedish furniture manufacturer IKEA doesn't just buy from suppliers. It involves them deeply in the process of delivering a stylish and affordable lifestyle to its customers worldwide.

Used with the permission of Inter IKEA Systems B.V.

suppliers. It involves them deeply in the process of delivering a stylish and affordable lifestyle to IKEA's customers:[2]

> IKEA, the world's largest furniture retailer, is the quintessential global cult brand. Each year, customers from Beijing to Moscow to Middletown, Ohio, flock to the Scandinavian retailer's more than 300 huge stores in 40 countries, snapping up more than $28 billion worth of IKEA's trendy but simple and practical furniture at affordable prices. But IKEA's biggest obstacle to growth isn't opening new stores and attracting customers. Rather, it's finding enough of the right kinds of suppliers to help design and make all the products that customers will carry out of its stores. IKEA currently relies on more than 2,000 suppliers in 50 countries to stock its shelves. IKEA can't just hope to find spot suppliers who might be available when needed. Instead, it must systematically develop a robust network of supplier-partners that reliably provide the more than 12,000 items it stocks. IKEA's designers start with a basic customer value proposition. Then they find and work closely with key suppliers to bring that proposition to market. Thus, IKEA does more than just buy from suppliers. It involves them deeply in questions of quality, design, and price to create the kinds of products that keep customers coming back.

Marketing Intermediaries

Marketing intermediaries help the company promote, sell, and distribute its products to final buyers. They include resellers, physical distribution firms, marketing services agencies, and financial intermediaries. *Resellers* are distribution channel firms that help the company find customers or make sales to them. These include wholesalers and retailers that buy and resell merchandise. Selecting and partnering with resellers is not easy. No longer do manufacturers have many small, independent resellers from which to choose. They now face large and growing reseller organizations, such as Walmart, Target, Home Depot, Costco, and Best Buy. These organizations frequently have enough power to dictate terms or even shut smaller manufacturers out of large markets.

Marketing intermediaries
Firms that help the company to promote, sell, and distribute its goods to final buyers.

Physical distribution firms help the company stock and move goods from their points of origin to their destinations. *Marketing services agencies* are the marketing research firms, advertising agencies, media firms, and marketing consulting firms that help the company target and promote its products to the right markets. *Financial intermediaries* include banks, credit companies, insurance companies, and other businesses that help finance transactions or insure against the risks associated with the buying and selling of goods.

Like suppliers, marketing intermediaries form an important component of the company's overall value delivery network. In its quest to create satisfying customer relationships, the company must do more than just optimize its own performance. It must partner effectively with marketing intermediaries to optimize the performance of the entire system.

Thus, today's marketers recognize the importance of working with their intermediaries as partners rather than simply as channels through which they sell their products. For example, when Coca-Cola signs on as the exclusive beverage provider for a fast-food chain, such as McDonald's, Wendy's, or Subway, it provides much more than just soft drinks. It also pledges powerful marketing support:[3]

> Coca-Cola assigns cross-functional teams dedicated to understanding the finer points of each retail partner's business. It conducts a staggering amount of research on beverage consumers and shares these insights with its partners. It analyzes the demographics of U.S. zip code areas and helps partners determine which Coke brands are preferred in their areas. Coca-Cola has even studied the design of drive-through menu boards to better understand which layouts, fonts, letter sizes, colors, and visuals induce consumers to order more food and drink. Based on such insights, the Coca-Cola Food Service group develops marketing programs and merchandising tools that help its retail partners improve their beverage sales and profits. Its Web site,

www.CokeSolutions.com, provides retailers with a wealth of information, business solutions, merchandising tips, and techniques on how to go green. "We know that you're passionate about delighting guests and enhancing their real experiences on every level," says Coca-Cola to its retail partners. "As your partner, we want to help in any way we can." Such intense partnering has made Coca-Cola a runaway leader in the U.S. fountain-soft-drink market.

Competitors

The marketing concept states that, to be successful, a company must provide greater customer value and satisfaction than its competitors do. Thus, marketers must do more than simply adapt to the needs of target consumers. They also must gain strategic advantage by positioning their offerings strongly against competitors' offerings in the minds of consumers.

No single competitive marketing strategy is best for all companies. Each firm should consider its own size and industry position compared to those of its competitors. Large firms with dominant positions in an industry can use certain strategies that smaller firms cannot afford. But being large is not enough. There are winning strategies for large firms, but there are also losing ones. And small firms can develop strategies that give them better rates of return than large firms enjoy.

Publics

Public
Any group that has an actual or potential interest in or impact on an organization's ability to achieve its objectives.

The company's marketing environment also includes various publics. A **public** is any group that has an actual or potential interest in or impact on an organization's ability to achieve its objectives. We can identify seven types of publics:

- *Financial publics:* This group influences the company's ability to obtain funds. Banks, investment analysts, and stockholders are the major financial publics.
- *Media publics:* This group carries news, features, editorial opinions, and other content. It includes television stations, newspapers, magazines, and blogs and other social media.
- *Government publics:* Management must take government developments into account. Marketers must often consult the company's lawyers on issues of product safety, truth in advertising, and other matters.
- *Citizen-action publics:* A company's marketing decisions may be questioned by consumer organizations, environmental groups, minority groups, and others. Its public relations department can help it stay in touch with consumer and citizen groups.
- *Local publics:* This group includes neighborhood residents and community organizations. Large companies usually create departments and programs that deal with local community issues and provide community support. >> For example, the Life is good company recognizes the importance of community publics in helping accomplish the brand's "spread optimism" mission (remember the Chapter 1 Life is good story in Marketing at Work 1.2?). Its Life is good Playmakers program promotes the philosophy that "Life can hurt, play can heal." It provides training and support for child-care professionals to use the power of play to help children overcome challenges ranging from violence and illness to extreme poverty in cities around the world, from Danbury, Connecticut, to

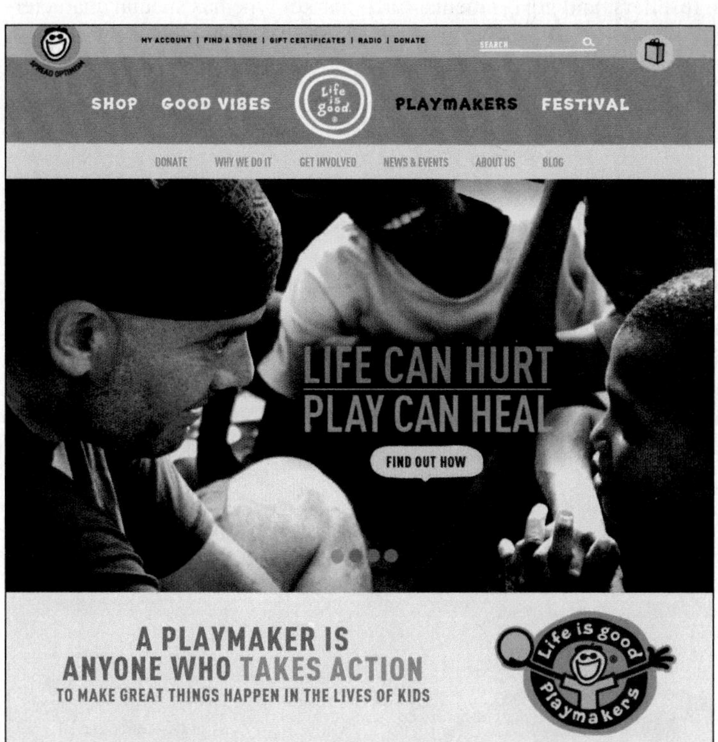

>> **Publics: The Life is good company recognizes the importance of community publics. Its Life is good Playmakers program provides training and support for child-care professionals in cities around the world to use the power of play to help children overcome challenges ranging from violence and illness to extreme poverty.**

The Life is good Company.

Port-au-Prince, Haiti. So far, the organization has raised more than $9 million to benefit children.[4]

- *General public:* A company needs to be concerned about the general public's attitude toward its products and activities. The public's image of the company affects its buying behavior.
- *Internal publics:* This group includes workers, managers, volunteers, and the board of directors. Large companies use newsletters and other means to inform and motivate their internal publics. When employees feel good about the companies they work for, this positive attitude spills over to the external publics.

A company can prepare marketing plans for these major publics as well as for its customer markets. Suppose the company wants a specific response from a particular public, such as goodwill, favorable word of mouth and social sharing, or donations of time or money. The company would have to design an offer to this public that is attractive enough to produce the desired response.

Customers

Customers are the most important actors in the company's microenvironment. The aim of the entire value delivery network is to serve target customers and create strong relationships with them. The company might target any or all of five types of customer markets. *Consumer markets* consist of individuals and households that buy goods and services for personal consumption. *Business markets* buy goods and services for further processing or use in their production processes, whereas *reseller markets* buy goods and services to resell at a profit. *Government markets* consist of government agencies that buy goods and services to produce public services or transfer the goods and services to others who need them. Finally, *international markets* consist of these buyers in other countries, including consumers, producers, resellers, and governments. Each market type has special characteristics that call for careful study by the seller.

Author Comment
The macroenvironment consists of broader forces that affect the actors in the microenvironment.

The Macroenvironment

The company and all of the other actors operate in a larger macroenvironment of forces that shape opportunities and pose threats to the company. **Figure 3.2** shows the six major forces in the company's macroenvironment. Even the most dominant companies can be vulnerable to the often turbulent and changing forces in the marketing environment. Some of these forces are unforeseeable and uncontrollable. Others can be predicted and handled through skillful management. Companies that understand and adapt well to their environments can thrive. Those that don't can face difficult times. One-time dominant market leaders such as Xerox, Sears, and Sony have learned this lesson the hard way (see Marketing at Work 3.1). In the remaining sections of this chapter, we examine these forces and show how they affect marketing plans.

Figure 3.2 Major Forces in the Company's Macroenvironment

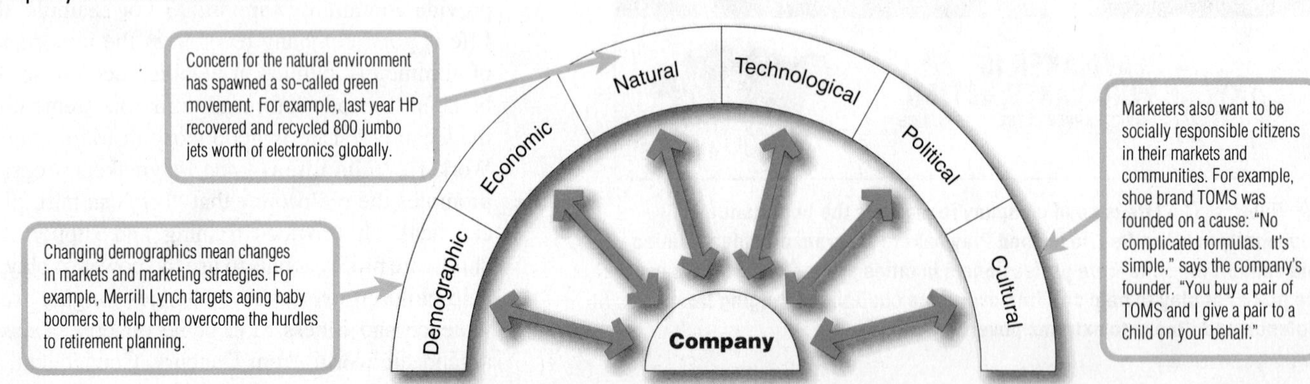

MARKETING AT WORK 3.1

Sony: Battling the Marketing Environment's "Perfect Storm"

After a decade of struggle, the year 2011 was supposed to be a comeback year for Sony. The consumer electronics and entertainment giant had one its best batches of new products ever heading for store shelves. Even more important, Sony was heading back into the digital big leagues with the launch of an iTunes-like global digital network that would combine Sony's strengths in movies, music, and video games for all its televisions, PCs, phones, game consoles, and tablets. Analysts forecasted a $2 billion profit. "I really and truly believed that I was going to have a year to remember," says Sony's chairman Sir Howard Stringer. "And I did, but in the wrong way."

Instead of a banner year, 2011 produced a near-perfect storm of environmental calamities for Sony. For starters, in March 2011, eastern Japan was devastated by a mammoth earthquake and tsunami. The disaster forced Sony to shutter 10 plants, disrupting operations and the flow of Sony products worldwide. In April, a hacking attack on the company's Internet entertainment services—the second-largest online data breach in U.S. history—forced the company to shut down its PlayStation Network. Only four months later, fires set by rioters in London destroyed a Sony warehouse and an estimated 25 million CDs and DVDs, gutting an inventory of 150 independent labels. To round out the year, floods in Thailand shut down component plants there.

When the rubble was cleared, Sony's projected $2 billion profit ended up as a $6.4 billion loss—the company's largest ever. That loss marked a three-year streak of losses that had begun with yet another environmental upheaval—the Great Recession and global financial meltdown of 2008. By mid-2013, a shell-shocked Sony was still looking for a return to profitability.

There's no doubt that environmental unforeseeables have dealt Sony some heavy blows. But not all the blame for Sony's woes goes to uncontrollable environmental forces. Sony's current difficulties began long before the recent string of events. More to blame than any natural disaster has been Sony's longer-term inability to adapt to one of the most powerful environmental forces of our time—dramatic changes in digital technology.

Interestingly, it was Sony's magical touch with technology that first built the company into a global powerhouse. Only a dozen years ago, Sony was a high-tech rock star, a veritable merchant of cool. Not only was it the world's largest consumer electronics company, its history of innovative products—such as Trinitron TVs, Walkman portable music players, Handycam video recorders, and PlayStation video-game consoles—had revolutionized entire industries. Sony's innovations drove pop culture, earned the adoration of the masses, and made money for the company. The Sony brand stood for innovation, style, and high quality.

Today, however, although still a $78 billion company, Sony is more a relic than a rock star, lost in the shadows of high-fliers such as Apple, Samsung, and Microsoft. Samsung overtook Sony as the world's largest consumer electronics maker nearly a decade ago. Samsung's sales last year more than tripled Sony's, and Samsung's profits surged as Sony's losses still mounted. Likewise, Apple has pounded Sony with one new product after another. "When I was young, I had to have a Sony product," summarizes one analyst, "but for the younger generation today it's Apple." All of this has turned Sony's current "Make. Believe." brand promise into more of a "make-believe" one.

How did Sony fall so hard so fast? It fell behind in technology. Sony built its once-mighty empire based on the innovative engineering and design of standalone electronics—TVs, CD players, and video-game consoles. As the Internet and digital technologies surged, however, creating a more connected and mobile world, standalone hardware was rapidly replaced by new connecting technologies, media, and content. As our entertainment lives swirled toward digital downloads and shared content accessed through PCs, iPods, smartphones, tablets, and Internet-ready TVs, Sony was late to adapt.

Behaving as though its market leadership could never be challenged, an arrogant Sony clung to successful old technologies rather than embracing new ones. For example, prior to the launch of Apple's first iPod in 2001, Sony had already developed devices that would download and play digital music files. Sony had everything it needed to create an iPod/iTunes-type world, including its own recording company. But it passed on

>> The marketing environment: Environmental unforeseeables have dealt Sony some heavy blows. But the company's inability to adapt to the changing technological environment has turned Sony's current "Make. Believe." brand promise into more of a "make-believe" one.

Bloomberg via Getty Images.

that idea in favor of continued emphasis on its then-highly successful CD business. "[Apple's] Steve Jobs figured it out, we figured it out, we didn't execute," says Sony chairman Stringer. "The music guys didn't want to see the CD go away."

Similarly, as the world's largest TV producer, Sony clung to its cherished Trinitron cathode-ray-tube technology. Meanwhile, Samsung, LG, and other competitors were moving rapidly ahead with flat screens. Sony eventually responded. But today, both Samsung and LG sell more TVs than Sony. Sony's TV business, once its main profit center, has suffered losses for the past eight years.

It was a similar story for Sony's PlayStation consoles, once the undisputed market leader and accounting for one-third of Sony's profits. Sony yawned when Nintendo introduced its innovative motion-sensing Nintendo Wii, dismissing it as a "niche game device." Instead, Sony engineers loaded up the PS3 with pricey technology that produced a loss of $300 per unit sold. Wii became a smash hit and the best-selling game console; the PS3 lost billions for Sony, dropping it from first place to third.

Even as a money loser, the PlayStation system, with its elegant blending of hardware and software, had all the right ingredients to make Sony a leader in the new world of digital entertainment distribution and social networking. Executives inside Sony even recognized the PlayStation platform as the "epitome of convergence," with the potential to create "a fusion of computers and entertainment." But that vision never materialized, and Sony has lagged in the burgeoning business of connecting people to digital entertainment.

To his credit, CEO Stringer made a credible effort to reignite Sony. After taking over in 2005, he drew up a turnaround plan aimed at changing the Sony mind-set and moving the company into the new connected and mobile digital age. Under his early leadership, the consumer electronics giant began to show renewed life as revenues and profits rose. Then came the Great Recession, once again knocking the bottom out of profits. And just as Sony began digging out from that disaster, it was struck by the string of 2011 environmental calamities.

Thus, environmental forces—whether unforeseeable natural and economic events or more predictable turns in technology—can heavily impact company strategy. Sony's difficult times provide a cautionary tale of what can happen when a company—even a dominant market leader—fails to adapt to its changing marketing environment. Despite the setbacks, however, giant Sony still has a lot going for it. It recently announced new plans to revitalize its core electronics businesses through renewed innovation. Now, if Sony can just get the economy and Mother Nature to cooperate. . . .

Sources: Bryan Gruley and Cliff Edwards, "Sony Needs a Hit," *Bloomberg Businessweek*, November 21, 2011, pp. 72–77; Hiroko Tabuchi, "Sony Revises Expected Loss to $6.40 Billion," *New York Times*, April 11, 2012, p. B3; Daisuke Wakabayashi, "Sony Posts Loss, Curbing Stock's Rally," *WallStreetJournal.com*, February 7, 2013, http://online.wsj.com/article/SB10001424127887324590904578289103990967408.html; Cliff Edwards and Mariko Yasu, "Sony's Search for Cool. The Old-Fashioned Way," *Bloomberg Businessweek*, February 24, 2013, pp. 20–21; and information from www.sony.net/SonyInfo/IR/, accessed November 2013.

Author Comment
Changes in demographics mean changes in markets, so they are very important to marketers. We first look at the biggest demographic trend—the changing age structure of the population.

The Demographic Environment

Demography is the study of human populations in terms of size, density, location, age, gender, race, occupation, and other statistics. The demographic environment is of major interest to marketers because it involves people, and people make up markets. The world population is growing at an explosive rate. It now exceeds 7 billion people and is expected to grow to more than 8 billion by the year 2030.[5] The world's large and highly diverse population poses both opportunities and challenges.

Changes in the world demographic environment have major implications for business. Thus, marketers keep a close eye on demographic trends and developments in their markets. They analyze changing age and family structures, geographic population shifts, educational characteristics, and population diversity. Here, we discuss the most important demographic trends in the United States.

Demography
The study of human populations in terms of size, density, location, age, gender, race, occupation, and other statistics.

The Changing Age Structure of the Population

The U.S. population currently stands at nearly 320 million and may reach almost 364 million by 2030.[6] The single most important demographic trend in the United States is the changing age structure of the population. The U.S. population contains several generational groups. Here, we discuss the three largest groups—the baby boomers, Generation X, and the Millennials—and their impact on today's marketing strategies.

Baby boomers
The 78 million people born during the years following World War II and lasting until 1964.

The Baby Boomers. The post–World War II baby boom produced 78 million **baby boomers**, who were born between 1946 and 1964. Over the years, the baby boomers have been one of the most powerful forces shaping the marketing environment. The youngest boomers are now moving into their fifties; the oldest are in their late sixties and entering retirement.

After years of prosperity, free spending, and saving little, the Great Recession hit many baby boomers hard, especially the preretirement boomers. A sharp decline in stock prices and home values ate into their nest eggs and retirement prospects. As a result, many boomers are now spending more carefully and are rethinking the purpose and value of their work, responsibilities, and relationships.

However, although some might still be feeling the postrecession pinch, the baby boomers are still the wealthiest generation in U.S. history. Today's baby boomers account for about 25 percent of the U.S. population but control an estimated 70 percent of the nation's disposable income. The 50-plus consumer segment now buys more than 47 percent of all consumer goods.[7] As they reach their peak earning and spending years, the boomers will continue to constitute a lucrative market for financial services, new housing and home remodeling, new cars, travel and entertainment, eating out, health and fitness products, and just about everything else.

In a recent campaign aimed at convincing companies to advertise in its magazine, the AARP (formerly the American Association of Retired Persons) advises that brands focusing on younger demographics groups are missing a big opportunity. The AARP ads feature people in their 50s and 60s, with headlines such as "I may be creased, but my money is crisp," and "I may be gray, but my money is as green as it gets." The ads continue: "Why is it all about 18–34, when they barely have a dime of their own? The story is simple, AARP . . . reaches the best boomers, and 68 percent of those over 50 give money to their adult kids."

It would be a mistake to think of the older boomers as phasing out or slowing down. Rather than viewing themselves as phasing out, many of today's boomer see themselves as entering new life phases. The more active boomers—sometimes called zoomers—have no intention of abandoning their youthful lifestyles as they age. For example, a recent study found that whereas 9 percent of baby boomers attended the symphony or opera during the previous 12 months, 12 percent attended a rock concert. Notes one expert, baby boomers "are showing the nation that their heyday is far from over by taking pleasure in life's adventures."[8]

For example, many travel companies—such as ElderTreks, 50PlusExpeditions, and Row Adventures—now design adventure travel expeditions for active baby boomers. ElderTreks, for instance, offers small-group, off-the-beaten-path tours designed exclusively for people 50 and over. Whether it's for wildlife and tribal African safari, active hiking in the Himalayas or Andes, or an expedition by icebreaker to the Artic or Antarctic, ElderTreks targets active boomers who have the time, resources, and passion for high-adventure travel but prefer to do it with others their own age—no young'uns allowed.[9]

Generation X. The baby boom was followed by a "birth dearth," creating another generation of 49 million people born between 1965 and 1976. Author Douglas Coupland calls them **Generation X** because they lie in the shadow of the boomers.

Generation X
The 49 million people born between 1965 and 1976 in the "birth dearth" following the baby boom.

Considerably smaller than the boomer generation that precedes them and the Millennials who follow, the Generation Xers are a sometimes overlooked consumer group. Although they seek success, they are less materialistic than the other groups; they prize experience, not acquisition. For many of the Gen Xers who are parents, family comes first—both children and their aging parents—and career second. From a marketing standpoint, the Gen Xers are a more skeptical bunch. They tend to research products before they consider a purchase, prefer quality to quantity, and tend to be less receptive to overt marketing pitches. They are more likely to be receptive to irreverent ad pitches that make fun of convention and tradition.

The first to grow up in the Internet era, Generation X is a connected generation that embraces the benefits of new technology. Some 49 percent own smartphones and 11 percent own tablets. Of the Xers on the Internet, 74 percent use the Internet for banking, 72 percent use it for researching companies or products, and 81 percent have made purchases online. Ninety-five percent have an active Facebook page.

The Gen Xers have now grown up and are taking over. They are increasingly displacing the lifestyles, culture, and values of the baby boomers. They are moving up in their careers, and many are proud homeowners with growing families. They are the most educated generation to date, and they possess hefty annual purchasing power. However, like the baby boomers, the Gen Xers now face growing economic pressures. Like almost everyone else these days, they are spending more carefully.[10]

Still, with so much potential, many brands and organizations are focusing on Gen Xers as a prime target segment. >> For example, Dairy Queen targets this segment directly, with a marketing campaign that fits the Gen Xer family situation and sense of humor:[11]

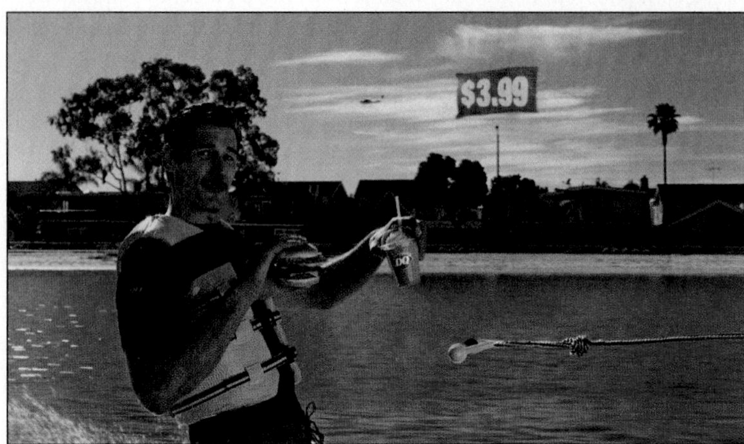

>> **Targeting Gen Xers: Dairy Queen's "So Good It's RiDQulous" campaign targets Gen Xers with irreverent humor and online ad placements.**

American Dairy Queen Corporation.

Generation X is Dairy Queen's new sweet spot. Its primary target market—parents roughly 34 to 44 years old with young children—falls squarely within the Gen X cohort. So what does that mean for DQ's marketing? A "So Good It's RiDQulous" advertising campaign loaded with irreverent Gen X humor—as in old-fashioned shaving bunnies, a guitar that sounds like a dolphin, fencing ninjas, and kittens in bubbles. In one ad, DQ's new pitchman—a mustachioed 30-something—touts Dairy Queen birthday cakes, then says, "And we don't just blow bubbles, we blow bubbles with kittens inside them [which he then does], because at Dairy Queen, good isn't good enough." To reach Gen X consumers better, DQ has shifted a batch of its ads from TV to the social media and online sites such as Hulu. "We're going where our Gen X customers' eyeballs are," says DQ's chief brand officer. An independent study last year found the "So Good It's RiDQulous" ads to be the most effective in the quick service restaurant segment.

Millennials (or Generation Y)
The 83 million children of the baby boomers born between 1977 and 2000.

Millennials. Both the baby boomers and Gen Xers will one day be passing the reins to the **Millennials** (also called **Generation Y** or the echo boomers). Born between 1977 and 2000, these children of the baby boomers number 83 million or more, dwarfing the Gen Xers and becoming larger even than the baby boomer segment. In the postrecession era, the Millennials are the most financially strapped generation. Facing higher unemployment and saddled with more debt, many of these young consumers have near-empty piggy banks. Still, because of their numbers, the Millennials make up a huge and attractive market, both now and in the future.

One thing that all Millennials have in common is their comfort with digital technology. They don't just embrace technology; it's a way of life. The Millennials were the first generation to grow up in a world filled with computers, mobile phones, satellite TV, iPods and iPads, and online social media. As a result, they engage with brands in an entirely new way, such as with mobile or social media. "They tend to expect one-to-one communication with brands," says one analyst, "and embrace the ability to share the good and bad about products and services with friends and strangers."[12]

>> **Targeting Millennials: The Kia Soul and its Hamster ads have been a smash hit with Millennials, helping to make the Kia one of the nation's fastest-growing car brands.**

KIA Motors America.

Many brands are now fielding specific products and marketing campaigns aimed at Millennial needs and lifestyles. >> For example, the Kia Soul targets young Millennial consumers. It's a funky but practical entry-level vehicle with an affordable price to match. Kia Soul "Hamstar" ads have a distinctly youthful appeal, featuring a trio of hamsters hip-hopping their way through scenes ranging from an apocalyptic landscape to an eighteenth-century

Generation Z
People born after 2000 (although many analysts include people born after 1995) who make up the kids, tweens, and teens markets.

opera house, accompanied by infectious soundtracks such as LMFAO's "Party Rock Anthem." The campaign—featuring everything from Super Bowl ads to online, mobile, and social media platforms—is built around what Kia's U.S. chief marketing officer calls "the four pillars of Millennial's lifestyles: music, sports, pop culture, and the 'connected life.'" Both the car and the marketing campaign have been a smash hit with targeted buyers.[13]

Generation Z. Hard on the heels of the Millennials is **Generation Z**, young people born after 2000 (although many analysts include people born after 1995 in this group). The Gen Zers make up important kids, tweens, and teens markets. For example, by themselves, U.S. "tweens" (ages 8–12) number 20 million girls and boys who spend an estimated $30 billion annually of their own money and influence another $150 billion of their parents' spending.[14] These young consumers also represent tomorrow's markets—they are now forming brand relationships that will affect their buying well into the future.

Even more than the Millennials, the defining characteristic of Gen Zers is their utter fluency and comfort with digital technologies. Generation Z take smartphones, tablets, iPods, Internet-connected game consoles, wireless Internet, and digital and social media for granted—they've always had them—making this group highly mobile, connected, and social. "If they're awake, they're online," quips one analyst. They have "digital in their DNA," says another.[15]

Gen Zers blend the online and offline worlds seamlessly as they socialize and shop. According to recent studies, despite their youth, more than half of all Generation Z tweens and teens do product research before buying a product, or having their parents buy it for them. Of those who shop online, more than half *prefer* shopping online in categories ranging from electronics, books, music, sports equipment, and beauty products to clothes, shoes, and fashion accessories.[16]

Companies in almost all industries market products and services aimed at Generation Z. For example, many retailers have created special lines or even entire stores appealing to Gen Z buyers and their parents—consider Abercrombie Kids, Gap Kids, Old Navy Kids, and Pottery Barn Kids. >> The Justice chain targets tween girls, with apparel and accessories laser-focused on their special preferences and lifestyles. Although these young buyers often have their mothers in tow, "the *last* thing a 10- or 12-year-old girl wants is to look like her mom," says Justice's CEO. Justice's stores, Web site, and social media pages are designed with tweens in mind. "You have to appeal to their senses," says the CEO. "They love sensory overload—bright colors, music videos, a variety of merchandise, the tumult of all of that." Fast-growing Justice now outsells even Walmart and Target in girl's apparel (that's impressive considering that Walmart has almost 4,000 U.S. stores compared to Justice's 920).[17]

>> Targeting Generation Z: Justice targets only tween girls, with apparel and accessories laser-focused on their special preferences and lifestyles.
Photo courtesy of Gary Armstrong.

Media companies and publishers are also targeting today's connected, tech-savvy Gen Zers and their parents. For example, Netflix has created a "Just for Kids" portal and app, by which children can experience Netflix on any or all of their screens—TVs, computers, and tablets or other mobile devices. "Just for Kids" is filled with movies and TV shows appropriate for children 12 and under, organized in a kid-friendly way with large images of their favorite characters and content categories.[18]

Marketing to Gen Zers and their parents presents special challenges. Traditional media are still important to this group. Magazines such as *J-14* and *Twist* are popular with some Gen Z segments, as are TV channels such as Nickelodeon and the Disney Channel. But marketers know they must meet Gen Zers where they hang out and shop. Increasingly, that's in the digital, online, and mobile worlds. Although the under-13 set remains barred from social media such as Facebook and Instagram, at least officially (half of all tweens say they use Facebook), the social media will play a crucial marketing role as the kids and tweens grow into teens.

Today's kids are notoriously hard to pin down, and they have short attention spans. Gen Zers "don't want to be hit over the head with ad messages," says one kid-marketing expert. They "don't want *products*, they want *experiences*. You want to engage them." Says another expert, "Today's tweens demand a more personal, more tactile, truly up-close-and-in-person connection to their favorite brands."[19]

Another Generation Z concern involves children's privacy and their vulnerability to marketing pitches. Companies marketing to this group must do so responsibly or risk the wrath of parents and public policy makers.

Generational Marketing. Do marketers need to create separate products and marketing programs for each generation? Some experts warn that marketers need to be careful about turning off one generation each time they craft a product or message that appeals effectively to another. Others caution that each generation spans decades of time and many socioeconomic levels. For example, marketers often split the baby boomers into three smaller groups—leading-edge boomers, core boomers, and trailing-edge boomers—each with its own beliefs and behaviors. Similarly, they split the Generaton Z into kids, tweens, and teens.

Thus, marketers need to form more precise age-specific segments within each group. More important, defining people by their birth date may be less effective than segmenting them by lifestyle, life stage, or the common values they seek in the products they buy. We will discuss many other ways to segment markets in Chapter 6.

The Changing American Family

The traditional household consists of a husband, wife, and children (and sometimes grandparents). Yet, the historic American ideal of the two-child, two-car suburban family has lately been losing some of its luster.

In the United States today, married couples with children represent only 20 percent of the nation's 121 million households, less than half that of 1970. Married couples without children represent 28 percent, and single parents are another 18 percent. A full 34 percent are nonfamily households—singles living alone or adults of one or both sexes living together.[20] More people are divorcing or separating, choosing not to marry, marrying later, or marrying without intending to have children. Marketers must increasingly consider the special needs of nontraditional households because they are now growing more rapidly than traditional households. Each group has distinctive needs and buying habits.

The number of working women has also increased greatly, growing from under 40 percent of the U.S. workforce in the late 1950s to 58 percent today. Among households made up of married couples with children, 58 percent are dual-income households; only the husband works in 28 percent. Meanwhile, more men are staying home with their children and managing the household while their wives go to work. Four percent of married couples with children in the United States have a full-time stay-at-home dad.[21]

The significant number of women in the workforce has spawned the child day-care business and increased the consumption of career-oriented women's clothing, convenience foods, financial services, and time-saving services. Royal Caribbean targets time-crunched working moms with budget-friendly family vacations that are easy to plan and certain to wow the family. Royal Caribbean estimates that, although vacations are a joint decision, 80 percent of all trips are planned and booked by women—moms who are pressed for time, whether they work or not. "We want to make sure that you're the hero, that when your family comes on our ship, it's going to be a great experience for all of them," says a senior marketer at Royal Caribbean, "and that you, mom, who has done all the planning and scheduling, get to enjoy that vacation."[22]

Geographic Shifts in Population

This is a period of great migratory movements between and within countries. Americans, for example, are a mobile people, with about 14 percent of all U.S. residents moving each year. Over the past two decades, the U.S. population has shifted toward the Sunbelt states. The West and South have grown, whereas the Midwest and Northeast states have lost population.[23] Such population shifts interest marketers because people in different regions buy differently. For example, people in the Midwest buy more winter clothing than people in the Southeast.

Also, for more than a century, Americans have been moving from rural to metropolitan areas. In the 1950s, they made a massive exit from the cities to the suburbs. Today, the migration to the suburbs continues. And more and more Americans are moving to "micropolitan areas," small cities located beyond congested metropolitan areas, such as Bozeman, Montana; Natchez, Mississippi; Traverse City, Michigan; and Torrington, Connecticut. These smaller micros offer many of the advantages of metro areas—jobs, restaurants, diversions, community organizations—but without the population crush, traffic jams, high crime rates, and high property taxes often associated with heavily urbanized areas.[24]

The shift in where people live has also caused a shift in where they work. For example, the migration toward micropolitan and suburban areas has resulted in a rapid increase in the number of people who "telecommute"—work at home or in a remote office and conduct their business by phone or the Internet. This trend, in turn, has created a booming SOHO (small office/home office) market. Increasing numbers of people are working from home with the help of electronic conveniences such as PCs, smartphones, and broadband Internet access. One recent study estimates that 24 percent of employed individuals do some or all of their work at home.[25]

Many marketers are actively courting the lucrative telecommuting market. For example, WebEx, the Web-conferencing division of Cisco, helps connect people who telecommute or work remotely. With WebEx, people can meet and collaborate online via computer or smartphone, no matter what their work location. And companies ranging from Salesforce.com to Google and IBM offer cloud computing applications that let people collaborate anywhere and everywhere through the Internet and mobile devices. >> Additionally, companies such as Regus or Grind rent out fully equipped shared office space by the day or month for telecommuters and others who work away from the main office.[26]

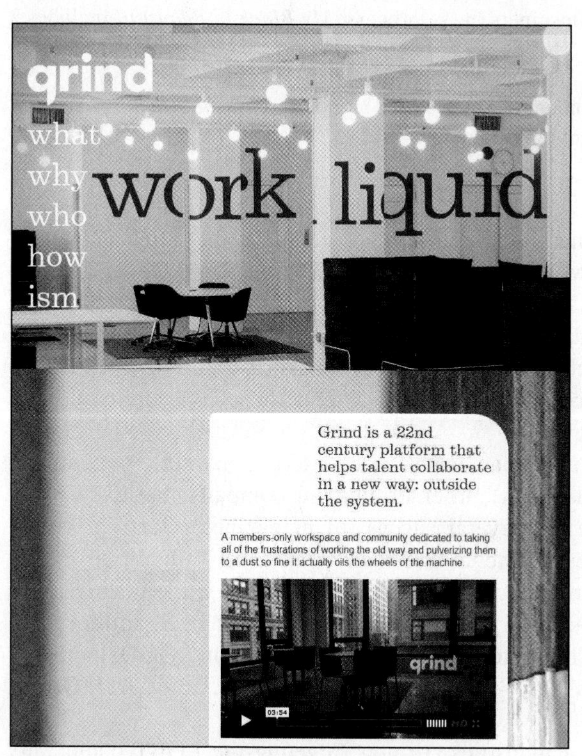

>> Serving the telecommuter market: Companies such as Grind rent out shared office space by the day or month to telecommuters and others who work away from the main office.

Grind, LLC.

A Better-Educated, More White-Collar, More Professional Population

The U.S. population is becoming better educated. For example, in 2012, 88 percent of the U.S. population over age 25 had completed high school and 30 percent had a bachelor's degree, compared with 66 percent and 16 percent, respectively, in 1980.[27] The workforce also is becoming more white collar. Job growth is now strongest for professional workers and weakest for manufacturing workers. Between 2010 and 2020, of 30 detailed occupations projected to have the fastest employment growth, 17 require some type of postsecondary education.[28] The rising number of educated professionals will affect not just what people buy but also how they buy.

Increasing Diversity

Countries vary in their ethnic and racial makeup. At one extreme is Japan, where almost everyone is Japanese. At the other extreme is the United States, with people from virtually all national origins. The United States has often been called a melting pot, where diverse groups from many nations and cultures have melted into a single, more homogenous whole. Instead, the United States seems to have become more of a "salad bowl" in which various groups have mixed together but have maintained their diversity by retaining and valuing important ethnic and cultural differences.

Marketers now face increasingly diverse markets, both at home and abroad, as their operations become more international in scope. The U.S. population is about 64 percent white, with Hispanics at almost 17 percent and African Americans at just over 13 percent. The U.S. Asian American population now totals more than 5 percent of the total U.S. population, with the remaining 1 percent being Native Hawaiian, Pacific Islander, American Indian, Eskimo, or Aleut. Moreover, one in eight people living in the United States—about 13 percent of the population—was born in another country. The nation's ethnic populations are expected to explode in coming decades. By 2050, Hispanics will be more than 30 percent of the population, African Americans will be almost 15 percent, and Asian Americans will increase to 8 percent.[29]

Most large companies, from P&G, Walmart, Allstate, and Bank of America to McDonald's and Levi Strauss, now target specially designed products, ads, and promotions to one or more of these groups. For example, Procter & Gamble has long been the leader in African American advertising, spending nearly 50 percent more than the second-place spender in Hispanic media. P&G also tailors products to the specific needs of black consumers. For instance, its CoverGirl Queen Collection is specially formulated "to celebrate the beauty of women of color." In addition to traditional product marketing efforts, P&G also supports a broader "My Black Is Beautiful" movement:[30]

> Created by a group of African American women at P&G, the movement aims "to ignite and support a sustained national conversation by, for, and about black women" and how they are reflected in popular culture. P&G discovered that black women spend three times more than the general market on beauty products yet feel they're portrayed worse than other women in media and advertising. Supported by brands such as Crest, Pantene, Always, Secret, the CoverGirl Queen Collection, and Olay Definity, the My Black Is Beautiful movement's goal is to empower African American women to embrace their beauty, health, and wellness and, of course, to forge a closer relationship between P&G brands and African American consumers in the process. *My Black Is Beautiful* includes a rich Web site, national media platforms, a TV series in its third season on BET, and a full slate of major social media such as Twitter, Facebook, and Pinterest. It maintains a presence at key events that allow women to interact with brands and the *My Black is Beautiful* movement in trusted and relevant environments.

Diversity goes beyond ethnic heritage. For example, many major companies explicitly target gay and lesbian consumers. According to one estimate, the 6 to 7 percent of U.S. adults who identify themselves as lesbian, gay, bisexual, or transgender (LGBT) have buying power of more than $790 billion.[31] As a result of TV shows such as *Modern Family* and *Glee,* movies like *Brokeback Mountain* and *The Perks of Being a Wallflower,* and openly gay celebrities and public figures such as Neil Patrick Harris, Ellen DeGeneres, David Sedaris, and former congressman Barney Frank, the LGBT community has increasingly emerged in the public eye.

Numerous media now provide companies with access to this market. For example, Planet Out Inc., a leading global media and entertainment company that exclusively serves the LGBT community, offers several successful magazines (*Out*, *The Advocate*, *Out Traveler*) and Web sites (Gay.com and PlanetOut.com). In addition, media giant Viacom's MTV Networks offers LOGO, a cable television network aimed at gays and lesbians and their friends and family. LOGO is now available in 51 million U.S. households. More than 100 mainstream marketers have advertised on LOGO, including Ameriprise Financial, Toyota, Anheuser-Busch, Dell, Levi Strauss, eBay, J&J, Orbitz, Sears, Sony, and Subaru.

Companies in a wide range of industries are now targeting the LGBT community with gay-specific ads and marketing efforts—from Amazon and Apple to household goods retailer Crate & Barrel. American Airlines has a dedicated LGBT sales team, sponsors gay community events, and offers a special gay-oriented Web site (www.aa.com/rainbow) that features travel deals, an e-newsletter, podcasts, and a gay events calendar. The airline's focus on gay consumers has earned it double-digit revenue growth from the LGBT community each year for more than a decade.[32]

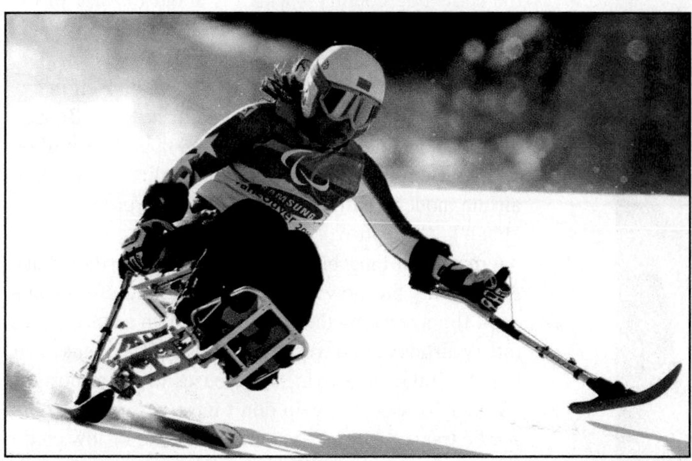

>> Targeting consumers with disabilities: Samsung features people with disabilities in its mainstream advertising and signs endorsement deals with Paralympic athletes.

GEPA/Imago/Icon SMI/Newscom.

Another attractive diversity segment is the 57 million U.S. adults with disabilities—a market larger than African Americans or Hispanics—representing more than $200 billion in annual spending power. Most individuals with disabilities are active consumers. For example, one study found that the segment spends $13.6 billion on 31.7 million business or leisure trips every year. And if certain needs were met, the amount spent on travel could double to $27 billion annually.[33]

How are companies trying to reach consumers with disabilities? Many marketers now recognize that the worlds of people with disabilities and those without disabilities are one in the same. Marketers such as McDonald's, Verizon Wireless, Nike, Samsung, and Honda have featured people with disabilities in their mainstream marketing. >> For instance, Samsung and Nike sign endorsement deals with Paralympic athletes and feature them in advertising.

As the population in the United States grows more diverse, successful marketers will continue to diversify their marketing programs to take advantage of opportunities in fast-growing segments.

SPEED BUMP LINKING THE CONCEPTS

Pull over here and think about how deeply these demographic factors impact all of us and, as a result, marketing strategies.

- Apply these demographic developments to your own life. Discuss some specific examples of how changing demographic factors affect you and your buying behavior.
- Identify a specific company that has done a good job of reacting to the shifting demographic environment—generational segments (baby boomers, Gen Xers, Millennials, or Gen Zers), the changing American family, and increased diversity. Compare this company to one that's done a poor job.

Economic environment
Economic factors that affect consumer purchasing power and spending patterns.

Author Comment
The economic environment can offer both opportunities and threats. For example, in the postrecession era of more sensible consumer spending, "value" has become the marketing watchword.

The Economic Environment

Markets require buying power as well as people. The **economic environment** consists of economic factors that affect consumer purchasing power and spending patterns. Marketers must pay close attention to major trends and consumer spending patterns both across and within their world markets.

Nations vary greatly in their levels and distribution of income. Some countries have *industrial economies*, which constitute rich markets for many different kinds of goods. At the other extreme are *subsistence economies*; they consume most of their own agricultural and industrial output and offer few market opportunities. In between are *developing economies* that can offer outstanding marketing opportunities for the right kinds of products.

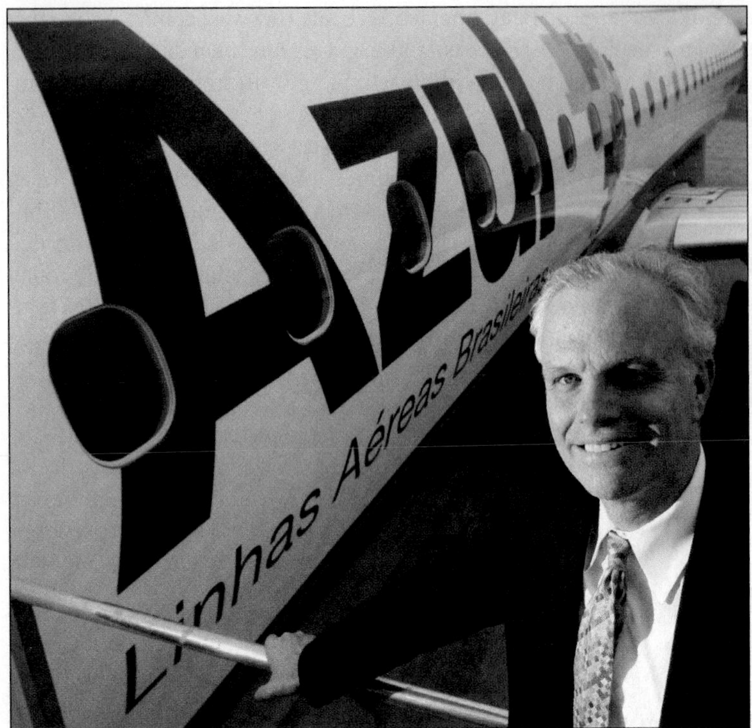

>> Economic environment: To tap Brazil's large and fast-growing middle class, former JetBlue founder David Neeleman, shown here, started low-fare Azul Brazilian Airlines, which provides a good-quality but affordable alternative to long bus rides across the sprawling country.

Associated Press.

Consider Brazil with its population of more than 196 million people. Until recently, only well-heeled Brazilians could afford to travel by air. >> Azul Brazilian Airlines has changed that:[34]

> For decades, Brazilians with lesser means traveled the sprawling country—which is about the size of the continental United States but with less-well-developed roads—mostly by bus. However, David Neeleman, founder and former CEO of JetBlue and himself native Brazilian, saw a real opportunity in serving Brazil's fast-growing middle class of more than 100 million people. He founded Azul Brazilian Airlines, a low-fare airline modeled after JetBlue ("azul" is Portuguese for "blue"). Azul provides a good-quality but affordable alternative to long bus rides—a trip that used to take 34 hours by bus now takes only 2 via Azul. And many Azul flights costing the same or less than a bus trip, the thrifty airline has converted millions of Brazilians to air travel. Azul even provides free buses to the airport for its many passengers who don't have cars or access to public transportation. Customers with no or low credit can pay for tickets with bank withdrawals or by installment. After only five years, Azul has grown rapidly to become Brazil's third-largest air carrier, with a more than 14 percent domestic travel market share.

Changes in Consumer Spending

Economic factors can have a dramatic effect on consumer spending and buying behavior. For example, until fairly recently, American consumers spent freely, fueled by income growth, a boom in the stock market, rapid increases in housing values, and other economic good fortunes. They bought and bought, seemingly without caution, amassing record levels of debt. However, the free spending and high expectations of those days were dashed by the Great Recession of 2008/2009.

As a result, as discussed in Chapter 1, consumers have now adopted a back-to-basics sensibility in their lifestyles and spending patterns that will likely persist for years to come. They are buying less and looking for greater value in the things that they do buy. In turn, *value marketing* has become the watchword for many marketers. Marketers in all industries are looking for ways to offer today's more financially frugal buyers greater value—just the right combination of product quality and good service at a fair price.

You'd expect value pitches from the sellers of everyday products. For example, as Target has shifted emphasis toward the "Pay less" side of its "Expect more. Pay less." slogan, the once-chic headlines at the Target.com Web site have been replaced by more practical appeals such as "Our lowest prices of the season," "Fun, sun, save," and "Free shipping, every day." However, these days, even luxury-brand marketers are emphasizing good value. For instance, upscale car brand Infiniti now promises to "make luxury affordable."

Income Distribution

Marketers should pay attention to *income distribution* as well as income levels. Over the past several decades, the rich have grown richer, the middle class has shrunk, and the poor have remained poor. The top 5 percent of American earners get over 22 percent of the country's adjusted gross income, and the top 20 percent of earners capture over 50 percent of all income. In contrast, the bottom 40 percent of American earners get just 12 percent of the total income.[35]

This distribution of income has created a tiered market. Many companies—such as Nordstrom and Neiman Marcus—aggressively target the affluent. Others—such as Dollar General and Family Dollar—target those with more modest means. In fact, dollar stores are now the fastest-growing retailers in the nation. Still other companies tailor their marketing offers across a range of markets, from the affluent to the less affluent. For example, Ford offers cars ranging from the low-priced Ford Fiesta, starting at $13,200, to the luxury Lincoln Navigator SUV, starting at $57,875.

Changes in major economic variables, such as income, cost of living, interest rates, and savings and borrowing patterns, have a large impact on the marketplace. Companies watch these variables by using economic forecasting. Businesses do not have to be wiped out by an economic downturn or caught short in a boom. With adequate warning, they can take advantage of changes in the economic environment.

Author Comment

Today's enlightened companies are developing environmentally sustainable strategies in an effort to create a world economy that the planet can support indefinitely.

The Natural Environment

Natural environment
The physical environment and the natural resources that are needed as inputs by marketers or that are affected by marketing activities.

The **natural environment** involves the physical environment and the natural resources that are needed as inputs by marketers or that are affected by marketing activities. At the most basic level, unexpected happenings in the physical environment—anything from weather to natural disasters—can affect companies and their marketing strategies. For example, a recent unexpectedly warm winter put the chill on sales of products ranging from cold-weather apparel to facial tissues and Campbell's soups. In contrast, the warmer weather boosted demand for products such as hiking and running shoes, house paint, and gardening supplies. Similarly, the damage caused by the recent earthquake and tsunami in Japan had a devastating effect on the ability of Japanese companies such as Sony and Toyota to meet worldwide demand for their products. Although companies can't prevent such natural occurrences, they should prepare contingency plans for dealing with them.[36]

At a broader level, environmental sustainability concerns have grown steadily over the past three decades. In many cities around the world, air and water pollution have reached dangerous levels. World concern continues to mount about the possibilities of global warming, and many environmentalists fear that we soon will be buried in our own trash.

Marketers should be aware of several trends in the natural environment. The first involves growing shortages of raw materials. Air and water may seem to be infinite resources, but some groups see long-run dangers. Air pollution chokes many of the world's large cities, and water shortages are already a big problem in some parts of the United States and the world. By 2030, more than one in three people in the world will not have enough water to drink.[37] Renewable resources, such as forests and food, also have to be used wisely. Nonrenewable resources, such as oil, coal, and various minerals, pose a serious problem. Firms making products that require these scarce resources face large cost increases, even if the materials remain available.

A second environmental trend is *increased pollution*. Industry will almost always damage the quality of the natural environment. Consider the disposal of chemical and nuclear wastes; the dangerous mercury levels in the ocean; the quantity of chemical pollutants in the soil and food supply; and the littering of the environment with nonbiodegradable bottles, plastics, and other packaging materials.

A third trend is *increased government intervention* in natural resource management. The governments of different countries vary in their concern and efforts to promote a clean environment. Some, such as the German government, vigorously pursue environmental quality. Others, especially many poorer nations, do little about pollution, largely because they lack the needed funds or political will. Even richer nations lack the vast funds and political accord needed to mount a worldwide environmental effort. The general hope is that companies around the world will accept more social responsibility and that less expensive devices can be found to control and reduce pollution.

In the United States, the Environmental Protection Agency (EPA) was created in 1970 to create and enforce pollution standards and conduct pollution research. In the

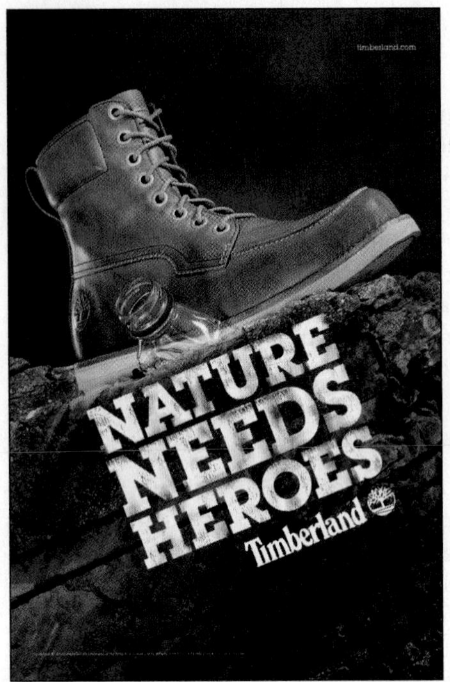

Environmental sustainability: Timberland is on a mission to do everything it can to reduce its impact on the planet while at the same time making better outdoor gear.

The Timberland Company.

future, companies doing business in the United States can expect continued strong controls from government and pressure groups. Instead of opposing regulation, marketers should help develop solutions to the materials and energy problems facing the world.

Concern for the natural environment has spawned the so-called green movement. Today, enlightened companies go beyond what government regulations dictate. They are developing strategies and practices that support **environmental sustainability**—an effort to create a world economy that the planet can support indefinitely. Environmental sustainability means meeting present needs without compromising the ability of future generations to meet their needs.

Environmental sustainability
Developing strategies and practices that create a world economy that the planet can support indefinitely.

Many companies are responding to consumer demands with more environmentally responsible products. Others are developing recyclable or biodegradable packaging, recycled materials and components, better pollution controls, and more energy-efficient operations. For example, Timberland's mission is about more than just making rugged, high-quality boots, shoes, clothes, and other outdoor gear. The brand is about doing everything it can to reduce the environmental footprint of its products and processes:[38]

> Timberland is on a mission to develop processes and products that cause less harm to the environment and to enlist consumers in the cause. For example, it has a solar-powered distribution center in California and a wind-powered factory in the Dominican Republic. It has installed energy-efficient lighting and equipment retrofits in its facilities and is educating workers about production efficiency. Timberland is constantly looking for and inventing innovative materials that allow it to reduce its impact on the planet while at the same time making better gear. Its Earthkeepers line of boots is made from recycled and organic materials, and the brand has launched footwear collections featuring outsoles made from recycled car tires. Plastic from recycled soda bottles goes into its breathable linings and durable shoe laces. Coffee grounds find a place in its odor-resistant jackets. Organic cotton without toxins makes it into its rugged canvas. To inspire consumers to make more sustainable decisions, Timberland puts Green Index tags on its products that rate each item's ecological footprint in terms of climate impact, chemicals used, and resources consumed. To pull it all together, Timberland launched an Earthkeeper's campaign, an online social networking effort that seeks to inspire people to take actions to lighten their environmental footprints.

Companies today are looking to do more than just good deeds. More and more, they are recognizing the link between a healthy ecology and a healthy economy. They are learning that environmentally responsible actions can also be good business.

Author Comment
Technological advances are perhaps the most dramatic forces affecting marketing today. Just think about the tremendous impact of digital technologies. You'll see examples of the exploding world of online, mobile, and social media marketing in every chapter and discussed in detail in Chapter 14.

The Technological Environment

Technological environment
Forces that create new technologies, creating new product and market opportunities.

The **technological environment** is perhaps the most dramatic force now shaping our destiny. Technology has released such wonders as antibiotics, robotic surgery, miniaturized electronics, smartphones, and the Internet. It also has released such horrors as nuclear missiles, chemical weapons, and assault rifles. It has released such mixed blessings as the automobile, television, and credit cards. Our attitude toward technology depends on whether we are more impressed with its wonders or its blunders.

New technologies can offer exciting opportunities for marketers. For example, what would you think about having tiny little transmitters implanted in all the products you buy, which would allow tracking of the products from their point of production through use and disposal? Or how about a bracelet with a chip inserted that would let you make and pay for purchases, receive personalized specials at retail locations, or even track your whereabouts or those of friends? On the one hand, such technology would provide many advantages to both buyers and sellers. On the other hand, it could be a bit scary.

Marketing technology: Disney is taking RFID technology to new levels with its cool new MagicBand RFID wristband.

Shelley Caran, OntheGoInMCO.com.

Either way, with the advent of radio-frequency identification (RFID) transmitters, it's already happening.

Many firms are already using RFID technology to track products through various points in the distribution channel. For example, Walmart has strongly encouraged suppliers shipping products to its distribution centers to apply RFID tags to their pallets. So far, more than 600 Walmart suppliers are doing so. And retailers such as American Apparel, Macy's, and Bloomingdales are now installing item-level RFID systems in their stores. Fashion and accessories maker Burberry even uses chips imbedded in items and linked to smartphones to provide personalized, interactive experiences for customers in its stores and at runway shows.[39]

Disney is taking RFID technology to new levels with its cool new MagicBand RFID wristband:[40]

> Wearing a MagicBand at The Walt Disney World Resort opens up a whole new level of Disney's famed magic. After registering for cloud-based MyMagic+ services, with the flick of your wrist you can enter a park or attraction, buy dinner or souvenirs, or even unlock your hotel room. But Disney has only begun to tap the MagicBand's potential for personalizing guest experiences. Future applications could be truly magical. Imagine, for example, the wonder of a child who receives a warm hug from Mickey Mouse, or a bow from Prince Charming, who then greets the child by name and wishes her a happy birthday. Imagine animatronics that interact with nearby guests based on personal information supplied in advance. You get separated from family or friends? No problem. A quick scan of your MagicBand at a nearby directory could pinpoint the locations of your entire party. Linked to your Disney phone app, the MagicBand could trigger in-depth information about park features, ride wait times, FastPass check-in alerts, and your reservations schedule. Of course, the MagicBand also offers Disney a potential motherload of digital data on guest activities and movements in minute detail, helping to improve guest logistics, services, and sales. If all this seems too big-brotherish, there will be privacy options—for example, letting parents opt out of things like characters knowing children's names. In all, such digital technologies promise to enrich the Disney experience for both guests and the company.

The technological environment changes rapidly. Think of all of today's common products that were not available 100 years ago—or even 30 years ago. Abraham Lincoln did not know about automobiles, airplanes, radios, or the electric light. Woodrow Wilson did not know about television, aerosol cans, automatic dishwashers, air conditioners, antibiotics, or computers. Franklin Delano Roosevelt did not know about xerography, synthetic detergents, birth control pills, jet engines, or earth satellites. John F. Kennedy did not know about PCs, the Internet, or Google, and Ronald Reagan knew nothing about smartphones or social media.

New technologies create new markets and opportunities. However, every new technology replaces an older technology. Transistors hurt the vacuum-tube industry, digital photography hurt the film business, and MP3 players and digital downloads are hurting the CD business. When old industries fought or ignored new technologies, their businesses declined. Thus, marketers should watch the technological environment closely. Companies that do not keep up will soon find their products outdated. If that happens, they will miss new product and market opportunities.

As products and technology become more complex, the public needs to know that these items are safe. Thus, government agencies investigate and ban potentially unsafe products. In the United States, the Food and Drug Administration (FDA) has created complex regulations for testing new drugs. The Consumer Product Safety Commission (CPSC) establishes safety standards for consumer products and penalizes companies that fail to meet them. Such regulations have resulted in much higher research costs and longer times between new product ideas and their introduction. Marketers should be aware of these regulations when applying new technologies and developing new products.

Author Comment

Even the strongest free-market advocates agree that the system works best with at least some regulation. But beyond regulation, most companies *want* to be socially responsible. We'll dig deeper into marketing and social responsibility in Chapter 16.

The Political and Social Environment

Marketing decisions are strongly affected by developments in the political environment. The **political environment** consists of laws, government agencies, and pressure groups that influence or limit various organizations and individuals in a given society.

Legislation Regulating Business

Even the strongest advocates of free-market economies agree that the system works best with at least some regulation. Well-conceived regulation can encourage competition and ensure fair markets for goods and services. Thus, governments develop *public policy* to guide commerce—sets of laws and regulations that limit business for the good of society as a whole. Almost every marketing activity is subject to a wide range of laws and regulations.

Legislation affecting business around the world has increased steadily over the years. The United States and many other countries have many laws covering issues such as competition, fair-trade practices, environmental protection, product safety, truth in advertising, consumer privacy, packaging and labeling, pricing, and other important areas (see **»Table 3.1**).

Political environment
Laws, government agencies, and pressure groups that influence and limit various organizations and individuals in a given society.

Understanding the public policy implications of a particular marketing activity is not a simple matter. In the United States, there are many laws created at the national, state, and local levels, and these regulations often overlap. For example, aspirin products sold in Dallas are governed by both federal labeling laws and Texas state advertising laws. Moreover, regulations are constantly changing; what was allowed last year may now be prohibited, and what was prohibited may now be allowed. Marketers must work hard to keep up with changes in regulations and their interpretations.

Business legislation has been enacted for a number of reasons. The first is to *protect companies* from each other. Although business executives may praise competition, they sometimes try to neutralize it when it threatens them. Therefore, laws are passed to define and prevent unfair competition. In the United States, such laws are enforced by the Federal Trade Commission (FTC) and the Antitrust Division of the Attorney General's office.

The second purpose of government regulation is to *protect consumers* from unfair business practices. Some firms, if left alone, would make shoddy products, invade consumer privacy, mislead consumers in their advertising, and deceive consumers through their packaging and pricing. Rules defining and regulating unfair business practices are enforced by various agencies.

The third purpose of government regulation is to *protect the interests of society* against unrestrained business behavior. Profitable business activity does not always create a better quality of life. Regulation arises to ensure that firms take responsibility for the social costs of their production or products.

International marketers will encounter dozens, or even hundreds, of agencies set up to enforce trade policies and regulations. In the United States, Congress has established federal regulatory agencies, such as the FTC, the FDA, the Federal Communications Commission, the Federal Energy Regulatory Commission, the Federal Aviation Administration, the Consumer Product Safety Commission, the Environmental Protection Agency, and hundreds of others. Because such government agencies have some discretion in enforcing the laws, they can have a major impact on a company's marketing performance.

New laws and their enforcement will continue to increase. Business executives must watch these developments when planning their products and marketing programs. Marketers need to know about the major laws protecting competition, consumers, and society. They need to understand these laws at the local, state, national, and international levels.

Increased Emphasis on Ethics and Socially Responsible Actions

Written regulations cannot possibly cover all potential marketing abuses, and existing laws are often difficult to enforce. However, beyond written laws and regulations, business is also governed by social codes and rules of professional ethics.

» Table 3.1 Major U.S. Legislation Affecting Marketing

Legislation	Purpose
Sherman Antitrust Act (1890)	Prohibits monopolies and activities (price-fixing, predatory pricing) that restrain trade or competition in interstate commerce.
Federal Food and Drug Act (1906)	Created the Food and Drug Administration (FDA). It forbids the manufacture or sale of adulterated or fraudulently labeled foods and drugs.
Clayton Act (1914)	Supplements the Sherman Act by prohibiting certain types of price discrimination, exclusive dealing, and tying clauses (which require a dealer to take additional products in a seller's line).
Federal Trade Commission Act (1914)	Established the Federal Trade Commission (FTC), which monitors and remedies unfair trade methods.
Robinson-Patman Act (1936)	Amends the Clayton Act to define price discrimination as unlawful. Empowers the FTC to establish limits on quantity discounts, forbid some brokerage allowances, and prohibit promotional allowances except when made available on proportionately equal terms.
Wheeler-Lea Act (1938)	Makes deceptive, misleading, and unfair practices illegal regardless of injury to competition. Places advertising of food and drugs under FTC jurisdiction.
Lanham Trademark Act (1946)	Protects and regulates distinctive brand names and trademarks.
National Traffic and Safety Act (1958)	Provides for the creation of compulsory safety standards for automobiles and tires.
Fair Packaging and Labeling Act (1966)	Provides for the regulation of the packaging and labeling of consumer goods. Requires that manufacturers state what the package contains, who made it, and how much it contains.
Child Protection Act (1966)	Bans the sale of hazardous toys and articles. Sets standards for child-resistant packaging.
Federal Cigarette Labeling and Advertising Act (1967)	Requires that cigarette packages contain the following statement: "Warning: The Surgeon General Has Determined That Cigarette Smoking Is Dangerous to Your Health."
National Environmental Policy Act (1969)	Establishes a national policy on the environment. The 1970 Reorganization Plan established the Environmental Protection Agency (EPA).
Consumer Product Safety Act (1972)	Establishes the Consumer Product Safety Commission (CPSC) and authorizes it to set safety standards for consumer products as well as exact penalties for failing to uphold those standards.
Magnuson-Moss Warranty Act (1975)	Authorizes the FTC to determine rules and regulations for consumer warranties and provides consumer access to redress, such as the class-action suit.
Children's Television Act (1990)	Limits the number of commercials aired during children's programs.
Nutrition Labeling and Education Act (1990)	Requires that food product labels provide detailed nutritional information.
Telephone Consumer Protection Act (1991)	Establishes procedures to avoid unwanted telephone solicitations. Limits marketers' use of automatic telephone dialing systems and artificial or prerecorded voices.
Americans with Disabilities Act (1991)	Makes discrimination against people with disabilities illegal in public accommodations, transportation, and telecommunications.
Children's Online Privacy Protection Act (2000)	Prohibits Web sites or online services operators from collecting personal information from children without obtaining consent from a parent and allowing parents to review information collected from their children.
Do-Not-Call Implementation Act (2003)	Authorizes the FTC to collect fees from sellers and telemarketers for the implementation and enforcement of a national Do-Not-Call Registry.
CAN-SPAM Act (2003)	Regulates the distribution and content of unsolicited commercial e-mail.
Financial Reform Law (2010)	Created the Bureau of Consumer Financial Protection, which writes and enforces rules for the marketing of financial products to consumers. It is also responsible for enforcement of the Truth-in-Lending Act, the Home Mortgage Disclosure Act, and other laws designed to protect consumers.

Socially Responsible Behavior. Enlightened companies encourage their managers to look beyond what the regulatory system allows and simply "do the right thing." These socially responsible firms actively seek out ways to protect the long-run interests of their consumers and the environment.

Almost every aspect of marketing involves ethics and social responsibility issues. Unfortunately, because these issues usually involve conflicting interests, well-meaning people can honestly disagree about the right course of action in a given situation. Thus, many industrial and professional trade associations have suggested codes of ethics. And more companies are now developing policies, guidelines, and other responses to complex social responsibility issues.

The boom in online, mobile, and social media marketing has created a new set of social and ethical issues. Critics worry most about online privacy issues. There has been an explosion in the amount of personal digital data available. Users, themselves, supply some of it. They voluntarily place highly private information on social media sites, such as Facebook or LinkedIn, or on genealogy sites that are easily searched by anyone with a computer or a smartphone.

However, much of the information is systematically developed by businesses seeking to learn more about their customers, often without consumers realizing that they are under the microscope. Legitimate businesses track consumers' Internet browsing and buying behavior and collect, analyze, and share digital data from every move consumers make at their online sites. Critics worry that these companies may now know *too* much and might use digital data to take unfair advantage of consumers. Although most companies fully disclose their Internet privacy policies and most try to use data to benefit their customers, abuses do occur. As a result, consumer advocates and policy makers are taking action to protect consumer privacy. In Chapter 16, we discuss these and other societal marketing issues in greater depth.

Cause-Related Marketing. To exercise their social responsibility and build more positive images, many companies are now linking themselves to worthwhile causes. These days, every product seems to be tied to some cause. For example, the P&G Tide Loads of Hope program provides mobile laundromats and loads of clean laundry to families in disaster-stricken areas—P&G washes, dries, and folds clothes for these families for free. Down the street, needy people will probably find the P&G Duracell Power Relief Trailer, which provides free batteries and flashlights as well as charging stations for phones and laptops. Walgreens sponsors a "Walk with Walgreens" program—do simple things like walk and log your steps, hit your goals, or just comment on other walkers' posts at the Web site, and you'll be rewarded with coupons and exclusive offers from Bayer, Vaseline, Degree, Slimfast, Dr. Scholls, or another program partner.

Some companies are founded on cause-related missions. Under the concept of "values-led business" or "caring capitalism," their mission is to use business to make the world a better place. >> For example, Warby Parker—the online marketer of low-priced prescription eyewear—was founded with the hope of bringing affordable eyewear to the masses. The company sells "eyewear with a purpose." For every pair of glasses Warby Parker sells, it distributes a free pair to someone in need. The company also works with not-for-profit organizations that train low-income entrepreneurs to sell affordable glasses. "We believe that everyone has the right to see," says the company.[41]

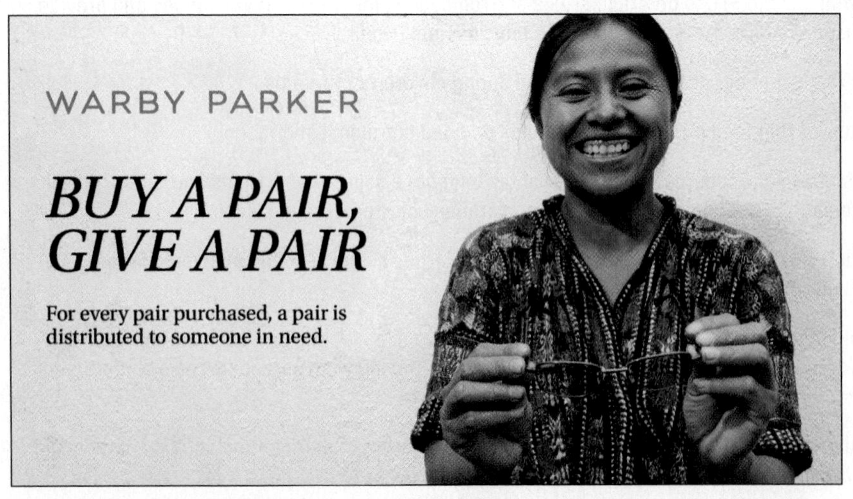

>> Cause-related marketing: Eyewear company Warby Parker offers designer glasses at a revolutionary low price while also leading the way for socially-conscious businesses. For every pair of glasses sold, Warby Parker distributes a pair to someone in need.

Warby Parker; photographer: Esther Havens.

Cause-related marketing has become a primary form of corporate giving. It lets companies "do well by doing good" by linking purchases of the company's products or services with benefiting worthwhile causes or charitable organizations. Beyond being socially admirable, Warby Parker's Buy a Pair, Give a Pair program also makes good economic sense, for both the company and its customers. "Companies can do good in the world while still being profitable," says Warby Parker co-founder Neil Blumenthal. "A single pair of reading glasses causes, on average, a 20 percent increase in income. Glasses are one of the most effective poverty alleviation tools in the world."[42]

Cause-related marketing has stirred some controversy. Critics worry that cause-related marketing is more a strategy for selling than a strategy for giving—that "cause-related" marketing is really "cause-exploitative" marketing. Thus, companies using cause-related marketing might find themselves walking a fine line between increased sales and an improved image and facing charges of exploitation. However, if handled well, cause-related marketing can greatly benefit both the company and the cause. The company gains an effective marketing tool while building a more positive public image. The charitable organization or cause gains greater visibility and important new sources of funding and support. Spending on cause-related marketing in the United States skyrocketed from only $120 million in 1990 to $1.78 billion in 2013.[43]

Author Comment
Cultural factors strongly affect how people think and how they consume. So marketers are keenly interested in the cultural environment.

The Cultural Environment

The **cultural environment** consists of institutions and other forces that affect a society's basic values, perceptions, preferences, and behaviors. People grow up in a particular society that shapes their basic beliefs and values. They absorb a worldview that defines their relationships with others. The following cultural characteristics can affect marketing decision making.

Cultural environment
Institutions and other forces that affect society's basic values, perceptions, preferences, and behaviors.

The Persistence of Cultural Values

People in a given society hold many beliefs and values. Their core beliefs and values have a high degree of persistence. For example, most Americans believe in individual freedom, hard work, getting married, and achievement and success. These beliefs shape more specific attitudes and behaviors found in everyday life. *Core* beliefs and values are passed on from parents to children and are reinforced by schools, businesses, religious institutions, and government.

Secondary beliefs and values are more open to change. Believing in marriage is a core belief; believing that people should get married early in life is a secondary belief. Marketers have some chance of changing secondary values but little chance of changing core values. For example, family-planning marketers could argue more effectively that people should get married later than not get married at all.

Shifts in Secondary Cultural Values

Although core values are fairly persistent, cultural swings do take place. Consider the impact of popular music groups, movie personalities, and other celebrities on young people's hairstyle and clothing norms. Marketers want to predict cultural shifts to spot new opportunities or threats. The major cultural values of a society are expressed in people's views of themselves and others, as well as in their views of organizations, society, nature, and the universe.

People's Views of Themselves. People vary in their emphasis on serving themselves versus serving others. Some people seek personal pleasure, wanting fun, change, and escape. Others seek self-realization through religion, recreation, or the avid pursuit of careers or other life goals. Some people see themselves as sharers and joiners; others see themselves as individualists. People use products, brands, and services as a means of self-expression, and they buy products and services that match their views of themselves.

For example, ads for Sherwin Williams paint—headlined "Make the most for your color with the very best paint"—seem to appeal to older, more practical do-it-yourselfers.

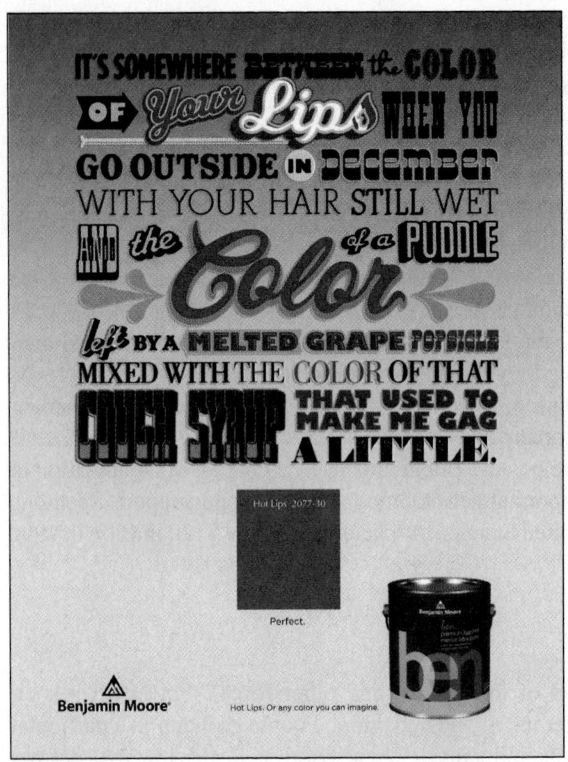

People's self-views: In its ads, Benjamin Moore appeals to people who view themselves as outgoing fashion individualists.

Courtesy of Benjamin Moore Paints.

By contrast, Benjamin Moore's ads, along with its several social media pitches, appeal to younger, more outgoing fashion individualists. One Benjamin Moore print ad—consisting of a single long line of text in a crazy quilt of fonts—describes Benjamin Moore's Hot Lips paint color this way: "It's somewhere between the color of your lips when you go outside in December with your hair still wet and the color of a puddle left by a melted grape popsicle mixed with the color of that cough syrup that used to make me gag a little. Hot lips. Perfect."

People's Views of Others. People's attitudes toward and interactions with others shift over time. In recent years, some analysts have voiced concerns that the Internet age would result in diminished human interaction, as people buried themselves in social media pages or e-mailed and texted rather than interacting personally. Instead, today's digital technologies seem to have launched an era of what one trend watcher calls "mass mingling." Rather than interacting less, people are using online social media and mobile communications to connect more than ever. Basically, the more people meet, network, tweet, and socialize online, the more likely they are to eventually meet up with friends and followers in the real world.[44]

However, these days, even when people are together, they are often "alone together." Groups of people sit or walk in their own little bubbles, intensely connected to tiny screens and keyboards. One expert describes the latest communication skill—"maintaining eye contact with someone while you text someone else; it's hard but it can be done," she says. "Technology-enabled, we are able to be with one another, and also elsewhere, connected to wherever we want to be."[45] Whether the new technology-driven communication is a blessing or a curse is a matter of much debate.

This new way of interacting strongly affects how companies market their brands and communicate with customers. "Consumers are increasingly tapping into their networks of friends, fans, and followers to discover, discuss, and purchase goods and services in ever-more sophisticated ways," says one analyst. "As a result, it's never been more important for brands to make sure they [tap into these networks] too."[46]

People's Views of Organizations. People vary in their attitudes toward corporations, government agencies, trade unions, universities, and other organizations. By and large, people are willing to work for major organizations and expect them, in turn, to carry out society's work.

The past two decades have seen a sharp decrease in confidence in and loyalty toward America's business and political organizations and institutions. In the workplace, there has been an overall decline in organizational loyalty. Waves of company downsizings bred cynicism and distrust. In just the last decade, major corporate scandals, rounds of layoffs resulting from the Great Recession, the financial meltdown triggered by Wall Street bankers' greed and incompetence, and other unsettling activities have resulted in a further loss of confidence in big business. Many people today see work not as a source of satisfaction but as a required chore to earn money to enjoy their nonwork hours. This trend suggests that organizations need to find new ways to win consumer and employee confidence.

People's Views of Society. People vary in their attitudes toward their society—patriots defend it, reformers want to change it, and malcontents want to leave it. People's orientation to their society influences their consumption patterns and attitudes toward the marketplace.

American patriotism has been increasing gradually for the past two decades. Marketers respond with renewed "Made in America" pitches and patriotic products and promotions, offering everything from orange juice to clothing to cars with patriotic themes. For example, ads for PepsiCo's Tropicana Pure Premium orange juice proclaim that the brand is "100% pure Florida orange juice—made from oranges grown, picked, and squeezed in Florida." And Chrysler's "Imported from Detroit" campaign, which declared that "the world's going to hear the roar of our engines," resonated strongly with American consumers.[47] Although most such marketing efforts are tasteful and well received, waving the red, white, and blue can sometimes prove tricky. Flag-waving promotions can be viewed as corny, or as attempts to cash in on the nation's triumphs or tragedies. Marketers must take care when responding to such strong national emotions.

People's Views of Nature. People vary in their attitudes toward the natural world—some feel ruled by it, others feel in harmony with it, and still others seek to master it. A long-term trend has been people's growing mastery over nature through technology and the belief that nature is bountiful. More recently, however, people have recognized that nature is finite and fragile; it can be destroyed or spoiled by human activities.

This renewed love of things natural has created a 41-million-person "lifestyles of health and sustainability" (LOHAS) market, consumers who seek out everything from natural, organic, and nutritional products to fuel-efficient cars and alternative medicine. This segment spends an estimated $290 billion annually on such products.[48]

Tom's of Maine caters to such consumers with sustainable, all-natural personal care products—toothpaste, deodorant, mouthwash, and soap—made with no artificial colors, flavors, fragrances, or preservatives.[49] The products are also "cruelty-free" (no animal testing or animal ingredients). Tom's makes sustainable practices a priority in every aspect of its business and strives to maximize the recycled content and recyclability of its packaging. Finally, Tom's donates 10 percent of its pretax profits to charitable organizations. >> In all, Tom's "makes uncommonly good products that serve the common good."

>> **Riding the trend toward all things natural: Tom's of Maine "makes uncommonly good products that serve the common good."**

Tom's of Maine.

Food producers have also found fast-growing markets for natural and organic products. In total, the U.S. organic food market generated $31 billion in sales last year, more than doubling over the past five years. Niche marketers, such as Whole Foods Market, have sprung up to serve this market, and traditional food chains, such as Kroger and Safeway, have added separate natural and organic food sections. Even pet owners are joining the movement as they become more aware of what goes into Fido's food. Almost every major pet food brand now offers several types of natural foods.[50]

People's Views of the Universe. Finally, people vary in their beliefs about the origin of the universe and their place in it. Although most Americans practice religion, religious conviction and practice have been dropping off gradually through the years. According to a recent poll, one-fifth of Americans now say they are not affiliated with any particular faith, double the percentage in 1990. Among Americans ages 18 to 29, one-third say they are not currently affiliated with any particular religion.[51]

However, the fact that people are dropping out of organized religion doesn't mean that they are abandoning their faith. Some futurists have noted a renewed interest in spirituality, perhaps as a part of a broader search for a new inner purpose. People have been moving away from materialism and dog-eat-dog ambition to seek more permanent values—family, community, earth, faith—and a more certain grasp of right and wrong. Rather than calling it "religion," they call it "spirituality."[52] This changing spiritualism affects consumers in everything from the television shows they watch and the books they read to the products and services they buy.

SPEED BUMP LINKING THE CONCEPTS

Slow down and cool your engine. How are all of the environmental factors you've read about in this chapter linked with each other? With company marketing strategy?

- How are major demographic forces linked with economic changes? With major cultural trends? How are the natural and technological environments linked? Think of an example of a company that has recognized one of these links and turned it into a marketing opportunity.
- Is the marketing environment uncontrollable? Where can companies be proactive in changing environmental factors? Think of a good example that makes your point, then read on.

Author Comment
Rather than simply watching and reacting to the marketing environment, companies should take proactive steps.

Responding to the Marketing Environment

Someone once observed, "There are three kinds of companies: those who make things happen, those who watch things happen, and those who wonder what's happened." Many companies view the marketing environment as an uncontrollable element to which they must react and adapt. They passively accept the marketing environment and do not try to change it. They analyze environmental forces and design strategies that will help the company avoid the threats and take advantage of the opportunities the environment provides.

Other companies take a *proactive* stance toward the marketing environment. Rather than assuming that strategic options are bounded by the current environment, these firms develop strategies to change the environment. Companies and their products often create and shape new industries and their structures, products such as Ford's Model T car, Apple's iPod and iPhone, and Google's search engine.

Even more, rather than simply watching and reacting to environmental events, proactive firms take aggressive actions to affect the publics and forces in their marketing environment. Such companies hire lobbyists to influence legislation affecting their industries and stage media events to gain favorable press coverage. They run "advertorials" (ads expressing editorial points of view) and blogs to shape public opinion. They press lawsuits and file complaints with regulators to keep competitors in line, and they form contractual agreements to better control their distribution channels.

By taking action, companies can often overcome seemingly uncontrollable environmental events. For example, whereas some companies try to hush up negative talk about their products, others proactively counter false information. Taco Bell did this when its brand fell victim to potentially damaging claims about the quality of the beef filling in its tacos:[53]

> When a California woman's class-action suit questioned whether Taco Bell's meat filling could accurately be labeled "beef," the company's reaction was swift and decisive. The suit claimed that Taco Bell's beef filling is 65 percent binders, extenders, preservatives, additives, and other agents. It wanted Taco Bell to stop calling it "beef." But Taco Bell fought back quickly with a major counterattack campaign, in print and on YouTube and Facebook. In full-page ads in the *Wall Street Journal,* the *New York Times,* and *USA Today,* the company boldly thanked those behind the lawsuit for giving it the opportunity to tell the "truth" about its "seasoned beef," which it claimed contains only quality beef with other ingredients added to maintain the product's flavor and quality. Taco Bell further announced that it would take legal action against those making the false statements. The company's proactive counter-campaign quickly squelched the false information in the lawsuit, which was voluntarily withdrawn only a few months later.

Marketing management cannot always control environmental forces. In many cases, it must settle for simply watching and reacting to the environment. For example, a company would have little success trying to influence geographic population shifts, the economic environment, or major cultural values. But whenever possible, smart marketing managers take a *proactive* rather than *reactive* approach to the marketing environment (see Marketing at Work 3.2).

MARKETING AT WORK 3.2

In the Social Media Age: When the Dialog Gets Nasty

Marketers have hailed the Internet and social media as the great new way to nurture customer relationships. Brands use social media to engage customers, gain insights into their needs, and create customer community. In turn, today's more-empowered consumers use the new digital media to share their brand experiences with companies and with each other. All of this back-and-forth helps both the company and its customers. But sometimes, the dialog can get nasty. Consider the following examples:

- Upon receiving a severely damaged computer monitor via FedEx, YouTube user goobie55 posts footage from his security camera. The video clearly shows a FedEx delivery man hoisting the monitor package over his head and tossing it over goobie55's front gate, without ever attempting to ring the bell, open the gate, or walk the package to the door. The video—with FedEx's familiar purple and orange logo prominently displayed on everything from the driver's shirt to the package and the truck—goes viral, with 5 million hits in just five days. TV news and talk shows go crazy discussing the clip.
- A young creative team at Ford's ad agency in India produces a Ford Figo print ad and releases it to the Internet without approval. The ad features three women—bound, gagged, and scantily clad—in the hatch of a Figo, with a caricature of a grinning Silvio Berlusconi (Italy's sex-scandal-plagued ex-prime minister) at the wheel. The ads tagline: "Leave your worries behind with Figo's extra-large boot (trunk)." Ford quickly pulls the ad, but not before it goes viral. Within days, millions of people around the world have viewed the ad, causing an online uproar and giving Ford a global black eye.
- When eight-year-old Harry Winsor sends a crayon drawing of an airplane he's designed to Boeing with a suggestion that the company might want to manufacture it, the company responds with a stern, legal-form letter. "We do not accept unsolicited ideas," the letter states. "We regret to inform you that we have disposed of your message and retain no copies." The embarrassing blunder would probably go unnoticed were it not for the fact that Harry's father—John Winsor, a prominent ad exec—blogs and tweets about the incident, making it instant national news.

Extreme events? Not anymore. The Internet and social media have turned the traditional power relationship between businesses and consumers upside down. In the good old days, disgruntled consumers could do little more than bellow at a company service rep or shout out their complaints from a street corner. Now, armed with only a laptop or smartphone, they can take it public, airing their gripes to millions on blogs, social media sites, or even hate sites devoted exclusively to their least favorite corporations.

"I hate" and "sucks" sites are almost commonplace. These sites target some highly respected companies with some highly disrespectful labels: Walmartblows.com, PayPalSucks.com (aka NoPayPal), IHateStarbucks.com, DeltaREALLYsucks.com, and UnitedPackageSmashers.com (UPS), to name only a few. "Sucks" videos on YouTube and other video sites also abound. For example, a search of "Apple sucks" on YouTube turns up more than 600,000 videos; a similar search for Microsoft finds 143,000 videos. An "Apple sucks" search on Facebook links to hundreds of groups. If you don't find one you like, try "Apple suks" or "Apple sux" for hundreds more.

Some of these sites, videos, and other online attacks air legitimate complaints that should be addressed. Others, however, are little more than anonymous, vindictive slurs that unfairly ransack brands and corporate reputations. Some of the attacks are only a passing nuisance; others can draw serious attention and create real headaches.

How should companies react to online attacks? The real quandary for targeted companies is figuring out how far they can go to protect their images without fueling the already raging fire. One point on which all experts seem to agree: Don't try to retaliate in kind. "It's rarely a good idea to lob bombs at the fire starters," says one analyst. "Preemption, engagement, and diplomacy are saner tools." Such criticisms are often based on real consumer concerns and unresolved anger. Hence, the best strategy might be to proactively monitor these sites and respond to the concerns they express.

For example, Boeing quickly took responsibility for mishandling aspiring Harry Winsor's designs, turning a potential PR disaster

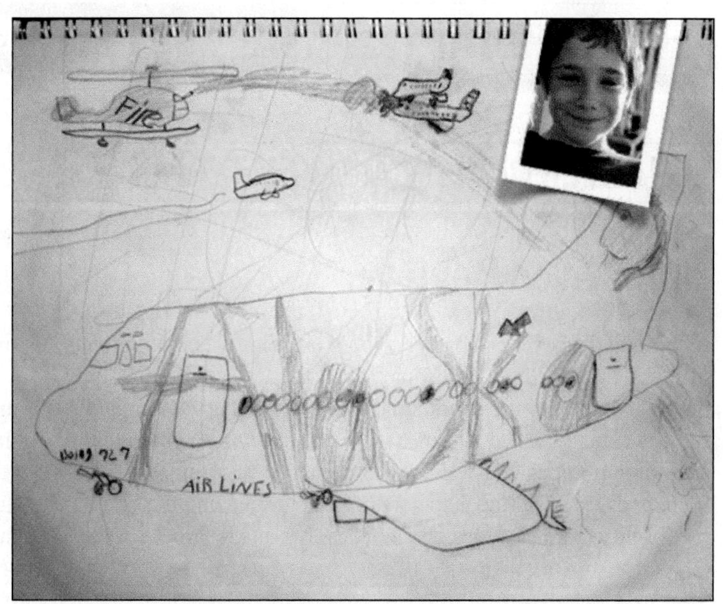

>> Today's empowered consumers: Boeing's embarrassing blunder over young Harry Winsor's airplane design made instant national news. However, Boeing quickly took responsibility and turned the potential public relations (PR) disaster into a positive.

John Winsor.

into a positive. It called and invited young Harry to visit Boeing's facilities. On its corporate Twitter site, it confessed "We're experts at airplanes but novices in social media. We're learning as we go." In response to its Figo ad fiasco, Ford's chief marketing officer issued a deep public apology, citing that Ford had not approved the ads and that it had modified its ad review process. Ford's ad agency promptly fired the guilty creatives. Similarly, FedEx drew praise by immediately posting its own YouTube video addressing the monitor-smashing incident. In the video, FedEx Senior Vice President of Operations Matthew Thornton stated that he had personally met with the aggrieved customer, who had accepted the company's apology. "This goes directly against all FedEx values," declared Thornton. The FedEx video struck a responsive chord. Numerous journalists and bloggers responded with stories about FedEx's outstanding package handling and delivering record.

Many companies have now created teams of specialists that monitor online conversations and engage unhappy consumers. For example, the social media team at Southwest Airlines includes a chief Twitter officer who tracks Twitter comments and monitors Facebook groups, an online representative who checks facts and interacts with bloggers, and another person who takes charge of the company's presence on sites such as YouTube, Instagram, Flickr, and LinkedIn. So if someone posts an online comment, the company can respond promptly in a personal way.

Not long ago, Southwest's team averted what could have been a major PR catastrophe when a hole popped open in a plane's fuselage on a flight from Phoenix to Sacramento. The flight had Wi-Fi, and the first passenger tweet about the incident, complete with a photo, was online in only 9 minutes—11 minutes before Southwest's official dispatch channel report. But Southwest's monitoring team picked up the social media chatter and was able to craft a blog post and other social media responses shortly after the plane made an emergency landing in Yuma, Arizona. By the time the story hit the major media, the passenger who had tweeted initially was back on Twitter praising the Southwest crew for its professional handling of the situation.

Thus, by monitoring and proactively responding to seemingly uncontrollable events in the environment, companies can prevent the negatives from spiraling out of control or even turn them into positives. Who knows? With the right responses, Walmartblows.com might even become Walmartrules.com. Then again, probably not.

Sources: Quotes, excerpts, and other information based on Matt Wilson, "How Southwest Airlines Wrangled Four Social Media Crises," *Ragan.com*, February 20, 2013, www.ragan.com/Main/Articles/How_Southwest_Airlines_wrangled_four_social_media_46254.aspx#; Vanessa Ko, "FedEx Apologizes after Video of Driver Throwing Fragile Package Goes Viral," *Time*, December 23, 2011, http://newsfeed.time.com/2011/12/23/fedex-apologizes-after-video-of-driver-throwing-fragile-package-goes-viral/; Michelle Conlin, "Web Attack," *BusinessWeek*, April 16, 2007, pp. 54–56; "Boeing's Social Media Lesson," May 3, 2010, http://mediadecoder.blogs.nytimes.com/2010/05/03/boeings-social-media-lesson/; Brent Snavely, "Ford Marketing Chief Apologizes for Ads," *USA Today*, March 27, 2013; and www.youtube.com/watch?v=C5uIH0VTg_o, accessed November 2013.

MyMarketingLab

Go to **mymktlab.com** to complete the problems marked with this icon .

END OF CHAPTER REVIEWING THE CONCEPTS

CHAPTER REVIEW AND KEY TERMS

Objectives Review

In this and the next two chapters, you'll examine the environments of marketing and how companies analyze these environments to better understand the marketplace and consumers. Companies must constantly watch and manage the *marketing environment* to seek opportunities and ward off threats. The marketing environment consists of all the actors and forces influencing the company's ability to transact business effectively with its target market.

 **OBJECTIVE 1 Describe the environmental forces that affect the company's ability to serve its customers. (pp 67–72)**

The company's *microenvironment* consists of actors close to the company that combine to form its value delivery network or that affect its ability to serve its customers. It includes the company's *internal environment*—its several departments and management levels—as it influences marketing decision making. *Marketing channel firms*—suppliers, marketing intermediaries, physical distribution firms, marketing services agencies, and financial intermediaries—cooperate to create customer value. *Competitors* vie with the company in an effort to serve customers better. Various *publics* have an actual or potential interest in or impact on the company's ability to meet its objectives. Finally, five types of customer *markets* exist: consumer, business, reseller, government, and international markets.

The *macroenvironment* consists of larger societal forces that affect the entire microenvironment. The six forces making up the company's macroenvironment are demographic, economic, natural, technological, political/social, and cultural forces. These forces shape opportunities and pose threats to the company.

OBJECTIVE 2 Explain how changes in the demographic and economic environments affect marketing decisions. (pp 72–81)

Demography is the study of the characteristics of human populations. Today's *demographic environment* shows a changing age structure, shifting family profiles, geographic population shifts, a better-educated and more white-collar population, and increasing diversity. The *economic environment* consists of factors that affect buying power and patterns. The economic environment is characterized by more frugal consumers who are seeking greater value—the right combination of good quality and service at a fair price. The distribution of income also is shifting. The rich have grown richer, the middle class has shrunk, and the poor have remained poor, leading to a two-tiered market.

OBJECTIVE 3 Identify the major trends in the firm's natural and technological environments. (pp 81–83)

The *natural environment* shows three major trends: shortages of certain raw materials, higher pollution levels, and more government intervention in natural resource management. Environmental concerns create marketing opportunities for alert companies. The *technological environment* creates both opportunities and challenges. Companies that fail to keep up with technological change will miss out on new product and marketing opportunities.

OBJECTIVE 4 Explain the key changes in the political and cultural environments. (pp 84–90)

The *political environment* consists of laws, agencies, and groups that influence or limit marketing actions. The political environment has undergone changes that affect marketing worldwide: increasing legislation regulating business, strong government agency enforcement, and greater emphasis on ethics and socially responsible actions. The *cultural environment* consists of institutions and forces that affect a society's values, perceptions, preferences, and behaviors. The environment shows trends toward new technology-enabled communication, a lessening trust of institutions, increasing patriotism, greater appreciation for nature, a changing spiritualism, and the search for more meaningful and enduring values.

OBJECTIVE 5 Discuss how companies can react to the marketing environment. (pp 90–92)

Companies can passively accept the marketing environment as an uncontrollable element to which they must adapt, avoiding threats and taking advantage of opportunities as they arise. Or they can take a *proactive* stance, working to change the environment rather than simply reacting to it. Whenever possible, companies should try to be proactive rather than reactive.

Key Terms

Objective 1
Marketing environment (p 66)
Microenvironment (p 67)
Macroenvironment (p 67)
Marketing intermediaries (p 68)
Public (p 69)

Objective 2
Demography (p 72)
Baby boomers (p 72)
Generation X (p 73)
Millennials (Generation Y) (p 74)
Generation Z (p 75)
Economic environment (p 79)

Objective 3
Natural environment (p 81)
Environmental sustainability (p 82)
Technological environment (p 82)

Objective 4
Political environment (p 84)
Cultural environment (p 87)

DISCUSSION AND CRITICAL THINKING

Discussion Questions

3-1. Name and briefly describe the elements of an organization's microenvironment and discuss how they affect marketing. (AACSB: Written and Oral Communication)

3-2. What is demography, and why is it so important for marketers? (AACSB: Written and Oral Communication; Reflective Thinking)

3-3. Who are the Millennials, and why are they of so much interest to marketers? (AACSB: Written and Oral Communication; Reflective Thinking)

3-4. Discuss trends in the natural environment of which marketers must be aware, and provide examples of companies' responses to them. (AACSB: Written and Oral Communication)

3-5. Compare and contrast core beliefs/values and secondary beliefs/values. Provide an example of each and discuss the potential impact marketers have on each. (AACSB: Written and Oral Communication; Reflective Thinking)

3-6. How should marketers respond to the changing environment? (AACSB: Written and Oral Communication)

Critical Thinking Exercises

3-7. Research a current or emerging change in the legal or regulatory environment affecting marketing. Explain its impact on marketing and how companies are reacting to the law or regulation. (AACSB: Written and Oral Communication; Reflective Thinking)

3-8. Cause-related marketing has grown considerably over the past 10 years. Visit www.causemarketingforum.com to learn about companies that have won Halo Awards for outstanding cause-related marketing programs. Present an award-winning case study to your class. (AACSB: Written and Oral Communication; Information Technology)

MINI CASES AND APPLICATIONS

Online, Mobile, and Social Media Marketing Crowdfunding

If you have a great product idea but no money, never fear, there's Kickstarter, an online crowdfunding site. Founded in 2008, Kickstarter enables companies to raise money from multiple individuals and has helped launch more than 60,000 projects. Pebble Technology Corporation created a "smart" wristwatch called Pebble, which works with iPhones or Android phones, but didn't have the funding to produce and market the device. So young CEO Eric Migicovsky turned to Kickstarter for crowdfunding. His modest goal was to raise $100,000, but the company raised $1 million in only one day and a total of $10.27 million in just over one month! Nearly 70,000 people pre-ordered the $115 watch, and Pebble now has to deliver on the promise. Kickstarter takes a 5 percent fee on the total funds raised, and Amazon Payments handles the processing of the funds. Kickstarter charges pledgers' credit cards and the project creator receives the funds within only a few weeks. The JOBS Act legislation signed into law in 2012 provides a legal framework for this type of financing, which is expected grow even faster as a result. However, Kickstarter and similar sites don't guarantee that the projects will be delivered as promised, and some people are concerned that crowd*funding* will beget crowd*frauding*.

3-9. Find another crowdfunding site and describe two projects featured on that site. (AACSB: Written and Oral Communication; Information Technology; Reflective Thinking)

3-10. Learn more about the JOBS Act and how it impacts crowdfunding for start-up businesses. What protections are in place for investors with regard to crowdfrauding? (AACSB: Written and Oral Communication; Information Technology; Reflective Thinking)

Marketing Ethics Targeting Children Online

The almost 24 percent of the U.S. population under 18 years old wields billions of dollars in purchasing power. Companies such as eBay and Facebook want to capitalize on those dollars—legitimately, that is. eBay is exploring ways to allow consumers under 18 years old to set up legitimate accounts to both buy and sell goods. Children already trade on the site, either through their parents' accounts or through accounts set up after they lie about their ages. Similarly, even though children under 13 are not allowed to set up Facebook accounts, about 7.5 million of them have accounts, and nearly 5 million account holders are under 10 years old. That translates to almost 20 percent of U.S. 10-year-olds and 70 percent of 13-year-olds active on Facebook. Many of these accounts were set up with parental knowledge and assistance. Both eBay and Facebook say that protections will be put in place on children's accounts and that parents will be able to monitor their children's accounts.

3-11. Debate the pros and cons of allowing these companies to target children. Are these efforts socially responsible behavior? (AACSB: Written and Oral Communication; Reflective Thinking; Ethical Understanding and Reasoning)

3-12. Review the Children's Online Privacy Protection Act at www.coppa.org/. Explain how eBay and Facebook can target this market and still comply with this act. (AACSB: Written and Oral Communication; Information Technology; Reflective Thinking)

Marketing by the Numbers Demographic Trends

Do you know of Danica from the Philippines, Peter from London, Nargis from India, Marina from Russia, Chieko from Japan, or Miran from the United States? These are some of the babies whose parents claimed they were the 7th billion human born into the world. The world population continues to grow, even though women are having fewer children than ever before. Markets are made up of people, and to stay competitive, marketers must know where populations are located and where they are going. The fertility rate in the United States is declining and the population is aging, creating opportunities as well as threats for marketers. That is why tracking and predicting demographic trends are so important in marketing. Marketers must plan to capitalize on opportunities and deal with the threats before it is too late.

3-13. Develop a presentation on a specific demographic trend in the United States. Explain the reasons behind this trend and discuss the implications for marketers. (AACSB: Written and Oral Communication; Analytical Thinking)

3-14. Discuss global demographic trends. What are the implications of those trends, and how should marketers respond to them? (AACSB: Written and Oral Communication; Reflective Thinking)

Video Case Ecoist

At least one company has taken the old phrase "One man's trash is another man's treasure" and turned it into a business model. Ecoist uses discarded packaging materials from multinational brands such as Coca-Cola, Frito-Lay, Disney, and Mars to craft high-end handbags that would thrill even the most discriminating fashionistas.

When the company first started in 2004, consumer perceptions of goods made from recycled materials weren't very positive. This video describes how Ecoist found its opportunity in a growing wave of environmentalism. Not only does Ecoist capitalize on low-cost materials and the brand images of some of the world's major brands, it comes out smelling like a rose as it saves a ton of trash from landfills.

After viewing the video featuring Ecoist, answer the following questions:

3-15. How engaged was Ecoist in analyzing the marketing environment before it launched its first company?

3-16. What trends in the marketing environment have contributed to the success of Ecoist?

3-17. Is Ecoist's strategy more about recycling or about creating value for customers? Explain.

Company Cases 3 Xerox / 7 Zipcar / 9 JCPenney

See Appendix 1 for cases appropriate for this chapter. **Case 3, Xerox: Adapting to the Turbulent Marketing Environment.** When the marketing environment changed and photocopying began to decline, Xerox created a new strategy that would allow it to succeed. **Case 7, Zipcar: "It's Not about Cars—It's about Urban Life."** A new company, a new concept, and a brand that transcends function. **Case 9, JCPenney: The Struggle to Find Optimum Price.** JCPenney tried to fix a pricing problem with a new strategy, only to create a new pricing problem.

MyMarketingLab

Go to **mymktlab.com** for Auto-graded writing questions as well as the following Assisted-graded writing questions:

3-18. Discuss the impact of current trends in the economic environment on consumer spending and buying behavior. (AACSB: Written and Oral Communication; Reflective Thinking)

3-19. Discuss a recent change in the technological environment that impacts marketing. How has it affected buyer behavior and how has it changed marketing? (AACSB: Written and Oral Communication; Reflective Thinking)

3-20. Mymktlab Only—comprehensive writing assignment for this chapter.

4 Managing Marketing Information to Gain Customer Insights

CHAPTER ROAD MAP

Objective Outline

- OBJECTIVE 1 **Explain the importance of information in gaining insights about the marketplace and customers.** Marketing Information and Customer Insights 98–100
- OBJECTIVE 2 **Define the marketing information system and discuss its parts.** Assessing Marketing Information Needs 100 Developing Marketing Information 100–103
- OBJECTIVE 3 **Outline the steps in the marketing research process.** Marketing Research 103–116
- OBJECTIVE 4 **Explain how companies analyze and use marketing information.** Analyzing and Using Marketing Information 116–120
- OBJECTIVE 5 **Discuss the special issues some marketing researchers face, including public policy and ethics issues.** Other Marketing Information Considerations 120–124

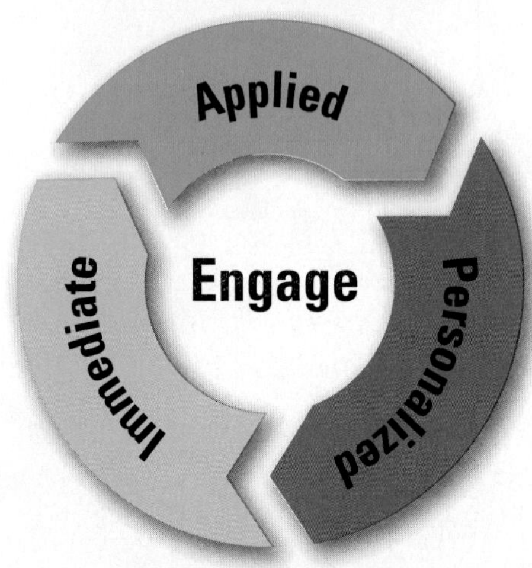

Previewing the Concepts

In this chapter, we continue our exploration of how marketers gain insights into consumers and the marketplace. We look at how companies develop and manage information about important marketplace elements: customers, competitors, products, and marketing programs. To succeed in today's marketplace, companies must know how to turn mountains of marketing information into fresh customer insights that will help them deliver greater value to customers.

Let's start with a good story about marketing research and customer insights in action. When Pepsi's market share and sales recently took an embarrassing dip, putting the iconic brand in third place behind archrival Coca-Cola's Coke and Diet Coke brands, Pepsi turned to consumer research for answers. It launched an exhaustive nine-month global search for fresh consumer insights about just what it is that makes Pepsi different from Coke. The answer: Whereas Coke is *timeless,* Pepsi is *timely.* This simple but powerful consumer insight resulted in Pepsi's global "Live for Now" marketing campaign.

---

*Over 10 million students improved their results using the Pearson MyLabs. Visit **mymktlab.com** for simulations, tutorials, and end-of-chapter problems.

First Stop

Pepsi's Marketing Insight: Pepsi Drinkers "Live for Now"

» After scouring the planet for fresh consumer insights, Pepsi launched its "Live for Now" campaign, which urges consumers to capture the excitement of now.

Pepsi-Cola North America.

Pepsi has long pitched itself to a now-generation of youthful cola drinkers, those young in mind and spirit. Almost 50 years ago, the brand invited consumers to "Come Alive! You're the Pepsi Generation!" Pepsi was different from Coca-Cola. "You've got a lot to live," went the jingle, "and Pepsi's got a lot to give."

But recently, PepsiCo's flagship cola brand began losing some of its youthful fizz. Partly to blame: U.S. soft drink consumption has been declining for the past seven years. But harder for PepsiCo to swallow, the Pepsi brand was losing ground in its century-long battle with archrival Coca-Cola, dropping from its perennial number-two position to number three, behind both Coca-Cola and Diet Coke. The embarrassing market-share slip sent a strong signal: The brand's positioning needed a pick-me-up.

To diagnose the issues behind the slide and find answers, PepsiCo launched an intense global consumer research effort. It set out to rediscover just what it is that makes Pepsi different from Coke. The company created a secretive, high-level research task force, located in an unmarked building in upstate New York. Charged with charting a new course for the Pepsi brand, the group embarked on an exhaustive nine-month worldwide search for new consumer insights.

The Pepsi task force left no stone unturned. It poured through reels of past Pepsi advertising. It fielded traditional focus groups, in-depth personal interviews, and lengthy quantitative surveys. Researchers and top executives participated in ethnographic studies, "moving in" with customers, observing them as they went about their daily lives, and immersing themselves in cultures throughout North and South America, Asia, Europe, Africa, and Australia.

Based on simple but powerful consumer insights gleaned from months of intensive consumer research, Pepsi's "Live for Now" marketing campaign has reenergized the Pepsi brand. "Live for Now" is "bringing back the roots of what Pepsi is all about."

The Pepsi research team discovered that the longtime iconic brand had lost sight of what it stands for and the role it plays in customers' lives. Top brands such as Nike, Disney, Starbucks, and Coca-Cola have a clear sense of their meaning. But Pepsi no longer had clear positioning that defined the essence of the brand, drove marketing and innovation, and fueled consumer engagement. In only the past few years, for example, Pepsi's positioning had jumped around from "Every Pepsi Refreshes the World" to "Summer Time Is Pepsi Time" to "Where There's Pepsi, There's Music."

So what does Pepsi mean to consumers? How does it differ from rival Coca-Cola in terms of consumer perceptions and feelings? The research task force boiled its extensive findings down to two simple but powerful customer insights. Whereas Coke is *timeless*, Pepsi is *timely*. Whereas Coca-Cola drinkers seek *happiness*, Pepsi drinkers seek *excitement*. According to Brad Jakeman, Pepsi's president of global enjoyment and chief creative officer, Coca-Cola stands for moments of joy and happiness, and for protecting the culture and status quo. In contrast, Pepsi stands for creating culture rather than preserving it, and Pepsi customers would rather lead an exciting life than a happy one. Whereas Coca-Cola means belonging, Pepsi embraces individuality. "Brands that are timeless want to have museums," says Jakeman. "Pepsi is not a brand that belongs in a museum."

Interestingly, such insights hark back to the old, youthful "choice of a new generation" positioning that built the Pepsi brand so powerfully decades ago. And despite its recent slide, Pepsi remains a formidable brand. Although it has never been the leading cola, Pepsi has always acted as if it were. According to Jakeman, Pepsi has done best when projecting the confidence and swagger of a leader, and Pepsi drinkers have always identified with that boldness. Looking forward, the key will be to regain that boldness and swagger. "This brand does not need to be reinvented," he asserts. "It needs to be reignited."

The "timely" versus "timeless" research insights—the idea of "capturing the excitement of now"—opened new creative doors for Pepsi. The result is a new global marketing campaign called "Live for Now." Giving a kind of modern twist to the brand's classic "Pepsi Generation" positioning, the campaign provides a new rallying cry for the next generation of Pepsi drinkers. "Live for Now" is designed to shape culture, capture the excitement of the moment, and reestablish Pepsi's connection with entertainment and pop culture. To back the new campaign, PepsiCo has increased its marketing budget by 50 percent, putting Pepsi's promotional spending at levels close to those of Coca-Cola.

"Live for Now" burst onto the scene with an abundance of traditional and digital media. The campaign has partnered with a full roster of music and sports stars, linking the brand with some of today's most exciting celebrities. For example, the first ads featured singer/rapper Nicki Minaj, whose hit "Moment 4 Life" contained lyrics made in heaven for Pepsi "Live for Now" commercials and videos ("I wish that I could have this moment for life. 'Cuz in this moment I just feel so alive"). Next, Pepsi inked a deal with Beyoncé that now has her pitching Pepsi's new message on everything from commercials and social media videos to Pepsi cans and a Super Bowl halftime extravaganza.

At the heart of the campaign, the interactive "Pepsi Pulse" Web site—what one analyst calls "a company-curated dashboard of pop culture"—serves as a portal to Pepsi's world of entertainment, featuring pop-culture information, entertainment news, and original content. Pepsi has also forged a music-related partnership with Twitter, and its Mi Pepsi Web site and Facebook page cater to Latino lifestyles and culture, urging customers to "Vive Hoy." Every aspect of the "Live for Now" campaign puts customers in the middle of the action. For example, during last year's Super Bowl XLVII, Pepsi commercials and the Pepsi-sponsored halftime show featured youthful consumers as participants. "It really begins with the insight that Pepsi consumers want to be active participants, not observers of life," says a Pepsi marketer.

Pepsi's extensive research also showed that Pepsi drinkers around the globe are remarkably similar, giving the "Live for Now" positioning worldwide appeal. For example, in India, Pepsi's consumer research revealed that the country's young people are among the most optimistic in the world but are impatient for the future to happen sooner. So Pepsi TV ads in India feature brand endorsers such as cricket captain MS Dhoni, actress-turned-pop-singer Priyanka Chopra, and Bollywood star Ranbir Kapoor overcoming moments of impatience, interspersed with images of young people doing exciting spur-of-the-moment things. The "Live for Now" campaign tells young consumers that "there's nothing wrong with wanting something now," says a senior PepsiCo India marketer.

It's still too soon to tell whether "Live for Now" will reverse Pepsi's fortunes. But it's clear that the folks at Pepsi have done their research homework. Based on what Pepsi's Jakeman describes as the "most-exhaustive and consumer-insights-led process" he's ever witnessed, the swagger is back at Pepsi. Backed by months and months of intensive consumer research, "Live for Now" is reenergizing the Pepsi brand, those who work on it, and those who drink it. According to one Pepsi bottler who cut his teeth in the industry back when the original "Pepsi Generation" campaign was in full stride, "Live for Now" is "bringing back the roots of what Pepsi is all about."[1]

As the Pepsi story highlights, good products and marketing programs begin with good customer information. Companies also need an abundance of information on competitors, resellers, and other actors and marketplace forces. But more than just gathering information, marketers must *use* the information to gain powerful *customer and market insights*.

Author Comment

Marketing information by itself has little value. The value is in the *customer insights* gained from the information and how marketers use these insights to make better decisions.

Marketing Information and Customer Insights

To create value for customers and build meaningful relationships with them, marketers must first gain fresh, deep insights into what customers need and want. Such customer insights come from good marketing information. Companies use these customer insights to develop a competitive advantage.

For example, Apple wasn't the first company to develop a digital music player. However, Apple's research uncovered two key insights: people wanted personal music players that let them take all of their music with them, and they wanted to be able to listen to it unobtrusively. » Based on these insights, Apple applied its design and usability magic to create the phenomenally successful iPod. The iPod now captures more than a 70 percent share of the global MP3 player market. Apple has sold more than 350 million iPods. "To put that in context," says Apple CEO Tim Cook, "it took Sony 30 years to sell just 230,000 Walkman cassette players."[2]

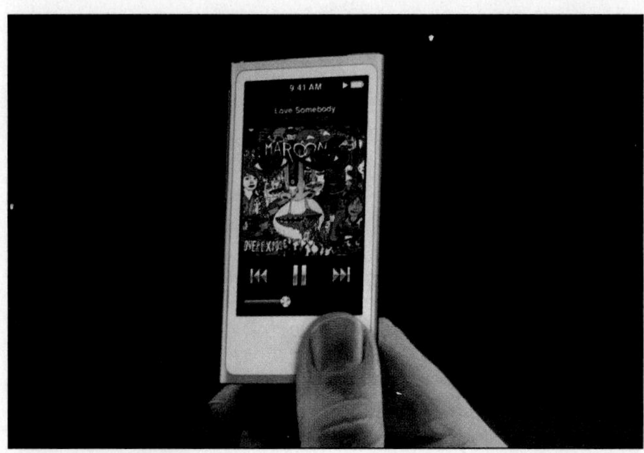

Key customer insights, plus a dash of Apple's design and usability magic, have made the iPod a blockbuster. It now captures a more than 78 percent market share and has spawned other Apple blockbusters such as the iPhone and iPad.

Beck Diefenbach/Reuters.

Although customer and market insights are important for building customer value and relationships, these insights can be very difficult to obtain. Customer needs and buying motives are often anything but obvious—consumers themselves usually can't tell you exactly what they need and why they buy. To gain good customer insights, marketers must effectively manage marketing information from a wide range of sources.

With the recent explosion of information technologies, companies can now generate marketing information in great quantities. Moreover, consumers themselves are now generating tons of marketing information. Through e-mail, text messaging, blogging, Facebook, Twitter, and other grassroots digital channels, consumers are now volunteering a tidal wave of bottom-up information to companies and to each other. Companies that tap into such information can gain rich, timely customer insights at lower cost.

Far from lacking information, most marketing managers are overloaded with data and often overwhelmed by it. For example, when a company such as Pepsi monitors online discussions about its brands by searching key words in tweets, blogs, posts, and other sources, its servers take in a stunning 6 million public conversations a day, more than 2 billion a year. That's far more information than any manager can digest. And for every Pepsi manager, a ton more information is only a Google search away. According to IBM, 90 percent of the data that companies collect from social media and other real-time sources isn't being used effectively.[3] Thus, marketers don't need *more* information; they need *better* information. And they need to make better *use* of the information they already have.

Customer insights
Fresh understandings of customers and the marketplace derived from marketing information that become the basis for creating customer value and relationships.

The real value of marketing research and marketing information lies in how it is used—in the **customer insights** that it provides. Based on such thinking, many companies are now restructuring their marketing research and information functions. They are creating *customer insights teams*, headed by a vice president of customer insights and composed of representatives from all of the firm's functional areas. For example, Coca-Cola's vice president of marketing strategy and insights heads up a team of 25 strategists who develop marketing strategy based on marketing research insights. This executive believes that marketing researchers need to do more than just provide data. They need to "tell the stories behind the data" and provide "now what" answers based on the insights gained.[4]

Customer insights groups collect customer and market information from a wide variety of sources, ranging from traditional marketing research studies to mingling with and observing consumers to monitoring social media conversations about the company and its products. Then they *use* this information to develop important customer insights from which the company can create more value for its customers.

Marketing information system (MIS)
People and procedures dedicated to assessing information needs, developing the needed information, and helping decision makers to use the information to generate and validate actionable customer and market insights.

Thus, companies must design effective marketing information systems that give managers the right information, in the right form, at the right time and help them to use this information to create customer value and stronger customer relationships. A **marketing information system (MIS)** consists of people and procedures dedicated to assessing information needs, developing the needed information, and helping decision makers use the information to generate and validate actionable customer and market insights.

Figure 4.1 shows that the MIS begins and ends with information users—marketing managers, internal and external partners, and others who need marketing information. First, it interacts with these information users to assess information needs. Next, it interacts with the marketing environment to develop needed information through internal company databases, marketing intelligence activities, and marketing research. Finally, the MIS helps users to analyze and use the information to develop customer insights, make marketing decisions, and manage customer relationships.

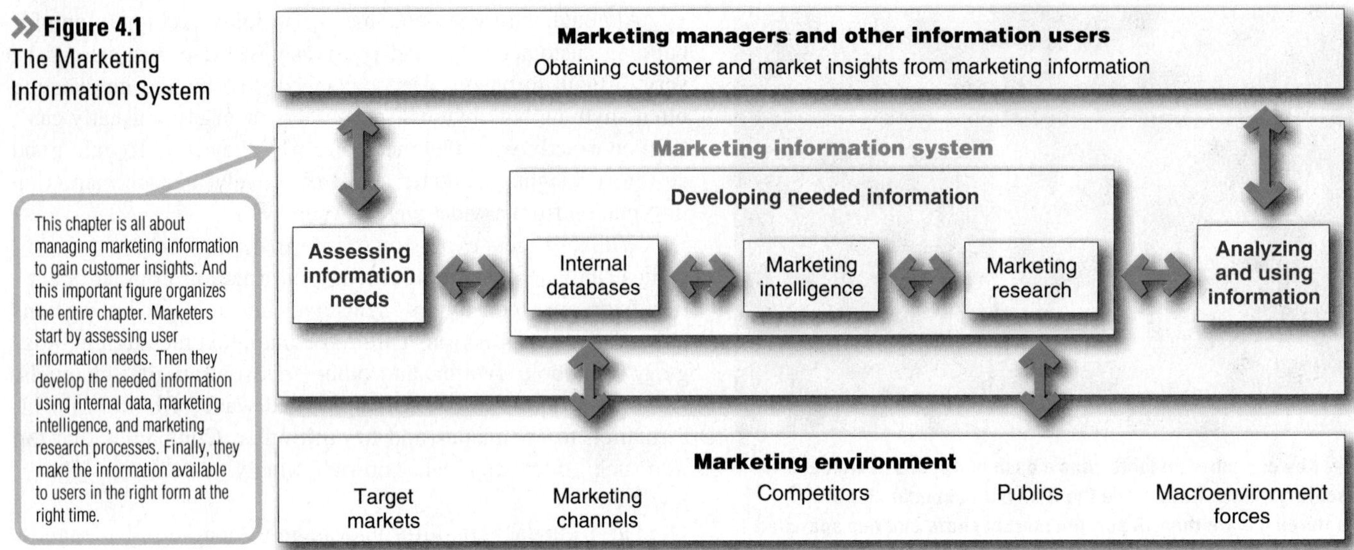
Marketing managers and other information users
Obtaining customer and market insights from marketing information
Marketing information system
Developing needed information
Assessing information needs
Internal databases
Marketing intelligence
Marketing research
Analyzing and using information
Marketing environment
Target markets
Marketing channels
Competitors
Publics
Macroenvironment forces
This chapter is all about managing marketing information to gain customer insights. And this important figure organizes the entire chapter. Marketers start by assessing user information needs. Then they develop the needed information using internal data, marketing intelligence, and marketing research processes. Finally, they make the information available to users in the right form at the right time.

Figure 4.1 The Marketing Information System

Author Comment The marketing information system begins and ends with users—assessing their information needs and then delivering information that meets those needs.

Assessing Marketing Information Needs

The marketing information system primarily serves the company's marketing and other managers. However, it may also provide information to external partners, such as suppliers, resellers, or marketing services agencies. For example, Walmart's Retail Link system gives key suppliers access to information on everything from customers' buying patterns and store inventory levels to how many items they've sold in which stores in the past 24 hours.[5]

A good MIS balances the information users would *like* to have against what they really *need* and what is *feasible* to offer. Some managers will ask for whatever information they can get without thinking carefully about what they really need. Too much information can be as harmful as too little. Other managers may omit things they ought to know, or they may not know to ask for some types of information they should have. For example, managers might need to know about surges in favorable or unfavorable consumer discussions about their brands on blogs or online social media. Because they do not know about these discussions, they do not think to ask about them. The MIS must monitor the marketing environment to provide decision makers with information they should have to better understand customers and make key marketing decisions.

Finally, the costs of obtaining, analyzing, storing, and delivering information can quickly mount. The company must decide whether the value of insights gained from additional information is worth the costs of providing it, and both value and cost are often hard to assess.

Author Comment The problem isn't *finding* information; the world is bursting with information from a glut of sources. The real challenge is to find the *right* information—from inside and outside sources—and turn it into customer insights.

Developing Marketing Information

Marketers can obtain the needed information from *internal data*, *marketing intelligence*, and *marketing research*.

Internal Data

Internal databases Electronic collections of consumer and market information obtained from data sources within the company network.

Many companies build extensive **internal databases**, electronic collections of consumer and market information obtained from data sources within the company's network. Information in an internal database can come from many sources. The marketing department furnishes information on customer characteristics, sales transactions, and Web site visits. The customer service department keeps records of customer satisfaction or service problems. The accounting department provides detailed records of sales, costs, and cash flows. Operations reports on production, shipments, and inventories. The sales force reports on reseller reactions and competitor activities, and marketing channel partners provide data on point-of-sale transactions. Harnessing such information can provide powerful customer insights and competitive advantage.

For example, >> financial services provider USAA uses its internal database to create an incredibly loyal customer base:[6]

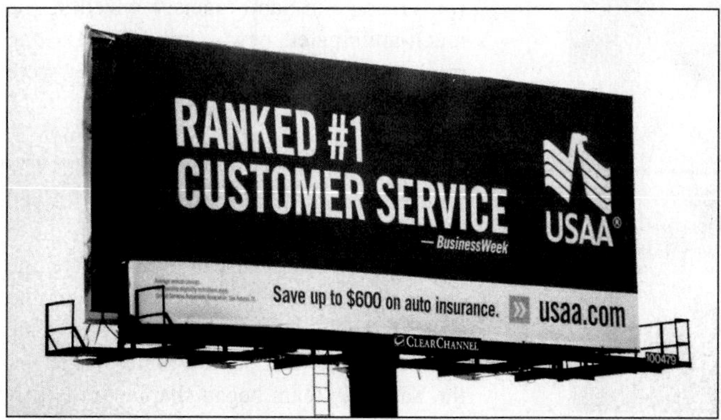

>> Internal data: Financial services provider USAA uses its extensive database to tailor its services to the specific needs of individual customers, creating incredible loyalty.

Courtney Young.

> USAA provides financial services to U.S. military personnel and their families, largely through direct marketing via the telephone, the Internet, and mobile channels. It maintains a huge customer database built from customer purchasing histories and information collected directly through customer surveys, transaction data, and browsing behavior at its online sites. USAA uses the database to tailor direct marketing offers to the needs of individual customers. For example, for customers looking toward retirement, it sends information on estate planning. If the family has college-age children, USAA sends those children information on how to manage their credit cards.
>
> One delighted reporter, a USAA customer, recounts how USAA even helped him teach his 16-year-old daughter to drive. Just before her birthday, but before she received her driver's license, USAA sent a "package of materials, backed by research, to help me teach my daughter how to drive, help her practice, and help us find ways to agree on what constitutes safe driving later on, when she gets her license." Through such skillful use of its database, USAA serves each customer uniquely, resulting in legendary levels of customer satisfaction and loyalty. More important, the $19 billion company retains 98 percent of its customers.

Internal databases usually can be accessed more quickly and cheaply than other information sources, but they also present some problems. Because internal information is often collected for other purposes, it may be incomplete or in the wrong form for making marketing decisions. Data also ages quickly; keeping the database current requires a major effort. Finally, managing the mountains of information that a large company produces requires highly sophisticated equipment and techniques.

Competitive Marketing Intelligence

Competitive marketing intelligence The systematic collection and analysis of publicly available information about consumers, competitors, and developments in the marketing environment.

Competitive marketing intelligence is the systematic collection and analysis of publicly available information about consumers, competitors, and developments in the marketplace. The goal of competitive marketing intelligence is to improve strategic decision making by understanding the consumer environment, assessing and tracking competitors' actions, and providing early warnings of opportunities and threats. Marketing intelligence techniques range from observing consumers firsthand to quizzing the company's own employees, benchmarking competitors' products, researching on the Internet, and monitoring social media buzz.

Good marketing intelligence can help marketers gain insights into how consumers talk about and connect with their brands. Many companies send out teams of trained observers to mix and mingle personally with customers as they use and talk about the company's products. Other companies routinely monitor consumers' online chatter. >> For example, PepsiCo's Gatorade brand has created an extensive control center to monitor real-time brand-related social media activity.[7] Whenever someone mentions anything related to Gatorade (including competitors, Gatorade athletes, and sports nutrition-related topics) on Twitter, Facebook, a blog, or in other social media, it pops up in various visualizations and dashboards on one of six big screens at Gatorade's Mission Control. Staffers also monitor online-ad and Web site traffic, producing a consolidated picture of the brand's Internet image. Gatorade uses what it sees and learns at Mission Control to improve its products, marketing, and interactions with customers.

Competitive marketing intelligence: PepsiCo's Gatorade brand has created an extensive control center to monitor real-time brand-related social media activity.

The Gatorade Company.

Samsung used intelligence gained from real-time monitoring of the social media activity surrounding the introduction of competitor Apple's new iPhone 5 to capture record-breaking sales of its own signature Galaxy S smartphone:[8]

> At the same time that Apple CEO Tim Cook was on stage in San Francisco unveiling the much-anticipated new iPhone 5, Samsung marketing and ad agency executives were huddled around their computers and TV screens in a Los Angeles war room hundreds of miles away watching events unfold. The Samsung strategists carefully monitored not only each new iPhone 5 feature as it was presented, but also the gush of online consumer commentary flooding blogs and social media channels. Even as the real-time consumer and competitive data surged in, the Samsung team began shaping a marketing response. By the time Cook had finished his iPhone 5 presentation two hours later, the Samsung team was already drafting a series on TV, print, and social media ads. The following week, just as the iPhone 5 was hitting store shelves, Samsung aired a 90-second "Fanboys" TV commercial. The ad mocked iPhone fans lined up outside Apple stores buzzing about the features of the new iPhone, only to be upstaged by two passersby and their Samsung Galaxy smartphones ("The next big thing is already here!"). Lines in the ad were based on thousands upon thousands of actual Tweets and other social media interactions poking fun at or complaining about specific iPhone 5 features. The real-time-insights-based ad became the tech-ad sensation of the year (grabbing more than 70 million online views), allowing Samsung to rechannel excitement surrounding the iPhone 5 debut to sell a record number of its own Galaxy S phones.

Many companies have even appointed *chief listening officers*, who are charged with sifting through online customer conversations and passing along key insights to marketing decision makers. Dell created a position called *Listening Czar* two years ago. "Our chief listener is critical to making sure that the right people in the organization are aware of what the conversations on the Web are saying about us, so the relevant people in the business can connect with customers," says a Dell marketing executive.[9]

Companies also need to actively monitor competitors' activities. Firms use competitive marketing intelligence to gain early warnings of competitor moves and strategies, new product launches, new or changing markets, and potential competitive strengths and weaknesses. Much competitor intelligence can be collected from people inside the company—executives, engineers and scientists, purchasing agents, and the sales force. The company can also obtain important intelligence information from suppliers, resellers, and key customers. It can monitor competitors' Web sites and use the Internet to search specific competitor names, events, or trends and see what turns up. And tracking consumer conversations about competing brands is often as revealing as tracking conversations about the company's own brands.

Intelligence seekers can also pour through any of thousands of online databases. Some are free. For example, the U.S. Security and Exchange Commission's database provides a huge stockpile of financial information on public competitors, and the U.S. Patent Office and Trademark database reveals patents that competitors have filed. For a fee, companies can also subscribe to any of the more than 3,000 online databases and information search services, such as Hoover's, LexisNexis, and Dun & Bradstreet. Today's marketers have an almost overwhelming amount of competitor information only a few keystrokes away.

The intelligence game goes both ways. Facing determined competitive marketing intelligence efforts by competitors, most companies are now taking steps to protect their own information. For example, Apple is obsessed with secrecy, and it passes that obsession along to its employees. "At Apple everything is a secret," says an insider. "Apple wants new products to remain in stealth mode until their release dates." Information leaks about new products before they are introduced gives competition time to respond, raises customer expectations, and can steal thunder and sales from current products. So Apple employees are taught a "loose-lips-sink-ships" mentality: A T-shirt for sale in the company store reads, "I visited the Apple campus, but that's all I'm allowed to say."[10]

One self-admitted corporate spy advises that companies should try conducting marketing intelligence investigations of themselves, looking for potentially damaging information leaks. They should start by "vacuuming up" everything they can find in the public record, including job postings, court records, company advertisements and blogs, Web pages, press releases, online business reports, social media postings by customers and employees, and other information available to inquisitive competitors.[11]

The growing use of marketing intelligence also raises ethical issues. Some intelligence-gathering techniques may involve questionable ethics. Clearly, companies should take advantage of publicly available information. However, they should not stoop to snoop. With all the legitimate intelligence sources now available, a company does not need to break the law or accepted codes of ethics to get good intelligence.

Author Comment
Whereas marketing intelligence involves actively scanning the general marketing environment, marketing research involves more focused studies to gain customer insights relating to specific marketing decisions.

Marketing Research

In addition to marketing intelligence information about general consumer, competitor, and marketplace happenings, marketers often need formal studies that provide customer and market insights for specific marketing situations and decisions. For example, Budweiser wants to know what appeals will be most effective in its Super Bowl advertising. Yahoo! wants to know how Web searchers will react to a proposed redesign of its site. Or Samsung wants to know how many and what kinds of people will buy its next-generation, ultrathin televisions. In such situations, managers will need marketing research.

Marketing research The systematic design, collection, analysis, and reporting of data relevant to a specific marketing situation facing an organization.

Marketing research is the systematic design, collection, analysis, and reporting of data relevant to a specific marketing situation facing an organization. Companies use marketing research in a wide variety of situations. For example, marketing research gives marketers insights into customer motivations, purchase behavior, and satisfaction. It can help them to assess market potential and market share or measure the effectiveness of pricing, product, distribution, and promotion activities.

Some large companies have their own research departments that work with marketing managers on marketing research projects. In addition, these companies—like their smaller counterparts—frequently hire outside research specialists to consult with management on specific marketing problems and to conduct marketing research studies. Sometimes firms simply purchase data collected by outside firms to aid in their decision making.

The marketing research process has four steps (see >> **Figure 4.2**): defining the problem and research objectives, developing the research plan, implementing the research plan, and interpreting and reporting the findings.

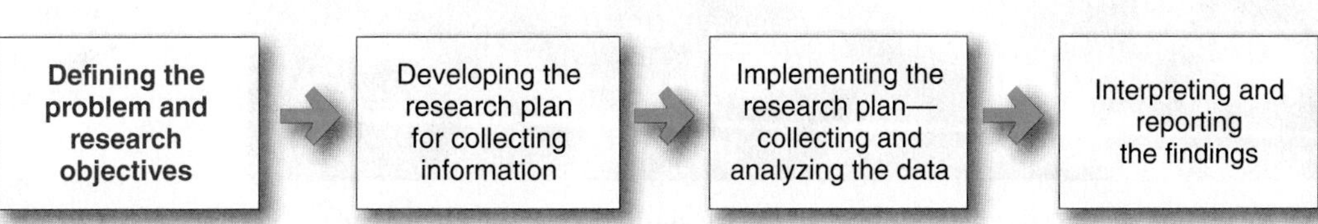
This first step is probably the most difficult but also the most important one. It guides the entire research process. It's frustrating to reach the end of an expensive research project only to learn that you've addressed the wrong problem!
Defining the problem and research objectives
Developing the research plan for collecting information
Implementing the research plan—collecting and analyzing the data
Interpreting and reporting the findings

>> **Figure 4.2** The Marketing Research Process

Defining the Problem and Research Objectives

Marketing managers and researchers must work closely together to define the problem and agree on research objectives. The manager best understands the decision for which information is needed, whereas the researcher best understands marketing research and how to obtain the information. Defining the problem and research objectives is often the hardest step in the research process. The manager may know that something is wrong, without knowing the specific causes.

After the problem has been defined carefully, the manager and the researcher must set the research objectives. A marketing research project might have one of three types of objectives. The objective of **exploratory research** is to gather preliminary information that will help define the problem and suggest hypotheses. The objective of **descriptive research** is to describe things, such as the market potential for a product or the demographics and attitudes of consumers who buy the product. The objective of **causal research** is to test hypotheses about cause-and-effect relationships. For example, would a 10 percent decrease in tuition at a private college result in an enrollment increase sufficient to offset the reduced tuition? Managers often start with exploratory research and later follow with descriptive or causal research.

Exploratory research
Marketing research to gather preliminary information that will help define problems and suggest hypotheses.

Descriptive research
Marketing research to better describe marketing problems, situations, or markets, such as the market potential for a product or the demographics and attitudes of consumers.

Causal research
Marketing research to test hypotheses about cause-and-effect relationships.

The statement of the problem and research objectives guides the entire research process. The manager and the researcher should put the statement in writing to be certain that they agree on the purpose and expected results of the research.

Developing the Research Plan

Once researchers have defined the research problem and objectives, they must determine the exact information needed, develop a plan for gathering it efficiently, and present the plan to management. The research plan outlines sources of existing data and spells out the specific research approaches, contact methods, sampling plans, and instruments that researchers will use to gather new data.

Research objectives must be translated into specific information needs. >> For example, suppose that Red Bull wants to know how consumers would react to a proposed new vitamin-enhanced water drink that would be available in several flavors and sold under the Red Bull name. Red Bull currently dominates the worldwide energy drink market with a more than 40 percent market share worldwide—it sold more than 4.6 billion cans last year alone. And the brand recently introduced Red Bull Total Zero, an energy drink for calorie-averse consumers.[12] A new line of enhanced, fizzless waters—akin to Glacéau's vitaminwater—might help Red Bull leverage its strong brand position even further. The proposed research might call for the following specific information:

>> **A decision by Red Bull to add a line of enhanced waters to its already successful mix of energy drinks would call for marketing research that provides lots of specific information.**
Jarrod Weaton/Weaton Digital, Inc.

- The demographic, economic, and lifestyle characteristics of current Red Bull customers. (Do current customers also consume enhanced-water products? Are such products consistent with their lifestyles? Or would Red Bull need to target a new segment of consumers?)
- The characteristics and usage patterns of the broader population of enhanced-water users: What do they need and expect from such products, where do they buy them, when and how do they use them, and what

existing brands and price points are most popular? (The new Red Bull product would need strong, relevant positioning in the crowded enhanced-water market.)

- Retailer reactions to the proposed new product line: Would they stock and support it? Where would they display it? (Failure to get retailer support would hurt sales of the new drink.)
- Forecasts of sales of both the new and current Red Bull products. (Will the new enhanced waters create new sales or simply take sales away from current Red Bull products? Will the new product increase Red Bull's overall profits?)

Red Bull's marketers will need these and many other types of information to decide whether or not to introduce the new product and, if so, the best way to do it.

The research plan should be presented in a *written proposal*. A written proposal is especially important when the research project is large and complex or when an outside firm carries it out. The proposal should cover the management problems addressed, the research objectives, the information to be obtained, and how the results will help management's decision making. The proposal also should include estimated research costs.

Secondary data
Information that already exists somewhere, having been collected for another purpose.

Primary data
Information collected for the specific purpose at hand.

To meet the manager's information needs, the research plan can call for gathering secondary data, primary data, or both. **Secondary data** consist of information that already exists somewhere, having been collected for another purpose. **Primary data** consist of information collected for the specific purpose at hand.

Gathering Secondary Data

Researchers usually start by gathering secondary data. The company's internal database provides a good starting point. However, the company can also tap into a wide assortment of external information sources.

Companies can buy secondary data from outside suppliers. For example, Nielsen sells shopper insight data from a consumer panel of more than 250,000 households in 25 countries worldwide, with measures of trial and repeat purchasing, brand loyalty, and buyer demographics. Experian Simmons carries out a full spectrum of consumer studies that provide a comprehensive view of the American consumer. The US Yankelovich MONITOR service by The Futures Company sells information on important social and lifestyle trends. These and other firms supply high-quality data to suit a wide variety of marketing information needs.[13]

Using *commercial online databases*, marketing researchers can conduct their own searches of secondary data sources. >> General database services such as Dialog, ProQuest, and LexisNexis put an incredible wealth of information at the fingertips of marketing decision makers. Beyond commercial Web sites offering information for a fee, almost every industry association, government agency, business publication, and news medium offers free information to those tenacious enough to find their Web sites or apps.

Internet search engines can also be a big help in locating relevant secondary information sources. However, they can also be very frustrating and inefficient. For example, a Red Bull marketer Googling "enhanced-water products" would come up with more than 50,000 hits. Still, well-structured, well-designed online searches can be a good starting point to any marketing research project.

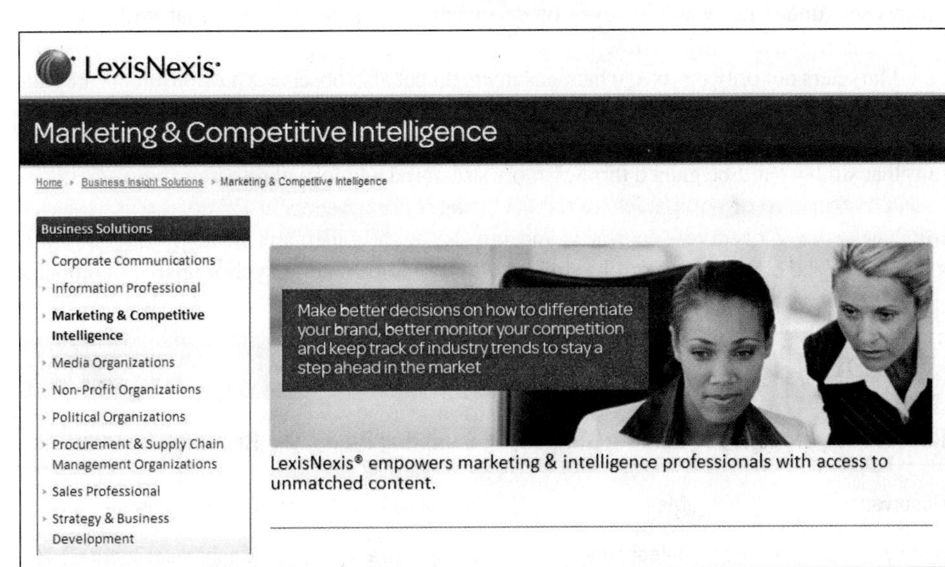

>> **Consumer database services such as LexisNexis put an incredible wealth of information at the fingertips of marketing decision makers.**

Secondary data can usually be obtained more quickly and at a lower cost than primary data. Also, secondary sources can sometimes provide data an individual company cannot collect on its own—information that either is not directly available or would be too expensive to collect. For example, it would be too expensive for Red Bull's marketers to conduct a continuing retail store audit to find out about the market shares, prices, and displays of competitors' brands. But those marketers can buy the InfoScan service from SymphonyIRI Group, which provides this information based on scanner and other data from 34,000 retail stores in markets around the nation.[14]

Secondary data can also present problems. Researchers can rarely obtain all the data they need from secondary sources. For example, Red Bull will not find existing information regarding consumer reactions about a new enhanced-water line that it has not yet placed on the market. Even when data can be found, the information might not be very usable. The researcher must evaluate secondary information carefully to make certain it is *relevant* (fits the research project's needs), *accurate* (reliably collected and reported), *current* (up to date enough for current decisions), and *impartial* (objectively collected and reported).

Primary Data Collection

Secondary data provide a good starting point for research and often help to define research problems and objectives. In most cases, however, the company must also collect primary data. **>> Table 4.1** shows that designing a plan for primary data collection calls for a number of decisions on *research approaches*, *contact methods*, the *sampling plan*, and *research instruments*.

Research Approaches

Research approaches for gathering primary data include observation, surveys, and experiments. We discuss each one in turn.

Observational research
Gathering primary data by observing relevant people, actions, and situations.

Observational Research. **Observational research** involves gathering primary data by observing relevant people, actions, and situations. For example, food retailer Trader Joe's might evaluate possible new store locations by checking traffic patterns, neighborhood conditions, and the locations of competing Whole Foods, Fresh Market, and other retail chains.

Researchers often observe consumer behavior to glean customer insights they can't obtain by simply asking customers questions. For instance, Fisher-Price has established an observation lab in which it can observe the reactions little tots have to new toys. The Fisher-Price Play Lab is a sunny, toy-strewn space where lucky kids get to test Fisher-Price prototypes, under the watchful eyes of designers who hope to learn what will get them worked up into a new-toy frenzy.

Marketers not only observe what consumers do but also observe what consumers are saying. As discussed earlier, marketers now routinely listen in on consumer conversations on blogs, social networks, and Web sites. Observing such naturally occurring feedback can provide inputs that simply can't be gained through more structured and formal research approaches.

Ethnographic research
A form of observational research that involves sending trained observers to watch and interact with consumers in their "natural environments."

A wide range of companies now use **ethnographic research**. Ethnographic research involves sending observers to watch and interact with consumers in their "natural environments." The observers might be trained anthropologists and psychologists or company

>> Table 4.1 Planning Primary Data Collection

Research Approaches	Contact Methods	Sampling Plan	Research Instruments
Observation	Mail	Sampling unit	Questionnaire
Survey	Telephone	Sample size	Mechanical instruments
Experiment	Personal	Sampling procedure	
	Online		

researchers and managers. For example, P&G uses extensive ethnographic research to gain deep insights into serving the world's poor. Three years ago, P&G launched the "$2-a-Day Project," named for the average income of the people it targets worldwide. The project sends ethnographic researchers trekking through the jungles of Brazil, the slums of India, and farming villages in rural China seeking insights into the needs of very-low-income consumers. >> As an example, P&G researchers recently spent time with poor Chinese potato farmer Wei Xiao Yan, observing in detail as she washed her long black hair using only three cups of water. Her family's water supply is a precious commodity—it comes from storing rainwater. P&G must find affordable and practical solutions that both work in Wei's harsh environment while also supporting her needs to feel attractive.[15]

Insights from P&G's $2-a-Day Project have already produced some successful new products for emerging markets—such as a skin-sensitive detergent for women who wash clothing by hand. In the works is a body cleanser formulated to clean without much water—it generates foam, which can be easily wiped away, instead of lather. Another product is a leave-in hair conditioner that requires no water at all. For underserved customers like Wei Xiao Yan, P&G has learned, it must develop products that are not just effective and affordable but are also aspirational.

Beyond conducting ethnographic research in physical consumer environments, many companies now routinely conduct *Netnography* research—observing consumers in a natural context on the Internet. Observing people as they interact and move about online can provide useful insights into both online and offline buying motives and behavior.[16]

>> **Ethnographic research: To better understand the needs of the world's poor, P&G sends researchers trekking through the jungles of Brazil, the slums of India, and farming villages in rural China to observe consumers in their "natural environments." Here, they watch Chinese potato farmer Wei Xiao Yan wash her long black hair with great care using only three cups of water.**

Benjamin Lowy/Getty Images.

Observational and ethnographic research often yield the kinds of details that just don't emerge from traditional research questionnaires or focus groups. Whereas traditional quantitative research approaches seek to test known hypotheses and obtain answers to well-defined product or strategy questions, observational research can generate fresh customer and market insights that people are unwilling or unable to provide. It provides a window into customers' unconscious actions and unexpressed needs and feelings.

In contrast, however, some things simply cannot be observed, such as attitudes, motives, or private behavior. Long-term or infrequent behavior is also difficult to observe. Finally, observations can be very difficult to interpret. Because of these limitations, researchers often use observation along with other data collection methods.

Survey research
Gathering primary data by asking people questions about their knowledge, attitudes, preferences, and buying behavior.

Survey Research. **Survey research**, the most widely used method for primary data collection, is the approach best suited for gathering descriptive information. A company that wants to know about people's knowledge, attitudes, preferences, or buying behavior can often find out by asking them directly.

The major advantage of survey research is its flexibility; it can be used to obtain many different kinds of information in many different situations. Surveys addressing almost any marketing question or decision can be conducted by phone or mail, in person, or online.

However, survey research also presents some problems. Sometimes people are unable to answer survey questions because they cannot remember or have never thought about what they do and why they do it. People may be unwilling to respond to unknown interviewers or about things they consider private. Respondents may answer survey questions even when they do not know the answer just to appear smarter or more informed. Or they may try to help the interviewer by giving pleasing answers. Finally, busy people may not take the time, or they might resent the intrusion into their privacy.

Experimental research
Gathering primary data by selecting matched groups of subjects, giving them different treatments, controlling related factors, and checking for differences in group responses.

Experimental Research. Whereas observation is best suited for exploratory research and surveys for descriptive research, **experimental research** is best suited for gathering causal information. Experiments involve selecting matched groups of subjects, giving them different treatments, controlling unrelated factors, and checking for differences in group responses. Thus, experimental research tries to explain cause-and-effect relationships.

For example, before adding a new sandwich to its menu, McDonald's might use experiments to test the effects on sales of two different prices it might charge. It could introduce the new sandwich at one price in one city and at another price in another city. If the cities are similar, and if all other marketing efforts for the sandwich are the same, then differences in sales in the two cities could be related to the price charged.

Contact Methods

Information can be collected by mail, telephone, personal interview, or online. **>>Table 4.2** shows the strengths and weaknesses of each contact method.

Mail, Telephone, and Personal Interviewing. *Mail questionnaires* can be used to collect large amounts of information at a low cost per respondent. Respondents may give more honest answers to more personal questions on a mail questionnaire than to an unknown interviewer in person or over the phone. Also, no interviewer is involved to bias respondents' answers.

However, mail questionnaires are not very flexible; all respondents answer the same questions in a fixed order. Mail surveys usually take longer to complete, and the response rate—the number of people returning completed questionnaires—is often very low. Finally, the researcher often has little control over the mail questionnaire sample. Even with a good mailing list, it is hard to control *who* at a particular address fills out the questionnaire. As a result of the shortcomings, more and more marketers are now shifting to faster, more flexible, and lower-cost e-mail and online surveys.

Telephone interviewing is one of the best methods for gathering information quickly, and it provides greater flexibility than mail questionnaires. Interviewers can explain difficult questions and, depending on the answers they receive, skip some questions or probe on others. Response rates tend to be higher than with mail questionnaires, and interviewers can ask to speak to respondents with the desired characteristics or even by name.

However, with telephone interviewing, the cost per respondent is higher than with mail or online questionnaires. Also, people may not want to discuss personal questions with an interviewer. The method introduces interviewer bias—the way interviewers talk, how they ask questions, and other differences that may affect respondents' answers. Finally, in this

>> Table 4.2 Strengths and Weaknesses of Contact Methods

	Mail	Telephone	Personal	Online
Flexibility	Poor	Good	Excellent	Good
Quantity of data that can be collected	Good	Fair	Excellent	Good
Control of interviewer effects	Excellent	Fair	Poor	Fair
Control of sample	Fair	Excellent	Good	Excellent
Speed of data collection	Poor	Excellent	Good	Excellent
Response rate	Poor	Poor	Good	Good
Cost	Good	Fair	Poor	Excellent

Source: Based on Donald S. Tull and Del I. Hawkins, *Marketing Research: Measurement and Method,* 7th ed. (New York: Macmillan Publishing Company, 1993). Adapted with permission of the authors.

age of do-not-call lists and promotion-harassed consumers, potential survey respondents are increasingly hanging up on telephone interviewers rather than talking with them.

Personal interviewing takes two forms: individual interviewing and group interviewing. *Individual interviewing* involves talking with people in their homes or offices, on the street, or in shopping malls. Such interviewing is flexible. Trained interviewers can guide interviews, explain difficult questions, and explore issues as the situation requires. They can show subjects actual products, advertisements, or packages and observe reactions and behavior. However, individual personal interviews may cost three to four times as much as telephone interviews.

Group interviewing consists of inviting 6 to 10 people to meet with a trained moderator to talk about a product, service, or organization. Participants normally are paid a small sum for attending. A moderator encourages free and easy discussion, hoping that group interactions will bring out actual feelings and thoughts. At the same time, the moderator "focuses" the discussion—hence the name **focus group interviewing**.

Focus group interviewing
Personal interviewing that involves inviting 6 to 10 people to gather for a few hours with a trained interviewer to talk about a product, service, or organization. The interviewer "focuses" the group discussion on important issues.

In traditional focus groups, researchers and marketers watch the focus group discussions from behind a one-way mirror and record comments in writing or on video for later study. Focus group researchers often use videoconferencing and Internet technology to connect marketers in distant locations with live focus group action. Using cameras and two-way sound systems, marketing executives in a far-off boardroom can look in and listen, using remote controls to zoom in on faces and pan the focus group at will.

Along with observational research, focus group interviewing has become one of the major qualitative marketing research tools for gaining fresh insights into consumer thoughts and feelings. In focus group settings, researchers not only hear consumer ideas and opinions, they can also observe facial expressions, body movements, group interplay, and conversational flows. However, focus group studies present some challenges. They usually employ small samples to keep time and costs down, and it may be hard to generalize from the results. Moreover, consumers in focus groups are not always open and honest about their real feelings, behavior, and intentions in front of other people.

To overcome these problems, many researchers are tinkering with the focus group design. Some companies use *immersion groups*—small groups of consumers who interact directly and informally with product designers without a focus group moderator present. Other researchers are changing the environments in which they conduct focus groups to help consumers relax and elicit more authentic responses. >> For example, Lexus recently hosted a series of "An Evening with Lexus" dinners with groups of customers in customers' homes:[17]

According to Lexus group vice president and general manager Mark Templin, the best way to find out why luxury car buyers did or didn't become Lexus owners is to dine with them—up close and personal in their homes. At the first dinner, 16 owners of Lexus, Mercedes, BMW, Audi, Land Rover, and other high-end cars traded their perceptions of the Lexus brand over a sumptuous meal prepared by a famous chef at a home in Beverly Hills. Templin gained many actionable insights. For example, some owners viewed Lexus vehicles as unexciting. "Everyone had driven a Lexus at some point and had a great experience," he says. "But the Lexus they [had] wasn't as fun to drive as the car they have now. It's our challenge to show that Lexus is more fun to drive today than it was 15 years ago." Templin was also surprised to learn the extent to which the grown children of luxury car buyers influence what car they purchase. Now, Templin says, future Lexus marketing will also target young adults who may not buy luxury cars but who influence their parents' decisions.

>> New focus group environments: Lexus USA general manager Mark Templin hosts "An Evening with Lexus" dinners with luxury car buyers to figure out why they did or didn't become Lexus owners.

Courtesy of Lexus.

Individual and focus group interviews can add a personal touch as opposed to more numbers-oriented research. "We get lots of research, and it tells us what we need to run our business, but I get more out of talking one-on-one," confirms Lexus's Templin. "It really comes to life when I hear people say it."

Online Marketing Research. The growth of the Internet has had a dramatic impact on how marketing research is conducted. Increasingly, researchers are collecting primary data through **online marketing research**: Internet surveys, online panels, experiments, and online focus groups and brand communities.

Online marketing research
Collecting primary data online through Internet surveys, online focus groups, Web-based experiments, or tracking consumers' online behavior.

Online research can take many forms. A company can use the Internet as a survey medium: It can include a questionnaire on its Web or social media sites or use e-mail to invite people to answer questions. It can create online panels that provide regular feedback or conduct live discussions or online focus groups. Researchers can also conduct online experiments. They can experiment with different prices, headlines, or product features on different Web or mobile sites or at different times to learn the relative effectiveness of their offers. They can set up virtual shopping environments and use them to test new products and marketing programs. Or a company can learn about the behavior of online customers by following their click streams as they visit the online site and move to other sites.

The Internet is especially well suited to *quantitative* research—for example, conducting marketing surveys and collecting data. More than 80 percent of all Americans now use the Internet, making it a fertile channel for reaching a broad cross-section of consumers.[18] As response rates for traditional survey approaches decline and costs increase, the Internet is quickly replacing mail and the telephone as the dominant data collection methodology.

Internet-based survey research offers many advantages over traditional phone, mail, and personal interviewing approaches. The most obvious advantages are speed and low costs. By going online, researchers can quickly and easily distribute Internet surveys to thousands of respondents simultaneously via e-mail or by posting them on selected online sites. Responses can be almost instantaneous, and because respondents themselves enter the information, researchers can tabulate, review, and share research data as the information arrives.

Online research also usually costs much less than research conducted through mail, phone, or personal interviews. Using the Internet eliminates most of the postage, phone, interviewer, and data-handling costs associated with the other approaches. Moreover, sample size has little impact on costs. Once the questionnaire is set up, there's little difference in cost between 10 respondents and 10,000 respondents on the Internet.

Its low cost puts online research well within the reach of almost any business, large or small. In fact, with the Internet, what was once the domain of research experts is now available to almost any would-be researcher. » Even smaller, less sophisticated researchers can use online survey services such as Snap Surveys (www.snapsurveys.com) and SurveyMonkey (www.surveymonkey.com) to create, publish, and distribute their own custom online or mobile surveys in minutes.

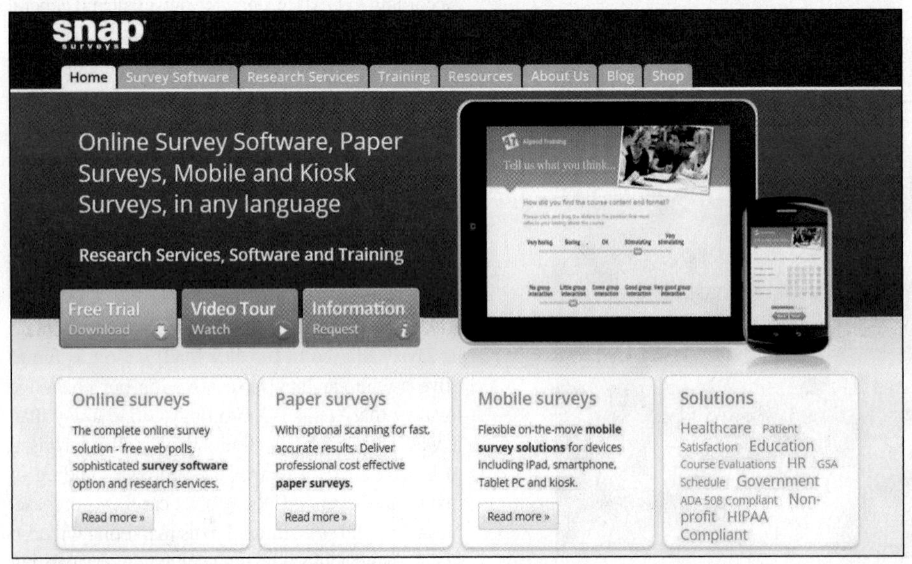

» Online research: Thanks to survey services such as Snap Surveys, almost any business, large or small, can create, publish, and distribute its own custom online or mobile surveys in minutes.

Snap Surveys.

Internet-based surveys also tend to be more interactive and engaging, easier to complete, and less intrusive than traditional phone or mail surveys. As a result, they usually garner higher response rates. The Internet is an excellent medium for reaching the hard-to-reach consumer—for example, the often-elusive teen, single, affluent, and well-educated audiences. It's also good for reaching people who lead busy lives, from working mothers to on-the-go executives. Such people are well represented online, and they can respond in their own space and at their own convenience.

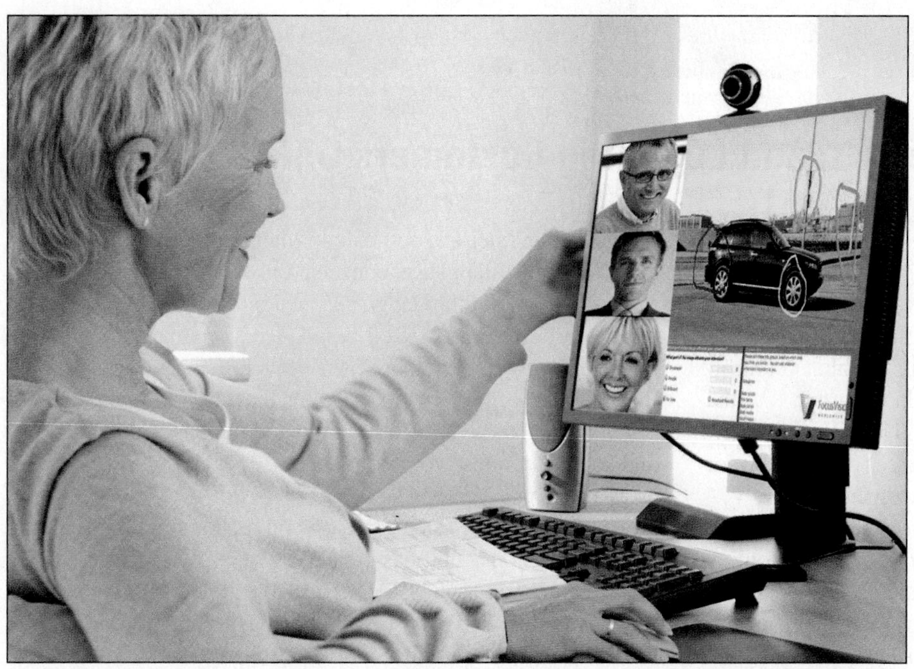

>> Online focus groups: FocusVision's InterVu service lets focus group participants at remote locations see, hear, and react to each other in real-time, face-to-face discussions.

FocusVision Worldwide, Inc.

Just as marketing researchers have rushed to use the Internet for quantitative surveys and data collection, they are now also adopting *qualitative* Internet-based research approaches, such as online focus groups, blogs, and social networks. The Internet can provide a fast, low-cost way to gain qualitative customer insights.

A primary qualitative Internet-based research approach is **online focus groups**. >> For example, online research firm FocusVision offers its InterVu service, which harnesses the power of Web conferencing to conduct focus groups with participants at remote locations, anywhere in the world, at any time. Using their own Webcams, InterVu participants can log on to focus sessions from their homes or offices and see, hear, and react to each other in real-time, face-to-face discussions.[19] Such focus groups can be conducted in any language and viewed with simultaneous translation. They work well for bringing together people from different parts of the country or world at low cost. Researchers can view the sessions in real time from just about anywhere, eliminating travel, lodging, and facility costs. Finally, although online focus groups require some advance scheduling, results are almost immediate.

Online focus groups
Gathering a small group of people online with a trained moderator to chat about a product, service, or organization and gain qualitative insights about consumer attitudes and behavior.

Although growing rapidly, both quantitative and qualitative Internet-based research have some drawbacks. One major problem is controlling who's in the online sample. Without seeing respondents, it's difficult to know who they really are. To overcome such sample and context problems, many online research firms use opt-in communities and respondent panels. Alternatively, many companies are now developing their own custom social networks and using them to gain customer inputs and insights. For example, in addition to picking customers' brains in face-to-face events such as "An Evening with Lexus" dinners in customers' homes, Lexus has built an extensive online research community called the Lexus Advisory Board, which consists of 20,000 invitation-only Lexus owners representing a wide range of demographics, psychographics, and model ownership. Lexus regularly surveys the group to obtain input on everything from perceptions of the brand to customer relationships with dealers.[20]

Online Behavioral and Social Tracking and Targeting. Thus, in recent years, the Internet has become an important tool for conducting research and developing customer insights. But today's marketing researchers are going even further—well beyond structured online surveys, focus groups, and Internet communities. Increasingly, they are listening to and watching consumers by actively mining the rich veins of unsolicited, unstructured, "bottom-up" customer information already coursing around the Internet. Whereas traditional marketing research provides more logical consumer responses to structured and intrusive research questions, online listening provides the passion and spontaneity of unsolicited consumer opinions.

Tracking consumers online might be as simple as scanning customer reviews and comments on the company's brand site or on shopping sites such as Amazon.com or BestBuy.com. Or it might mean using sophisticated online-analysis tools to deeply analyze the mountains of consumer brand-related comments and messages found in blogs or on social media sites, such as Facebook, Yelp, YouTube, or Twitter. Listening to and engaging customers online can provide valuable insights into what consumers are saying or feeling about a brand. It can also provide opportunities for building positive brand experiences and relationships. Companies like Dell excel at listening online and responding quickly and appropriately. (See Marketing at Work 4.1.)

MARKETING AT WORK 4.1

Dell Goes Social: Listening to and Engaging Customers Online

When it comes to listening, engaging, and responding to customers through online social media, Dell really gets it. The company has learned that good listening is an important part of building customer relationships. Similarly, not being a part of the social conversation can lead to serious missteps. It's not about controlling the online conversation; it's about making certain that the company knows what's being said about the brand and participates in the dialogue. Today, Dell has become a poster child for using social media to listen to and connect with customers.

But Dell learned its social media lessons through hard experience. It all started a few years ago with a painful online incident—dubbed "Dell Hell"—that dramatically demonstrated the power of the social media in giving voice to consumer opinions and concerns, often to a company's detriment. It began with a brief but scathing blog entry by well-known tech blogger Jeff Jarvis of BuzzMachine about the many failings of his Dell computer and his struggles with Dell's customer support. "I just got a new Dell laptop and paid a fortune for the four-year, in-home service," raged Jarvis. "The machine is a lemon and the service is a lie." After detailing his problems with the PC and the shortcomings of Dell's support, Jarvis signed off "DELL SUCKS. DELL LIES. Put that in your Google and smoke it, Dell."

In the old days, Jarvis's complaint, perhaps in the form of a letter to the editor in a local newspaper or a short commentary in an obscure technical journal, probably wouldn't have attracted much of an audience. But in today's superheated social media environment, Jarvis's blog post immediately went viral, becoming the third-most-linked-to post in the blogosphere the day it appeared. The ensuing online dialog unleashed a firestorm of complaints from customers who shared Jarvis's displeasure with Dell. Jarvis's headline—Dell Hell—became shorthand for the ability of a lone consumer using digital and social media to deliver a body blow to an unsuspecting business.

The Dell Hell incident opened Dell's eyes to the importance of the social media in shaping brand conversations and opinions. If consumers are talking about your brand online, you need to be there too. Beyond monitoring the social media to catch and deal with the rants of disgruntled consumers, Dell also saw opportunities to use social media to proactively engage consumers, learn from them, and build positive brand experiences. Even before "Dell Hell," Michael Dell had seen the social media as a perfect fit for a company with a deep heritage of working directly with customers. "Our customers have the best ideas and insights," says the company. So why not tap these insights and ideas as they fly around the social media?

In the aftermath of Dell Hell, Dell began to build an organization that actively and systematically listens to and interacts with customers online. At the heart of the effort is Dell's Social Media Listening Command Center, a state-of-the-art social media hub focused on monitoring, engaging, and responding to all things Dell online. The command center aggregates and analyzes 25,000 English-language conversations about Dell (and thousands more in 10 other languages) every day, looking for opportunities to reinforce the Dell brand. The Command Center isn't interested only in customer service or marketing matters. It sorts through oceans of online interactions that are important to all areas of Dell's business—from customer complaints, compliments, and support requests to product feedback and intelligence on an array of technology topics.

But beyond just listening in on and responding to social media conversations, Dell has created its own social media empire for engaging customers and other stakeholders. For example, the company now sponsors nine blogs, such as Direct2Dell.com, designed to provide "a direct exchange with Dell customers about the technology that connects us all." Dell's IdeaStorm site provides a forum where everyone from information technology professionals to regular folks can evaluate Dell's products and services and offer suggestions on how to improve them. Dell maintains an active presence on major public social media, ranging from Facebook, Twitter, LinkedIn, Google+, YouTube, Flickr, and Pinterest, to Brazil's Orkut, Germany's Xing, and China's Renren and YouKu social communities. Dell's participation in such social media goes well beyond the typical brand pages. All of Dell's social media efforts are designed to create and monitor consumer exchanges, gather feedback, provide customer service and support, and build customer relationships. Dell urges consumers to "get connected to Dell and let your voice be heard."

Dell's online listening and response culture pervades every aspect of its operations. At the top, Dell created the position of Listening Czar, an executive charged with making certain that the

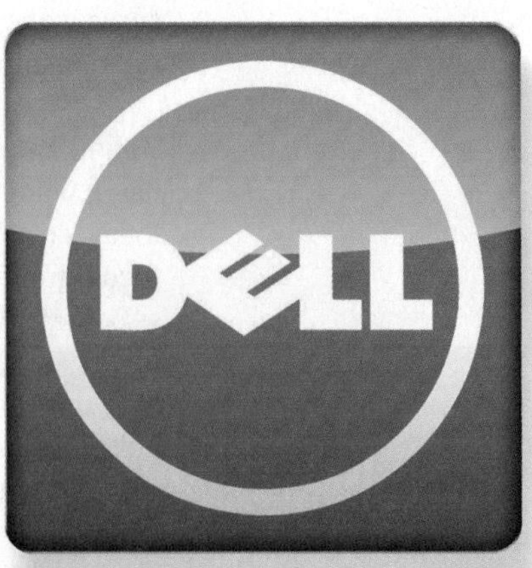

» When it comes to listening, engaging, and responding to customers through online social media, Dell really gets it.

social media are woven into the very fabric the organization. It established a Social Outreach Services group, comprised of scores of dedicated social media support people who form a frontline response team that is ready to pounce on any hot topic or customer need, turning online rants into raves. Dell even has a social media governance team that helps promote a company-wide social media mindset. And in an effort to turn every employee into an online brand advocate, Dell set up a social media certification program that trains employees on how to get social in their jobs, technical support, and customer care. More than 7,500 Dell employees worldwide have become Dell Certified Social Media and Community Professionals.

Finally, to engage online influencers in an off-line, in-person way, Dell now holds annual Consumer Advisory Panel (CAP) Days. During the two-day events, Dell invites 30 people active in social media to its headquarters to interact with Dell executives and discuss firsthand their thoughts about Dell's brand, products, Web site, and customer service. Dell teams take the feedback seriously—they know that the success of CAP Days depends on what happens after the customer advisors leave.

Thus, Dell has come a long way from its Dell Hell days. It now uses the social media skillfully to listen to, learn from, and engage its customers. Dell has become so good at social listening that it has formed a social media services group that helps clients such as Caterpillar, Aetna, Kraft Foods, the American Red Cross, and others to develop their own social media strategies. Dell understands that conversations in the social media can shape customer attitudes and experiences as powerfully as a big-budget advertising campaign or a high-powered customer service or sales force. "Social media is far more than a tool," agrees Karen Quintos, Dell's chief marketing officer. "It's an extension of our brand. If your [customers] are in the social space, they are talking about your brand—so either engage and be part of the conversation or be left behind."

Sources: Based on information from Jennifer Rooney, "In Dell Social-Media Journey, Lessons for Marketers about the Power of Listening," *Forbes*, September 25, 2012, www.forbes.com/sites/jenniferrooney/2012/09/25/in-dell-social-media-journey-lessons-for-marketers-about-the-power-of-listening/2/; Jason Falls, "Why Dell Is Still a Great Case Study," *Social Media Explorer*, December 13, 2011, www.socialmediaexplorer.com/social-media-marketing/why-dell-is-a-great-case-study/; Jeff Jarvis, "Dell Lies. Dell Sucks." *BuzzMachine*, June 21, 2005, http://buzzmachine.com/2005/06/21/dell-lies-dell-sucks/; "Dell Launches New Unit to Provide Social-Media Strategy to Brands," *Advertising Age*, December 4, 2012, http://adage.com/print/238594; "Dell Social Media," www.slideshare.net/dellsocialmedia, accessed March 2013; and http://content.dell.com/us/en/corp/about-dell-social-media.aspx and http://en.community.dell.com/dell-blogs/direct2dell/b/direct2dell/default.aspx, accessed October 2013.

Information about what consumers do while trolling the vast expanse of the Internet—what searches they make, the sites they visit, what music and programming they consume, how they shop, and what they buy—is pure gold to marketers. And today's marketers are busy mining that gold. Then, in a practice called **behavioral targeting**, marketers use the online data to target ads and offers to specific consumers. For example, if you place a mobile phone in your Amazon.com shopping cart but don't buy it, you might expect to see some ads for that very type of phone the next time you visit your favorite ESPN site to catch up on the latest sports scores.

Behavioral targeting
Using online consumer tracking data to target advertisements and marketing offers to specific consumers.

The newest wave of Web analytics and targeting takes online eavesdropping even further—from *behavioral* targeting to *social* targeting. Whereas behavioral targeting tracks consumer movements across online sites, social targeting also mines individual online social connections and conversations from social networking sites. Research shows that consumers shop a lot like their friends and are much more likely to respond to ads from brands friends use. So, instead of just having a Zappos.com ad for running shoes pop up because you've recently searched online for running shoes (behavioral targeting), an ad for a specific pair of running shoes pops up because a friend that you're connected to via Twitter just bought those shoes from Zappos.com last week (social targeting).

» Behavioral targeting: Marketers watch what consumers say and do online, then use the resulting insights to personalize online shopping experiences. Is it sophisticated Web research or "just a little creepy"?

Andresr/Shutterstock.com.

Online listening, behavioral targeting, and social targeting can help marketers to harness the massive amounts of consumer information swirling around the Internet. However, as marketers get more adept at trolling blogs, social networks, and other Internet domains, many critics worry about consumer privacy. » At what point does sophisticated online research cross the line into consumer stalking? Proponents claim that behavioral and social targeting benefit more than abuse consumers by feeding back ads and products that are more relevant to their interests. But to many consumers and public advocates, following consumers online and stalking them with ads feels more than just a little creepy. Regulators and others are stepping in. The Federal Trade Commission (FTC) has recommended the creation of a "Do Not Track" system (the Internet equivalent to the "Do Not Call" registry)—which would let people opt out of having their actions monitored online. Meanwhile, the major Internet browsers have heeded the concerns by adding "Do Not Track" features.[21]

Sampling Plan

Sample
A segment of the population selected for marketing research to represent the population as a whole.

Marketing researchers usually draw conclusions about large groups of consumers by studying a small sample of the total consumer population. A **sample** is a segment of the population selected for marketing research to represent the population as a whole. Ideally, the sample should be representative so that the researcher can make accurate estimates of the thoughts and behaviors of the larger population.

Designing the sample requires three decisions. First, *who* is to be studied (what *sampling unit*)? The answer to this question is not always obvious. For example, to learn about the decision-making process for a family automobile purchase, should the subject be the husband, the wife, other family members, dealership salespeople, or all of these? Second, *how many* people should be included (what *sample size*)? Large samples give more reliable results than small samples. However, larger samples usually cost more, and it is not necessary to sample the entire target market or even a large portion to get reliable results.

Finally, *how* should the people in the sample be *chosen* (what *sampling procedure*)? **>> Table 4.3** describes different kinds of samples. Using *probability samples*, each population member has a known chance of being included in the sample, and researchers can calculate confidence limits for sampling error. But when probability sampling costs too much or takes too much time, marketing researchers often take *nonprobability samples*, even though their sampling error cannot be measured. These varied ways of drawing samples have different costs and time limitations as well as different accuracy and statistical properties. Which method is best depends on the needs of the research project.

Research Instruments

In collecting primary data, marketing researchers have a choice of two main research instruments: *questionnaires* and *mechanical instruments*.

Questionnaires. The questionnaire is by far the most common instrument, whether administered in person, by phone, by e-mail, or online. Questionnaires are very flexible—there are many ways to ask questions. Closed-end questions include all the possible answers, and subjects make choices among them. Examples include multiple-choice questions and scale questions. Open-end questions allow respondents to answer in their own words. In a survey of airline users, Southwest Airlines might simply ask, "What is your opinion of Southwest Airlines?" Or it might ask people to complete a sentence: "When I choose an airline, the most important consideration is. . . ." These and other kinds of open-end questions often reveal more than closed-end questions because they do not limit respondents' answers.

>> Table 4.3 Types of Samples

Probability Sample	
Simple random sample	Every member of the population has a known and equal chance of selection.
Stratified random sample	The population is divided into mutually exclusive groups (such as age groups), and random samples are drawn from each group.
Cluster (area) sample	The population is divided into mutually exclusive groups (such as blocks), and the researcher draws a sample of the groups to interview.
Nonprobability Sample	
Convenience sample	The researcher selects the easiest population members from which to obtain information.
Judgment sample	The researcher uses his or her judgment to select population members who are good prospects for accurate information.
Quota sample	The researcher finds and interviews a prescribed number of people in each of several categories.

Open-end questions are especially useful in exploratory research, when the researcher is trying to find out *what* people think but is not measuring *how many* people think in a certain way. Closed-end questions, on the other hand, provide answers that are easier to interpret and tabulate.

Researchers should also use care in the *wording* and *ordering* of questions. They should use simple, direct, and unbiased wording. Questions should be arranged in a logical order. The first question should create interest if possible, and difficult or personal questions should be asked last so that respondents do not become defensive.

Mechanical Instruments. Although questionnaires are the most common research instrument, researchers also use mechanical instruments to monitor consumer behavior. Nielsen Media Research attaches people meters to television sets, cable boxes, and satellite systems in selected homes to record who watches which programs. Retailers likewise use checkout scanners to record shoppers' purchases. Other mechanical devices measure subjects' physical responses to marketing offerings. » Consider this example:[22]

» **Time Warner's MediaLab uses high-tech observation to capture the changing ways that today's viewers are using and reacting to television and Web content.**

© Time Warner 2012, photograph by Henrik Olund.

Time Warner's new MediaLab at its New York headquarters looks more like a chic consumer electronics store than a research lab. But the lab employs a nifty collection of high-tech observation techniques to capture the changing ways that today's viewers are using and reacting to television and Web content. The MediaLab uses biometric measures to analyze every show subjects watch, every site they visit, and every commercial they skip. Meanwhile, mechanical devices assess viewer engagement via physiological measures of skin temperature, heart rate, sweat level, leaning in, and facial and eye movements. Observers behind two-way mirrors or using cameras that peer over each subject's shoulder make real-time assessments of Web browsing behavior. In all, the deep consumer insights gained from MediaLab observations are helping Time Warner prepare for marketing in today's rapidly changing digital media landscape.

Still other researchers are applying *neuromarketing*, measuring brain activity to learn how consumers feel and respond. Marketing scientists using MRI scans and EEG devices have learned that tracking brain electrical activity and blood flow can provide companies with insights into what turns consumers on and off regarding their brands and marketing. "Companies have always aimed for the customer's heart, but the head may make a better target," suggests one neuromarketer. "Neuromarketing is reaching consumers where the action is: the brain."[23]

Companies ranging from PepsiCo and Disney to Google and Microsoft now hire neuromarketing research companies such as Sands Research, NeuroFocus, and EmSense to help figure out what people are really thinking. For example, PepsiCo's Frito-Lay worked with Nielsen's NeuroFocus to assess consumer motivations underlying the success of its Cheetos snack brand. After scanning the brains of carefully chosen consumers, NeuroFocus learned that part of what makes Cheetos a junk-food staple is the messy orange cheese dust—that's right, the neon stuff that gloms onto your fingers and then smears on your shirt or the couch cushions. As it turns out, the icky coating triggers a powerful brain response: a sense of "giddy subversion" that makes the messiness more than worth the trouble it causes. Using this finding, Frito-Lay successfully framed an entire advertising campaign around the mess Cheetos make. For its part, NeuroFocus won an award for outstanding advertising research.[24]

Although neuromarketing techniques can measure consumer involvement and emotional responses second by second, such brain responses can be difficult to interpret. Thus, neuromarketing is usually used in combination with other research approaches to gain a more complete picture of what goes on inside consumers' heads.

Implementing the Research Plan

The researcher next puts the marketing research plan into action. This involves collecting, processing, and analyzing the information. Data collection can be carried out by the company's marketing research staff or outside firms. Researchers should watch closely to make sure that the plan is implemented correctly. They must guard against problems of interacting with respondents, with the quality of participants' responses, and with interviewers who make mistakes or take shortcuts.

Researchers must also process and analyze the collected data to isolate important information and insight. They need to check data for accuracy and completeness and code it for analysis. The researchers then tabulate the results and compute statistical measures.

Interpreting and Reporting the Findings

The market researcher must now interpret the findings, draw conclusions, and report them to management. The researcher should not try to overwhelm managers with numbers and fancy statistical techniques. Rather, the researcher should present important findings and insights that are useful in the major decisions faced by management.

However, interpretation should not be left only to researchers. Although they are often experts in research design and statistics, the marketing manager knows more about the problem and the decisions that must be made. The best research means little if the manager blindly accepts faulty interpretations from the researcher. Similarly, managers may be biased. They might tend to accept research results that show what they expected and reject those that they did not expect or hope for. In many cases, findings can be interpreted in different ways, and discussions between researchers and managers will help point to the best interpretations. Thus, managers and researchers must work together closely when interpreting research results, and both must share responsibility for the research process and resulting decisions.

SPEED BUMP LINKING THE CONCEPTS

Whew! We've covered a lot of territory. Hold up a minute, take a breather, and see if you can apply the marketing research process you've just studied.

- What specific kinds of research can Red Bull's brand managers use to learn more about its customers' preferences and buying behaviors? Sketch out a brief research plan for assessing potential reactions to a new Red Bull enhanced-water line.
- Could you use the marketing research process to analyze your career opportunities and job possibilities? (Think of yourself as a "product" and employers as potential "customers.") If so, what would your research plan look like?

Author Comment
We've talked generally about managing customer relationships throughout the book. But here, "customer relationship management" (CRM) has a much narrower data-management meaning. It refers to capturing and using customer data from all sources to manage customer interactions, engage customers, and build customer relationships.

Analyzing and Using Marketing Information

Information gathered in internal databases and through competitive marketing intelligence and marketing research usually requires additional analysis. Managers may need help applying the information to gain customer and market insights that will improve their marketing decisions. This help may include advanced statistical analysis to learn more about the relationships within a set of data. Information analysis might also involve the application of analytical models that will help marketers make better decisions.

Once the information has been processed and analyzed, it must be made available to the right decision makers at the right time. In the following sections, we look deeper into analyzing and using marketing information.

Customer Relationship Management

The question of how best to analyze and use individual customer data presents special problems. Most companies are awash in information about their customers. In fact, smart companies capture information at every possible customer *touch point*. These touch points include customer purchases, sales force contacts, service and support calls, online site visits, satisfaction surveys, credit and payment interactions, market research studies—every contact between a customer and a company.

Unfortunately, this information is usually scattered widely across the organization. It is buried deep in the separate databases and records of different company departments. To overcome such problems, many companies are now turning to **customer relationship management (CRM)** to manage detailed information about individual customers and carefully manage customer touch points to maximize customer loyalty.

Customer relationship management (CRM)
Managing detailed information about individual customers and carefully managing customer touch points to maximize customer loyalty.

CRM consists of sophisticated software and analytical tools from companies such as Salesforce.com, Oracle, Microsoft, and SAS that integrate customer information from all sources, analyze it in depth, and apply the results to build stronger customer relationships. CRM integrates everything that a company's sales, service, and marketing teams know about individual customers, providing a 360-degree view of the customer relationship.

CRM analysts develop *data warehouses* and use sophisticated *data mining* techniques to unearth the riches hidden in customer data. A data warehouse is a company-wide electronic database of finely detailed customer information that needs to be sifted through for gems. The purpose of a data warehouse is not only to gather information but also to pull it together into a central, accessible location. Then, once the data warehouse brings the data together, the company uses high-powered data mining techniques to sift through the mounds of data and dig out interesting findings about customers.

These findings often lead to marketing opportunities. For example, Macy's digs deeply into customer data and uses the insights gained to personalize its customers' shopping experiences:

> Seventy percent of Americans visit a Macy's store or its Web site at least once a year. "We don't need more customers—we need the customers we have to spend more time with us," says Macy's chief marketing officer. To that end, Macy's has assembled a huge database of 30 million households, containing reams of data on individual households, including in-store and online purchases, style preferences and personal motivations, and even browsing patterns at Macy's Web sites. >> As part of its MyMacy's program, the retailer deeply analyzes the data and uses the resulting insights to hyper-personalize each customer's experience. "With a business this size, the data they have on their customers is mind-boggling," says an analyst. "They're [the ultimate in] one-to-one marketing."
>
> For example, Macy's now sends out up to 500,000 unique versions of a single direct mail catalogue. "My book might look very different from [someone else's]," says the Macy's CMO. "I'm not such a great homemaker, but I am a cosmetic, shoe, and jewelry person, so what you might see in my book would be all of those categories." Similarly, in the digital space, under its "Intelligent Display" initiative, Macy's can track what customers browse on the company Web site, then have a relevant display ad appear as they are browsing on another site. Future MyMacy's actions will include e-mail, mobile, and Web site customizations. The ultimate goal of the massive database effort, says the CMO, is to "put the customer at the center of all decisions."[25]

>> Through its MyMacy's program, Macy's digs deeply into its huge customer database and uses the resulting insights to hyper-personalize its customers' shopping experiences. "Happy Birthday, Keri!"

Courtesy of Gary Armstrong.

By using CRM to understand customers better, companies can provide higher levels of customer service and develop deeper customer relationships. They can use CRM to pinpoint high-value customers, target them more effectively, cross-sell the company's products, and create offers tailored to specific customer requirements. For example, Caesars Entertainment, the world's largest casino operator, maintains a vast customer database and uses its CRM system to manage day-to-day relationships with important customers at its 52 casino properties around the world (see Marketing at Work 4.2).

MARKETING AT WORK 4.2

Caesars Entertainment: Hitting the CRM Jackpot

Caesars Entertainment consists of a huge network of 52 casino resorts in seven countries, operating under well-known brands such as Caesars, Harrah's, Bally's, Paris, Flamingo, and Horseshoe. Each resort is a complex mix of gaming casinos, hotels, restaurants, shops, theaters, and other entertainment venues. "Our business has grown to encapsulate so much more than gaming," says Caesars Entertainment chairman and CEO Gary Loveman. "Every single one of our . . . resorts across the country provides a 360-degree entertainment experience."

What is it that holds this massive conglomeration of resorts together? Anyone at Caesars will tell you that it's all about managing customer relationships. When you get right down to it, in physical terms, most casinos are pretty much alike. Most customers can't distinguish one company's slot machines, game tables, restaurants, shows, and hotel rooms from another's. What sets Caesars apart is the way it relates to its customers and creates customer loyalty. During the past decade and a half, Caesars has become the model for CRM excellence.

At the heart of Caesars' CRM strategy is its pioneering card-based Total Rewards program, the gaming industry's first and by far most successful loyalty program. Total Rewards members receive points based on the amount they spend at Caesars facilities, whether through gaming, dining, a hotel stay, or any other type of entertainment spending. They can then redeem the points for a variety of perks, such as free play, food, merchandise, rooms, spa sessions, golfing, and show tickets. Total Rewards forms the basis for a two-part CRM process. First, the company uses the program to collect information about the types and amounts of activities that customers choose most often. Then, it mines this information to identify the best offerings for each customer's specific preferences, with an emphasis on the VIP guests who contribute most to the business.

Caesars maintains a vast database—more than 45 million members in all. Every time a member swipes a Total Rewards card to buy a meal, see a show, check into a hotel, or play at one of Caesars' 55,000 slot machines or 2,500 game tables, the data zips off into Caesars' bulging database. Once gathered, Caesars mines this information deeply to gain important customer insights into the characteristics and behavior of individual customers—who they are, how often they visit, how long they stay, and what forms of entertainment they enjoy most.

From its Total Rewards data, Caesars has learned that its best customers aren't always the "high rollers" that have long been the focus of the industry. Rather, they are often ordinary folks from all walks of life—middle-aged and retired teachers, bankers, and doctors who have discretionary income and time. More often than not, these customers visit casinos for an evening, rather than staying overnight at the hotel, and they are more likely to play at the slots than at tables. What motivates them? For many, it's the intense anticipation and excitement of gambling itself. For others, it's another form of entertainment, whether dining or shopping or golf or shows.

Using such insights, Caesars focuses its marketing and service development strategies on the needs of its best customers. For example, the company's advertising reflects the feeling of exuberance that target customers seek. The data insights also help Caesars do a better job of managing day-to-day customer relationships. After a day's gaming, by the next morning, it knows which customers should be rewarded with free show tickets, dinner vouchers, or room upgrades.

In fact, the sophisticated Total Rewards system now analyzes customer information in real time, from the moment customers swipe their rewards cards, creating the ideal link between data and the customer experience. Based on up-to-the-minute customer information, the clerk at a Caesars hotel can see a customer's history and determine whether that customer should get a room upgrade, based on hotel booking levels at that time and on the customer's past level of play. Or casino staff might

Caesars Entertainment maintains a vast customer database and uses its Total Rewards CRM program to manage day-to-day relationships with important customers at its casino properties around the world.

Courtesy of Caesars Entertainment Corporation. Used with permission.

walk up to regular customers as they are playing and offer them a free meal, $25 to play more slots, or maybe just wish them a happy birthday.

But Caesars doesn't just wait for customers to walk through its doors. It uses the insights gained from the Total Rewards system to craft personalized offers and promotions. For example, a good customer might receive as many as 150 pieces of direct mail from Caesars in a given year. That might sound like a junk-mail nightmare, but most Total Rewards members actually like it. Each personalized mailing delivers relevant information and rewards.

Taking its successful loyalty program a step further, Caesars recently expanded the Total Rewards network to include more than 500 online retailers such as Apple, Target, Best Buy, and Banana Republic, as well as travel partners such as Norwegian Cruise Lines and Hawaiian Airlines. Members who opt in can now earn Total Rewards points through these partner companies and redeem points there as well. And every time Total Rewards members do business with one of the partner companies, the Caesars database gets to know them even better.

Caesars' CRM efforts have paid off like a royal flush. The company has found that happy customers are much more loyal, and Caesars' Total Rewards customers appear to be a happier bunch today than ever before. Customer satisfaction scores reached an all-time high last year. Compared with nonmembers, Total Rewards members visit the company's casinos more frequently, stay longer, and spend a greater share of gaming and entertainment dollars in Caesars than in rival casinos. In fact, nearly two-thirds of Total Rewards members report that Total Rewards is their preferred loyalty program in the industry. Since setting up Total Rewards almost fifteen years ago, Caesars has seen its share of customers' average annual casino entertainment budgets rise 20 percent.

Caesars refers to Total Rewards as "the vertebrae of our business," claiming that 85 percent of its revenue is generated in some way by the program. CEO Loveman says that Caesars' CRM efforts are "constantly bringing us closer to our customers so we better understand their preferences, and from that understanding we are able to improve the entertainment experiences we offer." Another Caesars executive puts it even more simply: "It's no different from what a good retailer or grocery store does. We're trying to figure out which products sell, and we're trying to increase our customer loyalty." During a time when a weak economy and reduced consumer spending have wreaked havoc on Caesars and the gaming industry as a whole, the Total Rewards CRM program has emerged as Caesars' ace in the hole. Through smart CRM investments, Caesars has hit the customer-loyalty jackpot.

Sources: Howard Stutz, "Caesars Expands Total Rewards Program," *Las Vegas Review-Journal*, March 1, 2012; "Caesars Entertainment's 'Escape To Total Rewards' Concludes Its Multi-Million Dollar Campaign with Blowout Grand Finale Weekend," *PRNewswire,* May 18, 2012; "Caesar's Loveman: Customization Trumps Commoditization," *Hotel Management,* August 2012, p. 107; and www.caesars.com, and www.totalrewards.com, accessed October 2013.

CRM benefits don't come without costs or risk, either in collecting the original customer data or in maintaining and mining it. The most common CRM mistake is to view CRM as a technology and software process only. Yet technology alone cannot build profitable customer relationships. Companies can't improve customer relationships by simply installing some new software. Instead, marketers should start with the fundamentals of managing customer relationships and *then* employ high-tech solutions. They should focus first on the R—it's the *relationship* that CRM is all about.

Distributing and Using Marketing Information

Marketing information has no value until it is used to gain customer insights and make better marketing decisions. Thus, the marketing information system must make the information readily available to managers and others who need it, when they need it. In some cases, this means providing managers with regular performance reports, intelligence updates, and reports on the results of research studies.

But marketing managers may also need nonroutine information for special situations and on-the-spot decisions. For example, a sales manager having trouble with a large customer may want a summary of the account's sales and profitability over the past year. Or a brand manager may want to get a sense of the amount of the social media buzz surrounding the launch of a recent advertising campaign. These days, therefore, information distribution involves making information available in a timely, user-friendly way.

Many firms use company *intranet* and internal CRM systems to facilitate this process. These systems provide ready access to research and intelligence information, customer contact information, reports, shared work documents, and more. For example, the CRM system at phone and online gift retailer 1-800-Flowers.com gives customer-facing employees real-time access to customer information. When a repeat customer calls, the system immediately pulls up data on previous transactions and other contacts, helping reps make the customer's experience easier and more relevant. For instance, if a customer usually buys

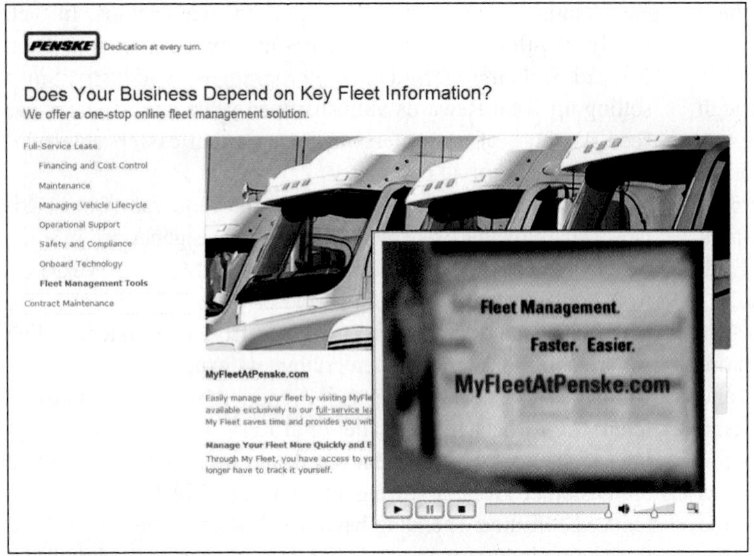

>> Extranets: Penske Truck Leasing's extranet site, MyFleetAtPenske.com, lets Penske customers access all of the data about their fleets in one spot and provides tools to help fleet managers manage their Penske accounts and maximize efficiency.

Penske Truck Leasing.

tulips for his wife, the rep can talk about the best tulip selections and related gifts. Such connections result in greater customer satisfaction and loyalty and greater sales for the company. "We can do it in real time," says a 1-800-Flowers.com executive, "and it enhances the customer experience."[26]

In addition, companies are increasingly allowing key customers and value-network members to access account, product, and other data on demand through *extranets*. Suppliers, customers, resellers, and select other network members may access a company's extranet to update their accounts, arrange purchases, and check orders against inventories to improve customer service. >> For example, Penske Truck Leasing's extranet site, MyFleetAtPenske.com, lets Penske business customers access all the data about their fleets in one spot and provides an array of tools and applications designed to help fleet managers manage their Penske accounts and maximize efficiency.[27]

Thanks to modern technology, today's marketing managers can gain direct access to a company's information system at any time and from virtually anywhere. They can tap into the system from a home office, hotel room, or the local Starbucks—anyplace they can connect on a laptop, tablet, or smartphone. Such systems allow managers to get the information they need directly and quickly and tailor it to their own needs.

SPEED BUMP LINKING THE CONCEPTS

Let's stop here, think back, and be certain that you've got the "big picture" concerning marketing information systems.

- What's the overall goal of an MIS? How are the individual components linked and what does each contribute? Take another look at Figure 4.1—it provides a good organizing framework for the entire chapter.
- Apply the MIS framework to Converse (a Nike company). How might Converse go about assessing marketing managers' information needs, developing the needed information, and helping managers to analyze and use the information to gain actionable customer and market insights?

Author Comment
We finish this chapter by examining three special marketing information topics.

Other Marketing Information Considerations

This section discusses marketing information in two special contexts: marketing research in small businesses and nonprofit organizations and international marketing research. Then, we look at public policy and ethics issues in marketing research.

Marketing Research in Small Businesses and Nonprofit Organizations

Just like larger firms, small organizations need market information and the customer insights that it can provide. Managers of small businesses and not-for-profit organizations often think that marketing research can be done only by experts in large companies with big research budgets. True, large-scale research studies are beyond the budgets of most small organizations. However, many of the marketing research techniques discussed in this chapter also can be used by smaller organizations in a less formal manner and at little or no expense. >> Consider how one small-business owner conducted market research on a shoestring before even opening his doors:[28]

>> **Before opening Bibbentuckers dry cleaner, owner Robert Byerly conducted research to gain insights into what customers wanted. First on the list: quality.**

Bibbentuckers.

After a string of bad experiences with his local dry cleaner, Robert Byerley decided to open his own dry-cleaning business. But before jumping in, he conducted plenty of market research. He needed a key customer insight: How would he make his business stand out from the others? To start, Byerley spent an entire week in the library and online, researching the dry-cleaning industry. To get input from potential customers, using a marketing firm, Byerley held focus groups on the store's name, look, and brochure. He also took clothes to the 15 best competing cleaners in town and had focus group members critique their work. Based on his research, he made a list of features for his new business. First on his list: quality. His business would stand behind everything it did. Not on the list: cheap prices. Creating the perfect dry-cleaning establishment simply didn't fit with a discount operation.

With his research complete, Byerley opened Bibbentuckers, a high-end dry cleaner positioned on high-quality service and convenience. It featured a bank-like drive-through area with curbside delivery. A computerized bar code system read customer cleaning preferences and tracked clothes all the way through the cleaning process. Byerley added other differentiators, such as decorative awnings, TV screens, and refreshments (even "candy for the kids and a doggy treat for your best friend"). "I wanted a place . . . that paired five-star service and quality with an establishment that didn't look like a dry cleaner," he says. The market research yielded results. Today, Bibbentuckers is a thriving eight-store operation.

Thus, small businesses and not-for-profit organizations can obtain good marketing insights through observation or informal surveys using small convenience samples. Also, many associations, local media, and government agencies provide special help to small organizations. For example, the U.S. Small Business Administration offers dozens of free publications and a Web site (www.sba.gov) that give advice on topics ranging from starting, financing, and expanding a small business to ordering business cards. Other excellent resources for small businesses include the U.S. Census Bureau (www.census.gov) and the Bureau of Economic Analysis (www.bea.gov). Finally, small businesses can collect a considerable amount of information at very little cost online. They can scour competitor and customer Web sites and use Internet search engines to research specific companies and issues.

In summary, secondary data collection, observation, surveys, and experiments can all be used effectively by small organizations with small budgets. However, although these informal research methods are less complex and less costly, they still must be conducted with care. Managers must think carefully about the objectives of the research, formulate questions in advance, recognize the biases introduced by smaller samples and less skilled researchers, and conduct the research systematically.[29]

International Marketing Research

International marketing research has grown tremendously over the past decade. International researchers follow the same steps as domestic researchers, from defining the research problem and developing a research plan to interpreting and reporting the results. However, these researchers often face more and different problems. Whereas domestic researchers deal with fairly homogeneous markets within a single country, international researchers deal with diverse markets in many different countries. These markets often vary greatly in their levels of economic development, cultures and customs, and buying patterns.

In many foreign markets, the international researcher may have a difficult time finding good secondary data. Whereas U.S. marketing researchers can obtain reliable secondary data from dozens of domestic research services, many countries have almost no research services at all. Some of the largest international research services operate in many countries. » For example, The Nielsen Company (the world's largest marketing research company) has offices in more than 100 countries, from Schaumburg, Illinois, to Hong Kong to Nicosia, Cyprus. However, most research firms operate in only a relative handful of countries.[30] Thus, even when secondary information is available, it usually must be obtained from many different sources on a country-by-country basis, making the information difficult to combine or compare.

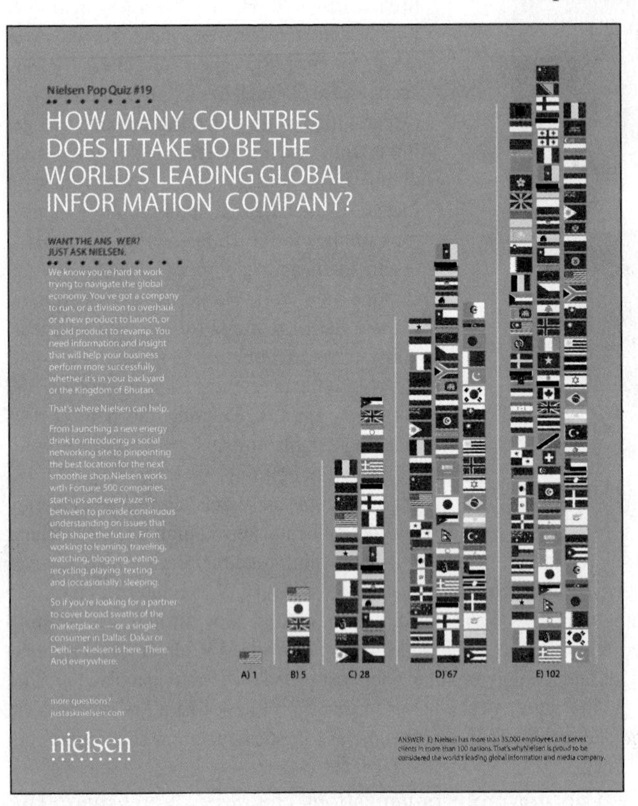

» **Some of the most successful research services firms have large international departments. Nielsen has offices in more than 100 countries.**

Because of the scarcity of good secondary data, international researchers often must collect their own primary data. However, obtaining primary data may be no easy task. For example, it can be difficult simply to develop good samples. U.S. researchers can use current telephone directories, e-mail lists, census tract data, and any of several sources of socioeconomic data to construct samples. However, such information is largely lacking in many countries.

Once the sample is drawn, the U.S. researcher usually can reach most respondents easily by telephone, by mail, online, or in person. However, reaching respondents is often not so easy in other parts of the world. Researchers in Mexico cannot rely on telephone, Internet, and mail data collection—most data collection is conducted door to door and concentrated in three or four of the largest cities. In some countries, few people have computers, let alone Internet access. For example, whereas there are 79 Internet users per 100 people in the United States, there are only 36 Internet users per 100 people in Mexico. In Madagascar, the number drops to 2 Internet users per 100 people. In some countries, the postal system is notoriously unreliable. In Brazil, for instance, an estimated 30 percent of the mail is never delivered; in Russia, mail delivery can take several weeks. In many developing countries, poor roads and transportation systems make certain areas hard to reach, making personal interviews difficult and expensive.[31]

Cultural differences from country to country cause additional problems for international researchers. Language is the most obvious obstacle. For example, questionnaires must be prepared in one language and then translated into the languages of each country researched. Responses then must be translated back into the original language for analysis and interpretation. This adds to research costs and increases the risks of error. Even within a given country, language can be a problem. For example, in India, English is the language of business, but consumers may use any of 14 "first languages," with many additional dialects.

Translating a questionnaire from one language to another is anything but easy. Many idioms, phrases, and statements mean different things in different cultures. For example, a Danish executive noted, "Check this out by having a different translator put back into English what you've translated from English. You'll get the shock of your life. I remember [an example in which] 'out of sight, out of mind' had become 'invisible things are insane.'"[32]

Consumers in different countries also vary in their attitudes toward marketing research. People in one country may be very willing to respond; in other countries, nonresponse can be a major problem. Customs in some countries may prohibit people from talking with strangers. In certain cultures, research questions often are considered too personal. For example, in many Muslim countries, mixed-gender focus groups are taboo, as is videotaping female-only focus groups. Even when respondents are *willing* to respond, they may not be *able* to because of high functional illiteracy rates.

Despite these problems, as global marketing grows, global companies have little choice but to conduct these types of international marketing research. Although the costs and problems associated with international research may be high, the costs of not doing it—in terms of missed opportunities and mistakes—might be even higher. Once recognized, many of the problems associated with international marketing research can be overcome or avoided.

Public Policy and Ethics in Marketing Research

Most marketing research benefits both the sponsoring company and its consumers. Through marketing research, companies gain insights into consumers' needs, resulting in more satisfying products and services and stronger customer relationships. However, the misuse of marketing research can also harm or annoy consumers. Two major public policy and ethics issues in marketing research are intrusions on consumer privacy and the misuse of research findings.

Intrusions on Consumer Privacy

Many consumers feel positive about marketing research and believe that it serves a useful purpose. Some actually enjoy being interviewed and giving their opinions. However, others strongly resent or even mistrust marketing research. They don't like being interrupted by researchers. They worry that marketers are building huge databases full of personal information about customers. Or they fear that researchers might use sophisticated techniques to probe our deepest feelings, peek over our shoulders as we shop, or track us as we browse and interact on the Internet and then use this knowledge to manipulate our buying.

There are no easy answers when it comes to marketing research and privacy. For example, is it a good or bad thing that marketers track and analyze consumers' online clicks and target ads to individuals based on their browsing and social networking behavior? Should we worry when marketers track consumer locations via their mobile phones to issue location-based ads and offers? Should we care that some retailers use mannequins with cameras hidden in one eye to record customer demographics and shopping behavior? Similarly, should we applaud or resent companies that monitor consumer discussions on YouTube, Facebook, Twitter, or other social media in an effort to be more responsive?[33]

For example, Dunkin' Donuts regularly eavesdrops on consumer online conversations as an important input to its customer relationship–building efforts. Take the case of customer Jeff Lerner, who recently tweeted about a loose lid that popped off his Dunkin' Donuts drive-through coffee and soaked his white shirt and new car. Within minutes, Dunkin' picked up Lerner's tweet, sent him a direct message asking for his phone number, called him to apologize, and sent him a $10 gift card. Lerner found Dunkin's actions laudable. "*This* is social media. This is listening. This is engagement," he stated in a later blog post. However, some disconcerted consumers might see Dunkin's Twitter monitoring as an invasion of their privacy.[34]

Increasing consumer privacy concerns have become a major problem for the marketing research industry. Companies face the challenge of unearthing valuable but potentially sensitive consumer data while also maintaining consumer trust. At the same time, consumers wrestle with the trade-offs between personalization and privacy. "The debate over online [privacy] stems from a marketing paradox," says a privacy expert. "Internet shoppers want to receive personalized, timely offers based on their wants and needs but they resent that companies track their online purchase and browsing histories."[35] The key question: When does a company cross the line in gathering and using customer data? A recent study shows that nearly half of U.S. adults worry that they have little or no control over the personal information that companies gather about them online.[36]

Failure to address privacy issues could result in angry, less cooperative consumers and increased government intervention. As a result, the marketing research industry is considering several options for responding to intrusion and privacy issues. One example is the Marketing Research Association's "Your Opinion Counts" and "Respondent Bill of Rights" initiatives to educate consumers about the benefits of marketing research and distinguish it from telephone selling and database building. The industry also has considered adopting broad standards, perhaps based on the International Chamber of Commerce's International Code of Marketing and Social Research Practice. This code outlines researchers' responsibilities to respondents and the general public. For example, it urges that researchers make their names and addresses available to participants and be open about the data they are collecting.[37]

Most major companies—including Facebook, Microsoft, IBM, Citigroup, American Express, and even the U.S. government—have now appointed a chief privacy officer (CPO), whose job is to safeguard the privacy of consumers who do business with the company. In the end, however, if researchers provide value in exchange for information, customers will gladly provide it. For example, Amazon.com's customers do not mind if the firm builds a database of products they buy as a way to provide future product recommendations. This saves time and provides value. The best approach is for researchers to ask only for the information they need, use it responsibly to provide customer value, and avoid sharing information without the customer's permission.

Misuse of Research Findings

Research studies can be powerful persuasion tools; companies often use study results as claims in their advertising and promotion. Today, however, many research studies appear to be little more than vehicles for pitching the sponsor's products. In fact, in some cases, research surveys appear to have been designed just to produce the intended effect. For example, a Black Flag survey once asked: "A roach disk . . . poisons a roach slowly. The dying roach returns to the nest and after it dies is eaten by other roaches. In turn these roaches become poisoned and die. How effective do you think this type of product would be in killing roaches?" Not surprisingly, 79 percent said effective.

However, few advertisers openly rig their research designs or blatantly misrepresent the findings—most abuses tend to be more subtle "stretches." Or disputes arise over the validity and use of research findings. >> Consider this example:

>> **Use of research findings: The FTC recently ruled against POM Wonderful's research-based advertising claims that the brand could improve a user's health. POM is appealing the ruling.**

Christopher Schall/Impact Photo.

> The FTC recently charged POM Wonderful—the pomegranate juice sold in the distinctive curvy bottle—and its parent company with making false and unsubstantiated health claims in its advertising. The disputed ads suggest that POM Wonderful Pomegranate Juice can prevent or treat heart disease, prostate cancer, and even erectile dysfunction. For instance, one ad boasted that POM has "Super Health Powers!" while another proclaimed "I'm off to save prostates!" POM has stood behind its ad claims, asserting that they are backed by $35 million worth of company research showing that antioxidant-rich pomegranate products are good for you. The brand even retaliated during two years of legal wrangling with ads disputing the FTC and its allegations. But the FTC isn't buying the research behind POM's claims—it recently issued a final ruling ordering the brand to refrain from making claims that its products could improve a user's health unless backed by more stringent research. "When a company touts scientific research in its advertising, the research must squarely support the claims made," says the agency. "Contrary to POM Wonderful's advertising, the available scientific information does not prove that POM Juice . . . effectively treats or prevents these illnesses." POM Wonderful is currently appealing the FTC ruling.[38]

Recognizing that surveys can be abused, several associations—including the American Marketing Association, the Marketing Research Association, and the Council of American Survey Research Organizations (CASRO)—have developed codes of research ethics and standards of conduct. For example, the CASRO Code of Standards and Ethics for Survey Research outlines researcher responsibilities to respondents, including confidentiality, privacy, and avoidance of harassment. It also outlines major responsibilities in reporting results to clients and the public.[39]

In the end, however, unethical or inappropriate actions cannot simply be regulated away. Each company must accept responsibility for policing the conduct and reporting of its own marketing research to protect consumers' best interests and its own.

MyMarketingLab

Go to **mymktlab.com** to complete the problems marked with this icon .

END OF CHAPTER REVIEWING THE CONCEPTS

CHAPTER REVIEW AND KEY TERMS

Objectives Review

To create value for customers and build meaningful relationships with them, marketers must first gain fresh, deep insights into what customers need and want. Such insights come from good marketing information. As a result of the recent explosion of marketing technology, companies can now obtain great quantities of information, sometimes even too much. The challenge is to transform today's vast volume of consumer information into actionable customer and market insights.

OBJECTIVE 1 Explain the importance of information in gaining insights about the marketplace and customers. (pp 98–100)

The marketing process starts with a complete understanding of the marketplace and consumer needs and wants. Thus, the company needs sound information to produce superior value and satisfaction for its customers. The company also requires information on competitors, resellers, and other actors and forces in the marketplace. Increasingly, marketers are viewing information not only as an input for making better decisions but also as an important strategic asset and marketing tool.

OBJECTIVE 2 Define the marketing information system and discuss its parts. (pp 100–103)

The *marketing information system* (*MIS*) consists of people and procedures for assessing information needs, developing the needed information, and helping decision makers use the information to generate and validate actionable customer and market insights. A well-designed information system begins and ends with users.

The MIS first *assesses information needs*. The MIS primarily serves the company's marketing and other managers, but it may also provide information to external partners. Then the MIS *develops information* from internal databases, marketing intelligence activities, and marketing research. *Internal databases* provide information on the company's own operations and departments. Such data can be obtained quickly and cheaply but often need to be adapted for marketing decisions. *Marketing intelligence* activities supply everyday information about developments in the external marketing environment. *Market research* consists of collecting information relevant to a specific marketing problem faced by the company. Last, the MIS helps users analyze and use the information to develop customer insights, make marketing decisions, and manage customer relationships.

OBJECTIVE 3 Outline the steps in the marketing research process. (pp 103–116)

The first step in the marketing research process involves *defining the problem and setting the research objectives*, which may be exploratory, descriptive, or causal research. The second step consists of *developing a research plan* for collecting data from primary and secondary sources. The third step calls for *implementing the marketing research plan* by gathering, processing, and analyzing the information. The fourth step consists of *interpreting and reporting the findings*. Additional information analysis helps marketing managers apply the information and provides them with sophisticated statistical procedures and models from which to develop more rigorous findings.

Both *internal* and *external* secondary data sources often provide information more quickly and at a lower cost than primary data sources, and they can sometimes yield information that a company cannot collect by itself. However, needed information might not exist in secondary sources. Researchers must also evaluate secondary information to ensure that it is *relevant*, *accurate*, *current*, and *impartial*.

Primary research must also be evaluated for these features. Each primary data collection method—*observational*, *survey*, and *experimental*—has its own advantages and disadvantages. Similarly, each of the various research contact methods—mail, telephone, personal interview, and online—has its own advantages and drawbacks.

OBJECTIVE 4 Explain how companies analyze and use marketing information. (pp 116–120)

Information gathered in internal databases and through marketing intelligence and marketing research usually requires more analysis. To analyze individual customer data, many companies have now acquired or developed special software and analysis techniques—called *customer relationship management (CRM)*—that integrate, analyze, and apply the mountains of individual customer data contained in their databases.

Marketing information has no value until it is used to make better marketing decisions. Thus, the MIS must make the information available to managers and others who make marketing decisions or deal with customers. In some cases, this means providing regular reports and updates; in other cases, it means making nonroutine information available for special situations and on-the-spot decisions. Many firms use company intranets and extranets to facilitate this process. Thanks to modern technology, today's marketing managers can gain direct access to marketing information at any time and from virtually any location.

OBJECTIVE 5 Discuss the special issues some marketing researchers face, including public policy and ethics issues. (pp 120–124)

Some marketers face special marketing research situations, such as those conducting research in small business, not-for-profit, or international situations. Marketing research can be conducted effectively by small businesses and nonprofit organizations with limited budgets. International marketing researchers follow the same steps as domestic researchers but often face more and different problems. All organizations need to act responsibly concerning major public policy and ethical issues surrounding marketing research, including issues of intrusions on consumer privacy and misuse of research findings.

Key Terms

Objective 1
Customer insights (p 99)
Marketing information system (MIS) (p 99)

Objective 2
Internal databases (p 100)
Competitive marketing intelligence (p 101)

Objective 3
Marketing research (p 103)
Exploratory research (p 104)
Descriptive research (p 104)
Causal research (p 104)
Secondary data (p 105)
Primary data (p 105)
Observational research (p 106)
Ethnographic research (p 106)
Survey research (p 107)
Experimental research (p 108)
Focus group interviewing (p 109)
Online marketing research (p 110)
Online focus groups (p 111)
Behavioral targeting (p 113)
Sample (p 114)

Objective 4
Customer relationship management (CRM) (p 117)

DISCUSSION AND CRITICAL THINKING

Discussion Questions

4-1. What is a marketing information system, and how is it used to create customer insights? (AACSB: Written and Oral Communication)

4-2. Explain how marketing intelligence differs from marketing research. (AACSB: Written and Oral Communication)

4-3. What is ethnographic research, and how is it conducted online? (AACSB: Written and Oral Communication)

4-4. How are marketers using customer relationship management (CRM) to reveal customer insights from the vast amounts of data gathered? (AACSB: Written and Oral Communication)

4-5. What is neuromarketing, and how is it useful in marketing research? Why is this research approach usually combined with other approaches? (AACSB: Written and Oral Communication)

4-6. What are the similarities and differences when conducting research in another country versus the domestic market? (AACSB: Written and Oral Communication)

Critical Thinking Exercises

4-7. In a small group, identify a problem faced by a local business or charitable organization and propose a research project addressing that problem. Develop a research proposal that implements each step of the marketing research process. Discuss how the research results will help the business or organization. (AACSB: Written and Oral Communication; Reflective Thinking)

4-8. Focus groups are commonly used during exploratory research. A focus group interview entails gathering a group of people to discuss a specific topic. In a small group, research how to conduct a focus group interview and then conduct one with 6 to 10 other students to learn what services your university could offer to better meet student needs. Assign one person in your group to be the moderator while the others observe and interpret the responses from the focus group participants. Present a report of what you learned from this research. (AACSB: Written and Oral Communication; Reflective Thinking)

4-9. Search "social media monitoring" on a search engine to find companies that specialize in monitoring social media. Discuss two of these companies. Next, find two more sites that allow free monitoring and describe how marketers can use these to monitor their brands. Write a brief report on your findings. (AACSB: Written and Oral Communication; Information Technology; Reflective Thinking)

MINICASES AND APPLICATIONS

Online, Mobile, and Social Media Marketing You Are What You Like

Marketers have always been interested in buyers' personality traits and how they influence behaviors, but it is difficult to measure personality. Until now, that is. Online, mobile, and social media technologies are now providing researchers with new tools to predict someone's personality traits and lifestyle activities. Microsoft and researchers from the University of Cambridge analyzed over 58,000 Facebook users' "Likes" and developed an algorithm that matched them with demographic information and personality profiles. The resulting personality profiles determined, with over 80 percent accuracy, factors such as users' gender, ethnicity, religion, sexual orientation, alcohol and drug use, and even whether their parents had separated before they turned 21 years old. Researchers even predicted IQ and found that users with higher IQs like curly fries and those with lower IQs like Harley-Davidson. All that and more can be predicted just from users' "Like"-clicking behavior on Web sites, social media, and mobile apps. This research gives marketers another tool that will help them customize their offerings and communications with greater accuracy.

4-10. Visit www.youarewhatyoulike.com to see what your "Likes" say about you. You will have to log on to Facebook to see the results. What characteristics are shown? Does the profile describe you accurately? (AACSB: Written and Oral Communication; Information Technology)

Marketing Ethics Research Ethics

As the Pepsi, P&G, and Lexus examples in the chapter illustrate, companies are increasingly using qualitative research methods such as observation, ethnography, and in-depth interviews to gain customer insights. However, qualitative research brings up ethical issues. Unlike quantitative data collection methods that use surveys or mechanical means, qualitative research puts researchers in close physical proximity to consumers—even in their homes—where the researchers may see or hear private and confidential things. Most research extends confidentiality to research subjects so they will be open in responding to questions, but what if a researcher learns something troublesome? For example, marketing research is advancing into more sensitive consumer behaviors related to product abuse and deviant behaviors, and consumers may reveal harmful or illegal behavior to the researcher. Alternatively, like all experiments, marketing research experiments, such as a researcher pretending to shoplift in a store to observe other customers' reactions, necessarily involve some type of deception. Such experiments can be conducted without customer knowledge, or customers may even be induced to participate in the deception. They may be told later and feel uncomfortable with their actions. These are just a few of the ethical issues related to qualitative marketing research.

4-11. What should marketing researchers do in situations such as those described? Visit www.iccindiaonline.org/policy_state/esomar.pdf and discuss whether the International Code of Marketing and Social Research Practice provides guidance in dealing with such issues. (AACSB: Written and Oral Communication; Ethical Understanding and Reasoning)

Marketing by the Numbers A Big Enough Sample?

Have you ever been disappointed when a television network cancelled one of your favorite television shows because of "low ratings"? The network didn't ask your opinion, did it? It probably didn't ask any of your friends, either. That's because estimates of television audience sizes are based on research done by The Nielsen Company, which uses a sample of only 9,000 households out of the more than 113 million households in the United States to determine national ratings for television programs. That doesn't seem like enough. But as it turns out, statistically, it's many more than enough.

4-12. Go to www.surveysystem.com/sscalc.htm to determine the appropriate sample size for a population of 113 million households. Briefly explain what is meant by *confidence interval* and *confidence level*. Assuming a confidence interval of 5, how large should the sample of households be when desiring a 95 percent confidence level? How large for a 99 percent confidence level? (AACSB: Written and Oral Communication; Information Technology; Analytical Thinking)

4-13. What sample sizes are necessary at population sizes of 1 billion, 10,000, and 100 with a confidence interval of 5 and a 95 percent confidence level? Explain the effect population size has on required sample size. (AACSB: Written and Oral Communication; Information Technology; Analytical Thinking)

Video Case Domino's

As a delivery company, no one delivers better than Domino's. Its reputation for hot pizza in 30 minutes or less is ingrained in customers' minds. But not long ago, Domino's began hearing its customers talking about how its pizza was horrible. As a company that has long focused on solid marketing intelligence to make decisions, Domino's went to work on how it could change consumer perceptions about its pizza.

Through marketing research techniques, Domino's soon realized that it had to take a very risky step and completely re-create the pizza that it had been selling for over 40 years. This video illustrates how research not only enabled Domino's to come up with a winning recipe, but led to a successful promotional campaign that has made fans of Domino's pizza in addition to its delivery service.

After viewing the video featuring Domino's, answer the following questions:

4-14. Explain the role that marketing research played in the creation and launch of Domino's new pizza.

4-15. Are there more effective ways that Domino's could have gone about its research process?

4-16. Why did it take so long for Domino's to realize that customers didn't like its pizza? Was it an accident that it made this realization?

Company Cases 4 Oracle/ 14 Pinterest

See Appendix 1 for cases appropriate for this chapter. **Case 4, Oracle: Getting a Grip on Big Data.** As technology allows for the gathering of more and more consumer data, Oracle is on the front line, helping companies harness Big Data as a means of forming stronger relationships with customers. **Case 14, Pinterest: Revolutionizing the Web—Again.** Pinterest has revolutionized Web design, and is influencing consumer purchase decisions in the process.

MyMarketingLab

Go to **mymktlab.com** for Auto-graded writing questions as well as the following Assisted-graded writing questions:

4-17. Describe an example in which marketing research could cause harm to participants. Many companies have a review process similar to that required for government-funded research to ensure research participant safety, with most following the government's "Common Rule." Write a brief report explaining this rule and how you would apply it your example. (AACSB: Written and Oral Communication; Reflective Thinking)

4-18. Critics claim that research activities such as this infringe on consumer privacy rights. Should marketers have access to such information? Discuss the advantages and disadvantages of such research for both marketers and consumers. (AACSB: Written and Oral Communication; Ethical Understanding and Reasoning)

4-19. Mymktlab Only—comprehensive writing assignment for this chapter.

5 Understanding Consumer and Business Buyer Behavior

CHAPTER ROAD MAP

Objective Outline

OBJECTIVE 1 Understand the consumer market and the major factors that influence consumer buyer behavior. Consumer Markets and Consumer Buyer Behavior 132; Model of Consumer Behavior 133; Characteristics Affecting Consumer Behavior 133–147

OBJECTIVE 2 Identify and discuss the stages in the buyer decision process. The Buyer Decision Process 147–149

OBJECTIVE 3 Describe the adoption and diffusion process for new products. The Buyer Decision Process for New Products 149–152

OBJECTIVE 4 Define the business market and identify the major factors that influence business buyer behavior. Business Markets and Business Buyer Behavior 152; Business Markets 152–154; Business Buyer Behavior 154–157

OBJECTIVE 5 List and define the steps in the business buying decision process. The Business Buying Process 157–159; E-Procurement and Online Purchasing 159–162

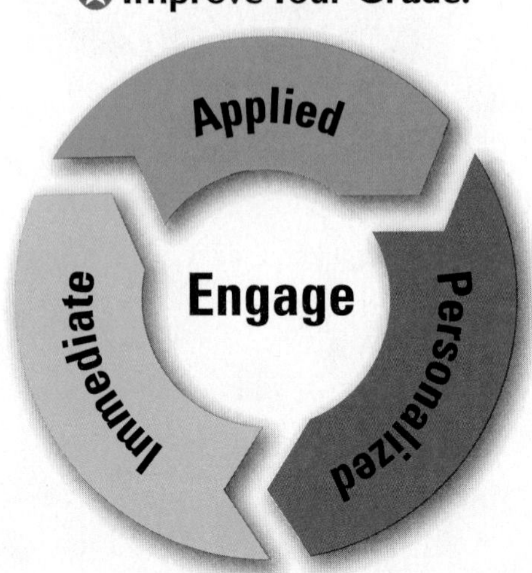

Previewing the Concepts

You've studied how marketers obtain, analyze, and use information to develop customer insights and assess marketing programs. In this chapter, we take a closer look at the most important element of the marketplace—customers. The aim of marketing is to affect how customers think and act. To affect the *whats*, *whens*, and *hows* of buyer behavior, marketers must first understand the *whys*. We first look at *final consumer* buying influences and processes and then at the buyer behavior of *business customers*. You'll see that understanding buyer behavior is an essential but very difficult task.

To get a better sense of the importance of understanding consumer behavior, we begin by looking at GoPro. You may never have heard of GoPro, the small but fast-growing company that makes tiny, wearable HD video cameras. Yet few brands can match the avid enthusiasm and intense loyalty that GoPro has created in the hearts and minds of its customers. GoPro knows that, deep down, it offers customers much more than just durable little video cameras. More than that, it gives them a way to share action-charged moments and emotions with friends.

---

*Over 10 million students improved their results using the Pearson MyLabs. Visit **mymktlab.com** for simulations, tutorials, and end-of-chapter problems.

» GoPro's amazing little cameras let even the rankest video amateurs take stunning videos, giving them a way to celebrate the action-charged moments and emotions of their lives with others.

GoPro.

First Stop

GoPro: Be a HERO!

A growing army of GoPro customers—many of them extreme sports enthusiasts—are now strapping amazing little GoPro cameras to their bodies, or mounting them on anything from the front bumpers of race cars to the heels of skydiving boots, in order to capture the extreme moments of their lives and lifestyles. Then, they can't wait to share those emotion-packed GoPro moments with friends. In fact, the chances are good that you've seen many GoPro-created videos on YouTube or Facebook, or even on TV.

Maybe it's the one shot by the skier who sets off an avalanche in the Swiss Alps and escapes by parachuting off a cliff—that amateur video received 2.6 million YouTube views in nine months. Or maybe you saw the one where a seagull picks up a tourist's camera and makes off with it, capturing a bird's-eye view of a castle in Cannes, France (3 million views in seven months). Or what about the video of the mountain biker in Africa who is ambushed by a full-grown gazelle (more than 13 million views in four months)? A recent promotional video featuring five minutes of clips videos captured by fans with the latest GoPro model snared more than 16 million YouTube videos in only three months.

GoPro's avid customers have become evangelists for the brand. On average, they upload a new video to YouTube every two minutes. In turn, the videos inspire new GoPro customers and even more video sharing. As a result, GoPro is growing explosively. Last year, the young company sold a cool 1 million cameras, generating revenues of $600 million—a seven-fold increase in the past two years—and an estimated 90 percent share of the wearable-camera market.

What makes GoPro so successful? Part of the formula is the cameras themselves: GoPro cameras are marvels of modern technology, especially given their affordable starting price of only $200 to $400. Only about 2 inches wide, a GoPro HD video camera looks like little more than a small gray box. But the lightweight, wearable or mountable GoPro is extremely versatile, and it packs amazing power for capturing stunning HD-quality video. A removable housing makes GoPro cameras waterproof to depths of 180 feet. And GoPro cameras are drop-proof from 3,000 feet (so claims one skydiver).

GoPro's runaway success comes from a deep-down understanding of what makes its customers tick. More than just selling tiny, wearable HD video cameras, GoPro helps people capture, share, and celebrate with others the most meaningful experiences in their lives.

But GoPro knows that consumer behavior is driven by much more than just high-quality products with innovative features. The brand is all about what its cameras let customers *do*. GoPro users don't just want to take videos. More than that, they want to tell the stories and share the adrenalin-pumped emotions of the extreme moments in their lifestyles. "Enabling you to share your life through incredible photos and video is what we do," says GoPro. We "help people capture and share their lives' most meaningful experiences with others—to celebrate them together."

When people view a stunning GoPro video clip—like the one of New Zealand's Jed Mildon landing the first-ever BMX triple backflip captured by his helmet camera—to some degree, they experience what the subject experiences. They feel the passion and adrenaline. And when that happens, GoPro creates an emotional connection between the GoPro storyteller and the audience.

Thus, making good cameras is only the start of GoPro's success. GoPro founder Nick Woodman, himself an extreme sports junkie, talks about helping customers through four essential steps in their storytelling and emotion-sharing journeys: capture, creation, broadcast, and recognition. *Capture* is what the cameras do—shooting pictures and videos. *Creation* is the editing and production process that turns raw footage into compelling videos. *Broadcast* involves distributing the video content to an audience. *Recognition* is the payoff for the content creator. Recognition might come in the form of YouTube views or "Likes" and Shares" on Facebook. More probably, it's the enthusiastic oohs and ahs that their videos evoke from friends and family. The company's slogan sums up pretty well the consumer's deeper motivations: GoPro—Be a HERO.

So far, GoPro has focused primarily on the capture step of the overall customer storytelling experience. GoPro bills itself as the "World's Most Versatile Camera. Wear It. Mount It. Love It." It offers a seemingly endless supply of rigs, mounts, harnesses, straps, and other accessories that make GoPro cameras wearable or mountable just about anywhere. Users can strap the little cameras to their wrists or mount them on helmets. They can attach them to the tip of a snow ski, the bottom of a skateboard, or the underside of an RC helicopter. The handy little GoPro lets even the rankest video amateur capture some pretty incredible footage.

But Woodman knows that to keep growing, GoPro must broaden its offer to address the full range of customer needs and motivations—not just capture, but also creation, broadcast, and recognition. For example, on the creation side, GoPro recently acquired a digital-video software company, CineForm, and now provides free software for creating 3D videos from footage shot by GoPro cameras rigged side-by-side and calibrated to shoot simultaneously. On the broadcast side, GoPro has partnered with YouTube to create a GoPro YouTube network offering a Wi-Fi plug-in that lets GoPro customers upload video directly from their cameras or using a mobile app. GoPro's YouTube channel long ago passed 200 million video views. As for recognition, GoPro now airs TV commercials created from the best videos submitted by customers at its Web site. GoPro's future lies in enabling and integrating the full user experience, from capturing video to sharing stories and life's emotions with others.

GoPro's rich understanding of what makes its customers tick is serving the young company well. Its enthusiastic customers are among the most loyal and engaged of any brand. For example, GoPro's Facebook fan base is more than 4 million and growing fast. To put that in perspective, much larger Canon USA has only 272,000 Facebook followers; Panasonic has 222,000. Beyond uploading nearly half a million videos a year, GoPro fans interact heavily across a broad range of social media. "I think we have the most socially engaged online audience of any consumer brand in the world," claims Woodman.

All that customer engagement and enthusiasm has made GoPro the fastest-growing camera company in the world. Today GoPro cameras are available in more than 30,000 stores in 100 or more countries, from small sports-enthusiast shops to REI, Best Buy, and Amazon .com. GoPro's remarkable little cameras have also spread beyond amateurs. They have become standard equipment for many professional filmmakers—whether it's the Discovery Channel or a news show team filming rescues, wildlife, and storms or the production crew of hit reality-TV shows such as *Deadliest Catch* taking pictures of underwater crab pots or the sides of ships in heavy seas. And GoPro recently teamed with ESPN to capture unprecedented angles and perspectives in its global X Games broadcasts. The use of GoPro equipment by professionals lends credibility that fuels even greater consumer demand.

The moral of this story: Success begins with understanding customer needs and motivations. GoPro knows that it doesn't just make cameras. More than that, it enables customers to share important moments and emotions. According to one industry expert, GoPro understands "how to wrap technology beautifully around human needs so that it matters to people." Says Woodman: "We spent a lot of time recently thinking about, What are we really doing here? We know that our cameras are arguably the most socially networked consumer devices of our time, so it's clear we're not just building hardware." GoPro customers know the truth, he asserts. "A GoPro really is that good for capturing and sharing their lives."[1]

Author Comment

In some ways, consumer and business markets are similar in their buyer behavior. But in many other ways, they differ a lot. We start by digging into consumer buyer behavior. Later in the chapter, we'll tackle business buyer behavior.

The GoPro example shows that factors at many levels affect consumer buying behavior. Buying behavior is never simple, yet understanding it is an essential task of marketing management. First we explore the dynamics of the consumer market and the consumer buyer behavior. We then examine business markets and the business buyer process.

Consumer Markets and Consumer Buyer Behavior

Consumer buyer behavior
The buying behavior of final consumers—individuals and households that buy goods and services for personal consumption.

Consumer market
All the individuals and households that buy or acquire goods and services for personal consumption.

Consumer buyer behavior refers to the buying behavior of final consumers—individuals and households that buy goods and services for personal consumption. All of these final consumers combine to make up the **consumer market**. The American consumer market consists of more than 314 million people who consume more than $15 trillion worth of goods and services each year, making it one of the most attractive consumer markets in the world.[2]

Consumers around the world vary tremendously in age, income, education level, and tastes. They also buy an incredible variety of goods and services. How these diverse consumers relate with each other and with other elements of the world around them impacts their choices among various products, services, and companies. Here we examine the fascinating array of factors that affect consumer behavior.

Author Comment
Despite the simple-looking model in Figure 5.1, understanding the *whys* of buying behavior is very difficult. Says one expert, "the mind is a whirling, swirling, jumbled mass of neurons bouncing around. . . ."

Model of Consumer Behavior

Consumers make many buying decisions every day, and the buying decision is the focal point of the marketer's effort. Most large companies research consumer buying decisions in great detail to answer questions about what consumers buy, where they buy, how and how much they buy, when they buy, and why they buy. Marketers can study actual consumer purchases to find out what they buy, where, and how much. But learning about the *whys* of consumer buying behavior is not so easy—the answers are often locked deep within the consumer's mind. Often, consumers themselves don't know exactly what influences their purchases.

The central question for marketers is this: How do consumers respond to various marketing efforts the company might use? The starting point is the stimulus-response model of buyer behavior shown in **»Figure 5.1**. This figure shows that marketing and other stimuli enter the consumer's "black box" and produce certain responses. Marketers must figure out what is in the buyer's black box.

Marketing stimuli consist of the four Ps: product, price, place, and promotion. Other stimuli include major forces and events in the buyer's environment: economic, technological, social, and cultural. All these inputs enter the buyer's black box, where they are turned into a set of buyer responses—the buyer's brand and company relationship behavior and what he or she buys, when, where, and how much.

Marketers want to understand how the stimuli are changed into responses inside the consumer's black box, which has two parts. First, the buyer's characteristics influence how he or she perceives and reacts to the stimuli. Second, the buyer's decision process itself affects his or her behavior. We look first at buyer characteristics as they affect buyer behavior and then discuss the buyer decision process.

Author Comment
Many levels of factors affect our buying behavior—from broad cultural and social influences to motivations, beliefs, and attitudes lying deep within us. For example, why *did* you buy *that* specific mobile phone you're carrying?

Characteristics Affecting Consumer Behavior

Consumer purchases are influenced strongly by cultural, social, personal, and psychological characteristics, as shown in **»Figure 5.2**. For the most part, marketers cannot control such factors, but they must take them into account.

Cultural Factors

Cultural factors exert a broad and deep influence on consumer behavior. Marketers need to understand the role played by the buyer's *culture*, *subculture*, and *social class*.

Culture
The set of basic values, perceptions, wants, and behaviors learned by a member of society from family and other important institutions.

Culture. **Culture** is the most basic cause of a person's wants and behavior. Human behavior is largely learned. Growing up in a society, a child learns basic values, perceptions, wants, and behaviors from his or her family and other important institutions. A child in the United States normally learns or is exposed to the following values: achievement and success, individualism, freedom, hard work, activity and involvement, efficiency and practicality, material comfort, youthfulness, and fitness and health. Every group or society has a culture, and cultural influences on buying behavior may vary greatly from both county to county and country to country.

Marketers are always trying to spot *cultural shifts* so as to discover new products that might be wanted. For example, the cultural shift toward greater concern about health and

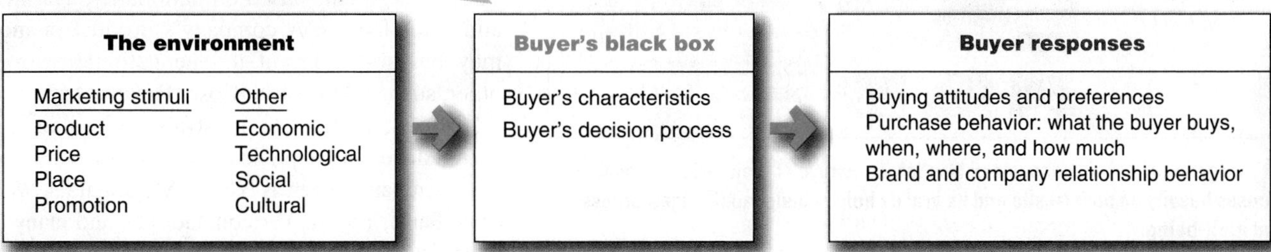
We can measure the whats, wheres, and whens of consumer buying behavior. But it's very difficult to "see" inside the consumer's head and figure out the whys of buying behavior (that's why it's called the black box). Marketers spend a lot of time and dollars trying to figure out what makes customers tick.
The environment
Marketing stimuli
Product
Price
Place
Promotion
Other
Economic
Technological
Social
Cultural
Buyer's black box
Buyer's characteristics
Buyer's decision process
Buyer responses
Buying attitudes and preferences
Purchase behavior: what the buyer buys, when, where, and how much
Brand and company relationship behavior

» Figure 5.1 Model of Buyer Behavior

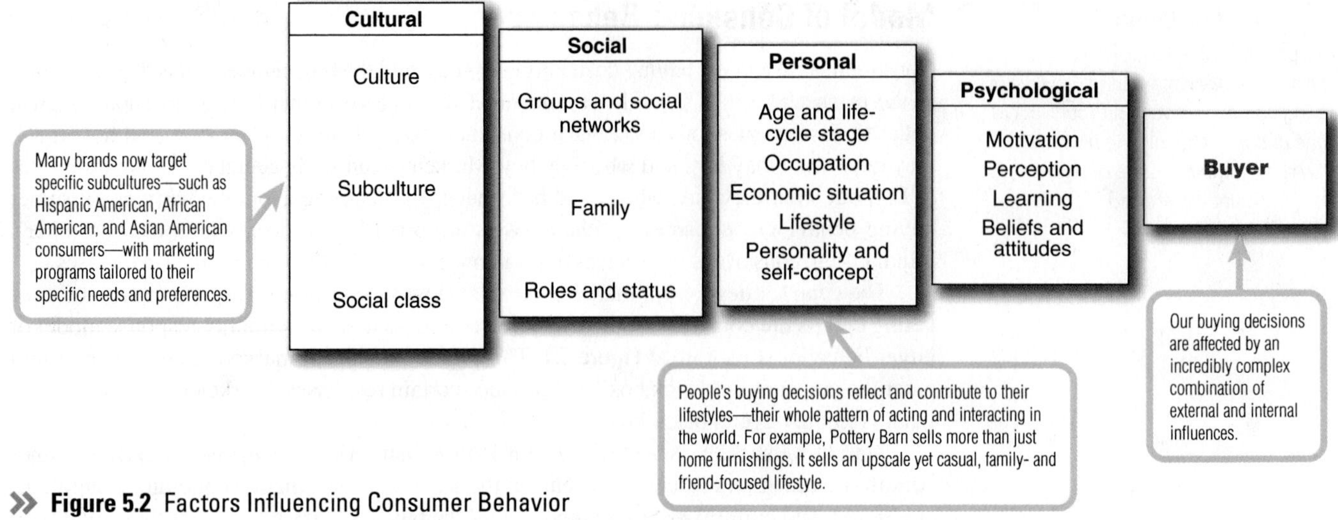

Figure 5.2 Factors Influencing Consumer Behavior

fitness has created a huge industry for health-and-fitness services, exercise equipment and clothing, organic foods, and a variety of diets.

Subculture
A group of people with shared value systems based on common life experiences and situations.

Subculture. Each culture contains smaller **subcultures**, or groups of people with shared value systems based on common life experiences and situations. Subcultures include nationalities, religions, racial groups, and geographic regions. Many subcultures make up important market segments, and marketers often design products and marketing programs tailored to their needs. Examples of three such important subculture groups are Hispanic American, African American, and Asian American consumers.

Hispanics represent a large, fast-growing market. The nation's more than 50 million Hispanic consumers will have total annual buying power of $1.6 trillion by 2015, accounting for 11 percent of the nation's total buying power. The U.S. Hispanic population will surge to more than 111 million by 2050, close to 30 percent of the total U.S. population.[3]

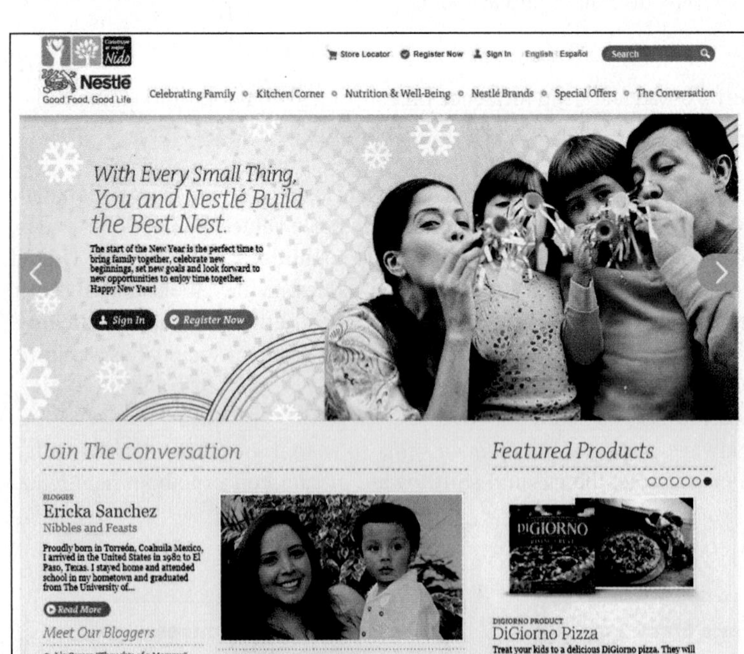

Targeting Hispanic consumers: Nestlé's Construye el Mejor Nido campaign focuses heavily on how Nestlé and its brands help to build family togetherness and well-being.

Although Hispanic consumers share many characteristics and behaviors with the mainstream buying public, there are also distinct differences. They tend to be deeply family oriented and make shopping a family affair—children have a big say in what brands they buy. Older, first-generation Hispanic consumers tend to be very brand loyal and to favor brands and sellers who show special interest in them. Younger Hispanics, however, have shown increasing price sensitivity in recent years and a willingness to switch to store brands.

Within the Hispanic market, there exist many distinct subsegments based on nationality, age, income, and other factors. A company's product or message may be more relevant to one nationality over another, such as Mexicans, Costa Ricans, Argentineans, or Cubans. Companies must also vary their pitches across different Hispanic economic segments.

Companies such as Nestlé, McDonald's, Walmart, State Farm, Toyota, Verizon, Google, and many others have developed special targeting efforts for this fast-growing consumer segment. For example, Google learned that 78 percent of U.S. Hispanics use the Internet as their primary information source and that Hispanics are 58 percent more likely than the general population to click on search ads, making the online Hispanic market too big to ignore. Hispanics are also more active on social networks than other segments. In response, Google created a "specialist team" that focuses on helping advertisers across all industries reach Hispanic consumers through online and mobile search and display advertising platforms.[4]

Similarly, Hispanic consumers shop for groceries three times more often than the general U.S. shopper, so Nestlé, General Mills, and other food companies compete heavily to get their brands into Hispanic shoppers' grocery carts. >> For example, Nestlé targets Hispanic family buyers with its extensive Construye el Mejor Nido (Create the Best Nest) marketing campaign, which connects Nestlé's products with family nutrition and wellness resources. The multipronged campaign includes a bilingual Web site (www.elmejornido.com), a Facebook page, Spanish-language television ads, sampling, and in-store marketing. No matter what the medium, the Construye el Mejor Nido campaign focuses heavily on how Nestlé and its brands help to build family togetherness and well-being. For example, four Hispanic mothers blog on the Web site, offering tips on parenting and healthy eating.[5]

The U.S. African American population is growing in affluence and sophistication. By 2015, the nation's more than 42 million black consumers will have a buying power of $1.1 trillion. Although more price conscious than other segments, blacks are also strongly motivated by quality and selection. Brands are important.[6]

Many companies develop special products, appeals, and marketing programs for African American consumers. For example, last year Ford spent more than $15 million in African American–targeted advertising media. >> As just one example, it recently launched a multicultural campaign—called "Brand New"—to introduce its redesigned Ford Escape to the African American small SUV market:[7]

> The campaign centers on the phrase "brand new," often used in the African American community to describe people who have tried something new or who have bettered themselves. "Brand New" also serves as an extension to the African American segment of Ford's brand-wide "Go Further" slogan. The humorous, documentary-style "Brand New" campaign creates a series of characters whose family lives are radically changed once they own an Escape. For instance, in the first commercial—aired during the finale of "The Game" on BET—the Brown family "gets all brand new" as their new Escape opens their eyes to new and exciting experiences such as kayaking, surfing, hiking, and even spelunking. Other ads introduce additional characters affected by the Brown's Ford Escape purchase, such as Stanley the gas station attendant who gets less business from the family thanks to the Escape's stingy EcoBoost feature, or Vince the Valet who loses out because the family uses the vehicle's Park Assist feature instead. The "Brand New" campaign—created by UniWorld, Ford's African American advertising agency—employs a full slate of black-oriented broadcast and print media, a campaign microsite (www.ford.com/brandnew), plus the Ford Escape YouTube channel and Facebook page and other social media. Ford has also created special African American campaigns for its Fusion and Focus models.

>> **Targeting African American consumers; Ford's "Brand New campaign introduces the redesigned Ford Escape into the African American small SUV market.**

Ford Motor Company.

Asian Americans are the most affluent U.S. demographic segment. They now number more than 16 million, with annual buying power approaching $775 billion by 2015. Asian Americans are the second-fastest-growing subsegment after Hispanic Americans. And like Hispanic Americans, they are a diverse group. Chinese Americans constitute the largest group, followed by Filipinos, Asian Indians, Vietnamese, Korean Americans, and Japanese Americans. Yet, unlike Hispanics who all speak various dialects of Spanish, Asians speak many different languages. For example, ads for the 2010 U.S. Census ran in languages ranging from Japanese, Cantonese, Khmer, Korean, and Vietnamese to Thai, Cambodian, Hmong, Hinglish, and Taglish.[8]

As a group, Asian American consumers shop frequently and are the most brand conscious of all the ethnic groups. They can be fiercely brand loyal. As a result, many firms now target the Asian American market. For example, State Farm actively targets these consumers:[9]

> A few years ago, State Farm discovered that, although it was a solid number one among older Asian American customers, it was losing market share among younger consumers to low-price direct-marketing competitors GEICO and Progressive. Young Asian Americans are tech-savvy buyers who often shop around online. However, State Farm learned that Asian youth often don't trust a digital quote or a faceless number given over the phone. Instead, they prefer to haggle over and finalize transactions face to face. Connections and relationships really matter to them. It's all summed up in the word "jeong"—an Asian concept of person-to-person feelings and connections.
>
> The "jeong" concept became the foundation for State Farm's award-winning "I'm connected" marketing campaign targeting young Asian Americans. The campaign played to one of State Farms major strengths—its existing corps of Asian agents who are already well respected and connected in their communities. These super-connected agents already connect customers not only with the right discounts, but also with each other and their communities. The youth-oriented "I'm connected" campaign featured comedy elements mixed with the pop song "Like a G6" by Far East Movement to make the topic of accident insurance more relatable to young consumers. The multi-platform campaign also pushed heavily online, including a YouTube video that went viral and a bilingual Chinese and English "I'm Connected" Facebook app that helped people connect to like-minded others. The app attracted 275,000 visitors monthly.

Cross-cultural marketing
Including ethnic themes and cross-cultural perspectives within a brand's mainstream marketing, appealing to consumer similarities across subcultures rather than differences.

Beyond targeting segments such as Hispanics, African Americans, and Asian Americans with specially tailored efforts, many marketers now embrace **cross-cultural marketing**—the practice of including ethnic themes and cross-cultural perspectives within their mainstream marketing. Cross-cultural marketing appeals to consumer similarities across subcultures rather than differences. Many marketers are finding that insights gleaned from ethnic consumers can influence their broader markets.

For example, today's youth-oriented lifestyle is influenced heavily by Hispanic and African American entertainers. So it follows that consumers expect to see many different cultures and ethnicities represented in the advertising and products they consume. For instance, McDonald's takes cues from African Americans, Hispanics, and Asians to develop menus and advertising in hopes of encouraging mainstream consumers to buy smoothies, mocha drinks, and snack wraps as avidly as they consume hip-hop and rock 'n' roll. "The ethnic consumer tends to set trends," says McDonald's chief marketing officer. "So they help set the tone for how we enter the marketplace." Thus, McDonald's might take an ad primarily geared toward African Americans and run it in general-market media. "The reality is that the new mainstream is multicultural," concludes one cross-cultural marketing expert.[10]

Social class
Relatively permanent and ordered divisions in a society whose members share similar values, interests, and behaviors.

Social Class. Almost every society has some form of social class structure. **Social classes** are society's relatively permanent and ordered divisions whose members share similar values, interests, and behaviors. Social scientists have identified the seven American social classes shown in >> **Figure 5.3**.

Social class is not determined by a single factor, such as income, but is measured as a combination of occupation, income, education, wealth, and other variables. In some social systems, members of different classes are reared for certain roles and cannot change their social positions. In the United States, however, the lines between social classes are not fixed and rigid; people can move to a higher social class or drop into a lower one.

Marketers are interested in social class because people within a given social class tend to exhibit similar buying behavior. Social classes show distinct product and brand preferences in areas such as clothing, home furnishings, travel and leisure activity, financial services, and automobiles.

Social Factors

A consumer's behavior also is influenced by social factors, such as the consumer's *small groups*, *social networks*, *family*, and *social roles and status*.

>> Figure 5.3 The Major American Social Classes

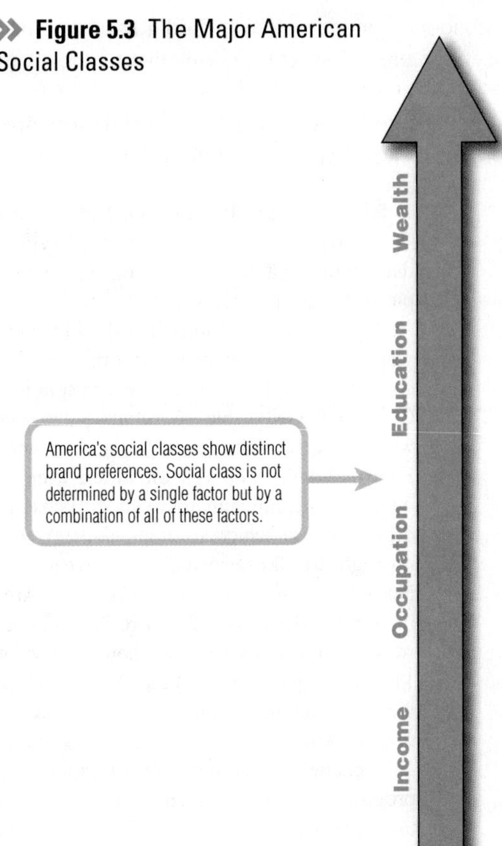
America's social classes show distinct brand preferences. Social class is not determined by a single factor but by a combination of all of these factors.
Wealth
Education
Occupation
Income

Upper Class

Upper Uppers (1 percent): The social elite who live on inherited wealth. They give large sums to charity, own more than one home, and send their children to the finest schools.

Lower Uppers (2 percent): Americans who have earned high income or wealth through exceptional ability. They are active in social and civic affairs and buy expensive homes, educations, and cars.

Middle Class

Upper Middles (12 percent): Professionals, independent businesspersons, and corporate managers who possess neither family status nor unusual wealth. They believe in education, are joiners and highly civic minded, and want the "better things in life."

Middle Class (32 percent): Average-pay white- and blue-collar workers who live on "the better side of town." They buy popular products to keep up with trends. Better living means owning a nice home in a nice neighborhood with good schools.

Working Class

Working Class (38 percent): Those who lead a "working-class lifestyle," whatever their income, school background, or job. They depend heavily on relatives for economic and emotional support, advice on purchases, and assistance in times of trouble.

Lower Class

Upper Lowers (9 percent): The working poor. Although their living standard is just above poverty, they strive toward a higher class. However, they often lack education and are poorly paid for unskilled work.

Lower Lowers (7 percent): Visibly poor, often poorly educated unskilled laborers. They are often out of work, and some depend on public assistance. They tend to live a day-to-day existence.

Group
Two or more people who interact to accomplish individual or mutual goals.

Groups and Social Networks. Many small **groups** influence a person's behavior. Groups that have a direct influence and to which a person belongs are called *membership groups*. In contrast, *reference groups* serve as direct (face-to-face interactions) or indirect points of comparison or reference in forming a person's attitudes or behavior. People often are influenced by reference groups to which they do not belong. For example, an *aspirational group* is one to which the individual wishes to belong, as when a young basketball player hopes to someday emulate basketball star LeBron James and play in the NBA.

Marketers try to identify the reference groups of their target markets. Reference groups expose a person to new behaviors and lifestyles, influence the person's attitudes and self-concept, and create pressures to conform that may affect the person's product and brand choices. The importance of group influence varies across products and brands. It tends to be strongest when the product is visible to others whom the buyer respects.

Word-of-mouth influence
The impact of the personal words and recommendations of trusted friends, associates, and other consumers on buying behavior.

Word-of-mouth influence can have a powerful impact on consumer buying behavior. The personal words and recommendations of trusted friends, associates, and other consumers tend to be more credible than those coming from commercial sources, such as advertisements or salespeople. One recent study showed that 92 percent of consumers trust recommendations from friends and family above any form of advertising.[11] Most word-of-mouth influence happens naturally: Consumers start chatting about a brand they use or feel strongly about one way or the other. Often, however, rather than leaving it to chance, marketers can help to create positive conversations about their brands.

Opinion leader
A person within a reference group who, because of special skills, knowledge, personality, or other characteristics, exerts social influence on others.

Marketers of brands subjected to strong group influence must figure out how to reach **opinion leaders**—people within a reference group who, because of special skills, knowledge, personality, or other characteristics, exert social influence on others. Some experts call this group the *influentials* or *leading adopters*. When these influentials talk, consumers listen. Marketers try to identify opinion leaders for their products and direct marketing efforts toward them.

Buzz marketing involves enlisting or even creating opinion leaders to serve as "brand ambassadors" who spread the word about a company's products. For example, Nike created a ton of buzz worldwide during the 2012 London Olympics when it shod 400 of its Nike-sponsored athletes in can't-miss incandescent green/yellow Volt Flyknit shoes. The shoes became the talk of the Olympics.

Many companies turn everyday customers into brand evangelists. >> For instance, Philips turned users into brand ambassadors for its novel Wake-up Light lighting system:[12]

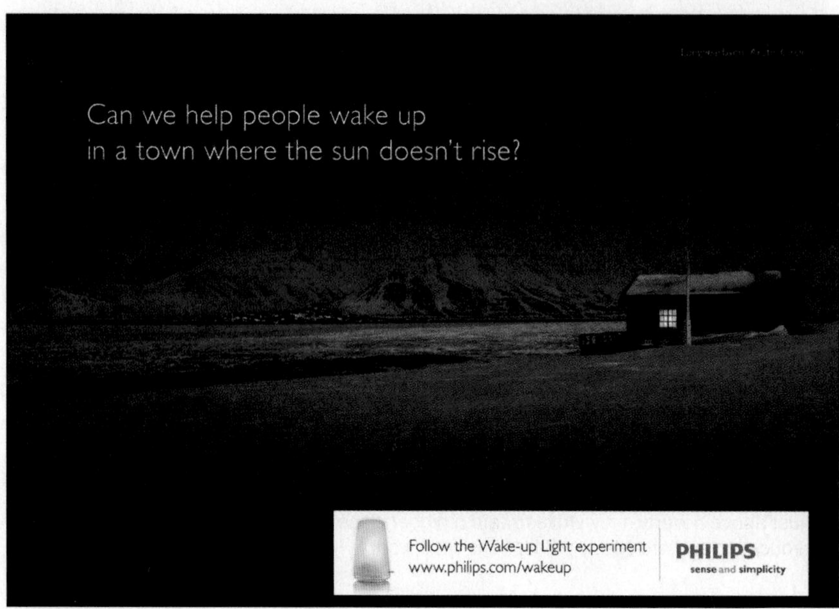

Can we help people wake up
in a town where the sun doesn't rise?
Follow the Wake-up Light experiment
www.philips.com/wakeup
PHILIPS
sense and simplicity

>> Creating word of mouth: Philips's award-winning "Wake up the Town" word-of-mouth campaign created knowledgeable consumers who helped explain the benefits of its complex Wake-up Light bedside lighting system to others.

Philips Consumer Lifestyle.

> A few years ago, Philips launched the first Wake-up Light—a bedside lighting system that simulated a natural sunrise, helping people to wake up more naturally and happily. At first, however, Philips had difficulty explaining the complex benefits of the wake-up concept to skeptical consumers. The solution: Create knowledgeable consumers advocates who could explain the product to others. Philips did this through an award-winning integrated media campaign called "Wake up the Town," in which it supplied the Wake-up Light to 200 residents in Longyearbyen, Norway—the northernmost town in the Arctic Circle. The town's 2,000 residents experience complete darkness 24 hours a day for 11 straight weeks each year. As you might imagine, waking up and starting the day in total darkness can be physically and mentally challenging. As the social experiment progressed, Philips asked consumers who used the Wake-up Light to honestly share their experiences on an interactive Web site, in blog posts, and on Facebook. Philips also arranged media interviews and posted video mini-documentaries on the site. The three-month word-of-mouth campaign paid off handsomely as potential buyers followed the stories of those using the light. Of the 200 participants in "Wake up the Town," 87 percent reported they were waking up feeling more refreshed, alert, and ready for the day; 98 percent reported that they would continue to use the Wake-up Light. During the campaign, purchase consideration in target markets in Sweden and the Netherlands grew by 17 percent and 45 percent, respectively. Unit demand grew by 29 percent.

Online social networks
Online social communities—blogs, social networking Web sites, and other online communities—where people socialize or exchange information and opinions.

More broadly, over the past several years, a new type of social interaction has exploded onto the scene—online social networking. **Online social networks** are online communities where people socialize or exchange information and opinions. Social networking media range from blogs (Consumerist, Gizmodo, Zenhabits) and message boards (Craigslist) to social media sites (Facebook, Twitter, Pinterest, and Foursquare) and virtual worlds (Second Life and Everquest). This form of consumer-to-consumer and business-to-consumer dialog has big implications for marketers.

Marketers are working to harness the power of these new social networks and other "word-of-Web" opportunities to promote their products and build closer customer relationships. Instead of throwing more one-way commercial messages at consumers, they hope to use the Internet and social networks to *interact* with consumers and become a part of their conversations and lives.

For example, Red Bull has an astounding 35 million friends on Facebook; Twitter and Facebook are the primary ways it communicates with college students. JetBlue listens in on customers on Twitter and often responds; one consumer recently tweeted "I'm getting on a JetBlue flight" and JetBlue tweeted back "You should try the smoked almonds [on board]." Dell sponsors nine blogs designed to provide "a direct exchange with Dell customers about the technology that connects us all." Even the Mayo Clinic uses social media extensively. It maintains Facebook, Flickr, and Twitter pages; a YouTube channel; smartphone patient apps that "put Mayo in your pocket wherever you are"; and a Sharing Mayo Clinic blog on which patients share their Mayo Clinic experiences and employees offer a behind-the-scenes view.

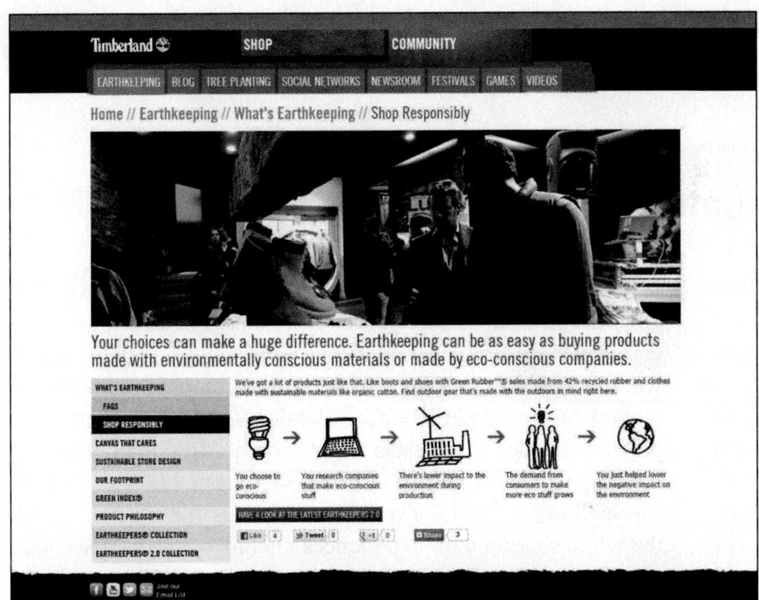

» **Using social networks: Timberland has created an extensive online community that connects like-minded "Earthkeepers" with each other and the brand through several Web sites, a Facebook page, a YouTube channel, a Bootmakers Blog, an e-mail newsletter, and several Twitter feeds.**

Courtesy of Timberland.

Most brands have built a comprehensive social media presence. » Eco-conscious outdoor shoe and gear maker Timberland, for instance, has created an online community (http://community.timberland.com) that connects like-minded "Earthkeepers" with each other and the brand through a network that includes several Web sites, a Facebook page, a YouTube channel, a Bootmakers Blog, an e-mail newsletter, and several Twitter feeds. We will dig deeper into online social networks as a marketing tool in Chapter 14.

However, although much of the current talk about tapping social influence focuses on the Internet and social media, some 90 percent of brand conversations still take place the old-fashioned way—face to face. So most effective word-of-mouth marketing programs begin with generating person-to-person brand conversations and integrating both offline and online social influence strategies. The goal is to create opportunities for customers to get involved with brands and then help them share their brand passions and experiences with others in both their real world and virtual social networks (see Marketing at Work 5.1).

Family. Family members can strongly influence buyer behavior. The family is the most important consumer buying organization in society, and it has been researched extensively. Marketers are interested in the roles and influence of the husband, wife, and children on the purchase of different products and services.

Husband–wife involvement varies widely by product category and by stage in the buying process. Buying roles change with evolving consumer lifestyles. For example, in the United States, the wife traditionally has been considered the main purchasing agent for the family in the areas of food, household products, and clothing. But with more women working outside the home and the willingness of husbands to do more of the family's purchasing, all this is changing. A recent survey of men ages 18 to 64 found that 52 percent identify themselves as primary grocery shoppers in their households, and 39 percent handle most of their household's laundry. At the same time, today women outspend men 3 to 2 on new technology purchases and influence two-thirds of all new car purchases.[13]

Such shifting roles signal a new marketing reality. Marketers in industries that have traditionally sold their products to only women or only men—from groceries and personal care products to cars and consumer electronics—are now carefully targeting the opposite sex. For example, P&G's "My Tide" campaign has a commercial featuring a stay-at-home dad who does the household laundry using Tide Boost. A General Mills ad shows a father packing Go-Gurt yogurt in his son's lunch as the child heads off to school in the morning, with the slogan "Dads who get it, get Go-Gurt."

Children may also have a strong influence on family buying decisions. The nation's 36 million children ages 9 to 12 wield an estimated $43 billion in disposable income. They also influence an additional $150 billion that their families spend on them in areas such as food, clothing, entertainment, and personal care items. One study found that kids significantly influence family decisions about everything from what cars they buy to where they eat out and take vacations.[14]

Roles and Status. A person belongs to many groups—family, clubs, organizations, online communities. The person's position in each group can be defined in terms of both role and status. A role consists of the activities people are expected to perform according to the people around them. Each role carries a status reflecting the general esteem given to it by society.

People usually choose products appropriate to their roles and status. Consider the various roles a working mother plays. In her company, she may play the role of a brand

MARKETING AT WORK 5.1

Word-of-Mouth Marketing: Sparking Brand Conversations and Helping Them Catch Fire

People love talking with others about things that make them happy—including their favorite products and brands. Say you really like JetBlue Airways—it flies with flair and gets you there at an affordable price. Or you just plain love your new little GoPro HERO3 Black Edition video camera—it's too cool to keep to yourself. So you spread the good word about your favorite brands to anyone who will listen. In the old days, you'd have chatted up these brands with a few friends and family members. But these days, thanks to the Internet, social media, and mobile technology, anyone can share brand experiences with thousands, even millions, of other consumers digitally.

In response, marketers are now feverishly working to harness today's newfound technologies and get people interacting with each other about their brands, both online and offline. The aim is inspire, nurture, and amplify brand conversations. Whether it entails seeding a product among high-potential consumers to get them talking, creating brand ambassadors, tapping into existing influentials and the social media, or developing conversation-provoking events and videos, the idea is to get people involved with and talking about the brand.

Generating successful word of mouth might be as simple as prompting Facebook Likes, Twitter streams, online reviews, blog commentaries, or YouTube videos. Even companies with small budgets can earn global exposure in the social media. For example, little-known startup DollarShaveClub.com—which ships quality razors directly to customers for as little as one dollar a month—became an overnight sensation thanks largely to a single YouTube video. Founder Michael Dubin scraped together $4,500 to produce a clever video featuring himself, some corny props, a guy in a bear suit, and very salty language to pitch the new service. "Are the blades any good?" Dubin asks in the video. "No. Our blades are f***ing great," he answers. "So stop forgetting where you're going to buy your blades every month and start deciding where you're going to stack all those dollar bills I'm saving you." The edgy video went viral, and the word-of-mouth firestorm quickly earned DollarShaveClub .com more than 9 million YouTube views, 23,000 Twitter followers, 73,000 Likes on Facebook, dozens of response videos, and $10 million in venture capital funding.

But most successful social influence campaigns go well beyond a YouTube video or Facebook Likes. For example, many companies start by creating their own brand evangelists. That's what Ford did to introduce its Fiesta subcompact model in the United States. Under its now classic Fiesta Movement campaign, it handed out Fiestas to 100 young Millennial drivers—the target audience for the car—selected from 4,000 applicants. These "Fiesta Agents" lived with their cars for six months, all the while sharing their experiences via blogs, tweets, Facebook updates, and YouTube and Flickr posts. The highly successful Fiesta Movement campaign generated 58 percent pre-launch brand awareness among Fiesta's under-30 target consumers. The Fiesta ambassadors posted 50,000 items, generating 28 million social media views, 52,000 test drives, and 10,000 online vehicle reservations.

Four years later, the Fiesta Movement is still rolling. Most recently, Ford recruited 100 new Fiesta agents to create a year's worth of advertising for the 2014 Fiesta, including video clips to be used as commercials, digital ads, ads for social media such as Facebook and YouTube, and even magazine and newspaper

>> **Creating brand buzz: Ford's highly successful Fiesta Movement campaign turned customers into brand evangelists, who shared their experiences via blogs, tweets, Facebook updates, and YouTube and Flickr posts.**

Ford Motor Company.

ads. The Fiesta Movement has been so successful that Ford created similar social media evangelist campaigns for the Ford Escape ("Escape Routes") and its latest generation Ford Fusion ("Random Acts of Fusion").

Beyond creating their own ambassadors, companies looking to harness influence can work with the army of self-made influencers already plying the Internet—independent bloggers. Believe it or not, there are now almost as many people making a living as bloggers as there are lawyers. No matter what the interest area, there are probably hundreds of bloggers covering it. Moreover, research shows that 90 percent of bloggers post about their favorite and least favorite brands.

As a result, most companies try to form relationships with influential bloggers and online personalities. The key is to find bloggers who have strong networks of relevant readers, a credible voice, and a good fit with the brand. For example, companies ranging from P&G and McDonald's to Walmart work closely with influential "mommy bloggers." And you'll no doubt cross paths with the likes of climbers and skiers blogging for Patagonia, bikers blogging for Harley-Davidson, and foodies blogging for Whole Foods Market or Trader Joe's. Sometimes, bloggers and other social media mavens focus exclusively on a given brand. For example, StarbucksMelody.com is "an unofficial fan site for any and all Starbucks enthusiasts everywhere." TUAW is "The Unofficial Apple Weblog—a resource for all things Apple and beyond." Thanks to their independence, such blogs often generate more trustworthy buzz than a company's own blogs or online sites can.

Much of the word-of-mouth marketing frenzy today seems to center on creating online buzz. However, the majority of brand conversations still take place offline. According to one expert, some 90 percent of brand conversations still happen in the real world rather than the virtual one. So many marketers work first to create good old face-to-face brand conversations.

For example, Kraft enlisted the help of word-of-mouth agency House Party to launch its Philadelphia Cooking Crème line of flavored cream cheeses. Kraft and House Party selected 10,000 cooking hobbyists from House Party's army of advocates to host Cooking Crème parties in their homes, where invited guests sampled recipes jazzed up with the flavorful new product. Kraft supplied kits filled with samples, recipes, coupons, and other incentives to help stage the parties and encourage invited guests to spread the good news afterward. The Philadelphia Cooking Crème word-of-mouth campaign was an overwhelming success. More than 138,000 people attended the dinner parties. And, of course, participants shared their in-person experiences on their social media channels. As a result, brand familiarity for the new product increased 39 percent while purchase intention rose 60 percent. Partygoers generated more than 22 million brand impressions, leading to 1 million product trials and 175 percent return on campaign investment.

Whether offline, online, or both, effective word-of-mouth marketing isn't something that just happens. And it's more than just building a following on Facebook. Marketers must build comprehensive programs that spark person-to-person brand conversations and then help them catch fire. The goal of word-of-mouth marketing is to "find and nurture true brand advocates [and to] encourage and amplify the narrative that naturally occurs," says one expert. It's about finding the company's best customers, giving them opportunities to become more involved, and helping them spread their brand passion and enthusiasm within their in-person and online social networks. "That's good advice to share with all your marketing friends and associates," advises another marketer.

Sources: Jack Neff, "Dollar Shave Club's Dubin Offers Tips for a Truly Viral Video," *Advertising Age*, July 18, 2012, http://adage.com/print/236099/; Stuart Feil, "Gift for Gab: What Marketers Are Doing to Encourage and Amplify Word-of-Mouth," *Adweek*, December 10, 2012, pp. W1–W2; Giselle Abramovich, "Why Ford Credits Social Media in Turnaround," *Digiday*, October 10, 2012, www.digiday.com/brands/why-ford-credits-social-media-in-turnaround/; Stuart Elliott, "Ford Turns to the Crowd for New Fiesta Ads," *New York Times*, February 19, 2013, http://mediadecoder.blogs.nytimes.com/2013/02/19/ford-turns-to-the-crowd-for-new-fiesta-ads/; and www.escaperoutes.com, www.randomactsoffusion.com, and www.fiestamovement.com, accessed October 2013.

manager; in her family, she plays the role of wife and mother; at her favorite sporting events, she plays the role of avid fan. As a brand manager, she will buy the kind of clothing that reflects her role and status in her company. At the game, she may wear clothing supporting her favorite team.

Personal Factors

A buyer's decisions also are influenced by personal characteristics such as the buyer's *age and life-cycle stage*, *occupation*, *economic situation*, *lifestyle*, and *personality and self-concept*.

Age and Life-Cycle Stage. People change the goods and services they buy over their lifetimes. Tastes in food, clothes, furniture, and recreation are often age related. Buying is also shaped by the stage of the family life cycle—the stages through which families might pass as they mature over time. Life-stage changes usually result from demographics and life-changing events—marriage, having children, purchasing a home, divorce, children going to college, changes in personal income, moving out of the house, and retirement. Marketers often define their target markets in terms of life-cycle stage and develop appropriate products and marketing plans for each stage.

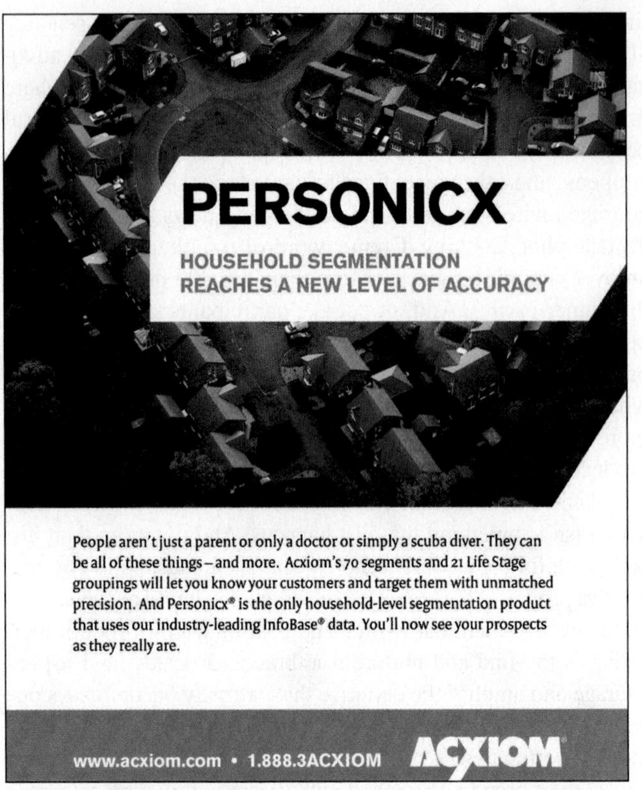

PERSONICX
HOUSEHOLD SEGMENTATION
REACHES A NEW LEVEL OF ACCURACY
People aren't just a parent or only a doctor or simply a scuba diver. They can be all of these things – and more. Acxiom's 70 segments and 21 Life Stage groupings will let you know your customers and target them with unmatched precision. And Personicx® is the only household-level segmentation product that uses our industry-leading InfoBase® data. You'll now see your prospects as they really are.
www.acxiom.com • 1.888.3ACXIOM
ACXIOM

Life-stage segmentation: Personicx's 21 life-stage groupings let marketers see customers as they really are and target them precisely. "People aren't just a parent or only a doctor or simply a scuba diver. They are all of these things."

Acxiom Corporation.

For example, consumer information giant Acxiom's Personicx life-stage segmentation system places U.S. households into one of 70 consumer segments and 21 life-stage groups, based on specific consumer behavior and demographic characteristics. Personicx includes life-stage groups with names such as *Beginnings, Taking Hold, Cash & Careers, Jumbo Families, Transition Time, Our Turn, Golden Years,* and *Active Elders*. The *Taking Hold* group consists of young, energetic, well-funded couples and young families who are busy with their careers, social lives, and interests, especially fitness and active recreation. *Transition Time* are blue-collar, less-educated, mid-income consumers who are transitioning to stable lives and talking about marriage and children.

"Consumers experience many life-stage changes during their lifetimes," says Acxiom. "As their life stages change, so do their behaviors and purchasing preferences." Armed with data about the timing and makeup of life-stage changes, marketers can create targeted, personalized campaigns.[15]

Occupation. A person's occupation affects the goods and services bought. Blue-collar workers tend to buy more rugged work clothes, whereas executives buy more business suits. Marketers try to identify the occupational groups that have an above-average interest in their products and services. A company can even specialize in making products needed by a given occupational group.

For example, Carhartt makes rugged, durable, no-nonsense work clothes—what it calls "original equipment for the American worker. From coats to jackets, bibs to overalls . . . if the apparel carries the name Carhartt, the performance will be legendary." Its Web site carries real-life testimonials of hard-working Carhartt customers. One electrician, battling the cold in Canada's arctic region, reports wearing Carhartt's lined Arctic bib overalls, Arctic jacket, and other clothing for more than two years without a single "popped button, ripped pocket seam, or stuck zipper." And a railroadman in northern New York, who's spent years walking rough railroad beds, climbing around trains, and switching cars in conditions ranging from extreme heat to frigid cold, calls his trusty brown Carhartt jacket part of his "survival gear—like a bulletproof vest is to a policeman."[16]

Economic Situation. A person's economic situation will affect his or her store and product choices. Marketers watch trends in personal income, savings, and interest rates. In the more frugal times following the Great Recession, most companies have taken steps to redesign, reposition, and reprice their products and services. For example, upscale discounter Target has replaced some of its "chic" with "cheap." It is putting more emphasis on the "Pay less" side of its "Expect more. Pay less." positioning promise.

Similarly, to become more competitive with discount competitors such as Target and Kohl's in the tighter economy, JCPenney announced sweeping changes in its marketing, including an everyday-low-price strategy featuring simpler pricing and an end to seemingly endless deals and sales. "Enough. Is. Enough." said the retailer's commercials that introduced the new strategy. Ads depicted shoppers screaming in frustration at having to clip coupons, rush to take advantage of sales, and stand in line for blowout promotions.[17]

Lifestyle
A person's pattern of living as expressed in his or her activities, interests, and opinions.

Lifestyle. People coming from the same subculture, social class, and occupation may have quite different lifestyles. **Lifestyle** is a person's pattern of living as expressed in his or her psychographics. It involves measuring consumers' major AIO dimensions—activities (work, hobbies, shopping, sports, social events), interests (food, fashion, family, recreation), and opinions (about themselves, social issues, business, products). Lifestyle captures something more than the person's social class or personality. It profiles a person's whole pattern of acting and interacting in the world.

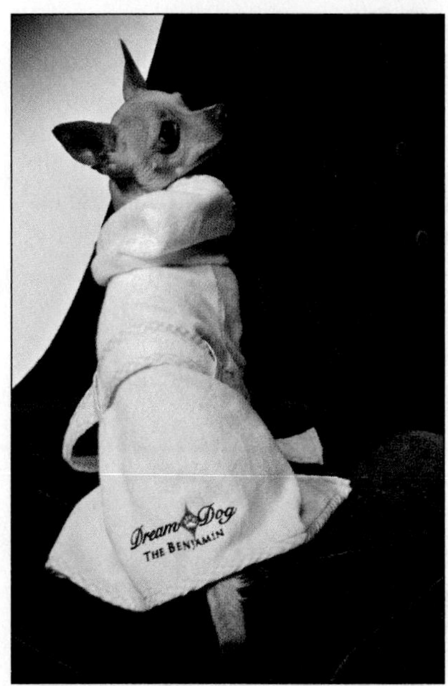

» **Catering to pet-owner lifestyles: The Benjamin Hotel's Dream Dog program "offers everything a pampered pooch needs to enjoy traveling in tail-wagging style, from grooming services to a lush bathrobe to a consultation with a pet psychic."**

The Benjamin Hotel.

When used carefully, the lifestyle concept can help marketers understand changing consumer values and how they affect buyer behavior. Consumers don't just buy products; they buy the values and lifestyles those products represent. For example, outdoor outfitter REI sells a lot more than just outdoor gear and clothing. It sells an entire outdoor lifestyle for active people who "love to get outside and play."[18] One REI ad shows a woman biking in the wide-open spaces, proclaiming "REI prefer hitting the trails over the snooze button, whatever that is." At the REI Web site, outdoor enthusiasts can swap outdoors stories, enroll in REI Outdoor School classes at local locations, or even sign up for any of dozens of REI-sponsored outdoor travel adventures around the world.

Marketers look for lifestyle segments with needs that can be served through special products or marketing approaches. Such segments might be defined by anything from family characteristics or outdoor interests to pet ownership. In fact, today's involved pet ownership lifestyles have created a huge and growing lifestyle segment of indulgent "pet parents":[19]

> For many devoted pet parents, having a pet affects just about every buying decision they make, from what car they buy or where they stay on vacation to even what TV channels they watch. » For example, The Benjamin Hotel in New York takes "pet friendly" to a whole new level. Its "Dream Dog" program offers "everything a pampered pet needs to enjoy travel in tail-wagging style." The program provides orthopedic dog beds, plush doggie bathrobes, canine room service, and DVDs for dogs, as well as access to pet spa treatments and a pet psychic. "We will ensure your furry friend never has to lift a paw," says the hotel.
>
> The list goes on and on. For owners of overweight dogs (40 percent of them are), there's the PetZen doggie treadmill ($500 to $900). For those who must leave their dogs behind while they work or play, there's DogTV, a cable channel "designed to keep your dog happy and contained while you're away." For owners who don't want their male pets to suffer the blow to their self-esteem that comes from being neutered, there are Neuticles, patented testicular implants for pets. Some 500,000 dogs, cats, monkeys, rats, and even a water buffalo sport a pair. And for a growing number of people who find it just too hard to part with their deceased pets, you can have them freeze-dried, stuffed, and preserved in a natural pose so that they'll always be around. Now that's the pet owner lifestyle.

Personality
The unique psychological characteristics that distinguish a person or group.

Personality and Self-Concept. Each person's distinct personality influences his or her buying behavior. **Personality** refers to the unique psychological characteristics that distinguish a person or group. Personality is usually described in terms of traits such as self-confidence, dominance, sociability, autonomy, defensiveness, adaptability, and aggressiveness. Personality can be useful in analyzing consumer behavior for certain product or brand choices.

The idea is that brands also have personalities, and consumers are likely to choose brands with personalities that match their own. A *brand personality* is the specific mix of human traits that may be attributed to a particular brand. One researcher identified five brand personality traits: *sincerity* (down-to-earth, honest, wholesome, and cheerful), *excitement* (daring, spirited, imaginative, and up to date), *competence* (reliable, intelligent, and successful), *sophistication* (glamorous, upper class, charming), and *ruggedness* (outdoorsy and tough). "Your personality determines what you consume, what TV shows you watch, what products you buy, and [most] other decisions you make," says one consumer behavior expert.[20]

» **Brand personality: Consumers are likely to choose brands with personalities that match their own. The Gucci brand is associated with "class" and "sophistication."**

Associated Press.

Most well-known brands are strongly associated with one particular trait: the Ford F150 with "ruggedness," Apple with "excitement," the *Washington Post* with "competence," Method with "sincerity," and » Gucci with "class" and "sophistication." Hence, these brands will attract persons who are high on the same personality traits.

Skullcandy, the performance headphone and audio accessory maker, projects a young, active, trendsetting, rebellious personality. The brand's leading-edge designs, vibrant colors, and unique styles provide "instant gratification for your ears." Skullcandy enhances its stylish, trendsetting persona through associations with a host of high-profile endorsers ranging from rappers Jay-Z, Snoop Dogg, and Wale to supermodels Kate Upton and Chanel Iman to NBA stars Kevin Durant and Derrick Rose to surfer Dane Reynolds and a whole team of skateboarders, including legend Eric Koston. Like-minded fans can keep track of their adventures, opinions, and interests on Skullcandy's Web site and blog.[21]

Many marketers use a concept related to personality—a person's *self-concept* (also called *self-image*). The idea is that people's possessions contribute to and reflect their identities—that is, "we are what we consume." Thus, to understand consumer behavior, marketers must first understand the relationship between consumer self-concept and possessions.

Psychological Factors

A person's buying choices are further influenced by four major psychological factors: *motivation*, *perception*, *learning*, and *beliefs and attitudes*.

Motive (drive)
A need that is sufficiently pressing to direct the person to seek satisfaction of the need.

Motivation. A person has many needs at any given time. Some are biological, arising from states of tension such as hunger, thirst, or discomfort. Others are psychological, arising from the need for recognition, esteem, or belonging. A need becomes a motive when it is aroused to a sufficient level of intensity. A **motive (or drive)** is a need that is sufficiently pressing to direct the person to seek satisfaction. Psychologists have developed theories of human motivation. Two of the most popular—the theories of Sigmund Freud and Abraham Maslow—carry quite different meanings for consumer analysis and marketing.

Sigmund Freud assumed that people are largely unconscious about the real psychological forces shaping their behavior. His theory suggests that a person's buying decisions are affected by subconscious motives that even the buyer may not fully understand. Thus, an aging baby boomer who buys a sporty BMW convertible might explain that he simply likes the feel of the wind in his thinning hair. At a deeper level, he may be trying to impress others with his success. At a still deeper level, he may be buying the car to feel young and independent again.

The term *motivation research* refers to qualitative research designed to probe consumers' hidden, subconscious motivations. Consumers often don't know or can't describe why they act as they do. Thus, motivation researchers use a variety of probing techniques to uncover underlying emotions and attitudes toward brands and buying situations.

Many companies employ teams of psychologists, anthropologists, and other social scientists to carry out motivation research. One ad agency routinely conducts one-on-one, therapy-like interviews to delve into the inner workings of consumers. Another company asks consumers to describe their favorite brands as animals or cars (say, a Mercedes versus a Chevy) to assess the prestige associated with various brands. Still others rely on hypnosis, dream therapy, or soft lights and mood music to plumb the murky depths of consumer psyches.

Such projective techniques seem pretty goofy, and some marketers dismiss such motivation research as mumbo jumbo. But many marketers use such touchy-feely approaches, now sometimes called *interpretive consumer research*, to dig deeper into consumer psyches and develop better marketing strategies.

Abraham Maslow sought to explain why people are driven by particular needs at particular times. Why does one person spend a lot of time and energy on personal safety and another on gaining the esteem of others? Maslow's answer is that human needs are arranged in a hierarchy, as shown in **»Figure 5.4**, from the most pressing at the bottom to the least pressing at the top.[22] They include *physiological* needs, *safety* needs, *social* needs, *esteem* needs, and *self-actualization* needs.

A person tries to satisfy the most important need first. When that need is satisfied, it will stop being a motivator, and the person will then try to satisfy the next most important need. For example, starving people (physiological need) will not take an interest in the latest happenings in the art world (self-actualization needs) nor in how they are seen or esteemed by others (social or esteem needs) nor even in whether they are breathing clean air (safety needs). But as each important need is satisfied, the next most important need will come into play.

Perception
The process by which people select, organize, and interpret information to form a meaningful picture of the world.

Perception. A motivated person is ready to act. How the person acts is influenced by his or her own perception of the situation. All of us learn by the flow of information through our five senses: sight, hearing, smell, touch, and taste. However, each of us receives, organizes, and interprets this sensory information in an individual way. **Perception** is the process by which people select, organize, and interpret information to form a meaningful picture of the world.

>> Figure 5.4 Maslow's Hierarchy of Needs

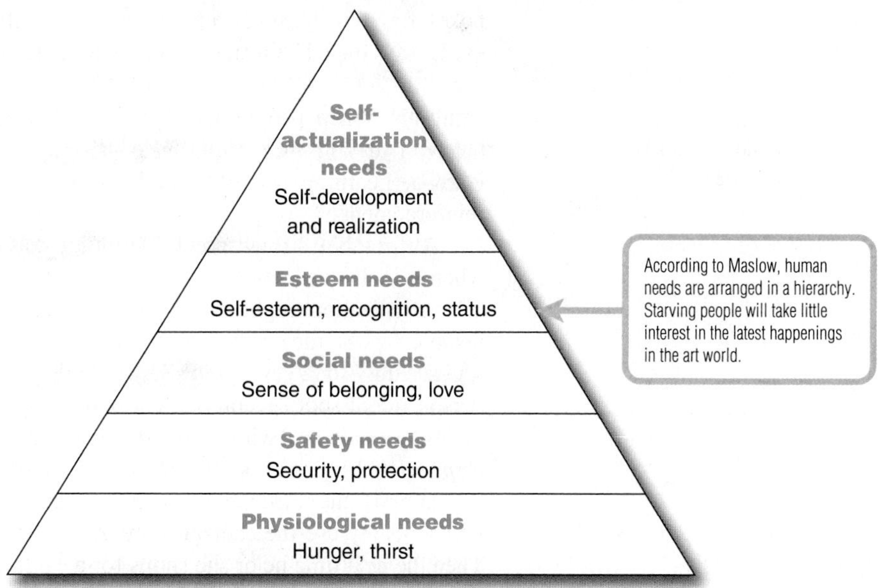

People can form different perceptions of the same stimulus because of three perceptual processes: selective attention, selective distortion, and selective retention. People are exposed to a great amount of stimuli every day. For example, people are exposed to an estimated 3,000 to 5,000 ad messages every day.[23] It is impossible for a person to pay attention to all these stimuli. *Selective attention*—the tendency for people to screen out most of the information to which they are exposed—means that marketers must work especially hard to attract the consumer's attention.

>> This classic ad from the American Association of Advertising Agencies pokes fun at subliminal advertising. "So-called 'subliminal advertising' simply doesn't exist," says the ad. "Overactive imaginations, however, most certainly do."

American Association of Advertising Agencies.

Even noticed stimuli do not always come across in the intended way. Each person fits incoming information into an existing mindset. *Selective distortion* describes the tendency of people to interpret information in a way that will support what they already believe. People also will forget much of what they learn. They tend to retain information that supports their attitudes and beliefs. *Selective retention* means that consumers are likely to remember good points made about a brand they favor and forget good points made about competing brands. Because of selective attention, distortion, and retention, marketers must work hard to get their messages through.

Interestingly, although most marketers worry about whether their offers will be perceived at all, some consumers worry that they will be affected by marketing messages without even knowing it—through *subliminal advertising*. More than 50 years ago, a researcher announced that he had flashed the phrases "Eat popcorn" and "Drink Coca-Cola" on a screen in a New Jersey movie theater every five seconds for 1/300th of a second. He reported that although viewers did not consciously recognize these messages, they absorbed them subconsciously and bought 58 percent more popcorn and 18 percent more Coke. Suddenly advertisers and consumer-protection groups became intensely interested in subliminal perception. Although the researcher later admitted to making up the data, the issue has not died. Some consumers still fear that they are being manipulated by subliminal messages.

Numerous studies by psychologists and consumer researchers have found little or no link between subliminal messages and consumer behavior. Recent brain-wave studies have found that in certain circumstances, our brains may register subliminal messages. However, it appears that subliminal advertising simply doesn't have the power attributed to it by its critics. >> One classic ad from the American Marketing Association pokes fun at subliminal advertising. "So-called 'subliminal advertising' simply doesn't exist," says the ad. "Overactive imaginations, however, most certainly do."[24]

Learning
Changes in an individual's behavior arising from experience.

Learning. When people act, they learn. **Learning** describes changes in an individual's behavior arising from experience. Learning theorists say that most human behavior is learned. Learning occurs through the interplay of drives, stimuli, cues, responses, and reinforcement.

A *drive* is a strong internal stimulus that calls for action. A drive becomes a motive when it is directed toward a particular *stimulus object*. For example, a person's drive for self-actualization might motivate him or her to look into buying a camera. The consumer's response to the idea of buying a camera is conditioned by the surrounding cues. *Cues* are minor stimuli that determine when, where, and how the person responds. For example, the person might spot several camera brands in a shop window, hear of a special sale price, or discuss cameras with a friend. These are all cues that might influence a consumer's *response* to his or her interest in buying the product.

Suppose the consumer buys a Nikon camera. If the experience is rewarding, the consumer will probably use the camera more and more, and his or her response will be *reinforced*. Then the next time he or she shops for a camera, or for binoculars or some similar product, the probability is greater that he or she will buy a Nikon product. The practical significance of learning theory for marketers is that they can build up demand for a product by associating it with strong drives, using motivating cues, and providing positive reinforcement.

Belief
A descriptive thought that a person holds about something.

Attitude
A person's consistently favorable or unfavorable evaluations, feelings, and tendencies toward an object or idea.

Beliefs and Attitudes. Through doing and learning, people acquire beliefs and attitudes. These, in turn, influence their buying behavior. A **belief** is a descriptive thought that a person holds about something. Beliefs may be based on real knowledge, opinion, or faith and may or may not carry an emotional charge. Marketers are interested in the beliefs that people formulate about specific products and services because these beliefs make up product and brand images that affect buying behavior. If some of the beliefs are wrong and prevent purchase, the marketer will want to launch a campaign to correct them.

People have attitudes regarding religion, politics, clothes, music, food, and almost everything else. **Attitude** describes a person's relatively consistent evaluations, feelings, and tendencies toward an object or idea. Attitudes put people into a frame of mind of liking or disliking things, of moving toward or away from them. Our camera buyer may hold attitudes such as "Buy the best," "The Japanese make the best electronics products in the world," and "Creativity and self-expression are among the most important things in life." If so, the Nikon camera would fit well into the consumer's existing attitudes.

Attitudes are difficult to change. A person's attitudes fit into a pattern; changing one attitude may require difficult adjustments in many others. Thus, a company should usually try to fit its products into existing attitudes rather than attempt to change attitudes. Of course, there are exceptions. For example, trying to convince parents that their children would actually like onions—that's right, onions—seems like an uphill battle against prevailing attitudes. Convincing the children themselves seems like an even bigger challenge. However, the Vidalia Onion Committee (VOC), formed to promote one of Georgia's most important agricultural products, managed to do just that:[25]

>> Attitudes and beliefs are difficult to change: The Vidalia Onion Committee's award-winning Ogres and Onions campaign made children believers and delighted their parents. Sales of bagged Vidalia onions shot up 30 percent.

Vidalia® is a registered certification mark of Georgia Department of Agriculture.

> It can be hard selling children on the idea of eating onions. Onions have a strong smell, they can make you cry, and many kids simply refuse to eat them. So to help change these attitudes, the VOC developed a unique plan. >> It employed Shrek, the famous ogre from the hugely popular animated films. The inspiration came from a scene in the first Shrek film, in which Shrek explains ogres to his friend, Donkey. "Onions have layers, ogres have layers," says Shrek. "Ogres are like onions. End of story."
>
> The result was a national "Ogres and Onions" marketing campaign, launched to coincide with both the onion harvest and the premier of the latest Shrek film. The campaign featured giant Shrek placards in grocery store aisles alongside bags of Vidalia onions on which Shrek asked, "What do ogres and onions have in common?" At the Vidalia Onion Web site, Shrek offered kid-friendly Vidalia onion recipes. The award-winning campaign soon had kids clamoring for onions, and surprised and delighted parents responded. Sales of bagged Vidalia onions increased almost 30 percent for the season.

» Figure 5.5 Buyer Decision Process

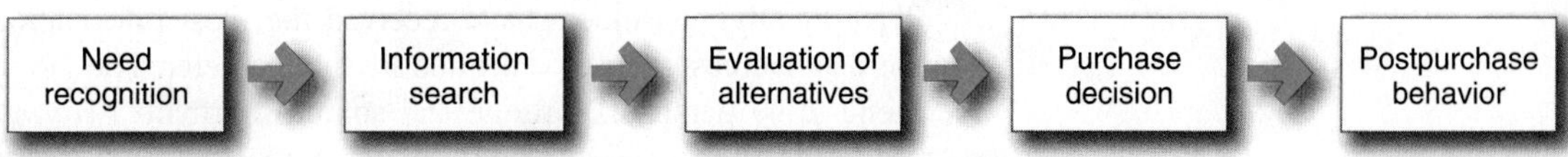

The buying process starts long before the actual purchase and continues long after. In fact, it might result in a decision not to buy. Therefore, marketers must focus on the entire buying process, not just the purchase decision.

We can now appreciate the many forces acting on consumer behavior. The consumer's choice results from the complex interplay of cultural, social, personal, and psychological factors.

Author Comment
The actual purchase decision is part of a much larger buying process—starting with need recognition through how you feel after making the purchase. Marketers want to be involved throughout the entire buyer decision process.

The Buyer Decision Process

Now that we have looked at the influences that affect buyers, we are ready to look at how consumers make buying decisions. **» Figure 5.5** shows that the buyer decision process consists of five stages: *need recognition, information search, evaluation of alternatives, purchase decision*, and *postpurchase behavior*. Clearly, the buying process starts long before the actual purchase and continues long after. Marketers need to focus on the entire buying process rather than on the purchase decision only.

Figure 5.5 suggests that consumers pass through all five stages with every purchase in a considered way. But buyers may pass quickly or slowly through the buying decision process. And in more routine purchases, consumers often skip or reverse some of the stages. Much depends on the nature of the buyer, the product, and the buying situation. A woman buying her regular brand of toothpaste would recognize the need and go right to the purchase decision, skipping information search and evaluation. However, we use the model in Figure 5.5 because it shows all the considerations that arise when a consumer faces a new and complex purchase situation.

» Need recognition can be triggered by advertising: Time for a snack?

SNICKERS and the parallelogram design are registered trademark of Mars, Incorporated. The trademark is used with permission. Mars, Incorporated is not associated with Pearson Education, Inc. The image of the SNICKERS advertisement is printed with permission of Mars, Incorporated.

Need Recognition

The buying process starts with *need recognition*—the buyer recognizes a problem or need. The need can be triggered by *internal stimuli* when one of the person's normal needs—for example, hunger or thirst—rises to a level high enough to become a drive. A need can also be triggered by *external stimuli*. » For example, an advertisement or a discussion with a friend might get you thinking about buying a new car. At this stage, the marketer should research consumers to find out what kinds of needs or problems arise, what brought them about, and how they led the consumer to this particular product.

Information Search

An interested consumer may or may not search for more information. If the consumer's drive is strong and a satisfying product is near at hand, he or she is likely to buy it then. If not, the consumer may store the need in memory or undertake an *information search* related to the need. For example, once you've decided you need a new car, at the least, you will probably pay more attention to car ads, cars owned by friends, and car conversations. Or you may actively search the Web, talk with friends, and gather information in other ways.

Consumers can obtain information from any of several sources. These include *personal sources* (family, friends, neighbors, acquaintances), *commercial sources* (advertising, salespeople, dealer Web sites, packaging, displays), *public sources* (mass media, consumer rating organizations, social media, online searches and peer reviews), and *experiential sources* (examining and using the product). The relative influence of these information sources varies with the product and the buyer.

Traditionally, consumers have received the most information about a product from commercial sources—those controlled by the marketer. The most effective sources, however, tend to be personal. Commercial sources normally *inform* the buyer, but personal sources *legitimize* or *evaluate* products for the buyer. Few advertising campaigns can be as effective as a next-door neighbor leaning over the fence and raving about a wonderful experience with a product you are considering.

Increasingly, that "neighbor's fence" is a digital one. Today, consumers share product opinions, images, and experiences freely across the social media. And buyers can find an abundance of user-generated reviews alongside the products they are considering at sites ranging from Amazon.com or BestBuy.com to Yelp, TripAdvisor, Epinions, and Epicurious. Although individual user reviews vary widely in quality, an entire body of reviews often provides a reliable product assessment—straight from the fingertips of people like you who've actually purchased and experienced the product.

As more information is obtained, the consumer's awareness and knowledge of the available brands and features increase. In your car information search, you may learn about several brands that are available. The information might also help you to drop certain brands from consideration. A company must design its marketing mix to make prospects aware of and knowledgeable about its brand. It should carefully identify consumers' sources of information and the importance of each source.

Evaluation of Alternatives

We have seen how consumers use information to arrive at a set of final brand choices. Next, marketers need to know about *alternative evaluation*, that is, how consumers process information to choose among alternative brands. Unfortunately, consumers do not use a simple and single evaluation process in all buying situations. Instead, several evaluation processes are at work.

How consumers go about evaluating purchase alternatives depends on the individual consumer and the specific buying situation. In some cases, consumers use careful calculations and logical thinking. At other times, the same consumers do little or no evaluating. Instead they buy on impulse and rely on intuition. Sometimes consumers make buying decisions on their own; sometimes they turn to friends, online reviews, or salespeople for buying advice.

Suppose you've narrowed your car choices to three brands. And suppose that you are primarily interested in four attributes—price, style, operating economy, and warranty. By this time, you've probably formed beliefs about how each brand rates on each attribute. Clearly, if one car rated best on all the attributes, the marketer could predict that you would choose it. However, the brands will no doubt vary in appeal. You might base your buying decision mostly on one attribute, and your choice would be easy to predict. If you wanted style above everything else, you would buy the car that you think has the most style. But most buyers consider several attributes, each with different importance. By knowing the importance that you assigned to each attribute, the marketer could predict your car choice more reliably.

Marketers should study buyers to find out how they actually evaluate brand alternatives. If marketers know what evaluative processes go on, they can take steps to influence the buyer's decision.

Purchase Decision

In the evaluation stage, the consumer ranks brands and forms purchase intentions. Generally, the consumer's *purchase decision* will be to buy the most preferred brand, but two factors can come between the purchase *intention* and the purchase *decision*. The first factor is the *attitudes of others*. If someone important to you thinks that you should buy the lowest-priced car, then the chances of you buying a more expensive car are reduced.

The second factor is *unexpected situational factors*. The consumer may form a purchase intention based on factors such as expected income, expected price, and expected product benefits. However, unexpected events may change the purchase intention. For example, the economy might take a turn for the worse, a close competitor might drop its price, or a friend might report being disappointed in your preferred car. Thus, preferences and even purchase intentions do not always result in an actual purchase choice.

Postpurchase Behavior

The marketer's job does not end when the product is bought. After purchasing the product, the consumer will either be satisfied or dissatisfied and will engage in *postpurchase behavior* of interest to the marketer. What determines whether the buyer is satisfied or dissatisfied with a purchase? The answer lies in the relationship between the *consumer's expectations* and the product's *perceived performance*. If the product falls short of expectations, the consumer is disappointed; if it meets expectations, the consumer is satisfied; if it exceeds expectations, the consumer is delighted. The larger the gap between expectations and performance, the greater the consumer's dissatisfaction. This suggests that sellers should promise only what their brands can deliver so that buyers are satisfied.

Cognitive dissonance
Buyer discomfort caused by postpurchase conflict.

Almost all major purchases, however, result in **cognitive dissonance**, or discomfort caused by postpurchase conflict. After the purchase, consumers are satisfied with the benefits of the chosen brand and are glad to avoid the drawbacks of the brands not bought. However, every purchase involves compromise. So consumers feel uneasy about acquiring the drawbacks of the chosen brand and about losing the benefits of the brands not purchased. >> Thus, consumers feel at least some postpurchase dissonance for every purchase.[26]

>> **Postpurchase cognitive dissonance: No matter what choice they make, consumers feel at least some postpurchase dissonance for every decision.**

Stephane Bidouze/Shutterstock.com.

Why is it so important to satisfy the customer? Customer satisfaction is a key to building profitable relationships with consumers—to keeping and growing consumers and reaping their customer lifetime value. Satisfied customers buy a product again, talk favorably to others about the product, pay less attention to competing brands and advertising, and buy other products from the company. Many marketers go beyond merely *meeting* the expectations of customers—they aim to *delight* customers.

A dissatisfied consumer responds differently. Bad word of mouth often travels farther and faster than good word of mouth. It can quickly damage consumer attitudes about a company and its products. But companies cannot simply wait for dissatisfied customers to volunteer their complaints. Most unhappy customers never tell the company about their problems. Therefore, a company should measure customer satisfaction regularly. It should set up systems that *encourage* customers to complain. In this way, the company can learn how well it is doing and how it can improve.

By studying the overall buyer decision process, marketers may be able to find ways to help consumers move through it. For example, if consumers are not buying a new product because they do not perceive a need for it, marketing might launch advertising messages that trigger the need and show how the product solves customers' problems. If customers know about the product but are not buying because they hold unfavorable attitudes toward it, marketers must find ways to change either the product or consumer perceptions.

New product
A good, service, or idea that is perceived by some potential customers as new.

Author Comment
Here we look at some special considerations in *new product* buying decisions.

The Buyer Decision Process for New Products

We now look at how buyers approach the purchase of new products. A **new product** is a good, service, or idea that is perceived by some potential customers as new. It may have been around for a while, but our interest is in how consumers learn about products for the

Adoption process
The mental process through which an individual passes from first hearing about an innovation to final adoption.

first time and make decisions on whether to adopt them. We define the **adoption process** as the mental process through which an individual passes from first learning about an innovation to final adoption. *Adoption* is the decision by an individual to become a regular user of the product.[27]

Stages in the Adoption Process

Consumers go through five stages in the process of adopting a new product:

Awareness: The consumer becomes aware of the new product but lacks information about it.

Interest: The consumer seeks information about the new product.

Evaluation: The consumer considers whether trying the new product makes sense.

Trial: The consumer tries the new product on a small scale to improve his or her estimate of its value.

Adoption: The consumer decides to make full and regular use of the new product.

CHEVY'S
LOVE IT OR RETURN IT
GUARANTEE*

Go to chevyconfidence.com for details.

>> The adoption process: To help buyers past the car-buying decision hurdle in a still-tight economy, Chevrolet offered a "Love It or Return It" guarantee giving uncertain buyers up to 60 days to reverse the buying decision.

General Motors LLC. Used with permission, GM Media Archives.

This model suggests that marketers should think about how to help consumers move through these stages. For example, to help customers past the car-purchase decision hurdle in a still-tight economy, >> Chevrolet last year launched a "Love It or Return It" guarantee. The program promised uncertain buyers of 2013 models up to 60 days to return cars that had been driven fewer than 4,000 miles and had no damage. Car maker Hyundai had offered a similar but even greater incentive program to help reduce purchasing barriers following the economic meltdown in 2008. Its Hyundai Assurance Plan promised to let buyers who financed or leased their new Hyundais to return them at no cost and with no harm to their credit rating if they lost their jobs or incomes within a year. Sales of the Hyundai Sonata surged 85 percent in the month following the start of the campaign.[28]

Individual Differences in Innovativeness

People differ greatly in their readiness to try new products. In each product area, there are "consumption pioneers" and early adopters. Other individuals adopt new products much later. People can be classified into the adopter categories shown in >> **Figure 5.6**.[29] As shown by the curve, after a slow start, an increasing number of people adopt the new product. As successive groups of consumers adopt the innovation, it eventually reaches its cumulative saturation level. Innovators are defined as the first 2.5 percent of buyers to adopt a new idea (those beyond two standard deviations from mean adoption time); the early adopters are the next 13.5 percent (between one and two standard deviations); and then come early mainstream, late mainstream, and lagging adopters.

The five adopter groups have differing values. *Innovators* are venturesome—they try new ideas at some risk. *Early adopters* are guided by respect—they are opinion leaders in their communities and adopt new ideas early but carefully. *Early mainstream* adopters are deliberate—although they rarely are leaders, they adopt new ideas before the average person. *Late mainstream* adopters are skeptical—they adopt an innovation only after a majority of people have tried it. Finally, *lagging adopters* are tradition bound—they are suspicious of changes and adopt the innovation only when it has become something of a tradition itself.

>> Figure 5.6 Adopter Categories Based on Relative Time of Adoption of Innovations

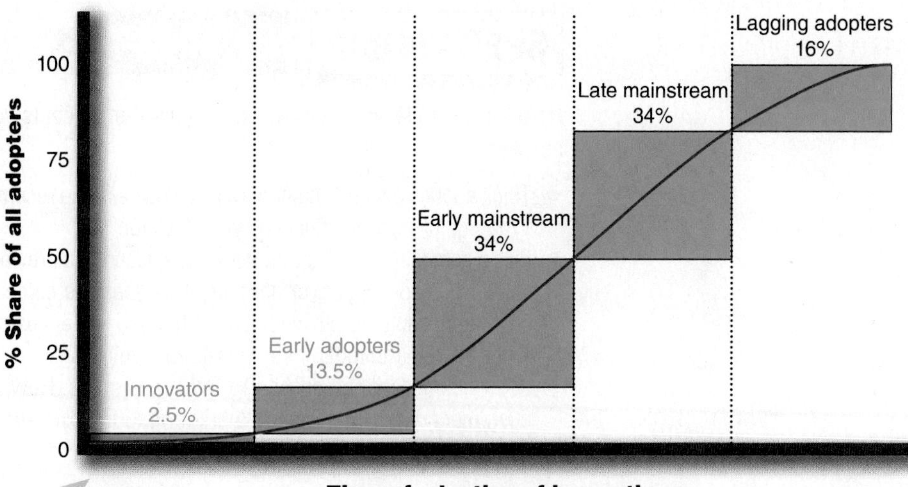

New product marketers often target innovators and early adopters, who in turn influence later adopters.

This adopter classification suggests that an innovating firm should research the characteristics of innovators and early adopters in their product categories and direct initial marketing efforts toward them.

Influence of Product Characteristics on Rate of Adoption

The characteristics of the new product affect its rate of adoption. Some products catch on almost overnight. For example, Apple's iPod, iPhone, and iPad flew off retailers' shelves at an astounding rate from the day they were first introduced. Others take a longer time to gain acceptance. For example, the first HDTVs were introduced in the United States in the 1990s, but the percentage of U.S. households owning a high-definition set stood at only 12 percent by 2007. By the end of 2012, HDTV penetration was more than 75 percent.[30]

Five characteristics are especially important in influencing an innovation's rate of adoption. For example, consider the characteristics of HDTV in relation to the rate of adoption:

Relative advantage: The degree to which the innovation appears superior to existing products. HDTV offers substantially improved picture quality. This accelerated its rate of adoption.

Compatibility: The degree to which the innovation fits the values and experiences of potential consumers. HDTV, for example, is highly compatible with the lifestyles of the TV-watching public. However, in the early years, HDTV was not yet compatible with programming and broadcasting systems, which slowed adoption. Now, as high-definition programs and channels have become the norm, the rate of HDTV adoption has increased rapidly.

Complexity: The degree to which the innovation is difficult to understand or use. HDTVs are not very complex. Therefore, as more programming has become available and prices have fallen, the rate of HDTV adoption has increased faster than that of more complex innovations.

Divisibility: The degree to which the innovation may be tried on a limited basis. Early HDTVs and HD cable and satellite systems were very expensive, which slowed the rate of adoption. As prices have fallen, adoption rates have increased.

Communicability: The degree to which the results of using the innovation can be observed or described to others. Because HDTV lends itself to demonstration and description, its use spread faster among consumers.

Other characteristics influence the rate of adoption, such as initial and ongoing costs, risk and uncertainty, and social approval. The new product marketer must research all these factors when developing the new product and its marketing program.

SPEED BUMP LINKING THE CONCEPTS

Here's a good place to pull over and apply the concepts you've examined in the first part of this chapter.

- Think about a specific major purchase you've made recently. What buying process did you follow? What major factors influenced your decision?
- Pick a company or brand that we've discussed in a previous chapter—Amazon.com, McDonald's, Nike, Microsoft, Pepsi, or another. How does the company you chose use its understanding of customers and their buying behavior to build better customer relationships?
- Think about a company such as Intel, which sells its products to computer makers and other businesses rather than to final consumers. How would Intel's marketing to business customers differ from Apple's marketing to final consumers? The second part of the chapter deals with this issue.

Author Comment
Now that we've looked at consumer markets and buyer behavior, let's dig into business markets and buyer behavior. Thinking ahead, how are they the same? How are they different?

Business Markets and Business Buyer Behavior

Business buyer behavior
The buying behavior of organizations that buy goods and services for use in the production of other products and services that are sold, rented, or supplied to others.

Business buying process
The decision process by which business buyers determine which products and services their organizations need to purchase and then find, evaluate, and choose among alternative suppliers and brands.

In one way or another, most large companies sell to other organizations. Companies such as Boeing, DuPont, IBM, Caterpillar, and countless other firms sell *most* of their products to other businesses. Even large consumer-products companies, which make products used by final consumers, must first sell their products to other businesses. For example, General Mills makes many familiar consumer brands—Big G cereals (Cheerios, Wheaties, Trix, Chex, Total, Fiber One), baking products (Pillsbury, Betty Crocker, Bisquick, Gold Medal flour), snacks (Nature Valley, Bugles, Chex Mix), Yoplait yogurt, Häagen-Dazs ice cream, and many others. But to sell these products to consumers, General Mills must first sell them to its wholesaler and retailer customers, who in turn serve the consumer market.

Business buyer behavior refers to the buying behavior of the organizations that buy goods and services for use in the production of other products and services that are sold, rented, or supplied to others. It also includes the behavior of retailing and wholesaling firms that acquire goods to resell or rent them to others at a profit. In the **business buying process**, business buyers determine which products and services their organizations need to purchase and then find, evaluate, and choose among alternative suppliers and brands. *Business-to-business (B-to-B) marketers* must do their best to understand business markets and business buyer behavior. Then, like businesses that sell to final buyers, they must build profitable relationships with business customers by creating superior customer value.

Author Comment
Business markets operate "behind the scenes" to most consumers. Most of the things you buy involve many sets of business purchases before you ever see them.

Business Markets

The business market is *huge*. In fact, business markets involve far more dollars and items than do consumer markets. For example, think about the large number of business transactions involved in the production and sale of a single set of Goodyear tires. Various suppliers sell Goodyear the rubber, steel, equipment, and other goods that it needs to produce tires. Goodyear then sells the finished tires to retailers, which in turn sell them to consumers. Thus, many sets of *business* purchases were made for only one set of *consumer* purchases. In addition, Goodyear sells tires as original equipment to manufacturers that install them on new vehicles and as replacement tires to companies that maintain their own fleets of company cars, trucks, or other vehicles.

In some ways, business markets are similar to consumer markets. Both involve people who assume buying roles and make purchase decisions to satisfy needs. However, business markets differ in many ways from consumer markets. The main differences are in *market structure and demand*, the *nature of the buying unit*, and the *types of decisions and the decision process* involved.

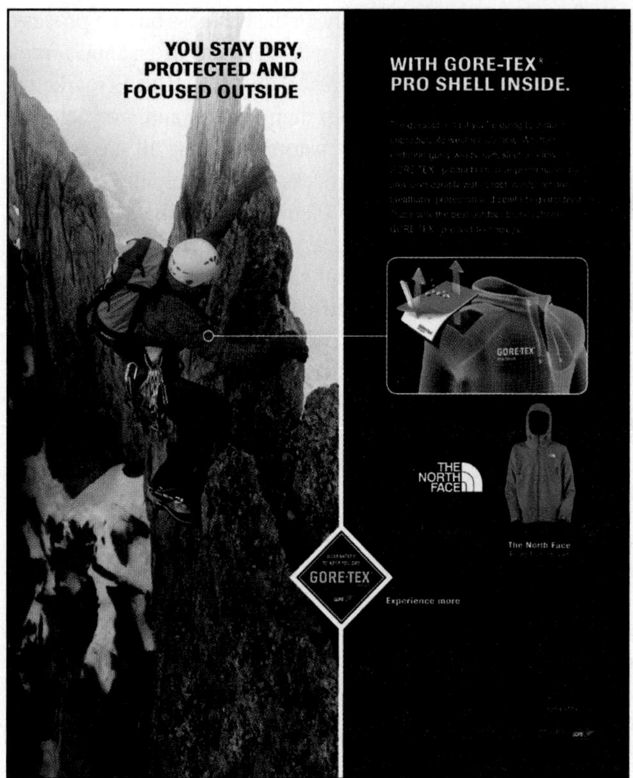

Derived demand: You can't buy anything directly from Gore, but to increase demand for Gore-Tex fabrics, the company markets directly to the buyers of outdoor apparel and other brands made from its fabrics. Both Gore and its partner brands—here, The North Face—win.

Courtesy of W. L. Gore & Associates, Inc.

Market Structure and Demand

The business marketer normally deals with *far fewer but far larger buyers* than the consumer marketer does. Even in large business markets, a few buyers often account for most of the purchasing. For example, when Goodyear sells replacement tires to final consumers, its potential market includes millions of car owners around the world. But its fate in business markets depends on getting orders from only a handful of large automakers.

Further, business demand is **derived demand**—it ultimately derives from the demand for consumer goods. For example, W. L. Gore & Associates sells its Gore-Tex brand to manufacturers who make and sell outdoor apparel brands made from Gore-Tex fabrics. If demand for these brands increases, so does demand for Gore-Tex fabrics. So to boost demand for Gore-Tex, Gore advertises to final consumers to educate them on the benefits of Gore-Tex fabrics in the brands they buy. It also directly markets brands containing Gore-Tex—from Arc'teryx, Marmot, and The North Face to Burton and L.L.Bean—on its own Web site (www.gore-tex.com).

To deepen its direct relationship with outdoor enthusiasts further, Gore even sponsors an "Experience More" online community in which members can share experiences and videos, connect with outdoor experts, and catch exclusive gear offers from partner brands. As a result, consumers around the world have learned to look for the familiar Gore-Tex brand label, and both Gore and its partner brands win. No matter what brand of apparel or footwear you buy, says the label, if it's made with Gore-Tex fabric, its "guaranteed to keep you dry."

Derived demand
Business demand that ultimately comes from (derives from) the demand for consumer goods.

Finally, many business markets have *inelastic and more fluctuating demand.* The total demand for many business products is not much affected by price changes, especially in the short run. A drop in the price of leather will not cause shoe manufacturers to buy much more leather unless it results in lower shoe prices that, in turn, increase consumer demand for shoes. And the demand for many business goods and services tends to change more—and more quickly—than does the demand for consumer goods and services. A small percentage increase in consumer demand can cause large increases in business demand.

Nature of the Buying Unit

Compared with consumer purchases, a business purchase usually involves *more decision participants* and a *more professional purchasing effort*. Often, business buying is done by trained purchasing agents who spend their working lives learning how to buy better. The more complex the purchase, the more likely it is that several people will participate in the decision-making process. Buying committees composed of technical experts and top management are common in the buying of major goods. Beyond this, B-to-B marketers now face a new breed of higher-level, better-trained supply managers. Therefore, companies must have well-trained marketers and salespeople to deal with these well-trained buyers.

Types of Decisions and the Decision Process

Business buyers usually face *more complex* buying decisions than do consumer buyers. Business purchases often involve large sums of money, complex technical and economic considerations, and interactions among people at many levels of the buyer's organization. The business buying process also tends to be *longer* and *more formalized*. Large business purchases usually call for detailed product specifications, written purchase orders, careful supplier searches, and formal approval.

DOW
Dow Performance Plastics
Think of Dow as the team...
behind your team.

» **Dow Performance Plastics isn't just selling commodity plastics—it's helping the businesses that buy its plastics to be heroes with their own customers. "We believe in a simple concept . . . if you win, we win."**

(logo) The Dow Chemical Company; (salespeople) © Bill Varie/Somos Images/Corbis.

Finally, in the business buying process, the buyer and seller are often much *more dependent* on each other. B-to-B marketers may roll up their sleeves and work closely with their customers during all stages of the buying process—from helping customers define problems, to finding solutions, to supporting after-sale operation. They often customize their offerings to individual customer needs. In the short run, sales go to suppliers who meet buyers' immediate product and service needs. In the long run, however, business-to-business marketers keep customers by meeting current needs *and* by partnering with them to help solve their problems.

For example, » Dow Performance Plastics doesn't just sell commodity plastics *to* its industrial customers—it works *with* these customers to help them succeed in their own markets. "Whether they're using Dow's plastics to make bags for Safeway or for complex [automotive] applications, we have to help them succeed in their markets," says a Dow spokesperson. "Think of Dow as the team behind your team," says Dow at its Web site. "We believe in a simple concept . . . if you win, we win."[31]

As in Dow's case, in recent years, relationships between most customers and suppliers have been changing from downright adversarial to close and chummy. In fact, many customer companies are now practicing **supplier development**, systematically developing networks of supplier-partners to ensure a dependable supply of the products and materials that they use in making their own products or reselling to others. For example, Walmart doesn't have a "Purchasing Department"; it has a "Supplier Development Department." The giant retailer knows that it can't just rely on spot suppliers who might be available when needed. Instead, Walmart manages a huge network of supplier-partners that help provide the hundreds of billions of dollars of goods that it sells to its customers each year.

Supplier development
Systematic development of networks of supplier-partners to ensure an appropriate and dependable supply of products and materials for use in making products or reselling them to others.

Author Comment
Business buying decisions can range from routine to incredibly complex, involving only a few or very many decision makers and buying influences.

Business Buyer Behavior

At the most basic level, marketers want to know how business buyers will respond to various marketing stimuli. » **Figure 5.7** shows a model of business buyer behavior. In this model, marketing and other stimuli affect the buying organization and produce certain buyer responses. To design good marketing strategies, marketers must understand what happens within the organization to turn stimuli into purchase responses.

Within the organization, buying activity consists of two major parts: the *buying center*, composed of all the people involved in the buying decision, and the *buying decision*

» **Figure 5.7** A Model of Business Buying Behavior

In some ways, business markets are similar to consumer markets—this model looks a lot like the model of consumer buyer behavior presented in Figure 5.1. But there are some major differences, especially in the nature of the buying unit, the types of decisions made, and the decision process.

The environment
Marketing stimuli
Other stimuli
Product
Economic
Price
Technological
Place
Political
Promotion
Cultural
Competitive

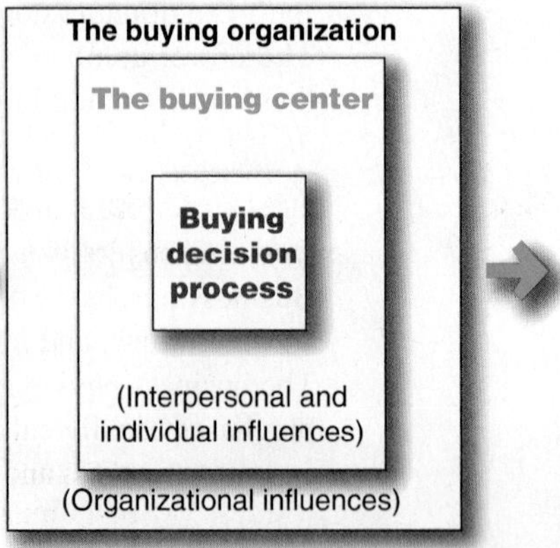

Buyer responses
Product or service choice
Supplier choice
Order quantities
Delivery terms and times
Service terms
Payment

process. The model shows that the buying center and the buying decision process are influenced by internal organizational, interpersonal, and individual factors as well as external environmental factors.

The model in Figure 5.7 suggests four questions about business buyer behavior: What buying decisions do business buyers make? Who participates in the business buying process? What are the major influences on buyers? How do business buyers make their buying decisions?

Major Types of Buying Situations

Straight rebuy
A business buying situation in which the buyer routinely reorders something without any modifications.

Modified rebuy
A business buying situation in which the buyer wants to modify product specifications, prices, terms, or suppliers.

New task
A business buying situation in which the buyer purchases a product or service for the first time.

Systems selling (or solutions selling)
Buying a packaged solution to a problem from a single seller, thus avoiding all the separate decisions involved in a complex buying situation.

There are three major types of buying situations.[32] In a **straight rebuy**, the buyer reorders something without any modifications. It is usually handled on a routine basis by the purchasing department. To keep the business, "in" suppliers try to maintain product and service quality. "Out" suppliers try to find new ways to add value or exploit dissatisfaction so that the buyer will consider them.

In a **modified rebuy**, the buyer wants to modify product specifications, prices, terms, or suppliers. The "in" suppliers may become nervous and feel pressured to put their best foot forward to protect an account. "Out" suppliers may see the modified rebuy situation as an opportunity to make a better offer and gain new business.

A company buying a product or service for the first time faces a **new task** situation. In such cases, the greater the cost or risk, the larger the number of decision participants and the greater the company's efforts to collect information. The new task situation is the marketer's greatest opportunity and challenge. The marketer not only tries to reach as many key buying influences as possible, but also provides help and information. The buyer makes the fewest decisions in the straight rebuy and the most in the new task decision.

Many business buyers prefer to buy a complete solution to a problem from a single seller rather than buying separate products and services from several suppliers and putting them together. The sale often goes to the firm that provides the most complete *system* for meeting the customer's needs and solving its problems. Such **systems selling** (or **solutions selling**) is often a key business marketing strategy for winning and holding accounts. Consider IBM and its customer Six Flags Entertainment Corporation:[33]

Six Flags operates 19 regional theme parks across the United States, Mexico, and Canada, featuring exciting rides and water attractions, world-class roller coasters, and special shows and concerts. » To deliver a fun and safe experience for guests, Six Flags must carefully and effectively manage thousands of park assets—from rides and equipment to buildings and other facilities. Six Flags needed a tool for managing all those assets efficiently and effectively across its far-flung collection of parks. So it turned to IBM, which has software—called Maximo Asset Management software—that handles that very problem well.

But IBM didn't just hand the software over to Six Flags with best wishes for a happy implementation. Instead, IBM's Maximo Professional Services group is combining the software with an entire set of services designed to get and keep the software up and running. IBM is working hand-in-hand with Six Flags to customize the application and strategically implement it across Six Flags's far-flung facilities, along with on-site immersion training and planning workshops. "We've implemented the solution at five parks to date, and as the implementation team completes each deployment, they move to the next property," says Six Flags's director of corporate project management. "We have one implementation team to make sure that all the deployments across our parks are consistent." IBM will work with Six Flags throughout the process. Thus, IBM isn't just selling the software, it's selling a complete solution to Six Flags's complex asset management problem.

» **Solutions selling: Delivering a fun and safe experience for Six Flags guests requires careful and effective management of thousands of park assets across its 19 regional theme parks. IBM works hand in hand with Six Flags to provide not just software, but a complete solution.**

WireImage.

Participants in the Business Buying Process

Who does the buying of the trillions of dollars' worth of goods and services needed by business organizations? The decision-making unit of a buying organization is called its

Buying center
All the individuals and units that play a role in the purchase decision-making process.

buying center. It consists of all the individuals and units that play a role in the business purchase decision-making process. This group includes the actual users of the product or service, those who make the buying decision, those who influence the buying decision, those who do the actual buying, and those who control buying information.

The buying center is not a fixed and formally identified unit within the buying organization. It is a set of buying roles assumed by different people for different purchases. Within the organization, the size and makeup of the buying center will vary for different products and for different buying situations. For some routine purchases, one person—say, a purchasing agent—may assume all the buying center roles and serve as the only person involved in the buying decision. For more complex purchases, the buying center may include 20 or 30 people from different levels and departments in the organization.

The buying center concept presents a major marketing challenge. The business marketer must learn who participates in the decision, each participant's relative influence, and what evaluation criteria each decision participant uses. This can be difficult.

The buying center usually includes some obvious participants who are involved formally in the buying decision. For example, the decision to buy a corporate jet will probably involve the company's CEO, the chief pilot, a purchasing agent, some legal staff, a member of top management, and others formally charged with the buying decision. It may also involve less obvious, informal participants, some of whom may actually make or strongly affect the buying decision. Sometimes, even the people in the buying center are not aware of all the buying participants. For example, the decision about which corporate jet to buy may actually be made by a corporate board member who has an interest in flying and who knows a lot about airplanes. This board member may work behind the scenes to sway the decision. Many business buying decisions result from the complex interactions of ever-changing buying center participants.

Major Influences on Business Buyers

Business buyers are subject to many influences when they make their buying decisions. Some marketers assume that the major influences are economic. They think buyers will favor the supplier who offers the lowest price or the best product or the most service. They concentrate on offering strong economic benefits to buyers. Such economic factors are very important to most buyers, especially in a tough economy. However, business buyers actually respond to both economic and personal factors. Far from being cold, calculating, and impersonal, business buyers are human and social as well. They react to both reason and emotion.

Today, most B-to-B marketers recognize that emotion plays an important role in business buying decisions. >> Consider this example:[34]

>> **Emotions play a role in business buying. The emotion-charged images in this B-to-B ad convey the message that the USG's Ultralight wallboard panels remove some of the weight from the backs and shoulders of its customers.**

USG Corporation.

USG Corporation is a leading manufacturer of gypsum wallboard and other building materials for the construction and remodeling industries. Given its construction contractor, dealer, and builder audience, you might expect USG's B-to-B ads to focus heavily on the performance features and benefits such as strength, impact resistance, ease of installation, and costs. USG does promote these benefits. However, a recent marketing campaign for USG's Sheetrock Ultralight wallboard panels also packed a decidedly more emotional wallop. Ultralight panels offer performance equal to or better than standard gypsum wallboard but are 30 percent lighter. That makes them easier to lift, carry, and install, reducing worker fatigue. Instead of just stating that Ultralight is lighter, USG's advertising campaign—called the "Weight

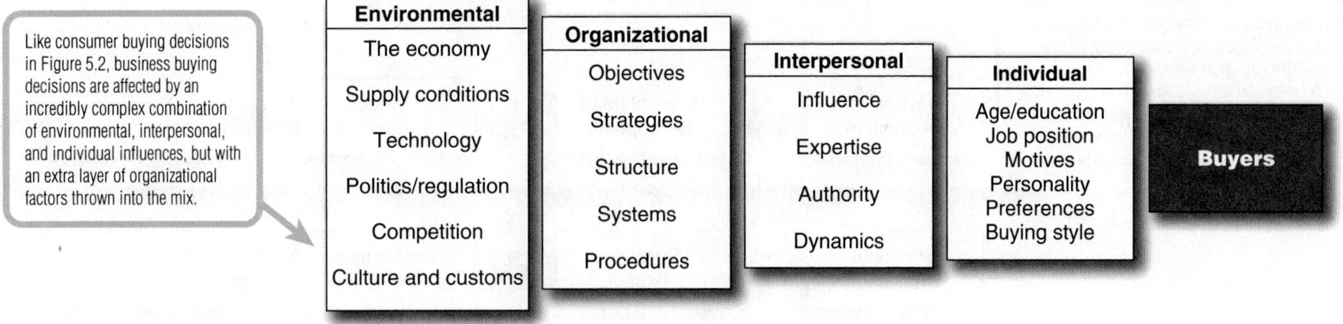

>> **Figure 5.8** Major Influences on Business Buying Behavior

Has Been Lifted"—visualized this benefit using dramatic, emotion-charged imagery showing that it's literally removing some weight from the backs and shoulders of its customers. Ads show contractors struggling to carry enormous objects such as a car, a giant anchor, a grand piano, or an elephant or dinosaur. The tagline: "If you're not lifting Ultralight Panels, what are you lifting?"

>> **Figure 5.8** lists various groups of influences on business buyers—environmental, organizational, interpersonal, and individual. Business buyers are heavily influenced by factors in the current and expected *economic environment*, such as the level of primary demand, the economic outlook, and the cost of money. Another environmental factor is the *supply* of key materials. Many companies now are more willing to buy and hold larger inventories of scarce materials to ensure adequate supply. Business buyers also are affected by *technological*, *political*, and *competitive* developments in the environment. Finally, *culture and customs* can strongly influence business buyer reactions to the marketer's behavior and strategies, especially in the international marketing environment. The business buyer must watch these factors, determine how they will affect the buyer, and try to turn these challenges into opportunities.

Organizational factors are also important. Each buying organization has its own objectives, strategies, structure, systems, and procedures, and the business marketer must understand these factors well. Questions such as these arise: How many people are involved in the buying decision? Who are they? What are their evaluative criteria? What are the company's policies and limits on its buyers?

The buying center usually includes many participants who influence each other, so *interpersonal factors* also influence the business buying process. However, it is often difficult to assess such interpersonal factors and group dynamics. Buying center participants do not wear tags that label them as "key decision maker" or "not influential." Nor do buying center participants with the highest rank always have the most influence. Participants may influence the buying decision because they control rewards and punishments, are well liked, have special expertise, or have a special relationship with other important participants. Interpersonal factors are often very subtle. Whenever possible, business marketers must try to understand these factors and design strategies that take them into account.

Each participant in the business buying decision process brings in personal motives, perceptions, and preferences. These *individual factors* are affected by personal characteristics such as age, income, education, professional identification, personality, and attitudes toward risk. Also, buyers have different buying styles. Some may be technical types who make in-depth analyses of competitive proposals before choosing a supplier. Other buyers may be intuitive negotiators who are adept at pitting the sellers against one another for the best deal.

The Business Buying Process

>> **Figure 5.9** lists the eight stages of the business buying process.[35] Buyers who face a new task buying situation usually go through all stages of the buying process. Buyers

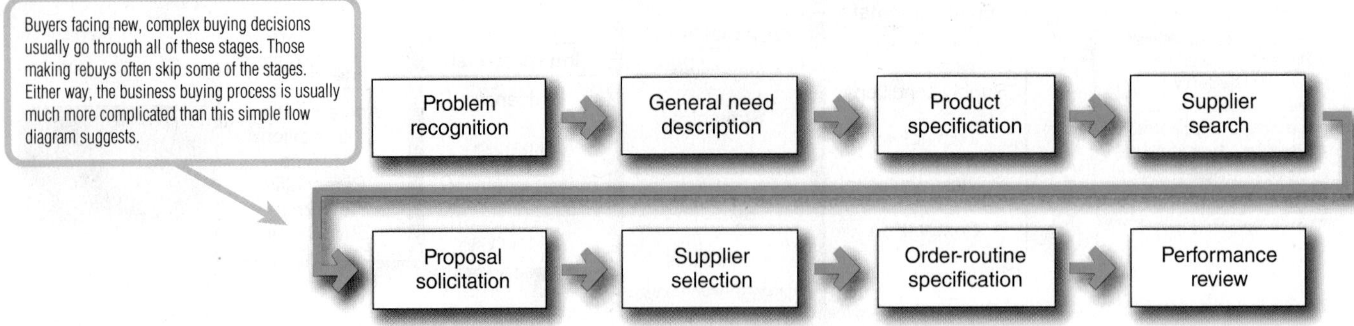

Figure 5.9 Stages of Business Buying Behavior

making modified or straight rebuys, in contrast, may skip some of the stages. We will examine these steps for the typical new task buying situation.

The buying process begins with *problem recognition*—when someone in the company recognizes a problem or need that can be met by acquiring a specific product or service. Problem recognition can result from internal or external stimuli. Business marketers use their sales forces or advertising to alert customers to potential problems and then show how their products provide solutions. For example, an award-winning ad from Quill.com, an online office products supplier that strives for strong customer service, highlights an important customer problem: what to do when your printer runs out of toner. The visual in the ad—which shows the headline fading then reappearing—effectively suggests both the problem and the solution. "If you run out of toner," says the ad, "we will replace it this quickly. At Quill.com, we are here whenever you need us."

Problem recognition: Quill.com uses this award-winning ad to alert customers to both an important problem and the solution. "At Quill.com, we're here whenever you need us."

Quill.com, agency—Euro RSCG Chicago, Creative Director, Blake Ebel.

Having recognized a need, the buyer next prepares a *general need description* that describes the characteristics and quantity of the needed items or solutions. For standard purchases, this process presents few problems. For complex items, however, the buyer may need to work with others—engineers, users, consultants—to define what's needed.

Once the buying organization has defined the need, it develops the item's technical *product specifications*, often with the help of a value analysis engineering team. **Product value analysis** is an approach to cost reduction in which the company carefully analyzes a product's or service's components to determine if they can be redesigned and made more effectively and efficiently to provide greater value. The team decides on the best product or service characteristics and specifies them accordingly. Sellers, too, can use value analysis as a tool to help secure new accounts and keep old ones. Improving customer value and helping customers find more cost-effective solutions gives the business marketer and important edge in keeping current customers loyal and winning new business.

In the next buying process step, the buyer conducts a *supplier search* to find the best vendors. The buyer can locate qualified suppliers through trade directories, computer searches, or recommendations from others. Today, more and more companies are turning to the Internet to find suppliers. For marketers, this has leveled the playing field—the Internet gives smaller suppliers many of the same advantages as larger competitors. The task of suppliers is to understand the search process and make certain that their firms are considered.

Product value analysis
Carefully analyzing a product's or service's components to determine if they can be redesigned and made more effectively and efficiently to provide greater value.

In the *proposal solicitation* stage of the business buying process, the buyer invites qualified suppliers to submit proposals. When the purchase is complex or expensive, the buyer will usually require detailed written proposals or formal presentations from each potential supplier. In response, business marketers must be skilled in researching, writing, and presenting proposals. The proposals should be marketing documents, not just technical documents. They should spell out how the seller's solution creates greater value for the customer than competing solutions.

The buyer next reviews the proposals and selects a supplier or suppliers. During *supplier selection*, the buyer will consider many supplier attributes and their relative importance. Such attributes include product and service quality, reputation, on-time delivery, ethical corporate behavior, honest communication, and competitive prices. In the end, buyers may select a single supplier or a few suppliers. Today's supplier development managers often want to develop a full network of supplier-partners that can help the company bring more value to its customers.

The buyer now prepares an *order-routine specification*. It includes the final order with the chosen supplier or suppliers and lists items such as technical specifications, quantity needed, expected time of delivery, return policies, and warranties. Many large buyers now practice *vendor-managed inventory*, in which they turn over ordering and inventory responsibilities to their suppliers. Under such systems, buyers share sales and inventory information directly with key suppliers. The suppliers then monitor inventories and replenish stock automatically as needed. For example, most major suppliers to large retailers such as Walmart, Target, Home Depot, and Lowe's assume vendor-managed inventory responsibilities.

The final stage of the business buying process is the supplier *performance review*, in which the buyer assesses the supplier's performance and provides feedback. For example, Home Depot has issued a set of supplier guidelines and policies and regularly evaluates each supplier in terms of quality, delivery, and other performance variables. It gives suppliers online performance scorecards that provide ongoing feedback that helps them improve their performance.[36] The supplier performance review may lead the buyer to continue, modify, or drop the arrangement. The seller's job is to monitor the same factors used by the buyer to make sure that the seller is giving the expected satisfaction.

The eight-stage buying process model provides a simple view of business buying as it might occur in a new task buying situation. The actual process is usually much more complex. In the modified rebuy or straight rebuy situation, some of these stages would be compressed or bypassed. Each organization buys in its own way, and each buying situation has unique requirements.

Different buying center participants may be involved at different stages of the process. Although certain buying process steps usually do occur, buyers do not always follow them in the same order, and they may add other steps. Often, buyers will repeat certain stages of the process. Finally, a customer relationship might involve many different types of purchases ongoing at a given time, all in different stages of the buying process. The seller must manage the total customer relationship, not just individual purchases.

E-Procurement and Online Purchasing

E-procurement
Purchasing through electronic connections between buyers and sellers—usually online.

Advances in information technology have changed the face of the B-to-B marketing process. Online purchasing, often called **e-procurement**, has grown rapidly in recent years. Virtually unknown a decade and a half ago, online purchasing is standard procedure for most companies today. E-procurement gives buyers access to new suppliers, lowers purchasing costs, and hastens order processing and delivery. In turn, business marketers can connect with customers online to share marketing information, sell products and services, provide customer support services, and maintain ongoing customer relationships.

Companies can do e-procurement in any of several ways. They can conduct *reverse auctions*, in which they put their purchasing requests online and invite suppliers to bid for the business. Or they can engage in online *trading exchanges*, through which companies work collectively to facilitate the trading process. Companies also can conduct e-procurement by setting up their own *company buying sites*. For example, GE operates a company trading site on which it posts its buying needs and invites bids, negotiates terms, and places orders. Or companies can create *extranet links* with key suppliers. For instance, they can create direct procurement accounts with suppliers such as Dell or Staples, through which company buyers can purchase equipment, materials, and supplies directly. Staples operates a business-to-business procurement division called Staples Advantage, which serves the office supplies and services buying needs of businesses of any size, from 20 employees to the Fortune 1000.

B-to-B marketers can help customers online and build stronger customer relationships by creating well-designed, easy-to-use Web sites. » For example, *BtoB* magazine recently rated the site of Shaw Floors—a market leader in flooring products—as one of its "10 great B-to-B Web sites." The site helps Shaw build strong links with its business and trade customers:[37]

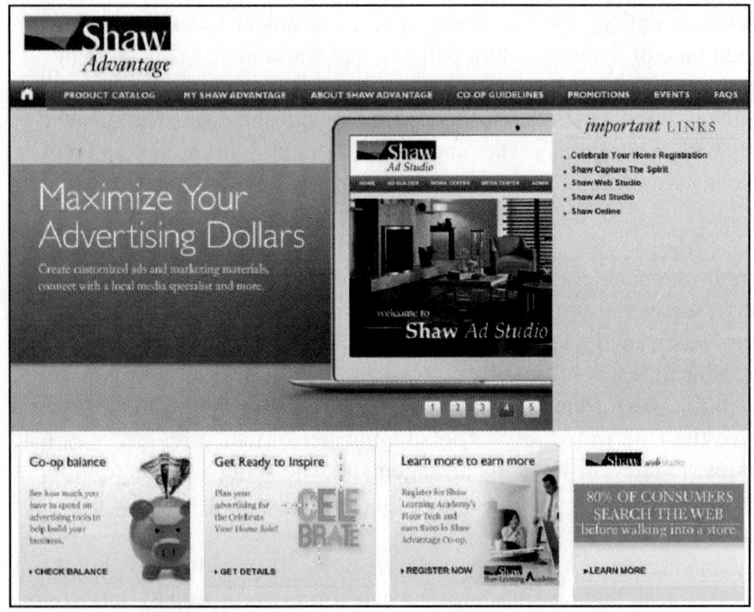

» **B-to-B Web sites: This Shaw Floors site builds strong links with Shaw's retailers. It provides marketing ideas and tools that make retailers more effective in selling Shaw's products to final customers.**

Shaw Industries, Inc.

At one time, flooring manufacturer Shaw Floors' Web site was nothing more than "brochureware." Today, however, the site is a true interactive experience. At the site, design and construction professionals as well as customers can "see"—virtually—the company's many product lines. At the popular "Try on a Floor" area, designers or retailers can even work with final buyers to upload digital images of an actual floor and put any of the company's many carpets on it to see how they look. They can select various lines and colors immediately without digging through samples. And the extremely detailed images can be rotated and manipulated so a designer, for example, can show a client what the pile of the carpet looks like and how deep it is.

The Shaw Floors site also provides a rich set of easy-to-navigate resources for Shaw retailers. The "For Retailers" area lets retail-partners search the company's products, make inventory checks, track order status, or order brochures for their stores. At the Shaw AdSource area, retailers can find resources to create their own ads. The Shaw Web Studio lets retailers—many of which are mom-and-pop stores—download the photography, catalog engines, and other tools they need to build their own Web sites. "So many retailers don't have the time or money to build their own online presence," says Shaw's interactive marketing manager, "so this really helps them."

More generally, today's business-to-business marketers are using a wide range of digital and social marketing approaches—from Web sites, blogs, and smartphone apps to mainstream social media such as Facebook, LinkedIn, YouTube, and Twitter to reach business customers and manage customer relationships anywhere, at any time. Digital and social media marketing has rapidly become *the* new space for engaging business customers (see Marketing at Work 5.2).

Business-to-business e-procurement yields many benefits. First, it shaves transaction costs and results in more efficient purchasing for both buyers and suppliers. E-procurement reduces the time between order and delivery. And an online-powered purchasing program eliminates the paperwork associated with traditional requisition and ordering procedures and helps an organization keep better track of all purchases. Finally, beyond the cost and time savings, e-procurement frees purchasing people from a lot of drudgery and paperwork. In turn, it frees them to focus on more-strategic issues, such as finding better supply sources and working with suppliers to reduce costs and develop new products.

The rapidly expanding use of e-procurement, however, also presents some problems. For example, at the same time that the Internet makes it possible for suppliers and customers to share business data and even collaborate on product design, it can also erode decades-old customer–supplier relationships. Many buyers now use the power of the Internet to pit suppliers against one another and search out better deals, products, and turnaround times on a purchase-by-purchase basis.

MARKETING AT WORK 5.2

B-to-B Social Marketing: The Space to Engage Business Customers

There's a hot new video on YouTube these days, featured at the Makino Machine Tools YouTube channel. It shows Makino's D500 five-axis vertical machining center in action, with metal chips flying as the machinery mills a new industrial part. Sound exciting? Probably not to you. But to the right industrial customer, the video is downright spellbinding. "Wow," says one viewer, "that's a new concept to have the saddle ride in Y rather than X. Is that a rigidity enhancement?" In all, the video has been viewed more than 33,000 times, mostly by current or prospective Makino customers. For B-to-B marketer Makino, that's great exposure.

When you think of digital marketing and social media, you most likely think of marketing to final consumers. But today, most business-to-business marketers, like Makino, have also upped their use of these new approaches to reach and engage business customers. The use of digital and social media channels in business marketing isn't just growing, it's exploding. Even as most major B-to-B marketers are cutting back on traditional media and event marketing, they are ramping up their use of everything from Web sites, blogs, mobile apps, and proprietary online networks to mainstream social media such as Facebook, LinkedIn, Google+, YouTube, and Twitter. Research shows that 79 percent of B-to-B companies now post articles online, 74 percent use existing social media, 65 percent blog, 63 percent send out e-newsletters, 52 percent post videos online, and 46 percent conduct webinars.

Digital and social media have become *the* space in which to engage B-to-B customers and strengthen customer relationships. Again, consider Makino, a leading manufacturer of metal cutting and machining technology:

> Makino employs a wide variety of social media initiatives that inform customers and enhance customer relationships. For example, it hosts an ongoing series of industry-specific webinars that position the company as an industry thought leader. Makino produces about three webinars each month and offers a library of more than 100 on topics ranging from optimizing machine tool performance to discovering new metal-cutting processes. Webinar content is tailored to specific industries, such as aerospace or medical, and is promoted through carefully targeted banner ads and e-mails. The webinars help to build Makino's customer database, generate leads, build customer relationships, and prepare the way for salespeople by providing relevant information and educating customers online.

Makino even uses Twitter, Facebook, and YouTube to inform customers and prospects about the latest Makino innovations and events and to vividly demonstrate the company's machines in action. The results have been gratifying. "We've shifted dramatically into the electronic marketing area," says Makino's marketing manager. "It speeds up the sales cycle and makes it more efficient—for both the company and the customer. The results have been outstanding."

Compared with traditional media and sales approaches, digital and social media approaches can create greater customer engagement and interaction. B-to-B marketers know that they aren't really targeting *businesses,* they are targeting *individuals* in those businesses who affect buying decisions. "We are selling business-to-people," notes one B-to-B marketer. And today's business buyers are always connected. They have their digital devices—whether PCs, tablets, or smartphones—hardwired to their brains. As one B-to-B marketer puts it, "Being at work is no longer a place; it is a state of mind."

Digital and social media can play an important role in engaging today's always-connected business buyers in a way that personal selling alone cannot. Instead of the old model

B-to-B social media: Machining tool manufacturer Makino engages its business customers through extensive digital and social marketing—everything from proprietary online communities and webinars to Facebook, YouTube, and Twitter.

Courtesy of Makino, Inc.; Facebook is a trademark of Facebook, Inc.

of sales reps calling on business customers at work or maybe meeting up with them at trade shows, the new digital approaches facilitate anytime, anywhere connections between a wide range of people in the selling and customer organizations. It gives both sellers and buyers more control of and access to important information. B-to-B marketing has always been social network marketing, but today's digital environment offers an exciting array of new networking tools and applications.

No company seems to grasp the new digital and social media opportunities more fully than one of the oldest companies around—IBM. At 115 years old and with 400,000 employees in 170 countries, Big Blue is as fresh and relevant—and profitable—as ever when it comes to social media. It uses a decentralized approach to social media. "We represent our brand online the way it always has been," says an IBM social media executive. "Our brand is largely shaped by the interactions that [IBMers] have with customers."

From that perspective, IBM encourages employees to talk publically in the social media—to each other and to customers—and lets them go about it with no intervention or oversight. And go about it they do. Thousands of IBMers are the voice of the company. There are 100,000 IBMers using 17,000 internal blogs and 53,000 members on SocialBlue (IBM's own internal Facebook-like network). "Run an online search for 'IBM blog' and you'll find countless IBMers posting publically on everything from service-oriented architecture to sales to parenthood," says one analyst. "If you want to blog at IBM, you simply start." IBM employees by the tens of thousands or even hundreds of thousands are also actively involved on Twitter, LinkedIn, Facebook, YouTube, and many other public social media.

All this IBMer-led social networking drives an incredible amount of interaction among IBM employees, customers, and suppliers. For example, an IBM "innovation jam" can include a diverse group of as many as 500,000 people inside and outside the company. Such online interactions helped spawn what is now a major IBM movement, Smarter Planet—an initiative that puts the collective minds and tools at IBM and outside the company toward solving issues ranging from rush-hour traffic to natural disaster response.

Whether it's IBM's decentralized approach to digital and social media or Makino's more focused and deliberate one, B-to-B marketers are discovering just how effective these new networking channels can be for engaging and interacting with business customers. Digital and social marketing aren't passing B-to-B fads; they signal a new way of doing business. Gone are the days when B-to-B marketers can just push out information about their products and services in a sales call or at a marketing event. Instead, marketers need to engage customers in meaningful and relevant ways, whenever and wherever customers demand it, 24 hours a day, 7 days a week. As one B-to-B social media director states, "Customer expectations have changed. Customers want, on demand, to have a say in how they interact with you as a company." Says another social media expert, "Social media is how the current and next generation of B-to-B customers is choosing to learn about new solutions and stay current on brands."

Sources: Kate Maddox, "Online Marketing Summit Focuses on Social, Search, Content," *btobonline.com*, February 13, 2012; Elizabeth Sullivan, "One to One," *Marketing News*, May 15, 2009, pp. 10–13; Sean Callahan, "Is B2B Marketing Really Obsolete?" *btobonline.com*, January 17, 2011; Casey Hibbard, "How IBM Uses Social Media to Spur Employee Innovation," *Socialmediaexaminer.com*, February 2, 2010; Joe Pulizzi, "2012 B2B Content Marketing Benchmarks, Budgets, and Trends," *contentmarketinginstitute.com*, December 5, 2011; "Analytics, Content, and Apps Are Hot Topics at 'BtoB's SF NetMarketing Breakfast," *BtoB*, February 17, 2012, www.btobonline.com/article/20120217/EVENT02/302179995/analytics-content-and-apps-are-hot-topics-at-btobs-sf-netmarketing; Louis Columbus, "B2B Marketers Need to Get Real about Social Media and Customer Engagement," *Forbes*, January 17, 2013, www.forbes.com/sites/louiscolumbus/2013/01/17/b2b-marketers-need-to-get-real-about-social-media-and-customer-engagement/print/; and www.youtube.com/user/MakinoMachineTools, accessed October 2013.

E-procurement can also create potential security concerns. Although home shopping transactions can be protected through basic encryption, the secure environment that businesses need to carry out confidential interactions is sometimes still lacking. Companies are spending millions for research on defensive strategies to keep hackers at bay. Cisco Systems, for example, specifies the types of routers, firewalls, and security procedures that its partners must use to safeguard extranet connections. In fact, the company goes even further; it sends its own security engineers to examine a partner's defenses and holds the partner liable for any security breach that originates from its computers.

MyMarketingLab

Go to **mymktlab.com** to complete the problems marked with this icon .

END OF CHAPTER REVIEWING THE CONCEPTS

CHAPTER REVIEW AND KEY TERMS

Objectives Review

This chapter is the last of three chapters that address understanding the marketplace and consumers. Here, we've looked closely at *consumer* and *business buyer behavior.* The American consumer market consists of more than 314 million people who consume more than $15 trillion worth of goods and services each year, making it one of the most attractive consumer markets in the world. The business market involves even more dollars and items than the consumer market. Understanding buyer behavior is one of the biggest challenges marketers face.

OBJECTIVE 1 Understand the consumer market and the major factors that influence consumer buyer behavior. (pp 132–147)

The *consumer market* consists of all the individuals and households that buy or acquire goods and services for personal consumption. A simple model of consumer behavior suggests that marketing stimuli and other major forces enter the consumer's "black box." This black box has two parts: buyer characteristics and the buyer's decision process. Once in the black box, the inputs result in buyer responses, such as buying attitudes and preferences and purchase behavior.

Consumer buyer behavior is influenced by four key sets of buyer characteristics: cultural, social, personal, and psychological. Understanding these factors can help marketers to identify interested buyers and to shape products and appeals to serve consumer needs better. *Culture* is the most basic determinant of a person's wants and behavior. People in different cultural, subcultural, and social class groups have different product and brand preferences. *Social factors*—such as small group, social network, and family influences—strongly affect product and brand choices, as do *personal characteristics,* such as age, lifecycle stage, occupation, economic circumstances, lifestyle, and personality. Finally, consumer buying behavior is influenced by four major sets of *psychological factors*—motivation, perception, learning, and beliefs and attitudes. Each of these factors provides a different perspective for understanding the workings of the buyer's black box.

OBJECTIVE 2 Identify and discuss the stages in the buyer decision process. (pp 147–149)

When making a purchase, the buyer goes through a decision process consisting of need recognition, information search, evaluation of alternatives, purchase decision, and postpurchase behavior. During *need recognition*, the consumer recognizes a problem or need that could be satisfied by a product or service. Once the need is recognized, the consumer moves into the *information search* stage. With information in hand, the consumer proceeds to *alternative evaluation* and assesses brands in the choice set. From there, the consumer makes a *purchase decision* and actually buys the product. In the final stage of the buyer decision process, *postpurchase behavior,* the consumer takes action based on satisfaction or dissatisfaction. The marketer's job is to understand the buyer's behavior at each stage and the influences that are operating.

OBJECTIVE 3 Describe the adoption and diffusion process for new products. (pp 149–152)

The product *adoption process* is made up of five stages: awareness, interest, evaluation, trial, and adoption. New product marketers must think about how to help consumers move through these stages. With regard to the *diffusion process* for new products, consumers respond at different rates, depending on consumer and product characteristics. Consumers may be innovators, early adopters, early majority, late majority, or laggards. Each group may require different marketing approaches. Marketers often try to bring their new products to the attention of potential early adopters, especially those who are opinion leaders.

OBJECTIVE 4 Define the business market and identify the major factors that influence business buyer behavior. (pp 152–157)

The *business market* comprises all organizations that buy goods and services for use in the production of other products and

services or for the purpose of reselling or renting them to others at a profit. As compared to consumer markets, business markets usually have fewer, larger buyers who are more geographically concentrated. Business demand is derived demand, and the business buying decision usually involves more, and more professional, buyers.

Business buyers make decisions that vary with the three types of *buying situations:* straight rebuys, modified rebuys, and new tasks. The decision-making unit of a buying organization—the *buying center*—can consist of many different persons playing many different roles. The business marketer needs to know the following: Who are the major buying center participants? In what decisions do they exercise influence and to what degree? What evaluation criteria does each decision participant use? The business marketer also needs to understand the major environmental, organizational, interpersonal, and individual influences on the buying process.

OBJECTIVE 5 List and define the steps in the business buying decision process. (pp 157–162)

The *business buying decision process* itself can be quite involved, with eight basic stages: problem recognition, general need description, product specification, supplier search, proposal solicitation, supplier selection, order-routine specification, and performance review. Buyers who face a new task buying situation usually go through all stages of the buying process. Buyers making modified or straight rebuys may skip some of the stages. Companies must manage the overall customer relationship, which often includes many different buying decisions in various stages of the buying decision process. Recent advances in information technology have given birth to "e-procurement," by which business buyers are purchasing all kinds of products and services online. Business marketers are increasingly connecting with customers online and through the social media to share marketing information, sell products and services, provide customer support services, and maintain ongoing customer relationships.

Key Terms

Objective 1
Consumer buyer behavior (p 132)
Consumer market (p 132)

Objective 2
Culture (p 133)
Subculture (p 134)
Cross-cultural marketing (p 136)
Social class (p 136)
Group (p 137)
Word-of-mouth influence (p 137)
Opinion leader (p 137)
Online social networks (p 138)
Lifestyle (p 142)
Personality (p 143)
Motive (drive) (p 144)
Perception (p 144)
Learning (p 146)
Belief (p 146)
Attitude (p 146)

Objective 3
Cognitive dissonance (p 149)
New product (p 149)
Adoption process (p 149)

Objective 4
Business buyer behavior (p 152)
Business buying process (p 152)
Derived demand (p 153)
Supplier development (p 154)
Straight rebuy (p 155)
Modified rebuy (p 155)
New task (p 155)
Systems selling (solutions selling) (p 155)
Buying center (p 156)

Objective 5
Product value analysis (p 158)
E-procurement (p 159)

DISCUSSION AND CRITICAL THINKING

Discussion Questions

5-1. Discuss the elements of culture that influence buyer behavior and give a personal example of how each has influenced a purchase decision you or your family made. (AACSB: Written and Oral Communication; Reflective Thinking)

5-2. What is an opinion leader? Describe how marketers attempt to use opinion leaders to help sell their products. (AACSB: Written and Oral Communication; Reflective Thinking)

5-3. How does the market structure and demand faced by business marketers differ from that faced by consumer marketers? (AACSB: Written and Oral Communication)

5-4. Explain what is meant by systems selling and discuss why it is a preferred approach to buying for many organizations. (AACSB: Written and Oral Communication; Reflective Thinking)

5-5. Describe how online purchasing has changed the business-to-business marketing process and discuss the advantages and disadvantages of electronic purchasing. (AACSB: Written and Oral Communication)

Critical Thinking Exercises

5-6. Form a small group of four or five students. Have each group member interview 10 consumers about if and when they purchased their first smartphone. Research when smartphones were first introduced, and based on each respondent's answer, identify which adopter category best describes that consumer. Create a chart similar to Figure 5.6 to present your results for all group members' interviews. How far along are smartphones in their adoption cycle? (AACSB: Written and Oral Communication; Diverse and Multicultural Work Environments; Reflective Thinking)

5-7. Malcolm Gladwell published a book entitled *The Tipping Point*. He describes the Law of the Few, Stickiness, and the Law of Context. Research these concepts and describe how understanding them helps marketers better understand and target consumers. (AACSB: Written and Oral Communication; Reflective Thinking)

5-8. Business buying occurs worldwide, so marketers need to be aware of cultural factors influencing business customers. In a small group, select a country and develop a multimedia presentation on proper business etiquette and manners, including appropriate appearance, behavior, and communication. Include a map showing the location of the country as well as a description of the country in terms of its demographics, culture, and economic history. (AACSB: Written and Oral Communication; Diverse and Multicultural Work Environments; Information Technology)

MINICASES AND APPLICATIONS

Online, Mobile, and Social Media Marketing Mourning 2.0

Every culture has rituals for mourning the dead, but technology is now changing many of our long-held cultural norms. The conservative funeral industry is slowly embracing new digital and social media technologies, resulting in new mourning behaviors. High-definition video screens play video homage to the deceased, live-streamed funerals reach all corners of the globe, digital guest books remain permanently active, e-mails remind the bereaved of the anniversary of a loved one's death, and digital candles remain perpetually "lit" on memorial pages. The deceased can now live on in cyberspace and friends can visit them on Facebook long after they have passed on. Quick-response code chips ("QR codes") affixed to tombstones can bring a person "back to life" virtually on a smartphone. With nearly half of all Americans owning smartphones, 20 percent owning tablets, 80 percent on the Internet, and almost 70 percent visiting social media sites, the time is now right for the funeral industry to capitalize on these digital trends. And with the still-sluggish economy and new competitors squeezing profit margins (for example, Walmart and Cosco now sell caskets online), the funeral industry is more open than ever to ways to satisfy consumers' mourning needs digitally.

5-9. Describe the characteristics of a new product that affect its rate of adoption. Which characteristics will impact how quickly the new digital services described above will be accepted by mourners in the United States? (AACSB: Written and Oral Communication; Reflective Thinking)

5-10. With new technologies, our digital lives can last much longer than our physical lives. Discuss how marketers might use social media such as Twitter, Facebook, YouTube, and Instagram to create social sharing and remembrance among mourners long after a loved one passes on. (AACSB: Written and Oral Communication; Information Technology; Reflective Thinking)

Marketing Ethics Pink Slime

In the early 1990s, Eldon Roth figured out a way to profit from slaughterhouse meat trimmings, by-products that were once used only in pet food and cooking oil. This cheap and safe beef product is called "lean, finely textured beef" (LFTB). The fatty bits of beef are heated and treated with a puff of ammonium hydroxide gas to kill bacteria. You've probably eaten many hamburgers that included LFTB prepared by fast-feeders, at school cafeterias, or even in your own kitchen. LFTB makes ground beef leaner and cheaper. Shortly after it was developed, a health safety inspector dubbed LFTB "pink slime," but the name didn't become public until the major "pink slime" media brouhaha erupted in 2012. Consumers were repulsed to learn that they were eating unappealing beef parts that were "soaked in ammonia." Sales of ground beef fell 11 percent in one month. Ground beef producer AFA Foods sought bankruptcy protection and Cargill lost 80 percent of its customers. The industry's leading LFTB manufacturer, Beef Products, Inc., shuttered 75 percent of its processing plants and laid off 650 workers. McDonald's and other fast-feeders, supermarkets, and institutional buyers such as schools and hospitals discontinued using beef products containing LFTB, even though the safe and inexpensive product has been around for many years.

5-11. Was the uproar over LFTB warranted, given the fact that it is a product deemed safe for consumption by the U.S. Food and Drug Administration? Research other types of products that are included in consumer products that could face a similar fate if consumers were aware of them. (AACSB: Written and Oral Communication; Reflective Thinking; Ethical Understanding and Reasoning)

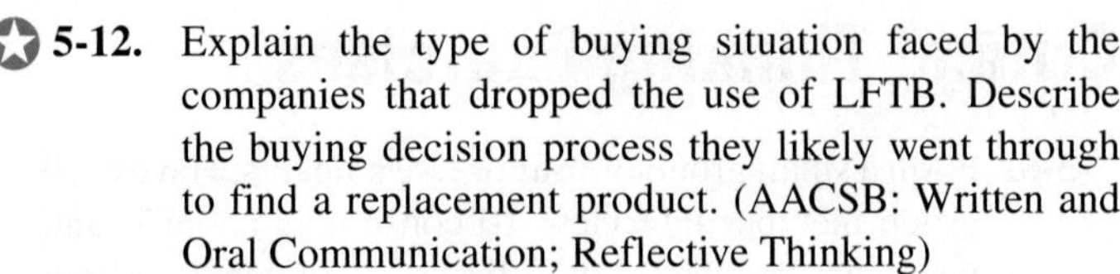

5-12. Explain the type of buying situation faced by the companies that dropped the use of LFTB. Describe the buying decision process they likely went through to find a replacement product. (AACSB: Written and Oral Communication; Reflective Thinking)

Marketing by the Numbers Evaluating Alternatives

One way consumers can evaluate alternatives is to identify important attributes and assess how purchase alternatives perform on those attributes. Consider the purchase of an automobile. Each attribute, such as gas mileage, is given a weight to reflect its level of importance to that consumer. Then the consumer evaluates each alternative on each attribute. For example, in the following table, gas mileage (weighted at 0.5) is the most important attribute for this consumer. The consumer believes that Brand C performs best on gas mileage, rating it 7 (higher ratings indicate higher performance). Brand B is perceived as performing the worst on this attribute (rating of 3). Styling and price are the consumer's next most important attributes. Warranty is least important.

	Importance	**Alternative Brands**		
Attributes	**Weight (e)**	**A**	**B**	**C**
Styling	0.2	4	6	2
Gas mileage	0.5	6	3	7
Warranty	0.1	5	5	4
Price	0.2	4	6	7

A score can be calculated for each brand by multiplying the importance weight for each attribute by the brand's score on that attribute. These weighted scores are then summed to determine the score for that brand. For example, $\text{Score}_{\text{Brand A}} = (0.2 \times 4) + (0.5 \times 6) + (0.1 \times 5) + (0.2 \times 4) = 0.8 + 3.0 + 0.5 + 0.8 = 5.1$. This consumer will select the brand with the highest score.

5-13. Calculate the scores for Brands B and C. Which brand would this consumer likely choose? (AACSB: Written and Oral Communication; Analytic Thinking)

5-14. Which brand is this consumer least likely to purchase? Discuss two ways the marketer of this brand can enhance consumer attitudes toward purchasing its brand. (AACSB: Written and Oral Communication; Reflective Thinking; Analytic Thinking)

Video Case Goodwill Industries

Since 1902, Goodwill Industries has funded job training and placement programs through its chain of thrift stores. Although selling used clothing, furniture, and other items may not seem like big business, for Goodwill, it amounts to over $3 billion in annual sales. You might think of thrift stores as musty, low-class operations. But Goodwill is putting an end to such perceptions by focusing on concepts of consumer behavior.

Like any good marketing company, Goodwill recognizes that not all customers are the same. This video demonstrates how Goodwill caters to different types of customers by recognizing the cultural, social, personal, and psychological factors that affect how customers make buying decisions. In this manner, Goodwill is able to maximize customer value by offering the right mix of goods at unbeatable bargains.

After viewing the video featuring Goodwill, answer the following questions:

5-15. Describe different types of Goodwill customers.

5-16. Which of the four sets of factors affecting consumer behavior do you believe most strongly affects consumers' purchase decisions from Goodwill?

5-17. How does Goodwill's recognition of consumer behavior principles affect its marketing mix?

Company Cases 5 Veterinary Pet Insurance / 1 In-N-Out Burger / 6 Dove

See Appendix 1 for cases appropriate for this chapter. **Case 5, Veterinary Pet Insurance: Health Insurance for Our Furry—or Feathery—Friends.** Consumer decisions are influenced by numerous factors that go way beyond dollars and cents. Veterinary Pet Insurance recognizes the value consumers place on emotional bonds. **Case 1, In-N-Out Burger: Customer Value the Old-Fashioned Way.** In-N-Out Burger provides value to customers by giving them exactly what they want, and never changing a thing. **Case 6, Dove: Building Customer Relationships Everywhere, One Gender at a Time.** Dove has long succeeded as a brand of soap and personal care products for women. Now, it's doing the same with men.

MyMarketingLab

Go to **mymktlab.com** for Auto-graded writing questions as well as the following Assisted-graded writing questions:

5-18. Discuss the stages of the consumer buyer decision process and describe how you or your family used this process to make a purchase. (AACSB: Written and Oral Communication; Reflective Thinking)

5-19. Describe the characteristics of a new product that affect its rate of adoption. Which characteristics will impact how quickly the new digital and social media services described above will be accepted by mourners in the United States? (AACSB: Written and Oral Communication; Reflective Thinking)

5-20. Mymktlab Only—comprehensive writing assignment for this chapter.

6 Customer-Driven Marketing Strategy

Creating Value for Target Customers

CHAPTER ROAD MAP

Objective Outline

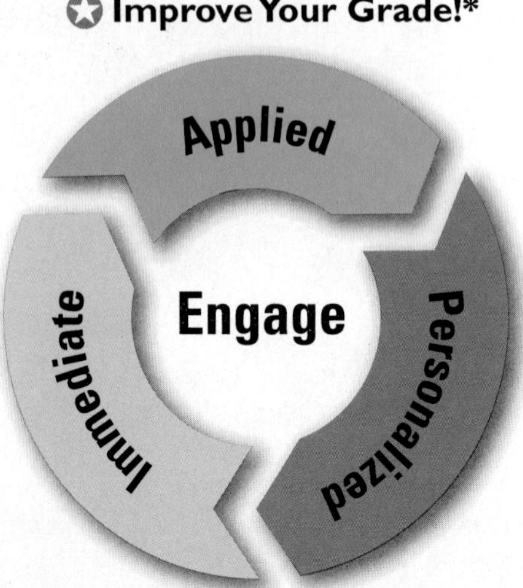

Previewing the Concepts

So far, you've learned what marketing is and about the importance of understanding consumers and the marketplace environment. With that as a background, you're now ready to delve deeper into marketing strategy and tactics. This chapter looks further into key customer-driven marketing strategy decisions—dividing up markets into meaningful customer groups (*segmentation*), choosing which customer groups to serve (*targeting*), creating market offerings that best serve targeted customers (*differentiation*), and positioning the offerings in the minds of consumers (*positioning*). The chapters that follow explore the tactical marketing tools—the four Ps—by which marketers bring these strategies to life.

To open our discussion of segmentation, targeting, differentiation, and positioning, let's look at master marketer Procter & Gamble (P&G). For more than 175 years, P&G has led the way in brand management and marketing. The consumer products giant now claims 25 brands with revenues exceeding $1 billion annually, more than triple the number of billion-dollar brands of its nearest competitor. Interestingly, many of P&G's blockbuster brands compete directly with one another on store shelves. How does that make sense? Careful segmentation and targeting—each brand offers a unique value proposition to a distinct segment of customers.

*Over 10 million students improved their results using the Pearson MyLabs. Visit **mymktlab.com** for simulations, tutorials, and end-of-chapter problems.

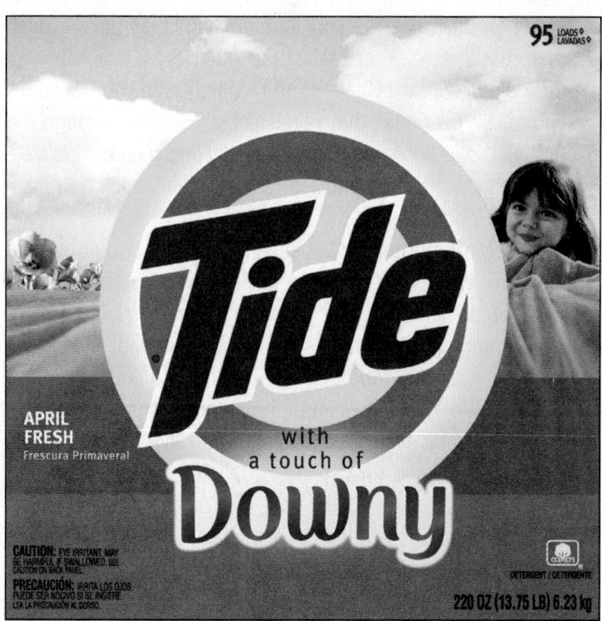

>> By offering brands and sub-brands that target specific segments of detergent preferences, Tide offers a unique value proposition to each distinct segment of customers.

The Procter & Gamble Company.

First Stop

P&G: Competing with Itself—and Winning

Procter & Gamble is the world's premier consumer products company. P&G invented brand management, and few companies do it better. The company markets more than 100 brands—most of them household names—to customers in over 180 countries around the world. An estimated 99 percent of all U.S. households use at least one P&G brand. And according to P&G, its brands now serve 4.6 billion of the planet's nearly 7 billion people.

P&G builds *big* brands. Just 50 of its brands account for 90 percent of the company's $84 billion in annual sales. Twenty-five of P&G's brands generate more than $1 billion annually, three times more billion-dollar brands than its nearest competitor and more than the total of the remaining competitors combined.

P&G brands flat-out dominate in many household and personal care categories. For example, in the United States, P&G sells a laundry room full of bestselling detergent and laundry care brands (including Tide, Gain, Cheer, Era, Dreft, Bold, Bounce, and Downy), alongside multiple brands of familiar household cleaning and homecare products (Mr. Clean, Swiffer, Febreze), dishwashing detergents (Dawn, Gain, Joy, and Cascade), and hand soaps and sanitizers (Safeguard, Olay, Ivory, and Camay). P&G markets more than a half-dozen each of shampoo and hair care brands (Head & Shoulders, Pantene, Herbal Essences, Pert, Vidal Sassoon, Wella, and Clairol) and fragrance brands (Old Spice, Gucci Fragrances, Hugo Boss, Lacoste, Puma, Dolce&Gabbana, and Escada). The list of iconic brands goes on and on, with megabrands in oral care (Crest, Oral-B, Scope), deodorants (Secret, Old Spice), shaving and grooming (Gillette, Braun), skin care (Olay, SK-II), cosmetics (Cover Girl, Max Factor), disposable diapers and baby care (Luvs, Pampers), and tissues and towels (Bounty, Charmin, Puffs).

Interestingly, many of these P&G brands compete directly with one another on the same supermarket shelves. But why would P&G introduce several brands in one category instead of concentrating its resources on a single leading brand? The answer lies in the concepts of segmentation and positioning, the fact that different people want different sets of benefits from the products they buy.

Take laundry detergents, for example. People use laundry detergents to get their clothes clean. But they also seek other benefits from their detergents—such as strength or mildness, stain removing, fabric softening, fresh scent, economy, and convenience. We all want *some* of every one of these detergent benefits, but we may have different *priorities* for each benefit. To some people, cleaning and bleaching power are most important; to others, fabric softening matters most. Still others want a mild, fresh-scented detergent. Thus, each segment of laundry detergent buyers seeks a special combination of benefits.

P&G's many brands often compete head to head on crowded supermarket shelves. But thanks to smart segmentation and positioning, when P&G competes against itself—it wins.

P&G has identified several important laundry detergent segments, along with numerous subsegments, and has developed distinct brands with value propositions to meet the needs of each. P&G's major U.S. detergent brands are positioned for different segments as follows:

- *Tide* is "a washing miracle." It's the original all-purpose, heavy-duty family detergent that gets out grime and tough stains. As we'll see shortly, Tide has branched into a dozen or more sub-brands that hone in on specific sets of laundry and fabric care needs.
- *Gain* leaves clothes smelling "irresistibly fresh. It's like sending your nose on a roller coaster and buying it a treat afterward."
- *Cheer* "helps you stay colorful." It "helps keep your pinks full of frolic and fancy, your yellows warm like the sun, and your blues brazenly beautiful."

- *Era* offers "a lot of fight for a little dough." It's an economical "concentrated liquid detergent that gives you stain-fighting power in a small convenient bottle."
- *Dreft* is "Mother-tested. Pediatrician-recommended. It's specially formulated to be gentle on baby's skin and tough on stains, bringing cuddle time to a whole new level of warm and fuzzy."

Such positionings are more than just brand-speak. Each brand is specially formulated to deliver the promised set of benefits.

Within each segment, P&G has identified even narrower niches. For example, you can buy Tide in any of more than 40 different formulations. Here's just a sampling:

- *Tide Original* is "the original Tide you love." It gives you "brilliant clean every time" in original or special scents such as Clean Breeze (the fresh scent of laundry line-dried in a clean breeze) or Mountain Spring (the scent of crisp mountain air and fresh wildflowers). Like many other Tide versions, you can buy it in either powder or liquid form.
- *Tide Coldwater* is specially formulated to deliver "brilliant clean at lower temperatures," saving you energy and money when you wash in cold water.
- *Ultra Tide* is a concentrated formula "with more stain-fighting power so you can use one-third less." *Tide HE* is specially formulated for use in high-efficiency washers. P&G now offers Ultra and HE versions of most of its major sub-brands.
- *Tide Free & Gentle* provides "a great clean that's gentle on your skin"—it's dye- and perfume-free.
- *Tide Vivid White + Bright* gives you "*white* whites and *bright* brights wash after wash." It contains no chlorine bleach and is safe for all your machine-washable clothes.
- *Tide plus Downy* gives you "outstanding clean plus a touch of softness, so clothes feel just as good as they look."
- *Tide plus Febreze* offers "great cleaning with the freshness you love," freshness that releases as you move through the day. *Tide plus Febreze Sport* is specially designed to eliminate sports apparel odors and fight tough stains such as grass, dirt, and blood.
- *TidePods* offer detergent + stain remover + brightener in a small, convenient, single-use packet—it's "reinventing the way you do laundry."
- Leveraging the strength of the Tide brand, P&G has launched several additional Tide-branded laundry products, such as *Tide To Go* stain removal pens and pads, *Tide Boost* in-wash stain booster, and *Tide Washing Machine Cleaner.*

P&G's brands and sub-brands do compete head to head in the crowded detergents market. But thanks to careful market segmentation and positioning, P&G has something special to offer consumers in each important preference group. Combined, its many detergent brands capture much more market share than any single brand could achieve on its own. As a result, P&G is really cleaning up in the $7 billion U.S. laundry detergent market. Incredibly, by itself, the Tide family of brands captures about one-third of all U.S. detergent sales; the Gain brand pulls in another 15 percent. Even more incredible, all P&G detergent brands combined capture an almost 70 percent market share. P&G's dominance has forced major competitors such as Unilever and Colgate to throw in the towel and sell off their U.S. laundry detergent brands. So by competing with itself, P&G wins.[1]

Companies today recognize that they cannot appeal to all buyers in the marketplace—or at least not to all buyers in the same way. Buyers are too numerous, widely scattered, and varied in their needs and buying practices. Moreover, companies themselves vary widely in their abilities to serve different market segments. Instead, like P&G, companies must identify the parts of the market they can serve best and most profitably. They must design customer-driven marketing strategies that build the right relationships with the right customers.

Market segmentation
Dividing a market into smaller segments of buyers with distinct needs, characteristics, or behaviors that might require separate marketing strategies or mixes.

Market targeting (targeting)
Evaluating each market segment's attractiveness and selecting one or more segments to enter.

Differentiation
Differentiating the market offering to create superior customer value.

Positioning
Arranging for a market offering to occupy a clear, distinctive, and desirable place relative to competing products in the minds of target consumers.

Thus, most companies have moved away from mass marketing and toward *target marketing:* identifying market segments, selecting one or more of them, and developing products and marketing programs tailored to each. Instead of scattering their marketing efforts (the "shotgun" approach), firms are focusing on the buyers who have greater interest in the values they create best (the "rifle" approach).

>> **Figure 6.1** shows the four major steps in designing a customer-driven marketing strategy. In the first two steps, the company selects the customers that it will serve. **Market segmentation** involves dividing a market into smaller segments of buyers with distinct needs, characteristics, or behaviors that might require separate marketing strategies or mixes. The company identifies different ways to segment the market and develops profiles of the resulting market segments. **Market targeting** (or **targeting**) consists of evaluating each market segment's attractiveness and selecting one or more market segments to enter.

In the final two steps, the company decides on a value proposition—how it will create value for target customers. **Differentiation** involves actually differentiating the firm's market offering to create superior customer value. **Positioning** consists of arranging for a market offering to occupy a clear, distinctive, and desirable place relative to competing products in the minds of target consumers. We discuss each of these steps in turn.

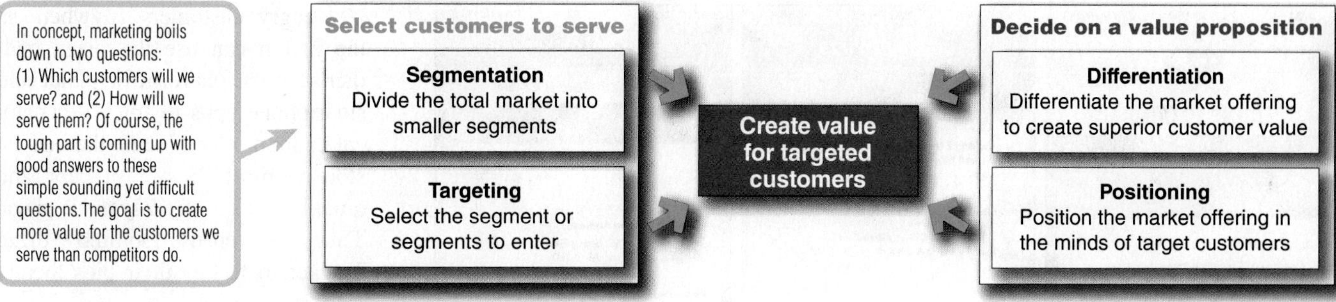
In concept, marketing boils down to two questions: (1) Which customers will we serve? and (2) How will we serve them? Of course, the tough part is coming up with good answers to these simple sounding yet difficult questions. The goal is to create more value for the customers we serve than competitors do.
Select customers to serve
Segmentation
Divide the total market into smaller segments
Targeting
Select the segment or segments to enter
Create value for targeted customers
Decide on a value proposition
Differentiation
Differentiate the market offering to create superior customer value
Positioning
Position the market offering in the minds of target customers

Figure 6.1 Designing a Customer-Driven Marketing Strategy

Author Comment
Market segmentation addresses the first simple-sounding marketing question: What customers will we serve?

Market Segmentation

Buyers in any market differ in their wants, resources, locations, buying attitudes, and buying practices. Through market segmentation, companies divide large, heterogeneous markets into smaller segments that can be reached more efficiently and effectively with products and services that match their unique needs. In this section, we discuss four important segmentation topics: segmenting consumer markets, segmenting business markets, segmenting international markets, and the requirements for effective segmentation.

Segmenting Consumer Markets

There is no single way to segment a market. A marketer has to try different segmentation variables, alone and in combination, to find the best way to view market structure. **Table 6.1** outlines variables that might be used in segmenting consumer markets. Here we look at the major *geographic, demographic, psychographic,* and *behavioral* variables.

Geographic Segmentation

Geographic segmentation
Dividing a market into different geographical units, such as nations, states, regions, counties, cities, or even neighborhoods.

Geographic segmentation calls for dividing the market into different geographical units, such as nations, regions, states, counties, cities, or even neighborhoods. A company may decide to operate in one or a few geographical areas or operate in all areas but pay attention to geographical differences in needs and wants.

Many companies today are localizing their products, advertising, promotion, and sales efforts to fit the needs of individual regions, cities, and neighborhoods. For example, Domino's Pizza is the nation's largest pizza delivery chain. But a customer ordering a pizza in Poughkeepsie, New York, doesn't care much about what's happening pizza-wise in Anaheim, California. So Domino's keeps its marketing and customer focus decidedly local.

Table 6.1 Major Segmentation Variables for Consumer Markets

Segmentation Variable	Examples
Geographic	Nations, regions, states, counties, cities, neighborhoods, population density (urban, suburban, rural), climate
Demographic	Age, life-cycle stage, gender, income, occupation, education, religion, ethnicity, generation
Psychographic	Social class, lifestyle, personality
Behavioral	Occasions, benefits, user status, usage rate, loyalty status

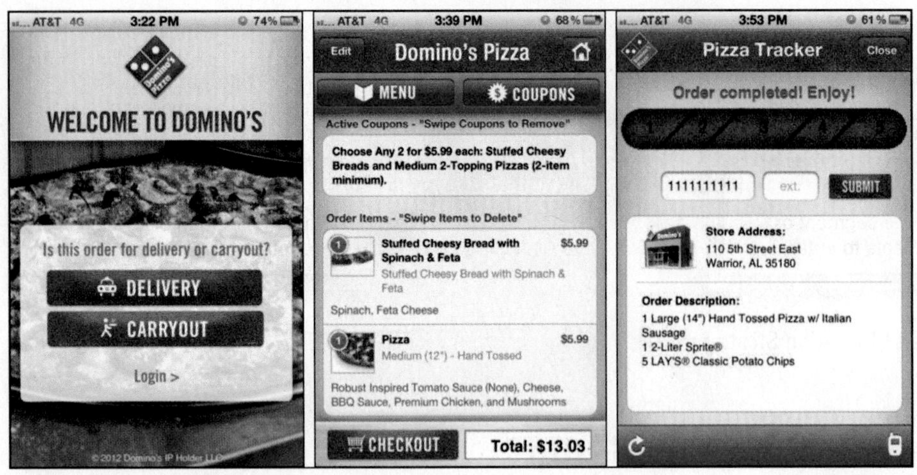

Geographic segmentation: Domino's keeps its marketing and customer focus decidedly local. Hungry customers anywhere can use the pizza peddler's smartphone app to locate the nearest store, order a pizza locally, and even track their pies store to door.

Dominos Pizza LLC.

Hungry customers anywhere in the nation can use the pizza peddler's online platform or tablet and smartphone apps to track down local coupon offers, locate the nearest store with a GPS store locator, and quickly receive a freshly made pizza. They can even use Domino's Pizza Tracker to follow their pies locally from store to door.[2]

Similarly, Marriott's Renaissance Hotels has rolled out its Navigator Program, which hyper-localizes guest experiences at each of its 145 lifestyle hotels around the world:

> Some hotels chains are large, faceless affairs delivering standardized experiences regardless of location. But Renaissance Hotels' Navigator Program puts a very personal, very local face on each location by "micro-localizing" guests' food, shopping, entertainment, and cultural experiences. The program hinges on "Navigators" at each hotel location. Whether it's Omar Bennett, a restaurant-loving Brooklynite at the Renaissance New York Times Square Hotel, or James Elliott at the St. Pancras Renaissance London Hotel, a history buff and local pub expert, Navigators are extensively trained locals who are deeply passionate about their cities. Based on personal experiences and never-ending research, they work one on one with guests to help them experience "the hidden gems around the unique neighborhood of each hotel through the eyes of those who know it best."
>
> The Renaissance even invites locals in each city to participate by following the local Navigator via the social media and adding their own favorite haunts to the hotel's database, creating each hotel's own version of Yelp. Navigators cull through submitted tips and feature the best ones alongside their own for sharing at the hotel's lobby advice desk or on its Web sites or social media channels. The hyper-localized Navigator Program has produced results. Since introducing the program as part of Renaissance Hotels' "Live Life to Discover" campaign two years ago, the hotel's Web site traffic has grown 82 percent, Facebook likes have exploded from 40,000 to more than 330,000, and Twitter followers have surged from 5,000 to 30,000.[3]

Demographic Segmentation

Demographic segmentation Dividing the market into segments based on variables such as age, life-cycle stage, gender, income, occupation, education, religion, ethnicity, and generation.

Demographic segmentation divides the market into segments based on variables such as age, life-cycle stage, gender, income, occupation, education, religion, ethnicity, and generation. Demographic factors are the most popular bases for segmenting customer groups. One reason is that consumer needs, wants, and usage rates often vary closely with demographic variables. Another is that demographic variables are easier to measure than most other types of variables. Even when marketers first define segments using other bases, such as benefits sought or behavior, they must know a segment's demographic characteristics to assess the size of the target market and reach it efficiently.

Age and life-cycle segmentation Dividing a market into different age and life-cycle groups.

Age and Life-Cycle Stage. Consumer needs and wants change with age. Some companies use **age and life-cycle segmentation**, offering different products or using different marketing approaches for different age and life-cycle groups. For example, Kraft promotes JELL-O to children as a fun snack, one that "taught the world to wiggle." For adults, it's a tasty, guilt-free indulgence—"the most sweet-tooth satisfaction 10 calories can hold."

Other companies offer brands that target specific age or life-stage groups. For example, whereas most tablet makers have been busy marketing their devices to grown-ups, Amazon has spotted a tinier tablet market. Feedback from parents suggested that they were handing their entertainment-packed Kindle Fire tablet over to their young children for entertainment, education, and babysitting purposes. To tap this young-family market, Amazon introduced FreeTime Unlimited, a multimedia subscription service targeted toward three- to eight-year-olds. Complete with parental controls, the service provides access to a treasure trove of G-rated movies, games, and books, including premium content from Nickelodeon, Disney, Sesame Street, and DC Comics. Not only does FreeTime Unlimited generate revenues for Amazon, it helps sell more Kindle Fire tablets to young families.[4]

Marketers must be careful to guard against stereotypes when using age and life-cycle segmentation. For example, although some 80-year-olds fit the stereotypes of doddering shut-ins with fixed incomes, others ski and play tennis. Similarly, whereas some 40-year-old couples are sending their children off to college, others are just beginning new families. Thus, age is often a poor predictor of a person's life cycle, health, work or family status, needs, and buying power.

Gender segmentation
Dividing a market into different segments based on gender.

Gender. **Gender segmentation** has long been used in clothing, cosmetics, toiletries, and magazines. For example, P&G was among the first to use gender segmentation with Secret, a brand specially formulated for a woman's chemistry, packaged and advertised to reinforce the female image. More recently, the men's cosmetics industry has exploded, and many cosmetics makers that previously catered primarily to women now successfully market men's lines. Just don't call them "cosmetics."[5]

> L'Oréal's Men's Expert line includes a host of products with decidedly unmanly names such as Men's Expert Vita Lift SPF 15 Anti-Wrinkle & Firming Moisturizer and Men's Expert Hydra-Energetic Ice Cold Eye Roller (for diminishing under-eye dark circles). Other brands, however, try to craft more masculine positions. >> For example, Mënaji promises "Skincare for the Confident Man." Manly men such as Tim McGraw, Kevin Bacon, and Kid Rock use it. Mënaji products come in discreet packaging such as old cigar boxes, and the line's "undetectable" foundation and concealer (or rather "Camo") come in easy-to-apply Chap Stick-style containers. Mënaji founder Michele Probst doesn't call any of it makeup. "The M word is cancer to us," she says. "We are skin care that looks good." Whatever you call it, Mënaji sales are up 70 percent in each of the past 4 years, as the U.S. men's grooming market has grown to $3 billion.

Similarly, Unilever's testosterone-heavy male body spray brand, Axe, is now waking up to new gender segments. It recently released a new scent, Anarchy, marketed in different versions to both men and women. Nearly one-quarter of Axe's 4 million Facebook and Twitter fans are women, and Unilever's research suggested that these women have been wanting an Axe scent of their very own. Past Axe commercials have featured young men spraying the brand on themselves to gain an edge in the mating game. "Now women also have something to spray on themselves," notes an Axe marketer, creating "more of an equilibrium between the sexes."[6]

Income segmentation
Dividing a market into different income segments.

Income. The marketers of products and services such as automobiles, clothing, cosmetics, financial services, and travel have long used **income segmentation**. Many companies target affluent consumers with luxury goods and convenience services. Other marketers use high-touch marketing programs to court the well-to-do:[7]

> Seadream Yacht Club, a small-ship luxury cruise line, calls select guests after every cruise and offers to have the CEO fly out to their home and host, at Seadream's expense, a brunch or reception for a dozen of the couple's best friends. The cruisers tell the story of their cruise. Seadream

>> **Gender segmentation: Many cosmetics makers now successfully market men's lines. Mënaji tells men to "Put your best face forward."**

Mënaji Skincare LLC.

offers a great rate to their guests and sells several cruises at $1,000 per person per night to the friends (and even friends of friends). Such highly personal marketing creates a community of "brand evangelists" who tell the story to prospective affluent buyers and friends—precisely the right target group. This has been so successful for Seadream that it has abandoned most traditional advertising.

However, not all companies that use income segmentation target the affluent. For example, many retailers—such as the Dollar General, Family Dollar, and Dollar Tree store chains—successfully target low- and middle-income groups. The core market for such stores is represented by families with incomes under $30,000. When Family Dollar real estate experts scout locations for new stores, they look for lower-middle-class neighborhoods where people wear less-expensive shoes and drive old cars that drip a lot of oil. With their low-income strategies, dollar stores are now the fastest-growing retailers in the nation.

Psychographic Segmentation

Psychographic segmentation Dividing a market into different segments based on social class, lifestyle, or personality characteristics.

Psychographic segmentation divides buyers into different segments based on social class, lifestyle, or personality characteristics. People in the same demographic group can have very different psychographic characteristics.

In Chapter 5, we discussed how the products people buy reflect their *lifestyles*. As a result, marketers often segment their markets by consumer lifestyles and base their marketing strategies on lifestyle appeals. For example, retailer Anthropologie, with its whimsical, "French flea market" store atmosphere, sells a Bohemian-chic lifestyle to which its young women customers aspire. And although W Hotels books out hotel rooms by the night, just like any other hotel chain, it doesn't see itself as a hotel company. Instead, it positions itself as "an iconic lifestyle brand," inviting guests to "step inside the worlds of design, music, and fashion." (See Marketing at Work 6.1.)

>> VF Corporation offers a closet full of more than 30 premium lifestyle brands that "fit the lives of consumers the world over, from commuters to cowboys, surfers to soccer moms, sports fans to rock bands":[8]

>> **Differentiated marketing: VF Corporation offers a closet full of over 30 premium lifestyle brands, each of which "taps into consumer aspirations to fashion, status, and well-being" in a well-defined segment.**

VF Corporation.

VF is the nation's number-one jeans maker, with brands such as Lee, Riders, Rustler, and Wrangler. But jeans are not the only focus for VF. The company's brands are carefully separated into five major lifestyle segments—Jeanswear, Imagewear (workwear), Outdoor and Action Sports, Sportswear, and Contemporary. The North Face and Timberland brands, both part of the Outdoor unit, offer top-of-the-line gear and apparel for outdoor enthusiasts. From the Sportswear unit, Nautica focuses on people who enjoy high-end casual apparel inspired by sailing and the sea. Vans began as a skate shoemaker, and Reef features surf-inspired footwear and apparel. In the Contemporary unit, Lucy features upscale active-wear, whereas 7 for All Mankind supplies premium denim and accessories sold in boutiques and high-end department stores such as Saks and Nordstrom. At the other end of the spectrum, Horace Small, part of the Imagewear unit, markets uniforms for police and fire departments and other first responders. No matter who you are, says the company, "We fit your life."

Marketers also use *personality* variables to segment markets. For example, different soft drinks target different personalities. On the one hand, Mountain Dew projects a youthful, rebellious, adventurous, go-your-own-way personality. Its ads remind customers that "It's different on the Mountain." By contrast, Coca-Cola Zero appears to target more mature, practical, and cerebral but good-humored personality types. Its subtly humorous ads promise "Real Coca-Cola taste and zero calories."

MARKETING AT WORK 6.1

W Hotels: Not Just a Room—It's a Trendsetter Lifestyle

You approach the glitzy, contemporary building in London, a 10-story structure encased in a translucent glass veil. Cameras mounted on the roof capture the surrounding skyline and project it onto the building's surface, creating a seamless blend of the building with its setting. Inside, you're greeted by thumping hip-hop music, large mirrored glitter balls, open fires, and a huge Chesterfield sofa that snakes around the lounge bar. You're in a nightclub perhaps, or the latest trendy restaurant. No, you're in the W London, a hotel that offers much more than just rooms for the night.

Starwood Hotels and Resorts operates nine different hotel chains—something for everyone, you might say. But its W Hotels brand stands out from all the rest. In fact, W Hotels doesn't really think of itself as just a hotel chain. Instead, it positions itself as "an iconic lifestyle brand." More than just rooms, W Hotels prides itself on "offering guests unprecedented insider access to a world of 'Wow' through contemporary cool design, fashion, music, nightlife, and entertainment." W Hotels exudes a youthful, outgoing, jet-setting life style that fits its ultrahip, trendsetter clientele—mostly from the media, music, fashion, entertainment, and consulting industries. For these patrons, W provides an unmatched sense of belonging.

W Hotels' lifestyle positioning starts with unique design. Whereas most hotel chains churn out cookie-cutter locations in search of a consistent brand image, W Hotels's 54 properties worldwide look nothing alike. W's patrons view themselves as unique, so they demand the same from the hotels they choose. Every W Hotel projects a common "energetic, vibrant, forward-thinking attitude," and an appreciation for fashion, art, and music befitting its lifestyle image. But in terms of design, each W Hotel is "uniquely inspired by its destination, mixing cutting-edge design with local influences."

For example, the W Taipei in Taiwan, located in the Xinyi district near Taipei 101, the city's tallest skyscraper, is designed around the theme of "nature electrified," blending soft wooden walls; geometric, box-shaped shelves; and lighting inspired by Chinese lanterns. The W Koh Samui (in Thailand), an all-villa beach resort, treats guests to the concept of "day and night"—relaxing by the pool by day and partying by night—with modern interiors accented by bright flashes of red, off-white terrazzo floors, and wooden decks for private guest pools. The W Bali features an "inside and outside" theme, with grass-like green pillows that bring a bit of outdoors into the rooms and bed headboards made from the skin of stingrays.

With each unique design, however, W maintains a consistent ambiance that leaves no question in guests' minds that they are living the W lifestyle. The W Paris, for example, blends the facade of its historic and elegant 1870s building with the theme of Paris as the "City of Light," all wrapped in W's signature contemporary energy:

> The hotel design revolves around an oversized backlit digital undulating wall that defines the central core of the building and weaves through the public and private spaces. "Our design feeds off the elegance, richness, and radiance of Paris . . . and W's DNA for infusing a sense of energy" says the head of the hotel's design group. In true W fashion, it brings the historic building to life with a glowing vibrancy.

But unique design is only part of W Hotels' lifestyle formula. The brand also bridges connections with the worlds of fashion, music, and art. For example, the chain acquired a fashion director, Jenné Lombardo, who has been hosting cutting-edge fashion events in New York for years. Lombardo heads up W's ongoing *Fashion Next* program, which forges relationships with up-and-coming designers. W sponsors the young design talent by paying for fees and space at major runway events, supplying a W DJ to help with music, and providing hair and makeup, catering, and other services. In return, the designers participate in shows, art exhibitions, luncheons, and other events that attract fashion-conscious guests at W hotels around the world. Such events provide "insider access" for W's patrons, contributing further to the hotel's lifestyle appeal.

W Hotels works with music in the same way that it works with fashion. Under the direction of a global music director,

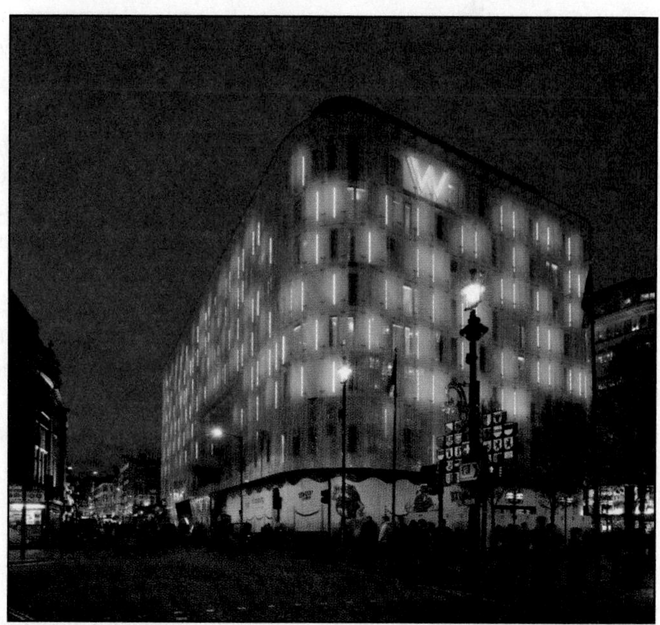

>> Lifestyle segmentation: W Hotels positions itself as "an iconic lifestyle brand," inviting guests to "step inside the worlds of design, music, and fashion."

W's long-running *Symmetry Live* concert series offers guests access to exclusive performances by some of the world's hottest, just-discovered acts, such as Cee Lo Green, Janelle Monae, Ellie Goulding, and Theophilus London. This year, W is sponsoring an exclusive traveling exhibition of the photography of Madonna, curated by Rock Paper Photo and sponsored by vitaminwater. The exhibit features never seen before photos of pop star Madonna from the 1980s. The exclusive exhibition celebrates music and fashion, two of the W brand's core passions.

Beyond its passion for art, fashion, and entertainment, as you might expect, another constant at W Hotels is first-class service—what W calls "Whatever-Whenever" service. "We aim to provide whatever, whenever, as long as it is legal—something that is very much consistent throughout the W brand," explains one W Hotel manager. W Hotels don't have concierges; instead, they have "W Insiders." The Insiders go a step beyond. Rather than waiting to be asked for advice, they proactively seek out things they can do to enhance the stay of each guest. In keeping with the brand's lifestyle positioning, insiders stay in tune with special need-to-know happenings and advise guests on all the latest places to see and be seen.

Adding even more luster to W's lifestyle allure, the chain's hotels attract a star-studded list of celebrities. The W South Beach in Miami, for example, in addition to its modern art collection, is known for guests like Sean Penn and Leonardo DiCaprio. The hotel has a basketball court where NBA players are often seen shooting hoops. LeBron James held a party there after announcing that he was taking his "talents to South Beach," and Dwyane Wade celebrates birthdays there. New York Knicks forward Amar'e Stoudemire and Italian soccer sensation Alessandro Nesta paid millions to become residents of the elite W South Beach property.

Staying at a W Hotel isn't cheap. The basic W room runs about $450 a night, with top suites running up to five figures. But a W Hotel isn't just a place where you rent a room and get a good night's sleep. It's the design of the place, the contemporary ambiance, what's hanging on the walls, the music that's playing, the other guests who stay there—all of these things contribute mightily to the W's lifestyle positioning and allure to its young, hip, upscale W clientele. It's not just a room—it's part of an entire trendsetter lifestyle.

Sources: Janet Harmer, "W London—A Hotel That Dares to Be Different," *Caterer & Hotelkeeper*, March 4–10, 2011, pp. 26–28; Nancy Keates, "The Home Front: His Hotel, His Hangout," *Wall Street Journal*, June 3, 2011, p. D6; Christina Binkley, "Putting the Hot Back in Hotel," *Wall Street Journal*, August 18, 2011, accessed at http://online.wsj.com/article/SB10001424053111903596904576514293384502896.html; "W Hotels Unveils Innovative Design Concept of the Soon-to-Open W Paris-Opéra by Acclaimed Rockwell Group Europe," Starwood press release, December 14, 2011, http://development.starwoodhotels.com/news/7/336-w_hotels_unveils_innovative_design_concept_of_the_soon-to-open_w_paris-opera_by_acclaimed_rockwell_group_europe; and information and press releases from www.starwoodhotels.com/whotels/about/index.html, accessed September 2013.

Behavioral Segmentation

Behavioral segmentation
Dividing a market into segments based on consumer knowledge, attitudes, uses of a product, or responses to a product.

Behavioral segmentation divides buyers into segments based on their knowledge, attitudes, uses, or responses concerning a product. Many marketers believe that behavior variables are the best starting point for building market segments.

Occasion segmentation
Dividing the market into segments according to occasions when buyers get the idea to buy, actually make their purchase, or use the purchased item.

Occasions. Buyers can be grouped according to occasions when they get the idea to buy, actually make their purchases, or use the purchased items. **Occasion segmentation** can help firms build up product usage. Campbell's advertises its soups more heavily in the cold winter months, and Home Depot runs special springtime promotions for lawn and garden products. Other marketers prepare special offers and ads for holiday occasions. For example, M&M's runs ads throughout the year but prepares special ads and packaging for holidays and events such as Christmas, Easter, and the Super Bowl.

Still other companies try to boost consumption by promoting usage during nontraditional occasions. For example, most consumers drink orange juice in the morning, but orange growers have promoted drinking orange juice as a cool, healthful refresher at other times of the day. And Taco Bell's First Meal campaign attempts to build business by promoting the chain's A.M. Crunchwrap, Mtn Dew A.M., and other items as a great way to start the day.

Benefit segmentation
Dividing the market into segments according to the different benefits that consumers seek from the product.

Benefits Sought. A powerful form of segmentation is grouping buyers according to the different *benefits* that they seek from a product. **Benefit segmentation** requires finding the major benefits people look for in a product class, the kinds of people who look for each benefit, and the major brands that deliver each benefit.

For example, people buying bikes are looking for any of numerous benefits, from competitive racing and sports performance to recreation, fitness, touring, transportation, and just plain fun. To meet varying benefit preferences, Trek makes bikes in three major benefit

Benefit segmentation: Trek makes a bike to fit every bike benefit segment. For example, its popular FX model is a fitness and transportation bike, a favorite for "roadies, commuters, fitness fans, errand runners, and Sunday riders."

Jarrod Weaton/Weaton Digital, Inc.

groups: road bikes, mountain bikes, and town bikes.[9] *Road bikes* are "fast bikes designed to fly over pavement—for racing, recreating, or both." Trek further divides the road bike segment into six benefit subsegments, such as race performance ("train, race, win"), fitness ("from fitness to fun and all points in between"), and touring ("escapism at its finest). Trek's *mountain bikes* are for people seeking rugged competition or recreational trail bikes. These bikes are "sure-footed off-road bikes built to conquer any trail, from tame to treacherous," including cross-country, off-road sport, and single-track trail bikes. Finally, Trek's *town bikes* are for people seeking recreation, fitness, and urban utility. They "let you live the two-wheeled life—haul, commute, get fit, have fun."

In all, Trek makes some 40 different families of bikes, each designed for a specific benefit segment or subsegment. For example, the high-tech Trek Madone 7 (priced at $4,000 to $12,000) is a race performance bike—"the road racing bike champions have dreamed of. The lightest. The fastest. Incredibly aero. Built by hand to win it all." In contrast, Trek's most popular bike is the Trek FX (at a more affordable $600 to $1,300), a fitness and transportation bike that gives riders a great bike for everyday exercise or getting around. "Roadies, commuters, fitness fans, errand runners, Sunday riders . . . everybody loves FX," says the company.

User Status. Markets can be segmented into nonusers, ex-users, potential users, first-time users, and regular users of a product. Marketers want to reinforce and retain regular users, attract targeted nonusers, and reinvigorate relationships with ex-users. Included in the potential users group are consumers facing life-stage changes—such as new parents and newlyweds—who can be turned into heavy users. For example, to get new parents off to the right start, P&G makes certain that its Pampers Swaddlers are the diaper most U.S. hospitals provide for newborns. And to capture newly engaged couples who will soon be equipping their new kitchens, upscale kitchen and cookware retailer Williams-Sonoma takes the usual bridal registry a step further. Through a program called "The Store Is Yours," it opens its stores after hours, by appointment, exclusively for individual couples to visit and make their wish lists. About half the people who register are new to the Williams-Sonoma brand.

Targeting heavy users: Sister chains Hardee's and Carl's, Jr. focus on a target of "young, hungry men" who fully embrace the chains' "If you're gonna eat, eat like you mean it" positioning.

Fuse.

Usage Rate. Markets can also be segmented into light, medium, and heavy product users. Heavy users are often a small percentage of the market but account for a high percentage of total consumption. For instance, Carl's Jr. and Hardee's restaurants, both owned by parent company CKE Restaurants, focus on a target of "young, hungry men." These young male customers, ages 18 to 34, fully embrace the chain's "If you're gonna eat, eat like you mean it" positioning. That means they wolf down a lot more Thickburgers and other indulgent items featured on the chains' menus. To attract this audience, the company is known for its steamy hot-models-in-bikinis commercials, featuring models such as Kate Upton, Padma Lakshmi, and Nina Agdal to heat up the brands' images. Such ads clearly show "what our target audience of young, hungry guys like," says CKE's chief executive.[10]

Loyalty Status. A market can also be segmented by consumer loyalty. Consumers can be loyal to brands (Tide), stores (Target), and companies (Apple). Buyers can be divided into groups according to their degree of loyalty. Some consumers are completely loyal—they buy one brand all the time and can't wait to tell others about it. For example, whether they own a MacBook computer, an iPhone, or an iPad, Apple devotees are granite-like in their devotion to the brand. At one end are the quietly satisfied Apple users, folks who own one or several Apple devices and use them for e-mail, browsing, texting, and social networking. At the other extreme, however, are the Apple zealots—the so-called MacHeads or Macolytes—who can't wait to tell anyone within earshot of their latest Apple gadget. Such loyal Apple devotees helped keep Apple afloat during the lean years a decade ago, and they are now at the forefront of Apple's huge iPod, iTunes, and iPad empire.

Other consumers are somewhat loyal—they are loyal to two or three brands of a given product or favor one brand while sometimes buying others. Still other buyers show no loyalty to any brand—they either want something different each time they buy, or they buy whatever's on sale.

A company can learn a lot by analyzing loyalty patterns in its market. It should start by studying its own loyal customers. Highly loyal customers can be a real asset. They often promote the brand through personal word of mouth and social media. Some companies actually put loyalists to work for the brand. For example, Patagonia relies on its most tried-and-true customers—what it calls Patagonia ambassadors—to field test products in harsh environments, provide input for "ambassador-driven" lines of apparel and gear, and share their product experiences with others.[11] In contrast, by studying its less-loyal buyers, a company can detect which brands are most competitive with its own. By looking at customers who are shifting away from its brand, the company can learn about its marketing weaknesses and take actions to correct them.

Using Multiple Segmentation Bases

Marketers rarely limit their segmentation analysis to only one or a few variables. Rather, they often use multiple segmentation bases in an effort to identify smaller, better-defined target groups. Several business information services—such as Nielsen, Acxiom, and Experian—provide multivariable segmentation systems that merge geographic, demographic, lifestyle, and behavioral data to help companies segment their markets down to zip codes, neighborhoods, and even households.

One of the leading segmentation systems is the Nielsen PRIZM system operated by The Nielsen Company. >> PRIZM classifies every American household based on a host of demographic factors—such as age, education, income, occupation, family composition, ethnicity, and housing—and behavioral and lifestyle factors, such as purchases, free-time activities, and media preferences. PRIZM classifies U.S. households into 66 demographically and behaviorally distinct segments, organized into 14 different social groups. PRIZM segments carry such exotic names as "Kids & Cul-de-Sacs," "Gray Power," "Mayberry-ville," "Shotguns & Pickups," "Old Glories," "Multi-Culti Mosaic," "Big City Blues," and "Brite Lites L'il City." The colorful names help to bring the segments to life.[12]

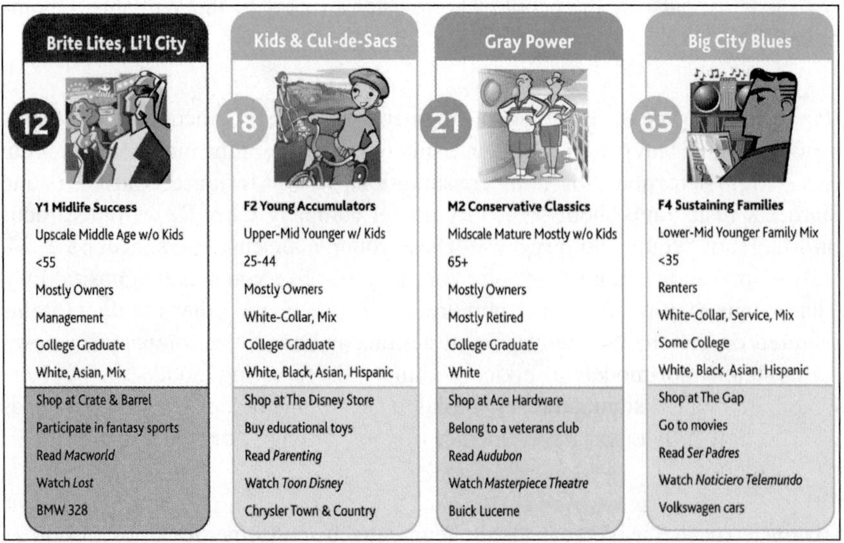

>> Using Nielsen's PRIZM system, marketers can paint a surprisingly precise picture of who you are and what you might buy. PRIZM segments carry such exotic names as "Brite Lites, L'il City," "Kids & Cul-de-Sacs," "Gray Power," and "Big City Blues."

PRIZM and other such systems can help marketers segment people and locations into marketable groups of like-minded consumers. Each segment has its own pattern of likes, dislikes, lifestyles, and purchase behaviors. For example, *Winner's Circle* neighborhoods, part of the Elite Suburbs social group, are suburban areas populated by well-off couples, between the ages of 35 and 54, with large families in new-money neighborhoods. People in this segment are more likely to own a Mercedes GL Class, go jogging, shop at Neiman Marcus, and read the *Wall Street Journal*. In contrast, the *Bedrock America* segment, part of the Rustic

Living social group, is populated by young, economically challenged families in small, isolated towns located throughout the nation's heartland. People in this segment are more likely to order from Avon, buy toy cars, and read *Parents Magazine*.

Such segmentation provides a powerful tool for marketers of all kinds. It can help companies identify and better understand key customer segments, reach them more efficiently, and tailor market offerings and messages to their specific needs.

Segmenting Business Markets

Consumer and business marketers use many of the same variables to segment their markets. Business buyers can be segmented geographically, demographically (industry, company size), or by benefits sought, user status, usage rate, and loyalty status. Yet, business marketers also use some additional variables, such as customer *operating characteristics*, *purchasing approaches*, *situational factors*, and *personal characteristics*.

Almost every company serves at least some business markets. For example, Starbucks has developed distinct marketing programs for each of its two business segments: the office coffee and food service segments. In the office coffee and vending segment, Starbucks Office Coffee Solutions markets a variety of workplace coffee services to businesses of any size, helping them to make Starbucks coffee and related products available to their employees in their workplaces. Starbucks helps these business customers design the best office solutions involving its coffees (the Starbucks or Seattle's Best brands), teas (Tazo), syrups, and branded paper products and methods of serving them—portion packs, single cups, or vending. The Starbucks Foodservice division teams up with businesses and other organizations—ranging from airlines, restaurants, colleges, and hospitals to baseball stadiums—to help them serve the well-known Starbucks brand to their own customers. Starbucks provides not only the coffee, tea, and paper products to its food service partners, but also equipment, training, and marketing and merchandising support.[13]

Many companies establish separate systems for dealing with larger or multiple-location customers. For example, Steelcase, a major producer of office furniture, first divides customers into seven segments: biosciences, higher education, U.S. and Canadian governments, state and local governments, health care, professional services, and retail banking. Next, company salespeople work with independent Steelcase dealers to handle smaller, local, or regional Steelcase customers in each segment. But many national, multiple-location customers, such as ExxonMobil or IBM, have special needs that may reach beyond the scope of individual dealers. Therefore, Steelcase uses national account managers to help its dealer networks handle national accounts.

Segmenting International Markets

Few companies have either the resources or the will to operate in all, or even most, of the countries that dot the globe. Although some large companies, such as Coca-Cola or Sony, sell products in more than 200 countries, most international firms focus on a smaller set. Operating in many countries presents new challenges. Different countries, even those that are close together, can vary greatly in their economic, cultural, and political makeup. Thus, just as they do within their domestic markets, international firms need to group their world markets into segments with distinct buying needs and behaviors.

Companies can segment international markets using one or a combination of several variables. They can segment by *geographic location*, grouping countries by regions such as Western Europe, the Pacific Rim, South Asia, or Africa. Geographic segmentation assumes that nations close to one another will have many common traits and behaviors. Although this is often the case, there are many exceptions. For example, some U.S. marketers lump all Central and South American countries together. However, the Dominican Republic is no more like Brazil than Italy is like Sweden. Many Central and South Americans don't even speak Spanish, including more than 200 million Portuguese-speaking Brazilians and the millions in other countries who speak a variety of Indian dialects.

World markets can also be segmented based on *economic factors*. Countries might be grouped by population income levels or by their overall level of economic development.

A country's economic structure shapes its population's product and service needs, and therefore the marketing opportunities it offers. For example, many companies are now targeting the BRIC countries—Brazil, Russia, India, and China—which are fast-growing developing economies with rapidly increasing buying power.

Countries can also be segmented by *political and legal factors* such as the type and stability of government, receptivity to foreign firms, monetary regulations, and amount of bureaucracy. *Cultural factors* can also be used, grouping markets according to common languages, religions, values and attitudes, customs, and behavioral patterns.

Intermarket (cross-market) segmentation
Forming segments of consumers who have similar needs and buying behaviors even though they are located in different countries.

Segmenting international markets based on geographic, economic, political, cultural, and other factors presumes that segments should consist of clusters of countries. However, as new communications technologies, such as satellite TV and the Internet, connect consumers around the world, marketers can define and reach segments of like-minded consumers no matter where in the world they are. Using **intermarket segmentation** (also called **cross-market segmentation**), they form segments of consumers who have similar needs and buying behaviors even though they are located in different countries.

>> Intermarket segmentation: Retailer H&M targets fashion-conscious but frugal shoppers in 43 countries with its low-priced, trendy apparel and accessories.

REUTERS/Toru Hanai.

For example, Lexus targets the world's well-to-do—the "global elite" segment—regardless of their country. >> Retailer H&M targets fashion-conscious but frugal shoppers in 43 countries with its low-priced, trendy apparel and accessories. And Coca-Cola creates special programs to target teens, core consumers of its soft drinks the world over. By 2020, one-third of the world's population—some 2.5 billion people—will be under 18 years of age. Coca-Cola reaches this important market through the universal language of music:

> Two years ago, Coca-Cola launched a Coca-Cola Music campaign to engage the world's teen in more than 100 global markets. The brand extended these efforts with a highly successful "Move to the Beat" teen-focused campaign centered on the London 2012 Olympics, inspired by the sounds, spirit, and culture of the host city. Most recently, Coca-Cola Music joined forces with Spotify to provide a global music network that helps teens discover new music, connect with other music-loving teens, and share their experiences with friends worldwide both online and offline. "The number one passion point for teens is music," says a Coca-Cola global marketing executive. Coca-Cola's CEO agrees: "Our success . . . today depends on our ability to grow and connect with teens, the generation of tomorrow."[14]

Requirements for Effective Segmentation

Clearly, there are many ways to segment a market, but not all segmentations are effective. For example, buyers of table salt could be divided into blonde and brunette customers. But hair color obviously does not affect the purchase of salt. Furthermore, if all salt buyers bought the same amount of salt each month, believed that all salt is the same, and wanted to pay the same price, the company would not benefit from segmenting this market.

To be useful, market segments must be

- ***Measurable:*** The size, purchasing power, and profiles of the segments can be measured.
- ***Accessible:*** The market segments can be effectively reached and served.
- ***Substantial:*** The market segments are large or profitable enough to serve. A segment should be the largest possible homogeneous group worth pursuing with a tailored marketing program. It would not pay, for example, for an automobile manufacturer to develop cars especially for people whose height is greater than seven feet.
- ***Differentiable:*** The segments are conceptually distinguishable and respond differently to different marketing mix elements and programs. If men and women

respond similarly to marketing efforts for soft drinks, they do not constitute separate segments.

- ***Actionable:*** Effective programs can be designed for attracting and serving the segments. For example, although one small airline identified seven market segments, its staff was too small to develop separate marketing programs for each segment.

SPEED BUMP LINKING THE CONCEPTS

Pause for a bit and think about segmentation. How do the companies you do business with employ the segmentation concepts you're reading about here?

- Can you identify specific companies, other than the examples already mentioned, that practice the different types of segmentation just discussed?
- Using the segmentation bases you've just read about, segment the U.S. footwear market. Describe each of the major segments and subsegments. Keep these segments in mind as you read the next section on market targeting.

Author Comment
After dividing the market into segments, it's time to answer that first seemingly simple marketing strategy question we raised in Figure 6.1: Which customers will the company serve?

Market Targeting

Market segmentation reveals the firm's market segment opportunities. The firm now has to evaluate the various segments and decide how many and which segments it can serve best. We now look at how companies evaluate and select target segments.

Evaluating Market Segments

In evaluating different market segments, a firm must look at three factors: segment size and growth, segment structural attractiveness, and company objectives and resources. First, a company wants to select segments that have the right size and growth characteristics. But "right size and growth" is a relative matter. The largest, fastest-growing segments are not always the most attractive ones for every company. Smaller companies may lack the skills and resources needed to serve larger segments. Or they may find these segments too competitive. Such companies may target segments that are smaller and less attractive, in an absolute sense, but that are potentially more profitable for them.

The company also needs to examine major structural factors that affect long-run segment attractiveness.[15] For example, a segment is less attractive if it already contains many strong and aggressive *competitors* or if it is easy for *new entrants* to come into the segment. The existence of many actual or potential *substitute products* may limit prices and the profits that can be earned in a segment. The relative *power of buyers* also affects segment attractiveness. Buyers with strong bargaining power relative to sellers will try to force prices down, demand more services, and set competitors against one another—all at the expense of seller profitability. Finally, a segment may be less attractive if it contains *powerful suppliers* that can control prices or reduce the quality or quantity of ordered goods and services.

Even if a segment has the right size and growth and is structurally attractive, the company must consider its own objectives and resources. Some attractive segments can be dismissed quickly because they do not mesh with the company's long-run objectives. Or the company may lack the skills and resources needed to succeed in an attractive segment. For example, the economy segment of the automobile market is large and growing. But given its objectives and resources, it would make little sense for luxury-performance carmaker BMW to enter this segment. A company should only enter segments in which it can create superior customer value and gain advantages over its competitors.

Selecting Target Market Segments

Target market
A set of buyers sharing common needs or characteristics that the company decides to serve.

After evaluating different segments, the company must decide which and how many segments it will target. A **target market** consists of a set of buyers who share common needs

Figure 6.2 Market-Targeting Strategies

This figure covers a broad range of targeting strategies, from mass marketing (virtually no targeting) to individual marketing (customizing products and programs to individual customers). An example of individual marketing: At mymms.com you can order a batch of M&M's with your face and personal message printed on each little candy.

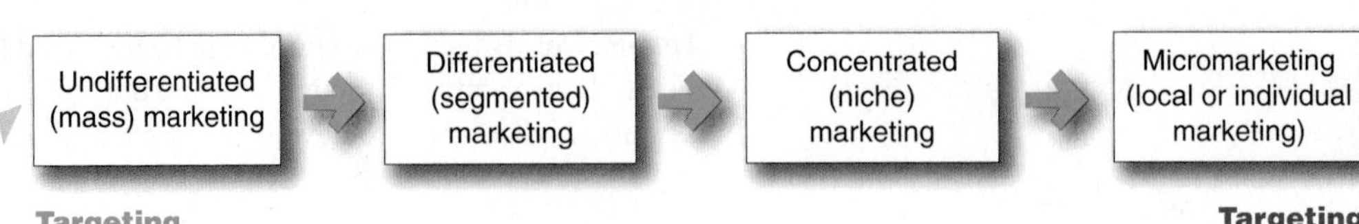

or characteristics that the company decides to serve. Market targeting can be carried out at several different levels. **Figure 6.2** shows that companies can target very broadly (*undifferentiated marketing*), very narrowly (*micromarketing*), or somewhere in between (*differentiated or concentrated marketing*).

Undifferentiated Marketing

Undifferentiated (mass) marketing A market-coverage strategy in which a firm decides to ignore market segment differences and go after the whole market with one offer.

Using an **undifferentiated marketing** (or **mass marketing**) strategy, a firm might decide to ignore market segment differences and target the whole market with one offer. Such a strategy focuses on what is *common* in the needs of consumers rather than on what is *different*. The company designs a product and a marketing program that will appeal to the largest number of buyers.

As noted earlier in the chapter, most modern marketers have strong doubts about this strategy. Difficulties arise in developing a product or brand that will satisfy all consumers. Moreover, mass marketers often have trouble competing with more-focused firms that do a better job of satisfying the needs of specific segments and niches.

Differentiated Marketing

Differentiated (segmented) marketing A market-coverage strategy in which a firm decides to target several market segments and designs separate offers for each.

Using a **differentiated marketing** (or **segmented marketing**) strategy, a firm decides to target several market segments and designs separate offers for each. As we saw in the chapter-opening story, P&G markets at least six different laundry detergent brands in the United States (Tide, Gain, Cheer, Era, Dreft, and Bold), which compete with each other on supermarket shelves. Then, P&G further segments each detergent brand to serve even narrower niches. For example, you can buy any of dozens of versions of Tide—from original Tide, Tide Coldwater, or TidePods to Tide Free & Gentle, Tide plus Febreze, or Tide plus Downy.

Perhaps no brand practices differentiated marketing like Hallmark Cards:[16]

> Hallmark vigorously segments the greeting card market. In addition to its broad Hallmark card line and popular sub-branded lines such as the humorous Shoebox Greetings, Hallmark has introduced lines targeting a dozen or more specific segments. Fresh Ink targets 18- to 39-year-old women. Hallmark Warm Wishes offers hundreds of affordable 99-cent cards. Hallmark's three ethnic lines—Mahogany, Sinceramente Hallmark, and Tree of Life—target African-American, Hispanic, and Jewish consumers, respectively. Hallmark's newer Journeys line of encouragement cards focuses on such challenges as fighting cancer, coming out, and battling depression. Hallmark's Signature Collection—with its quality papers, unique textures, fun embellishments, and relevant messages—targets buyers with more sophisticated tastes. Specific greeting cards also benefit charities such as (PRODUCT) RED, UNICEF, and the Susan G. Komen Race for the Cure. Hallmark has also embraced technology. Musical greeting cards incorporate

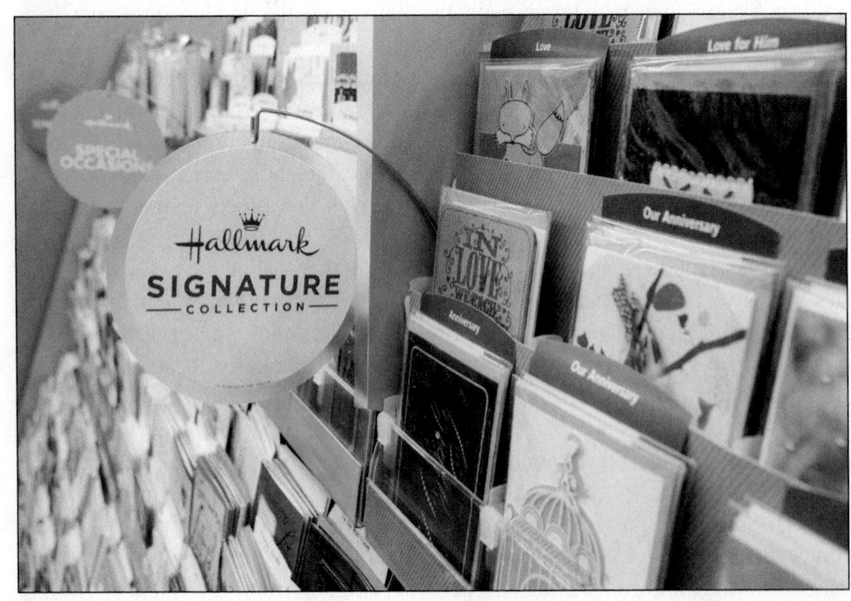

Differentiated marketing: In addition to its broad Hallmark card line, Hallmark vigorously segments the greeting card market, with shelves full of popular sub-branded lines.

sound clips from popular movies, TV shows, and songs. Recordable storybooks let people record each page of a book and have it played back as the recipient turns the pages. Online, Hallmark offers e-cards as well as personalized printed greeting cards that it mails for consumers. For business needs, Hallmark Business Expressions offers personalized corporate holiday cards and greeting cards for all occasions and events.

By offering product and marketing variations to segments, companies hope for higher sales and a stronger position within each market segment. Developing a stronger position within several segments creates more total sales than undifferentiated marketing across all segments. Thanks to its differentiated approach, Hallmark's brands account for more than 44 percent of the greeting cards purchased in the United States. Similarly, P&G's multiple detergent brands capture four times the market share of its nearest rival.[17]

But differentiated marketing also increases the costs of doing business. A firm usually finds it more expensive to develop and produce, say, 10 units of 10 different products than 100 units of a single product. Developing separate marketing plans for separate segments requires extra marketing research, forecasting, sales analysis, promotion planning, and channel management. And trying to reach different market segments with different advertising campaigns increases promotion costs. Thus, the company must weigh increased sales against increased costs when deciding on a differentiated marketing strategy.

Concentrated Marketing

Concentrated (niche) marketing
A market-coverage strategy in which a firm goes after a large share of one or a few segments or niches.

When using a **concentrated marketing** (or **niche marketing**) strategy, instead of going after a small share of a large market, a firm goes after a large share of one or a few smaller segments or niches. For example, Whole Foods Market has more than 340 stores and over $11 billion in sales, compared with goliaths such as Kroger (more than 3,600 stores and sales of $90 billion) and Walmart (close to 10,000 stores and sales of $446 billion).[18] Yet, over the past five years, the smaller, more upscale retailer has grown faster and more profitably than either of its giant rivals. Whole Foods thrives by catering to affluent customers who the Walmarts of the world can't serve well, offering them "organic, natural, and gourmet foods, all swaddled in Earth Day politics." In fact, a typical Whole Foods customer is more likely to boycott the local Walmart than to shop at it.

Through concentrated marketing, the firm achieves a strong market position because of its greater knowledge of consumer needs in the niches it serves and the special reputation it acquires. It can market more *effectively* by fine-tuning its products, prices, and programs to the needs of carefully defined segments. It can also market more *efficiently*, targeting its products or services, channels, and communications programs toward only consumers that it can serve best and most profitably.

» **Concentrated marketing: Thanks to the reach and power of online marketing, online women's clothing nicher ModCloth.com has attracted a devoted following.**

Modcloth Inc.

Niching lets smaller companies focus their limited resources on serving niches that may be unimportant to or overlooked by larger competitors. Many companies start as nichers to get a foothold against larger, more resourceful competitors and then grow into broader competitors. For example, Southwest Airlines began by serving intrastate, no-frills commuters in Texas but is now one of the nation's largest airlines. And Enterprise Rent-A-Car began by building a network of neighborhood offices rather than competing with Hertz and Avis in airport locations. Enterprise is now the nation's largest car rental company.

Today, the low cost of setting up shop on the Internet makes it even more profitable to serve seemingly miniscule niches. Small businesses, in particular, are realizing riches from serving small niches on the Web. » Consider online women's clothing nicher Modcloth.com:[19]

While her high-school classmates were out partying with friends or shopping at the mall, Susan Gregg Koger was squirreled away in her bedroom, sorting through vintage clothing she'd found at local thrift shops and dreaming up her own online business. At the tender age of 17, she and her boyfriend, now husband, Eric Koger, launched ModCloth.com out of their Carnegie Mellon dorm rooms. Despite these modest beginnings, thanks to the power of the Internet, the fledgling company soared. Today, only a decade later, ModCloth.com boasts more than 370 employees, 700 independent designers, and a closet full of one-of-a-kind finds. ModCloth.com's unique selection of indie clothing, engaging promotions on The ModCloth blog and various social media, and Web interactivity—such as letting customers play a big role in selecting featured apparel and even its design direction—have attracted a devoted following. ModCloth's revenues have grown to more than $50 million a year and the site draws more than 2 million visitors per month.

Concentrated marketing can be highly profitable. At the same time, it involves higher-than-normal risks. Companies that rely on one or a few segments for all of their business will suffer greatly if the segment turns sour. Or larger competitors may decide to enter the same segment with greater resources. For these reasons, many companies prefer to diversify in several market segments.

Micromarketing

Differentiated and concentrated marketers tailor their offers and marketing programs to meet the needs of various market segments and niches. At the same time, however, they do not customize their offers to each individual customer. **Micromarketing** is the practice of tailoring products and marketing programs to suit the tastes of specific individuals and locations. Rather than seeing a customer in every individual, micromarketers see the individual in every customer. Micromarketing includes *local marketing* and *individual marketing*.

Micromarketing
Tailoring products and marketing programs to the needs and wants of specific individuals and local customer segments; it includes *local marketing* and *individual marketing*.

Local marketing
Tailoring brands and marketing to the needs and wants of local customer segments—cities, neighborhoods, and even specific stores.

Local Marketing. **Local marketing** involves tailoring brands and promotions to the needs and wants of local customer groups—cities, neighborhoods, and even specific stores. For example, department store chain Macy's has rolled out a localization program called MyMacy's in which merchandise is customized under 69 different geographical districts. At stores around the country, Macy's sales clerks record local shopper requests and pass them along to district managers. In turn, blending the customer requests with store transaction data, the district managers customize the mix of merchandise in their stores. So, for instance, Macy's stores in Michigan stock more locally made Sanders chocolate candies. In Orlando, Macy's carries more swimsuits in stores near waterparks and more twin bedding in stores near condominium rentals. The chain stocks extra coffee percolators in its Long Island stores, where it sells more of the 1960s must-haves than anywhere else in the country. In all, the "MyMacy's" strategy is to meet the needs of local markets, making the giant retailer seem smaller and more in touch.[20]

Advances in communications technology have given rise to new high-tech versions of location-based marketing. Using location-based social networks such as Foursquare or Shopkick and local-marketing deal-of-the-day services such as Groupon or LivingSocial, retailers can engage consumers with local online or mobile phone deals (see Marketing at Work 6.2). Increasingly, location-based marketing is going mobile, reaching on-the-go consumers as they come and go in key local market areas. It's called *SoLoMo (social+local+mobile)* marketing:[21]

> With the rise of smartphones and tablets that integrate geo-location technology such as GPS, marketers are now tapping into what experts call the Social Local Mobile (SoLoMo) revolution. SoLoMo refers to the ability of on-the-go consumers to get local information fast, wherever they may be. Services such as Foursquare and Groupon, and retailers ranging from REI to Starbucks, have jumped onto the SoLoMo bandwagon, primarily in the form of smartphone and tablet apps.
>
> Mobile app Shopkick excels at SoLoMo. It sends special offers and rewards to shoppers simply for checking into client stores such as Target, American

Increasingly, local marketing is going mobile. Mobile app Shopkick excels at SoLoMo (social+local+mobile) by sending rewards and special offers to shoppers for simply walking into client stores such as Target, American Eagle, Best Buy, or Crate&Barrel.

Shopkick.

MARKETING AT WORK 6.2

Location-Based Micromarketing Equals Macro Opportunities

Marketers use a host of factors to target customers—from demographics and psychographics to detailed purchase histories. However, today's marketers are increasingly adding an important new targeting variable: location—where you are, right now. Thanks to the explosion in net-connected smartphones with GPS capabilities and location-based social networks, companies can now track your whereabouts closely and gear their offers accordingly.

Today's high-tech location-based marketing takes two major forms. One is mobile "check-in" services—such as Foursquare, Shopkick, and Scvngr—where people check in on their smartphones to reveal their locations and obtain special retail offers. The other is "deal-of-the-day" online marketers—such as Groupon and LivingSocial—that partner with local businesses to offer local shopping deals to subscribers based on where they live and what they like.

The location-based check-in services bridge the gap between the digital world and the real brick-and-mortar world. For example, Foursquare's location-based mobile app lets its more than 30 million users visit participating retail locations such as Starbucks, their favorite local pizza place, or any of more than 1 million other businesses. They check in by pushing buttons on their mobile phones and reap special rewards. That typically means discount e-coupons. But most check-in services add additional incentives with an addictive game-like twist. For example, location-based gaming platform Scvngr designs smartphone-enabled scavenger hunts, granting discounts for completing certain tasks, such as taking in-store pictures. And Foursquare members compete to become the "mayor" of a given retail location by having the highest number of check-ins there, earn badges by checking in to specific locations, or gain status designations by making helpful contributions to the Foursquare community.

But more than just passing out e-coupons and other rewards, Foursquare and the other check-in services are becoming full-fledged, location-based lifestyle networks. The aim is to enrich people's lives by helping them to learn the whereabouts of friends, share location-related experiences, and discover new places, all while linking them to sponsoring locations that match their interests.

Foursquare co-founder Dennis Crowley envisions a futuristic scenario in which your phone checks the calendars and locations of friends on a late Friday afternoon, learns who is available that evening, and suggests a nearby restaurant that everyone has wanted to try. It even notes what tables are available and the restaurant's dinner specials. Foursquare is getting closer and closer to making this scenario a reality. At its Web site, it already promises: "Foursquare makes the real world easier to use. Our app helps you keep up with friends, discover what's nearby, save money, and unlock deals. When you're looking for inspiration on what to do next, we'll give you personalized recommendations and deals based on where you, your friends, and people with your tastes have been."

Mobile app Shopkick combines location-based technologies to "make shopping better" with its own seamless, intuitive, and personalized version of a retailer rewards program. It's automatic. When Shopkickers walk into their favorite retail stores, the app automatically checks them in and they rack up rewards points or "kicks." If they buy something, they get even more kicks. Users can use their kicks for discounted or free merchandise of their own choosing. Shopkick helps users get the most out of their efforts by mapping out potential kicks in a given geographic area. Shopkick has grown quickly to become one of the nation's top five shopping apps, with more than 3 million users.

The second major form of location-based marketing—"deal-of-the-day" services—has become one of the hottest-ever online crazes. Market leader Groupon dominates with more than 36 million active users in hundreds of cities worldwide. Groupon partners with retailers in each city to craft attractive offers promoting their goods and services to area customers. Most of Groupon's local partners are small businesses, but global giants such as Starbucks, Best Buy, Barnes & Noble, Gap, and PepsiCo have also gotten into the Groupon act.

Groupon offers subscribers at least one deal each day in their city—such as paying \$40 for an \$80 voucher at a local restaurant. But the coupon deals kick in only if enough people

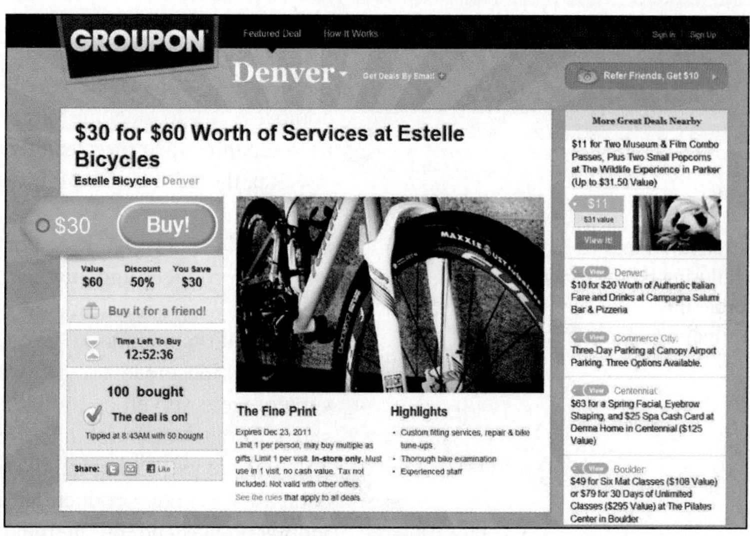

>> Location-based marketing: "Deal-of-the-day" Web marketers—such as Groupon—partner with local businesses to offer shopping deals to subscribers based on where they live and what they like.

Groupon Inc.

sign up, encouraging subscribers to spread word of the deal to friends and neighbors and via social media such as Twitter and Facebook. Hence, the name Groupon—*group* plus *coupon*. When a deal "tips," Groupon shares the revenue roughly 50–50 with the retailer. Nearly all of Groupon's deals tip.

To further personalize its deals, the location-based marketer now incorporates factors such as gender, age, neighborhood, and a host of interests and preferences members can select in order to narrow the types of deals they receive. Groupon has also expanded its "deal-of-the-day" model to include Groupon Getaways (travel bargains), Groupon Goods (product deals from national brands), and Groupon Now (a mobile app that targets deals based on user location).

Working with Groupon can transform a local business in as little as 24 hours. For example, when the Joffrey Ballet in Chicago offered highly discounted season subscriptions through Groupon, 2,334 people signed up, doubling the performing group's subscription base in a single day. Sometimes, Groupon's deals can work too well. Retailer Gap's server crashed when 445,000 people bought $50 merchandise cards for only $25. Groupon works to minimize such cases by coaching businesses through the deal process and recommending appropriate deal caps. And its new Merchant Impact Report gives merchants clear and accurate assessments of return patronage and profits.

Groupon may have entered Internet stardom faster than any other dot.com. Its average subscriber is a target marketer's dream: female, between the ages of 18 and 34, single, and making more than $70,000 a year. Before Groupon was even two years old, *Forbes* crowned it "the fastest growing company ever." Its revenues have shot up from $14 million in 2009 to $1.6 billion last year, making it the youngest company of any kind to hit $1 billion in total revenue.

More generally, the growth of location-based services has been nothing short of astounding. Whereas no such companies even existed just six years ago, today there are more than 6,000 location-based smartphone apps alone. Online giants Google and Facebook have experimented with their own location-based services and have integrated check-in and deal-of-the-day features into their core products. Similarly, Amazon.com owns a significant chunk of deal-of-the-day service LivingSocial.

With so much competition, the industry is currently working its way through growing pains, and a shake-out seems likely. But one thing is clear. When the dust settles, there will be macro potential for location-based micromarketing.

Sources: Based on quotes and other information from Ingrid Lunden, "Shopkick Says It's Now Profitable, with Its Shopping App Adding $200M in Sales for Target, Best Buy, and Others in 2012," *Techcrunch*, January 16, 2013, http://techcrunch.com/2013/01/16/shopkick-says-its-now-profitable-with-its-shopping-app-adding-200m-in-sales-for-target-best-buy-and-other-partners/; Diane Brady, "Social Media's New Mantra: Location, Location, Location," *Bloomberg Businessweek*, May 10–May 16, 2010, pp. 34–36; Bob Krummert, "Do Your Groupon Offers Make Money?" *Restaurant Hospitality*, January 17, 2013, http://restaurant-hospitality.com/marketing/do-your-groupon-offers-make-money; and http://investor.groupon.com/annuals.cfm, www.groupon.com, www.foursquare.com, and www.shopkick.com, accessed October 2013.

Eagle, Best Buy, or Crate&Barrel. When shoppers are near a participating store, the Shopkick app on their phone picks up a signal from the store and spits out store coupons, deal alerts, and product information. Similarly, shopping center operator DDR Corporation, which operates 27 open-air malls across 16 markets, uses technology that detects nearby shoppers and sends real-time text messages about various store sales and promotions to customers who have opted in. Such geo-targeting benefits both marketers and consumers. It helps merchants get out their messages while at the same time personalizing the customer's shopping experience.

Local marketing has some drawbacks, however. It can drive up manufacturing and marketing costs by reducing the economies of scale. It can also create logistics problems as companies try to meet the varied requirements of different regional and local markets. Still, as companies face increasingly fragmented markets, and as new supporting technologies develop, the advantages of local marketing often outweigh the drawbacks.

Individual marketing
Tailoring products and marketing programs to the needs and preferences of individual customers.

Individual Marketing. In the extreme, micromarketing becomes **individual marketing**—tailoring products and marketing programs to the needs and preferences of individual customers. Individual marketing has also been labeled one-to-one marketing, mass customization, and markets-of-one marketing.

The widespread use of mass marketing has obscured the fact that for centuries consumers were served as individuals: The tailor custom-made a suit, the cobbler designed shoes for an individual, and the cabinetmaker made furniture to order. Today, new technologies are permitting many companies to return to customized marketing. More detailed databases, robotic production and flexible manufacturing, and interactive media such as mobile phones and the Internet have combined to foster mass customization. *Mass customization* is the process by which firms interact one to one with masses of customers to design products and services tailor-made to individual needs.

Individual marketing has made relationships with customers more important than ever. Just as mass production was the marketing principle of the twentieth century, interactive

Individual marketing: Nike's NikeID program lets users choose shoe materials, personalize colors, imprint text on the heels, and even size the left and right shoes differently.

Getty Images for Nike.

marketing is becoming a marketing principle for the twenty-first century. The world appears to be coming full circle—from the good old days when customers were treated as individuals to mass marketing when nobody knew your name, and then back again.

Companies these days are hyper-customizing everything from food to artwork, earphones, sneakers, and motorcycles.[22] At mymms.com, candylovers can buy M&M's embossed with images of their kids or pets. JH Audio in Orlando makes music earphones based on molds of customers' ears to provide optimized fit and better and safer sound. The company even laser prints designs on the tiny ear buds—some people request a kid for each ear; others prefer a dog. Nike's NikeID program lets users choose materials for their shoes' tread (say, for trail or street) and upper (Gore-Tex, mesh, or other), pick the color of the swoosh symbol and stitching, and even imprint text on the heels. Different-sized right and left feet? That, too, can be retooled. On a much larger scale, Harley-Davidson's H-D1 factory customization program lets customers go online, design their own Harley, and get it in as little as four weeks. It invites customers to explore some 8,000 ways to create their own masterpiece. "You dream it. We build it," says the company.

Business-to-business marketers are also finding new ways to customize their offerings. For example, John Deere manufactures seeding equipment that can be configured in more than 2 million versions to individual customer specifications. The seeders are produced one at a time, in any sequence, on a single production line. Mass customization provides a way to stand out against competitors.

Choosing a Targeting Strategy

Companies need to consider many factors when choosing a market-targeting strategy. Which strategy is best depends on the company's resources. When the firm's resources are limited, concentrated marketing makes the most sense. The best strategy also depends on the degree of product variability. Undifferentiated marketing is more suited for uniform products, such as grapefruit or steel. Products that can vary in design, such as cameras and cars, are more suited to differentiation or concentration. The product's life-cycle stage also must be considered. When a firm introduces a new product, it may be practical to launch one version only, as undifferentiated marketing or concentrated marketing may make the most sense. In the mature stage of the product life cycle, however, differentiated marketing often makes more sense.

Another factor is *market variability*. If most buyers have the same tastes, buy the same amounts, and react the same way to marketing efforts, undifferentiated marketing is appropriate. Finally, *competitors' marketing strategies* are important. When competitors use differentiated or concentrated marketing, undifferentiated marketing can be suicidal. Conversely, when competitors use undifferentiated marketing, a firm can gain an advantage by using differentiated or concentrated marketing, focusing on the needs of buyers in specific segments.

Socially Responsible Target Marketing

Smart targeting helps companies become more efficient and effective by focusing on the segments that they can satisfy best and most profitably. Targeting also benefits consumers—companies serve specific groups of consumers with offers carefully tailored to their needs. However, target marketing sometimes generates controversy and concern. The biggest issues usually involve the targeting of vulnerable or disadvantaged consumers with controversial or potentially harmful products.

For example, cigarette, beer, and fast-food marketers have generated controversy over the years by their attempts to target inner-city minority consumers. For example, fast-food chains have drawn criticism for pitching their high-fat, salt-laden fare to low-income, urban residents who are much more likely than suburbanites to be heavy consumers. Similarly, big banks and mortgage lenders have been criticized for targeting consumers in poor urban areas with attractive adjustable-rate home mortgages that they can't really afford.

Children are seen as an especially vulnerable audience. Marketers in a wide range of industries—from cereal, soft drinks, and fast food to toys and fashion—have been heavily criticized for their marketing efforts directed toward children. Critics worry that premium offers and high-powered advertising appeals presented through the mouths of lovable animated characters will overwhelm children's defenses. In recent years, for instance, McDonald's has been criticized by various health advocates and parent groups that are concerned that its popular Happy Meals offers—featuring trinkets and other items tied in with children's movies such as *Toy Story*—create a too-powerful connection between children and the often fat- and calorie-laden meals. Some critics have even asked McDonald's to retire its iconic Ronald McDonald character. McDonald's has responded by putting the Happy Meal on a diet, cutting the overall calorie count by 20 percent and adding fruit to every meal.[23]

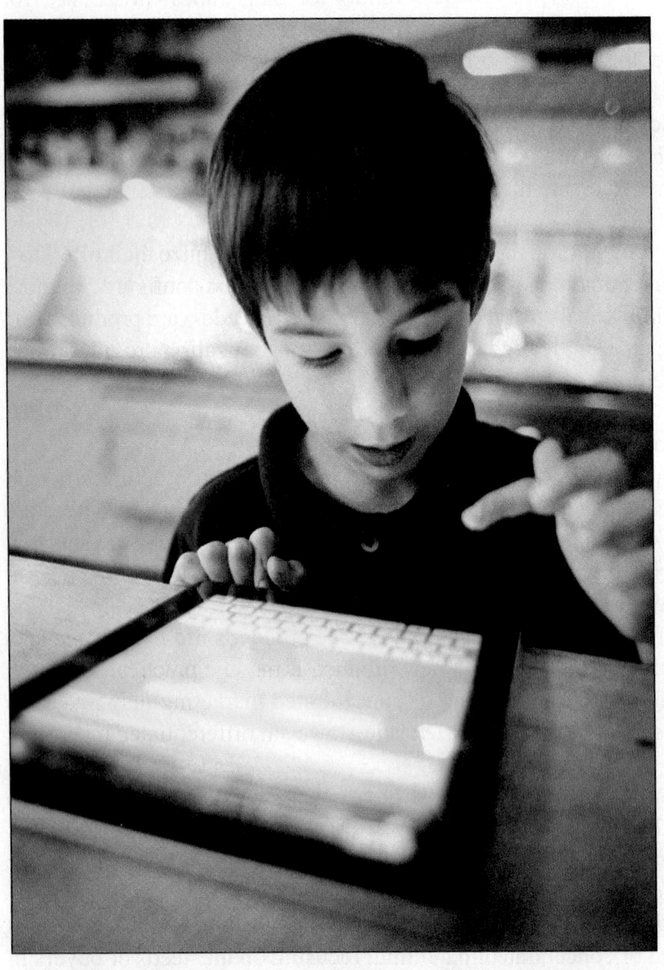

>> Socially responsible targeting: Critics worry that children may be especially vulnerable to targeted marketing messages subtly embedded within digital content and viewed on personal, small-screen devices that are beyond even the most watchful parent's eye.

The digital era may make children even more vulnerable to targeted marketing messages. Traditional child-directed TV and print ads usually contain obvious pitches that are easily detected and controlled by parents. >> However, marketing in digital media may be subtly embedded within the content and viewed by children on personal, small-screen devices that are beyond even the most watchful parent's eye. Such marketing might take the form of immersive "advergames"—video games specifically designed to engage children with products. Or they might consist of embedded ads, quizzes, or product placements that let marketers cross-promote branded products, TV shows, popular characters, or other marketable entities.

For example, free video games offered at Barbie.com let children help Barbie "build 'n style" her "perf mansion" or play "princess charm school games" with her. At Nickelodeon's The Club—an "online virtual word for kids"—young children can create an avatar and immerse themselves in "Super Spongy Square Games" with SpongeBob SquarePants or browse the Power Rangers Samurai store. Kraft's free "Jiggle-It" app engages kids by letting them watch a JELL-O cube dance to their favorite songs; the brand's "Dinner, Not Art" app lets them create digital macaroni art, helping to promote the company's Kraft Macaroni and Cheese. Some watchers see such marketing as adding value for both the children and the marketers—promoting child creativity and entertainment while engaging child in brand-related experiences. Others, however, worry that it constitutes "stealth marketing" that takes advantage of children who can't yet tell the difference between commercial and entertainment or educational content. "Kids are not as savvy to the methods and motives of advertisers," concludes one analyst. "Young kids are more gullible."[24]

To encourage responsible children's advertising, the Children's Advertising Review Unit, the advertising industry's self-regulatory agency, has published extensive children's advertising guidelines that recognize the special needs of child audiences. Still, critics feel that more should been done, especially concerning online and digital marketing. Some have even called for a complete ban on advertising to children.

More broadly, the growth of the Internet and other carefully targeted direct media has raised fresh concerns about potential targeting abuses. The Internet allows more precise targeting, letting the makers of questionable products or deceptive advertisers zero in on the most vulnerable audiences. Unscrupulous marketers can now send tailor-made, deceptive messages by e-mail directly to millions of unsuspecting consumers. For example, the Federal Bureau of Investigation's Internet Crime Complaint Center Web site alone received more than 310,000 complaints last year.[25]

Not all attempts to target children, minorities, or other special segments draw such criticism. In fact, most provide benefits to targeted consumers. For example, Pantene markets Relaxed and Natural hair products to women of color. Samsung markets the Jitterbug, an easy-to-use phone, directly to seniors who need a simpler mobile phone with bigger buttons, large screen text, and a louder speaker. And Colgate makes a large selection of toothbrush shapes and toothpaste flavors for children—from Colgate SpongeBob SquarePants Mild Bubble Fruit toothpaste to Colgate Dora the Explorer character toothbrushes. Such products help make tooth brushing more fun and get children to brush longer and more often.

Thus, in target marketing, the issue is not really *who* is targeted but rather *how* and for *what*. Controversies arise when marketers attempt to profit at the expense of targeted segments—when they unfairly target vulnerable segments or target them with questionable products or tactics. Socially responsible marketing calls for segmentation and targeting that serve not just the interests of the company but also the interests of those targeted.

SPEED BUMP LINKING THE CONCEPTS

It's time to pause and take stock.

- At the last Linking the Concepts, you segmented the U.S. footwear market. Refer to Figure 6.2 and select two companies that serve the footwear market. Describe their segmentation and targeting strategies. Can you come up with a company that targets many different segments versus another that focuses on only one or a few segments?
- How does each company you chose differentiate its market offering and image? Has each done a good job of establishing this differentiation in the minds of targeted consumers? The final section in this chapter deals with such positioning issues.

Author Comment
At the same time that the company is answering the first simple-sounding question (Which customers will we serve?), it must be asking the second question (How will we serve them?).

Differentiation and Positioning

Beyond deciding which segments of the market it will target, the company must decide on a *value proposition*—how it will create differentiated value for targeted segments and what positions it wants to occupy in those segments. A **product position** is the way a product is *defined by consumers* on important attributes—the place the product occupies in consumers' minds relative to competing products. Products are made in factories, but brands happen in the minds of consumers.

Product position
The way a product is defined by consumers on important attributes—the place the product occupies in consumers' minds relative to competing products.

Method laundry detergent is positioned as a smarter, easier, and greener detergent; Dreft is positioned as the gentle detergent for baby clothes. At IHOP, you "Come hungry. Leave happy."; at Olive Garden, "When You're Here, You're Family." In the automobile market, the Nissan Versa and Honda Fit are positioned on economy, Mercedes and Cadillac on luxury, and Porsche and BMW on performance. Folger's Coffee is "The best part of wakin' up"; Honest Tea is positioned as "Refreshingly Honest," with "Brewed organic tea leaves. Real ingredients."

Consumers are overloaded with information about products and services. They cannot reevaluate products every time they make a buying decision. To simplify the buying process, consumers organize products, services, and companies into categories and "position" them in their minds. A product's position is the complex set of perceptions, impressions, and feelings that consumers have for the product compared with competing products.

>> **Positioning: Honest Tea is positioned as "Refreshingly Honest," with "Brewed organic tea leaves. Real ingredients."**
Coca-Cola Company.

Consumers position products with or without the help of marketers. But marketers do not want to leave their products' positions to chance. They must *plan* positions that will give their products the greatest advantage in selected target markets, and they must design marketing mixes to create these planned positions.

Positioning Maps

In planning their differentiation and positioning strategies, marketers often prepare *perceptual positioning maps* that show consumer perceptions of their brands versus those of competing products on important buying dimensions. >> **Figure 6.3** shows a positioning map for the U.S. large luxury SUV market.[26] The position of each circle on the map indicates the brand's perceived positioning on two dimensions: price and orientation (luxury versus performance). The size of each circle indicates the brand's relative market share.

Thus, customers view the market-leading Cadillac Escalade as a moderately priced, large, luxury SUV with a balance of luxury and performance. The Escalade is positioned on urban luxury, and, in its case, "performance" probably means power and safety performance. You'll find no mention of off-road adventuring in an Escalade ad.

By contrast, the Range Rover and the Land Cruiser are positioned on luxury with nuances of off-road performance. For example, the Toyota Land Cruiser began in 1951 as a four-wheel-drive, Jeep-like vehicle designed to conquer the world's most grueling terrains and climates. In recent years, the Land Cruiser has retained this adventure and performance positioning but with luxury added. Its Web site brags of "legendary off-road capability," with off-road technologies such as an Acoustic Control Induction System to get the most out of the RPMs, "so you can make molehills out of mountains." Despite its ruggedness, however, the company notes that "its available Bluetooth hands-free technology, DVD entertainment, and a sumptuous interior have softened its edges."

Choosing a Differentiation and Positioning Strategy

Some firms find it easy to choose a differentiation and positioning strategy. For example, a firm well known for quality in certain segments will go after this position in a new segment if there are enough buyers seeking quality. But in many cases, two or more firms will go after the same position. Then each will have to find other ways to set itself apart. Each firm must differentiate its offer by building a unique bundle of benefits that appeals to a substantial group within the segment.

>> **Figure 6.3** Positioning Map: Large Luxury SUVs
Source: Based on data provided by WardsAuto.com and Edmunds.com, 2013.

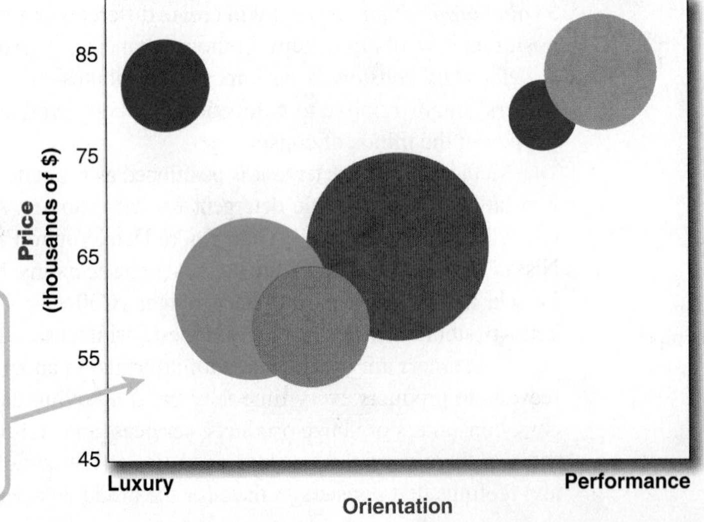

The location of each circle shows where consumers position a brand on two dimensions: price and luxury-performance orientation. The size of each circle indicates the brand's relative market share in the segment. Thus, Toyota's Land Cruiser is a niche brand that is perceived to be relatively expensive and more performance oriented.

Above all else, a brand's positioning must serve the needs and preferences of well-defined target markets. For example, although both Dunkin' Donuts and Starbucks are coffee shops, they target very different customers, who want very different things from their favorite coffee seller. Starbucks targets more upscale professionals, positioning itself as a sort of high-brow "third place"—outside the home and office—featuring couches, eclectic music, WIFI, and art-splashed walls. Dunkin' Donuts targets the "average Joe" with a decidedly more low-brow, "everyman" kind of positioning. Yet each brand succeeds because it creates just the right value proposition for its unique mix of customers.

The differentiation and positioning task consists of three steps: identifying a set of differentiating competitive advantages on which to build a position, choosing the right competitive advantages, and selecting an overall positioning strategy. The company must then effectively communicate and deliver the chosen position to the market.

Identifying Possible Value Differences and Competitive Advantages

To build profitable relationships with target customers, marketers must understand customer needs and deliver more customer value better than competitors do. To the extent that a company can differentiate and position itself as providing superior customer value, it gains **competitive advantage**.

Competitive advantage
An advantage over competitors gained by offering greater customer value, either by having lower prices or providing more benefits that justify higher prices.

But solid positions cannot be built on empty promises. If a company positions its product as *offering* the best quality and service, it must actually differentiate the product so that it *delivers* the promised quality and service. Companies must do much more than simply shout out their positions with slogans and taglines. They must first *live* the slogan. For example, online shoes and accessories seller Zappos' "powered by service" positioning would ring hollow if not backed by truly outstanding customer care. Zappos aligns its entire organization and all of its people around providing the best possible customer service. At Zappos, says the company, "customer service isn't just a department." The online seller's number-one core value: "Deliver WOW through service."[27]

To find points of differentiation, marketers must think through the customer's entire experience with the company's product or service. An alert company can find ways to differentiate itself at every customer contact point. In what specific ways can a company differentiate itself or its market offer? It can differentiate along the lines of *product*, *services*, *channels*, *people*, or *image*.

Through *product differentiation*, brands can be differentiated on features, performance, or style and design. Thus, Bose positions its speakers on their striking design and sound characteristics. By gaining the approval of the American Heart Association as an approach to a healthy lifestyle, Subway differentiates itself as the healthy fast-food choice. >> And SodaStream positions itself as an alternative to bottled carbonated waters and soft drinks. It promises a simple, convenient, ecofriendly process for turning home tap water into fresh, homemade soda with no heavy bottles to carry, store, and recycle. SodaStream gives you "smart. simple. soda."

>> Product differentiation: SodaStream promises a simple, convenient, ecofriendly alternative for turning home tap water into fresh, homemade soda. It gives you "smart. simple. soda."

Image provided courtesy of SodaStream, © 2013.

Beyond differentiating its physical product, a firm can also differentiate the services that accompany the product. Some companies gain *services differentiation* through speedy, convenient, or careful delivery. For example, First Convenience Bank of Texas offers "Real Hours for Real People"; it is open seven days a week, including evenings. Others differentiate their service based on high-quality customer care. In an age where customer satisfaction with airline service is in constant decline, Singapore Airlines sets itself apart through extraordinary customer care and the grace of its flight attendants. "Everyone expects excellence from us," says the international airline. "[So even] in the smallest details of flight, we rise to each occasion and deliver the Singapore Airlines experience."[28]

Firms that practice *channel differentiation* gain competitive advantage through the way they design their channel's coverage, expertise, and performance. Amazon.com and GEICO, for example, set themselves apart with their smooth-functioning direct channels. Companies can also gain a strong competitive advantage through *people differentiation*—hiring and training better people than their competitors do. People differentiation requires that a company select its customer-contact people carefully and train them well. For example, Disney World trains its theme park people thoroughly to ensure that they are competent, courteous, friendly, and upbeat—from the hotel check-in agents, to the monorail drivers, to the ride attendants, to the people who sweep Main Street USA. Each employee is carefully trained to understand customers and to "make people happy."

Even when competing offers look the same, buyers may perceive a difference based on company or brand *image differentiation*. A company or brand image should convey a product's distinctive benefits and positioning. Developing a strong and distinctive image calls for creativity and hard work. A company cannot develop an image in the public's mind overnight by using only a few ads. If Ritz-Carlton means quality, this image must be supported by everything the company says and does.

Symbols, such as the McDonald's golden arches, the colorful Google logo, the Nike swoosh, or Apple's "bite mark" logo, can provide strong company or brand recognition and image differentiation. The company might build a brand around a famous person, as Nike did with its Michael Jordan, Kobe Bryant, and LeBron James basketball shoe and apparel collections. Some companies even become associated with colors, such as Coca-Cola (red), IBM (blue), or UPS (brown). The chosen symbols, characters, and other image elements must be communicated through advertising that conveys the company's or brand's personality.

Choosing the Right Competitive Advantages

Suppose a company is fortunate enough to discover several potential differentiations that provide competitive advantages. It now must choose the ones on which it will build its positioning strategy. It must decide how many differences to promote and which ones.

How Many Differences to Promote. Many marketers think that companies should aggressively promote only one benefit to the target market. Advertising executive Rosser Reeves, for example, said a company should develop a *unique selling proposition (USP)* for each brand and stick to it. Each brand should pick an attribute and tout itself as "number one" on that attribute. Buyers tend to remember number one better, especially in this overcommunicated society. Thus, Walmart promotes its unbeatable low prices and Burger King promotes personal choice—"have it your way."

Other marketers think that companies should position themselves on more than one differentiator. This may be necessary if two or more firms are claiming to be best on the same attribute. Today, in a time when the mass market is fragmenting into many small segments, companies and brands are trying to broaden their positioning strategies to appeal to more segments. >> For example, whereas Gatorade originally offered a sports drink positioned only on performance hydration, the brand now offers an entire G Series of sports drinks that provide at least three primary benefits. G Series "fuels your body before, during, and after practice, training, or competition." Gatorade Prime 01 is positioned as "pre-game fuel" that provides energy *before* exercise. Gatorade G2 Thirst Quencher is for use "in the moment of activity" *during* exercise. Finally, Gatorade Recover 03 is positioned as a post-game recovering beverage that provides protein for recovery *after* exercise. Clearly, many buyers want these multiple benefits. The challenge is to convince them that one brand can do it all.

>> Positioning on multiple competitive advantages: The Gatorade G Series "fuels your body before, during, and after" exercise.

Pepsi-Cola North America, Inc.

Which Differences to Promote. Not all brand differences are meaningful or worthwhile, and each difference has the potential to create company costs as well as customer benefits. A difference is worth establishing to the extent that it satisfies the following criteria:

- *Important:* The difference delivers a highly valued benefit to target buyers.
- *Distinctive:* Competitors do not offer the difference, or the company can offer it in a more distinctive way.
- *Superior:* The difference is superior to other ways that customers might obtain the same benefit.
- *Communicable:* The difference is communicable and visible to buyers.
- *Preemptive:* Competitors cannot easily copy the difference.
- *Affordable:* Buyers can afford to pay for the difference.
- *Profitable:* The company can introduce the difference profitably.

Many companies have introduced differentiations that failed one or more of these tests. When the Westin Stamford Hotel in Singapore once advertised itself as the world's tallest hotel, it was a distinction that was not important to most tourists; in fact, it turned many off. Polaroid's Polarvision, which produced instantly developed home movies, bombed too. Although Polarvision was distinctive and even preemptive, it was inferior to another way of capturing motion—namely, camcorders.

Thus, choosing competitive advantages on which to position a product or service can be difficult, yet such choices may be crucial to success. Choosing the right differentiators can help a brand stand out from the pack of competitors. For example, when carmaker Nissan introduced its novel little Cube, it didn't position the car only on attributes shared with competing models, such as affordability and customization. It positioned it as a "mobile device" that fits today's digital lifestyles.

Selecting an Overall Positioning Strategy

Value proposition
The full positioning of a brand—the full mix of benefits on which it is positioned.

The full positioning of a brand is called the brand's **value proposition**—the full mix of benefits on which a brand is differentiated and positioned. It is the answer to the customer's question "Why should I buy your brand?" BMW's "ultimate driving machine" value proposition hinges on performance but also includes luxury and styling, all for a price that is higher than average but seems fair for this mix of benefits.

>> **Figure 6.4** shows possible value propositions on which a company might position its products. In the figure, the five blue cells on the top and right represent winning value propositions—differentiation and positioning that give the company a competitive advantage. The pink cells at the lower left, however, represent losing value propositions. The center green cell represents at best a marginal proposition. In the following sections, we discuss the five winning value propositions: more for more, more for the same, the same for less, less for much less, and more for less.

>> **Figure 6.4** Possible Value Propositions

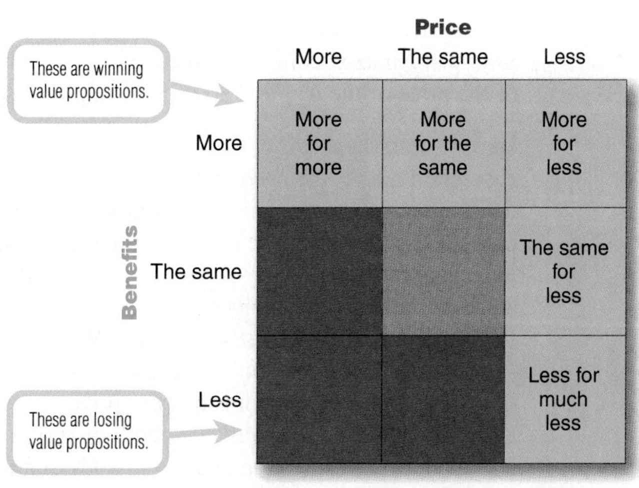

More for More. *More-for-more* positioning involves providing the most upscale product or service and charging a higher price to cover the higher costs. A more-for-more market offering not only offers higher quality, it also gives prestige to the buyer. It symbolizes status and a loftier lifestyle. Four Seasons hotels, Rolex watches, Mercedes automobiles, SubZero appliances—each claims superior quality, craftsmanship, durability, performance, or style, and therefore charges a higher price. When Apple premiered its iPhone, it offered higher-quality features than a traditional mobile phone, with a hefty price tag to match.

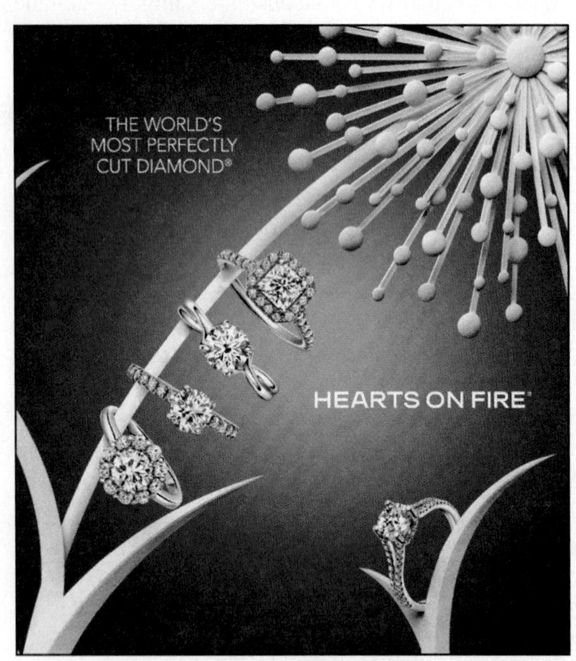

» **More-for-more positioning: Hearts On Fire diamonds have created a more-for-more niche as "The World's Most Perfectly Cut Diamond—for those who expect more and give more in return."**

Used with permission of Hearts On Fire Company, LLC.

Similarly, the marketers of Hearts On Fire diamonds have created a more-for-more niche as "The World's Most Perfectly Cut Diamond." Hearts On Fire diamonds have a unique "hearts and arrow" design. When viewed under magnification from the bottom, a perfect ring of eight hearts appears; from the top comes a perfectly formed Fireburst of light. » Hearts On Fire diamonds aren't for everyone, says the company. "Hearts On Fire is for those who expect more and give more in return." The brand commands a 15 to 20 percent price premium over comparable competing diamonds.[29]

Although more-for-more can be profitable, this strategy can also be vulnerable. It often invites imitators who claim the same quality but at a lower price. For example, more-for-more brand Starbucks now faces "gourmet" coffee competitors ranging from Dunkin' Donuts to McDonald's. Also, luxury goods that sell well during good times may be at risk during economic downturns when buyers become more cautious in their spending. The recent gloomy economy hit premium brands, such as Starbucks, the hardest.

More for the Same. Companies can attack a competitor's more-for-more positioning by introducing a brand offering comparable quality at a lower price. For example, Toyota introduced its Lexus line with a *more-for-the-same* value proposition versus Mercedes and BMW. Its first headline read: "Perhaps the first time in history that trading a $72,000 car for a $36,000 car could be considered trading up." It communicated the high quality of its new Lexus through rave reviews in car magazines and a widely distributed video showing side-by-side comparisons of Lexus and Mercedes automobiles. It published surveys showing that Lexus dealers were providing customers with better sales and service experiences than were Mercedes dealerships. Many Mercedes owners switched to Lexus, and the Lexus repurchase rate has been 60 percent, twice the industry average.

The Same for Less. Offering *the same for less* can be a powerful value proposition—everyone likes a good deal. Discount stores such as Walmart and "category killers" such as Best Buy, PetSmart, David's Bridal, and DSW Shoes use this positioning. They don't claim to offer different or better products. Instead, they offer many of the same brands as department stores and specialty stores but at deep discounts based on superior purchasing power and lower-cost operations. Other companies develop imitative but lower-priced brands in an effort to lure customers away from the market leader. For example, Amazon.com offers the Kindle Fire tablet, which sells for less than 40 percent of the price of the Apple iPad or Samsung Galaxy.

Less for Much Less. A market almost always exists for products that offer less and therefore cost less. Few people need, want, or can afford "the very best" in everything they buy. In many cases, consumers will gladly settle for less-than-optimal performance or give up some of the bells and whistles in exchange for a lower price. For example, many travelers seeking lodgings prefer not to pay for what they consider unnecessary extras, such as a pool, an attached restaurant, or mints on the pillow. Hotel chains such as Ramada Limited, Holiday Inn Express, and Motel 6 suspend some of these amenities and charge less accordingly.

Less-for-much-less positioning involves meeting consumers' lower performance or quality requirements at a much lower price. For example, Family Dollar and Dollar General stores offer more affordable goods at very low prices. Costco warehouse stores offer less merchandise selection and consistency and much lower levels of service; as a result, they charge rock-bottom prices.

More for Less. Of course, the winning value proposition would be to offer *more for less*. Many companies claim to do this. And, in the short run, some companies can actually achieve such lofty positions. For example, when it first opened for business, Home Depot had arguably the best product selection, the best service, *and* the lowest prices compared to local hardware stores and other home improvement chains.

Yet in the long run, companies will find it very difficult to sustain such best-of-both positioning. Offering more usually costs more, making it difficult to deliver on the "for-less" promise. Companies that try to deliver both may lose out to more focused competitors. For example, facing determined competition from Lowe's stores, Home Depot must now decide whether it wants to compete primarily on superior service or on lower prices.

All said, each brand must adopt a positioning strategy designed to serve the needs and wants of its target markets. *More for more* will draw one target market, *less for much less* will draw another, and so on. Thus, in any market, there is usually room for many different companies, each successfully occupying different positions. The important thing is that each company must develop its own winning positioning strategy, one that makes the company special to its target consumers.

Developing a Positioning Statement

Positioning statement
A statement that summarizes company or brand positioning using this form: To (target segment and need) our (brand) is (concept) that (point of difference).

Company and brand positioning should be summed up in a **positioning statement**. The statement should follow the form: To (target segment and need) our (brand) is (concept) that (point of difference).[30] >> Here is an example using the popular digital information management application Evernote: "To busy multitaskers who need help remembering things, Evernote is digital content management application that makes it easy to capture and remember moments and ideas from your everyday life using your computer, phone, tablet, and the Web."

Note that the positioning statement first states the product's membership in a category (digital content management application) and then shows its point of difference from other members of the category (easily capture moments and ideas and remember them later). Evernote helps you "remember everything" by letting you take notes, capture photos, create to-do lists, and record voice reminders, and then makes them easy to find and access using just about any device, anywhere—at home, at work, or on the go.

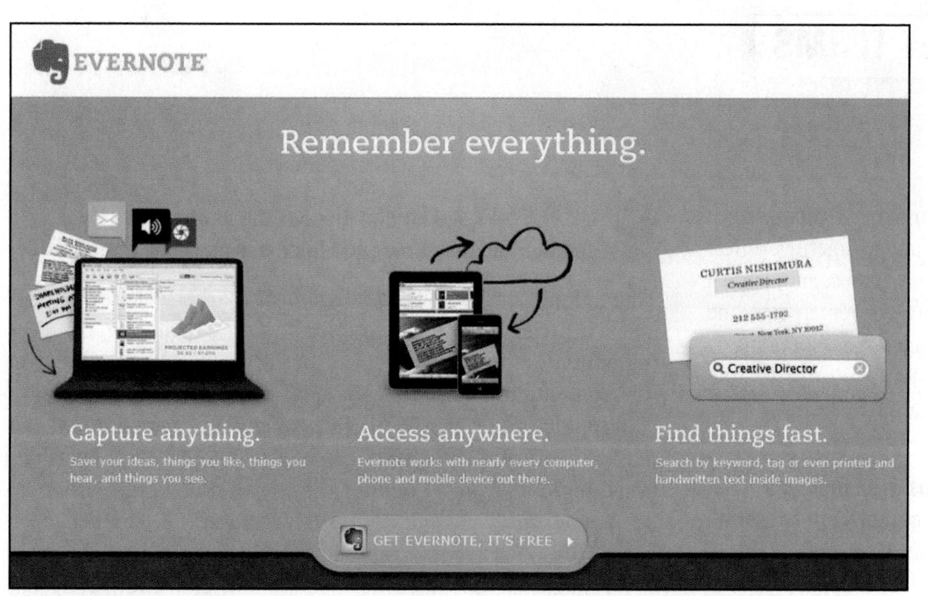

>> **Positioning statement: Evernote is positioned as a digital content management application that helps busy people to capture and remember moments and ideas and find them fast later.**

Evernote Corporation.

Placing a brand in a specific category suggests similarities that it might share with other products in the category. But the case for the brand's superiority is made on its points of difference. For example, the U.S. Postal Service ships packages just like UPS and FedEx, but it differentiates its Priority Mail from competitors with convenient, low-price, flat-rate shipping boxes and envelopes. "If it fits, it ships," promises the Post Office.

Communicating and Delivering the Chosen Position

Once it has chosen a position, the company must take strong steps to deliver and communicate the desired position to its target consumers. All the company's marketing mix efforts must support the positioning strategy.

Positioning the company calls for concrete action, not just talk. If the company decides to build a position on better quality and service, it must first *deliver* that position. Designing the marketing mix—product, price, place, and promotion—involves working out the tactical details of the positioning strategy. Thus, a firm that seizes on a more-for-more position knows that it must produce high-quality products, charge a high price, distribute through high-quality dealers, and advertise in high-quality media. It must hire and train more service people, find retailers that have a good reputation for service, and develop sales and advertising messages that broadcast its superior service. This is the only way to build a consistent and believable more-for-more position.

Companies often find it easier to come up with a good positioning strategy than to implement it. Establishing a position or changing one usually takes a long time. In contrast, positions that have taken years to build can quickly be lost. Once a company has built the desired position, it must take care to maintain the position through consistent performance and communication. It must closely monitor and adapt the position over time to match changes in consumer needs and competitors' strategies. However, the company should avoid abrupt changes that might confuse consumers. Instead, a product's position should evolve gradually as it adapts to the ever-changing marketing environment.

MyMarketingLab

Go to **mymktlab.com** to complete the problems marked with this icon .

END OF CHAPTER REVIEWING THE CONCEPTS

CHAPTER REVIEW AND KEY TERMS

Objectives Review

In this chapter, you learned about the major elements of a customer-driven marketing strategy: segmentation, targeting, differentiation, and positioning. Marketers know that they cannot appeal to all buyers in their markets, or at least not to all buyers in the same way. Therefore, most companies today practice *target marketing*—identifying market segments, selecting one or more of them, and developing products and marketing mixes tailored to each.

OBJECTIVE 1 Define the major steps in designing a customer-driven marketing strategy: market segmentation, targeting, differentiation, and positioning. (pp 168–171)

A customer-driven marketing strategy begins with selecting which customers to serve and determining a value proposition that best serves the targeted customers. It consists of four steps. *Market segmentation* is the act of dividing a market into distinct segments of buyers with different needs, characteristics, or behaviors who might require separate products or marketing mixes. Once the groups have been identified, *market targeting* evaluates each market segment's attractiveness and selects one or more segments to serve. *Differentiation* involves actually differentiating the market offering to create superior customer value. *Positioning* consists of positioning the market offering in the minds of target customers. A customer-driven marketing strategy seeks to build the *right relationships* with the *right customers*.

OBJECTIVE 2 List and discuss the major bases for segmenting consumer and business markets. (pp 171–181)

There is no single way to segment a market. Therefore, the marketer tries different variables to see which give the best segmentation opportunities. For consumer marketing, the major segmentation variables are geographic, demographic, psychographic, and behavioral. In *geographic segmentation*, the market is divided into different geographical units, such as nations, regions, states, counties, cities, or even neighborhoods. In *demographic segmentation*, the market is divided into groups based on demographic variables, including age, life-cycle stage, gender, income, occupation, education, religion, ethnicity, and generation. In *psychographic segmentation*, the market is divided into different groups based on social class, lifestyle, or personality characteristics. In *behavioral segmentation*, the market is divided into groups based on consumers' knowledge, attitudes, uses, or responses concerning a product.

Business marketers use many of the same variables to segment their markets. But business markets also can be segmented by business *demographics* (industry, company size), *operating characteristics*, *purchasing approaches*, *situational factors*, and *personal characteristics*. The effectiveness of the segmentation analysis depends on finding segments that are *measurable*, *accessible*, *substantial*, *differentiable*, and *actionable*.

OBJECTIVE 3 Explain how companies identify attractive market segments and choose a market-targeting strategy. (pp 181–189)

To target the best market segments, the company first evaluates each segment's size and growth characteristics, structural attractiveness, and compatibility with company objectives and resources. It then chooses one of four market-targeting strategies—ranging from very broad to very narrow targeting. The seller can ignore segment differences and target broadly using *undifferentiated* (or *mass*) *marketing*. This involves mass producing, mass distributing, and mass promoting the same product in about the same way to all consumers. Or the seller can adopt *differentiated marketing*—developing different market offers for several segments. *Concentrated marketing* (or *niche marketing*) involves focusing on one or a few market segments only. Finally, *micromarketing* is the practice of tailoring products and marketing programs to suit the tastes of specific individuals and locations. Micromarketing includes *local marketing* and *individual marketing*. Which targeting strategy is best depends on company resources, product variability, product life-cycle stage, market variability, and competitive marketing strategies.

OBJECTIVE 4 Discuss how companies differentiate and position their products for maximum competitive advantage. (pp 189–196)

Once a company has decided which segments to enter, it must decide on its *differentiation and positioning strategy*. The differentiation and positioning task consists of three steps: identifying a set of possible differentiations that create competitive advantage, choosing advantages on which to build a position, and selecting an overall positioning strategy.

The brand's full positioning is called its *value proposition*—the full mix of benefits on which the brand is positioned. In general, companies can choose from one of five winning value propositions on which to position their products: more for more, more for the same, the same for less, less for much less, or more for less. Company and brand positioning are summarized in positioning statements that state the target segment and need, the positioning concept, and specific points of difference. The company must then effectively communicate and deliver the chosen position to the market.

Key Terms

Objective 1
Market segmentation (p 170)
Market targeting (targeting) (p 170)
Differentiation (p 170)
Positioning (p 170)

Objective 2
Geographic segmentation (p 171)
Demographic segmentation (p 172)
Age and life-cycle segmentation (p 172)
Gender segmentation (p 173)
Income segmentation (p 173)
Psychographic segmentation (p 174)
Behavioral segmentation (p 176)
Occasion segmentation (p 176)
Benefit segmentation (p 176)
Intermarket (cross-market) segmentation (p 180)

Objective 3
Target market (p 181)
Undifferentiated (mass) marketing (p 182)
Differentiated (segmented) marketing (p 182)
Concentrated (niche) marketing (p 183)
Micromarketing (p 184)
Local marketing (p 184)
Individual marketing (p 186)

Objective 4
Product position (p 189)
Competitive advantage (p 191)
Value proposition (p 193)
Positioning statement (p 195)

DISCUSSION AND CRITICAL THINKING

Discussion Questions

6-1. How does market segmentation differ from market targeting? (AACSB: Written and Oral Communication)

6-2. How can marketers use behavioral segmentation in consumer markets? Discuss, using an example for each method of behavioral segmentation. (AACSB: Written and Oral Communication; Reflective Thinking)

6-3. Compare and contrast consumer market segmentation and business market segmentation. (AACSB: Written and Oral Communication)

6-4. How do marketers use local marketing and individual marketing? Do these terms mean the same thing? (AACSB: Written and Oral Communication; Reflective Thinking)

6-5. How can a company gain competitive advantage through differentiation? Describe an example of a company that illustrates each type of differentiation discussed in the chapter. (AACSB: Written and Oral Communication)

6-6. Discuss the criteria that should be evaluated in determining which differences a company should promote in its products. (AACSB: Written and Oral Communication)

Critical Thinking Exercises

6-7. Advertisers use market segmentation when promoting products to consumers. For each major consumer segmentation variable, find an example of a print ad that appears to be based on that variable. For each ad, identify the target market and explain why you think the advertiser is using the segmentation variable you identified for that ad. (AACSB: Written and Oral Communication; Reflective Thinking)

6-8. Perceptual positioning maps are useful for showing consumer perceptions of brands in a product category. Search the Internet for guides on creating perceptual maps and create a map of your perceptions of brands in a product category of your choice. How can the brand you perceived least favorably improve? (AACSB: Written and Oral Communication; Reflective Thinking)

6-9. In a small group, create an idea for a new business. Using the steps described in the chapter, develop a customer-driven marketing strategy. Describe your strategy and conclude with a positioning statement for this business. (AACSB: Written and Oral Communication; Reflective Thinking)

MINICASES AND APPLICATIONS

Online, Mobile, and Social Media Marketing Google Glass

Consumers enjoy having Google's search power at their fingertips, but if things go as planned, they'll have that Google power right before their very eyes, no fingers necessary. "Augmented reality"—the ability to project information in front of our eyes—is now being used in commercial and military operations. For example, the U.S. Air Force uses it to display weapons information in fighter pilot helmets. However, the technology has yet to take off in the consumer market. That's because the required headgear has been uncomfortable, unattractive, and expensive. But Google is peering into the future and has tentative plans to sell its Google Glass device to consumers soon. The sleek wraparound glasses place a single lens above a person's right eye that displays digital information that can be voice and gesture controlled. Connecting the device to a smartphone opens up a world of possibilities. The only product close to Google Glass currently on the consumer market is a GPS device that skiers and snowboarders insert into goggles that displays speed information.

6-10. Research "augmented reality" on the Internet. Discuss the most appropriate variables for segmenting the consumer market for products based on this technology. Explain why those variables are appropriate. (AACSB: Written and Oral Communication; Reflective Thinking)

Marketing Ethics K.G.O.Y.

K.G.O.Y. stands for "kids getting older younger," and marketers are getting much of the blame. Kids today see all types of messages, especially on the Internet, that they would never have seen in the past. Whereas boys may give up their G.I. Joe's at an earlier age to play war games on their xBox 360s, the greater controversy seems to surround claims of how girls have changed, or rather, how marketers have changed girls. Critics describe clothing designed for young girls aged 8 to 11 as "floozy" and sexual, with department stores selling youngsters thongs and T-shirts that say "Naughty Girl!" Although Barbie's sexuality has never been subtle, she was originally targeted to girls 9 to 12 years old. Now, Barbie dolls target primarily 3- to 7-year-old girls! And Barbie's competitor, Bratz dolls, has an "in-your-face" attitude that has some parents complaining that they are too sexual.

6-11. Do you think marketers are to blame for kids getting older younger? Give some other examples that could support marketing's responsibility in K.G.O.Y. (AACSB: Written and Oral Communication; Ethical Understanding and Reasoning)

6-12. Give an example of a company that is countering this trend by offering age-appropriate products for children. (AACSB: Written and Oral Communication; Reflective Thinking)

Marketing by the Numbers Man's Furry Friends

Americans love their pets, with 62 percent of households spending more than $50 billion on them last year. You may have one or more furry, feathery, or scaly friends yourself, so you know how much money you spend each year. Marketers need to know that information to estimate the size of a potential market segment, and past market sales are often used as a baseline to estimate next year's market sales. The National Pet Products Manufacturers Association (NPPMA) conducts a yearly survey of pet owners that provides useful information for estimating market size and potential.

6-13. Refer to Appendix 3: Marketing by the Numbers and use the information available from the NPPMA survey (www.americanpetproducts.org/press_industrytrends.asp) to develop an estimate of the market potential for dog food in the United States. Do the same for cat food. (AACSB: Written and Oral Communication; Information Technology; Analytical Thinking)

6-14. Evaluate the usefulness of these market segments. (AACSB: Written and Oral Communication; Information Technology; Reflective Thinking)

Video Case Boston Harbor Cruises

Since 1926, Boston Harbor Cruises has been providing customers with memorable experiences on ocean-going vessels in and around the Boston area. But these days, the term "cruise" has different meanings to the four-generation family business. To thrive in strong economic times and in bad, Boston Harbor Cruises has progressively targeted various types of customers with its different boats and different services.

Sight-seeing trips around Boston Harbor, whale-watching tours, fast ferry service to Cape Cod, dinner and wedding cruises, and a high-speed thrill ride are among the offerings of Boston Harbor Cruises. It even offers commuter services and off-shore construction support. Targeting this diverse customer base has become even more challenging as Boston Harbor Cruises has further differentiated the market into local customers, domestic vacationers, and international travelers.

After viewing the video featuring Boston Harbor Cruises, answer the following questions:

6-15. On what main variables had Boston Harbor Cruises focused in segmenting its markets?

6-16. Which target-marketing strategy best describes the efforts of Boston Harbor Cruises? Support your choice.

6-17. How does Boston Harbor Cruises use the concepts of differentiation and positioning to build relationships with the right customers?

Company Cases 6 Dove / 7 Zipcar / 11 Dollar General

See Appendix 1 for cases appropriate for this chapter. **Case 6, Dove: Building Customer Relationships Everywhere, One Gender at a Time.** Dove has long succeeded as a brand of soap and personal care products for women. Now, it's doing the same with men.

Case 7, Zipcar: "It's Not about Cars—It's about Urban Life." A new company, a new concept, and a brand that transcends function. **Case 11, Dollar General: Today's Hottest Retailing Format.** By taking advantage of a gap in the market, Dollar General is growing faster than other forms of retail.

MyMarketingLab

Go to **mymktlab.com** for Auto-graded writing questions as well as the following Assisted-graded writing questions:

6-18. How can marketers use behavioral segmentation in consumer markets? Discuss, using an example for each method of behavioral segmentation. (AACSB: Written and Oral Communication; Reflective Thinking)

6-19. Discuss ideas for applications of the Google Glass device among the business and institutional markets. How can these applications be incorporated into online, mobile, and social media marketing? (AACSB: Written and Oral Communication; Information Technology; Reflective Thinking)

6-20. Mymktlab Only—comprehensive writing assignment for this chapter.

7 Products, Services, and Brands

Building Customer Value

CHAPTER ROAD MAP

Objective Outline

OBJECTIVE 1 **Define *product* and describe the major classifications of products and services.** What Is a Product? 202–207

OBJECTIVE 2 **Describe the decisions companies make regarding their individual products and services, product lines, and product mixes.** Product and Service Decisions 207–214

OBJECTIVE 3 **Identify the four characteristics that affect the marketing of services and the additional marketing considerations that services require.** Services Marketing 214–221

OBJECTIVE 4 **Discuss branding strategy—the decisions companies make in building and managing their brands.** Branding Strategy: Building Strong Brands 221–231

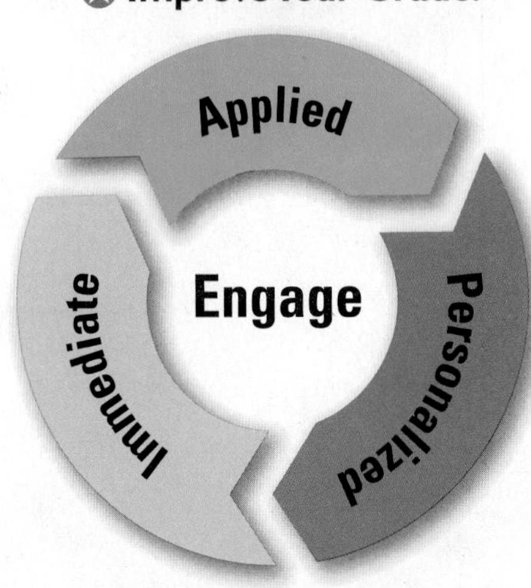

Previewing the Concepts

After examining customer-driven marketing strategy, we now take a deeper look at the marketing mix: the tactical tools that marketers use to implement their strategies and deliver superior customer value. In this and the next chapter, we will study how companies develop and manage products and brands. Then, in the chapters that follow, we look at pricing, distribution, and marketing communication tools. The product and brand are usually the first and most basic marketing consideration. We start with a seemingly simple question: What *is* a product? As it turns out, the answer is not so simple.

Before starting into the chapter, let's look at an interesting brand story. Marketing is all about building brands that connect deeply with customers. So, when you think about top brands, which ones pop up first? Maybe it's traditional megabrands such as Coca-Cola, Nike, or McDonald's. Or maybe a trendy tech brand such as Google, Facebook, or GoPro. But if we asked you to focus on sports entertainment, you'd probably name ESPN. When it comes to your life and sports, ESPN probably has it covered.

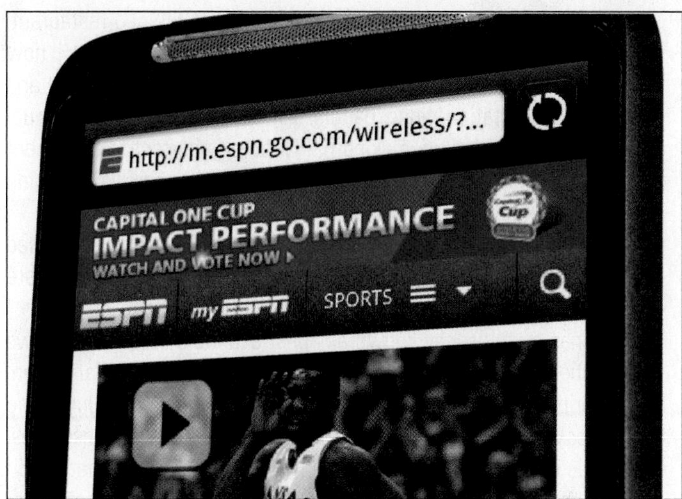

» ESPN is more than just a collection of cable networks, online and mobile sites, and publications. The ESPN brand is synonymous with sports entertainment, inexorably linked with consumers' sports memories, realities, and anticipations.

First Stop

The ESPN Brand: Every Sport Possible—Now

When you think about ESPN, you probably don't think of it as a "brand." You think of it as a cable TV network, a Web site or mobile app, or perhaps a magazine. ESPN is all of those things. But more than that, ESPN is a brand experience—a meaningful part of customers' lives that goes well beyond the cable networks, publications, and other media entities it comprises. To consumers, ESPN is synonymous with sports entertainment, inexorably linked with their sports memories, realities, and anticipations.

In 1979, entrepreneur Bill Rasmussen took a daring leap and founded the round-the-clock sports network ESPN (Entertainment and Sports Programming Network). The rest, as they say, is history. Despite many early skeptics—a 24-hour sports network?—ESPN is now a multibillion-dollar sports empire and a "can't-live-without-it" part of the daily routine for hundreds of millions of people worldwide.

Today, ESPN is as much recognized and revered as iconic megabrands such as Coca-Cola, Nike, or Google. No matter who you are, chances are good that ESPN has touched you in some meaningful way. And no matter what the sport or where, ESPN seems to be everywhere at once. Here's a brief summary of the incredible variety of entities tied together under the ESPN brand:

Television: From its original groundbreaking cable network, the ESPN brand has sprouted seven additional networks—ESPN3D, ESPN2, ESPN Classic, ESPNEWS, ESPNU, ESPN Deportes (Spanish language), and the Longhorn Network. With its signal now flowing into more than 100 million U.S. households at an industry-topping cost of $4.69 per household per month—TNT is a distant second at $1.16—ESPN is by far the most-sought cable network. Additionally, ESPN International serves fans through 48 international networks in more than 200 countries on every continent. ESPN is the home of the NBA Finals, WNBA, Monday Night Football, NASCAR, IndyCar, the NHRA, college football and the BCS, college basketball, tennis's Grand Slam events, golf's Masters, the U.S. Open and British Open, World Cup Soccer, the Little League World Series, and more. This list grows every year as ESPN outbids the major broadcast networks to capture the rights to major sports events. ESPN has certainly answered the question of whether cable TV has the mass appeal needed to support major sports events.

The ever-expanding ESPN brand is as much recognized and revered as iconic megabrands such as Coca-Cola, Nike, or Google. When it comes to your life and sports, chances are good that ESPN plays a meaningful role.

Radio: Sports radio is thriving, and ESPN operates the largest sports radio network, broadcasting more than 9,000 hours of content annually to 24 million listeners through 700 U.S. affiliates plus 45 Spanish-language ESPN Deportes stations in major markets. Overseas, ESPN has radio and syndicated radio programs in 11 countries.

Online: ESPN.com is the leading sports Web site, with more than 41 million unique visitors spending 3.3 billion minutes on the site each month. Its video offerings capture 35 percent of all sports-related video streams. ESPNRadio.com is the most-listened-to online sports destination, with 35 original podcasts each week. With literally dozens of global and market-specific sites, ESPN more than dominates.

With access to content from television, radio, and print, ESPN has a plentiful supply of material to feed its digital efforts. But ESPN is also leading the game in the exploding mobile arena. It employs a "mobile first" strategy, in which it orients all of its Web sites around mobile, thus optimizing performance. Now, ESPN delivers mobile sports content via all major U.S. wireless providers—including real-time scores, stats, late-breaking news, and video-on-demand. The digital strategy has led to ESPN3, a multi-screen live 24/7 sports network available at no cost to 70 million homes that receive their high-speed Internet connection from an affiliated service provider. ESPN3 viewers can stream ESPN coverage on their computers, tablets, or smartphones.

Publishing: When ESPN first published *ESPN The Magazine* in 1998, critics gave it little chance against mighty *Sports Illustrated.* Yet, with its bold look, bright colors, and unconventional format, the ESPN publication now serves more than 16 million readers each month and continues to grow. By comparison, a relatively stagnant *Sports Illustrated* is struggling to make the shift to a digital world.

As if all this weren't enough, ESPN also manages events, including the X Games, Winter X Games, ESPN Outdoors (featuring the Bassmaster Classic), the Skins Games, the Jimmy V Classic, and several football bowl games. It also develops ESPN-branded consumer products and services, including CDs, DVDs, video games, apparel, and even golf schools. If reading all this makes you hungry, you may be near an ESPN Zone, which includes a sports-themed restaurant, interactive games, and sports-related merchandise sales. You'll now find ESPN content in airports and on planes, in health clubs, and even on gas station video panels. All this translates into annual revenues of $8.5 billion, making ESPN more important to the parent Walt Disney Company than the Disneyland and Disney World theme parks combined.

What ties it all together? The ESPN brand's customer-focused mission: It wants to serve sports enthusiasts "wherever sports are watched, listened to, discussed, debated, read about, or played." ESPN has a philosophy known as "best available screen." It knows that when fans are at home, they'll watch the big 50-inch flat screen. But during the morning hours, smartphones light up more. During the day, desktops dominate, and in the evening, tablet activity increases. ESPN is on a crusade to know when, where, and under what conditions fans will reach for which device, and to provide the most seamless, high-quality experience for them.

It's no surprise, then, that sports fans around the world love their ESPN. To consumers everywhere, ESPN means sports. Tech savvy, creative, and often irreverent, the well-managed, ever-extending brand continues to build meaningful customer experiences and relationships. If it has to do with your life and sports—large or small—ESPN covers it for you, anywhere you are, 24/7. Perhaps the company should rename ESPN to stand for Every Sport Possible—Now.[1]

As the ESPN story shows, in their quest to create customer relationships, marketers must build and manage products and brands that connect with customers. This chapter begins with a deceptively simple question: *What is a product?* After addressing this question, we look at ways to classify products in consumer and business markets. Then we discuss the important decisions that marketers make regarding individual products, product lines, and product mixes. Next, we examine the characteristics and marketing requirements of a special form of product—services. Finally, we look into the critically important issue of how marketers build and manage product and service brands.

Author Comment
As you'll see, this is a deceptively simple question with a very complex answer. For example, think back to the opening ESPN story. What is the ESPN "product"?

What Is a Product?

We define a **product** as anything that can be offered to a market for attention, acquisition, use, or consumption that might satisfy a want or need. Products include more than just tangible objects, such as cars, computers, or mobile phones. Broadly defined, *products* also include services, events, persons, places, organizations, and ideas, or a mixture of these. Throughout this text, we use the term *product* broadly to include any or all of these entities. Thus, an Apple iPhone, a Toyota Camry, and a Caffé Mocha at Starbucks are products. But so are a trip to Las Vegas, Schwab online investment services, your Facebook page, and advice from your family doctor.

Product
Anything that can be offered to a market for attention, acquisition, use, or consumption that might satisfy a want or need.

Because of their importance in the world economy, we give special attention to services. **Services** are a form of product that consists of activities, benefits, or satisfactions offered for sale that are essentially intangible and do not result in the ownership of anything. Examples include banking, hotel, airline travel, retail, wireless communication, and home-repair services. We will look at services more closely later in this chapter.

Service
An activity, benefit, or satisfaction offered for sale that is essentially intangible and does not result in the ownership of anything.

Products, Services, and Experiences

Products are a key element in the overall *market offering*. Marketing mix planning begins with building an offering that brings value to target customers. This offering becomes the basis on which the company builds profitable customer relationships.

A company's market offering often includes both tangible goods and services. At one extreme, the market offer may consist of a *pure tangible good*, such as soap, toothpaste, or salt; no services accompany the product. At the other extreme are *pure services*, for which the market offer consists primarily of a service. Examples include a doctor's exam and financial services. Between these two extremes, however, many goods-and-services combinations are possible.

Today, as products and services become more commoditized, many companies are moving to a new level in creating value for their customers. To differentiate their offers, beyond simply making products and delivering services, they are creating and managing customer *experiences* with their brands or companies.

Experiences have always been an important part of marketing for some companies. Disney has long manufactured dreams and memories through its movies and theme parks—it wants theme park cast members to deliver a thousand "small wows" to every customer. And Nike has long declared, "It's not so much the shoes but where they take you." Today, however, all kinds of firms are recasting their traditional goods and services to create experiences. >> For example, Starbucks serves up more than just a hot cup of coffee:[2]

>> Creating customer experiences: Starbucks doesn't sell just coffee, it sells "The Starbucks Experience"—what it calls a "third place"—away from home and away from work, a place for conversation and a sense of community.

© Daily Mail/Rex/Alamy.

Three decades ago, Howard Schultz hit on the idea of bringing a European-style coffeehouse to America. He believed that people needed to slow down, to "smell the coffee" and enjoy life a little more. The result was Starbucks. This coffeehouse doesn't sell just coffee, it sells The Starbucks Experience—one that enriches customers' lives. The smells, the hissing steam, the comfy chairs—all contribute to the Starbucks ambience. Starbucks gives customers what it calls a "third place"—away from home and away from work—a place for conversation and a sense of community. As a result, Starbucks has transformed coffee from a commodity to a $4 splurge and the company's sales and profits have risen like steam off a mug of hot java.

Companies that market experiences realize that customers are really buying much more than just products and services. They are buying what those offers will *do* for them. A recent BMW ad puts it this way: "We realized a long time ago that what you make people feel is just as important as what you make."

Levels of Product and Services

Product planners need to think about products and services on three levels (see **>> Figure 7.1**). Each level adds more customer value. The most basic level is the *core customer value*, which addresses the question: *What is the buyer really buying?* When designing products, marketers must first define the core, problem-solving benefits or services that consumers seek. A woman buying lipstick buys more than lip color. Charles Revson of Revlon saw this early: "In the factory, we make cosmetics; in the store, we sell hope." >> And people who buy an Apple iPad are buying much more than just a tablet computer. They are buying entertainment, self-expression, productivity, and connectivity with friends and family—a mobile and personal window to the world.

At the second level, product planners must turn the core benefit into an *actual product*. They need to develop product and service features, a design, a quality level, a brand name,

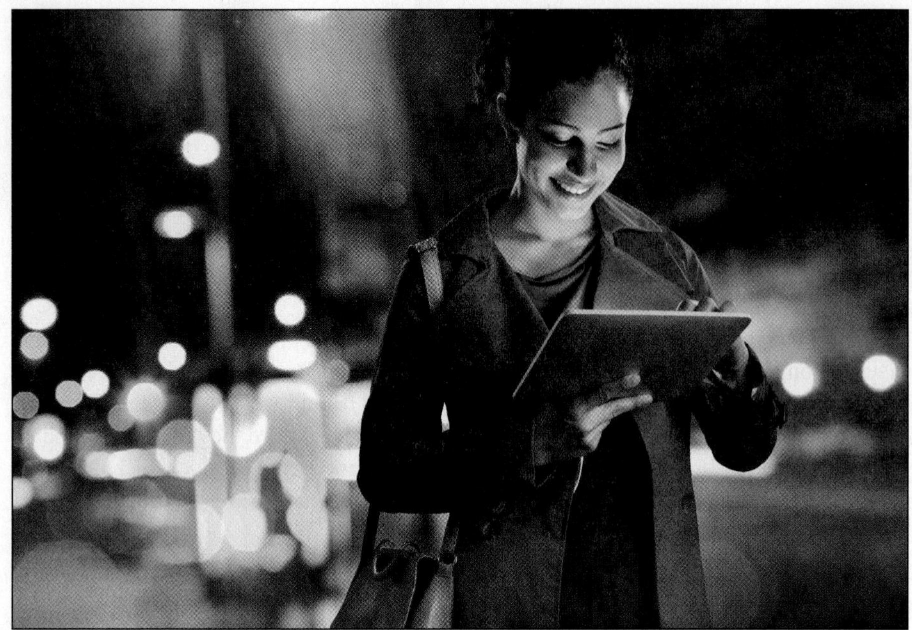

>> Core, actual, and augmented product: People who buy an iPad are buying much more than a tablet computer. They are buying entertainment, self-expression, productivity, and connectivity—a mobile and personal window to the world.

Betsie Van der Meer/Getty Images.

and packaging. For example, the iPad is an actual product. Its name, parts, styling, operating system, features, packaging, and other attributes have all been carefully combined to deliver the core customer value of staying connected.

Finally, product planners must build an *augmented product* around the core benefit and actual product by offering additional consumer services and benefits. The iPad is more than just a digital device. It provides consumers with a complete connectivity solution. Thus, when consumers buy an iPad, Apple and its resellers also might give buyers a warranty on parts and workmanship, quick repair services when needed, and a Web site to use if they have problems or questions. Apple also provides access to a huge assortment of apps and accessories, along with an iCloud service that integrates buyers' photos, music, documents, apps, calendars, contacts, and other content across all of their devices from any location.

Consumers see products as complex bundles of benefits that satisfy their needs. When developing products, marketers first must identify the *core customer value* that consumers seek from the product. They must then design the *actual* product and find ways to *augment* it to create customer value and a full and satisfying brand experience.

Product and Service Classifications

Products and services fall into two broad classes based on the types of consumers who use them: *consumer products* and *industrial products*. Broadly defined, products also include other marketable entities such as experiences, organizations, persons, places, and ideas.

>> Figure 7.1 Three Levels of Product

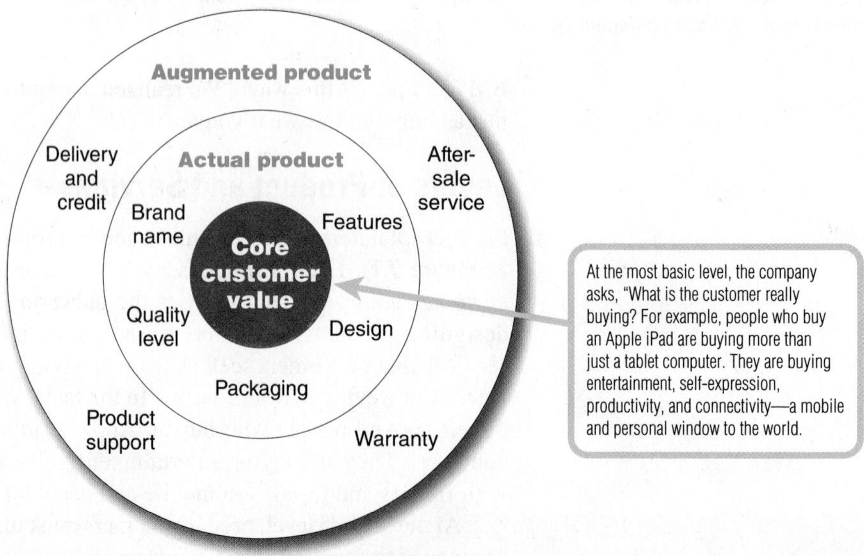
Augmented product
Delivery and credit
Actual product
After-sale service
Brand name
Features
Core customer value
Quality level
Design
Packaging
Product support
Warranty
At the most basic level, the company asks, "What is the customer really buying? For example, people who buy an Apple iPad are buying more than just a tablet computer. They are buying entertainment, self-expression, productivity, and connectivity—a mobile and personal window to the world.

Consumer Products

Consumer product
A product bought by final consumers for personal consumption.

Convenience product
A consumer product that customers usually buy frequently, immediately, and with minimal comparison and buying effort.

Shopping product
A consumer product that the customer, in the process of selecting and purchasing, usually compares on such attributes as suitability, quality, price, and style.

Specialty product
A consumer product with unique characteristics or brand identification for which a significant group of buyers is willing to make a special purchase effort.

Unsought product
A consumer product that the consumer either does not know about or knows about but does not normally consider buying.

Consumer products are products and services bought by final consumers for personal consumption. Marketers usually classify these products and services further based on how consumers go about buying them. Consumer products include *convenience products*, *shopping products*, *specialty products*, and *unsought products*. These products differ in the ways consumers buy them and, therefore, in how they are marketed (see » **Table 7.1**).

Convenience products are consumer products and services that customers usually buy frequently, immediately, and with minimal comparison and buying effort. Examples include laundry detergent, candy, magazines, and fast food. Convenience products are usually low priced, and marketers place them in many locations to make them readily available when customers need or want them.

Shopping products are less frequently purchased consumer products and services that customers compare carefully on suitability, quality, price, and style. When buying shopping products and services, consumers spend much time and effort in gathering information and making comparisons. Examples include furniture, clothing, major appliances, and hotel and airline services. Shopping product marketers usually distribute their products through fewer outlets but provide deeper sales support to help customers in their comparison efforts.

Specialty products are consumer products and services with unique characteristics or brand identifications for which a significant group of buyers is willing to make a special purchase effort. Examples include specific brands of cars, high-priced photography equipment, designer clothes, gourmet foods, and the services of medical or legal specialists. A Lamborghini automobile, for example, is a specialty product because buyers are usually willing to travel great distances to buy one. Buyers normally do not compare specialty products. They invest only the time needed to reach dealers carrying the wanted products.

Unsought products are consumer products that the consumer either does not know about or knows about but does not normally consider buying. Most major new innovations are unsought until the consumer becomes aware of them through advertising. Classic examples of known but unsought products and services are life insurance, preplanned funeral services, and blood donations to the Red Cross. By their very nature, unsought products require a lot of advertising, personal selling, and other marketing efforts.

» Table 7.1 Marketing Considerations for Consumer Products

	Type of Consumer Product			
Marketing Considerations	**Convenience**	**Shopping**	**Specialty**	**Unsought**
Customer buying behavior	Frequent purchase; little planning, little comparison or shopping effort; low customer involvement	Less frequent purchase; much planning and shopping effort; comparison of brands on price, quality, and style	Strong brand preference and loyalty; special purchase effort; little comparison of brands; low price sensitivity	Little product awareness or knowledge (or, if aware, little or even negative interest)
Price	Low price	Higher price	High price	Varies
Distribution	Widespread distribution; convenient locations	Selective distribution in fewer outlets	Exclusive distribution in only one or a few outlets per market area	Varies
Promotion	Mass promotion by the producer	Advertising and personal selling by both the producer and resellers	More carefully targeted promotion by both the producer and resellers	Aggressive advertising and personal selling by the producer and resellers
Examples	Toothpaste, magazines, and laundry detergent	Major appliances, televisions, furniture, and clothing	Luxury goods, such as Rolex watches or fine crystal	Life insurance and Red Cross blood donations

Industrial Products

Industrial product
A product bought by individuals and organizations for further processing or for use in conducting a business.

Industrial products are those products purchased for further processing or for use in conducting a business. Thus, the distinction between a consumer product and an industrial product is based on the *purpose* for which the product is purchased. If a consumer buys a lawn mower for use around home, the lawn mower is a consumer product. If the same consumer buys the same lawn mower for use in a landscaping business, the lawn mower is an industrial product.

The three groups of industrial products and services are materials and parts, capital items, and supplies and services. *Materials and parts* include raw materials as well as manufactured materials and parts. Raw materials consist of farm products (wheat, cotton, livestock, fruits, vegetables) and natural products (fish, lumber, crude petroleum, iron ore). Manufactured materials and parts consist of component materials (iron, yarn, cement, wires) and component parts (small motors, tires, castings). Most manufactured materials and parts are sold directly to industrial users. Price and service are the major marketing factors; branding and advertising tend to be less important.

Capital items are industrial products that aid in the buyer's production or operations, including installations and accessory equipment. Installations consist of major purchases such as buildings (factories, offices) and fixed equipment (generators, drill presses, large computer systems, elevators). Accessory equipment includes portable factory equipment and tools (hand tools, lift trucks) and office equipment (computers, fax machines, desks). These types of equipment have shorter lives than do installations and simply aid in the production process.

The final group of industrial products is *supplies and services*. Supplies include operating supplies (lubricants, coal, paper, pencils) and repair and maintenance items (paint, nails, brooms). Supplies are the convenience products of the industrial field because they are usually purchased with a minimum of effort or comparison. Business services include maintenance and repair services (window cleaning, computer repair) and business advisory services (legal, management consulting, advertising). Such services are usually supplied under contract.

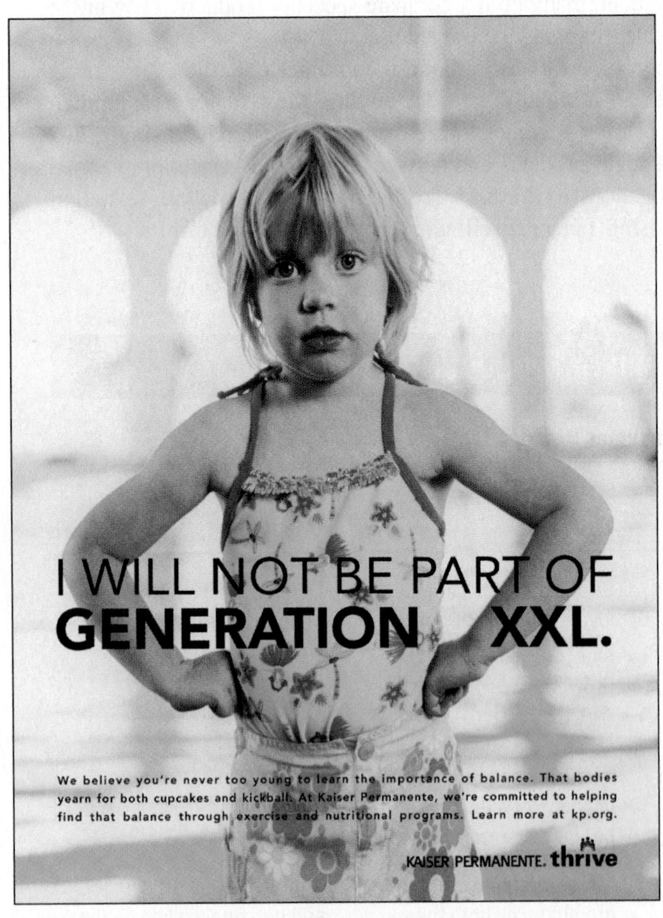

I WILL NOT BE PART OF
GENERATION XXL.
We believe you're never too young to learn the importance of balance. That bodies yearn for both cupcakes and kickball. At Kaiser Permanente, we're committed to helping find that balance through exercise and nutritional programs. Learn more at kp.org.
KAISER PERMANENTE. thrive

>> Organization marketing: Kaiser Permanente's "Thrive" campaign markets the organization as a total health advocate that helps its members get healthy, stay healthy, and thrive.

Organizations, Persons, Places, and Ideas

In addition to tangible products and services, marketers have broadened the concept of a product to include other market offerings: organizations, persons, places, and ideas.

Organizations often carry out activities to "sell" the organization itself. *Organization marketing* consists of activities undertaken to create, maintain, or change the attitudes and behavior of target consumers toward an organization. Both profit and not-for-profit organizations practice organization marketing. Business firms sponsor public relations or *corporate image marketing* campaigns to market themselves and polish their images.

For example, Kaiser Permanente's long-running "Thrive" campaign markets the health maintenance organization (HMO) not just as a health-care company, but as a total health advocate. Whereas "competitors [stand] for health care," says the company, "Kaiser Permanente [stands] for health." The award-winning "Thrive" campaign promotes prevention and wellness through healthy lifestyles that will help Kaiser Permanente members and their families get healthy, stay healthy, and thrive. Some ads show people exercising or focus on healthy eating choices ("I scream, You Scream. We all scream for green beans."). >> Another ad shows a determined, trim, and fit young girl who declares, "I will not be part of Generation XXL." Still other ads show how Kaiser Permanente accomplishes major health-care breakthroughs behind the scenes so that its members can thrive and enjoy the everyday moments of their lives to the fullest.[3]

People can also be thought of as products. *Person marketing* consists of activities undertaken to create, maintain, or change attitudes or behavior toward particular people. People ranging from presidents, entertainers, and sports figures to professionals such as doctors, lawyers, and architects use person marketing to build their reputations. And businesses, charities, and other organizations use well-known personalities to help sell their products or causes. For example, P&G's Cover Girl brand is represented by well-known celebrities such as Ellen DeGeneres, P!NK, and Sofia Vergara. The skillful use of marketing can turn a person's name into a powerhouse brand. For example, The Food Network's celebrity chef Rachael Ray is a one-woman marketing phenomenon, with her own daytime talk show, cookware and cutlery brands, dog food brand (Nutrish), and even her own brand of EVOO (extra virgin olive oil, for those not familiar with Rayisms).

Place marketing involves activities undertaken to create, maintain, or change attitudes or behavior toward particular places. Cities, states, regions, and even entire nations compete to attract tourists, new residents, conventions, and company offices and factories. The New Orleans city Web site shouts "Go NOLA" and markets annual events such as Mardi Gras festivities and the New Orleans Jazz and Heritage Festival. Michigan invites visitors to experience Pure Michigan: unspoiled nature, lakes that feel like oceans, miles of cherry orchards, glorious sunsets, and nighttime skies scattered with stars. And Brand USA, a public–private marketing partnership created by a recent act of Congress, promotes the United States as a tourist destination to international travelers. Its mission is to "represent the true greatness of America—from sea to shining sea" through country-by-country ads and promotions and a DiscoverAmerica.com Web site that features destinations, U.S. travel information and tips, and travel planning tools.[4]

Ideas can also be marketed. In one sense, all marketing is the marketing of an idea, whether it is the general idea of brushing your teeth or the specific idea that Crest toothpastes create "healthy, beautiful smiles for life." Here, however, we narrow our focus to the marketing of *social ideas*. This area has been called **social marketing** and consists of using traditional business marketing concepts and tools to create behaviors that will create individual and societal well-being.

Social marketing
The use of commercial marketing concepts and tools in programs designed to influence individuals' behavior to improve their well-being and that of society.

Social marketing programs cover a wide range of issues. The Ad Council of America (www.adcouncil.org), for example, has developed dozens of social advertising campaigns involving issues ranging from health care, education, and environmental sustainability to human rights and personal safety. But social marketing involves much more than just advertising. It involves a broad range of marketing strategies and marketing mix tools designed to bring about beneficial social change.[5]

Author Comment
Now that we've answered the "What is a product?" question, we dig into the specific decisions that companies must make when designing and marketing products and services.

Product and Service Decisions

Marketers make product and service decisions at three levels: individual product decisions, product line decisions, and product mix decisions. We discuss each in turn.

Individual Product and Service Decisions

Figure 7.2 shows the important decisions in the development and marketing of individual products and services. We will focus on decisions about *product attributes*, *branding*, *packaging*, *labeling*, and *product support services*.

Figure 7.2 Individual Product Decisions

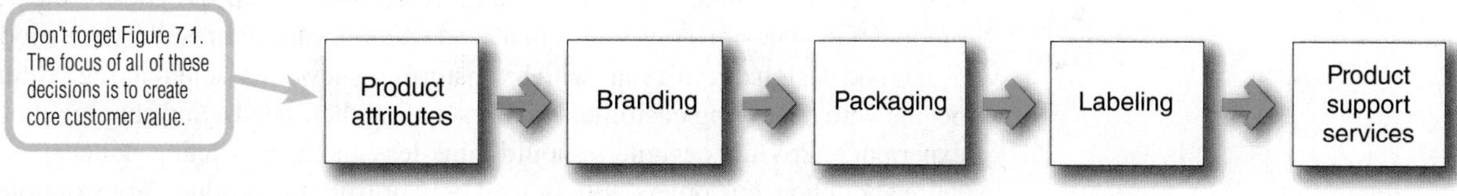
Don't forget Figure 7.1. The focus of all of these decisions is to create core customer value.
Product attributes
Branding
Packaging
Labeling
Product support services

Product and Service Attributes

Developing a product or service involves defining the benefits that it will offer. These benefits are communicated and delivered by product attributes such as *quality*, *features*, and *style and design*.

Product quality
The characteristics of a product or service that bear on its ability to satisfy stated or implied customer needs.

Product Quality. **Product quality** is one of the marketer's major positioning tools. Quality affects product or service performance; thus, it is closely linked to customer value and satisfaction. In the narrowest sense, quality can be defined as "freedom from defects." But most marketers go beyond this narrow definition. Instead, they define quality in terms of creating customer value and satisfaction. The American Society for Quality defines quality as the characteristics of a product or service that bear on its ability to satisfy stated or implied customer needs. Similarly, Siemens defines quality this way: "Quality is when our customers come back and our products don't."[6]

Total quality management (TQM) is an approach in which all of the company's people are involved in constantly improving the quality of products, services, and business processes. For most top companies, customer-driven quality has become a way of doing business. Today, companies are taking a *return-on-quality* approach, viewing quality as an investment and holding quality efforts accountable for bottom-line results.

Product quality has two dimensions: level and consistency. In developing a product, the marketer must first choose a *quality level* that will support the product's positioning. Here, product quality means *performance quality*—the product's ability to perform its functions. For example, a Rolls-Royce provides higher performance quality than a Chevrolet: It has a smoother ride, provides more luxury and "creature comforts," and lasts longer. Companies rarely try to offer the highest possible performance quality level; few customers want or can afford the high levels of quality offered in products such as a Rolls-Royce automobile, a Viking range, or a Rolex watch. Instead, companies choose a quality level that matches target market needs and the quality levels of competing products.

Beyond quality level, high quality also can mean high levels of quality consistency. Here, product quality means *conformance quality*—freedom from defects and *consistency* in delivering a targeted level of performance. All companies should strive for high levels of conformance quality. In this sense, a Chevrolet can have just as much quality as a Rolls-Royce. Although a Chevy doesn't perform at the same level as a Rolls-Royce, it can just as consistently deliver the quality that customers pay for and expect.

Product Features. A product can be offered with varying features. A stripped-down model, one without any extras, is the starting point. The company can then create higher-level models by adding more features. Features are a competitive tool for differentiating the company's product from competitors' products. Being the first producer to introduce a valued new feature is one of the most effective ways to compete.

How can a company identify new features and decide which ones to add to its product? It should periodically survey buyers who have used the product and ask these questions: How do you like the product? Which specific features of the product do you like most? Which features could we add to improve the product? The answers to these questions provide the company with a rich list of feature ideas. The company can then assess each feature's *value* to customers versus its *cost* to the company. Features that customers value highly in relation to costs should be added.

Product Style and Design. Another way to add customer value is through distinctive *product style and design*. Design is a larger concept than style. *Style* simply describes the appearance of a product. Styles can be eye catching or yawn producing. A sensational style may grab attention and produce pleasing aesthetics, but it does not necessarily make the product *perform* better. Unlike style, *design* is more than skin deep—it goes to the very heart of a product. Good design contributes to a product's usefulness as well as to its looks.

Good design doesn't start with brainstorming new ideas and making prototypes. Design begins with observing customers, understanding their needs, and shaping their product-use experience. Product designers should think less about technical product specifications and more about how customers will use and benefit from the product. For example, using smart design based on deep insights into consumer needs, >> Nest Labs created a home heating and cooling thermostat that's not just pretty to look at but also packed with easy-to-access customer benefits:[7]

> The Nest learning thermostat looks great—its sleek, clean, curved design and neutral brushed-silver finish create a chameleon effect that grounds Nest within its environment. But Nest's beauty is more than just skin deep. Before Nest, programmable thermostats developed in the 1970s were supposed to both improve comfort and conserve energy. But research showed that 89 percent of owners rarely or never programmed them. The programmable thermostats were just too complicated. Moreover, the old programmable units looked clunky and antiquated.
>
> So Nest Labs assembled a corps of Silicon Valley designers who reinvented the thermostat to fit the needs of today's smartphone generation. The result is Nest, a "learning thermostat" that—all by itself—learns from your preferences, behaviors, and surroundings and then optimizes your heating and cooling schedule to keep you comfortable while you're at home while saving energy while you're away. "Nest remembers the temperatures you like and builds a schedule for you," says the company. "Teach it well and Nest can lower your heating and cooling bills up to 20 percent." Users can also control the device simply via WIFI, at home or away using a laptop, tablet, or smartphone app. Thus, Nest Labs has transformed the lowly home thermostat into a device that you're not only proud to hang on your wall but also a cool, connected device that's easy, fun, and effective to use. Thanks to good design, the nifty little Nest sold out for months shortly after launch.

>> Through award-winning, consumer-driven design, Nest Labs created the Nest learning thermostat, a sleek device that both looks good and is easy, fun, and effective to use.

Handout/MCT/Newscom.

Branding

Brand
A name, term, sign, symbol, or design, or a combination of these, that identifies the products or services of one seller or group of sellers and differentiates them from those of competitors.

Perhaps the most distinctive skill of professional marketers is their ability to build and manage brands. A **brand** is a name, term, sign, symbol, or design, or a combination of these, that identifies the maker or seller of a product or service. Consumers view a brand as an important part of a product, and branding can add value to a consumer's purchase. Customers attach meanings to brands and develop brand relationships. As a result, brands have meaning well beyond a product's physical attributes. For example, consider Coca-Cola:[8]

> In an interesting taste test of Coca-Cola versus Pepsi, 67 subjects were connected to brain-wave-monitoring machines while they consumed both products. When the soft drinks were unmarked, consumer preferences were split down the middle. But when the brands were identified, subjects chose Coke over Pepsi by a margin of 75 percent to 25 percent. When drinking the identified Coke brand, the brain areas that lit up most were those associated with cognitive control and memory—a place where culture concepts are stored. That didn't happen as much when drinking Pepsi. Why? According to one brand strategist, it's because of Coca-Cola's long-established brand imagery—the almost 100-year-old contour bottle, the bright red cans, the cursive font, and its association with iconic images ranging from the Polar Bears to Santa Claus. Pepsi's imagery isn't quite as deeply rooted. People apparently don't link Pepsi to the strong and emotional American icons associated with Coke. The conclusion? Plain and simple: Consumer preference isn't based on taste alone. Coke's iconic brand associations appear to make a difference.

Branding has become so strong that today hardly anything goes unbranded. Salt is packaged in branded containers, common nuts and bolts are packaged with a distributor's label, and automobile parts—spark plugs, tires, filters—bear brand names that differ from those of the automakers. Even fruits, vegetables, dairy products, and poultry are branded—Cuties mandarin oranges, Dole Classic iceberg salads, Horizon Organic milk, Perdue chickens, and Eggland's Best eggs.

Branding helps buyers in many ways. Brand names help consumers identify products that might benefit them. Brands also say something about product quality and consistency—buyers who always buy the same brand know that they will get the same features, benefits, and quality each time they buy. Branding also gives the seller several advantages. The seller's brand name and trademark provide legal protection for unique product features that otherwise might be copied by competitors. Branding helps the seller to segment markets. For example, rather than offering just one general product to all consumers, Toyota can offer the different Lexus, Toyota, and Scion brands, each with numerous sub-brands—such as Camry, Corolla, Prius, Matrix, Yaris, Tundra, and Land Cruiser. Finally, a brand name becomes the basis on which a whole story can be built about a product's special qualities. For example, the Cuties brand of pint-sized mandarins sets itself apart from ordinary oranges by promising "Kids love Cuties because Cuties are made for kids." They are a healthy snack that's "perfect for little hands": sweet, seedless, kid-sized, and easy to peel.[9] Building and managing brands are perhaps the marketer's most important tasks. We will discuss branding strategy in more detail later in the chapter.

Packaging

Packaging
The activities of designing and producing the container or wrapper for a product.

Packaging involves designing and producing the container or wrapper for a product. Traditionally, the primary function of the package was to hold and protect the product. In recent times, however, packaging has become an important marketing tool as well. Increased competition and clutter on retail store shelves means that packages must now perform many sales tasks—from attracting buyers, to communicating brand positioning, to closing the sale. Not every customer will be see a brand's advertising, social media pages, or other promotions. However, all consumers who buy and use a product will interact regularly with its packaging. Thus, the humble package represents prime marketing space.

Companies are realizing the power of good packaging to create immediate consumer recognition of a brand. For example, an average supermarket stocks about 38,700 items; the average Walmart supercenter carries 142,000 items. The typical shopper makes 70 percent of all purchase decisions in stores and passes by some 300 items per minute. In this highly competitive environment, the package may be the seller's last and best chance to influence buyers. So the package itself has become an important promotional medium.[10]

Poorly designed packages can cause headaches for consumers and lost sales for the company. Think about all those hard-to-open packages, such as DVD cases sealed with impossibly sticky labels, packaging with finger-splitting wire twist-ties, or sealed plastic clamshell containers that cause "wrap rage" and send about 6,000 people to the hospital each year with lacerations and puncture wounds. Another packaging issue is overpackaging—as when a tiny USB flash drive in an oversized cardboard and plastic display package is delivered in a giant corrugated shipping carton. Overpackaging creates an incredible amount of waste, frustrating those who care about the environment.[11]

By contrast, innovative packaging can give a company an advantage over competitors and boost sales. >> For example, Puma recently replaced the traditional shoebox with an attractive and functional yet environmentally friendly alternative—the Clever Little Bag:[12]

>> **Innovative packaging: Puma's next-generation shoe packaging—The Clever Little Bag—is more than just friendly to the environment, it's also very friendly to consumers' sensibilities and the company's bottom line. Pretty clever, huh?**

PUMA.

In their search for the next generation of shoe packaging, Puma's designers spent 21 months road testing 40 shoebox prototypes, checking on their potential environmental impact from production and transport through use and future reuse. They came up with what Puma calls the Clever Little Bag with a big impact. The new container—which consists of a light cardboard insert that slides seamlessly into a colorful, reusable red bag—uses 65 percent less paper to make and reduces water, energy, and fuel consumption during manufacturing by more than 60 percent a year. Because it takes up less space and weight, the new container also reduces carbon emissions during shipping by 10,000 tons a year. What's more, everything is 100 percent recyclable. In all, Puma's Clever Little Bag is more than just friendly to the environment, it's also very friendly to consumers' likes and the company's bottom line. Pretty clever, huh?

In recent years, product safety has also become a major packaging concern. We have all learned to deal with hard-to-open "childproof" packaging. Due to the rash of product tampering scares in the 1980s, most drug producers and food makers now put their products in tamper-resistant packages. In making packaging decisions, the company also must heed growing environmental concerns. Fortunately, like Puma, many companies have gone "green" by reducing their packaging and using environmentally responsible packaging materials.

Labeling

Labels range from simple tags attached to products to complex graphics that are part of the packaging. They perform several functions. At the very least, the label *identifies* the product or brand, such as the name Sunkist stamped on oranges. The label might also *describe* several things about the product—who made it, where it was made, when it was made, its contents, how it is to be used, and how to use it safely. Finally, the label might help to *promote* the brand, support its positioning, and connect with customers. For many companies, labels have become an important element in broader marketing campaigns.

Labels and brand logos can support the brand's positioning and add personality to the brand. For example, although similar to the familiar red, white, and blue logo that customers would have seen 60 years ago, Pepsi recently introduced a new, more uplifting smiling logo. "It feels like the same Pepsi we know and love," says a brand expert, "but it's more adventurous, more youthful, with a bit more personality to it." It presents a "spirit of optimism and youth," says a Pepsi marketer.[13]

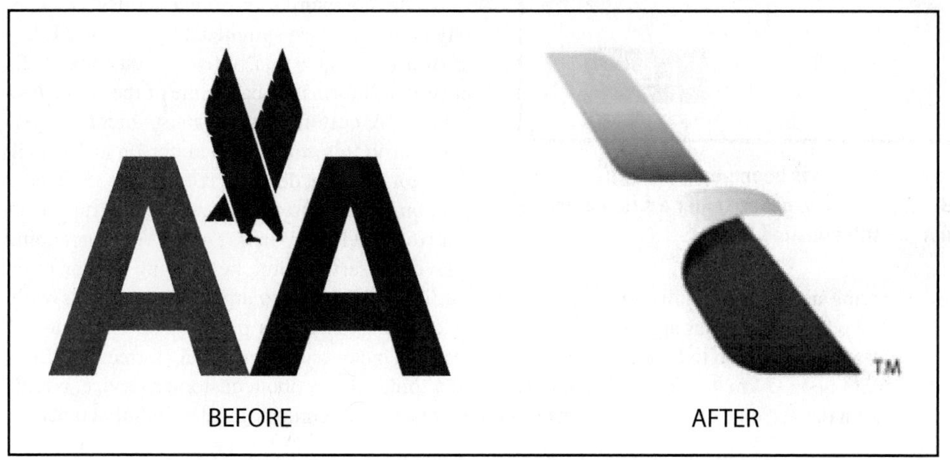

Brand labels and logos: When American Airlines modernized its familiar old "AA eagle" logo, the new logo became a flashpoint for both brand fans and detractors.

Mark Fairhurst/ZUMA Press/Newscom (old); Associated Press (new).

In fact, brand labels and logos can become a crucial element in the brand–customer connection. For example, when Gap recently introduced a more contemporary redesign of its familiar old logo—the well-known white text on a blue square—customers went ballistic and imposed intense online pressure. Gap reinstated the old logo after only one week. Similarly, when American Airlines replaced its familiar 45-year-old "AA eagle" logo with a more modern version, the new logo became a flashpoint for both brand fans and detractors. Although the brand redesign was probably overdue, fans lamented the loss of the classic design, whereas detractors claimed that the millions spent on repainting all of American's planes should have been invested in improving the airline's customer service. Such examples "highlight a powerful connection people have to the visual representations of their . . . brands," says an analyst.[14]

Along with the positives, there has been a long history of legal concerns about packaging and labels. The Federal Trade Commission Act of 1914 held that false, misleading, or deceptive labels or packages constitute unfair competition. Labels can mislead customers, fail to describe important ingredients, or fail to include needed safety warnings. As a result, several federal and state laws regulate labeling. The most prominent is the Fair Packaging and Labeling Act of 1966, which set mandatory labeling requirements, encouraged voluntary industry packaging standards, and allowed federal agencies to set packaging regulations in specific industries.

Labeling has been affected in recent times by *unit pricing* (stating the price per unit of a standard measure), *open dating* (stating the expected shelf life of the product), and *nutritional labeling* (stating the nutritional values in the product). The Nutritional Labeling and Educational Act of 1990 requires sellers to provide detailed nutritional information on food products, and recent sweeping actions by the Food and Drug Administration (FDA) regulate the use of health-related terms such as *low fat*, *light*, and *high fiber*. Sellers must ensure that their labels contain all the required information.

Product Support Services

Customer service is another element of product strategy. A company's offer usually includes some support services, which can be a minor part or a major part of the total offering. Later in this chapter, we will discuss services as products in themselves. Here, we discuss services that augment actual products.

Support services are an important part of the customer's overall brand experience. For example, L.L.Bean—the iconic American outdoor apparel and equipment retailer—knows good marketing doesn't stop with making the sale. Keeping customers happy *after* the sale is the key to building lasting relationships.[15]

NOTICE

I do not consider a sale complete until goods are worn out and customer still satisfied.

We will thank anyone to return goods that are not perfectly satisfactory.

Should the person reading this notice know of anyone who is not satisfied with our goods, I will consider it a favor to be notified.

Above all things we wish to avoid having a dissatisfied customer.

L.L.Bean

Customer service: For more than 100 years, L.L.Bean has been going the extra mile for customers. As founder Leon Leonwood Bean put it: "I do not consider a sale complete until the goods are worn out and the customer [is] still satisfied."

L.L.Bean Inc.

Year after year, L.L.Bean lands in the top ten of virtually every list of top service companies, including J.D. Power's most recent list of "customer service champions." The customer-service culture runs deep at L.L.Bean. More than 100 years ago, Leon Leonwood Bean founded the company on a philosophy of complete customer satisfaction, expressed in the following guarantee: "I don't consider a sale complete until the goods are worn out and the customer [is] still satisfied." To this day, customers can return any item, no questions asked, even decades after purchase.

The company's customer-service philosophy is perhaps best summed up in founder L.L.'s answer to the question, What is a customer? His answer still forms the backbone of the company's values: "A customer is the most important person ever in this company—in person or by mail. A customer is not dependent on us, we are dependent on him. A customer is not an interruption of our work, he is the purpose of it. We are not doing a favor by serving him, he is doing us a favor by giving us the opportunity to do so. A customer is not someone to argue or match wits with. Nobody ever won an argument with a customer. A customer is a person who brings us his wants. It is our job to handle them profitably to him and to ourselves." Adds former L.L.Bean CEO Leon Gorman: "A lot of people have fancy things to say about customer service, but it's just a day-in, day-out, ongoing, never-ending, persevering, compassionate kind of activity."

The first step in designing support services is to survey customers periodically to assess the value of current services and obtain ideas for new ones. Once the company has assessed the quality of various support services to customers, it can take steps to fix problems and add new services that will both delight customers and yield profits to the company.

Many companies now use a sophisticated mix of phone, e-mail, Internet, and interactive voice and data technologies to provide support services that were not possible before. For example, AT&T offers a complete set of after-sale services for all of its products, from wireless to digital TV. Customers can access 24/7 tech support via an AT&T Live Agent, either by phone or online. In addition, its online support pages offer troubleshooting, virtual tours, and online live chat. Other companies are adding a more personal service touch. For example, under its "BMW Genius Everywhere" program, BMW hires young, tech-savvy employees—often college students—who patrol dealership showrooms with iPods in hand, offering expert advice to customers. The BMW geniuses don't sell cars or even try to, but they do have deep knowledge of BMW models and features that customers find helpful.[16]

Product line
A group of products that are closely related because they function in a similar manner, are sold to the same customer groups, are marketed through the same types of outlets, or fall within given price ranges.

Product Line Decisions

Beyond decisions about individual products and services, product strategy also calls for building a product line. A **product line** is a group of products that are closely related because they function in a similar manner, are sold to the same customer groups, are marketed through the same types of outlets, or fall within given price ranges. For example,

Nike produces several lines of athletic shoes and apparel, and Marriott offers several lines of hotels.

The major product line decision involves *product line length*—the number of items in the product line. The line is too short if the manager can increase profits by adding items; the line is too long if the manager can increase profits by dropping items. Managers need to analyze their product lines periodically to assess each item's sales and profits and understand how each item contributes to the line's overall performance.

A company can expand its product line in two ways: by *line filling* or *line stretching*. *Product line filling* involves adding more items within the present range of the line. There are several reasons for product line filling: reaching for extra profits, satisfying dealers, using excess capacity, being the leading full-line company, and plugging holes to keep out competitors. However, line filling is overdone if it results in cannibalization and customer confusion. The company should ensure that new items are noticeably different from existing ones.

Product line stretching occurs when a company lengthens its product line beyond its current range. The company can stretch its line downward, upward, or both ways. Companies located at the upper end of the market can stretch their lines *downward*. A company may stretch downward to plug a market hole that otherwise would attract a new competitor or to respond to a competitor's attack on the upper end. Or it may add low-end products because it finds faster growth taking place in the low-end segments. Companies can also stretch their product lines *upward*. Sometimes, companies stretch upward to add prestige to their current products. Or they may be attracted by a faster growth rate or higher margins at the higher end.

To broaden its market appeal and boost growth, BMW has in recent years stretched its line in *both directions* while at the same time filling the gaps in between:[17]

> Over the past decade, BMW has morphed from a one-brand, five-model carmaker into a powerhouse with three brands, 14 "Series," and more than 30 distinct models. Not only has the carmaker stretched its product line downward, with MINI Cooper and its compact 1-Series models, but it has also stretched it upward with the addition of Rolls-Royce. The company has filled the gaps in between with Z4 roadsters, 6-Series coupe, X-Series crossovers and sports activity vehicles, and M-Series high-performance models. Next up: a growing selection of hybrids and all-electric cars. As a result, BMW has boosted its appeal to the rich, the super-rich, and the wannabe-rich, all without departing from its pure premium positioning.

Product Mix Decisions

Product mix (or product portfolio)
The set of all product lines and items that a particular seller offers for sale.

An organization with several product lines has a product mix. A **product mix** (or **product portfolio**) consists of all the product lines and items that a particular seller offers for sale. Campbell Soup Company's product mix consists of three major product lines: healthy beverages, baked snacks, and simple meals.[18] Each product line consists of several sublines. For example, the simple meals line consists of soups, sauces, and pastas. Each line and subline has many individual items. Altogether, Campbell's product mix includes hundreds of items.

A company's product mix has four important dimensions: width, length, depth, and consistency. Product mix *width* refers to the number of different product lines the company carries. >> For example, Campbell Soup Company has a fairly contained product mix that fits its mission of "nourishing people's lives everywhere, every day." By contrast, GE manufactures as many as 250,000 items across a broad range of categories, from light bulbs to medical equipment, jet engines, and diesel locomotives.

Product mix *length* refers to the total number of items a company carries within its product lines. Campbell Soup carries several brands within each line. For example, its simple meals line includes Campbell's soups, Wolfgang Puck soups and broths, Prego tomato sauce, Pace salsas, and Swanson broths, plus other international brands.

Product mix *depth* refers to the number of versions offered for each product in the line. Campbell's soups come in seven varieties, ranging from Campbell's Condensed soups and Campbell's Chunky soups to Campbell's Select Harvest soups and Campbell's Healthy Request soups. Each variety offers a number of forms and formulations. For example, you can buy Campbell's Chunky Hearty Beef Noodle soup, Chunky Chicken & Dumplings soup,

Campbell's
Healthy Beverages
Baked Snacks
Simple Meals
A Winning Combination
At Campbell, we are focused on three large and growing categories: Healthy Beverages, Baked Snacks and Simple Meals. Our brands are market leaders in their principal geographies. We have world-class product technologies, an experienced, talented team and the financial strength to invest in growth. It all adds up to a focused food company with a winning portfolio for nourishing people's lives everywhere, every day.

The product mix: Campbell Soup Company has a nicely contained product line consistent with its mission of "nourishing people's lives everywhere, every day."

Campbell Soup Company.

and Chunky Steak & Potato soup, in either cans or microwavable containers.

Finally, the *consistency* of the product mix refers to how closely related the various product lines are in end use, production requirements, distribution channels, or some other aspect. Campbell Soup Company's product lines are consistent insofar as they are consumer products and go through the same distribution channels. The lines are less consistent insofar as they perform different functions for buyers.

These product mix dimensions provide the handles for defining the company's product strategy. The company can increase its business in four ways. It can add new product lines, widening its product mix. In this way, its new lines build on the company's reputation in its other lines. The company can lengthen its existing product lines to become a more full-line company. It can add more versions of each product and thus deepen its product mix. Finally, the company can pursue more product line consistency—or less—depending on whether it wants to have a strong reputation in a single field or in several fields.

From time to time, a company may also have to streamline its product mix to pare out marginally performing lines and to regain its focus. For example, as discussed in the previous chapter, P&G pursues a megabrand strategy built around 25 billion-dollar brands in the household care and beauty and grooming categories. During the past decade, the consumer products giant has sold off dozens of major brands that no longer fit either its evolving focus or the billion-dollar threshold, ranging from Jif peanut butter, Crisco shortening, Folgers coffee, Pringles snack chips, and Sunny Delight drinks to Noxema skin care products, Right Guard deodorant, and Aleve pain reliever. Such pruning is essential for maintaining a focused, healthy product mix.

SPEED BUMP LINKING THE CONCEPTS

Slow down for a minute. To get a better sense of how large and complex a company's product offering can become, investigate Procter & Gamble's product mix.

- Using P&G's Web site (www.pg.com), its annual report, or other sources, develop a list of all the company's product lines and individual products. What surprises you about this list of products?
- Is P&G's product mix consistent? What overall strategy or logic appears to have guided the development of this product mix?

Author Comment
As noted at the start of this chapter, services are "products," too—intangible ones. So all the product topics we've discussed so far apply to services as well as to physical products. However, in this section, we focus on the special characteristics and marketing needs that set services apart.

Services Marketing

Services have grown dramatically in recent years. Services now account for close to 80 percent of the U.S. gross domestic product (GDP), and the service industry is growing. By 2014, it is estimated that more than four out of five jobs in the United States will be in service industries. Services are growing even faster in the world economy, making up almost 64 percent of the gross world product.[19]

Service industries vary greatly. *Governments* offer services through courts, employment services, hospitals, military services, police and fire departments, the postal service, and schools. *Private not-for-profit organizations* offer services through museums, charities,

Figure 7.3 Four Service Characteristics

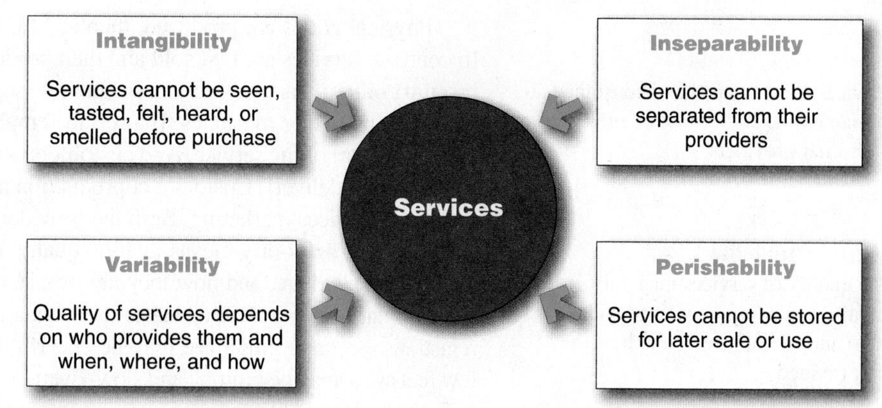

Although services are "products" in a general sense, they have special characteristics and marketing needs. The biggest differences come from the fact that services are essentially intangible and that they are created through direct interactions with customers. Think about your experiences with an airline versus Nike or Apple.

churches, colleges, foundations, and hospitals. In addition, a large number of *business organizations* offer services—airlines, banks, hotels, insurance companies, consulting firms, medical and legal practices, entertainment and telecommunications companies, real estate firms, retailers, and others.

The Nature and Characteristics of a Service

Service intangibility
Services cannot be seen, tasted, felt, heard, or smelled before they are bought.

A company must consider four special service characteristics when designing marketing programs: intangibility, inseparability, variability, and perishability (see **Figure 7.3**).

Service intangibility means that services cannot be seen, tasted, felt, heard, or smelled before they are bought. For example, people undergoing cosmetic surgery cannot see the result before the purchase. Airline passengers have nothing but a ticket and a promise that they and their luggage will arrive safely at the intended destination, hopefully at the same time. To reduce uncertainty, buyers look for *signals* of service quality. They draw conclusions about quality from the place, people, price, equipment, and communications that they can see.

Therefore, the service provider's task is to make the service tangible in one or more ways and send the right signals about quality. The Mayo Clinic does this well:[20]

When it comes to hospitals, most patients can't really judge "product quality." It's a very complex product that's hard to understand, and you can't try it out before buying it. So when considering a hospital, most people unconsciously search for evidence that the facility is caring, competent, and trustworthy. The Mayo Clinic doesn't leave these things to chance. Rather, it offers patients organized and honest evidence of its dedication to "providing the best care to every patient every day."

Inside, staff is trained to act in a way that clearly signals Mayo Clinic's concern for patient wellbeing. For example, doctors regularly follow up with patients at home to see how they are doing, and they work with patients to smooth out scheduling problems. The clinic's physical facilities also send the right signals. They've been carefully designed to offer a place of refuge, show caring and respect, and signal competence. Looking for external confirmation? Go online and hear directly from those who've been to the clinic or work there. The Mayo Clinic now uses social networking—everything from blogs to Facebook and YouTube—to enhance the patient experience. For example, on the Sharing Mayo Clinic blog (http://sharing.mayoclinic.org), patients and their families retell their Mayo experiences, and Mayo employees offer behind-the-scenes views. The result? Highly loyal customers who willingly spread the good word to others, building one of the most powerful brands in health care.

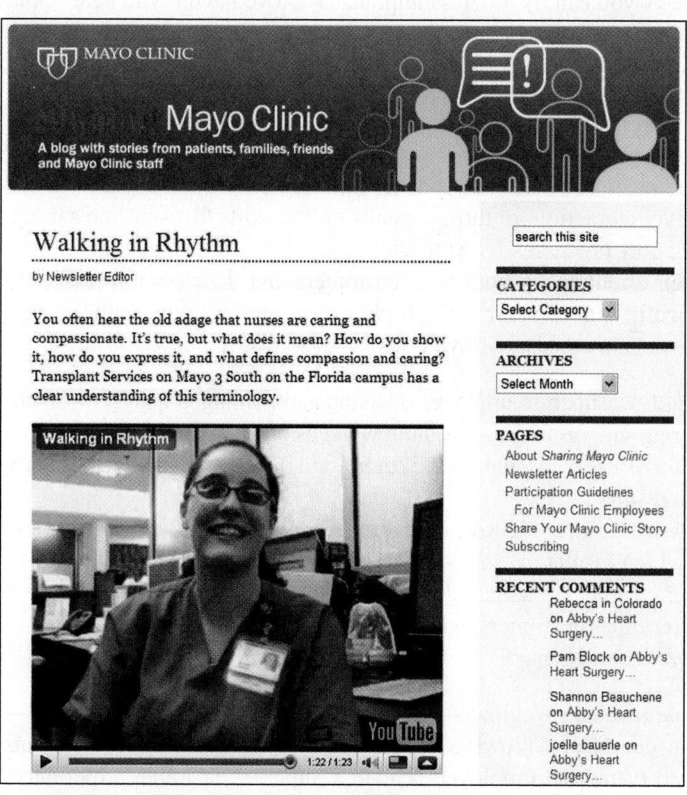

By providing customers with organized, honest evidence of its capabilities, the Mayo Clinic has built one of the most powerful brands in health care. Its Sharing Mayo Clinic blog lets you hear directly from those who have been to the clinic or who work there.

Mayo Clinic.

Service inseparability
Services are produced and consumed at the same time and cannot be separated from their providers.

Physical goods are produced, then stored, then later sold, and then still later consumed. In contrast, services are first sold and then produced and consumed at the same time. **Service inseparability** means that services cannot be separated from their providers, whether the providers are people or machines. If a service employee provides the service, then the employee becomes a part of the service. And customers don't just buy and use a service, they play an active role in its delivery. Customer coproduction makes *provider–customer interaction* a special feature of services marketing. Both the provider and the customer affect the service outcome.

Service variability
The quality of services may vary greatly depending on who provides them and when, where, and how they are provided.

Service variability means that the quality of services depends on who provides them as well as when, where, and how they are provided. For example, some hotels—say, Marriott—have reputations for providing better service than others. Still, within a given Marriott hotel, one registration-counter employee may be cheerful and efficient, whereas another standing just a few feet away may be grumpy and slow. Even the quality of a single Marriott employee's service varies according to his or her energy and frame of mind at the time of each customer encounter.

Service perishability
Services cannot be stored for later sale or use.

Service perishability means that services cannot be stored for later sale or use. Some doctors charge patients for missed appointments because the service value existed only at that point and disappeared when the patient did not show up. The perishability of services is not a problem when demand is steady. However, when demand fluctuates, service firms often have difficult problems. For example, because of rush-hour demand, public transportation companies have to own much more equipment than they would if demand were even throughout the day. Thus, service firms often design strategies for producing a better match between demand and supply. Hotels and resorts charge lower prices in the off-season to attract more guests. And restaurants hire part-time employees to serve during peak periods.

Marketing Strategies for Service Firms

Just like manufacturing businesses, good service firms use marketing to position themselves strongly in chosen target markets. FedEx promises to take your packages "faster, farther"; Angie's List offers "Reviews you can trust." At Hampton, "We love having you here." And St. Jude Children's Hospital is "Finding cures. Saving children." These and other service firms establish their positions through traditional marketing mix activities. However, because services differ from tangible products, they often require additional marketing approaches.

The Service Profit Chain

In a service business, the customer and the front-line service employee *interact* to cocreate the service. Effective interaction, in turn, depends on the skills of front-line service employees and on the support processes backing these employees. Thus, successful service companies focus their attention on both their customers and their employees. They understand the **service profit chain**, which links service firm profits with employee and customer satisfaction. This chain consists of five links:[21]

Service profit chain
The chain that links service firm profits with employee and customer satisfaction.

- *Internal service quality:* superior employee selection and training, a quality work environment, and strong support for those dealing with customers, which results in . . .
- *Satisfied and productive service employees:* more satisfied, loyal, and hardworking employees, which results in . . .
- *Greater service value:* more effective and efficient customer value creation and service delivery, which results in . . .
- *Satisfied and loyal customers:* satisfied customers who remain loyal, make repeat purchases, and refer other customers, which results in . . .
- *Healthy service profits and growth:* superior service firm performance.

For example, supermarket chain Wegmans—a perennial customer service champion—has developed a cult-like customer following by putting its employees first. Wegmans believes that happy, superbly trained employees create a superior customer experience. The resulting happy customers are tremendously loyal, give the firm more business, and convince other customers to do the same. That, in turn, results in happy investors. "Our employees are our number one asset, period," says a Wegmans executive. "The first question [we] ask is 'Is this the best thing for employees?'"[22] Similarly, Four Seasons Hotels and Resorts, a chain legendary for its outstanding customer service, is also legendary for its motivated and satisfied employees (see Marketing at Work 7.1).

MARKETING AT WORK 7.1

Four Seasons: Taking Care of Those Who Take Care of Customers

At Four Seasons Hotels & Resorts, every guest is a somebody. Other exclusive resorts pamper their guests, but Four Seasons has perfected the art of high-touch, carefully crafted service. Whether it's at the elegantly "re-imagined" Four Seasons London, the regally attentive Four Seasons Hotel Riyadh in Saudi Arabia, the tropical island paradise at the Four Seasons Resort Mauritius, or the luxurious Sub-Saharan "camp" at the Four Seasons Safari Lodge Serengeti, guests paying $1,000 or more a night expect to have their minds read. For these guests, Four Seasons doesn't disappoint. Its mission is to perfect the travel experience through the highest standards of hospitality. "From elegant surroundings of the finest quality, to caring, highly personalized 24-hour service," says the company, "Four Seasons embodies a true home away from home for those who know and appreciate the best."

As a result, Four Seasons has a cult-like customer clientele, making it one of the most-decorated hotel chains in the world. For example, TripAdvisor recently named the Hawaiian beachfront resort Four Seasons Resort Hualalai the number-one hotel in the world based on reviews from the Web site's millions of international users. As one Four Seasons Maui guest recently told a manager, "If there's a heaven, I hope it's run by Four Seasons."

But what makes Four Seasons so special? It's really no secret. Just ask anyone who works there. From the CEO to the doorman, they'll tell you—it's the quality of the Four Seasons staff. Its people are "the heart and soul of what makes this company succeed," says Four Seasons founder Isadore Sharp. "When we say people are our most important asset—it's not just talk." Just as it does for customers, Four Seasons respects and pampers its employees. It knows that happy, satisfied employees make for happy, satisfied customers.

The Four Seasons customer service legacy is deeply rooted in the company's culture, which in turn is grounded in the Golden Rule. In all of its dealings with both guests and staff, the luxury resort chain seeks to treat others as it wishes to be treated. "How you treat your employees is a reflection of how you expect them to treat customers," says Sharp.

Four Seasons brings this customer service culture to life by hiring the best people, orienting them carefully, instilling in them a sense of pride, and motivating them by recognizing and rewarding outstanding service deeds. It all starts with hiring the right people—those who fit the Four Seasons culture. Every applicant—whether it's a potential receptionist, a hopeful pool manager, or a would-be backroom financial manager—undergoes multiple job interviews. "We look for employees who share that Golden Rule—people who, by nature, believe in treating others as they would have them treat us," says Sharp.

Once on board, all new employees receive three months of training, including improvisation exercises, that help them to fully understand customer needs and behavior. At Four Seasons, the training never stops. But even more important is the people themselves and the culture under which they work. The most important cultural guideline: the good-old Golden Rule. "That's not a gimmick," Sharp insists. As a result, Four Seasons employees know what good service is and are highly motivated to give it.

Most important, once it has the right people in place, Four Seasons treats them as it would its most important guests. Compared with the competition, Four Seasons salaries are in the 75th to 90th percentile, with generous retirement and profit-sharing plans. All employees—from the maids who make up the rooms to the general manager—dine together (free of charge) in the hotel cafeteria. Perhaps best of all, every employee receives free stays at other Four Seasons resorts, starting at three free nights per year after six months with the company, then six free nights or more after one year.

The room stays make employees feel as important and pampered as the guests they serve, and they motivate employees to achieve even higher levels of service in their own jobs. Kanoe Braun, a pool attendant at the Four Seasons Maui, has visited several other Four Seasons resorts in his 10 years with the

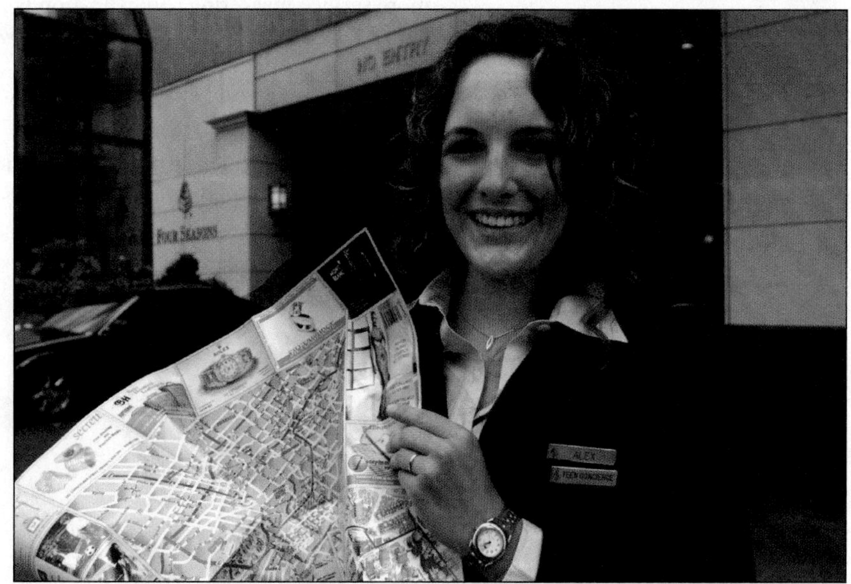

>> Four Seasons' happy, dedicated, and energetic employees—from the pool manager to the concierge to the backroom financial manager—create unparalleled customer experiences. Says one customer, "If there's a heaven, I hope it's run by Four Seasons."

Toronto Star via Getty Images.

company. "I've been to the one in Bali. That was by far my favorite," he proclaims. "You walk in, and they say, 'How are you, Mr. Braun?' and you say, 'Yeah, I'm somebody!'" Adds another Four Seasons staffer, "You're never treated like just an employee. You're a guest. You come back from those trips on fire. You want to do so much for the guests."

As a result, the Four Seasons staff loves the hotel just as much as customers do. Although guests can check out anytime they like, employees never want to leave. The annual turnover for full-time employees is only 18 percent, half the industry average. Four Seasons has been included for 16 straight years on *Fortune* magazine's list of 100 Best Companies to Work For. And that's the biggest secret to Four Seasons' success. Creating customer satisfaction and value involves more than just crafting a lofty competitive marketing strategy and handing it down from the top. At Four Seasons, creating customer value is everybody's business. And it all starts with taking care of those who take care of customers.

Sources: Based on information from "TripAdvisor Names Four Seasons Resort Hualalai #1 Hotel in the World," January 18, 2013, http://press.fourseasons.com/hualalai/hotel-news/tripadvisor-names-four-seasons-resort-hualalai-1-hotel-in-the-world/#image---KON_039; Jeffrey M. O'Brien, "A Perfect Season," *Fortune*, January 22, 2008, pp. 62–66; "The 100 Best Companies to Work For," *Fortune*, February 4, 2013, p. 85; and http://jobs.fourseasons.com/Pages/Home.aspx and www.fourseasons.com/about_us/, accessed October 2013.

Service marketing requires more than just traditional external marketing using the four Ps. **>> Figure 7.4** shows that service marketing also requires *internal marketing* and *interactive marketing*. **Internal marketing** means that the service firm must orient and motivate its customer-contact employees and supporting service people to work as a *team* to provide customer satisfaction. Marketers must get everyone in the organization to be customer centered. In fact, internal marketing must *precede* external marketing. For example, Four Seasons Hotels and Resorts starts by hiring the right people and carefully orienting and inspiring them to give unparalleled customer service. The idea is to make certain that employees themselves believe in the brand so that they can authentically deliver the brand's promise to customers.

Internal marketing
Orienting and motivating customer-contact employees and supporting service employees to work as a team to provide customer satisfaction.

Interactive marketing means that service quality depends heavily on the quality of the buyer–seller interaction during the service encounter. In product marketing, product quality often depends little on how the product is obtained. But in services marketing, service quality depends on both the service deliverer and the quality of delivery. Service marketers, therefore, have to master interactive marketing skills. Thus, Four Seasons selects only people with an innate "passion to serve" and instructs them carefully in the fine art of interacting with customers to satisfy their every need. All new hires complete a three-month training regimen, including improvisation exercises, to help them improve their customer-interaction skills.

Interactive marketing
Training service employees in the fine art of interacting with customers to satisfy their needs.

Today, as competition and costs increase, and as productivity and quality decrease, more service marketing sophistication is needed. Service companies face three major marketing tasks: They want to increase their *service differentiation*, *service quality*, and *service productivity*.

Managing Service Differentiation

In these days of intense price competition, service marketers often complain about the difficulty of differentiating their services from those of competitors. To the extent that customers view the services of different providers as similar, they care less about the provider than the price. The solution to price competition is to develop a differentiated offer, delivery, and image.

>> Figure 7.4 Three Types of Service Marketing

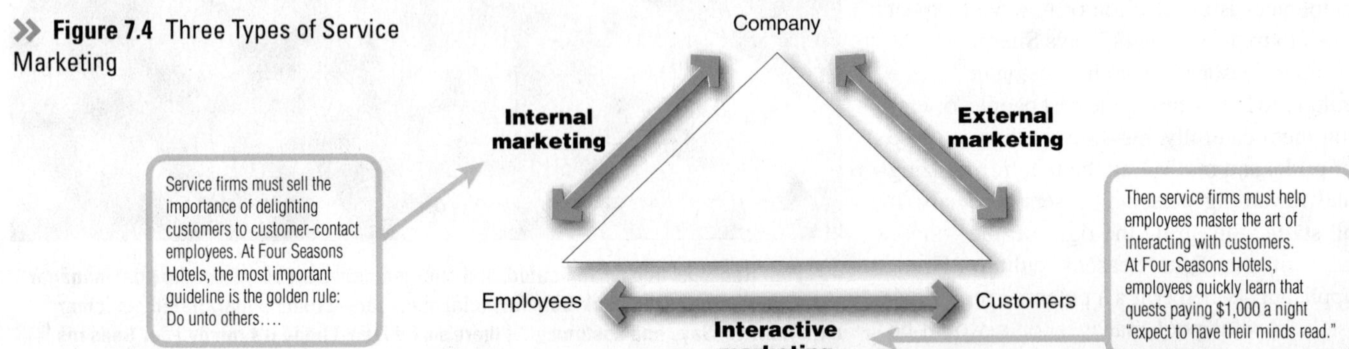
Company
Internal marketing
External marketing
Employees
Customers
Interactive marketing
Service firms must sell the importance of delighting customers to customer-contact employees. At Four Seasons Hotels, the most important guideline is the golden rule: Do unto others....
Then service firms must help employees master the art of interacting with customers. At Four Seasons Hotels, employees quickly learn that guests paying $1,000 a night "expect to have their minds read."

Service differentiation: Dick's Sporting Goods differentiates itself by offering services that go well beyond the products it stocks.

© Ian Dagnall/Alamy.

The *offer* can include innovative features that set one company's offer apart from competitors' offers. For example, some retailers differentiate themselves by offerings that take you well beyond the products they stock. Dick's Sporting Goods has grown from a single bait-and-tackle store in Binghamton, New York, into a 510-store, $5.2 billion sporting goods megaretailer in 44 states by offering interactive services that set it apart from ordinary sporting goods stores. Customers can sample shoes on Dick's indoor footwear track, test golf clubs with an on-site golf swing analyzer and putting green, shoot bows in its archery range, and receive personalized fitness product guidance from an in-store team of fitness trainers. Such differentiated services help make Dick's "the ultimate sporting goods destination store for core athletes and outdoor enthusiasts."[23]

Service companies can differentiate their service *delivery* by having more able and reliable customer-contact people, developing a superior physical environment in which the service product is delivered, or designing a superior delivery process. For example, many grocery chains now offer online shopping and home delivery as a better way to shop than having to drive, park, wait in line, and tote groceries home. And most banks offer mobile phone apps that allow you to more easily transfer money and check account balances. Many even allow mobile check deposits. "Sign, snap a photo, and submit a check from anywhere," says one Citibank ad. "It's easier than running to the bank."

Finally, service companies also can work on differentiating their *images* through symbols and branding. Aflac adopted the duck as its advertising symbol. Today, the duck is immortalized through stuffed animals, golf club covers, and free ringtones and screensavers. The well-known Aflac duck helped make the big but previously unknown insurance company memorable and approachable. Other well-known service characters and symbols include the GEICO gecko, Progressive Insurance's Flo, McDonald's golden arches, Allstate's "good hands," and the Twitter bird.

Service differentiation: Service companies can differentiate their images using unique characters or symbols. Do you recognize this familiar symbol?

© 2013 Twitter.

Managing Service Quality

A service firm can differentiate itself by delivering consistently higher quality than its competitors provide. Like manufacturers before them, most service industries have now joined the customer-driven quality movement. And like product marketers, service providers need to identify what target customers expect in regard to service quality.

Unfortunately, service quality is harder to define and judge than product quality. For instance, it is harder to agree on the quality of a haircut than on the quality of a hair dryer. Customer retention is perhaps the best measure of quality; a service firm's ability to hang onto its customers depends on how consistently it delivers value to them.

Top service companies set high service-quality standards. They watch service performance closely, both their own and that of competitors. They do not settle for merely good service—they strive for 100 percent defect-free service. A 98 percent performance standard may sound good, but using this standard, the U.S. Postal Service would lose or misdirect 391,000 pieces of mail each hour, and U.S. pharmacies would misfill more than 72.4 million prescriptions each week.[24]

Unlike product manufacturers who can adjust their machinery and inputs until everything is perfect, service quality will always vary, depending on the interactions between employees and customers. As hard as they may try, even the best companies will have an occasional late delivery, burned steak, or grumpy employee. However, good *service recovery* can turn angry customers into loyal ones. In fact, good recovery can win more customer purchasing and loyalty than if things had gone well in the first place. For example, Southwest Airlines has a proactive customer communications team whose job is to find the situations in which something went wrong—a mechanical delay, bad weather, a medical emergency, or a berserk passenger—then remedy the bad experience quickly, within 24 hours, if possible.[25] The team's communications to passengers, usually e-mails these days, have three basic components: a sincere apology, a brief explanation of what happened, and a gift to make it up, usually a voucher in dollars that can be used on their next Southwest flight. Surveys show that when Southwest handles a delay situation well, customers score it 14 to 16 points higher than on regular on-time flights.

These days, social media such as Facebook and Twitter can help companies to root out and remedy customer dissatisfaction with service. Consider Marriott International:[26]

> John Wolf, Marriott Hotel's director of public relations, heads a team of Marriott people who work full-time monitoring the company's Twitter feed and other social media. The team seeks out people who are complaining about problems they've had at Marriott. "We'd rather know that there's an issue than not know it, and we'd rather be given the opportunity to solve the problem," Wolf says. This strategy helps Marriott to solve customer problems as they arise and to recover previously dissatisfied customers. For example, when the team discovered an unhappy Marriott regular tweeting and blogging about an experience at a Marriott hotel that resulted in a ruined pair of shoes and big dry cleaning bill, they contacted him directly via Twitter, asking for his contact information. The next day, the disgruntled customer received a personal call from Marriott offering an explanation, a sincere apology, and a generous amount of reward points added to his account to be applied to future stays at Marriott. The result: a once-again happy and loyal customer who now blogged and tweeted to others about his positive experience.

Managing Service Productivity

With their costs rising rapidly, service firms are under great pressure to increase service productivity. They can do so in several ways. They can train current employees better or hire new ones who will work harder or more skillfully. Or they can increase the quantity of their service by giving up some quality. Finally, a service provider can harness the power of technology. Although we often think of technology's power to save time and costs in manufacturing companies, it also has great—and often untapped—potential to make service workers more productive.

However, companies must avoid pushing productivity so hard that doing so reduces quality. Attempts to streamline a service or cut costs can make a service company more efficient in the short run. But that can also reduce its longer-run ability to innovate, maintain service quality, or respond to consumer needs and desires. >> For example, some airlines have learned this lesson the hard way as they attempt to economize in the face of rising costs. Passengers on most airlines now encounter "time-saving" check-in kiosks rather than personal counter service. And most airlines have stopped offering even the little things for free—such as in-flight snacks—and now charge extra for everything from luggage to aisle seats. The result is a plane full of resentful customers. In their attempts to improve productivity, many airlines have mangled customer service.

>> Managing service productivity: Companies should be careful not to take things too far. For example, in their attempts to improve productivity, some airlines have mangled customer service.

AP Photo/Rick Bowmer.

Thus, in attempting to improve service productivity, companies must be mindful of how they create and deliver customer value. They should be careful not to take *service* out of the service. In fact, a company may purposely lower service productivity in order to improve service quality, in turn allowing it to maintain higher prices and profit margins.[27]

SPEED BUMP LINKING THE CONCEPTS

Let's pause here for a moment. We've said that although services are "products" in a general sense, they have special characteristics and marketing needs. To get a better grasp of this concept, select a traditional product brand, such as Nike or Honda. Next, select a service brand, such as Southwest Airlines or McDonald's. Then compare the two.

- How are the characteristics and marketing needs of the product and service brands you selected similar?
- How do the characteristics and marketing needs of the two brands differ? How are these differences reflected in each brand's marketing strategy? Keep these differences in mind as we move into the final section of the chapter.

Author Comment
A brand represents everything that a product or service *means* to consumers. As such, brands are valuable assets to a company. For example, when you hear someone say "Coca-Cola," what do you think, feel, or remember? What about "Target"? Or "Google"?

Branding Strategy: Building Strong Brands

Some analysts see brands as *the* major enduring asset of a company, outlasting the company's specific products and facilities. John Stewart, former CEO of Quaker Oats, once said, "If this business were split up, I would give you the land and bricks and mortar, and I would keep the brands and trademarks, and I would fare better than you." A former CEO of McDonald's declared, "If every asset we own, every building, and every piece of equipment were destroyed in a terrible natural disaster, we would be able to borrow all the money to replace it very quickly because of the value of our brand. . . . The brand is more valuable than the totality of all these assets."[28]

Thus, brands are powerful assets that must be carefully developed and managed. In this section, we examine the key strategies for building and managing product and service brands.

Brand Equity

Brands are more than just names and symbols. They are a key element in the company's relationships with consumers. Brands represent consumers' perceptions and feelings about a product and its performance—everything that the product or the service *means* to consumers. In the final analysis, brands exist in the heads of consumers. As one well-respected marketer once said, "Products are created in the factory, but brands are created in the mind." Adds Jason Kilar, former CEO of the online video service Hulu, "A brand is what people say about you when you're not in the room."[29]

Brand equity
The differential effect that knowing the brand name has on customer response to the product or its marketing.

A powerful brand has high *brand equity*. **Brand equity** is the differential effect that knowing the brand name has on customer response to the product and its marketing. It's a measure of the brand's ability to capture consumer preference and loyalty. A brand has positive brand equity when consumers react more favorably to it than to a generic or unbranded version of the same product. It has negative brand equity if consumers react less favorably than to an unbranded version.

Brands vary in the amount of power and value they hold in the marketplace. Some brands—such as Coca-Cola, Nike, Disney, GE, McDonald's, Harley-Davidson, and others—become larger-than-life icons that maintain their power in the market for years, even generations. Other brands—such as Google, Facebook, Apple, ESPN, and Wikipedia—create fresh consumer excitement and loyalty. These brands win in the marketplace not simply because they deliver unique benefits or reliable service. Rather, they succeed because they forge deep connections with customers. People really do have relationships with brands. For example, to a devoted Converse fan, the brand stands for much more than just shoes. It stands for a youthful, rebellious lifestyle. The Converse brand and shoes represent a canvas for self-expression.

Ad agency Young & Rubicam's BrandAsset Valuator measures brand strength along four consumer perception dimensions: *differentiation* (what makes the brand stand out), *relevance* (how consumers feel it meets their needs), *knowledge* (how much consumers know about the brand), and *esteem* (how highly consumers regard and respect the brand). Brands with strong brand equity rate high on all four dimensions. The brand must be distinct, or consumers will have no reason to choose it over other brands. However, the fact that a brand is highly differentiated doesn't necessarily mean that consumers will buy it. The brand must stand out in ways that are relevant to consumers' needs. Even a differentiated, relevant brand is far from a shoe-in. Before consumers will respond to the brand, they must first know about and understand it. And that familiarity must lead to a strong, positive consumer–brand connection.[30]

Consumers sometimes bond very closely with specific brands. Perhaps the ultimate expression of brand devotion: tattooing the brand on your body.

Kristoffer Tripplaar/Alamy.

Thus, positive brand equity derives from consumer feelings about and connections with a brand. Consumers sometimes bond *very* closely with specific brands. As perhaps the ultimate expression of brands devotion, a surprising number of people—and not just Harley-Davidson fans—have their favorite brand tattooed on their bodies. Whether its contemporary new brands such as Facebook or Amazon or old classics like Harley or Converse, strong brands are built around an ideal of building trust and improving consumers' lives in some relevant way (see Marketing at Work 7.2).

A brand with high brand equity is a very valuable asset. *Brand valuation* is the process of estimating the total financial value of a brand. Measuring such value is difficult. However, according to one estimate, the brand value of Apple is a whopping $182 billion, with IBM at $115 billion, Google at $107 billion, McDonald's at $95 billion, Microsoft at $76 billion, and Coca-Cola at $74 billion. Other brands rating among the world's most valuable include AT&T, China Mobile, GE, Walmart, and Amazon.com.[31]

High brand equity provides a company with many competitive advantages. A powerful brand enjoys a high level of consumer brand awareness and loyalty. Because consumers expect stores to carry the particular brand, the company has more leverage in bargaining with resellers. Because a brand name carries high credibility, the company can more easily launch line and brand extensions. A powerful brand also offers the company some defense against fierce price competition.

Above all, however, a powerful brand forms the basis for building strong and profitable customer relationships. The fundamental asset underlying brand equity is *customer equity*—the value of customer relationships that the brand creates. A powerful brand is important, but what it really represents is a profitable set of loyal customers. The proper focus of marketing is building customer equity, with brand management serving as a major marketing tool. Companies need to think of themselves not as portfolios of brands but as portfolios of customers.

MARKETING AT WORK 7.2

Breakaway Brands: Connecting with Consumers and Building Trust

What does Facebook—the contemporary, social media powerhouse—have in common with Foster Farms—a family-owned poultry company? Not much, it would seem. Yet both brands landed in brand consultancy Landor Associates' most recent annual Top Ten Breakaway Brands list, a list of top brands based on a comprehensive survey that measures brand strength.

Each year, the Breakway Brands survey identifies the brands with the greatest percentage gains in brand health and business value as a result of superb brand strategy and execution over the previous three-year period. The survey taps Young & Rubicam's BrandAsset Valuator—a database of responses from 15,000 consumers evaluating 2,500 brands measured across 48 metrics—which looks at consumer brand measures such as differentiation, relevance, esteem, and knowledge. The survey also taps a second set of measures, "Economic Value Added" by BrandEconomics, which assesses the financial performance of each brand. Combined, the BrandAsset Valuator and Economic Value Added models provide a comprehensive brand valuation based on both consumer and financial measures.

Ideas about what constitutes brand strength, that elusive blend of consumer and financial performance, have changed in the past decade. The most recent Breakaway Brands list is dominated by contemporary Internet and high-tech brands—such as Facebook, YouTube, Apple, Samsung, Amazon, and Netflix—which have shattered and redefined their categories or built new categories altogether. However, mixed in with these contemporary brands are some decidedly lower-tech brands, such as Foster Farms, Kobalt Tools, and, of all things, the U.S. Marine Corps, which stand out in the list like a couple of old geezers in a glass-and-chrome Apple store.

Top Breakaway Brands

1. Facebook	**7.** YouTube
2. Keurig	**8.** Netflix
3. Skype	**9.** USMC
4. Amazon	**10.** Apple
5. Vizio	**11.** Kobalt Tools
6. Samsung	**12.** Foster Farms

Missing altogether are some brand titans such as Coca-Cola, McDonald's, and Disney—huge brands that grace many "top brands" lists but aren't growing nearly fast enough to be crowned Breakaway Brands.

Just what do these diverse Breakaway Brands have in common? According to Landor Associates, the seemingly diverse brands in this year's list share three important common values: connection, convenience, and confidence. The current survey measured brand performance in the aftermath of the Great Recession, an era characterized by persistent unemployment, tight finances, and reduced consumer confidence. It's no surprise, then, that in these less-certain times, consumer relationships with brands are based on more pragmatic, day-to-day concerns. "From tech brands that help people stay in touch globally while keeping the phone bill down, to packaged goods brands that offer healthy choices and convenient coffee breaks," says Landor, "this year's Breakaway list includes names that were singled out by consumers as those they turn to and rely on to make life better."

When it comes to connection, convenience, and confidence, the technology firms on the Breakaway list seem like naturals. Amazon.com cuts through life's clutter, reliably connects people to the things they want, sells to them at the click of a button, and delivers goods direct to their doorsteps, in some urban areas as fast as the same day of purchase. Apple and Samsung make the phones, tablets, other hardware devices that create reliable anytime, anywhere mobile connections. Netflix connects customers dependably and instantly to the entertainment they crave through high-definition streaming for a low monthly price.

Facebook provides a convenient platform that connects people to others—friends, family, celebrities, organizations—and keeps them in the know about important happenings. During the three-year period of the most recent Breakaway Brands assessment, total time spent per month on Facebook increased by more than 2,000 percent, from 33.9 billion minutes per month to 700 billion minutes (that's 1,330,928 people-years per month!). Similarly, under the guidance of parent company Google, YouTube has expanded beyond a mere video hosting site to become a full-fledged social network that connects 100 million users. And as the market leader in international long distance, Skype has helped people connect globally while keeping their phone bills at a minimum. With slogans such as "Upgrade from a wall post to a first class conversation" and "140 characters doesn't equal staying in touch," Skype has made old-school phone connections hip again.

But it's not just the high-tech brands that are breaking away through connections, convenience, and confidence. Mixed in with the Facebooks, Amazons, and Apples on the list are less-glamorous but still-valued brands such as Keurig and Foster Farms. Keurig's single-serve home coffee maker connects consumers through "convenience with a conscience." Users get a good cup of their favorite coffee easily and with no waste, and Keurig's one-use K-Cup packs and filters are BPA free, recyclable, and filled with fair-trade-certified coffee. Keurig gives you "brewing excellence one cup at a time."

Similarly, Foster Farms has been quietly and reliably making people's lives easier and more convenient since 1939. Its broad line of poultry products includes frozen chicken parts that don't require thawing before cooking, fully cooked poultry products that require only reheating, and pre-prepared entrées and appetizers. Foster Farms has also built customer trust and confidence—the brand is closely associated with healthy eating, community service, and environmental responsibility, establishing itself as the leading brand of locally sourced, all-natural, hormone- and steroid-free poultry.

So, again, what is it that ties this diverse set of brands together? It all boils down to building meaningful connections with consumers and adding value to their lives. Whether it's an omnipresent online retailer like Amazon.com, a social media powerhouse like Facebook, a sustainable poultry processor like Foster Farms, or a maker of dependable, affordable tools like Kobalt Tools, consumers trust these brands to connect their lives and make life easier and better. According to Landor, brands must be trusted companions:

> The Breakaway Brands list reveals a simple but powerful truth: To flourish in today's environment, brands must excel at being a trustworthy and helpful companion. Connect people. Make their lives simpler. Give them a deep sense of confidence. Most importantly, don't squander that trust. More than ever, to demand brand loyalty requires that a brand is loyal to its own values and its customers. After all, [companionship] is a two-way street.

Sources: Based on information from Jennifer Rooney, "Facebook Maintains Hold as Leading 'Breakaway Brand' for 2012," *Forbes*, September 4, 2012, www.forbes.com/sites/onmarketing/2011/09/08/facebook-apple-netflix-top-2011-breakaway-brands-list/; "Breakaway Brands of 2012," Landor Associates, September 6, 2012, http://landor.com/#!/talk/articles-publications/articles/breakaway-brands-of-2012/; Jack Neff, "Just How Well-Defined Is Your Brand's Ideal?" *Advertising Age,* January 16, 2012, p. 4; and www.youtube.com/yt/press/index.html, www.facebook.com/facebook/info, and www.fosterfarms.com, accessed July, 2013.

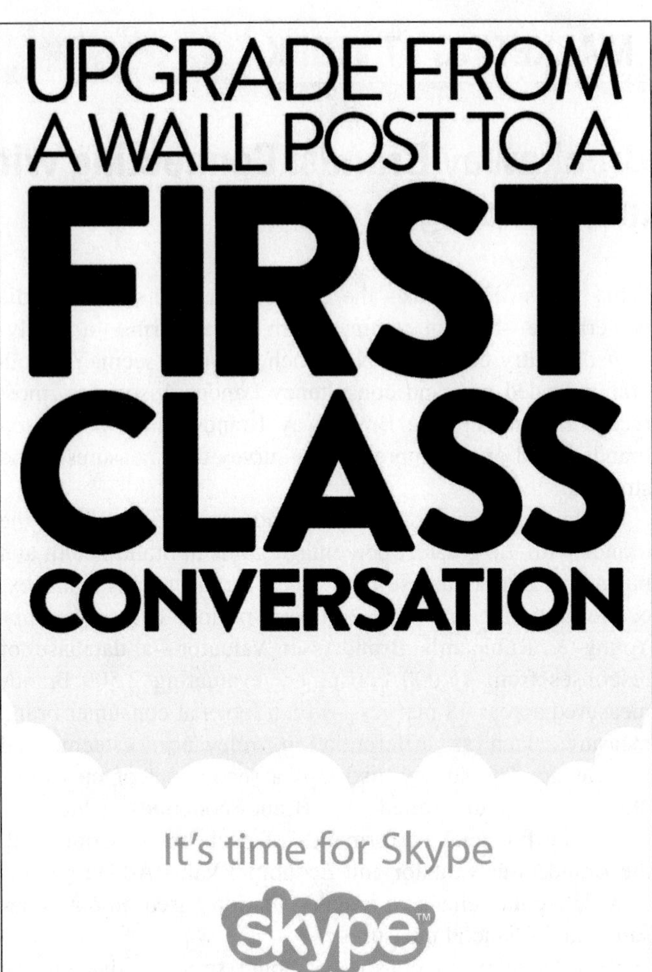

» Breakaway brands: Strong and trusting brand relationships are built around connection, convenience, and confidence. With slogans such as "Upgrade from a wall post to a first class conversation," Skype has made old-school phone connections hip again.

Building Strong Brands

Branding poses challenging decisions to the marketer. » **Figure 7.5** shows that the major brand strategy decisions involve *brand positioning*, *brand name selection*, *brand sponsorship*, and *brand development*.

Brand Positioning

Marketers need to position their brands clearly in target customers' minds. They can position brands at any of three levels.[32] At the lowest level, they can position the brand on *product attributes*. For example, P&G invented the disposable diaper category with its Pampers brand. Early Pampers marketing focused on attributes such as fluid absorption, fit, and disposability. In general, however, attributes are the least desirable level for brand positioning. Competitors can easily copy attributes. More important, customers are not interested in attributes as such—they are interested in what the attributes will do for them.

A brand can be better positioned by associating its name with a desirable *benefit*. Thus, Pampers can go beyond technical product attributes and talk about the resulting containment and skin-health benefits from dryness. Some successful brands positioned on benefits are FedEx (guaranteed on-time delivery), Nike (performance), Walmart (low prices), and Facebook (connections and sharing).

» **Figure 7.5** Major Brand Strategy Decisions

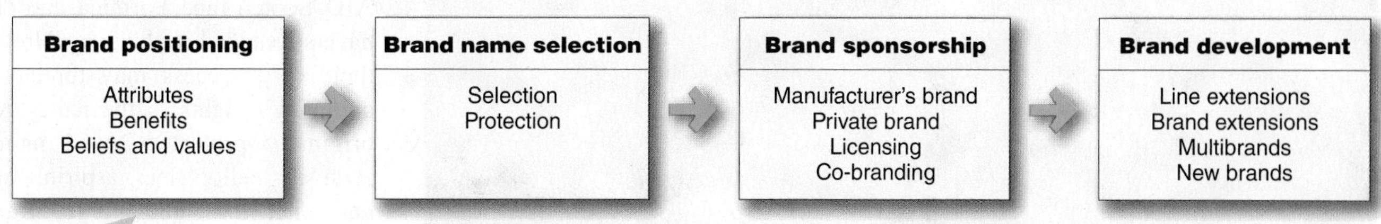

Brands are powerful assets that must be carefully developed and managed. As this figure suggests, building strong brands involves many challenging decisions.

The strongest brands go beyond attribute or benefit positioning. They are positioned on strong *beliefs and values,* engaging customers on a deep, emotional level. For example, to parents, Pampers mean much more than just containment and dryness. The "Pampers village" Web site (www.pampers.com) positions Pampers as a "where we grow together" brand that's concerned about happy babies, parent–child relationships, and total baby care. Says a former P&G executive, "Our baby care business didn't start growing aggressively until we changed Pampers from being about dryness to helping mom with her baby's development."[33]

Successful brands engage customers on a deep, emotional level. Advertising agency Saatchi & Saatchi suggests that brands should strive to become *lovemarks*, products or services that "inspire loyalty beyond reason." Brands ranging from Apple, Google, Disney, and Coca-Cola to Nike, Trader Joe's, Facebook, In-N-Out Burger, and Hallmark have achieved this status with many of their customers. Lovemark brands pack an emotional wallop. Customers don't just like these brands, they have strong emotional connections with them and love them unconditionally.[34]

When positioning a brand, the marketer should establish a mission for the brand and a vision of what the brand must be and do. A brand is the company's promise to deliver a specific set of features, benefits, services, and experiences consistently to buyers. The brand promise must be simple and honest. Motel 6, for example, offers clean rooms, low prices, and good service but does not promise expensive furnishings or large bathrooms. In contrast, The Ritz-Carlton offers luxurious rooms and a truly memorable experience but does not promise low prices.

Brand Name Selection

A good name can add greatly to a product's success. However, finding the best brand name is a difficult task. It begins with a careful review of the product and its benefits, the target market, and proposed marketing strategies. After that, naming a brand becomes part science, part art, and a measure of instinct.

Desirable qualities for a brand name include the following: (1) It should suggest something about the product's benefits and qualities: Beautyrest, Lean Cuisine, Mop & Glo. (2) It should be easy to pronounce, recognize, and remember: iPad, Tide, Jelly Belly, Facebook, JetBlue. (3) The brand name should be distinctive: Panera, Flickr, Swiffer, Zappos. (4) It should be extendable—Amazon.com began as an online bookseller but chose a name that would allow expansion into other categories. (5) The name should translate easily into foreign languages. Before changing its name to Exxon, Standard Oil of New Jersey rejected the name Enco, which it learned meant a stalled engine when pronounced in Japanese. (6) It should be capable of registration and legal protection. A brand name cannot be registered if it infringes on existing brand names.

Choosing a new brand name is hard work. After a decade of choosing quirky names (Yahoo!, Google) or trademark-proof made-up names (Novartis, Aventis, Accenture), today's style is to build brands around names that have real meaning. For example, names like Silk (soy milk), Method (home products), Smartwater (beverages), and Blackboard (school software) are simple and make intuitive sense. But with trademark applications soaring, *available* new names can be hard to find. Try it yourself. Pick a product and see if you can come up with a better name for it. How about Moonshot? Tickle? Vanilla? Treehugger? Simplicity? Google them and you'll find that they're already taken.

Once chosen, the brand name must be protected. Many firms try to build a brand name that will eventually become identified with the product category. Brand names such

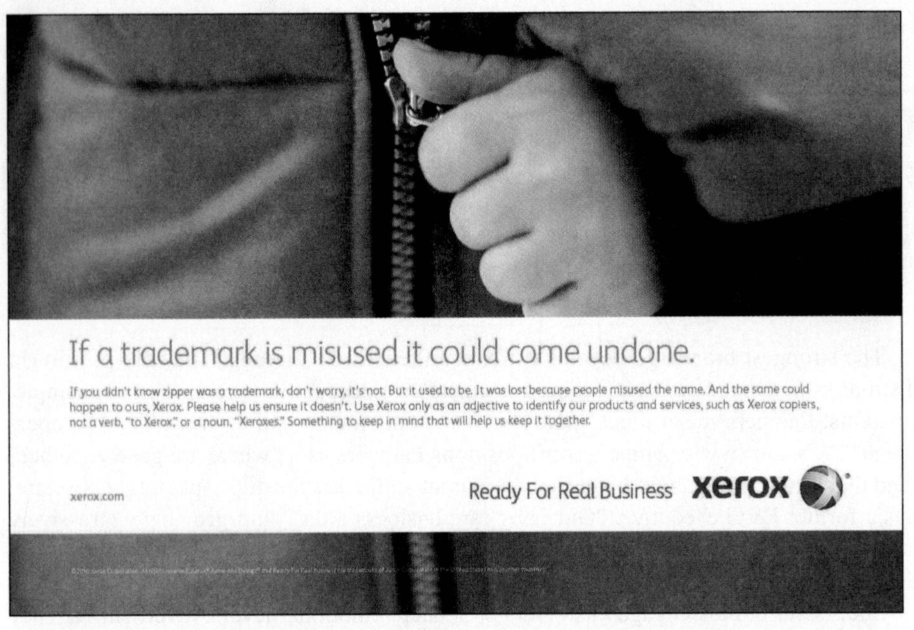

If a trademark is misused it could come undone.
If you didn't know zipper was a trademark, don't worry, it's not. But it used to be. It was lost because people misused the name. And the same could happen to ours, Xerox. Please help us ensure it doesn't. Use Xerox only as an adjective to identify our products and services, such as Xerox copiers, not a verb, "to Xerox," or a noun, "Xeroxes." Something to keep in mind that will help us keep it together.
xerox.com
Ready For Real Business
xerox

Protecting a brand name: This ad asks people to use the Xerox name only as an adjective to identify its products and services (such as "Xerox copiers"), not as a verb ("to Xerox" something) or a noun ("I'll make a Xerox").

Associated Press.

as Kleenex, Levi's, JELL-O, BAND-AID, Scotch Tape, Formica, and Ziploc have succeeded in this way. However, their very success may threaten the company's rights to the name. Many originally protected brand names—such as cellophane, aspirin, nylon, kerosene, linoleum, yo-yo, trampoline, escalator, thermos, and shredded wheat—are now generic names that any seller can use.

To protect their brands, marketers present them carefully using the word brand and the registered trademark symbol, as in "BAND-AID® Brand Adhesive Bandages." Even the long-standing "I am stuck on BAND-AID 'cause BAND-AID's stuck on me" jingle has now become "I am stuck on BAND-AID brand 'cause BAND-AID's stuck on me." Similarly, a recent Xerox advertisement notes that a brand name can be lost if people misuse it. The ad asks people to use the Xerox name only as an adjective to identify its products and services (such as "Xerox copiers"), not as a verb ("to Xerox" something) or a noun ("I'll make a Xerox").

Brand Sponsorship

A manufacturer has four sponsorship options. The product may be launched as a *national brand* (or *manufacturer's brand*), as when Samsung and Kellogg sell their output under their own brand names (the Samsung Galaxy tablet or Kellogg's Frosted Flakes). Or the manufacturer may sell to resellers who give the product a *private brand* (also called a *store brand* or *distributor brand*). Although most manufacturers create their own brand names, others market *licensed brands*. Finally, two companies can join forces and *co-brand* a product. We discuss each of these options in turn.

Store brand (or private brand)
A brand created and owned by a reseller of a product or service.

National Brands versus Store Brands. National brands (or manufacturers' brands) have long dominated the retail scene. In recent times, however, increasing numbers of retailers and wholesalers have created their own **store brands** (or **private brands**). Store brands have been gaining strength for more than two decades, but recent tighter economic times have created a store-brand boom. Studies show that consumers are now buying even more private brands, which on average yield a 25 percent savings. "[Thrifty] times are good times for private labels," says a brand expert. "As consumers become more price-conscious, they also become less brand-conscious."[35]

In fact, store brands are growing much faster than national brands. Over the past six years, whereas most food categories have been struggling, private labels have grown at a rate of 6 percent per year. Over the past decade, annual sales of private-brand goods have increased more than 40 percent in supermarkets and an incredible 96 percent in drug stores. Private labels now account for almost 18 percent of supermarket dollar sales. Similarly, for apparel sales, private-label brands—such as Hollister, The Limited, Arizona Jean Company (JCPenney), and Xhilaration (Target)—now capture a 50 percent share of all U.S. apparel sales, up from 25 percent a decade ago.[36]

Many large retailers skillfully market a deep assortment of store-brand merchandise. For example, Walmart's private brands account for a whopping 25 percent of its sales: brands such as Great Value food products; Sam's Choice beverages; Equate pharmacy, health, and beauty products; White Cloud brand toilet tissue and diapers; Simple Elegance laundry products; and Canopy outdoor home products. Its private-label brands alone generate nearly twice the sales of all P&G brands combined, and Walmart's Great Value is

The popularity of store brands has soared recently. Walmart's store brands account for a whopping 25 percent of its sales, and its Great Value brand is the nation's largest single food brand.

Photo courtesy of Gary Armstrong.

the nation's largest single food brand. At the other end of the grocery spectrum, upscale Whole Foods Market offers an array of store-brand products under its 365 Everyday Value brand, from organic Canadian maple syrup and frozen chicken Caesar pizza to chewy children's multivitamins and organic whole-wheat pasta.[37]

Once known as "generic" or "no-name" brands, today's store brands are shedding their image as cheap knockoffs of national brands. Store brands now offer much greater selection, and they are rapidly achieving name-brand quality. In fact, retailers such as Target and Trader Joe's are out-innovating many of their national-brand competitors. As a result, consumers are becoming loyal to store brands for reasons besides price. Recent research showed that 44 percent of grocery shoppers believe that store brands are produced in the same factory as national brands, and 59 percent think that national brands are more expensive because of advertising costs, not better quality.[38] In some cases, consumers are even willing to pay more for store brands that have been positioned as gourmet or premium items.

In the so-called *battle of the brands* between national and private brands, retailers have many advantages. They control what products they stock, where they go on the shelf, what prices they charge, and which ones they will feature in local promotions. Retailers often price their store brands lower than comparable national brands and feature the price differences in side-by-side comparisons on store shelves. Although store brands can be hard to establish and costly to stock and promote, they also yield higher profit margins for the reseller. And they give resellers exclusive products that cannot be bought from competitors, resulting in greater store traffic and loyalty. Fast-growing retailer Trader Joe's, which carries 80 percent store brands, largely controls its own brand destiny, rather than relying on producers to make and manage the brands it needs to serve its customers best.

To compete with store brands, national brands must sharpen their value propositions, especially when appealing to today's more frugal consumers. Many national brands are fighting back by rolling out more discounts and coupons to defend their market share. In the long run, however, leading brand marketers must compete by investing in new brands, new features, and quality improvements that set them apart. They must design strong advertising programs to maintain high awareness and preference. And they must find ways to partner with major distributors to find distribution economies and improve joint performance.

For example, in response to the recent surge in private-label sales, consumer product giant Procter & Gamble has redoubled its efforts to develop and promote new and better products, particularly at lower price points. "We invest $2 billion a year in research and development, $400 million on consumer knowledge, and about 10 percent of sales on advertising," says P&G's CEO, Bob McDonald. "Store brands don't have that capacity." As a result, P&G brands such as Tide and Gain still dominate in their categories, with combined sales of more than $6.5 billion worldwide.[39]

Licensing. Most manufacturers take years and spend millions to create their own brand names. However, some companies license names or symbols previously created by other manufacturers, names of well-known celebrities, or characters from popular movies and books. For a fee, any of these can provide an instant and proven brand name.

Apparel and accessories sellers pay large royalties to adorn their products—from blouses to ties and linens to luggage—with the names or initials of well-known fashion innovators such as Calvin Klein, Tommy Hilfiger, Gucci, or Armani. Sellers of children's products attach an almost endless list of character names to clothing, toys, school supplies, linens, dolls, lunch boxes, cereals, and other items. Licensed character names range from classics such as Sesame Street, Disney, Barbie, Star Wars, Scooby Doo, Hello Kitty, and Dr. Seuss characters to the more recent Dora the Explorer, Go, Diego, Go!, Angry Birds,

Licensing: Disney is the world's largest licensor with a studio full of hugely popular characters, from the Disney Princesses to the heroes from Cars.

and Ben 10. And currently, numerous top-selling retail toys are products based on television shows and movies.

Name and character licensing has grown rapidly in recent years. Annual retail sales of licensed products worldwide have grown from only $4 billion in 1977 to $55 billion in 1987 and more than $182 billion today. Licensing can be a highly profitable business for many companies. >> For example, Disney is the world's biggest licensor with a studio full of hugely popular characters, from the Disney Princesses and Disney Fairies to heroes from *Toy Story* and *Cars*, to classic characters such as Mickey and Minnie Mouse. Disney characters reaped a reported $37.5 billion in worldwide merchandise sales last year. By themselves, the Disney Princesses made $1.6 billion in North American retail sales and more than $3 billion worldwide.[40]

Co-branding
The practice of using the established brand names of two different companies on the same product.

Co-branding. **Co-branding** occurs when two established brand names of different companies are used on the same product. Co-branding offers many advantages. Because each brand dominates in a different category, the combined brands create broader consumer appeal and greater brand equity. For example, Pillsbury and Cinnabon joined forces to create Pillsbury Cinnabon cinnamon rolls. Benjamin Moore and Pottery Barn teamed up to create a special collection of Benjamin Moore paint colors designed to perfectly coordinate with Pottery Barn's unique furnishings and accents. And Dairy Queen and the Girl Scouts teamed up to create Girl Scout limited edition cookie-filled Blizzards. The Thin Mint Blizzard is the most popular DQ limited edition to date, selling more than 10 million in one month.

Co-branding can take advantage of the complementary strengths of two brands. For example, the Tim Hortons coffee chain has established co-branded Tim Hortons–Cold Stone Creamery shops. Tim Hortons is strong in the morning and midday periods, with coffee and baked goods, soups, and sandwiches. By contrast, Cold Stone Creamery's ice cream snacks are strongest in the afternoon and evening, which are Tim Hortons's nonpeak periods. The co-branded locations offer customers a reason to visit morning, noon, and night.[41]

Co-branding also allows a company to expand its existing brand into a category it might otherwise have difficulty entering alone. For example, Nike and Apple co-branded the Nike+iPod Sport Kit, which lets runners link their Nike shoes with their iPods to track and enhance running performance in real time. "Your iPod Nano [or iPod Touch] becomes your coach. Your personal trainer. Your favorite workout companion." The Nike+iPod arrangement gives Apple a presence in the sports and fitness market. At the same time, it helps Nike bring new value to its customers.[42]

Co-branding can also have limitations. Such relationships usually involve complex legal contracts and licenses. Co-branding partners must carefully coordinate their advertising, sales promotion, and other marketing efforts. Finally, when co-branding, each partner must trust that the other will take good care of its brand. If something damages the reputation of one brand, it can tarnish the co-brand as well.

Brand Development

A company has four choices when it comes to developing brands (see >> **Figure 7.6**). It can introduce *line extensions*, *brand extensions*, *multibrands*, or *new brands*.

Line extension
Extending an existing brand name to new forms, colors, sizes, ingredients, or flavors of an existing product category.

Line Extensions. **Line extensions** occur when a company extends existing brand names to new forms, colors, sizes, ingredients, or flavors of an existing product category. Thus, the

Figure 7.6 Brand Development Strategies

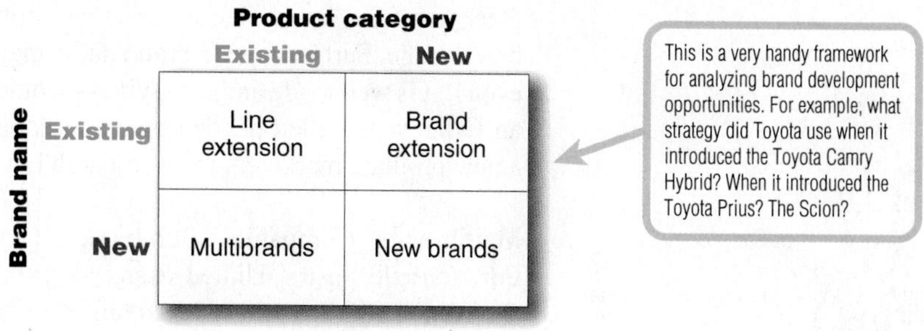

Cheerios line of cereals includes Honey Nut, Frosted, Yogurt Burst, MultiGrain, Banana Nut, and several other variations.

A company might introduce line extensions as a low-cost, low-risk way to introduce new products. Or it might want to meet consumer desires for variety, use excess capacity, or simply command more shelf space from resellers. However, line extensions involve some risks. An overextended brand name might cause consumer confusion or lose some of its specific meaning. For example, Tide offers so many different versions in its popular detergent line that consumers might be baffled as to which one to pick. Not to worry—the Tide Web site provides a four-step selection guide that helps customers "find the Tide that's right for you" based on the laundry challenges they face.

At some point, additional extensions might add little value to a line. For instance, the original Doritos Tortilla Chips have morphed into a U.S. roster of more than 20 different types of chips and flavors, plus dozens more in foreign markets. Flavors include everything from Nacho Cheese and Pizza Supreme to Blazin' Buffalo & Ranch, Fiery Fusion, and Salsa Verde. Or how about duck-flavored Gold Peking Duck Chips or wasabi-flavored Mr. Dragon's Fire Chips (Japan)? Although the line seems to be doing well with global sales of nearly $5 billion, the original Doritos chips seem like just another flavor.[43] And how much would adding yet another flavor steal from Doritos' own sales versus those of competitors? A line extension works best when it takes sales away from competing brands, not when it "cannibalizes" the company's other items.

Brand extension
Extending an existing brand name to new product categories.

Brand Extensions. A **brand extension** extends a current brand name to new or modified products in a new category. For example, Kellogg's has extended its Special K cereal brand into a full line of cereals plus lines of crackers, fruit crisps, snack and nutrition bars, breakfast shakes, protein waters, and other health and nutrition products. Starbucks extended its retail coffee shops by adding packaged supermarket coffees and even a single-serve home coffee, espresso, and latte machine—the Verismo. Furniture retailer IKEA recently launched a line of prefabricated houses under the IKEA Aktiv brand (let's see how that works out!). And P&G has leveraged the strength of its Mr. Clean household cleaner brand to launch several new lines: cleaning pads (Magic Eraser), bathroom cleaning tools (Magic Reach), and home auto cleaning kits (Mr. Clean AutoDry). It even launched Mr. Clean–branded car washes.

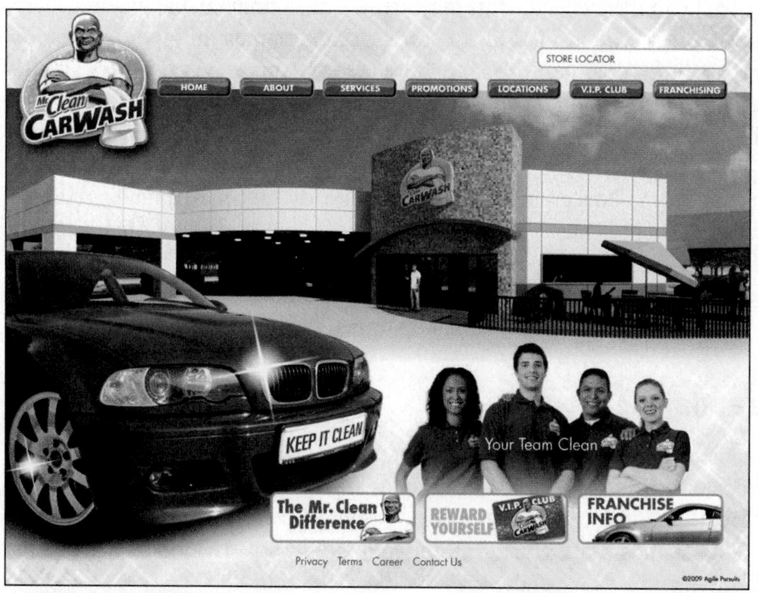

Brand extensions: P&G has leveraged the strength of its Mr. Clean brand to launch new lines, including Mr. Clean–branded car washes.

The Procter & Gamble Company.

A brand extension gives a new product instant recognition and faster acceptance. It also saves the high advertising costs usually required to build a new brand name. At the same time, a brand extension strategy involves some risk. The extension may confuse the image of the main brand—for example, how about Zippo perfume or Dr. Pepper marinades? Brand extensions such as Cheetos lip balm, Heinz pet food, and Life Savers gum met early deaths.[44] And if a brand extension fails, it may harm consumer attitudes toward other products carrying the same brand name. Furthermore, a brand name may not be appropriate to a particular new product, even if it is well made and satisfying—would you consider flying on Hooters Air or wearing an Evian water-filled padded bra (both failed)? Thus, before transferring a brand name to a new product, marketers must research how well the product fits the brand's associations.

Multibrands. Companies often market many different brands in a given product category. For example, in the United States, PepsiCo markets at least five brands of soft drinks (Pepsi, Sierra Mist, Slice, Mountain Dew, and Mug root beer), four brands of sports and energy drinks (Gatorade, No Fear, Propel, and AMP Energy), five brands of bottled teas and coffees (Lipton, SoBe, Seattle's Best, Starbucks, and Tazo), two brands of bottled waters (Aquafina and SoBe), and two brands of fruit drinks (Tropicana and Ocean Spray). Each brand includes a long list of sub-brands. For instance, SoBe consists of SoBe Teas & Elixers, SoBe Lifewater, SoBe Lean, and SoBe Lifewater with Purevia. Aquafina includes regular Aquafina, Aquafina Flavorsplash, and Aquafina Sparkling.

Multibranding offers a way to establish different features that appeal to different customer segments, lock up more reseller shelf space, and capture a larger market share. For example, although PepsiCo's many brands of beverages compete with one another on supermarket shelves, the combined brands reap a much greater overall market share than any single brand ever could. Similarly, by positioning multiple brands in multiple segments, Pepsi's five soft drink brands combine to capture much more market share than any single brand could capture by itself.

A major drawback of multibranding is that each brand might obtain only a small market share, and none may be very profitable. The company may end up spreading its resources over many brands instead of building a few brands to a highly profitable level. These companies should reduce the number of brands they sell in a given category and set up tighter screening procedures for new brands. This happened to GM, which in recent years has cut numerous brands from its portfolio, including Saturn, Oldsmobile, Pontiac, Hummer, and Saab. Similarly, as part of its recent turnaround, Ford dropped its Mercury line, sold off Volvo, and pruned the number of Ford nameplates from 97 to fewer than 20. Says Ford CEO Alan Mulally, "I mean, we had 97 of [models, for goodness] sake! How you gonna make 'em all cool? You gonna come in at 8 a.m. and say 'from 8 until noon I'm gonna make No. 64 cool? And then I'll make No. 17 cool after lunch?' It was ridiculous."[45]

New Brands. A company might believe that the power of its existing brand name is waning, so a new brand name is needed. Or it may create a new brand name when it enters a new product category for which none of its current brand names are appropriate. For example, Toyota created the separate Lexus brand aimed at luxury car consumers and the Scion brand, targeted toward Millennial consumers.

As with multibranding, offering too many new brands can result in a company spreading its resources too thin. And in some industries, such as consumer packaged goods, consumers and retailers have become concerned that there are already too many brands, with too few differences between them. Thus, P&G, PepsiCo, Kraft, and other large marketers of consumer products are now pursuing megabrand strategies—weeding out weaker or slower-growing brands and focusing their marketing dollars on brands that can achieve the number-one or number-two market share positions with good growth prospects in their categories.

Managing Brands

Companies must manage their brands carefully. First, the brand's positioning must be continuously communicated to consumers. Major brand marketers often spend huge amounts on advertising to create brand awareness and build preference and loyalty. For example, worldwide, Coca-Cola spends almost $2.9 billion annually to advertise its many brands, GM spends $3.3 billion, and P&G spends an astounding $9.3 billion.[46]

Such advertising campaigns can help create name recognition, brand knowledge, and perhaps even some brand preference. However, the fact is that brands are not maintained by advertising but by customers' *brand experiences*. Today, customers come to know a

» **Managing brands requires managing "touch points." Says a former Disney executive: "A brand is a living entity, and it is enriched or undermined cumulatively over time, the product of a thousand small gestures."**

Joe Raedle/Getty Images.

brand through a wide range of contacts and touch points. These include advertising but also personal experience with the brand, word of mouth and social media, company Web pages and mobile apps, and many others. The company must put as much care into managing these touch points as it does into producing its ads. » As one former Disney top executive put it: "A brand is a living entity, and it is enriched or undermined cumulatively over time, the product of a thousand small gestures."[47]

The brand's positioning will not take hold fully unless everyone in the company lives the brand. Therefore, the company needs to train its people to be customer centered. Even better, the company should carry on internal brand building to help employees understand and be enthusiastic about the brand promise. Many companies go even further by training and encouraging their distributors and dealers to serve their customers well.

Finally, companies need to periodically audit their brands' strengths and weaknesses. They should ask: Does our brand excel at delivering benefits that consumers truly value? Is the brand properly positioned? Do all of our consumer touch points support the brand's positioning? Do the brand's managers understand what the brand means to consumers? Does the brand receive proper, sustained support? The brand audit may turn up brands that need more support, brands that need to be dropped, or brands that must be rebranded or repositioned because of changing customer preferences or new competitors.

MyMarketingLab

Go to **mymktlab.com** to complete the problems marked with this icon .

END OF CHAPTER REVIEWING THE CONCEPTS

CHAPTER REVIEW AND KEY TERMS

Objectives Review

A product is more than a simple set of tangible features. Each product or service offered to customers can be viewed on three levels. The *core customer value* consists of the core problem-solving benefits that consumers seek when they buy a product. The *actual product* exists around the core and includes the quality level, features, design, brand name, and packaging. The *augmented product* is the actual product plus the various services and benefits offered with it, such as a warranty, free delivery, installation, and maintenance.

OBJECTIVE 1 Define *product* and describe the major classifications of products and services. (pp 202–207)

Broadly defined, a *product* is anything that can be offered to a market for attention, acquisition, use, or consumption that might satisfy a want or need. Products include physical objects but also services, events, persons, places, organizations, ideas, or mixtures of these entities. *Services* are products that consist of activities, benefits, or satisfactions offered for sale that are essentially intangible, such as banking, hotel, tax preparation, and home-repair services.

Products and services fall into two broad classes based on the types of consumers who use them. *Consumer products*—those bought by final consumers—are usually classified according to consumer shopping habits (convenience products, shopping products, specialty products, and unsought products). *Industrial products*—those purchased for further processing or for use in conducting a business—include materials and parts, capital items, and supplies and services. Other marketable entities—such as organizations, persons, places, and ideas—can also be thought of as products.

OBJECTIVE 2 Describe the decisions companies make regarding their individual products and services, product lines, and product mixes. (pp 207–214)

Individual product decisions involve product attributes, branding, packaging, labeling, and product support services. *Product attribute* decisions involve product quality, features, and style and design. *Branding* decisions include selecting a brand name and developing a brand strategy. *Packaging* provides many key benefits, such as protection, economy, convenience, and promotion. Package decisions often include designing *labels*, which identify, describe, and possibly promote the product. Companies also develop *product support services* that enhance customer service and satisfaction and safeguard against competitors.

Most companies produce a product line rather than a single product. A *product line* is a group of products that are related in function, customer-purchase needs, or distribution channels. All product lines and items offered to customers by a particular seller make up the *product mix*. The mix can be described by four dimensions: width, length, depth, and consistency. These dimensions are the tools for developing the company's product strategy.

OBJECTIVE 3 Identify the four characteristics that affect the marketing of services and the additional marketing considerations that services require. (pp 214–221)

Services are characterized by four key aspects: they are *intangible*, *inseparable*, *variable*, and *perishable*. Each characteristic poses problems and marketing requirements. Marketers work to find ways to make the service more tangible, increase the productivity of providers who are inseparable from their products, standardize quality in the face of variability, and improve demand movements and supply capacities in the face of service perishability.

Good service companies focus attention on *both* customers and employees. They understand the *service profit chain*, which links service firm profits with employee and customer satisfaction. Services marketing strategy calls not only for external marketing but also for *internal marketing* to motivate employees and *interactive marketing* to create service delivery skills among service providers. To succeed, service marketers must create *competitive differentiation*, offer high *service quality*, and find ways to increase *service productivity*.

OBJECTIVE 4 Discuss branding strategy—the decisions companies make in building and managing their brands. (pp 221–231)

Some analysts see brands as *the* major enduring asset of a company. Brands are more than just names and symbols; they embody everything that the product or the service *means* to consumers. *Brand equity* is the positive differential effect that knowing the brand name has on customer response to the product or the service. A brand with strong brand equity is a very valuable asset.

In building brands, companies need to make decisions about brand positioning, brand name selection, brand sponsorship, and brand development. The most powerful *brand positioning* builds around strong consumer beliefs and values. *Brand name selection* involves finding the best brand name based on a careful review of product benefits, the target market, and proposed marketing strategies. A manufacturer has four *brand sponsorship* options: it can launch a *national brand* (or manufacturer's brand), sell to resellers that use a *private brand*, market *licensed brands*, or join forces with another company to *co-brand* a product. A company also has four choices when it comes to developing brands. It can introduce *line extensions*, *brand extensions*, *multibrands*, or *new brands*.

Companies must build and manage their brands carefully. The brand's positioning must be continuously communicated to consumers. Advertising can help. However, brands are not maintained by advertising but by customers' *brand experiences*. Customers come to know a brand through a wide range of contacts and interactions. The company must put as much care into managing these touch points as it does into producing its ads. Companies must periodically audit their brands' strengths and weaknesses.

Key Terms

Objective 1

Product (p 202)
Service (p 202)
Consumer product (p 205)
Convenience product (p 205)
Shopping product (p 205)
Specialty product (p 205)
Unsought product (p 205)
Industrial product (p 206)
Social marketing (p 207)

Objective 2

Product quality (p 208)
Brand (p 209)
Packaging (p 210)
Product line (p 212)
Product mix (product portfolio) (p 213)

Objective 3

Service intangibility (p 215)
Service inseparability (p 216)
Service variability (p 216)
Service perishability (p 216)
Service profit chain (p 216)
Internal marketing (p 218)
Interactive marketing (p 218)

Objective 4

Brand equity (p 221)
Store brand (private brand) (p 226)
Co-branding (p 228)
Line extension (p 228)
Brand extension (p 229)

DISCUSSION AND CRITICAL THINKING

Discussion Questions

7-1. What is a product? How do consumer products differ from industrial products? (AACSB: Written and Oral Communication; Reflective Thinking)

7-2. Name and briefly describe the important decisions in developing and marketing individual products and services. (AACSB: Written and Oral Communication)

7-3. What is a brand? How does branding help both buyers and sellers? (AACSB: Written and Oral Communication)

7-4. What is a product line? Discuss the various product line decisions marketers make and how a company can expand its product line. (AACSB: Written and Oral Communication)

7-5. What is a product mix? Name and describe the four important dimensions of a product mix. (AACSB: Written and Oral Communication)

7-6. Discuss the four special characteristics of services. In terms of these characteristics, how do the services offered by a doctor's office differ from those offered by a bank? (AACSB: Written and Oral Communication; Reflective Thinking)

Critical Thinking Exercises

7-7. The 2009 Family Smoking Prevention and Tobacco Control Act requires the addition of graphic warning labels on cigarette packaging and advertising. Research this act and the subsequent controversy and write a report of your findings. Also research and include in your report a discussion of whether such labels would reduce smoking in the United States. (AACSB: Written and Oral Communication; Reflective Thinking)

7-8. List the names of the store brands found in the following stores: Walmart, Best Buy, and Whole Foods. Identify the private-label brands of another retailer of your choice and compare the price and quality of one of the products to those of a comparable national brand. (AACSB: Written and Oral Communication; Reflective Thinking)

MINICASES AND APPLICATIONS

Online, Mobile, and Social Media Marketing Mobile Hotspot

You've heard of mobile Wi-Fi hotspots, but one is truly mobile—your car. Automobile manufacturers Audi, Ford, Nissan, and General Motors are equipping cars with 10-inch screens and Internet access. Cadillac's XTS includes an iPad-like touchscreen and voice commands so you can keep in touch with your friends on Facebook. In 2014 General Motors will offer 4G mobile broadband technology in all of its brands, transforming these vehicles into virtual smartphones. The government is concerned that Web access will cause a spike in accidents due to increased driver distraction and wants the devices to only work when the car is in park. Such guidelines are only suggestions, however, leaving car manufacturers to include whatever they think customers want in their vehicles. The industry's argument is that these new gadgets are safer than the handheld ones drivers are already using in their cars. Automakers claim that there will be even fewer buttons than currently found in cars, possibly resulting in greater safety for drivers and passengers.

7-9. Describe the core, actual, and augmented levels of product associated with an automobile. What level does the mobile Wi-Fi system represent? Explain. (AACSB: Written and Oral Communication; Reflective Thinking)

Marketing Ethics $450 Starbucks Gift Card

Just in time for the holidays, Starbucks offered the Limited Edition Medal Starbucks Card for $450, entitling the holder to $400 of Starbucks drinks, goodies, and gold-level Starbucks membership status. The other $50 was to cover the cost to make the steel card. Sounds crazy, doesn't it? Well, the 5,000 super-premium cards, which could only be purchased at the luxury goods Web site Gilt.com, sold out within minutes. Then they popped up on eBay with opening bids starting at $480 and one selling for $1,000! The premium cards are refillable, allowing the owner elite exclusivity. Some criticized Starbucks, claiming it is a card "for the 1 percent" and saying it is "all about status" and that holders of the premium card have something others don't. Starbucks also rolled out a pricey brew for the other 99 percent, charging $7 a cup.

7-10. What is it about Starbucks that the company could sell a gift card for $50 more than the $400 in merchandise the card could purchase? Should a brand be allowed to do that? (AACSB: Written and Oral Communication; Reflective Thinking; Ethical Understanding and Reasoning)

7-11. How has Starbucks positioned its brand? Could this premium gift card offer or $7 cup of coffee harm Starbucks' brand image? (AACSB: Written and Oral Communication; Reflective Thinking)

Marketing by the Numbers Beauty Balm Cannibalization

The newest product in the cosmetic beauty market is BB cream, which combines multiple skin care benefits into one product. BB stands for "beauty balm," and it is heralded as a "worldwide phenomenon" and a "multitasking miracle" by companies in the industry. But rather than creating new demand, this all-in-one product could cannibalize sales of existing products such as moisturizers, sunscreens, anti-aging creams, primers, and foundations offered by cosmetic manufacturers. With BB cream sales reaching $9 million in the United States in less than a year and promising to go much higher, skin care and cosmetic products maker Clinique does not want to miss out on this opportunity. It is introducing a new BB cream product under the Clinique brand name. Although the new BB cream will garner a higher price for the manufacturer ($10.00 per ounce for the BB cream versus $8.00 per ounce for the moisturizer product), it also comes with higher variable costs ($6.00 per ounce for the BB cream versus $3.00 per ounce for the moisturizer product).

7-12. What brand development strategy is Clinique undertaking? (AACSB: Written and Oral Communication; Reflective Thinking)

7-13. Assume Clinique expects to sell 3 million ounces of BB cream within the first year after introduction but expects that half of those sales will come from buyers who would otherwise purchase Clinique's moisturizer (that is, cannibalized sales). Assuming that Clinique normally sells 10 million ounces of moisturizer per year and that the company will incur an increase in fixed costs of $2 million during the first year of production for the BB cream, will the new product be profitable for the company? Refer to the discussion of cannibalization in Appendix 3: Marketing by the Numbers for an explanation of how to conduct this analysis. (AACSB: Written and Oral Communication; Analytical Thinking)

Video Case Life Is Good

You're probably familiar with the Life is good apparel brand. The company features its cheerful logo prominently on everything from T-shirts to dog collars and seems to exude a positive vibe. While this company has found considerable success in selling its wares based on a happy brand image, consumers still aren't getting the complete image that the Life is good founders intended. This video illustrates the challenges a company faces in balancing the customer's role with that of the company in determining a brand's meaning.

After viewing the video featuring Life is good, answer the following questions:

7-14. What are people buying when they purchase a Life is good product?

7-15. What factors have contributed to the Life is good brand image?

7-16. What recommendations would you make to Life is good regarding brand development strategies?

Company Cases 7 Zipcar / 16 Warby Parker / 10 Corning

See Appendix 1 for cases appropriate for this chapter. **Case 7, Zipcar: "It's Not about Cars—It's about Urban Life."** A new company, a new concept, and a brand that transcends function. **Case 16, Warby Parker: Eyewear with a Purpose.** Warby Parker makes high-quality, fashionable eyeglasses at a revolutionary price point—and distributes a free pair of glasses to a person in need for every pair purchased. **Case 10: Corning: Feeding Innovation through the Supply Chain.** As an innovator in glass products, Corning relies on relationships with suppliers and customers to develop new technologies.

MyMarketingLab

Go to **mymktlab.com** for Auto-graded writing questions as well as the following Assisted-graded writing questions:

7-17. A product's package must satisfy many criteria, such as sustainability, convenience, safety, efficiency, functionality, and marketing. Research "packaging awards" and develop a presentation analyzing an award-winning product packaging effort. Describe the organization hosting the award competition, the criteria for selecting winners, and one of the award-winning packages. (AACSB: Written and Oral Communication; Information Technology)

7-18. Suggest ways automobile makers can use social media through new digital devices in today's cars to safely create customer engagement and customer-managed relationships. (AACSB: Written and Oral Communication; Information Technology; Reflective Thinking)

7-19. Mymktlab Only–comprehensive writing assignment for this chapter.

PART 1: DEFINING MARKETING AND THE MARKETING PROCESS (CHAPTERS 1–2)
PART 2: UNDERSTANDING THE MARKETPLACE AND CUSTOMER VALUE (CHAPTERS 3–5)
PART 3: DESIGNING A CUSTOMER VALUE–DRIVEN STRATEGY AND MIX (CHAPTERS 6–14)
PART 4: EXTENDING MARKETING (CHAPTERS 15–16)

8 New Product Development and **Product Life-Cycle Strategies**

CHAPTER ROAD MAP

Objective Outline

- OBJECTIVE 1 **Explain how companies find and develop new product ideas.** New Product Development Strategy 238–239
- OBJECTIVE 2 **List and define the steps in the new product development process and the major considerations in managing this process.** The New Product Development Process 239–248; Managing New Product Development 248–250
- OBJECTIVE 3 **Describe the stages of the product life cycle and how marketing strategies change during a product's life cycle.** Product Life-Cycle Strategies 250–257
- OBJECTIVE 4 **Discuss two additional product issues: socially responsible product decisions and international product and services marketing.** Additional Product and Service Considerations 257–259

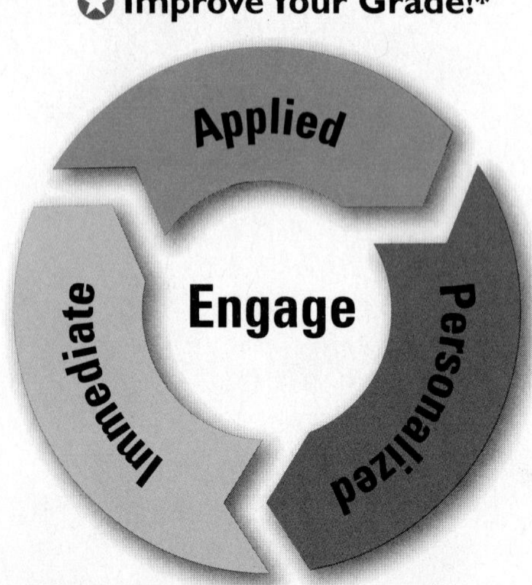

Previewing the Concepts

In previous chapters, you've learned how marketers manage and develop products and brands. In this chapter, we examine two additional product topics: developing new products and managing products through their life cycles. New products are the lifeblood of an organization. However, new product development is risky, and many new products fail. So, the first part of this chapter lays out a process for finding and growing successful new products. Once introduced, marketers then want their products to enjoy long and happy lives. In the second part of this chapter, you'll see that every product passes through several life-cycle stages, and each stage poses new challenges requiring different marketing strategies and tactics. Finally, we wrap up our product discussion by looking at two additional considerations: social responsibility in product decisions and international product and services marketing.

For openers, consider Samsung, the world's leading consumer electronics maker and one of the world's most innovative companies. Over the past two decades, Samsung has transformed itself by creating a culture of customer-focused innovation and a seemingly endless flow of inspired new products that feature stunning design, innovative technology, life-enriching features, and a big dose of "Wow!"

*Over 10 million students improved their results using the Pearson MyLabs. Visit **mymktlab.com** for simulations, tutorials, and end-of-chapter problems.

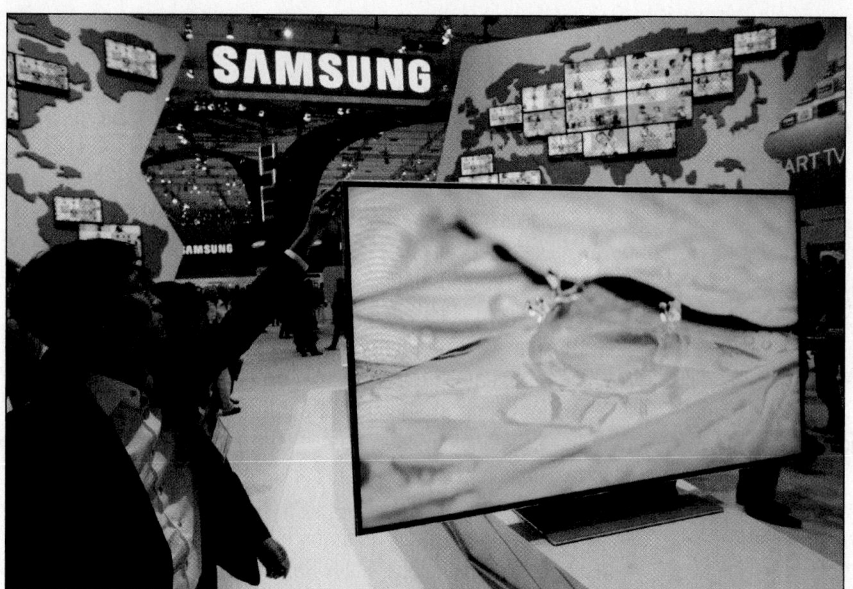

» Beyond cutting-edge technology and stylish design, Samsung puts the customer at the core of its innovation movement. Its new products "bring genuine change to people's lives."

Sean Gallup/Getty Images.

First Stop

Samsung: Enriching Customers' Lives through New Product Innovation

You're probably familiar with the Samsung brand. Maybe you own one of Samsung's hot new Galaxy smartphones that tracks your eye movements to help you navigate the screen, or maybe you've seen one of those dazzling new Samsung slim bezel Smart TVs. You might even be reading this story on a smart new Samsung Galaxy Note or tablet. Samsung, the world's largest consumer electronics manufacturer, produces "gotta-have" electronics in just about every category, from TVs and Blu-ray players, tablets and mobile phones, and laptops and laser printers to digital camcorders and even a full range of home appliances. Chances are good that you or someone you know owns a Samsung product.

But little more than 20 years ago, Samsung was barely known, and it was anything but cutting-edge. Back then, Samsung was a Korean copycat brand that you bought off a shipping pallet at Costco if you couldn't afford a Sony, then the world's most coveted consumer electronics brand. However, in 1993 Samsung made an inspired decision. It turned its back on cheap knock-offs and set out to overtake rival Sony. To dethrone the consumer electronics giant, however, Samsung first had to change its entire culture, from copycat to leading-edge. To out-*sell* Sony, Samsung decided, it first had to out-*innovate* Sony.

Samsung's dramatic shift began with a top-down mandate for reform. Samsung set out to become a premier brand and a trailblazing product leader. The company hired a crop of fresh, young designers and managers, who unleashed a torrent of new products—not humdrum, me-too products, but sleek, bold, and beautiful products targeted to high-end users. Samsung called them "lifestyle works of art." Every new product had to pass the "Wow!" test: If it didn't get a "Wow!" reaction during market testing, it went straight back to the design studio.

Samsung has become the world's leading consumer electronics company through customer-focused innovation and new products that enrich customers' lives. At Samsung, every new product has to pass the consumer "Wow!" test.

Beyond cutting-edge technology and stylish designs, Samsung put the customer at the core of its innovation movement. Its primary innovation goal was to improve the customer experience and bring genuine change to people's lives in everything it did.

With its fresh customer-centered new product focus, Samsung overtook Sony in less than 10 years. Today, Samsung's annual revenues of $185 billion are more than two and one-half times Sony's revenues. And over the past three years, whereas Sony's sales have fallen and losses have mounted in a difficult economy, Samsung's sales and profits have seen double-digit growth. According to brand tracker Interbrand, Samsung is now the world's ninth most valuable brand—ahead of megabrands such as Disney, Pepsi, Nike, and Toyota—and one of the fastest-growing brands in the world.

But more than just being biggest, Samsung has now achieved the new product Wow! factor it sought. For example, Samsung was a dominant force at the two most recent International Design Excellence Awards (IDEA) presentations—the Academy Awards of the design world—which judge new products based on appearance, functionality, and inspirational thinking. Samsung came away as the top corporate winner, claiming seven awards each year, more than twice as many as the next runner-up. Samsung's award-winning products were deemed both stylish and functional, such as a pocket projector that plugs into a USB port, an HD camcorder with a SwitchGrip design for both lefties and righties, and a compact, silicone-rubber-covered external hard drive that protects user's data from impact.

Despite its success, Samsung isn't resting on its innovation laurels. Whatever's next in consumer electronics, Samsung wants to be the first company that finds and develops it. To that end, last year Samsung made an incredible $41 billion technology investment for research and development (R&D), capital expenditures, and new plants and equipment—more than two and one-half times the combined investments of rivals Sony, Toshiba, Hitachi, and Sharp. Further, Samsung's market intelligence and product innovation teams around the globe continually research product usage, purchase behavior, and lifestyle trends, looking for consumer insights and innovative new ways to meet consumer needs.

These days, as consumer technologies become more connected and mobile, Samsung competes less with the Sonys of the world and more with innovation pacesetters like Apple. And against Apple, Samsung is more than holding its own. In mobile devices, for example, Samsung has surged to the top of the market. Just a few years ago, Samsung's goal was to double its market share of smartphones from 5 percent to 10 percent. But the success of its Galaxy line catapulted Samsung's global share to more than 30 percent, well ahead of Apple worldwide.

In its favor, Samsung holds a piece of the technology puzzle that Apple doesn't—big screens. In fact, Samsung has been the global leader in television sales for seven straight years. Its new Smart TVs not only offer gesture control, voice control, and face recognition, but also provide seamless Web connectivity that has TV users Facebooking, Skyping, streaming online content, and using their favorite apps with a wave of the hand. Such features are attractive not just to consumers but also to advertisers wanting to reach them. Samsung hopes to take in lots of advertising dollars from companies eager to pitch their products on screens up to 25 times the size of an iPhone's or iPad's. If successful, Samsung will threaten not just Apple but also cable and satellite companies.

Beyond TVs and mobile devices, Samsung is applying its new product Wow! to categories ranging from household appliances to digital imaging and notebook PCs. Hot off the assembly lines are washing machines with Eco Bubble technology that reduces energy consumption by up to 70 percent; digital cameras with multi-view/multi-angle technology, making it easier for users to capture life's important moments; and Samsung's Series 7 Chronos laptops that start faster, perform faster, and stay charged longer. "All of these are examples of new products that are enriching our customers' lives with innovative technology," says Samsung's CMO.

Twenty years ago, few would have predicted that Samsung could have transformed itself so quickly and completely from a low-cost copycat manufacturer into a world-leading innovator of stylish, high-performing, premium products. But through a dedication to customer-focused new product innovation, that's exactly what Samsung has done. "[We] win by giving consumers what they want," says Samsung Electronics America's president of consumer electronics. "Maybe even . . . features they didn't know they wanted." Whatever gets that "Wow!"[1]

As the Samsung story suggests, companies that excel at developing and managing new products reap big rewards. Every product seems to go through a life cycle: It is born, goes through several phases, and eventually dies as newer products come along that create new or greater value for customers.

This product life cycle presents two major challenges: First, because all products eventually decline, a firm must be good at developing new products to replace aging ones (the challenge of *new product development*). Second, a firm must be good at adapting its marketing strategies in the face of changing tastes, technologies, and competition as products pass through stages (the challenge of *product life-cycle strategies*). We first look at the problem of finding and developing new products and then at the problem of managing them successfully over their life cycles.

New product development
The development of original products, product improvements, product modifications, and new brands through the firm's own product development efforts.

New Product Development Strategy

Author Comment
New products are the lifeblood of a company. As old products mature and fade away, companies must develop new ones to take their place. For example, the iPhone and iPad have been around for less than seven years but are now Apple's two top-selling products.

A firm can obtain new products in two ways. One is through *acquisition*—by buying a whole company, a patent, or a license to produce someone else's product. The other is through the firm's own **new product development** efforts. By *new products* we mean original products, product improvements, product modifications, and new brands that the firm develops through its own research and development (R&D) efforts. In this chapter, we concentrate on new product development.

New products are important to both customers and the marketers who serve them: They bring new solutions and variety to customers' lives, and they are a key source of growth for companies. In today's fast-changing environment, many companies rely on new products for the majority of their growth. For example, new products have almost completely transformed Apple in recent years. The iPhone and iPad—neither of which was available just seven years ago—are now the company's two biggest-selling products, with the iPhone bringing in more than half of Apple's total revenues.[2]

Yet innovation can be very expensive and very risky. New products face tough odds. By one estimate, 66 percent of all new products introduced by established companies fail within two years. By another, 96 percent of all innovations fail to return their development costs.[3] Why do so many new products fail? There are several reasons. Although an idea may be good, the company may overestimate market size. The actual product may be poorly designed. Or it might be incorrectly positioned, launched at the wrong time, priced too high, or poorly advertised. A high-level executive might push a favorite idea despite poor marketing research findings. Sometimes the costs of product development are higher than expected, and sometimes competitors fight back harder than expected.

So, companies face a problem: They must develop new products, but the odds weigh heavily against success. To create successful new products, a company must understand its consumers, markets, and competitors and develop products that deliver superior value to customers.

Author Comment
Companies can't just hope that they'll stumble across good new products. Instead, they must develop a systematic new product development process.

The New Product Development Process

Rather than leaving new products to chance, a company must carry out strong new product planning and set up a systematic, customer-driven *new product development process* for finding and growing new products. **>> Figure 8.1** shows the eight major steps in this process.

Idea Generation

Idea generation
The systematic search for new product ideas.

New product development starts with **idea generation**—the systematic search for new product ideas. A company typically generates hundreds—even thousands—of ideas to find a few good ones. Major sources of new product ideas include internal sources and external sources such as customers, competitors, distributors and suppliers, and others.

Internal Idea Sources

Using *internal sources*, the company can find new ideas through formal R&D. However, in a recent study, only 33 percent of companies surveyed rated traditional R&D as a leading source of innovation ideas. In contrast, 41 percent of companies identified customers as a key source, followed by heads of company business units (35 percent), employees (33 percent), and the sales force (17 percent).[4]

Thus, beyond its internal R&D process, a company can pick the brains of its own people—from executives to salespeople to scientists, engineers, and manufacturing staff. Many companies have developed successful internal social networks and *intrapreneurial* programs that encourage employees to develop new product ideas. For example, Twitter hosts a quarterly "Hack Week: Let's Hack Together" event, which actively promotes

New-product development starts with good new-product ideas—lots of them. For example, Cisco's I-Prize crowdsourcing challenge attracted 824 ideas from 2,900 innovators representing more than 156 countries.

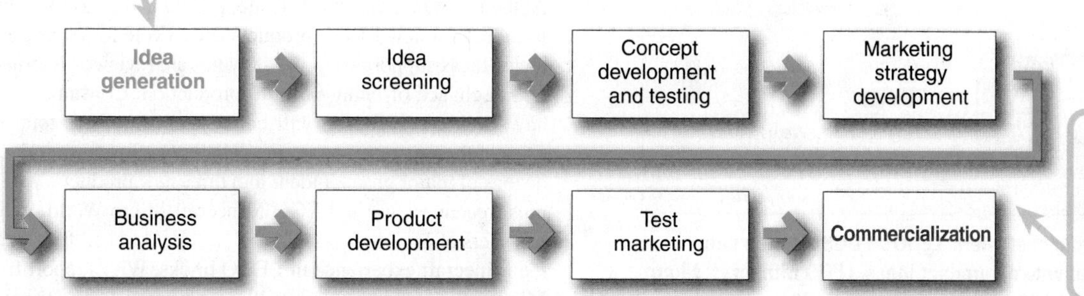

The remaining steps reduce the number of ideas and develop only the best ones into profitable products. Of the 824 ideas from Cisco's I-Prize challenge, only a handful are being developed.

>> Figure 8.1 Major Stages in New Product Development

internal innovation through experimentation around the company:[5]

During Hack Week, a wide range of Twitter folks take time away from their day-to-day work to collaborate and see what crazy cool new things they can develop. Says one employee, "No meetings for a week. No releases for a week. And almost no rules. Go Hack Week!" During the most recent Hack Week, some 100 teams worked on wide-ranging projects, from developing new Twitter products and features to improving the Twitter user experience. "Some projects were technical and strategic; some were simply fun and off the wall, giving people a chance to stretch their creative muscles," says Twitter. Some of the ideas developed during Hack Week will become blockbuster additions; others will fall quietly by the wayside. It's still too soon to tell. "We can't wait to find out," says Twitter. But "one thing we do know: We'll have a bunch of awesome new products, features, and ideas."

Internal product ideas: Twitter hosts an annual "Hack Week: Let's Hack Together" event, which actively promotes internal innovation through experimentation around the company.

External Idea Sources

Companies can also obtain good new product ideas from any of a number of external sources. For example, *distributors and suppliers* can contribute ideas. Distributors are close to the market and can pass along information about consumer problems and new product possibilities. Suppliers can tell the company about new concepts, techniques, and materials that can be used to develop new products.

Competitors are another important source. Companies watch competitors' ads to get clues about their new products. They buy competing new products, take them apart to see how they work, analyze their sales, and decide whether they should bring out a new product of their own. Other idea sources include trade magazines, shows, Web sites, and seminars; government agencies; advertising agencies; marketing research firms; university and commercial laboratories; and inventors.

Perhaps the most important sources of new product ideas are *customers* themselves. The company can analyze customer questions and complaints to find new products that better solve consumer problems. Or it can invite customers to share suggestions and ideas. For example, the Danish-based LEGO Group, maker of the classic LEGO plastic bricks that have been fixtures in homes around the world for more than 60 years, systematically taps users for new product ideas and input:[6]

At the LEGO CUUSOO Web site, LEGO invites users to submit ideas for new LEGO products and to vote for other users' ideas. Ideas supported by 10,000 votes are reviewed internally with a chance of being put into production. Consumers who have their ideas chosen will earn 1 percent of the total net sales of the product. So far, the CUUSOO effort has produced dozens of major product ideas and three new products. The most recent release is LEGO Minecraft Micro World, which lets users of Mojang's popular videogame, Minecraft, recreate the Minecraft experience in LEGO bricks. With support from Minecraft's more than 20 million registered users, the new idea pulled in the required 10,000 votes on CUUSOO in less than 48 hours.

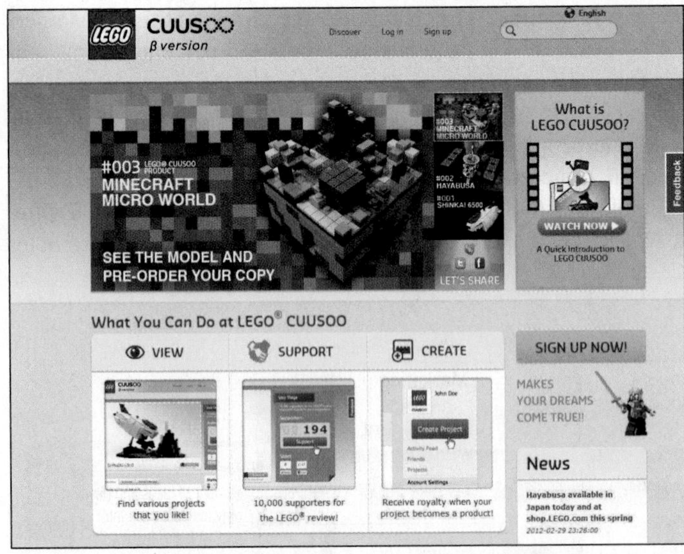

New product ideas from customers: LEGO's CUUSOO Web site invites users to submit and vote on product ideas. LEGO Minecraft Micro World racked up the required 10,000 votes in less than 48 hours.

On a broader level, in developing new product ideas, LEGO actively taps into the AFOL (adult fans of LEGO) community. It has created a roster of customer ambassadors who provide regular input, and it even invites customers to participate directly in the idea-development process. For example, it invited 250 LEGO train-set enthusiasts to visit its New York office to assess new designs. The result was the LEGO Santa Fe Super Chief set, which sold out the first 10,000 units in less than two weeks with virtually no additional marketing. Thus, listening to consumers makes good business sense. "If our fans can tell us there's demand for [something], then why wouldn't we consider it?" asks a LEGO senior product-development executive. "And if we can take something like that and turn it into a runaway success for the business, then that will show the value of listening to our consumers."

Crowdsourcing

Crowdsourcing
Inviting broad communities of people—customers, employees, independent scientists and researchers, and even the public at large—into the new product innovation process.

More broadly, many companies are now developing crowdsourcing or open-innovation new product idea programs. **Crowdsourcing** throws the innovation doors wide open, inviting broad communities of people—customers, employees, independent scientists and researchers, and even the public at large—into the new product innovation process. Tapping into a breadth of sources—both inside and outside the company—can produce unexpected and powerful new ideas. For example, rather than relying only on its own R&D labs to produce all of the new product innovations needed to support growth, Procter & Gamble developed its Connect + Develop crowdsourcing process. Through Connect + Develop, the company uncovers promising innovations from entrepreneurs, scientists, engineers, and other researchers—even consumers themselves—that will help it meet its goal of improving consumers' lives (see Marketing at Work 8.1).

Rather than creating and managing their own crowdsourcing platforms, companies can use third-party crowdsourcing networks, such as InnoCentive, TopCoder, Hypios, and Jovoto. For example, organizations ranging from Facebook and PayPal to ESPN, NASA, and the Salk Institute tap into TopCoder's network of nearly 400,000 mathematicians, engineers, software developers, and designers for ideas and solutions, offering prizes of $100 to $100,000. PayPal recently posted a challenge to the TopCoder community seeking the development of an innovative Android or iPhone app that would successfully and securely run its checkout process, awarding the winners $5,000 each. After only four weeks of competition and two weeks of review, PayPal had its solutions. The Android app came from a programmer in the United States; the iPhone app from a programmer in Colombia.[7]

Crowdsourcing can produce a flood of innovative ideas. In fact, opening the floodgates to anyone and everyone can overwhelm the company with ideas—some good and some bad. For example, when Cisco Systems sponsored an open-innovation effort called I-Prize, soliciting ideas from external sources, it received more than 820 distinct ideas from more than 2,900 innovators from 156 countries. "The evaluation process was far more labor-intensive than we'd anticipated," says Cisco's chief technology officer. It required "significant investments of time, energy, patience, and imagination . . . to discern the gems hidden within rough stones." In the end, a team of six Cisco people worked full-time for three months to carve out 32 semifinalist ideas, as well as nine teams representing 14 countries in six continents for the final phase of the competition.[8]

Truly innovative companies don't rely only on one source or another for new product ideas. Instead, they develop extensive innovation networks that capture ideas and inspiration from every possible source, from employees and customers to outside innovators and multiple points beyond.

Idea Screening

Idea screening
Screening new product ideas to spot good ones and drop poor ones as soon as possible.

The purpose of idea generation is to create a large number of ideas. The purpose of the succeeding stages is to *reduce* that number. The first idea-reducing stage is **idea screening**, which helps spot good ideas and drop poor ones as soon as possible. Product development costs rise greatly in later stages, so the company wants to go ahead only with those product ideas that will turn into profitable products.

Many companies require their executives to write up new product ideas in a standard format that can be reviewed by a new product committee. The write-up describes the product or the service, the proposed customer value proposition, the target market, and the competition. It makes some rough estimates of market size, product price, development

MARKETING AT WORK 8.1

Crowdsourcing: P&G's Connect + Develop

Since its founding more than 175 years ago, Procter & Gamble has set the gold standard for breakthrough innovation and new product development in its industry. P&G's Tide detergent, introduced in the late 1940s, was the first synthetic laundry detergent for automatic washing machines. Its Pampers brand was the first successful disposable diaper, and Crest was the first fluoride toothpaste that really did prevent cavities. Febreze was the first air freshener that eliminated odors rather than just covering them up. And P&G's Olay ProX erases wrinkles more effectively than much-more-expensive prescription anti-aging products. Such breakthrough innovations have been a pivotal element in P&G's incredible growth and success.

Until recently, most of the company's innovations came from within P&G's own R&D labs. P&G invests $2 billion a year in R&D, 50 percent more than its largest competitor and more than most of its other competitors combined. The consumer products giant employs more than 8,000 R&D researchers in 26 facilities around the globe, some of the best research talent in the world. But even with this hefty investment, P&G's own research labs simply can't provide the quantity of innovation required to meet all the growth needs of the $84 billion company.

So about 10 years ago, P&G shook up its research process. It transitioned from an internal R&D model that relied on P&G's own labs to produce needed innovation to an open-innovation model that invites outside partners to help develop new products and technologies that will delight customers.

P&G doesn't want to replace its 8,000 researchers; it wants to leverage them better. The company realized that much of today's important innovation is happening at entrepreneurial companies, universities, and government labs all around the world. For every researcher working at P&G, there are hundreds of scientists and engineers working elsewhere—millions in all. Moreover, thanks to the Internet, the world's talent markets are increasingly linked. P&G needed to change from its old "not-invented-here" culture to one that embraced ideas found elsewhere. "We needed to change how we defined, and perceived, our R&D organization—from [8,000 people inside to 8,000 inside plus millions outside], with a permeable boundary between them," says P&G's vice president for innovation and knowledge.

With this objective in mind, P&G launched Connect + Develop, a major crowdsourcing program for uncovering promising innovation ideas from outside sources anywhere in the world. The Connect + Develop Web site invites entrepreneurs, scientists, engineers, and other researchers—even consumers themselves—to submit ideas for new technologies, product design, packaging, marketing models, research methods, engineering, or promotion—anything that has the potential to create better products and services that will help P&G meet its goal of "improving more consumers' lives." At the site, P&G also provides a list of already-identified innovation needs for which it is seeking solutions. Through Connect + Develop, "we share our R&D, consumer understanding, marketing expertise, and brand equity with our partners, bringing great innovations to market and into the lives of consumers faster," says P&G at the Connect + Develop site. "Together, we can do more than either of us could do alone."

Launched in 2001 with a goal of delivering 50 percent of P&G's innovation through external collaboration, Connect + Develop has far surpassed that objective. Today, P&G collaborates with a truly global innovation network—more than 50 percent of its innovations involve some kind of external partner. So far, Connect + Develop has resulted in more than 2,000 successful agreements. The long list of successful new products brought to market through Connect + Develop includes, among many others, Tide Pods, Tide Total Care, Olay Regenerist, Swiffer Dusters, Glad ForceFlex Bags, Clairol Perfect 10, CoverGirl Eyewear, the Oral B Pulsonic toothbrush, Febreze Candles, and Mr. Clean Magic Eraser.

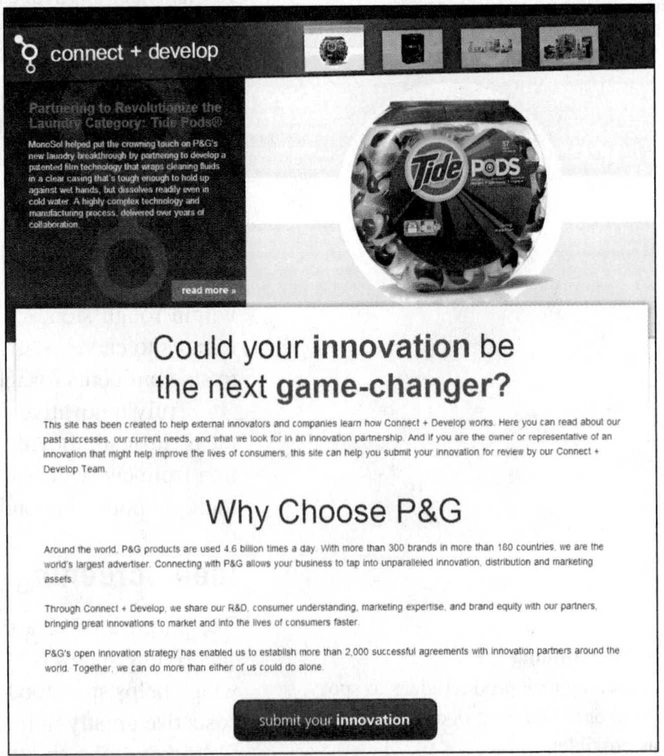

>> P&G's highly successful Connect + Develop crowdsourcing program invites outside innovation partners to help develop new technologies and products that will delight customers.

The Procter & Gamble Company.

Under Connect + Develop, innovative ideas and technologies roll in from a wide diversity of sources, saving P&G both time and money. For example, the new peptide for P&G's blockbuster Olay Regenerist, a $2 billion brand, came from a small French company. The Oral B Pulsonic sonic toothbrush came from a partnership with a Japanese firm—it was in the market less than a year after the first meeting.

Connect + Develop was the source of the idea behind Febreze Candles, which give off a warm glow and pleasing scent as they neutralize pet odors, cooking smells, or other unwanted household odors. P&G provided the Febreze odor-care technology but worked with an external candle company to develop the candles. In turn, Febreze Candles led to the development of the entire Febreze Home Collection—a line of decorative candles, scented reed diffusers, and flameless scented luminaries—that has helped make Febreze another one of P&G's 25-billion-dollar brands.

Similarly, P&G's popular Mr. Clean Magic Eraser—the self-cleaning pads that act like an eraser to lift away tough dirt, including difficult scuff and crayon marks—got its start when an independent technology entrepreneur discovered a stain-removing sponge already on the market in Osaka, Japan, and alerted P&G via Connect + Develop. The product's magic ingredient was a packing foam made by German chemical company BASF, which happened already to be a major P&G supplier. P&G introduced the new product within a year, and it quickly became yet another blockbuster P&G brand.

The Connect + Develop crowdsourcing program has produced big benefits for P&G. Connect + Develop "opened our minds and doors to external collaboration," says Bruce Brown, P&G's chief technology officer. "It changed our culture from 'invented here' to 'partnering for greater value.'" As a result of the program, P&G's R&D productivity has increased 60 percent, and its innovation success rate has more than doubled, even as the cost of innovation has fallen. "Connect + Develop has created a culture of open innovation that has already generated sustainable growth," says P&G CEO Bob McDonald, "but we know we can do more. We want the best minds in the world to work with us to create big ideas that can touch and improve the lives of more consumers, in more parts of the world, more completely."

Sources: Based on quotes and other information in "P&G Connect + Develop Launches New Open Innovation Website," February 7, 2013, http://news.pg.com/press-release/pg-corporate-announcements/pg-connectdevelop-launches-new-open-innovation-website; "P&G Adapts R&D Model," *warc*, January 31, 2012, www.warc.com/LatestNews/News/PG_adapts_RD_model.news?ID=29389; Larry Huston and Nabil Sakkab, "Connect and Develop: Inside Procter & Gamble's New Model for Innovation," *Harvard Business Review*, March 2006, pp. 2–9; Bruce Brown, "Why Innovation Matters," *Technology Management*, November–December 2010, pp. 18–23; "P&G Sets Two New Goals for Open Innovation Partnerships," *PR Newswire*, October 28, 2010; Issie Lapowsky, "Why Every Company Is Now an Incubator," *Inc.*, December 21, 2012, www.inc.com/issie-lapowsky/why-everyone-is-an-incubator-now.html; and the P&G Connect + Develop Web site at www.pgconnectdevelop.com/, accessed October 2013.

---

time and costs, manufacturing costs, and rate of return. The committee then evaluates the idea against a set of general criteria.

One marketing expert describes an R-W-W ("real, win, worth doing") new product screening framework that asks three questions. First, *Is it real?* Is there a real need and desire for the product and will customers buy it? Is there a clear product concept and will such a product satisfy the market? Second, *Can we win?* Does the product offer a sustainable competitive advantage? Does the company have the resources to make such a product a success? Finally, *Is it worth doing?* Does the product fit the company's overall growth strategy? Does it offer sufficient profit potential? The company should be able to answer yes to all three R-W-W questions before developing the new product idea further.[9]

Concept Development and Testing

Product concept
A detailed version of the new product idea stated in meaningful consumer terms.

An attractive idea must then be developed into a **product concept**. It is important to distinguish between a product idea, a product concept, and a product image. A *product idea* is an idea for a possible product that the company can see itself offering to the market. A *product concept* is a detailed version of the idea stated in meaningful consumer terms. A *product image* is the way consumers perceive an actual or potential product.

Concept Development

Suppose a car manufacturer has developed a practical battery-powered, all-electric car. Its initial prototype is a sleek, sporty roadster convertible that sells for more than $100,000.[10] » However, it plans to introduce more-affordable, mass-market versions that will compete with recently introduced hybrid-electric or all-electric cars such as the Chevy Volt and Nissan Leaf. This 100 percent electric car will accelerate from 0 to 60 miles per hour in 4 seconds, travel up to 300 miles on a single charge, recharge in 45 minutes from a normal 120-volt electrical outlet, and cost about one penny per mile to power.

>> Tesla is introducing more-affordable all-electric mass-market models that will travel more than 300 miles on a single charge, recharge in 45 minutes from a normal 120-volt electrical outlet, and cost about one penny per mile to power.

AFP/Getty Images.

Looking ahead, the marketer's task is to develop this new product into alternative product concepts, find out how attractive each concept is to customers, and choose the best one. It might create the following product concepts for this electric car:

- *Concept 1:* An affordably priced midsize car designed as a second family car to be used around town for running errands and visiting friends.
- *Concept 2:* A mid-priced sporty compact appealing to young singles and couples.
- *Concept 3:* A "green" car appealing to environmentally conscious people who want practical, no-polluting transportation.
- *Concept 4:* A high-end midsize utility vehicle appealing to those who love the space SUVs provide but lament the poor gas mileage.

Concept Testing

Concept testing
Testing new product concepts with a group of target consumers to find out if the concepts have strong consumer appeal.

Concept testing calls for testing new product concepts with groups of target consumers. The concepts may be presented to consumers symbolically or physically. Here, in more detail, is concept 3:

> An efficient, fun-to-drive, battery-powered compact car that seats four. This 100 percent electric wonder provides practical and reliable transportation with no pollution. It goes 300 miles on a single charge and costs pennies per mile to operate. It's a sensible, responsible alternative to today's pollution-producing gas-guzzlers. Its fully equipped price is $30,000.

Many firms routinely test new product concepts with consumers before attempting to turn them into actual new products. For some concept tests, a word or picture description might be sufficient. However, a more concrete and physical presentation of the concept will increase the reliability of the concept test. After being exposed to the concept, consumers then may be asked to react to it by answering questions similar to those in **>> Table 8.1**.

The answers to such questions will help the company decide which concept has the strongest appeal. For example, the last question asks about the consumer's intention to buy. Suppose 2 percent of consumers say they "definitely" would buy, and another 5 percent say "probably." The company could project these figures to the full population in this target

>> Table 8.1 Questions for the All-Electric Car Concept Test

1. Do you understand the concept of a battery-powered electric car?
2. Do you believe the claims about the car's performance?
3. What are the major benefits of an all-electric car compared with a conventional car?
4. What are its advantages compared with a gas-electric hybrid car?
5. What improvements in the car's features would you suggest?
6. For what uses would you prefer an all-electric car to a conventional car?
7. What would be a reasonable price to charge for the car?
8. Who would be involved in your decision to buy such a car? Who would drive it?
9. Would you buy such a car (definitely, probably, probably not, definitely not)?

group to estimate sales volume. Even then, however, the estimate is uncertain because people do not always carry out their stated intentions.

Marketing Strategy Development

Marketing strategy development
Designing an initial marketing strategy for a new product based on the product concept.

Suppose the carmaker finds that concept 3 for the electric car tests best. The next step is **marketing strategy development**, designing an initial marketing strategy for introducing this car to the market.

The *marketing strategy statement* consists of three parts. The first part describes the target market; the planned value proposition; and the sales, market-share, and profit goals for the first few years. Thus:

> The target market is younger, well-educated, moderate- to high-income individuals, couples, or small families seeking practical, environmentally responsible transportation. The car will be positioned as more fun to drive and less polluting than today's internal combustion engine or hybrid cars. The company will aim to sell 50,000 cars in the first year, at a loss of not more than $15 million. In the second year, the company will aim for sales of 90,000 cars and a profit of $25 million.

The second part of the marketing strategy statement outlines the product's planned price, distribution, and marketing budget for the first year:

> The battery-powered all-electric car will be offered in three colors—red, white, and blue—and will have a full set of accessories as standard features. It will sell at a retail price of $30,000, with 15 percent off the list price to dealers. Dealers who sell more than 10 cars per month will get an additional discount of 5 percent on each car sold that month. A marketing budget of $50 million will be split 40-30-30 among a national media campaign, online and social media marketing, and local event marketing. Advertising, the Web site, and various social media content will emphasize the car's fun spirit and low emissions. During the first year, $100,000 will be spent on marketing research to find out who is buying the car and what their satisfaction levels are.

The third part of the marketing strategy statement describes the planned long-run sales, profit goals, and marketing mix strategy:

> We intend to capture a 3 percent long-run share of the total auto market and realize an after-tax return on investment of 15 percent. To achieve this, product quality will start high and be improved over time. Price will be raised in the second and third years if competition and the economy permit. The total marketing budget will be raised each year by about 10 percent. Marketing research will be reduced to $60,000 per year after the first year.

Business Analysis

Business analysis
A review of the sales, costs, and profit projections for a new product to find out whether these factors satisfy the company's objectives.

Once management has decided on its product concept and marketing strategy, it can evaluate the business attractiveness of the proposal. **Business analysis** involves a review of the sales, costs, and profit projections for a new product to find out whether they satisfy the company's objectives. If they do, the product can move to the product development stage.

To estimate sales, the company might look at the sales history of similar products and conduct market surveys. It can then estimate minimum and maximum sales to assess the range of risk. After preparing the sales forecast, management can estimate the expected costs and profits for the product, including marketing, R&D, operations, accounting, and finance costs. The company then uses the sales and costs figures to analyze the new product's financial attractiveness.

Product Development

Product development
Developing the product concept into a physical product to ensure that the product idea can be turned into a workable market offering.

For many new product concepts, a product may exist only as a word description, a drawing, or perhaps a crude mock-up. If the product concept passes the business test, it moves into **product development**. Here, R&D or engineering develops the product concept into a physical product. The product development step, however, now calls for a huge jump in investment. It will show whether the product idea can be turned into a workable product.

The R&D department will develop and test one or more physical versions of the product concept. R&D hopes to design a prototype that will satisfy and excite consumers and that can be produced quickly and at budgeted costs. Developing a successful prototype can take days, weeks, months, or even years depending on the product and prototype methods.

Often, products undergo rigorous tests to make sure that they perform safely and effectively, or that consumers will find value in them. Companies can do their own product testing or outsource testing to other firms that specialize in testing.

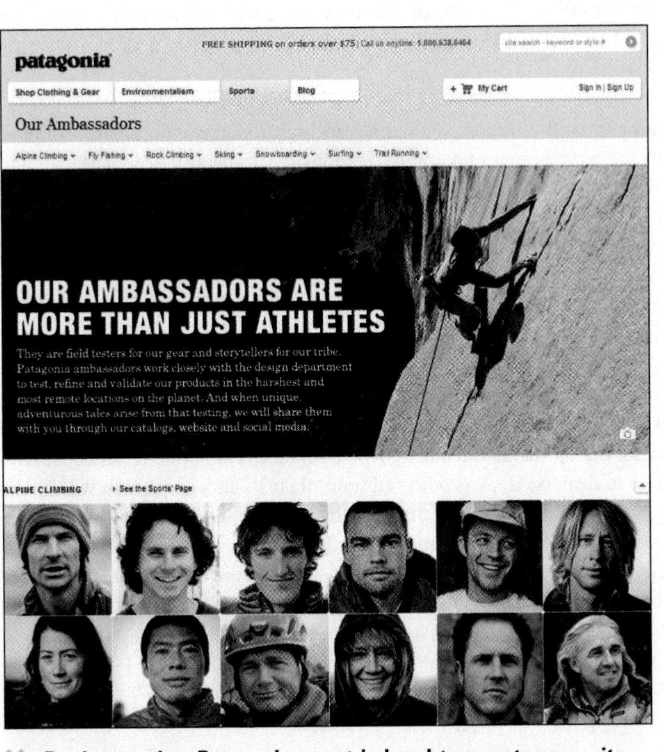

>> Product testing: Patagonia uses tried-and-true customers—its Patagonia Ambassadors—to help field test its products under harsh conditions and help designers refine them.

Patagonia, Inc.

Marketers often involve actual customers in product testing. >> For example, Patagonia selects tried-and-true customers—called Patagonia Ambassadors—to work closely with its design department to field test and refine its products under harsh conditions. Similarly, New Balance's Weartest Program engages consumers throughout the product development process to field test new shoe designs under real-life conditions. Consumer testers attend The New Balance Tester School to learn how to analyze the fit, function, and durability of their assigned test shoes. As they test shoes over an eight-week period, they log on to their Wear Test accounts and complete online surveys and feedback forms documenting their experiences with the test product. Says New Balance, "We believe that subjecting our product line to rigorous field testing ensures that all of our products perform at their peak—so you can too."[11]

A new product must have the required functional features and also convey the intended psychological characteristics. The all-electric car, for example, should strike consumers as being well built, comfortable, and safe. Management must learn what makes consumers decide that a car is well built. To some consumers, this means that the car has "solid-sounding" doors. To others, it means that the car is able to withstand a heavy impact in crash tests. Consumer tests are conducted in which consumers test-drive the car and rate its attributes.

Test Marketing

Test marketing
The stage of new product development in which the product and its proposed marketing program are tested in realistic market settings.

If the product passes both the concept test and the product test, the next step is **test marketing**, the stage at which the product and its proposed marketing program are introduced into realistic market settings. Test marketing gives the marketer experience with marketing a product before going to the great expense of full introduction. It lets the company test the product and its entire marketing program—targeting and positioning strategy, advertising, distribution, pricing, branding and packaging, and budget levels.

The amount of test marketing needed varies with each new product. When introducing a new product requires a big investment, when the risks are high, or when management is not sure of the product or its marketing program, a company may do a lot of test marketing. For instance, Starbucks VIA instant coffee was one of the company's biggest, most risky product rollouts ever. The company spent 20 years developing the coffee and several months testing the product in Starbucks shops in Chicago and Seattle before releasing the product nationally.[12]

However, test marketing costs can be high, and testing takes time that may allow market opportunities to slip by or competitors to gain advantages. A company may do little or no test marketing when the costs of developing and introducing a new product are low, or when management is already confident about the new product. For example, companies often do not test market simple line extensions or copies of competitors' successful products. Companies may also shorten or skip testing to take advantage of fast-changing market developments. That's what Post Foods did when it launched its Honey Bunches of Oats Greek Honey Crunch cereal:[13]

Companies sometimes shorten or skip test marketing to take advantage of fast-changing market developments, as Post did in launching Post Honey Bunches of Oats Greek Honey Crunch cereal in record time.

> When a Post Foods cereal executive informally mentioned to buyers from Walmart and Target that the company was considering a new cereal concept—mixing trendy Greek yogurt with breakfast cereal—the buyers loved the idea. In fact, they loved it so much that they wanted the product on their shelves within six months to take advantage of the Greek yogurt trend. The problem: Post still hadn't invented or market tested the cereal, a process that usually takes a year or more. "We had the nation's biggest retailer and No. 2 retailer give us a slot to deliver this," says a Post product-development executive. And deliver it they did. Post undertook a crash program to overcome technical development challenges while at the same time developing packaging and marketing programs for the new cereal. The result: Post Honey Bunches of Oats Greek Honey Crunch cereal went from concept to store shelf in less than six months, the fastest rollout in Post history. That left almost no time for market testing before launch. However, given the market opportunity, the risks of launching the new product without testing were well worth taking. "Luckily, the product [ended up testing] very well," says the Post executive.

As an alternative to extensive and costly standard test markets, companies can use controlled test markets or simulated test markets. In *controlled test markets*, such as SymphonyIRI's BehaviorScan, new products and tactics are tested among controlled panels of shoppers and stores.[14] By combining information on each test consumer's purchases with consumer demographic and TV viewing information, BehaviorScan can provide store-by-store, week-by-week reports on the sales of tested products and the impact of in-store and in-home marketing efforts. Using *simulated test markets*, researchers measure consumer responses to new products and marketing tactics in laboratory stores or simulated online shopping environments. Both controlled test markets and simulated test markets reduce the costs of test marketing and speed up the process.

Commercialization

Commercialization
Introducing a new product into the market.

Test marketing gives management the information needed to make a final decision about whether to launch the new product. If the company goes ahead with **commercialization**—introducing the new product into the market—it will face high costs. For example, the company may need to build or rent a manufacturing facility. And, in the case of a major new consumer product, it may spend hundreds of millions of dollars for advertising, sales promotion, and other marketing efforts in the first year. For instance, to introduce the Surface tablet, Microsoft spent close to $400 million on an advertising blitz that spanned TV, print, radio, outdoor, the Internet, events, public relations, and sampling. Similarly, Tide spent $150 million on a campaign to launch its Tide Pods in the highly competitive U.S. laundry detergent market.[15]

A company launching a new product must first decide on introduction *timing*. If the new product will eat into the sales of other company products, the introduction may be delayed. If the product can be improved further, or if the economy is down, the company may wait until the following year to launch it. However, if competitors are ready to introduce their own competing products, the company may push to introduce its new product sooner.

Customer-centered new product development
New product development that focuses on finding new ways to solve customer problems and create more customer-satisfying experiences.

Next, the company must decide *where* to launch the new product—in a single location, a region, the national market, or the international market. Some companies may quickly introduce new models into the full national market. Companies with international distribution systems may introduce new products through swift global rollouts. For example, Microsoft launched its Windows 8 operating system with a massive $1 billion global marketing campaign spanning 42 countries. The initial launch featured a series of events that began with preview parties in Shanghai and New York City and the opening of 31 pop-up stores worldwide.[16]

Author Comment
Above all else, new product development must focus on creating customer value. Says a senior Samsung executive, "We get our ideas from the market. The market is the driver."

Managing New Product Development

The new product development process shown in Figure 8.1 highlights the important activities needed to find, develop, and introduce new products. However, new product development involves more than just going through a set of steps. Companies must take a holistic approach to managing this process. Successful new product development requires a customer-centered, team-based, and systematic effort.

Customer-Centered New Product Development

Above all else, new product development must be customer centered. When looking for and developing new products, companies often rely too heavily on technical research in their R&D laboratories. But like everything else in marketing, successful new product development begins with a thorough understanding of what consumers need and value. **Customer-centered new product development** focuses on finding new ways to solve customer problems and create more customer-satisfying experiences.

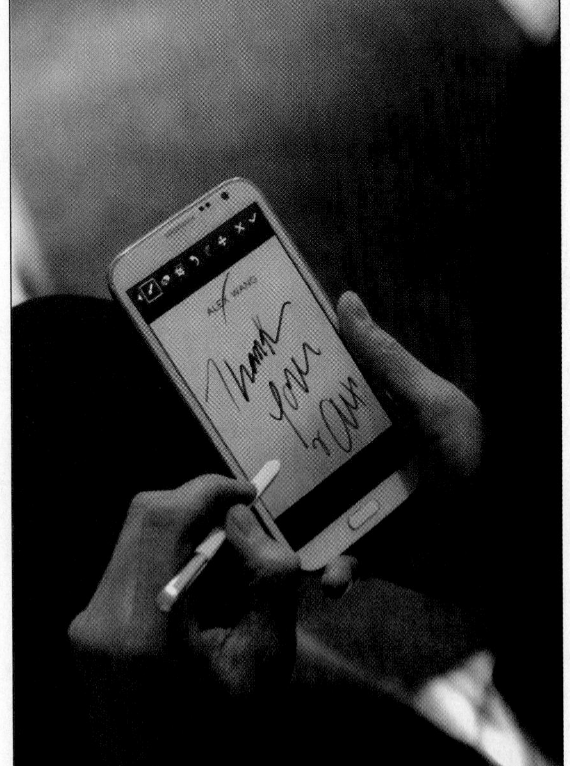

Customer-centered new product development: The idea for Samsung's Galaxy Note "phablet" came from intensive consumer research showing that mobile phone users wanted a device that allows drawing, handwriting, and sharing notes.
PR NEWSWIRE.

One study found that the most successful new products are ones that are differentiated, solve major customer problems, and offer a compelling customer value proposition. Another study showed that companies that directly engage their customers in the new product innovation process had twice the return on assets and triple the growth in operating income of firms that did not. Thus, customer involvement has a positive effect on the new product development process and product success.[17]

As discussed in the chapter-opening story, Samsung is a strong proponent of customer-driven new product development. The company's new product prowess stems from listening to consumers and giving them what they want. Samsung spends nearly 6 percent of revenues on research and development, three times what Apple spends. It regularly polls consumers, pours through piles of consumer data, and even embeds researchers in local markets to study trends and consumer needs and attitudes. For example, the idea for Samsung's Galaxy Note phone (sometimes dubbed a "phablet," with a 5.5-inch display that makes it larger than a phone but smaller than a tablet) came through intensive consumer research. Through surveys, focus groups, and other customer interactions, Samsung learned that many phone users—especially Asians—wanted a device that allows drawing, handwriting, and sharing notes. Such customer insights resulted in the Note's larger screen and digital pen. "We get our ideas from the market," says a senior Samsung executive. "The market is the driver."[18]

Thus, today's innovative companies get out of the research lab and connect with customers in search of fresh ways to meet customer needs. Customer-centered new product development begins and ends with understanding customers and involving them in the process.

Team-Based New Product Development

Good new product development also requires a total-company, cross-functional effort. Some companies organize their new product development process into the orderly sequence of steps shown in Figure 8.1, starting with idea generation and ending with commercialization. Under this *sequential product development* approach, one company department works individually to complete its stage of the process before passing the new product along to the next department and stage. This orderly, step-by-step process can help bring control to complex and risky projects. But it can also be dangerously slow. In fast-changing, highly competitive markets, such slow-but-sure product development can result in product failures, lost sales and profits, and crumbling market positions.

Team-based new product development
New product development in which various company departments work closely together, overlapping the steps in the product development process to save time and increase effectiveness.

To get their new products to market more quickly, many companies use a **team-based new product development** approach. Under this approach, company departments work closely together in cross-functional teams, overlapping the steps in the product development process to save time and increase effectiveness. Instead of passing the new product from department to department, the company assembles a team of people from various departments that stays with the new product from start to finish. Such teams usually include people from the marketing, finance, design, manufacturing, and legal departments and even supplier and customer companies. In the sequential process, a bottleneck at one phase can seriously slow an entire project. In the team-based approach, however, if one area hits snags, it works to resolve them while the team moves on.

The team-based approach does have some limitations, however. For example, it sometimes creates more organizational tension and confusion than the more orderly sequential approach. However, in rapidly changing industries facing increasingly shorter product life cycles, the rewards of fast and flexible product development far exceed the risks. Companies that combine a customer-centered approach with team-based new product development gain a big competitive edge by getting the right new products to market faster.

Systematic New Product Development

Finally, the new product development process should be holistic and systematic rather than compartmentalized and haphazard. Otherwise, few new ideas will surface, and many good ideas will sputter and die. To avoid these problems, a company can install an *innovation management system* to collect, review, evaluate, and manage new product ideas.

The company can appoint a respected senior person to be its innovation manager. It can set up Web-based idea management software and encourage all company stakeholders—employees, suppliers, distributors, dealers—to become involved in finding and developing new products. It can assign a cross-functional innovation management committee to evaluate proposed new product ideas and help bring good ideas to market. It can also create recognition programs to reward those who contribute the best ideas.

The innovation management system approach yields two favorable outcomes. First, it helps create an innovation-oriented company culture. It shows that top management supports, encourages, and rewards innovation. Second, it will yield a larger number of new product ideas, among which will be found some especially good ones. The good new ideas will be more systematically developed, producing more new product successes. No longer will good ideas wither for the lack of a sounding board or a senior product advocate.

Thus, new product success requires more than simply thinking up a few good ideas, turning them into products, and finding customers for them. It requires a holistic approach for finding new ways to create valued customer experiences, from generating and screening new product ideas to creating and rolling out want-satisfying products to customers.

More than this, successful new product development requires a whole-company commitment. At companies known for their new product prowess, such as Google, Apple, 3M, P&G, and GE, the entire culture encourages, supports, and rewards innovation. Consider Google:

> Google is wildly innovative. At many companies, new-product development is a cautious, step-by-step affair. In contrast, Google's new-product development moves at the speed of light. Its famously chaotic innovation process has unleashed a seemingly unending flurry of diverse products, ranging from an e-mail service (Gmail), a blog search engine (Google Blog Search), and a photo sharing service (Google Picasa) to a universal platform for mobile-phone applications (Google Android), a fast and cloud-friendly Web browser (Chrome), projects for mapping and exploring the world (Google Maps and Google Earth), a news channel

» Google is spectacularly successful and wildly innovative. At Google, innovation is more than just a process—"it's in the air, in the spirit of the place."

Felipe Trueba/ZUMAPRESS/Newscom.

(Google News), a social media network (Google+), an ultrahigh-speed Internet service (FiberSpace), and even an early warning system for flu outbreaks (FluTrends). What ties it all together is the company's passion for helping people find and use information.

Innovation is the responsibility of every Google employee. Google engineers are encouraged to spend 20 percent of their time developing their own "cool and wacky" new-product ideas. The company often asks potential employees how they'd change the world if they worked for Google. Google really wants to know—that's how the company operates. "Thinking—and building—on that scale is what Google does" observes one analyst. "This, after all, is the company that wants to make available online every page of every book ever published. Smaller-gauge ideas die of disinterest." » In the end, at Google, innovation is more than a process—it's part of the company's DNA. "It's in the air," says the analyst, "in the spirit of the place."[19]

New Product Development in Turbulent Times

When tough economic times hit, or when a company faces financial difficulties, management may be tempted to reduce spending on new product development. However, such thinking is usually shortsighted. By cutting back on new products, the company may make itself less competitive during or after the downturn. In fact, tough times might call for even greater new product development, as the company struggles to better align its market offerings with changing consumer needs and tastes. In difficult times, innovation more often helps than hurts in making the company more competitive and positioning it better for the future.

Companies such as Apple, Google, Samsung, and Amazon keep the innovations flowing during down economic times. For example, Apple created its blockbuster iPod, iPhone, and iTunes innovations in the midst of some very difficult times it faced more than a decade ago. Those innovations not only saved the company, they propelled in into the innovative powerhouse it is today. Thus, rain or shine, good times or bad, a company must continue to innovate and develop new products if it wants to grow and prosper.

SPEED BUMP LINKING THE CONCEPTS

Take a break. Think about new products and how companies find and develop them.

- Suppose that you're on a panel to nominate the "best new products of the year." What products would you nominate and why? See what you can learn about the new product development process for one of these products.
- Applying the new product development process you've just studied, develop an idea for an innovative new snack-food product and sketch out a brief plan for bringing it to market. Loosen up and have some fun with this.

Author Comment
A company's products are born, grow, mature, and then decline, just as living things do. To remain vital, the firm must continually develop new products and manage them effectively throughout their life cycles.

Product Life-Cycle Strategies

After launching the new product, management wants that product to enjoy a long and happy life. Although it does not expect that product to sell forever, the company wants to earn a decent profit to cover all the effort and risk that went into launching it. Management

Figure 8.2 Sales and Profits over the Product's Life from Inception to Decline

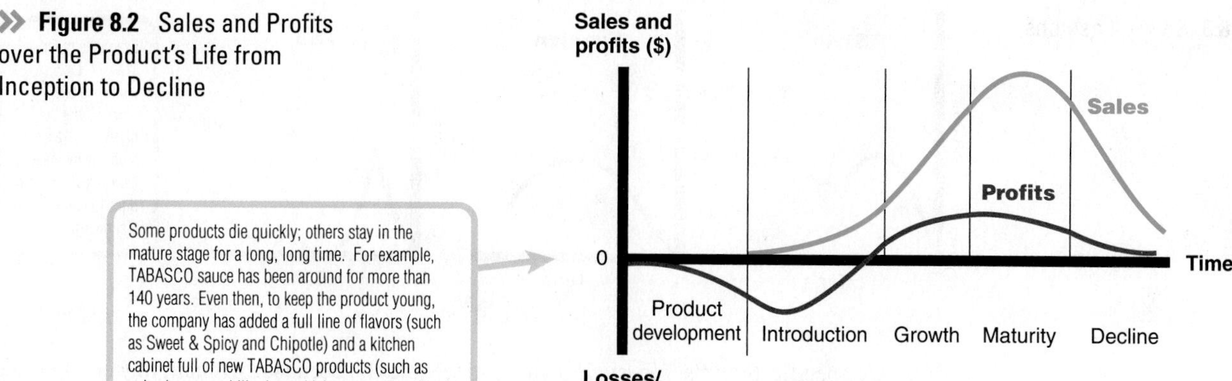

Sales and profits ($)
Sales
Profits
0
Time
Product development
Introduction
Growth
Maturity
Decline
Losses/ investment ($)
Some products die quickly; others stay in the mature stage for a long, long time. For example, TABASCO sauce has been around for more than 140 years. Even then, to keep the product young, the company has added a full line of flavors (such as Sweet & Spicy and Chipotle) and a kitchen cabinet full of new TABASCO products (such as spicy beans, a chili mix, and jalapeno nacho slices).

is aware that each product will have a life cycle, although its exact shape and length is not known in advance.

Product life cycle (PLC) The course of a product's sales and profits over its lifetime.

Figure 8.2 shows a typical **product life cycle (PLC)**, the course that a product's sales and profits take over its lifetime. The PLC has five distinct stages:

1. *Product development* begins when the company finds and develops a new product idea. During product development, sales are zero, and the company's investment costs mount.
2. *Introduction* is a period of slow sales growth as the product is introduced in the market. Profits are nonexistent in this stage because of the heavy expenses of product introduction.
3. *Growth* is a period of rapid market acceptance and increasing profits.
4. *Maturity* is a period of slowdown in sales growth because the product has achieved acceptance by most potential buyers. Profits level off or decline because of increased marketing outlays to defend the product against competition.
5. *Decline* is the period when sales fall off and profits drop.

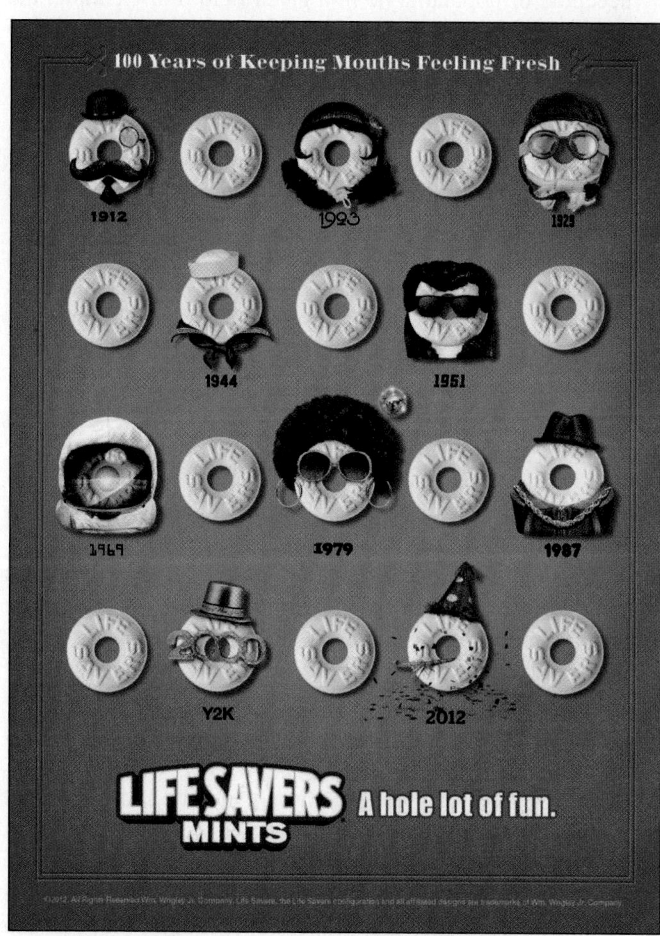

100 Years of Keeping Mouths Feeling Fresh
1912
1923
1929
1944
1951
1969
1979
1987
Y2K
2012
LIFE SAVERS MINTS
A hole lot of fun.

Product life cycle: Some brands stay in the mature stage for a long, long time. Life Savers mints recently celebrated "100 years of keeping your mouth fresh."

The Wrigley Company.

Not all products follow all five stages of the PLC. Some products are introduced and die quickly; others stay in the mature stage for a long, long time. Some enter the decline stage and are then cycled back into the growth stage through strong promotion or repositioning. It seems that a well-managed brand could live forever. Venerable brands like Coca-Cola, Gillette, Budweiser, Guinness, American Express, Wells Fargo, Kikkoman, and TABASCO sauce, for instance, are still going strong after more than 100 years. Guinness beer has been around for more than 250 years, Life Savers mints recently celebrated "100 years of keeping your mouth fresh," and TABASCO sauce brags that it's "over 140 years old and still able to totally whup your butt!"

The PLC concept can describe a *product class* (gasoline-powered automobiles), a *product form* (SUVs), or a *brand* (the Ford Escape). The PLC concept applies differently in each case. Product classes have the longest life cycles; the sales of many product classes stay in the mature stage for a long time. Product forms, in contrast, tend to have the standard PLC shape. Product forms such as "dial telephones" and "VHS tapes" passed through a regular history of introduction, rapid growth, maturity, and decline.

>> Figure 8.3 Styles, Fashions, and Fads

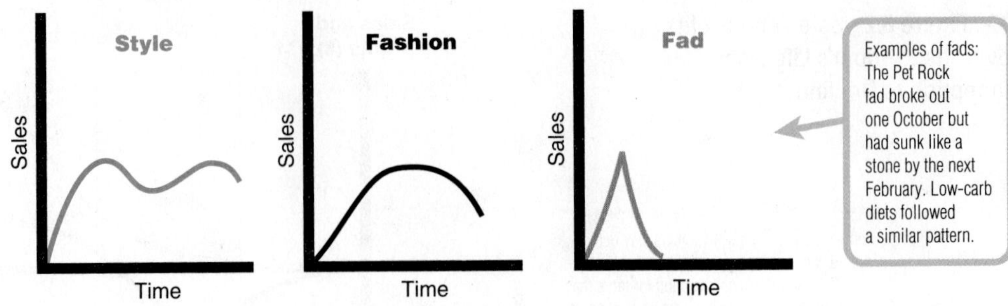
Style
Fashion
Fad
Sales
Sales
Sales
Time
Time
Time
Examples of fads: The Pet Rock fad broke out one October but had sunk like a stone by the next February. Low-carb diets followed a similar pattern.

A specific brand's life cycle can change quickly because of changing competitive attacks and responses. For example, although laundry soaps (product class) and powdered detergents (product form) have enjoyed fairly long life cycles, the life cycles of specific brands have tended to be much shorter. Today's leading U.S. brands of powdered laundry soap are Tide and Gain; the leading brands almost 100 years ago were Fels-Naptha, Octagon, and Kirkman.

Style
A basic and distinctive mode of expression.

Fashion
A currently accepted or popular style in a given field.

Fad
A temporary period of unusually high sales driven by consumer enthusiasm and immediate product or brand popularity.

The PLC concept also can be applied to what are known as styles, fashions, and fads. Their special life cycles are shown in **>> Figure 8.3**. A **style** is a basic and distinctive mode of expression. For example, styles appear in homes (colonial, ranch, transitional), clothing (formal, casual), and art (realist, surrealist, abstract). Once a style is invented, it may last for generations, passing in and out of vogue. A style has a cycle showing several periods of renewed interest.

A **fashion** is a currently accepted or popular style in a given field. For example, the more formal "business attire" look of corporate dress of the 1980s and 1990s gave way to the "business casual" look of the 2000s and 2010s. Fashions tend to grow slowly, remain popular for a while, and then decline slowly.

Fads are temporary periods of unusually high sales driven by consumer enthusiasm and immediate product or brand popularity.[20] A fad may be part of an otherwise normal life cycle, as in the case of recent surges in the sales of poker chips and accessories. Or the fad may comprise a brand's or product's entire life cycle. Pet Rocks are a classic example. Upon hearing his friends complain about how expensive it was to care for their dogs, advertising copywriter Gary Dahl joked about his pet rock. He soon wrote a spoof of a dog-training manual for it, titled "The Care and Training of Your Pet Rock." Soon Dahl was selling some 1.5 million ordinary beach pebbles at $4 a pop. Yet the fad, which broke one October, had sunk like a stone by the next February. Dahl's advice to those who want to succeed with a fad: "Enjoy it while it lasts." Other examples of fads include Silly Bandz, Crocs, and Pogs.[21]

Marketers can apply the product life-cycle concept as a useful framework for describing how products and markets work. And when used carefully, the PLC concept can help in developing good marketing strategies for the different life-cycle stages. However, using the PLC concept for forecasting product performance or developing marketing strategies presents some practical problems. For example, in practice, it is difficult to forecast the sales level at each PLC stage, the length of each stage, and the shape of the PLC curve. Using the PLC concept to develop marketing strategy also can be difficult because strategy is both a cause and a result of the PLC. The product's current PLC position suggests the best marketing strategies, and the resulting marketing strategies affect product performance in later stages.

Moreover, marketers should not blindly push products through the traditional product life-cycle stages. Instead, marketers often defy the "rules" of the life cycle and position or reposition their products in unexpected ways. By doing this, they can rescue mature or declining products and return them to the growth phase of the life cycle. Or they can leapfrog obstacles that slow consumer acceptance and propel new products forward into the growth phase.

The moral of the product life cycle is that companies must continually innovate; otherwise, they risk extinction. No matter how successful its current product lineup, a company must skillfully manage the life cycles of existing products for future success. And to grow, the company must develop a steady stream of new products that bring new value to customers.

We looked at the product development stage of the PLC in the first part of this chapter. We now look at strategies for each of the other life-cycle stages.

Introduction Stage

Introduction stage
The PLC stage in which a new product is first distributed and made available for purchase.

The **introduction stage** starts when a new product is first launched. Introduction takes time, and sales growth is apt to be slow. Well-known products such as frozen foods and HDTVs lingered for many years before they entered a stage of more rapid growth.

In this stage, as compared to other stages, profits are negative or low because of the low sales and high distribution and promotion expenses. Much money is needed to attract distributors and build their inventories. Promotion spending is relatively high to inform consumers of the new product and get them to try it. Because the market is not generally ready for product refinements at this stage, the company and its few competitors produce basic versions of the product. These firms focus their selling on those buyers who are the most ready to buy.

A company, especially the *market pioneer*, must choose a launch strategy that is consistent with the intended product positioning. It should realize that the initial strategy is just the first step in a grander marketing plan for the product's entire life cycle. If the pioneer chooses its launch strategy to make a "killing," it may be sacrificing long-run revenue for the sake of short-run gain. The pioneer has the best chance of building and retaining market leadership if it plays its cards correctly from the start.

Growth Stage

Growth stage
The PLC stage in which a product's sales start climbing quickly.

If the new product satisfies the market, it will enter a **growth stage**, in which sales will start climbing quickly. The early adopters will continue to buy, and later buyers will start following their lead, especially if they hear favorable word of mouth. Attracted by the opportunities for profit, new competitors will enter the market. They will introduce new product features, and the market will expand. The increase in competitors leads to an increase in the number of distribution outlets, and sales jump just to build reseller inventories. Prices remain where they are or decrease only slightly. Companies keep their promotion spending at the same or a slightly higher level. Educating the market remains a goal, but now the company must also meet the competition.

Profits increase during the growth stage as promotion costs are spread over a large volume and as unit manufacturing costs decrease. The firm uses several strategies to sustain rapid market growth as long as possible. It improves product quality and adds new product features and models. It enters new market segments and new distribution channels. It shifts some advertising from building product awareness to building product conviction and purchase, and it lowers prices at the right time to attract more buyers.

In the growth stage, the firm faces a trade-off between high market share and high current profit. By spending a lot of money on product improvement, promotion, and distribution, the company can capture a dominant position. In doing so, however, it gives up maximum current profit, which it hopes to make up in the next stage.

Maturity Stage

Maturity stage
The PLC stage in which a product's sales growth slows or levels off.

At some point, a product's sales growth will slow down, and it will enter the **maturity stage.** This maturity stage normally lasts longer than the previous stages, and it poses strong challenges to marketing management. Most products are in the maturity stage of the life cycle, and therefore most of marketing management deals with the mature product.

The slowdown in sales growth results in many producers with many products to sell. In turn, this overcapacity leads to greater competition. Competitors begin marking down prices, increasing their advertising and sales promotions, and upping their product development budgets to find better versions of the product. These steps lead to a drop in profit.

Some of the weaker competitors start dropping out, and the industry eventually contains only well-established competitors.

Although many products in the mature stage appear to remain unchanged for long periods, most successful ones are actually evolving to meet changing consumer needs. Product managers should do more than simply ride along with or defend their mature products—a good offense is the best defense. They should consider modifying the market, product offering, and marketing mix.

In *modifying the market*, the company tries to increase consumption by finding new users and new market segments for its brands. For example, brands such as Harley-Davidson and Axe fragrances, which have typically targeted male buyers, are introducing products and marketing programs aimed at women. Conversely, Weight Watchers and Bath & Body Works, which have typically targeted women, have created products and programs aimed at men.

The company may also look for ways to increase usage among present customers. » For example, 3M recently ran a marketing campaign to inspire more usage of its Post-it Products:[22]

» Inspiring more usage: The Post-it Brand's "Go Ahead" campaign portrays Post-it products as good for much more than just scribbling temporary notes and reminders. Instead, they are a means of self-expression.

Courtesy of 3M Company. Post-it® is a registered trademark of 3M Company.

> The Post-it Brand's "Go Ahead" campaign hopes to convince customers that their products are good for much more than just scribbling temporary notes and reminders. Instead, it positions Post-it Notes as a means of self-expression by showing creative, nontraditional ways that consumers around the world use them. In the past, 3M promoted mostly functional uses of Post-it products but research showed that consumers have a surprisingly strong emotional relationship with the brand. "They're using it to communicate, using it to collaborate, using it to organize themselves," says a 3M marketing executive. The "Go Ahead" campaign was motivated by customers' "quirky and inspired uses of our product."
>
> An initial ad shows people on a college campus blanketing a wall outside a building with Post-it Notes answering the question, "What inspires you?" "Share on a real wall," the announcer explains. Other scenes show a young man filling a wall with mosaic artwork created from multiple colors of Post-it Notes, teachers using Post-it Notes to enliven their classrooms, and a man posting a "Morning, beautiful" note on the bathroom mirror as his wife is brushing her teeth. "Go ahead," says the announcer, "keep the honeymoon going." The ad ends with a hand pealing Post-it Notes off a pad one by one to reveal new, unexpected uses: "Go Ahead, Connect," "Go Ahead, Inspire," and "Go Ahead, Explore."

The company might also try *modifying the product*—changing characteristics such as quality, features, style, packaging, or technology platforms to retain current users or attract new ones. Thus, to freshen up their products for today's technology-obsessed children, many classic toy and game makers are creating new digital versions or add-ons for old favorites. More than a third of children eight years old and younger now use devices such as tablets and smartphones. So toy makers are souping up their products to meet the tastes of the new generation. For example, the electronic banking edition of Monopoly uses bank cards instead of paper money, Hot Wheels cars can zoom across an iPad using the Hot Wheels Apptivity app, and the Barbie Photo Fashion doll has a digital camera built in. "We know the kids are going to play with technology," says a Mattel executive. "If you can't fix it, feature it."[23]

Finally, the company can try *modifying the marketing mix*—improving sales by changing one or more marketing mix elements. The company can offer new or improved services to buyers. It can cut prices to attract new users and competitors' customers. It can launch a better advertising campaign or use aggressive sales promotions—trade deals, cents-off, premiums, and contests. In addition to pricing and promotion, the company can also move into new marketing channels to help serve new users.

Kellogg used all of these market, product, and marketing mix modification approaches to keep its 50+-year-old Special K brand from sinking into decline. Introduced in 1957 as a healthful, high-protein cereal, Special K had matured by the 1990s—sales were flat and the brand had lost its luster. To reinvigorate the brand, Kellogg first extended the cereal line to include a variety of cereal flavors, such as Red Berries, Vanilla Almond, and Chocolatey Delight. Then, it stretched Special K beyond cereals, turning it into a healthful, slimming lifestyle brand. The expanded line now includes meal and snack bars, protein waters and shakes, crackers and chips, and fruit crisps. To attract new users and more usage, Kellogg promotes the Special K Challenge, a weight-management plan built around Special K products. "Whether your goal is to finally slip into those skinny jeans or you're just looking to become a little more fit and fabulous, the Special K Challenge is a great way to kick-start a better you!" The Special K brand-rejuvenation efforts paid off. The Special K line has grown steadily over the past decade and now accounts for more than $2 billion in annual sales.[24]

Decline Stage

The sales of most product forms and brands eventually dip. The decline may be slow, as in the cases of stamps and oatmeal cereal, or rapid, as in the cases of VHS tapes. Sales may plunge to zero, or they may drop to a low level where they continue for many years. This is the **decline stage**.

Decline stage
The PLC stage in which a product's sales fade away.

Sales decline for many reasons, including technological advances, shifts in consumer tastes, and increased competition. As sales and profits decline, some firms withdraw from the market. Those remaining may prune their product offerings. In addition, they may drop smaller market segments and marginal trade channels, or they may cut the promotion budget and reduce their prices further.

Carrying a weak product can be very costly to a firm, and not just in profit terms. There are many hidden costs. A weak product may take up too much of management's time. It often requires frequent price and inventory adjustments. It requires advertising and sales-force attention that might be better used to make "healthy" products more profitable. A product's failing reputation can cause customer concerns about the company and its other products. The biggest cost may well lie in the future. Keeping weak products delays the search for replacements, creates a lopsided product mix, hurts current profits, and weakens the company's foothold on the future.

For these reasons, companies must identify products in the decline stage and decide whether to maintain, harvest, or drop them. Management may decide to *maintain* its brand, repositioning or reinvigorating it in hopes of moving it back into the growth stage of the product life cycle. P&G has done this with several brands, including Mr. Clean and Old Spice. And Converse found fresh strategies for breathing new life into the venerable old Converse All Stars brand (see Marketing at Work 8.2.)

Management may decide to *harvest* the product, which means reducing various costs (plant and equipment, maintenance, R&D, advertising, sales force), hoping that sales hold up. If successful, harvesting will increase the company's profits in the short run. Finally, management may decide to *drop* the product from its line. The company can sell the product to another firm or simply liquidate it at salvage value. In recent years, P&G has sold off several lesser or declining brands, such as Folgers coffee, Crisco oil, Comet cleanser, Sure deodorant, Duncan Hines cake mixes, and Jif peanut butter. If the company plans to find a buyer, it will not want to run down the product through harvesting.

MARKETING AT WORK 8.2

Converse: An Old Brand Story with a New Beginning

The Converse brand has had a long, eventful product life cycle. The company invented basketball shoes, and in 1923 it introduced the first pair of Chuck Taylor All Stars—known around the world as Cons, Connies, Convics, Verses, or just plain Chucks. Throughout the '30s, '40s, '50s, and '60s, Chucks were *the* shoes to have. The first Olympic basketball team wore them, and they dominated basketball courts—amateur and professional—for more than 50 years. By the mid-1970s, 70 to 80 percent of basketball players still wore Converse.

However, every story has a beginning, a middle, and an end, and that holds true for most brand stories as well. For Converse, the story almost came to an end a little more than a decade ago. As the sneaker market exploded in the 1980s and 1990s, Converse failed to keep up with the times. Aggressive new competitors like Nike, adidas, and Reebok took the market by storm with new high-performance shoes and even higher-performing marketing schemes. By 2001, Converse's market share had dwindled to only 1 percent and the once-dominant brand declared Chapter 11 bankruptcy.

The Converse story would likely have ended right there if not for the foresight of an unlikely suitor. In 2003, market leader Nike stepped in and quietly bought Converse on the cheap. Nike still saw promise in the venerable-though-depleted old brand. However, it faced a perplexing product life-cycle question: How does a megabrand like Nike bring a fading icon like Converse back to life? To find answers, Nike assigned a new management team to Converse, gave it a fresh infusion of cash, and left the brand alone to shape its own strategy outside the shadow of the swoosh.

The new team discovered that, despite its dwindling market share, the Converse brand had acquired a small but fiercely loyal following. During the 1990s, street kids had begun wearing affordable Converse shoes as an expression of individuality. Soon to follow were emerging artists, designers, and musicians, who wore Chucks because of their simplicity and classic looks. Converse became a favorite of the anti-establishment, anti-corporate crowd, those tired of trendy fashions. Individualistic Converse fans would take a pair of cheap but comfy All Stars, trash them, scribble on them, and customize them as a canvas for personal expression.

This small but loyal following provided a lifeline for rejuvenating the aging brand. Building on that niche, in the years that followed, Converse would transform the classic yesteryear brand into a fresh, expressive lifestyle brand befitting current times. Today's young consumers don't want a brand that's neatly packaged and handed to them; they want to experience a brand and help shape it. So rather than forcing a new brand story onto the market, Converse decided to turn the brand over to consumers themselves and let them write the next chapter.

To be sure, Converse has been very strategic in its "stand-back" approach. For example, it has taken the original Chuck Taylor All Star shoe and branched out with new designs and new channels. The One Star variant is a low-priced line available at Target. Thousands of higher-priced versions of All Stars, created by fashion designers, are now sold through upscale retailers like Saks and Bloomingdales. And the brand has been extended to offer everything from kids' shoes, work shoes, sandals, and boots to Converse-branded eyewear and watches.

But Converse sees its role simply as making great products that customers want to wear. Beyond that, it participates in the brand story rather than dictating it. At the heart of the rekindled Converse brand is the philosophy that customers control brands, not companies. In the eyes of consumers, Converse today is less about the shoes and more about self-expression and the Converse experience. According to Converse Chief Marketing Officer Geoff Cottrill, largely on their own, consumers have come to define the Converse brand around five ideas: "American, sneaker, youthful, rebellious, and a blank canvas."

Accordingly, the Converse Web site is all about designing your own shoes and using Chucks as your own personal canvas. Also,

» Product life cycle: The venerable old Converse brand has begun a new life as a small but thriving lifestyle brand. Consumers themselves are helping to write the new Converse story.

Blend Images/Moxie Productions.

in recent years, Converse has focused its brand identity on one of the ultimate forms of youthful self-expression—rock n' roll music. For example, the company has released several popular lines of All Stars designed by legendary rock artists. It has even built its own music studio—Converse Rubber Tracks—where undiscovered artists can have free access to high-end equipment and lay down tracks that might land them record deals elsewhere. More than 300 artists, signed and unsigned, used the studio in the first 12 months. Converse's focus on self-expression and music has helped it create real and relevant brand conversations with and among people who might wear its sneakers.

Converse has also embraced social media, an ideal forum for engaging young consumers and letting them help to define the brand. Converse now spends more than 90 percent of its marketing dollars on emerging media. Consider this: Converse has become the most popular sneaker brand on Facebook, with more than 35 million fans on its Facebook page, three times the number for parent company and market leader Nike, and eight times as many as number-two ranked adidas. Converse also has 118,000 Twitter followers. That's amazing for a niche brand that still captures only 3 percent of the U.S. market.

In using social media, however, Converse is careful to stand back and let customers give voice to the brand. Its approach is to create positive brand experiences and interactions, and then step aside and let customers themselves talk about the brand and share their understanding of the brand with friends. As a result, Converse has now become one of the most democratic brands of all time—a brand of the people, by the people, and for the people. "This brand is a unique brand in that consumers really do own it, and really do direct it, and really do take it into interesting places," says Cottrill. "It's been inspiring to see this brand go into all the places it has gone simply because the consumers have taken us there."

In all, Converse appears now to have begun a new life cycle as a small but thriving lifestyle brand. In the decade or so since being acquired by Nike, Converse's revenues have more than quadrupled to $1.3 billion. At its Web site, Converse provides a fitting summary of its product life-cycle story, the end of which has yet to be written. "The best stories are the ones that don't end—the ones you just keep adding to and adding to—all the while marveling at the creative, disruptive, optimistic, courageous ways things evolve from being what they were, to what they are, to what they will become."

Sources: Based on information from Jeffrey Summers, "Why Converse Has 42 Million Facebook Fans," *Forbes* video interview, February 22, 2012, accessed at www.youtube.com/watch?v=BV1ilkKoy1o; Todd Wasserman, "How Converse Became the Biggest Little Sneaker Brand on Facebook," *Mashable*, May 4, 2011; Doug Schumacher, "TopTen: On Converse's Facebook Page, the Fans Do the Selling," *iMedia Connection*, March 13, 2012, http://blogs.imediaconnection.com/blog/2012/03/13/topten-on-converses-facebook-page-the-fans-do-the-selling/; Robert Klara, "Chuck's Big Comeback," *Adweek*, October 4, 2012, www.adweek.com/print/144059; and www.converse.com and www.converse.com/About/, accessed October 2013.

>> **Table 8.2** summarizes the key characteristics of each stage of the PLC. The table also lists the marketing objectives and strategies for each stage.[25]

Author Comment
Let's look at just a few more product topics, including regulatory and social responsibility issues and the special challenges of marketing products internationally.

Additional Product and Service Considerations

We wrap up our discussion of products and services with two additional considerations: social responsibility in product decisions and issues of international product and services marketing.

Product Decisions and Social Responsibility

Marketers should carefully consider public policy issues and regulations regarding acquiring or dropping products, patent protection, product quality and safety, and product warranties.

Regarding new products, the government may prevent companies from adding products through acquisitions if the effect threatens to lessen competition. Companies dropping products must be aware that they have legal obligations, written or implied, to their suppliers, dealers, and customers who have a stake in the dropped product. Companies must also obey U.S. patent laws when developing new products. A company cannot make its product illegally similar to another company's established product.

Manufacturers must comply with specific laws regarding product quality and safety. The Federal Food, Drug, and Cosmetic Act protects consumers from unsafe and adulterated food, drugs, and cosmetics. Various acts provide for the inspection of sanitary conditions in the meat- and poultry-processing industries. Safety legislation has been passed to regulate fabrics, chemical substances, automobiles, toys, and drugs and poisons. The Consumer Product Safety Act of 1972 established the Consumer Product Safety Commission, which has the authority to ban or seize potentially harmful products and set severe penalties for violation of the law.

If consumers have been injured by a product with a defective design, they can sue manufacturers or dealers. A recent survey of manufacturing companies found that product liability

» Table 8.2 Summary of Product Life-Cycle Characteristics, Objectives, and Strategies

	Introduction	Growth	Maturity	Decline
Characteristics				
Sales	Low sales	Rapidly rising sales	Peak sales	Declining sales
Costs	High cost per customer	Average cost per customer	Low cost per customer	Low cost per customer
Profits	Negative	Rising profits	High profits	Declining profits
Customers	Innovators	Early adopters	Middle majority	Laggards
Competitors	Few	Growing number	Stable number beginning to decline	Declining number
Marketing Objectives				
	Create product awareness and trial	Maximize market share	Maximize profit while defending market share	Reduce expenditure and milk the brand
Strategies				
Product	Offer a basic product	Offer product extensions, service, and warranty	Diversify brand and models	Phase out weak items
Price	Use cost-plus	Price to penetrate market	Price to match or beat competitors	Cut price
Distribution	Build selective distribution	Build intensive distribution	Build more intensive distribution	Go selective: phase out unprofitable outlets
Advertising	Build product awareness among early adopters and dealers	Build awareness and interest in the mass market	Stress brand differences and benefits	Reduce to level needed to retain hard-core loyals
Sales Promotion	Use heavy sales promotion to entice trial	Reduce to take advantage of heavy consumer demand	Increase to encourage brand switching	Reduce to minimal level

Source: Philip Kotler and Kevin Lane Keller, *Marketing Management*, 14th ed. (Upper Saddle River, NJ: Prentice Hall, 2012), p. 317. © 2012. Printed and Electronically reproduced by permission of Pearson Education, Inc., Upper Saddle River, New Jersey.

was the second-largest litigation concern, behind only labor and employment matters. Tens of thousands of product liability suits are now tried in U.S. district courts each year. Although manufacturers are found to be at fault in only a small percentage of all product liability cases, when they are found guilty, awards can run into the tens or even hundreds of millions of dollars. Class-action suits can run into the billions. For example, after it recalled some 7 million vehicles for acceleration-pedal-related issues, Toyota faced more than 100 class-action and individual lawsuits that could end up costing the company \$3 billion or more.[26]

This litigation phenomenon has resulted in huge increases in product liability insurance premiums, causing big problems in some industries. Some companies pass these higher rates along to consumers by raising prices. Others are forced to discontinue high-risk product lines. Some companies are now appointing *product stewards*, whose job is to protect consumers from harm and the company from liability by proactively ferreting out potential product problems.

International Product and Services Marketing

International product and services marketers face special challenges. First they must figure out what products and services to introduce and in which countries. Then they must decide how much to standardize or adapt their products and services for world markets.

On the one hand, companies would like to standardize their offerings. Standardization helps a company develop a consistent worldwide image. It also lowers the product design, manufacturing, and marketing costs of offering a large variety of products. On the other hand, markets and consumers around the world differ widely. Companies must usually respond to these differences by adapting their product offerings. For example, by carefully adapting its menu and operations to local tastes and eating styles, YUM! Brands—parent company of quintessential fast-food restaurants KFC, Pizza Hut, and Taco Bell—has become the largest restaurant company in mainland China. Consider KFC:[27]

Global product adaptation: By adapting to local tastes and eating styles, KFC has achieved finger-lickin' good success in China.

Gan jun—Imaginechina.

A typical Kentucky Fried Chicken meal in the United States features original, extra crispy, and a Pepsi. What do you get at a KFC in China? Of course, you can get some good old Kentucky fried, but more popular items include chicken with Sichuan spicy sauce and rice, egg soup, or a "dragon twister" (KFC's version of a traditional Beijing duck wrap), all washed down with some soybean milk. Also on the menu: egg tarts, fried dough sticks, wraps with local sauces, fish and shrimp burgers on fresh buns, and congee, a popular rice porridge that is KFC's number one seller at breakfast. The Chinese menu also offers a large selection—some 50 items compared with 29 in the United States—meant to appeal to the Chinese style of eating, in which groups of people share several dishes. And whereas KFC outlets in the United States are designed primarily for takeout and eating at home, outlets in China are about twice the size of their U.S. counterparts, providing more space for eat-in diners, who like to linger with friends and family. Through such adaptation, KFC and YUM!'s other brands in China have positioned themselves not as a foreign presence but as a part of the local community. The result: YUM! Brands has achieved finger lickin' good success in China. Its 4,000 KFC restaurants in more than 800 cities in China earned more revenue last year than all 19,000 of its restaurants in the United States combined, including KFC, Pizza Hut, and Taco Bell.

Service marketers also face special challenges when going global. Some service industries have a long history of international operations. For example, the commercial banking industry was one of the first to grow internationally. Banks had to provide global services to meet the foreign exchange and credit needs of their home-country clients who wanted to sell overseas. In recent years, many banks have become truly global. Germany's Deutsche Bank, for example, serves more than 19 million customers through 3,078 branches in more than 70 countries. For its clients around the world who wish to grow globally, Deutsche Bank can raise money not only in Frankfurt but also in Zurich, London, Paris, Tokyo, and Moscow.[28]

Professional and business services industries, such as accounting, management consulting, and advertising, have also globalized. The international growth of these firms followed the globalization of the client companies they serve. For example, as more clients employ worldwide marketing and advertising strategies, advertising agencies have responded by globalizing their own operations. McCann Worldgroup, a large U.S.-based advertising and marketing services agency, operates in more than 110 countries. It serves international clients such as Coca-Cola, GM, ExxonMobil, Microsoft, MasterCard, Johnson & Johnson, and Unilever in markets ranging from the United States and Canada to Korea and Kazakhstan. Moreover, McCann Worldgroup is one company in the Interpublic Group of Companies, an immense, worldwide network of advertising and marketing services companies.[29]

Retailers are among the latest service businesses to go global. As their home markets become saturated, American retailers such as Walmart, Office Depot, and Saks Fifth Avenue are expanding into faster-growing markets abroad. For example, since 1991, Walmart has entered 27 countries outside the United States; its international division's sales account for 28 percent of total sales. Foreign retailers are making similar moves. Asian shoppers can now buy American products in French-owned Carrefour stores. Carrefour, the world's second-largest retailer behind Walmart, now operates more than 15,500 stores in more than 35 countries. It is the leading retailer in Europe, Brazil, and Argentina and the largest foreign retailer in China.[30]

The trend toward growth of global service companies will continue, especially in banking, airlines, telecommunications, and professional services. Today, service firms are no longer simply following their manufacturing customers. Instead, they are taking the lead in international expansion.

MyMarketingLab

Go to **mymktlab.com** to complete the problems marked with this icon .

END OF CHAPTER REVIEWING THE CONCEPTS

CHAPTER REVIEW AND KEY TERMS

Objectives Review

A company's current products face limited life spans and must be replaced by newer products. But new products can fail—the risks of innovation are as great as the rewards. The key to successful innovation lies in a customer-focused, holistic, total-company effort; strong planning; and a systematic new product development process.

OBJECTIVE 1 Explain how companies find and develop new product ideas. (pp 238–239)

Companies find and develop new product ideas from a variety of sources. Many new product ideas stem from *internal sources*. Companies conduct formal R&D, or they pick the brains of their employees, urging them to think up and develop new product ideas. Other ideas come from *external sources*. Companies track *competitors'* offerings and obtain ideas from *distributors and suppliers* who are close to the market and can pass along information about consumer problems and new product possibilities.

Perhaps the most important sources of new product ideas are customers themselves. Companies observe customers, invite them to submit their ideas and suggestions, or even involve customers in the new product development process. Many companies are now developing *crowdsourcing* or *open-innovation* new product idea programs, which invite broad communities of people—customers, employees, independent scientists and researchers, and even the general public—into the new product innovation process. Truly innovative companies do not rely only on one source or another for new product ideas.

OBJECTIVE 2 List and define the steps in the new product development process and the major considerations in managing this process. (pp 239–250)

The new product development process consists of eight sequential stages. The process starts with *idea generation*. Next comes *idea screening*, which reduces the number of ideas based on the company's own criteria. Ideas that pass the screening stage continue through *product concept development*, in which a detailed version of the new product idea is stated in meaningful consumer terms. This stage includes *concept testing*, in which new product concepts are tested with a group of target consumers to determine whether the concepts have strong consumer appeal. Strong concepts proceed to *marketing strategy development*, in which an initial marketing strategy for the new product is developed from the product concept. In the *business-analysis* stage, a review of the sales, costs, and profit projections for a new product is conducted to determine whether the new product is likely to satisfy the company's objectives. With positive results here, the ideas become more concrete through *product development* and *test marketing* and finally are launched during *commercialization*.

New product development involves more than just going through a set of steps. Companies must take a systematic, holistic approach to managing this process. Successful new product development requires a customer-centered, team-based, systematic effort.

OBJECTIVE 3 Describe the stages of the product life cycle and how marketing strategies change during a product's life cycle. (pp 250–257)

Each product has a *life cycle* marked by a changing set of problems and opportunities. The sales of the typical product follow an S-shaped curve made up of five stages. The cycle begins with the *product development* stage in which the company finds and develops a new product idea. *The introduction stage* is marked by slow growth and low profits as the product is distributed to the market. If successful, the product enters a *growth stage*, which offers rapid sales growth and increasing profits. Next comes a *maturity stage* in which the product's sales growth slows down and profits stabilize. Finally, the product enters a *decline stage* in which sales and profits dwindle. The company's task during this stage is to recognize the decline and decide whether it should maintain, harvest, or drop the product. The different stages of the PLC require different marketing strategies and tactics.

OBJECTIVE 4 Discuss two additional product issues: socially responsible product decisions and international product and services marketing. (pp 257–259)

Marketers must consider two additional product issues. The first is *social responsibility*. This includes public policy issues and regulations involving acquiring or dropping products, patent protection, product quality and safety, and product warranties. The second involves the special challenges facing international product and services marketers. International marketers must decide how much to standardize or adapt their offerings for world markets.

Key Terms

Objective 1
New product development (p 238)

Objective 2
Idea generation (p 239)
Crowdsourcing (p 241)
Idea screening (p 241)
Product concept (p 243)
Concept testing (p 244)
Marketing strategy development (p 245)
Business analysis (p 245)
Product development (p 245)
Test marketing (p 246)
Commercialization (p 247)
Customer-centered new product development (p 248)
Team-based new product development (p 249)

Objective 3
Product life cycle (PLC) (p 251)
Style (p 252)
Fashion (p 252)
Fad (p 252)
Introduction stage (p 253)
Growth stage (p 253)
Maturity stage (p 253)
Decline stage (p 255)

DISCUSSION AND CRITICAL THINKING

Discussion Questions

8-1. Define *crowdsourcing* and describe an example not already presented in the chapter. (AACSB: Written and Oral Communication; Reflective Thinking)

8-2. What activities are performed in the marketing strategy development step of the new product development process? What is required in a good marketing strategy statement? (AACSB: Written and Oral Communication; Reflective Thinking)

8-3. What is test marketing? Explain why companies may or may not test market products, and discuss alternatives to full test markets. (AACSB: Written and Oral Communication)

8-4. Compare and contrast styles, fashions, and fads. (AACSB: Written and Oral Communication)

8-5. Discuss how a company can maintain success for products in the mature stage of the product life cycle and give examples not already described in the chapter. (AACSB: Written and Oral Communication)

Critical Thinking Exercises

8-6. Visit the Product Development and Management Association's Web site (www.pdma.org) to learn about this organization. Click on "OCI Award" in the "About PDMA" dropdown menu. Describe this award and the criteria used when granting it, and discuss one company that has received the OCI Award. (AACSB: Written and Oral Communication; Information Technology)

8-7. Find an example of a company that launched a new consumer product within the last five years. Develop a presentation showing how the company implemented the 4 P's in launching the product and report on the product's success since the launch. (AACSB: Written and Oral Communication; Reflective Thinking)

MINICASES AND APPLICATIONS

Online, Mobile, and Social Media Marketing Reading Rainbow

You may have grown up watching LeVar Burton on PBS's *Reading Rainbow* show. He hosted the children's educational show for 26 years and now is taking it mobile. Burton purchased the rights to the show and launched a Reading Rainbow mobile app. The app is free to try, but a $9.99 per month or $29.99 per six-month subscription allows kids unlimited access to the library and adventures on themed islands such as the Animal Kingdom and others from the iconic television show, as well as new adventure field trips. Audio and video storytelling brings books to life for children, and interactive elements encourage curiosity and learning. Adventures incorporate segments from the TV show as well as new video. Up to five children in a household can customize their own reading adventures, and reading lists are suggested based on their abilities and interests. The parent dashboard lets parents monitor their child's reading progress. LeVar Burton personally starts each day with a "Good morning, y'all" tweet followed by

15 to 20 more tweets each day to his followers. The service is always expanding, offering new adventures that are often based on user feedback through social media.

8-8. In what stage of the product life cycle is the *Reading Rainbow* television program? Has the mobile app changed that? Explain. (AACSB: Written and Oral Communication; Reflective Thinking)

8-9. Discuss other existing products that have created new life for the product by embracing Internet, mobile, or social media platforms. Suggest an app for another tangible product or service that does not currently use online, mobile, or social media, along with ways to encourage customer engagement and social sharing. (AACSB: Written and Oral Communication; Information Technology; Reflective Thinking)

Marketing Ethics Orphan Drugs

For years, rare diseases—those affecting fewer than 200,000 patients—were unattractive markets for pharmaceutical companies. That changed in 1983 when Congress created the "orphan drug" designation. The Food and Drug Administration (FDA) now offers incentives such as faster approval, tax breaks, and longer patent protections to companies developing drugs for rare diseases, and patient groups raise millions of dollars to aid in their development. Now, more than 200 orphan drugs a year enter development, and about a third of them gain FDA approval. But these drugs are expensive to users. For example, Isis Pharmaceutical's cholesterol drug for a rare condition costs $235,000 to $295,000 per year. NPS Pharmaceuticals has a drug for a rare bowel condition, Gattex, that costs patients $295,000 per year. In Europe, Sanofi's enzyme-replacement therapy drug, Mynozyme, costs €700,000 (over $900,000) per year. These high prices fetched more than $1 billion in annual sales for a third of orphan drug makers, and the category has more than $50 billion in worldwide sales that grow more than 20 percent per year. According to the U.S. National Institutes of Health, there are almost 7,000 rare diseases affecting 30 million Americans, making this an attractive market segment for pharmaceutical companies that have seen many of their blockbuster drugs go off-patent and are looking for new revenue streams. But who pays for these expensive orphan drugs? Right now, private health plans and governments foot the bill.

8-10. Discuss the ethical issues surrounding orphan drugs. Should pharmaceutical companies be allowed to charge such high prices for these drugs? (AACSB: Written and Oral Communication; Ethical Understanding and Reasoning)

8-11. Discuss the impact of austerity measures in Europe and the implementation of health-care reform in the United States on the future of orphan drugs. (AACSB: Written and Oral Communication; Reflective Thinking)

Marketing by the Numbers Kei Cars

The U.S. government fuel-economy regulations require carmakers to achieve a fleet average of 54.5 miles per gallon by 2025. Smaller vehicles can help car companies meet those standards. Tiny vehicles in Japan, known as *kei* cars (from "kei-jidosha" or "light automobile"), achieve 55-mpg ratings. Kei cars are not new in Japan. They began as a tax and insurance break to stimulate the Japanese economy after World War II. However, the typical kei buyer in Japan is close to 50 years old, causing concern for Japanese automakers focusing only on the Japanese market. The U.S. regulations provide an opportunity for these automobiles in the United States. However, profit margins are almost as tiny as the cars themselves, causing carmakers to wonder if they can make an adequate profit when exporting to the United States. Of the big-three Japanese carmakers—Honda, Toyota, and Nissan—Honda is the only one making kei cars. It is considering bringing its new Honda N Box to the United States. Its closest competitor would be Daimler's Smart car, which made a profit of $108.3 million on sales of $10.7 billion in the United States last year. Smart cars sell for around $13,000 but seat only two people. In comparison, Honda's N Box holds four people and would be priced at $16,000, making it an alternative for small-car-minded families. To answer the following questions, refer to Appendix 3, Marketing by the Numbers.

8-12. What is the profit margin for Daimler's Smart car? (AACSB: Written and Oral Communication; Analytical Thinking)

8-13. If the unit variable cost for each N Box is $14,000 and Honda has fixed costs totaling $20 million for this car, how many N Box cars must Honda sell to break even? How many must it sell to realize a profit margin similar to that of the Smart car? (AACSB: Written and Oral Communication; Analytical Thinking)

Video Case Subaru

When a company has a winning product, everything else falls into place. Or does it? Subaru is a winning company (one of the few automotive companies to sustain growth and profits in hard economic times) with various winning products, including the Impreza, Legacy, Forester, and Outback. But what happens when any one product starts to decline in popularity?

This video demonstrates how Subaru constantly engages in new-product development as part of its efforts to manage the product life cycle for each of its models. Subaru is focused on both developing the next version of each existing model and developing possible new models to boost its product portfolio.

After viewing the video featuring Subaru, answer the following questions:

8-14. How would you describe the product life cycle in relation to one Subaru product?

8-15. How do shifting consumer trends affect Subaru's products?

8-16. How does Subaru remain customer-oriented in its new product efforts?

Company Cases 8 Google / 2 Dyson / 6 Dove

See Appendix 1 for cases appropriate for this chapter. **Case 8, Google: New Product Innovation at the Speed of Light.** When it comes to developing new products, Google bucks all convention with a process that churns things out in weeks and months, not years. **Case 2, Dyson: Solving Customer Problems in Ways They Never Imagined.** Dyson focuses on ho-hum product lines that haven't changed in decades, infusing them with technology that solves consumers' long-accepted problems. **Case 6, Dove: Building Customer Relationships Everywhere, One Gender at a Time.** Dove has long succeeded as a brand of soap and personal care products for women. Now, it's doing the same with men.

MyMarketingLab

Go to **mymktlab.com** for Auto-graded writing questions as well as the following Assisted-graded writing questions:

8-17. What decisions must be made once a company decides to go ahead with commercialization for a new product? (AACSB: Written and Oral Communication).

8-18. Visit creatingminds.org/tools/tools_ideation.htm to learn about idea-generation techniques. Form a small group and have each group member explain a different technique to the rest of the group. Apply one or more of the techniques to generate four new product ideas. Present your ideas to the rest of the class with an explanation of the techniques your group applied to generate them. (AACSB: Written and Oral Communication; Information Technology; Reflective Thinking)

8-19. Mymktlab Only—comprehensive writing assignment for this chapter.

9 Pricing
Understanding and Capturing Customer Value

CHAPTER ROAD MAP

Objective Outline

- OBJECTIVE 1 **Identify the three major pricing strategies and discuss the importance of understanding customer value perceptions, company costs, and competitor strategies when setting prices.** What Is a Price? 266–267; Major Pricing Strategies 267–274
- OBJECTIVE 2 **Identify and define the other important external and internal factors affecting a firm's pricing decisions.** Other Internal and External Considerations Affecting Price Decisions 274–279
- OBJECTIVE 3 **Describe the major strategies for pricing new products.** New Product Pricing Strategies 280–281
- OBJECTIVE 4 **Explain how companies find a set of prices that maximizes the profits from the total product mix.** Product Mix Pricing Strategies 281–283
- OBJECTIVE 5 **Discuss how companies adjust their prices to take into account different types of customers and situations.** Price-Adjustment Strategies 283–289
- OBJECTIVE 6 **Discuss the key issues related to initiating and responding to price changes.** Price Changes 289–294; Public Policy and Pricing 294–296

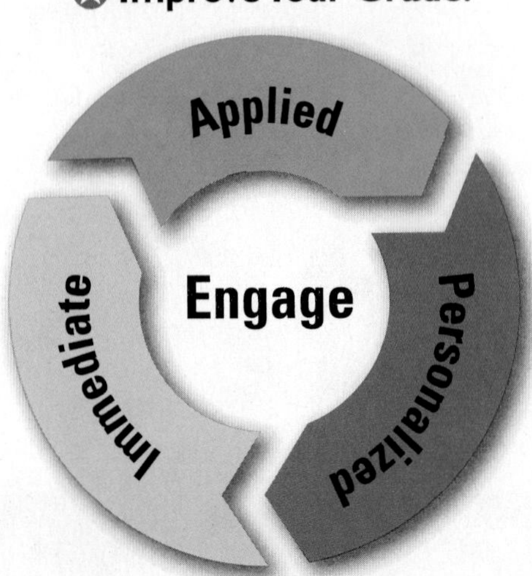

Previewing the Concepts

We now look at the second major marketing mix tool—pricing. If effective product development, promotion, and distribution sow the seeds of business success, effective pricing is the harvest. Firms successful at creating customer value with the other marketing mix activities must still capture some of this value in the prices they earn. In this chapter, we discuss the importance of pricing, dig into three major pricing strategies, and look at internal and external considerations that affect pricing decisions. In the next chapter, we examine some additional pricing considerations and approaches.

For openers, let's look at Trader Joe's, whose unique price and value strategy has made it one of the nation's fastest-growing, most popular food stores. Trader Joe's understands that success comes not just from what products you offer customers, or from the prices you charge. It comes from offering the combination of products and prices that produces the greatest customer *value*—what customers get for the prices they pay.

---

*Over 10 million students improved their results using the Pearson MyLabs. Visit **mymktlab.com** for simulations, tutorials, and end-of-chapter problems.

» **Trader Joe's unique price–value strategy has earned it an almost cult-like following of devoted customers who love what they get for the prices they pay.**

Michael Nagle/Getty Images USA, Inc.

First Stop

Trader Joe's: A Special Twist on the Price–Value Equation—Cheap Gourmet

On an early July morning in Manhattan's Chelsea neighborhood, a large and enthusiastic crowd has already gathered. The occasion: Trader Joe's is opening a new store, and waiting shoppers are sharing their joy over the arrival of the trendy retailer in their neighborhood. Trader Joe's is more than a grocery store—it's a cultural experience. Its shelves are packed with goods that are at the same time both exotic luxuries and affordable. Whether it's organic creamy Valencia peanut butter or cage-free eggs, Thai lime-and-chili cashews, or Belgian butter waffle cookies, you'll find them only at Trader Joe's. Within moments of the new store's opening, the deluge of customers makes it almost impossible to navigate the aisles. They line up 10 deep at checkouts with carts full of Trader Joe's exclusive $2.99 Charles Shaw wine—aka "Two-Buck Chuck"—and an assortment of other exclusive gourmet products at impossibly low prices. All of this has made Trader Joe's one of the nation's hottest retailers.

Trader Joe's isn't really a gourmet food store. Then again, it's not a discount food store either. It's actually a bit of both. Trader Joe's has put its own special twist on the food price–value equation—call it "cheap gourmet." It offers gourmet-caliber, one-of-a-kind products at bargain prices, all served up in a festive, vacation-like atmosphere that makes shopping fun. However you define it, Trader Joe's inventive price–value positioning has earned it an almost cult-like following of devoted customers who love what they get from Trader Joe's for the prices they pay.

Trader Joe's describes itself as an "island paradise" where "value, adventure, and tasty treasures are discovered, every day." Shoppers bustle and buzz amid cedar-plank-lined walls and fake palm trees as a ship's bell rings out occasionally at checkout, alerting them to special announcements. Unfailingly helpful and cheery associates in aloha shirts chat with customers about everything from the weather to menu suggestions for dinner parties. At the Chelsea store opening, workers greeted customers with high-fives and free cookies. Customers don't just shop at Trader Joe's; they experience it.

Trader Joe's understands that success comes not only from what products you offer customers or the prices you charge. It comes from offering the combination of products and prices that produces the greatest customer value.

Shelves bristle with an eclectic assortment of gourmet-quality grocery items. Trader Joe's stocks only a limited assortment of about 4,000 products (compared with the 50,000 items found in a typical grocery store). However, the assortment is uniquely Trader Joe's, including special concoctions of gourmet packaged foods and sauces, ready-to-eat soups, fresh and frozen entrees, snacks, and desserts—all free of artificial colors, flavors, and preservatives. Trader Joe's is a gourmet foodie's delight, featuring everything from kettle corn cookies, organic strawberry lemonade, creamy Valencia peanut butter, and fair-trade coffees to kimchi fried rice and triple-ginger gingersnaps.

Another thing that makes Trader Joe's products so special is that you just can't get most of them elsewhere. For example, try finding Ginger Cats cookies or quinoa-and-black-bean tortilla chips at some other store. More than 80 percent of the store's brands are private-label goods, sold exclusively by Trader Joe's. If asked, almost any customer can tick off a ready list of Trader Joe's favorites that they just can't live without—a list that quickly grows. People come in intending to buy a few favorites and quickly fill a cart. "They just seem to turn their customers on," says one food industry analyst.

A special store atmosphere, exclusive gourmet products, helpful and attentive associates—this all sounds like a recipe for high prices. Not so at Trader Joe's. Whereas upscale competitors such as Whole Foods Market charge upscale prices to match their wares ("Whole Foods, Whole Paycheck"), Trader Joe's amazes customers with its relatively frugal prices. The prices aren't all that low in absolute terms, but they're a real bargain compared with what you'd pay for the same quality and coolness elsewhere. "At Trader Joe's, we're as much about value as we are about great food," says the company. "So you can afford to be adventurous without breaking the bank."

How does Trader Joe's keep its gourmet prices so low? It carefully shapes nonprice elements to support its overall price–value strategy. For starters, Trader Joe's has lean operations and a near-fanatical focus on saving money. To keep costs down, Trader Joe's typically locates its stores in low-rent, out-of-the-way locations, such as suburban strip malls. Its small store size with small back rooms and limited product assortment result in reduced facilities and inventory costs. Trader Joe's stores save money by eliminating large produce sections and expensive on-site bakery, butcher, deli, and seafood shops. And for its private-label brands, Trader Joe's buys directly from suppliers and negotiates hard on price.

Finally, the frugal retailer saves money by spending almost nothing on advertising, and it offers no coupons, discount cards, or special promotions of any kind. Trader Joe's unique combination of quirky products and low prices produces so much word-of-mouth promotion and buying urgency that the company doesn't really need to advertise or price promote. The closest thing to an official promotion is the company's Web site or *The Fearless Flyer*, a newsletter mailed out monthly to people who opt in to receive it. Trader Joe's most potent promotional weapon is its army of faithful followers. Trader Joe's customers have even started their own fan Web site, www.traderjoesfan.com, where they discuss new products and stores, trade recipes, and swap their favorite Trader Joe's stories.

Thus, building the right price–value formula has made Trader Joe's one of the nation's fastest-growing and most popular food stores. Its more than 400 stores in 32 states now reap annual sales of an estimated $10.5 billion, more than double its sales five years ago. Trader Joe's stores pull in an amazing $1,750 per square foot, more than twice the supermarket industry average. *Consumer Reports* recently ranked Trader Joe's, along with Wegmans, as the best supermarket chain in the nation.

It's all about value and price—what you get for what you pay. Just ask Trader Joe's regular Chrissi Wright, found early one morning browsing her local Trader Joe's in Bend, Oregon:

> Chrissi expects she'll leave Trader Joe's with eight bottles of the popular Charles Shaw wine priced at $2.99 each tucked under her arms. "I love Trader Joe's because they let me eat like a yuppie without taking all my money," says Wright. "Their products are gourmet, often environmentally conscientious and beautiful . . . and, of course, there's Two-Buck Chuck—possibly the greatest innovation of our time."[1]

Pricing: No matter what the state of the economy, companies should sell value, not price.

magicoven/Shutterstock.com.

Price
The amount of money charged for a product or service, or the sum of the values that customers exchange for the benefits of having or using the product or service.

Companies today face a fierce and fast-changing pricing environment. Value-seeking customers have put increased pricing pressure on many companies. Thanks to tight economic times in recent years, the pricing power of the Internet, and value-driven retailers such as Walmart, today's more frugal consumers are pursuing spend-less strategies. In response, it seems that almost every company has been looking for ways to cut prices.

Yet, cutting prices is often not the best answer. Reducing prices unnecessarily can lead to lost profits and damaging price wars. It can cheapen a brand by signaling to customers that price is more important than the customer value a brand delivers. Instead, in both good economic times and bad, companies should sell value, not price. In some cases, that means selling lesser products at rock-bottom prices. But in most cases, it means persuading customers that paying a higher price for the company's brand is justified by the greater value they gain.

What Is a Price?

In the narrowest sense, **price** is the amount of money charged for a product or a service. More broadly, price is the sum of all the values that customers give up to gain the benefits of having or using a product or service. Historically, price has been the major factor affecting buyer choice. In recent decades, however, nonprice factors have gained increasing importance. Even so, price remains one of the most important elements that determine a firm's market share and profitability.

Price is the only element in the marketing mix that produces revenue; all other elements represent costs. Price is also one of the most flexible marketing mix elements. Unlike product features and channel commitments, prices can be changed quickly. At the same time, pricing is the number-one problem facing many marketing executives, and many companies do not handle pricing well. Some managers view pricing as a big headache, preferring instead to focus on other marketing mix elements.

However, smart managers treat pricing as a key strategic tool for creating and capturing customer value. Prices have a direct impact on a firm's bottom line. A small percentage improvement in price can generate a large percentage increase in profitability. More important, as part of a company's overall value proposition, price plays a key role in creating customer value and building customer relationships. So, instead of shying away from pricing, smart marketers are embracing it as an important competitive asset.[2]

Author Comment
Setting the right price is one of the marketer's most difficult tasks. A host of factors will come into play. But finding and implementing the right price strategy is critical to success.

Major Pricing Strategies

The price the company charges will fall somewhere between one that is too low to produce a profit and one that is too high to produce any demand. >> **Figure 9.1** summarizes the major considerations in setting prices. Customer perceptions of the product's value set the ceiling for its price. If customers perceive that the product's price is greater than its value, they will not buy the product. Likewise, product costs set the floor for a product's price. If the company prices the product below its costs, the company's profits will suffer. In setting its price between these two extremes, the company must consider several external and internal factors, including competitors' strategies and prices, the overall marketing strategy and mix, and the nature of the market and demand.

Figure 9.1 suggests three major pricing strategies: customer value–based pricing, cost-based pricing, and competition-based pricing.

Author Comment
Like everything else in marketing, good pricing starts with *customers* and their perceptions of value.

Customer Value–Based Pricing

In the end, the customer will decide whether a product's price is right. Pricing decisions, like other marketing mix decisions, must start with customer value. When customers buy a product, they exchange something of value (the price) to get something of value (the benefits of having or using the product). Effective customer-oriented pricing involves understanding how much value consumers place on the benefits they receive from the product and setting a price that captures that value.

Customer value–based pricing
Setting price based on buyers' perceptions of value rather than on the seller's cost.

Customer value–based pricing uses buyers' perceptions of value as the key to pricing. Value-based pricing means that the marketer cannot design a product and marketing program and then set the price. Price is considered along with all other marketing mix variables *before* the marketing program is set.

>> **Figure 9.2** compares value-based pricing with cost-based pricing. Although costs are an important consideration in setting prices, cost-based pricing is often product driven. The company designs what it considers to be a good product, adds up the costs of making the product, and sets a price that covers costs plus a target profit. Marketing must then convince buyers that the product's value at that price justifies its purchase. If the price turns out to be too high, the company must settle for lower markups or lower sales, both resulting in disappointing profits.

Value-based pricing reverses this process. The company first assesses customer needs and value perceptions. It then sets its target price based on customer perceptions of value. The targeted value and price drive decisions about what costs can be incurred and the resulting product design. As a result, pricing begins with analyzing consumer needs and value perceptions, and the price is set to match perceived value.

>> **Figure 9.1** Considerations in Setting Price

If customers perceive that a product's price is greater than its value, they won't buy it. If the company prices the product below its costs, profits will suffer. Between the two extremes, the "right" pricing strategy is one that delivers both value to the customer and profits to the company.

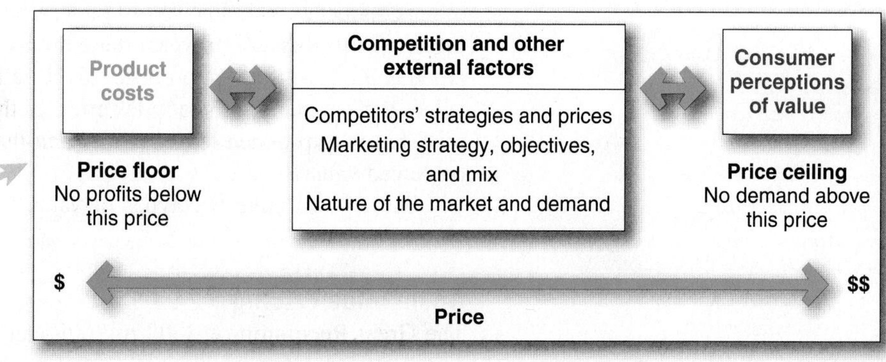

Figure 9.2 Value-Based Pricing versus Cost-Based Pricing

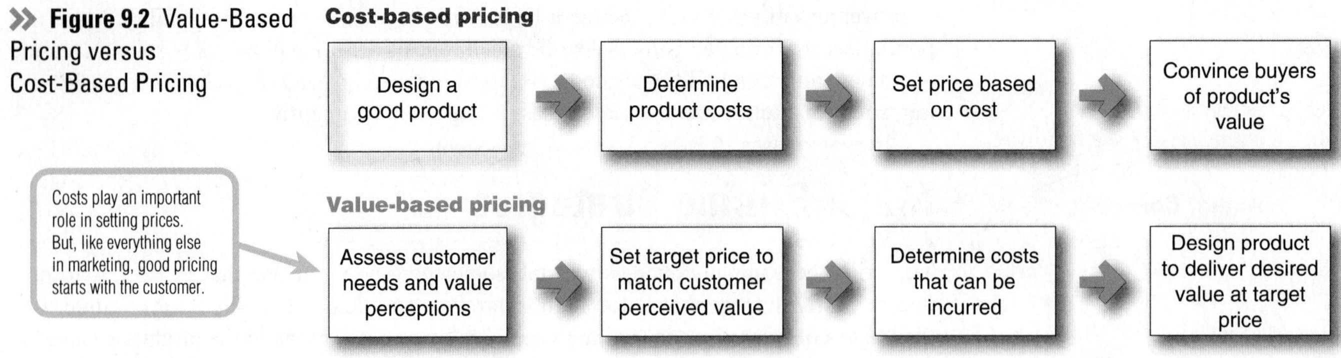

It's important to remember that "good value" is not the same as "low price." For example, a Steinway piano—any Steinway piano—costs a lot. But to those who own one, a Steinway is a great value:[3]

Perceived value: A Steinway piano—any Steinway piano—costs a lot. But to those who own one, price is nothing; the Steinway experience is everything.

ROBERT CAPLIN/The New York Times.

A Steinway grand piano typically runs anywhere from $55,000 to as high as several hundred thousand dollars. The most popular model sells for around $87,000. But ask anyone who owns a Steinway grand piano, and they'll tell you that, when it comes to Steinway, price is nothing; the Steinway experience is everything. Steinway makes very high quality pianos—handcrafting each Steinway requires up to one full year. But, more importantly, owners get the Steinway mystique. The Steinway name evokes images of classical concert stages and the celebrities and performers who've owned and played Steinway pianos across more than 160 years.

But Steinways aren't just for world-class pianists and the wealthy. Ninety-nine percent of all Steinway buyers are amateurs who perform only in their dens. To such customers, whatever a Steinway costs, it's a small price to pay for the value of owning one. "A Steinway takes you places you've never been," says an ad. As one Steinway owner puts it, "My friendship with the Steinway piano is one of the most important and beautiful things in my life." Who can put a price on such feelings?

A company will often find it hard to measure the value customers attach to its product. For example, calculating the cost of ingredients in a meal at a fancy restaurant is relatively easy. But assigning value to other measures of satisfaction such as taste, environment, relaxation, conversation, and status is very hard. Such value is subjective; it varies both for different consumers and different situations.

Still, consumers will use these perceived values to evaluate a product's price, so the company must work to measure them. Sometimes, companies ask consumers how much they would pay for a basic product and for each benefit added to the offer. Or a company might conduct experiments to test the perceived value of different product offers. According to an old Russian proverb, there are two fools in every market—one who asks too much and one who asks too little. If the seller charges more than the buyers' perceived value, the company's sales will suffer. If the seller charges less, its products sell very well, but they produce less revenue than they would if they were priced at the level of perceived value.

We now examine two types of value-based pricing: *good-value pricing* and *value-added pricing*.

Good-Value Pricing

The Great Recession of 2008 to 2009 caused a fundamental and lasting shift in consumer attitudes toward price and quality. In response, many companies have changed their pricing approaches to bring them in line with changing economic conditions and consumer price perceptions. More and more, marketers have adopted the strategy of **good-value pricing**—offering the right combination of quality and good service at a fair price.

Good-value pricing
Offering just the right combination of quality and good service at a fair price.

In many cases, this has involved introducing less-expensive versions of established, brand name products. For example, fast-food restaurants such as Taco Bell and McDonald's offer value menu and dollar menu items. Every car company now offers small, inexpensive models better suited to tighter consumer budgets and thriftier spending habits. P&G has introduced "Basic" versions of its Bounty and Charmin brands that sell for less and recently launched bargain-priced Gain dish soap, its first new dish soap in almost 40 years. The company has also reduced the size of some Tide laundry detergent packages from 100 ounces to 75 ounces and sells the smaller-size packages for 20 percent less at Walmart and other discount stores. "Today, when you ask the consumer, 'What is value?' the No. 1 answer is 'brand names for less,'" says a pricing expert.[4]

In other cases, good-value pricing has involved redesigning existing brands to offer more quality for a given price or the same quality for less. Some companies even succeed by offering less value but at very low prices. For example, passengers flying low-cost European airline Ryanair won't get much in the way of free amenities, but they'll like the airline's unbelievably low prices (see Marketing at Work 9.1). >> Similarly, the ALDI supermarket chain has established a good-value pricing position by which it gives customers "more 'mmm' for the dollar":[5]

> ALDI promises customers "Simply Smarter Shopping." The rapidly expanding, 1,200-store chain is driven by a long list of "ALDI Truths" by which it delivers "impressively high quality at impossibly low prices." (ALDI Truth #1: When deciding between eating well and saving money, always choose both.) ALDI has redesigned the food shopping experience to reduce costs and give customers prices it claims are up to 50 percent lower than those of other supermarkets. To keep costs down, ALDI operates smaller, energy-saving stores that carry only about 1,400 of the fastest-moving grocery items (the typical supermarket carries about 30,000 items). Almost 95 percent of its items are ALDI store brands. So, ALDI claims, customers are paying for the product itself, not national brand advertising and marketing. Also, ALDI does no promotional pricing or price matching—it just sticks with its efficient everyday very low prices (ALDI Truth #12: We don't match other stores' prices because that would mean raising ours). Even customers themselves help to keep costs low: They bring their own bags (ALDI doesn't provide any), bag their own groceries (no baggers at ALDI), return shopping carts on their own (to get back a 25-cent deposit), and pay with cash or a debit card (no credit cards accepted). But to ALDI fans, the savings make it all worthwhile. At ALDI, "Your wallet and taste buds are in for a treat" (Truth #34).

>> **Good-value pricing: ALDI keeps costs low so that it can offer customers "impressively high quality at impossibly low prices" every day.**

Photo courtesy of Keri Miksza.

ALDI practices an important type of good-value pricing at the retail level called *everyday low pricing (EDLP)*. EDLP involves charging a constant, everyday low price with few or no temporary price discounts. Retailers such as Costco and Lumber Liquidators practice EDLP. However, the king of EDLP is Walmart, which practically defined the concept. Except for a few sale items every month, Walmart promises everyday low prices on everything it sells. In contrast, *high-low pricing* involves charging higher prices on an everyday basis but running frequent promotions to lower prices temporarily on selected items. Department stores such as Kohl's and Macy's practice high-low pricing by having frequent sale days, early-bird savings, and bonus earnings for store credit-card holders.

MARKETING AT WORK 9.1

Ryanair: Really Good-Value Pricing—Fly for Free!

The major airlines are struggling with difficult pricing strategy decisions in these tough air-travel times. Pricing strategies vary widely. One airline, however, appears to have found a radical new pricing solution, one that customers are sure to love: Make flying *free*! That's right. Michael O'Leary, CEO of Dublin-based Ryanair, has a dream that someday all Ryanair passengers will fly for free. And with a current average price of $42 per ticket (compared to $87 for closest competitor easyJet and a whopping $130 for "discount airline" Southwest), Ryanair is getting closer.

Even without completely free flights, Ryanair has become Europe's most popular carrier. Last year Ryanair flew 76 million passengers to more than 155 European destinations in 26 countries. The budget airline is also Europe's most profitable one. Over the past decade, even as the global airline industry collectively lost nearly $50 billion, Ryanair has turned healthy net profits in 10 out of 11 years. Given the prospects of rising fuel costs, collapsing European economies, and other troubled times ahead for the airline industry, Ryanair seems well positioned to weather the turbulence.

What's the secret? Ryanair's frugal cost structure makes even cost-conscious Southwest look like a reckless spender. In addition, the Irish airline makes money on everything *but* the ticket, from charging for baggage check-in to revenues from seat-back advertising space. Ryanair's low-cost strategy is modeled after Southwest's. Twenty years ago, when Ryanair was just another struggling European carrier, Ryanair's O'Leary went to Dallas to meet with Southwest executives and see what he could learn. The result was a wholesale revamping of the Irish carrier's business model. Following Southwest's lead, to economize, Ryanair began employing only a single type of aircraft—the good-old Boeing 737. Also like Southwest, it began focusing on smaller, secondary airports and offering unassigned passenger seating.

But Ryanair has since taken Southwest's low-cost pricing model even further. When it comes to keeping costs down, O'Leary—who wears jeans, sneakers, and off-the-rack short-sleeved shirts—is an absolute fanatic. He wants Ryanair to be known as the Walmart of flying. Like the giant retailer, Ryanair is constantly on the lookout for new ways to cut costs—for example, hard plastic seats with no seat-back pockets reduce both weight and cleaning expense. Ryanair flight crews even buy their own uniforms, and headquarters staff members supply their own pens.

O'Leary equates every cost reduction with the benefit to customers in terms of lower ticket prices. Removing all but one toilet from each plane would cut 5 percent off the average ticket price. Replacing the last 10 rows with a standing cabin—another 20 to 25 percent off. O'Leary's sometimes nutty proposals for cost-cutting—deliberately provocative so that they're sure to gain free publicity—have even included flying planes with only one pilot ("Let's take out the second pilot. Let the bloody computer fly it.") and having customers place their own bags in the belly of Ryanair planes ("You take your own bag with you. You bring it down. You put it on."). It all sounds crazy, but think again about those zero-dollar ticket prices.

O'Leary's dream of customers flying free rests on the eventuality that, someday, all of Ryanair's revenues will come from "ancillary" fees. The penny-pinching airline currently takes in only 20 percent of its revenue from such nonticket charges. But Ryanair is the industry leader in charging passengers for virtually every optional amenity they consume. The brash airline brags about being the first to charge for checked bags and in-flight refreshments. Such tactics, once shunned by the industry, are now standard procedure and bring in billions in airline revenues. But Ryanair takes it much further. It now charges customers for printing boarding passes, paying with a debit or credit card, or using wheelchairs. It has even proposed charging for overweight customers, or charging a fee for using that proposed one remaining toilet.

In addition to charging customers for every aspect of the flight, Ryanair also envisions big revenues from selling products for other companies. The interiors of Ryanair planes are

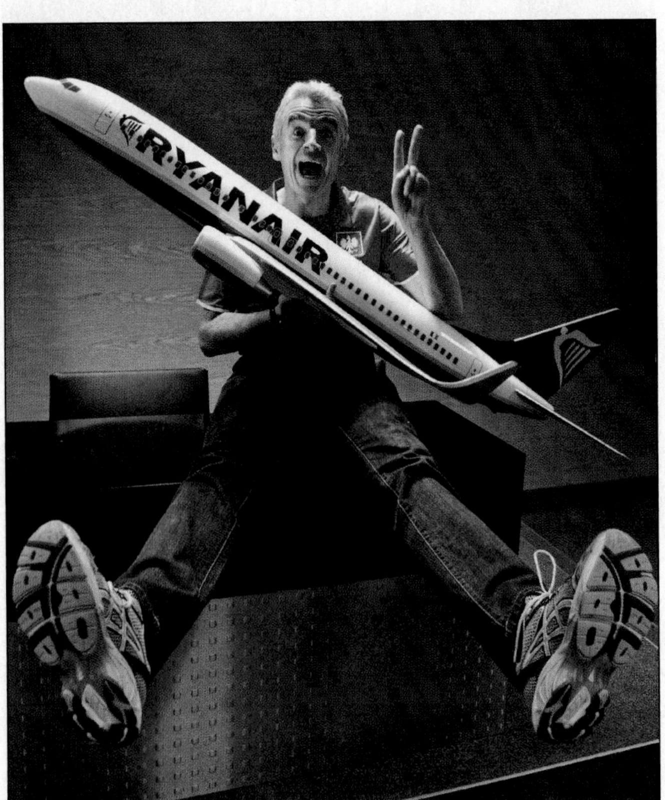

>> Good-value pricing: Ryanair's sometimes outrageous CEO, Michael O'Leary, hopes one day to "make flying free."

Maciej Kulczynski/EPA/News.com.

almost as littered with advertising as Time Square. Once in the air, flight attendants hawk everything from scratch-card games to digital cameras to their captive audience. They peddle croissants and cappuccino; digital gadgets and perfumes; raffle tickets for the airline's sponsored charity; and even smokeless cigarettes for €6 a pack.

Upon arrival at a usually out-of-the-way airport, Ryanair will sell passengers bus or train tickets into town. The company also gets commissions from rental cars, hotel rooms, ski packages, and travel insurance. Every chance it gets, Ryanair tries to squeeze just a little more out of its passengers.

Ryanair makes no excuses for both the additional charges and the absence of creature comforts. In fact, it sees its "less-for-less" value-pricing approach as long overdue in the airline industry. "In many ways, travel is pleasant and enriching," O'Leary states. But "the physical process of getting from point A to point B shouldn't be pleasant, nor enriching. It should be quick, efficient, affordable, and safe." As Ryanair's success suggests, customers seem to agree. Passengers are getting exactly what they want—outrageously low prices. And the additional purchases are discretionary.

Despite the lack of amenities, most passengers seem to appreciate rather than resent Ryanair's open and straightforward approach to pricing. Compared with the so-called "sophisticated" approaches of other airlines, proclaims one passenger, "I prefer [Ryanair's] crude ways, with its often dirt-cheap tickets and shameless [but plain-speaking] efforts to get its hand in my purse." And commenting on what some analysts have referred to as Ryanaire's "cattle-car" approach to passengers, another good-humored flier observes, "Only O'Leary will call you a cow, lick his chops, and explain how he plans to carve you up for dinner."

O'Leary's philosophy that commercial air passengers don't need to be coddled to make them loyal appears to fly in the face of modern marketing's focus on providing an exceptional customer experience. But Ryanair is proving that companies can provide customer value in more ways than one. When you look at Ryanair's falling prices and rising profits, O'Leary's dream of flying for free doesn't seem so far-fetched after all. With Ryanair's knack for good-value pricing, not even the sky's the limit.

Sources: Quotes and other information from Cecilia Rodriguez, "Airlines Look to Raise Revenue the Ryanair Way," *Forbes*, March 5, 2012, www.forbes.com/sites/ceciliarodriguez/2012/03/05/105/; Jane Leung, "Ryanair's Five 'Cheapest' Money-Saving Schemes," *CNNTravel*, October 17, 2011 www.cnn.com/2011/10/17/travel/ryanair-money-saving-schemes/index.htm; Felix Gillette, "Ryanair's O'Leary: The Duke of Discomfort," *Businessweek*, September 2, 2010, www.businessweek.com/magazine/content/10_37/b4194058006755.htm; Helen Thomas, "Ryanair Increases Profit Outlook," *Financial Times,* January 29, 2013, p. 16; and www.ryanair.com/en/investor/investor-relations-news, accessed October 2013.

Value-Added Pricing

Value-based pricing doesn't mean simply charging what customers want to pay or setting low prices to meet competition. Instead, many companies adopt **value-added pricing** strategies. Rather than cutting prices to match competitors, they attach value-added features and services to differentiate their offers and thus support their higher prices. For example, even as frugal consumer spending habits linger, some movie theater chains are *adding* amenities and charging *more* rather than cutting services to maintain lower admission prices:[6]

Value-added pricing
Attaching value-added features and services to differentiate a company's offers and charging higher prices.

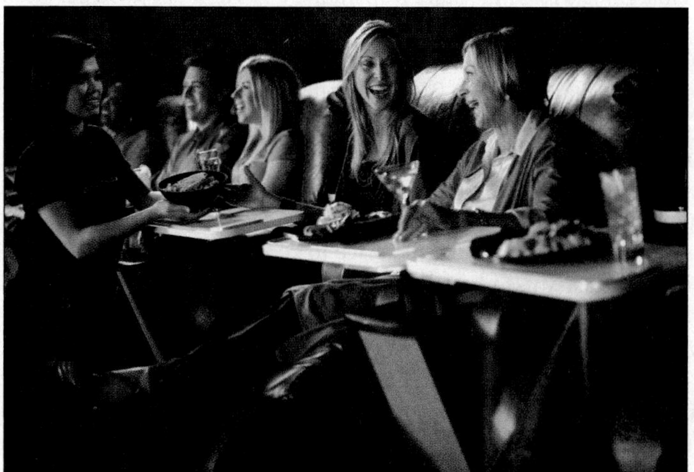

Value-added pricing: Rather than cutting services to maintain lower admission prices, premium theaters such as AMC's Cinema Suites are adding amenities and charging more. "Once people experience it, . . . they don't want to go anywhere else."

Courtesy of AMC Theaters.

Some theater chains are turning their multiplexes into smaller, roomier luxury outposts. The new premium theaters offer value-added features such as online reserved seating, high-backed leather executive or rocking chairs with armrests and footrests, the latest in digital sound and super-wide screens, dine-in restaurants serving fine food and drinks, and even valet parking. For example, AMC Theatres (the second-largest American theater chain) operates more than 50 theaters with some kind of enhanced food and beverage amenities, including Fork & Screen (upgraded leather seating, seat-side service, extensive menu including dinner offerings, beer, wine, and cocktails) and Cinema Suites (additional upscale food offerings in addition to premium cocktails and an extensive wine list, seat-side service, red leather reclining chairs, and eight to nine feet of spacing between rows).

So at the Cinema Suites at the AMC Easton 30 with IMAX in Columbus, Ohio, bring on the mango margaritas! For $9 to $15 a ticket (depending on the time and day), moviegoers are treated to reserved seating, a strict 21-and-over-only policy, reclining leather seats, and the opportunity to pay even more to have dinner and drinks brought to their seats. Such theaters are so successful that AMC plans to add more. "Once people experience it," says a company spokesperson, "more often than not they don't want to go anywhere else."

Author Comment

Costs set the floor for price, but the goal isn't always to *minimize* costs. In fact, many firms invest in higher costs so that they can claim higher prices and margins (think about Steinway pianos). The key is to manage the *spread* between costs and prices—how much the company makes for the customer value it delivers.

Cost-Based Pricing

Whereas customer value perceptions set the price ceiling, costs set the floor for the price that the company can charge. **Cost-based pricing** involves setting prices based on the costs of producing, distributing, and selling the product plus a fair rate of return for the company's effort and risk. A company's costs may be an important element in its pricing strategy.

Some companies, such as Walmart or Southwest Airlines, work to become the *low-cost producers* in their industries. Companies with lower costs can set lower prices that result in smaller margins but greater sales and profits. However, other companies—such as Apple, BMW, and Steinway—intentionally pay higher costs so that they can add value and claim higher prices and margins. For example, it costs more to make a "hand-crafted" Steinway piano than a Yamaha production model. But the higher costs result in higher quality, justifying that eye-popping $87,000 price. The key is to manage the spread between costs and prices—how much the company makes for the customer value it delivers.

Cost-based pricing
Setting prices based on the costs of producing, distributing, and selling the product plus a fair rate of return for effort and risk.

Types of Costs

A company's costs take two forms: fixed and variable. **Fixed costs** (also known as **overhead**) are costs that do not vary with production or sales level. For example, a company must pay each month's bills for rent, heat, interest, and executive salaries regardless of the company's level of output. **Variable costs** vary directly with the level of production. Each PC produced by HP involves a cost of computer chips, wires, plastic, packaging, and other inputs. Although these costs tend to be the same for each unit produced, they are called variable costs because the total varies with the number of units produced. **Total costs** are the sum of the fixed and variable costs for any given level of production. Management wants to charge a price that will at least cover the total production costs at a given level of production.

Fixed costs (overhead)
Costs that do not vary with production or sales level.

Variable costs
Costs that vary directly with the level of production.

Total costs
The sum of the fixed and variable costs for any given level of production.

The company must watch its costs carefully. If it costs the company more than its competitors to produce and sell a similar product, the company will need to charge a higher price or make less profit, putting it at a competitive disadvantage.

Cost-Plus Pricing

Cost-plus pricing (markup pricing)
Adding a standard markup to the cost of the product.

The simplest pricing method is **cost-plus pricing** (or **markup pricing**)—adding a standard markup to the cost of the product. For example, an electronics retailer might pay a manufacturer $20 for a flash drive and mark it up to sell at $30, a 50 percent markup on cost. The retailer's gross margin is $10. If the store's operating costs amount to $8 per flash drive sold, the retailer's profit margin will be $2. The manufacturer that made the flash drive probably used cost-plus pricing, too. If the manufacturer's standard cost of producing the flash drive was $16, it might have added a 25 percent markup, setting the price to the retailers at $20.

Does using standard markups to set prices make sense? Generally, no. Any pricing method that ignores consumer demand and competitor prices is not likely to lead to the best price. Still, markup pricing remains popular for many reasons. First, sellers are more certain about costs than about demand. By tying the price to cost, sellers simplify pricing. Second, when all firms in the industry use this pricing method, prices tend to be similar and price competition is minimized.

Break-even pricing (target return pricing)
Setting price to break even on the costs of making and marketing a product, or setting price to make a target return.

Another cost-oriented pricing approach is **break-even pricing**, or a variation called **target return pricing**. The firm tries to determine the price at which it will break even or make the target return it is seeking. Target return pricing uses the concept of a *break-even chart,* which shows the total cost and total revenue expected at different sales volume levels. >> **Figure 9.3** shows a break-even chart for the flash drive manufacturer discussed previously. Fixed costs are $6 million regardless of sales volume, and variable costs are $5 per unit. Variable costs are added to fixed costs to form total costs, which rise with volume. The slope of the total revenue curve reflects the price. Here, the price is $15 (for example, the company's revenue is $12 million on 800,000 units, or $15 per unit).

>> Figure 9.3 Break-Even Chart for Determining Target Return Price and Break-Even Volume

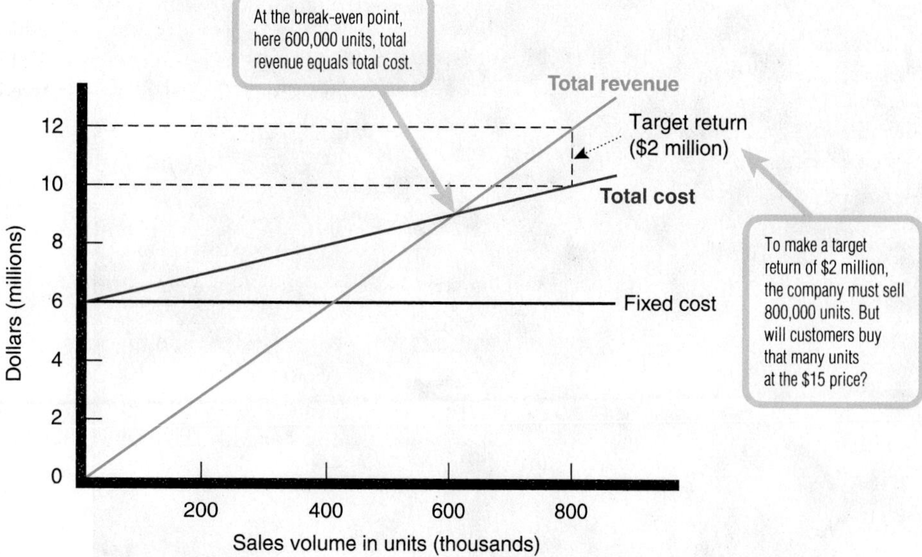

At the $15 price, the manufacturer must sell at least 600,000 units to *break even* (break-even volume = fixed costs ÷ (price − variable costs) = $6,000,000 ÷ ($15 − $5) = 600,000). That is, at this level, total revenues will equal total costs of $9 million, producing no profit. If the flash drive manufacturer wants a target return of $2 million, it must sell at least 800,000 units to obtain the $12 million of total revenue needed to cover the costs of $10 million plus the $2 million of target profits. In contrast, if the company charges a higher price, say $20, it will not need to sell as many units to break even or to achieve its target profit. In fact, the higher the price, the lower the manufacturer's break-even point will be.

The major problem with this analysis, however, is that it fails to consider customer value and the relationship between price and demand. As the *price* increases, *demand* decreases, and the market may not buy even the lower volume needed to break even at the higher price. For example, suppose the flash drive manufacturer calculates that, given its current fixed and variable costs, it must charge a price of $30 for the product in order to earn its desired target profit. But marketing research shows that few consumers will pay more than $25. In this case, the company must trim its costs in order to lower the break-even point so that it can charge the lower price consumers expect.

Thus, although break-even analysis and target return pricing can help the company to determine the minimum prices needed to cover expected costs and profits, they do not take the price–demand relationship into account. When using this method, the company must also consider the impact of price on the sales volume needed to realize target profits and the likelihood that the needed volume will be achieved at each possible price.

Author Comment
In setting prices, the company must also consider competitors' prices. No matter what price it charges—high, low, or in between—the company must be certain to give customers superior value for that price.

Competition-Based Pricing

Competition-based pricing involves setting prices based on competitors' strategies, costs, prices, and market offerings. Consumers will base their judgments of a product's value on the prices that competitors charge for similar products.

Competition-based pricing
Setting prices based on competitors' strategies, prices, costs, and market offerings.

In assessing competitors' pricing strategies, the company should ask several questions. First, how does the company's market offering compare with competitors' offerings in terms of customer value? If consumers perceive that the company's product or service provides greater value, the company can charge a higher price. If consumers perceive less value relative to competing products, the company must either charge a lower price or change customer perceptions to justify a higher price.

Next, how strong are current competitors and what are their current pricing strategies? If the company faces a host of smaller competitors charging high prices relative to the value they deliver, it might charge lower prices to drive weaker competitors from the market. If the market is dominated by larger, lower-price competitors, the company may decide

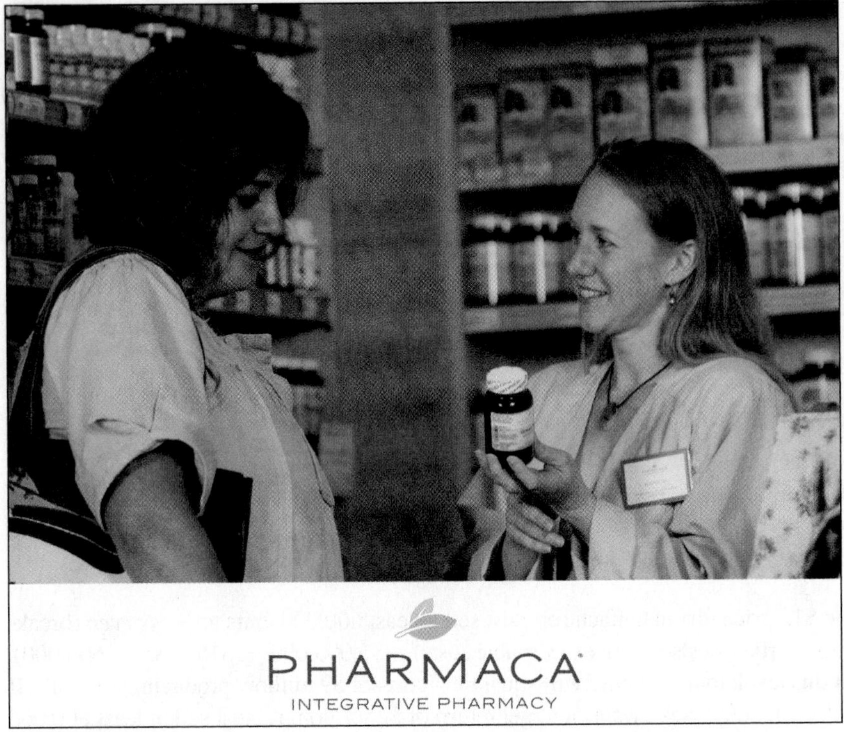

Pricing against larger, lower-price competitors: Pharmaca targets small niches with value-added services at higher prices. It's the relationships with Pharmaca's highly qualified professional staff, not low prices, that bring customers back.

Photo courtesy Pharmaca Integrative Pharmacy.

to target unserved market niches with value-added products and services at higher prices. For example, consider Pharmaca Integrative Pharmacy:[7]

> In a market saturated with CVSs, Rite-Aids, and Walgreens, pharmacy nicher Pharmaca wants to be much more than a traditional drug store. Instead, at its two dozen and growing brick-and-mortar stores and its robust online site, Pharmaca positions itself as an upscale total wellness resource center. Sometimes dubbed "the Whole Foods of pharmacies," Pharmaca carries only a limited sprinkling of mainstream consumer brands amidst a much broader assortment of high-end natural, organic, and alternative products, everything from organic chocolates to spa skin care brands to mineral makeup lines. Like a typical drugstore, Pharmaca fills prescriptions for traditional medicines. But what sets it apart from a Walgreens or CVS is its highly-skilled staff of integrative health-care professionals—nutritionists, herbalists, aestheticians, homeopaths, and naturopathic doctors—all dressed in lab coats, milling the aisles, and ready to assist customers. Their goal is to get to know customers and help them take charge of their own wellness by treating the whole person—from the skin to the bones to the mind. Pharmaca's high-end products and professional staff mean higher prices; a typical customer receipt is three times greater than in a traditional drugstore. But Pharmaca customers aren't looking for low prices. "When customers develop faith in a practitioner, they become much more loyal to the store," says CEO Mark Panzer says. It's those relationships, not low prices, that keep customers coming back.

What principle should guide decisions about what price to charge relative to those of competitors? The answer is simple in concept but often difficult in practice: No matter what price you charge—high, low, or in between—be certain to give customers superior value for that price.

Author Comment
Now that we've looked at the three general pricing strategies—value-, cost-, and competitor-based pricing—let's dig into some of the many other factors that affect pricing decisions.

Other Internal and External Considerations Affecting Price Decisions

Beyond customer value perceptions, costs, and competitor strategies, the company must consider several additional internal and external factors. Internal factors affecting pricing include the company's overall marketing strategy, objectives, and marketing mix, as well as other organizational considerations. External factors include the nature of the market and demand and other environmental factors.

Overall Marketing Strategy, Objectives, and Mix

Price is only one element of the company's broader marketing strategy. So, before setting price, the company must decide on its overall marketing strategy for the product or service. Sometimes, a company's overall strategy is built around its price and value story. For example, as we saw in the chapter-opening story, grocery retailer Trader Joe's unique "cheap gourmet" price–value positioning has made it one of the nation's fastest-growing, most popular food stores.

If a company has selected its target market and positioning carefully, then its marketing mix strategy, including price, will be fairly straightforward. For example, Amazon positions its Kindle Fire tablet as offering the same (or even more) for less, and prices it at 40 percent less than Apple's iPad and Samsung's Galaxy tablets. It recently began targeting families with young children, positioning the Kindle Fire as the "Perfect family tablet," with models priced as low as $159, bundled with Kindle Freetime, a $4.99-per-month all-in-one subscription service that brings together books, games, educational apps, movies, and TV shows for kids ages three through eight. Thus, the Kindle pricing strategy is largely determined by decisions on market positioning.

Pricing may play an important role in helping to accomplish company objectives at many levels. A firm can set prices to attract new customers or profitably retain existing ones. It can set prices low to prevent competition from entering the market or set prices at competitors' levels to stabilize the market. It can price to keep the loyalty and support of resellers or avoid government intervention. Prices can be reduced temporarily to create excitement for a brand. Or one product may be priced to help the sales of other products in the company's line.

Target costing
Pricing that starts with an ideal selling price, then targets costs that will ensure that the price is met.

Price decisions must be coordinated with product design, distribution, and promotion decisions to form a consistent and effective integrated marketing mix program. Decisions made for other marketing mix variables may affect pricing decisions. For example, a decision to position the product on high-performance quality will mean that the seller must charge a higher price to cover higher costs. And producers whose resellers are expected to support and promote their products may have to build larger reseller margins into their prices.

Companies often position their products on price and then tailor other marketing mix decisions to the prices they want to charge. Here, price is a crucial product-positioning factor that defines the product's market, competition, and design. Many firms support such price-positioning strategies with a technique called **target costing**. Target costing reverses the usual process of first designing a new product, determining its cost, and then asking, "Can we sell it for that?" Instead, it starts with an ideal selling price based on customer value considerations and then targets costs that will ensure that the price is met. For example, when Honda initially designed the Honda Fit, it began with a $13,950 starting price point and highway mileage of 33 miles per gallon firmly in mind. It then designed a stylish, peppy little car with costs that allowed it to give target customers those values.

>> Nonprice positioning: Luxury smartphone maker Vertu puts very high value into its products and charges premium prices to match that value. Average price: nearly $6,000.

Vertu.

Other companies deemphasize price and use other marketing mix tools to create *nonprice* positions. Often, the best strategy is not to charge the lowest price but rather to differentiate the marketing offer to make it worth a higher price. >> For example, luxury smartphone maker Vertu puts very high value into its products and charges premium prices to match that value. Vertu phones are made from high-end materials such as titanium and sapphire crystal, and each phone is hand-assembled by a single craftsman in England. Phones come with additional services such as Vertu Concierge, which helps create personal, curated user experiences and recommendations. Vertu phones sell for an average price of $6,000, with top models going for more than $10,000. But target customers recognize Vertu's very high quality and are willing to pay more to get it.[8]

Some marketers even position their products on *high* prices, featuring high prices as part of their product's allure. For example, Grand Marnier offers a $225 bottle of Cuvée du Cent Cinquantenaire cognac that's marketed with the tagline "Hard to find, impossible to pronounce, and prohibitively expensive." And Titus Cycles, a premium bicycle manufacturer, features its high prices in its advertising. One ad humorously shows a man giving his girlfriend a "cubic zirconia" engagement ring so that he can purchase a Titus Vuelo for himself. Suggested retail price: $7,750.00.

Thus, marketers must consider the total marketing strategy and mix when setting prices. But again, even when featuring price, marketers need to remember that customers rarely buy on price alone. Instead, they seek products that give them the best value in terms of benefits received for the prices paid.

Organizational Considerations

Management must decide who within the organization should set prices. Companies handle pricing in a variety of ways. In small companies, prices are often set by top management rather than by the marketing or sales departments. In large companies, pricing is typically handled by divisional or product managers. In industrial markets, salespeople may be allowed to negotiate with customers within certain price ranges. Even so, top management sets the pricing objectives and policies, and it often approves the prices proposed by lower-level management or salespeople.

In industries in which pricing is a key factor (airlines, aerospace, steel, railroads, oil companies), companies often have pricing departments to set the best prices or help others set them. These departments report to the marketing department or top management. Others who have an influence on pricing include sales managers, production managers, finance managers, and accountants.

The Market and Demand

As noted earlier, good pricing starts with an understanding of how customers' perceptions of value affect the prices they are willing to pay. Both consumer and industrial buyers balance the price of a product or service against the benefits of owning it. Thus, before setting prices, the marketer must understand the relationship between price and demand for the company's product. In this section, we take a deeper look at the price–demand relationship and how it varies for different types of markets. We then discuss methods for analyzing the price–demand relationship.

Pricing in Different Types of Markets

The seller's pricing freedom varies with different types of markets. Economists recognize four types of markets, each presenting a different pricing challenge.

Under *pure competition*, the market consists of many buyers and sellers trading in a uniform commodity, such as wheat, copper, or financial securities. No single buyer or seller has much effect on the going market price. In a purely competitive market, marketing research, product development, pricing, advertising, and sales promotion play little or no role. Thus, sellers in these markets do not spend much time on marketing strategy.

Under *monopolistic competition*, the market consists of many buyers and sellers trading over a range of prices rather than a single market price. A range of prices occurs because sellers can differentiate their offers to buyers. Because there are many competitors, each firm is less affected by competitors' pricing strategies than in oligopolistic markets. Sellers try to develop differentiated offers for different customer segments and, in addition to price, freely use branding, advertising, and personal selling to set their offers apart. » Thus, Honda sets its Odyssey minivan apart through strong branding and advertising, reducing the impact of price. Its tongue-in-cheek "Van of Your Dreams" advertisements tell parents "the new Odyssey has everything one would dream about in a van, if one had dreams about vans." Beyond the standard utility features you'd expect in a van, Honda tells them, you'll also find yourself surrounded by a dazzling array of technology, a marvel of ingenuity. "Hook up your MP3 player and summon music like a rock god. Call out a song name and it plays through an audio system that can split the heavens!"

odyssey.honda.com
THE VAN OF YOUR DREAMS.
Introducing the all-new Honda ODYSSEY

>> Pricing in monopolistic competition: Honda sets its Odyssey minivan apart through strong branding and advertising, reducing the impact of price. Its tongue-in-cheek "Van of Your Dreams" ads tell parents "the new Odyssey has everything one would dream about in a van, if one had dreams about vans."

Print advertisement provided courtesy of American Honda Motor Co., Inc.

Under *oligopolistic competition*, the market consists of only a few large sellers. For example, only four companies—Verizon, AT&T, Sprint, and T-Mobile—control more than 90 percent of the U.S. wireless service provider market. Because there are few sellers, each seller is alert and responsive to competitors' pricing strategies and marketing moves. In a *pure monopoly*, the market is dominated by one seller. The seller may be a government monopoly (the U.S. Postal Service), a private regulated monopoly (a power company), or a private unregulated monopoly (De Beers and diamonds). Pricing is handled differently in each case.

Analyzing the Price–Demand Relationship

Each price the company might charge will lead to a different level of demand. The relationship between the price charged and the resulting demand level is shown in the **demand curve** in **>> Figure 9.4**. The demand curve shows the number of units the market will buy in a given time period at different prices that might be charged. In the normal case, demand and price are inversely related—that is, the higher the price, the lower the demand. Thus, the company would sell less if it raised its price from P_1 to P_2. In short, consumers with limited budgets probably will buy less of something if its price is too high.

Demand curve
A curve that shows the number of units the market will buy in a given time period, at different prices that might be charged.

Understanding a brand's price–demand curve is crucial to good pricing decisions. ConAgra Foods learned this lesson when pricing its Banquet frozen dinners:[9]

> When ConAgra tried to cover higher commodity costs by raising list price of Banquet dinners from $1 to $1.25, consumers turned up their noses to the higher price. Sales dropped, forcing ConAgra to sell off excess dinners at discount prices. It turns out that "the key component for Banquet dinners—the key attribute—is you've got to be at $1," says ConAgra's CEO Gary Rodkin. "Everything else pales in comparison to that." Banquet dinner prices are now back to a buck a dinner. To make money at that price, ConAgra is doing a better job of managing costs by shrinking portions and substituting less expensive ingredients for costlier ones. More than just Banquet dinners, ConAgra prices all of its frozen and canned products at under $1 per serving. Consumers are responding well to the brand's efforts to keep prices down. After all, where else can you find dinner for $1?

Most companies try to measure their demand curves by estimating demand at different prices. The type of market makes a difference. In a monopoly, the demand curve shows the total market demand resulting from different prices. If the company faces competition,

>> Figure 9.4 Demand Curve

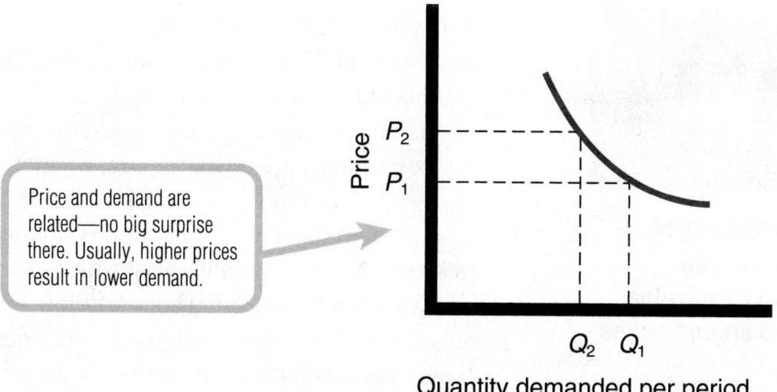
Price and demand are related—no big surprise there. Usually, higher prices result in lower demand.
Price
P2
P1
Q2 Q1
Quantity demanded per period

its demand at different prices will depend on whether competitors' prices stay constant or change with the company's own prices.

Price Elasticity of Demand

Price elasticity
A measure of the sensitivity of demand to changes in price.

Marketers also need to know **price elasticity**—how responsive demand will be to a change in price. If demand hardly changes with a small change in price, we say demand is *inelastic*. If demand changes greatly, we say the demand is *elastic*.

If demand is elastic rather than inelastic, sellers will consider lowering their prices. A lower price will produce more total revenue. This practice makes sense as long as the extra costs of producing and selling more do not exceed the extra revenue. At the same time, most firms want to avoid pricing that turns their products into commodities. In recent years, forces such as deregulation and the instant price comparisons afforded by the Internet and other technologies have increased consumer price sensitivity, turning products ranging from telephones and computers to new automobiles into commodities in some consumers' eyes.

The Economy

Economic conditions can have a strong impact on the firm's pricing strategies. Economic factors such as a boom or recession, inflation, and interest rates affect pricing decisions because they affect consumer spending, consumer perceptions of the product's price and value, and the company's costs of producing and selling a product.

In the aftermath of the recent Great Recession, many consumers have rethought the price–value equation. They have tightened their belts and become more value conscious. Consumers will likely continue their thriftier ways well beyond any economic recovery. As a result, many marketers have increased their emphasis on value-for-the-money pricing strategies.

The most obvious response to the new economic realities is to cut prices and offer discounts. Thousands of companies have done just that. Lower prices make products more affordable and help spur short-term sales. However, such price cuts can have undesirable long-term consequences. Lower prices mean lower margins. Deep discounts may cheapen a brand in consumers' eyes. And once a company cuts prices, it's difficult to raise them again when the economy recovers.

Rather than cutting prices, many companies have instead shifted their marketing focus to more affordable items in their product mixes. For example, whereas its previous promotions emphasized high-end products and pricey concepts such as creating dream kitchens, Home Depot's more recent advertising pushes items like potting soil and hand tools under the tagline: "More saving. More doing. That's the power of Home Depot."

Other companies are holding prices but redefining the "value" in their value propositions. >> Consider upscale grocery retailer Whole Foods Market:[10]

> Whole Foods Market grew rapidly by serving up high-quality grocery items to upscale customers who were willing and able to pay more for the extra value they got. Then came the Great Recession of 2008, and even relatively affluent customers began cutting back and spending less. All of a sudden, Whole Foods Market faced a difficult question: Should it hold the line on its premium price positioning, or should it cut prices and reposition itself to fit the leaner times? Whole Foods decided to stick with its core up-market positioning, but it also began to subtly realign its value proposition. Rather than dropping everyday prices across the board, Whole Foods lowered prices on selected basic items and offered significant sales on others. It also started emphasizing its lower-price private-label brand, 365 Everyday Value.

>> When the economy dipped, rather than cutting everyday prices, Whole Foods set out to convince shoppers that it was, in fact, an affordable place to shop. It even assigned workers to serve as "value tour guides," like the one shown here, to escort shoppers around stores pointing out value items.

© Elise Amendola/AP Wide World.

At the same time, however, Whole Foods Market launched a new marketing program that did more than simply promote more affordable merchandise. It convinced shoppers that, for what you get, Whole Foods's regular products and prices offer good value as well. When it comes to quality food, price isn't everything. The upscale retailer even assigned workers to serve as "value tour guides" to escort shoppers around stores and point out the value in both sale and regular items. As one tour guide notes, "Value means getting a good exchange for your money." As a result of subtle shifts in its value strategy, Whole Foods Market is now back on track in the post-recession economy. It is meeting the challenges of more frugal times in a way that preserves all the things that have made it special to customers through the years.

Remember, even in tough economic times, consumers do not buy based on prices alone. They balance the price they pay against the value they receive. For example, despite selling its shoes for as much as $150 a pair, Nike commands the highest consumer loyalty of any brand in the footwear segment. Customers perceive the value of Nike's products and the Nike ownership experience to be well worth the price. Thus, no matter what price they charge—low or high—companies need to offer great *value for the money*.

Other External Factors

Beyond the market and the economy, the company must consider several other factors in its external environment when setting prices. It must know what impact its prices will have on other parties in its environment. How will *resellers* react to various prices? The company should set prices that give resellers a fair profit, encourage their support, and help them to sell the product effectively. The *government* is another important external influence on pricing decisions. Finally, *social concerns* may need to be taken into account. In setting prices, a company's short-term sales, market share, and profit goals may need to be tempered by broader societal considerations. We will examine public policy issues later in the chapter.

SPEED BUMP LINKING THE CONCEPTS

The concept of customer value is critical to good pricing and to successful marketing in general. Pause for a minute and be certain that you appreciate what value really means.

- An earlier example states that although the average Steinway piano costs $87,000, to those who own one, a Steinway is a great value. Does this fit your idea of value?
- Pick two competing brands from a familiar product category (watches, perfume, consumer electronics, restaurants)—one low priced and the other high priced. Which, if either, offers the greatest value?
- Does "value" mean the same thing as "low price"? How do these concepts differ?

We've now seen that pricing decisions are subject to a complex array of customer, company, competitive, and environmental forces. To make things even more complex, a company sets not a single price but rather a *pricing structure* that covers different items in its line. This pricing structure changes over time as products move through their life cycles. The company adjusts its prices to reflect changes in costs and demand and to account for variations in buyers and situations. As the competitive environment changes, the company considers when to initiate price changes and when to respond to them.

We now examine additional pricing approaches used in special pricing situations or to adjust prices to meet changing situations. We look in turn at *new product pricing* for products in the introductory stage of the product life cycle, *product mix pricing* for related products in the product mix, *price-adjustment tactics* that account for customer differences and changing situations, and strategies for initiating and responding to *price changes*.

Author Comment
Pricing new products can be especially challenging. Just think about all the things you'd need to consider in pricing a new mobile phone, say the first Apple iPhone. Even more, you need to start thinking about the price—along with many other marketing considerations—at the very beginning of the design process.

New Product Pricing Strategies

Pricing strategies usually change as the product passes through its life cycle. The introductory stage is especially challenging. Companies bringing out a new product face the challenge of setting prices for the first time. They can choose between two broad strategies: *market-skimming pricing* and *market-penetration pricing*.

Market-Skimming Pricing

Market-skimming pricing (price skimming)
Setting a high price for a new product to skim maximum revenues layer by layer from the segments willing to pay the high price; the company makes fewer but more profitable sales.

Many companies that invent new products set high initial prices to *skim* revenues layer by layer from the market. Apple frequently uses this strategy, called **market-skimming pricing** (or **price skimming**). When Apple first introduced the iPhone, its initial price was as much as $599 per phone. The phones were purchased only by customers who really wanted the sleek new gadget and could afford to pay a high price for it. Six months later, Apple dropped the price to $399 for an 8-GB model and $499 for the 16-GB model to attract new buyers. Within a year, it dropped prices again to $199 and $299, respectively, and you can now buy a basic 8-GB model for $49. In this way, Apple has skimmed the maximum amount of revenue from the various segments of the market.

Market skimming makes sense only under certain conditions. First, the product's quality and image must support its higher price, and enough buyers must want the product at that price. Second, the costs of producing a smaller volume cannot be so high that they cancel the advantage of charging more. Finally, competitors should not be able to enter the market easily and undercut the high price.

Market-Penetration Pricing

Market-penetration pricing
Setting a low price for a new product in order to attract a large number of buyers and a large market share.

Rather than setting a high initial price to skim off small but profitable market segments, some companies use **market-penetration pricing**. Companies set a low initial price to *penetrate* the market quickly and deeply—to attract a large number of buyers quickly and win a large market share. The high sales volume results in falling costs, allowing companies to cut their prices even further. For example, the giant Swedish retailer IKEA used penetration pricing to boost its success in the Chinese market:[11]

> When IKEA first opened stores in China in 2002, people crowded in but not to buy home furnishings. Instead, they stopped by to lounge around, enjoy the free toilets and air conditioning, or even just take a short snooze on a comfy chair or bed on display. Chinese consumers are famously frugal. When it came time to actually buy, they shopped instead at local stores just down the street that offered knockoffs of IKEA's designs at a much lower price. So to turn finicky Chinese consumers into paying customers, IKEA in China cut costs by boosting the proportion of China-made products on its showroom floors and then slashed its prices. Prices on some merchandise dropped to as low as 70 percent below prices in IKEA stores in other parts of the world. The penetration pricing strategy worked. IKEA now captures a 43 percent market share of China's fast-growing home wares market alone, and the sales at its 11 mammoth Chinese stores surged 20 percent last year. >> One store alone in Beijing draws nearly six million visitors annually and 28,000 patrons on an average Saturday. Weekend crowds in many of IKEA's Chinese stores are so big that employees use megaphones to keep shoppers under control.

>> Penetration pricing: To lure famously frugal Chinese customers, IKEA slashed its prices. The strategy worked. Weekend crowds in many of IKEA's Chinese stores are so big that employees use megaphones to keep shoppers under control.

Author Comment
Most individual products are part of a broader product mix and must be priced accordingly. For example, Gillette prices its Fusion razors low. But once you buy the razor, you're a captive customer for its higher-margin replacement cartridges.

Several conditions must be met for this low-price strategy to work. First, the market must be highly price sensitive so that a low price produces more market growth. Second, production and distribution costs must decrease as sales volume increases. Finally, the low price must help keep out the competition, and the penetration pricer must maintain its low-price position. Otherwise, the price advantage may be only temporary.

Product Mix Pricing Strategies

The strategy for setting a product's price often has to be changed when the product is part of a product mix. In this case, the firm looks for a set of prices that maximizes its profits on the total product mix. Pricing is difficult because the various products have related demand and costs and face different degrees of competition. We now take a closer look at the five product mix pricing situations summarized in **»Table 9.1**: *product line pricing*, *optional-product pricing*, *captive-product pricing*, *by-product pricing*, and *product bundle pricing*.

» **Product line pricing: Mr. Clean car washes offer a complete line of wash packages priced from $5 for the basic Bronze wash to $27 for the feature-loaded Mr. Clean Signature Shine package.**

The Procter & Gamble Company.

Product Line Pricing

Companies usually develop product lines rather than single products. For example, Rossignol offers seven different collections of alpine skis of all designs and sizes, at prices that range from $150 for its junior skis, such as Fun Girl, to more than $1,100 for a pair from its Radical racing collection. It also offers lines of Nordic and backcountry skis, snowboards, and ski-related apparel. In **product line pricing**, management must determine the price steps to set between the various products in a line.

The price steps should take into account cost differences between products in the line. More important, they should account for differences in customer perceptions of the value of different features. » For example, at a Mr. Clean car wash, you can choose from any of six wash packages, ranging from a basic exterior-clean-only "Bronze" wash for $5; to an exterior clean, shine, and protect "Gold" package for $12; to an interior-exterior "Signature Shine" package for $27 that includes the works, from a thorough cleaning inside and out to a tire shine, underbody rust inhibitor, surface protectant, and even air freshener. The car wash's task is to establish perceived value differences that support the price differences.

» Table 9.1 Product Mix Pricing

Pricing Situation	Description
Product line pricing	Setting prices across an entire product line
Optional-product pricing	Pricing optional or accessory products sold with the main product
Captive-product pricing	Pricing products that must be used with the main product
By-product pricing	Pricing low-value by-products to get rid of or make money on them
Product bundle pricing	Pricing bundles of products sold together

Product line pricing
Setting the price steps between various products in a product line based on cost differences between the products, customer evaluations of different features, and competitors' prices.

Optional-Product Pricing

Optional-product pricing
The pricing of optional or accessory products along with a main product.

Many companies use **optional-product pricing**—offering to sell optional or accessory products along with the main product. For example, a car buyer may choose to order a navigation system and premium entertainment system. Refrigerators come with optional ice makers. And when you order a new computer, you can select from a bewildering array of processors, hard drives, docking systems, software options, and service plans. Pricing these options is a sticky problem. Companies must decide which items to include in the base price and which to offer as options.

Captive-Product Pricing

Captive-product pricing
Setting a price for products that must be used along with a main product, such as blades for a razor and games for a video-game console.

Companies that make products that must be used along with a main product are using **captive-product pricing**. Examples of captive products are razor blade cartridges, video games, printer cartridges, and e-books. Producers of the main products (razors, video-game consoles, printers, and tablet computers) often price them low and set high markups on the supplies. For example, Amazon loses an estimated $8 per machine on its $199 Kindle Fire HD tablet. It hopes to more than make up for the loss through sales of digital books, music, movies, subscription services, and other content for the devices.[12]

However, companies that use captive-product pricing must be careful. Finding the right balance between the main-product and captive-product prices can be tricky. Even more, consumers trapped into buying expensive captive products may come to resent the brand that ensnared them. Just ask about any customer how he feels after buying a Gillette Fusion ProGlide razor at a giveaway price only to learn later how expensive the replacements cartridge are. The cartridges are so pricy that they've become a high-value target for professional thieves for black-market resale. Moreover, Gillette's captive pricing strategy has invited direct price challenges from competitors such as Schick and the Dollar Shave Club. Recent Schick ads proclaimed that the Schick Hydro 5 is "Preferred over Fusion ProGlide at a better price." And the direct-response Dollar Shave Club asks, "Do you like spending $20 a month on brand-name razors?" As an alternative, it offers twin-blade razors for $1 a month ($3, including shipping and handling), and four- and six-blade models for $6 to $9, shipping and handling included.[13]

By-product pricing
Setting a price for by-products in order to make the main product's price more competitive.

In the case of services, captive-product pricing is called *two-part pricing*. The price of the service is broken into a *fixed fee* plus a *variable usage rate*. Thus, at Six Flags and other amusement parks, you pay a daily ticket or season pass charge plus additional fees for food and other in-park features.

By-Product Pricing

Producing products and services often generates by-products. If the by-products have no value and if getting rid of them is costly, this will affect the pricing of the main product. Using **by-product pricing**, the company seeks a market for these by-products to help offset the costs of disposing of them and help make the price of the main product more competitive.

The by-products themselves can even turn out to be profitable—turning trash into cash. For example, Coca-Cola converts waste from its beverage-making operations into profitable by-products. Nothing goes to waste, not even orange peels:[14]

> To make its Simply Orange, Minute Maid, and other orange juice brands, Coca-Cola and its fruit-procuring partner, Cutrale, squeeze a lot of oranges. Together each year, the two companies buy and process some 50 million boxes of oranges from Florida growers alone. That's a lot of orange juice, but it also leaves behind a lot of orange peels. Rather than paying to have the peels hauled way, however, Coca-Cola and Cutrale

>> By-product pricing: Coca-Cola converts waste from its beverage-making operations into profitable by-products. Nothing goes to waste, not even orange peels.
Igor Dutina/Shutterstock.

turn them into valuable by-products. Every part of the orange is put to good use. Essential oils are extracted, bottled, and sold for everything from food flavorings to household cleaners. What's left is pressed into pellets sold for livestock feed. Even the Simply Orange bottles you buy at your supermarket might soon be made in part from left-over orange peels. Coca-Cola's newly developed bio-PET Plant Bottles contain orange peels and other agricultural by-products from the company's food processing operations.

Product Bundle Pricing

Product bundle pricing
Combining several products and offering the bundle at a reduced price.

Using **product bundle pricing**, sellers often combine several products and offer the bundle at a reduced price. For example, fast-food restaurants bundle a burger, fries, and a soft drink at a "combo" price. Bath & Body Works offers "three-fer" deals on its soaps and lotions (such as three antibacterial soaps for $10). And Comcast, Time Warner, Verizon, and other telecommunications companies bundle TV service, phone service, and high-speed Internet connections at a low combined price. Price bundling can promote the sales of products consumers might not otherwise buy, but the combined price must be low enough to get them to buy the bundle.

Author Comment
Setting the base price for a product is only the start. The company must then adjust the price to account for customer and situational differences. When was the last time you paid the full suggested retail price for something?

Price-Adjustment Strategies

Companies usually adjust their basic prices to account for various customer differences and changing situations. Here we examine the seven price adjustment strategies summarized in **» Table 9.2**: *discount and allowance pricing*, *segmented pricing*, *psychological pricing*, *promotional pricing*, *geographical pricing*, *dynamic pricing*, and *international pricing*.

Discount and Allowance Pricing

Most companies adjust their basic price to reward customers for certain responses, such as paying bills early, volume purchases, and off-season buying. These price adjustments—called *discounts* and *allowances*—can take many forms.

Discount
A straight reduction in price on purchases during a stated period of time or in larger quantities.

One form of **discount** is a *cash discount*, a price reduction to buyers who pay their bills promptly. A typical example is "2/10, net 30," which means that although payment is due within 30 days, the buyer can deduct 2 percent if the bill is paid within 10 days. A *quantity discount* is a price reduction to buyers who buy large volumes. A seller offers a *functional discount* (also called a *trade discount*) to trade-channel members who perform certain functions, such as selling, storing, and record keeping. A *seasonal discount* is a price reduction to buyers who buy merchandise or services out of season.

» Table 9.2 Price Adjustments

Strategy	Description
Discount and allowance pricing	Reducing prices to reward customer responses such as paying early or promoting the product
Segmented pricing	Adjusting prices to allow for differences in customers, products, or locations
Psychological pricing	Adjusting prices for psychological effect
Promotional pricing	Temporarily reducing prices to spur short-run sales
Geographical pricing	Adjusting prices to account for the geographic location of customers
Dynamic pricing	Adjusting prices continually to meet the characteristics and needs of individual customers and situations
International pricing	Adjusting prices for international markets

Allowance
Promotional money paid by manufacturers to retailers in return for an agreement to feature the manufacturer's products in some way.

Allowances are another type of reduction from the list price. For example, *trade-in allowances* are price reductions given for turning in an old item when buying a new one. Trade-in allowances are most common in the automobile industry but are also given for other durable goods. *Promotional allowances* are payments or price reductions that reward dealers for participating in advertising and sales-support programs.

Segmented Pricing

Segmented pricing
Selling a product or service at two or more prices, where the difference in prices is not based on differences in costs.

Companies will often adjust their basic prices to allow for differences in customers, products, and locations. In **segmented pricing**, the company sells a product or service at two or more prices, even though the difference in prices is not based on differences in costs.

Segmented pricing takes several forms. Under *customer-segment pricing*, different customers pay different prices for the same product or service. Museums and movie theaters, for example, may charge a lower admission for students and senior citizens. Under *product form pricing*, different versions of the product are priced differently but not according to differences in their costs. For instance, a round-trip economy seat on a flight from New York to London might cost $1,000, whereas a business-class seat on the same flight might cost $4,500 or more. Although business-class customers receive roomier, more comfortable seats and higher-quality food and service, the differences in costs to the airlines are much less than the additional prices to passengers. >> However, to passengers who can afford it, the additional comfort and services are worth the extra charge.

>> Product form pricing: A roomier business-class seat on a flight from New York to London is many times the price of an economy seat on the same flight. To customers who can afford it, the extra comfort and service are worth the extra charge.

© Index Stock Imagery.

Using *location-based pricing*, a company charges different prices for different locations, even though the cost of offering each location is the same. For instance, state universities charge higher tuition for out-of-state students, and theaters vary their seat prices because of audience preferences for certain locations. Finally, using *time-based pricing*, a firm varies its price by the season, the month, the day, and even the hour. For example, movie theaters charge matinee pricing during the daytime, and resorts give weekend and seasonal discounts.

For segmented pricing to be an effective strategy, certain conditions must exist. The market must be segmentable, and segments must show different degrees of demand. The costs of segmenting and reaching the market cannot exceed the extra revenue obtained from the price difference. Of course, the segmented pricing must also be legal.

Most important, segmented prices should reflect real differences in customers' perceived value. Consumers in higher price tiers must feel that they're getting their extra money's worth for the higher prices paid. By the same token, companies must be careful not to treat customers in lower price tiers as second-class citizens. Otherwise, in the long run, the practice will lead to customer resentment and ill will. For example, in recent years, the airlines have incurred the wrath of frustrated customers at both ends of the airplane. Passengers paying full fare for business- or first-class seats often feel that they are being gouged. At the same time, passengers in lower-priced coach seats feel that they're being ignored or treated poorly.

Psychological Pricing

Price says something about the product. For example, many consumers use price to judge quality. A $100 bottle of perfume may contain only $3 worth of scent, but some people are willing to pay the $100 because this price indicates something special.

Psychological pricing
Pricing that considers the psychology of prices and not simply the economics; the price is used to say something about the product.

In using **psychological pricing**, sellers consider the psychology of prices, not simply the economics. For example, consumers usually perceive higher-priced products as having higher quality. When they can judge the quality of a product by examining it or by calling on past experience with it, they use price less to judge quality. But when they cannot judge quality because they lack the information or skill, price becomes an important quality signal. For instance, who's the better lawyer, one who charges $50 per hour or one who charges $500 per hour? You'd have to do a lot of digging into the respective lawyers' credentials to answer this question objectively; even then, you might not be able to judge accurately. Most of us would simply assume that the higher-priced lawyer is better.

Reference prices
Prices that buyers carry in their minds and refer to when they look at a given product.

Another aspect of psychological pricing is **reference prices**—prices that buyers carry in their minds and refer to when looking at a given product. The reference price might be formed by noting current prices, remembering past prices, or assessing the buying situation. Sellers can influence or use these consumers' reference prices when setting price. For example, a grocery retailer might place its store brand of bran flakes and raisins cereal priced at $2.49 next to Kellogg's Raisin Bran priced at $3.79. Or a company might offer more expensive models that don't sell very well to make its less expensive but still-high-priced models look more affordable by comparison. For example, Williams-Sonoma once offered a fancy bread maker at the steep price of $279. However, it then added a $429 model. The expensive model flopped but sales of the cheaper model doubled.[15]

For most purchases, consumers don't have all the skill or information they need to figure out whether they are paying a good price. They don't have the time, ability, or inclination to research different brands or stores, compare prices, and get the best deals. Instead, they may rely on certain cues that signal whether a price is high or low. Interestingly, such pricing cues are often provided by sellers, in the form of sales signs, price-matching guarantees, loss-leader pricing, and other helpful hints.

Even small differences in price can signal product differences. For example, in one study, people were asked how likely they were to choose among LASIK eye surgery providers based only on the prices they charged: $299 or $300. The actual price difference was only $1, but the study found that the psychological difference was much greater. Preference ratings for the providers charging $300 were much higher. Subjects perceived the $299 price as significantly less, but the lower price also raised stronger concerns about quality and risk. Some psychologists even argue that each digit has symbolic and visual qualities that should be considered in pricing. Thus, eight (8) is round and even and creates a soothing effect, whereas seven (7) is angular and creates a jarring effect.[16]

Promotional Pricing

Promotional pricing
Temporarily pricing products below the list price, and sometimes even below cost, to increase short-run sales.

With **promotional pricing**, companies will temporarily price their products below list price—and sometimes even below cost—to create buying excitement and urgency. >>Promotional pricing takes several forms. A seller may simply offer *discounts* from normal prices to increase sales and reduce inventories. Sellers also use *special-event pricing* in certain seasons to draw more customers. Thus, TVs and other consumer electronics are promotionally priced in November and December to attract holiday shoppers into the stores. *Limited-time offers*, such as online *flash sales*, can create buying urgency and make buyers feel lucky to have gotten in on the deal.

Manufacturers sometimes offer *cash rebates* to consumers who buy the product from dealers within a specified time; the manufacturer sends the rebate directly to the customer. Rebates have been popular with automakers and producers of mobile phones and small appliances, but they are also used with consumer packaged goods. Some manufacturers offer *low-interest financing*, *longer warranties*, or *free maintenance* to reduce the consumer's "price." This practice has become another favorite of the auto industry.

Promotional pricing, however, can have adverse effects. During most holiday seasons, for example, it's an all-out bargain war. Marketers carpet-bomb consumers with deals, causing buyer wear-out and pricing confusion. Used too frequently, price promotions can create "deal-prone" customers who wait until brands go on sale before buying them. In addition, constantly reduced prices can erode a brand's value in the eyes of customers.

Marketers sometimes become addicted to promotional pricing, especially in tight economic times. They use price promotions as a quick fix instead of sweating through

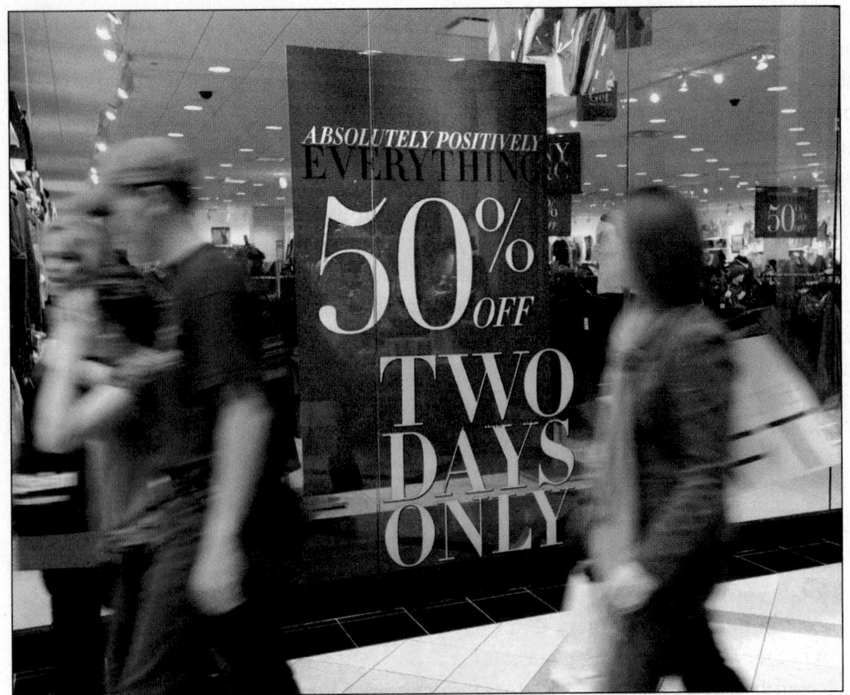

Promotional pricing: Companies offer promotional prices to create buying excitement and urgency.

Bloomberg via Getty Images.

the difficult process of developing effective longer-term strategies for building their brands. For example, before announcing its turnaround pricing strategy, JCPenney's developed an unhealthy reliance on coupons, markdowns, and nonstop sales, which accounted for the vast majority of its revenues. But companies must be careful to balance short-term sales incentives against long-term brand building. As JCPenney has learned, although a steady diet of promotional pricing can be destructive to a brand's image and profitability, some promotional pricing is often needed to generate sales.

Geographical Pricing

A company also must decide how to price its products for customers located in different parts of the United States or the world. Should the company risk losing the business of more-distant customers by charging them higher prices to cover the higher shipping costs? Or should the company charge all customers the same prices regardless of location? We will look at five *geographical pricing* strategies for the following hypothetical situation:

> The Peerless Paper Company is located in Atlanta, Georgia, and sells paper products to customers all over the United States. The cost of freight is high and affects the companies from which customers buy their paper. Peerless wants to establish a geographical pricing policy. It is trying to determine how to price a $10,000 order to three specific customers: Customer A (Atlanta), Customer B (Bloomington, Indiana), and Customer C (Compton, California).

One option is for Peerless to ask each customer to pay the shipping cost from the Atlanta factory to the customer's location. All three customers would pay the same factory price of $10,000, with Customer A paying, say, $100 for shipping; Customer B, $150; and Customer C, $250. Called *FOB-origin pricing,* this practice means that the goods are placed *free on board* (hence, *FOB*) a carrier. At that point the title and responsibility pass to the customer, who pays the freight from the factory to the destination. Because each customer picks up its own cost, supporters of FOB pricing feel that this is the fairest way to assess freight charges. The disadvantage, however, is that Peerless will be a high-cost firm to distant customers.

Uniform-delivered pricing is the opposite of FOB pricing. Here, the company charges the same price plus freight to all customers, regardless of their location. The freight charge is set at the average freight cost. Suppose this is $150. Uniform-delivered pricing therefore results in a higher charge to the Atlanta customer (who pays $150 freight instead of $100) and a lower charge to the Compton customer (who pays $150 instead of $250). Although the Atlanta customer would prefer to buy paper from another local paper company that uses FOB-origin pricing, Peerless has a better chance of capturing the California customer.

Zone pricing falls between FOB-origin pricing and uniform-delivered pricing. The company sets up two or more zones. All customers within a given zone pay a single total price; the more distant the zone, the higher the price. For example, Peerless might set up an East Zone and charge $100 freight to all customers in this zone, a Midwest Zone in which it charges $150, and a West Zone in which it charges $250. In this way, the customers within a given price zone receive no price advantage from the company. For example, customers in Atlanta and Boston pay the same total price to Peerless. The complaint, however, is that the Atlanta customer is paying part of the Boston customer's freight cost.

Using *basing-point pricing,* the seller selects a given city as a "basing point" and charges all customers the freight cost from that city to the customer location, regardless of the city from which the goods are actually shipped. For example, Peerless might set Chicago as the basing point and charge all customers $10,000 plus the freight from Chicago to their locations. This means that an Atlanta customer pays the freight cost from Chicago to Atlanta, even though the goods may be shipped from Atlanta. If all sellers used the same basing-point city, delivered prices would be the same for all customers, and price competition would be eliminated.

Finally, the seller who is anxious to do business with a certain customer or geographical area might use *freight-absorption pricing.* Using this strategy, the seller absorbs all or part of the actual freight charges to get the desired business. The seller might reason that if it can get more business, its average costs will decrease and more than compensate for its extra freight cost. Freight-absorption pricing is used for market penetration and to hold on to increasingly competitive markets.

Dynamic and Internet Pricing

Throughout most of history, prices were set by negotiation between buyers and sellers. *Fixed-price* policies—setting one price for all buyers—is a relatively modern idea that arose with the development of large-scale retailing at the end of the nineteenth century. Today, most prices are set this way. However, some companies are now reversing the fixed-pricing trend. They are using **dynamic pricing**—adjusting prices continually to meet the characteristics and needs of individual customers and situations.

Dynamic pricing
Adjusting prices continually to meet the characteristics and needs of individual customers and situations.

Dynamic pricing is especially prevalent online, where the Internet seems to be taking us back to a new age of fluid pricing. Such pricing offers many advantages for marketers. For example, Internet sellers such as L.L.Bean, Amazon.com, or Dell can mine their databases to gauge a specific shopper's desires, measure his or her means, instantaneously tailor offers to fit that shopper's behavior, and price products accordingly. Also, most retailers today—both online and offline—monitor each other's prices and quickly adjust their own prices accordingly. For example, when Target recently advertised plans to sell a Dyson Ball vacuum cleaner at a low sale price in its stores, Best Buy beat it to the punch with an even lower online price. Fast-growing retailer Kohl's even uses electronic price tags on products throughout its stores that allow it to quickly change prices on individual items based on competitive and other market requirements.[17]

Thus, services ranging from retailers, airlines, and hotels to sports teams change prices on the fly according to changes in demand, costs, or competitor pricing, adjusting what they charge for specific items on a day-by-day or even hour-by-hour basis. And many direct marketers monitor inventories, costs, and demand at any given moment and adjust prices instantly.

In the extreme, some companies customize their offers and prices based on the specific characteristics and behaviors of individual customers, mined from online browsing and purchasing histories. These days, online offers and prices might well be based on what specific customers search for and buy, how much they pay for other purchases, and whether they might be willing and able to spend more. For example, a consumer who recently went online to purchase a first-class ticket to London or customize a new Mercedes coupe might later get a higher quote on a new Bose Wave Radio. By comparison, a friend with a more modest online search and purchase history might receive an offer of 5 percent off and free shipping on the same radio.[18]

Although such dynamic pricing practices seem legally questionable, they're not. Dynamic pricing is legal as long as companies do not discriminate based on age, gender, location, or other similar characteristics. Dynamic pricing makes sense in many contexts—it adjusts prices according to market forces and consumer preferences. But marketers need to be careful not to use dynamic pricing to take advantage of certain customer groups, thereby damaging important customer relationships.

The practice of online pricing, however, goes both ways, and consumers often benefit from online and dynamic pricing. Thanks to the Internet, the centuries-old art of haggling is suddenly back in vogue. For example, consumers can negotiate prices at online auction sites and exchanges. Want to sell that antique pickle jar that's been collecting dust for generations? Post it on eBay or Craigslist. Want to name your own price for a hotel room or rental car? Visit Priceline.com or another reverse auction site. Want to bid on a ticket to a Katy Perry concert? Check out Ticketmaster.com, which offers an online auction service for concert tickets.

Also thanks to the Internet, consumers can get instant product and price comparisons from thousands of vendors at price comparison sites such as Yahoo! Shopping, Epinions.com, PriceGrabber.com, and PriceScan.com, or using mobile apps such as TheFind, eBay's RedLaser, Google's Barcode Scanner, or Amazon.com's PriceCheck. » For example, the RedLaser mobile app lets customers scan barcodes or QR codes (or search by voice or image) while shopping in stores. It then searches online and at nearby stores to provide thousands of reviews and comparison prices, and even offers buying links for immediate online purchasing. Armed with this information, consumers can often negotiate better in-store prices.

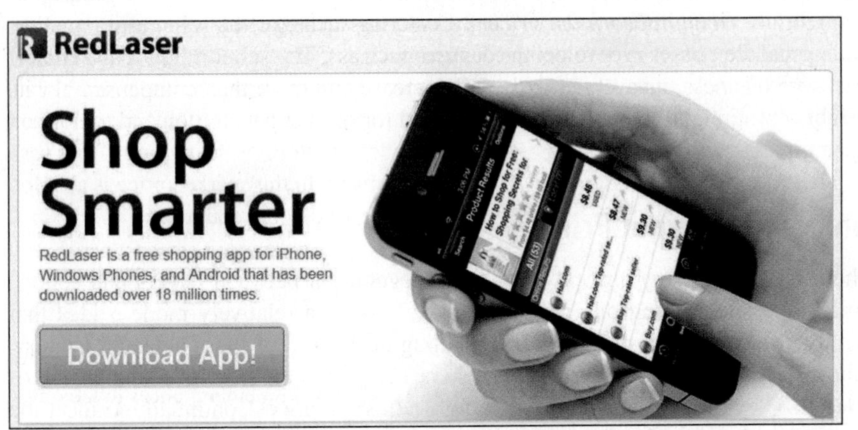

» **Dynamic and Internet pricing: Using mobile apps such as eBay's RedLaser, consumers can scan barcodes or QR codes while shopping in stores and receive product reviews, availability information, and comparison prices for online and nearby stores.**

In fact, many retailers are finding that ready online access to comparison prices is giving consumers *too* much of an edge. Store retailers ranging from Target and Best Buy to Brookstone and GNC are now devising strategies to combat the consumer practice of *showrooming*. Increasingly, consumers armed with smartphones come to stores to see an item, compare prices online while in the store, and then buy the item online at a lower price. Such behavior is called *showrooming* because consumers use store retailers as de facto "showrooms" for online resellers such as Amazon.com. In fact, Amazon.com encourages showrooming: It recently ran a promotion on its PriceCheck shopping app that gave customers discounts on qualifying items if they checked the prices for those items at Amazon.com while browsing at a physical store. To counter showrooming, store retailers must either match online prices or work with manufacturers to develop exclusive or store-branded merchandise on which price comparisons cannot be made. Or they must leverage the advantages of buying from their showroom floors, such as expert advice, easy returns, and immediate purchase gratification.[19]

International Pricing

Companies that market their products internationally must decide what prices to charge in different countries. In some cases, a company can set a uniform worldwide price. For example, Boeing sells its jetliners at about the same price everywhere, whether the buyer is in the United States, Europe, or a third-world country. However, most companies adjust their prices to reflect local market conditions and cost considerations.

The price that a company should charge in a specific country depends on many factors, including economic conditions, competitive situations, laws and regulations, and the nature of the wholesaling and retailing system. Consumer perceptions and preferences also may vary from country to country, calling for different prices. Or the company may have different marketing objectives in various world markets, which require changes in pricing strategy. For example, Nokia might introduce sophisticated, feature-rich mobile phones into carefully segmented mature markets in highly developed countries—this would call for a market-skimming pricing strategy. By contrast, it might enter sizable but less affluent markets in developing countries with more basic phones, supported by a penetration-pricing strategy.

Costs play an important role in setting international prices. Travelers abroad are often surprised to find that goods that are relatively inexpensive at home may carry outrageously higher price tags in other countries. A pair of Levi's selling for $30 in the United States might go for $63 in Tokyo and $88 in Paris. A McDonald's Big Mac selling for a modest $4.20 in the United States might cost $7.85 in Norway or $5.65 in Brazil, and an Oral-B toothbrush selling for $2.49 at home may cost $10 in China. Conversely, a Gucci handbag going for only $140 in Milan, Italy, might fetch $240 in the United States. In some cases, such *price escalation* may result from differences in selling strategies or market conditions. In most instances, however, it is simply a result of the higher costs of selling in another country—the additional costs of operations, product modifications, shipping and insurance, import tariffs and taxes, exchange-rate fluctuations, and physical distribution.

Price has become a key element in the international marketing strategies of companies attempting to enter emerging markets. Typically, entering such markets has meant targeting the exploding middle classes in developing countries such as China, India, Russia, and Brazil, whose economies have been growing rapidly. More recently, however, as the weakened global economy has slowed growth in both domestic and emerging markets, many companies are shifting their sights to include a new target—the so-called "bottom of the pyramid," the vast untapped market consisting of the world's poorest consumers. In this market, price is a major consideration. » Consider Unilever's pricing strategy for developing countries:[20]

» International pricing: To lower prices in emerging markets, such as Indonesia shown here, Unilever developed smaller, single-use packets of its Sunsilk, Ponds, Dove, and other brands that sell at prices even the world's poorest consumers can afford.

Bloomberg via Getty Images.

Not long ago, the preferred way for many Western companies to market their products in developing markets such as India or Indonesia was to paste new labels on them and sell them at premium prices to the privileged few who could afford them. However, when Unilever—the maker of such brands as Dove, Sunsilk, Lipton, and Vaseline—realized that such pricing put its products out of the reach of tens of millions of consumers in emerging markets, it forged a different approach. It shrunk its packaging and set low prices that even the world's poorest consumers could afford. By developing single-use packages of its shampoo, laundry detergent, face cream, and other products, Unilever can make a profit while selling its brands for just pennies a pack. As a result, today, more than 55 percent of Unilever's revenues come from emerging economies.

Although this strategy has been successful for Unilever, most companies are learning that selling profitably to the bottom of the pyramid requires more than just repackaging or stripping down existing products and selling them at low prices. Just like more well-to-do consumers, low-income buyers want products that are both functional *and* aspirational. Thus, companies today are innovating to create products that not only sell at very low prices but also give bottom-of-the-pyramid consumers more for their money, not less (see Marketing at Work 9.2).

International pricing presents many special problems and complexities. We discuss international pricing issues in more detail in Chapter 15.

Author Comment

When and how should a company change its price? What if costs rise, putting the squeeze on profits? What if the economy sags and customers become more price sensitive? Or what if a major competitor raises or drops its prices? As Figure 9.5 suggests, companies face many price-changing options.

Price Changes

After developing their pricing structures and strategies, companies often face situations in which they must initiate price changes or respond to price changes by competitors.

Initiating Price Changes

In some cases, the company may find it desirable to initiate either a price cut or a price increase. In both cases, it must anticipate possible buyer and competitor reactions.

MARKETING AT WORK 9.2

International Pricing: Targeting the Bottom of the Pyramid

Many companies are now waking up to a shocking statistic. Of the roughly 7 billion people on this planet, 4 billion of them (that's 57 percent) live in poverty. Known as the "bottom of the pyramid," the world's poor might not seem like a promising market. However, despite their paltry incomes, as a group, these consumers represent an eye-popping $5 trillion in annual purchasing power. Moreover, this vast segment is largely untapped. The world's poor often have little or no access to even the most basic products and services taken for granted by more affluent consumers. As the weakened global economy has flattened domestic markets and slowed the growth of emerging middle-class markets, companies are increasingly looking to the bottom of the pyramid for fresh growth opportunities.

But how can a company sell profitably to consumers with incomes below the poverty level? For starters, the *price* has got to be right. And in this case, says one analyst, "right" means "lower than you can imagine." With this in mind, many companies have made their products more affordable simply by offering smaller package sizes or lower-tech versions of current products. For example, in Nigeria, P&G sells a Gillette razor for 23 cents, a 1-ounce package of Ariel detergent for about 10 cents, and a 10-count pack of one-diaper-a-night Pampers for $2.30. Although there isn't much margin on products selling for pennies apiece, P&G is succeeding through massive volume.

Consider Pampers: Nigeria alone produces some 6 million newborns each year, almost 50 percent more than the United States, a country with twice the population. Nigeria's astounding birthrate creates a huge, untapped market for Pampers diapers, P&G's top-selling brand. However, the typical Nigerian mother spends only about 5,000 naira a month, about $30, on household purchases. P&G's task is to make Pampers affordable to this mother and to convince her that Pampers are worth some of her scarce spending. To keep costs and prices low in markets like Nigeria, P&G invented an absorbent but fewer-featured diaper. Although much less expensive, the diaper still functions at a high level. When creating such affordable new products, says an R&D manager at P&G, "Delight, don't dilute." That is, the diaper needs to be priced low, but it also has to do what other cheap diapers don't—keep a baby comfortable and dry for 12 hours.

Even with the right diaper at the right price, selling Pampers in Nigeria presents a challenge. In the West, babies typically go through numerous disposable diapers a day. In Nigeria, however, most babies are in cloth diapers. To make Pampers more acceptable and even more affordable for Nigerians, P&G markets the diapers as a one-a-day item. According to company ads, "One Pampers equals one dry night." The campaign tells mothers that keeping babies dry at night helps them to get a good night's sleep, which in turn helps them to grow and achieve. The message taps into a deep sentiment among Nigerians, unearthed by P&G researchers, that their children will have a better life than they do. Thus, thanks to affordable pricing, a product that meets customers' needs, and relevant positioning, Pampers sales are booming. In Nigeria, the name Pampers is now synonymous with diapers.

As P&G has learned, in most cases, selling profitably to the bottom of the pyramid takes much more than just developing single-use packets and pennies-apiece pricing. It requires broad-based innovation that produces not just lower prices but also new products that give people in poverty more for their money, not less. As another example, consider how Indian appliance company Godrej & Boyce used customer-driven

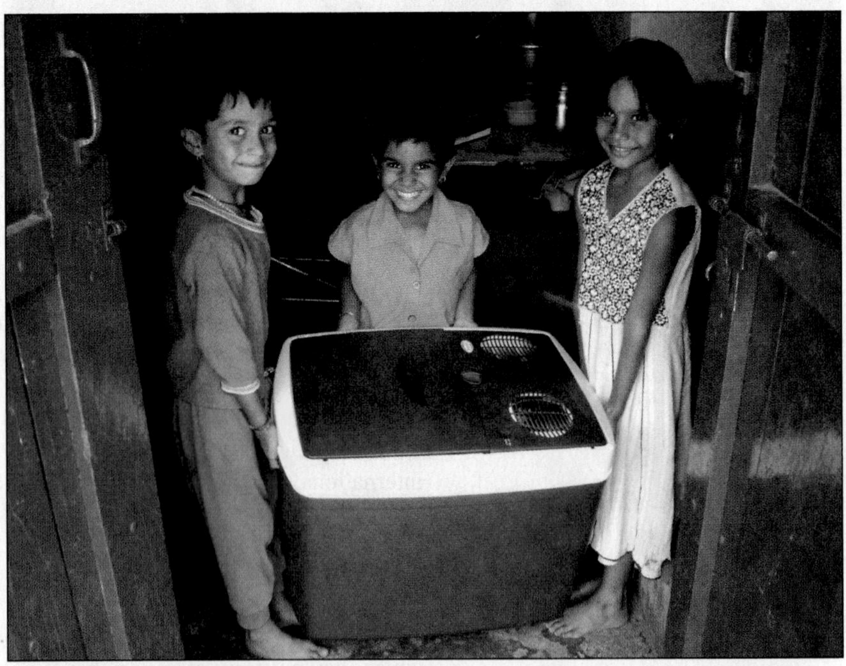

>> Selling to the world's poor: At only $69, Godrej's ChotuKool ("little cool") does a better job of meeting the needs of low-end Indian consumers at half the price of even the most basic conventional refrigerator.

Courtesy Godrej & Boyce Mfg. Co. Ltd.

innovation to successfully tap the market for low-priced refrigerators in India:

> Because of their high cost to both buy and operate, traditional compressor-driven refrigerators had penetrated only 18 percent of the Indian market. But rather than just produce a cheaper, stripped-down version of its higher-end refrigerators, Godrej assigned a team to study the needs of Indian consumers with poor or no refrigeration. The semi-urban and rural people the team observed typically earned 5,000 to 8,000 rupees (about $125 to $200) a month, lived in single-room dwellings with four or five family members, and changed residences frequently. Unable to afford conventional refrigerators, these consumers were making do with communal, usually second-hand ones. But even the shared fridges usually contained only a few items. Their users tended to shop daily and buy only small quantities of vegetables and milk. Moreover, electricity was unreliable, putting even the little food they wanted to keep cool at risk.
>
> Godrej concluded that the low-end segment had little need for a conventional high-end refrigerator; it needed a fundamentally new product. So Godrej invented the ChotuKool ("little cool"), a candy red, top-opening, highly-portable, dorm-size unit that has room for the few items users want to keep fresh for a day or two. Rather than a compressor and refrigerant, the miserly little unit uses a chip that cools when current is applied, and its top-opening design keeps cold air inside when the lid is opened. In all, the ChotuKool uses less than half the energy of a conventional refrigerator and can run on a battery during the power outages common in rural villages. The best part: At only $69, "little cool" does a better job of meeting the needs of low-end consumers at half the price of even the most basic traditional refrigerator.

Thus, the bottom of the pyramid offers huge untapped opportunities to companies that can develop the right products at the right prices. And companies such as P&G are moving aggressively to capture these opportunities. P&G has set a lofty goal of 1 billion new customers by 2015, moving the company's emphasis from the developed West, where it currently gets most of its revenue, to the developing economies of Asia and Africa.

But successfully tapping these new developing markets will require more than just shipping out cheaper versions of existing products. "Our innovation strategy is not just diluting the top-tier product for the lower-end consumer," says P&G's CEO. "You have to discretely innovate for every one of those consumers on that economic curve, and if you don't do that, you'll fail."

Sources: Quotes, extracts, and other information from or based on David Holthaus, "Pampers: P&G's No. 1 Growth Brand," *Cincinnati.com*, April 17, 2011, http://news.cincinnati.com/article/20110417/BIZ01/104170337/; Mya Frazier, "How P&G Brought the Diaper Revolution to China," *CBS News*, January 7, 2010, www.cbsnews.com/8301-505125_162-51379838/; David Holthaus, "Health Talk First, Then a Sales Pitch," April 17, 2011, *Cincinnati.com*, http://news.cincinnati.com/article/20110417/BIZ01/104170344/; Matthew J. Eyring, Mark W. Johnson, and Hari Nair, "New Business Models in Emerging Markets," *Harvard Business Review*, January–February 2011, pp. 89–95; C. K. Prahalad, "Bottom of the Pyramid as a Source of Breakthrough Innovations," *Journal of Product Innovation Management*, January 2012, pp. 6–12; Erik Simanis, "Reality Check at the Bottom of the Pyramid," *Harvard Business Review*, June 2012, pp. 120–125; and "The State of Consumption Today," *Worldwatch Institute*, www.worldwatch.org/node/810, accessed July 2013.

Initiating Price Cuts

Several situations may lead a firm to consider cutting its price. One such circumstance is excess capacity. Another is falling demand in the face of strong price competition or a weakened economy. In such cases, the firm may aggressively cut prices to boost sales and market share. But as the airline, fast-food, automobile, and other industries have learned in recent years, cutting prices in an industry loaded with excess capacity may lead to price wars as competitors try to hold on to market share.

A company may also cut prices in a drive to dominate the market through lower costs. Either the company starts with lower costs than its competitors, or it cuts prices in the hope of gaining market share that will further cut costs through larger volume. For example, Lenovo uses an aggressive low-cost, low-price strategy to increase its share of the PC market in developing countries.

Initiating Price Increases

A successful price increase can greatly improve profits. For example, if the company's profit margin is 3 percent of sales, a 1 percent price increase will boost profits by 33 percent if sales volume is unaffected. A major factor in price increases is cost inflation. Rising costs squeeze profit margins and lead companies to pass cost increases along to customers. Another factor leading to price increases is over-demand: When a company cannot supply all that its customers need, it may raise its prices, ration products to customers, or both—consider today's worldwide oil and gas industry.

When raising prices, the company must avoid being perceived as a *price gouger*. >> For example, when gasoline prices rise rapidly, angry customers often accuse the major oil companies of enriching themselves at the expense of consumers. Customers have long memories, and they will eventually turn away from companies or even whole industries

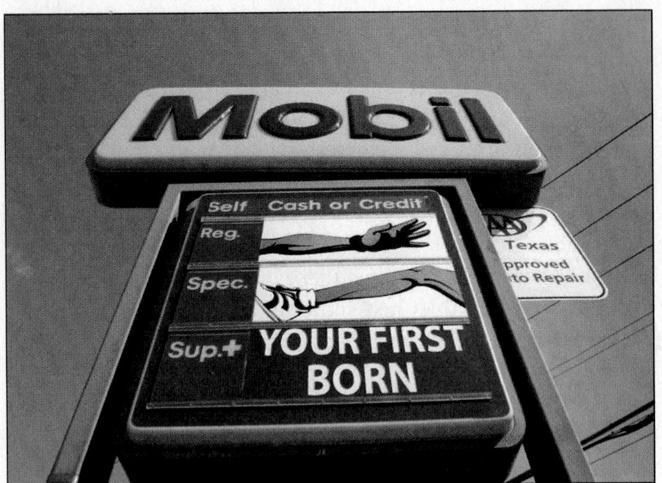

» **Initiating price increases: When gasoline prices rise rapidly, angry consumers often accuse the major oil companies of enriching themselves by gouging customers.**

Louis DeLuca/Dallas Morning News/Corbis.

that they perceive as charging excessive prices. In the extreme, claims of price gouging may even bring about increased government regulation.

There are some techniques for avoiding these problems. One is to maintain a sense of fairness surrounding any price increase. Price increases should be supported by company communications telling customers why prices are being raised.

Wherever possible, the company should consider ways to meet higher costs or demand without raising prices. For example, it might consider more cost-effective ways to produce or distribute its products. It can shrink the product or substitute less-expensive ingredients instead of raising the price, as ConAgra did in an effort to hold its Banquet frozen dinner prices at $1. Or it can "unbundle" its market offering, removing features, packaging, or services and separately pricing elements that were formerly part of the offer.

Buyer Reactions to Price Changes

Customers do not always interpret price changes in a straightforward way. A price *increase*, which would normally lower sales, may have some positive meanings for buyers. For example, what would you think if Rolex *raised* the price of its latest watch model? On the one hand, you might think that the watch is even more exclusive or better made. On the other hand, you might think that Rolex is simply being greedy by charging what the traffic will bear.

Similarly, consumers may view a price *cut* in several ways. For example, what would you think if Rolex were to suddenly cut its prices? You might think that you are getting a better deal on an exclusive product. More likely, however, you'd think that quality had been reduced, and the brand's luxury image might be tarnished. A brand's price and image are often closely linked. A price change, especially a drop in price, can adversely affect how consumers view the brand.

Competitor Reactions to Price Changes

A firm considering a price change must worry about the reactions of its competitors as well as those of its customers. Competitors are most likely to react when the number of firms involved is small, when the product is uniform, and when the buyers are well informed about products and prices.

How can the firm anticipate the likely reactions of its competitors? The problem is complex because, like the customer, the competitor can interpret a company price cut in many ways. It might think the company is trying to grab a larger market share or that it's doing poorly and trying to boost its sales. Or it might think that the company wants the whole industry to cut prices to increase total demand.

The company must guess each competitor's likely reaction. If all competitors behave alike, this amounts to analyzing only a typical competitor. In contrast, if the competitors do not behave alike—perhaps because of differences in size, market shares, or policies—then separate analyses are necessary. However, if some competitors will match the price change, there is good reason to expect that the rest will also match it.

Responding to Price Changes

Here we reverse the question and ask how a firm should respond to a price change by a competitor. The firm needs to consider several issues: Why did the competitor change the price? Is the price change temporary or permanent? What will happen to the company's market share and profits if it does not respond? Are other competitors going to respond? Besides these issues, the company must also consider its own situation and strategy and possible customer reactions to price changes.

» **Figure 9.5** Assessing and Responding to Competitor Price Changes

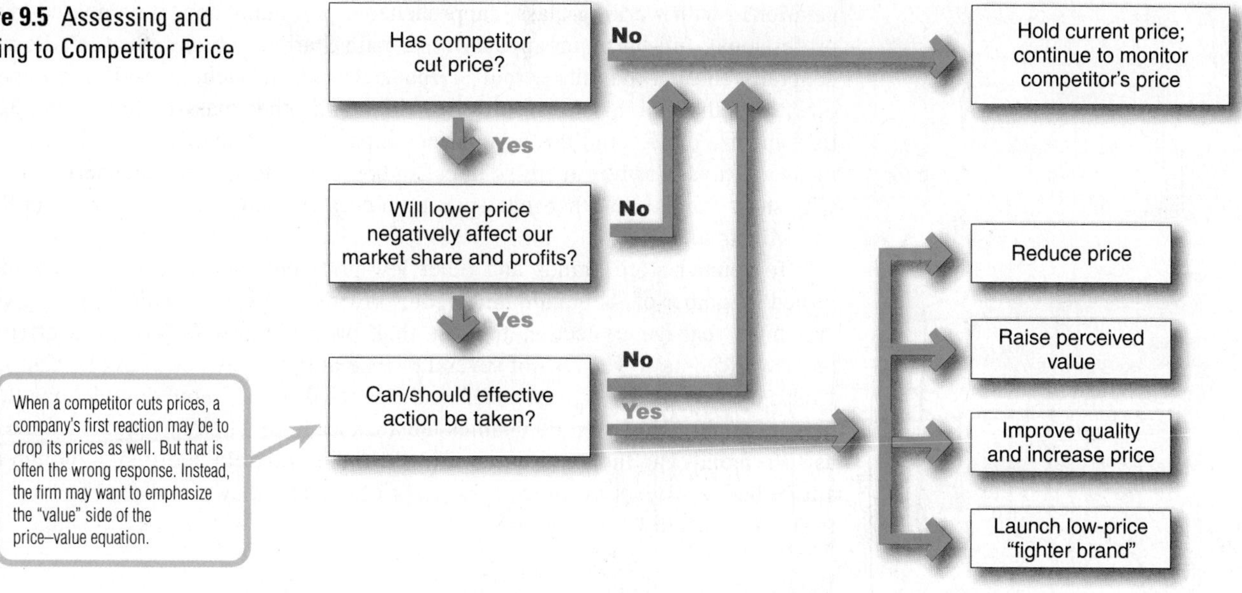

» **Figure 9.5** shows the ways a company might assess and respond to a competitor's price cut. Suppose the company learns that a competitor has cut its price and decides that this price cut is likely to harm its sales and profits. It might simply decide to hold its current price and profit margin. The company might believe that it will not lose too much market share, or that it would lose too much profit if it reduced its own price. Or it might decide that it should wait and respond when it has more information on the effects of the competitor's price change. However, waiting too long to act might let the competitor get stronger and more confident as its sales increase.

If the company decides that effective action can and should be taken, it might make any of four responses. First, it could *reduce its price* to match the competitor's price. It may decide that the market is price sensitive and that it would lose too much market share to the lower-priced competitor. However, cutting the price will reduce the company's profits in the short run. Some companies might also reduce their product quality, services, and marketing communications to retain profit margins, but this will ultimately hurt long-run market share. The company should try to maintain its quality as it cuts prices.

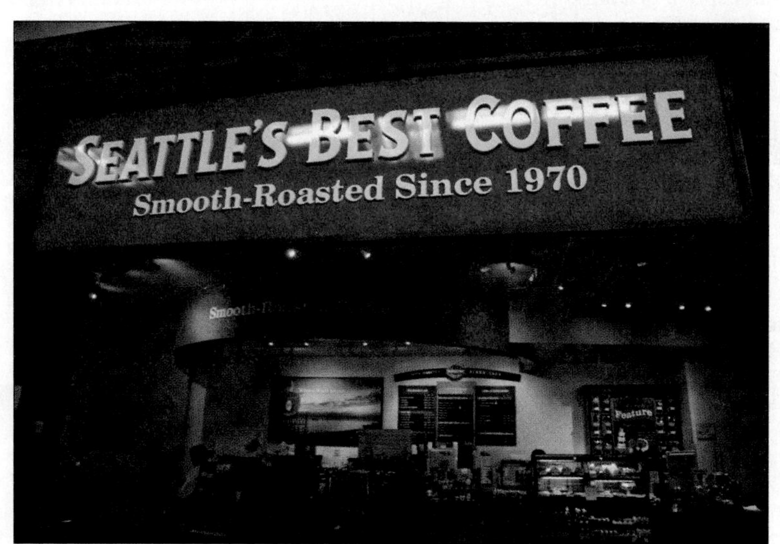

» **Fighter brands: Starbucks has positioned its Seattle's Best Coffee unit to compete more directly with the "mass-premium" brands sold buy Dunkin' Donuts, McDonald's, and other lower-priced competitors.**

AP Images/Eric Risberg.

Alternatively, the company might maintain its price but *raise the perceived value* of its offer. It could improve its communications, stressing the relative value of its product over that of the lower-price competitor. The firm may find it cheaper to maintain price and spend money to improve its perceived value than to cut price and operate at a lower margin. Or, the company might *improve quality and increase price*, moving its brand into a higher price–value position. The higher quality creates greater customer value, which justifies the higher price. In turn, the higher price preserves the company's higher margins.

Finally, the company might *launch a low-price "fighter brand"*—adding a lower-price item to the line or creating a separate lower-price brand. This is necessary if the particular market segment being lost is price sensitive and will not respond to arguments of higher quality. » Starbucks did this when it acquired Seattle's Best Coffee, a brand positioned with working-class, "approachable-premium" appeal compared to the more professional, full-premium appeal of the main Starbucks brand. Seattle's Best coffee is generally cheaper than the parent Starbucks brand. As such, at retail, it competes more directly with Dunkin' Donuts, McDonald's, and other mass-premium brands through its franchise outlets and through partnerships with Subway, Burger King, Delta, AMC theaters, Royal Caribbean cruise lines, and others. On supermarket shelves, it competes with store brands and other mass-premium coffees such as Folgers Gourmet Selections and Millstone.[21]

To counter store brands and other low-price entrants in a tighter economy, P&G turned a number of its brands into fighter brands. Luvs disposable diapers give parents "premium leakage protection for less than pricier brands." And P&G offers popular budget-priced basic versions of several of its major brands. For example, Charmin Basic "holds up at a great everyday price," and Bounty Basic is "more durable than the leading bargain brand." However, companies must use caution when introducing fighter brands, as such brands can tarnish the image of the main brand. In addition, although they may attract budget buyers away from lower-priced rivals, they can also take business away from the firm's higher-margin brands.

Author Comment
Pricing decisions are often constrained by social and legal issues. For example, think about the pharmaceuticals industry. Are rapidly rising prescription drug prices justified? Or are the drug companies unfairly lining their pockets by gouging consumers who have few alternatives? Should the government step in?

Public Policy and Pricing

Price competition is a core element of our free-market economy. In setting prices, companies usually are not free to charge whatever prices they wish. Many federal, state, and even local laws govern the rules of fair play in pricing. In addition, companies must consider broader societal pricing concerns. In setting their prices, for example, pharmaceutical firms must balance their development costs and profit objectives against the sometimes life-and-death needs of drug consumers.

The most important pieces of legislation affecting pricing are the Sherman Act, the Clayton Act, and the Robinson-Patman Act, initially adopted to curb the formation of monopolies and regulate business practices that might unfairly restrain trade. Because these federal statutes can be applied only to interstate commerce, some states have adopted similar provisions for companies that operate locally.

>> **Figure 9.6** shows the major public policy issues in pricing. These include potentially damaging pricing practices within a given level of the channel (price-fixing and predatory pricing) and across levels of the channel (retail price maintenance, discriminatory pricing, and deceptive pricing).[22]

>> **Figure 9.6** Public Policy Issues in Pricing

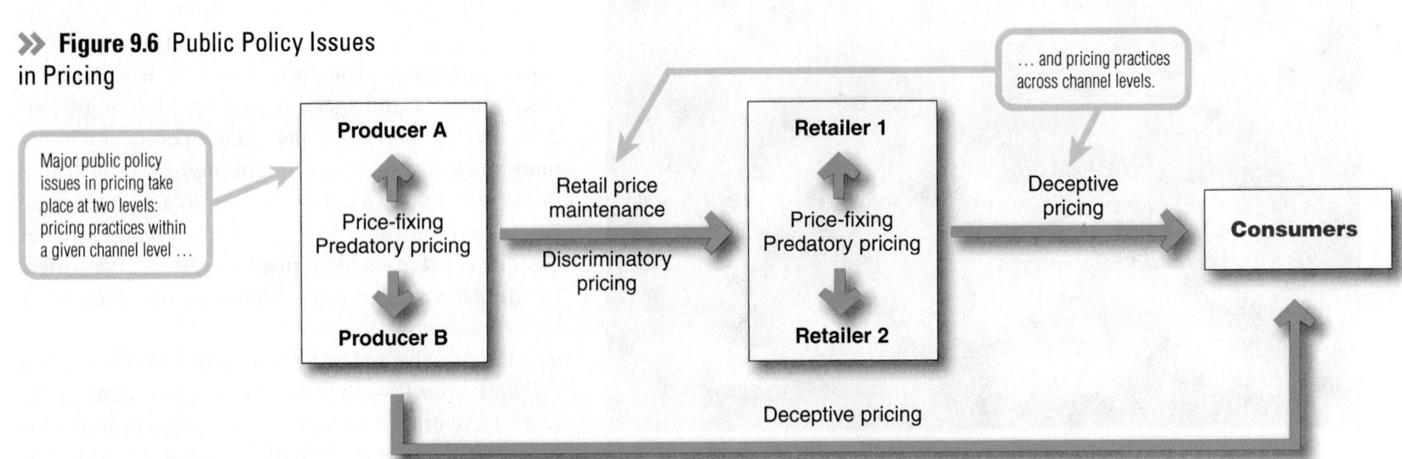

Pricing within Channel Levels

Federal legislation on *price-fixing* states that sellers must set prices without talking to competitors. Otherwise, price collusion is suspected. Price-fixing is illegal per se—that is, the government does not accept any excuses for price-fixing. As such, companies found guilty of these practices can receive heavy fines. Recently, governments at the state and national levels have been aggressively enforcing price-fixing regulations in industries ranging from gasoline, insurance, and concrete to credit cards, CDs, and computer chips. Price-fixing is also prohibited in many international markets. For example, European Union regulators recently fined electronics companies Philips, LG Electronics, Panasonic, Toshiba, Samsung SDI, and Technicolor a combined $1.9 billion after finding they had schemed to rig the prices of cathode ray tubes, used in both computer monitors and television screens before flat screens.[23]

Sellers are also prohibited from using *predatory pricing*—selling below cost with the intention of punishing a competitor or gaining higher long-run profits by putting competitors out of business. This protects small sellers from larger ones that might sell items below cost temporarily or in a specific locale to drive them out of business. The biggest problem is determining just what constitutes predatory pricing behavior. Selling below cost to unload excess inventory is not considered predatory; selling below cost to drive out competitors is. Thus, a given action may or may not be predatory depending on intent, and intent can be very difficult to determine or prove.

In recent years, several large and powerful companies have been accused of predatory pricing. However, turning an accusation into a lawsuit can be difficult. »For example, many publishers and booksellers have expressed concerns about Amazon.com's predatory practices, especially its book pricing:[24]

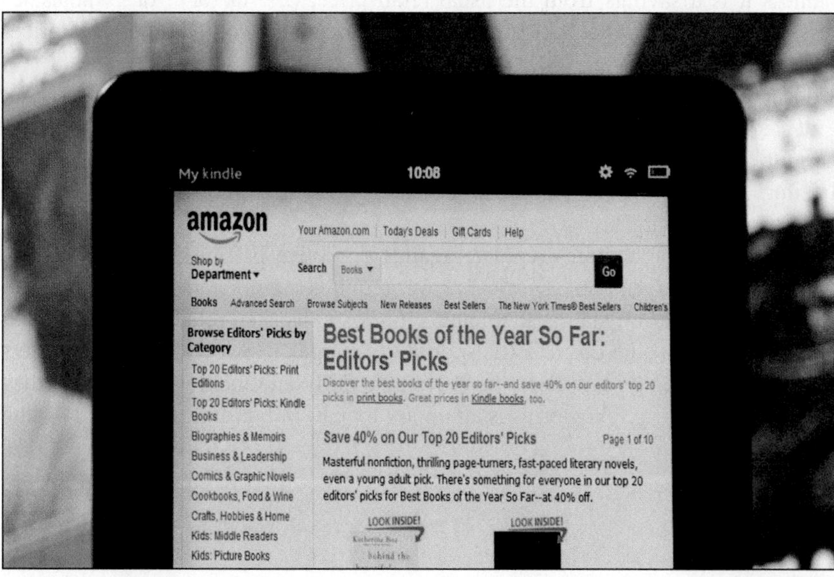

» **Predatory pricing: Some industry critics have accused Amazon.com of pricing books at fire-sale prices that harm competing booksellers. But is it predatory pricing or just plain good competitive marketing?**

Christopher Schall/Impact Photo.

Many booksellers and publishers complain that Amazon.com's book pricing policies are destroying their industry. During past holiday seasons, Amazon has sold top-10 bestselling hardback books as loss leaders at cut-rate prices of less than $10 each. And Amazon now sells e-books at fire-sale prices in order to win customers for its Kindle e-reader. Such very low book prices have caused considerable damage to competing booksellers, many of whom view Amazon's pricing actions as predatory. Says one observer, "The word 'predator' is pretty strong, and I don't use it loosely, but . . . I could have sworn we had laws against predatory pricing. I just don't understand why [Amazon's pricing] is not an issue." Still, no predatory pricing charges have ever been filed against Amazon. It would be extremely difficult to prove that such loss-leader pricing is purposefully predatory as opposed to just plain good competitive marketing.

Pricing across Channel Levels

The Robinson-Patman Act seeks to prevent unfair *price discrimination* by ensuring that sellers offer the same price terms to customers at a given level of trade. For example, every retailer is entitled to the same price terms from a given manufacturer, whether the retailer is REI or a local bicycle shop. However, price discrimination is allowed if the seller can prove that its costs are different when selling to different retailers—for example, that it costs less per unit to sell a large volume of bicycles to REI than to sell a few bicycles to the local dealer.

The seller can also discriminate in its pricing if the seller manufactures different qualities of the same product for different retailers. The seller has to prove that these differences are proportional. Price differentials may also be used to "match competition" in "good faith," provided the price discrimination is temporary, localized, and defensive rather than offensive.

Laws also prohibit *retail (or resale) price maintenance*—a manufacturer cannot require dealers to charge a specified retail price for its product. Although the seller can propose a manufacturer's *suggested* retail price to dealers, it cannot refuse to sell to a dealer that takes independent pricing action, nor can it punish the dealer by shipping late or denying advertising allowances. For example, the Florida attorney general's office investigated Nike for allegedly fixing the retail price of its shoes and clothing. It was concerned that Nike might be withholding items from retailers who were not selling its most expensive shoes at prices the company considered suitable.

Deceptive pricing occurs when a seller states prices or price savings that mislead consumers or are not actually available to consumers. This might involve bogus reference or comparison prices, as when a retailer sets artificially high "regular" prices and then announces "sale" prices close to its previous everyday prices. For example, Overstock.com recently came under scrutiny for inaccurately listing manufacturer's suggested retail prices, often quoting them higher than the actual prices. Such comparison pricing is widespread.

Although comparison pricing claims are legal if they are truthful, the Federal Trade Commission's "Guides against Deceptive Pricing" warn sellers not to advertise (1) a price reduction unless it is a savings from the usual retail price, (2) "factory" or "wholesale" prices unless such prices are what they are claimed to be, and (3) comparable value prices on imperfect goods.[25]

Other deceptive pricing issues include *scanner fraud* and price confusion. The widespread use of scanner-based computer checkouts has led to increasing complaints of retailers overcharging their customers. Most of these overcharges result from poor management, such as a failure to enter current or sale prices into the system. Other cases, however, involve intentional overcharges.

Many federal and state statutes regulate against deceptive pricing practices. For example, the Automobile Information Disclosure Act requires automakers to attach a statement on new vehicle windows stating the manufacturer's suggested retail price, the prices of optional equipment, and the dealer's transportation charges. However, reputable sellers go beyond what is required by law. Treating customers fairly and making certain that they fully understand prices and pricing terms is an important part of building strong and lasting customer relationships.

MyMarketingLab

Go to **mymktlab.com** to complete the problems marked with this icon .

END OF CHAPTER REVIEWING THE CONCEPTS

CHAPTER REVIEW AND KEY TERMS

Objectives Review

Price can be defined as the sum of all the values that customers give up in order to gain the benefits of having or using a product or service. Pricing decisions are subject to an incredibly complex array of company, environmental, and competitive forces.

 **OBJECTIVE 1 Identify the three major pricing strategies and discuss the importance of understanding customer value perceptions, company costs, and competitor strategies when setting prices. (pp 266–274)**

A price is the sum of all the values that customers give up in order to gain the benefits of having or using a product or service. The three major pricing strategies are customer value–based pricing, cost-based pricing, and competition-based pricing. Good pricing begins with a complete understanding of the value that a product or service creates for customers and setting a price that captures that value.

Customer perceptions of the product's value set the ceiling for prices. If customers perceive that the price is greater than the product's value, they will not buy the product. At the other extreme, company and product costs set the floor for prices. If the company prices the product below its costs, its profits will suffer. Between these two extremes, consumers will base their judgments of a product's value on the prices that competitors charge for similar products. Thus, in setting prices, companies need to consider all three factors, customer perceived value, costs, and competitors' pricing strategies.

Costs are an important consideration in setting prices. However, cost-based pricing is often product driven. The company designs what it considers to be a good product and sets a price that covers costs plus a target profit. If the price turns out to be too high, the company must settle for lower markups or lower sales, both resulting in disappointing profits. Value-based pricing reverses this process. The company assesses customer needs and value perceptions and then sets a target price to match the targeted value. The targeted value and price then drive decisions about product design and what costs can be incurred. As a result, price is set to match customers' perceived value.

 **OBJECTIVE 2 Identify and define the other important external and internal factors affecting a firm's pricing decisions. (pp 274–279)**

Other *internal* factors that influence pricing decisions include the company's overall marketing strategy, objectives, and marketing mix, as well as organizational considerations. Price is only one element of the company's broader marketing strategy. If the company has selected its target market and positioning carefully, then its marketing mix strategy, including price, will be fairly straightforward. Common pricing objectives might include customer retention and building profitable customer relationships, preventing competition, supporting resellers and gaining their support, or avoiding government intervention. Price decisions must be coordinated with product design, distribution, and promotion decisions to form a consistent and effective marketing program. Finally, in order to coordinate pricing goals and decisions, management must decide who within the organization is responsible for setting price.

Other *external* pricing considerations include the nature of the market and demand and environmental factors such as the economy, reseller needs, and government actions. Ultimately, the customer decides whether the company has set the right price. The customer weighs the price against the perceived values of using the product—if the price exceeds the sum of the values, consumers will not buy. So the company must understand such concepts as demand curves (the price–demand relationship) and price elasticity (consumer sensitivity to prices).

Economic conditions can have a major impact on pricing decisions. The Great Recession caused consumers to rethink the price–value equation. Marketers have responded by increasing their emphasis on value-for-the-money pricing strategies. Even in tight economic times, however, consumers do not buy based on prices alone. Thus, no matter what price they charge—low or high—companies need to offer superior value for the money.

OBJECTIVE 3 Describe the major strategies for pricing new products. (pp 280–281)

Pricing is a dynamic process. Companies design a *pricing structure* that covers all of their products. They change this structure over time and adjust it to account for different customers and situations. Pricing strategies usually change as a product passes through its life cycle. In pricing innovative new products, a company can use *market-skimming pricing* by initially setting high prices to "skim" the maximum amount of revenue from various segments of the market. Or it can use *market-penetrating pricing* by setting a low initial price to penetrate the market deeply and win a large market share.

OBJECTIVE 4 Explain how companies find a set of prices that maximizes the profits from the total product mix. (pp 281–283)

When the product is part of a product mix, the firm searches for a set of prices that will maximize the profits from the total mix. In *product line pricing*, the company decides on price steps for the entire set of products it offers. In addition, the company must set prices for *optional products* (optional or accessory products included with the main product), *captive products* (products that are required for use of the main product), *by-products* (waste or residual products produced when making the main product), and *product bundles* (combinations of products at a reduced price).

OBJECTIVE 5 Discuss how companies adjust their prices to take into account different types of customers and situations. (pp 283–289)

Companies apply a variety of *price-adjustment strategies* to account for differences in consumer segments and situations. One is *discount and allowance pricing*, whereby the company establishes cash, quantity, functional, or seasonal discounts, or varying types of allowances. A second strategy is *segmented pricing*, where the company sells a product at two or more prices to accommodate different customers, product forms, locations, or times. Sometimes companies consider more than economics in their pricing decisions, using *psychological pricing* to better communicate a product's intended position. In *promotional pricing*, a company offers discounts or temporarily sells a product below list price as a special event, sometimes even selling below cost as a loss leader. Another approach is *geographical pricing*, whereby the company decides how to price to near or distant customers. In *dynamic pricing*, companies adjust prices continually to meet the characteristics and needs of individual customers and situations. Finally, *international pricing* means that the company adjusts its price to meet different conditions and expectations in different world markets.

OBJECTIVE 6 Discuss the key issues related to initiating and responding to price changes. (pp 289–296)

When a firm considers initiating a *price change*, it must consider customers' and competitors' reactions. There are different implications to *initiating price cuts* and *initiating price increases*. Buyer reactions to price changes are influenced by the meaning customers see in the price change. Competitors' reactions flow from a set reaction policy or a fresh analysis of each situation.

There are also many factors to consider in responding to a competitor's price changes. The company that faces a price change initiated by a competitor must try to understand the competitor's intent as well as the likely duration and impact of the change. If a swift reaction is desirable, the firm should preplan its reactions to different possible price actions by competitors. When facing a competitor's price changes, the company might sit tight, reduce its own price, raise perceived quality, improve quality and raise price, or launch a fighting brand.

Key Terms

Objective 1
Price (p 266)
Customer value–based pricing (p 267)
Good-value pricing (p 269)
Value-added pricing (p 271)
Cost-based pricing (p 272)
Fixed costs (overhead) (p 272)
Variable costs (p 272)
Total costs (p 272)
Cost-plus pricing (markup pricing) (p 272)
Break-even pricing (target return pricing) (p 272)
Competition-based pricing (p 273)

Objective 2
Target costing (p 275)
Demand curve (p 277)
Price elasticity (p 278)

Objective 3
Market-skimming pricing (price skimming) (p 280)
Market-penetration pricing (p 280)

Objective 4
Product line pricing (p 281)
Optional-product pricing (p 282)
Captive-product pricing (p 282)
By-product pricing (p 282)
Product bundle pricing (p 283)

Objective 5
Discount (p 283)
Allowance (p 284)
Segmented pricing (p 284)
Psychological pricing (p 285)
Reference prices (p 285)
Promotional pricing (p 285)
Dynamic pricing (p 287)

DISCUSSION AND CRITICAL THINKING

Discussion Questions

9-1. Name and describe the two types of value-based pricing methods. (AACSB: Written and Oral Communication)

9-2. Describe the cost-plus pricing method and discuss why marketers use it even if it is not the best method for setting prices. (AACSB: Written and Oral Communication)

9-3. What is price elasticity? Why is it important for marketers to consider price elasticity when making pricing decisions? (AACSB: Written and Oral Communication; Reflective Thinking)

9-4. Name and describe the two broad new product pricing strategies. When would each be appropriate? (AACSB: Written and Oral Communication)

9-5. How do marketers use psychological pricing to communication something about the product? (AACSB: Written and Oral Communication)

Critical Thinking Exercises

9-6. You can turn your hobby into profits at online sites such as Etsy. In a small group, create ideas for a craft product to sell on Etsy, an online community of buyers and creative businesses. Using the resources available at www.etsy.com as a guide to setting prices, determine the price for your product. Justify that price and provide a link to the resources you found most useful on the Etsy site. (AACSB: Written and Oral Communication; Information Technology; Analytical Thinking)

9-7. What is the Consumer Price Index (CPI)? Select one of the reports available at www.bls.gov/cpi/home.htm and create a presentation on price changes over the past two years. Discuss reasons for those changes. (AACSB: Written and Oral Communication; Information Technology; Reflective Thinking)

MINICASES AND APPLICATIONS

Online, Mobile, and Social Media Marketing HOT Lanes

If you have traveled in a big city, you know how congested traffic can get. Many major cities now have HOV lanes (high-occupancy vehicle lanes) that allow vehicles with two or more occupants to sail past all the other vehicles in single-occupancy lanes. The lanes are usually barricaded off between the opposing-direction lanes and switch directions from morning to evening to cater to the flow of heavy traffic. Mobile technology has resulted in a new opportunity for communities by converting these lanes to HOT lanes (high-occupancy toll lanes). For example, travelers in Houston can drive in these lanes for free if more than two people are in the car, but single riders can jump in these lanes as well for a toll. But the toll varies depending on the volume of traffic. The "dynamic pricing" lanes now appear in about a dozen cities, with digital signs indicating the fluctuating prices. Tolls range from 25 cents to $1.40 per mile, depending on the speed of traffic, and are charged to drivers' toll tags.

9-8. Suggest another example of how dynamic pricing can be applied based on information obtained from consumers' digital behavior on the Internet, use of social media, or through mobile technology usage. (AACSB: Written and Oral Communication; Information Technology; Reflective Thinking)

9-9. Is dynamic pricing ethical? (AACSB: Written and Oral Communication; Ethical Understanding and Reasoning)

Marketing Ethics The Price of a Song

Country music stars such as Taylor Swift, Rascal Flatts, and Tim McGraw will be the first artists to be paid every time their songs are played on the radio. In the United States, only songwriters and music publishers receive royalties from radio airplay or when a song is played in a movie, television program, commercial, or even as hold music on telephones. This dates back to a 1917 Supreme Court ruling that composers of copyrighted music are due a royalty every time the music is played or performed through commercial means. But performing artists or recording companies do not receive such royalties. The rationale is that radio play promotes record sales, where the artists earn royalties ranging from 8 to 25 percent of the price of a CD. But thanks to the Internet and music download sites such as iTunes, sales of traditional recorded music have dropped almost 50 percent. In 2011, digital music sales surpassed traditional CD sales. Listeners have also tuned in to Internet sites such as Pandora, Spotify, and Rdio to listen to music. Recording artists did get some relief through the Digital Performance Rights in Sound Recording Act of 1995. The act gave performers their first royalties when their songs are played in a digital format, such as in a Webcast or on satellite radio, where listeners subscribe but cannot select specific songs. Pandora, the online radio company, claims that such royalty payments, equivalent to about 60 percent of revenues, are the reason the company is unprofitable.

9-10. Research how music royalties work to learn more about the cost and pricing of music. Write a report of what you learned. (AACSB: Written and Oral Communication; Reflective Thinking)

9-11. Should artists and record labels be paid royalties every time their music is played? What type of cost does this represent for a radio station? (AACSB: Written and Oral Communication; Reflective Thinking)

Marketing by the Numbers Louis Vuitton Price Increase

One way to maintain exclusivity for a brand is to raise its price. That's what the makers of Louis Vuitton, the luxury fashion and leather goods brand, did. The company does not want the brand to become overexposed and too common, so it raised prices 10 percent and is slowing its expansion in China. The Louis Vuitton brand is the largest contributor to the company's $13.3 billion revenue from its fashion and leather division, accounting for $8 billion of those sales. It might seem counterintuitive to want to encourage fewer customers to purchase a company's products, but when price increases, so does the product's contribution margin, making each sale more profitable. Thus, sales can drop and the company can still maintain the same profitability as before the price hike.

9-12. If the company's original contribution margin was 40 percent, calculate the new contribution margin if price is increased 10 percent. Refer to Appendix 3, Marketing by the Numbers, paying attention to endnote 6 on the price change explanation in which the analysis is done by setting price equal to $1.00. (AACSB: Written and Oral Communication; Analytic Thinking)

9-13. Determine by how much sales can drop while still allowing the company to maintain the total contribution it had when the contribution margin was 40 percent. (AACSB: Written and Oral Communication; Analytical Thinking)

Video Case Hammerpress

Printing paper goods may not sound like the best business to get into these days, but Hammerpress is nonetheless carving out a niche in this old industry. And they're doing it by returning to old technology. Most of today's printing firms use computer-driven graphic design techniques and printing processes. But Hammerpress creates greeting cards, calendars, and business cards that are hand-crafted by professional artists and printed using traditional letterpress technology.

When it comes to competing, this old-fashioned process presents both opportunities and challenges. While Hammerpress's products certainly stand out as works of art, the cost for producing such goods is considerably higher than the industry average. This video illustrates how Hammerpress employs dynamic pricing techniques to meet the needs of various customer segments and thrive in a competitive environment.

After viewing the video featuring Hammerpress, answer the following questions:

9-14. How does Hammerpress employ the concept of dynamic pricing?

9-15. Discuss Hammerpress in relation to the three major pricing strategies. Which of these three strategies is the company's core strategy?

9-16. Does it make sense for Hammerpress to compete in product categories where the market dictates a price that is not profitable for the company? Explain.

Company Cases 9 JCPenney / 11 Dollar General / 16 Warby Parker

See Appendix 1 for cases appropriate for this chapter. **Case 9, JCPenney: The Struggle to Find Optimum Price.** JCPenney tried to fix a pricing problem with a new strategy, only to create a new pricing problem. **Case 11, Dollar General: Today's Hottest Retailing Format.** By taking advantage of a gap in the market, Dollar General is growing faster than other forms of retail. **Case 16, Warby Parker: Eyewear with a Purpose.** Warby Parker makes high-quality, fashionable eyeglasses at a revolutionary price point—and distributes a free pair of glasses to a person in need for every pair purchased.

MyMarketingLab

Go to **mymktlab.com** for Auto-graded writing questions as well as the following Assisted-graded writing questions:

9-17. Compare and contrast fixed costs and variable costs and discuss their importance in setting prices. (AACSB: Written and Oral Communication; Reflective Thinking)

9-18. In a small group, discuss your perceptions of value and how much you are willing to pay for the following products: automobiles, frozen dinners, jeans, and athletic shoes. Are there differences of opinion among members of your group? If so, explain why those differences exist. Discuss some examples of brands of these products that are positioned to deliver different value to consumers. (AACSB: Written and Oral Communication; Reflective Thinking)

9-19. Mymktlab Only—comprehensive writing assignment for this chapter.

10 Marketing Channels

Delivering Customer Value

CHAPTER ROAD MAP

Objective Outline

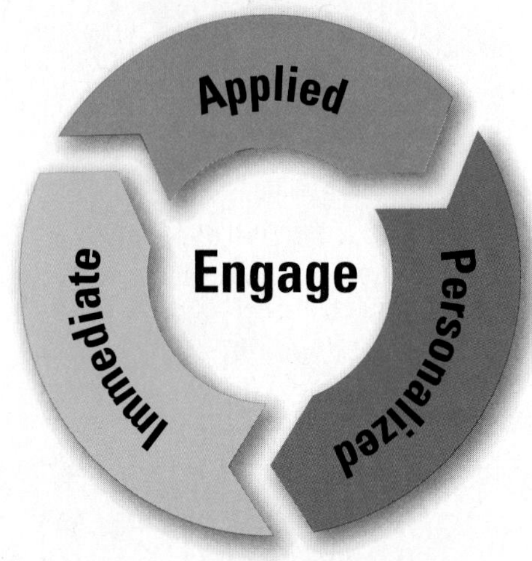

Previewing the Concepts

We now arrive at the third marketing mix tool—distribution. Companies rarely work alone in creating value for customers and building profitable customer relationships. Instead, most are only a single link in a larger supply chain and marketing channel. As such, a firm's success depends not only on how well *it* performs but also on how well its *entire marketing channel* competes with competitors' channels. The first part of this chapter explores the nature of marketing channels and the marketer's channel design and management decisions. We then examine physical distribution—or logistics—an area that is growing dramatically in importance and sophistication. In the next chapter, we'll look more closely at two major channel intermediaries: retailers and wholesalers.

We start by looking at Netflix. Through innovative distribution, Netflix has become the world's largest video subscription service. But as baseball great Yogi Berra, known more for his mangled phrasing than for his baseball prowess, once said, "The future ain't what it used to be." To stay atop of the churning video distribution industry, Netflix must continue to innovate at a break-neck pace or risk being pushed aside.

*Over 10 million students improved their results using the Pearson MyLabs. Visit **mymktlab.com** for simulations, tutorials, and end-of-chapter problems.

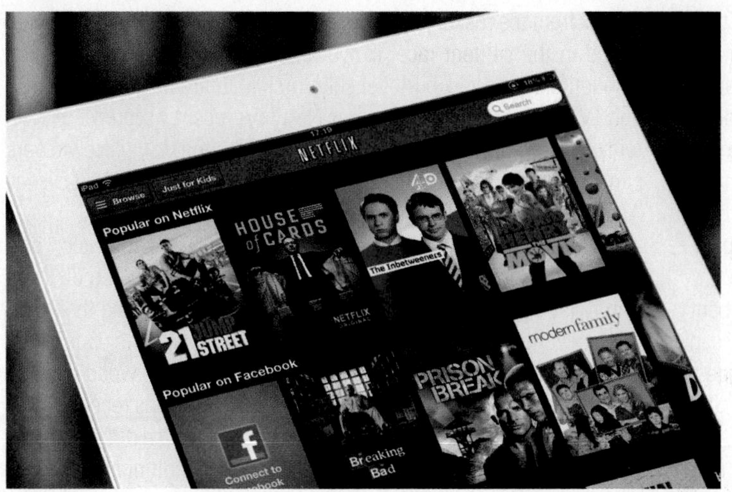

›› Netflix's innovative distribution strategy: Netflix is bent on speeding up its leap from success in DVD rentals to success in digital streaming. What's next?

© IanDagnall Computing/Alamy.

First Stop

Netflix's Channel Innovation: Finding the Future by Abandoning the Past

Time and again, Netflix has innovated its way to the top in the distribution of video entertainment. In the early 2000s, Netflix's revolutionary DVD-by-mail service put all but the most powerful movie-rental stores out of business. In 2007, Netflix's then ground-breaking move into digital streaming once again revolutionized how people accessed movies and other video content. Now, with Netflix leading the pack, video distribution has become a boiling, roiling pot of emerging technologies and high-tech competitors, one that offers both mind-bending opportunities and stomach-churning risks.

Just ask Blockbuster. Only a few years ago, the giant brick-and-mortar movie-rental chain flat-out owned the industry. Then along came Netflix, the fledgling DVD-by-mail service. First thousands then millions of subscribers were drawn to Netflix's innovative distribution model—no more trips to the video store, no more late fees, and a selection of more than 100,000 titles that dwarfed anything Blockbuster could offer. Even better, Netflix's $5-a-month subscription rate cost little more than renting a single video from Blockbuster. In 2010, as Netflix surged, once-mighty Blockbuster fell into bankruptcy.

The Blockbuster riches-to-rags story underscores the turmoil that typifies today's video distribution business. In only the past few years, a glut of video access options has materialized. At the same time that Netflix ascended and Blockbuster plunged, Coinstar's Redbox came out of nowhere to build a novel national network of $1-a-day DVD-rental kiosks. Then high-tech start-ups such as Hulu—with its high-quality, ad-supported free access to movies and current TV shows—began pushing digital streaming via the Internet.

All along the way, Netflix has acted boldly to stay ahead of the competition. For example, in 2007, rather than sitting on the success of its still-hot DVD-by-mail business, Netflix and its CEO, Reed Hastings, set their sights on a then-revolutionary new video distribution model: Deliver the Netflix service to every Internet-connected screen, from laptops to Internet-ready TVs to mobile phones and other Wi-Fi-enabled devices. Netflix began by launching its Watch Instantly service, which let Netflix members stream movies instantly to their computers as part of their monthly membership fee, even if it came at the expense of Netflix's still-booming DVD business.

Time and again, Netflix has innovated its way to the top in the distribution of video entertainment. But to stay atop its boiling, roiling industry, Netflix must keep the distribution innovation pedal to the metal.

Although Netflix didn't pioneer digital streaming, it poured resources into improving the technology and building the largest streaming library. It built a customer base of nearly 25 million subscribers, and sales and profits soared. With its massive physical DVD library and a streaming library of more than 20,000 high-definition movies accessible via 200 different Internet-ready devices, it seemed that nothing could stop Netflix.

But Netflix's stunning success drew a slew of resourceful competitors. In 2010, video giants such as Google's YouTube and Apple's iTunes began renting movie downloads, and Hulu introduced subscription-based Hulu Plus. To stay ahead, even to survive, Netflix needed to keep the innovation pedal to the metal. So in the summer of 2011, in an ambitious but risky move, CEO Hastings made an all-in bet on digital streaming. He split off Netflix's still-thriving DVD-by-mail service into a separate business named Qwikster and required separate subscriptions for DVD rentals and streaming (at a startling 60 percent price increase for customers using both). The Netflix name would now stand for nothing but digital streaming, which would be the primary focus of the company's future growth.

Although perhaps visionary, Netflix's abrupt changes didn't sit well with customers. Some 800,000 subscribers dropped the service and Netflix's stock price plummeted by almost two-thirds. To repair the damage, Netflix quickly admitted its blunder and reversed its decision to set up a separate Qwikster operation. However, despite the setback, Netflix retained its separate, higher pricing for DVDs by mail. Netflix rebounded quickly, replacing all of its lost subscribers and then some. What's more, with a 60 percent higher price, revenues and profits rose as well. Netflix's stock price was once again skyrocketing.

With the quick recovery, now more than ever, Hastings seems bent on speeding up the company's leap from success in DVDs to success in streaming. Although customers can still access Netflix's world's-biggest DVD library, the company's promotions and Web site barely mention that option. The focus is now squarely on streaming video.

Despite its continuing success, Netflix knows that it can't rest its innovation machine. Competition continues to move at a blurring rate. For example, Amazon's Prime Instant Video offers instant streaming of thousands of movies and TV shows to Amazon Prime members at no extra cost. Google has moved beyond its YouTube rental service with Google Play, an all-media entertainment portal for movies, music, e-books, and apps. Comcast offers Xfinity Streampix, which lets subscribers stream older movies and television programs via their TVs, laptops, tablets, or smartphones. Coinstar and Verizon have now joined forces to form Redbox Instant by Verizon, which offers subscription-based streaming of older movies and newer pay-per-view content. And Apple and Samsung are creating smoother integration with streaming content via smart TVs.

Moving ahead, as the industry settles into streaming as the main delivery model, content—not just delivery—will be a key to distancing Netflix from the rest of pack. Given its head start, Netflix remains well ahead in the content race. However, Amazon, Hulu Plus, and other competitors are working feverishly to sign contracts with big movie and TV content providers. But so is Netflix. It recently scored a big win with a Disney exclusive—soon, Netflix will be the only place viewers can stream Disney's deep catalog and new releases from Walt Disney Animation, Marvel, Pixar, and Lucasfilm.

But as content-licensing deals with movie and television studios become harder to get, in yet another innovative video distribution twist, Netflix and its competitors are now developing their own original content. Once again, Netflix appears to have the upper hand with *House of Cards,* a new series produced by Hollywood bigwigs David Fincher and Kevin Spacey. The Netflix series has received rave reviews and sets a number of industry "firsts." *House of Cards* is the first major TV show to completely bypass the traditional broadcast and cable networks. With its $100 million price tag, it's by far the most expensive series to air on a streaming network. And it marks the first time a series has released an entire season all at once. With *House of Cards*, Netflix has left the rest of the video industry scrambling to keep up.

Thus, from DVDs by mail, to Watch Instantly, to video streaming on almost any device, to developing original content, Netflix has stayed ahead of the howling pack by doing what it does best—innovate and revolutionize distribution. What's next? No one really knows. But one thing seems certain: Whatever's coming, if Netflix doesn't lead the change, it risks being left behind—and quickly. In this fast-changing business, new tricks grow old in a hurry. To stay ahead, as one headline suggests, Netflix must "find its future by abandoning its past."[1]

As the Netflix story shows, good distribution strategies can contribute strongly to customer value and create competitive advantage for a firm. But firms cannot bring value to customers by themselves. Instead, they must work closely with other firms in a larger value delivery network.

Author Comment

These are pretty hefty terms for a really simple concept: A company can't go it alone in creating customer value. It must work within a broader network of partners to accomplish this task. Individual companies and brands don't compete; their entire value delivery networks do.

Supply Chains and the Value Delivery Network

Producing a product or service and making it available to buyers requires building relationships not only with customers but also with key suppliers and resellers in the company's *supply chain*. This supply chain consists of upstream and downstream partners. Upstream from the company is the set of firms that supply the raw materials, components, parts, information, finances, and expertise needed to create a product or service. Marketers, however, have traditionally focused on the downstream side of the supply chain—the *marketing channels* (or *distribution channels*) that look toward the customer. Downstream marketing channel partners, such as wholesalers and retailers, form a vital link between the firm and its customers.

The term *supply chain* may be too limited, as it takes a *make-and-sell* view of the business. It suggests that raw materials, productive inputs, and factory capacity should serve as the starting point for market planning. A better term would be *demand chain* because it suggests a *sense-and-respond* view of the market. Under this view, planning starts by identifying the needs of target customers, to which the company responds by organizing a chain of resources and activities with the goal of creating customer value.

Yet, even a demand chain view of a business may be too limited because it takes a step-by-step, linear view of purchase-production-consumption activities. Instead, most large

Value delivery network: In making and marketing even just its adidas originals line, adidas manages a huge network of people within the company plus thousands of outside suppliers, resellers, and marketing firms that must work together to create customer value and establish the line's "unite all originals" positioning.

adidas.

companies today are engaged in building and managing a complex, continuously evolving value delivery network. As defined in Chapter 2, a **value delivery network** is made up of the company, suppliers, distributors, and, ultimately, customers who "partner" with each other to improve the performance of the entire system. For example, adidas makes great sports shoes and apparel. But to make and market just one of its many lines—say its new adidas originals line of retro shoes and vintage street wear—adidas manages a huge network of people within the company. It also coordinates the efforts of thousands of suppliers, retailers ranging from Foot Locker to online seller Zappos, and advertising agencies and other marketing service firms that must work together to create customer value and establish the line's "unite all originals" positioning.

This chapter focuses on marketing channels—on the downstream side of the value delivery network. We examine four major questions concerning marketing channels: What is the nature of marketing channels and why are they important? How do channel firms interact and organize to do the work of the channel? What problems do companies face in designing and managing their channels? What role do physical distribution and supply chain management play in attracting and satisfying customers? In the next chapter, we will look at marketing channel issues from the viewpoints of retailers and wholesalers.

Author Comment

In this section, we look at the downstream side of the value delivery network—the marketing channel organizations that connect the company and its customers. To understand their value, imagine life without retailers—say, without grocery stores or department stores.

The Nature and Importance of Marketing Channels

Few producers sell their goods directly to final users. Instead, most use intermediaries to bring their products to market. They try to forge a **marketing channel** (or **distribution channel**)—a set of interdependent organizations that help make a product or service available for use or consumption by the consumer or business user.

A company's channel decisions directly affect every other marketing decision. Pricing depends on whether the company works with national discount chains, uses high-quality specialty stores, or sells directly to consumers online. The firm's sales force and communications decisions depend on how much persuasion, training, motivation, and support its channel partners need. Whether a company develops or acquires certain new products may depend on how well those products fit the capabilities of its channel members.

Value delivery network
A network composed of the company, suppliers, distributors, and, ultimately, customers who partner with each other to improve the performance of the entire system in delivering customer value.

Marketing channel (or distribution channel)
A set of interdependent organizations that help make a product or service available for use or consumption by the consumer or business user.

Companies often pay too little attention to their distribution channels—sometimes with damaging results. In contrast, many companies have used imaginative distribution systems to gain a competitive advantage. Enterprise Rent-A-Car revolutionized the car-rental business by setting up off-airport rental offices. Apple turned the retail music business on its head by selling music for the iPod via the Internet on iTunes. FedEx's creative and imposing distribution system made it a leader in express package delivery. And Amazon.com forever changed the face of retailing and became the Walmart of the Internet by selling anything and everything without using physical stores.

Distribution channel decisions often involve long-term commitments to other firms. For example, companies such as Ford, McDonald's, or Nike can easily change their advertising, pricing, or promotion programs. They can scrap old products and introduce new ones as market tastes demand. But when they set up distribution channels through contracts with franchisees, independent dealers, or large retailers, they cannot readily replace these channels with company-owned stores or Internet sites if the conditions change. Therefore, management must design its channels carefully, with an eye on both today's likely selling environment and tomorrow's as well.

How Channel Members Add Value

Why do producers give some of the selling job to channel partners? After all, doing so means giving up some control over how and to whom they sell their products. Producers use intermediaries because they create greater efficiency in making goods available to target markets. Through their contacts, experience, specialization, and scale of operation, intermediaries usually offer the firm more than it can achieve on its own.

>> **Figure 10.1** shows how using intermediaries can provide economies. Figure 10.1A shows three manufacturers, each using direct marketing to reach three customers. This system requires nine different contacts. Figure 10.1B shows the three manufacturers working through one distributor, which contacts the three customers. This system requires only six contacts. In this way, intermediaries reduce the amount of work that must be done by both producers and consumers.

From the economic system's point of view, the role of marketing intermediaries is to transform the assortments of products made by producers into the assortments wanted by consumers. Producers make narrow assortments of products in large quantities, but consumers want broad assortments of products in small quantities. Marketing channel members buy large quantities from many producers and break them down into the smaller quantities and broader assortments desired by consumers.

For example, Unilever makes millions of bars of Lever 2000 hand soap each week. However, you most likely only want to buy a few bars at a time. Therefore, big food, drug, and discount retailers, such as Safeway, Walgreens, and Target, buy Lever 2000 by the truckload and stock it on their stores' shelves. In turn, you can buy a single bar of Lever 2000, along with a shopping cart full of small quantities of toothpaste, shampoo, and other related products, as you need them. Thus, intermediaries play an important role in matching supply and demand.

In making products and services available to consumers, channel members add value by bridging the major time, place, and possession gaps that separate goods and services from those who use them. Members of the marketing channel perform many key functions. Some help to complete transactions:

- *Information:* Gathering and distributing information about consumers, producers, and other actors and forces in the marketing environment needed for planning and aiding exchange.
- *Promotion:* Developing and spreading persuasive communications about an offer.

>> **Figure 10.1** How a Distributor Reduces the Number of Channel Transactions

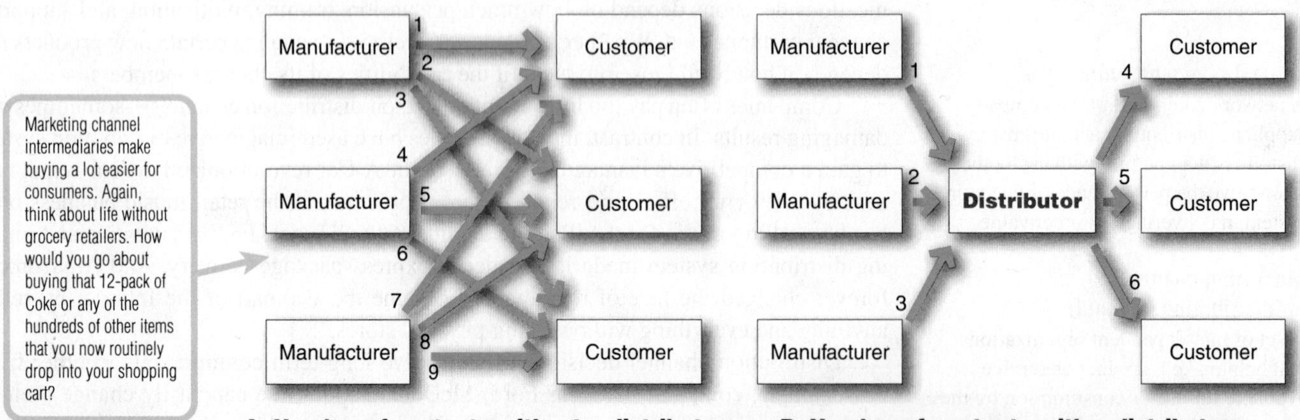

- *Contact:* Finding and communicating with prospective buyers.
- *Matching:* Shaping offers to meet the buyer's needs, including activities such as manufacturing, grading, assembling, and packaging.
- *Negotiation:* Reaching an agreement on price and other terms so that ownership or possession can be transferred.

Others help to fulfill the completed transactions:

- *Physical distribution:* Transporting and storing goods.
- *Financing:* Acquiring and using funds to cover the costs of the channel work.
- *Risk taking:* Assuming the risks of carrying out the channel work.

The question is not *whether* these functions need to be performed—they must be—but rather *who* will perform them. To the extent that the manufacturer performs these functions, its costs go up; therefore, its prices must be higher. When some of these functions are shifted to intermediaries, the producer's costs and prices may be lower, but the intermediaries must charge more to cover the costs of their work. In dividing the work of the channel, the various functions should be assigned to the channel members that can add the most value for the cost.

Number of Channel Levels

Channel level
A layer of intermediaries that performs some work in bringing the product and its ownership closer to the final buyer.

Direct marketing channel
A marketing channel that has no intermediary levels.

Companies can design their distribution channels to make products and services available to customers in different ways. Each layer of marketing intermediaries that performs some work in bringing the product and its ownership closer to the final buyer is a **channel level**. Because both the producer and the final consumer perform some work, they are part of every channel.

The *number of intermediary levels* indicates the *length* of a channel. >> **Figure 10.2** shows both consumer and business channels of different lengths. Figure 10.2A shows several common consumer distribution channels. Channel 1, called a **direct marketing channel**, has no intermediary levels—the company sells directly to consumers. For example, Mary Kay Cosmetics and Amway sell their products through home and office

>> **Figure 10.2** Consumer and Business Marketing Channels

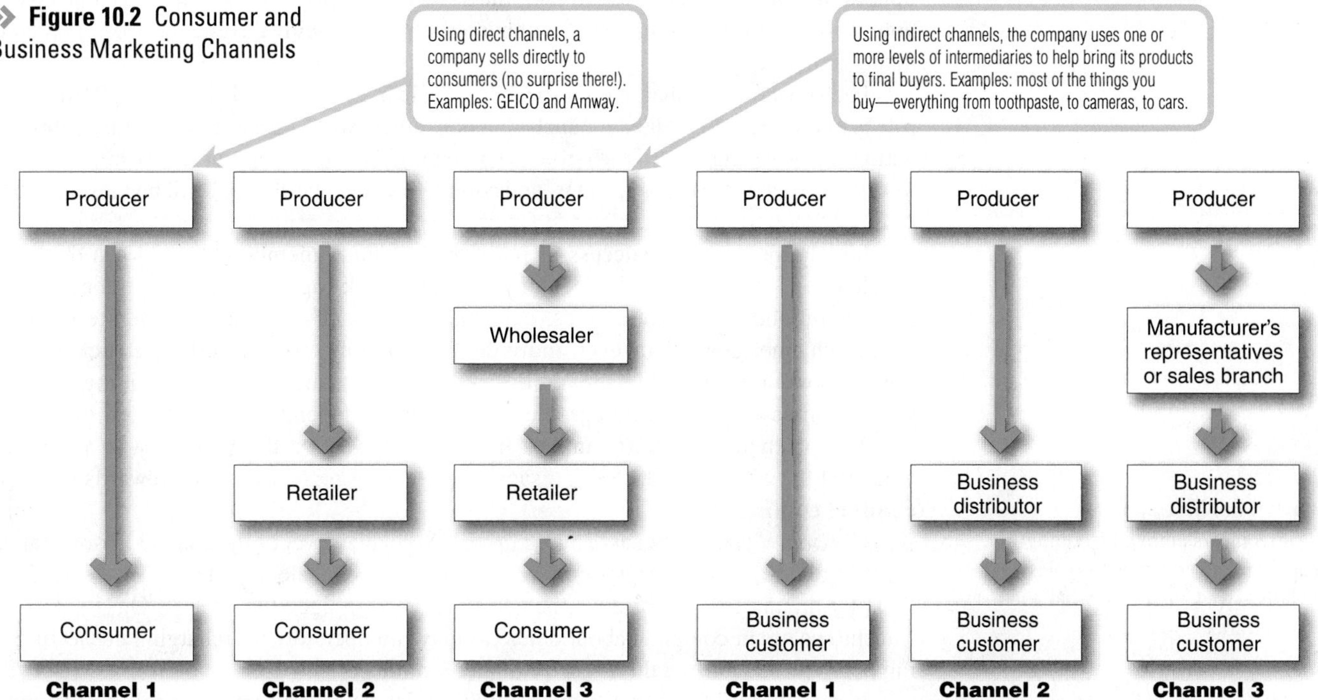

sales parties and online Web sites and social networks; companies ranging from GEICO insurance to Omaha Steaks sell directly to customers via the Internet and telephone. The remaining channels in Figure 10.2A are **indirect marketing channels**, containing one or more intermediaries.

Indirect marketing channel
A marketing channel containing one or more intermediary levels.

Figure 10.2B shows some common business distribution channels. The business marketer can use its own sales force to sell directly to business customers. Or it can sell to various types of intermediaries, which in turn sell to these customers. Although consumer and business marketing channels with even more levels can sometimes be found, these are less common. From the producer's point of view, a greater number of levels means less control and greater channel complexity. Moreover, all the institutions in the channel are connected by several types of *flows*. These include the *physical flow* of products, the *flow of ownership*, the *payment flow*, the *information flow*, and the *promotion flow*. These flows can make even channels with only one or a few levels very complex.

Author Comment
Channels are made up of more than just boxes and arrows on paper. They are behavioral systems made up of real companies and people who interact to accomplish their individual and collective goals. Like groups of people, sometimes they work well together and sometimes they don't.

Channel Behavior and Organization

Distribution channels are more than simple collections of firms tied together by various flows. They are complex behavioral systems in which people and companies interact to accomplish individual, company, and channel goals. Some channel systems consist of only informal interactions among loosely organized firms. Others consist of formal interactions guided by strong organizational structures. Moreover, channel systems do not stand still—new types of intermediaries emerge and whole new channel systems evolve. Here we look at channel behavior and how members organize to do the work of the channel.

Channel Behavior

A marketing channel consists of firms that have partnered for their common good. Each channel member depends on the others. For example, a Ford dealer depends on Ford to design cars that meet customer needs. In turn, Ford depends on the dealer to attract customers, persuade them to buy Ford cars, and service the cars after the sale. Each Ford dealer also depends on other dealers to provide good sales and service that will uphold the brand's reputation. In fact, the success of individual Ford dealers depends on how well the entire Ford marketing channel competes with the channels of other auto manufacturers.

Each channel member plays a specialized role in the channel. For example, Samsung's role is to produce electronics products that consumers will like and create demand through national advertising. Best Buy's role is to display these Samsung products in convenient locations, answer buyers' questions, and complete sales. The channel will be most effective when each member assumes the tasks it can do best.

Ideally, because the success of individual channel members depends on the overall channel's success, all channel firms should work together smoothly. They should understand and accept their roles, coordinate their activities, and cooperate to attain overall channel goals. However, individual channel members rarely take such a broad view. Cooperating to achieve overall channel goals sometimes means giving up individual company goals. Although channel members depend on one another, they often act alone in their own short-run best interests. They often disagree on who should do what and for what rewards. Such disagreements over goals, roles, and rewards generate **channel conflict**.

Channel conflict
Disagreements among marketing channel members on goals, roles, and rewards—who should do what and for what rewards.

Horizontal conflict occurs among firms at the same level of the channel. For instance, some Ford dealers in Chicago might complain that other dealers in the city steal sales from them by pricing too low or advertising outside their assigned territories. Or Holiday Inn franchisees might complain about other Holiday Inn operators overcharging guests or giving poor service, hurting the overall Holiday Inn image.

Vertical conflict, conflict between different levels of the same channel, is even more common. >> For example, KFC and its franchisees came into conflict over the company's

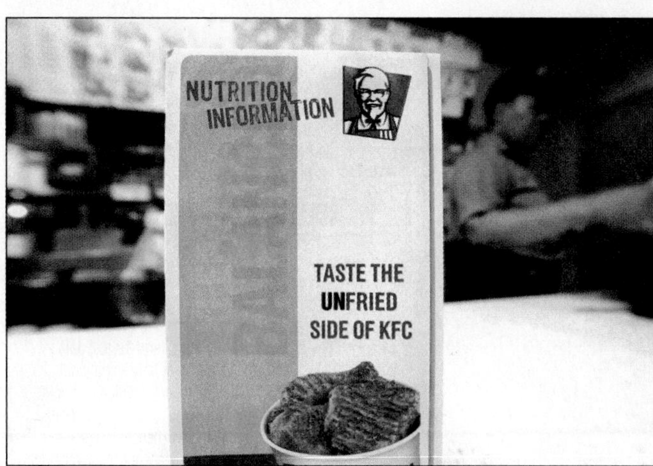

Channel conflict: KFC came into conflict with its franchisees over the brand's "Unthink KFC" repositioning, which emphasized grilled chicken over its traditional Kentucky fried. "We ought to be shooting the competition," says one franchisee. "Instead, we're shooting one another."

Joshua Lutz/Redux.

decision to emphasize grilled chicken and sandwiches over the brand's traditional fried chicken:[2]

> KFC claimed that it must reposition the brand around grilled chicken rather than fried to reach today's increasingly health-conscious, on-the-go consumers. However, a sizable group of the company's more than 4,000 U.S. franchisees cried "foul" when the chain introduced grilled chicken, supported by a major marketing campaign with the slogan "Unthink KFC." The franchisees were concerned that abandoning the brand's Southern fried chicken legacy would confuse consumers and hurt sales. It "tells our customers not to think of us as a fried chicken chain," complained one franchisee who operates 60 franchises in five states. Soon after the "Unthink" campaign began, the KFC National Council & Advertising Cooperative, which represents all U.S. KFC franchisees, sued KFC to halt it. And the Association of Kentucky Fried Chicken Franchises, which represents two-thirds of U.S. franchisees, developed its own local marketing campaign emphasizing good old Kentucky fried. KFC eventually dropped "Unthink KFC." However, that and others have left a bad aftertaste in mouths on both sides. "We ought to be walking arm in arm to figure out a way out of [the current] sales decline. We ought to be shooting the competition," says one franchisee. "Instead, we're shooting one another."

Some conflict in the channel takes the form of healthy competition. Such competition can be good for the channel; without it, the channel could become passive and noninnovative. For example, KFC's conflict with its franchisees might represent normal give-and-take over the respective rights of the channel partners. However, severe or prolonged conflict can disrupt channel effectiveness and cause lasting harm to channel relationships. KFC should manage the channel conflict carefully to keep it from getting out of hand.

Vertical Marketing Systems

For the channel as a whole to perform well, each channel member's role must be specified, and channel conflict must be managed. The channel will perform better if it includes a firm, agency, or mechanism that provides leadership and has the power to assign roles and manage conflict.

Conventional distribution channel
A channel consisting of one or more independent producers, wholesalers, and retailers, each a separate business seeking to maximize its own profits, perhaps even at the expense of profits for the system as a whole.

Vertical marketing system (VMS)
A channel structure in which producers, wholesalers, and retailers act as a unified system. One channel member owns the others, has contracts with them, or has so much power that they all cooperate.

Corporate VMS
A vertical marketing system that combines successive stages of production and distribution under single ownership—channel leadership is established through common ownership.

Historically, *conventional distribution channels* have lacked such leadership and power, often resulting in damaging conflict and poor performance. One of the biggest channel developments over the years has been the emergence of *vertical marketing systems* that provide channel leadership. **Figure 10.3** contrasts the two types of channel arrangements.

A **conventional distribution channel** consists of one or more independent producers, wholesalers, and retailers. Each is a separate business seeking to maximize its own profits, perhaps even at the expense of the system as a whole. No channel member has much control over the other members, and no formal means exists for assigning roles and resolving channel conflict.

In contrast, a **vertical marketing system (VMS)** consists of producers, wholesalers, and retailers acting as a unified system. One channel member owns the others, has contracts with them, or wields so much power that they must all cooperate. The VMS can be dominated by the producer, the wholesaler, or the retailer.

We look now at three major types of VMSs: *corporate*, *contractual*, and *administered*. Each uses a different means for setting up leadership and power in the channel.

Corporate VMS

A **corporate VMS** integrates successive stages of production and distribution under single ownership. Coordination and conflict management are attained through regular organizational channels. For example, the grocery giant Kroger owns and operates 39 manufacturing

Figure 10.3 Comparison of Conventional Distribution Channel with Vertical Marketing System

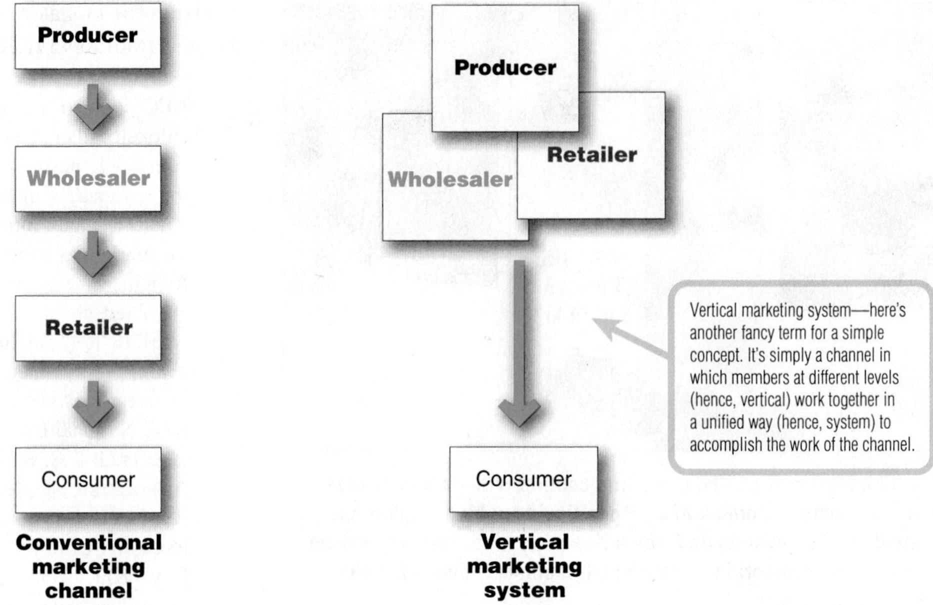
Producer
Wholesaler
Retailer
Consumer
Conventional marketing channel
Producer
Retailer
Wholesaler
Consumer
Vertical marketing system
Vertical marketing system—here's another fancy term for a simple concept. It's simply a channel in which members at different levels (hence, vertical) work together in a unified way (hence, system) to accomplish the work of the channel.

plants—15 dairies, 7 bakery plants, 5 grocery plants, 3 beverage plants, 3 deli plants, 2 frozen dough and cake plants, 2 ice cream plants, 2 cheese plants, and 2 meat plants—that give it factory-to-store channel control over 40 percent of the more than 11,000 private-label items found on its shelves.[3]

And integrating the entire distribution chain—from its own design and manufacturing operations to distribution through its own managed stores—has turned Spanish clothing chain Zara into the world's fastest-growing fast-fashion retailer:[4]

> In recent years, fashion retailer Zara has attracted a near cultlike clientele of shoppers swarming to buy its "cheap chic"—stylish designs that resemble those of big-name fashion houses but at moderate prices. However, Zara's amazing success comes not just from *what* it sells, but from *how fast* its cutting-edge distribution system *delivers* what it sells. Zara delivers fast fashion—*really* fast fashion. Thanks to vertical integration, Zara can take a new fashion concept through design, manufacturing, and store-shelf placement in as little as three weeks, whereas competitors such as Gap, Benetton, or H&M often take six months or more. And the resulting low costs let Zara offer the very latest midmarket chic at down-market prices.
>
> Speedy design and distribution allows Zara to introduce a copious supply of new fashions—at three times the rate of competitor introductions. Then, Zara's distribution system supplies its stores with small shipments of new merchandise twice a week, compared with competing chains' outlets, which get large shipments seasonally, usually just four to six times per year. The combination of a large number of timely new fashions delivered in frequent small batches gives Zara stores a continually updated merchandise mix that brings customers back more often. Fast turnover also results in less outdated and discounted merchandise. "Instead of betting on tomorrow's hot look," says one analyst, "Zara can wait to see what customers are actually buying—and make that."

Contractual VMS
A vertical marketing system in which independent firms at different levels of production and distribution join together through contracts.

Franchise organization
A contractual vertical marketing system in which a channel member, called a franchisor, links several stages in the production-distribution process.

Contractual VMS

A **contractual VMS** consists of independent firms at different levels of production and distribution that join together through contracts to obtain more economies or sales impact than each could achieve alone. Channel members coordinate their activities and manage conflict through contractual agreements.

The **franchise organization** is the most common type of contractual relationship. In this system, a channel member called a *franchisor* links several stages in the production-distribution process. In the United States alone, some 3,000 franchisors and 757,000 franchise outlets account for more than $800 billion of economic output. Industry analysts estimate that a new franchise outlet opens somewhere in the United States every eight minutes and

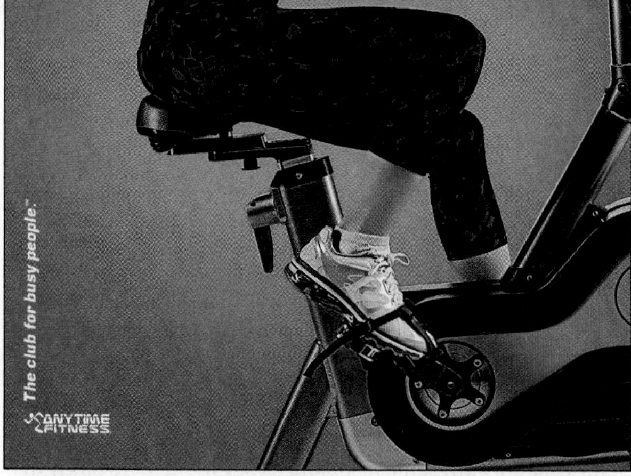

>> Franchising systems: Almost every kind of business has been franchised. For example, Anytime Fitness, "The club for busy people," brings convenient, affordable, and fun fitness to nearly 2 million members through 2,100 franchise outlets around the nation and world.

Courtesy of Anytime Fitness.

that about one out of every 12 retail business outlets is a franchised business.[5]

Almost every kind of business has been franchised—from motels and fast-food restaurants to dental centers and dating services, from wedding consultants and handyman services to funeral homes and fitness centers. >> For example, Anytime Fitness, "The club for busy people," grew quickly through franchising. Only a decade or so after its founding, Anytime Fitness now operates more than 2,100 clubs with nearly 2 million members in all 50 states and 15 countries.

There are three types of franchises. The first type is the *manufacturer-sponsored retailer franchise system*—for example, Ford and its network of independent franchised dealers. The second type is the *manufacturer-sponsored wholesaler franchise system*—Coca-Cola licenses bottlers (wholesalers) in various world markets that buy Coca-Cola syrup concentrate and then bottle and sell the finished product to retailers locally. The third type is the *service-firm-sponsored retailer franchise system*—for example, Burger King and its nearly 12,300 franchisee-operated restaurants around the world. Other examples can be found in everything from auto rentals (Hertz, Avis), apparel retailers (The Athlete's Foot, Plato's Closet), and motels (Holiday Inn, Hampton Inn) to supplemental education (Huntington Learning Center, Kumon) and personal services (Great Clips, Mr. Handyman, Anytime Fitness).

The fact that most consumers cannot tell the difference between contractual and corporate VMSs shows how successfully the contractual organizations compete with corporate chains. The next chapter presents a fuller discussion of the various contractual VMSs.

Administered VMS

In an **administered VMS**, leadership is assumed not through common ownership or contractual ties but through the size and power of one or a few dominant channel members. Manufacturers of a top brand can obtain strong trade cooperation and support from resellers. For example, GE, P&G, and Kraft can command unusual cooperation from many resellers regarding displays, shelf space, promotions, and price policies. In turn, large retailers such as Walmart, Home Depot, and Kohl's can exert strong influence on the many manufacturers that supply the products they sell.

Administered VMS
A vertical marketing system that coordinates successive stages of production and distribution through the size and power of one of the parties.

For example, with commodity prices increasing, many consumer goods manufacturers want to pass these costs along to Walmart and other retailers in the form of higher prices. However, Walmart wants to hold the line on its own costs and prices in order to maintain its low-price positioning with customers in tighter times. This creates push and pull between Walmart and its suppliers, a tussle in which Walmart—the biggest grocery seller in the United States—usually gets its way. Take Clorox Company, for instance. Although the company's strong consumer brand preference gives it significant negotiating power, Walmart simply holds more cards. Sales to Walmart make up 26 percent of Clorox's sales, so maintaining a strong relationship with the giant retailer is crucial.[6]

Horizontal Marketing Systems

Horizontal marketing system
A channel arrangement in which two or more companies at one level join together to follow a new marketing opportunity.

Another channel development is the **horizontal marketing system**, in which two or more companies at one level join together to follow a new marketing opportunity. By working together, companies can combine their financial, production, or marketing resources to accomplish more than any one company could alone.

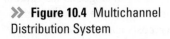

Horizontal marketing channels: McDonald's places "express" versions of its restaurants in Walmart stores. McDonald's benefits from Walmart's heavy store traffic and Walmart keeps hungry shoppers from needing to go elsewhere to eat.

Gary Armstrong.

Companies might join forces with competitors or noncompetitors. They might work with each other on a temporary or permanent basis, or they may create a separate company. For example, Walmart also partners with McDonald's to place "express" versions of McDonald's restaurants in Walmart stores. McDonald's benefits from Walmart's heavy store traffic, and Walmart keeps hungry shoppers from needing to go elsewhere to eat.

Such channel arrangements also work well globally. For example, competitors General Mills and Nestlé operate a joint venture—Cereal Partners Worldwide—to market General Mills BigG cereal brands in 130 countries outside North America. General Mills supplies a kitchen cabinet full of quality cereal brands, whereas Nestlé contributes its extensive international distribution channels and local market knowledge. The 30-year-old alliance produces more than \$1.1 billion in revenues for General Mills.[7]

Multichannel Distribution Systems

In the past, many companies used a single channel to sell to a single market or market segment. Today, with the proliferation of customer segments and channel possibilities, more and more companies have adopted **multichannel distribution systems**. Such multichannel marketing occurs when a single firm sets up two or more marketing channels to reach one or more customer segments.

Multichannel distribution system
A distribution system in which a single firm sets up two or more marketing channels to reach one or more customer segments.

Figure 10.4 shows a multichannel marketing system. In the figure, the producer sells directly to consumer segment 1 using catalogs, telemarketing, and the Internet and reaches consumer segment 2 through retailers. It sells indirectly to business segment 1 through distributors and dealers and to business segment 2 through its own sales force.

These days, almost every large company and many small ones distribute through multiple channels. For example, John Deere sells its familiar green-and-yellow lawn and garden tractors, mowers, and outdoor power products to consumers and commercial users through several channels, including John Deere retailers, Lowe's home improvement stores, and online. It sells and services its tractors, combines, planters, and other agricultural equipment through its premium John Deere dealer network. And it sells large construction and forestry equipment through selected large, full-service John Deere dealers and their sales forces.

Figure 10.4 Multichannel Distribution System

Most large companies distribute through multiple channels. For example, you could buy a familiar green-and-yellow John Deere lawn tractor from a neighborhood John Deere dealer or from Lowe's. A large farm or forestry business would buy larger John Deere equipment from a premium full-service John Deere dealer and its sales force.

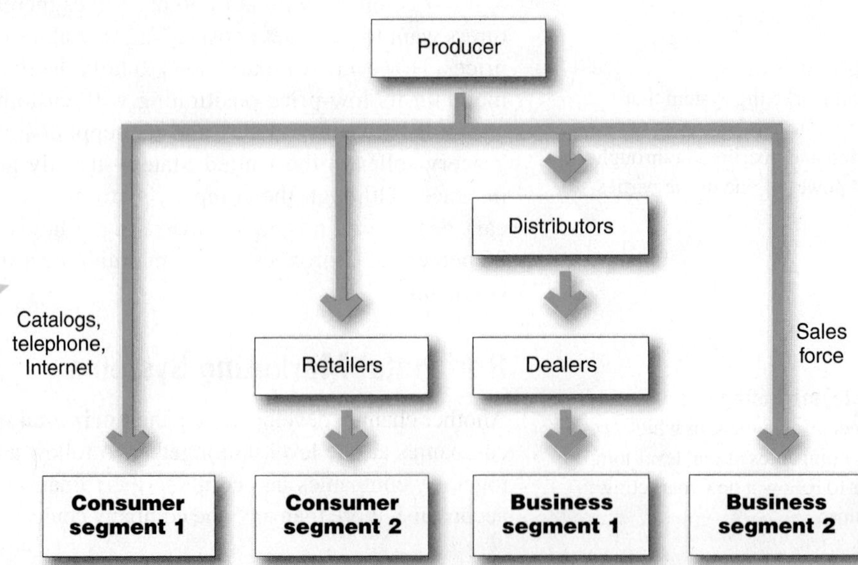

Multichannel distribution systems offer many advantages to companies facing large and complex markets. With each new channel, the company expands its sales and market coverage and gains opportunities to tailor its products and services to the specific needs of diverse customer segments. But such multichannel systems are harder to control, and they can generate conflict as more channels compete for customers and sales. For example, when John Deere first began selling selected consumer products through Lowe's home improvement stores, many of its dealers complained loudly. To avoid such conflicts in its Internet marketing channels, the company routes all of its Web site sales to John Deere dealers.

Changing Channel Organization

Disintermediation
The cutting out of marketing channel intermediaries by product or service producers or the displacement of traditional resellers by radical new types of intermediaries.

Changes in technology and the explosive growth of direct and online marketing are having a profound impact on the nature and design of marketing channels. One major trend is toward **disintermediation**—a big term with a clear message and important consequences. Disintermediation occurs when product or service producers cut out intermediaries and go directly to final buyers or when radically new types of channel intermediaries displace traditional ones.

Thus, in many industries, traditional intermediaries are dropping by the wayside, as is the case with online marketers taking business from traditional brick-and-mortar retailers. For example, online music download services such as iTunes and Amazon MP3 have pretty much put traditional music-store retailers out of business. And Amazon.com almost single-handedly bankrupted the nation's number-two bookseller, Borders, in less than 10 years. The burgeoning online-only merchant has recently forced highly successful store retailers such as Best Buy to dramatically rethink their entire operating models. In fact, many retailing experts question whether stores like Best Buy can compete in the long run against online rivals.[8]

Disintermediation presents both opportunities and problems for producers and resellers. Channel innovators who find new ways to add value in the channel can displace traditional resellers and reap the rewards. In turn, traditional intermediaries must continue to innovate to avoid being swept aside. For example, superstore booksellers Borders and Barnes & Noble pioneered huge book selections and low prices, sending most small independent bookstores into ruin. Then, along came Amazon.com, which threatened even the largest brick-and-mortar bookstores through online book sales. Now, both offline and online sellers of physical books are being threatened by digital book downloads and e-readers. Rather than being threatened by these digital developments, however, Amazon.com is leading them with its highly successful Kindle e-readers. » By contrast, Barnes & Noble—the giant that helped put so many independent bookstores out of business—is a latecomer with its Nook e-reader and now finds itself locked in a battle for survival.[9]

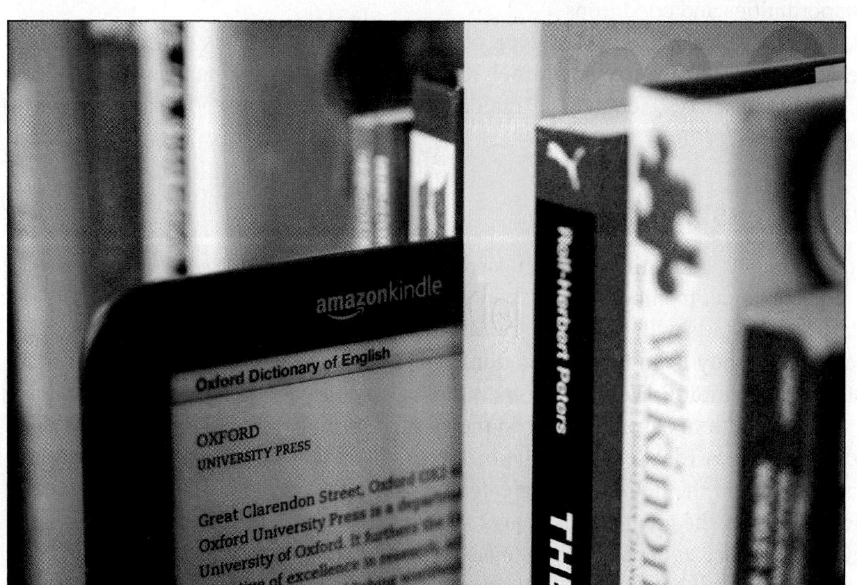

» **Disintermediation: Resellers must innovate or risk being swept aside. For example, Barnes & Noble, the giant that helped put so many independent booksellers out of business, now faces disintermediation at the hands of online booksellers and digital e-book downloads.**

Bloomberg via Getty Images.

Like resellers, to remain competitive, product and service producers must develop new channel opportunities, such as the Internet and other direct channels. However, developing these new channels often brings them into direct competition with their established channels, resulting in conflict. To ease this problem, companies often look for ways to make going direct a plus for the entire channel. For example, guitar and amp maker Fender knows that many customers would prefer to buy its guitars, amps, and accessories online. But selling directly through its Web site would create conflicts with retail partners, from large chains such as Guitar Center, Sam Ash, and Best Buy to small shops scattered throughout the world, such as the Musician's Junkyard in Windsor, Vermont, or Freddy for Music in Amman, Jordan. So Fender's Web site provides detailed information about the company's products, but you can't buy a new Fender Stratocaster or Acoustasonic guitar there. Instead, the Fender Web site refers you to its resellers' Web sites and stores. Thus, Fender's direct marketing helps both the company and its channel partners.

SPEED BUMP LINKING THE CONCEPTS

Stop here for a moment and apply the distribution channel concepts we've discussed so far.

- Compare the Zara and Ford channels. Draw a diagram that shows the types of intermediaries in each channel. What kind of channel system does each company use?
- What are the roles and responsibilities of the members in each channel? How well do these channel members work together toward overall channel success?

Author Comment
Like everything else in marketing, good channel design begins with analyzing customer needs. Remember, marketing channels are really *customer value-delivery networks.*

Channel Design Decisions

We now look at several channel design decisions manufacturers face. In designing marketing channels, manufacturers struggle between what is ideal and what is practical. A new firm with limited capital usually starts by selling in a limited market area. In this case, deciding on the best channels might not be a problem: The problem might simply be how to convince one or a few good intermediaries to handle the line.

If successful, the new firm can branch out to new markets through existing intermediaries. In smaller markets, the firm might sell directly to retailers; in larger markets, it might sell through distributors. In one part of the country, it might grant exclusive franchises; in another, it might sell through all available outlets. Then it might add an Internet store that sells directly to hard-to-reach customers. In this way, channel systems often evolve to meet market opportunities and conditions.

For maximum effectiveness, however, channel analysis and decision making should be more purposeful. **Marketing channel design** calls for analyzing consumer needs, setting channel objectives, identifying major channel alternatives, and evaluating those alternatives.

Marketing channel design
Designing effective marketing channels by analyzing customer needs, setting channel objectives, identifying major channel alternatives, and evaluating those alternatives.

Analyzing Consumer Needs

As noted previously, marketing channels are part of the overall *customer value–delivery network.* Each channel member and level adds value for the customer. Thus, designing the marketing channel starts with finding out what target consumers want from the channel. Do consumers want to buy from nearby locations or are they willing to travel to more distant and centralized locations? Would customers rather buy in person, by phone, or online? Do they value breadth of assortment or do they prefer specialization? Do consumers want many add-on services (delivery, installation, repairs), or will they obtain these services elsewhere? The faster the delivery, the greater the assortment provided, and the more add-on services supplied, the greater the channel's service level.

Providing the fastest delivery, the greatest assortment, and the most services may not be possible or practical, however. The company and its channel members may not have the resources or skills needed to provide all the desired services. Also, providing higher levels of service results in higher costs for the channel and higher prices for consumers. >> For example, your local independent hardware store probably provides more personalized service, a more convenient location, and less shopping hassle than the nearest huge Home Depot or Lowe's store. But it may also charge higher prices. The company must balance

>> **Meeting customers' channel service needs: Your local hardware store probably provides more personalized service, a more convenient location, and less shopping hassle than a huge Home Depot or Lowe's store. But it may also charge higher prices.**

DAVID WALTER BANKS/The New York Times/Redux Pictures.

consumer needs not only against the feasibility and costs of meeting these needs but also against customer price preferences. The success of discount retailing shows that consumers will often accept lower service levels in exchange for lower prices.

Setting Channel Objectives

Companies should state their marketing channel objectives in terms of targeted levels of customer service. Usually, a company can identify several segments wanting different levels of service. The company should decide which segments to serve and the best channels to use in each case. In each segment, the company wants to minimize the total channel cost of meeting customer service requirements.

The company's channel objectives are also influenced by the nature of the company, its products, its marketing intermediaries, its competitors, and the environment. For example, the company's size and financial situation determine which marketing functions it can handle itself and which it must give to intermediaries. Companies selling perishable products, for example, may require more direct marketing to avoid delays and too much handling.

In some cases, a company may want to compete in or near the same outlets that carry competitors' products. For example, Maytag and other appliance makers want their products displayed alongside competing brands to facilitate comparison shopping. In other cases, companies may avoid the channels used by competitors. Mary Kay Cosmetics, for example, sells directly to consumers through its corps of more than 2.4 million independent beauty consultants in more than 35 markets worldwide rather than going head-to-head with other cosmetics makers for scarce positions in retail stores.[10] GEICO primarily markets auto and homeowner's insurance directly to consumers via the telephone and the Internet rather than through agents.

Finally, environmental factors such as economic conditions and legal constraints may affect channel objectives and design. For example, in a depressed economy, producers will want to distribute their goods in the most economical way, using shorter channels and dropping unneeded services that add to the final price of the goods.

Identifying Major Alternatives

When the company has defined its channel objectives, it should next identify its major channel alternatives in terms of the *types* of intermediaries, the *number* of intermediaries, and the *responsibilities* of each channel member.

Types of Intermediaries

A firm should identify the types of channel members available to carry out its channel work. Most companies face many channel member choices. For example, until recently, Dell sold directly to final consumers and business buyers only through its sophisticated phone and Internet marketing channel. It also sold directly to large corporate, institutional, and government buyers using its direct sales force. However, to reach more consumers and match competitors such as Samsung and Apple, Dell now sells indirectly through retailers such as Best Buy, Staples, and Walmart. It also sells indirectly through value-added resellers, independent distributors and dealers that develop computer systems and applications tailored to the special needs of small- and medium-sized business customers.

Using many types of resellers in a channel provides both benefits and drawbacks. For example, by selling through retailers and value-added resellers in addition to its own direct channels, Dell can reach more and different kinds of buyers. However, the new channels will be more difficult to manage and control. In addition, the direct and indirect channels will compete with each other for many of the same customers, causing potential conflict.

In fact, Dell often finds itself "stuck in the middle," with its direct sales reps complaining about competition from retail stores, whereas its value-added resellers complain that the direct sales reps are undercutting their business.

Number of Marketing Intermediaries

Intensive distribution
Stocking the product in as many outlets as possible.

Exclusive distribution
Giving a limited number of dealers the exclusive right to distribute the company's products in their territories.

Companies must also determine the number of channel members to use at each level. Three strategies are available: intensive distribution, exclusive distribution, and selective distribution. Producers of convenience products and common raw materials typically seek **intensive distribution**—a strategy in which they stock their products in as many outlets as possible. These products must be available where and when consumers want them. For example, toothpaste, candy, and other similar items are sold in millions of outlets to provide maximum brand exposure and consumer convenience. Kraft, Coca-Cola, Kimberly-Clark, and other consumer goods companies distribute their products in this way.

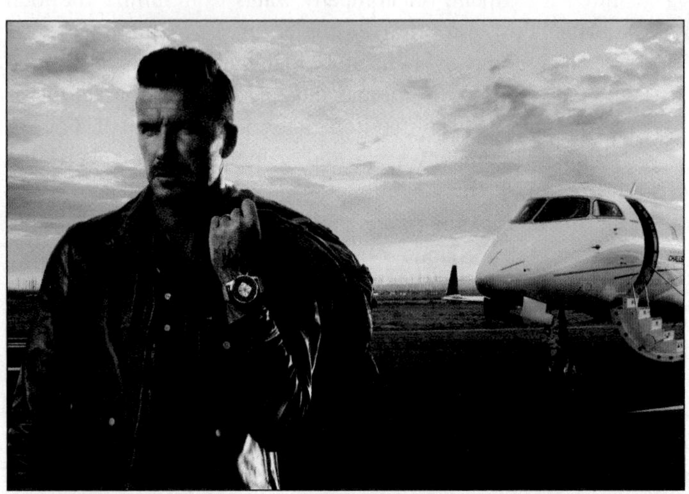

>> **Exclusive distribution: Breitling watches—positioned as "Instruments for Professionals" (here David Beckham) and with prices to match—are sold by only a few authorized dealers in any given market area.**

Associated Press.

By contrast, some producers purposely limit the number of intermediaries handling their products. The extreme form of this practice is **exclusive distribution**, in which the producer gives only a limited number of dealers the exclusive right to distribute its products in their territories. Exclusive distribution is often found in the distribution of luxury brands. >> For example, Breitling watches—positioned as "Instruments for Professionals" and selling at prices from $5,000 to more than $100,000—are sold by only a few authorized dealers in any given market area. Exclusive distribution enhances Breitling's distinctive positioning and earns greater dealer support and customer service.

Selective distribution
The use of more than one but fewer than all of the intermediaries that are willing to carry the company's products.

Between intensive and exclusive distribution lies **selective distribution**—the use of more than one but fewer than all of the intermediaries who are willing to carry a company's products. Most television, furniture, and home appliance brands are distributed in this manner. For example, Whirlpool and GE sell their major appliances through dealer networks and selected large retailers. By using selective distribution, they can develop good working relationships with selected channel members and expect a better-than-average selling effort. Selective distribution gives producers good market coverage with more control and less cost than does intensive distribution.

Responsibilities of Channel Members

The producer and the intermediaries need to agree on the terms and responsibilities of each channel member. They should agree on price policies, conditions of sale, territory rights, and the specific services to be performed by each party. The producer should establish a list price and a fair set of discounts for the intermediaries. It must define each channel member's territory, and it should be careful about where it places new resellers.

Mutual services and duties need to be spelled out carefully, especially in franchise and exclusive distribution channels. For example, McDonald's provides franchisees with promotional support, a record-keeping system, training at Hamburger University, and general management assistance. In turn, franchisees must meet company standards for physical facilities and food quality, cooperate with new promotion programs, provide requested information, and buy specified food products.

Evaluating the Major Alternatives

Suppose a company has identified several channel alternatives and wants to select the one that will best satisfy its long-run objectives. Each alternative should be evaluated against economic, control, and adaptability criteria.

Using *economic criteria*, a company compares the likely sales, costs, and profitability of different channel alternatives. What will be the investment required by each channel alternative, and what returns will result? The company must also consider *control issues*. Using intermediaries usually means giving them some control over the marketing of the product, and some intermediaries take more control than others. Other things being equal, the company prefers to keep as much control as possible. Finally, the company must apply *adaptability criteria*. Channels often involve long-term commitments, yet the company wants to keep the channel flexible so that it can adapt to environmental changes. Thus, to be considered, a channel involving long-term commitments should be greatly superior on economic and control grounds.

Designing International Distribution Channels

International marketers face many additional complexities in designing their channels. Each country has its own unique distribution system that has evolved over time and changes very slowly. These channel systems can vary widely from country to country. Thus, global marketers must usually adapt their channel strategies to the existing structures within each country.

In some markets, the distribution system is complex and hard to penetrate, consisting of many layers and large numbers of intermediaries. For example, many Western companies find Japan's distribution system difficult to navigate. It's steeped in tradition and very complex, with many distributors touching the product before it arrives on the store shelf.

At the other extreme, distribution systems in developing countries may be scattered, inefficient, or altogether lacking. For example, China and India are huge markets—each with a population well over 1 billion people. However, because of inadequate distribution systems, most companies can profitably access only a small portion of the population located in each country's most affluent cities. Rural markets in both countries are highly decentralized, made of many distinct submarkets, each with its own subculture. China's distribution system is so fragmented that logistics costs to wrap, bundle, load, unload, sort, reload, and transport goods amount to 18 percent of the nation's GDP, far higher than in most other countries. (In comparison, U.S. logistics costs account for about 8.5 percent of the nation's GDP.) After years of effort, even Walmart executives admit that they have been unable to assemble an efficient supply chain in China.[11]

Sometimes local conditions can greatly influence how a company distributes products in global markets. For example, in low-income neighborhoods in Brazil where consumers have limited access to supermarkets, Nestlé supplements its distribution with thousands of self-employed salespeople who sell Nestlé products from refrigerated carts door to door. And in crowded cities in Asia and Africa, fast-food restaurants such as McDonald's and KFC offer delivery:[12]

> Whereas Americans who want a quick meal delivered to their homes are likely to order in Chinese, people in China and elsewhere around the world are now ordering in from McDonald's or KFC. In big cities such as Beijing, Cairo, and Tokyo, where crowded streets and high real estate costs make drive-thrus impractical, delivery is becoming an important part of fast-food strategy. >> In these markets, McDonald's and KFC now dispatch legions of motorbike delivery drivers in colorful uniforms to dispense Big Macs and buckets of chicken to customers who call in. In McDonald's Asia/Pacific, Middle East, and Africa division, more than 1,500 of its 8,800 restaurants now offer "McDelivery." "We've used the slogan, 'If you can't come to us, we'll come to you,'" says the division's president. More than 30 percent of McDonald's total sales in Egypt and 12 percent of its Singapore sales come from delivery. Similarly, for KFC, delivery accounts for nearly half of all sales in Kuwait and a third of sales in Egypt.

>> **The McDonald's delivery guy: In cities like Beijing, Seoul, and Cairo, armies of motorbike delivery drivers outfitted in colorful uniforms and bearing food in specially designed boxes strapped to their backs make their way through bustling traffic to deliver Big Macs.**

Li shengli Imaginechina.

Thus, international marketers face a wide range of channel alternatives. Designing efficient and effective channel systems between and within various country markets poses a difficult challenge. We discuss international distribution decisions further in Chapter 15.

Author Comment
Now it's time to implement the chosen channel design and work with selected channel members to manage and motivate them.

Channel Management Decisions

Once the company has reviewed its channel alternatives and determined the best channel design, it must implement and manage the chosen channel. **Marketing channel management** calls for selecting, managing, and motivating individual channel members and evaluating their performance over time.

Marketing channel management
Selecting, managing, and motivating individual channel members and evaluating their performance over time.

Selecting Channel Members

Producers vary in their ability to attract qualified marketing intermediaries. Some producers have no trouble signing up channel members. For example, when Toyota first introduced its Lexus line in the United States, it had no trouble attracting new dealers. In fact, it had to turn down many would-be resellers.

At the other extreme are producers that have to work hard to line up enough qualified intermediaries. For example, when Timex first tried to sell its inexpensive watches through regular jewelry stores, most jewelry stores refused to carry them. The company then managed to get its watches into mass-merchandise outlets. This turned out to be a wise decision because of the rapid growth of mass merchandising.

Even established brands may have difficulty gaining and keeping their desired distribution, especially when dealing with powerful resellers. For example, you won't find P&G's Pampers diapers in a Costco store. After P&G declined to manufacture Costco's Kirkland store brand diapers a few years ago, Costco gave Pampers the boot and now only carries Huggies and its own Kirkland brand (manufactured by Huggies maker Kimberly-Clark). The removal by Costco, the number-two diaper retailer after Walmart, has cost P&G an estimated $150 million to $200 million in annual sales. In a similar dispute, Costco temporarily stopped carrying Coca-Cola products, and it recently swapped out Coke for Pepsi in the beloved hot dog and soft drink combo sold in its food courts. That's a big loss for Coca-Cola: Costco serves up 100 million hot dog combos a year, more than four times the combined hot dog sales of at all Major League Baseball parks last year.[13]

When selecting intermediaries, the company should determine what characteristics distinguish the better ones. It will want to evaluate each channel member's years in business, other lines carried, location, growth and profit record, cooperativeness, and reputation.

Managing and Motivating Channel Members

Once selected, channel members must be continuously managed and motivated to do their best. The company must sell not only *through* the intermediaries but also *to* and *with* them. Most companies see their intermediaries as first-line customers and partners. They practice strong *partner relationship management* to forge long-term partnerships with channel members. This creates a value delivery system that meets the needs of both the company *and* its marketing partners.

In managing its channels, a company must convince suppliers and distributors that they can succeed better by working together as a part of a cohesive value delivery system. Thus, P&G works closely with Target to create superior value for final consumers. The two jointly plan merchandising goals and strategies, inventory levels, and advertising and promotion programs. Similarly, Toyota works to create supplier satisfaction, which in turn helps to create greater customer satisfaction. Whether it's heavy-equipment manufacturer Caterpillar partnering with its network of large dealers or cosmetics maker L'Oréal building mutually beneficial relationships with its network of suppliers, companies must work in close harmony with others in the channel to find better ways to bring value to customers (see Marketing at Work 10.1).

Many companies are now installing integrated high-tech partnership relationship management (PRM) systems to coordinate their whole-channel marketing efforts. Just as they use customer relationship management (CRM) software systems to help manage relationships with important customers, companies can now use PRM and supply chain management (SCM) software to help recruit, train, organize, manage, motivate, and evaluate relationships with channel partners.

MARKETING AT WORK 10.1

Working with Channel Partners to Create Value for Customers

Today's successful companies know that they can't go it alone in creating value for customers. Instead they must create effective value delivery systems, consisting of suppliers, producers, and distributors that work together to get the job done. Partnering with suppliers and distributors can yield big competitive advantages. Consider these examples.

Caterpillar

Heavy-equipment manufacturer Caterpillar produces innovative, high-quality industrial equipment products. But ask anyone at Caterpillar and they'll tell you that the most important reason for Caterpillar's dominance is its outstanding distribution network of 189 independent dealers in more than 180 countries. "Our dealers [have] been the source of our Cat brand advantage more than most people really understand," says Caterpillar CEO Doug Oberhelman.

According to Oberhelman, dealers are the ones on the front line. Once the product leaves the factory, the dealers take over. They're the ones that customers see. So rather than selling to or through its dealers, Caterpillar treats dealers as inside partners. When a big piece of Caterpillar equipment breaks down, customers know that they can count on both Caterpillar and its dealer network for support. On a deeper level, dealers play a vital role in almost every aspect of Caterpillar's operations, from product design and delivery to service and support.

Dealers are a key element in what Caterpillar insiders call the "Caterpillar flywheel"—a kind of virtuous circle of success. Big, healthy dealers help Caterpillar sell the most machines. In turn, all those machines in the field bring dealers lots of parts and service revenues, so much that they can survive even in lean years when they don't sell many new machines. That financial stability helps dealers grow bigger, attracting even more customers who buy machines from Caterpillar.

In sum, a strong dealer network makes for a strong Caterpillar, and the other way around. So it makes sense that Caterpillar really knows its dealers and cares about their success. In fact, high on Cat's 13-point list of priorities is "dealer health." The company closely monitors each dealership's sales, market position, service capabilities, and financial situation. When it sees a problem, it jumps in to help.

In addition to more formal business ties, Caterpillar also forms close personal ties with dealers in a kind of family relationship. This leads to a deep sense of pride among dealers at what they are accomplishing together—a feeling that they are an important part of an organization that makes, sells, and tends to the machines that make the world work.

As a result of its close partnership with dealers, the big Cat is purring. Caterpillar dominates the world's markets for heavy construction, mining, and logging equipment. Its familiar yellow tractors, crawlers, loaders, bulldozers, and trucks capture well over a third of the worldwide heavy-equipment business, more than twice that of number two Komatsu.

Toyota

Achieving satisfying supplier relationships has been a cornerstone of Toyota's stunning success. Historically, Toyota's U.S. competitors often alienated their suppliers through self-serving, heavy-handed dealings. "The [U.S. automakers] set annual cost-reduction targets [for the parts they buy]," said one supplier. "To realize those targets, they'll do anything. [They've unleashed] a reign of terror, and it gets worse every year." Says another, "[One automaker] seems to send its people to 'hate school' so that they learn how to hate suppliers."

By contrast, Toyota has long known the importance of building close relationships with suppliers. In fact, it even includes the phrase "achieve supplier satisfaction" in its mission statement. Rather than bullying suppliers, Toyota partners with them and helps them to meet its very high expectations. It learns about their businesses, conducts joint improvement activities,

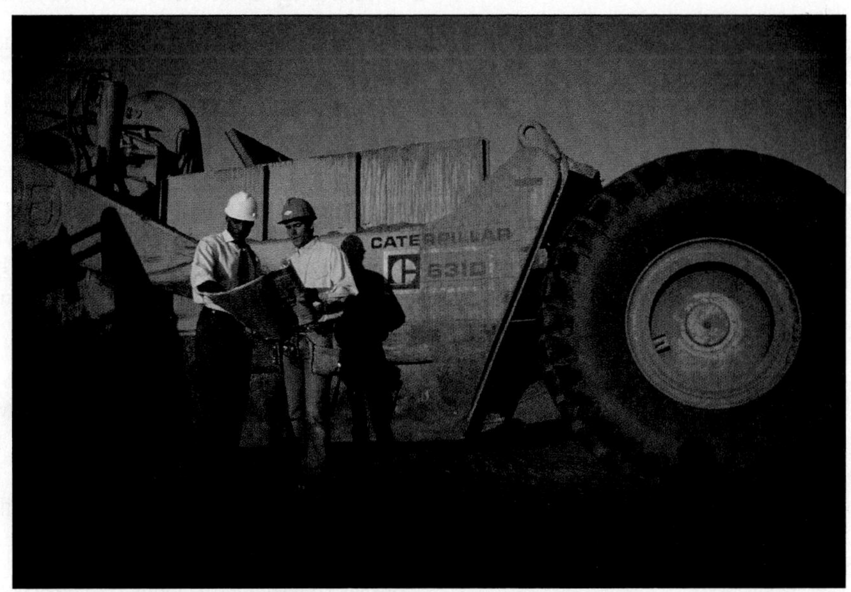

» Caterpillar partners closely with its worldwide network of independent dealers to bring value to customers. When a big piece of Caterpillar equipment breaks down, customers know that they can count on both Caterpillar and its outstanding dealer network for support.

helps train supplier employees, gives daily performance feedback, and actively seeks out supplier concerns. It even recognizes top suppliers with annual performance awards.

In a recent annual survey of auto parts makers—which measured items such as trust, open and honest communication, help given to reduce costs, and opportunities to make a profit—Toyota scored higher than any other automaker. The survey showed that Toyota suppliers consider themselves true partners with the automotive giant.

Such high supplier satisfaction means that Toyota can rely on suppliers to help it improve its own quality, reduce costs, and develop new products quickly. For example, when Toyota recently launched a program to reduce prices by 30 percent on 170 parts that it would buy for its next generation of cars, suppliers didn't complain. Instead, they pitched in, trusting that Toyota would help them achieve the targeted reductions, in turn making them more competitive and profitable in the future. In all, creating satisfied suppliers helps Toyota produce lower-cost, higher-quality cars, which in turn results in more satisfied customers.

L'Oréal

L'Oréal is the world's largest cosmetics maker, with 34 global brands ranging from Maybelline and Kiehl's to Lancôme and The Body Shop. What does a cosmetics maker have in common with down-and-dirty industrial giants like Caterpillar and Toyota? Like both of those companies, L'Oréal's extensive supplier network—which supplies everything from polymers and fats to spray cans and packaging to production equipment and office supplies—is crucial to its success.

As a result, L'Oréal treats suppliers as respected partners. On the one hand, it expects a lot from suppliers in terms of design innovation, quality, and socially responsible actions. The company carefully screens new suppliers and regularly assesses the performance of current suppliers. On the other hand, L'Oréal works closely with suppliers to help them meet its exacting standards. Whereas some companies make unreasonable demands of their suppliers and "squeeze" them for short-term gains, L'Oréal builds long-term supplier relationships based on mutual benefit and growth.

According to the company's supplier Web site, it treats suppliers with "fundamental respect for their business, their culture, their growth, and the individuals who work there." Each relationship is based on "dialogue and joint efforts. L'Oréal seeks not only to help its suppliers meet its expectations but also to contribute to their growth, through opportunities for innovation and competitiveness." As a result, more than 75 percent of L'Oréal's supplier partners have been working with the company for 10 years or more, and the majority of them for several decades. Says the company's head of purchasing, "The CEO wants to make L'Oréal a top performer and one of the world's most respected companies. Being respected also means being respected by our suppliers."

Sources: Geoff Colvin, "Caterpillar Is Absolutely Crushing It," *Fortune*, May 12, 2011, pp. 136–144; Jeffery K. Liker and Thomas Y. Choi, "Building Deep Supplier Relationships," *Harvard Business Review*, 2004, pp. 104–113; "Year in Review: Rock Solid," Caterpillar Annual Report, February 2013, www.caterpillar.com/cda/files/2674611/7/2012_Year_in_Review.pdf, p. 47; Paul Eisensten, "Toyota Tops in Supplier Relations—Just Barely," *The Detroit Bureau*, May 23, 2011, www.thedetroitbureau.com/2011/05/toyota-tops-in-supplier-relations-but-just-barely/; and www.caterpillar.com, www.toyotasupplier.com, www.loreal.com/_en/_ww/brands-l-oreal.aspx, and www.loreal.com/_en/_ww/html/suppliers/, accessed November 2013.

Evaluating Channel Members

The company must regularly check channel member performance against standards such as sales quotas, average inventory levels, customer delivery time, treatment of damaged and lost goods, cooperation in company promotion and training programs, and services to the customer. The company should recognize and reward intermediaries that are performing well and adding good value for consumers. Those that are performing poorly should be assisted or, as a last resort, replaced.

Finally, companies need to be sensitive to the needs of their channel partners. Those that treat their partners poorly risk not only losing their support but also causing some legal problems. The next section describes various rights and duties pertaining to companies and other channel members.

SPEED BUMP | LINKING THE CONCEPTS

Time for another pause. This time, compare the Caterpillar and KFC channel systems.

- Diagram the Caterpillar and KFC channel systems. How do they compare in terms of channel levels, types of intermediaries, channel member roles and responsibilities, and other characteristics? How well is each system designed?
- Assess how well Caterpillar and KFC have managed and supported their channels. With what results?

Public Policy and Distribution Decisions

For the most part, companies are legally free to develop whatever channel arrangements suit them. In fact, the laws affecting channels seek to prevent the exclusionary tactics of some companies that might keep another company from using a desired channel. Most channel law deals with the mutual rights and duties of channel members once they have formed a relationship.

Many producers and wholesalers like to develop exclusive channels for their products. When the seller allows only certain outlets to carry its products, this strategy is called *exclusive distribution*. When the seller requires that these dealers not handle competitors' products, its strategy is called *exclusive dealing*. Both parties can benefit from exclusive arrangements: The seller obtains more loyal and dependable outlets, and the dealers obtain a steady source of supply and stronger seller support. But exclusive arrangements also exclude other producers from selling to these dealers. This situation brings exclusive dealing contracts under the scope of the Clayton Act of 1914. They are legal as long as they do not substantially lessen competition or tend to create a monopoly and as long as both parties enter into the agreement voluntarily.

Exclusive dealing often includes *exclusive territorial agreements*. The producer may agree not to sell to other dealers in a given area, or the buyer may agree to sell only in its own territory. The first practice is normal under franchise systems as a way to increase dealer enthusiasm and commitment. It is also perfectly legal—a seller has no legal obligation to sell through more outlets than it wishes. The second practice, whereby the producer tries to keep a dealer from selling outside its territory, has become a major legal issue.

Producers of a strong brand sometimes sell it to dealers only if the dealers will take some or all of the rest of its line. This is called *full-line forcing*. Such *tying agreements* are not necessarily illegal, but they violate the Clayton Act if they tend to lessen competition substantially. The practice may prevent consumers from freely choosing among competing suppliers of these other brands.

Finally, producers are free to select their dealers, but their right to terminate dealers is somewhat restricted. In general, sellers can drop dealers "for cause." However, they cannot drop dealers if, for example, the dealers refuse to cooperate in a doubtful legal arrangement, such as exclusive dealing or tying agreements.

Author Comment
Marketers used to call this plain-old "physical distribution." But as these titles suggest, the topic has grown in importance, complexity, and sophistication.

Marketing Logistics and Supply Chain Management

In today's global marketplace, selling a product is sometimes easier than getting it to customers. Companies must decide on the best way to store, handle, and move their products and services so that they are available to customers in the right assortments, at the right time, and in the right place. Logistics effectiveness has a major impact on both customer satisfaction and company costs. Here we consider the nature and importance of logistics management in the supply chain, the goals of the logistics system, major logistics functions, and the need for integrated supply chain management.

Nature and Importance of Marketing Logistics

Marketing logistics (or physical distribution)
Planning, implementing, and controlling the physical flow of materials, final goods, and related information from points of origin to points of consumption to meet customer requirements at a profit.

To some managers, marketing logistics means only trucks and warehouses. But modern logistics is much more than this. **Marketing logistics**—also called **physical distribution**—involves planning, implementing, and controlling the physical flow of goods, services, and related information from points of origin to points of consumption to meet customer requirements at a profit. In short, it involves getting the right product to the right customer in the right place at the right time.

In the past, physical distribution planners typically started with products at the plant and then tried to find low-cost solutions to get them to customers. However, today's

>> **Logistics: As this huge stockpile of shipping containers suggests, American companies spent $1.28 trillion last year—8.5 percent of U.S. GDP—to bundle, load, unload, sort, reload, and transport goods.**

E.G. Pors/Shutterstock.com.

customer-centered logistics starts with the marketplace and works backward to the factory or even to sources of supply. Marketing logistics involves not only *outbound logistics* (moving products from the factory to resellers and ultimately to customers) but also *inbound logistics* (moving products and materials from suppliers to the factory) and *reverse logistics* (reusing, recycling, refurbishing, or disposing of broken, unwanted, or excess products returned by consumers or resellers). That is, it involves the entirety of **supply chain management**—managing upstream and downstream value-added flows of materials, final goods, and related information among suppliers, the company, resellers, and final consumers, as shown in >> **Figure 10.5**.

The logistics manager's task is to coordinate the activities of suppliers, purchasing agents, marketers, channel members, and customers. These activities include forecasting, information systems, purchasing, production planning, order processing, inventory, warehousing, and transportation planning.

Companies today are placing greater emphasis on logistics for several reasons. First, companies can gain a powerful competitive advantage by using improved logistics to give customers better service or lower prices. Second, improved logistics can yield tremendous cost savings to both a company and its customers. As much as 20 percent of an average product's price is accounted for by shipping and transport alone. This far exceeds the cost of advertising and many other marketing costs. >> American companies spend $1.28 trillion each year—about 8.5 percent of GDP—to wrap, bundle, load, unload, sort, reload, and transport goods. That's more than the national GDPs of all but 13 countries worldwide.[14]

Shaving off even a small fraction of logistics costs can mean substantial savings. For example, Walmart is currently implementing a program of logistics improvements through more efficient sourcing, better inventory management, and greater supply chain productivity that will reduce supply chain costs by 5 to 15 percent over five years—that's a whopping $4 billion to $12 billion.[15]

Supply chain management
Managing upstream and downstream value-added flows of materials, final goods, and related information among suppliers, the company, resellers, and final consumers.

Third, the explosion in product variety has created a need for improved logistics management. For example, in 1916 the typical Piggly Wiggly grocery store carried only 605 items. Today, a Piggly Wiggly carries a bewildering stock of between 20,000 and 35,000 items, depending on store size. A Walmart Supercenter store carries more than 100,000 products, 30,000 of which are grocery products.[16] Ordering, shipping, stocking, and controlling such a variety of products presents a sizable logistics challenge.

Improvements in information technology have also created opportunities for major gains in distribution efficiency. Today's companies are using sophisticated supply chain management software, Internet-based logistics systems, point-of-sale scanners, RFID

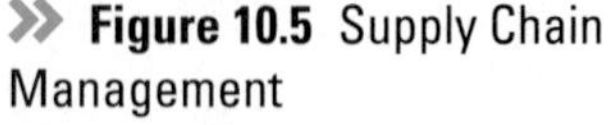

>> **Figure 10.5** Supply Chain Management

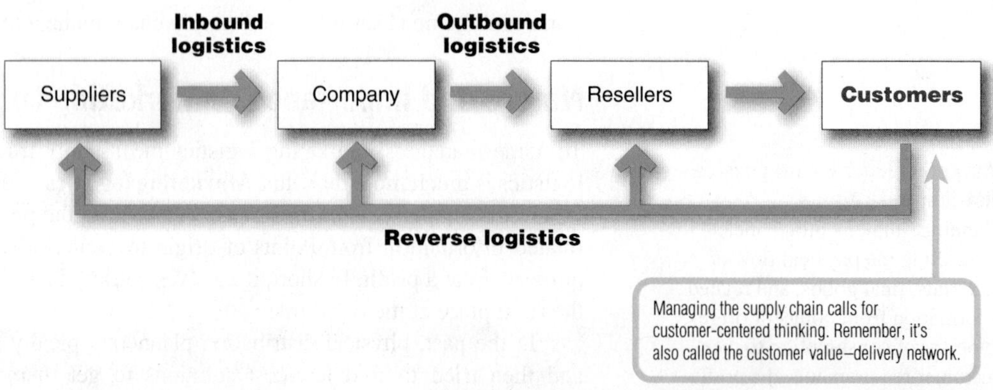
Inbound logistics
Outbound logistics
Suppliers
Company
Resellers
Customers
Reverse logistics
Managing the supply chain calls for customer-centered thinking. Remember, it's also called the customer value–delivery network.

tags, satellite tracking, and electronic transfer of order and payment data. Such technology lets them quickly and efficiently manage the flow of goods, information, and finances through the supply chain. Finally, more than almost any other marketing function, logistics affects the environment and a firm's environmental sustainability efforts. Transportation, warehousing, packaging, and other logistics functions are typically the biggest supply chain contributors to the company's environmental footprint. At the same time, they also provide one of the most fertile areas for cost savings. In other words, developing a *green supply chain* is not only environmentally responsible but can also be profitable (see Marketing at Work 10.2). Here's a simple example:[17]

> Consumer package goods maker SC Johnson made a seemingly simple but smart—and profitable—change in the way it packs its trucks. Under the old system, a load of its Ziploc products filled a truck trailer before reaching the maximum weight limit. In contrast, a load of Windex glass cleaner hit the maximum weight before the trailer was full. By strategically mixing the two products, SC Johnson found it could send the same amount of products with 2,098 fewer shipments, while burning 168,000 fewer gallons of diesel fuel and eliminating 1,882 tons of greenhouse gasses. Thus, smart supply chain thinking not only helped the environment, it also saved the company money. Says the company's director of environmental issues, "Loading a truck may seem simple, but making sure that a truck is truly full is a science. Consistently hitting a trailer's maximum weight provided a huge opportunity to reduce our energy consumption, cut our greenhouse gas emissions, and save money [in the bargain.]" Green supply chains aren't just something companies have to do, they make good business sense. "Sustainability shouldn't be about Washington jamming green stuff down your throat," concludes one supply chain expert. "This is a lot about money, about reducing costs."

Goals of the Logistics System

Some companies state their logistics objective as providing maximum customer service at the least cost. Unfortunately, as nice as this sounds, no logistics system can *both* maximize customer service *and* minimize distribution costs. Maximum customer service implies rapid delivery, large inventories, flexible assortments, liberal returns policies, and other services—all of which raise distribution costs. In contrast, minimum distribution costs imply slower delivery, smaller inventories, and larger shipping lots—which represent a lower level of overall customer service.

The goal of marketing logistics should be to provide a *targeted* level of customer service at the least cost. A company must first research the importance of various distribution services to customers and then set desired service levels for each segment. The objective is to maximize *profits*, not sales. Therefore, the company must weigh the benefits of providing higher levels of service against the costs. Some companies offer less service than their competitors and charge a lower price. Other companies offer more service and charge higher prices to cover higher costs.

Major Logistics Functions

Given a set of logistics objectives, the company designs a logistics system that will minimize the cost of attaining these objectives. The major logistics functions are *warehousing*, *inventory management*, *transportation*, and *logistics information management*.

Warehousing

Production and consumption cycles rarely match, so most companies must store their goods while they wait to be sold. For example, Snapper, Toro, and other lawn mower manufacturers run their factories all year long and store up products for the heavy spring and summer buying seasons. The storage function overcomes differences in needed quantities and timing, ensuring that products are available when customers are ready to buy them.

Distribution center
A large, highly automated warehouse designed to receive goods from various plants and suppliers, take orders, fill them efficiently, and deliver goods to customers as quickly as possible.

A company must decide on *how many* and *what types* of warehouses it needs and *where* they will be located. The company might use either *storage warehouses* or *distribution centers*. Storage warehouses store goods for moderate to long periods. In contrast, **distribution centers** are designed to move goods rather than just store them. They are

MARKETING AT WORK 10.2

Greening the Supply Chain: It's the Right Thing to Do—and It's Profitable Too

You may remember the old song in which Kermit the Frog laments, "it's not easy bein' green." That's often as true for a company's supply chains as it is for the Muppet. Greening up a company's channels often takes substantial commitment, ingenuity, and investment. Although challenging, however, today's supply channels are getting ever greener.

Companies have many reasons for reducing the environmental impact of their supply chains. For one thing, in the not-too-distant future, if companies don't green up voluntarily, a host of "green laws" and sustainability regulations enacted around the world will require them to do so. For another, many large customers—from Nike to Walmart to the federal government—are demanding it. Environmental sustainability has become an important factor in supplier selection and performance evaluation, so suppliers need to think green or put their relationships with prime customers at risk. Perhaps even more important than *having* to do it, designing more environmentally responsible supply chains is simply the *right* thing to do. It's one more way that companies can contribute to saving our world for future generations.

But that's all pretty heady stuff. As it turns out, companies have a more immediate and practical reason for turning their supply chains green. Not only are green channels good for the world, they're also good for a company's bottom line. Companies green their supply chains through greater efficiency, and greater efficiency means lower costs and higher profits. This cost-savings side of environmental responsibility makes good sense. The very logistics activities that create the biggest environmental footprint—such as transportation, warehousing, and packaging—are also the ones that account for a lion's share of logistics costs, especially in an age of scarce resources and soaring energy prices. Although it may require an up-front investment, in the long run, greening up channels usually costs less.

Here are just a few examples of how creating greener supply chains can benefit both the environment and a company's bottom line:

- *Stonyfield Farm.* As the world's largest yogurt maker grew over the years, inefficiencies crept into its distribution system. So Stonyfield worked with Ryder Systems, the large transportation and logistics services firm, to design a new logistics system that cut distribution costs at the same time that it improved customer service levels and dramatically reduced the company's carbon footprint. After evaluating the Stonyfield network, Ryder helped Stonyfield set up a small, dedicated truck fleet, including fuel-efficient hybrid vehicles, to make regional deliveries in New England. It then replaced Stonyfield's national less-than-truckload distribution network with a regional multistop truckload system. As a result, Stonyfield now moves more product in fewer but fuller trucks, cutting in half the number of miles traveled. In all, the changes produced a 40-percent reduction in transportation-related carbon dioxide emissions while knocking an eye-popping 14 percent off Stonyfield's transportation costs. Says Stonyfield's director of logistics, "We're surprised. We understand that environmental responsibility can be profitable. We expected some savings, but not really in this range."
- *Nike.* The iconic sports shoe and apparel company has developed a sweeping strategy for greening every phase of its supply chain. For example, Nike recently teamed with Levi's, REI, Target, and other members of the Sustainable Apparel Coalition to develop the Higg Index—a tool that measures how a single apparel product impacts the environment across the entire supply chain. Based in part on Nike's years-old Materials Sustainability Index, the Higg Index lets Nike work with suppliers and distributors to reduce the supply chain's environmental footprint. For instance, during just the past three years, the more than 900 contract factories that make Nike footwear worldwide have reduced their carbon emissions by 6 percent, despite production increases of 20 percent. That's equivalent to an emissions savings equal to more than 1 billion car-miles.

Nike has found that even seemingly simple supply chain adjustments can produce big benefits. For example, Nike sources its shoes in Asia, but most are sold in North America. Until about a decade ago, the shoes were shipped from factory to store by air freight. After analyzing distribution costs more

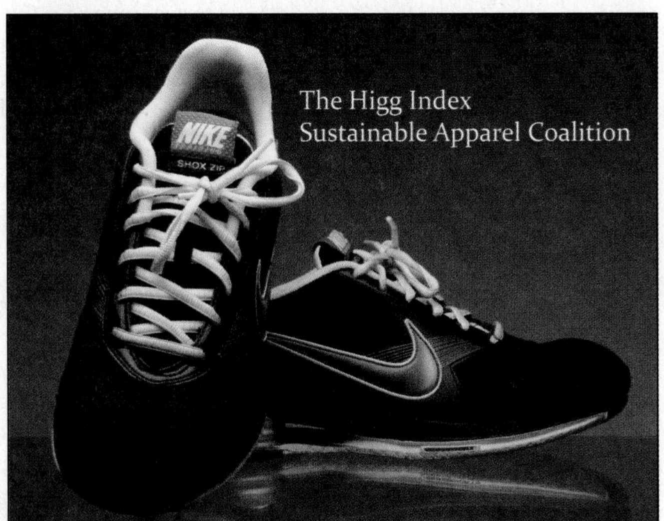

>> Green supply chains: Nike has developed a sweeping strategy for greening its supply chain. The Higg Index lets Nike work with suppliers and distributors to reduce the supply chain's environmental footprint.

carefully, Nike shifted a sizable portion of its cargo to ocean freight. That simple shoes-to-ships shift reduced emissions per product by 4 percent, making environmentalists smile. But it also put a smile on the faces of Nike's accountants by saving the company some $8 million a year in shipping costs.

- *Walmart.* The world's largest retailer is often criticized for its huge carbon footprint. But it turns out that Walmart is perhaps the world's biggest green-channels champion. Among dozens of other major greening initiatives, the giant retailer has worked diligently to reduce the environmental impact of its huge fleet of more than 7,000 trucks. It has installed more efficient tires and hybrid engines, adopted alternative fuels, and developed more effective load-management and routing systems. As a result, during the past five years, Walmart's fleet has delivered 361 million more cases of product in 287 million fewer miles, reducing carbon emissions by 25 percent and cutting a big chunk out of distribution costs.

Walmart also works with its throng of suppliers to help them clean up their environmental acts. For example, it recently set a goal to reduce overall supplier packaging by 5 percent. Given Walmart's size, even small changes make a substantial impact. For instance, a slight change in the design of one supplier's shoeboxes resulted in a 43 percent reduction in the amount of paper required to make them. In only 10 months, that Walmart-led design improvement cut out 692 tons of paper from shoeboxes crossing Walmart's check-out scanners. That equates to saving 2,500 trees, 400,000 pounds of solid waste, 2.4 million gallons of water, and 14.5 billion BTUs. The change also resulted in a 28 percent reduction in supply chain costs.

So when it comes to supply chains, Kermit might be right—it's not easy bein' green. But it's now more necessary than ever, and it can pay big returns. It's a challenging area, says one supply chain expert, "but if you look at it from a pure profit-and-loss perspective, it's also a rich one." Another expert concludes, "It's now easier than ever to build a green supply chain without going into the red, while actually saving cash along the way."

Sources: Based on information from Ryan Boccelli and Mark Swenson, "Improving Transportation and Supply Chain Efficiency while Reducing Your Carbon Footprint," http://investors.ryder.com/files/doc_downloads/stonyfield_ryder_carbon.pdf, accessed May 2013; Jessica Stillman, "Green Cred: Sustainability a Cost-Cutting Move for Suppliers," *Forbes,* December 11, 2012, www.forbes.com/sites/ups/2012/12/11/green-cred-sustainability-a-cost-cutting-move-for-suppliers/; William Hoffman, "Supplying Sustainability," *Traffic World,* April 7, 2008; "Supply Chain Standard: Going Green without Going into the Red," *Logistics Manager,* March 2009, p. 22; Amy Westervelt, "Target, Nike, Levi's Join Forces on Sustainable Clothing," *Forbes,* July 26, 2012, www.forbes.com/sites/amywestervelt/2012/07/26/target-nike-levis-join-forces-on-sustainable-clothing/; and www.nikeresponsibility.com/, www.nikeresponsibility.com/report/content/chapter/manufacturing, and http://corporate.walmart.com/global-responsibility/environment-sustainability, accessed September, 2013.

---

large and highly automated warehouses designed to receive goods from various plants and suppliers, take orders, fill them efficiently, and deliver goods to customers as quickly as possible.

For example, Home Depot operates 18 giant Rapid Deployment Centers (RDCs)—huge, highly mechanized distribution centers that supply almost all of the daily needs of Home Depot's more than 2,200 stores around the country. The RDC in Westfield, Massachusetts, covers 657,000 square feet under a single roof (13 football fields) and serves some 115 Home Depot stores throughout New England. Nothing is stored at the RDCs. Instead, they are "pass-through" centers at which product shipments are received from suppliers, processed, and efficiently redistributed to individual Home Depot stores. The RDCs provide a maximum 72-hour turnaround from the time products reach the center until their delivery to stores, where 80 percent go directly to the sales floor. With such rapid and accurate delivery, individual Home Depot stores can improve merchandise availability to customers while at the same time carrying less in-store stock and reducing inventory costs.[18]

>> High-tech distribution centers: Staples employs a team of super-retrievers—in day-glo orange—to keep its warehouse humming.

Brent Humphreys/Redux Pictures.

Like almost everything else these days, warehousing has seen dramatic changes in technology in recent years. Outdated materials-handling methods are steadily being replaced by newer, computer-controlled systems requiring few employees. Computers and scanners read orders and direct lift trucks, electric hoists, or robots to gather goods, move them to loading docks, and issue invoices. >> For example, office supplies retailer Staples now employs teams of day-glo orange robots in its warehouses around the country. The robots work tirelessly 16 hours a day, seven days a week, carrying racks of pens, paper clips, pads of paper, and other items to packing stations, where humans fill and pack customer orders. The super-efficient robots, which never complain about the workload or ask for pay raises, are pretty much maintenance free. "When they run low on power, they head to battery-charging terminals," notes one observer, "or, as warehouse personnel say, 'They get themselves a drink of water.'" At Staples' huge Chambersburg, Pennsylvania, distribution center, some 150 robots have helped improve average daily output by 60 percent.[19]

Inventory Management

Inventory management also affects customer satisfaction. Here, managers must maintain the delicate balance between carrying too little inventory and carrying too much. With too little stock, the firm risks not having products when customers want to buy. To remedy this, the firm may need costly emergency shipments or production. Carrying too much inventory results in higher-than-necessary inventory-carrying costs and stock obsolescence. Thus, in managing inventory, firms must balance the costs of carrying larger inventories against resulting sales and profits.

Many companies have greatly reduced their inventories and related costs through *just-in-time* logistics systems. With such systems, producers and retailers carry only small inventories of parts or merchandise, often enough for only a few days of operations. New stock arrives exactly when needed, rather than being stored in inventory until being used. Just-in-time systems require accurate forecasting along with fast, frequent, and flexible delivery so that new supplies will be available when needed. However, these systems result in substantial savings in inventory-carrying and inventory-handling costs.

Marketers are always looking for new ways to make inventory management more efficient. In the not-too-distant future, handling inventory might even become fully automated. For example, in Chapter 3 we discussed RFID or "smart tag" technology, by which small transmitter chips are embedded in or placed on products and packaging for everything from flowers and razors to tires. "Smart" products could make the entire supply chain—which accounts for nearly 75 percent of a product's cost—intelligent and automated.

Companies using RFID know, at any time, exactly where a product is located physically within the supply chain. "Smart shelves" would not only tell them when it's time to reorder but also place the order automatically with their suppliers. Such exciting new information technology is revolutionizing distribution as we know it. Many large and resourceful marketing companies, such as Walmart, P&G, Kraft, and IBM, are investing heavily to make the full use of RFID technology a reality.[20]

Transportation

The choice of transportation carriers affects the pricing of products, delivery performance, and the condition of goods when they arrive—all of which will affect customer satisfaction. In shipping goods to its warehouses, dealers, and customers, the company can choose among five main transportation modes: truck, rail, water, pipeline, and air, along with an alternative mode for digital products—the Internet.

Trucks have increased their share of transportation steadily and now account for 40 percent of total cargo ton-miles moved in the United States. U.S. trucks travel more than 397 billion miles a year—more than double the distance traveled 25 years ago—carrying 9.2 billion tons of freight. According to the American Trucking Association, 80 percent of U.S. communities depend solely on trucks for their goods and commodities. Trucks are highly flexible in their routing and time schedules, and they can usually offer faster service than railroads. They are efficient for short hauls of high-value merchandise. Trucking firms have evolved in recent years to become full-service providers of global transportation services. For example, large trucking firms now offer everything from satellite tracking, Internet-based shipment management, and logistics planning software to cross-border shipping operations.[21]

Railroads account for another 40 percent of the total cargo ton-miles moved. They are one of the most cost-effective modes for shipping large amounts of bulk products—coal, sand, minerals, and farm and forest products—over long distances. In recent years, railroads have increased their customer services by designing new equipment to handle special categories of goods, providing flatcars for carrying truck trailers by rail (piggyback), and providing in-transit services such as the diversion of shipped goods to other destinations en route and the processing of goods en route.

Water carriers, which account for less than 5 percent of the cargo ton-miles, transport large amounts of goods by ships and barges on U.S. coastal and inland waterways. Although the cost of water transportation is very low for shipping bulky, low-value, nonperishable products such as sand, coal, grain, oil, and metallic ores, water transportation is the slowest mode and may be affected by the weather. *Pipelines*, which account for less than 1 percent of the cargo ton-miles, are a specialized means of shipping petroleum, natural gas, and chemicals from sources to markets. Most pipelines are used by their owners to ship their own products.

Although *air* carriers transport less than 1 percent of the cargo ton-miles of the nation's goods, they are an important transportation mode. Airfreight rates are much higher than rail or truck rates, but airfreight is ideal when speed is needed or distant markets have to be reached. Among the most frequently airfreighted products are perishables (such as fresh fish, cut flowers) and high-value, low-bulk items (technical instruments, jewelry). Companies find that airfreight also reduces inventory levels, packaging costs, and the number of warehouses needed.

Multimodal transportation
Combining two or more modes of transportation.

The *Internet* carries digital products from producer to customer via satellite, cable, phone wire, or wireless signal. Software firms, the media, music and video companies, and education all make use of the Internet to transport digital products. The Internet holds the potential for lower product distribution costs. Whereas planes, trucks, and trains move freight and packages, digital technology moves information bits.

Shippers also use **multimodal transportation**—combining two or more modes of transportation. Twelve percent of the total cargo ton-miles are moved via multiple modes. *Piggyback* describes the use of rail and trucks; *fishyback*, water and trucks; *trainship*, water and rail; and *airtruck*, air and trucks. Combining modes provides advantages that no single mode can deliver. Each combination offers advantages to the shipper. For example, not only is piggyback cheaper than trucking alone, but it also provides flexibility and convenience.

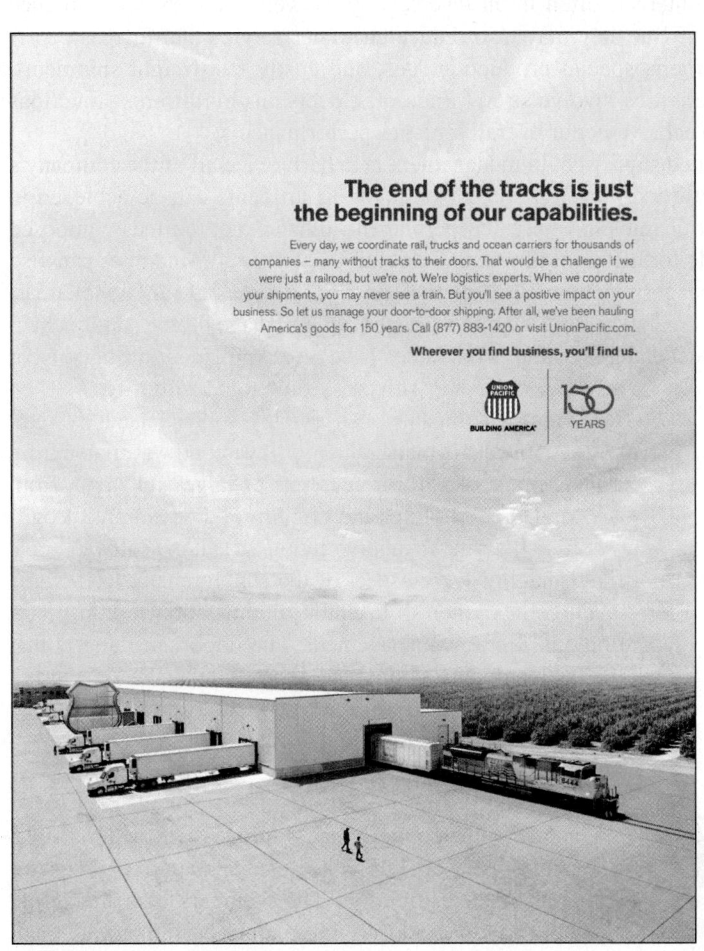

The end of the tracks is just
the beginning of our capabilities.
Every day, we coordinate rail, trucks and ocean carriers for thousands of companies – many without tracks to their doors. That would be a challenge if we were just a railroad, but we're not. We're logistics experts. When we coordinate your shipments, you may never see a train. But you'll see a positive impact on your business. So let us manage your door-to-door shipping. After all, we've been hauling America's goods for 150 years. Call (877) 883-1420 or visit UnionPacific.com.
Wherever you find business, you'll find us.
UNION PACIFIC
BUILDING AMERICA
150
YEARS

Multimodal transportation: Although it's primarily a rail carrier, Union Pacific coordinates rail, trucks, and ocean carriers for its customers to give the "door-to-door shipping" logistics services. At Union Pacific, "The end of the tracks is just the beginning of our capabilities."

Courtesy of Union Pacific. Photographer: Tom Nagy.

Most logistics carriers now recognize the importance of multimodal transportation, regardless of their main line of activity. For example, Union Pacific, primarily a rail carrier, offers "door-to-door shipping" coordination for its business customers. According to one Union Pacific ad: "The end of the tracks is just the beginning of our capabilities. Every day, we coordinate rail, trucks, and ocean carriers for thousands of companies—many without tracks to their doors. That would be a challenge if we were just a railroad, but we're not. We're logistics experts."

Logistics Information Management

Companies manage their supply chains through information. Channel partners often link up to share information and make better joint logistics decisions. From a logistics perspective, flows of information, such as customer transactions, billing, shipment and inventory levels, and even customer data, are closely linked to channel performance. Companies need simple, accessible, fast, and accurate processes for capturing, processing, and sharing channel information. Information can be shared and managed in many ways, but most sharing takes place through *electronic data interchange (EDI)*, the digital exchange of data between organizations, which primarily is transmitted via the Internet. Walmart, for example, requires EDI links with its more than 100,000 suppliers through its Retail Link sales data system. If new suppliers don't have EDI capability, Walmart will work with them to find and implement the needed tools.[22]

In some cases, suppliers might actually be asked to generate orders and arrange deliveries for their customers. Many large retailers—such as Walmart and Home Depot—work closely with major suppliers such as P&G or Moen to set up *vendor-managed inventory (VMI)* systems or *continuous inventory replenishment* systems. Using VMI, the customer shares real-time data on sales and current inventory levels with the supplier. The supplier then takes full responsibility for managing inventories and deliveries. Some retailers even go so far as to shift inventory and delivery costs to the supplier. Such systems require close cooperation between the buyer and seller.

Integrated Logistics Management

Integrated logistics management
The logistics concept that emphasizes teamwork—both inside the company and among all the marketing channel organizations—to maximize the performance of the entire distribution system.

Today, more and more companies are adopting the concept of **integrated logistics management**. This concept recognizes that providing better customer service and trimming distribution costs require *teamwork*, both inside the company and among all the marketing channel organizations. Inside, the company's various departments must work closely together to maximize its own logistics performance. Outside, the company must integrate its logistics system with those of its suppliers and customers to maximize the performance of the entire distribution network.

Cross-Functional Teamwork inside the Company

Most companies assign responsibility for various logistics activities to many different departments—marketing, sales, finance, operations, and purchasing. Too often, each function tries to optimize its own logistics performance without regard for the activities of the other functions. However, transportation, inventory, warehousing, and information management activities interact, often in an inverse way. Lower inventory levels reduce inventory-carrying costs. But they may also reduce customer service and increase costs from stockouts, backorders, special production runs, and costly fast-freight shipments. Because distribution activities involve strong trade-offs, decisions by different functions must be coordinated to achieve better overall logistics performance.

The goal of integrated supply chain management is to harmonize all of the company's logistics decisions. Close working relationships among departments can be achieved in several ways. Some companies have created permanent logistics committees composed of managers responsible for different physical distribution activities. Companies can also create supply chain manager positions that link the logistics activities of functional areas. For example, P&G has created product supply managers who manage all the supply chain activities for each product category. Many companies have a vice president of logistics or a supply chain VP with cross-functional authority.

Finally, companies can employ sophisticated, system-wide supply chain management software, now available from a wide range of software enterprises large and small, from SAP and Oracle to Infor and Logility. >> For example, Logility offers Logility Voyager Solutions, a suite of software tools for managing every aspect of the supply chain, from value chain collaboration to inventory optimization to transportation and logistics management. The important thing is that the company must coordinate its logistics, inventory investments, demand forecasting, and marketing activities to create high market satisfaction at a reasonable cost.

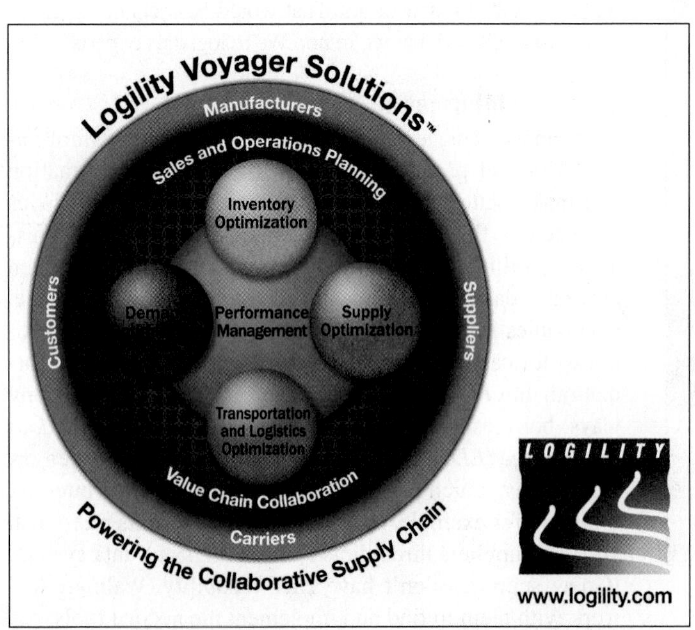

>> **Integrated logistics management: Logility's Voyager Solutions software offers tools for managing every aspect of the supply chain, from value chain collaboration to inventory optimization to transportation and logistics management.**

Logility, Inc.

Building Logistics Partnerships

Companies must do more than improve their own logistics. They must also work with other channel partners to improve whole-channel distribution. The members of a marketing channel are linked closely in creating customer value and building customer relationships. One company's distribution system is another company's supply system. The success of each channel member depends on the performance of the entire supply chain. For example, IKEA can create its stylish but affordable furniture and deliver the "IKEA lifestyle" only if its entire supply chain—consisting of thousands of merchandise designers and suppliers, transport companies, warehouses, and service providers—operates at maximum efficiency and with customer-focused effectiveness.

Smart companies coordinate their logistics strategies and forge strong partnerships with suppliers and customers to improve customer service and reduce channel costs. Many companies have created *cross-functional, cross-company teams*. For example, Nestlé's Purina pet food unit has a team of dozens of people working in Bentonville, Arkansas, the home base of Walmart. The Purina Walmart team members work jointly with their counterparts at Walmart to find ways to squeeze costs out of their distribution system. Working together benefits not only Purina and Walmart but also their shared, final consumers.

Other companies partner through *shared projects*. For example, many large retailers conduct joint in-store programs with suppliers. Home Depot allows key suppliers to use its stores as a testing ground for new merchandising programs. The suppliers spend time at Home Depot stores watching how their product sells and how customers relate to it. They then create programs specially tailored to Home Depot and its customers. Clearly, both the supplier and the customer benefit from such partnerships. The point is that all supply chain members must work together in the cause of bringing value to final consumers.

Third-Party Logistics

Although most big companies love to make and sell their products, many loathe the associated logistics "grunt work." They detest the bundling, loading, unloading, sorting, storing, reloading, transporting, customs clearing, and tracking required to supply their factories and get products to their customers. They hate it so much that a growing number of firms now outsource some or all of their logistics to **third-party logistics (3PL) providers** such as Ryder, Penske Logistics, BAX Global, DHL Logistics, FedEx Logistics, and UPS Business Solutions.

Third-party logistics (3PL) provider
An independent logistics provider that performs any or all of the functions required to get a client's product to market.

For example, UPS knows that, for many companies, logistics can be a real nightmare. But logistics is exactly what UPS does best. To UPS, logistics is today's most powerful force for creating competitive advantage. "We ♥ logistics," proclaims UPS. "It makes running your business easier. It can make your customers happier. It's a whole new way of thinking." As one UPS ad concludes: "We love logistics. Put UPS to work for you and you'll love logistics too."

At one level, UPS can simply handle a company's package shipments. But on a deeper level, UPS can help businesses sharpen their own logistics systems to cut costs and serve customers better. At a still deeper level, companies can let UPS take over and manage part or all of their logistics operations. For example, consumer electronics maker Toshiba lets UPS handle its entire laptop PC repair process—lock, stock, and barrel:[23]

> UPS's logistics prowess was the answer to one of Toshiba's biggest challenges—turnaround time on laptop repairs. Toshiba once used UPS only to ship its finished PCs from the factory to customers. But when the two companies worked together to examine the entire supply chain, including parts management and the PC repair process, they forged a much broader logistics relationship. Now, customers ship laptops needing repair to a special UPS facility near the Worldport air hub in Louisville. There, UPS employees receive the units, run diagnostics to assess the repairs needed, pick the necessary parts, quickly complete the service, and return the laptops to their owners. UPS can now fix and ship a laptop in a single day, shortening a door-to-door repair process that once took two to three weeks down to four or fewer days. Together, UPS and Toshiba greatly improved the customer repair experience while at the same time reducing Toshiba's costs. More than just delivering packages for Toshiba, UPS has become a strategic logistics partner. Says Toshiba America's CEO, "They really understand the overall experience we're trying to create for the customers."

3PL providers like UPS can help clients tighten up sluggish, overstuffed supply chains; slash inventories; and get products to customers more quickly and reliably. According to a survey of chief logistics executives at *Fortune 500* companies, 82 percent of these companies use 3PL (also called *outsourced logistics* or *contract logistics*) services. In all, North American shippers spend 47 percent of their logistics budget on outsourced logistics.[24]

Companies use third-party logistics providers for several reasons. First, because getting the product to market is their main focus, using these providers makes the most sense, as they can often do it more efficiently and at lower cost. Outsourcing typically results in a 15 to 30 percent cost savings. Second, outsourcing logistics frees a company to focus more intensely on its core business. Finally, integrated logistics companies understand increasingly complex logistics environments.

MyMarketingLab

Go to **mymktlab.com** to complete the problems marked with this icon .

END OF CHAPTER REVIEWING THE CONCEPTS

CHAPTER REVIEW AND KEY TERMS

Objectives Review

Some companies pay too little attention to their distribution channels; others, however, have used imaginative distribution systems to gain a competitive advantage. A company's channel decisions directly affect every other marketing decision. Management must make channel decisions carefully, incorporating today's needs with tomorrow's likely selling environment.

OBJECTIVE 1 Explain why companies use marketing channels and discuss the functions these channels perform. (pp 304–308)

In creating customer value, a company can't go it alone. It must work within an entire network of partners—a value delivery network—to accomplish this task. Individual companies and brands don't compete, their entire value delivery networks do.

Most producers use intermediaries to bring their products to market. They forge a *marketing channel* (or *distribution channel*)—a set of interdependent organizations involved in the process of making a product or service available for use or consumption by the consumer or business user. Through their contacts, experience, specialization, and scale of operation, intermediaries usually offer the firm more than it can achieve on its own.

Marketing channels perform many key functions. Some help *complete transactions* by gathering and distributing *information* needed for planning and aiding exchange, developing and spreading persuasive *communications* about an offer, performing *contact* work (finding and communicating with prospective buyers), *matching* (shaping and fitting the offer to the buyer's needs), and entering into *negotiation* to reach an agreement on price and other terms of the offer so that ownership can be transferred. Other functions help to *fulfill* the completed transactions by offering *physical distribution* (transporting and storing goods), *financing* (acquiring and using funds to cover the costs of the channel work), and *risk taking* (assuming the risks of carrying out the channel work.

OBJECTIVE 2 Discuss how channel members interact and how they organize to perform the work of the channel. (pp 308–314)

The channel will be most effective when each member assumes the tasks it can do best. Ideally, because the success of individual channel members depends on overall channel success, all channel firms should work together smoothly. They should understand and accept their roles, coordinate their goals and activities, and cooperate to attain overall channel goals. By cooperating, they can more effectively sense, serve, and satisfy the target market.

In a large company, the formal organization structure assigns roles and provides needed leadership. But in a distribution channel composed of independent firms, leadership and power are not formally set. Traditionally, distribution channels have lacked the leadership needed to assign roles and manage conflict. In recent years, however, new types of channel organizations have appeared that provide stronger leadership and improved performance.

OBJECTIVE 3 Identify the major channel alternatives open to a company. (pp 314–318)

Channel alternatives vary from direct selling to using one, two, three, or more intermediary *channel levels*. Marketing channels face continuous and sometimes dramatic change. Three of the most important trends are the growth of *vertical*, *horizontal*, and *multichannel marketing systems*. These trends affect channel cooperation, conflict, and competition.

Channel design begins with assessing customer channel service needs and company channel objectives and constraints. The company then identifies the major channel alternatives in terms of the *types* of intermediaries, the *number* of intermediaries, and the *channel responsibilities* of each. Each channel alternative must be evaluated according to economic, control, and adaptive criteria. *Channel management* calls for selecting qualified intermediaries and motivating them. Individual channel members must be evaluated regularly.

OBJECTIVE 4 Explain how companies select, motivate, and evaluate channel members. (pp 318–321)

Producers vary in their ability to attract qualified marketing intermediaries. Some producers have no trouble signing up channel members, whereas others have to work hard to line up enough qualified intermediaries. When selecting intermediaries, the company should evaluate each channel member's qualifications and select those that best fit its channel objectives.

Once selected, channel members must be continuously motivated to do their best. The company must sell not only *through* the intermediaries but also *with* them. It should forge strong partnerships with channel members to create a marketing system that meets the needs of both the manufacturer *and* the partners.

 **OBJECTIVE 5 Discuss the nature and importance of marketing logistics and integrated supply chain management. (pp 321–329)**

Marketing logistics (or *physical distribution*) is an area of potentially high cost savings and improved customer satisfaction. Marketing logistics addresses not only *outbound logistics* but also *inbound logistics* and *reverse logistics*. That is, it involves the entire *supply chain management*—managing value-added flows between suppliers, the company, resellers, and final users. No logistics system can both maximize customer service and minimize distribution costs. Instead, the goal of logistics management is to provide a *targeted* level of service at the least cost. The major logistics functions are *warehousing*, *inventory management*, *transportation*, and *logistics information management*.

The *integrated supply chain management concept* recognizes that improved logistics requires teamwork in the form of close working relationships across functional areas inside the company and across various organizations in the supply chain. Companies can achieve logistics harmony among functions by creating cross-functional logistics teams, integrative supply manager positions, and senior-level logistics executive positions with cross-functional authority. Channel partnerships can take the form of cross-company teams, shared projects, and information-sharing systems. Today, some companies are outsourcing their logistics functions to third-party logistics (3PL) providers to save costs, increase efficiency, and gain faster and more effective access to global markets.

Key Terms

Objective 1
Value delivery network (p 305)
Marketing channel (or distribution channel) (p 305)
Channel level (p 307)
Direct marketing channel (p 307)
Indirect marketing channel (p 308)

Objective 2
Channel conflict (p 308)
Conventional distribution channel (p 309)
Vertical marketing system (VMS) (p 309)
Corporate VMS (p 309)
Contractual VMS (p 310)
Franchise organization (p 310)
Administered VMS (p 311)
Horizontal marketing system (p 311)
Multichannel distribution system (p 312)
Disintermediation (p 313)

Objective 3
Marketing channel design (p 314)
Intensive distribution (p 316)
Exclusive distribution (p 316)
Selective distribution (p 316)

Objective 4
Marketing channel management (p 318)

Objective 5
Marketing logistics (physical distribution) (p 321)
Supply chain management (p 322)
Distribution center (p 323)
Multimodal transportation (p 327)
Integrated logistics management (p 328)
Third-party logistics (3PL) provider (p 329)

DISCUSSION AND CRITICAL THINKING

Discussion Questions

10-1. Describe how marketing channel members add value in the channel of distribution between manufacturers and consumers. (AACSB: Written and Oral Communication)

10-2. Compare direct marketing channels and indirect marketing channels. Name the various types of resellers in marketing channels. (AACSB: Written and Oral Communication)

10-3. Explain how a vertical marketing system differs from a conventional marketing system. (AACSB: Written and Oral Communication)

10-4. What types of exclusive arrangements do manufacturers develop with resellers? Are these arrangements legal? (AACSB: Written and Oral Communication; Reflective Thinking)

10-5. List and briefly describe the major logistics functions. Provide an example of a decision a logistics manager would make for each major function. (AACSB: Written and Oral Communication; Reflective Thinking)

10-6. What are third-party logistics providers, and why do companies use them? (AACSB: Written and Oral Communication)

Critical Thinking Exercises

10-7. The most common type of contractual vertical marketing system is the franchise organization. Visit the International Franchise Association at www.franchise.org and find a franchise that interests you. Write a report describing the franchise. Identify what type of franchise it represents and research the market opportunities for that product or service. (AACSB: Written and Oral Communication; Information Technology; Reflective Thinking)

10-8. Form a small group and research the distribution challenges faced by companies expanding into emerging international markets such as China, Africa, and India. Develop a multimedia presentation on how one company overcame these challenges. (AACSB: Written and Oral Communication; Reflective Thinking; Information Technology)

10-9. Distribution channel concerns for pharmaceutical drugs—especially the problem of counterfeit drugs—can be a matter of life and death. The Prescription Drug Marketing Act of 1987 requires a record of the chain of custody ("pedigree") from manufacturer through resellers to point of dispensing, and some states are requiring an electronic pedigree using serialization and track-and-trace systems. Write a report on this act and the current status of track-and-trace systems in the pharmaceutical drug distribution channel as well as other initiatives to fight counterfeit drugs. (AACSB: Written and Oral Communication; Reflective Thinking)

MINICASES AND APPLICATIONS

Online, Mobile, and Social Media Marketing Slow-Motion Video

Movie and television program distribution technology is changing fast. Consumers can now watch movies and TV shows on demand on TVs, computers, tablets, and smartphones. This has caused a surge in demand for online video-streaming services such as Netflix and Hulu. However, it's causing problems for subscription-TV services such as Comcast Cable, which offer scheduled programming and face increased competition from the video-streaming services. Interestingly, however, as one of the country's largest Internet service providers, Comcast is also the distribution channel for competitors such as Netflix and Hulu. The fact that Comcast has control over its competitors' distribution channel causes uncomfortable conflicts. It has invested billions building its scheduled programming network, and it doesn't want to become a mere conduit as its subscribers drop cable in favor of streamed programming from one of the competing services. And because it controls the Internet channel, it can cause problems for those competitors. For example, the U.S. Justice Department is investigating whether cable companies such as Comcast are attempting to squash competition from video-streaming providers such as Netflix by limiting the amount of data their Internet service subscribers can download. Comcast has also countered with its own online video-streaming app called Xfinity, by which subscribers can stream programming using game consoles, tablets, and smartphones. Video content streamed through Xfinity is not counted against Comcast's data limits the way that videos streamed through other services such as Netflix are.

10-10. What types of channel conflict are present in this channel of distribution? Explain. (AACSB: Written and Oral Communication; Reflective Thinking)

Marketing Ethics Supplier Safety

Fast-fashion retailers such as Zara, H&M, and others demand short lead times and quick changes from suppliers to feed consumers' demand for changing fashions. Retailers used to place orders almost a year in advance and suppliers produced high volumes cheaply. But fast-fashion retailers now offer new inventory in their stores almost weekly to get customers coming back. Additionally, many retailers are placing small initial orders, and if styles take off with consumers, they quickly re-order—a tactic known as "chasing." Appropriate inventory levels in the apparel industry have always been difficult to predict, but it appears that retailers are pushing this worry back onto suppliers. Bangladesh is the second-largest apparel producer for North American and European brands and retailers. However, recent fires and building collapses due to lax safety concerns are killing thousands of workers and even some of the factory executives. Unlike in more developed countries, the industry is loosely regulated in Bangladesh. That, coupled with the demands to feed the fast-fashion industry, is alleged to be the cause of these tragedies. As a result, U.S. and European brands and retailers are coming under greater scrutiny concerning supplier issues. IndustriALL, a Geneva-based international union, organized a proposal to enhance supplier safety in Bangladesh that many, but not all, Western retailers/brands accepted.

10-11. Write a brief report on the Bangladesh Accord on Fire and Building Safety proposed by IndustriALL. Which retailers signed the agreement, and why have some U.S. retailers refused to sign the pact? (AACSB: Written and Oral Communication; Reflective Thinking)

Marketing by the Numbers Reseller Margins

One external factor manufacturers must consider when setting prices is reseller margins. Manufacturers do not have the final say concerning the price to consumers—retailers do. So, manufacturers must start with their suggested retail prices and work back, subtracting out the markups required by resellers that sell the product to consumers. Once that is considered, manufacturers know at what price to sell their products to resellers, and they can determine what volume they must sell to break even at that price and cost combination. To answer the following questions, refer to Appendix 2, Marketing by the Numbers.

10-12. A consumer purchases a flat iron to straighten her hair for $150 from a salon at which she gets her hair cut. If the salon's markup is 40 percent and the wholesaler's markup is 15 percent, both based on their selling prices, for what price does the manufacturer sell the product to the wholesaler? (AACSB: Written and Oral Communication; Analytical Thinking)

10-13. If the unit variable costs for each flat iron are $40 and the manufacturer has fixed costs totaling $200,000, how many flat irons must this manufacturer sell to break even? How many must it sell to realize a profit of $800,000? (AACSB: Written and Oral Communication; Analytical Thinking)

Video Case Gaviña Gourmet Coffee

These days, there seems to be plenty of coffee to go around. So how does a small time coffee roaster like Gaviña make it in an industry dominated by big players? By carefully crafting a distribution strategy that moves its products into the hands of consumers.

Without a big advertising budget, Gaviña has creatively pursued channel partners in the grocery, restaurant, and hospitality industries. Now, major chains like McDonald's and Publix make Gaviña's coffees available to the public. This video also illustrates the impact of distribution strategy on supply chain and product development issues.

After viewing the video featuring Gaviña, answer the following questions:

10-14. Apply the concept of the supply chain to Gaviña.

10-15. Sketch out as many consumer and business channels for Gaviña as you can. How does each of these channels meet distinct customer needs?

10-16. How has Gaviña's distribution strategy affected its product mix?

Company Cases 10 Corning / 15 IKEA / 16 Warby Parker

See Appendix 1 for cases appropriate for this chapter. **Case 10: Corning: Feeding Innovation through the Supply Chain.** As an innovator in glass products, Corning relies on relationships with suppliers and customers to develop new technologies. **Case 15, IKEA: Making Life Better for the World's Many People.** IKEA manages to sell the same couch in 41 different countries by creating the perfect balance between standardization and adaptation. **Case 16, Warby Parker: Eyewear with a Purpose.** Warby Parker makes high-quality, fashionable eyeglasses at a revolutionary price point—and distributes a free pair of glasses to a person in need for every pair purchased.

MyMarketingLab

Go to **mymktlab.com** for Auto-graded writing questions as well as the following Assisted-graded writing questions:

10-17. Experts are predicting that cable and satellite television will become obsolete because of the Internet. Discuss what this trend reflects with respect to the channel of distribution. (AACSB: Written and Oral Communication; Reflective Thinking)

10-18. Should retailers be responsible for safety conditions in garment factories in other countries? Discuss. (AACSB: Written and Oral Communication; Reflective Thinking; Ethical Understanding and Reasoning)

10-19. Mymktlab Only—comprehensive writing assignment for this chapter.

11 Retailing and Wholesaling

CHAPTER ROAD MAP

Objective Outline

OBJECTIVE 1 Explain the role of retailers in the distribution channel and describe the major types of retailers. Retailing 336–343

OBJECTIVE 2 Describe the major retailer marketing decisions. Retailer Marketing Decisions 343–349

OBJECTIVE 3 Discuss the major trends and developments in retailing. Retailing Trends and Developments 349–356

OBJECTIVE 4 Explain the major types of wholesalers and their marketing decisions. Wholesaling 356–361

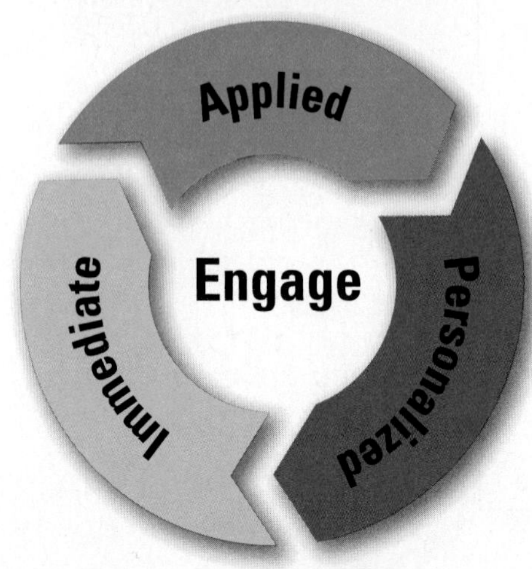

Previewing the Concepts

We now look more deeply into the two major intermediary marketing channel functions: retailing and wholesaling. You already know something about retailing—retailers of all shapes and sizes serve you every day. However, you probably know much less about the hoard of wholesalers working behind the scenes. In this chapter, we examine the characteristics of different kinds of retailers and wholesalers, the marketing decisions they make, and trends for the future.

When it comes to retailers, you have to start with Walmart. This megaretailer's phenomenal success has resulted from an unrelenting focus on bringing value to its customers. Day in and day out, Walmart lives up to its promise: "Save money. Live better." That focus on customer value has made Walmart the world's largest retailer, with sales almost double those of its next six competitors combined. Yet, despite its huge success, Walmart still faces plenty of fresh opportunities and daunting challenges.

*Over 10 million students improved their results using the Pearson MyLabs. Visit **mymktlab.com** for simulations, tutorials, and end-of-chapter problems.

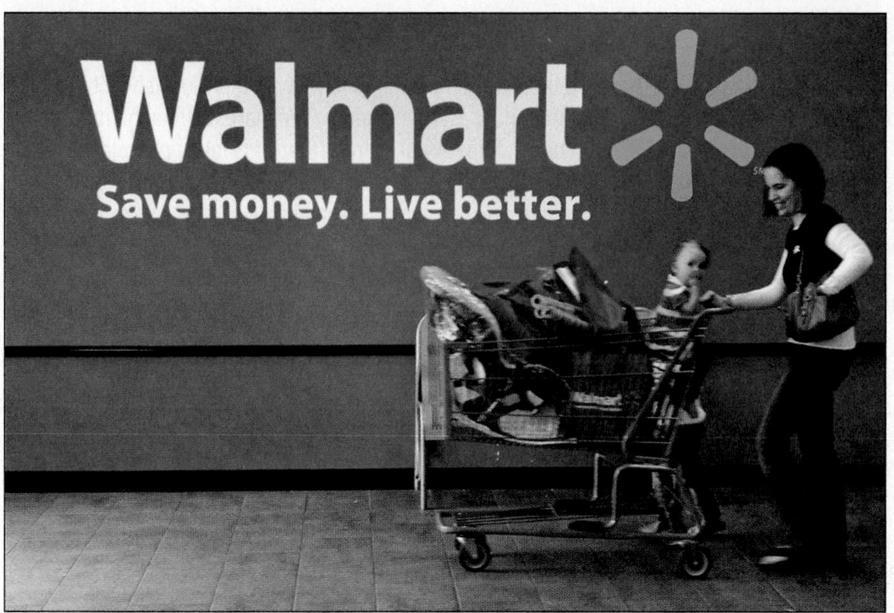
Walmart
Save money. Live better.

>> At Walmart: "Save money. Live better." Says Walmart's CEO, "We're obsessed with delivering value to customers."

Bloomberg via Getty Images.

First Stop

Walmart: The World's Largest *Retailer*—the World's Second-Largest *Company*

Walmart is almost unimaginably big. It's the world's largest retailer—the world's second-largest company. It rang up an incredible $469 billion in sales last year—more than 1.8 times the sales of competitors Costco, Target, Sears/Kmart, Macy's, JCPenney, and Kohl's combined.

Walmart is the number-one seller in many categories of consumer products, including groceries, clothing, toys, DVDs, and pet care products. It sells nearly 2.5 times as many groceries as Kroger, the leading grocery-only food retailer, and its clothing and shoe sales alone exceed the total revenues of Macy's Inc., parent of both Macy's and Bloomingdale's department stores. Incredibly, Walmart sells an estimated 30 percent of the disposable diapers purchased in the United States each year, 30 percent of the hair care products, 30 percent of all health and beauty products, 26 percent of the toothpaste, and 20 percent of the pet food. On average, worldwide, Walmart serves more than 200 million customers per week through more than 10,000 stores in 27 countries and on Web sites in 10 countries.

It's also hard to fathom Walmart's impact on the U.S. economy. It's the nation's largest employer—one out of every 225 men, women, and children in the United States is a Walmart associate. Its average *daily* sales of $1.32 billion exceed the *annual* GDPs of 22 countries. By one estimate, through its own low prices and impact on competitors' prices, Walmart saves the average American household $2,500 each year, equivalent to more than six months' worth of groceries for the average family.

Day in and day out, giant Walmart lives up to its promise: "Save money. Live better." Its obsession with customer value has made Walmart not only the world's largest retailer but also the world's second-largest company.

What's behind this spectacular success? First and foremost, Walmart is passionately dedicated to its long-time, low-price value proposition and what its low prices mean to customers: "Save money. Live better." To accomplish this mission, Walmart offers a broad selection of goods at "unbeatable low prices," day in and day out. No other retailer has come nearly so close to mastering the concepts of everyday low prices and one-stop shopping. Sam Walton himself summed up Walmart's mission best when he said, "If we work together, we'll lower the cost of living for everyone . . . we'll give the world an opportunity to see what it's like to save and have a better life."

How does Walmart make money with such low prices? Walmart is a lean, mean, distribution machine—it has the lowest cost structure in the industry. Low costs let the giant retailer charge lower prices while remaining profitable. Lower prices attract more shoppers, producing more sales, making the company more efficient, and enabling it to lower prices even more.

Walmart's low costs result from superior operations management, sophisticated information technology, and good-old "tough buying." Its huge, fully automated distribution centers supply stores efficiently. It employs an information technology system that the U.S. Department of Defense would envy, giving managers around the world instant access to sales and operating information. And Walmart is known for using its massive scale to wring low prices from suppliers. "Don't expect a greeter and don't expect friendly," said one supplier's sales executive after a visit to Walmart's buying offices. "Once you are ushered into one of the spartan little buyers' rooms, expect a steely eye across the table and be prepared to cut your price. They are very, very focused people, and they use their buying power more forcefully than anyone else in America."

Despite its incredible success over the past five decades, mighty Walmart faces some weighty challenges ahead. Having grown so big, the maturing giant is having difficulty maintaining the rapid growth rates of its youth. Think about this: To grow just 7 percent next year, Walmart will have to add nearly $33 billion in new sales. That's a sales *increase* greater than the *total* sales of all but the top 92 companies on the *Fortune* 500, including companies such as American Express, Allstate, Macy's, McDonald's, 3M, and Nike. The bigger Walmart gets, the harder it is to maintain a high rate of growth.

To keep growing, Walmart has pushed into new, faster-growing product and service lines, including organic foods, store brands, in-store health clinics, and consumer financial services. To combat trendier competitors such as Target, Walmart even gave itself a modest image face-lift. It spruced up its stores with a cleaner, brighter, more open look and less clutter to make them more shopper friendly. In search of broader appeal, it has added new, higher-quality products. Many Walmart stores now carry a selection of higher-end consumer electronics products, from Samsung ultra-thin televisions to Dell and Toshiba laptops to Apple iPhones and iPads. The retailer has also dressed up its apparel racks with more-stylish fashion lines.

Despite its massive presence, Walmart still has room to expand geographically. Believe it or not, there are plenty of places in the United States that still don't have a Walmart. And the giant retailer is expanding rapidly in international markets, where sales grew more than 7.5 percent last year to $135 billion. Walmart also faces substantial growth opportunities—and challenges—in e-commerce. Its online sales of an estimated $9 billion account for less than 2 percent of total sales, making it a distant online also-ran next to Amazon .com, which last year topped $61 billion in online sales. Walmart lists "winning in global e-commerce" as one of its top priorities for the future.

As Walmart continues to adapt and grow, however, one thing seems certain. The giant retailer may add new products lines and services. It might go digital and global. It might brush up its look and image. But Walmart has no intention of ever giving up its core low-price value proposition. After all, Walmart is and always will be a discounter. "I don't think Walmart's . . . ever going to be edgy," says a Walmart marketer. "I don't think that fits our brand. Our brand is about saving people money" so that they can live better.[1]

The Walmart story sets the stage for examining the fast-changing world of today's resellers. This chapter looks at *retailing* and *wholesaling*. In the first section, we look at the nature and importance of retailing, the major types of store and nonstore retailers, the decisions retailers make, and the future of retailing. In the second section, we discuss these same topics as they apply to wholesalers.

Author Comment
You already know a lot about retailers. You deal with them every day—store retailers, service retailers, online retailers, and others.

Retailing

What is retailing? We all know that Costco, Home Depot, Macy's, and Target are retailers, but so are Amazon.com, the local Hampton Inn, and a doctor seeing patients. **Retailing** includes all the activities involved in selling products or services directly to final consumers for their personal, nonbusiness use. Many institutions—manufacturers, wholesalers, and retailers—do retailing. But most retailing is done by **retailers**, businesses whose sales come *primarily* from retailing.

Retailing plays a very important role in most marketing channels. Last year, retailers accounted for more than $4.8 trillion of sales to final consumers. They play an important role in connecting brands to consumers in what marketing agency OgilvyAction calls "the last mile"—the final stop in the consumer's path to purchase. It's the "distance a consumer travels between an attitude and an action," explains OgilvyAction's CEO. Some 40 percent of all consumer decisions are made in or near the store. Thus, retailers "reach consumers at key moments of truth, ultimately [influencing] their actions at the point of purchase."[2]

In fact, many marketers are now embracing the concept of **shopper marketing**, using point-of-purchase promotions and advertising to extend brand equity to "the last mile" and encourage favorable point-of-purchase decisions. Shopper marketing involves focusing the entire marketing process—from product and brand development to logistics, promotion, and merchandising—toward turning shoppers into buyers at the point of sale.

Of course, every well-designed marketing effort focuses on customer buying behavior. What differentiates the concept of shopper marketing is the suggestion that these efforts should be coordinated around the shopping process itself. For example, P&G follows a "store back" concept, in which all marketing ideas need to be effective at the store-shelf

Retailing
All the activities involved in selling goods or services directly to final consumers for their personal, nonbusiness use.

Retailer
A business whose sales come *primarily* from retailing.

Shopper marketing
Using in-store promotions and advertising to extend brand equity to "the last mile" and encourage favorable point-of-purchase decisions.

level and work back from there. The strategy builds around what P&G calls the "First Moment of Truth"—the critical three to seven seconds that a shopper considers a product on a store shelf. "We are now brand-building from the eyes of the consumer toward us," says a P&G executive.[3]

The dramatic growth of digital shopping, or combined digital and in-store shopping, has added a new dimension to shopper marketing. >> The "last mile" or "first moment of truth" no longer takes place only in stores. Instead, Google defines a "zero moment of truth," when consumers begin the buying process by researching and searching for products online. Most consumers now make at least some of their purchases online, without even setting foot into a retail store. Alternatively, they may research a purchase on the Internet before—or even during—a store visit. For example, it's not uncommon to see a consumer looking at new TVs in a Best Buy while at the same time using a mobile app to check product reviews and prices at Amazon .com. Thus, shopper marketing isn't just about in-store buying these days. Influencing consumers' buying decisions as they shop involves efforts aimed at online search and in-store, online, and mobile shopping.[4]

>> Shopper marketing: The dramatic growth of digital shopping has added a new dimension to "point of purchase." Influencing consumers' buying decisions as they shop now involves efforts aimed at in-store, online, and mobile shopping.

Inmagine.

Although most retailing is still done in retail stores, in recent years direct and online retailing have been growing much faster than store retailing. We discuss direct and online retailing in detail later in this chapter and in Chapter 14. For now, we will focus on store retailing.

Types of Retailers

Retail stores come in all shapes and sizes—from your local hairstyling salon or family-owned restaurant to national specialty chain retailers such as REI or Williams-Sonoma to megadiscounters such as Costco or Walmart. The most important types of retail stores are described in **>> Table 11.1** and discussed in the following sections. They can be classified in terms of several characteristics, including the *amount of service* they offer, the breadth and depth of their *product lines,* the *relative prices* they charge, and how they are *organized.*

Amount of Service

Different types of customers and products require different amounts of service. To meet these varying service needs, retailers may offer one of three service levels: self-service, limited service, and full service.

Self-service retailers serve customers who are willing to perform their own *locate-compare-select* process to save time or money. Self-service is the basis of all discount operations and is typically used by retailers selling convenience goods (such as supermarkets) and nationally branded, fast-moving shopping goods (such as Target or Kohl's). *Limited-service retailers*, such as Sears or JCPenney, provide more sales assistance because they carry more shopping goods about which customers need information. Their increased operating costs result in higher prices.

Full-service retailers, such as high-end specialty stores (for example, Tiffany or Williams-Sonoma) and first-class department stores (such as Nordstrom or Neiman Marcus) assist customers in every phase of the shopping process. Full-service stores usually carry more specialty goods for which customers need or want assistance or advice. They provide more services, which results in much higher operating costs. These higher costs are passed along to customers as higher prices.

Specialty store
A retail store that carries a narrow product line with a deep assortment within that line.

Product Line

Retailers can also be classified by the length and breadth of their product assortments. Some retailers, such as **specialty stores**, carry narrow product lines with deep assortments

» Table 11.1 Major Store Retailer Types

Type	Description	Examples
Specialty store	A store that carries a narrow product line with a deep assortment, such as apparel stores, sporting-goods stores, furniture stores, florists, and bookstores.	REI, Radio Shack, Williams-Sonoma
Department store	A store that carries several product lines—typically clothing, home furnishings, and household goods—with each line operated as a separate department managed by specialist buyers or merchandisers.	Macy's, Sears, Neiman Marcus
Supermarket	A relatively large, low-cost, low-margin, high-volume, self-service operation designed to serve the consumer's total needs for grocery and household products.	Kroger, Safeway, SuperValu, Publix
Convenience store	A relatively small store located near residential areas, open long hours seven days a week, and carrying a limited line of high-turnover convenience products at slightly higher prices.	7-Eleven, Stop-N-Go, Circle K, Sheetz
Discount store	A store that carries standard merchandise sold at lower prices with lower margins and higher volumes.	Walmart, Target, Kohl's
Off-price retailer	A store that sells merchandise bought at less-than-regular wholesale prices and sold at less than retail. These include *factory outlets* owned and operated by manufacturers; *independent off-price retailers* owned and run by entrepreneurs or by divisions of larger retail corporations; and *warehouse (or wholesale) clubs* selling a limited selection of goods at deep discounts to consumers who pay membership fees.	Mikasa (factory outlet); TJ Maxx (independent off-price retailer); Costco, Sam's Club, BJ's (warehouse clubs)
Superstore	A very large store that meets consumers' total needs for routinely purchased food and nonfood items. This includes *supercenters*, combined supermarket and discount stores, and *category killers*, which carry a deep assortment in a particular category.	Walmart Supercenter, SuperTarget, Meijer (discount stores); Best Buy, PetSmart, Staples, Barnes & Noble (category killers)

within those lines. Today, specialty stores are flourishing. The increasing use of market segmentation, market targeting, and product specialization has resulted in a greater need for stores that focus on specific products and segments.

Department store
A retail store that carries a wide variety of product lines, each operated as a separate department managed by specialist buyers or merchandisers.

By contrast, **department stores** carry a wide variety of product lines. In recent years, department stores have been squeezed between more focused and flexible specialty stores on the one hand and more efficient, lower-priced discounters on the other. In response, many have added promotional pricing to meet the discount threat. Others have stepped up the use of store brands and single-brand *designer shops* to compete with specialty stores. Still others are trying direct and online selling. Service remains the key differentiating factor. Retailers such as Nordstrom, Saks, Neiman Marcus, and other high-end department stores are doing well by emphasizing exclusive merchandise and high-quality service.

Supermarket
A large, low-cost, low-margin, high-volume, self-service store that carries a wide variety of grocery and household products.

Supermarkets are the most frequently visited type of retail store. Today, however, they are facing slow sales growth because of slower population growth and an increase in competition from discounters (Walmart, Costco, and Dollar General) on the one hand and specialty food stores (Whole Foods Market, Trader Joe's, Sprouts) on the other. Supermarkets also have been hit hard by the rapid growth of out-of-home eating over the past two decades. In fact, supermarkets' share of the groceries and food market plunged from 66 percent in 2000 to 48 percent last year.[5]

In the battle for "share of stomachs," some supermarkets have moved upscale, providing improved store environments and higher-quality food offerings, such as from-scratch bakeries, gourmet deli counters, natural foods, and fresh seafood departments. Others, however, are attempting to compete head-on with food discounters such as Costco and Walmart by cutting costs, establishing more-efficient operations, and lowering prices.

Publix, the nation's largest employee-owned supermarket chain, has done this successfully:[6]

Despite recent belt-tightening by consumers, the Publix supermarket chain has succeeded by lowering prices and helping customers get the most out of today's tighter food budgets.

Lannis Waters/ZUMA Press/Newscom.

> Despite recent belt-tightening by consumers, while other Southeast grocery chains have struggled, Publix has grown steadily and profitably. The $27 billion chain has opened and acquired more new stores than any other supermarket during the past five years, and it boasts the second-highest annualized sales per square foot in the industry, behind only Whole Foods. Publix's success comes from its focus on helping customers get the most out of today's tighter food budgets. Despite its own rapidly rising purchasing and transportation costs, the chain introduced Publix Essentials, a consumer program that reduced its prices for basics such as bread, milk, and laundry detergent by as much as 20 percent. In addition, Publix began a Savings Made Easy program that offers Meal Deal and Thrifty Tips advice to customers trying to stretch their shopping dollars. "In today's economy, Publix is working hard to help," says the chain. "In addition to lowering prices on groceries you need most, we're giving you simple strategies for saving." Says one retail consultant, "Publix is always at its best when the economy is at its worst." Customers seem to agree. According to the American Customer Satisfaction Index (ACSI), for the 19th consecutive year, Publix is the highest-ranking supermarket for customer satisfaction.

Convenience store
A small store, located near a residential area, that is open long hours seven days a week and carries a limited line of high-turnover convenience goods.

Convenience stores are small stores that carry a limited line of high-turnover convenience goods. After several years of stagnant sales, these stores are now experiencing growth. Many convenience store chains have tried to expand beyond their primary market of young, blue-collar men by redesigning their stores to attract female shoppers. They are shedding the image of a "truck stop" where men go to buy gas, beer, cigarettes, or shriveled hotdogs on a roller grill and are instead offering freshly prepared foods and cleaner, safer, more-upscale environments.

For example, consider 7-Eleven, which is providing new reasons to say "Oh thank heaven—it's 7-Eleven":[7]

> Long known as a haven for Slurpees, Big Gulps, hot dogs spinning on a roller, self-serve nachos with cheese and chili, smokes, beer, and bags of chips, 7-Eleven is changing both its fare and its image. To meet evolving consumer tastes and stiffer competition from the likes of Dunkin Donuts and Starbucks—which now offer fresh food to on-the-go customers—7-Eleven is stocking its shelves with healthier options, developed by a company team of culinary and food science experts. More health-conscious customers will now find an expanding menu of snack and meal items under 400 calories, such as yogurt parfaits, salads, bags of carrots and celery, fresh subs, Smart turkey sandwiches on whole wheat bread, and a Bistro Snack Protein Pack—carrots, hummus, pita rounds, cheddar cheese, and grapes in a meal-to-go box. The chain is also resizing and single-sizing existing products. Over the next three years, 7-Eleven plans to boost its sales of high-margin fresh foods to 20 percent, twice the current level. The goal is to offer "what the consumer now wants, which is tasty, healthy, fresh food choices," says 7-Eleven's CEO. The change means less reliance on decreasing cigarette sales and aligns the chain with the latest consumer buying trends. "We used to be a place for people to buy beer, wine, cigarettes, candy and chips, and people would occasionally ask where they could go to get something to eat," says a 7-Eleven franchisee. "We're no longer getting that question because now you can get something to eat right here."

Convenience stores: 7-Eleven now stocks "tasty, healthy, fresh food choices." Here, 7-Eleven's Corporate Dietitian shows a selection of the store chain's healthier options.

7-Eleven, Inc.

Superstores are much larger than regular supermarkets and offer a large assortment of routinely purchased food products, nonfood items, and services. Walmart, Target, Meijer, and other discount retailers offer *supercenters*, very large combination food and discount stores. Whereas a traditional grocery store brings in about $385,000 a week in sales, a supercenter brings in about $1.42 million a week. Walmart, which opened its first supercenter in 1988, now has more than 3,000 supercenters in North America and is opening new ones at a rate of about 125 per year.[8]

Recent years have also seen the rapid growth of superstores that are actually giant specialty stores, the so-called **category killers** (for example, Best Buy,

Superstore
A store much larger than a regular supermarket that offers a large assortment of routinely purchased food products, nonfood items, and services.

Category killer
A giant specialty store that carries a very deep assortment of a particular line.

Service retailer
A retailer whose product line is actually a service; examples include hotels, airlines, banks, colleges, and many others.

Discount store
A retail operation that sells standard merchandise at lower prices by accepting lower margins and selling at higher volume.

Home Depot, and PetSmart). They feature stores the size of airplane hangars that carry a very deep assortment of a particular line. Category killers are found in a wide range of categories, including electronics, home-improvement products, books, baby gear, toys, linens and towels, party goods, sporting goods, and even pet supplies.

Finally, for many retailers, the product line is actually a service. **Service retailers** include hotels and motels, banks, airlines, restaurants, colleges, hospitals, movie theaters, tennis clubs, bowling alleys, repair services, hair salons, and dry cleaners. Service retailers in the United States are growing faster than product retailers.

Relative Prices

Retailers can also be classified according to the prices they charge (see Table 11.1). Most retailers charge regular prices and offer normal-quality goods and customer service. Others offer higher-quality goods and service at higher prices. Retailers that feature low prices are discount stores and "off-price" retailers.

Discount Stores. A **discount store** (for example, Target, Kohl's, or Walmart) sells standard merchandise at lower prices by accepting lower margins and selling higher volume. The early discount stores cut expenses by offering few services and operating in warehouse-like facilities in low-rent, heavily traveled districts. Today's discounters have improved their store environments and increased their services, while at the same time keeping prices low through lean, efficient operations.

Leading "big-box" discounters, such as Walmart, Costco, and Target, now dominate the retail scene. However, even "small-box" discounters are thriving in the current economic environment. For example, dollar stores are now today's fastest-growing retail format. Back in the day, dollar stores sold mostly odd-lot assortments of novelties, factory overruns, closeouts, and outdated merchandise—most priced at $1. Not anymore. >> Dollar General, the nation's largest small-box discount retailer, makes a powerful value promise for the times: "Save time. Save money. Every day":[9]

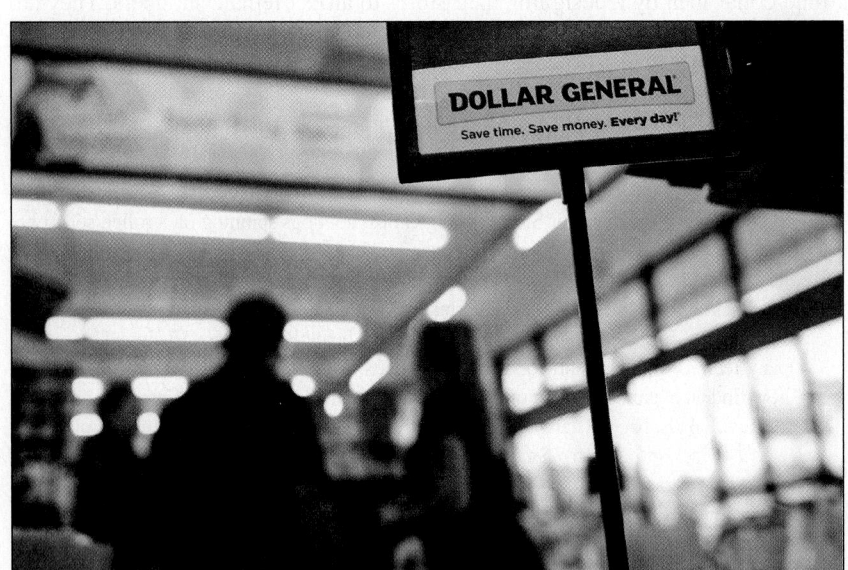

>> Discounter Dollar General, the nation's largest small-box discount retailer, makes a powerful value promise for the times: "Save time. Save money. Every day."
Bloomberg via Getty Images.

> Dollar General's slogan isn't just for show. It's a careful statement of the store's value promise. The retailer's goal is to keep shopping simple by offering only a selected assortment of popular brands at everyday low prices in small and convenient locations. Dollar General's slimmed-down product line and smaller stores (you could fit more than 25 Dollar General stores inside the average Walmart supercenter) add up to a quick trip—the average customer is in and out of the store in less than 10 minutes. And its prices on the popular brand-name products it carries are an estimated 20 to 40 percent lower than grocery store prices. Put it all together, and things are sizzling right now at Dollar General. Moreover, the fast-growing retailer is well positioned for the future. We "see signs of a new consumerism," says Dollar General's CEO, as people shift where they shop, switch to lower-cost brands, and stay generally more frugal." Convenience and low prices, it seems, never go out of style.

Off-price retailer
A retailer that buys at less-than-regular wholesale prices and sells at less than retail.

Independent off-price retailer
An off-price retailer that is either independently owned and run or is a division of a larger retail corporation.

Off-Price Retailers. As the major discount stores traded up, a new wave of **off-price retailers** moved in to fill the ultralow-price, high-volume gap. Ordinary discounters buy at regular wholesale prices and accept lower margins to keep prices down. By contrast, off-price retailers buy at less-than-regular wholesale prices and charge consumers less than retail. Off-price retailers can be found in all areas, from food, clothing, and electronics to no-frills banking and discount brokerages.

The three main types of off-price retailers are *independents*, *factory outlets*, and *warehouse clubs*. **Independent off-price retailers** either are independently owned and run or are divisions of larger retail corporations. Although many off-price operations are run by smaller independents, most large off-price retailer operations are owned by bigger retail chains. Examples include store retailers such as TJ Maxx and Marshalls, which are owned by TJX Companies, and online sellers such as Overstock.com.

Factory outlet
An off-price retailing operation that is owned and operated by a manufacturer and normally carries the manufacturer's surplus, discontinued, or irregular goods.

Factory outlets—manufacturer-owned and operated stores by firms such as J. Crew, Gap, Levi Strauss, and others—sometimes group together in *factory outlet malls* and *value-retail centers.* At these centers, dozens of outlet stores offer prices as much as 50 percent below retail on a wide range of mostly surplus, discounted, or irregular goods. Whereas outlet malls consist primarily of manufacturers' outlets, value-retail centers combine manufacturers' outlets with off-price retail stores and department store clearance outlets.

These malls in general are now moving upscale—and even dropping *factory* from their descriptions. A growing number of outlet malls now feature luxury brands such as Coach, Polo Ralph Lauren, Dolce&Gabbana, Giorgio Armani, Burberry, and Versace. As consumers become more value-minded, even upper-end retailers are accelerating their factory outlet strategies, placing more emphasis on outlets such as Nordstrom Rack, Neiman Marcus Last Call, Bloomingdale's Outlets, and Saks Off 5th. Many companies now regard outlets not simply as a way of disposing of problem merchandise but as an additional way of gaining business for fresh merchandise. The combination of highbrow brands and lowbrow prices found at outlets provides powerful shopper appeal, especially in thriftier times.

Warehouse club
An off-price retailer that sells a limited selection of brand name grocery items, appliances, clothing, and other goods at deep discounts to members who pay annual membership fees.

Warehouse clubs (also known as *wholesale clubs* or *membership warehouses*), such as Costco, Sam's Club, and BJ's, operate in huge, drafty, warehouse-like facilities and offer few frills. However, they offer ultralow prices and surprise deals on selected branded merchandise. Warehouse clubs have grown rapidly in recent years. These retailers appeal not only to low-income consumers seeking bargains on bare-bones products but also to all kinds of customers shopping for a wide range of goods, from necessities to extravagances.

Consider Costco, now the nation's third-largest discount retailer, behind Walmart and Target. Low price is an important part of Costco's equation, but what really sets Costco apart is the products it carries and the sense of urgency that it builds into the Costco shopper's store experience:[10]

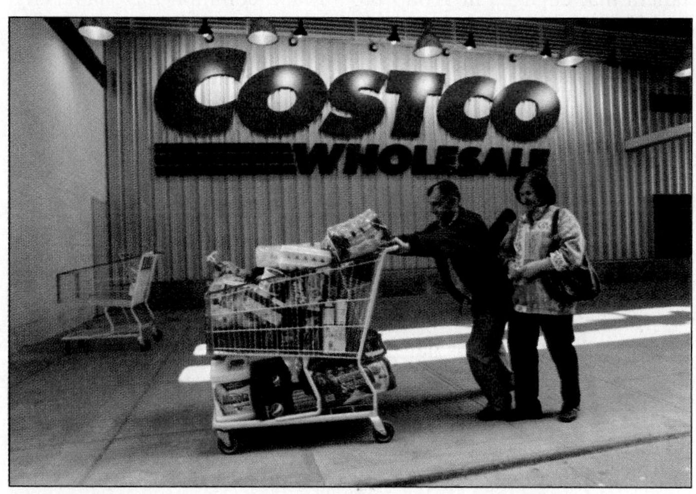

>> Warehouse clubs: Costco is a retail treasure hunt, where one's shopping cart could contain a $50,000 diamond ring resting on top of a vat of mayonnaise.

Suzanne Dechillo/The New York Times.

>> Costco is a retail treasure hunt, where both low-end and high-end products meet deep-discount prices. Alongside the gallon jars of peanut butter and 2,250-count packs of Q-Tips, Costco offers an ever-changing assortment of high-quality products—even luxuries—all at tantalizingly low margins. Last year, Costco sold more than 100 million hot dog and soda combinations (still only $1.50 as they have been for more than 25 years). At the same time, it sold more than 100,000 carats of diamonds at up to $100,000 per item. It is the nation's biggest baster of poultry (more than 70,000 rotisserie chickens a day at $4.99) but also the country's biggest seller of fine wines (including the likes of a Chateau Cheval Blanc Premier Grand Cru Classe at $1,750 a bottle).

Each Costco store is a theater of retail that creates buying urgency and excitement. Mixed in with its regular stock of staples, Costco features a glittering, constantly shifting array of one-time specials, such as discounted Prada bags, Calloway golf clubs, or Kenneth Cole bags—deals you just won't find anywhere else. In fact, of the 4,000 items that Costco carries, 1,000 are designated as "treasure items" (Costco's words). The changing assortment and great prices keep people of all kinds coming back, wallets in hand. There was a time when only the great, unwashed masses shopped at off-price retailers, but Costco has changed all that. Now, even people who don't have to pinch pennies shop there.

Organizational Approach

Although many retail stores are independently owned, others band together under some form of corporate or contractual organization. **>> Table 11.2** describes four major types of retail organizations—*corporate chains*, *voluntary chains*, *retailer cooperatives*, and *franchise organizations.*

» Table 11.2 Major Types of Retail Organizations

Type	Description	Examples
Corporate chain	Two or more outlets that are commonly owned and controlled. Corporate chains appear in all types of retailing but they are strongest in department stores, discount stores, food stores, drugstores, and restaurants.	Macy's (department stores), Target (discount stores), Kroger (grocery stores), CVS (drugstores)
Voluntary chain	Wholesaler-sponsored group of independent retailers engaged in group buying and merchandising.	Independent Grocers Alliance (IGA), Do-It Best (hardware), Western Auto (auto supply), True Value (hardware)
Retailer cooperative	Group of independent retailers who jointly establish a central buying organization and conduct joint promotion efforts.	Associated Grocers (groceries), Ace Hardware (hardware)
Franchise organization	Contractual association between a franchisor (a manufacturer, wholesaler, or service organization) and franchisees (independent businesspeople who buy the right to own and operate one or more units in the franchise system).	McDonald's, Subway, Pizza Hut, Jiffy Lube, Meineke Mufflers, 7-Eleven

Corporate chains
Two or more outlets that are commonly owned and controlled.

Franchise
A contractual association between a manufacturer, wholesaler, or service organization (a franchisor) and independent businesspeople (franchisees) who buy the right to own and operate one or more units in the franchise system.

Corporate chains are two or more outlets that are commonly owned and controlled. They have many advantages over independents. Their size allows them to buy in large quantities at lower prices and gain promotional economies. They can hire specialists to deal with areas such as pricing, promotion, merchandising, inventory control, and sales forecasting.

The great success of corporate chains caused many independents to band together in one of two forms of contractual associations. One is the *voluntary chain*—a wholesaler-sponsored group of independent retailers that engages in group buying and common merchandising. Examples include the Independent Grocers Alliance (IGA), Western Auto, and Do-It Best hardware stores. The other type of contractual association is the *retailer cooperative*—a group of independent retailers that bands together to set up a jointly owned, central wholesale operation and conduct joint merchandising and promotion efforts. Examples are Associated Grocers and Ace Hardware. These organizations give independents the buying and promotion economies they need to meet the prices of corporate chains.

Another form of contractual retail organization is a **franchise**. The main difference between franchise organizations and other contractual systems (voluntary chains and retail cooperatives) is that franchise systems are normally based on some unique product or service; a method of doing business; or the trade name, goodwill, or patent that the franchisor has developed. Franchising has been prominent in fast-food restaurants, motels, health and fitness centers, auto sales and service dealerships, and real estate agencies.

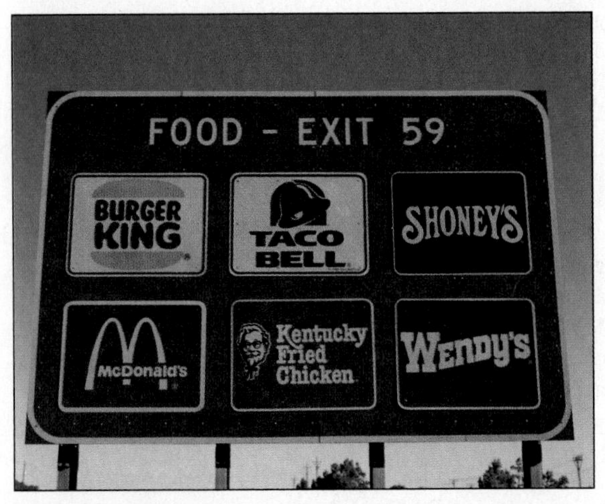

» **Franchising: These days, it's nearly impossible to stroll down a city block or drive on a suburban street without seeing an abundance of franchise businesses.**

However, franchising covers a lot more than just burger joints and fitness centers. Franchises have sprung up to meet just about any need. For example, Mad Science Group franchisees put on science programs for schools, scout troops, and birthday parties. H&R Block provides tax-preparation services, and Supercuts offers affordable, anytime, walk-in haircuts. Mr. Handyman provides repair services for homeowners, while Merry Maids tidies up their houses.

Franchises now command 40 percent of all retail sales in the United States. » These days, it's nearly impossible to stroll down a city block or drive on a city street without seeing a McDonald's, Subway, Jiffy Lube, or Holiday Inn. One of the best-known and most successful franchisers, McDonald's, now has more than 34,000 stores in 119 countries, including more than 14,000 in the United States. It serves 69 million customers a day and racks up more than $95 billion in annual system-wide sales. More than 80 percent of McDonald's restaurants worldwide are owned and operated by franchisees. Gaining fast is Subway, one of the fastest-growing franchise restaurants, with system-wide sales of $16.6 billion and almost 39,000 shops in 100 countries, including nearly 25,000 in the United States.[11]

SPEED BUMP LINKING THE CONCEPTS

Pause here and think about all the different kinds of retailers you deal with regularly, many of which overlap in the products they carry.

- Pick a familiar product: a camera, microwave oven, lawn tool, or something else. Shop for this product at two very different store types, say a discount store or category killer on the one hand, and a department store or smaller specialty store on the other. Then shop for it online. Compare the three shopping outlets on product assortment, services, and prices. If you were going to buy the product, where would you buy it and why?
- What does your shopping trip suggest about the futures of the competing store formats that you sampled?

Retailer Marketing Decisions

Retailers are always searching for new marketing strategies to attract and hold customers. In the past, retailers attracted customers with unique product assortments and more or better services. Today, the assortments and services of various retailers are looking more and more alike. You can find most consumer brands not only in department stores but also in mass-merchandise discount stores, off-price discount stores, and all over the Internet. Thus, it's now more difficult for any one retailer to offer exclusive merchandise.

Service differentiation among retailers has also eroded. Many department stores have trimmed their services, whereas discounters have increased theirs. In addition, customers have become smarter and more price sensitive. They see no reason to pay more for identical brands, especially when service differences are shrinking. For all these reasons, many retailers today are rethinking their marketing strategies.

As shown in >> **Figure 11.1**, retailers face major marketing decisions about *segmentation and targeting*, *store differentiation and positioning*, and the *retail marketing mix*.

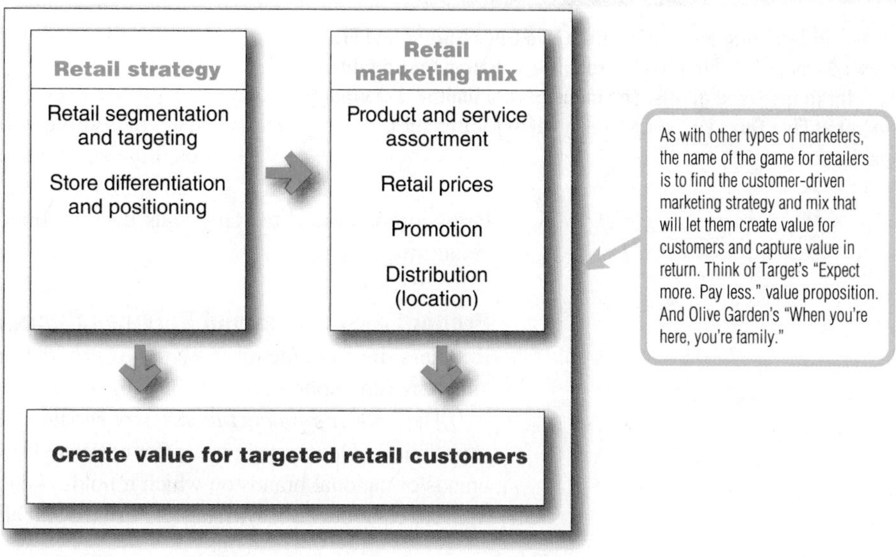

>> **Figure 11.1** Retailer Marketing Strategies

Segmentation, Targeting, Differentiation, and Positioning Decisions

Retailers must first segment and define their target markets and then decide how they will differentiate and position themselves in these markets. Should the store focus on upscale, midscale, or downscale shoppers? Do target shoppers want variety, depth of assortment, convenience, or low prices? Until they define and profile their markets, retailers cannot make consistent decisions about product assortment, services, pricing, advertising, store décor, or any of the other decisions that must support their positions.

Too many retailers, even big ones, fail to clearly define their target markets and positions. For example, what market does Sears target? For what is the department store known? What is its value proposition versus, say, Walmart on one hand and Macy's or Nordstrom on the other? If you're having trouble answering those questions, you're not alone—so is Sears's management (see Marketing at Work 11.1).

By contrast, successful retailers define their target markets well and position themselves strongly. For example, Trader Joe's positions itself strongly with its "cheap gourmet" value proposition. Walmart is strongly positioned on low prices and what those always-low prices mean to its customers. And highly successful outdoor products retailer Bass Pro Shops positions itself powerfully as being "as close to the Great Outdoors as you can get indoors!"

With solid targeting and positioning, a retailer can compete effectively against even the largest and strongest competitors. For example, compare little Five Guys Burger and Fries to giant McDonald's. Five Guys has only about 1,000 stores and $1 billion in sales; McDonald's has more than 34,000 stores worldwide and system-wide sales of $95 billion. McDonald's has 27.7 million Facebook Likes; Five Guys has only 834,000. How does this smaller burger chain compete with Big Mac? It doesn't—at least not directly. >> Five Guys succeeds by carefully positioning itself *away* from McDonald's:[12]

>> Retail targeting and positioning: Five Guys Burger and Fries succeeds by positioning itself strongly away from McDonald's and other large fast-food giants. The menu is very limited, but what you can get at Five Guys you simply can't get at McDonald's.

© Radharc Images/Alamy.

> Five Guys' menu is limited—really limited. Aside from hamburgers, the chain has only hot dogs and grilled cheese or veggie sandwiches (which hardly anyone buys). You won't find salads or breakfasts or Chicken McBites at Five Guys, or even a chocolate milk shake. But what you *can* get at Five Guys you simply *can't* get at McDonald's—such as a mouthwatering Five Guys cheeseburger consisting of two patties and 840 gluttonous calories, piled high with cheese, lettuce, tomatoes, pickles, jalapenos, grilled mushrooms, or any of 11 free toppings, made to order with all-fresh ingredients and buried under an absurdly large serving of just-cooked hand-cut fries. The chain claims that there are more than 250,000 ways to order a Five Guys burger, recently crowned Zagat's "Best Burger." What's more, it's all very fresh—there are no freezers in any Five Guys locations, just coolers. The small burger joint's unique offerings and generous portions set it apart, allowing it to charge more than regular fast-food places.

Five Guys can't match McDonald's massive economies of scale, incredible volume purchasing power, ultraefficient logistics, diverse menu, and low prices. But then again, it doesn't even try. By positioning itself away from McDonald's and other large competitors, Five Guys has become one of the nation's fastest-growing fast-casual restaurant chains.

Product Assortment and Services Decision

Retailers must decide on three major product variables: product assortment, services mix, and store atmosphere.

The retailer's *product assortment* should differentiate it while matching target shoppers' expectations. One strategy is to offer merchandise that no other competitor carries, such as store brands or national brands on which it holds exclusive rights. For example, Saks gets exclusive rights to carry a well-known designer's labels. It also offers its own private-label lines—the Saks

MARKETING AT WORK 11.1

Positioning Sears: Why Should You Shop There?

If you're like many Americans, you probably don't shop much at Sears. And when you do shop there, it's probably to catch a sale on appliances or tools, or maybe to browse the selection of Lands' End apparel, a brand owned by Sears since 2002. Even then, the merchandise and brands at your local Sears probably seem a bit stale, and the store itself feels a little old and run down. Shopping at Sears just doesn't provide the modern, feel-good shopping experience that you get at competing retailers such as Macy's or Nordstrom, or even Target or Walmart.

Today's successful retailers position themselves strongly—customers know what the store stands for and how it delivers value. Mention Walmart and people think "Save money. Live better." Bring up Target, and they know to "Expect more. Pay less." Successful discounter Kohl's tells customers to "Expect great things." At Macy's you get "the magic of Macy's," and Nordstrom promises to "take care of customers no matter what it takes." But mention Sears and people are stumped. They are left wondering, "Why should I shop at Sears?"

Founded in 1886, over the next century, Sears grew to become America's iconic retailer. It began as a mail-order catalog company in the 1880s, grew into a national chain of urban department stores during the early- to mid-1900s, and became an important anchor store in the fast-growing suburban malls of the 1960s and 1970s. Through the 1980s, Sears was the nation's largest retail chain—the Walmart of its time. Its then-well-known slogan, "Where America Shops," was more than just an advertising tagline—it was a meaningful positioning statement. Almost every American relied on Sears for everything from basic apparel and home goods to appliances and tools.

But during the past two decades, as the retail landscape has shifted, once-mighty Sears has lost its way. Squeezed between lower-priced big-box discount stores on the one hand, and trendier, more targeted upscale department and specialty stores on the other, Sears has gotten lost in the murky middle. Its old "Where America shops" positioning has little meaning these days for a store with only about one-twelfth the sales of competitor Walmart. And Sears has failed to refresh its positioning to make itself relevant in today's marketplace.

A look at Sears advertising or a visit to the Sears Web site testifies to the retailer's almost complete lack of current positioning. Headlines scream "Buy more, save more on appliances," "50% off your favorite apparel brands," "Lowest prices on Craftsman lawn and garden," and "Big brand sale: great values, top brands." It seems that about the only thing Sears has going for it these days is that everything it sells is always on sale. However, price is not a convincing value proposition for Sears, which has trouble matching the low prices of competitors such as Walmart, Target, or Kohl's.

In 2005, a struggling Sears merged with an even more distressed Kmart to become Sears Holding Corporation. The merger of the two failing retailers left analysts scratching their heads and customers even more confused about the value propositions of the respective chains. Following the merger, the corporation jumped from one questionable tactic to another. For example, Kmart stores began carrying well-known Sears brands such as Craftsman tools, Kenmore appliances, and Diehard batteries, diluting one of Sears's only remaining differentiating assets.

Sears Holding has also tried a variety of store formats. For instance, it converted 400 Kmart stores to Sears Essentials stores, which it later changed to Sears Grand stores—Walmart-like outlets that carry regular Sears merchandise plus everything from health and beauty brands, toys, and baby products to party supplies and groceries. It has also dabbled with a confusing assortment of other formats carrying the Sears name, such as Sears Hometown stores (a franchised smaller version of full-sized Sears stores), Sears Hardware stores, Sears Home Appliance Showrooms, Sears Outlet stores, and Sears Auto Centers.

Despite all the new store formats, Sears has done little to refresh its positioning. "A lot of traditional department stores have reinvigorated themselves through merchandising. You haven't seen that from Sears," says one analyst. To make matters worse, whereas most competing retailers have invested heavily to spruce up their stores, Sears has spent less than one-quarter of the industry average on store maintenance and renovation, leaving many of its outlets looking old and shabby. "There's no reason to shop at Sears," concludes a retailing expert. "It offers a depressing shopping experience and uncompetitive prices."

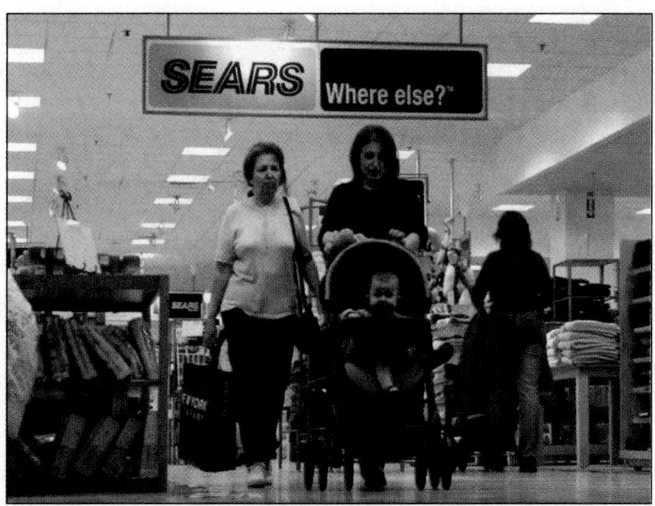

>> To once again position Sears as the place "Where America Shops," the retailer must first answer the question, "Why should people shop at Sears?"

TANNEN MAURY/EPA/Newscom.

Many critics place the blame for Sears's lack of sound marketing and positioning on Sears Holding Company chairman Edward Lampert, a hedge fund manager and the driving force behind the Sears/Kmart merger. Lampert and his funds own about 60 percent of Sears Holding's stock. Critics claim that since the 2005 merger, Lampert has run the company more as a portfolio of financial assets than as a retail chain. Indeed, Lampert has hired four CEOs since the merger, not a single one with any retailing experience. Most recently, he assumed CEO responsibilities himself. "Being a successful hedge fund manager doesn't make you a good retailer," says one Sears watcher.

Sears's lack of customer and marketing thinking has taken a big toll. Sears Holding Corporation revenues have fallen every year since the Sears/Kmart merger, ending last year down 4.1 percent at $39.8 billion, with losses of $930 million. Sears's stock price has fallen 70 percent since 2007. With no cogent marketing plan and seemingly no way out of its financial tailspin, some analysts even predict that once-dominant Sears will soon disappear entirely. "They are letting . . . Sears die on the vine," says one doubter. "As strong as a brand is, and it has huge familiarity and favorability over the years, you can't continue to have a lack of focus without causing long-term damage."

Sears does have some strengths. One bright spot is online sales, which account for nearly 10 percent of Sears's total revenues, compared with only the 1 to 2 percent of sales that Walmart and Target have struggled to achieve online. Another positive is Sears's enduring store brands. Craftsman tools and Kenmore appliances still lead their categories, and the DieHard brand of automotive batteries remains strong. And the company has announced that it will license its brands to makers of related products. Thus, we might soon see Craftsman work apparel, Kenmore kitchenware, and DieHard flashlights and household batteries.

However, creating more online business and renting out its store brands will not overcome what one industry expert characterizes as "the horror show that is the . . . Sears stores themselves." Restoring Sears's relevance and luster will require nothing short of a complete strategic turnaround that positions Sears and its brands on differentiated customer value. To once again position Sears as the place "Where America Shops," the retailer must first answer the question, "Why should people shop at Sears?"

Sources: Based on quotes and other information from Lauren Coleman-Lochner and Carol Hymowitz, "A Money Man's Trials in Retailing," *Businessweek*, January 5, 2012, pp. 24–25; "Prediction: These Famous Brands Will Disappear in 2012," *The Business Insider*, January 5, 2012, http://finance.yahoo.com/blogs/daily-ticker/prediction-famous-brands-disappear-2012-010414512.html; Phil Wahba, "Sears Closing More Stores as Holiday Sales Slide," *Reuters*, December 27, 2011, www.reuters.com/article/2011/12/27/us-sears-sales-idUSTRE7BQ0AV20111227; Jeff Macke, "Sears Done Pretending It's a Retailer," *Yahoo! Finance*, August 16, 2012, http://finance.yahoo.com/blogs/breakout/sears-done-pretending-retailer-162848190.html; Karen Talley, "Sears to License Names of Kenmore, Craftsman Brands," *Wall Street Journal*, April 5, 2012, http://online.wsj.com/article/SB10001424052702303299604577325643404448050.html; Karen Talley and Saabira Chaudhuri, "Sears Loss Narrows; Kohl's Net Falls," *Wall Street Journal*, March 1, 2013, p. B3; and various pages at www.sears.com, accessed November 2013.

Fifth Avenue Signature, Classic, and Sport collections. Alternatively, a retailer can differentiate itself by offering a highly targeted product assortment: Lane Bryant carries plus-size clothing, Brookstone offers an unusual assortment of gadgets and gifts, and BatteryDepot.com offers about every imaginable kind of replacement battery.

The *services mix* can also help set one retailer apart from another. For example, some retailers invite customers to ask questions or consult service representatives in person or via phone or keyboard. Home Depot offers a diverse mix of services to do-it-yourselfers, from "how-to" classes and "do-it-herself" and kid workshops to a proprietary credit card. Nordstrom delivers top-notch service and promises to "take care of the customer, no matter what it takes."

The *store's atmosphere* is another important element in the reseller's product arsenal. Retailers want to create a unique store experience, one that suits the target market and moves customers to buy. Many retailers practice *experiential retailing*. For example, L.L.Bean has turned its flagship retail store in Freeport, Maine, into an adventure center, where customers can experience the store's goods before buying them:[13]

Experiential retailing: L.L.Bean has turned its flagship retail store in Freeport, Maine, into an adventure center, where customers can experience goods before buying them.

Photos courtesy of L.L.Bean.

Customers don't just shop at L.L.Bean's flagship store in Freeport, they *experience* it. Sure, the company's several stores on the Freeport campus offer a full assortment of outdoor apparel and gear, but more than that, they create outdoor experiences. For example, along with selling camping, fishing, hiking,

> boating, home furnishings, and other goods, L.L.Bean offers a slate of free in-store, hands-on clinics, in which knowledgeable experts share tips and techniques to help customers prepare for their own outdoor adventures. Clinics cover everything from tying knots and fishing flies to roadside bike repair to compass navigation and even stargazing. Customers seeking more depth can sign up for one of L.L.Bean's Outdoor Discovery Schools programs in snowshoeing, cross-country skiing, stand-up paddleboarding, fly fishing, biking, birdwatching, canoeing, hunting, or any of a dozen other outdoor activities. L.L.Bean plans to turn the Freeport campus into a full-fledged outdoor adventure center, where customers can hike, bike, golf, kayak, or even go seal watching or fishing at nearby Cisco Bay. The adventure center pulls in more customers, who in turn buy more goods. L.L.Bean's flagship store and Freeport campus attract more than 3 million visitors a year, making them Maine's second-most popular tourist destination behind Acadia National Park. The Freeport campus may soon become a model for additional L.L.Bean adventure centers in other states. The company plans to open 35 new stores in the next five years.[14]

Today's successful retailers carefully orchestrate virtually every aspect of the consumer store experience. The next time you step into a retail store—whether it sells consumer electronics, hardware, or high fashion—stop and carefully consider your surroundings. Think about the store's layout and displays. Listen to the background music. Check out the colors. Smell the smells. Chances are good that everything in the store, from the layout and lighting to the music and even the colors and smells, has been carefully orchestrated to help shape the customers' shopping experiences—and open their wallets.

For example, retailers choose the colors in their logos and interiors carefully: Black suggests sophistication, orange is associated with fairness and affordability, white signifies simplicity and purity (think Apple stores), and blue connotes trust and dependability (financial institutions use it a lot). And most large retailers have developed signature scents that you smell only in their stores:[15]

> Bloomingdale's uses different essences in different departments: the soft scent of baby powder in the baby store, coconut in the swimsuit area, lilacs in intimate apparel, and sugar cookies and evergreen scent during the holiday season. Abercrombie and Fitch uses a scent called "Fierce," a "woody" aroma that's a combination of orange, fir resin, and Brazilian rosewood, among others. Anytime Fitness pipes in "Inspire," a eucalyptus-mint fragrance to create a uniform scent from store to store and mask that "gym" smell. Sheraton Hotels employs Welcoming Warmth, a mix of fig, Jasmine, and freesia; whereas Westin Hotel & Resorts disperses White Tea, which attempts to provide the indefinable "Zen-retreat" experience. Says the founder of ScentAir, a company that produces such scents, "Developing a signature fragrance is much like how you develop a message in print or radio: What do you want to communicate to consumers and how often?"

Such *experiential retailing* confirms that retail stores are much more than simply assortments of goods. They are environments to be experienced by the people who shop in them. In fact, retail establishments sometimes become small communities in themselves—places where people get together. For example, today's bookstores have become part bookstore, part library, part living room, and part coffeehouse. On an early evening at your local Barnes & Noble, you'll likely find backpack-toting high school students doing homework with friends in the coffee bar. Nearby, retirees sit in cushy chairs thumbing through travel or gardening books while parents read aloud to their children. In the corner, there's a local book club discussing the latest best seller. Barnes & Noble sells more than just books—it sells comfort, relaxation, and a community meeting place.

Price Decision

A retailer's price policy must fit its target market and positioning, product and service assortment, the competition, and economic factors. All retailers would like to charge high markups and achieve high volume, but the two seldom go together. Most retailers seek *either* high markups on lower volume (most specialty stores) *or* low markups on higher volume (mass merchandisers and discount stores).

Thus, 110-year-old Bergdorf Goodman caters to the upper crust by selling apparel, shoes, and jewelry created by designers such as Chanel, Prada, and Hermes. The up-market retailer pampers its customers with services such as a personal shopper and in-store showings of

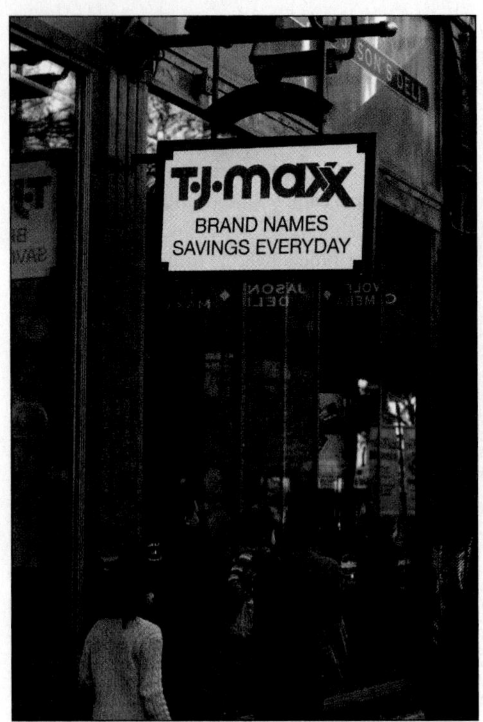

Retailer pricing: Discounter TJ Maxx provides a treasure hunt for bargain shoppers. "No sales. No gimmicks." says the retailer. "Just brand name and designer fashions for you . . . for up to 60 percent off department store prices."

Bloomberg via Getty Images.

the upcoming season's trends with cocktails and hors d'oeuvres. By contrast, TJ Maxx sells brand-name clothing at discount prices aimed at middle-class Americans. As it stocks new products each week, the discounter provides a treasure hunt for bargain shoppers. "No sales. No gimmicks." says the retailer. "Just brand name and designer fashions for you . . . for up to 60 percent off department store prices."

Retailers must also decide on the extent to which they will use sales and other price promotions. Some retailers use no price promotions at all, competing instead on product and service quality rather than on price. For example, it's difficult to imagine Bergdorf Goodman holding a two-for-the-price-of-one sale on Chanel handbags, even in a tight economy. Other retailers—such as Walmart, Costco, Aldi, and Family Dollar—practice *everyday low pricing (EDLP)*, charging constant, everyday low prices with few sales or discounts.

Still other retailers practice *high-low pricing*—charging higher prices on an everyday basis, coupled with frequent sales and other price promotions, to increase store traffic, create a low-price image, or attract customers who will buy other goods at full prices. The recent economic downturn caused a rash of high-low pricing, as retailers poured on price cuts and promotions to coax bargain-hunting customers into their stores. Which pricing strategy is best depends on the retailer's overall marketing strategy, the pricing approaches of its competitors, and the economic environment.

Promotion Decision

Retailers use any or all of the five promotion tools—advertising, personal selling, sales promotion, public relations (PR), and direct marketing—to reach consumers. They advertise in newspapers and magazines and on radio and television. Advertising may be supported by newspaper inserts and catalogs. Store salespeople greet customers, meet their needs, and build relationships. Sales promotions may include in-store demonstrations, displays, sales, and loyalty programs. PR activities, such as new-store openings, special events, newsletters and blogs, store magazines, and public service activities, are also available to retailers.

Most retailers also interact digitally with customers via Web sites and digital catalogs, online ads and video, social media, mobile ads and apps, blogs, and e-mail. Almost every retailer, large or small, maintains a full social media presence. For example, giant Walmart leads the way with a whopping 27 million Facebook Likes, 19.6 million Pinterest followers, 314,000 Twitter followers, and 6,195 YouTube subscribers. By contrast, Sprouts Farmers Market, the small but very-fast-growing Southwest U.S. grocery chain featuring the feel of an old-fashioned farmers market, has only 202,000 Facebook Likes. But Sprouts isn't complaining—that's more than three times the Facebook Likes per million dollars of sales than mighty Walmart.[16]

Place Decision

Retailers often point to three critical factors in retailing success: location, location, and location! It's very important that retailers select locations that are accessible to the target market in areas that are consistent with the retailer's positioning. For example, Apple locates its stores in high-end malls and trendy shopping districts—such as the "Magnificent Mile" on Chicago's Michigan Avenue or Fifth Avenue in Manhattan—not low-rent strip malls on the edge of town. By contrast, to keep costs down and support its "cheap gourmet" positioning, Trader Joe's places its stores in low-rent, out-of-the-way locations. Small retailers may have to settle for whatever locations they can find or afford. Large retailers, however, usually employ specialists who use advanced methods to select store locations.

Most stores today cluster together to increase their customer pulling power and give consumers the convenience of one-stop shopping. Central business districts were the main form of retail cluster until the 1950s. Every large city and town had a central business district with department stores, specialty stores, banks, and movie theaters. When people began moving to the suburbs, however, many of these central business districts, with their traffic, parking, and crime problems, began to lose business. In recent years, many cities have joined with merchants to revive downtown shopping areas, generally with only mixed success.

Shopping center
A group of retail businesses built on a site that is planned, developed, owned, and managed as a unit.

A **shopping center** is a group of retail businesses built on a site that is planned, developed, owned, and managed as a unit. A *regional shopping center*, or *regional shopping mall*, the largest and most dramatic shopping center, has from 50 to more than 100 stores, including two or more full-line department stores. It is like a covered mini-downtown and attracts customers from a wide area. A *community shopping center* contains between 15 and 50 retail stores. It normally contains a branch of a department store or variety store, a supermarket, specialty stores, professional offices, and sometimes a bank. Most shopping centers are *neighborhood shopping centers* or *strip malls* that generally contain between 5 and 15 stores. These centers, which are close and convenient for consumers, usually contain a supermarket, perhaps a discount store, and several service stores—dry cleaner, drugstore, hardware store, local restaurant, or other stores.[17]

A newer form of shopping center is the so-called power center. *Power centers* are huge unenclosed shopping centers consisting of a long strip of retail stores, including large, free-standing anchors such as Walmart, Home Depot, Costco, Best Buy, Michaels, PetSmart, and OfficeMax. Each store has its own entrance with parking directly in front for shoppers who wish to visit only one store.

In contrast, *lifestyle centers* are smaller, open-air malls with upscale stores, convenient locations, and nonretail activities, such as a playground, skating rink, hotel, dining establishments, and a movie theater. "Think of lifestyle centers as part Main Street and part Fifth Avenue," comments an industry observer. In fact, the original power center and lifestyle center concepts are now morphing into hybrid lifestyle-power centers that combine the convenience and community feel of a neighborhood center with the brute force of a power center. In all, today's centers are more places to hang out than just places to shop.[18]

The past few years have brought hard times for shopping centers. With more than 100,000 centers in the United States, many experts suggest that the country has been "overmalled." Not surprisingly, the recent Great Recession hit shopping malls hard. Consumer spending cutbacks forced many retailers—small and large—out of business, increasing mall vacancy rates. Power centers were especially hard hit as their big-box retailer tenants suffered during the downturn. Some of the pizzazz has also gone out of lifestyle centers, whose upper-middle-class shoppers suffered most during the recession. Many lifestyle centers are even adding lower-price retailers to replace classier tenants that have folded. "We've learned that lifestyle centers have to adapt to a changing environment to survive," says one mall developer.[19]

Retailing Trends and Developments

Retailers operate in a harsh and fast-changing environment, which offers threats as well as opportunities. Consumer demographics, lifestyles, and spending patterns are changing rapidly, as are retailing technologies. To be successful, retailers need to choose target segments carefully and position themselves strongly. They need to take the following retailing developments into account as they plan and execute their competitive strategies.

Tighter Consumer Spending

Following many years of good economic times for retailers, the Great Recession turned many retailers' fortunes from boom to bust. Even as the economy has recovered, retailers will feel the effects of changed consumer spending patterns well into the future.

Some retailers actually benefit from a down economy. For example, as consumers cut back and looked for ways to spend less on what they bought, big discounters such as Costco scooped up new business from bargain-hungry shoppers. Similarly, lower-priced fast-food chains, such as McDonald's, took business from their pricier eat-out competitors.

For most retailers, however, tighter consumer spending has meant tough times. During and following the recent recession, several large and familiar retailers declared bankruptcy or closed their doors completely—including household names such as Linens 'n Things, Circuit City, KB Toys, Borders Books, and Sharper Image, to name a few. Other retailers, from Macy's and Home Depot to Starbucks, laid off employees, cut their costs, and offered deep price discounts and promotions aimed at luring cash-strapped customers back into their stores.

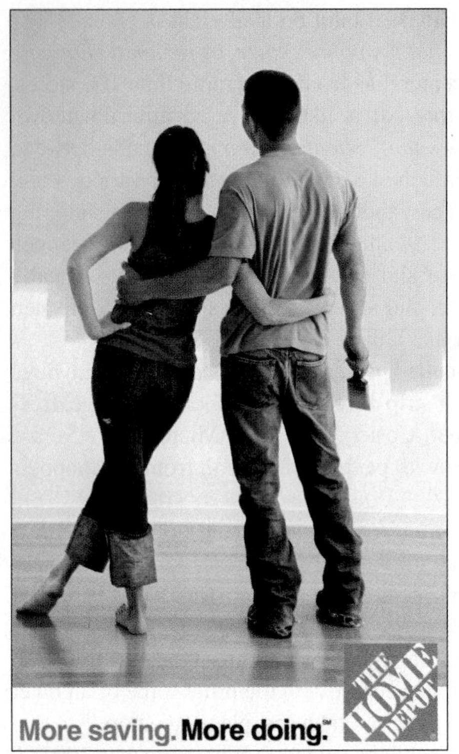

Value positioning: Facing tighter consumer spending, Home Depot adopted a thriftier theme: "More saving. More doing."

(logo) The Home Depot,/(photo)iofoto/Shutterstock.com.

Beyond cost-cutting and price promotions, many retailers also added new value pitches to their positioning. For example, Home Depot replaced its older "You can do it. We can help." theme with a thriftier one: "More saving. More doing." Similarly, Whole Foods Market kicked up the promotion of its 365 Everyday Value private-label brand with ads sporting headlines such as "Sticker shock, but in a good way" and "No wallets were harmed in the buying of our 365 Everyday Value products." And following significant declines in same-store sales caused by the recession, Target, for the first time in its history, introduced TV ads featuring more practical price and savings appeals, putting increased emphasis on the "Pay less" part of its "Expect more. Pay less" promise.

When reacting to economic difficulties, retailers must be careful that their short-run actions don't damage their long-run images and positions. For example, drastic price discounting can increase immediate sales but damage brand loyalty. Instead of relying on cost-cutting and price reductions, retailers should focus on building greater customer value within their long-term store positioning strategies. For example, although it makes sense to boost the "Pay less" part of Target's positioning, Target has not abandoned the quality and design that differentiate it from Walmart and other discounters. As the economy has recovered, although it has shifted the balance a bit toward lower prices, Target still asserts its "Target-ness" by continuing to support the "Expect more" side of its value equation as well.

New Retail Forms, Shortening Retail Life Cycles, and Retail Convergence

New retail forms continue to emerge to meet new situations and consumer needs, but the life cycle of new retail forms is getting shorter. Department stores took about 100 years to reach the mature stage of the life cycle; more recent forms, such as warehouse stores, reached maturity in about 10 years. In such an environment, seemingly solid retail positions can crumble quickly. Of the top 10 discount retailers in 1962 (the year that the first Walmart, Kmart, Target, and Kohl's stores opened), not one exists today. Even the most successful retailers can't sit back with a winning formula. To remain successful, they must keep adapting.

New retail forms are always emerging. The most recent blockbuster retailing trend is the advent of online retailing, by both online-only and brick-and-mortar retailers, via Web sites, mobile apps, and the social media. But lesser innovations occur regularly. For example, many retailers are now experimenting with limited-time *pop-up stores* that let them promote their brands to seasonal shoppers and create buzz in busy areas. During the last holiday season, for instance, Toys "R" Us set up approximately 150 temporary pop-up toy boutiques, many located in malls that formerly housed recently bankrupt KB Toys stores. Likewise, Target recently opened pop-up stores to celebrate limited-run collections by Jason Wu in Toronto and Missoni in New York. The online and mobile equivalent is *flash sales* sites, such as Nordstrom's HauteLook and Amazon's MyHabit, which host time-limited sales events on top fashion and lifestyle brands.[20]

New retail forms: Many retailers—such as Toys "R" Us—are setting up limited-time "pop-up" stores that let them promote their brands to seasonal shoppers and create buzz in busy areas.

Courtesy Toys "R" Us, Inc.

Today's retail forms appear to be converging. Increasingly, different types of retailers now sell the same products at the same prices to the same consumers. For example, you can buy brand name home appliances at department stores, discount stores, home-improvement stores, off-price retailers, electronics superstores, and a slew of online sites that all compete for the same customers. If you can't find the microwave oven you want at Sears, you can step across the street and find one for a better price at Lowe's or Best Buy—or just order one online from Amazon.com or even RitzCamera.com. This merging of consumers, products, prices, and retailers is called *retail convergence*. Such convergence means greater competition for retailers and greater difficulty in differentiating the product assortments of different types of retailers.

The Rise of Megaretailers

The rise of huge mass merchandisers and specialty superstores, the formation of vertical marketing systems, and a rash of retail mergers and acquisitions have created a core of superpower megaretailers. With their size and buying power, these giant retailers can offer better merchandise selections, good service, and strong price savings to consumers. As a result, they grow even larger by squeezing out their smaller, weaker competitors.

The megaretailers have shifted the balance of power between retailers and producers. A small handful of retailers now controls access to enormous numbers of consumers, giving them the upper hand in their dealings with manufacturers. For example, you may never have heard of specialty coatings and sealants manufacturer RPM International, but you've probably used one or more of its many familiar do-it-yourself brands—such as Rust-Oleum paints, Plastic Wood and Dap fillers, Mohawk and Watco finishes, and Testors hobby cements and paints—all of which you can buy at your local Home Depot store. Home Depot is a very important customer to RPM, accounting for a significant share of its consumer sales. However, Home Depot's sales of $70 billion are almost 20 times RPM's sales of $3.8 billion. As a result, the giant retailer can, and often does, use this power to wring concessions from RPM and thousands of other smaller suppliers.[21]

Growth of Direct, Online, Mobile, and Social Media Retailing

Most consumers still make a majority of their purchases the old-fashioned way: They go to a store, find what they want, wait patiently in line to plunk down their cash or credit cards, and bring home the goods. However, consumers now have a broad array of nonstore alternatives, including direct and digital shopping via Web sites, mobiles apps, and the social media. As we'll discuss in Chapter 14, direct and digital marketing are currently the fastest-growing forms of marketing.

Today, thanks to advanced technologies, easier-to-use and enticing online sites and mobile apps, improved online services, and the increasing sophistication of search technologies, online retailing is thriving. In fact, although it currently accounts for only about 5.2 percent of total U.S. retail sales, online buying is growing at a much brisker pace than retail buying as a whole. Last year's U.S. online retail sales reached an estimated $225 billion, up 16 percent over the previous year, and will reach an estimated $327 billion by 2016.[22]

Showrooming
The shopping practice of coming into retail store showrooms to check out merchandise and prices but instead buying from an online-only rival, sometimes while in the store.

Retailer online sites, mobile apps, and online social media also influence a large amount of in-store buying. One recent survey revealed that more than 60 percent of shoppers say they look for deals online before at least half of all shopping trips. In another survey, nearly 20 percent of online holiday shoppers made at least some purchases based on personal connections or promotions on Facebook. What's more, to the dismay of store retailers, many shoppers now check out merchandise at brick-and-mortar store showrooms but then buy it online, sometimes while in the store—a process called **showrooming**. Today, half of shoppers who buy products online first check them out at a traditional store. Large retailers such as Target, Best Buy, Bed Bath & Beyond, and Toys "R" Us have been hardest hit by showrooming and are busy devising strategies designed to thwart such shopping behavior (see Marketing at Work 11.2).[23]

Thus, it's no longer a matter of customers deciding whether to shop in the store *or* shop online. Increasingly, customers are merging store, online Web sites, social media, and mobile outlets into a single shopping process. The Internet and digital devices have spawned a whole new breed of shopper and way of shopping. >> Whether shopping for cars, homes, electronics, consumer products, or medical care, many people just can't buy anything unless they first look it up online and get the lowdown. And they've gotten used to buying anywhere, anytime—whether it's in the store, online, or even online while in the store.

>> The digital age has spawned a whole new breed of shopper—people who just can't buy anything unless they first look it up online and get the lowdown.

Ariwasabi/Shutterstock.

All types of retailers now employ direct and online channels. The Web and mobile online sales of large

MARKETING AT WORK 11.2

Showrooming: Shopping in Stores but Buying Online

At the local Best Buy, a helpful sales associate in the familiar blue shirt patiently assists a customer who's itching to buy a new computer monitor. After 20 minutes, the customer settles on a beautiful new 27-inch Samsung LED monitor, priced at $399. Everyone seems happy and it looks like the associate has earned a well-deserved sale.

However, instead of reaching for his credit card, the customer whips out his smartphone. With the salesperson looking on, he uses an app called TheFind to scan the Samsung's barcode. The app spouts out a list of eight online retailers who sell the same model, along with their prices. Amazon.com has the best price—only $349, and with his Amazon Prime membership, says the customer, he can have it delivered to his doorstep in two days, with no shipping fee and no sales tax. Best Buy doesn't price-match online competitors. So with apologies to the helpful sales associate, the customer pushes the Amazon.com "Buy Now" button and walks out of the store empty-handed.

This now-common shopping practice of coming into store showrooms to scope out merchandise and prices but instead buying it from an online-only rival—a practice called *showrooming*—has become the bane of many store retailers. According to one recent survey, half of shoppers who buy products online now check them out first in a traditional store. Another survey shows that about 40 percent of shoppers have used an in-store shopping app—such as TheFind, eBay's RedLaser, or Amazon's Price Check—to find better prices online and purchase from an online retailer while still in the store.

Showrooming has wreaked damage to many store retailers, especially those selling consumer electronics, which are easy to order online and expensive enough to make price comparisons worthwhile. For example, Target's sales during the most recent holiday season fell short of expectations, with the greatest fallout in electronics, movies, books, music, and toys—products experiencing the biggest shift in sales to e-tailers. It's no surprise, then, that Best Buy—still the largest consumer electronics retailer—has recently been posting losses, closing stores, and laying off workers. But store retailers in all categories—from electronics retailers such as Best Buy to general discounters such as Target and Walmart to specially stores such as GNC, Brookstone, and Toys "R" Us—are now looking for ways to keep smartphone-wielding shoppers from defecting. Says one store retailing executive, who refers to Amazon.com as "the A-word," comparison shopping in the post-smartphone and tablet era has "amped up to a whole 'nother level."

Price-matching is one way to thwart showrooming, but it's often not a realistic option. Online sellers have significant cost advantages—they don't bear the expense of running physical store locations and they aren't required to collect sales taxes in most states. One recent study found that, even before the "no-sales-tax" benefit, Amazon.com's average prices were 8 to 14 percent lower than those of major store retailers, including Target, Walmart, and Best Buy. Most major brick-and-mortar retailers aggressively track online competitor pricing and do their best to match it. For example, Target and Best Buy recently announced that they would price-match Amazon and other online sellers. But store retailers have already trimmed costs and are running on paper-thin margins. So, in most cases, they simply can't match online prices and remain profitable.

With so little room to maneuver on price, store retailers are exploring nonprice tactics to combat showrooming. One tactic is to shift toward exclusive products and store-branded merchandise that don't allow direct comparisons. For example, 56 percent of the products offered by health-and-wellness retailer GNC are either exclusives or GNC-branded items. At specialty retailer Brookstone, many best sellers, such as a $229 smartphone projector, are developed internally. Similarly, Target recently sent an urgent letter to suppliers requesting that they create exclusive Target-only lines and models that would shield it from showrooming price comparisons. It suggested that such exclusives could include all-new products or modifications in packaging and model numbers that would make direct comparisons difficult.

However, rather than just side-stepping the issue of showrooming—or online shopping more generally—many store retailers are trying to ride the trend by boosting their own online and digital options as an alternative or enhancement to shopping in their stores. For example, Target recently upgraded its Web site and quadrupled the number of items it sells online. Walmart has upped its emphasis on in-store pickups for online

» Showrooming: The now-common shopping practice of viewing products in stores but buying them online has become the bane of store retailers. But what can they do about it?

ZUMA Press/Newscom.

orders. It tells customers that they can order from its Walmart.com site, sometimes pick up items on the same day, avoid shipping fees, and easily return items to the store if not satisfied. Customers now pick up half of all Walmart.com purchases in stores, often buying additional merchandise during the visit.

Both Walmart and Target are also testing digital apps that pull customers to both their Web sites and stores, let them prepare shopping lists, and, in Target's case, receive personalized daily-alert deals and exclusive discounts sent to their mobile phones. To help keep customers in the store once they arrive, Walmart has adopted a new strategy that it calls the "endless aisle," by which in-store clerks help customers to order immediately from Walmart.com when they can't find particular items in the store. Both retailers are working feverishly to provide multichannel strategies that merge the advantages of digital shopping with the unique advantages of in-store shopping, such as instant buying gratification, easy returns, and personal sales assistance.

Best Buy is looking for additional ways to make in-store buying more attractive. In a strategy patterned after the "Genius Bars" at Apple stores, Best Buy has tested what it calls "Connected Stores," which feature tech support, wireless connections, and a large customer-assistance hub at the center, as well as new areas and checkout lanes to speed pickup on items purchased online. The hope is that additional in-store services will make higher shelf prices more palatable.

Despite such tactics to combat showrooming and digital buying, many experts remain skeptical about the future of store retailers such as Best Buy. Online retailers like Amazon have transformed how people buy, and when it comes to online commerce, traditional retailers have a lot of catching up to do. Online sales account for only 1 to 2 percent of Target's and Walmart's total sales. And although online sales currently represent only about 8 percent of total retail buying, they are growing at a breathtaking rate. For example, Amazon.com, with sales of $61 billion, is growing at an average annual rate of 34 percent. The world's leading online retailer recently surged past Best Buy, whose sales have stagnated at about $50 billion for the past three years.

For now, although it's a clear and present danger to Best Buy and certain other specialty retailers, showrooming is little more than a nuisance to the Targets and Walmarts of the world. But showrooming sales have more than doubled in just the past year, and as more and more shoppers are leaving stores empty-handed, brick-and-mortar retailers are rising to meet the threat. Target laid out the challenge in its petition to suppliers: "What we aren't willing to do is let online-only retailers use our brick-and-mortar stores as a showroom for their products and undercut our prices without making investments, as we do, to proudly display your brands." The key question for Target, however, is this: "What are you going to do about it?"

Sources: Based on information from "Consumers Visit Retailers, Then Go Online for Cheaper Sources," *Adweek,* March 14, 2013, www.adweek.com/print/147777; Ann Zimmerman, "Can Retailers Halt 'Showrooming'?" *Wall Street Journal*, April 11, 2012, p. B1; Dana Mattioli, "Retailers Try to Thwart Price Apps," *Wall Street Journal*, December 23, 2011, http://online.wsj.com/article/SB10001424052970203686204577114901480554444.html; Ann Zimmerman, "Showdown over 'Showrooming,'" *Wall Street Journal*, January 23, 2012, p. B1; Laurie Sullivan, "Online Content Discovery Heightens Traditional Shopping," *MediaPost News,* November 15, 2012, www.mediapost.com/publications/article/187303/; and Bob Ankosko, "Retailers Embrace Showrooming," *Dealerscope,* January 2013, www.dealerscope.com/article/mobile-shopping-seen-opportunity-engage-customers/1#.

brick-and-mortar retailers, such as Walmart, Target, Staples, and Best Buy, are increasing rapidly. Many large online-only retailers—Amazon.com, Zappos.com, Netflix, online travel companies such as Travelocity.com and Expedia.com, and others—have made it big on the Internet. At the other extreme, hordes of niche marketers have used the Internet to reach new markets and expand their sales.

Still, much of the anticipated growth in online sales will go to multichannel retailers—the click-and-brick marketers who can successfully merge the virtual and physical worlds. In a recent ranking of the top 25 online retail sites, 16 were owned by store-based retail chains.[24] For example, thanks largely to rapid growth in online sales, upscale home products retailer Williams-Sonoma now captures more than 47 percent of its total revenues from its direct-to-consumer channel. Online sales accounted for three-quarters of the retailer's growth last year. Like many retailers, Williams-Sonoma has discovered that many of its best customers visit and shop both online and offline. Beyond just offering online shopping, the retailer engages customers through online communities, social media, mobile apps, a blog, and special online programs. "The Internet has changed the way our customers shop," says Williams-Sonoma CEO Laura Alber, "and the online brand experience has to be inspiring and seamless."[25]

Growing Importance of Retail Technology

Retail technologies have become critically important as competitive tools. Progressive retailers are using advanced information technology (IT) and software systems to produce better forecasts, control inventory costs, interact electronically with suppliers, send information between stores, and even sell to customers within stores. They have adopted sophisticated systems for checkout scanning, RFID inventory tracking, merchandise handling, information sharing, and customer interactions.

Perhaps the most startling advances in retail technology concern the ways in which retailers are connecting with consumers. Today's customers have gotten used to the speed and convenience of buying online and to the control that the Internet gives them over the buying process. The Internet lets consumers shop when they like and where they like, with instant access to gobs of information about competing products and prices. At the same time, Web sites, blogs, social media, and mobile apps give retailers a whole new avenue for establishing brand connections and community with customers. No real-world store can do all that.

Increasingly, retailers are bringing online and digital technologies into their physical stores. Many retailers now routinely use technologies ranging from touchscreen kiosks, mobile handheld shopping assistants, and customer-loyalty apps to interactive dressing-room mirrors and virtual sales associates. But the future of technology in retailing lies in merging online and offline shopping into a seamless shopping experience. It's not a matter of online retailing growing while physical retailing declines. Instead, both will be important, and the two must be integrated. >> For example, Eastern Mountain Sports uses an iPad app to assist in outfitting shoppers for their next adventure with items available both in the store and on the company's Web site. "No longer are we constrained by square footage as to what we can sell," says an EMS marketer.[26]

>> Retail technology: The future belongs to retailers who can blend in-store and online technologies into a seamless shopping experience. Here, an Eastern Mountain Sports associate uses an iPad app to help outfit a shopper for his next adventure.

Eastern Mountain Sports.

Similarly, Walmart's goal is to merge online, social media, and mobile innovations with physical stores to give customers an "anytime, anywhere" shopping experience. To augment in-store shopping, Walmart formed @WalmartLabs, which develops mobile and social media platforms that make shopping easier, more accessible, and more fun. For example, Walmart's Shopycat gift finder app applies data from users' Facebook activities to recommend the best products for customers and gifts for their friends. The retailer's feature-rich mobile apps let customers create smart shopping lists, scan barcodes and check prices, access product information, and scan coupons in real time—all from a smartphone or tablet, at home, at work, in the store, or anywhere in between. Customers will soon be able to use their smartphones in self-checkout lines. The Walmart Social-Store team at @WalmartLabs is exploring other new in-store social media, mobile, and kiosk technologies that will both assist customers as they shop and help stores get to know and serve their customers better.[27]

Green Retailing

Today's retailers are increasingly adopting environmentally sustainable practices. They are greening up their stores and operations, promoting more environmentally responsible products, launching programs to help customers be more responsible, and working with channel partners to reduce their environmental impact.

At the most basic level, most large retailers are making their stores more environmentally friendly through sustainable building design, construction, and operations. For example, all new Kohl's stores are constructed with recycled and regionally sourced building materials, water-efficient landscaping and plumbing fixtures, and ENERGY STAR-rated roofs that reduce energy usage. Inside, new Kohl's stores use occupancy sensor lighting for stockrooms, dressing rooms, and offices; energy management systems to control heating and cooling; and a recycling program for cardboard boxes, packaging, and hangers. "Kohl's cares," says the store. "From large-scale initiatives like constructing environmentally friendly buildings to everyday practices like recycling hangers, we're taking big steps to ensure we leave a smaller footprint."[28]

Green retailing: Safeway offers its own Bright Green line of home care products, including cleaning and laundry products made from biodegradable and naturally derived ingredients.

Safeway, Inc.

Retailers are also greening up their product assortments. For example, Safeway offers its own Bright Green line of home care products, featuring cleaning and laundry soaps made with biodegradable and naturally derived ingredients, energy-efficient light bulbs, and paper products made from a minimum of 60 percent recycled content. Such products can both boost sales and lift the retailer's image as a responsible company.

Many retailers have also launched programs that help consumers make more environmentally responsible decisions. Staples' Easy on the Planet program "makes it easier to make a difference" by helping customers to identify green products sold in its stores and to recycle printer cartridges, mobile phones, computers, and other office technology products. Staples recycles some 30 million printer cartridges and 10 million pounds of old technology each year.[29]

Finally, many large retailers are joining forces with suppliers and distributors to create more sustainable products, packaging, and distribution systems. For example, Amazon.com works closely with the producers of many of the products it sells to reduce and simplify their packaging. And beyond its own substantial sustainability initiatives, Walmart wields its huge buying power to urge its army of suppliers to improve their environmental impact and practices. The retailer has even developed a worldwide Sustainable Product Index, by which it rates suppliers. It plans to translate the index into a simple rating for consumers to help them make more sustainable buying choices.

Green retailing yields both top- and bottom-line benefits. Sustainable practices lift a retailer's top line by attracting consumers looking to support environmentally friendly sellers and products. They also help the bottom line by reducing costs. For example, Amazon.com's reduced-packaging efforts increase customer convenience and eliminate "wrap rage" while at the same time saving packaging costs. And Kohl's earth-friendly and environmentally friendly buildings not only appeal to customers and help save the planet but also cost less to operate.

Global Expansion of Major Retailers

Retailers with unique formats and strong brand positions are increasingly moving into other countries. Many are expanding internationally to escape saturated home markets. Over the years, some giant U.S. retailers, such as McDonald's, have become globally prominent as a result of their marketing prowess. Others, such as Walmart, are rapidly establishing a global presence. Walmart, which now operates more than 6,100 stores in 26 non-U.S. markets, sees exciting global potential. Its international division alone last year racked up sales of more than $135 billion, 85 percent more than rival Target's *total* sales of $73 billion.[30]

However, most U.S. retailers are still significantly behind Europe and Asia when it comes to global expansion. Although 8 of the world's top 20 retailers are U.S. companies, only 4 of these retailers have set up stores outside North America (Walmart, Home Depot, Costco, and Best Buy). Of the 12 non-U.S. retailers in the world's top 20, 8 have stores in at least 10 countries. Foreign retailers that have gone global include France's Carrefour and Auchan chains, Germany's Metro and Aldi chains, Britain's Tesco, and Japan's Seven & I.[31]

International retailing presents challenges as well as opportunities. Retailers can face dramatically different retail environments when crossing countries, continents, and cultures. Simply adapting the operations that work well in the home country is usually not enough to create success abroad. Instead, when going global, retailers must understand and meet the needs of local markets.

SPEED BUMP LINKING THE CONCEPTS

Time out! So-called experts have long predicted that online retailing eventually will replace store retailing as our primary way to shop. What do you think?

- Shop for a good book at the Barnes & Noble Web site (www.bn.com), taking time to browse the site and see what it has to offer. Next, shop at a nearby Barnes & Noble or other bookstore. Compare the two shopping experiences. Where would you rather shop? On what occasions? Why?
- A Barnes & Noble store creates an ideal "community" where people can "hang out." How does its Web site compare on this dimension?
- Do Barnes & Noble's various social media efforts create community for the retailer and its customers? For example, see www.facebook.com/barnesandnoble, https://twitter.com/bnbooks, http://pinterest.com/barnesandnoble/followers/.

Author Comment
Because wholesalers operate behind the scenes, they are largely unknown to final consumers. But they are very important to their business customers.

Wholesaling

Wholesaling
All the activities involved in selling goods and services to those buying for resale or business use.

Wholesaler
A firm engaged *primarily* in wholesaling activities.

Wholesaling includes all the activities involved in selling goods and services to those buying them for resale or business use. Firms engaged *primarily* in wholesaling activities are called **wholesalers**.

Wholesalers buy mostly from producers and sell mostly to retailers, industrial consumers, and other wholesalers. As a result, many of the nation's largest and most important wholesalers are largely unknown to final consumers. >> For example, you may never have heard of Grainger, even though it's very well known and much valued by its more than 2 million business and institutional customers in 157 countries:[32]

> Grainger may be the biggest market leader you've never heard of. It's a $9 billion business that offers more than 1 million maintenance, repair, and operating (MRO) products from 3,500 manufacturers in 30 countries to 2 million active customers. Through its branch network, service centers, sales reps, catalog, and online and social media sites, Grainger links customers with the supplies they need to keep their facilities running smoothly—everything from light bulbs, cleaners, and display cases to nuts and bolts, motors, valves, power tools, test equipment, and safety supplies. Grainger's 711 branches, 28 strategically located distribution centers, nearly 21,500 employees, and innovative Web sites handle more than 115,000 transactions a day. Grainger's customers include organizations ranging from factories, garages, and grocers to schools and military bases.
>
> Grainger operates on a simple value proposition: to make it easier and less costly for customers to find and buy MRO supplies. It starts by acting as a one-stop shop for products needed to maintain facilities. On a broader level, it builds lasting relationships with customers by helping them find *solutions* to their overall MRO problems. Acting as consultants, Grainger sales reps help buyers with everything from improving their supply chain management to reducing inventories and streamlining warehousing operations.
>
> So, how come you've never heard of Grainger? Perhaps it's because the company operates in the not-so-glamorous world of MRO supplies, which are important to every business but not so important to consumers. More likely, it's because Grainger is a wholesaler. And like most wholesalers, it operates behind the scenes, selling mostly to other businesses.

GRAINGER
"Service Delivered"

>> **Wholesaling: Many of the nation's largest and most important wholesalers—like Grainger—are largely unknown to final consumers. But they are very well known and much valued by the business customers they serve.**

W. W. Grainger, Inc.

Why are wholesalers important to sellers? For example, why would a producer use wholesalers rather than selling directly to retailers or consumers? Simply put, wholesalers add value by performing one or more of the following channel functions:

- *Selling and promoting:* Wholesalers' sales forces help manufacturers reach many small customers at a low cost. The wholesaler has more contacts and is often more trusted by the buyer than the distant manufacturer.

- *Buying and assortment building:* Wholesalers can select items and build assortments needed by their customers, thereby saving much work.
- *Bulk breaking:* Wholesalers save their customers money by buying in carload lots and breaking bulk (breaking large lots into small quantities).
- *Warehousing:* Wholesalers hold inventories, thereby reducing the inventory costs and risks of suppliers and customers.
- *Transportation:* Wholesalers can provide quicker delivery to buyers because they are closer to buyers than are producers.
- *Financing:* Wholesalers finance their customers by giving credit, and they finance their suppliers by ordering early and paying bills on time.
- *Risk bearing:* Wholesalers absorb risk by taking title and bearing the cost of theft, damage, spoilage, and obsolescence.
- *Market information:* Wholesalers give information to suppliers and customers about competitors, new products, and price developments.
- *Management services and advice:* Wholesalers often help retailers train their salesclerks, improve store layouts and displays, and set up accounting and inventory control systems.

Types of Wholesalers

Wholesalers fall into three major groups (see **>>Table 11.3**): *merchant wholesalers*, *brokers and agents*, and *manufacturers' and retailers' branches and offices*. **Merchant wholesalers** are the largest single group of wholesalers, accounting for roughly 50 percent of all wholesaling. Merchant wholesalers include two broad types: full-service wholesalers and limited-service wholesalers. *Full-service wholesalers* provide a full set of services, whereas the various *limited-service wholesalers* offer fewer services to their suppliers and customers. The different types of limited-service wholesalers perform varied specialized functions in the distribution channel.

Brokers and *agents* differ from merchant wholesalers in two ways: They do not take title to goods, and they perform only a few functions. Like merchant wholesalers, they generally specialize by product line or customer type. A **broker** brings buyers and sellers together and assists in negotiation. **Agents** represent buyers or sellers on a more permanent basis. *Manufacturers' agents* (also called *manufacturers' representatives*) are the most common type of agent wholesaler. The third major type of wholesaling is that done in **manufacturers' and retailers' branches and offices** by sellers or buyers themselves rather than through independent wholesalers.

Merchant wholesaler
An independently owned wholesale business that takes title to the merchandise it handles.

Broker
A wholesaler who does not take title to goods and whose function is to bring buyers and sellers together and assist in negotiation.

Agent
A wholesaler who represents buyers or sellers on a relatively permanent basis, performs only a few functions, and does not take title to goods.

Manufacturers' and retailers' branches and offices
Wholesaling by sellers or buyers themselves rather than through independent wholesalers.

Wholesaler Marketing Decisions

Wholesalers now face growing competitive pressures, more-demanding customers, new technologies, and more direct-buying programs on the part of large industrial, institutional, and retail buyers. As a result, they have taken a fresh look at their marketing strategies. As with retailers, their marketing decisions include choices of segmentation and targeting, differentiation and positioning, and the marketing mix—product and service assortments, price, promotion, and distribution (see **>>Figure 11.2**).

Segmentation, Targeting, Differentiation, and Positioning Decisions

Like retailers, wholesalers must segment and define their target markets and differentiate and position themselves effectively—they cannot serve everyone. They can choose a target group by size of customer (for example, large retailers only), type of customer (convenience stores only), the need for service (customers who need credit), or other factors. Within the target group, they can identify the more profitable customers, design stronger offers, and build better relationships with them. They can propose automatic reordering systems, establish management-training and advisory systems, or even sponsor a voluntary chain. They can discourage less-profitable customers by requiring larger orders or adding service charges to smaller ones.

» Table 11.3 Major Types of Wholesalers

Type	Description
Merchant Wholesalers	Independently owned businesses that take title to all merchandise handled. There are full-service wholesalers and limited-service wholesalers.
Full-Service Wholesalers	Provide a full line of services: carrying stock, maintaining a sales force, offering credit, making deliveries, and providing management assistance. Full-service wholesalers include wholesale merchants and industrial distributors.
Wholesale merchants	Sell primarily to retailers and provide a full range of services. General merchandise wholesalers carry several merchandise lines, whereas general line wholesalers carry one or two lines in great depth. Specialty wholesalers specialize in carrying only part of a line.
Industrial distributors	Sell to manufacturers rather than to retailers. Provide several services, such as carrying stock, offering credit, and providing delivery. May carry a broad range of merchandise, a general line, or a specialty line.
Limited-Service Wholesalers	Offer fewer services than full-service wholesalers. Limited-service wholesalers are of several types:
Cash-and-carry wholesalers	Carry a limited line of fast-moving goods and sell to small retailers for cash. Normally do not deliver.
Truck wholesalers (or truck jobbers)	Perform primarily a selling and delivery function. Carry a limited line of semiperishable merchandise (such as milk, bread, snack foods), which is sold for cash as deliveries are made to supermarkets, small groceries, hospitals, restaurants, factory cafeterias, and hotels.
Drop shippers	Do not carry inventory or handle the product. On receiving an order, drop shippers select a manufacturer, who then ships the merchandise directly to the customer. Drop shippers operate in bulk industries, such as coal, lumber, and heavy equipment.
Rack jobbers	Serve grocery and drug retailers, mostly in nonfood items. Rack jobbers send delivery trucks to stores, where the delivery people set up toys, paperbacks, hardware items, health and beauty aids, or other items. Rack jobbers price the goods, keep them fresh, set up point-of-purchase displays, and keep inventory records.
Producers' cooperatives	Farmer-owned members that assemble farm produce for sale in local markets. Producers' cooperatives often attempt to improve product quality and promote a co-op brand name, such as Sun-Maid raisins, Sunkist oranges, or Diamond nuts.
Mail-order or Web wholesalers	Send catalogs to or maintain Web sites for retail, industrial, and institutional customers featuring jewelry, cosmetics, specialty foods, and other small items. Its primary customers are businesses in small outlying areas.
Brokers and Agents	Do not take title to goods. Main function is to facilitate buying and selling, for which they earn a commission on the selling price. Generally specialize by product line or customer type.
Brokers	Bring buyers and sellers together and assist in negotiation. Brokers are paid by the party who hired the broker and do not carry inventory, get involved in financing, or assume risk. Examples include food brokers, real estate brokers, insurance brokers, and security brokers.
Agents	Represent either buyers or sellers on a more permanent basis than brokers do. There are four types:
Manufacturers' agents	Represent two or more manufacturers of complementary lines. Often used in such lines as apparel, furniture, and electrical goods. A manufacturer's agent is hired by small manufacturers who cannot afford their own field sales forces and by large manufacturers who use agents to open new territories or cover territories that cannot support full-time salespeople.
Selling agents	Have contractual authority to sell a manufacturer's entire output. The selling agent serves as a sales department and has significant influence over prices, terms, and conditions of sale. Found in product areas such as textiles, industrial machinery and equipment, coal and coke, chemicals, and metals.

Type	Description
Purchasing agents	Generally have a long-term relationship with buyers and make purchases for them, often receiving, inspecting, warehousing, and shipping the merchandise to buyers. Purchasing agents help clients obtain the best goods and prices available.
Commission merchants	Take physical possession of products and negotiate sales. Used most often in agricultural marketing by farmers who do not want to sell their own output. Take a truckload of commodities to a central market, sell it for the best price, deduct a commission and expenses, and remit the balance to the producers.
Manufacturers' and Retailers' Branches and Offices	Wholesaling operations conducted by sellers or buyers themselves rather than operating through independent wholesalers. Separate branches and offices can be dedicated to either sales or purchasing.
Sales Branches and Offices	Set up by manufacturers to improve inventory control, selling, and promotion. Sales branches carry inventory and are found in industries such as lumber and automotive equipment and parts. Sales offices do not carry inventory and are most prominent in the dry goods and notions industries.
Purchasing Offices	Perform a role similar to that of brokers or agents but are part of the buyer's organization. Many retailers set up purchasing offices in major market centers, such as New York and Chicago.

Marketing Mix Decisions

Like retailers, wholesalers must decide on product and service assortments, prices, promotion, and place. Wholesalers add customer value though the *products and services* they offer. They are often under great pressure to carry a full line and stock enough for immediate delivery. But this practice can damage profits. Wholesalers today are cutting down on the number of lines they carry, choosing to carry only the more profitable ones. They are also rethinking which services count most in building strong customer relationships and which should be dropped or paid for by the customer. The key for companies is to find the mix of services most valued by their target customers.

Price is also an important wholesaler decision. Wholesalers usually mark up the cost of goods by a standard percentage—say, 20 percent. Expenses may run 17 percent of the gross margin, leaving a profit margin of 3 percent. In grocery wholesaling, the average profit margin is often less than 2 percent. The recent recession put heavy pressure on wholesalers to cut their costs and prices. As their retail and industrial customers face sales and margin declines, these customers turn to wholesalers, looking for lower prices. Wholesalers may, in turn, cut their margins on some lines to keep important customers. They may also ask suppliers for special price breaks in cases when they can turn them into an increase in the supplier's sales.

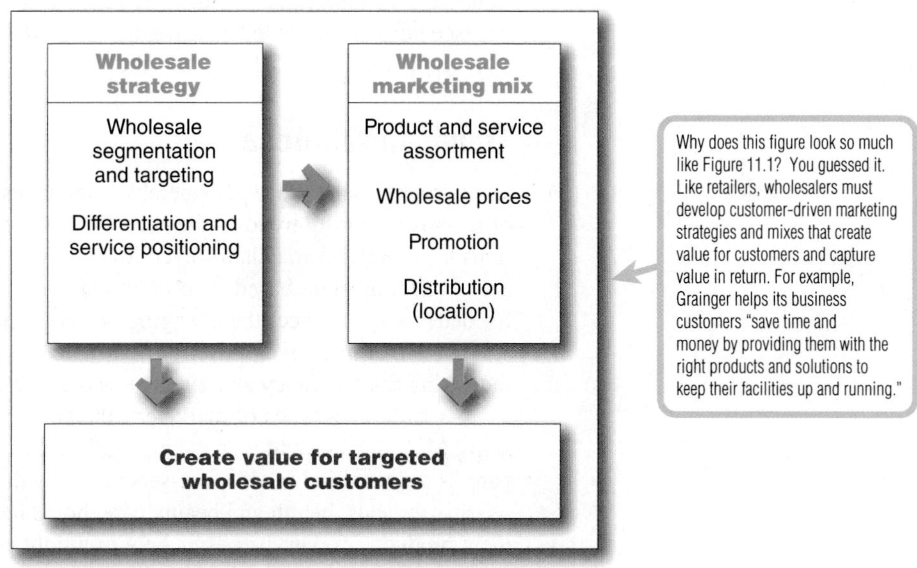
Wholesale strategy
Wholesale segmentation and targeting
Differentiation and service positioning
Wholesale marketing mix
Product and service assortment
Wholesale prices
Promotion
Distribution (location)
Create value for targeted wholesale customers
Why does this figure look so much like Figure 11.1? You guessed it. Like retailers, wholesalers must develop customer-driven marketing strategies and mixes that create value for customers and capture value in return. For example, Grainger helps its business customers "save time and money by providing them with the right products and solutions to keep their facilities up and running."

>> **Figure 11.2** Wholesaler Marketing Strategies

Although *promotion* can be critical to wholesaler success, most wholesalers are not promotion minded. They use largely scattered and unplanned trade advertising, sales promotion, personal selling, and public relations. Many are behind the times in personal selling; they still see selling as a single salesperson talking to a single customer instead of as a team effort to sell, build, and service major accounts. Wholesalers also need to adopt some of the nonpersonal promotion techniques used by retailers. They need to develop an overall promotion strategy and make greater use of supplier promotion materials and programs. Digital and social media are playing an increasingly important role. For example, Grainger maintains an active presence on Facebook, YouTube, Twitter, LinkedIn, and Google+. It also provides a feature-rich mobile app. >> On its YouTube channel, Grainger lists more than 500 videos on topics ranging from the company and its products and services to keeping down inventory costs.

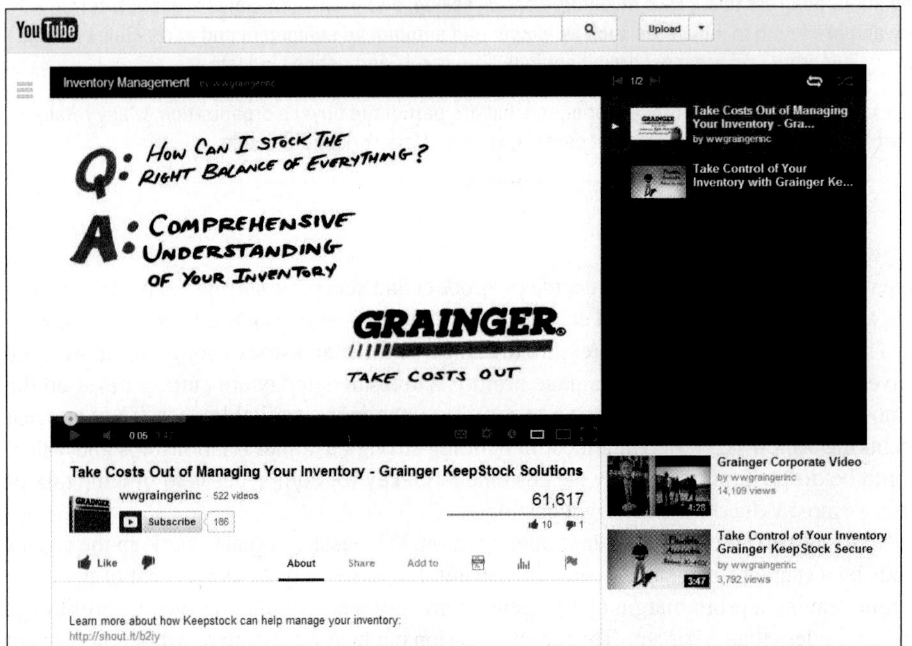

>> Wholesaler marketing: Progressive wholesalers like Grainger maintain an active presence in the social media. For example, on its YouTube channel, Grainger offers more than 500 videos on topics ranging from the company and its products and services to keeping inventory costs down.

W. W. Grainger, Inc.

Finally, *distribution* (location) is important. Wholesalers must choose their locations, facilities, and Web locations carefully. There was a time when wholesalers could locate in low-rent, low-tax areas and invest little money in their buildings, equipment, and systems. Today, however, as technology zooms forward, such behavior results in outdated systems for material handling, order processing, and delivery.

Instead, today's large and progressive wholesalers have reacted to rising costs by investing in automated warehouses and IT systems. Orders are fed from the retailer's information system directly into the wholesaler's, and the items are picked up by mechanical devices and automatically taken to a shipping platform where they are assembled. Most large wholesalers use technology to carry out accounting, billing, inventory control, and forecasting. Modern wholesalers are adapting their services to the needs of target customers and finding cost-reducingmethods of doing business. They are also transacting more business online. For example, e-commerce is Grainger's fastest-growing sales channel, making Grainger the 15th largest e-tailer in the United States and Canada. Online purchasing now accounts for more than 30 percent of the wholesaler's total sales.[33]

Trends in Wholesaling

Today's wholesalers face considerable challenges. The industry remains vulnerable to one of its most enduring trends—the need for ever-greater efficiency. Recent economic conditions have led to demands for even lower prices and the winnowing out of suppliers who are not adding value based on cost and quality. Progressive wholesalers constantly watch for better ways to meet the changing needs of their suppliers and target customers. They recognize that their only reason for existence comes from adding value, which occurs by increasing the efficiency and effectiveness of the entire marketing channel.

As with other types of marketers, the goal is to build value-adding customer relationships. McKesson provides an example of progressive, value-adding wholesaling. The company is a diversified health-care-services provider and the nation's leading wholesaler of pharmaceuticals, health and beauty care, home health care, and medical supply and equipment products. To survive, especially in a tight economic environment, McKesson has to be more cost effective than manufacturers' sales branches. Thus, the company has built efficient automated warehouses, established direct computer links with drug manufacturers, and created extensive online supply management and accounts receivable systems for customers. It offers retail pharmacists a wide range of online resources, including supply management assistance, catalog searches, real-time order tracking, and an account management system. It has also created solutions such as automated pharmaceutical-dispensing machines that assist pharmacists by reducing costs and improving accuracy. Retailers can even use the McKesson systems to maintain prescription histories and medical profiles on their customers.

McKesson's medical-surgical supply and equipment customers receive a rich assortment of online solutions and supply management tools, including an online order management system and real-time information on products and pricing, inventory availability, and order status. According to McKesson, it adds value in the channel by providing "supply, information, and health care management products and services designed to reduce costs and improve quality across healthcare."[34]

The distinction between large retailers and large wholesalers continues to blur. Many retailers now operate formats such as wholesale clubs and supercenters that perform many wholesale functions. In return, some large wholesalers are setting up their own retailing operations. For example, SuperValu is the nation's largest food wholesaler, and it's also one of the country's largest food retailers. Almost half of the company's sales comes from its Cub Foods, Save-A-Lot, Farm Fresh, Hornbacher's, Shop 'n Save, and Shoppers stores. In fact, SuperValu now bills itself as "America's neighborhood grocer."[35]

Wholesalers will continue to increase the services they provide to retailers—retail pricing, cooperative advertising, marketing and management information services, accounting services, online transactions, and others. However, both the recently tight economy and the demand for increased services have put the squeeze on wholesaler profits. Wholesalers that do not find efficient ways to deliver value to their customers will soon drop by the wayside. Fortunately, the increased use of computerized, automated, and Internet-based systems will help wholesalers contain the costs of ordering, shipping, and inventory holding, thus boosting their productivity.

MyMarketingLab

Go to **mymktlab.com** to complete the problems marked with this icon .

END OF CHAPTER REVIEWING THE CONCEPTS

CHAPTER REVIEW AND KEY TERMS

Objectives Review

Retailing and wholesaling consist of many organizations bringing goods and services from the point of production to the point of use. In this chapter, we examined the nature and importance of retailing, the major types of retailers, the decisions retailers make, and the future of retailing. We then examined these same topics for wholesalers.

OBJECTIVE 1 Explain the role of retailers in the distribution channel and describe the major types of retailers. (pp 336–343)

Retailing includes all the activities involved in selling goods or services directly to final consumers for their personal, nonbusiness use. Retailers play an important role in connecting brands to consumers in the final phases of the buying process. *Shopper marketing* involves focusing the entire marketing process on turning shoppers into buyers at the point of sale, whether it's in-store, online, or mobile shopping.

Retail stores come in all shapes and sizes, and new retail types keep emerging. Store retailers can be classified by the *amount of service* they provide (self-service, limited service, or full service), *product line sold* (specialty stores, department stores, supermarkets, convenience stores, superstores, and service businesses), and *relative prices* (discount stores and off-price retailers). Today, many retailers are banding together in corporate and contractual *retail organizations* (corporate chains, voluntary chains, retailer cooperatives, and franchise organizations).

OBJECTIVE 2 Describe the major retailer marketing decisions. (pp 343–349)

Retailers are always searching for new marketing strategies to attract and hold customers. They face major marketing decisions about segmentation and targeting, store differentiation and positioning, and the retail marketing mix.

Retailers must first segment and define their target markets and then decide how they will differentiate and position themselves in these markets. Those that try to offer "something for everyone" end up satisfying no market well. By contrast, successful retailers define their target markets well and position themselves strongly.

Guided by strong targeting and positioning, retailers must decide on a retail marketing mix—product and services assortment, price, promotion, and place. Retail stores are much more than simply an assortment of goods. Beyond the products and services they offer, today's successful retailers carefully orchestrate virtually every aspect of the consumer store experience. A retailer's price policy must fit its target market and positioning, products and services assortment, and competition. Retailers use any or all of the five promotion tools—advertising, personal selling, sales promotion, PR, and direct marketing—to reach consumers. Finally, it's very important that retailers select locations that are accessible to the target market in areas that are consistent with the retailer's positioning.

OBJECTIVE 3 Discuss the major trends and developments in retailing. (pp 349–356)

Retailers operate in a harsh and fast-changing environment, which offers threats as well as opportunities. Following years of good economic times for retailers, the Great Recession turned many retailers' fortunes from boom to bust. New retail forms continue to emerge. At the same time, however, different types of retailers are increasingly serving similar customers with the same products and prices (retail convergence), making differentiation more difficult. Other trends in retailing include the rise of megaretailers; the rapid growth of direct, online, and social media retailing; the growing importance of retail technology; a surge in green retailing; and the global expansion of major retailers.

OBJECTIVE 4 Explain the major types of wholesalers and their marketing decisions. (pp 356–361)

Wholesaling includes all the activities involved in selling goods or services to those who are buying for the purpose of resale or business use. Wholesalers fall into three groups. First, *merchant wholesalers* take possession of the goods. They include *full-service wholesalers* (wholesale merchants and industrial distributors) and *limited-service wholesalers* (cash-and-carry wholesalers, truck wholesalers, drop shippers, rack jobbers, producers' cooperatives, and mail-order wholesalers). Second, *brokers* and *agents* do not take possession of the goods but are paid a commission for aiding companies in buying and selling. Finally, *manufacturers' and retailers' branches and offices* are wholesaling operations conducted by non-wholesalers to bypass the wholesalers.

Like retailers, wholesalers must target carefully and position themselves strongly. And, like retailers, wholesalers must decide on product and service assortments, prices, promotion, and place. Progressive wholesalers constantly watch for better ways to meet the changing needs of their suppliers and target customers. They recognize that, in the long run, their only reason for existence comes from adding value, which occurs by increasing the efficiency and effectiveness of the entire marketing channel. As with other types of marketers, the goal is to build value-adding customer relationships.

Key Terms

Objective 1
Retailing (p 336)
Retailer (p 336)
Shopper marketing (p 336)
Specialty store (p 337)
Department store (p 338)
Supermarket (p 338)
Convenience store (p 339)
Superstore (p 339)
Category killer (p 339)
Service retailer (p 340)
Discount store (p 340)
Off-price retailer (p 340)
Independent off-price retailer (p 340)
Factory outlet (p 341)
Warehouse club (p 341)
Corporate chains (p 342)
Franchise (p 342)

Objective 2
Shopping center (p 349)

Objective 3
Showrooming (p 351)

Objective 4
Wholesaling (p 356)
Wholesaler (p 356)
Merchant wholesaler (p 357)
Broker (p 357)
Agent (p 357)
Manufacturers' and retailers' branches and offices (p 357)

DISCUSSION AND CRITICAL THINKING

Discussion Questions

11-1. Explain how retailers can be classified based on the amount of service offered and give an example of each retailer type. (AACSB: Written and Oral Communication; Reflective Thinking)

11-2. Name and describe the types of corporate or contractual retail store organizations and the advantages of each. (AACSB: Written and Oral Communication)

11-3. List the major trends in retailing. (AACSB: Written and Oral Communication)

11-4. Describe the types of shopping centers and identify specific examples in your community or a nearby city. (AACSB: Written and Oral Communication; Reflective Thinking)

11-5. Explain how wholesalers add value in the channel of distribution. (AACSB: Written and Oral Communication)

11-6. Name and describe the three major groups of wholesalers. (AACSB: Written and Oral Communication; Reflective Thinking)

Critical Thinking Exercises

11-7. Retailers that accept credit cards pay a "swipe fee" to credit-card issuers such as Visa and Mastercard ranging from 1 to 3 percent of the purchase. The credit-card companies prohibited retailers from passing that fee on to consumers, but a recent lawsuit settlement proposal lifted that restriction. Under the settlement, retailers can charge 2.5 to 3 percent on each transaction. Discuss this issue and develop a report on the pros and cons of retailers adding a surcharge to credit purchases. (AACSB: Written and Oral Communication; Reflective Thinking)

11-8. In 2012, JCPenney changed its pricing strategy from one in which it charged relatively high prices and aggressively discounted them to one in which it charges lower but constant everyday "fair and square prices." Evaluate the effectiveness of this pricing strategy change. (AACSB: Written and Oral Communication; Reflective Thinking)

MINICASES AND APPLICATIONS

Online, Mobile, and Social Media Marketing Tracking Customers

According to Nielsen, more than 50 percent of mobile phone consumers own smartphones. Many of them use free Wi-Fi when available for faster connections and to reduce data usage charges. But even when they don't log on to the Wi-Fi, the device continues to search, giving information on users' locations. By using the signals emitted by shoppers' smartphones, retailers can keep tabs on shoppers, knowing where they are and what they are searching for on their phones' browsers. Retailers can learn in which aisles shoppers are most likely to check online prices at retailers such as Amazon.com and can send an alert to a sales representative. "Heat mapping" identifies traffic patterns and locations attracting the greatest number of shoppers checking the Internet. This gives retailers an idea of which products are most vulnerable to showrooming—the practice of shoppers visiting stores to learn about and try products and later purchasing them for less online.

11-9. What is *shopper marketing,* and how might retailers use Wi-Fi technology to implement it? (AACSB: Written and Oral Communication; Information Technology; Reflective Thinking)

11-10. What will be the likely response as more shoppers learn that retailers gather information without their knowledge? (AACSB: Written and Oral Communication; Reflective Thinking)

Marketing Ethics Marketplace Fairness Act of 2013

The Marketplace Fairness Act of 2013 would allow states to require online retailers to collect sales taxes. Most consumers purchase online knowing that they may not have to pay sales tax, which essentially lowers prices for consumers. This results from a 1992 Supreme Court ruling stipulating that catalog and online sellers need only collect sales taxes for states in which they have a physical presence. Consumers are supposed to remit taxes to their state if an online retailer does not collect them, but consumers often do not pay the taxes, causing states to miss out on millions of dollars of tax revenues. Online giant Amazon saw this as a competitive advantage and was very careful regarding how its employees behaved when conducting business in certain states to avoid the "physical presence" requirement. Amazon opposed any initiatives to require online resellers to collect sales taxes. Brick-and-mortar retailers cried foul, claiming online sellers have an unfair competitive price advantage. The Marketplace Fairness Act will supposedly eliminate that advantage. But will it? With more than 9,000 different tax jurisdictions, can a small retailer that also has an online presence compete with the Amazons and Walmarts online? Although Amazon was initially against such legislation, the online reseller is now supporting the act.

11-11. Why has Amazon changed its position regarding online sales taxes—why is it now in favor of the Marketplace Fairness Act? (AACSB: Written and Oral Communication; Reflective Thinking)

Marketing by the Numbers Stockturn Rate

Retailers need merchandise to make sales. In fact, a retailer's inventory is its biggest asset. Not stocking enough merchandise can result in lost sales, but carrying too much inventory increases costs and lowers margins. Both circumstances reduce profits. One measure of a reseller's inventory management effectiveness is its *stockturn rate* (also called *inventory turnover rate* for manufacturers). The key to success in retailing is realizing a large volume of sales on as little inventory as possible while maintaining enough stock to meet customer demands.

11-12. Refer to Appendix 3, Marketing by the Numbers, and determine the stockturn rate of a retailer carrying an average inventory at a cost of $350,000, with a cost of goods sold of $800,000. (AACSB: Written and Oral Communication; Analytical Thinking)

11-13. If this company's stockturn rate was 3.5 last year, is the stockturn rate calculated in the previous question better or worse? Discuss. (AACSB: Written and Oral Communication; Reflective Thinking)

Video Case Home Shopping Network

Shopping on television has been around almost as long as television itself. The Home Shopping Network (HSN) made it a full-time endeavor in 1982, giving birth to a new retail outlet. Since then, HSN has been a pioneer in products, presentation, and order taking. The company has sold millions of products and has been known for giving an outlet to legitimate products that otherwise would not reach customers.

But what does a company do when the very retail channel that it depends upon starts to fizzle out? This video illustrates how HSN has met the challenges of a changing marketplace to continue its innovative methods for reaching its customer base.

After viewing the video featuring HSN, answer the following questions:

11-14. How has HSN differentiated itself from other retailers through each element of the retail marketing mix?

11-15. Discuss the concept of the retail life cycle as it relates to HSN.

11-16. Do you think HSN has a bright future? Why or why not?

Company Cases 11 Dollar General/ 15 IKEA/ 16 Warby Parker

See Appendix 1 for cases appropriate for this chapter. **Case 11, Dollar General: Today's Hottest Retailing Format.** By taking advantage of a gap in the market, Dollar General is growing faster than other forms of retail. **Case 15, IKEA: Making Life Better for the World's Many People.** IKEA manages to sell the same couch in 41 different countries by creating the perfect balance between standardization and adaptation. **Case 16, Warby Parker: Eyewear with a Purpose.** Warby Parker makes high-quality, fashionable eyeglasses at a revolutionary price point—and gives a free pair of glasses away for every pair purchased.

MyMarketingLab

Go to **mymktlab.com** for Auto-graded writing questions as well as the following Assisted-graded writing questions:

11-17. The atmosphere in a retail store is carefully crafted to influence shoppers. Select a retailer that has both a physical store and an online store. Describe the elements of the physical store's atmosphere, such as the colors, lighting, music, scents, and décor. What image is the store's atmosphere projecting? Is that image appropriate given the merchandise assortment and target market of the store? Which elements of the physical store's atmosphere are part of its online store atmosphere? Does the retailer integrate the physical store's atmosphere with its online presence? Explain. (AACSB: Written and Oral Communication; Information Technology; Reflective Thinking)

11-18. Discuss the impact the Marketplace Fairness Act will have on small retailers. Is it fair that small retailers should have to collect sales taxes on online sales to customers outside of their state? (AACSB: Written and Oral Communication; Ethical Understanding and Reasoning; Reflective Thinking)

11-19. Mymktlab Only—comprehensive writing assignment for this chapter.

12 Engaging **Consumers** and Communicating **Customer Value**

Advertising and **Public Relations**

CHAPTER ROAD MAP

Objective Outline

- OBJECTIVE 1 **Define the five promotion mix tools for communicating customer value.** The Promotion Mix 368–369
- OBJECTIVE 2 **Discuss the changing communications landscape and the need for integrated marketing communications.** Integrated Marketing Communications 369–377
- OBJECTIVE 3 **Describe and discuss the major decisions involved in developing an advertising program.** Advertising 377–393
- OBJECTIVE 4 **Explain how companies use public relations to communicate with their publics.** Public Relations 393–397

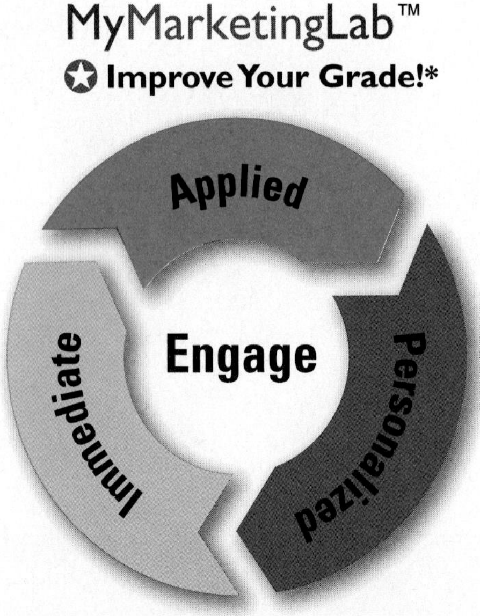

Previewing the Concepts

In this and the next two chapters, we'll examine the last of the marketing mix tools—promotion. Companies must do more than just create customer value. They must also clearly and persuasively communicate that value. Promotion is not a single tool but rather a mix of several tools. Ideally, under the concept of *integrated marketing communications,* a company will carefully coordinate these promotion elements to engage customers and build a clear, consistent, and compelling message about the organization and its products. We'll begin by introducing the various promotion mix tools. Next, we'll examine the rapidly changing communications environment—especially the addition of new digital and social media—and the need for integrated marketing communications. Finally, we'll look more closely at two of the promotion tools—advertising and public relations. In the next chapter, we'll visit two other promotion mix tools—sales promotion and personal selling. Then, in Chapter 14, we'll explore direct, online, mobile, and social media marketing.

Let's start by looking at a good integrated marketing communications campaign. In an industry characterized by constantly shifting promotional themes, Chick-fil-A's remarkably enduring "Eat Mor Chikin" campaign—featuring an unlikely herd of quirky cows—has successfully engaged customers, communicated the brand's personality and positioning, and made Chick-fil-A one of America's most successful quick-service restaurant chains.

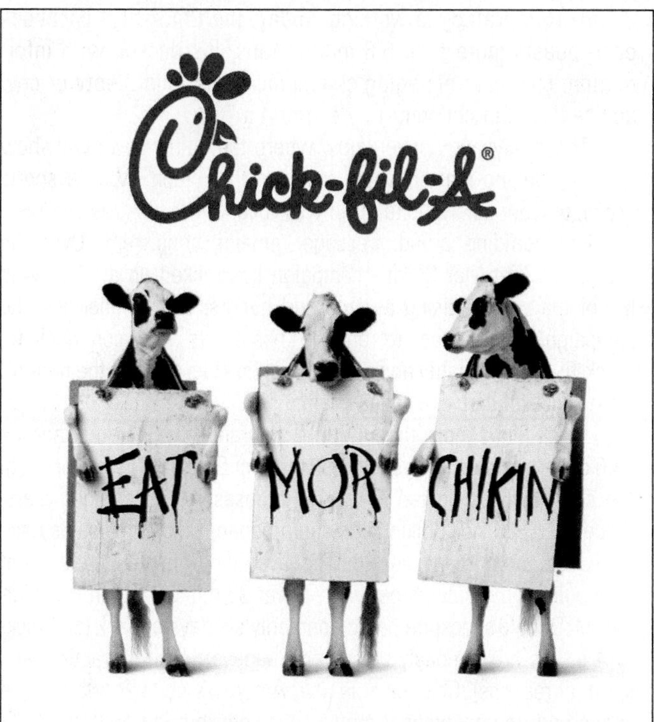

>> For nearly two decades, Chick-fil-A has stuck steadfastly to its simple but potent "Eat Mor Chikin" message, and the brand's rascally cows have now become pop culture icons.

PR Newswire.

First Stop

Chick-fil-A: A Remarkably Enduring Integrated Marketing Communications Campaign

Nearly two decades ago, regional fast-food chain Chick-fil-A set out in search of a promotion strategy that would set it apart from its big-three fast-food competitors—burger joints McDonald's, Burger King, and Wendy's. Chick-fil-A's strength had always been its signature fried chicken sandwich—you still won't find anything but chicken on the menu. But somehow, just saying "we make good chicken sandwiches" wasn't enough. Chick-fil-A needed a creative "big idea"—something memorable that would communicate the brand's unique value proposition.

What it came up with—of all things—was an improbable herd of renegade black-and-white cows that couldn't spell. Their message: "Eat Mor Chikin." Their goal: to convince consumers to switch from hamburgers to chicken. Acting in their own self-interest, the fearless cows realized that when people eat chicken, they don't eat beef. So in 1995, the first mischievous cow, paintbrush in mouth, painted "Eat Mor Chikin" on a billboard. From that first billboard, the effort has now grown to become one of the most consistent and enduring integrated marketing communications campaigns in history, a full multimedia campaign that has forever changed the burger-eating landscape.

The key to the "Eat Mor Chikin" campaign's success lies in its remarkable consistency. As industry publication *Advertising Age* pointed out when it recently crowned Chick-fil-A as its runner-up marketer of the year, "Often, the smartest marketing is the most patient marketing." And few promotion campaigns have been more persistently patient than this one. For more than 17 years, Chick-fil-A has stuck steadfastly to its simple but potent "Eat Mor Chikin" message, and the brand's racscally cows have now become pop culture icons.

Chick-fil-A's remarkably enduring "Eat Mor Chikin" integrated marketing communications campaign is more than just an advertising campaign. The renegade cows have "become part of our passion and our brand."

Building on the basic "Eat Mor Chikin" message, Chick-fil-A keeps the campaign fresh with an ever-changing mix of clever message executions and innovative media placements. Today, you find the cows just about anywhere and everywhere—from traditional television, print, and radio ads, to imaginative sales promotions and event sponsorships, to online social media and smartphone apps, with an occasional water tower still thrown in.

For example, in a TV ad promoting Chick-fil-A's growing breakfast menu, the pesky cows set off car alarm after car alarm, awakening an apartment building full of tenants to the message, "Wake up—itz chikin time." In print ads, the cows promote menu staples with taglines like "Milk shakes—the after chikin dinner drink." Billboards sport quotes such as "Lose that burger belly." During election years, the cows show their nonpartisanship with phrases like "Vote chikin. Itz not right wing or left." The ubiquitous cows even pull zany stunts, such as parachuting into football stadiums with signs reading "Du the wave. Eat the chikin."

Although the "Eat Mor Chikin" campaign has made plentiful use of the traditional media, it is perhaps the nontraditional promotional tactics that have won the cows a special place in the hearts of Chick-fil-A's fiercely loyal customers. Shortly after the start of the campaign, the company began its now-packed promotional merchandise catalogue with an annual cow-themed calendar. This year, it offered the first ever digital calendar, titled "Royal T-Bones," and paid tribute to some of the brand's more famous bovine royalty, such as Queen Elizabrisket—"though her appearance was soft, this skirt steak could be counted on to lead calfkind through tough times"—and Emperor Napoloin Bovinapart, the cow that "wasn't just a two-time emperor—he was also great commander of the militeryaki." Today, Chick-fil-A loyalists snap up large quantities of cow-themed mugs, T–shirts, stuffed animals, refrigerator magnets, laptop cases, and dozens of other items. These promotional items not only generate revenue, they also help to strengthen company–customer engagement while at the same time spreading the brand's "Eat Mor Chikin" message.

Chick-fil-A further engages customers through an assortment of in-store promotional events. Every July, for example, the company promotes "Cow Appreciation Day," on which customers who show up at any Chick-fil-A store dressed as a cow get a free meal. Last year, nearly 600,000 cow-clad customers cashed in on the event. And when a new Chick-fil-A restaurant opens, under the chain's "First 100" promotion, fans who camp out for 24 hours in advance of the opening get a chance to be one of the lucky 100 who win free Chick-fil-A meals for a year. While waiting, they'll likely meet Chick-fil-A CEO Dan Cathy—known for his customer-centered leadership style—who often camps out overnight with customers, signing T-shirts, posing for pictures, and ultimately handing out those vouchers for a free year's worth of Chick-fil-A.

Most recently, Chick-fil-A has taken its "Eat Mor Chikin" message to the social media, including Facebook, YouTube, Pinterest, and Twitter. When the company first plotted its social media strategy a few years back, it discovered that it already had a robust Facebook fan page with some 25,000 fans. The page was created by customer Brandy Bitzer, a true Chick-fil-A brand evangelist. In a genuine gesture of customer appreciation, Chick-fil-A joined forces with Bitzer, who continues to administer the page while the company provides assets to fuel enthusiasm for the brand. The strategy is working. Today, the Chick-fil-A Facebook page boasts more than 6.6 million fans. It's packed with information, customer-engaging communications, and plenty of cow advice like "Eat chikin or I'll de-friend u."

These days, you never know where the quirky cows will show up next. But no matter where you see them—on TV, in a sports arena, on your smartphone, or in your local Chick-fil-A restaurant—the long-standing brand message remains consistent. Over the years, the "Eat Mor Chikin" campaign has racked up a who's who list of major advertising awards and honors. More important, the campaign has helped to engage customers and communicate Chick-fil-A's personality and positioning, making it one of the nation's most successful quick-service chains.

Chick-fil-A's more than 1,700 restaurants in 39 states rang up $4.6 billion in sales last year. Since the first Chick-fil-A store opened, the company has posted revenue increases for 45 straight years. Since the "Eat Mor Chikin" campaign began, Chick-fil-A sales have increased more than six-fold. The average Chick-fil-A restaurant now pulls in more sales per year—over $3 million—than the average McDonald's, despite being open only six days a week (all Chick-fil-A stores are famously closed on Sundays for both practical and spiritual reasons). Chick-fil-A is now America's number-two chicken chain, and its phenomenal growth has contributed greatly to KFC's plummeting market share in the category.

In all, Chick-fil-A's now-classic but still-contemporary integrated marketing communications campaign "has been more successful than we ever imagined it could be," concludes the company's senior vice president of marketing. "The Cows started as part of our advertising campaign, and now they have become part of our passion and our brand." Who knows what the cows can accomplish in yet another 5 or 10 years. Whatever the future brings, the Chick-fil-A message will still be loud and clear: Eat Mor Chikin![1]

Author Comment
The promotion mix is the marketer's bag of tools for engaging and communicating with customers and other stakeholders. To deliver a clear and compelling message, each tool must be carefully coordinated under the concept of integrated marketing communications (IMC).

Building good customer relationships calls for more than just developing a good product, pricing it attractively, and making it available to target customers. Companies must also *communicate* their value propositions to customers, and what they communicate should not be left to chance. All communications must be planned and blended into carefully integrated programs. Just as good communication is important in building and maintaining any other kind of relationship, it is a crucial element in a company's efforts to engage customers and build profitable customer relationships.

The Promotion Mix

Promotion mix (or marketing communications mix)
The specific blend of promotion tools that the company uses to engage consumers, persuasively communicate customer value, and build customer relationships.

A company's total **promotion mix**—also called its **marketing communications mix**—consists of the specific blend of advertising, public relations, personal selling, sales promotion, and direct marketing tools that the company uses to engage consumers, persuasively communicate customer value, and build customer relationships. The five major promotion tools are defined as follows:[2]

- **Advertising**: Any paid form of nonpersonal presentation and promotion of ideas, goods, or services by an identified sponsor.
- **Sales promotion**: Short-term incentives to encourage the purchase or sale of a product or service.

Advertising
Any paid form of nonpersonal presentation and promotion of ideas, goods, or services by an identified sponsor.

Sales promotion
Short-term incentives to encourage the purchase or sale of a product or service.

Personal selling
Personal customer interactions by the firm's sales force for the purpose of making sales and building customer relationships.

Public relations (PR)
Building good relations with the company's various publics by obtaining favorable publicity, building up a good corporate image, and handling or heading off unfavorable rumors, stories, and events.

- **Personal selling**: Personal customer interactions by the firm's sales force for the purpose of making sales and building customer relationships.
- **Public relations**: Building good relations with the company's various publics by obtaining favorable publicity, building up a good corporate image, and handling or heading off unfavorable rumors, stories, and events.
- **Direct and digital marketing**: Engaging directly with carefully targeted individual consumers and customer communities to both obtain an immediate response and build lasting customer relationships.

Each category involves specific promotional tools that are used to communicate with customers. For example, *advertising* includes broadcast, print, Internet, mobile, outdoor, and other forms. *Sales promotion* includes discounts, coupons, displays, and demonstrations. *Personal selling* includes sales presentations, trade shows, and incentive programs. *Public relations (PR)* includes press releases, sponsorships, events, and Web pages. And *direct and digital marketing* includes direct mail, catalogs, online and social media, mobile marketing, and more.

At the same time, marketing communication goes beyond these specific promotion tools. The product's design, its price, the shape and color of its package, and the stores that sell it—*all* communicate something to buyers. Thus, although the promotion mix is the company's primary communications and engagement activity, the entire marketing mix—promotion, *as well as* product, price, and place—must be coordinated for greatest impact.

Author Comment
IMC is a *really* hot marketing topic these days. No other area of marketing is changing so quickly and profoundly. A big part of the reason is the huge surge in customer engagement through digital media—online, mobile, and social media marketing.

Integrated Marketing Communications

In past decades, marketers perfected the art of mass marketing: selling highly standardized products to masses of customers. In the process, they developed effective mass-media communications techniques to support these strategies. Large companies now routinely invest millions or even billions of dollars in television, magazine, or other mass-media advertising, reaching tens of millions of customers with a single ad. Today, however, marketing managers face some new marketing communications realities. Perhaps no other area of marketing is changing so profoundly as marketing communications, creating both exciting and anxious times for marketing communicators.

Direct and social-media marketing
Engaging and interacting directly with carefully targeted individual consumers and consumer communities to both obtain an immediate response and cultivate lasting customer relationships.

The New Marketing Communications Model

Several major factors are changing the face of today's marketing communications. First, *consumers* are changing. In this digital, wireless consumers are better informed and more communications empowered. Rather than relying on marketer-supplied information, they can use the Internet, social media, and other technologies to find information on their own. They can connect easily with other consumers to exchange brand-related information or even create their own brand messages.

Second, *marketing strategies* are changing. As mass markets have fragmented, marketers are shifting away from mass marketing. More and more, they are developing focused marketing programs designed to build closer relationships with customers in more narrowly defined micromarkets.

Finally, sweeping advances in *digital technology* are causing remarkable changes in the ways companies and customers communicate with each other. The digital age has spawned a host of new information and communication tools—from smartphones and tablets to satellite and cable television systems to the many faces of the Internet (brand Web sites, e-mail, blogs, social media and online communities, the mobile Web, and so much more). These explosive developments have had a dramatic impact on marketing communications. Just as mass marketing once gave rise to a new generation of mass-media communications, the new digital and social media have given birth to a more targeted, social, and engaging marketing communications model.

Although network television, magazines, newspapers, and other traditional mass media remain very important, their dominance is declining. In their place, advertisers are now adding a broad selection of more-specialized and highly targeted media to engage smaller customer segments with more-personalized, interactive content. The new media range from specialty cable television channels and made-for-the-Web videos to online display ads, Internet catalogs, e-mail and texting, blogs, mobile coupons and other content, and social media such as Twitter, Facebook, and Google+. Such new media have taken marketing by storm.

Some advertising industry experts even predict that the old mass-media communications model will eventually become obsolete. Mass-media costs are rising, audiences are shrinking, ad clutter is increasing, and viewers are gaining control of message exposure through technologies such as video streaming or DVRs that let them skip disruptive television commercials. As a result, the skeptics suggest, marketers are shifting ever-larger portions of their marketing budgets away from old-media mainstays and moving them to online, social, mobile, and other new-age media. In recent years, although TV still dominates as an advertising medium with a 40 percent share of global ad spending, its growth has stagnated. Spending in magazines, newspapers, and radio has lost considerable ground. Meanwhile, digital media have come from nowhere during the past few years to account for more than 18 percent of global advertising spending, second only to TV. By far the fastest-growing ad-spending category, digital's share is expected to grow to 23.4 percent by 2015.[3]

In some cases, marketers are skipping traditional media altogether. » For example, when Rovio Entertainment introduced the Angry Birds Space version of its popular game, it used only online video. It began by posting a 20-second video teaser containing only the game title and launch date—that video landed 2.2 million views. Next, in an inspired move, Rovio Entertainment teamed with NASA and astronaut Don Pettit to do a video in outer space on the International Space Station, which demonstrated the actual physics a stuffed Angry Bird in space—that video went viral. Six millions views and a few days later, Rovio Entertainment released a video trailer briefly introducing the game's characters, which grabbed another cool 1 million views in only two days. Finally, at launch time, Rovio Entertainment posted a two-minute video fully introducing the new game. In total, the award-winning video campaign reaped an astonishing 134 million views and 168,570 social shares.[4]

» The new marketing communications model: Rovio Entertainment introduced the Angry Birds Space version of its popular game using only an online video campaign. The campaign reaped an astonishing 134 million views and 168,570 social shares.

Similarly, eco-friendly household products maker Method recently employed a full but digital-only promotional campaign themed "Clean happy":[5]

Method is known for offbeat campaigns using slogans like "People against dirty" and "For the love of clean." But the most notable thing about the "Clean happy" campaign is that, unlike previous Method campaigns, it at first used zero ads in traditional media like TV or magazines. Instead, the centerpiece of the campaign was a two-minute brand video that could be watched only on YouTube and on the Method Facebook page. That video was followed at monthly intervals by four other clips that focused on individual Method products. The campaign also employed online media ads, as well as a major presence in social media that included, in addition to YouTube and Facebook, the Method Twitter feed and blogs.

The "Clean happy" campaign fit both Method's personality and its budget. "Method is the type of brand that benefits from word-of-mouth—from "the moms in mom groups telling each other about it," says a Method ad agency executive. Moreover, "Clean happy" ran a first-year budget of only about $3.5 million, compared with the whopping $150 million or so that rival P&G might spend to bring out a new product, such as its Tide Pods detergent packets. "We're embracing this grass-roots movement," says the Method ad executive. "When you don't have $150 million bucks, that's what you have to do." Method ran the digital-only campaign for a full year before beginning to bring it to TV.

In the new marketing communications world, rather than using old approaches that interrupt customers and force-feed them mass messages, new media formats let marketers reach smaller communities of consumers in more interactive, engaging ways. For example, think about television viewing these days. Consumers can now watch their favorite programs on just about anything with a screen—on televisions but also laptops, mobile phones, or tablets. And they can choose to watch programs whenever and wherever they wish, often without commercials. Increasingly, some programs, ads, and videos are being produced only for Internet viewing.

Despite the shift toward new digital media, however, traditional mass media still capture a lion's share of the promotion budgets of most major marketing firms, a fact that probably won't change quickly. For example, P&G, a leading proponent of digital media, still spends the majority of its huge advertising budget on mass media. Although P&G's digital outlay amounted to more than $173 million last year, digital still accounts for less than 5 percent of the company's annual advertising budget.[6]

Thus, rather than the old-media model rapidly collapsing, most industry insiders see a more gradual blending of new and traditional media. The new marketing communications model will consist of a shifting mix of both traditional mass media and a wide array of online, mobile, and social media that engage more-targeted consumer communities in a more-personalized, interactive way.

Many advertisers and ad agencies are still grappling with this transition. In the end, however, regardless of the communications channel, the key is to integrate all of these media in a way that best engages customers, communicates the brand message, and enhances the customer's brand experience. As the marketing communications environment shifts, so will the role of marketing communicators. Rather than just creating and placing "TV ads" or "print ads" or "Facebook display ads," many marketers now view themselves more broadly as **brand content managers**. As such, they create, inspire, and share brand messages and conversations with and among customers across a fluid mix of *paid, owned, earned,* and *shared* communications channels. These channels include media that are both traditional and new, and controlled and not controlled (see Marketing at Work 12.1).

Brand content management
Creating, inspiring, and sharing brand messages and conversations with and among consumers across a fluid mix of paid, owned, earned, and shared channels.

The Need for *Integrated* Marketing Communications

The shift toward a richer mix of media and communication approaches poses a problem for marketers. Consumers today are bombarded by commercial messages from a broad range of sources. But consumers don't distinguish between message sources the way marketers do. In the consumer's mind, messages from different sources and promotional approaches—whether it's a Super Bowl ad, store display, or a friend's social media post—all become part of a single message about the company. Conflicting messages from these different sources can result in confused company images, brand positions, and customer relationships.

All too often, companies fail to integrate their various communications channels. The result is a hodgepodge of communications to consumers. Mass-media ads say one thing, whereas an in-store promotion sends a different signal, and the company's Internet site, e-mails, Facebook page, or videos posted on YouTube say something altogether different. The problem is that these communications often come from different parts of the company. Advertising messages are planned and implemented by the advertising department or an ad agency. Other company departments or agencies are responsible for public relations (PR), sales promotion events, and online or social media efforts. However, whereas companies may have separated their communications tools, customers don't. Mixed communications from these sources result in blurred brand perceptions by consumers.

The new world of online and social media marketing, tablet computers, smartphones, and apps presents tremendous opportunities but also big challenges. It can "give companies increased access to their customers, fresh insights into their preferences, and a broader creative palette to work with," says one marketing executive. But "the biggest issue is complexity and fragmentation . . . the amount of choice out there," says another. The challenge is to "make it come together in an organized way."[7]

MARKETING AT WORK 12.1

Brand Content Management: Paid, Owned, Earned, and Shared

In the good old days, life seemed so simple for advertisers: Come up with a good creative idea, develop a media plan, produce and run a set of TV commercials and magazine ads, and maybe issue a press release to stir up some news. But today's marketing communications landscape seems more complex, characterized by a spate of new digital and social media and rapidly blurring lines within and between traditional and new channels. The old practice of placing "advertisements" in well-defined "media," within the tidy framework of a carefully managed promotional campaign, doesn't work as well as it once did.

Traditional message and media classifications just don't fit like they used to. For example, a TV ad isn't really just a TV ad anymore. Instead, it's "video content" that might be seen anywhere—on a consumer's TV screen but also on a PC, tablet, or phone. Other brand video content looks a lot like TV advertising but was never intended for TV, such as made-for-the-Web videos posted on YouTube, Facebook, or other social media. Video content about the brand may even be prepared by consumers and shared with others online.

Similarly, printed brand messages and pictures no longer appear only in carefully crafted ads placed in magazines, newspapers, or direct mail pieces. Instead, such content, created by a variety of sources, pops up in anything from formal advertisements and brand Web pages to consumer posts on online social media and editorials by independent bloggers. In the hands of today's empowered consumers, the creation and distribution of brand messages can—and often does—take on a life of its own, beyond the design or control of the brand's marketers.

As a result, as the message and media environments are changing, so are the old notions about placing "ads" in well-defined "media." Instead of creating "TV ads" or "print ads" or "PR press releases," many marketers now view themselves more broadly as creating, sharing, and managing "brand content" and leveraging it across a wealth of integrated communications channels—both traditional and new, controlled and not controlled. This new thinking has led to a new marketing communications framework. Rather than classifying communications by traditional media breakdowns, the new framework builds on the broader concept of how and by whom brand content is created, controlled, and distributed. The new classification identifies four major types of media: paid, owned, earned, and shared (POES):

Paid media—includes promotional channels paid for by the sponsor, including traditional media (such as TV, radio, print, or outdoor) and online and digital media (paid search ads, Web and social media display ads, mobile ads, or e-mail marketing).

Owned media—includes promotional channels owned and controlled by the company, including company Web sites, corporate blogs, owned social media pages, proprietary brand communities, sales forces, and events.

Earned media—includes PR media channels, such as television, newspapers, blogs, online video sites, and other media not directly paid for or controlled by the marketer but that include the content because of viewer, reader, or user interest.

Shared media—includes media shared by consumers with other consumers, such as social media, blogs, mobile media, and viral channels, as well as traditional word of mouth.

In the past, marketers have focused on traditional paid (broadcast, print) or earned (public relations) media. Now, however, they are rapidly adding the new generation of owned (Web sites, blogs, brand communities) and shared (online social networks, mobile, e-mail) media. Whereas a successful paid ad or PR piece used to be an end in itself, marketers are now asking "What else can I do with this content?" The marketer's goal is to leverage the combined power of all the POES channels. "The important thing is to be in all streams—paid, owned, earned, and shared—so the message is heard," says one expert.

Careful integration across the POES channels can produce striking communications results. A now-classic example is the highly successful Old Spice "The Man Your Man Could Smell Like" campaign, featuring football player Isaiah Mustafa. The campaign began with TV commercials (paid), which Old Spice then posted to its Web site and its YouTube and Facebook pages (owned). The campaign quickly went viral, as consumers by the millions buzzed about the ads through e-mail, Facebook, and Twitter (shared). In turn, Old Spice received seemingly endless media coverage on everything from network TV to professional blog editorials (earned). In all, the campaign was viewed and discussed hundreds of millions of times across dozens of channels, all voicing the same integrated brand message.

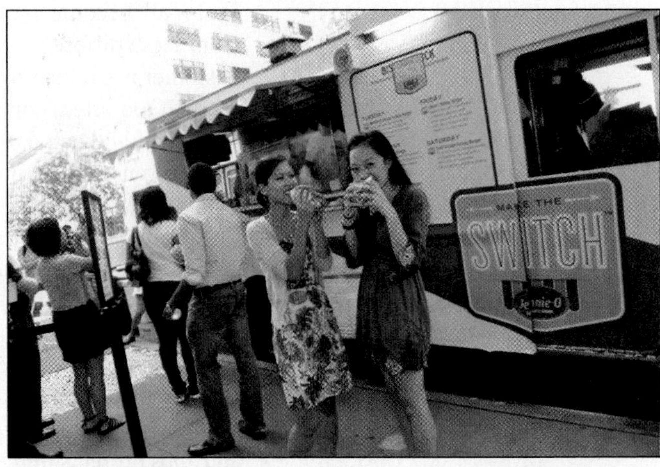

>> Hormel's JENNIE-O turkey brand successfully leveraged its imaginative "Make the Switch" campaign across paid, owned, earned, and shared media.

Here's another example of a brand that successfully leveraged its campaign across paid, owned, earned, and shared media:

> Hormel's wholly-owned subsidiary JENNIE-O Turkey Store wanted to find a way to get consumers to appreciate how easy—and tasty—it was to substitute JENNIE-O ground turkey in recipes that called for ground beef. To get things cooking, it staged an imaginative "Make the Switch" marketing event (owned media). For five days, JENNIE-O took over the Bistro Truck, a popular Manhattan food truck, wrapping it with "Make the Switch" banners. Instead of ground beef, the truck's burgers were made from ground turkey. Each day, courtesy of JENNIE-O, the truck gave away 500 free gourmet turkey burgers at lunch. The truck's location and menu were previewed to local foodies and bloggers (earned media), and posted daily on Facebook, Twitter, Pinterest, and a special microsite (owned media). Then, the social media universe took over (shared media). About 450,000 tweets and retweets mentioned the "Make the Switch" promotion and locations. People lined up for thousands of free JENNIE-O burgers. Within five days the Facebook page had 23,000 "likes," and ground turkey sales rose 7 percent in New York. The "Make the Switch" takeover was so successful it has been extended to other cities and has become the subject of JENNIE-O TV commercials (paid).

Thus, today's shifting and sometimes chaotic marketing communications environment calls for more than simply creating and placing some ads in well-defined and controlled media spaces. Rather, it calls for inspired brand content management, an integrated effort to create, inspire, and share the right brand content, whatever the sources, and help it catch fire. Today's marketing communicators must be more than just advertising copywriters or media analysts. They must be brand content strategists, creators, connectors, and catalysts who manage brand conversations with and among customers across a fluid mix of message channels. That's a tall order, but with today's new communications thinking, anything is POES–ible!

Sources: Extract example and quotes from Julie Liesse, "The Big Idea," *Advertising Age*, November 28, 2011, pp. C4–C6; with additional information from Julie Liesse, "Top Trends for 2012," *Advertising Age*, November 28, 2011, p. C8; Peter Himler, "Paid, Earned & Owned: Revisited," Theflack.blogspot.com, June 21, 2011; Natalie Zmuda, "Solving the Content Creation Conundrum," *Advertising Age*, January 14, 2013, pp. 12–13; and www.hormelfoods.com/brands/jennie0/, www.switchtoturkey.com, and www.facebook.com/jennieoturkey/app_175338739199041, accessed October 2013. JENNIE-O® and "Make the Switch®" are registered trademarks of JENNIE-O Turkey Store, LLC.

Integrated marketing communications (IMC)
Carefully integrating and coordinating the company's many communications channels to deliver a clear, consistent, and compelling message about the organization and its products.

To that end, more companies today are adopting the concept of **integrated marketing communications (IMC)**. Under this concept, as illustrated in >> **Figure 12.1**, the company carefully integrates its many communications channels to deliver a clear, consistent, and compelling message about the organization and its brands.

Integrated marketing communications calls for recognizing all touch points where the customer may encounter the company and its brands. Each contact with the brand will deliver a message—whether good, bad, or indifferent. The company's goal should be to deliver a consistent and positive message at each contact. Integrated marketing communications ties together all of the company's messages and images. Its television and print ads have the same message, look, and feel as its e-mail and personal selling communications. And its PR materials project the same image as its Web site, online social media, or mobile marketing efforts. Often, different media play unique roles in attracting, informing, and

>> **Figure 12.1** Integrated Marketing Communications

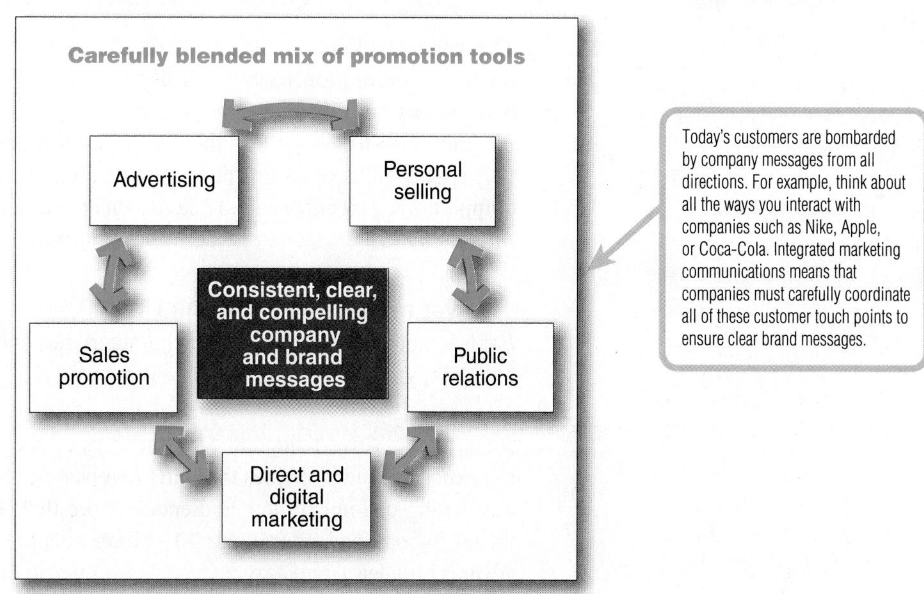
Carefully blended mix of promotion tools
Advertising
Personal selling
Consistent, clear, and compelling company and brand messages
Sales promotion
Public relations
Direct and digital marketing
Today's customers are bombarded by company messages from all directions. For example, think about all the ways you interact with companies such as Nike, Apple, or Coca-Cola. Integrated marketing communications means that companies must carefully coordinate all of these customer touch points to ensure clear brand messages.

persuading consumers; these roles must be carefully coordinated under the overall marketing communications plan.

A great example of a well-integrated marketing communications effort is Coca-Cola's recent "Mirage" campaign. Built around two Super Bowl XLVII ads, the campaign integrated the clout of traditional big-budget TV advertising with the interactive power of social media to create real-time customer engagement with the Coke brand:[8]

Integrated marketing communications: Coca-Cola's "Mirage" campaign. The campaign integrated the clout of traditional big-budget TV advertising with the social power of the social media to create real-time customer engagement with the Coke brand.

Associated Press.

Coca-Cola's "Mirage" tells the story of three bands of desert vagabonds—Cowboys, Showgirls, and *Mad Max*-inspired "Badlanders"—as they trek through the blazing-hot desert pursuing the same elusive mirage—a frosty bottle of Coca-Cola. The Mirage campaign began two weeks before the Super Bowl with a 30-second teaser ad on *American Idol* and posted on YouTube and other online destinations inviting fans to visit CokeChase.com to get to know the story and teams. Then, during the game, a 60-second Mirage ad set up the exciting chase, with a cliff-hanging close that urged viewers to visit CokeChase.com, where they could help decide the outcome by casting votes for their favorite team and throwing obstacles in front of rival teams. During the rest of the game, Coca-Cola listening teams monitored related activity on major social media, and put fans in the middle of the action by posting real-time chase updates on Facebook, YouTube, and Twitter and chase photos on Tumblr and Instagram. After the end of the game, a second Mirage ad announced the chase team with the most viewer votes—the Showgirls, in their glam pink and silver outfits, won the Coke. But the real winner was Coca-Cola. The Mirage campaign exceeded all expectations. In addition to the usual huge Super Bowl audience numbers, during the game, the campaign captured an eye-popping 8.2 million online and social-media interactions and 910,000 votes, far exceeding the brand's internal goals of 1.6 million interactions and 400,000 votes.

In the past, no one person or department was responsible for thinking through the communication roles of the various promotion tools and coordinating the promotion mix. To help implement integrated marketing communications, some companies have appointed a marketing communications director who has overall responsibility for the company's communications efforts. This helps to produce better communications consistency and greater sales impact. It places the responsibility in someone's hands—where none existed before—to unify the company's image as it is shaped by thousands of company activities.

Author Comment

In this section, we'll look at how marketers blend the various marketing communication tools into a smooth-functioning integrated promotion mix.

Shaping the Overall Promotion Mix

The concept of integrated marketing communications suggests that the company must blend the promotion tools carefully into a coordinated *promotion mix*. But how does it determine what mix of promotion tools to use? Companies within the same industry differ greatly in the design of their promotion mixes. For example, cosmetics maker Mary Kay spends most of its promotion funds on personal selling and direct marketing, whereas competitor CoverGirl spends heavily on consumer advertising. We now look at factors that influence the marketer's choice of promotion tools.

The Nature of Each Promotion Tool

Each promotion tool has unique characteristics and costs. Marketers must understand these characteristics in shaping the promotion mix.

Advertising. Advertising can reach masses of geographically dispersed buyers at a low cost per exposure, and it enables the seller to repeat a message many times. For example, television advertising can reach huge audiences. More than 108 million Americans watched the most recent Super Bowl, more than 40 million people watched at least part of the last Academy Awards broadcast, and as many as 23 million avid fans tuned in each week for the latest season of *NCIS*. What's more, a popular TV ad's reach can be extended through online and social media. For example, in addition to the 100+ plus million TV viewers, Tide's popular Super Bowl XLVII ad featuring a "miracle" Joe Montana–shaped salsa stain on a San Francisco 49er fan's jersey (his wife, a Baltimore Ravens fan, washed it out with Tide!) garnered an estimated 1.5 billion free impressions in the form of online and social media views, tweets, and posts. For companies that want to reach a mass audience, TV is the place to be.[9]

Beyond its reach, large-scale advertising says something positive about the seller's size, popularity, and success. Because of advertising's public nature, consumers tend to view advertised products as more legitimate. Advertising is also very expressive; it allows the company to dramatize its products through the artful use of visuals, print, sound, and color. On the one hand, advertising can be used to build up a long-term image for a product (such as Coca-Cola ads). On the other hand, advertising can trigger quick sales (as when Kohl's advertises weekend specials).

Advertising also has some shortcomings. Although it reaches many people quickly, advertising is impersonal and lacks the direct persuasiveness of company salespeople. For the most part, advertising can carry on only a one-way communication with an audience, and the audience does not feel that it has to pay attention or respond. In addition, advertising can be very costly. Although some advertising forms, such as newspaper and radio advertising, can be done on smaller budgets, other forms, such as network TV advertising, require very large budgets.

Personal Selling. Personal selling is the most effective tool at certain stages of the buying process, particularly in building up buyers' preferences, convictions, and actions. It involves personal interaction between two or more people, so each person can observe the other's needs and characteristics and make quick adjustments. Personal selling also allows all kinds of customer relationships to spring up, ranging from matter-of-fact selling relationships to personal friendships. An effective salesperson keeps the customer's interests at heart to build a long-term relationship by solving a customer's problems. >> Finally, with personal selling, the buyer usually feels a greater need to listen and respond, even if the response is a polite "No thank-you."

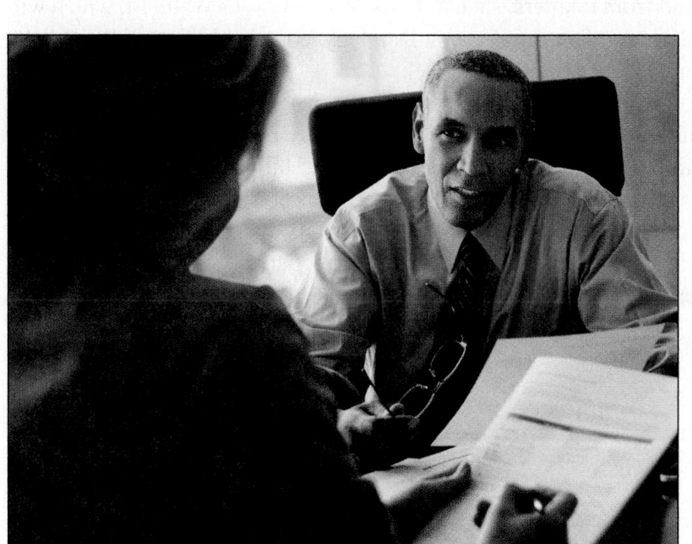

>> With personal selling, the customer feels a greater need to listen and respond, even if the response is a polite "No thank you."

SelectStock.

These unique qualities come at a cost, however. A sales force requires a longer-term commitment than does advertising—although advertising can be turned up or down, the size of a sales force is harder to change. Personal selling is also the company's most expensive promotion tool, costing companies on average $600 or more per sales call, depending on the industry.[10] U.S. firms spend up to three times as much on personal selling as they do on advertising.

Sales Promotion. Sales promotion includes a wide assortment of tools—coupons, contests, discounts, premiums, and others—all of which have many unique qualities. They attract consumer attention, offer strong incentives to purchase, and can be used to dramatize product offers and boost sagging sales. Sales promotions invite and reward quick response. Whereas advertising says, "Buy our product," sales promotion says, "Buy it now." Sales promotion effects are often short lived, however, and often are not as effective as advertising or personal selling in building long-run brand preference and customer relationships.

Public Relations. Public relations is very believable—news stories, features, sponsorships, and events seem more real and believable to readers than ads do. PR can also reach many prospects who avoid salespeople and advertisements—the message gets to buyers as "news" rather than as a sales-directed communication. And, as with advertising, public relations can dramatize a company or product. Marketers tend to underuse public relations or use it as an afterthought. Yet a well-thought-out public relations campaign used with other promotion mix elements can be very effective and economical.

Direct and Digital Marketing. The many forms of direct and digital marketing—from direct mail, catalogs, and telephone marketing to online, mobile, and social media—all share some distinctive characteristics. Direct marketing is more targeted: It's usually directed to a specific customer or customer community. Direct marketing is immediate and personalized: Messages can be prepared quickly—even in real time—and tailored to appeal to specific consumers or brand groups. Finally, direct marketing is interactive: It allows a dialogue between the marketing team and the consumer, and messages can be altered depending on the consumer's response. Thus, direct and digital marketing are well suited to highly targeted marketing efforts, creating customer engagement, and building one-to-one customer relationships.

Promotion Mix Strategies

Marketers can choose from two basic promotion mix strategies: *push* promotion or *pull* promotion. **Figure 12.2** contrasts the two strategies. The relative emphasis given to the specific promotion tools differs for push and pull strategies. A **push strategy** involves "pushing" the product through marketing channels to final consumers. The producer directs its marketing activities (primarily personal selling and trade promotion) toward channel members to induce them to carry the product and promote it to final consumers. For example, John Deere does very little promoting of its lawn mowers, garden tractors, and other residential consumer products to final consumers. Instead, John Deere's sales force works with Lowe's, Home Depot, independent dealers, and other channel members, who in turn push John Deere products to final consumers.

Push strategy
A promotion strategy that calls for using the sales force and trade promotion to push the product through channels. The producer promotes the product to channel members, which in turn promote it to final consumers.

Using a **pull strategy**, the producer directs its marketing activities (primarily advertising, consumer promotion, and direct and digital media) toward final consumers to induce them to buy the product. For example, Unilever promotes its Axe grooming products directly to its young male target market using TV and print ads, a brand Web site, its YouTube channel and Facebook page, and other channels. If the pull strategy is effective, consumers will then demand the brand from retailers, such as CVS, Walgreens, or Walmart, which will in turn demand it from Unilever. Thus, under a pull strategy, consumer demand "pulls" the product through the channels.

Pull strategy
A promotion strategy that calls for spending a lot on consumer advertising and promotion to induce final consumers to buy the product, creating a demand vacuum that "pulls" the product through the channel.

Some industrial-goods companies use only push strategies; likewise, some direct marketing companies use only pull strategies. However, most large companies use some combination of both. For example, Unilever spends more than $8.5 billion worldwide each year on consumer marketing and sales promotions to create brand preference and pull customers into stores that carry its products.[11] At the same time, it uses its own and distributors' sales forces and trade promotions to push its brands through the channels, so that they will be available on store shelves when consumers come calling.

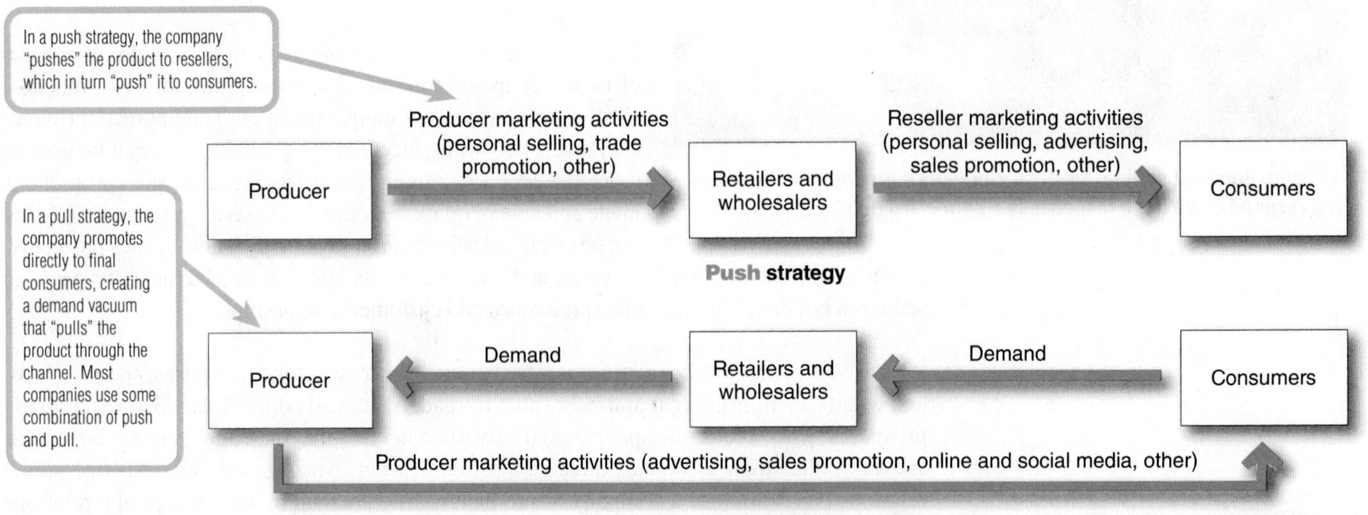

Figure 12.2 Push versus Pull Promotion Strategy

Companies consider many factors when designing their promotion mix strategies, including the type of product and market. For example, the importance of different promotion tools varies between consumer and business markets. Business-to-consumer companies usually pull more, putting more of their funds into advertising, followed by sales promotion, personal selling, and then public relations. In contrast, business-to-business marketers tend to push more, putting more of their funds into personal selling, followed by sales promotion, advertising, and public relations.

Now that we've examined the concept of integrated marketing communications and the factors that firms consider when shaping their promotion mixes, let's look more closely at the specific marketing communications tools.

SPEED BUMP LINKING THE CONCEPTS

Pause here for a few minutes. Flip back through and link the parts of the chapter you've read so far.

- How do the *integrated marketing communications (IMC)* and *promotion mix* concepts relate to one another?
- How has the changing communications environment affected the ways in which companies communicate with you about their products and services? If you were in the market for a new car, where might you hear about various available models? Where would you *search* for information?

Author Comment
You already know a lot about advertising—you are exposed to it every day. But here we'll look behind the scenes at how companies make advertising decisions.

Advertising

Advertising can be traced back to the very beginnings of recorded history. Archaeologists working in countries around the Mediterranean Sea have dug up signs announcing various events and offers. The Romans painted walls to announce gladiator fights and the Phoenicians painted pictures on large rocks to promote their wares along parade routes. During the golden age in Greece, town criers announced the sale of cattle, crafted items, and even cosmetics. An early "singing commercial" went as follows: "For eyes that are shining, for cheeks like the dawn/For beauty that lasts after girlhood is gone/For prices in reason, the woman who knows/Will buy her cosmetics from Aesclyptos."

Modern advertising, however, is a far cry from these early efforts. U.S. advertisers now run up an estimated annual bill of almost $140 billion on measured advertising media; worldwide ad spending is an estimated $557 billion. P&G, the world's largest advertiser, last year spent almost $5 billion on U.S. advertising and $11.2 billion worldwide.[12]

Although advertising is used mostly by business firms, a wide range of not-for-profit organizations, professionals, and social agencies also use advertising to promote their causes to various target publics. In fact, the 56th largest advertising spender is a not-for-profit organization—the U.S. government, which advertises in many ways. For example, its Centers for Disease Control spent $48 million on the second year of an anti-smoking advertising campaign titled "A Tip from a Former Smoker," showing people who have paid dearly due to smoking-related diseases.[13] Advertising is a good way to inform and persuade, whether the purpose is to sell Coca-Cola worldwide or educate people in developing nations on how to lead healthier lives.

Marketing management must make four important decisions when developing an advertising program (see >> **Figure 12.3**): *setting advertising objectives, setting the advertising budget, developing advertising strategy (message decisions and media decisions), and evaluating advertising campaigns.*

Setting Advertising Objectives

The first step is to set *advertising objectives*. These objectives should be based on past decisions about the target market, positioning, and the marketing mix, which define the job

>> Figure 12.3 Major Advertising Decisions

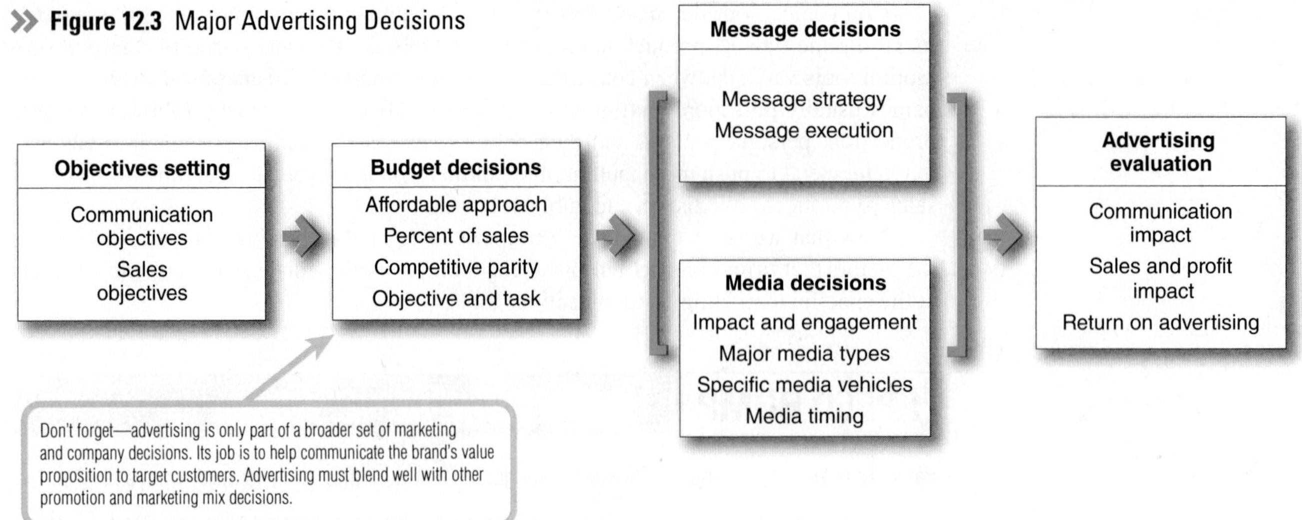

that advertising must do in the total marketing program. The overall advertising objective is to help engage customers and build customer relationships by communicating customer value. Here, we discuss specific advertising objectives.

Advertising objective
A specific communication task to be accomplished with a specific target audience during a specific period of time.

An **advertising objective** is a specific communication *task* to be accomplished with a specific *target* audience during a specific period of *time*. Advertising objectives can be classified by their primary purpose—to *inform*, *persuade*, or *remind*. **>>Table 12.1** lists examples of each of these specific objectives.

Informative advertising is used heavily when introducing a new product category. In this case, the objective is to build primary demand. Thus, early producers of HDTVs first had to inform consumers of the image quality and size benefits of the new product. *Persuasive advertising* becomes more important as competition increases. Here, the

>> Table 12.1 Possible Advertising Objectives

Informative Advertising	
Communicating customer value	Suggesting new uses for a product
Building a brand and company image	Informing the market of a price change
Telling the market about a new product	Describing available services and support
Explaining how a product works	Correcting false impressions
Persuasive Advertising	
Building brand preference	Persuading customers to purchase now
Encouraging switching to a brand	Creating customer engagement
Changing customer perceptions of product value	Building brand community
Reminder Advertising	
Maintaining customer relationships	Reminding consumers where to buy the product
Reminding consumers that the product may be needed in the near future	Keeping the brand in a customer's mind during off-seasons

» Microsoft's "Bing It On" campaign urged consumers to make side-by-side comparisons of the search results from its Bing search engine versus Google's. It claims that people making the comparison chose Bing by nearly 2 to 1.

Microsoft.

company's objective is to build selective demand. For example, once HDTVs became established, Samsung began trying to persuade consumers that *its* brand offered the best quality for their money. Such advertising wants to engage customers and create brand community.

Some persuasive advertising has become *comparative advertising* (or *attack advertising*), in which a company directly or indirectly compares its brand with one or more other brands. You see examples of comparative advertising in almost every product category, ranging from sports drinks and soup to car rentals, credit cards, wireless phone services, and even retail pricing. For example, Walmart recently ran reality-type local TV ads directly comparing its prices against those on shopper cash-register receipts from specific competitors such as Best Buy, Toys 'R' Us, Kroger, and other supermarket rivals.[14] » And Microsoft ran a campaign directly comparing its Bing search engine to Google's search engine. The "Bing It On" campaign challenged consumers to make side-by-side comparisons of search results without knowing which results were from which search engine. According to Microsoft, to the surprise of many people, those making the comparison choose Bing over Google by a 2-to-1 margin. Microsoft backed the "Bing It On" challenge with an advertising campaign claiming that "people prefer Bing over Google 2–1."[15]

Advertisers should use comparative advertising with caution. All too often, such ads invite competitor responses, resulting in an advertising war that neither competitor can win. Upset competitors might also take more drastic action, such as filing complaints with the self-regulatory National Advertising Division of the Council of Better Business Bureaus or even filing false-advertising lawsuits. For example, Sara Lee's Ball Park brand hot dogs and Kraft's Oscar Mayer brand recently waged a nearly two-year "weiner war." It started when Sara Lee sued Kraft, challenging advertising claims that Oscar Mayer franks had won a national taste test over Ball Park and other brands and that they were "100% beef." Kraft, in turn, filed a countersuit, accusing Sara Lee of making similar advertising misstatements about its own "all-beef" Ball Park hot dogs, along with claims touting Ball Park as "America's best." By the time the lawsuits were settled, about all that the competitors had accomplished was to publicly call into question the taste and contents of both hot dog brands.[16]

Reminder advertising is important for mature products; it helps to maintain customer relationships and keep consumers thinking about the product. Expensive Coca-Cola television ads primarily build and maintain the Coca-Cola brand relationship rather than inform consumers or persuade them to buy it in the short run.

Advertising's goal is to help move consumers through the buying process. Some advertising is designed to move people to immediate action. For example, a direct-response television ad by Weight Watchers urges consumers to go online and sign up right away, and a Best Buy newspaper insert for a weekend sale encourages immediate store visits. However, many ads focus on building or strengthening long-term customer relationships. For example, a Nike television ad in which well-known athletes work through extreme challenges in their Nike gear never directly asks for a sale. Instead, the goal is to somehow change the way the customers think or feel about the brand.

Setting the Advertising Budget

Advertising budget
The dollars and other resources allocated to a product or a company advertising program.

After determining its advertising objectives, the company next sets its **advertising budget** for each product. Here, we look at four common methods used to set the total budget for advertising: the *affordable method*, the *percentage-of-sales method*, the *competitive-parity method*, and the *objective-and-task method*.[17]

Affordable Method

Affordable method
Setting the promotion budget at the level management thinks the company can afford.

Some companies use the **affordable method**: They set the promotion budget at the level they think the company can afford. Small businesses often use this method, reasoning that a company cannot spend more on advertising than it has. They start with total revenues, deduct operating expenses and capital outlays, and then devote some portion of the remaining funds to advertising.

Unfortunately, this method of setting budgets completely ignores the effects of promotion on sales. It tends to place promotion last among spending priorities, even in situations in which advertising is critical to the firm's success. It leads to an uncertain annual promotion budget, which makes long-range market planning difficult. Although the affordable method can result in overspending on advertising, it more often results in underspending.

Percentage-of-Sales Method

Percentage-of-sales method
Setting the promotion budget at a certain percentage of current or forecasted sales or as a percentage of the unit sales price.

Other companies use the **percentage-of-sales method**, setting their promotion budget at a certain percentage of current or forecasted sales. Or they budget a percentage of the unit sales price. The percentage-of-sales method has advantages. It is simple to use and helps management think about the relationships between promotion spending, selling price, and profit per unit.

Despite these claimed advantages, however, the percentage-of-sales method has little to justify it. It wrongly views sales as the *cause* of promotion rather than as the *result*. Although studies have found a positive correlation between promotional spending and brand strength, this relationship often turns out to be effect and cause, not cause and effect. Stronger brands with higher sales can afford the biggest ad budgets.

Thus, the percentage-of-sales budget is based on availability of funds rather than on opportunities. It may prevent the increased spending sometimes needed to turn around falling sales. Because the budget varies with year-to-year sales, long-range planning is difficult. Finally, the method does not provide any basis for choosing a *specific* percentage, except what has been done in the past or what competitors are doing.

Competitive-Parity Method

Competitive-parity method
Setting the promotion budget to match competitors' outlays.

Still other companies use the **competitive-parity method**, setting their promotion budgets to match competitors' outlays. They monitor competitors' advertising or get industry promotion spending estimates from publications or trade associations, and then set their budgets based on the industry average.

Two arguments support this method. First, competitors' budgets represent the collective wisdom of the industry. Second, spending what competitors spend helps prevent promotion wars. Unfortunately, neither argument is valid. There are no grounds for believing that the competition has a better idea of what a company should be spending on promotion than does the company itself. Companies differ greatly, and each has its own special promotion needs. Finally, there is no evidence that budgets based on competitive parity prevent promotion wars.

Objective-and-Task Method

Objective-and-task method
Developing the promotion budget by (1) defining specific objectives, (2) determining the tasks that must be performed to achieve these objectives, and (3) estimating the costs of performing these tasks. The sum of these costs is the proposed promotion budget.

The most logical budget-setting method is the **objective-and-task method**, whereby the company sets its promotion budget based on what it wants to accomplish with promotion. This budgeting method entails (1) defining specific promotion objectives, (2) determining the tasks needed to achieve these objectives, and (3) estimating the costs of performing these tasks. The sum of these costs is the proposed promotion budget.

The advantage of the objective-and-task method is that it forces management to spell out its assumptions about the relationship between dollars spent and promotion results. But it is also the most difficult method to use. Often, it is hard to figure out which specific tasks will achieve stated objectives. For example, suppose Microsoft wants 75 percent awareness for the latest version of its Surface tablet during the three-month introductory period. What specific advertising messages and media schedules should Microsoft use to attain this objective? How much would these messages and media schedules cost? Microsoft management must consider such questions, even though they are hard to answer.

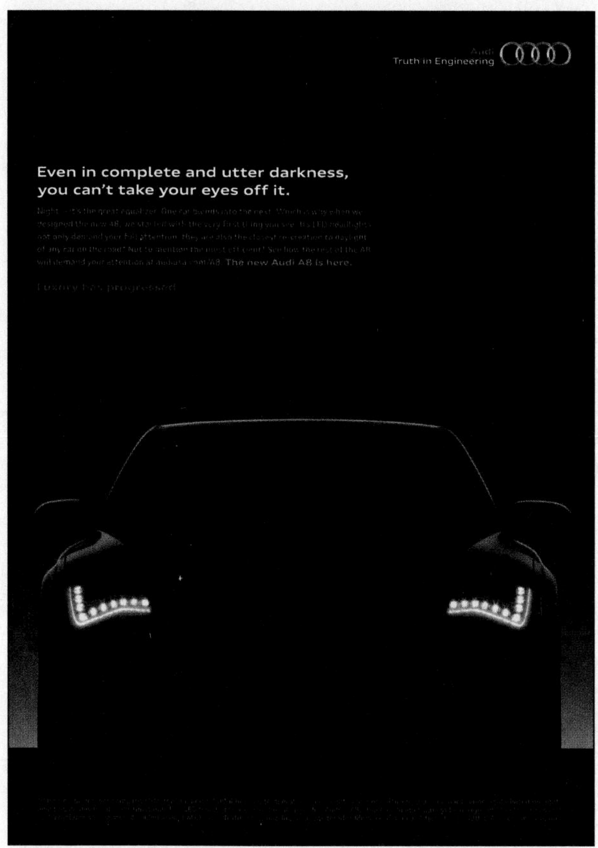
Audi
Truth in Engineering
Even in complete and utter darkness,
you can't take your eyes off it.
The new Audi A8 is here.

» Setting the promotion budget: Promotion spending is one of the easiest items to cut in tough economic times. But Audi gained competitive advantage by keeping its foot on the promotion pedal as competitors retrenched.

Used with permission of Audi of America.

No matter what method is used, setting the advertising budget is no easy task. John Wanamaker, the department store magnate, once said, "I know that half of my advertising is wasted, but I don't know which half. I spent $2 million for advertising, and I don't know if that is half enough or twice too much."

As a result of such thinking, advertising is one of the easiest budget items to cut when economic times get tough. Cuts in brand-building advertising appear to do little short-term harm to sales. For example, in the wake of the recent Great Recession, U.S. advertising expenditures plummeted 12 percent over the previous year. In the long run, however, slashing ad spending risks long-term damage to a brand's image and market share. In fact, companies that can maintain or even increase their advertising spending while competitors are decreasing theirs can gain competitive advantage.

»For example, during the recent Great Recession, while competitors were cutting back, car maker Audi actually increased its marketing and advertising spending. Audi "kept its foot on the pedal while everyone else is pulling back," said an Audi ad executive at the time. "Why would we go backwards now when the industry is generally locking the brakes and cutting spending?" As a result, Audi's brand awareness and buyer consideration reached record levels during the recession, outstripping those of BMW, Mercedes, and Lexus, and positioning Audi strongly for the post-recession era. In the post-recession economy, Audi is now one of the hottest auto brands on the market.[18]

Developing Advertising Strategy

Advertising strategy consists of two major elements: creating advertising *messages* and selecting advertising *media*. In the past, companies often viewed media planning as secondary to the message-creation process. After the creative department created good advertisements, the media department then selected and purchased the best media for carrying those advertisements to the desired target audiences. This often caused friction between creatives and media planners.

Advertising strategy
The strategy by which the company accomplishes its advertising objectives. It consists of two major elements: creating advertising messages and selecting advertising media.

Today, however, soaring media costs, more-focused target marketing strategies, and the blizzard of new online, mobile, and social media have promoted the importance of the media-planning function. The decision about which media to use for an ad campaign—television, newspapers, magazines, a Web site or online social media, mobile devices, or e-mail—is now sometimes more critical than the creative elements of the campaign. Also, brand content and messages are now often co-created through interactions with and among consumers. As a result, more and more advertisers are orchestrating a closer harmony between their messages and the media that deliver them. As discussed earlier, the goal is to create and manage brand content across a full range of media, whether they are paid, owned, earned, or shared.

Creating the Advertising Message

No matter how big the budget, advertising can succeed only if it gains attention, engages consumers, and communicates well. Good advertising messages and content are especially important in today's costly and cluttered advertising environment. In 1950, the average U.S. household received only three network television channels and a handful of major national magazines. Today, the average household receives about 135 channels, and consumers have more than 20,000 magazines from which to choose.[19] Add in the countless radio stations and a continuous barrage of catalogs, direct mail, out-of-home media, e-mail, and online, mobile, and social media exposures, and consumers are being bombarded with ads at home, work, and all points in between.

Breaking through the Clutter. If all this advertising clutter bothers some consumers, it also causes huge headaches for advertisers. Take the situation facing network television advertisers. They pay an average of $354,000 to produce a single 30-second commercial. Then, each time they show it, they pay an average of $122,000 for 30 seconds of advertising time during a popular primetime program. They pay even more if it's an especially popular program, such as *American Idol* ($341,000), *Sunday Night Football* ($545,000), *Modern Family* ($331,000), or a mega-event such as the Super Bowl ($3.8 million to $4 million per 30 seconds!).[20]

Then their ads are sandwiched in with a clutter of other commercials, announcements, and network promotions, totaling nearly 20 minutes of nonprogram material per primetime hour, with commercial breaks coming every six minutes on average. Such clutter in television and other ad media has created an increasingly hostile advertising environment. According to one study, more than 70 percent of Americans think there are too many ads on TV, and another study shows that 69 percent of national advertisers themselves agree.[21]

Advertising clutter: Today's consumers, armed with an arsenal of weapons, can choose what they watch and don't watch. Increasingly, they are choosing not to watch ads.

iStockphoto.com.

Until recently, television viewers were pretty much a captive audience for advertisers. But today's digital wizardry has given consumers a rich new set of information and entertainment choices. With the growth in cable and satellite TV, the Internet, video streaming, tablets, and smartphones, today's viewers have many more options.

Digital technology has also armed consumers with an arsenal of weapons for choosing what they watch or don't watch. Increasingly, thanks to the growth of DVR systems, consumers are choosing *not* to watch ads. Forty-six percent of American TV households now have DVRs, triple the number reached only five years earlier. One ad agency executive calls these DVR systems "electronic weedwhackers" when it comes to viewing commercials. It is estimated that DVR owners view only about 44 percent of the commercials during DVR playback. At the same time, video downloads and streaming are exploding, letting viewers watch entertainment on their own time—with or without commercials.[22]

Thus, advertisers can no longer force-feed the same old cookie-cutter message content to captive consumers through traditional media. Just to gain and hold attention, today's content must be better planned, more imaginative, more entertaining, and more emotionally engaging. Simply interrupting or disrupting consumers no longer works. Unless ads provide information that is interesting, useful, or entertaining, many consumers will simply skip by them.

Madison & Vine
A term that has come to represent the merging of advertising and entertainment in an effort to break through the clutter and create new avenues for reaching customers with more engaging messages.

Merging Advertising and Entertainment. To break through the clutter, many marketers have subscribed to a new merging of advertising and entertainment, dubbed "**Madison & Vine**." You've probably heard of Madison Avenue, the New York City street that houses the headquarters of many of the nation's largest advertising agencies. You may also have heard of Hollywood & Vine, the intersection of Hollywood Avenue and Vine Street in Hollywood, California, long the symbolic heart of the U.S. entertainment industry. Now, Madison Avenue and Hollywood & Vine have come together to form a new intersection—Madison & Vine—that represents the merging of advertising and entertainment in an effort to create new avenues for reaching consumers with more engaging messages.

This merging of advertising and entertainment takes one of two forms: advertainment or branded entertainment. The aim of *advertainment* is to make ads themselves so entertaining, or so useful, that people *want* to watch them. There's no chance that you'd watch ads on purpose, you say? Think again. For example, the Super Bowl has become an annual advertainment showcase. Tens of millions of people tune in to the Super Bowl each year, as much to watch the entertaining ads as to see the game.

In fact, DVR systems can actually *improve* viewership of a really *good* ad. For example, most Super Bowl ads are typically viewed more in DVR households than non-DVR households. Rather than zipping past the ads, many people skip back to re-watch them during halftime and following the game.

These days, it's not unusual to see an entertaining ad or other brand message on YouTube before you see it on TV. And you might well seek it out at a friend's suggestion rather than having it forced on you by the advertiser. Moreover, beyond making their regular ads more entertaining, advertisers are also creating new advertising forms that look less like ads and more like short films or shows. A range of new brand messaging platforms—from Webisodes and blogs to viral videos and apps—now blur the line between ads and entertainment. For example, T-Mobile created an entertaining two-minute video ad based on the royal wedding between Prince William and Kate Middleton, using impressive lookalikes of British royal family members dancing down the aisle to a funky pop song. The fun ad was never shown on TV but pulled down more than 26 million views on YouTube.

Branded entertainment (or *brand integrations*) involves making the brand an inseparable part of some other form of entertainment. The most common form of branded entertainment is product placements—embedding brands as props within other programming. It might be a brief glimpse of the latest LG phone on *Grey's Anatomy* or of Starbucks' coffee products on *Morning Joe* on MSNBC. Or the product placement might be scripted into an episode, as when *Big Bang Theory* character Sheldon Cooper uses Purell hand sanitizer after putting a live snake in his friend's desk drawer, spitting out the memorable line, "Oh dear. Oh dear. Purell, Purell, Purell, Purell. . . ." An entire episode of *The Middle* centered on the show's Heck family coveting their neighbor's new VW Passat. Similarly, one memorable episode of *Modern Family* was built around the Dunphy family trying to find the recently released, hard-to-find Apple iPad their father, Phil, coveted as his special birthday present. Other episodes have featured brands ranging from Oreos to Target to Toyota Prius, all carefully integrated with the show's theme.

Originally created with TV in mind, branded entertainment has spread quickly into other sectors of the entertainment industry. For example, it is widely used in movies. Last year's top 34 films contained 397 identifiable brand placements—*Ted* alone had 38 placements.[23] If you look carefully, you'll also see product placements in video games, comic books, Broadway musicals, and even pop music. For example, in *Call of Duty: Modern Warfare 3,* a Jeep Wrangler is prominently featured. Chrysler even sells a Call of Duty: MW3 limited edition Jeep Wrangler.

» **Madison & Vine: IKEA produces its own branded entertainment in the form of the Web-only comedy "Easy to Assemble," set inside an IKEA store. In its four seasons, the show has captured a cult following and millions of online and social media views and shares.**

Many companies are even producing their own branded entertainment. For example, Ford created "Random Acts of Fusion," a Web-only show that followed TV celebrities Joel McHale and Ryan Seacrest as they hosted video contests and free food festivals across America, letting people interact with the latest-model Ford Fusion as they went. The show increased traffic to the Ford Fusion Web site by 20 percent. » Similarly, IKEA sponsors "Easy to Assemble," a tongue-in-cheek Web-only comedy series. The show, now in its fourth season, follows the adventures of Illeana Douglas, who left Hollywood for a job at an IKEA store in Burbank, California. The IKEA store serves as the show's set. IKEA's goal is to communicate the brand's fun, cheerful, and sophisticated image and values. The show has achieved near cult status and has been shared more than 1.5 million times by social media users. "Our content resonates because it's produced by entertainers, not salespeople," says IKEA's media manager.[24]

So, Madison & Vine is now the meeting place for the advertising and entertainment industries. The goal is for brand messages to become a part of the entertainment rather than interrupting it. As advertising agency JWT puts it, "We believe advertising needs to stop *interrupting* what people are interested in and *be* what people are interested in." However, advertisers must be careful that the new intersection itself doesn't become too congested. With all the new ad formats and product placements, Madison & Vine threatens to create even more of the very clutter that it was designed to break through. At that point, consumers might decide to take yet a different route.

Message Strategy. The first step in creating effective advertising messages is to plan a *message strategy*—the general message that will be communicated to consumers. The purpose of advertising is to get consumers to engage with or react to the product or company in a certain way. People will engage and react only if they believe they will benefit from doing so. Thus, developing an effective message strategy begins with identifying customer *benefits* that can be used as advertising appeals. Ideally, the message strategy will follow directly from the company's broader positioning and customer value–creation strategies.

Creative concept
The compelling "big idea" that will bring an advertising message strategy to life in a distinctive and memorable way.

Execution style
The approach, style, tone, words, and format used for executing an advertising message.

Message strategy statements tend to be plain, straightforward outlines of benefits and positioning points that the advertiser wants to stress. The advertiser must next develop a compelling **creative concept**—or *big idea*—that will bring the message strategy to life in a distinctive and memorable way. At this stage, simple message ideas become great ad campaigns. Usually, a copywriter and an art director will team up to generate many creative concepts, hoping that one of these concepts will turn out to be the big idea. The creative concept may emerge as a visualization, a phrase, or a combination of the two.

The creative concept will guide the choice of specific appeals to be used in an advertising campaign. *Advertising appeals* should have three characteristics. First, they should be *meaningful,* pointing out benefits that make the product more desirable or interesting to consumers. Second, appeals must be *believable*. Consumers must believe that the product or service will deliver the promised benefits.

However, the most meaningful and believable benefits may not be the best ones to feature. Appeals should also be *distinctive*. They should tell how the product is better than competing brands. For example, the most meaningful benefit of using a body wash or fragrance is that it makes you feel cleaner or smell better. >> But Axe's new Anarchy brand for men and women sets itself apart by the extreme nature of the "Axe Effect" it promises to create—Axe Anarchy for Him + for Her will "Unleash the Chaos." Similarly, the most meaningful benefit of owning a wristwatch is that it keeps accurate time, yet few watch ads feature this benefit. Instead, watch advertisers might select any of a number of advertising themes. For years, Timex has been the affordable watch that "takes a licking and keeps on ticking." In contrast, Rolex ads talk about the brand's "obsession with perfection" and the fact that "Rolex has been the preeminent symbol of performance and prestige for more than a century."

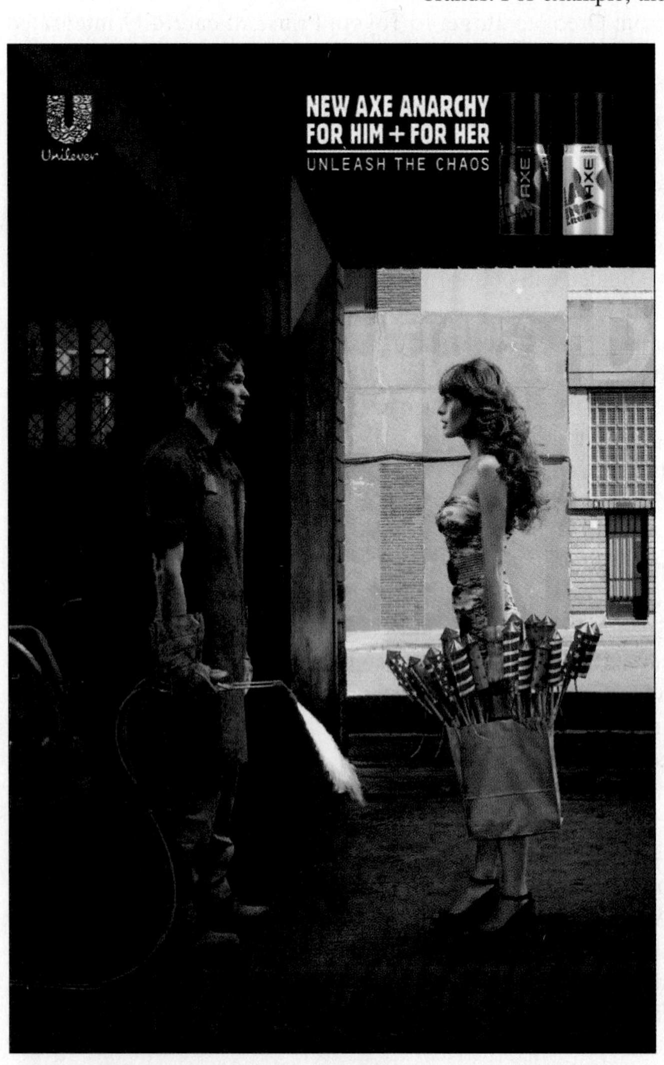

>> Distinctive advertising appeals: Axe Anarchy For Him + For Her sets itself apart by the extreme nature of the "Axe Effect" it promises to create—Anarchy will "Unleash the Chaos."

Message Execution. The advertiser now must turn the big idea into an actual ad execution that will capture the target market's attention and interest. The creative team must find the best approach, style, tone, words, and format for executing the message. The message can be presented in various **execution styles**, such as the following:

- *Slice of life:* This style shows one or more "typical" people using the product in a normal setting. For example, a Silk Soymilk "Rise and Shine" ad shows a young professional starting the day with a healthier breakfast and high hopes.
- *Lifestyle:* This style shows how a product fits in with a particular lifestyle. For example, an ad for Athleta active wear shows a woman in a complex yoga pose and states: "If your body is your temple, build it one piece at a time."
- *Fantasy:* This style creates a fantasy around the product or its use. For example, recent IKEA ads show consumers creating fanciful room designs with IKEA furniture, such as "a bedroom for a queen made by Bree and her sister, designed by IKEA."
- *Mood or image:* This style builds a mood or image around the product or service, such as beauty, love, intrigue, or serenity. Few claims are made about the product or service

except through suggestion. For example, a Nestlé Toll House ad shows a daughter hugging her mother after surprising her with an unexpected weekend home from college. The mother responds, "So I baked her the cookies she's loved since she was little."

- *Musical:* This style shows people or cartoon characters singing about the product. For example, M&Ms "Love Ballad" ad, part of the Better with M campaign, featured Red singing Meatloaf's "I would do anything for love," showcasing his commitment to actress Naya Rivera. Red has second thoughts, however, when Rivera can't resist adding Red to some of her favorite treats, including cookies, cake, and ice cream. To all of that, Red answers with the lyric "But I won't do that . . . or that . . . or that . . . or that."
- *Personality symbol:* This style creates a character that represents the product. The character might be animated (Mr. Clean, the GEICO Gecko, or the Michelin Man) or real (perky Progressive Insurance spokeswoman Flo, Allstate's Mayhem, Ronald McDonald).
- *Technical expertise:* This style shows the company's expertise in making the product. Thus, natural foods maker Kashi shows its buyers carefully selecting ingredients for its products, and Jim Koch of the Boston Beer Company tells about his many years of experience in brewing Samuel Adams beer.
- *Scientific evidence:* This style presents survey or scientific evidence that the brand is better or better liked than one or more other brands. For years, Crest toothpaste has used scientific evidence to convince buyers that Crest is better than other brands at fighting cavities.
- *Testimonial evidence or endorsement:* This style features a highly believable or likable source endorsing the product. It could be ordinary people saying how much they like a given product. For example, Subway's spokesman Jared is a customer who lost 245 pounds on a diet of Subway sandwiches. » Or it might be a celebrity presenting the product, such as Beyoncé speaking for Pepsi.

» Message execution styles: Using celebrity endorsers to represent brands—Beyoncé speaks for Pepsi.

Pepsi-Cola North America, Inc.

The advertiser also must choose a *tone* for the ad. For example, P&G always uses a positive tone: Its ads say something very positive about its products. Other advertisers now use edgy humor to break through the commercial clutter. Bud Light commercials are famous for this.

The advertiser must use memorable and attention-getting *words* in the ad. For example, rather than claiming simply that its laundry detergent is "superconcentrated," Method asks customers, "Are you jug addicted?" The solution: "Our patent-pending formula that's so fricken' concentrated, 50 loads fits in a teeny bottle. . . . With our help, you can get off the jugs and get clean."

Finally, *format* elements make a difference in an ad's impact as well as in its cost. A small change in an ad's design can make a big difference in its effect. In a print ad, the *illustration* is the first thing the reader notices—it must be strong enough to draw attention. Next, the *headline* must effectively entice the right people to read the copy. Finally, the *copy*—the main block of text in the ad—must be simple but strong and convincing. Moreover, these three elements must effectively work *together* to persuasively present customer value. However, novel formats can help an ad stand out from the clutter. For example, striking Benjamin Moore paint ads consist mostly of a single long headline in mixed fonts balanced against a color swatch and background that illustrate the color discussed in the headline.

Consumer-Generated Content. Taking advantage of today's digital and social media technologies, many companies are now tapping consumers for marketing content, message ideas, or even actual ads. Sometimes the results are outstanding; sometimes they are forgettable. If done well, however, user-generated content can incorporate the voice of the customer into brand messages and generate greater customer engagement.

>> **Consumer-generated messages: In Super Bowl XLVI, two Doritos "Crash the Super Bowl" ads took first place in *USA Today*'s AdMeter/Facebook ratings, including this "Sling Baby" ad.**

Frito-Lay, Inc.

Many brands hold contests that invite consumers to submit ad message ideas and videos. For example, for the past several years, PepsiCo's Doritos brand has held its annual "Crash the Super Bowl Challenge" contest that invites consumers to create their own 30-second video ads about the tasty triangular corn chips. A Doritos brand team whittles down the thousands of entries and posts the finalists on Facebook, where consumers vote for their favorites. The winners receive large cash awards and have their ads run during the Super Bowl.

Past "Crash the Super Bowl" campaigns have produced numerous top awards. For example, in Super Bowl XLVI, user-created Doritos ads earned two first-place finishes, one for the top ranking in the traditional *USA Today* AdMeter rankings and another for finishing first in a new *USA Today*/Facebook social media version of the AdMeter rankings. Both ads earned their creators a cool $1 million cash award from Doritos. >>The favorite ad with online voters that year was one called "Sling Baby," created by 31-year-old Jonathan Friedman of Virginia Beach, Virginia, in which a grandmother slingshots a baby across the yard to nab a bag of Doritos chips from a taunting neighbor kid. For Doritos, "Crash the Super Bowl" has been an advertising and social media touchdown, triggering consumer involvement over several months before, during, and the Super Bowl.[25]

The Super bowl is one thing, but many marketers employ consumer-generated content in a simpler way. For example, Yogawear company Lululemon recently launched its #TheSweatLife campaign, in which it invited customers to tweet or Instagram photos of themselves "getting their sweat on" in Lululemon gear. "Your perspiration is our inspiration," said the brand at its Web site. "We want to see you living #thesweatlife." Within only a few months, the brand had received more than 7,000 photos, which it featured in a #thesweatlife online gallery, quickly drawing more than 40,000 unique visitors. The user-generated content campaign created substantial customer engagement for Lululemon. "We created the program as a way to connect with our guests and showcase how they're authentically sweating in our product offline," says a Lululemon brand manager. "We see it as a unique way to bring their offline experiences into our online community."[26]

Not all consumer-generated advertising efforts, however, are so successful. As many big companies have learned, ads made by amateurs can be . . . well, pretty amateurish. If done well, however, consumer-generated content efforts can produce new creative ideas and fresh perspectives on the brand from consumers who actually experience it. Such campaigns can boost consumer involvement and get customer talking and thinking about a brand and its value to them. "For those willing to give up control and trust the wisdom of the crowd," says one analyst, "collaboration on . . . marketing campaigns can bear amazing results."[27]

Selecting Advertising Media

Advertising media
The vehicles through which advertising messages are delivered to their intended audiences.

The major steps in **advertising media** selection are (1) determining *reach, frequency,* and *impact;* (2) choosing among major *media types;* (3) selecting specific *media vehicles;* and (4) choosing *media timing.*

Determining Reach, Frequency, Impact, and Engagement. To select media, the advertiser must determine the reach and frequency needed to achieve the advertising objectives. *Reach* is a measure of the *percentage* of people in the target market who are exposed to the ad campaign during a given period of time. For example, the advertiser might try to reach

70 percent of the target market during the first three months of the campaign. *Frequency* is a measure of how many *times* the average person in the target market is exposed to the message. For example, the advertiser might want an average exposure frequency of three.

But advertisers want to do more than just reach a given number of consumers a specific number of times. The advertiser also must determine the desired *media impact*—the *qualitative value* of message exposure through a given medium. For example, the same message in one magazine (say, *Time*) may be more believable than in another (say, the *National Enquirer*). For products that need to be demonstrated, messages on television or in an online video may have more impact than messages on radio because they use sight, motion, *and* sound. Products for which consumers provide input on design or features might be better promoted at an interactive Web site or social media page than in a direct mailing.

More generally, the advertiser wants to choose media that will *engage* consumers rather than simply reach them. In any medium, the relevance of ad content for its audience is often much more important than how many people it reaches. For example, Home Depot has learned that although it lacks the broad reach of local TV or print ads, a combination of mobile and online media can engage customers more deeply and personally. >> For example, it now runs ads on the Weather Channel's mobile app. When customers tap on the Home Depot banner ad, they're sent to the retailer's mobile Web site, which highlights products matching their local weather conditions and forecast. Expecting snow in your area? You'll likely see special deals on snow shovels and snow blowers. Such focused and engaging media placements nicely supplement Home Depot's broader advertising efforts.[28]

>> To engage consumers, Home Depot runs ads on Weather Channel's mobile app.

Provided by The Weather Channel.

Although Nielsen is beginning to measure *media engagement* levels for some television, radio, and social media, such measures are still hard to find in most cases. Current media measures are things such as ratings, readership, listenership, and click-through rates. However, engagement happens inside the consumer. Notes one expert, "Just measuring the number of eyeballs in front of a television set is hard enough without trying to measure the intensity of those eyeballs doing the viewing."[29] Still, marketers need to know how customers connect with an ad and brand idea as a part of the broader brand relationship.

Engaged consumers are more likely to act upon brand messages and even share them with others. Thus, rather than simply tracking *consumer impressions* for a media placement—how many people see, hear, or read an ad—Coca-Cola now also tracks the *consumer expressions* that result, such as a comment, a "Like," uploading a photo or video, or sharing brand content on social networks. Today's empowered consumers often generate more messages about a brand than a company can. Through engagement, "instead of having to always pay for their message to run somewhere, [marketers] can 'earn' media for free, via consumer spreading YouTube clips, Groupons, and tweets," says an advertising consultant.[30]

For example, Coca-Cola estimates that on YouTube there are about 146 million views of content related to Coca-Cola. However, only about 26 million of those are of content that Coca-Cola created. The other 120 million are of content created by engaged consumers. "We can't match the volume of our consumers' output," says Coca-Cola's chief marketing officer, "but we can spark it with the right type [and placement] of content."[31]

Choosing among Major Media Types. As summarized in **>> Table 12.2**, the major media types are television, digital and social media, newspapers, direct mail, magazines, radio, and outdoor. Each medium has its advantages and its limitations. Media planners want to choose media that will effectively and efficiently present the advertising message to target customers. Thus, they must consider each medium's impact, message effectiveness, and cost. As discussed earlier in the chapter, it's typically not a question of which one medium to use. Rather, the advertiser selects a mix of media and blends them into a fully integrated marketing communications campaign.

The mix of media must be reexamined regularly. For a long time, television and magazines dominated the media mixes of national advertisers, with other media often neglected. However, as mass-media costs rise, audiences shrink, and exciting new digital and social media emerge, many advertisers are finding new ways to reach consumers. They are supplementing the traditional mass media with more-specialized and highly targeted digital media that cost less, target more effectively, and engage consumers more fully.

» Table 12.2 Profiles of Major Media Types

Medium	Advantages	Limitations
Television	Good mass-marketing coverage; low cost per exposure; combines sight, sound, and motion; appealing to the senses	High absolute costs; high clutter; fleeting exposure; less audience selectivity
Online, mobile, and social media	Focus on individuals and customer communities; immediacy; personalization, interaction, and engagement capabilities; social sharing power; low cost	Potentially narrow impact; difficult to administer and control; the audience often controls content and exposure
Newspapers	Flexibility; timeliness; good local market coverage; broad acceptability; high believability	Short life; poor reproduction quality; small pass-along audience
Direct mail	High audience selectivity; flexibility; no ad competition within the same medium; allows personalization	Relatively high cost per exposure; "junk mail" image
Magazines	High geographic and demographic selectivity; credibility and prestige; high-quality reproduction; long life and good pass-along readership	Long ad purchase lead time; high cost; no guarantee of position
Radio	Good local acceptance; high geographic and demographic selectivity; low cost	Audio only; fleeting exposure; low attention ("the half-heard" medium); fragmented audiences
Outdoor	Flexibility; high repeat exposure; low cost; low message competition; good positional selectivity	Little audience selectivity; creative limitations

As discussed earlier, today's marketers want to assemble a full mix of *paid, owned, earned,* and *shared media* that create and deliver involving brand content to target consumers.

In addition to the explosion of online, mobile, and social media, cable and satellite television systems are thriving. Such systems allow narrow programming formats, such as all sports, all news, nutrition, arts, home improvement and gardening, cooking, travel, history, finance, and others that target select groups. Time Warner, Comcast, and other cable operators are even testing systems that will let them target specific types of ads to TVs in specific neighborhoods or individually to specific types of customers. For example, ads for a Spanish-language channel would run in only Hispanic neighborhoods, or only pet owners would see ads from pet food companies. Advertisers can take advantage of such *narrowcasting* to "rifle in" on special market segments rather than use the "shotgun" approach offered by network broadcasting.

Finally, in their efforts to find less costly and more highly targeted ways to reach consumers, advertisers have discovered a dazzling collection of *alternative media*. These days, no matter where you go or what you do, you will probably run into some new form of advertising.

> Tiny billboards attached to shopping carts urge you to buy JELL-O Pudding Pops or Pampers, while ads roll by on the store's checkout conveyor touting your local Chevy dealer. Step outside and there goes a city trash truck sporting an ad for Glad trash bags or a school bus displaying a Little Caesar's pizza ad. A nearby fire hydrant is emblazoned with advertising for KFC's "fiery" chicken wings. You escape to the ballpark, only to find billboard-size video screens running Budweiser ads while a blimp with an electronic message board circles lazily overhead. » In mid-winter, you wait in a city bus shelter that looks like an oven—with heat coming from the coils—introducing Caribou Coffee's line-up of hot breakfast sandwiches.
>
> These days, you're likely to find ads—well—anywhere. Taxi cabs sport electronic messaging signs tied to GPS location sensors that can pitch local stores and restaurants wherever they roam. Ad space is being sold on DVD cases, parking-lot tickets, airline boarding passes, subway turnstiles, highway toll booth gates, golf scorecards, ATMs, municipal garbage cans, and even police cars, doctors' examining tables, and church bulletins. One company even sells space

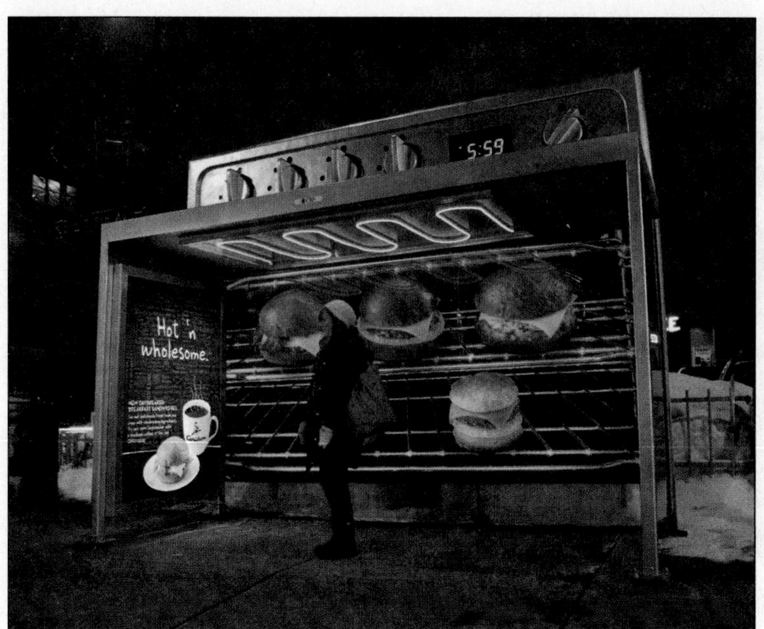

Marketers have discovered a dazzling array of alternative media, like this heated Caribou Coffee bus shelter.

Caribou Coffee.

on toilet paper furnished free to restaurants, stadiums, and malls—the paper carries advertiser logos, coupons, and codes you can scan with your smartphone to download digital coupons or link to advertisers' social media pages. Now that's a captive audience.

Such alternative media seem a bit far-fetched, and they sometimes irritate consumers who resent it all as "ad nauseam." But for many marketers, these media can save money and provide a way to hit selected consumers where they live, shop, work, and play.

Another important trend affecting media selection is the rapid growth in the number of *media multitaskers*, people who absorb more than one medium at a time. For example, it's not uncommon to find someone watching TV with a smartphone in hand, tweeting, snapchatting with friends, and chasing down product information on Google. One recent survey found that a whopping 88 percent of tablet owners and 86 percent of smartphone owners use the devices while watching TV. Although some users of this multitasking is related to TV viewing—such as looking up related product and program information—most multitasking involves tasks unrelated to the shows being watched. Marketers need to take such media interactions into account when selecting the types of media they will use.[32]

Selecting Specific Media Vehicles. Media planners must also choose the best media vehicles—specific media within each general media type. For example, television vehicles include *Modern Family* and *ABC World News Tonight*. Magazine vehicles include *Time*, *Real Simple*, and *ESPN The Magazine*. Online and mobile vehicles include Twitter, Facebook, Pinterest, and YouTube.

Media planners must compute the cost per 1,000 persons reached by a vehicle. For example, if a full-page, four-color advertisement in the U.S. national edition of *Forbes* costs $135,730 and *Forbes's* readership is 900,000 people, the cost of reaching each group of 1,000 persons is about $150. The same advertisement in *Bloomberg Businessweek's* Northeast U.S. regional edition may cost only $48,100 but reach only 155,000 people—at a cost per 1,000 of about $310.[33] The media planner ranks each magazine by cost per 1,000 and favors those magazines with the lower cost per 1,000 for reaching target consumers. In the above case, if a marketer is targeting Northeast business managers, *BusinessWeek* might be the more cost-effective buy, even at a higher cost per thousand.

Media planners must also consider the costs of producing ads for different media. Whereas newspaper ads may cost very little to produce, flashy television ads can be very costly. Many online and social media ads cost little to produce, but costs can climb when producing made-for-the-Web videos and ad series.

In selecting specific media vehicles, media planners must balance media costs against several media effectiveness factors. First, the planner should evaluate the media vehicle's audience quality. For a Huggies disposable diapers advertisement, for example, *Parents* magazine would have a high exposure value; *Maxim* would have a low exposure value. Second, the media planner should consider audience engagement. Readers of *Vogue*, for example, typically pay more attention to ads than do *Time* readers. Third, the planner should assess the vehicle's editorial quality. *Time* and the *Wall Street Journal* are more believable and prestigious than *Star* or the *National Enquirer*.

Deciding on Media Timing. An advertiser must also decide how to schedule the advertising over the course of a year. Suppose sales of a product peak in December and drop in March (for winter outdoor gear, for instance). The firm can vary its advertising to follow the seasonal pattern, oppose the seasonal pattern, or be the same all year. Most firms do some seasonal advertising. For example, Mars currently runs M&M's special ads for almost

Media timing: Vicks NyQuil runs ads like this only during the cold and flu season.

The Procter & Gamble Company.

every holiday and "season," from Easter, Fourth of July, and Halloween to the Super Bowl season and the Oscar season. The Picture People, the national chain of portrait studios, advertises more heavily before major holidays, such as Christmas, Easter, Valentine's Day, and Halloween. Some marketers do *only* seasonal advertising: For instance, P&G advertises its Vicks NyQuil only during the cold and flu season.

Finally, the advertiser must choose the pattern of the ads. *Continuity* means scheduling ads evenly within a given period. *Pulsing* means scheduling ads unevenly over a given time period. Thus, 52 ads could either be scheduled at one per week during the year or pulsed in several bursts. The idea behind pulsing is to advertise heavily for a short period to build awareness that carries over to the next advertising period. Those who favor pulsing feel that it can be used to achieve the same impact as a steady schedule but at a much lower cost. However, some media planners believe that although pulsing achieves minimal awareness, it sacrifices depth of advertising communications. Several companies turned the power blackout in Super Bowl XLVII into advertising opportunities with quick-reaction social media ads.

Today's online and social media let advertisers create ads that respond to events in real time. For example, Lexus recently introduced a new model through live streaming from the North American International Auto Show via Facebook's News Feed. Some 100,000 people watched the introduction live in only the first 10 minutes; another 600,000 viewed it online within the next few days. As another example, Oreos reacted to a power outage during Super Bowl XLVII with an outage-related "You can still dunk in the dark" tweet. The fast-reaction ad was retweeted and favorited thousands of times in only 15 minutes. Similarly, drugstore retailer Walgreens tweeted "We do carry candles" and ". . . we also sell lights," messages that also drew thousands of quick retweets and faves.[34]

Evaluating Advertising Effectiveness and the Return on Advertising Investment

Return on advertising investment The net return on advertising investment divided by the costs of the advertising investment.

Measuring advertising effectiveness and the **return on advertising investment** has become a hot issue for most companies, especially in a challenging economic environment. Even in a recovering economy with marketing budgets again on the rise, like consumers, advertisers are still pinching their pennies and spending conservatively. That leaves top management at many companies asking their marketing managers, "How do we know that we're spending the right amount on advertising?" and "What return are we getting on our advertising investment?"

Advertisers should regularly evaluate two types of advertising results: the communication effects and the sales and profit effects. Measuring the *communication effects* of an ad or ad campaign tells whether the ads and media are communicating the ad message well. Individual ads can be tested before or after they are run. Before an ad is placed, the advertiser can show it to consumers, ask how they like it, and measure message recall or attitude changes resulting from it. After an ad is run, the advertiser can measure how the ad affected consumer recall or product awareness, knowledge, and preference. Pre- and post-evaluations of communication effects can be made for entire advertising campaigns as well.

Advertisers have gotten pretty good at measuring the communication effects of their ads and ad campaigns. However, *sales and profit* effects of advertising are often much harder to measure. For example, what sales and profits are produced by an ad campaign that increases brand awareness by 20 percent and brand preference by 10 percent? Sales and profits are affected by many factors other than advertising—such as product features, price, and availability.

One way to measure the sales and profit effects of advertising is to compare past sales and profits with past advertising expenditures. Another way is through experiments. For example, to test the effects of different advertising spending levels, Coca-Cola could vary the amount it spends on advertising in different market areas and measure the differences in the resulting sales and profit levels. More complex experiments could be designed to include other variables, such as differences in the ads or media used.

However, because so many factors affect advertising effectiveness, some controllable and others not, measuring the results of advertising spending remains an inexact science. Managers often must rely on large doses of judgment along with quantitative analysis when assessing advertising performance.

Other Advertising Considerations

In developing advertising strategies and programs, the company must address two additional questions. First, how will the company organize its advertising function—who will perform which advertising tasks? Second, how will the company adapt its advertising strategies and programs to the complexities of international markets?

Organizing for Advertising

Different companies organize in different ways to handle advertising. In small companies, advertising might be handled by someone in the sales department. Large companies have advertising departments whose job it is to set the advertising budget, work with the ad agency, and handle other advertising not done by the agency. However, most large companies use outside advertising agencies because they offer several advantages.

Advertising agency
A marketing services firm that assists companies in planning, preparing, implementing, and evaluating all or portions of their advertising programs.

How does an **advertising agency** work? Advertising agencies originated in the mid- to late 1800s from salespeople and brokers who worked for the media and received a commission for selling advertising space to companies. As time passed, the salespeople began to help customers prepare their ads. Eventually, they formed agencies and grew closer to the advertisers than to the media.

Today's agencies employ specialists who can often perform advertising tasks better than the company's own staff can. Agencies also bring an outside point of view to solving the company's problems, along with lots of experience from working with different clients and situations. So, today, even companies with strong advertising departments of their own use advertising agencies.

Some ad agencies are huge; the largest U.S. agency, Y&R, has annual gross U.S. revenues of $1.86 billion. In recent years, many agencies have grown by gobbling up other agencies, thus creating huge agency holding companies. The largest of these megagroups, WPP, includes several large advertising, PR, and promotion agencies, with combined worldwide revenues of more than $16 billion.[35] Most large advertising agencies have the staff and resources to handle all phases of an advertising campaign for their clients, from creating a marketing plan to developing ad campaigns and preparing, placing, and evaluating ads and other brand content. Large brands commonly employ several agencies that handle everything from mass-media advertising campaigns to shopper marketing and social media content.

International Advertising Decisions

International advertisers face many complexities not encountered by domestic advertisers. The most basic issue concerns the degree to which global advertising should be adapted to the unique characteristics of various country markets.

Some advertisers have attempted to support their global brands with highly standardized worldwide advertising, with campaigns that work as well in Bangkok as they do in Baltimore. For example, McDonald's unifies its creative elements and brand presentation under the familiar "i'm lovin' it" theme in all its 100-plus markets worldwide. Visa coordinates worldwide advertising for its debit and credit cards under the "more people go with Visa" creative platform, which works as well in Korea as it does in the United States or Brazil.

Ads from colorful Brazilian flip-flops maker Havaianas make the same outrageously colorful splash worldwide, no matter what the country, here the United States and Brazil.

MANOLO MORAN FOTOGRAFIA LTDA and ALPARGATAS S.A.

And ads from Brazilian flip-flops maker Havaianas make the same outrageously colorful splash worldwide, no matter what the country.

In recent years, the increased popularity of online marketing and social media sharing has boosted the need for advertising standardization for global brands. Most big marketing and advertising campaigns include a large online presence. Connected consumers can now zip easily across borders via the Internet and social media, making it difficult for advertisers to roll out adapted campaigns in a controlled, orderly fashion. As a result, at the very least, most global consumer brands coordinate their Web sites internationally. For example, check out the McDonald's Web sites from Germany to Jordan to China. You'll find the golden arches logo, the "i'm lovin' it" logo and jingle, a Big Mac equivalent, and maybe even Ronald McDonald himself.

Standardization produces many benefits—lower advertising costs, greater global advertising coordination, and a more consistent worldwide image. But it also has drawbacks. Most important, it ignores the fact that country markets differ greatly in their cultures, demographics, and economic conditions. Thus, most international advertisers "think globally but act locally." They develop global advertising *strategies* that make their worldwide efforts more efficient and consistent. Then they adapt their advertising *programs* to make them more responsive to consumer needs and expectations within local markets. For example, although Visa employs its "more people go with Visa" theme globally, ads in specific locales employ local language and inspiring local imagery that make the theme relevant to the local markets in which they appear.

Global advertisers face several special problems. For instance, advertising media costs and availability differ vastly from country to country. Countries also differ in the extent to which they regulate advertising practices. Many countries have extensive systems of laws restricting how much a company can spend on advertising, the media used, the nature of advertising claims, and other aspects of the advertising program. Such restrictions often require advertisers to adapt their campaigns from country to country.

Thus, although advertisers may develop global strategies to guide their overall advertising efforts, specific advertising programs must usually be adapted to meet local cultures and customs, media characteristics, and regulations.

SPEED BUMP LINKING THE CONCEPTS

Think about what goes on behind the scenes for the ads we all tend to take for granted.

- Pick a favorite print or television ad. Why do you like it? Do you think that it's effective? Can you think of an ad that people like that may not be effective?
- Dig a little deeper and learn about the campaign *behind* your ad. What are the campaign's objectives? What is its budget? Assess the campaign's message and media strategies. Looking beyond your own feelings about the ad, is the campaign likely to be effective?

Author Comment
Not long ago, public relations was considered a marketing stepchild because of its limited marketing use. That situation is changing fast, however, as more marketers recognize PR's brand-building, customer engagement, and social power.

Public Relations

Another major mass-promotion tool, public relations, consists of activities designed to engage and build good relations with the company's various publics. PR departments may perform any or all of the following functions:[36]

- *Press relations or press agency:* Creating and placing newsworthy information in the news media to attract attention to a person, product, or service.
- *Product publicity:* Publicizing specific products.
- *Public affairs:* Building and maintaining national or local community relationships.
- *Lobbying:* Building and maintaining relationships with legislators and government officials to influence legislation and regulation.
- *Investor relations:* Maintaining relationships with shareholders and others in the financial community.
- *Development:* Working with donors or members of nonprofit organizations to gain financial or volunteer support.

Public relations is used to promote products, people, places, ideas, activities, organizations, and even nations. Companies use PR to build good relations with consumers, investors, the media, and their communities. Trade associations have used PR to rebuild interest in commodities, such as eggs, apples, potatoes, milk, and even onions. For example, the Vidalia Onion Committee built a PR campaign around the DreamWorks character Shrek—complete with Shrek images on packaging and in-store displays with giant inflatable Shreks—that successfully promoted onions to children. Even government organizations use PR to build awareness. For example, the National Heart, Lung, and Blood Institute (NHLBI) of the National Institutes of Health sponsors a long-running PR campaign that builds awareness of heart disease in women:[37]

> Heart disease is the number one killer of women; it kills more women each year than all forms of cancer combined. But a 2000 survey by the NHLBI showed that only 34 percent of women knew this, and that most people thought of heart disease as a problem mostly affecting men. So with the help of Ogilvy Public Relations Worldwide, the NHLBI set out to "create a personal and urgent wakeup call to American women." In 2002, it launched a national PR campaign—"The Heart Truth"—to raise awareness of heart disease among women and get women to discuss the issue with their doctors.
>
> »The centerpiece of the campaign is the Red Dress, now the national symbol for women and heart disease awareness. The campaign creates awareness through an interactive Web site; mass media placements; Facebook, Twitter, YouTube, and Pinterest pages; and campaign materials—everything from brochures, DVDs, and posters to speaker's kits and airport dioramas. It also sponsors several major national events, such as the National Wear Red Day, an annual Red Dress Collection Fashion Show, and The Heart Truth Road Show, featuring heart disease risk factor screenings in major U.S. cities. Finally, the campaign works with more than three dozen corporate sponsors, such as Diet Coke, St. Joseph aspirin, Tylenol, Cheerios, CVS Pharmacy, Swarovski, and Bobbi Brown Cosmetics. So far, some 2.65 billion product packages have carried the Red Dress symbol.

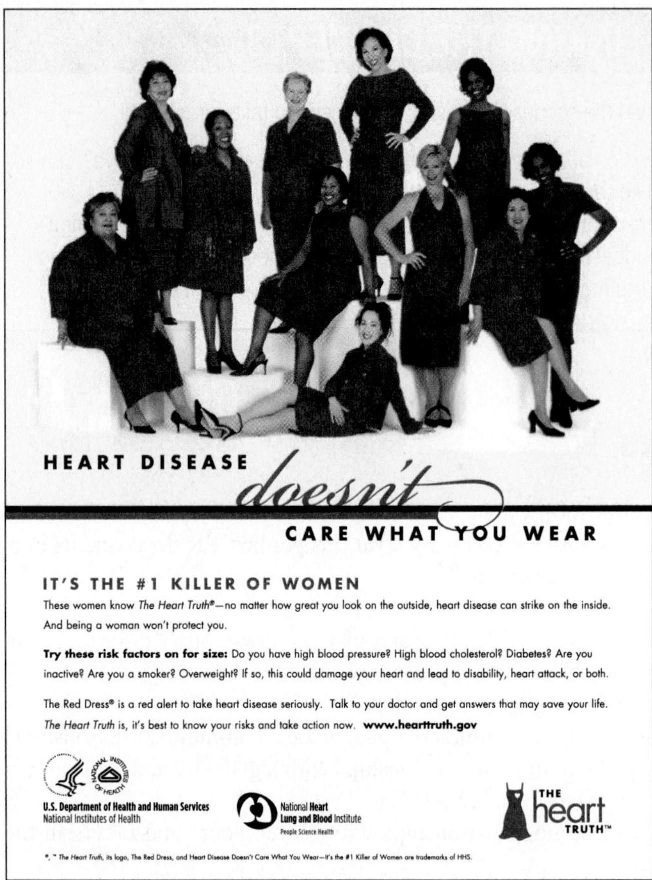

Public relations campaigns: The NHLBI's "The Heart Truth" campaign has produced impressive results in raising awareness of the risks of heart disease in women.

Courtesy of the National Heart, Lung, and Blood Institute. The Heart Truth and Red Dress are trademarks of DHHS.

The results are impressive: Awareness among American women of heart disease as the number one killer of women has increased to 57 percent, and the number of heart disease deaths in women has declined steadily from one in three women to one in four. The American Heart Association has also adopted the Red Dress symbol and introduced its own complementary campaign.

The Role and Impact of PR

Public relations can have a strong impact on public awareness at a much lower cost than advertising can. When using public relations, the company does not pay for the space or time in the media. Rather, it pays for a staff to develop and circulate information and manage events. If the company develops an interesting story or event, it could be picked up by several different media and have the same effect as advertising that would cost millions of dollars. What's more, public relations has the power to engage consumers and make them a part of the brand story and its telling (see Marketing at Work 12.2).

PR results can sometimes be spectacular. Consider the launches of Apple's iPad and iPad 2:[38]

> Apple's iPad was one of the most successful new-product launches in history. The funny thing: Whereas most big product launches are accompanied by huge prelaunch advertising campaigns, Apple pulled this one off with no advertising. None at all. Instead, it simply fed the PR fire. It built buzz months in advance by distributing iPads for early reviews, feeding the offline and online press with tempting tidbits, and offering fans an early online peek at thousands of new iPad apps that would be available. At launch time, it fanned the flames with a cameo on the TV sitcom *Modern Family*, a flurry of launch-day appearances on TV talk shows, and other launch-day events. In the process, through PR alone, the iPad launch generated unbounded consumer excitement, a media frenzy, and long lines outside retail stores on launch day. Apple sold more than 300,000 of the sleek gadgets on the first day alone and more than two million in the first two months—even as demand outstripped supply. Apple repeated the feat a year later with the equally successful launch of iPad 2, which sold close to one million devices the weekend of its launch.

Despite its potential strengths, public relations is occasionally described as a marketing stepchild because of its sometimes limited and scattered use. The PR department is often located at corporate headquarters or handled by a third-party agency. Its staff is so busy dealing with various publics—stockholders, employees, legislators, and the press—that PR programs to support product marketing objectives may be ignored. Moreover, marketing managers and PR practitioners do not always speak the same language. Whereas many PR practitioners see their jobs as simply communicating, marketing managers tend to be much more interested in how advertising and PR affect brand building, sales and profits, and customer engagement and relationships.

This situation is changing, however. Although public relations still captures only a small portion of the overall marketing budgets of most firms, PR can be a powerful brand-building tool. Especially in this digital age, the lines between advertising and PR are becoming more and more blurred. For example, are brand Web sites, blogs, viral brand videos, and social media activities advertising or PR efforts? All are both. And as the use of earned and shared digital content grows rapidly, PR may play a bigger role in marketing content management. More than any other department, PR has always been responsible for creating relevant marketing content that draws consumers to a brand rather than pushing messages out. "Knowing where influence and conversations are to be found is PR's stock in trade," says one expert. "PR pros are an organization's master storytellers. In a word, they *do* content."[39] The point is that PR should work hand in hand with advertising within

MARKETING AT WORK 12.2

PR and Customer Engagement at Coca-Cola: From Impressions to Expressions to Transactions

Coca-Cola aims to do much more with public relations than just create passive "impressions." It's looking to create customer engagement and inspire customer "expressions." According to Coca-Cola's chief marketing officer, Joe Tripodi, the PR goal is to develop "strongly sharable pieces of communication information that generate huge numbers of impressions online—and then, crucially, lead to expressions from consumers, who join the story and extend it, and then finally to transactions." That is, Coca-Cola uses PR to engage consumers and start customer conversations that will inspire consumers themselves to extend the brand's theme of open happiness and optimism.

Consider Coca-Cola's recent "Hug Me" campaign, in which the company installed a "happiness" vending machine overnight at a university in Singapore. The machine had a solid red front and trademark wavy white stripe, but it contained no Coca-Cola logo, no coin slot, and no soda selection buttons. Only the words "Hug Me" were visible in large white letters printed in Coca-Cola's famous script. With hidden cameras rolling, Coca-Cola captured the quizzical reactions of passersby as they first scratched their heads, then slowly approached the machine, and, finally, with smiles on their faces, gave it a big hug. Responding to that simple act of happiness, the machine magically dispensed a cold can of Coca-Cola, free of charge.

>> The power of PR: Coca-Cola's "Hug Me" campaign created 112 million impressions in only one week's time. More important, it created countless customer expressions that extended the brand's theme of happiness and optimism.

Coca-Cola's "Hug Me" video shows one person after another hugging the machine, receiving a Coke, and sharing their delight with others. Coca-Cola placed the video online, then stepped back and let the media and consumers carry the story forward. Within only one week's time, the video generated 112 million impressions. Given the low costs of the free Cokes and producing the video, the "Hug Me" campaign resulted in an amazingly low cost per impression. But even more valuable were the extensive customer expressions that followed, such as "Liking" the video and forwarding it to others. "The Coca Cola Hug Machine is a simple idea to spread some happiness," says a Coca-Cola marketer. Our strategy is to deliver doses of happiness in an unexpected, innovative way . . . and happiness is contagious."

The "Hug Me" campaign was only the most recent in a long line of similar conversation-starting PR tactics by Coca-Cola. This past Valentine's Day, the company placed a modified vending machine in the middle of a busy shopping mall that dispensed free Cokes to folks who confirmed their "couple" status with a hug or a kiss. A few years ago, another Coca-Cola Happiness machine placed at a university dispensed everything from free Cokes to popcorn, pizza, flowers, handshakes, and Polaroid photos. Making periodic "jackpot" sounds, the machine dispensed dozens of Cokes and a long plank layered with colorful cupcakes. These unexpected actions not only prompted smiles and cheers, but recipients could hardly wait to share their bounty and the story with anyone and everyone, extending Coke's happiness positioning.

Coca-Cola has fielded many other PR campaigns that employ its "impressions-expressions-transactions" model to inspire brand conversations. In its "Project Connect" campaign, the company printed 150 common first names on Coke bottles, an exploit that had consumers by the hundreds of thousands rifling through Coca-Cola displays in retail stores looking for their names. In its "Move to the Beat" project, Coca-Cola brought music, youth, and sports together for the London 2012 Olympics through an original music track by British music producer Mark Ronson, which wrapped the live sounds of five different Olympic sports around the vocals of Katy B.

Coca-Cola's long-running Arctic Home campaign employs the power of publicity and shared media to create engagement by connecting the company's brands to a culturally relevant cause. In that campaign, Coca-Cola has partnered with the World Wildlife Fund (WWF) to protect the habitat of polar bears—a cause that fits perfectly with Coke's longstanding use of digitally produced polar bears as spokes-critters in its ads. The Arctic Home campaign goes well beyond clever seasonal ads by integrating PR efforts with virtually every aspect of promotion and marketing. The campaign includes a dedicated Web site, a smartphone app, a pledge of $3 million to the WWF, advertisements and online videos featuring footage from the IMAX film *To the Arctic 3D*, and attention-grabbing white Coke cans highlighting the plight of polar bears. In its first year, Arctic Home produced an astounding 1.3 billion impressions, which in turn inspired untold customer engagement and expressions.

Coca-Cola's "BHAG," or "big hairy audacious goal," is not just to hold its market share in the soft drink category, where sales have been flat for years, but to double its business by the end of the decade. Public relations and the social media will play a central role in achieving this goal by making customers a part of the brand story and turning them into an army of brand advocates who will carry the Coca-Cola Open Happiness message forward. "It's not just about pushing stuff out as we've historically done," says CMO Tripodi. "We have to create experiences that perhaps are had only by a few but are compelling enough to fuel conversations with many."

Sources: Tim Nudd, "Coca-Cola Joins the Revolution in a World Where the Mob Rules," *Adweek*, June 19, 2012, www.adweek.com/print/141217; Thomas Pardee, "Olympics Campaigns Go Big on the Viral Video Chart," *Advertising Age*, May 17, 2012, http://adage.com/print/234790/; Natalie Zmuda, "Coca-Cola Gets Real with Polar Bears," *Advertising Age*, October 25, 2011, http://adage.com/print/230632/; Emma Hall, "Coca-Cola Launches Global 2012 Olympics Campaign with Mark Ronson," *Advertising Age*, September 29, 2011, http://adage.com/print/230107/; Anthony Wing Kosner, "Hug Me: Coca-Cola Introduces Gesture Based Marketing in Singapore," *Forbes*, April 11, 2012, www.forbes.com/sites/anthonykosner/2012/04/11/hug-me-coca-cola-introduces-gesture-based-marketing-in-singapore/; "Cannes Lions 2012: Five-Points to a Great Marketing Strategy," afaqs.com, June 20, 2012, www.afaqs.com/news/story/34444; and www.youtube.com/watch?feature=endscreen&NR=1&v=-A-7H4aOhq0, accessed November 2013.

an integrated marketing communications program to help build customer engagement and relationships.

Major Public Relations Tools

Public relations uses several tools. One of the major tools is *news*. PR professionals find or create favorable news about the company and its products or people. Sometimes news stories occur naturally; sometimes the PR person can suggest events or activities that would create news. Another common PR tool is *special events*, ranging from news conferences and speeches, brand tours, and grand openings to laser light shows, multimedia presentations, or educational programs designed to reach and interest target publics.

Public relations people also prepare *written materials* to reach and influence their target markets. These materials include annual reports, brochures, articles, and company newsletters and magazines. *Audiovisual materials*, such as DVDs and online videos, are being used increasingly as communication tools. *Corporate identity materials* can also help create a corporate identity that the public immediately recognizes. Logos, stationery, brochures, signs, business forms, business cards, buildings, uniforms, and company cars and trucks all become marketing tools when they are attractive, distinctive, and memorable. Finally, companies can improve public goodwill by contributing money and time to *public service activities*.

As previously discussed, the Web and social media are also important PR channels. Web sites, blogs, and social media such as YouTube, Facebook, Pinterest, Storify, and Twitter are providing new ways to reach and engage people. As noted earlier, storytelling and engagement are core PR strengths, and that plays well into the use of online and social media. Consider the Wrangler NextBlue PR campaign:[40]

> Wrangler wanted to reach out beyond its core consumers—to a young, metropolitan mindset. But rather than using ads or standard PR approaches, it created NextBlue, an online project giving consumers and fledgling designers a chance to create the next style of Wrangler jeans. Working with its PR agency, Wrangler created a microsite that asked consumers to create videos of themselves and their jeans designs. The campaign was promoted on Wrangler's Web site and Facebook page and in its e-mails to Wrangler subscribers. The brand also used a mix of traditional PR media, along with paid ads on Facebook and social media promotions on YouTube and Twitter, allowing the public to comment and vote on the submitted designs.
>
> The rich integration of paid, owned, earned, and shared PR media produced the desired results. Within just two weeks, Wrangler received 50 video submissions. The winning entry, created by Song Ahn Nguyen, was then sold on Wrangler.com as the first design in the NextBlue line. But in addition to the new design, Wrangler also signed up 19 young designers to blog for its NextBlue site, garnered 5,000 new subscribers to its e-mail database, and counted more than 80,000 views of the finalist videos. "The heart of the NextBlue [PR] project was a brand

collaboration with consumers," says a Wrangler marketing communications executive. "The social media are a natural fit for [that]."

As with the other promotion tools, in considering when and how to use product public relations, management should set PR objectives, choose the PR messages and vehicles, implement the PR plan, and evaluate the results. The firm's PR should be blended smoothly with other promotion activities within the company's overall integrated marketing communications effort.

MyMarketingLab

Go to **mymktlab.com** to complete the problems marked with this icon .

END OF CHAPTER

REVIEWING THE CONCEPTS

CHAPTER REVIEW AND KEY TERMS

Objectives Review

In this chapter, you've learned how companies use integrated marketing communications (IMC) to engage customers and communicate customer value. You've also explored two of the major marketing communications mix elements—advertising and public relations. Modern marketing calls for more than just creating customer value by developing a good product, pricing it attractively, and making it available to target customers. Companies also must clearly and persuasively *communicate* that value to current and prospective customers. To do this, they must blend five communication mix tools, guided by a well-designed and implemented IMC strategy.

OBJECTIVE 1 Define the five promotion mix tools for communicating customer value. (pp 368–369)

A company's total *promotion mix*—also called its *marketing communications mix*—consists of the specific blend of *advertising, personal selling, sales promotion, public relations,* and *direct and digital marketing* tools that the company uses to persuasively communicate customer value and build customer relationships. Advertising includes any paid form of nonpersonal presentation and promotion of ideas, goods, or services by an identified sponsor. In contrast, public relations focuses on building good relations with the company's various publics. Personal selling is personal presentation by the firm's sales force for the purpose of making sales and building customer relationships. Firms use sales promotion to provide short-term incentives to encourage the purchase or sale of a product or service. Finally, firms seeking immediate response from targeted individual consumers and consumer communities use direct, digital, and social media marketing tools to engage consumers and cultivate relationships with them.

OBJECTIVE 2 Discuss the changing communications landscape and the need for integrated marketing communications. (pp 369–377)

The explosive developments in communications technology and changes in marketer and customer communication strategies have had a dramatic impact on marketing communications. The new digital and social media have given birth to a more targeted, social, and engaging marketing communications model. Along with traditional communications tools, advertisers are now adding a broad selection of more-specialized and highly targeted media to engage smaller customer segments with more-personalized, interactive content. As they adopt richer but more fragmented media and promotion mixes to reach their diverse markets, they risk creating a communications hodgepodge for consumers. To prevent this, companies are adopting the concept of *integrated marketing communications (IMC)*. Guided by an overall IMC strategy, the company works out the roles that the various promotional tools will play and the extent to which each will be used. It carefully coordinates the promotional activities and the timing of when major campaigns take place.

OBJECTIVE 3 Describe and discuss the major decisions involved in developing an advertising program. (pp 377–393)

Advertising—the use of paid, owned, earned, and shared media by a seller to inform, persuade, and remind about its products or organization—is a strong promotion tool that takes many forms and has many uses. *Advertising decision making* involves decisions about the objectives, the budget, the message, the media, and, finally, the evaluation of results. Advertisers should set clear *objectives* as to whether the advertising is supposed to inform, persuade, or remind buyers. The advertising *budget* can be based on what is affordable, on sales, on competitors' spending, or on advertising objectives and tasks. The *message decision* calls for planning a "big idea" and message strategy and executing it effectively. The *media decision* involves defining reach, frequency, impact, and engagement goals; choosing major media types; selecting media vehicles; and deciding on media timing. Message and media decisions must be closely coordinated for maximum campaign effectiveness. Finally, *evaluation* calls for evaluating the communication and sales effects of advertising before, during, and after the advertising is placed and measuring advertising return on investment.

OBJECTIVE 4 Explain how companies use public relations to communicate with their publics. (pp 393–397)

Public relations involves building good relations with the company's various publics. Its functions include *press agentry, product publicity, public affairs, lobbying, investor relations,* and *development.* Public relations can have a strong impact on public awareness at a much lower cost than advertising can, and PR results can sometimes be spectacular. Despite its potential strengths, however, PR sometimes sees only limited and scattered use. Public relations tools include *news, special events, written materials, audiovisual materials, corporate identity materials,* and *public service activities*. A company's Web site and online social media can be good PR vehicles. In considering when and how to use product PR, management should set PR objectives, choose the PR messages and vehicles, implement the PR plan, and evaluate the results. Public relations should be blended smoothly with other promotion activities within the company's overall IMC effort.

Key Terms

Objective 1

Promotion mix (marketing communications mix) (p 368)
Advertising (p 368)
Sales promotion (p 368)
Personal selling (p 369)
Public relations (PR) (p 369)
Direct and digital marketing (p 369)

Objective 2

Brand content management (p 371)
Integrated marketing communications (IMC) (p 373)
Push strategy (p 376)
Pull strategy (p 376)

Objective 3

Advertising objective (p 378)
Advertising budget (p 379)
Affordable method (p 380)
Percentage-of-sales method (p 380)
Competitive-parity method (p 380)
Objective-and-task method (p 380)
Advertising strategy (p 381)
Madison & Vine (p 382)
Creative concept (p 384)
Execution style (p 384)
Advertising media (p 386)
Return on advertising investment (p 390)
Advertising agency (p 391)

DISCUSSION AND CRITICAL THINKING

Discussion Questions

12-1. Discuss the factors changing the face of today's marketing communications. (AACSB: Written and Oral Communication)

12-2. What is integrated marketing communications (IMC), and how does a company go about implementing it? (AACSB: Written and Oral Communication)

12-3. How do marketers measure the effectiveness of advertising? (AACSB: Written and Oral Communication)

12-4. What are the role and functions of public relations within an organization? (AACSB: Written and Oral Communication)

12-5. Discuss the major public relations tools and the role played by the Internet and social media. (AACSB: Written and Oral Communication)

Critical Thinking Exercises

12-6. Any message can be presented using different execution styles. Select a brand and target audience and design two advertisements, each using a different execution style to deliver the same message to the target audience but in a different way. Identify the types of execution styles you are using and present your advertisements. (AACSB: Written and Oral Communication; Reflective Thinking)

12-7. The Public Relations Society of America (PRSA) awards the best public relations campaigns with Silver Anvil Awards. Visit www.prsa.org/Awards/Search and review several case reports of previous winners. What does the field of public relations encompass? Write a report on one of the award winners focusing on marketing-related activities. (AACSB: Written and Oral Communication; Information Technology; Reflective Thinking)

MINICASES AND APPLICATIONS

Online, Mobile, and Social Media Marketing Twitter—Media Friend or Foe?

Visit any media outlet's Internet site and you'll see the familiar Facebook and Twitter icons. Traditional news media have migrated to online versions and beyond through social media. But social media have become a major source of news for many people. Sixty percent of respondents in one study indicated Facebook as a source of news, and 20 percent used Twitter to learn what's happening in the world. Twitter might have a growing advantage because of the nature of short tweets and how quickly they spread. Most news outlets have a presence on Twitter, promoting their content and directing audiences to their online sites. But Twitter has found a way to make money through advertising and is hiring editorial personnel to produce and manage content. It appears that Twitter is moving away from being just a media platform to becoming a media entity, which concerns traditional media outlets. Twitter has been a partner with traditional media, but now it's becoming more of a competitor. Twitter's NASCAR and Olympics Hub editorial offerings were just the beginning. Part of Twitter's success is because of the relationships it has fostered with these outlets, but now Twitter is building a digital media business on content provided by its media partners as well as eye-witness input from people located where the news is happening.

12-8. Explain how Twitter makes money through advertising. Find examples of companies using Twitter as a promotional tool. (AACSB: Written and Oral Communication; Reflective Thinking)

12-9. How does social media advertising spending compare to traditional mass-media advertising spending? How likely is it that Twitter can become a media entity rather than just a media platform, and what are the implications for advertisers? (AACSB: Written and Oral Communication; Reflective Thinking)

Marketing Ethics Don't Say That!

If you like a restaurant . . . Yelp about it! If you don't . . . Yelp about it! Yelp is an online guide that posts customers' reviews of local businesses such as restaurants, spas, and even doctors. Businesses are rated based on the reviews posted about them, with a 5-star rating being the best. Although almost 60 percent are 4- or 5-star reviews, the remaining reviews are less positive. Bad reviews can be the kiss of death for a small business. Businesses do not put this information on the Yelp site—others do. This is creating a problem for many businesses. Some customers demand something in return for posting a positive review, or worse, for not posting a negative review. One restaurant owner claimed a customer threatened to post a "scathing" review after allegedly getting food poisoning from eating at the restaurant unless he received a $100 gift card. This is not much different than the unethical customers who put glass shards or a dead cockroach on their plates and demand their meal for free (conveniently when they've almost finished the dish). Most restaurants capitulate to avoid a scene. But a negative Yelp or other online review is more ominous, with "word-of-mouse" having such far-reaching and lasting consequences. Some medical professionals have gone so far as to require new patients to sign anti-defamation contracts called "medical gag-orders" before receiving treatment. These waivers attempt to prevent patients from posting negative reviews online and often include signing over copyrights of any reviews posted in an attempt to gain leverage in removing any negative content from rating sites. Some sites, such as Angie's List, flag physicians requiring such waivers, and one state—Michigan—has introduced a bill deeming such waivers illegal.

12-10. Visit Yelp and other sites such as Angie's List, RateMDs.com, and Rate My Professor. Are reviewers limited in any way regarding what they can say on such sites? Should they be limited? (AACSB: Written and Oral Communication; Ethical Understanding and Reasoning; Reflective Thinking)

12-11. Discuss the arguments for and against doctors' rights to require medical gag-orders. Recommend how doctors should handle this situation. (AACSB: Written and Oral Communication; Ethical Understanding and Reasoning; Reflective Thinking)

Marketing by the Numbers C3, CPM, and CPP

Nielsen ratings are very important to both advertisers and television programmers because the cost of television advertising time is based on these ratings. A show's *rating* is the number of households in Nielsen's sample that are tuned to that show divided by the number of television-owning households—115 million in the United States. One rating point represents 1 percent of the TV market, so one point equals 1.15 million households. Nielson's TV ratings are referred to as C3 and measure viewers who watch commercials live or watch recorded commercials up to three days later. A common measure of advertising efficiency is cost per thousand (CPM), which is the ad cost per thousand potential audience contacts. Advertisers also assess the cost per rating point by dividing the ad cost by the rating. These numbers are used to assess the efficiency of a media buy. Use the following average price and rating information to answer the questions:

Program	Cost Per :30 Spot	C3 Rating
Sunday Night Football	$425,000	11.8
American Idol	$475,000	9.0
Grey's Anatomy	$225,000	5.3
Two and a Half Men	$215,000	6.0
The Vampire Diaries	$75,000	1.2

12-12. How many households are expected to watch each program? (AACSB: Written and Oral Communication; Analytical Thinking)

12-13. Calculate the cost per thousand (CPM) and cost per point (CPP) for each program. How should advertisers use these measures when planning a television media buy? (AACSB: Written and Oral Communication; Analytical Thinking; Reflective Thinking)

Video Case OXO

For over 20 years, OXO has put its well-known kitchen gadgets into almost every home in the United States through word-of-mouth, product placement, and other forms of nontraditional promotional techniques. Although OXO is a leading national brand, it competes in product categories that are small in size. With its tight advertising budgets, mass-media promotions are not feasible.

This video demonstrates how OXO is moving forward with its promotional mix through online and social media campaigns. For its Good Grips, SteeL, Candela, Tot, and Staples/OXO brands, OXO is making extensive use of the major social networks, expanding into the blogosphere, developing online ad campaigns, and more.

After viewing the video featuring OXO, answer the following questions:

12-14. How would you describe OXO's overall advertising strategy?

12-15. Why has OXO chosen to change its promotional strategy at this time?

12-16. Is OXO abandoning its old promotional methods? How is OXO blending a new advertising strategy with its promotional techniques that have made it a success?

Company Cases 12 The Super Bowl / 9 JCPenney

See Appendix 1 for cases appropriate for this chapter. **Case 12, The Super Bowl: More Than a Single Advertising Event—a Social Media Frenzy.** Super Bowl advertising illustrates that traditional media and new social media go hand-in-hand.

Case 9, JCPenney: The Struggle to Find Optimum Price. JCPenney tried to fix a pricing problem with a new strategy, only to create a new pricing problem.

MyMarketingLab

Go to **mymktlab.com** for Auto-graded writing questions as well as the following Assisted-graded writing questions:

12-17. Discuss the major advertising objectives and describe an advertisement that is attempting to achieve each objective. (AACSB: Written and Oral Communication; Reflective Thinking)

12-18. According to a recently released study, mascots create more social media buzz than do celebrity endorsers. For example, the Pillsbury Doughboy scored 10 (highest on the scale) and LeBron James scored 1. In a small group, find an example of another company using a mascot to create social media buzz and suggest ways the company can create even more buzz. How is social media buzz measured? (AACSB: Written and Oral Communication; Information Technology; Reflective Thinking)

12-19. Mymktlab Only—comprehensive writing assignment for this chapter.

13 Personal Selling and Sales Promotion

CHAPTER ROAD MAP

Objective Outline

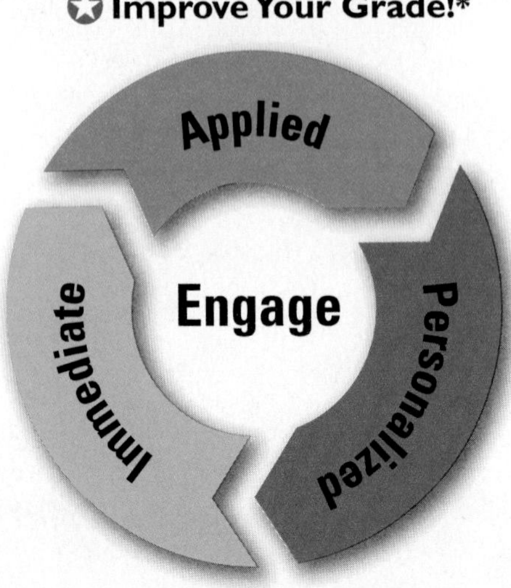

Previewing the Concepts

In the previous two chapters, you learned about communicating customer value through integrated marketing communications (IMC) and two elements of the promotion mix: advertising and public relations. In this chapter, we examine two more IMC elements: personal selling and sales promotion. Personal selling is the interpersonal arm of marketing communications, in which the sales force engages customers and prospects to build relationships and make sales. Sales promotion consists of short-term incentives to encourage the purchase or sale of a product or service. As you read, remember that although this chapter presents personal selling and sales promotion as separate tools, they must be carefully integrated with the other elements of the promotion mix.

To start, what is your first reaction when you think of a salesperson or a sales force? Perhaps you think of pushy retail sales clerks, "yell-and-sell" TV pitchmen, or the stereotypical glad-handing "used-car salesman." In reality, such stereotypes simply don't fit most of today's salespeople. Instead, today's sales professionals succeed not by taking advantage of customers but by listening to their needs and helping them to forge solutions. Consider IBM, whose customer-focused sales force has been the model for modern personal selling for nearly a century.

*Over 10 million students improved their results using the Pearson MyLabs. Visit **mymktlab.com** for simulations, tutorials, and end-of-chapter problems.

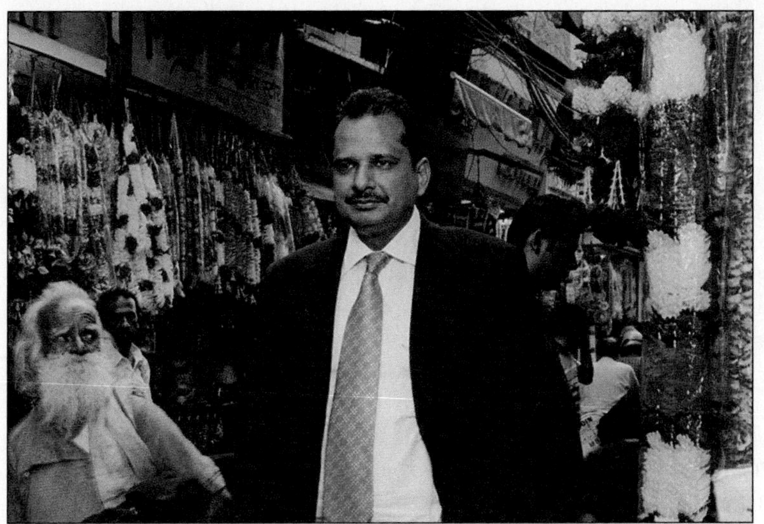

>> Vivek Gupta became IBM's top salesperson in its fastest-growing marketing division (telecommunications) and fastest-growing market (India). He wins business by patiently listening, observing, and identifying how IBM can solve customers' problems.

First Stop

IBM: A Classic Model for Modern Customer-Focused Selling

When Thomas J. Watson Sr. became president of the young Computing Tabulating Recording Corporation—as IBM was known in 1915—sales was considered by many to be a barely reputable profession. Back then, in the minds of most folks, salespeople were slick, fast-talking men who employed hard-sell tactics and fast-and-loose claims to peddle whatever they thought would make them a buck. Watson was a salesman at heart—he'd cut his teeth selling pianos off the back of a horse-drawn wagon to farmers in upstate New York. But he had a different vision for selling. By the time his company was renamed IBM in 1924, he had already put in place a sales force template that would forever change the face of professional sales.

At IBM, Watson hired only top-performing graduates from Ivy League universities, and he insisted that they wear conservative suits and white dress shirts. He demanded the highest ethical standards. IBM provided intensive sales training that focused on developing a deep knowledge of the company and its customers. Above all, Watson stressed, "be a good listener, observe, study through observation." This advice became the foundation of what the company later came to call "solutions selling." By the time Watson handed over the reins of IBM to his son in the 1950s, his forward-looking sales principles were firmly engrained in the company's culture, and IBM had become the model for modern customer-centered selling.

Now a $105 billion company, IBM has survived and prospered for nearly 100 years—something no other *Fortune* top-25 company can claim. During that time, *what* IBM sells has changed dramatically, from cash registers to typewriters to mainframe computers and PCs to its current complex mix of information technology hardware, software, and services. What hasn't changed is *how* IBM sells. IBM salespeople have always been customer relationship developers and solutions providers.

Over the past 100 years, *what* IBM sells has changed dramatically. What hasn't changed is *how* IBM sells. IBM's customer-focused salespeople have always been customer relationship developers and solution providers.

Consider Vivek Gupta, who became IBM's top salesperson in its fastest-growing industry (telecommunications) and fastest-growing market (India). When Gupta first joined IBM in 2003, his sales strengths and philosophies were a perfect fit for the company. IBM was a newcomer in India, struggling to gain a foothold in a market where more than 70 percent of corporations are family controlled, where relationships, trust, and family ties trump almost everything else. In addition to his formal IBM training, Gupta launched his own extensive investigative effort, getting to know people, learning about IBM and its customers, and developing a rock-solid knowledge of how the company's products and services fit customer needs.

When Gupta first approached potential customer Vodafone—the dominant firm in India's exploding mobile phone market—the managing director there told him, "I don't do any business with IBM and I don't intend to." But the quietly determined Gupta kept at it, getting to know Vodafone's key decision makers and patiently listening, observing, and identifying how IBM might be able to help Vodafone succeed in its volatile and competitive markets. Gupta came to know more about Vodafone than many people who worked there. It took him nearly four years, but Gupta finally sold Vodafone—the same people who vowed never to do business with IBM—on a gigantic five-year, $600-million turn-key contract to handle everything from Vodafone's customer service to its finances. Gupta became such a well-known figure at Vodafone's offices in

Mumbai that many people there were surprised that his badge said "IBM" not "Vodafone."

Gupta thrives on rooting out customer problems to solve. "You have to understand [customers'] pain points," he explains. "And they are not going to spell them out." For example, when another big prospect told him "Thanks, but we don't need anything," Gupta asked for permission to study the potential customer's business anyway, no strings attached. When chatting with the company's engineers, he learned that the microwave radio technology they were using in their mobile phone towers was crashing their network six or seven times each week, a very costly problem that greatly annoyed mobile customers. Returning to make a second sales call on the decision maker who'd snubbed him initially, Gupta explained that he understood the network reliability problem and that IBM had a relatively inexpensive fix. That call resulted in a small contract for new microwave radios—not much to brag about. But within a year, the small foothold had led to additional business worth more than $100 million.

Flush with success, Gupta set his sights on still bigger targets. He realized that many big Indian telecoms were so busy simply hammering out their basic back-office operating systems that they had little money and brainpower left for strategy, branding, and marketing. However, IBM had all the technology and expertise required to build and maintain such systems. What if IBM were to take over managing the system innards, freeing the customer to attend to strategy and marketing? Gupta proposed just such a novel solution to Bharti Airtel, then a relative newcomer to India's wireless industry. The result: IBM now runs the bulk of Bharti Airtel's back-office operations, while Bharti Airtel focuses on taking care of its own customers. In the first five years, the deal produced an incredible $1 billion for IBM. Bharti Airtel is now India's wireless industry leader, and the deal is a staple "how-to" case study in IBM's emerging-markets sales training.

IBM's culture has always dictated that its salespeople be "part teacher, part psychologist, and part glad-hander," observes one IBM watcher. But Vivek Gupta's success demonstrates that, to be really good in sales today, they also must be "part diplomat, part entrepreneur, and part inventor"—complete customer problem solvers. Gupta doesn't just sell IBM computer hardware and software—he sells the people and systems that will make the hardware and software come to life. He sells the essential concepts behind the entire system of IBM people and products that will deliver results for the customer. "It's at once radically simple and just plain radical," says the analyst. "He wants to convince you that IBM can run your business—your entire business, save for strategy and marketing—better than you can."

Thus, over the past 100 years, many things have changed as IBM has adapted to the turbulent technological environment. But one thing has remained constant—IBM salespeople are still inspired by Watson's founding principles of selling. Today, IBM still asks aspiring prospective sales candidates, "Can you sell a solution? Can you sell change? Can you create value through industry knowledge?" Vivek Gupta is all about solutions. That's what made him a sales superstar at Big Blue. "I don't remember a single deal in my career which I pursued and I lost," he says. "It's just a question of time. If I play very smart, I can crack the nuts very quickly. If I don't play smart, it might take some time."[1]

In this chapter, we examine two more promotion mix tools: *personal selling* and *sales promotion*. Personal selling consists of interpersonal interactions with customers and prospects to make sales and maintain customer relationships. Sales promotion involves using short-term incentives to encourage customer purchasing, reseller support, and sales force efforts.

Author Comment
Personal selling is the interpersonal arm of the promotion mix. A company's sales force creates and communicates customer value by personally engaging customers and building customer relationships.

Personal Selling

Robert Louis Stevenson once noted, "Everyone lives by selling something." Companies around the world use sales forces to sell products and services to business customers and final consumers. But sales forces are also found in many other kinds of organizations. For example, colleges use recruiters to attract new students, and churches use membership committees to attract new members. Museums and fine arts organizations use fundraisers to contact donors and raise money. Even governments use sales forces. The U.S. Postal Service, for instance, uses a sales force to sell Express Mail and other shipping and mailing solutions to corporate customers. In the first part of this chapter, we examine personal selling's role in the organization, sales force management decisions, and the personal selling process.

The Nature of Personal Selling

Personal selling
Personal presentations by the firm's sales force for the purpose of making sales and building customer relationships.

Personal selling is one of the oldest professions in the world. The people who do the selling go by many names, including salespeople, sales representatives, agents, district managers, account executives, sales consultants, and sales engineers.

People hold many stereotypes of salespeople—including some unfavorable ones. *Salesman* may bring to mind the image of Dwight Schrute, the opinionated Dunder Mifflin paper salesman from the old TV show *The Office*, who lacks both common sense and social skills. Or they may think of the real-life "yell-and-sell" TV pitchmen, who hawk everything from the ShamWow to the INSANITY Workout and the Swivel Sweeper in infomercials. However, the majority of salespeople are a far cry from these unfortunate stereotypes.

As the opening IBM story shows, most salespeople are well-educated and well-trained professionals who add value for customers and maintain long-term customer relationships. They listen to their customers, assess customer needs, and organize the company's efforts to solve customer problems. The best salespeople are the ones who work closely with customers for mutual gain. >> Consider Boeing, the aerospace giant competing in the rough-and-tumble worldwide commercial aircraft market. It takes more than fast talk and a warm smile to sell expensive airplanes:

>> **Professional selling: It takes more than fast talk and a warm smile to sell expensive airplanes. Boeing's real challenge is to win business by building partnerships—day in, day out, year in, year out—with its customers.**

Boeing.

> Selling high-tech aircraft at $150 million or more a copy is complex and challenging. A single big sale to an airline, air-freight carrier, government, and military customer can easily run into billions of dollars. Boeing salespeople head up an extensive team of company specialists—sales and service technicians, financial analysts, planners, engineers—all dedicated to finding ways to satisfy a large customer's needs. On the customer side, buying a batch of jetliners involves dozens or even hundreds of decision makers from all levels of the buying organization, and layer upon layer of subtle and not-so-subtle buying influences. The selling process is nerve-rackingly slow—it can take two or three years from the first sales presentation to the day the sale is announced. After getting the order, salespeople then must stay in almost constant touch to keep track of the account's equipment needs and to make certain the customer stays satisfied. The real challenge is to win buyers' business by building day-in, day-out, year-in, year-out partnerships with them based on superior products and close collaboration.

Salesperson
An individual who represents a company to customers by performing one or more of the following activities: prospecting, communicating, selling, servicing, information gathering, and relationship building.

The term **salesperson** covers a wide range of positions. At one extreme, a salesperson might be largely an *order taker*, such as the department store salesperson standing behind the counter. At the other extreme are *order getters*, whose positions demand *creative selling, social selling,* and *relationship building* for products and services ranging from appliances, industrial equipment, and airplanes to insurance and IT services. In this chapter, we focus on the more creative types of selling and the process of building and managing an effective sales force.

The Role of the Sales Force

Personal selling is the interpersonal arm of the promotion mix. Advertising consists largely of nonpersonal communication with large groups of consumers. By contrast, personal selling involves interpersonal interactions between salespeople and individual customers—whether face to face, by phone, via e-mail or Twitter, through video or online conferences, or by other means. Personal selling can be more effective than advertising in more complex selling situations. Salespeople can probe customers to learn more about their problems and then adjust the marketing offer and presentation to fit each customer's special needs.

The role of personal selling varies from company to company. Some firms have no salespeople at all—for example, companies that sell only online, or companies that sell through manufacturers' reps, sales agents, or brokers. In most firms, however, the sales force plays a major role. In companies that sell business products and services, such as IBM, DuPont, or Boeing, salespeople work directly with customers. In consumer product companies such as Nestlé or Nike, the sales force plays an important behind-the-scenes role. It works with wholesalers and retailers to gain their support and help them be more effective in selling the company's products to final buyers.

Linking the Company with Its Customers

The sales force serves as a critical link between a company and its customers. »In many cases, salespeople serve two masters—the seller and the buyer. First, they *represent the company to customers*. They find and develop new customers and communicate information about the company's products and services. They sell products by approaching and engaging customers, presenting their offerings, answering objections, negotiating prices and terms, closing sales, and servicing accounts.

» Salespeople link the company with its customers. To many customers, the salesperson *is* the company.

Digital Vision.

At the same time, salespeople *represent customers to the company*, acting inside the firm as "champions" of customers' interests and managing the buyer–seller relationship. Salespeople relay customer concerns about company products and actions back inside to those who can handle them. They learn about customer needs and work with other marketing and nonmarketing people in the company to develop greater customer value.

In fact, to many customers, the salesperson *is* the company—the only tangible manifestation of the company that they see. Hence, customers may become loyal to salespeople as well as to the companies and products they represent. This concept of *salesperson-owned loyalty* lends even more importance to the salesperson's customer-relationship-building abilities. Strong relationships with the salesperson will result in strong relationships with the company and its products. Conversely, poor salesperson relationships will probably result in poor company and product relationships.

Given its role in linking the company with its customers, the sales force must be strongly customer-solutions focused. In fact, such a customer-solutions focus is a must not only for the sales force but also for the entire organization.

Coordinating Marketing and Sales

Ideally, the sales force and other marketing functions (marketing planners, brand managers, and researchers) should work together closely to jointly create value for customers. Unfortunately, however, some companies still treat sales and marketing as separate functions. When this happens, the separate sales and marketing groups may not get along well. When things go wrong, marketers blame the sales force for its poor execution of what they see as an otherwise splendid strategy. In turn, the sales team blames the marketers for being out of touch with what's really going on with customers. Neither group fully values the other's contributions. However, if not repaired, such disconnects between marketing and sales can damage customer relationships and company performance.

A company can take several actions to help bring its marketing and sales functions closer together. At the most basic level, it can increase communications between the two groups by arranging joint meetings and spelling out communications channels. It can create opportunities for salespeople and marketers to work together. Brand managers and researchers can tag along on sales calls or sit in on sales planning sessions. In turn, salespeople can sit in on marketing planning sessions and share their firsthand customer knowledge.

A company can also create joint objectives and reward systems for sales and marketing teams or appoint marketing–sales liaisons—people from marketing who "live with the sales force" and help coordinate marketing and sales force programs and efforts. Finally, it can appoint a high-level marketing executive to oversee both marketing and sales. Such a person can help infuse marketing and sales with the common goal of creating value for customers to capture value in return.[2]

Author Comment
Here's another definition of sales force management: "planning, organizing, leading, and controlling personal contact programs designed to achieve profitable customer relationships." Once again, the goal of every marketing activity is to create customer value and build customer relationships.

Managing the Sales Force

We define **sales force management** as analyzing, planning, implementing, and controlling sales force activities. It includes designing sales force strategy and structure, as well as recruiting, selecting, training, compensating, supervising, and evaluating the firm's salespeople. These major sales force management decisions are shown in **Figure 13.1** and discussed in the following sections.

Sales force management
Analyzing, planning, implementing, and controlling sales force activities.

Designing the Sales Force Strategy and Structure

Marketing managers face several sales force strategy and design questions. How should salespeople and their tasks be structured? How big should the sales force be? Should salespeople sell alone or work in teams with other people in the company? Should they sell in the field, by phone, or on the Internet? We address these issues next.

The Sales Force Structure

A company can divide sales responsibilities along any of several lines. The structure decision is simple if the company sells only one product line to one industry with customers in many locations. In that case the company would use a *territorial sales force structure*. However, if the company sells many products to many types of customers, it might need a *product sales force structure*, a *customer sales force structure*, or a combination of the two.

Territorial sales force structure
A sales force organization that assigns each salesperson to an exclusive geographic territory in which that salesperson sells the company's full line.

In the **territorial sales force structure**, each salesperson is assigned to an exclusive geographic area and sells the company's full line of products or services to all customers in that territory. This organization clearly defines each salesperson's job and fixes accountability. It also increases the salesperson's desire to build local customer relationships that, in turn, improve selling effectiveness. Finally, because each salesperson travels within a limited geographic area, travel expenses are relatively small. A territorial sales organization is often supported by many levels of sales management positions. For example, individual territory sales reps may report to area managers, who in turn report to regional managers who report to a director of sales.

Product sales force structure
A sales force organization in which salespeople specialize in selling only a portion of the company's products or lines.

If a company has numerous and complex products, it can adopt a **product sales force structure**, in which the sales force specializes along product lines. For example, GE employs different sales forces within different product and service divisions of its major businesses. Within GE Infrastructure, for instance, the company has separate sales forces for aviation, energy, transportation, and water processing products and technologies. No single salesperson can become expert in all of these product categories, so product specialization is required. Similarly, GE Healthcare employs different sales forces for diagnostic imaging, life sciences, and integrated IT products and services. In all, a company as large and complex as GE might have dozens of separate sales forces serving its diverse product and service portfolio.

Customer (or market) sales force structure
A sales force organization in which salespeople specialize in selling only to certain customers or industries.

Using a **customer** (or **market**) **sales force structure**, a company organizes its sales force along customer or industry lines. Separate sales forces may be set up for different

Figure 13.1 Major Steps in Sales Force Management

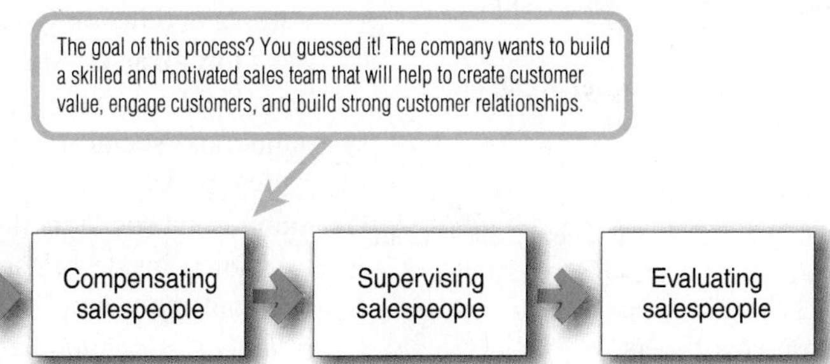
The goal of this process? You guessed it! The company wants to build a skilled and motivated sales team that will help to create customer value, engage customers, and build strong customer relationships.
Designing sales force strategy and structure
Recruiting and selecting salespeople
Training salespeople
Compensating salespeople
Supervising salespeople
Evaluating salespeople

Sales force structure: Whirlpool specializes its sales force by customer and by territory for each key customer group.

Paul Sancya/Associated Press.

industries, serving current customers versus finding new ones, and serving major accounts versus regular accounts. Organizing the sales force around customers can help a company build closer relationships with important customers. Many companies even have special sales forces to handle the needs of individual large customers. For example, appliance maker Whirlpool assigns individual teams of salespeople to big retail customers such as Sears, Lowe's, Best Buy, and Home Depot. Each Whirlpool sales team aligns with the large customer's buying team.[3]

When a company sells a wide variety of products to many types of customers over a broad geographic area, it often employs a *complex sales force structure,* which combines several types of organization. Salespeople can be specialized by customer and territory; product and territory; product and customer; or territory, product, and customer. For example, Whirlpool specializes its sales force by customer (with different sales teams for Sears, Lowe's, Best Buy, Home Depot, and smaller independent retailers) *and* by territory for each key customer group (territory representatives, territory managers, regional managers, and so on). No single structure is best for all companies and situations. Each company should select a sales force structure that best serves the needs of its customers and fits its overall marketing strategy.

Sales Force Size

Once the company has set its structure, it is ready to consider *sales force size*. Sales forces may range in size from only a few salespeople to tens of thousands. Some sales forces are huge—for example, in the United States, PepsiCo employs 36,000 salespeople; American Express, 23,400; GE, 16,400; and Xerox, 15,000.[4] Salespeople constitute one of the company's most productive—and most expensive—assets. Therefore, increasing their numbers will increase both sales and costs.

Many companies use some form of *workload approach* to set sales force size. Using this approach, a company first groups accounts into different classes according to size, account status, or other factors related to the amount of effort required to maintain the account. It then determines the number of salespeople needed to call on each class of accounts the desired number of times.

The company might think as follows: Suppose we have 1,000 A-level accounts and 2,000 B-level accounts. A-level accounts require 36 calls per year, and B-level accounts require 12 calls per year. In this case, the sales force's *workload*—the number of calls it must make per year—is 60,000 calls [(1,000 × 36) + (2,000 × 12) = 36,000 + 24,000 = 60,000]. Suppose our average salesperson can make 1,000 calls a year. Thus, we need 60 salespeople (60,000 ÷ 1,000).

Other Sales Force Strategy and Structure Issues

Sales management must also determine who will be involved in the selling effort and how various sales and sales support people will work together.

Outside sales force (or field sales force)
Salespeople who travel to call on customers in the field.

Inside sales force
Salespeople who conduct business from their offices via telephone, online and social media interactions, or visits from prospective buyers.

Outside and Inside Sales Forces. A company may have an **outside sales force** (or **field sales force**), an **inside sales force**, or both. Outside salespeople travel to call on customers in the field. In contrast, inside salespeople conduct business from their offices via telephone, online and social media interactions, or visits from buyers. The use of inside sales has grown in recent years as a result of increased outside selling costs and the surge in online, mobile, and social media technologies.

Some inside salespeople provide support for the outside sales force, freeing them to spend more time selling to major accounts and finding new prospects. For example, *technical sales support people* provide technical information and answers to customers' questions. *Sales assistants* provide research and administrative backup for outside salespeople. They track down sales leads, call ahead and confirm appointments, follow up on deliveries, and answer customers' questions when outside salespeople cannot be reached. Using such combinations of inside and outside salespeople can help serve important customers better. The inside rep provides daily access and support, whereas the outside rep provides face-to-face collaboration and relationship building.

Other inside salespeople do more than just provide support. *Telemarketers* and *online sellers* use the phone, Internet, and social media to find new leads, learn about customers and their business, or sell and service accounts directly. Telemarketing and online selling can be very effective, less costly ways to sell to smaller, harder-to-reach customers. Depending on the complexity of the product and customer, for example, a telemarketer can make from 20 to 33 decision-maker contacts a day, compared to the average of 4 that an outside salesperson can make. In addition, whereas an average business-to-business (B-to-B) field sales call can average close to $600, a routine industrial telemarketing or online contact might average only $20 to $30.[5]

Although the federal government's Do Not Call Registry put a dent in telephone sales to consumers, telemarketing remains a vital tool for most B-to-B marketers. For some smaller companies, telephone and Internet selling may be the primary sales approaches. However, larger companies also use these tactics, either to sell directly to small and midsize customers or help out with larger ones.

In addition to costs savings, in today's digital, mobile, and social media environments, many buyers are more receptive to—or even prefer—phone and online contact versus the high level of face-to-face contact once required. Many customers are more inclined to gather information online and use the phone, Internet meetings, and social media interactions to engage sellers and close deals. "With virtual meeting software such as GoToMeeting .com and WebEx, communications tools such as Skype, and social media sites such as Twitter, Facebook, and LinkedIn, it's become easier to sell with few if any face-to-face meetings," says an inside sales consultant.[6]

As a result of these trends, telephone and online selling are growing much faster than in-person selling. One study also notes the emergence of the "hybrid sales rep," a modern cross between a field sales rep and an inside rep, who often works from a remote location. Some 41 percent of outside sales activity is now done over the phone or a mobile device, from either a home office, a company office, or on the go.[7]

For many types of products and selling situations, » phone or online selling can be as effective as a personal sales call:[8]

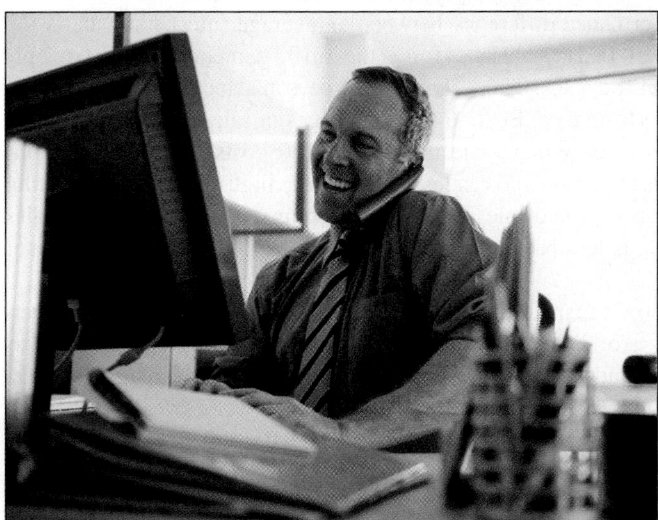

» **For many types of selling situations, phone or Web selling can be as effective as a personal sales call. At Climax Portable Machine Tools, phone reps build surprisingly strong and personal customer relationships.**

© Tetra Images/Alamy.

> Climax Portable Machining and Welding Systems, which manufactures portable maintenance tools for the metal cutting industry, has proven that telephone and online marketing can save money and still lavish attention on buyers. Under the old system, Climax sales engineers spent one-third of their time on the road, training distributor salespeople and accompanying them on calls. They could make about four contacts a day. Now, each of five sales engineers on Climax's inside sales team calls about 30 prospects a day, following up on leads generated by ads, e-mails, and the company's Facebook, Twitter, YouTube, and other social-media sites. Because it takes about five calls to close a sale, the sales engineers update a prospect's profile after each contact, noting the degree of commitment, requirements, next call date, and personal comments. "If anyone mentions he's going on a fishing trip, our sales engineer enters that in the sales information system and uses it to personalize the next call," says Climax's president, noting that this is one way to build good relations.
>
> Another is that the first contact with a prospect includes the sales engineer's business card with his or her picture on it. Climax's customer sales system also gives inside reps instant access to customer information entered by the outside sales force and service people. Armed with all the information, inside reps can build surprisingly strong and personal customer relationships.

Of course, it takes more than friendliness to sell $15,000 machine tools over the phone (special orders may run $200,000), but the telephone and online approach works well. When Climax customers were asked, "Do you see the sales engineer often enough?" the response was overwhelmingly positive. Obviously, many people didn't realize that the only contact they had with Climax had been on the phone or Internet.

Team selling
Using teams of people from sales, marketing, engineering, finance, technical support, and even upper management to service large, complex accounts.

Team Selling. As products become more complex, and as customers grow larger and more demanding, a single salesperson simply can't handle all of a large customer's needs. Instead, most companies now use **team selling** to service large, complex accounts. Sales teams can unearth problems, solutions, and sales opportunities that no individual salesperson could. Such teams might include experts from any area or level of the selling firm—sales, marketing, technical and support services, research and development (R&D), engineering, operations, finance, and others.

In many cases, the move to team selling mirrors similar changes in customers' buying organizations. Many large customer companies have implemented team-based purchasing, requiring marketers to employ equivalent team-based selling. When dealing with large, complex accounts, one salesperson can't be an expert in everything the customer needs. Instead, selling is done by strategic account teams, quarterbacked by senior account managers or customer business managers.

Some companies, such as IBM, Xerox, and P&G, have used teams for a long time. As we will discuss again later in the chapter, P&G sales reps are organized into Customer Business Development (CBD) teams. Each CBD team is assigned to a major P&G customer, such as Walmart, Safeway, or CVS Pharmacy. The CBD organization places the focus on serving the complete needs of each major customer. It lets P&G "grow business by working as a 'strategic partner' with our accounts," not just as a supplier.[9]

Team selling does have some pitfalls, however. For example, salespeople are by nature competitive and have often been trained and rewarded for outstanding individual performance. Salespeople who are used to having customers all to themselves may have trouble learning to work with and trust others on a team. In addition, selling teams can confuse or overwhelm customers who are used to working with only one salesperson. Finally, difficulties in evaluating individual contributions to the team-selling effort can create some sticky compensation issues.

Recruiting and Selecting Salespeople

At the heart of any successful sales force operation is the recruitment and selection of good salespeople. The performance difference between an average salesperson and a top salesperson can be substantial. In a typical sales force, the top 30 percent of the salespeople might bring in 60 percent of the sales. Thus, careful salesperson selection can greatly increase overall sales force performance. Beyond the differences in sales performance, poor selection results in costly turnover. When a salesperson quits, the costs of finding and training a new salesperson—plus the costs of lost sales—can be very high. One sales consulting firm calculates the total costs of a bad sales hire at a whopping $616,000.[10] Also, a sales force with many new people is less productive, and turnover disrupts important customer relationships.

What sets great salespeople apart from all the rest? In an effort to profile top sales performers, Gallup Consulting, a division of the well-known Gallup polling organization, has interviewed hundreds of thousands of salespeople. Its research suggests that the best salespeople possess four key talents: intrinsic motivation, a disciplined work style, the ability to close a sale, and, perhaps most important, the ability to build relationships with customers.[11]

Super salespeople are motivated from within—they have an unrelenting drive to excel. Some salespeople are driven by money, a desire for recognition, or the satisfaction of competing and winning. Others are driven by the desire to provide service and build relationships. The best salespeople possess some of each of these motivations. They also have a disciplined work style. They lay out detailed, organized plans and then follow through in a timely way.

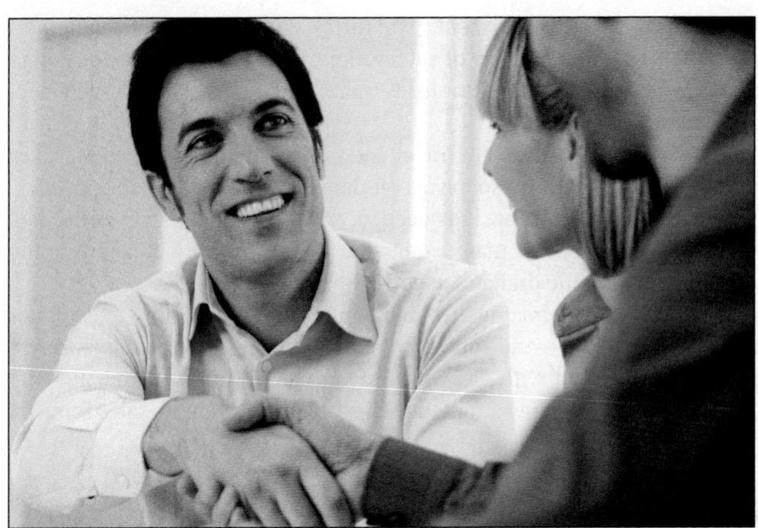

Great salespeople: The best salespeople possess intrinsic motivation, disciplined work style, the ability to close a sale, and, perhaps most important, the ability to build relationships with customers.

© Rido.

But motivation and discipline mean little unless they result in closing more sales and building better customer relationships. Super salespeople build the skills and knowledge they need to get the job done. Perhaps most important, top salespeople are excellent customer problem solvers and relationship builders. They understand their customers' needs. Talk to sales executives and they'll describe top performers in these terms: good listeners, empathetic, patient, caring, and responsive. Top performers can put themselves on the buyer's side of the desk and see the world through their customers' eyes. They don't want just to be liked; they want to add value for their customers.

That said, there is no one right way to sell. Each successful salesperson uses a different approach, one that best applies his or her unique strengths and talents. For example, some salespeople enjoy the thrill of a harder sell in confronting challenges and winning people over. Others might apply "softer" talents to reach the same goal. "The key is for sales reps to understand and nurture their innate talents so they can develop their own personal approach and win business *their* way," says a selling expert.[12]

When recruiting, a company should analyze the sales job itself and the characteristics of its most successful salespeople to identify the traits needed by a successful salesperson in their industry. Then it must recruit the right salespeople. The human resources department looks for applicants by getting names from current salespeople, using employment agencies, searching the Internet and online social media, posting ads and notices on its Web site and industry media, and working through college placement services. Another source is to attract top salespeople from other companies. Proven salespeople need less training and can be productive immediately.

Recruiting will attract many applicants from which the company must select the best. The selection procedure can vary from a single informal interview to lengthy testing and interviewing. Many companies give formal tests to sales applicants. Tests typically measure sales aptitude, analytical and organizational skills, personality traits, and other characteristics. But test scores provide only one piece of information in a set that includes personal characteristics, references, past employment history, and interviewer reactions.

Training Salespeople

New salespeople may spend anywhere from a few weeks or months to a year or more in training. After the initial training ends, most companies provide continuing sales training via seminars, sales meetings, and Internet e-learning throughout the salesperson's career. According to one source, North American firms spent more than nearly $2 billion on sales training last year. Although training can be expensive, it can also yield dramatic returns. For instance, one recent study showed that sales training conducted by ADP, an administrative services firm, resulted in a return on investment of nearly 338 percent in only 90 days.[13]

Training programs have several goals. First, salespeople need to know about customers and how to build relationships with them. Therefore, the training program must teach them about different types of customers and their needs, buying motives, and buying habits. It must also teach them how to sell effectively and train them in the basics of the selling process. Salespeople also need to know and identify with the company, its products, and its competitors. Therefore, an effective training program teaches them about the company's objectives, organization, products, and the strategies of major competitors.

Today, many companies are adding digital e-learning to their sales training programs. Online training may range from simple text- and video-based product training and Internet-based sales exercises that build sales skills to sophisticated simulations that re-create the dynamics of real-life sales calls. One of the most basic forms is virtual instructor-led training (VILT). Using this method, a small group of salespeople at remote locations logs on to a Web conferencing site, where a sales instructor leads training sessions using online video, audio, and interactive learning tools.

Training online instead of on-site can cut travel and other training costs, and it takes up less of a salesperson's selling time. It also makes on-demand training available to salespeople, letting them train as little or as much as needed, whenever and wherever needed. Although most e-learning is Web-based, many companies now offer on-demand training from anywhere via almost any mobile digital device.

Many companies are now using imaginative and sophisticated e-learning techniques to make sales training more efficient—and sometimes even more fun. For example, Bayer HealthCare Pharmaceuticals worked with Concentric Pharma Advertising, a health-care marketing agency, to create a role-playing simulation video game to train its sales force on a new drug marketing program:[14]

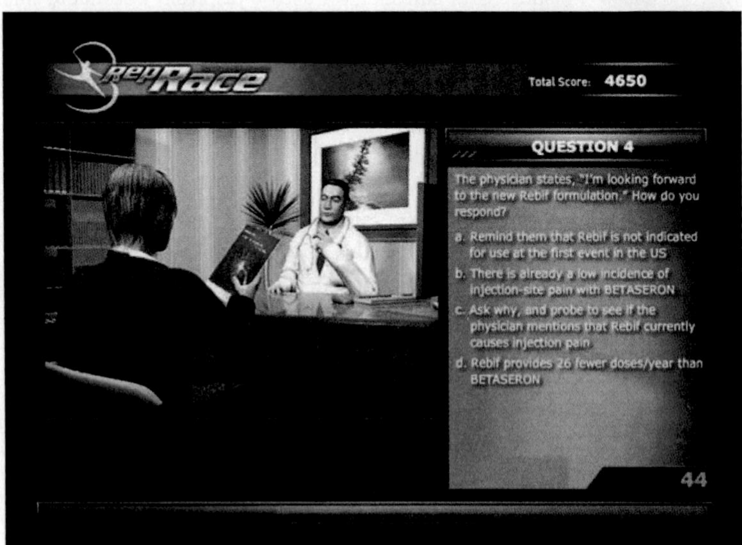

E-training can make sales training more efficient—and more fun. Bayer HealthCare Pharmaceuticals' role-playing video game—Rep Race—helped improve sales rep effectiveness by 20 percent.

Concentric Pharma Advertising.

Most people don't usually associate fast-paced rock music and flashy graphics with online sales training tools. But Concentric Pharma Advertising's innovative role-playing video game—Rep Race: The Battle for Office Supremacy—has all that and a lot more. Rep Race gives Bayer sales reps far more entertainment than the staid old multiple-choice skills tests it replaces. The game was created to help breathe new life into a mature Bayer product—Betaseron, an 18-year-old multiple sclerosis (MS) therapy treatment. The aim was to find a fresh, more active way to help Bayer sales reps apply the in-depth information they learned about Betaseron to actual selling and objections-handling situations. Bayer also wanted to increase rep engagement through interactive learning and feedback through real-time results. Bayer reps liked Rep Race from the start. According to Bayer, when the game was first launched, reps played it as many as 30 times. In addition to its educational and motivational value, Rep Race allowed Bayer to measure sales reps' individual and collective performance. In the end, Bayer calculated that the Rep Race simulation helped improve the Betaseron sales team's effectiveness by 20 percent.

Compensating Salespeople

To attract good salespeople, a company must have an appealing compensation plan. Compensation consists of four elements: a fixed amount, a variable amount, expenses, and fringe benefits. The fixed amount, usually a salary, gives the salesperson some stable income. The variable amount, which might be commissions or bonuses based on sales performance, rewards the salesperson for greater effort and success.

Management must determine what *mix* of these compensation elements makes the most sense for each sales job. Different combinations of fixed and variable compensation give rise to four basic types of compensation plans: straight salary, straight commission, salary plus bonus, and salary plus commission. According to one study of sales force compensation, 18 percent of companies pay straight salary, 19 percent pay straight commission, and 63 percent pay a combination of salary plus incentives. A study showed that the average salesperson's pay consists of about 67 percent salary and 33 percent incentive pay.[15]

A sales force compensation plan can both motivate salespeople and direct their activities. Compensation should direct salespeople toward activities that are consistent with the overall sales force and marketing objectives. For example, if the strategy is to acquire new business, grow rapidly, and gain market share, the compensation plan might include a larger commission component, coupled with a new-account bonus to encourage high sales performance and new account development. In contrast, if the goal is to maximize current account profitability, the compensation plan might contain a larger base-salary component with additional incentives for current account sales or customer satisfaction.

In fact, more and more companies are moving away from high-commission plans that may drive salespeople to make short-term grabs for business. They worry that a salesperson who is pushing too hard to close a deal may ruin the customer relationship. Instead, companies are designing compensation plans that reward salespeople for building customer relationships and growing the long-run value of each customer.

When times get tough economically, some companies are tempted to cut costs by reducing sales compensation. However, although some cost-cutting measures make sense when business is sluggish, cutting sales force compensation across the board is usually an action of last resort. Top salespeople are always in demand, and paying them less might mean losing them at a time when they are most needed. Thus, short-changing key salespeople can result in short-changing important customer relationships. If the company must reduce its compensation expenses, rather than making across-the-board cuts, companies should continue to pay top performers well while turning loose low performers.

Supervising and Motivating Salespeople

New salespeople need more than a territory, compensation, and training—they need supervision and motivation. The goal of *supervision* is to help salespeople "work smart" by doing the right things in the right ways. The goal of *motivation* is to encourage salespeople to "work hard" and energetically toward sales force goals. If salespeople work smart and work hard, they will realize their full potential—to their own and the company's benefit.

Supervising Salespeople

Companies vary in how closely they supervise their salespeople. Many help salespeople identify target customers and set call objectives. Some may also specify how much time the sales force should spend prospecting for new accounts and set other time management priorities. One tool is the weekly, monthly, or annual *call plan* that shows which customers and prospects to call on and which activities to carry out. Another tool is *time-and-duty analysis*. In addition to time spent selling, the salesperson spends time traveling, waiting, taking breaks, and doing administrative chores.

» **Figure 13.2** shows how salespeople spend their time. On average, active selling time accounts for only 11 percent of total working time! If selling time could be raised from 11 percent to 33 percent, this would triple the time spent selling.[16] Companies are always looking for ways to save time—simplifying administrative duties, developing better sales-call and routing plans, supplying more and better customer information, and using phone, e-mail, or Internet conferencing instead of traveling.

Many firms have adopted *sales force automation systems*: computerized, digitized sales force operations that let salespeople work more effectively anytime, anywhere. Companies

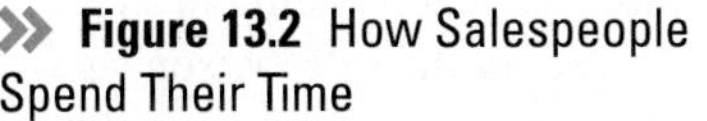

» **Figure 13.2** How Salespeople Spend Their Time

Source: Proudfoot Consulting. Data used with permission.

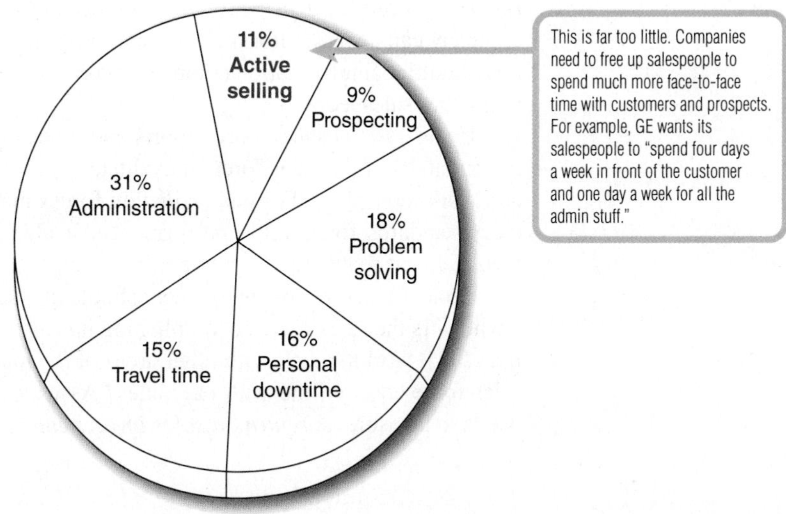

now routinely equip their salespeople with laptops or tablets, smartphones, wireless connections, videoconferencing technologies, and customer-contact and relationship management software. Armed with these technologies, salespeople can more effectively and efficiently profile customers and prospects, analyze and forecast sales, engage customers, make presentations, prepare sales and expense reports, and manage account relationships. The result is better time management, improved customer service, lower sales costs, and higher sales performance. In all, technology has reshaped the ways in which salespeople carry out their duties and engage customers.

Motivating Salespeople

Beyond directing salespeople, sales managers must also motivate them. Some salespeople will do their best without any special urging from management. To them, selling may be the most fascinating job in the world. But selling can also be frustrating. Salespeople often work alone, and they must sometimes travel away from home. They may also face aggressive competing salespeople and difficult customers. Therefore, salespeople often need special encouragement to do their best.

Management can boost sales force morale and performance through its organizational climate, sales quotas, and positive incentives. *Organizational climate* describes the feeling that salespeople have about their opportunities, value, and rewards for a good performance. Some companies treat salespeople as if they are not very important, so performance suffers accordingly. Other companies treat their salespeople as valued contributors and allow virtually unlimited opportunity for income and promotion. Not surprisingly, these companies enjoy higher sales force performance and less turnover.

Sales quota
A standard that states the amount a salesperson should sell and how sales should be divided among the company's products.

Many companies motivate their salespeople by setting **sales quotas**—standards stating the amount they should sell and how sales should be divided among the company's products. Compensation is often related to how well salespeople meet their quotas. Companies also use various *positive incentives* to increase the sales force effort. *Sales meetings* provide social occasions, breaks from the routine, chances to meet and talk with "company brass," and opportunities to air feelings and identify with a larger group. Companies also sponsor *sales contests* to spur the sales force to make a selling effort above and beyond what is normally expected. Other incentives include honors, merchandise and cash awards, trips, and profit-sharing plans.

Evaluating Salespeople and Sales Force Performance

We have thus far described how management communicates what salespeople should be doing and how it motivates them to do it. This process requires good feedback, which means getting regular information about salespeople to evaluate their performance.

Management gets information about its salespeople in several ways. The most important source is *sales reports*, including weekly or monthly work plans and longer-term territory marketing plans. Salespeople also write up their completed activities on *call reports* and turn in *expense reports* for which they are partly or wholly reimbursed. The company can also monitor the sales and profit performance data in the salesperson's territory. Additional information comes from personal observation, customer surveys, and talks with other salespeople.

Using various sales force reports and other information, sales management evaluates the members of the sales force. It evaluates salespeople on their ability to "plan their work and work their plan." Formal evaluation forces management to develop and communicate clear standards for judging performance. It also provides salespeople with constructive feedback and motivates them to perform well.

On a broader level, management should evaluate the performance of the sales force as a whole. Is the sales force accomplishing its customer relationship, sales, and profit objectives? Is it working well with other areas of the marketing and company organization? Are sales force costs in line with outcomes? As with other marketing activities, the company wants to measure its *return on sales investment*.

Author Comment
Like just about everything else these days, the digital technologies have impacted selling big time. Today's sales forces are mastering the use of online, mobile, and social media tools to engage business customers, build relationships, and make sales.

Selling Digitally: Online, Mobile, and Social Media Tools

The fastest-growing sales trend is the exploding use of online, mobile, and social media tools in selling. New digital sales force technologies are creating exciting new avenues for connecting with and engaging customers in the digital and social media age. Some analysts even predict that the Internet will mean the death of person-to-person selling, as salespeople are ultimately replaced by Web sites, online social media, mobile apps, video and conferencing technologies, and other tools that allow direct customer contact. "Don't believe it," says one sales expert (see Marketing at Work 13.1).[17] Used properly, online and social media technologies won't make salespeople obsolete; they will make salespeople more productive and effective.

The new digital technologies are providing salespeople with powerful tools for identifying and learning about prospects, engaging customers, creating customer value, closing sales, and nurturing customer relationships. Internet-based technologies can produce big organizational benefits for sales forces. They help conserve salespeople's valuable time, save travel dollars, and give salespeople new vehicles for selling and servicing accounts.

Using the Internet hasn't really changed the fundamentals of selling. "The way to sell is to touch, listen to, and engage customers," says one sales force expert. "Now we do [more of] it online." However, the Internet and social media are dramatically changing the customer buying process. As a result, they are also changing the selling process. In today's digital world, many customers no longer rely as much as they once did on information and assistance provided by salespeople. Instead, they carry out more of the buying process on their own—especially the early stages. Increasingly, they use online and social media resources to analyze their own problems, research solutions, get advice from colleagues, and rank buying options before ever speaking to a salesperson. One recent study of more than 1,400 business buyers found that, on average, buyers completed nearly 60 percent of the buying process before contacting a supplier.[18]

Thus, today's customers have much more control over the sales process than they had in the days when brochures, pricing, and product advice were only available from a sales rep. Customers can now browse corporate Web sites, blogs, and YouTube videos to identify and qualify sellers. They can hobnob with others buyers on social media such as LinkedIn, Twitter, or Facebook to share experiences, identify solutions, and evaluate products they are considering. According to one study, 55 percent of business buyers now turn to social media when searching for information.[19]

As a result, if and when salespeople do enter the buying process, customers often know almost as much about a company's products as the salespeople do. "It's not just that buyers start the sales process without you," says an analyst, "they typically complete most of the purchase journey before having any contact with sales. And by that point they are far more informed about your business than you are about theirs."[20]

In response to this new digital buying environment, sellers are reorienting their selling processes around the new customer buying process. They are "going where customers are"—social media, Web forums, online communities, blogs—in order to engage customers earlier. They are engaging customers not just where and when they are buying, but also where and when they are learning about and evaluating what they will buy. Salespeople now routinely use digital tools to monitor customer social media exchanges to spot trends, identify prospects, and learn what customers would like to buy, how they feel about a vendor, and what it would take to make a sale. They generate lists of prospective customers from online databases and social networking sites, such as InsideView, Hoovers, and LinkedIn. They create dialogs when prospective customers visit their Web and social media sites through live chats with the sales team. » They use Internet conferencing tools such as WebEx, GoToMeeting, or TelePresence to talk live with customers about products and services. They provide videos and other information on their YouTube channels and Facebook pages.

MARKETING AT WORK 13.1

B-to-B Salespeople: In This Digital and Social Media Age, Who Needs Them Anymore?

It's hard to imagine a world without salespeople. But according to some analysts, there will be a lot fewer of them a decade from now. With the explosion of the Internet, mobile devices, social media, and other technologies that link customers directly with companies, they reason, who needs face-to-face selling anymore? According to the doubters, salespeople are rapidly being replaced by Web sites, e-mail, blogs, mobile apps, video sharing, virtual trade shows, social media such as LinkedIn and Facebook, and a host of other digital-age interaction tools.

Research firm Gartner predicts that by 2020, 85 percent of all interactions between businesses will be executed without human intervention, requiring fewer salespeople. Of the 18 million salespeople now employed in the United States, the firm says, there will be only about 4 million left. "The world no longer needs salespeople," one doomsayer boldly proclaims. "Sales is a dying profession and soon will be as outmoded as oil lamps and the rotary phone." Says another, "If we don't find and fill a need faster than a computer, we won't be needed."

So, is business-to-business selling really dying? Will the Internet, mobile technologies, and social media replace the age-old art of selling face to face? To answer these questions, *SellingPower* magazine called together a panel of five sales experts and asked them to weigh in on the future of B-to-B sales. The panel members agreed that technology is radically transforming the selling profession. Today's revolutionary changes in how people communicate are affecting every aspect of business, and selling is no exception.

But is B-to-B selling dead in this Internet age? Don't believe it, says the *SellingPower* panel. Technology, the Internet, and social media won't soon be replacing person-to-person buying and selling. Selling has changed, agrees the panel, and the technology can greatly enhance the selling process. But it can't replace many of the functions that salespeople perform. "The Internet can take orders and disseminate content, but what it can't do is discover customer needs," says one panelist. "It can't build relationships, and it can't prospect on its own." Adds another panelist, "Someone must define the company's value proposition and unique message and communicate it to the market, and that person is the sales rep."

What is dying, however, is what one panelist calls the account-maintenance role—the order taker who stops by the customer's office on Friday and says, "Hey, got anything for me?" Such salespeople are not creating value and can easily be replaced by automation. However, salespeople who excel at new customer acquisition, relationship management, and account growth with existing customers will always be in high demand.

There's no doubt about it—technology is transforming the profession of selling. Instead of relying on salespeople for basic information and education, customers can now do much of their own prepurchase research via Web sites, online searches, social media contacts, and other venues. Many customers now start the sales process online and do their homework about competing products and suppliers before the first sales meeting ever takes place. They don't need basic information or product education; they need solutions. So today's salespeople need "to move into the discovery and relationship-building phase, uncovering pain points and focusing on the prospect's business," says a panelist.

Rather than replacing salespeople, however, technology is augmenting them. Today's salespeople aren't really doing anything fundamentally new. They've always done customer research and social networking. Today, however, they are "doing it on steroids," using a new kit of high-tech digital tools and applications.

For example, many companies are moving rapidly into online-community-based selling. Case in point: enterprise-software company SAP, which has set up EcoHub, its own online, community-powered social media marketplace consisting of customers, partners, and almost anyone else who wants to join. The EcoHub community (ecohub.sap.com) has 2 million users in 200 countries and extends across a broad Internet spectrum—a dedicated Web site, Twitter channels, LinkedIn groups, Facebook fan pages, YouTube channels, Flickr groups, mobile apps, and more. It includes 600 "solution storefronts" where visitors can

» Online selling tools, such as SAP's EcoHub online community-based social media marketplace, are coming into their own in helping to build customer awareness and generate consideration, purchase interest, and sales. But rather than replacing salespeople, such efforts extend their reach and effectiveness.

"easily discover, evaluate, and initiate the purchase of software solutions and services from SAP and its partners." EcoHub also lets users rate the solutions and advice they get from other community members.

SAP was surprised to learn that what it had originally seen as a place for customers to discuss issues, problems, and solutions has turned into a significant point of sale. The information, give-and-take discussions, and conversations at the site draw in customers, even for big-ticket sales. "Some customers are spending $20 to $30 million due to EcoHub," says the SAP vice president who heads up the community.

However, although EcoHub draws in new potential customers and takes them through many of the initial stages of product discovery and evaluation, it doesn't replace SAP's or its partners' salespeople. Instead, it extends their reach and effectiveness. The real value of EcoHub is the flood of sales leads it creates for the SAP and partner sales forces. Once prospective customers have discovered, discussed, and evaluated SAP solutions on EcoHub, SAP invites them to "initiate contact, request a proposal, or start the negotiation process." That's where the person-to-person selling begins.

All this suggests that B-to-B selling isn't dying, it's just changing. The tools and techniques may be different as selling leverages and adapts to selling in the digital and social media age. But the panelists agree strongly that B-to-B marketers will never be able to do without strong sales teams. Salespeople who can discover customer needs, solve customer problems, and build relationships will be needed and successful, regardless of what else changes. Especially for those big-ticket B-to-B sales, "all the new technology may make it easier to sell by building strong ties to customers even before the first sit-down, but when the signature hits the dotted line, there will be a sales rep there."

Sources: Quotes and other information from Robert McGarvey, "All about Us," *SellingPower,* March 7, 2011, p. 48; Lain Chroust Ehmann, "Sales Up!" *SellingPower*, January/February 2011, p. 40; James Ledbetter, "Death of a Salesman. Of Lots of Them, Actually," *Slate*, September 21, 2010, www.slate.com/id/2268122/; Sean Callahan, "Is B-to-B Marketing Really Obsolete?" *BtoB,* January 17, 2011, p. 1; Gerhared Gschwandtner, "How Many Salespeople Will Be Left by 2020?" *SellingPower,* May/June 2011, p. 7; Brent Adamson, Matthew Dixon, and Nicholas Toman, "The End of Solution Sales," *HBR,* July–August 2012, pp. 61–68; Scott Gillum, "The Disappearing Sales Process," *Forbes,* January 7, 2013, www.forbes.com/sites/gyro/2013/01/07/the-disappearing-sales-process/; Matt Dixon and Steve Richard, "Solution Selling Is Dead: Why 2013 Is the Year of B@B Insight Selling," *Openview,* January 4, 2013, http://labs.openviewpartners.com/solution-selling-is-dead-2013-year-of-b2b-insight-selling/; and "Getting Started with SAP EcoHub," http://ecohub.sap.com/getting-started, accessed November 2013.

Today's sales forces are also ramping up their own use of social media to engage customers throughout the buying process. A recent survey of business-to-business marketers found that, although they have recently cut back on traditional media and event spending, 68 percent are investing more in social media, ranging from proprietary online customer communities to webinars and Twitter, Facebook, LinkedIn, and YouTube applications. Consider Makino, a leading manufacturer of metal cutting and machining technology:[21]

Selling and the Internet: Companies use Internet collaboration tools such as Cisco's TelePresence to talk live with customers about products and services.

Courtesy of Cisco.

> Makino complements its sales force efforts through a wide variety of social media initiatives that inform customers and enhance customer relationships. For example, it hosts an ongoing series of industry-specific webinars that position the company as an industry thought leader. Makino produces about three webinars each month and has archived more than 100 on topics ranging from how to get the most out of your machine tools to how metal-cutting processes are done. Webinar content is tailored to specific industries, such as aerospace or medical, and is promoted through carefully targeted banner ads and e-mail invitations. The webinars help to build Makino's customer database, generate leads, build customer relationships, and prepare the way for salespeople by serving up relevant information and educating customers online. Makino also uses Twitter, Facebook, and YouTube to inform customers and prospects about the latest Makino innovations and events and demonstrate the company's machines in action. "We've shifted dramatically into the electronic marketing area," says Makino's marketing manager. "It speeds up the sales cycle and makes it more efficient—for both the company and the customer. The results have been 'outstanding.'"

Ultimately, online and social media technologies are helping to make sales forces more efficient, cost-effective, and productive. The technologies help salespeople do what good salespeople have always done—build customer relationships by solving customer problems—but do it better, faster, and cheaper.

However, the technologies also have some drawbacks. For starters, they're not cheap. In addition, such systems can intimidate low-tech salespeople or clients. Even more, there are some things you just can't present or teach via the Internet—things that require personal interactions. For these reasons, some high-tech experts recommend that sales executives use online and social media technologies to spot opportunities, provide information, maintain customer contact, and make preliminary client sales presentations but resort to old-fashioned, face-to-face meetings when the time draws near to close a big deal.

SPEED BUMP LINKING THE CONCEPTS

Take a break and reexamine your thoughts about salespeople and sales management.

- Again, when someone says "salesperson," what image comes to mind? Have your perceptions of salespeople changed after what you've read in the chapter so far? If so, how? Be specific.
- Find and talk with someone employed in professional sales. Ask about and report on how this salesperson's company designs its sales force and recruits, selects, trains, compensates, supervises, and evaluates its salespeople. Would you like to work as a salesperson for this company?

Author Comment
So far, we've examined how sales management develops and implements overall sales force strategies and programs. In this section, we'll look at how individual salespeople and sales teams sell to customers and build relationships with them.

The Personal Selling Process

We now turn from designing and managing a sales force to the personal selling process. The **selling process** consists of several steps that salespeople must master. These steps focus on the goal of getting new customers and obtaining orders from them. However, most salespeople spend much of their time maintaining existing accounts and building long-term customer *relationships*. We will discuss the relationship aspect of the personal selling process in a later section.

Steps in the Selling Process

As shown in **Figure 13.3**, the selling process consists of seven steps: prospecting and qualifying, preapproach, approach, presentation and demonstration, handling objections, closing, and follow-up.

Figure 13.3 Steps in the Selling Process

As shown here, these steps are transaction-oriented—aimed at closing a specific sale with the customer...

...but remember that in the long run, a single sale is only one element of a long-term customer relationship. So the selling process steps must be understood in the broader context of maintaining profitable customer relationships.

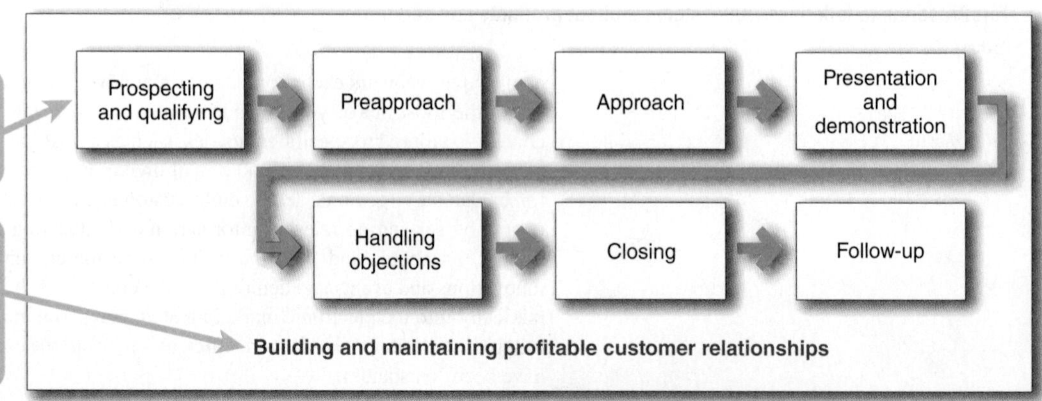

Selling process
The steps that salespeople follow when selling, which include prospecting and qualifying, preapproach, approach, presentation and demonstration, handling objections, closing, and follow-up.

Prospecting and Qualifying

The first step in the selling process is **prospecting**—identifying qualified potential customers. Approaching the right customers is crucial to selling success. Salespeople don't want to call on just any potential customers. They want to call on those who are most likely to appreciate and respond to the company's value proposition—those the company can serve well and profitably.

A salesperson must often approach many prospects to get only a few sales. Although the company supplies some leads, salespeople need skill in finding their own. The best source is referrals. Salespeople can ask current customers for referrals and cultivate other referral sources, such as suppliers, dealers, noncompeting salespeople, and Web or other social media contacts. They can also search for prospects in directories or on the Internet and track down leads using the telephone, e-mail, and social media. Or, as a last resort, they can drop in unannounced on various offices (a practice known as *cold calling*).

Prospecting
The sales step in which a salesperson or company identifies qualified potential customers.

Salespeople also need to know how to *qualify* leads—that is, how to identify the good ones and screen out the poor ones. Prospects can be qualified by looking at their financial ability, volume of business, special needs, location, and possibilities for growth.

Preapproach

Before calling on a prospect, the salesperson should learn as much as possible about the organization (what it needs, who is involved in the buying) and its buyers (their characteristics and buying styles). This step is known as **preapproach**. A successful sale begins long before the salesperson makes initial contact with a prospect. Preapproach begins with good research and preparation. The salesperson can consult standard industry and online sources, acquaintances, and others to learn about the company. He or she can scour the prospect's Web and social media sites for information about its products, buyers, and buying processes. Then the salesperson must apply the research gathered to develop a customer strategy.

Preapproach
The sales step in which a salesperson learns as much as possible about a prospective customer before making a sales call.

The salesperson should set *call objectives*, which may be to qualify the prospect, gather information, or make an immediate sale. Another task is to determine the best approach, which might be a personal visit, a phone call, an e-mail, or a text or tweet. The ideal timing should be considered carefully because many prospects are busiest at certain times of the day or week. Finally, the salesperson should give thought to an overall sales strategy for the account.

Approach

Approach
The sales step in which a salesperson meets the customer for the first time.

During the **approach** step, the salesperson should know how to meet and greet the buyer and get the relationship off to a good start. The approach might take place offline or online, in-person or via digital conferencing or social media. This step involves the salesperson's appearance, opening lines, and follow-up remarks. The opening lines should be positive to build goodwill from the outset. This opening might be followed by some key questions to learn more about the customer's needs or by showing a display or sample to attract the buyer's attention and curiosity. As in all stages of the selling process, listening to the customer is crucial.

Presentation and Demonstration

Presentation
The sales step in which a salesperson tells the "value story" to the buyer, showing how the company's offer solves the customer's problems.

During the **presentation** step of the selling process, the salesperson tells the "value story" to the buyer, showing how the company's offer solves the customer's problems. The *customer-solution approach* fits better with today's relationship marketing focus than does a hard sell or glad-handing approach. The goal should be to show how the company's products and services fit the customer's needs. Buyers today want insights and solutions, not smiles; results, not razzle-dazzle. Moreover, they don't want just products. More than ever in today's economic climate, buyers want to know how those products will add value to their businesses. They want salespeople who listen to their concerns, understand their needs, and respond with the right products and services.

But before salespeople can *present* customer solutions, they must *develop* solutions to present. The solutions approach calls for good listening and problem-solving

Listening to customer needs: Great salespeople know how to sell, but more important, they know how to listen and build strong customer relationships.

Tony Garcia/Getty Images.

skills. The qualities that buyers *dislike most* in salespeople include being pushy, late, deceitful, unprepared, disorganized, or overly talkative. The qualities they *value most* include good listening, empathy, honesty, dependability, thoroughness, and follow-through. Great salespeople know how to sell, but more important, they know how to listen and build strong customer relationships. According to an old sales adage, "You have two ears and one mouth. Use them proportionally." A classic ad from office products maker Boise Cascade makes the listening point. It shows a Boise salesperson with huge ears drawn on. "With Boise, you'll notice a difference right away, especially with our sales force," says the ad. "At Boise . . . our account representatives have the unique ability to listen to your needs."

Finally, salespeople must also plan their presentation methods. Good interpersonal communication skills count when it comes to making effective sales presentations. However, the current media-rich and cluttered communications environment presents many new challenges for sales presenters. Today's information-overloaded customers demand richer presentation experiences. For their part, presenters now face multiple distractions during presentations from mobile phones, text messages, and other digital competition. As a result, salespeople must deliver their messages in more engaging and compelling ways.

Thus, today's salespeople are employing advanced presentation technologies that allow for full multimedia presentations to only one or a few people. The venerable old sales presentation flip chart has been replaced with sophisticated presentation software, online presentation technologies, interactive whiteboards, digital projectors, and tablet computers.

Handling Objections

Handling objections
The sales step in which a salesperson seeks out, clarifies, and overcomes any customer objections to buying.

Customers almost always have objections during the presentation or when asked to place an order. The objections can be either logical or psychological, and are often unspoken. In **handling objections**, the salesperson should use a positive approach, seek out hidden objections, ask the buyer to clarify any objections, take objections as opportunities to provide more information, and turn the objections into reasons for buying. Every salesperson needs training in the skills of handling objections.

Closing

Closing
The sales step in which a salesperson asks the customer for an order.

After handling the prospect's objections, the salesperson next tries to close the sale. However, some salespeople do not get around to **closing** or don't handle it well. They may lack confidence, feel guilty about asking for the order, or fail to recognize the right moment to close the sale. Salespeople should know how to recognize closing signals from the buyer, including physical actions, comments, and questions. For example, the customer might sit forward and nod approvingly or ask about prices and credit terms.

Salespeople can use any of several closing techniques. They can ask for the order, review points of agreement, offer to help write up the order, ask whether the buyer wants this model or that one, or note that the buyer will lose out if the order is not placed now. The salesperson may offer the buyer special reasons to close, such as a lower price, an extra quantity at no charge, or additional services.

Follow-Up

Follow-up
The sales step in which a salesperson follows up after the sale to ensure customer satisfaction and repeat business.

The last step in the selling process—**follow-up**—is necessary if the salesperson wants to ensure customer satisfaction and repeat business. Right after closing, the salesperson should complete any details on delivery time, purchase terms, and other matters. The salesperson then should schedule a follow-up call after the buyer receives the initial order to make sure proper installation, instruction, and servicing occur. This visit would reveal any problems, assure the buyer of the salesperson's interest, and reduce any buyer concerns that might have arisen since the sale.

Personal Selling and Managing Customer Relationships

The steps in the just-described selling process are *transaction oriented*—their aim is to help salespeople close a specific sale with a customer. But in most cases, the company is not simply seeking a sale. Rather, it wants to engage the customer over the long haul in a mutually profitable *relationship*. The sales force usually plays an important role in customer relationship building. Thus, as shown in Figure 13.3, the selling process must be understood in the context of building and maintaining profitable customer relationships. Moreover, as discussed in a previous section, today's buyers are increasingly moving through the early stages of the buying process themselves, before ever engaging sellers. Salespeople must adapt their selling process to match the new buying process. That means discovering and engaging customers on a relationship basis rather than a transaction basis.

Successful sales organizations recognize that winning and keeping accounts requires more than making good products and directing the sales force to close lots of sales. If the company wishes only to close sales and capture short-term business, it can do this by simply slashing its prices to meet or beat those of competitors. Instead, most companies want their salespeople to practice *value selling*—demonstrating and delivering superior customer value and capturing a return on that value that is fair for both the customer and the company. For example, companies like Procter & Gamble understand that they aren't just selling products to and through their retailer customers. They are partnering with these retail accounts to create more value for final consumers to their mutual benefit. P&G knows that it can succeed only if its retail partners succeed (see Marketing at Work 13.2).

Unfortunately, in the heat of closing sales, salespeople too often take the easy way out by cutting prices rather than selling value. Sales management's challenge is to transform salespeople from customer advocates for price cuts into company advocates for value. Here's how Rockwell Automation sells value and relationships rather than price:[22]

> Under pressure from Walmart to lower its prices, a condiment producer asked several competing supplier representatives—including Rockwell Automation sales rep Jeff Policicchio—to help it find ways to reduce its operating costs. After spending a day in the customer's plant, Policicchio quickly put his finger on the major problem: Production was suffering because of down time due to poorly performing pumps on the customer's 32 large condiment tanks. Quickly gathering cost and usage data, Policicchio used his Rockwell Automation laptop value-assessment tool to develop an effective solution for the customer's pump problem.
>
> The next day, as he and competing reps presented their cost-reduction proposals to plant management, Policicchio offered the following value proposition: "With this Rockwell Automation pump solution, through less downtime, reduced administrative costs in procurement, and lower spending on repair parts, your company will save at least $16,268 per pump—on up to 32 pumps—relative to our best competitor's solution." Compared with competitors' proposals, Policicchio's solution carried a higher initial price. However, no competing rep offered more than fuzzy promises about possible cost savings. Most simply lowered their prices.
>
> Impressed by Policicchio's value proposition—despite its higher initial price—the plant managers opted to buy and try one Rockwell Automation pump. When the pump performed even better than predicted, the customer ordered all of the remaining pumps. By demonstrating tangible value rather than simply selling on price, Policicchio not only landed the initial sale but also earned a loyal future customer.

Thus, value selling requires listening to customers, understanding their needs, and carefully coordinating the whole company's efforts to create lasting relationships based on customer value.

MARKETING AT WORK 13.2

P&G: It's Not Sales, It's Customer Business Development

For decades, Procter & Gamble has been at the top of almost every expert's A-list of outstanding marketing companies. The experts point to P&G's stable of top-selling consumer brands, or to the fact that year in and year out, P&G is the world's largest advertiser. Consumers seem to agree. You'll find at least one of P&G's blockbuster brands in 99 percent of all American households; in many homes, you'll find a dozen or more familiar P&G products. But P&G is also highly respected for something else—its top-notch, customer-focused sales force.

P&G's sales force has long been an American icon for personal selling at its very best. When it comes to selecting, training, and managing salespeople, P&G sets the gold standard. The company employs a massive sales force of more than 5,000 salespeople worldwide. At P&G, however, they rarely call it "sales." Instead, it's "Customer Business Development" (CBD). And P&G sales reps aren't "salespeople"; they're "CBD managers" or "CBD account executives." All this might seem like just so much "corp-speak," but at P&G the distinction goes to the very core of how selling works.

P&G understands that if its customers don't do well, neither will the company. To grow its own business, therefore, P&G must first grow the business of the retailers that sell its brands to final consumers. And at P&G, the primary responsibility for helping customer companies grow falls to the sales force. In P&G's own words, "CBD is more than mere 'selling'—it's a P&G-specific approach which enables us to grow our business by working as a 'strategic partner' (as opposed to just a supplier) with those who ultimately sell our products to consumers." Says one CBD manager, "We depend on them as much as they depend on us." By partnering with each other, P&G and its customers create "win-win" relationships that help both to prosper.

Most P&G customers are huge and complex businesses—such as Walgreens, Walmart, or Dollar General—with thousands of stores and billions of dollars in revenues. Working with and selling to such customers can be a very complex undertaking, more than any single salesperson or sales team could accomplish. Instead, P&G assigns a full CBD team to every large customer account. Each CBD team contains not only salespeople but also a full complement of specialists in every aspect of selling P&G's consumer brands at the retail level.

CBD teams vary in size depending on the customer. For example, P&G's largest customer, Walmart, which accounts for an amazing 20 percent of the company's sales, commands a 350-person CBD team. By contrast, the P&G Dollar General team consists of about 30 people. Regardless of size, every CBD team constitutes a complete, multifunctional customer service unit. Each team includes a CBD manager and several CBD account executives (each responsible for a specific P&G product category), supported by specialists in marketing strategy, product development, operations, information systems, logistics, finance, and human resources.

To deal effectively with large accounts, P&G salespeople must be smart, well trained, and strategically grounded. They deal daily with high-level retail category buyers who may purchase hundreds of millions of dollars' worth of P&G and competing brands annually. It takes a lot more than a friendly smile and a firm handshake to interact with such buyers. Yet, individual P&G salespeople can't know everything, and thanks to the CBD sales structure, they don't have to. Instead, as members of a full CBD team, P&G salespeople have at hand all the resources they need to resolve even the most challenging customer problems. "I have everything I need right here," says a household care account executive. "If my customer needs help from us with in-store promotions, I can go right down the hall and talk with someone on my team in marketing about doing some kind of promotional deal. It's that simple."

Customer Business Development involves partnering with customers to jointly identify strategies that create shopper value and satisfaction and drive profitable sales at the store level. When it comes to profitably moving Tide, Pampers, Gillette, or other P&G brands off store shelves and into consumers' shopping carts, P&G reps and their teams often know more than the retail buyers they advise. In fact, P&G's retail partners often rely on CBD teams to help them manage not only the P&G

>> P&G Customer Business Development managers know that to grow P&G's business, they must first help their retail partners to sell P&G's brands.

Jin Lee/Getty Images USA, Inc.

brands on their shelves but also entire product categories, including competing brands.

Wait a minute. Does it make sense to let P&G advise on the stocking and placement of competitors' brands as well as its own? Would a P&G CBD rep ever tell a retail buyer to stock fewer P&G products and more of a competing brand? Believe it or not, it happens all the time. The CBD team's primary goal is to help the customer win in each product category. Sometimes, analysis shows that the best solution for the customer is "more of the other guy's product." For P&G, that's okay. It knows that creating the best situation for the retailer ultimately pulls in more customer traffic, which in turn will likely lead to increased sales for other P&G products in the same category. Because most of P&G's brands are market-share leaders, it stands to benefit more from the increased traffic than competitors do. Again, what's good for the customer is good for P&G—it's a win-win situation.

Honest and open dealings also help to build long-term customer relationships. P&G salespeople become trusted advisors to their retailer-partners, a status they work hard to maintain. "It took me four years to build the trust I now have with my buyer," says a veteran CBD account executive. "If I talk her into buying P&G products that she can't sell or out of stocking competing brands that she should be selling, I could lose that trust in a heartbeat."

Finally, collaboration is usually a two-way street—P&G gives and customers give back in return. "We'll help customers run a set of commercials or do some merchandising events, but there's usually a return-on-investment," explains another CBD manager. "Maybe it's helping us with distribution of a new product or increasing space for fabric care. We're very willing if the effort creates value for us as well as for the customer and the final consumer."

According to P&G, "Customer Business Development is selling and a whole lot more. It's a P&G-specific approach [that lets us] grow business by working as a 'strategic partner' with our accounts, focusing on mutually beneficial business building opportunities. All customers want to improve their business; it's [our] role to help them identify the biggest opportunities."

Thus, P&G salespeople aren't the stereotypical glad-handers that some people have come to expect when they think of selling. P&G's "salespeople"—its CBD managers—are talented, well-educated, well-trained sales professionals who do all they can to help customers succeed. They know that good selling involves working with customers to solve their problems for mutual gain. They know that if customers succeed, they succeed.

Sources: Based on information from numerous P&G managers; with information from "500 Largest Sales Forces in America," *Selling Power*, September 2012, pp. 34, 40; "Then and Now: Going to Great Lengths to Get P&G Products into the Hands of Consumers," http://news.pg.com/blog/company-strategy/then-and-now-going-great-lengths-get-pg-products-hands-consumers, accessed June 2013; Cassandra Jowett, "Schulich Grand Finds Her Calling in Customer Business Development at P&G," *TalentEgg*, January 8, 2013, http://talentegg.ca/incubator/2013/01/08/schulich-grad-finds-calling-customer-business-development-pg/; and www.experiencepg.com/jobs/customer-business-development-sales.aspx, accessed November 2013.

Author Comment
Sales promotion is the most short-term of the promotion mix tools. Whereas advertising or personal selling says "buy," sales promotions say "buy now."

Sales Promotion

Personal selling and advertising often work closely with another promotion tool, sales promotion. **Sales promotion** consists of short-term incentives to encourage the purchase or sales of a product or service. Whereas advertising offers reasons to buy a product or service, sales promotion offers reasons to buy *now*.

Sales promotion
Short-term incentives to encourage the purchase or sale of a product or a service.

Examples of sales promotions are found everywhere. A freestanding insert in the Sunday newspaper contains a coupon offering $1 off Meow Mix Tender Centers food for your cat. >> A Bed Bath & Beyond ad in your favorite magazine offers 20 percent off on any single item. The end-of-the-aisle display in the local supermarket tempts impulse buyers with a wall of Coca-Cola cases—four 12-packs for $12. Buy a new Samsung laptop and get a free memory upgrade. A hardware store chain receives a 10 percent discount on selected Stihl power lawn and garden tools if it agrees to advertise them in local newspapers. Sales promotion includes a wide variety of promotion tools designed to stimulate earlier or stronger market response.

The Rapid Growth of Sales Promotion

Sales promotion tools are used by most organizations, including manufacturers, distributors, retailers, and not-for-profit institutions. They are targeted toward final buyers (*consumer promotions*), retailers and wholesalers (*trade promotions*), business customers (*business promotions*), and members of the sales force (*sales force promotions*). Today, in the average consumer packaged-goods company, sales promotion accounts for 60 percent of all marketing budgets.[23]

How much do you love saving 20%?
20% OFF
One single item!
BED BATH & BEYOND
CHOOSE FROM ONE OF OUR HUNDREDS OF THOUSANDS OF ITEMS.
CUT COUPON ALONG DOTTED LINE
BED BATH & BEYOND
SIGN UP AT bedbathandbeyond.com/TheNest.asp
to keep the savings coming all year long

>> **Sales promotions are found everywhere. For example, your favorite magazine is loaded with offers like this one that promote a strong and immediate response.**

Bed Bath & Beyond, Inc.

Several factors have contributed to the rapid growth of sales promotion, particularly in consumer markets. First, inside the company, product managers face greater pressures to increase current sales, and they view promotion as an effective short-run sales tool. Second, externally, the company faces more competition, and competing brands are less differentiated. Increasingly, competitors are using sales promotion to help differentiate their offers. Third, advertising efficiency has declined because of rising costs, media clutter, and legal restraints. Finally, consumers have become more deal oriented. In the current economy, consumers are demanding lower prices and better deals. Sales promotions can help attract today's more thrift-oriented consumers.

The growing use of sales promotion has resulted in *promotion clutter*, which is similar to advertising clutter. According to one recent study, 37 percent of all groceries were sold with some sort of promotional support.[24] A given promotion runs the risk of being lost in a sea of other promotions, weakening its ability to trigger an immediate purchase. Manufacturers are now searching for ways to rise above the clutter, such as offering larger coupon values, creating more dramatic point-of-purchase displays, or delivering promotions through new digital media—such as the Internet or mobile phones. According to one study, 88 percent of retailers now see digital promotions—such as mobile coupons, shopper e-mails, and online deals—as an important part of their shopper marketing efforts.[25]

In developing a sales promotion program, a company must first set sales promotion objectives and then select the best tools for accomplishing these objectives.

Sales Promotion Objectives

Sales promotion objectives vary widely. Sellers may use *consumer promotions* to urge short-term customer buying or boost customer brand involvement. Objectives for *trade promotions* include getting retailers to carry new items and more inventory, buy ahead, or promote the company's products and give them more shelf space. *Business promotions* are used to generate business leads, stimulate purchases, reward customers, and motivate salespeople. For the sales force, objectives include getting more sales force support for current or new products and getting salespeople to sign up new accounts.

Sales promotions are usually used together with advertising, personal selling, direct marketing, or other promotion mix tools. Consumer promotions must usually be advertised and can add excitement and pulling power to ads. Trade and business sales promotions support the firm's personal selling process.

When the economy tightens and sales lag, it's tempting to offer deep promotional discounts to spur consumer spending. In general, however, rather than creating only short-term sales or temporary brand switching, sales promotions should help to reinforce the product's position and build long-term customer relationships. If properly designed, every sales promotion tool has the potential to build both short-term excitement and long-term consumer engagement and relationships. Marketers should avoid "quick fix," price-only promotions in favor of promotions that are designed to build brand equity. Examples include the various *frequency marketing programs* and loyalty cards that have mushroomed in popularity in recent years. Most hotels, supermarkets, and airlines offer frequent-guest/buyer/flyer programs that give rewards to regular customers to keep them coming back. All kinds of companies now offer rewards programs. Such promotional programs can build loyalty through added value rather than discounted prices.

Consumer promotions
Sales promotion tools used to boost short-term customer buying and engagement or enhance long-term customer relationships.

For example, Kroger Plus Card holders receive the usual frequent shopper perks—special in-store discounts on selected items, exclusive e-mail offers and coupons, and the ability to create and save their shopping lists online. But the grocery chain also keeps customers coming back by linking cumulative food purchases to discounts on gasoline prices. >> Shoppers who use the company's loyalty card when they shop can accrue 10 cents

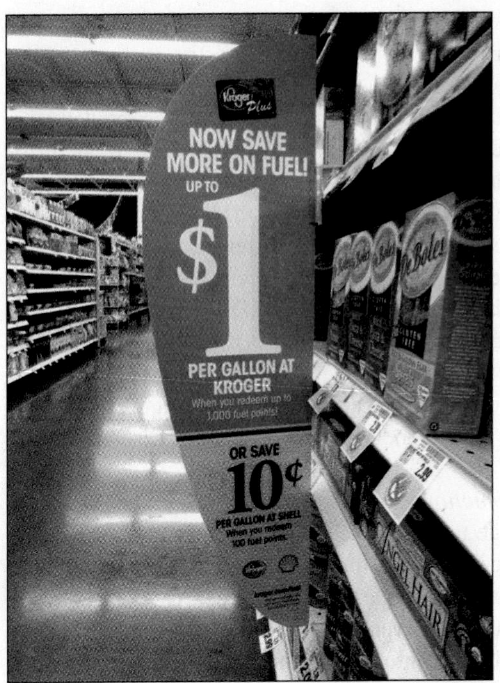

Customer loyalty programs: Kroger keeps its Plus Card holders coming back by linking food purchases to discounts on gasoline prices.

Gary Armstrong.

off each gallon of gas for every $100 spent in the store, up to a $1-per-gallon discount when they fill up their tanks. "We're delighted to offer [customers] more control at the pump," says a Kroger marketing executive. "This is another way we're rewarding our customers for choosing to shop with us."[26]

Major Sales Promotion Tools

Many tools can be used to accomplish sales promotion objectives. Descriptions of the main consumer, trade, and business promotion tools follow.

Consumer Promotions

Consumer promotions include a wide range of tools—from samples, coupons, refunds, premiums, and point-of-purchase displays to contests, sweepstakes, and event sponsorships.

Samples are offers of a trial amount of a product. Sampling is the most effective—but most expensive—way to introduce a new product or create new excitement for an existing one. Some samples are free; for others, the company charges a small amount to offset its cost. The sample might be sent by mail, handed out in a store or at a kiosk, attached to another product, or featured in an ad, e-mail, or mobile offer. Samples are sometimes combined into sample packs, which can then be used to promote other products and services. Sampling can be a powerful promotional tool.

Coupons are certificates that save buyers money when they purchase specified products. Most consumers love coupons. U.S. consumer packaged goods companies distributed 305 billion coupons with an average face value of $1.53 last year. Consumers redeemed more than 2.9 billion of them for a total savings of about $3.7 billion, 27.6 percent higher than five years ago.[27] Coupons can promote early trial of a new brand or stimulate sales of a mature brand. However, to combat the increase in coupon clutter, most major consumer goods companies are issuing fewer coupons and targeting them more carefully.

Marketers are also cultivating new outlets for distributing coupons, such as supermarket shelf dispensers, electronic point-of-sale coupon printers, and online and mobile coupon programs. Digital coupons represent today's fastest-growing coupon segment. Digital coupons can be individually targeted and personalized in ways that print coupons can't. Digital coupons accounted for nearly 9 percent of all coupons redeemed last year; 5.6 percent of all coupons were printed from a computer at home and 1.3 percent were redeemed via smartphone or other mobile devices. According to one study, the number of mobile phone coupon users rose by 66 percent last year, following 100 percent growth rates in each of the previous two years.[28] As mobile phones become appendages that many people can't live without, businesses are increasingly eyeing them as prime real estate for coupons, offers, and other marketing messages. For example, drugstore chain Walgreens makes coupons available to its customers through several mobile channels:[29]

Mobile coupons: Drug store chain Walgreens makes coupons available to its customers through several mobile channels.

Walgreens Digital Marketing & Emerging Media Team. Rich Lesperance, Director.

> Using the Walgreens smartphone app, customers can instantly download coupons ranging in value from 50 cents to $5, good toward anything from health and beauty products to everyday essentials such as diapers. The coupons are conveniently scannable—no clipping or printing required. Customers simply pull up the coupons on the Walgreens app and cashiers scan them straight from the customer's phone. Walgreens also tweets mobile coupons to customers who check in to any of its 8,000 stores nationwide using check-in apps such as Foursquare, Yelp, or Facebook Places. Walgreens has mobile scanning capabilities available at all of its stores, giving it the nation's largest retail mobile coupon program. "Through our mobile application, no matter where people are, they can find an easy way to save next time they come to Walgreens," says the company's president of e-commerce.

Rebates (or *cash refunds*) are like coupons except that the price reduction occurs after the purchase rather than at the retail outlet. The customer sends proof of purchase to the manufacturer, which then refunds part of the purchase price by mail. For example, Toro ran a clever preseason promotion on some of its snowblower models, offering a rebate if the snowfall in the buyer's market area turned out to be below average. Competitors were not able to match this offer on such short notice, and the promotion was very successful.

Price packs (also called *cents-off deals*) offer consumers savings off the regular price of a product. The producer marks the reduced prices directly on the label or package. Price packs can be single packages sold at a reduced price (such as two for the price of one) or two related products banded together (such as a toothbrush and toothpaste). Price packs are very effective—even more so than coupons—in stimulating short-term sales.

Premiums are goods offered either free or at low cost as an incentive to buy a product, ranging from toys included with kids' products to phone cards and DVDs. A premium may come inside the package (in-pack), outside the package (on-pack), or through the mail. For example, over the years, McDonald's has offered a variety of premiums in its Happy Meals—from *Madagascar* characters to Beanie Babies and *Pokémon* toy figures. Customers can visit www.happymeal.com to play games and watch commercials associated with the current Happy Meal sponsor.[30]

Advertising specialties, also called *promotional products*, are useful articles imprinted with an advertiser's name, logo, or message that are given as gifts to consumers. Typical items include T-shirts and other apparel, pens, coffee mugs, calendars, key rings, mouse pads, tote bags, coolers, golf balls, and caps. U.S. marketers spent nearly $18 billion on advertising specialties last year. Such items can be very effective. The "best of them stick around for months, subtly burning a brand name into a user's brain," notes a promotional products expert.[31]

Point-of-purchase (POP) promotions include displays and demonstrations that take place at the point of sale. Think of your last visit to the local Safeway, Costco, CVS, or Bed Bath & Beyond. Chances are good that you were tripping over aisle displays, promotional signs, "shelf talkers," or demonstrators offering free tastes of featured food products. Unfortunately, many retailers do not like to handle the hundreds of displays, signs, and posters they receive from manufacturers each year. Manufacturers have therefore responded by offering better POP materials, offering to set them up, and tying them in with television, print, or online messages.

Contests, *sweepstakes*, and *games* give consumers the chance to win something, such as cash, trips, or goods, by luck or through extra effort. A *contest* calls for consumers to submit an entry—a jingle, guess, suggestion—to be judged by a panel that will select the best entries. A *sweepstakes* calls for consumers to submit their names for a drawing. A *game* presents consumers with something—bingo numbers, missing letters—every time they buy, which may or may not help them win a prize.

All kinds of companies use sweepstakes and contests to create brand attention and boost consumer involvement. For example, Outback's Kick Back with the Guys Sweepstakes offers chances to win a dinner for four of "crave-able appetizers and juicy steaks." The O'Reilly Auto Parts Win Free Gas for a Year Giveaway promises to let you "forget about gas prices for a year." Enter the Coleman Great American Family Vacation Sweepstakes and you could win a family trip to Yellowstone and a Coleman camping package. And separate Chevrolet Race to Win sweepstakes recently offered either a new Corvette 427 convertible plus a trip to the 24 Hours of Le Mans, France, or a new Camaro plus a weekend at the Indy 500.

Event marketing (or event sponsorships)
Creating a brand-marketing event or serving as a sole or participating sponsor of events created by others.

Finally, marketers can promote their brands through **event marketing** (or **event sponsorships**). They can create their own brand-marketing events or serve as sole or participating sponsors of events created by others. The events might include anything from mobile brand tours to festivals, reunions, marathons, concerts, or other sponsored gatherings. Event marketing is huge, and it may be the fastest-growing area of promotion. Effective event marketing links events and sponsorships to a brand's value proposition.

All kinds of brands now hold events. One week, it might be the National Football League (NFL) filling the southern tip of Times Square with NFL players to promote new NFL jersey designs. The next week, it's a mob of Russian models on the 45th street island between Broadway and Seventh Avenue in New York City, using it as a fashion runway for

Maybelline. But according to one business reporter, energy drink maker Red Bull is the "mother of all event marketers":[32]

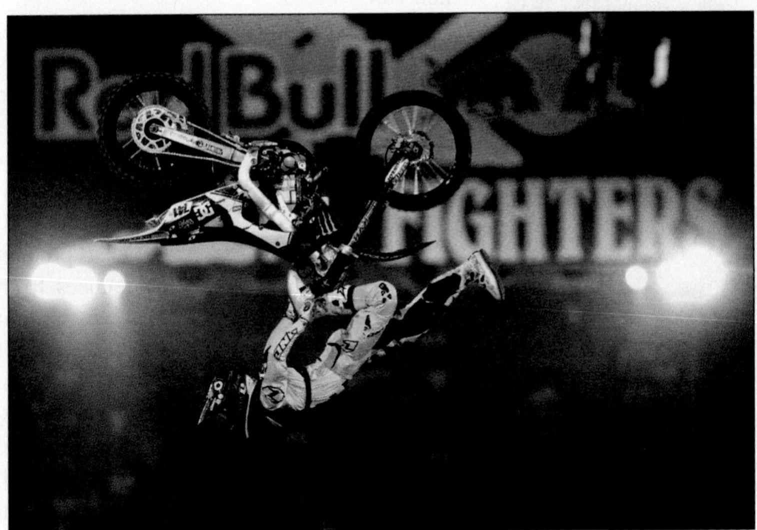

Event marketing: Red Bull hosts hundreds of events each year in dozens of sports around the world, designed to bring the high-octane world of Red Bull to its community of enthusiasts.

REUTERS/Max Rossi.

Event pioneer Red Bull holds hundreds of events each year in dozens of sports around the world. Each event features off-the-grid experiences designed to bring the high-octane world of Red Bull to its community of enthusiasts. The brand even hosts a "Holy S**t" tab on its Web site, featuring videos of everything from 27-meter ocean cliff dives at its Cliff Diving Series event in Grimstad, Norway, to dare-devil freeskiing feats at its Red Bull Cold Rush event in the Colorado mountain peaks, to absolutely breathtaking wing suit flights at Red Bull events staged in exotic locations from Monterrey, Mexico, to Hunan Province, China. The Red Bull Final Descent series is a mountain biking challenge that pushes riders to the brink and back, over some of the most technically challenging terrain in North America. Red Bull events draw large crowds and plenty of media coverage. But it's about more than just the events—it's about customer engagement. It's about creating face-to-face experiences in which customers can actually feel the excitement and live the brand. "It's about deepening and enhancing relationships," says one analyst.

Trade Promotions

Trade promotions
Sales promotion tools used to persuade resellers to carry a brand, give it shelf space, and promote it in advertising.

Manufacturers direct more sales promotion dollars toward retailers and wholesalers (79 percent of all promotions dollars) than to final consumers (21 percent).[33] **Trade promotions** can persuade resellers to carry a brand, give it shelf space, promote it in advertising, and push it to consumers. Shelf space is so scarce these days that manufacturers often have to offer price-offs, allowances, buy-back guarantees, or free goods to retailers and wholesalers to get products on the shelf and, once there, to keep them on it.

Manufacturers use several trade promotion tools. Many of the tools used for consumer promotions—contests, premiums, displays—can also be used as trade promotions. Or the manufacturer may offer a straight *discount* off the list price on each case purchased during a stated period of time (also called a *price-off*, *off-invoice*, or *off-list*). Manufacturers also may offer an *allowance* (usually so much off per case) in return for the retailer's agreement to feature the manufacturer's products in some way. For example, an advertising allowance compensates retailers for advertising the product, whereas a display allowance compensates them for using special displays.

Manufacturers may offer *free goods*, which are extra cases of merchandise, to resellers who buy a certain quantity or who feature a certain flavor or size. They may also offer *push money*—cash or gifts to dealers or their sales forces to "push" the manufacturer's goods. Manufacturers may give retailers free *specialty advertising items* that carry the company's name, such as pens, calendars, memo pads, flashlights, and tote bags.

Business Promotions

Business promotions
Sales promotion tools used to generate business leads, stimulate purchases, reward customers, and motivate salespeople.

Companies spend billions of dollars each year on promotion geared toward industrial customers. **Business promotions** are used to generate business leads, stimulate purchases, reward customers, and motivate salespeople. Business promotions include many of the same tools used for consumer or trade promotions. Here, we focus on two additional major business promotion tools: conventions and trade shows and sales contests.

Many companies and trade associations organize *conventions and trade shows* to promote their products. Firms selling to the industry show their products at the trade show. Vendors at these shows receive many benefits, such as opportunities to find new sales leads, contact customers, introduce new products, meet new customers, sell more to present customers, and educate customers with publications and audiovisual materials.

Some trade shows are huge. At this year's Bauma mining and construction equipment trade show in Munich, Germany, more than 3,400 exhibitors from 57 countries presented their latest product innovations to over 530,000 attendees from more than 200 countries.

Messe München.

Trade shows also help companies reach many prospects that are not reached through their sales forces.

Some trade shows are huge. For example, at this year's International Consumer Electronics Show, 3,100 exhibitors attracted some 156,000 professional visitors. Even more impressive, at the Bauma mining and construction equipment trade show in Munich, Germany, more than 3,400 exhibitors from 57 countries presented their latest product innovations to over 530,000 attendees from more than 200 countries. Total exhibition space equaled about 6.1 million square feet (more than 127 football fields).[34]

A *sales contest* is a contest for salespeople or dealers to motivate them to increase their sales performance over a given period. Sales contests motivate and recognize good company performers, who may receive trips, cash prizes, or other gifts. Some companies award points for performance, which the receiver can turn in for any of a variety of prizes. Sales contests work best when they are tied to measurable and achievable sales objectives (such as finding new accounts, reviving old accounts, or increasing account profitability).

Developing the Sales Promotion Program

Beyond selecting the types of promotions to use, marketers must make several other decisions in designing the full sales promotion program. First, they must determine the *size of the incentive*. A certain minimum incentive is necessary if the promotion is to succeed; a larger incentive will produce more sales response. The marketer also must set *conditions for participation*. Incentives might be offered to everyone or only to select groups.

Marketers must determine how to *promote and distribute the promotion* program itself. For example, a $2-off coupon could be given out in a package, in an advertisement, at the store, via the Internet, or in a mobile download. Each distribution method involves a different level of reach and cost. Increasingly, marketers are blending several media into a total campaign concept. The *length of the promotion* is also important. If the sales promotion period is too short, many prospects (who may not be buying during that time) will miss it. If the promotion runs too long, the deal will lose some of its "act now" force.

Evaluation is also very important. Marketers should work to measure the returns on their sales promotion investments, just as they should seek to assess the returns on other marketing activities. The most common evaluation method is to compare sales before, during, and after a promotion. Marketers should ask: Did the promotion attract new customers or more purchasing from current customers? Can we hold onto these new customers and purchases? Will the long-run customer relationship and sales gains from the promotion justify its costs?

Clearly, sales promotion plays an important role in the total promotion mix. To use it well, the marketer must define the sales promotion objectives, select the best tools, design the sales promotion program, implement the program, and evaluate the results. Moreover, sales promotion must be coordinated carefully with other promotion mix elements within the overall IMC program.

MyMarketingLab

Go to **mymktlab.com** to complete the problems marked with this icon .

END OF CHAPTER REVIEWING THE CONCEPTS

CHAPTER REVIEW AND KEY TERMS

Objectives Review

This chapter is the second of three chapters covering the final marketing mix element—promotion. The previous chapter dealt with overall integrated marketing communications and with advertising and public relations. This one chapter investigated personal selling and sales promotion. Personal selling is the interpersonal arm of the communications mix. Sales promotion consists of short-term incentives to encourage the purchase or sale of a product or service.

OBJECTIVE 1 Discuss the role of a company's salespeople in creating value for customers and building customer relationships. (pp 404–407)

Most companies use salespeople, and many companies assign them an important role in the marketing mix. For companies selling business products, the firm's sales force works directly with customers. Often, the sales force is the customer's only direct contact with the company and therefore may be viewed by customers as representing the company itself. In contrast, for consumer product companies that sell through intermediaries, consumers usually do not meet salespeople or even know about them. The sales force works behind the scenes, dealing with wholesalers and retailers to obtain their support and helping them become more effective in selling the firm's products.

As an element of the promotion mix, the sales force is very effective in achieving certain marketing objectives and carrying out such activities as prospecting, communicating, selling and servicing, and information gathering. But with companies becoming more market oriented, a customer-focused sales force also works to produce both customer satisfaction and company profit. The sales force plays a key role in developing and managing profitable customer relationships.

OBJECTIVE 2 Identify and explain the six major sales force management steps. (pp 407–418)

High sales force costs necessitate an effective sales management process consisting of six steps: designing sales force strategy and structure, recruiting and selecting, training, compensating, supervising, and evaluating salespeople and sales force performance.

In designing a sales force, sales management must address various issues, including what type of sales force structure will work best (territorial, product, customer, or complex structure), sales force size, who will be involved in selling, and how various salespeople and sales support people will work together (inside or outside sales forces and team selling).

Salespeople must be recruited and selected carefully. In recruiting salespeople, a company may look to the job duties and the characteristics of its most successful salespeople to suggest the traits it wants in new salespeople. It must then look for applicants through recommendations of current salespeople, ads, and the Internet and social media, as well as college recruitment/placement centers. After the selection process is complete, training programs familiarize new salespeople not only with the art of selling but also with the company's history, its products and policies, and the characteristics of its customers and competitors.

The sales force compensation system helps to reward, motivate, and direct salespeople. In addition to compensation, all salespeople need supervision, and many need continuous encouragement because they must make many decisions and face many frustrations. Periodically, the company must evaluate their performance to help them do a better job. In evaluating salespeople, the company relies on information gathered from sales reports, personal observations, customer surveys, and conversations with other salespeople.

The fastest-growing sales trend is the exploding use of online, mobile, and social media tools in selling. New digital sales force technologies are creating exciting new avenues for connecting with and engaging customers in the digital and social media age. Today's sales forces are mastering the use of online, mobile, and social media tools to identify and learn about prospects, engage customers, create customer value, close sales, and nurture customer relationships. Rather than reducing the need for sales people, online and social media technologies are helping to make sales forces more efficient, cost-effective, and productive. The technologies help salespeople do what good salespeople have always done—build customer relationships by solving customer problems—but do it better, faster, and cheaper.

 **OBJECTIVE 3 Discuss the personal selling process, distinguishing between transaction-oriented marketing and relationship marketing. (pp 418–423)**

Selling involves a seven-step process: prospecting and qualifying, preapproach, approach, presentation and demonstration, handling objections, closing, and follow-up. These steps help marketers close a specific sale and, as such, are transaction oriented. However, a seller's dealings with customers should be guided by the larger concept of relationship marketing. The company's sales force should help to orchestrate a whole-company effort to develop profitable long-term relationships with key customers based on superior customer value and satisfaction.

The fastest-growing sales trend is the exploding use of online, mobile, and social media tools in selling. The new digital technologies are providing salespeople with powerful tools for identifying and learning about prospects, engaging customers, creating customer value, closing sales, and nurturing customer relationships. Many of today's customers no longer rely as much on assistance provided by salespeople. Instead, increasingly, they use online and social media resources to analyze their own problems, research solutions, get advice from colleagues, and rank buying options before ever speaking to a salesperson. In response, sellers are reorienting their selling processes around the new customer buying process. They are using social media, Web forums, online communities, blogs, and other digital tools to engage customers earlier and more fully. Ultimately, online and social media technologies are helping to make sales forces more efficient, cost effective, and productive.

 **OBJECTIVE 4 Explain how sales promotion campaigns are developed and implemented. (pp 423–428)**

Sales promotion campaigns call for setting sales promotion objectives (in general, sales promotions should be *consumer relationship building*); selecting tools; and developing and implementing the sales promotion program by using *consumer promotion tools* (from coupons, refunds, premiums, and point-of-purchase promotions to contests, sweepstakes, and events), *trade promotion tools* (from discounts and allowances to free goods and push money), and *business promotion tools* (conventions, trade shows, and sales contests), as well as determining such things as the size of the incentive, the conditions for participation, how to promote and distribute the promotion package, and the length of the promotion. After this process is completed, the company must evaluate its sales promotion results.

Key Terms

Objective 1
Personal selling (p 404)
Salesperson (p 405)

Objective 2
Sales force management (p 407)
Territorial sales force structure (p 407)
Product sales force structure (p 407)
Customer (or market) sales force structure (p 407)
Outside sales force (or field sales force) (p 408)
Inside sales force (p 408)
Team selling (p 410)
Sales quota (p 414)

Objective 3
Selling process (p 418)
Prospecting (p 419)
Preapproach (p 419)
Approach (p 419)
Presentation (p 419)
Handling objections (p 420)
Closing (p 420)
Follow-up (p 420)

Objective 4
Sales promotion (p 423)
Consumer promotions (p 425)
Event marketing (or event sponsorships) (p 426)
Trade promotions (p 427)
Business promotions (p 427)

DISCUSSION AND CRITICAL THINKING

Discussion Questions

13-1. Describe the roles a salesperson and the sales force perform in marketing. (AACSB: Written and Oral Communication; Reflective Thinking)

13-2. Compare and contrast the three sales force structures outlined in the chapter. Which structure is most effective? (AACSB: Written and Oral Communication; Reflective Thinking)

13-3. Compare an inside sales force and an outside sales force. Why might a company have both? (AACSB: Written and Oral Communication; Reflective Thinking)

13-4. Discuss how online, mobile, and social media tools are changing the selling function. (AACSB: Written and Oral Communication; Reflective Thinking)

13-5. Define *sales promotion* and discuss its objectives. (AACSB: Written and Oral Communication)

13-6. Discuss the different types of trade sales promotions and distinguish these types of promotions from business promotions. (AACSB: Written and Oral Communication)

Critical Thinking Exercises

13-7. Hiring the right people for sales jobs is an important sales management function. Aptitude tests are used often to assist in assessing a candidate's abilities and traits. Search the Internet for information on sales assessment tests and present the characteristics and traits most often assessed. (AACSB: Written and Oral Communication; Information Technology; Reflective Thinking)

13-8. Select a product or service and role-play a sales call—from the approach to the close—with another student. Have one member of the team act as the salesperson with the other member acting as the customer, raising at least three objections. Select another product or service and perform this exercise again with your roles reversed. (AACSB: Written and Oral Communication; Reflective Thinking)

13-9. Find an example of each type of consumer sales promotion tool. Explain how you obtained the promotion (that is, how did the marketer distribute it to consumers?) and what you think the marketer was trying to achieve with the sales promotion tool. (AACSB: Written and Oral Communication; Reflective Thinking)

MINICASES AND APPLICATIONS

Online, Mobile, and Social Media Marketing Sales Promotion

Sales promotion has always been an effective tool for influencing behavior and providing a means for measuring effectiveness. Marketers can measure how many buyers redeem a coupon, enter a contest, receive a premium, or buy bonus packs. But now, new technologies are taking sales promotion to a new level—generating consumer engagement. When AMC Theaters wanted to encourage movie goers to watch a movie on Sunday, typically a slow day for AMC, the company offered a coupon for $1.00 popcorn and fountain drinks on Facebook for the week prior to a specific Sunday and encouraged respondents to invite their friends to claim a coupon as well. The result? More than 200,000 takers in six days and almost 50,000 of them driving their friends to AMC's fan page as well. Similarly, when Edible Arrangements wanted to acquire fans for its Facebook page and increase awareness for the company, it offered free boxes of chocolate-covered fruit to consumers who entered and "Liked" the page. When the company quickly ran out of free samples, it changed the offer to a coupon and experienced double-digit growth as tens of thousands of customers flooded the stores to redeem the coupon—all in less than a week. When Nintendo Wii wanted to raise awareness and generate excitement for its NBA Jam game, it used an essay contest of "jamisms," with voting done in a bracket style like the NBA playoffs. In addition to the 3,000 entries, the contest generated buzz and thousands of impressions and new Facebook fans.

13-10. Design a sales promotion campaign using online, mobile, and social media marketing for a small business or organization in your community. Develop a presentation to pitch your campaign to the business or organization and incorporate what you've learned about the selling process. (AACSB: Written and Oral Communication; Reflective Thinking)

Marketing Ethics Off-Label Marketing

Johnson & Johnson agreed to a $2.2 billion settlement over the marketing of its antipsychotic drug Risperdal. Pfizer agreed to a $2.3 billion settlement and Eli Lilly paid $1.4 billion to settle disputes with the U.S. government. GlaxoSmithKline agreed to a $3 million settlement—its fourth settlement with the government over the marketing of its products. By law, pharmaceutical companies are allowed to market their drugs only for uses approved by the Food and Drug Administration (FDA), but doctors may prescribe any approved drug as they see fit. Drug manufacturers have been training their sales forces to educate doctors on non-approved uses and dosages, called "off-label" marketing. Almost 75 percent of the largest pharmaceutical settlements with the government are for off-label marketing. GlaxoSmithKline even went so far as to have a questionable article ghostwritten by a company and later published in a medical journal under the names of academic authors to convince doctors that Paxil was proven effective in treating depression in children, a use that the FDA has not approved. The reported clinical trial was later criticized by the medical community, but doctors probably are not aware of that because a majority of them rely on pharmaceutical companies for information on drugs. Most unlawful practices by the pharmaceutical industry come to light only because an insider—someone in management or a sales rep—blows the whistle. Fortunately, the Federal False Claim Act provides protection and even incentive for employees to come forward. Pharmaceutical companies settle these types of investigations because even if they plead guilty to criminal charges, which J&J and GlaxoSmithKline did, they don't lose the ability to sell drugs as they would if found guilty after a trial.

13-11. What would you do if you were a pharmaceutical sales rep and were told to promote a drug for off-label use? What protections and incentives are available under the Federal False Claim Act to encourage employees to report illegal behavior? (AACSB: Written and Oral Communication; Ethical Understanding and Reasoning; Reflective Thinking)

Marketing by the Numbers Sales Force Analysis

Brown, Inc. manufactures furniture sold through retail furniture outlets in the southeastern United States. The company has two salespeople that do more than just sell the products—they manage relationships with retail customers to enable them to better meet consumers' needs. The company's sales reps visit retail customers several times per year, often for hours at a time. Brown is considering expanding to other regions of the country and would like to have distribution through 1,000 retail customer accounts. To do so, however, the company would have to hire more salespeople. Each salesperson earns $50,000 plus 2 percent commission on all sales. Another alternative is to use the services of sales agents instead of its own sales force. Sales agents would be paid 10 percent of sales.

13-12. Refer to Appendix 2 to answer this question. Determine the number of salespeople Brown needs if it has 1,000 retail customer accounts that need to be called on five times per year. Each sales call lasts approximately 2.5 hours, and each sales rep has approximately 1,250 hours per year to devote to customers. (AACSB: Written and Oral Communication; Analytical Thinking)

13-13. At what level of sales would it be more cost efficient for Brown to use its own sales force compared to sales agents? To determine this, consider the fixed and variable costs for each alternative. What are the pros and cons of using a company's own sales force over independent sales agents? (AACSB: Written and Oral Communication; Analytical Thinking; Reflective Thinking)

Video Case MedTronic

Many companies sell products that most customers can live without. But MedTronic's devices are literally a matter of life and death. Patient well-being depends upon the insulin delivery devices, implantable defibrillators, and cardiac pacemakers designed and manufactured by MedTronic. In some markets, seven out of eight medical devices in use are MedTronic devices.

But what happens when MedTronic has a product that it knows will help a given business or institutional customer in terms of cost, time, and end-user well-being, but it can't get a foot in the door to communicate that information? This video demonstrates how MedTronic sales representatives maintain a customer-centered approach to the personal selling process as a means for effectively communicating their product benefits.

After viewing the video featuring MedTronic, answer the following questions:

13-14. How is the sales force at MedTronic structured?

13-15. Can you identify the selling process for MedTronic? Give an example of each step.

13-16. Is MedTronic effective at building long-term customer relationships through its sales force? If so, how? If not, how could its process be improved?

Company Cases 13 Salesforce.com / 16 Warby Parker

See Appendix 1 for cases appropriate for this chapter. **Case 13, Salesforce.com: Helping Companies Super-Charge the Selling Process.** Salesforce.com invented cloud computing as a platform for customer relationship management (CRM) products and services. **Case 16, Warby Parker: Eyewear with a Purpose.** Warby Parker makes high-quality, fashionable eyeglasses at a revolutionary price point—and distributes a free pair of glasses to a person in need for every pair purchased.

MyMarketingLab

Go to **mymktlab.com** for Auto-graded writing questions as well as the following Assisted-graded writing questions:

13-17. What traits and behaviors should an ethical salesperson possess? What role does the sales manager play in ethical selling behavior? (AACSB: Ethical Understanding and Reasoning)

13-18. Businesses large and small are using online, mobile, and social media marketing to influence buyer behavior and generate customer engagement. Research tips for offering an online promotion. What should marketers consider when designing and launching online sales promotions? (AACSB: Analytical Thinking)

13-19. Mymktlab Only—comprehensive writing assignment for this chapter.

14 Direct, Online, Social Media, and Mobile **Marketing**

CHAPTER ROAD MAP

Objective Outline

OBJECTIVE 1 **Define *direct and digital marketing* and discuss their rapid growth and benefits to customers and companies.** The New Direct Marketing Model 437; Rapid Growth of Direct and Digital Marketing 437–438; Benefits of Direct and Digital Marketing to Buyers and Sellers 438

OBJECTIVE 2 **Identify and discuss the major forms of direct and digital marketing.** Forms of Direct and Digital Marketing 438–440

OBJECTIVE 3 **Explain how companies have responded to the Internet and the digital age with various online marketing strategies.** Marketing, the Internet, and the Digital Age 441–442; Online Marketing 442–446

OBJECTIVE 4 **Discuss how companies use social media and mobile marketing to engage consumers and create brand community.** Social Media Marketing 446–449; Mobile Marketing 449–452

OBJECTIVE 5 **Identify and discuss the traditional direct marketing forms and overview public policy and ethical issues presented by direct marketing.** Traditional Direct Marketing Forms 453–457; Public Policy Issues in Direct and Digital Marketing 457–460

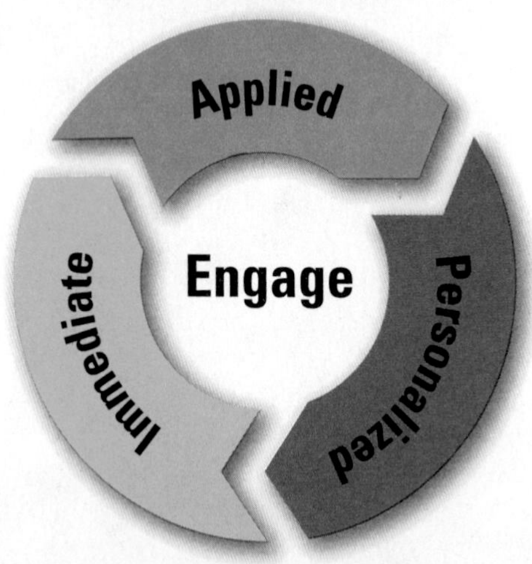

Previewing the Concepts

In the previous two chapters, you learned about engaging consumers and communicating customer value through integrated marketing communication, and about four elements of the marketing communications mix: advertising, publicity, personal selling, and sales promotion. In this chapter, we examine direct marketing and its fastest-growing form, digital marketing (online, social media, and mobile marketing). Today, spurred by the surge in Internet usage and buying, and by rapid advances in digital technologies—from smartphones, tablets, and other digital devices to the spate of online social and mobile media—direct marketing has undergone a dramatic transformation. As you read this chapter, remember that although direct and digital marketing are presented as separate tools, they must be carefully integrated with each other and with other elements of the promotion and marketing mixes.

Let's start by looking at Facebook, a company that markets *only* directly and digitally. The giant online social media network promises to become one of the world's most powerful and profitable digital marketers. Yet, as a marketing company, Facebook is just getting started.

---

*Over 10 million students improved their results using the Pearson MyLabs. Visit **mymktlab.com** for simulations, tutorials, and end-of-chapter problems.

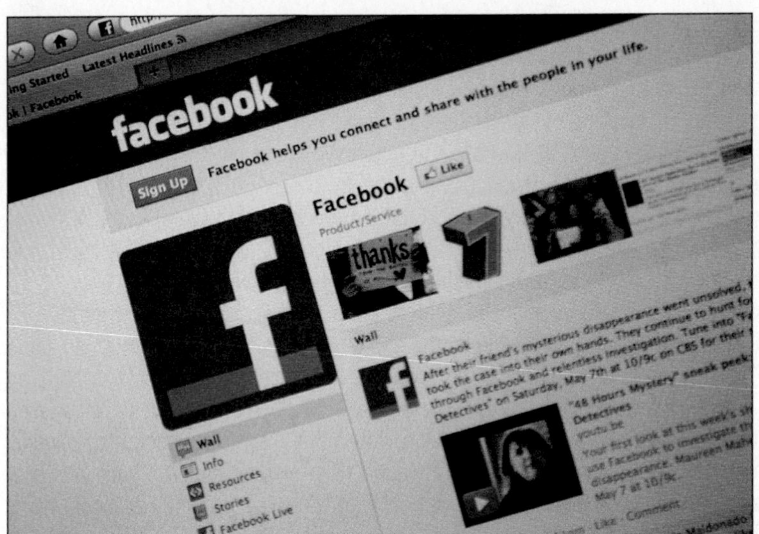

>> The burgeoning young Facebook online social media network is only now beginning to realize its staggering marketing potential. It "helps you connect and share with the people in your life."

Justin Sullivan/Getty Images.

First Stop

Facebook: Going Online, Social, and Mobile—and Making Money Doing It

The world is rapidly going online, social, and mobile. And no company is more online, social, and mobile than Facebook. The huge social media network has a deep and daily impact on the lives of hundreds of millions of members around the world. Yet Facebook is now grappling with a crucial question: How can it profitably tap the marketing potential of its massive community to make money without driving off its legions of loyal users?

Facebook is humongous. In little more than nine years, it has signed up more than 1.1 billion members—one-seventh of the world's population—who combine for 150 billion friend connections. Some 665 million Facebook members access the site daily and 751 million access it on a mobile device at least once monthly. Together, this army uploads 350 million photos, "Likes" 4.5 billion items, and shares 4.75 billion pieces of content daily.

With that many eyeballs glued to one virtual space for that much time, Facebook has tremendous impact and influence, not just as a sharing community but also as an Internet and mobile gateway. Facebook's power comes not just from its size and omnipresence. Rather, it lies in the deep social connections between users. Facebook's mission is "to give people the power to share and make the world more open and connected." It's a place where friends and family meet, share their stories, display their photos, and chronicle their lives. Hordes of people have made Facebook their digital home 24/7.

By wielding all of that influence, Facebook has the potential to become one of the world's most powerful and profitable online marketers. Yet the burgeoning social network is only now beginning to realize that potential. Although Facebook's membership exploded from the very start, CEO Mark Zuckerberg and the network's other idealistic young co-founders gave little thought to making money. They actually opposed running ads or other marketing, worried that marketing might damage Facebook's free (and commercial-free) sharing culture.

Giant social media network Facebook is grappling with a crucial question: How can it profitably tap into its massive marketing potential to make money without driving off its legions of loyal users?

In fact, without any help from Facebook, companies themselves were first to discover the social medium's commercial value. Most brands—small and large—have now built their own Facebook Pages, gaining free and relatively easy access to the gigantic community's word-of-Web potential. And with the massive number of likes clicked every day, companies large and small want a piece of that action. At one extreme, the Runcible Spoon Bakery in Nyack, New York, has 400 Facebook fans. At other extremes, Life is good boasts nearly 2 million fans, and Coca-Cola—the most "Liked" brand on Facebook—has 66 million and rising.

As the company has matured, however, Facebook has come to realize it must make its own marketing and moneymaking moves. If it doesn't make money, it can't continue to serve its members. And now that it is a public company, it must grow and turn a profit for investors. So Facebook has changed its philosophy on advertising. Today, companies can place display or video ads on users' home, profile, or photo pages. Facebook maintains one of the richest collections of user profile data in the world. So ads there can be carefully targeted based on user location, gender, age, likes and interests, relationship status, workplace, and education.

But taking advantage of the social sharing power of the site, Facebook's ads are designed to do far more than simply capture the right eyeballs. They are "engagement ads," designed to harness the power of social connections and move people to action. Facebook ads blend in with regular user activities, and users can interact with ads by leaving comments, making recommendations, clicking the "Like" button, or following a link to a brand-sponsored Facebook page.

Advertising is proving to be a real moneymaker for Facebook. Its ad revenues increased 40 percent last year, helping boost Facebook's overall revenue by 37 percent to more than $5 billion. Facebook charges companies nothing to create and maintain fan pages, but the fan pages and paid advertising interact as a part of a brand's integrated Facebook presence. Brands advertise on Facebook to spark consumer conversations and draw attention to the experiences created on the brand sites.

But advertising is only one potential moneymaking venture for Facebook. As a global gathering place where people spend time with friends, Facebook is also a natural for selling entertainment. For instance, take social gaming, one of the most popular activities on Facebook. More than 250 million people log on each month to play games from developers such as King, Geewa, Wooga, and Zynga. Users play the games for free, but the developers make money by selling virtual goods that enhance the playing experience and by selling ad space within games. For every dollar game developers make, Facebook keeps 30 percent.

Facebook hopes to duplicate its gaming successes with other forms of entertainment. For example, recognizing that members often exit the Facebook environment to listen to music or watch movies, the social network is now providing more of these services to keep people at the site. As one example, Facebook has partnered with Spotify, the ultra-hot online music service. Spotify flows so seamlessly with Facebook that it appears to be in-house. Activities on the Facebook and Spotify sites synchronize so well that friends can share their music listening activities while on Facebook, on Spotify, or both. Such integration has led to the sharing of 110 million songs, albums, and online radio stations.

In line with its goal to keep everything within the community, Facebook has even entered the banking business. That's right, banking. Facebook Payments—an official Facebook subsidiary—lets businesses and customers make purchase transactions by exchanging various world currencies. Facebook's banking activities over the past few years amount to a declaration of war on payment providers such as PayPal and Google Wallet. In only four years, Facebook Payments' revenues have grown to over $800 million. That's only a fraction of PayPal's $5.6 billion revenues, but with Facebook's massive membership and growing e-commerce presence, it could one day pass PayPal as the online payments leader.

One financial analyst predicts that Facebook's revenues will more than double by the end of 2016. Part of this growth will come from increases in ad revenues and Facebook Payments. Mobile ad revenues are also rising quickly—Facebook's app recently surpassed Google Maps as the top U.S. mobile app. Facebook also expects to generate growing revenue from new businesses such as Facebook Gifts (a service for giving gifts to friends) and Facebook Offers (a discount deal service for companies).

Will increased marketing and commercialization on Facebook alienate loyal Facebook fans? Not if it's done right. Research shows that online users readily accept—even welcome—well-targeted online advertising and marketing. Tasteful and appropriately targeted offers can enhance rather than detract from the Facebook user experience. "We've found, frankly, that users are getting more value [because of our marketing efforts]," says a Facebook marketing executive, so that companies are "getting value by putting more [marketing] in."

It's too soon to say whether Facebook will eventually challenge the likes of Google in online advertising or whether its ability to sell entertainment to users will ever expand into selling other types of products on a large scale. But Facebook's immense, closely knit social network gives it staggering potential. As a marketing company, Facebook is just getting started. Carolyn Everson, Facebook's vice president of global sales, sums up Facebook's growth potential this way: "I'm not sure the marketing community understands our story yet. We evolve so quickly. We have a saying here: 'We are one percent done with our mission.'"[1]

Many of the marketing and promotion tools that we've examined in previous chapters were developed in the context of *mass marketing*: targeting broad markets with standardized messages and offers distributed through intermediaries. Today, however, with the trend toward narrower targeting and the surge in digital and social media technologies, many companies are adopting *direct marketing*, either as a primary marketing approach or as a supplement to other approaches. In this section, we explore the exploding world of direct marketing and its fastest-growing form—digital marketing using online, social media, and mobile marketing channels.

Direct and Digital Marketing

Direct and digital marketing
Engaging directly with carefully targeted individual consumers and customer communities to both obtain an immediate response and build lasting customer relationships.

Direct and digital marketing involve engaging directly with carefully targeted individual consumers and customer communities to both obtain an immediate response and build lasting customer relationships. Companies use direct marketing to tailor their offers and content to the needs and interests of narrowly defined segments or individual buyers. In this way, they build customer engagement, brand community, and sales.

For example, Amazon.com interacts directly with customers via its Web site or mobile app to help them discover and buy almost anything and everything online. Similarly, GEICO interacts directly with customers—by telephone, through its Web site or phone app, or on its Facebook, Twitter, and YouTube pages—to build individual brand relationships, give insurance quotes, sell policies, or service customer accounts.

Author Comment
For most companies, direct and digital marketing are supplemental channels or media. But for many other companies today—such as Amazon, GEICO, and Facebook—direct marketing is a complete way of doing business.

The New Direct Marketing Model

Early direct marketers—catalog companies, direct mailers, and telemarketers—gathered customer names and sold goods mainly by mail and telephone. Today, however, spurred by the surge in Internet usage and buying, and by rapid advances in digital technologies—from smartphones, tablets, and other digital devices to the spate of online social and mobile media—direct marketing has undergone a dramatic transformation.

In previous chapters, we discussed direct marketing as direct distribution—as marketing channels that contain no intermediaries. We also included direct and digital marketing as elements of the promotion mix—as an approach for engaging consumers directly and creating brand community. In actuality, direct marketing is both of these things and much more.

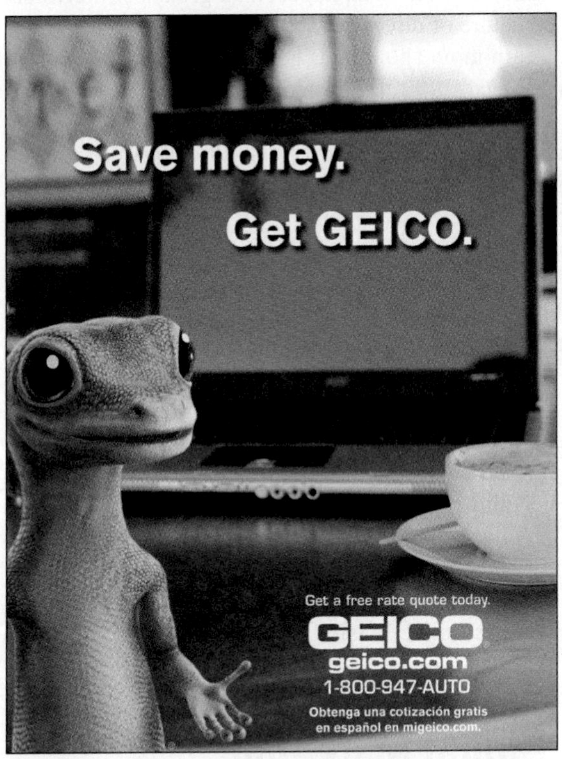

The new direct marketing model: Companies such as GEICO have built their entire approach to the marketplace around direct and digital marketing. Just call 1-800-947-AUTO, or visit geico.com or any of the brand's many social media sites.

Most companies still use direct marketing as a supplementary channel or medium. Thus, most department stores, such as Sears or Macy's, sell the majority of their merchandise off their store shelves, but they also sell through direct mail, online catalogs, and social media pages. Pepsi's Mountain Dew brand markets heavily through mass-media advertising and its retail partners channel. However, it also supplements these channels with direct marketing. It uses its several brand Web sites and a long list of social media to engage its customer community in everything from designing their own Mountain Dew lifestyle pages to co-creating advertising campaigns and deciding which limited-edition flavors should be launched or retired. Through such direct interactions, Mountain Dew has created one of the most passionately loyal fan bases of any brand. By one estimate, simply letting fans pick flavors has generated $200 million in incremental revenues per year for Mountain Dew.[2]

However, for many companies today, direct and digital marketing are more than just supplementary channels or advertising media—they constitute a complete model for doing business. Firms employing this direct model use it as the *only* approach. Companies such as Facebook, Amazon, Google, eBay, Priceline, Netflix, and GEICO have built their entire approach to the marketplace around direct and digital marketing. Many, like Amazon.com, have employed this model with tremendous success.

Rapid Growth of Direct and Digital Marketing

Direct and digital marketing have become the fastest-growing form of marketing. According to the Direct Marketing Association (DMA), U.S. companies spent almost $168.5 billion on direct and digital marketing last year. As a result, direct-marketing-driven sales now amount to more than $2 trillion, accounting for 13 percent of the U.S. economy. The DMA estimates that direct marketing sales will grow 4.9 percent annually through 2016, compared with a projected 4.1 percent annual growth for total U.S. sales.[3]

Direct marketing continues to become more Internet-based, and digital direct marketing is claiming a surging share of marketing spending and sales. For example, U.S. marketers spent an estimated $37 billion on online advertising alone last year, a 15 percent increase over the previous year. These efforts generated more than $231 billion in online consumer spending. Total digital marketing spending—including online display and search advertising, video, social media, mobile, e-mail, and other—now accounts for the second-largest share of media spending, behind only television. Over the next five years, digital marketing expenditures and digitally-driven sales are expected to grow at a blistering 9 percent a year.[4]

Benefits of Direct and Digital Marketing to Buyers and Sellers

For buyers, direct and digital marketing are convenient, easy, and private. They give buyers anywhere, anytime access to an almost unlimited assortment of goods and a wealth of products and buying information. For example, on its Web site and mobile app, Amazon.com offers more information than most of us can digest, ranging from top-10 product lists, extensive product descriptions, and expert and user product reviews to recommendations based on customers' previous purchases. Through direct marketing, buyers can interact with sellers by phone or on the seller's Web site or app to create exactly the configuration of information, products, or services they want and then order them on the spot. Finally, for consumers who want it, digital marketing through online, mobile, and social media provides a sense of brand engagement and community—a place to share brand information and experiences with other brand fans.

For sellers, direct marketing often provides a low-cost, efficient, speedy alternative for reaching their markets. Today's direct marketers can target small groups or individual customers. Because of the one-to-one nature of direct marketing, companies can interact with customers by phone or online, learn more about their needs, and personalize products and services to specific customer tastes. In turn, customers can ask questions and volunteer feedback.

Direct and digital marketing also offer sellers greater flexibility. They let marketers make ongoing adjustments to prices and programs, or make immediate, timely, and personal announcements and offers. For example, when Winter Storm Nemo hit the Northeastern United States with heavy snowfall and hurricane-force winds in early 2013, Starbucks placed direct, real-time Facebook and Twitter "Snow Day" ads in affected areas from New York City to Maine. As the storm approached, the ads urged customers to stock up on Starbucks. After the storm, Starbucks Twitter and Facebook promotions offered free coffee to customers in areas where the weather had forced their local Starbucks to close. "We wanted to make a grand [and timely] gesture," said a Starbucks digital marketer.[5]

Especially in today's digital environment, direct marketing is a powerful tool for moving customers through the buying process and for building customer engagement, community, and relationships. The new direct marketing tools provide rich opportunities for building close, personalized, interactive customer relationships. For example, Southwest Airlines uses a full range of high-tech direct marketing tools—including a desktop widget (DING!), smartphone apps, e-mail, texting, a blog (Nuts About Southwest), and a heavy social media presence—to inject itself directly into customers' everyday lives (see Marketing at Work 14.1).

Author Comment
Direct marketing is rich in tools, from traditional favorites such as direct mail and catalogs to dazzling new digital tools—online, social media, and mobile.

Forms of Direct and Digital Marketing

The major forms of direct and digital marketing are shown in **Figure 14.1**. Traditional direct marketing tools include face-to-face selling, direct-mail marketing, catalog marketing, telemarketing, direct-response television marketing, and kiosk marketing. In recent

Digital and social media marketing
Online marketing
(Web sites, online advertising, e-mail, online videos, blogs)
Social media marketing
Mobile marketing

→ **Build direct customer engagement and community** ←

Traditional direct marketing
Face-to-face selling
Direct-mail marketing
Catalog marketing
Telemarketing
Direct-response TV marketing
Kiosk marketing

Figure 14.1 Forms of Direct and Digital Marketing

MARKETING AT WORK 14.1

Southwest Airlines: Engaging Customers Directly via Online, Social Media, and Mobile Marketing

For decades, Southwest Airlines has communicated directly with customers through traditional direct marketing approaches. And the company still uses lots of direct mail, sending promotional messages directly to customers through the good old U.S. Postal Service. But in recent years, Southwest has expanded its direct marketing strategy to take advantage of the surging digital opportunities for direct, up-close-and-personal interactions with customers. Today, Southwest's new-age direct marketing capability makes the passenger-centered company the envy of its industry.

When it comes to building direct customer relationships, Southwest Airlines is "the undisputed ruler of the social atmosphere," declares one travel expert. In addition to standard direct marketing tools, such as direct mail and its Web site, Southwest's broad-based direct marketing strategy employs a wide range of cutting-edge digital tools to engage customers. Consider these examples:

- *DING!* Available as a desktop widget or a smartphone app, DING! offers exclusive, limited-time airfare deals. When an enticing new deal becomes available, DING! emits the familiar in-flight seatbelt-light bell-dinging sound. The deep discounts last only 6 to 12 hours and can be accessed only online through the application. DING! lets Southwest Airlines bypass the reservations system and pass bargain fares directly to interested customers. Eventually, DING! may even allow Southwest Airlines to customize fare offers based on each customer's unique characteristics and travel preferences.
- *Smartphone app.* In addition to the DING! app, Southwest's regular smartphone app lets customers book reservations directly, arrange car rentals, check in for flights, check flight status, access their Rapid Rewards accounts, and view flight schedules at any time from any location. "You asked for it," says the company. "The Southwest Airlines app is here to make traveling with Southwest Airlines even more convenient."
- *E-mail.* With their high response rates, Web and mobile e-mail are effective ways to build long-term, one-to-one relationships with carefully targeted customers. Working from its huge opt-in database, Southwest tailors e-mails—the design, message, offer, and even copy length—to the characteristics and needs of specific customers. Most important, Southwest's e-mails offer real value. For example, recent Southwest mobile ads in smartphone apps such as Pandora and Draw with Friends promised, "Only people who sign up get the e-mails—Click 'N Save." The enticing message worked and customers signed up in droves to start saving money by receiving e-mails from Southwest.
- *Texting.* With more than 3,200 flights every day, some of those flights are bound to be delayed, rescheduled, or canceled because of weather or other unforeseen circumstances. Because most of its customers carry a mobile device when they travel, Southwest now communicates with customers via text messaging to save them time, ensure they get important information, and provide them with peace of mind. "As more passengers adopt mobile devices, [they] are starting to expect information at their fingertips, and waiting in line to speak to customer service agents is not always acceptable," says Fred Taylor, senior manager of proactive customer service communications at Southwest. By providing customers with up-to-date information instantly, Southwest has created sky-high customer awareness, satisfaction, and loyalty.
- *Nuts About Southwest blog.* Written by Southwest employees, this creative blog allows for a two-way customer–employee dialogue that gives customers a look inside the company's culture and operations. At the same time, it lets Southwest talk directly with and get feedback from customers.
- *The social networking media.* Finally, of course, Southwest's customers interact directly with the company and with each other at the airline's many Web and mobile-based social media sites, from Facebook, Twitter, and YouTube to Pinterest and Flickr. "Southwest is an incredibly social company," says a social media analyst. "Its Twitter feed, which abounds with 'thank you' tweets and @mentions, has [more than 1.5 million] followers. More than [3.8 million] people

» Digital direct marketing: Southwest's broad-based direct marketing strategy employs a wide range of cutting-edge digital tools to connect directly with customers.

Southwest Airlines; Facebook is a trademark of Facebook, Inc.

'like' the airline's comment-packed Facebook page, and its Nuts About Southwest blog is an industry standard." Another analyst agrees: "It's no surprise to find Southwest at the forefront of social media marketing. Southwest . . . has always been a leader in passenger and public engagement. Social media fits the Southwest culture perfectly, where older airlines seem to be playing catch-up in this powerful modern marketing arena."

Southwest's creative, energetic, and super-friendly employees have long been an important competitive advantage. You might worry that with all of these new digital direct marketing tools, Southwest might lose some of its human touch. Not at all. First, the digital touch points are only one option—customers are still only a phone call away from a human voice, and they still interact face-to-face with Southwest employees during flights. More important, the new digital approaches actually enhance customer contact with Southwest's people rather than substitute for it. In many of its direct marketing efforts, Southwest lets its employees do the talking. For example, at its Nuts About Southwest blog, flight attendants, pilots, mechanics, and other employees armed with Flip cams tell insider stories. The company also encourages employees to create local Facebook pages to connect with their communities and lets them be creative in their approaches. As a result, Southwest's direct marketing communications are loaded with employee personality. "You should sound like you're talking to a person," says a Southwest direct marketer. "People embrace our quirkiness."

Thus, Southwest's high-tech direct marketing strategy hasn't changed the company's people orientation. In fact, digital direct marketing brings Southwest's people and customers closer together than ever.

Sources: Lauren Johnson, "Southwest Airlines Builds Email Database via Mobile Initiative," *Mobile Marketer*, June 26, 2012, www.mobilemarketer.com/cms/news/email/13177.html; "Southwest Airlines Taps SMS to Streamline Customer Service," *Mobile Marketer*, May 6, 2010, www.mobilemarketer.com/cms/news/database-crm/6174.html; Samantha Hosenkamp, "How Southwest Manages Its Popular Social Media Sites," *Ragan's PR Daily*, February 10, 2012, www.prdaily.com/Main/Articles/How_Southwest_manages_its_popular_social_media_sit_10788.aspx; "Southwest Airlines Rules the Social Atmosphere, Dominating Facebook and Twitter," *PRWeb*, May 23, 2012, www.prweb.com/releases/2012/5/prweb9536405.htm; and information from "Nuts About Southwest," www.blogsouthwest.com; "What Is DING!?," www.southwest.com/ding; and www.southwest.com/iphone/, accessed November 2013.

---

years, however, a dazzling new set of direct digital marketing tools has burst onto the marketing scene, including online marketing (Web sites, online ads and promotions, e-mail, online videos, and blogs), social media marketing, and mobile marketing. We'll begin by examining the new direct digital and social media marketing tools that have received so much attention lately. Then, we'll look at the still heavily used and very important traditional direct marketing tools. As always, however, it's important to remember that all of these tools—both the new digital and the more traditional forms—must be blended into a fully integrated marketing communications program.

SPEED BUMP LINKING THE CONCEPTS

Hold up a moment and think about the impact of direct and digital marketing on your life.

- When was last time that you bought something via direct or digital marketing? What did you buy and why did you buy it direct? When was the last time that you *rejected* a direct or digital marketing offer? Why did you reject it? Based on these experiences, what advice would you give to direct marketers?
- For the next week, keep track of all the direct and digital marketing offers that come your way via direct mail and catalogs, e-mail and mobile ads, online and social media marketing offers, and others. Then analyze the offers by type, source, and what you liked or disliked about each offer and the way it was delivered. Which offer best hit its target (you)? Which missed by the widest margin?

Digital and social media marketing
Using digital marketing tools such as Web sites, social media, mobile apps and ads, online video, e-mail, and blogs that engage consumers anywhere, anytime via their digital devices.

Author Comment
Direct digital and social media are surging and grabbing all the headlines these days, so we'll start with them. But the traditional direct marketing tools are still heavily used. We'll dig into them later in the chapter.

Digital and Social Media Marketing

As noted earlier, **digital and social media marketing** is the fastest-growing form of direct marketing. It uses digital marketing tools such as Web sites, online video, e-mail, blogs, social media, mobile ads and apps, and other digital platforms to directly engage consumers anywhere, anytime via their computers, smartphones, tablets, Internet-ready TVs, and other digital devices. The widespread use of the Internet and digital technologies is having a dramatic impact on both buyers and the marketers who serve them.

Marketing, the Internet, and the Digital Age

Much of the world's business today is carried out over digital networks that connect people and companies. These days, people connect digitally with information, brands, and each other at almost any time and from almost anywhere. The digital age has fundamentally changed customers' notions of convenience, speed, price, product information, service, and brand interactions. As a result, it has given marketers a whole new way to create customer value, engage customers, and build customer relationships.

Digital usage and impact continues to grow steadily. More than 80 percent of all U.S. households now use the Internet, and the average U.S. Internet user spends some 32 hours a month online. Moreover, more than 41 percent of people in the United States access the Internet via their smartphones or other mobile devices. Worldwide, 34 percent of the population has Internet access. And 16 percent have access to the mobile Internet, a number that's expected to double over the next five years as mobile becomes an ever-more-popular way to get online.[6]

As a result, more than half of all U.S. households now regularly shop online, and digital buying continues to grow at a healthy double-digit rate. U.S. online retail sales were an estimated $231 billion last year and are expected to grow 10 percent each year to $370 billion by 2017 as consumers shift their spending from physical to digital stores. Perhaps even more important, although online and digital shopping currently capture some 7 percent of total U.S. retail sales, by one estimate, the Internet influences a staggering 50 percent of total sales—including sales transacted online plus those made in stores but encouraged by online research.[7] And a growing number of consumers armed with smartphones and tablets use them as they shop to find better deals and score price-matching offers.

To reach this burgeoning market, most companies now market online. Some companies operate *only* online. They include a wide array of firms, from *e-tailers* such as Amazon.com and Expedia.com that sell products and services directly to final buyers via the Internet to *search engines and portals* (such as Google, Yahoo!, and Bing), *transaction sites* (eBay, Craigslist), *content sites* (the *New York Times* on the Web, ESPN.com, and *Encyclopædia Britannica*), and *online social media* (Facebook, YouTube, Pinterest, Instagram, Twitter, and Flickr).

Multichannel marketing
Marketing both through stores and other traditional offline channels and through digital, online, social media, and mobile channels.

Today, however, it's hard to find a company that doesn't have a substantial online presence. Even companies that have traditionally operated offline have now created their own online sales, marketing, and brand community channels. In fact, **multichannel marketing** companies are having more online success than their online-only competitors. A recent ranking of the world's 10 largest online retail sites contained only three online-only retailers (Amazon.com, which was ranked number one, Netflix, and CDW). All the others were multichannel retailers.[8]

For example, number two on the list of online retail sites is Staples, the $24 billion office supply retailer. Staples operates more than 2,295 superstores worldwide. » But you might be surprised to learn that more than 43 percent of Staples' sales come from its online marketing operations, including its Web site and mobile app; its presence on social media such as Facebook, Google+, Twitter, YouTube, and LinkedIn; and its own Staples .com community.[9]

» Multichannel marketing: More than 43 percent of Staples' sales come from its online marketing operations, including its Web site and mobile app, its presence on social media, and its own Staples.com community.

Staples the Office Superstore, LLC & Staples, Inc.

Selling online lets Staples build deeper, more personalized relationships with customers large and small. A large customer, such as GE or P&G, can create lists of approved office products at discount prices and then let company departments or even individuals do their own online and mobile purchasing. This reduces ordering costs, cuts through the red tape, and speeds up the ordering process for customers. At the same time, it encourages companies to use Staples as a sole source for office supplies. Even the smallest companies and individual consumers find 24-hour-a-day online ordering via the Web, Staples mobile app, or social media sites easier and more efficient.

In addition, Staples' online operations complement store sales. The Staples.com site, mobile app, and social media pages build store traffic by offering hot deals and by helping customers find a local store and check stock and prices. In return, the local store promotes online buying through in-store kiosks. If customers don't find what they need on the shelves, they can quickly order it via the kiosk. Thus, Staples backs its "that was easy" positioning by offering a full range of contact points and delivery modes—online, social media, mobile, catalogs, phone, and in the store. No online-only or store-only seller can match that kind of call, click, or visit convenience and support.

Direct digital and social media marketing takes any of the several forms shown in Figure 14.1. These forms include online marketing, social media marketing, and mobile marketing. We discuss each in turn, starting with online marketing.

Online Marketing

Online marketing
Marketing via the Internet using company Web sites, online ads and promotions, e-mail, online video, and blogs.

By **online marketing**, we refer to marketing via the Internet using company Web sites, online advertising and promotions, e-mail marketing, online video, and blogs. Social media and mobile marketing also take place online and must be closely coordinated with other forms of digital marketing. However, because of their special characteristics, we discuss these fast-growing digital marketing approaches in separate sections.

Web Sites and Branded Web Communities

For most companies, the first step in conducting online marketing is to create a Web site. Web sites vary greatly in purpose and content. Some Web sites are primarily **marketing Web sites**, designed to interact with customers to move them closer to a direct purchase or other marketing outcome. >> For example, MINI USA operates a marketing Web site at www.MINIUSA.com. Once a potential customer clicks in, the carmaker wastes no time trying to turn the inquiry into a sale, and then into a long-term relationship. The site offers a garage full of useful information and interactive selling features, including detailed and fun descriptions of current MINI models, tools for designing your very own MINI, information on dealer locations and services, and even tools for tracking your new MINI from factory to delivery. After delivery, new owners can check into the MINI online owner's lounge to access technology guides, instructional videos, mobile apps, and service information.

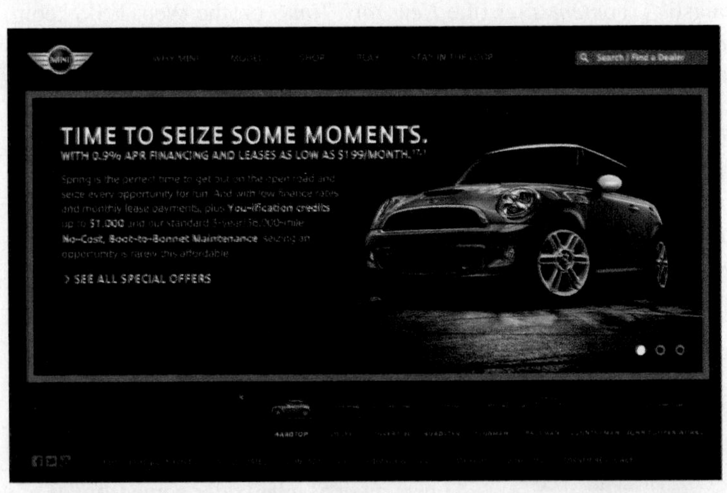

>> Marketing Web sites: Once a potential customer clicks onto the MINI Web site, the carmaker wastes no time trying to turn the inquiry into a sale, and then into a long-term relationship.
MINI USA.

In contrast, **branded community Web sites** don't try to sell anything at all. Instead, their primary purpose is to present brand content that engages consumers and creates customer–brand community. Such sites typically offer a rich variety of brand information, videos, blogs, activities, and other features that build closer customer relationships and generate engagement with and between the brand and its customers.

For example, consider ESPN's Web site. You can't buy anything at ESPN.com. Instead, the site creates a vast branded sports community:[10]

Marketing Web site
A Web site that interacts with consumers to move them closer to a direct purchase or other marketing outcome.

Branded community Web site
A Web site that presents brand content that engages consumers and creates customer community around a brand.

At ESPN.com, sports fans can access an almost overwhelming repository of sports information, statistics, and game updates. They can customize site content by sport, team, players, and authors to match their own special sports interests and team preferences. The site engages fans in contests and fantasy games (everything from fantasy football, baseball, and basketball to hockey and poker). Sports fans from around the world can participate in discussions with other fans and celebrities before, during, and after sporting events. They can friend and message other users and post comments on message boards and blogs. By downloading various widgets and apps, fans can customize their ESPN experience and carry it with them wherever they go. In all, ESPN's Web site creates a virtual brand community without walls, a must-have experience that keeps fans coming back again and again.

Creating a Web site is one thing; getting people to *visit* the site is another. To attract visitors, companies aggressively promote their Web sites in offline print and broadcast advertising and through ads and links on other sites. But today's Web users are quick to abandon any Web site that doesn't measure up. The key is to create enough value and engagement to get consumers to come to the site, stick around, and come back again.

At the very least, a Web site should be easy to use and visually appealing. Ultimately, however, Web sites must also be *useful*. When it comes to Web browsing and shopping, most people prefer substance over style and function over flash. For example, ESPN's site isn't all that flashy, and it's pretty heavily packed and congested. But it connects customers quickly and effectively to all the sports information and involvement they are seeking. Thus, effective Web sites contain deep and useful information, interactive tools that help find and evaluate content of interest, links to other related sites, changing promotional offers, and entertaining features that lend relevant excitement.

Online advertising
Advertising that appears while consumers are browsing online, including display ads, search-related ads, online classifieds, and other forms.

E-mail marketing
Sending highly targeted, highly personalized, relationship-building marketing messages via e-mail.

Online Advertising

As consumers spend more and more time online, companies are shifting more of their marketing dollars to **online advertising** to build brand sales or attract visitors to their Internet, mobile, and social media sites. Online advertising has become a major promotional medium.

The main forms of online advertising are display ads and search-related ads. Together, display and search-related ads account of the largest portion of firms' digital marketing budgets, capturing more than 23 percent of all digital marketing spending.[11]

Online display ads might appear anywhere on an Internet user's screen and are often related to the information being viewed. For instance, while browsing vacation packages on Travelocity.com, you might encounter a display ad offering a free upgrade on a rental car from Enterprise Rent-A-Car. Online display ads have come a long way in recent years in terms of attracting and holding consumer attention. Today's *rich media* ads incorporate animation, video, sound, and interactivity. >> For example, while browsing sports-related content on your computer or phone, you might see a bright orange Gatorade G Series banner emerge to take over your screen. Your favorite football player then bursts through the banner before the action settles on a stationary click-through display ad showing how some of the world's biggest sports stars use Gatorade Prime to pre-fuel their bodies before games. The action-packed "takeover" ad takes only a few seconds but delivers major impact.[12]

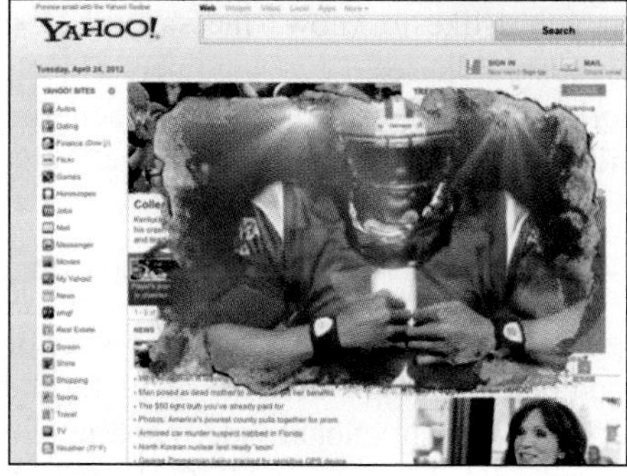

>> **Online display advertising: Gatorade's online "takeover" ad lasts only a few seconds but delivers major impact.**

Pepsi-Cola North America, Inc. Reproduced with permission of Yahoo! Inc. ©2012 Yahoo! Inc. YAHOO! and the YAHOO! logo are registered trademarks of Yahoo! Inc.

The largest form of online advertising is *search-related ads* (or *contextual advertising*), which accounted for nearly half of all online advertising spending last year. In search advertising, text-based ads and links appear alongside search engine results on sites such as Google, Yahoo!, and Bing. For example, search Google for "LCD TVs." At the top and side of the resulting search list, you'll see inconspicuous ads for 10 or more advertisers, ranging from Samsung and Dell to Best Buy, Sears, Amazon.com, Walmart.com, and Nextag.com. Ninety-five percent of Google's $50 billion in revenues last year came from ad sales. Search is an always-on kind of medium, and the results are easily measured.[13]

A search advertiser buys search terms from the search site and pays only if consumers click through to its site. For instance, type "Coke" or "Coca-Cola" or even just "soft drinks" or "rewards" into your search engine and almost without fail "My Coke Rewards" comes up as one of the top options, perhaps along with a display ad and link to Coca-Cola's official Google+ page. This is no coincidence. Coca-Cola supports its popular online loyalty program largely through search buys. The soft drink giant started first with traditional TV and print advertising but quickly learned that search was the most effective way to bring consumers to its www.mycokerewards.com Web site to register. Now, any of dozens of purchased search terms will return MyCokeRewards.com at or near the top of the search list.

E-Mail Marketing

E-mail marketing is an important and growing digital marketing tool. E-mail is a much-used communication tool; by one estimate, there are more than 3.6 billion e-mail accounts worldwide. What's more, e-mail is no longer limited to PCs and workstations; more than half of all e-mails are now opened on mobile devices. Not surprisingly, then, a recent study found that 78 percent of all digital direct marketing campaigns involved e-mail. Despite all the e-mail clutter, thanks to its low costs, e-mail marketing still brings one of the highest marketing returns on investment. According to the Direct Marketing Association, marketers get a return of $40 on every $1 they spend on e-mail. U.S. companies spent $1.15 billion on e-mail marketing last year, up from only $243 million 10 years earlier.[14]

When used properly, e-mail can be the ultimate direct marketing medium. Most blue-chip marketers use it regularly and with great success. E-mail lets these marketers send highly targeted, tightly personalized, relationship-building messages. For example, the National Hockey League (NHL) sends hypertargeted e-newsletters to fans based on their team affiliations and locations. It sends 62 versions of the e-newsletter weekly—two for each of the 30 teams, tailored to fans in the United States and Canada, respectively, and two generic league e-newsletters for the two countries. Another highly targeted NHL e-mail campaign promotes single-game ticket sales. The e-mailing consists of 900 different versions covering each of 30 recipient locations and 30 team preferences. So a Boston Bruin's fan living in Philadelphia receives an e-mail with Bruins imagery and information when the Bruins are scheduled to play the Flyers in Philadelphia. Last year, the e-mail campaign boosted single-game NHL ticket sales by 31 percent over the previous season.[15]

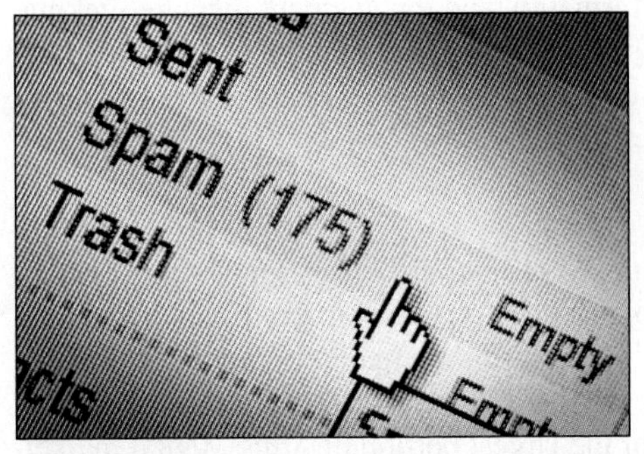

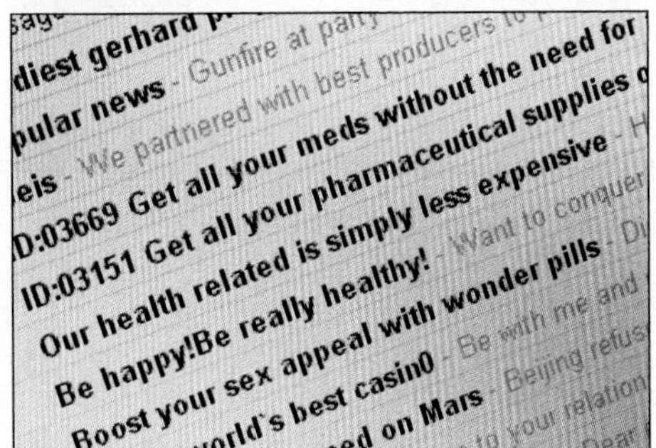

>> **E-mail can be an effective marketing tool. But there's a dark side—spam, unwanted commercial e-mail that clogs up our inboxes and causes frustration.**

© Yong Hian Lim/istockphoto; © adimas/Fotolia.

But there's a dark side to the growing use of e-mail marketing. >> The explosion of **spam**—unsolicited, unwanted commercial e-mail messages that clog up our e-mail boxes—has produced consumer irritation and frustration. According to one research company, spam now accounts for 70 percent of all e-mail sent.[16] E-mail marketers walk a fine line between adding value for consumers and being intrusive.

To address these concerns, most legitimate marketers now practice *permission-based e-mail marketing*, sending e-mail pitches only to customers who "opt in." Many companies use configurable e-mail systems that let customers choose what they want to get. Amazon.com targets opt-in customers with a limited number of helpful "we thought you'd like to know" messages based on their expressed preferences and previous purchases. Few customers object, and many actually welcome such promotional messages. Amazon.com benefits through higher return rates and by avoiding alienating customers with e-mails they don't want.

Spam
Unsolicited, unwanted commercial e-mail messages.

Online Videos

Another form of online marketing is posting digital video content on brand Web sites or social media sites such as YouTube, Facebook, and others. Some videos are made for the Web and social media. Such videos range from "how-to" instructional videos and public relations (PR) pieces to brand promotions and brand-related entertainment. Other videos are ads that a company makes primarily for TV and other media but posts online before or after an advertising campaign to extend their reach and impact.

Good online videos can engage consumers by the millions. The online video audience is soaring, with 58 percent of the U.S. population and 75 percent of Internet users now streaming video.[17] Marketers hope that some of their videos will go viral. **Viral marketing**, the digital version of word-of-mouth marketing, involves creating videos, ads, and other marketing content that is so infectious that customers will seek them out or pass them along to their friends. Because customers find and pass along the message or promotion, viral marketing can be very inexpensive. And when video or other information comes from a friend, the recipient is much more likely to view or read it.

Viral marketing
The digital version of word-of-mouth marketing: videos, ads, and other marketing content that is so infectious that customers will seek it out or pass it along to friends.

All kinds of videos can go viral, producing engagement and positive exposure for a brand. For example, in one simple but honest McDonald's video, the director of marketing at McDonald's Canada answers an online viewer's question about why McDonald's products look better in ads than in real life by conducting a behind-the-scenes tour of how a McDonald's ad is made. The award-winning 3½-minute video pulled almost 9 million views and 19,000 shares, earning the company praise for its honesty and transparency. As another example, in association with the 2012 London Olympics, P&G produced three heart-warming two-minute "Proud Sponsors of Moms" videos thanking the moms who helped the athletes reach Olympic heights. Those videos garnered more than 28 million views and 220,000 shares. They also formed the basis for TV ads shown during the Olympics.[18]

At the other extreme, to promote its Shop Your Way rewards program with its free shipping benefit, >> Kmart posted a TV ad-like video featuring shoppers of all ages exclaiming "ship my pants" (try saying that out loud). "Ship my pants? Right here?" says one surprised shopper. "I just shipped my pants, and it's very convenient," says another. The humorous video wasn't initially aired on TV. But after it pulled in nearly 8 million YouTube views and 38,000 Facebook likes in only one week, Kmart ran the commercial on selected TV channels.[19]

>> **Viral marketing: Kmart's TV ad-like video featuring shoppers of all ages exclaiming "ship my pants" (try saying that out loud) pulled in nearly 8 million YouTube views and 38,000 Facebook likes in only one week.**

Image courtesy of Sears Brands, LLC and © 2013 Sears Brands, LLC.

Sometimes a well-made regular ad can go viral with the help of targeted "seeding." For example, Volkswagen's clever "The Force" Super Bowl LXV ad, featuring a pint-sized Darth Vader using The Force to start a VW Passat, turned viral after a team at VW's ad agency seeded it to selected auto, pop culture, and Star Wars sites the week before the sporting event. By the time the ad aired during the Super Bowl, it had received more than 18 million hits online. By the end of the year, "The Force" had received more than 80 million online views.[20]

However, marketers usually have little control over where their viral messages end up. They can seed content online, but that does little good unless the message itself strikes a chord with consumers. For example, why did the seeded VW Darth Vader ad explode virally? Because the sentimental ad appealed to parents—the car's target demographic—who want a responsible suburban family ride. And it appealed to the child inside the parent, who may have once been wowed by *Star Wars* and now wanted a car with a little bit of magic. Says one creative director, "you hope that the creative is at a high enough mark where the seeds grow into mighty oaks. If they don't like it, it ain't gonna move. If they like it, it'll move a little bit; and if they love it, it's gonna move like a fast-burning fire through the Hollywood hills."[21]

Blogs and Other Online Forums

Blogs
Online journals where people and companies post their thoughts and other content, usually related to narrowly defined topics.

Brands also conduct online marketing through various digital forums that appeal to specific special-interest groups. **Blogs** (or Web logs) are online journals where people and companies post their thoughts and other content, usually related to narrowly defined topics. Blogs can be about anything, from politics or baseball to haiku, car repair, or the latest television series. According to one study, there are now more than 31 million blogs in the United States. Many bloggers use social networks such as Twitter and Facebook to promote their blogs, giving them huge reach. Such numbers can give blogs—especially those with large and devoted followings—substantial influence.[22]

Most marketers are now tapping into the blogosphere as a medium for reaching their customer communities. For example, on the Netflix Blog, members of the Netflix team (themselves rabid movie fans) tell about the latest Netflix features, share tricks for getting the most out of the Netflix experience, and collect feedback from subscribers. The Disney Parks Blog is a place to learn about and discuss all things Disney, including a Behind the Scenes area with posts about dance rehearsals, sneak peeks at new construction sites, interviews with employees, and more. Whole Foods Market's Whole Story Blog features videos, images, and posts about healthy eating, recipes, and what's happening inside the

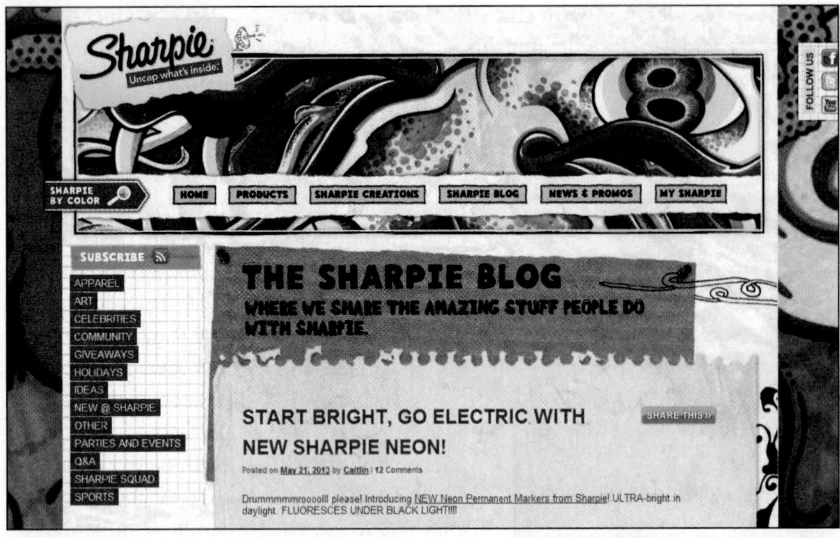

Most marketers are now tapping into the blogosphere as a medium for reaching their customer communities. For example, the Sharpie Blog shares "all the amazing stuff" that people do with Sharpie markers.

Sharpie®.

store. Clorox's Dr. Laundry blog discusses everything from laundry basics to removing melted crayon from children's clothes, and the Sharpie Blog shares "all the amazing stuff" that people do with Sharpie markers.

Dell has a dozen or more blogs that facilitate "a direct exchange with Dell customers about the technology that connects us all." The blogs include Direct2Dell (the official Dell corporate blog), Dell TechCenter (information technology brought into focus), DellShares (insights for investor relations), Health Care (about the health-care technology that connects us all), and Education (insights on using technology to enhance teaching, learning, and educational administration). Dell also has a very active and successful YouTube presence that it calls DellVlog, with 1,700 videos and more than 13 million video views. Dell bloggers often embed these YouTube videos into blog posts.[23]

One recent survey found that 54 percent of marketers had used third-party blogs to help get their messages out.[24] For example, McDonald's systematically reaches out to key "mommy bloggers," those who influence the nation's homemakers, who in turn influence their families' eating-out choices:[25]

> McDonald's recently hosted 15 bloggers on an all-expenses-paid tour of its headquarters in Oak Brook, Illinois. The bloggers toured the facilities (including the company's test kitchens), met McDonald's USA president Jan Fields, and had their pictures taken with Ronald at a nearby Ronald McDonald House. McDonald's knows that these mommy bloggers are very important. They have loyal followings and talk a lot about McDonald's in their blogs. So McDonald's is turning the bloggers into believers by giving them a behind-the-scenes view. McDonald's doesn't try to tell the bloggers what to say in their posts about the visit. It simply asks them to write one honest recap of their trip. However, the resulting posts (each acknowledging the blogger's connection with McDonald's) were mostly very positive. Thanks to this and many other such efforts, mommy bloggers around the country are now more informed about and connected with McDonald's. "I know they have smoothies and they have yogurt and they have other things that my kids would want," says one prominent blogger. "I really couldn't tell you what Burger King's doing right now," she adds. "I have no idea."

As a marketing tool, blogs offer some advantages. They can offer a fresh, original, personal, and cheap way to enter into consumer online conversations. However, the blogosphere is cluttered and difficult to control. And although companies can sometimes leverage blogs to engage customers in meaningful relationships, blogs remain largely a consumer-controlled medium. Whether or not they actively participate in the blogs, companies should monitor and listen to them. Marketers can use insights from consumer online conversations to improve their marketing programs.

Author Comment
As in about every other area of our lives, social media and mobile technologies have taken the marketing world by storm. They offer some amazing marketing possibilities. But truth be told, many marketers are still sweating over how to use them effectively.

Social Media Marketing

As we've discussed throughout the text so far, the surge in Internet usage and digital technologies and devices has spawned a dazzling array of online **social media** and digital communities. Countless independent and commercial social networks have arisen that give consumers online places to congregate, socialize, and exchange views and information. These days, it seems, almost everyone is buddying up on Facebook or Google+, checking in with Twitter, tuning into the day's hottest videos at YouTube, pinning images on social

Social media
Independent and commercial online communities where people congregate, socialize, and exchange views and information.

scrapbooking site Pinterest, or sharing photos with Instagram. And, of course, wherever consumers congregate, marketers will surely follow. Most marketers are now riding the huge social media wave. According to one survey, nearly 90 percent of U.S. companies now use social media networks as part of their marketing mixes.[26]

Using Social Media

Marketers can engage in social media in two ways: They can use existing social media or they can set up their own. Using existing social media seems the easiest. Thus, most brands—large and small—have set up shop on a host of social media sites. Check the Web sites of brands ranging from Coca-Cola and Nike to Victoria's Secret or even the NFL's San Francisco 49ers and you'll find links to each brand's Facebook, Google+, Twitter, YouTube, Flickr, Instagram, or other social media pages. Such social media can create substantial brand communities. For example, the 49ers have 1.85 million Facebook fans; Coca-Cola has an eye-popping 66 million fans.

Some of the major social networks are huge. More than 50 percent of Internet users in the United States and Canada use Facebook. That rivals the 55 percent who watch any TV channel and trounces the percentage listening to radio (37 percent) and reading newspapers (22 percent) daily. Facebook now reaches more than 1.1 billion members worldwide, almost 2.5 times the combined populations of the United States and Canada. Similarly, Twitter has more than 500 million registered users, and more than 1 billion unique users visit YouTube each month, watching more than 4 billion hours of video.[27]

Although these large social media networks grab most of the headlines, countless niche social media have also emerged. Niche online social networks cater to the needs of smaller communities of like-minded people, making them ideal vehicles for marketers who want to target special interest groups. There's at least one social media network for just about every interest or hobby. Yub.com and Kaboodle.com are for shopaholics, whereas moms share advice and commiseration at CafeMom.com. GoFISHn, a community of 4,000 anglers, features maps that pinpoint where fish are biting and a photo gallery where members can show off their catches. » At Dogster, 700,000 members set up profiles of their four-legged friends, read doggy diaries, or just give a dog a (virtual) bone. FarmersOnly.com provides online dating for down-to-earth "country folks" who enjoy "blue skies, living free and at peace in wide open spaces, raising animals, and appreciating nature"—"because city folks just don't get it." myTransponder.com is an online community where pilots find work, students locate flight instructors, and trade-specific advertisers hone in on a hard-to-reach audience of more than 2,000 people who love aviation.[28]

» **Thousands of social networking sites have popped up to cater to specific interests, backgrounds, professions, and age groups. At Dogster, 700,000 members set up profiles of their four-legged friends, read doggy diaries, or just give a dog a bone.**

Dogster.com.

Beyond these independent social media, many companies have created their own online brand communities. For example, in Nike's Nike+ running community—consisting of more than 7 million runners who have logged more than 873 million running miles worldwide—members join together online to upload, track, and compare their performances. Due to its success, Nike has expanded Nike+ to both basketball and general training, each with its own unique community site, app, and corresponding products.[29]

Social Media Marketing Advantages and Challenges

Using social media presents both advantages and challenges. On the plus side, social media are *targeted* and *personal*—they allow marketers to create and share tailored brand content with individual consumers and customer communities. Social media are *interactive,* making them ideal for starting and participating in customer conversations and listening to customer feedback. For example, Volvo uses its #Swedespeak Tweetchat platform as a kind of digital focus group to engage customers and obtain immediate input on everything from product features to creating ads. The regular Twitter chats are "creating good conversations," says Volvo's head marketer. "People enjoy being part of [the process]."[30]

Social media are also *immediate* and *timely*. They can be used to reach customers anytime, anywhere with timely and relevant content regarding brand happenings and activities. And social media can be very *cost effective*. Although creating and administering social media content can be costly, many social media are free or inexpensive to use. Thus, returns on social media investments are often high compared with those of expensive traditional media such as television or print. The low cost of social media puts them within easy reach of even small businesses and brands that can't afford the high costs of big-budget marketing campaigns.

Perhaps the biggest advantage of social media is their *engagement and social sharing capabilities*. Social media are especially well suited to creating customer engagement and community—for getting customers involved with the brand and with each other. More than any other channels, social media can involve customers in shaping and sharing brand content and experiences. Consider the recent Oreo Cookies vs. Crème Instagram campaign:[31]

> The two-month Oreo Cookies vs. Crème campaign began with a Super Bowl XLVII ad called "Whisper Fight," in which two men argued in a library over which part of an Oreo cookie they like best—the cookies or the crème. The ad invited consumers to take sides by posting photos they love on social scrapbooking site Instagram with the hashtag #cookiethis or #cremethis. Oreo then selected a number of the photos and worked with artists to create sculptures of the photos made of either cookies or crème. The campaign really got people buzzing about what they like best about Oreos. Prior to the Super Bowl airing, Oreo had about 2,200 Instagram followers. Immediately following the game, that number had jumped to about 22,000 followers and is now up to more than 87,000. The contest yielded nearly 32,000 fan submissions and 122 sculptures. More than just launching an Instagram page, Oreo launched "an engagement experience," says an Oreo brand manager. Oreo wrapped up the campaign with a series of short, funny online videos accessed by submitting votes for which you like best: cookies or crème. Oreo's answer to the which is best question? Not surprisingly, Oreo says it's both.

Social media marketing is an excellent way to create brand communities, places where brand loyalists can share experiences, information, and ideas. For example, Whole Foods Market uses a host of social media to create a Whole Foods lifestyle community where customers can research foods, access recipes, connect with other customers, discuss relevant food-related topics, and link to in-store events. » In addition to its very active Facebook, Twitter, YouTube, and Google+ pages, Whole Foods engages nearly 120,000 brand followers with 46 boards on social scrapbooking site Pinterest. Board topics range from "Food Tips and Tricks," "Delicious Art," and "Edible Celebrations" to Super HOT Kitchens, which is loaded with pictures of captivating kitchens. Whole Foods isn't in the kitchen remodeling business, but cooking and kitchens are a big part of the Whole Foods customer lifestyle.[32]

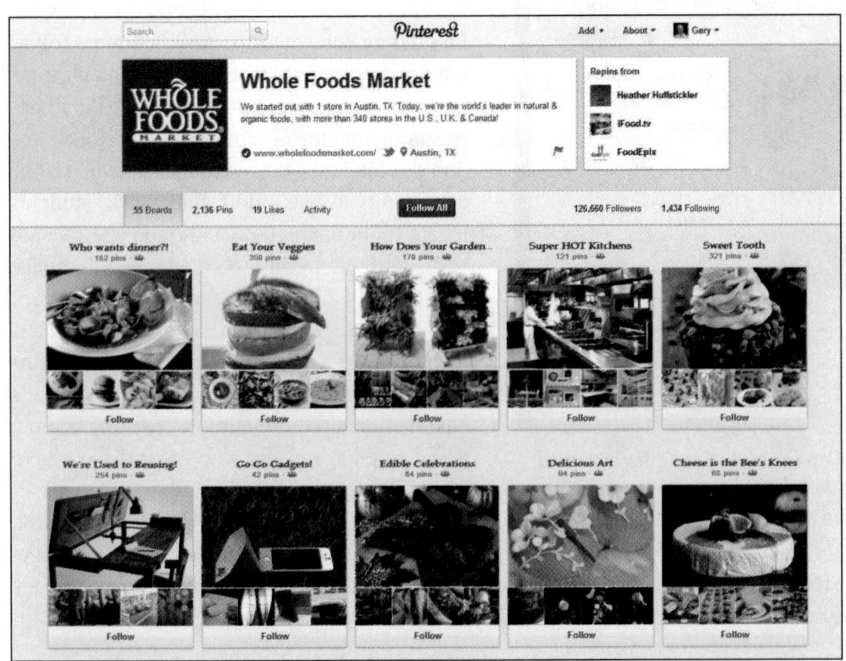

» **Whole Foods Market uses a host of social media to create a Whole Foods lifestyle community. For example, it engages nearly 120,000 brand followers with 46 boards on social scrapbooking site Pinterest.**

Courtesy of Whole Foods Market. "Whole Foods Market" is a registered trademark of Whole Foods Market IP, L.P.

Social media marketing also present challenges. First, most companies are still experimenting with how to use them effectively, and results are hard to measure. Second, such social networks are largely user controlled. The company's goal in using social media is to make the brand a part of consumers' conversations and their lives. However, marketers can't simply muscle their way into consumers' digital interactions—they need to earn the right to be there. Rather than intruding, marketers must learn to become a valued part of the online experience.

Because consumers have so much control over social media content, even the seemingly most harmless social media campaign can backfire. For example, McDonald's recently launched a Twitter campaign using the hashtag #McDStories, hoping that it would inspire heart-warming stories about Happy Meals. Instead, the effort was hijacked by Twitter users, who turned the hashtag into a "bashtag" by posting less-than-appetizing messages about their bad experiences with the fast-food chain. McDonald's pulled the campaign within only two hours, but the hashtag was still churning weeks later. "You're going into the consumer's backyard. This is their place," warns one social marketer. "Social media is a pressure cooker," says another. "The hundreds of thousands, or millions, of people out there are going to take your idea, and they're going to try to shred it or tear apart and find what's weak or stupid in it."[33]

Integrated Social Media Marketing

Using social media might be as simple as posting some messages and promotions on a brand's Facebook or Twitter pages or creating brand buzz with videos or images on YouTube or Pinterest. However, most large companies are now designing full-scale social media efforts that blend with and support other elements of a brand's marketing strategy and tactics. More than making scattered efforts and chasing "likes" and tweets, companies that use social media successfully are integrating a broad range of diverse media to create brand-related social sharing, engagement, and customer community.

Managing a brand's social media efforts can be a major undertaking. For example, Starbucks, one of the most successful social media marketers, manages 51 Facebook pages (including 43 in other countries); 31 Twitter handles (19 of them international); 22 Instagram names (14 international); plus Google+, Pinterest, YouTube, and Foursquare accounts. Managing and integrating all that social media content is challenging, but the results are worth the investment. Customers can engage with Starbucks digitally without ever setting foot in a store—and engage they do. With more than 34.5 million fans on its main U.S. page alone, Starbucks is the fifth-largest brand on Facebook. It ranks fourth on Twitter with 3.8 million followers.

But more than just creating online engagement and community, the Starbucks' social media presence also drives customer into its stores. For example, in its first big social media promotion four years ago, Starbucks offered a free pastry with a morning drink purchase. A million people showed up. Social media "are not just about engaging and telling a story and connecting," says Starbucks' head of global digital marketing. "They can have a material impact on the business."[34]

Mobile Marketing

Mobile marketing
Marketing messages, promotions, and other content delivered to on-the-go consumers through mobile phones, smartphones, tablets, and other mobile devices.

Mobile marketing features marketing messages, promotions, and other content delivered to on-the-go consumers through their mobile devices. Marketers use mobile marketing to engage customers anywhere, anytime during the buying and relationship-building processes. The widespread adoption of mobile devices and the surge in mobile Web traffic have made mobile marketing a must for most brands.

With the recent proliferation of mobile phones, smartphone, and tablets, mobile device penetration is now greater than 100 percent in the United States (many people possess more than one mobile device). Thirty-six percent of U.S. households are currently mobile-only households with no landline phone. Almost 60 percent of people in the United States own a smartphone, and about 81 percent of smartphone users use it to access the mobile Internet. They not only browse the mobile Internet but are also avid mobile app users. The mobile apps market has exploded: There are more than 2.7 million apps available and the average smartphone has 41 apps installed on it.[35]

Most people love their phones and rely heavily on them. According to one study, nearly 90 percent of consumers who own smartphones, tablets, computers, and TVs would give up all of those other screens before giving up their phones. On average, Americans check their phones 150 times a day—once every six-and-one-half minutes—and spend 58 minutes a day on their smartphones talking, texting, and visiting Web sites. Thus, although TV is still a big part of people's lives, mobile is rapidly becoming their "first screen." Away from home, it's their only screen.[36]

For consumers, a smartphone or tablet can be a handy shopping companion. It can provide on-the-go product information, price comparison, advice and reviews from other consumers, and access to instant deals and digital coupons. Not surprisingly, then, mobile devices provide a rich platform for engaging consumers more deeply as they move through the buying process with tools ranging mobile ads, coupons, and texts to apps and mobile Web sites.

Mobile advertising spending in the United States is surging; it more than doubled last year alone. Almost every major marketer—from P&G and Macy's to your local bank or supermarket to nonprofits such as the ASPCA—is now integrating mobile marketing into its direct marketing programs. Such efforts can produce very positive outcomes. For example, 49 percent of mobile users search for more information after seeing a mobile ad.[37]

Companies use mobile marketing to stimulate immediate buying, make shopping easier, enrich the brand experience, or all of these. It lets marketers provide consumers with information, incentives, and choices at the moment they are expressing an interest or when they are in a position to make a buying choice. For example, McDonald's uses mobile marketing to promote new menu items, announce special promotions, and drive immediate traffic at its restaurants. One recent interactive ad on Pandora's mobile app read "Taste buds. Any size soft drink or sweet tea for $1. Tap to visit site." A tap on the mobile ad took customers to a mobile site promoting McDonald's ongoing summer promotion. Another McDonald's mobile campaign used a word scrabble game to entice customers to try the fast feeder's dollar menu items. Such efforts create both customer engagement and store traffic. Using a game "inside a mobile campaign is all about finding and maintaining engagement," says a McDonald's marketer.[38]

Today's rich media mobile ads can create substantial impact and engagement. For example, HBO ran engaging mobile ads for the season premiere of its *True Blood* series. As consumers browsed their Flixter apps looking for good movies or their Variety apps seeking the latest entertainment news, touches on their screens turned into bloody fingerprints. Blood quickly filled their screens, followed by a tap-to-watch trailer invitation. The spine-chilling *True Blood* mobile ad campaign helped draw 5.1 million viewers to the show's season premiere and increased viewership by 38 percent.[39]

Retailers can use mobile marketing to enrich the customer's shopping experience at the same time they stimulate buying. » For example, Macy's built its recent "Brasil: A Magical Journey" promotion around a popular and imaginative smartphone app. The campaign featured apparel from Brazilian designers and in-store experiences celebrating Brazilian culture. By using their smartphones to scan Quick Response (QR) codes throughout the store, shoppers could learn about featured fashions and experience Brazilian culture through virtual tours, such as a trip to the Amazon, a visit to Rio de Janeiro during Carnival, or attending a Brazilian soccer match. "Mobile ads aim for 'of-the-moment' targeting, anywhere and everywhere," says one expert, whether it's at the time of a mobile search or in a store during the purchase decision.[40]

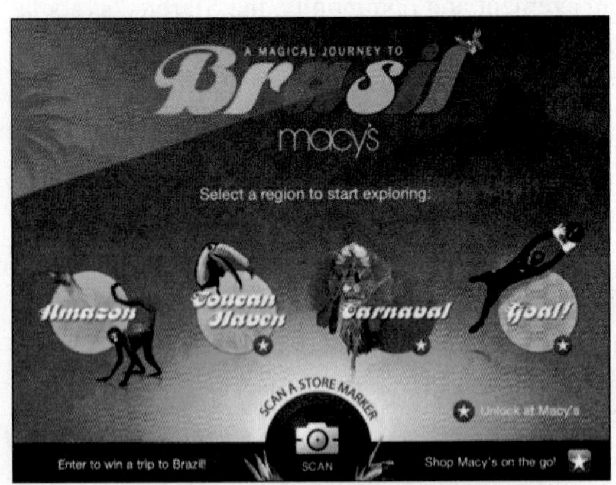

» **Mobile marketing: Macy's recent "Brasil: A Magical Journey" promotion, built around a popular and imaginative smartphone app, enriched the customer shopping experience while stimulating buying.**

Macy's Inc.

Many marketers have created their own mobile online sites, optimized for specific phones and mobile service providers. Others have created useful or entertaining mobile apps to engage customers with their brands and help them shop (see Marketing at Work 14.2). For example, Clorox offers a myStain app that targets young moms with useful on-the-go stain removal solutions. Schwab offers "Schwab to Go," a mobile app that lets customers get up-to-the-minute investment news, monitor their accounts, and make trades at any time from any location. And Starbucks' mobile app lets customers use their phones as a Starbucks card to make fast and easy purchases.

As with other forms of direct marketing, however, companies must use mobile marketing responsibly or risk angering already ad-weary consumers. "If you were interrupted every two minutes by advertising, not many people want that," says a mobile marketing expert. "The industry needs to work out smart and clever ways to engage people on mobiles." The key is to provide genuinely useful information and offers that will make consumers want to engage.

MARKETING AT WORK 14.2

Mobile Marketing: Customers Come Calling

You're at the local Best Buy checking out portable GPS navigation systems. You've narrowed it down to the latest Garmin nüvi versus a less-expensive competing model, but you're not certain that Best Buy has the best prices. Also, you'd love to know how other consumers rate the two brands. No problem. Just pull out your smartphone and launch your Amazon Mobile app, which lets you browse the brands you're considering, read customer reviews, and compare prices of portable GPS systems sold by Amazon.com and its retail partners. The application even lets you snap a photo or scan a barcode from an item; Amazon.com will then search for a similar item available from Amazon. If Amazon.com offers a better deal, you can make the purchase directly from the app with 1-Click ordering, then track the order until it reaches your doorstep.

Welcome to the world of mobile marketing. Today's smartphones and other mobile devices are changing the way we live—including the way we shop. And as they change how we shop, they also change how marketers sell to us. A growing number of consumers are using their mobile phones as a kind of digital Swiss Army Knife—as a preferred device for texting, browsing the mobile Internet, checking e-mail, watching videos and TV shows, playing games, listening to music, accessing news and information, and socializing. Mobile devices currently account for 37 percent of all Internet time, a number that will grow to 50 percent by the end of 2014.

For some, mobile domination has already arrived. For example, for U.S. Facebook members who use both its mobile and Web interfaces, time spent per month on the social network's mobile site far exceeds time spent on its classic Web site. In fact, all by itself, the Facebook app consumes 18 percent of all time spent on mobile devices. Similarly, for Twitter, 60 percent of all traffic is mobile. In all, U.S. consumers spend an average of 2 hours and 38 minutes a day socializing and accessing the Internet on their mobile devices—twice the amount of time they spend eating and about one-third the amount of time they spend sleeping.

Marketers are responding to this massive growth in mobile access and use. Mobile ad spending is expected to quadruple in the next four years, and corporate use of mobile Internet sites more than doubled last year. Mobile phones, tablets, and other mobile devices have become today's brave new marketing frontier, especially for brands courting younger consumers. Mobile devices are very personal, ever-present, and always on. That makes them an ideal medium for obtaining quick responses to individualized, time-sensitive offers. Mobile marketing reaches consumers with the right message in the right place at the right time.

Marketers large and small are weaving mobile marketing into their direct marketing mixes. And the successful campaigns go beyond just giving people a link to buy. They attract attention by providing helpful services, useful information, and entertainment. For example, Tide's Stain Brain app helps customers find ways to remove stains while out and about. A Sit or Squat app that directs people to nearby public restrooms opens with a splash page for Charmin bathroom tissue. And REI's The Snow Report app gives ski slope information for locations throughout the United States and Canada, such as snow depth, snow conditions, and the number of open lifts. The app helps you share resort information with friends via Twitter and Facebook, and it links you to "Shop REI" for times "when you decide you can't live without a new set of K2 skis or a two-man Hubba Hubba tent."

Beyond helping customers buy, mobile apps provide other helpful services. For example, Target's mobile app lets you keep shopping lists and sends out scannable mobile coupons for groceries and other merchandise: Just hold up your mobile phone at the checkout, and the cashier will scan the barcode off the screen. Zipcar's app lets members find and reserve a Zipcar, honk the

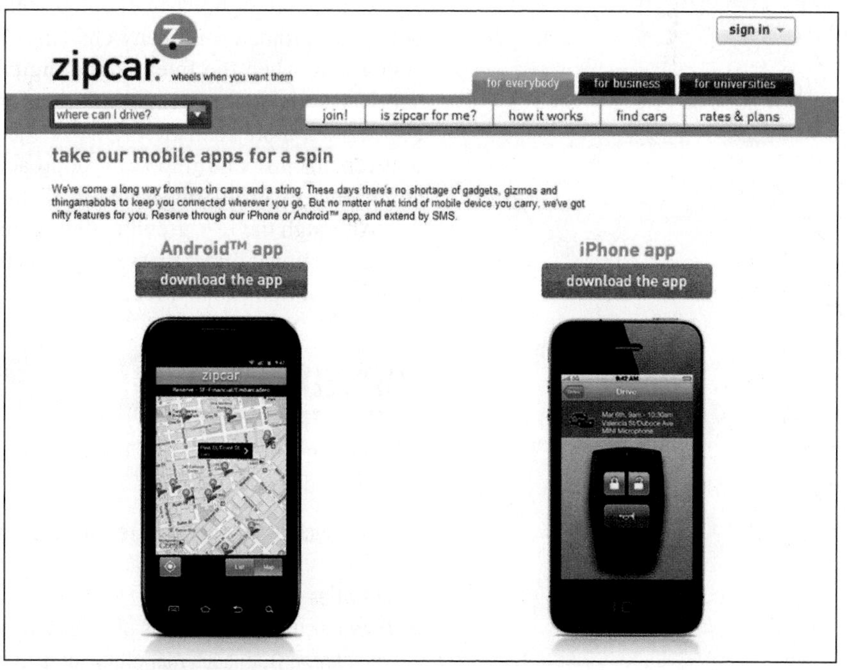

>> Mobile marketing: Zipcar's iPhone app lets members find and book a Zipcar, honk the horn (so they can find it in a crowd), and even lock and unlock the doors—all from their phones.

Zipcar.

horn (so they can find it in a crowd), and even lock and unlock the doors—all from their phones. And with MasterCard's PayPass app, cardholders can pay instantly and securely with their phones at any participating retailer—just "tap, pay, and be on your way."

One of the most effective mobile marketing apps is Kraft's iFood Assistant, which puts "delicious at your fingertips" in the form of easy-to-prepare recipes for food shoppers on the go, how-to videos, a recipe box, and a built-in shopping list. The iFood Assistant app supplies advice on how to prepare thousands of simple but satisfying meals—literally decades worth of recipes. The app will even give you directions to local stores. Of course, most of the meals call for ingredients that just happen to be Kraft brands. The iFood Assistant app cost Kraft less than $100,000 to create but has engaged millions of shoppers, providing great marketing opportunities for Kraft and its brands.

As the Amazon example suggests, consumers are increasingly using their phones as in-store shopping aids, and retailers are responding accordingly. For example, Walgreens has created the mobile equivalent of the local newspaper circular. Using new technology, Walgreens knows when participating customers check in to one of its 8,000 stores via Foursquare, Yelp, Twitter, Facebook, and a host of other location-based services. The retailer then tweets or texts the customers, sending mobile coupons or directing them to in-store deals with a message such as "Check out the specials on Halls new cough drops in the cold aisle." It's like taking shoppers by the hand and guiding them through the store.

According to one mobile marketing expert, the real advantage to targeting shoppers while they are out and about is the ability to reach consumers when they are closest to buying. "Ask yourself," he says, "are your customers more likely to leave their homes and their pantries . . . to go out and get a sub sandwich . . . or [is it more likely] when they've been out running errands all day, missed lunch, and you sent them a text with an offer for a half-price sub [at a nearby] shop?"

Many consumers are initially skeptical about mobile marketing. But they often change their minds if mobile marketers deliver value in the form of useful brand and shopping information, entertaining content, or discounted prices and coupons for their favorite products and services. Most mobile marketing efforts target only consumers who voluntarily opt in or who download apps. In the increasingly cluttered mobile marketing space, customers just won't do that unless they see real value in it. The challenge for marketers: Develop useful and engaging mobile marketing apps that make customers come calling.

Sources: Chuck Jones, "Mobile Ad Spending Forecast to Increase 4X over the Next 4 Years," *Forbes*, January 4, 2013, www.forbes.com/sites/chuckjones/2013/01/04/mobile-ad-spending-forecast-to-increase-4x-over-the-next-4-years/; Greg Sterling, "Report: Nearly 40 Percent of Internet Time Now on Mobile Devices," February 26, 2013, http://marketingland.com/report-nearly-40-percent-of-internet-time-now-on-mobile-devices-34639; Jichél Stewart, "8 Mobile Marketing Trends You Should Track in 2012," *Business 2 Community*, December 18, 2011, www.business2community.com/mobile-apps/8-mobile-marketing-trends-you-should-track-in-2012-0108821; Kunur Patel, "At Walgreens, a Mobile Check-In Acts Like Circular," *Advertising Age*, February 8, 2012, http://adage.com/print/232584/; and John Koetsier, "The Mobile War Is Over and the App Has Won," April 3, 2013, http://venturebeat.com/2013/04/03/the-mobile-war-is-over-and-the-app-has-won-80-of-mobile-time-spent-in-apps/.

In all, digital direct marketing—online, social media, and mobile marketing—offers both great promise and many challenges for the future. Its most ardent apostles still envision a time when the Internet and digital marketing will replace magazines, newspapers, and even stores as sources for information, engagement, and buying. Most marketers, however, hold a more realistic view. For most companies, digital and social media marketing will remain just one important approach to the marketplace that works alongside other approaches in a fully integrated marketing mix.

Although the fast-growing digital marketing tools have grabbed most of the headlines lately, traditional direct marketing tools are very much alive and still heavily used. We now examine the traditional direct marketing approaches shown on the right side of Figure 14.1.

SPEED BUMP LINKING THE CONCEPTS

Stop now and think about how online, social media, and mobile marketing affect your brand buying behavior and preferences.

- How much of your product research, shopping, and actual buying take place online? How much of that is conducted on a mobile device? How and how much do your in-store and digital buying activities interact?
- How much and what kinds of online, social media, and mobile marketing do you encounter? Do you benefit from such marketing, or is it more of an unwelcome intrusion? In what ways?
- Do you engage directly with any brands or brand communities through online sites, social media, or phone apps? Do your online, social media, or mobile interactions influence your brand preferences and buying? Discuss.

Author Comment
Again, although online, social media, and mobile direct marketing seem to be getting much of the attention these days, traditional direct media still carry a lot of the direct marketing freight. Just think about your often overstuffed mailbox.

Traditional Direct Marketing Forms

The major traditional forms of direct marketing—as shown in Figure 14.1—are face-to-face or personal selling, direct-mail marketing, catalog marketing, telemarketing, direct-response television (DRTV) marketing, and kiosk marketing. We examined personal selling in depth in Chapter 13. Here, we look into the other forms of traditional direct marketing.

Direct-Mail Marketing

Direct-mail marketing
Marketing that occurs by sending an offer, announcement, reminder, or other item directly to a person at a particular address.

Direct-mail marketing involves sending an offer, announcement, reminder, or other item to a person at a particular address. Using highly selective mailing lists, direct marketers send out millions of mail pieces each year—letters, catalogs, ads, brochures, samples, videos, and other "salespeople with wings." The Direct Marketing Association reports that U.S. marketers spent more than $50 billion on direct mail last year (including both catalog and noncatalog mail), which accounted for 30 percent of all direct marketing spending and generated 31 percent of all direct marketing sales. According to the DMA, every dollar spent on direct mail generates $12.57 in sales.[41]

Direct mail is well suited to direct, one-to-one communication. It permits high target-market selectivity, can be personalized, is flexible, and allows the easy measurement of results. Although direct mail costs more per thousand people reached than mass media such as television or magazines, the people it reaches are much better prospects. Direct mail has proved successful in promoting all kinds of products, from books, insurance, travel, gift items, gourmet foods, clothing, and other consumer goods to industrial products of all kinds. Charities also use direct mail heavily to raise billions of dollars each year.

Some analysts predict a decline in the use of traditional forms of direct mail in coming years, as marketers switch to newer digital forms, such as e-mail and online marketing, social media marketing, and mobile marketing. The newer digital direct marketing approaches deliver messages at incredible speeds and lower costs compared to the U.S. Post Office's "snail mail" pace.

However, even though new digital forms of direct marketing are bursting onto the scene, traditional direct mail is still heavily used by most marketers. Mail marketing offers some distinct advantages over digital forms. It provides something tangible for people to hold and keep and it can be used to send samples. "Mail makes it real," says one analyst. It "creates an emotional connection with customers that digital cannot. They hold it, view it, and engage with it in a manner entirely different from their [digital] experiences." In contrast, e-mail and other digital forms are easily filtered or trashed. "[With] spam filters and spam folders to keep our messaging away from consumers' inboxes," says a direct marketer, "sometimes you have to lick a few stamps."[42]

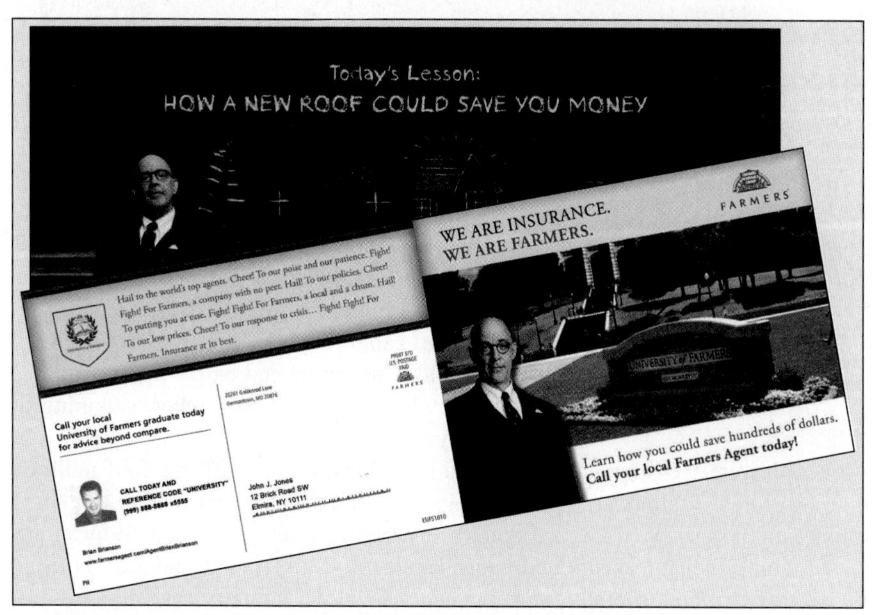

>> **Direct mail marketing: Insurance companies like Farmers Insurance rely heavily on TV advertising to establish broad customer awareness. However, they also use lots of good old direct mail to communicate with consumers in a more direct and personalized way.**

Farmers Group, Inc.

Traditional direct mail can be an effective component of a broader integrated marketing campaign. For example, most large insurance companies rely heavily on TV advertising to establish broad customer awareness and positioning. However, the insurance companies also use lots of good old direct mail to break through the glut of insurance advertising on TV. Whereas

TV advertising talks to broad audiences, direct mail communicates in a more direct and personal way. "Mail is a channel that allows all of us to find the consumer with a very targeted, very specific message that you can't do in broadcast," says John Ingersoll, vice president of marketing communications for Farmers Insurance. And "most people are still amenable to getting marketing communications in their mailbox, which is why I think direct mail will grow."[43]

Direct mail may be resented as *junk mail* or if sent to people who have no interest in it. For this reason, smart marketers are targeting their direct mail carefully so as not to waste their money and recipients' time. They are designing permission-based programs that send direct mail only to those who want to receive it.

Catalog Marketing

Catalog marketing
Direct marketing through print, video, or digital catalogs that are mailed to select customers, made available in stores, or presented online.

Advances in technology, along with the move toward personalized, one-to-one marketing, have resulted in exciting changes in **catalog marketing**. *Catalog Age* magazine used to define a *catalog* as "a printed, bound piece of at least eight pages, selling multiple products, and offering a direct ordering mechanism." Today, this definition is sadly out of date.

With the stampede to the Internet and digital marketing, more and more catalogs are going digital. A variety of online-only catalogers have emerged, and most print catalogers have added Web-based catalogs and smartphone catalog shopping apps to their marketing mixes. >> For example, apps such as Catalog Spree put a mall full of classic catalogs from retailers such as Macy's, Anthropologie, L.L.Bean, Hammacher Schlemmer, ColdwaterCreek, or West Elm only a swipe of the finger away on a smartphone or tablet. And days before the latest Lands' End catalog arrives in the mail, customers can access it digitally at landsend.com, at social media outlets such as Facebook, or via the Lands' End mobile app. With Lands' End Mobile, says the company, "You're carrying every item we carry."[44]

>> **Digital catalogs: Apps such as Catalog Spree put a mall full of classic catalogs from retailers such as Macy's, Best Buy, Anthropologie, L.L.Bean, Hammacher Schlemmer, or Coldwater Creek only a swipe of the finger away on a smartphone or tablet.**

Catalog Spree, the #1 catalog shopping app for the iPad and iPhone. www.catalogspree.com.

Digital catalogs eliminate printing and mailing costs. And whereas space is limited in a print catalog, online catalogs can offer an almost unlimited amount of merchandise. They also offer a broader assortment of presentation formats, including search and video. Finally, online catalogs allow real-time merchandising; products and features can be added or removed as needed, and prices can be adjusted instantly to match demand. Customers can carry digital catalogs anywhere they go, even when shopping at physical stores.

However, despite the advantages of digital catalogs, as your overstuffed mailbox may suggest, printed catalogs are still thriving. U.S. direct marketers mailed out some 12.5 billion catalogs last year—more than 100 per American household. Why aren't companies ditching their old-fashioned paper catalogs in this new digital era? For one thing, paper catalogs create emotional connections with customers that digital sales spaces simply can't. "Glossy catalog pages still entice buyers in a way that computer images don't," says an analyst.[45]

In addition, printed catalogs are one of the best ways to drive online and mobile sales, making them more important than ever in the digital era. According to one study, 70 percent of online purchases are driven by catalogs. Another study found that 60 percent of consumers who receive a catalog from a company go online to make a purchase within a week. Catalog users look at more than double the number of Web pages per visit to the company's site than the average visitor and spend twice the amount of time there.[46]

Telemarketing

Telemarketing
Using the telephone to sell directly to customers.

Telemarketing involves using the telephone to sell directly to consumers and business customers. Last year, telemarketing accounted for almost 14.9 percent of all direct-marketing-driven sales. We're all familiar with telephone marketing directed toward consumers, but business-to-business (B-to-B) marketers also use telemarketing extensively, accounting for nearly 56 percent of all telephone marketing sales.[47] Marketers use *outbound* telephone marketing to sell directly to consumers and businesses. » They also use *inbound* toll-free numbers to receive orders from television and print ads, direct mail, or catalogs.

Careful...you might sprain a taste bud.
Don't wait another day! Call now to place an order or request a catalog. Also, go on line at www.carolinacookie.com to place an order, request a catalog or view our entire selection of products.
1-800-447-5797
CAROLINA COOKIE
JUST BAKED
COMPANY

» **Marketers use inbound toll-free 800 numbers to receive orders garnered from television and print ads, direct mail, or catalogs. Here, the Carolina Cookie Company urges, "Don't wait another day. Call now to place an order or request a catalog."**

Carolina Cookie Company.

Properly designed and targeted telemarketing provides many benefits, including purchasing convenience and increased product and service information. However, the explosion in unsolicited outbound telephone marketing over the years annoyed many consumers, who objected to the almost daily "junk phone calls." In 2003, U.S. lawmakers responded with the National Do Not Call Registry, which is managed by the Federal Trade Commission (FTC). The legislation bans most telemarketing calls to registered phone numbers (although people can still receive calls from nonprofit groups, politicians, and companies with which they have recently done business). Consumers responded enthusiastically. To date, more than 217 million home and mobile phone numbers have been registered at www.donotcall.gov or by calling 888-382-1222. Businesses that break do-not-call laws can be fined up to $16,000 per violation. As a result, reports an FTC spokesperson, the program "has been exceptionally successful."[48]

Do-not-call legislation has hurt parts of the consumer telemarketing industry. However, two major forms of telemarketing—inbound consumer telemarketing and outbound B-to-B telemarketing—remain strong and growing. Telemarketing also remains a major fundraising tool for nonprofit and political groups. Interestingly, do-not-call regulations appear to be helping some direct marketers more than it's hurting them. Rather than making unwanted calls, many of these marketers are developing "opt-in" calling systems, in which they provide useful information and offers to customers who have invited the company to contact them by phone or e-mail. The opt-in model provides better returns for marketers than the formerly invasive one.

Direct-Response Television Marketing

Direct-response television (DRTV) marketing
Direct marketing via television, including direct-response television advertising (or infomercials) and interactive television (iTV) advertising.

Direct-response television (DRTV) marketing takes one of two major forms: direct-response television advertising and interactive TV (iTV) advertising. Using *direct-response television advertising*, direct marketers air television spots, often 60 or 120 seconds in length, which persuasively describe a product and give customers a toll-free number or a Web site for ordering. It also includes full 30-minute or longer advertising programs, called *infomercials*, for a single product.

Successful direct-response television advertising campaigns can ring up big sales. For example, little-known infomercial maker Guthy-Renker has helped propel its Proactiv Solution acne treatment and other "transformational" products into power brands that pull in $1.8 billion in sales annually to 5 million active customers (compare that to only about $150 million in annual drugstore sales of acne products in the United States). Guthy-Renker now combines DRTV with social media campaigns using Twitter and

YouTube to create a powerful integrated direct marketing channel that builds consumer involvement and buying.[49]

DRTV ads are often associated with somewhat loud or questionable pitches for cleaners, stain removers, kitchen gadgets, and nifty ways to stay in shape without working very hard at it. For example, over the past few years yell-and-sell TV pitchmen like Anthony Sullivan (Swivel Sweeper, Awesome Auger) and Vince Offer (ShamWow, SlapChop) have racked up billions of dollars in sales of "As Seen on TV" products. Brands like OxiClean, ShamWow, and the Snuggie (a blanket with sleeves) have become DRTV cult classics. And infomercial viral sensation PajamaJeans ("Pajamas you live in, Jeans you sleep in") created buzz on everything from YouTube to *The Tonight Show,* selling more than 2 million pairs at $39.95 each, plus $7.95 shipping and handling.[50]

In recent years, however, a number of large companies—from P&G, Disney, Revlon, Apple, and Kodak to Toyota, Coca-Cola, Anheuser-Busch, and even the U.S. Navy—have begun using infomercials to sell their wares, refer customers to retailers, recruit members, or attract buyers to their online, mobile, and social media sites.

A more recent form of direct-response television marketing is *interactive TV (iTV),* which lets viewers interact with television programming and advertising. Thanks to technologies such as interactive cable systems, Internet-ready smart TVs, and smartphones and tablets, consumers can now use their TV remotes, phones, or other devices to obtain more information or make purchases directly from TV ads. Also, increasingly, as the lines continue to blur between TV screens and other video screens, interactive ads and infomercials are appearing not just on TV, but also on mobile, online, and social media platforms, adding even more TV-like interactive direct marketing venues.

Kiosk Marketing

As consumers become more and more comfortable with digital and touchscreen technologies, many companies are placing information and ordering machines—called *kiosks* (good old-fashioned vending machines but so much more)—in stores, airports, hotels, college campuses, and other locations. Kiosks are everywhere these days, from self-service hotel and airline check-in devices, to unmanned product and information kiosks in malls, to in-store ordering devices that let you order merchandise not carried in the store. "Vending machines, which not long ago had mechanical levers and coin trays, now possess brains," says one analyst. Many modern "smart kiosks" are now wireless-enabled. And some machines can even use facial recognition software that lets them guess gender and age and make product recommendations based on that data.[51]

In-store Kodak, Fuji, and HP kiosks let customers transfer pictures from memory cards, mobile phones, and other digital storage devices; edit them; and make high-quality color prints. Seattle's Best kiosks in grocery, drug, and mass merchandise stores grind and brew fresh coffee beans and serve coffee, mochas, and lattes to on-the-go customers around the clock. Redbox operates more than 35,000 DVD rental kiosks in McDonald's, Walmart, Walgreens, CVS, Family Dollar, and other retail outlets—customers make their selections on a touchscreen, then swipe a credit or debit card to rent DVDs for less than $2 a day.

>> Kiosk marketing: ZoomShop kiosks across the country automatically dispense an assortment of popular consumer electronics products. This ZoomShop is located in a Macy's store and features Apple products, among others.

ZoomSystems.

ZoomSystems creates small, free-standing kiosks called ZoomShops for retailers ranging from Apple, Sephora, and The Body Shop to Macy's and Best Buy. For example, 100 Best Buy Express ZoomShop kiosks across the country—conveniently located in airports, busy malls, military bases, and resorts—automatically dispense an assortment of portable media players, digital cameras, gaming consoles, headphones, phone chargers, travel gadgets, and other popular products. According to ZoomSystems, today's automated retailing "offers [consumers] the convenience of online shopping with the immediate gratification of traditional retail."[52]

Author Comment

Although we mostly benefit from direct and digital marketing, like most other things in life, they have a dark side as well. Marketers and customers alike must guard against irritating or harmful direct and digital marketing practices.

Public Policy Issues in Direct and Digital Marketing

Direct marketers and their customers usually enjoy mutually rewarding relationships. Occasionally, however, a darker side emerges. The aggressive and sometimes shady tactics of a few direct marketers can bother or harm consumers, giving the entire industry a black eye. Abuses range from simple excesses that irritate consumers to instances of unfair practices or even outright deception and fraud. The direct marketing industry has also faced growing privacy concerns, and online marketers must deal with Internet security issues.

Irritation, Unfairness, Deception, and Fraud

Direct marketing excesses sometimes annoy or offend consumers. For example, most of us dislike direct-response TV commercials that are too loud, long, and insistent. Our mailboxes fill up with unwanted junk mail, our e-mailboxes bulge with unwanted spam, and our computer, phone, and tablet screens flash with unwanted online or mobile display ads, pop-ups, or pop-unders.

Beyond irritating consumers, some direct marketers have been accused of taking unfair advantage of impulsive or less-sophisticated buyers. Television shopping channels, enticing Web sites, and program-long infomercials targeting television-addicted shoppers seem to be the worst culprits. They feature smooth-talking hosts, elaborately staged demonstrations, claims of drastic price reductions, "while they last" time limitations, and unequaled ease of purchase to inflame buyers who have low sales resistance.

Fraudulent schemes, such as investment scams or phony collections for charity, have also multiplied in recent years. *Internet fraud*, including identity theft and financial scams, has become a serious problem. According to the FBI's Internet Crime Complaint Center, since 2005, Internet scam complaints have more than tripled to 300,000 per year. The monetary loss of scam complaints exceeds $300 million per year.[53]

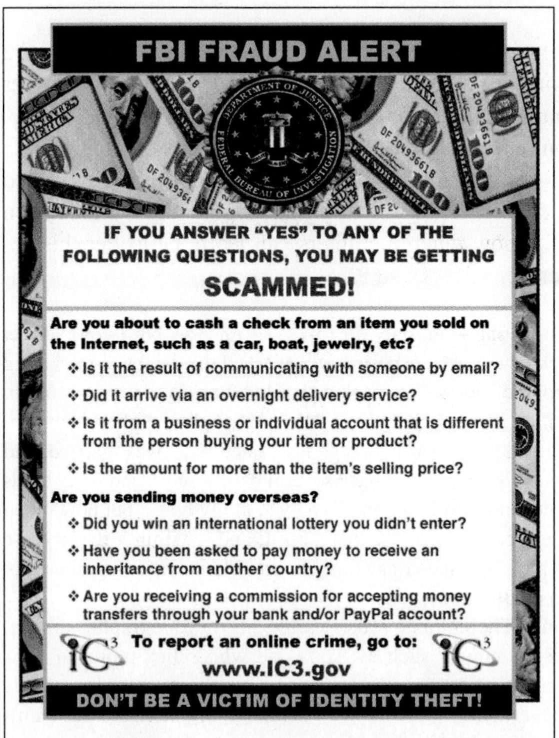

Internet fraud has multiplied in recent years. The FBI's Internet Crime Complaint Center provides consumers with a convenient way to alert authorities to suspected violations.

FBI.

One common form of Internet fraud is *phishing*, a type of identity theft that uses deceptive e-mails and fraudulent online sites to fool users into divulging their personal data. For example, consumers may receive an e-mail, supposedly from their bank or credit card company, saying that their account's security has been compromised. The sender asks them to log on to a provided Web address and confirm their account number, password, and perhaps even their social security number. If they follow the instructions, users are actually turning this sensitive information over to scam artists. Although many consumers are now aware of such schemes, phishing can be extremely costly to those caught in the net. It also damages the brand identities of legitimate online marketers who have worked to build user confidence in Web, e-mail, and other digital transactions.

Many consumers also worry about *online and digital security*. They fear that unscrupulous snoopers will eavesdrop on their online transactions and social media posting, picking up personal information or intercepting credit and debit card numbers. Although online shopping has grown rapidly, one study showed that 59 percent of participants were still concerned about identity theft.[54]

Another Internet marketing concern is that of *access by vulnerable or unauthorized groups*. For example, marketers of adult-oriented materials and sites have found it difficult to restrict access by minors. Although Facebook allows no children under age 13 to have a profile, and estimated 40 percent of under-18 Facebook users are actually under 13. Facebook removes 200,000 underage accounts every day. And it's not just Facebook. Young users are logging onto social media such as Formspring, tweeting their locations to the Web, and making friends with strangers on Disney and other games sites. Concerned state and national lawmakers are currently debating bills that would help better protect children online. Unfortunately, this requires the development of technology solutions, and as Facebook puts it, "That's not so easy."[55]

Consumer Privacy

Invasion of privacy is perhaps the toughest public policy issue now confronting the direct marketing industry. Consumers often benefit from database marketing; they receive more offers that are closely matched to their interests. However, many critics worry that marketers may know *too* much about consumers' lives and that they may use this knowledge to take unfair advantage of consumers. At some point, they claim, the extensive use of databases intrudes on consumer privacy. Consumers, too, worry about their privacy. Although they are now much more willing to share personal information and preferences with marketers via the digital and social media, they are still nervous about it. In one recent survey, some three-quarters of consumers agreed with the statement, "No one should ever be allowed to have access to my personal data or Web behavior."[56]

These days, it seems that almost every time consumers post something on social media or send a tweet, visit a Web site, enter a sweepstakes, apply for a credit card, or order products by phone or online, their names are entered into some company's already bulging database. Using sophisticated computer technologies, direct marketers can mine these databases to "microtarget" their selling efforts. Most marketers have become highly skilled at collecting and analyzing detailed consumer information both online and offline. Even the experts are sometimes surprised by how much marketers can learn. Consider this account by one *Advertising Age* reporter:[57]

> I'm no neophyte when it comes to targeting—not only do I work at *Ad Age*, but I cover direct marketing. Yet even I was taken aback when, as an experiment, we asked the database-marketing company to come up with a demographic and psychographic profile of me. Was it ever spot-on. Using only publicly available information, it concluded my date of birth, home phone number, and political-party affiliation. It gleamed that I was a college graduate, that I was married, and that one of my parents had passed away. It found that I have several bank, credit, and retail cards at "low-end" department stores. It knew not just how long I've lived at my house but how much it costs, how much it was worth, the type of mortgage that's on it, and—within a really close ballpark guess—how much is left to pay on it. It estimated my household income—again nearly perfectly—and determined that I am of British descent.
>
> But that was just the beginning. The company also nailed my psychographic profile. It correctly placed me into various groupings such as: someone who relies more on their own opinions than the recommendations of others when making a purchase; someone who is turned off by loud and aggressive advertising; someone who is family-oriented and has an interest in music, running, sports, computers, and is an avid concert-goer; someone who is never far from an Internet connection, generally used to peruse sports and general news updates; and someone who sees health as a core value. Scary? Certainly.

Some consumers and policy makers worry that the ready availability of information may leave consumers open to abuse. For example, they ask, should online sellers be allowed to plant cookies in the browsers of consumers who visit their sites and use tracking information to target ads and other marketing efforts? Should credit card companies be allowed to make data on their millions of cardholders worldwide available to merchants who accept their cards? Or is it right for states to sell the names and addresses of driver's license holders, along with height, weight, and gender information, allowing apparel retailers to target tall or overweight people with special clothing offers?

A Need for Action

To curb direct marketing excesses, various government agencies are investigating not only do-not-call lists but also do-not-mail lists, do-not-track online lists, and Can Spam legislation. In response to online privacy and security concerns, the federal government has considered numerous legislative actions to regulate how online, social media, and mobile operators obtain and use consumer information. For example, Congress is drafting legislation that would give consumers more control over how online information is used. In addition, the FTC is taking a more active role in policing online privacy.

All of these concerns call for strong actions by marketers to monitor and prevent privacy abuses before legislators step in to do it for them. For example, to head off increased government regulation, six advertiser groups—the American Association of Advertising Agencies, the American Advertising Federation, the Association of National Advertisers, the Direct Marketing Association, the Interactive Advertising Bureau, and the Network Advertising Initiative—recently issued a set of online advertising principles through the Digital Advertising Alliance. Among other measures, the self-regulatory principles call for online marketers to provide transparency and choice to consumers if Web viewing data is collected or used for targeting interest-based advertising. The ad industry has agreed on an *advertising option icon*—a little "i" inside a triangle—that it will add to most behaviorally targeted online ads—those targeted using third-party information—to tell consumers why they are seeing a particular ad and allowing them to opt out.[58]

Consumer privacy: The ad industry has agreed on an *advertising option icon*—a little "i" inside a triangle—that will tell consumers why they are seeing a particular ad and allow them to opt out.

Digital Advertising Alliance.

Of special concern are the privacy rights of children. In 2000, Congress passed the Children's Online Privacy Protection Act (COPPA), which requires online operators targeting children to post privacy policies on their sites. They must also notify parents about any information they're gathering and obtain parental consent before collecting personal information from children under age 13. With the subsequent advent of online social media, mobile phones, and other digital technologies, privacy groups are now urging the U.S. Senate to extend COPPA to include both the new technologies and teenagers.The main concern is the amount of data mined by third parties from social media as well as the social medias' own hazy privacy policies.[59]

Many companies have responded to consumer privacy and security concerns with actions of their own. Still others are taking an industry-wide approach. For example, TRUSTe, a nonprofit self-regulatory organization, works with many large corporate sponsors, including Microsoft, Yahoo!, AT&T, Facebook, Disney, and Apple, to audit privacy and security measures and help consumers navigate the Internet safely. According to the company's Web site, "TRUSTe believes that an environment of mutual trust and openness will help make and keep the Internet a free, comfortable, and richly diverse community for everyone." To reassure consumers, the company lends its TRUSTe privacy seal to Web sites, mobile apps, e-mail marketing, and other online and social media channels that meet its privacy and security standards.[60]

The direct marketing industry as a whole is also addressing public policy issues. For example, in an effort to build consumer confidence in shopping direct, the

Direct Marketing Association—the largest association for businesses practicing direct, database, and interactive marketing, including nearly half of the *Fortune* 100 companies—launched a "Privacy Promise to American Consumers." The Privacy Promise requires that all DMA members adhere to a carefully developed set of consumer privacy rules. Members must agree to notify customers when any personal information is rented, sold, or exchanged with others. They must also honor consumer requests to opt out of receiving further solicitations or having their contact information transferred to other marketers. Finally, they must abide by the DMA's Preference Service by removing the names of consumers who do not wish to receive mail, phone, or e-mail offers.[61]

Direct marketers know that, if left untended, such direct marketing abuses will lead to increasingly negative consumer attitudes, lower response and engagement rates, and calls for more restrictive state and federal legislation. Most direct marketers want the same things that consumers want: honest and well-designed marketing offers targeted only toward consumers who will appreciate and respond to them. Direct marketing is just too expensive to waste on consumers who don't want it.

MyMarketingLab

Go to **mymktlab.com** to complete the problems marked with this icon .

END OF CHAPTER REVIEWING THE CONCEPTS

CHAPTER REVIEW AND KEY TERMS

Objectives Review

This chapter is the last of three chapters covering the final marketing mix element—promotion. The previous chapters dealt with advertising, public relations, personal selling, and sales promotion. This one investigates the burgeoning field of direct and digital marketing.

OBJECTIVE 1 Define *direct and digital marketing* and discuss their rapid growth and benefits to customers and companies. (pp 437–438)

Direct and digital marketing involve engaging directly with carefully targeted individual consumers and customer communities to both obtain an immediate response and build lasting customer relationships. Companies use direct marketing to tailor their offers and content to the needs and interests of narrowly defined segments or individual buyers to build direct customer engagement, brand community, and sales. Today, spurred by the surge in Internet usage and buying, and by rapid advances in digital technologies—from smartphones, tablets, and other digital devices to the spate of online social and mobile media—direct marketing has undergone a dramatic transformation.

For buyers, direct and digital marketing are convenient, easy to use, and private. They give buyers anywhere, anytime access to an almost unlimited assortment of products and buying information. Direct marketing is also immediate and interactive, allowing buyers to create exactly the configuration of information, products, or services they desire and then order them on the spot. Finally, for consumers who want it, digital marketing through online, mobile, and social media provides a sense of brand engagement and community—a place to share brand information and experiences with other brand fans. For sellers, direct and digital marketing are powerful tools for building customer engagement and close, personalized, interactive customer relationships. They also offer greater flexibility, letting marketers make ongoing adjustments to prices and programs, or make immediate, timely, and personal announcements and offers.

OBJECTIVE 2 Identify and discuss the major forms of direct and digital marketing. (pp 438–440)

The main forms of direct and digital marketing include traditional direct marketing tools and the new direct digital marketing tools. Traditional direct approaches are face-to-face personal selling, direct-mail marketing, catalog marketing, telemarketing, DRTV marketing, and kiosk marketing. These traditional tools are still heavily used and very important in most firm's direct marketing efforts. In recent years, however, a dazzling new set of direct digital marketing tools has burst onto the marketing scene, including online marketing (Web sites, online ads and promotions, e-mail, online videos, and blogs), social media marketing, and mobile marketing. The chapter first discusses the fast-growing new digital direct marketing tools and then examines the traditional tools.

OBJECTIVE 3 Explain how marketers have responded to the Internet and the digital age with various online marketing strategies. (pp 441–446)

The Internet and digital age have fundamentally changed customers' notions of convenience, speed, price, product information, service, and brand interactions. As a result, they have given marketers a whole new way to create customer value, engage customers, and build customer relationships. The Internet now influences a staggering 50 percent of total sales—including sales transacted online plus those made in stores but encouraged by online research. To reach this burgeoning market, most companies now market online.

Online marketing takes several forms, including company Web sites, online advertising and promotions, e-mail marketing, online video, and blogs. Social media and mobile marketing also take place online. But because of their special characteristics, we discuss these fast-growing digital marketing approaches in separate sections. For most companies, the first step in conducting online marketing is to create a Web site. The key to a successful Web site is to create enough value and engagement to get consumers to come to the site, stick around, and come back again.

Online advertising has become a major promotional medium. The main forms of online advertising are display ads and search-related ads. E-mail marketing is also an important form of digital marketing. Used properly, e-mail lets marketers send highly targeted, tightly personalized, relationship-building messages. Another important form of online marketing is posting digital video content on brand Web sites or social media. Marketers hope that some of their videos will go viral, engaging consumers by the millions. Finally, companies can use blogs as effective means of reaching customer communities. They can create their own blogs and advertise on existing blogs or influence content there.

OBJECTIVE 4 Discuss how companies use social media and mobile marketing to engage consumers and create brand community. (pp 446–452)

In the digital age, countless independent and commercial social media have arisen that give consumers online places to congregate, socialize, and exchange views and information. Most marketers are now riding this huge social media wave. Brands can use existing social media or they can set up their own. Using existing social media seems the easiest. Thus, most brands—large and small—have set up shop on a host of social media sites. Some of the major social networks are huge; other niche social media cater to the needs of smaller communities of like-minded people. Beyond these independent social media, many companies have created their own online brand communities. More than making just scattered efforts and chasing "Likes" and tweets, most companies are integrating a broad range of diverse media to create brand-related social sharing, engagement, and customer community.

Using social media presents both advantages and challenges. On the plus side, social media are targeted and personal, interactive, immediate and timely, and cost effective. Perhaps the biggest advantage is their engagement and social sharing capabilities, making them ideal for creating customer community. On the down side, consumers control over social media content make social media difficult to control.

Mobile marketing features marketing messages, promotions, and other content delivered to on-the-go consumers through their mobile devices. Marketers use mobile marketing to engage customers anywhere, anytime during the buying and relationship-building processes. The widespread adoption of mobile devices and the surge in mobile Web traffic have made mobile marketing a must for most brands, and almost every major marketer is now integrating mobile marketing into its direct marketing programs. Many marketers have created their own mobile online sites. Others have created useful or entertaining mobile apps to engage customers with their brands and help them shop.

OBJECTIVE 5 Identify and discuss the traditional direct marketing forms and overview the public policy and ethical issues presented by direct marketing. (pp 453–460)

Although the fast-growing digital marketing tools have grabbed most of the headlines lately, traditional direct marketing tools are very much alive and still heavily used. The major forms are face-to-face or personal selling, direct-mail marketing, catalog marketing, telemarketing, direct-response television (DRTV) marketing, and kiosk marketing

Direct-mail marketing consists of the company sending an offer, announcement, reminder, or other item to a person at a specific address. Some marketers rely on catalog marketing—selling through catalogs mailed to a select list of customers, made available in stores, or accessed online. Telemarketing consists of using the telephone to sell directly to consumers. DRTV marketing has two forms: direct-response advertising (or infomercials) and interactive television (iTV) marketing. Kiosks are information and ordering machines that direct marketers place in stores, airports, hotels, and other locations.

Direct marketers and their customers usually enjoy mutually rewarding relationships. Sometimes, however, direct marketing presents a darker side. The aggressive and sometimes shady tactics of a few direct marketers can bother or harm consumers, giving the entire industry a black eye. Abuses range from simple excesses that irritate consumers to instances of unfair practices or even outright deception and fraud. The direct marketing industry has also faced growing concerns about invasion-of-privacy and Internet security issues. Such concerns call for strong action by marketers and public policy makers to curb direct marketing abuses. In the end, most direct marketers want the same things that consumers want: honest and well-designed marketing offers targeted only toward consumers who will appreciate and respond to them.

Key Terms

Objective 1
Direct and digital marketing (p 436)

Objective 2
Digital and social media marketing (p 440)

Objective 3
Multichannel marketing (p 441)
Online marketing (p 442)
Marketing Web site (p 442)
Branded community Web site (p 442)
Online advertising (p 443)
E-mail marketing (p 443)
Spam (p 444)
Viral marketing (p 444)
Blogs (p 445)

Objective 4
Social media (p 446)
Mobile marketing (p 449)

Objective 5
Direct-mail marketing (p 453)
Catalog marketing (p 454)
Telemarketing (p 455)
Direct-response television (DRTV) marketing (p 455)

DISCUSSION AND CRITICAL THINKING

Discussion Questions

14-1. List and briefly describe the various forms of direct digital and social media marketing. (AACSB: Written and Oral Communication)

14-2. Compare and contrast a marketing Web site and a branded community Web site. (AACSB: Written and Oral Communication)

14-3. Name and describe the two main forms of online advertising. (AACSB: Written and Oral Communication)

14-4. List and briefly describe the major traditional forms of direct marketing. (AACSB: Written and Oral Communication)

14-5. What public policy issues are related to direct and digital marketing? (AACSB: Written and Oral Communication; Reflective Thinking)

Critical Thinking Exercises

14-6. In a small group, design and deliver a direct-response television ad (DRTV) for a national brand not normally associated with this type of promotion, such as an athletic shoe, automobile, or food product. (AACSB: Written and Oral Communication; Reflective Thinking)

14-7. Develop a presentation about phishing. In your presentation, define phishing, show three examples (search Google Images for phishing examples), and discuss how consumers and businesses used in scams can protect themselves. (AACSB: Written and Oral Communication; Information Technology; Reflective Thinking)

MINICASES AND APPLICATIONS

Online, Mobile, and Social Media Marketing Big Business for Small Business

Mobile marketing is the place to be for small businesses. When rain pounded New Orleans right before its famous Jazz & Heritage Festival, the owner of a local shoe store saw an opportunity. She tweeted about rain boots available at her store, Feet First, and sold out in two hours. Feet First is no stranger to online marketing with a Web site, online shopping cart, and a Facebook page, but mobile is where the action is. Employees update the store's Facebook, Twitter, Instagram, Pinterest, Tumblr, and Snapette—a local fashion app—accounts frequently. Consumers are increasingly turning to mobile devices to find information and purchase products. The Polkadot Alley, an online store, found that 90 percent of orders come from mobile phones. Even though Yelp's app traffic is a fraction of the overall Web site's traffic, 45 percent of all Yelp searches come from its mobile app. Local retailers see the advantages of mobile marketing. As a result, Google changed its ad platform to accommodate the growth in mobile ad campaigns. Advertisers not only bid for search words, but also on the searcher's device used to search, their location, and time of day. If it's Saturday before Mother's Day and you use your phone to search for a florist, Emily's Flower Shop a half a mile away probably bid 30 percent higher to get its ad at the top of your results list.

14-8. What local businesses in your community are using online, social media, and/or mobile marketing? Interview the owner or manager of one of the businesses to learn how the business uses these marketing activities and the overall level of satisfaction with these activities. (AACSB: Written and Oral Communication; Reflective Thinking)

14-9. Mobile marketing can be confusing for a small business owner. Develop a presentation to present to small business owners that describes mobile marketing, its advantages and disadvantages, and examples of how small businesses are using mobile marketing. (AACSB: Written and Oral Communication; Reflective Thinking)

Marketing Ethics Online Advertising Auctions

Advertisers pay to have ads placed based on your keyword searches, track your Web-surfing behavior, and even monitor what you post on Facebook or write in Gmail messages. While concerns over privacy mount, the online tracking industry just keeps ramping up. Krux Digital reports that the average visit to a Web page generated 56 instances of data collection, representing a five-fold increase from the previous year. A 2010 investigation by *The Wall Street Journal* found that the 50 most popular U.S. Web sites installed more than 3,000 tracking files on the computer used in the study. The total was even higher—4,123 tracking files—for the top 50 sites that are popular with children and teens. Many sites installed more than 100 tracking tools each during the tests. Tracking tools include files placed on users' computers and on Web sites. Marketers use this information to target online advertisements. But this wouldn't be possible without online-ad auctions. When a user visits a Web page, that information is auctioned among computers to the highest bidder. Bids are based on the user's Internet browsing behavior. The bidder in such an auction is a technology broker acting on behalf of the advertiser. Real-time bidding makes up 18 percent of the online display ad market, and bids sell for less than $1 per thousand viewers. Web-tracking provides the user data to sell in the auction, and more than 300 companies are gathering this data. Data collectors often share information with each other, called "piggybacking," so they have more information about a Web site's user than the owner—the ad seller—of a Web site has. The practice has spread to mobile ads where consumers receive tailored ads for services in their vicinity. It will eventually spread to Web-enabled televisions as well.

14-10. Write a report explaining how online-ad auctions work and the impact they have on Internet advertising. (AACSB: Written and Oral Communication; Reflective Thinking)

14-11. Critics claim that Internet tracking infringes consumer privacy rights and that the industry is out of control. Should marketers have access to such information? Discuss the advantages and disadvantages of this activity for both marketers and consumers. (AACSB: Written and Oral Communication; Ethical Understanding and Reasoning; Reflective Thinking)

Marketing by the Numbers Field Sales vs. Telemarketing

Many companies are realizing the efficiency of telemarketing in the face of soaring sales-force costs. Whereas an average cost of a business-to-business sales call by an outside salesperson is more than $300, the cost of a telemarketing sales call can be as little as $5 to $20. And telemarketers can make 20 to 33 decision-maker contacts per day to a salesperson's four per day. This has gotten the attention of many business-to-business marketers, where telemarketing can be very effective.

14-12. Refer to Appendix 3, Marketing by the Numbers, to determine the marketing return on sales (marketing ROS) and return on marketing investment (marketing ROI) for Company A and Company B in the chart below. Which company is performing better? Explain. (AACSB: Written and Oral Communication; Analytical Thinking; Reflective Thinking)

	Company A (sales force only)	Company B (telemarketing only)
Net sales	$2,000,000	$1,000,000
Cost of goods sold	$ 800,000	$ 500,000
Sales expenses	$ 700,000	$ 200,000

14-13. Should all companies consider reducing their sales forces in favor of telemarketing? Discuss the pros and cons of this action. (AACSB: Written and Oral Communication; Reflective Thinking)

Video Case Home Shopping Network

Long ago, television marketing was associated with low-quality commercials broadcast in the wee hours of the morning that offered obscure merchandise. But Home Shopping Network (HSN) has played an instrumental role in marking television shopping a legitimate outlet. Around the clock, top-quality programming featuring name-brand merchandise is now the norm.

But just like any other retailer, HSN has had its share of challenges. This video illustrates how HSN has focused on principles of direct marketing in order to overcome these challenges and form strong customer relationships. As market conditions continue to shift, HSN explores new ways to form and strengthen direct relationships with customers.

After viewing the video featuring HSN, answer the following questions:

14-14. What are the different ways that HSN engages in direct marketing?

14-15. What advantages does HSN specifically have over brick-and-mortar retailers?

14-16. What recommendations would you suggest for how HSN could make better use of its role as a direct marketer?

Company Cases 14 Pinterest / 8 Google / 12 Super Bowl / 13 Salesforce.com / 4 Oracle

See Appendix 1 for cases appropriate for this chapter. **Case 14, Pinterest: Revolutionizing the Web—Again**. Pinterest has revolutionized Web design, and is influencing consumer purchase decisions in the process. **Case 8, Google: New Product Innovation at the Speed of Light**. When it comes to developing new products, Google bucks all convention with a process that churns things out in weeks and months, not years. **Case 12, The Super Bowl: More Than a Single Advertising Event—A Social Media Frenzy**. Super Bowl advertising illustrates that traditional media and new social media go hand-in-hand. **Case 13, Salesforce.com: Helping Companies Super-Charge the Selling Process**. Salesforce.com invented cloud computing as a platform for customer relationship management (CRM) products and services. **Case 4, Oracle: Getting a Grip on Big Data**. As technology allows for the gathering of more and more consumer data, Oracle is on the front line, helping companies harness Big Data as a means of forming stronger relationships with customers.

MyMarketingLab

Go to **mymktlab.com** for Auto-graded writing questions as well as the following Assisted-graded writing questions:

14-17. Discuss the advantages and challenges of social media marketing. (AACSB: Written and Oral Communication)

14-18. Review the FTC's guidelines on disclosure in online, social media, and mobile advertisements at www.ftc.gov/os/2013/03/130312dotcomdisclosures.pdf. Will the FTC's requirements regarding ads and endorsers make Twitter less effective as an advertising medium? (AACSB: Written and Oral Communication; Information Technology; Reflective Thinking)

14-19. Mymktlab Only—comprehensive writing assignment for this chapter.

15 The Global Marketplace

CHAPTER ROAD MAP

Objective Outline

OBJECTIVE 1 Discuss how the international trade system and the economic, political-legal, and cultural environments affect a company's international marketing decisions. Global Marketing Today 468–470; Looking at the Global Marketing Environment 470–478; Deciding Whether to Go Global 478; Deciding Which Markets to Enter 478–479

OBJECTIVE 2 Describe three key approaches to entering international markets. Deciding How to Enter the Market 479–482

OBJECTIVE 3 Explain how companies adapt their marketing strategies and mixes for international markets. Deciding on the Global Marketing Program 482–489

OBJECTIVE 4 Identify the three major forms of international marketing organization. Deciding on the Global Marketing Organization 489–490

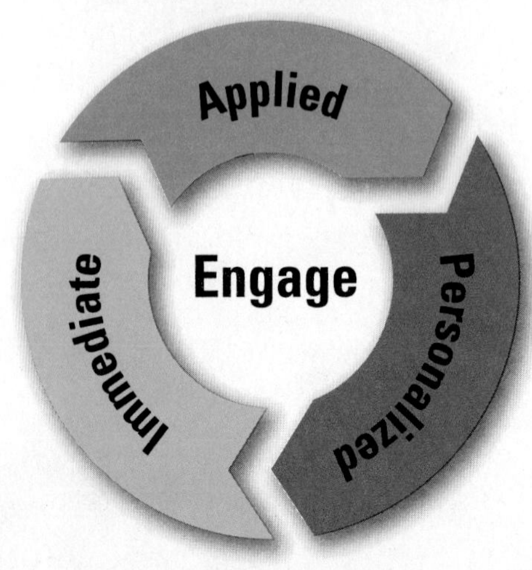

Previewing the Concepts

You've now learned the fundamentals of how companies develop competitive marketing strategies to create customer value and build lasting customer relationships. In this chapter, we extend these fundamentals to global marketing. Although we discussed global topics in each previous chapter—it's difficult to find an area of marketing that doesn't contain at least some international elements—here we'll focus on special considerations that companies face when they market their brands globally. Advances in communication, transportation, and digital technologies have made the world a much smaller place. Today, almost every firm, large or small, faces international marketing issues. In this chapter, we will examine six major decisions marketers make in going global.

To start our exploration of global marketing, let's look at Coca-Cola, a truly global operation. You'll find a Coca-Cola product within arm's length of almost anyone, anywhere in the world. "We sell moments of happiness, for cents at a time, more than 1.7 billion times a day in more than 200 countries," says the company in its annual report. Like many companies, Coca-Cola's greatest growth opportunities lie in international markets. Here, we examine the company's odyssey into Africa.

---

*Over 10 million students improved their results using the Pearson MyLabs. Visit **mymktlab.com** for simulations, tutorials, and end-of-chapter problems.

First Stop

Coca-Cola in Africa: "Everything Is Right There to Have It Happen."

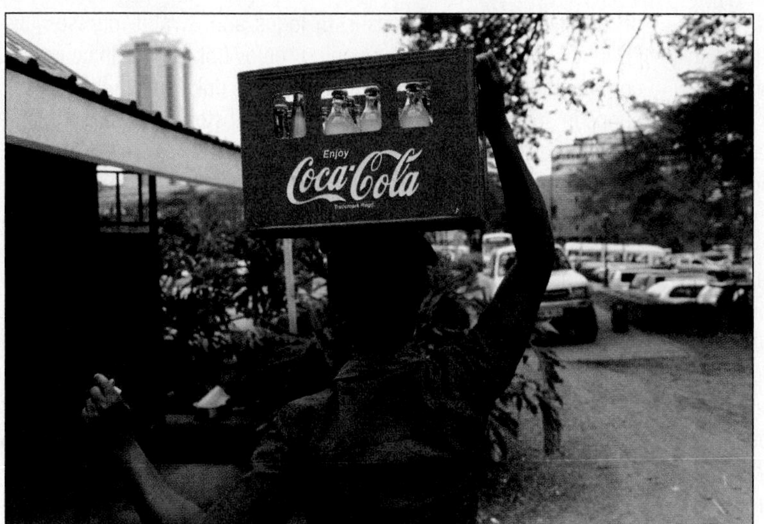

» With sales stagnating in its mature markets, Coca-Cola is looking to emerging markets—such as Africa—to meet its ambitious growth goals. Its African distribution network is rudimentary but effective.

Marco Di Lauro/Getty Images.

Coca-Cola is one of the world's truly iconic brands—a $48-billion global powerhouse. It puts Coke products within "an arm's length" of 98 percent of the world's population. Already the world's number-one soft drink maker, Coca-Cola is in the middle of a 12-year plan to double its global system revenues by 2020. But achieving such growth won't be easy. The major problem: Soft drink sales growth has lost its fizz in North America and Europe, two of Coca-Cola's largest and most profitable markets. In fact, the U.S. soft drink market has shrunk for five straight years. With sales stagnating in its mature markets, Coca-Cola must look elsewhere to meet its ambitious growth goals.

In recent years, Coca-Cola has sought growth primarily in developing global markets such as China and India, which boast large emerging middle classes but relatively low per capita consumption of Coke. However, both China and India are now crowded with competitors and notoriously difficult for outsiders to navigate. So while Coca-Cola will continue to compete heavily in those countries, it has set its sights on an even more promising long-term growth opportunity—Africa.

Many Western companies view Africa as an untamed final frontier—a kind of no man's land plagued by poverty, political corruption and instability, unreliable transportation, and shortages of fresh water and other essential resources. But Coca-Cola sees plenty of opportunity in Africa to justify the risks. Africa has a growing population of more than 1 billion people and a just-emerging middle class. The number of African households earning at least $5,000—the income level where families begin to spend at least half their income on nonfood items—has tripled over the past 30 years to more than a third of the population. "You've got an incredibly young population, a dynamic population," says Coca-Cola CEO Muhtar Kent, "[and] huge disposable income. I mean $1.6 trillion of GDP, which is bigger than Russia, bigger than India."

With its home markets losing their fizz, Coca-Cola is looking for growth in emerging markets such as Africa. But in Africa, "Coke is, in a sense, sticking its hand into a bees' nest to get some honey."

Coca-Cola is no stranger to Africa. It has operated there since 1929, and it's the only multinational that offers its products in every African country. The company has a dominant 29 percent market share in Africa and the Middle East, as compared with Pepsi's 15 percent share. Coca-Cola's revenues in Africa and the Middle East grew by 11 percent last year, far greater than the 2 percent growth in North America and 1 percent decline in Europe.

But there's still plenty of room for Coca-Cola to grow in Africa. For example, annual per capita consumption of Coke in Kenya is just 40 servings, compared with more developed countries like Mexico, where consumption runs at an eye-popping 728 servings per year. So the stage is set for Coca-Cola on the African continent, not just for its flagship Coke brand but also for its large stable of other soft drinks, waters, and juices. Whereas the beverage giant invested $6 billion in the African market over the past decade, it plans to invest twice that amount during the next 10 years—an effort that includes bottling plants, distribution networks, retailer support, and an Africa-wide promotional campaign called "One Billion Reasons to Believe in Africa."

Marketing in Africa is a very different proposition from marketing in more developed regions. "Africa . . . is not Atlanta," observes one analyst, "and Coke is, in a sense, sticking its hand into a bees' nest to get some honey." To grow its sales in Africa, beyond just marketing through traditional channels in larger African cities, Coca-Cola is now invading smaller communities with more grassroots tactics. "[Just] being in a country is very easy; you can go and set up a depot in every capital city," says CEO Kent. But in Africa, "that's not what we're about. There's nowhere in Africa that we don't go. We go to every town, every village, every community, every township." In Africa, every small shop in every back alley has become important, as Coca-Cola launches what another analyst describes as "a street-by-street campaign to win drinkers . . . not yet used to guzzling Coke by the gallon."

For example, take the Mamakamau Shop in Uthiru, a poor community outside Nairobi, Kenya. Piles of trash burn outside the shop and sewage trickles by in an open trench. Besides Coca-Cola products, the shop—known as a duka—also carries everything from mattresses to plastic buckets, all in a room about the size of a small bedroom. Still, proprietor Mamakamau Kingori has earned Coca-Cola's "Gold" vendor status, its highest level, for selling about 72 cola products a day, priced at 30 Kenyan shillings (37 U.S. cents) for a 500-milliliter bottle. Most customers drink the soda in the store while sitting on overturned red crates—they can't afford to pay the bottle deposit. Coca-Cola's Kenyan bottler will reuse the glass bottles up to 70 times.

To earn her "Gold" status, Kingori follows carefully prescribed selling techniques. She uses a red, Coke-provided, refrigerated cooler by the front entrance, protected by a blue cage. Like other mom-and-pop stores in her area, she keeps the cooler fully stocked with Coke on top, Fanta in the middle, and large bottles on the bottom. Inside the store, she posts red menu signs provided by Coca-Cola that push combo meals, such as a 300-milliliter Coke and a ndazi, a type of local donut, for 25 Kenyan shillings.

In Kabira, another poor Nairobi neighborhood, the crowded streets are lined with shops painted Coke red. The local bottler hires an artist to paint the shops with logos and Swahili phrases like "Burudika na Coke Baridi," meaning "enjoy Coke cold." In countless communities across Africa, whether it's the dukas in Nairobi or tuck shops in Johannesburg, South Africa, small stores play a big role in helping Coca-Cola grow.

Such shops are supplied by a rudimentary but effective network of Coca-Cola distributors. For example, in downtown Nairobi, men in red lab coats load hand-pulled trolleys with 22 to 40 crates of Coke and other soft drinks from Rosinje Distributors, one of 3,200 Micro Distribution Centers (MDCs) that Coca-Cola operates in Africa. These centers are the spine of Coca-Cola's African distribution network. For example, the Nairobi plant ships Coke, Fanta, Stoney Ginger Beer, and other Coca-Cola brands to almost 400 area MDCs. From there, crews hustle the products—sometimes a case at a time carried on their heads—to local shops and beverage kiosks. Because of the poor roads crowded with traffic, moving drinks by hand is often the best method. The MDCs help Coca-Cola to get its products into remote areas, making them available as people develop a taste for soft drinks and have the income to buy them.

Despite their elemental nature, Coca-Cola's marketing approaches in Africa are proving effective. The company's first rule is to get its products "cold and close." "If they don't have roads to move products long distances on trucks, we will use boats, canoes, or trolleys," says the president of Coca-Cola South Africa. For example, in Nigeria's Makako district—a maze of stilt houses on the Lagos lagoon—women criss-cross the waterways selling Coca-Cola directly from canoes to residents.

There's little doubt that Coca-Cola's increased commitment to Africa will be key to its achieving its global goals. As CEO Muhtar Kent concludes: "Africa is the untold story and could be the big story of the next decade, like India and China were this past decade. . . . Everything is right there to have it happen."[1]

In the past, U.S. companies paid little attention to international trade. If they could pick up some extra sales via exports, that was fine. But the big market was at home, and it teemed with opportunities. The home market was also much safer. Managers did not need to learn other languages, deal with strange and changing currencies, face political and legal uncertainties, or adapt their products to different customer needs and expectations. Today, however, the situation is much different. Organizations of all kinds, from Coca-Cola and HP to Google, MTV, and even the NBA, have gone global.

Author Comment

The rapidly changing global environment provides both opportunities and threats. It's difficult to find a marketer today that isn't affected in some way by global developments.

Global Marketing Today

The world is shrinking rapidly with the advent of faster digital communication, transportation, and financial flows. Products developed in one country—Samsung electronics, McDonald's hamburgers, Zara fashions, Caterpillar construction equipment, German BMWs, Facebook social networking—have found enthusiastic acceptance in other countries. It would not be surprising to hear about a German businessman wearing an Italian suit meeting an English friend at a Japanese restaurant who later returns home to drink Russian vodka while watching *American Idol* on TV and checking Facebook posts from friends around the world.

International trade has boomed over the past three decades. Since 1990, the number of multinational corporations in the world has more than doubled to more than 63,000.

Many American companies have now made the world their market. Nearly 60 percent of Apple's sales come from outside the Americas.

AFP/Getty Images.

Some of these multinationals are true giants. In fact, of the largest 150 economies in the world, only 77 are countries. The remaining 73 are multinational corporations. Walmart, the world's largest company (based on a weighted average of sales, profits, assets, and market value), has annual revenues greater than the gross domestic product (GDP) of all but the world's 27 largest countries.[2] Despite a dip in world trade caused by the recent worldwide recession, the world trade of products and services last year was valued at more than $18.3 trillion, about 31.8 percent of GDP worldwide.[3]

Many U.S. companies have long been successful at international marketing: Coca-Cola, McDonald's, Starbucks, Nike, GE, IBM, Apple, Colgate, Caterpillar, Boeing, and dozens of other American firms have made the world their market. In the United States, names such as Toyota, Nestlé, IKEA, Canon, Adidas, and Samsung have become household words. Other products and services that appear to be American are, in fact, produced or owned by foreign companies, such as Ben & Jerry's ice cream, Budweiser beer, 7-Eleven, GE and RCA televisions, Carnation milk, Universal Studios, and Motel 6. Michelin, the oh-so-French tire manufacturer, now does 36 percent of its business in North America; J&J, the maker of quintessentially all-American products such as BAND-AIDs and Johnson's Baby Shampoo, does nearly 56 percent of its business abroad. And America's own Caterpillar belongs more to the wider world, with 69 percent of its sales coming from outside the United States.[4]

But as global trade grows, global competition is also intensifying. Foreign firms are expanding aggressively into new international markets, and home markets are no longer as rich in opportunity. Few industries are currently safe from foreign competition. If companies delay taking steps toward internationalizing, they risk being shut out of growing markets in Western and Eastern Europe, China and the Pacific Rim, Russia, India, Brazil, and elsewhere. Firms that stay at home to play it safe might not only lose their chances to enter other markets but also risk losing their home markets. Domestic companies that never thought about foreign competitors suddenly find these competitors in their own backyards.

Ironically, although the need for companies to go abroad is greater today than in the past, so are the risks. Companies that go global may face highly unstable governments and currencies, restrictive government policies and regulations, and high trade barriers. The recently dampened global economic environment has also created big global challenges. In addition, corruption is an increasing problem; officials in several countries often award business not to the best bidder but to the highest briber.

Global firm
A firm that, by operating in more than one country, gains R&D, production, marketing, and financial advantages in its costs and reputation that are not available to purely domestic competitors.

A **global firm** is one that, by operating in more than one country, gains marketing, production, research and development (R&D), and financial advantages that are not available to purely domestic competitors. Because the global company sees the world as one market, it minimizes the importance of national boundaries and develops global brands. The global company raises capital, obtains materials and components, and manufactures and markets its goods wherever it can do the best job.

For example, U.S.-based Otis Elevator, the world's largest elevator maker, is headquartered in Farmington, Connecticut. However, it offers products in more than 200 countries and achieves 82 percent of its sales from outside the United States. It gets elevator door systems from France, small geared parts from Spain, electronics from Germany, and special motor drives from Japan. It operates manufacturing facilities in the Americas, Europe, and Asia, and engineering and test centers in the United States, Austria, Brazil, China, Czech Republic, France, Germany, India, Italy, Japan, Korea, and Spain. In turn, Otis Elevator is a wholly owned subsidiary of global commercial and aerospace giant United Technologies

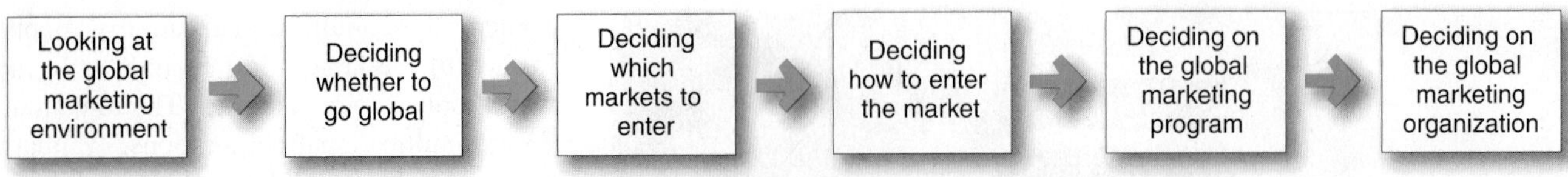

Figure 15.1 Major International Marketing Decisions

It's a big and beautiful but threatening world out there for marketers! Most large American firms have made the world their market. For example, once all-American McDonald's now captures 66 percent of its sales from outside the United States.

Corporation.[5] Many of today's global corporations—both large and small—have become truly borderless.

This does not mean, however, that every firm must operate in a dozen countries to succeed. Smaller firms can practice global niching. But the world is becoming smaller, and every company operating in a global industry—whether large or small—must assess and establish its place in world markets.

The rapid move toward globalization means that all companies will have to answer some basic questions: What market position should we try to establish in our country, in our economic region, and globally? Who will our global competitors be and what are their strategies and resources? Where should we produce or source our products? What strategic alliances should we form with other firms around the world?

As shown in **Figure 15.1**, a company faces six major decisions in international marketing. We discuss each decision in detail in this chapter.

Author Comment

Going global adds many layers of complexities. For example, Coca-Cola markets its products in hundreds of countries around the globe. It must understand the varying trade, economic, cultural, and political environments in each market.

Looking at the Global Marketing Environment

Before deciding whether to operate internationally, a company must understand the international marketing environment. That environment has changed a great deal in recent decades, creating both new opportunities and new problems.

Nontariff trade barriers: Walmart and other foreign businesses in China appear to receive unusually close scrutiny and harsh treatment from Chinese authorities, aimed at boosting the fortunes of local Chinese competitors.

REUTERS/Jason Lee.

The International Trade System

U.S. companies looking abroad must start by understanding the international *trade system*. When selling to another country, a firm may face restrictions on trade between nations. Governments may charge *tariffs* or *duties*, taxes on certain imported products designed to raise revenue or protect domestic firms. Tariffs and duties are often used to force favorable trade behaviors from other nations. For example, the European Union (EU) recently placed import duties on Chinese solar panels after determining that Chinese companies were selling the panels in EU countries at under-market prices. To retaliate, the very next day, the Chinese government launched an investigation into putting similar duties on EU wine exports to China. The investigation targeted the wine countries of Spain, France, and Italy but spared Germany, which had taken China's side in the solar panel dispute. The message was clear, says an international trade expert: "You don't like our cheap solar panels? Well, we'll make your wine even more expensive."[6]

Countries may set *quotas*, limits on the amount of foreign imports that they will accept in certain product categories. The purpose of a quota is to conserve on foreign exchange and protect local industry and employment. Firms may also encounter *exchange controls*, which limit the amount of foreign exchange and the exchange rate against other currencies.

A company also may face *nontariff trade barriers*, such as biases against its bids, restrictive product standards, or excessive host-country regulations or enforcement. For example, foreign businesses in China appear to receive unusually close scrutiny and harsh treatment from Chinese authorities, aimed at boosting the fortunes of local competitors. For instance, national and local Chinese regulators recently launched what appeared to be a new wave of protectionism, with the goal of shielding Chinese brands from their Western rivals in a slowing economy. The harshest treatment was reserved for Western retailers such as Walmart. The retailer was first fined for misleading pricing in several of its stores. Next, it paid fines for allegedly selling expired products in the city of Changsha. Then, Chinese regulators in Chongqing accused Walmart of selling regular pork improperly labeled as organic, forcing the chain to temporarily close 13 stores and pay a $573,000 fine. The motives behind these protectionist moves appeared to be more to hinder Walmart's operations in China than to improve the operations of local retailers. As one analyst puts it, "Why go to the effort of getting your own guys to raise their game when you can tear down a foreign guy instead?"[7]

At the same time, certain other forces can *help* trade between nations. Examples include the World Trade Organization (WTO) and various regional free trade agreements.

The World Trade Organization

The General Agreement on Tariffs and Trade (GATT), established in 1947 and modified in 1994, was designed to promote world trade by reducing tariffs and other international trade barriers. » It established the World Trade Organization (WTO), which replaced GATT in 1995 and now oversees the original GATT provisions. WTO and GATT member nations (currently numbering 159) have met in eight rounds of negotiations to reassess trade barriers and establish new rules for international trade. The WTO also imposes international trade sanctions and mediates global trade disputes. Its actions have been productive. The first seven rounds of negotiations reduced the average worldwide tariffs on manufactured goods from 45 percent to just 5 percent.[8]

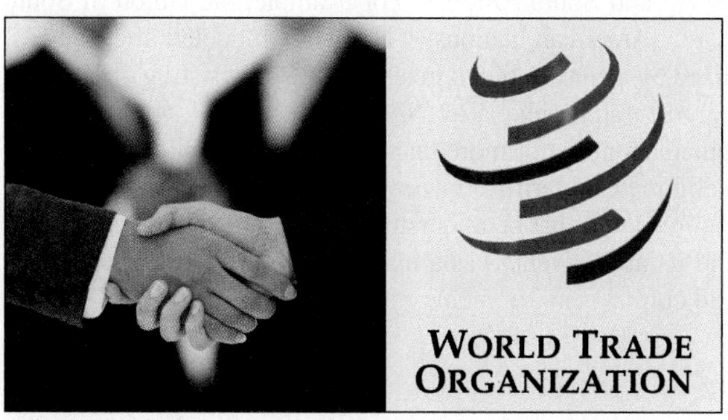

» The WTO promotes trade by reducing tariffs and other international trade barriers. It also imposes international trade sanctions and mediates global trade disputes.

(left) Corbis Images; (right) Donald Stampfli/Associated Press.

The most recently completed negotiations, dubbed the Uruguay Round, dragged on for seven long years before concluding in 1994. The benefits of the Uruguay Round will be felt for many years, as the accord promoted long-term global trade growth, reduced the world's remaining merchandise tariffs by 30 percent, extended the WTO to cover trade in agriculture and a wide range of services, and toughened the international protection of copyrights, patents, trademarks, and other intellectual property. A new round of global WTO trade talks, the Doha Round, began in Doha, Qatar, in late 2001 and was set to conclude in 2005; however, the discussions still continued through 2013.[9]

Regional Free Trade Zones

Economic community
A group of nations organized to work toward common goals in the regulation of international trade.

Certain countries have formed *free trade zones* or **economic communities**. These are groups of nations organized to work toward common goals in the regulation of international trade. One such community is the *European Union (EU)*. Formed in 1957, the EU set out to create a single European market by reducing barriers to the free flow of products, services, finances, and labor among member countries and developing policies on trade with nonmember nations. Today, the EU represents one of the world's largest single markets. » Currently, it has 27 member countries containing more than half a billion consumers and accounting for almost 20 percent of the world's exports.[10] The EU offers tremendous trade opportunities for U.S. and other non-European firms.

Over the past decade and a half, 17 EU member nations have taken a significant step toward unification by adopting the euro as a common currency. Widespread adoption of the euro has decreased much of the currency risk associated with doing business in Europe, making member countries with previously weak currencies more attractive markets. However, the adoption of a common currency has also caused problems as European economic powers such as Germany and France have had to step in recently to prop up weaker economies such as those of Greece, Portugal, and Cyprus. This recent "euro crisis" has led some analysts to predict the possible break-up of the euro zone as it is now set up.[11]

It is unlikely that the EU will ever go against 2,000 years of tradition and become the "United States of Europe." A community with more than two dozen different languages and

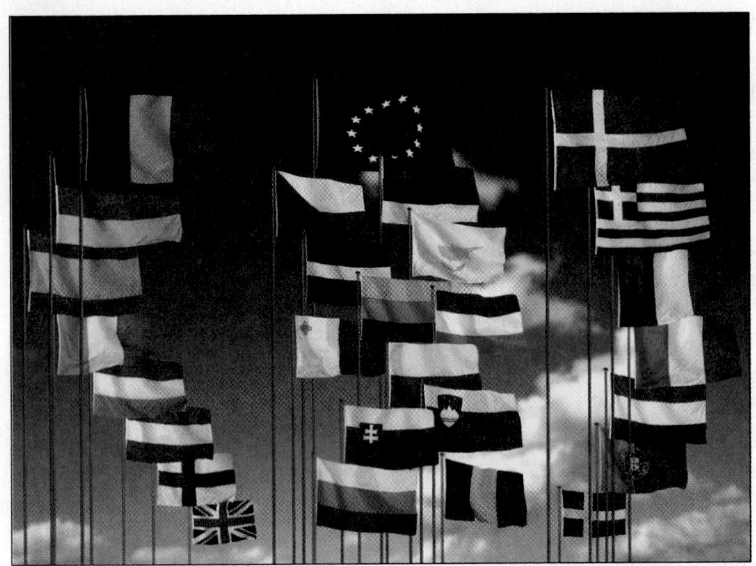

Economic communities: The European Union represents one of the world's single largest markets. Its current member countries contain more than half a billion consumers and account for 20 percent of the world's exports.

cultures will always have difficulty coming together and acting as a single entity. Still, with a combined annual GDP of more than $15 trillion, the EU has become a potent economic force.[12]

In 1994, the *North American Free Trade Agreement (NAFTA)* established a free trade zone among the United States, Mexico, and Canada. The agreement created a single market of 453 million people who produce and consume $17.8 trillion worth of goods and services annually. Over the past 18 years, NAFTA has eliminated trade barriers and investment restrictions among the three countries. Total trade among the NAFTA countries nearly tripled from $288 billion in 1993 to $1 trillion in 2011.[13]

Following the apparent success of NAFTA, in 2005 the Central American Free Trade Agreement (CAFTA-DR) established a free trade zone between the United States and Costa Rica, the Dominican Republic, El Salvador, Guatemala, Honduras, and Nicaragua. Other free trade areas have formed in Latin America and South America. For example, the Union of South American Nations (UNASUR), modeled after the EU, was formed in 2004 and formalized by a constitutional treaty in 2008. Consisting of 12 countries, UNASUR makes up the largest trading bloc after NAFTA and the EU, with a population of 387 million and a combined economy of more than $4.1 trillion. Similar to NAFTA and the EU, UNASUR aims to eliminate all tariffs between nations by 2019.[14]

Each nation has unique features that must be understood. A nation's readiness for different products and services and its attractiveness as a market to foreign firms depend on its economic, political-legal, and cultural environments.

Economic Environment

The international marketer must study each country's economy. Two economic factors reflect the country's attractiveness as a market: its industrial structure and its income distribution.

The country's *industrial structure* shapes its product and service needs, income levels, and employment levels. The four types of industrial structures are as follows:

- *Subsistence economies:* In a subsistence economy, the vast majority of people engage in simple agriculture. They consume most of their output and barter the rest for simple goods and services. These economies offer few market opportunities. Many African countries fall into this category.
- *Raw material exporting economies:* These economies are rich in one or more natural resources but poor in other ways. Much of their revenue comes from exporting these resources. Some examples are Chile (tin and copper) and the Democratic Republic of the Congo (copper, cobalt, and coffee). These countries are good markets for large equipment, tools and supplies, and trucks. If there are many foreign residents and a wealthy upper class, they are also a market for luxury goods.
- *Emerging economies (industrializing economies):* In an emerging economy, fast growth in manufacturing results in rapid overall economic growth. Examples include the BRIC countries—Brazil, Russia, India, and China. As manufacturing increases, the country needs more imports of raw textile materials, steel, and heavy machinery, and fewer imports of finished textiles, paper products, and automobiles. Industrialization typically creates a new rich class and a growing middle class, both demanding new types of imported goods. As more developed markets stagnate and become increasingly competitive, many marketers are now targeting growth opportunities in emerging markets (see Marketing at Work 15.1).

MARKETING AT WORK 15.1

Brazil: An Emerging Market or Already Emerged?

When it comes to talk of the world's emerging economies, China and India seem to ink most of the headlines. But ask Brazilians what they think of their country and they'll likely respond that it's "O pais maior do mundo"—"The greatest country in the world." And based on the strength of Brazil's growing consumer markets, many global marketers would agree.

South America's largest country, Brazil also boasts the world's sixth-largest economy; it's expected to pass France to take the number five spot within the next decade. And although both India and China each have more than six times Brazil's population of 200 million, Brazil bests both countries by a wide margin in per capita purchasing power. In fact, Brazil's GDP is 200 percent larger than India's.

Thanks to historically low unemployment, rising wages, and an influx of foreign direct investment, Brazil's consumer markets are soaring. And the world's marketers are beginning to covet Brazil's rapidly exploding middle class—a group that has grown by 40 million in just the past five years. The growing prosperity and aspirations of this segment have resulted in rapidly growing demand for higher-value brands in categories ranging from soft drinks to mobile phones to imported luxury goods.

The world's largest retailers are now setting up shop in Brazil. They are finding success through innovative formats that target mixed segments of the middle-class consumers, small businesses, and wealthier shoppers. France's Carrefour is a market leader with its Costco-like Atacadao warehouse stores. Like Costco, Atacadao stores offer premium brands in large quantities in a modern warehouse-like store environment combined with enticing promotions and low prices. Walmart is also experiencing big growth in Brazil with 561 stores, including Walmart Supercenters, Sam's Clubs, and its fast-growing chain TodoDia—low-price supermarkets featuring the assortment of national brands and private labels that Walmart is known for around the world, but served up in a way that appeals to Brazilians.

One product category showing strong growth among Brazil's increasingly affluent middle class is child's play—literally. With Brazilian disposable income on the rise, spending on traditional toys and games has grown by more than 25 percent annually in recent years. Mattel leads the market with a substantial 30 percent share, followed by Hasbro. Brazil's toy market looks a lot like the U.S. toy market, with Brazilian tots and preteens clamoring not only for Hot Wheels and Barbies but also for other North American favorites ranging from Disney's princesses, Shrek, and Toy Story characters to Nickelodeon's "Dora la Exploradora."

Just as it offers opportunities, Brazil also presents challenges. Although its market infrastructure is light years ahead of what it was even a decade ago, the country's still-fragmented social classes and regional variances create difficulties for multinational marketers. For example, southern and southeastern Brazil contain some of the country's wealthiest, most-populated, and easiest-to-reach areas, such as Sao Paulo, Brazil's richest state. In contrast, the northeast region is Brazil's poorest, and many residents there lack access to basics such as roads and running water. This region historically prefers local markets over supermarkets and regional brands over global brands. With more mouths to feed in every household, northeastern Brazilian consumers are also sticklers for low prices.

But as it happens, northeast Brazil is also the region with the greatest growth in household income. So as Brazil's more affluent regions become increasingly competitive, marketers are finding innovative ways to meet the distribution challenges in regions like the northeast to capture the growing potential there. For example, Nestlé developed its "Ate Voce" ("Reaching You") program, by which its reps go door-to-door with push carts—a method residents find very appealing—selling "kits" full of dairy products, cookies, yogurt, and desserts. More than just selling products, these Nestlé vendors are trained to serve as nutrition consultants, helping customers to develop healthier diets.

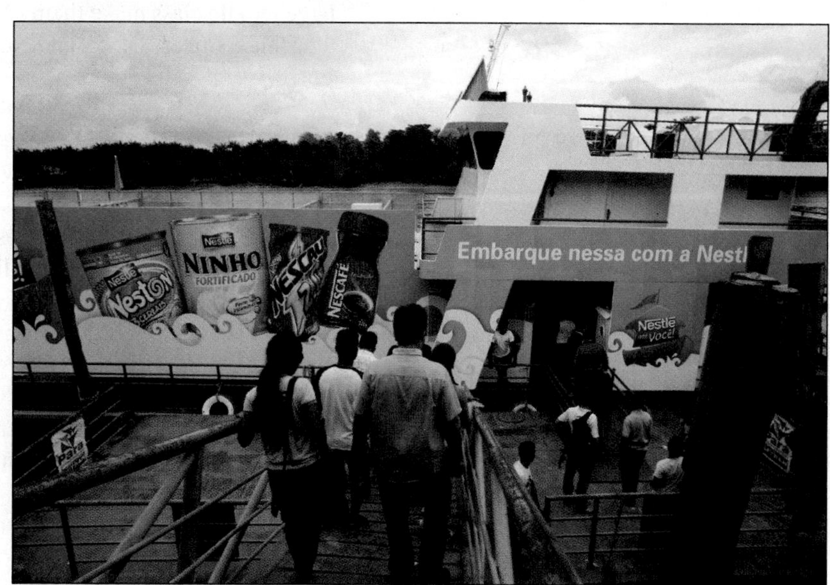

>> Marketing in Brazil presents both opportunities and challenges. Nestlé's "Ate Voce" ("Reaching You") program includes innovative distribution approaches, such as this floating supermarket that serves customers in northeast Brazil's Amazon River basin.

Bloomberg via Getty Images.

To serve consumers in northeast Brazil's Amazon River basin, which lacks a solid network of roads and highways, Nestlé has even launched a floating supermarket that takes goods directly to consumers. Setting sail from Belem, Brazil's biggest city along the Amazon, the boat serves 1.5 million consumers in 27 riverside towns with 300 different Nestlé products. It spends one day at each stop. Customers can check the floating store's schedule at nestleatevoce.com.br, call a toll-free number, or text for more information and plan their shopping accordingly. This and other innovative Ate Voce marketing initiatives are paying off for Nestlé. "Demand for our products has more than doubled in the north and northeast compared to other Brazilian regions," says Nestlé's marketing manager in Brazil.

Many companies are adapting their products to meet local northeastern Brazilian tastes. For example, Nestlé makes a cookie based on a popular local sweet-corn dish that it sells only in northeast Brazil. Huge multinational agribusiness firm Bunge has developed a best-selling Brazilian version of its Primor margarine—a firmer, saltier version that doesn't melt in northeast Brazil's searing heat. Even Nike scored a hit with the launch of a regional sneaker—the Lanceiro—a shoe designed to appeal to northeastern Brazilians by evoking images of a state flag.

Keeping up with local brands can be challenging, even for the biggest global brands. For example, Coca-Cola has long been the number one soft drink brand in Brazil. However, a local beverage brand—Guaraná Jesus—runs a close second. Named for the druggist who formulated it from extracts of Brazil's guarana plant in 1920, the local favorite was giving Coca-Cola a real run for its money. The solution: Coca-Cola bought the brand. Now, in Brazil, the company makes and sells both the world's favorite global soft drink brand (Coca-Cola) and the country's favorite local brand (Guaraná Jesus). In the words of Coca-Cola's marketing slogan, that's "Open Happiness."

As Brazil's poverty fades and its middle class continues to burst its boundaries, more and more global marketers will find fertile ground for growing their brands there. As Brazil prepares to host the 2014 Football World Cup and the 2016 Olympics, foreign investment and business activity in Brazil are booming. Global marketers that can tap into the unique tastes of Brazil's growing middle class will reap the benefits. Many global marketers are now asking: Does Brazil still belong among the ranks of the world's emerging economies? Or has it already emerged?

Sources: Kenneth Rapoza, "Brazil's 'Poor' Middle Class, and the Poor That No Longer Serve Them," *Forbes*, January 22, 2013, www.forbes.com/sites/kenrapoza/2013/01/22/brazils-poor-middle-class-and-the-poor-that-no-longer-serve-them/print/; Claudia Penteado, "Brazil's Northeast Goes from 'Land of Laziness' to Next China," *Advertising Age*, June 13, 2011, http://adage.com/print/228070/; Richard Wallace, "Middle-Classes on the Up: Why Brazil Is Growing," IGD, September 15, 2011, www.igd.com/index.asp?id=1&fid=1&sid=7&tid=10&cid=2128; "Brazil Fact Sheet," www.walmartstores.com/AboutUs/259.aspx, accessed October 2013 and Giedrius Daujotas, "Brazil's Emerging Middle-Class Offers Opportunities for Toymakers," *Euromonitor*, February 27, 2012, http://blog.euromonitorcom/2012/02/brazils-emerging-middle-class-offers-opportunities-for-toymakers.html.

- *Industrial economies:* Industrial economies are major exporters of manufactured goods, services, and investment funds. They trade goods among themselves and also export them to other types of economies for raw materials and semifinished goods. The varied manufacturing activities of these industrial nations and their large middle class make them rich markets for all sorts of goods. Examples include the United States, Japan, and Norway.

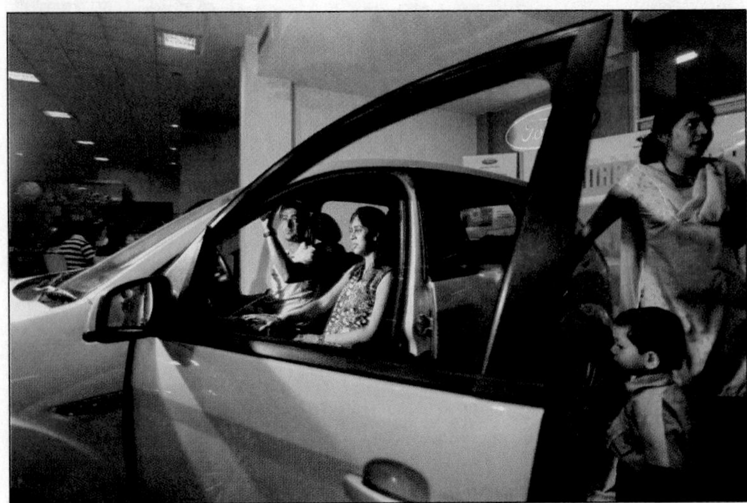

Economic environment: In India, Ford's $6,600 Figo targets low- to middle-income consumers who are only now able to afford their first car.

Namas Bhojani/Namas Bhojani Photography.

The second economic factor is the country's *income distribution*. Industrialized nations may have low-, medium-, and high-income households. In contrast, countries with subsistence economies consist mostly of households with very low family incomes. Still other countries may have households with either very low or very high incomes. Even poor or emerging economies may be attractive markets for all kinds of goods. These days, companies in a wide range of industries—from cars to computers to candy—are increasingly targeting even low- and middle-income consumers in emerging economies.

For example, in India, Ford introduced a new model targeted to consumers who are only now able to afford their first car. In an effort to boost its presence in Asia's third-largest auto market behind Japan and China, Ford introduced the Figo, a successful $6,600 hatchback designed for a hypothetical twenty-something Indian consumer named Sandeep. Sandeep is a young professional who currently drives a motorcycle.

But given his improving means and pending family, he now wants something bigger. "There are huge numbers of people wanting to move off their motorbikes," says Ford's India general manager. As a result, demand is booming in India for cars in the Figo's size and price range. After just two years, the diminutive Figo has become Ford's best-selling car in India and is now also selling well in 50 other emerging markets across Asia and Africa.[15]

Political-Legal Environment

Nations differ greatly in their political-legal environments. In considering whether to do business in a given country, a company should consider factors such as the country's attitudes toward international buying, government bureaucracy, political stability, and monetary regulations.

Some nations are very receptive to foreign firms; others are less accommodating. For example, India has tended to bother foreign businesses with import quotas, currency restrictions, and other limitations that make operating there a challenge. In contrast, neighboring Asian countries, such as Singapore and Thailand, court foreign investors and shower them with incentives and favorable operating conditions. Political and regulatory stability is another issue. For example, Russia is consumed by corruption and governmental red tape, which the government finds difficult to control, increasing the risk of doing business there. Although most international marketers still find the Russian market attractive, the corrupt climate will affect how they handle business and financial matters.[16]

Companies must also consider a country's monetary regulations. Sellers want to take their profits in a currency of value to them. Ideally, the buyer can pay in the seller's currency or in other world currencies. Short of this, sellers might accept a blocked currency—one whose removal from the country is restricted by the buyer's government—if they can buy other goods in that country that they need or can sell elsewhere for a needed currency. In addition to currency limits, a changing exchange rate also creates high risks for the seller.

Most international trade involves cash transactions. Yet many nations have too little hard currency to pay for their purchases from other countries. They may want to pay with other items instead of cash. *Barter* involves the direct exchange of goods or services. For example, Venezuela regularly barters oil, which it produces in surplus quantities, for food on the international market—rice from Guyana; coffee from El Salvador; sugar, coffee, meat, and more from Nicaragua; and beans and pasta from the Dominican Republic. Venezuela has even struck a deal to supply oil to Cuba in exchange for Cuban doctors and medical care for Venezuelans.[17]

Cultural Environment

Each country has its own folkways, norms, and taboos. When designing global marketing strategies, companies must understand how culture affects consumer reactions in each of its world markets. In turn, they must also understand how their strategies affect local cultures.

The Impact of Culture on Marketing Strategy

Sellers must understand the ways that consumers in different countries think about and use certain products before planning a marketing program. There are often surprises. For example, the average French man uses almost twice as many cosmetics and grooming aids as his wife. The Germans and the French eat more packaged, branded spaghetti than Italians do. Some 49 percent of Chinese eat on the way to work. Most American women let down their hair and take off makeup at bedtime, whereas 15 percent of Chinese women style their hair at bedtime and 11 percent put *on* makeup.[18]

Companies that ignore cultural norms and differences can make some very expensive and embarrassing mistakes. Here are two examples:

> Nike inadvertently offended Chinese officials when it ran an ad featuring LeBron James crushing a number of culturally revered Chinese figures in a kung fu–themed television ad. The Chinese government found that the ad violated regulations to uphold national dignity and respect the "motherland's culture" and yanked the multimillion-dollar campaign. With egg on

its face, Nike released a formal apology. Burger King made a similar mistake when it created in-store ads in Spain showing Hindu goddess Lakshmi atop a ham sandwich with the caption "a snack that is sacred." Cultural and religious groups worldwide objected strenuously—Hindus are vegetarian. Burger King apologized and pulled the ads.[19]

Business norms and behaviors also vary from country to country. For example, American executives like to get right down to business and engage in fast and tough face-to-face bargaining. However, Japanese and other Asian businesspeople often find this behavior offensive. They prefer to start with polite conversation, and they rarely say no in face-to-face conversations. As another example, firm handshakes are a common and expected greeting in most Western countries; in some Middle Eastern countries, however, handshakes might be refused if offered. Microsoft founder Bill Gates recently set off a flurry of international controversy when he shook the hand of South Korea's president with his right hand while keeping his left hand in his pocket, something that Koreans consider highly disrespectful. In some countries, when being entertained at a meal, not finishing all the food implies that it was somehow substandard. In other countries, in contrast, wolfing down every last bite might be taken as a mild insult, suggesting that the host didn't supply enough quantity.[20] American business executives need to understand these kinds of cultural nuances before conducting business in another country.

By the same token, companies that understand cultural nuances can use them to their advantage in the global markets. For example, furniture retailer IKEA's stores are a big draw for up-and-coming Chinese consumers. But IKEA has learned that customers in China want a lot more from its stores then just affordable Scandinavian-designed furniture:[21]

» The impact of culture on marketing strategy: IKEA customers in China want a lot more from its stores than just affordable Scandinavian-designed furniture.

Lou Linwei/Alamy.

In Chinese, IKEA is known as Yi Jia. Translated, it means "comfortable home," a concept taken literally by the millions of consumers who visit one of IKEA's 11 huge Chinese stores each year. "Customers come on family outings, hop into display beds and nap, pose for snapshots with the décor, and hang out for hours to enjoy the air conditioning and free soda refills," notes one observer. » On a typical Saturday afternoon, for example, display beds and other furniture in a huge Chinese IKEA store are occupied, with customers of all ages lounging or even fast asleep. IKEA managers encourage such behavior, figuring that familiarity with the store will result in later purchasing when shoppers' incomes eventually rise to match their aspirations. "Maybe if you've been visiting IKEA, eating meatballs, hot dogs, or ice cream for 10 years, then maybe you will consider IKEA when you get yourself a sofa," says the company's Asia-Pacific president. Thanks to such cultural understandings, IKEA already captures about 7 percent of the surging Chinese home-furnishings market, and its sales in China increased 20 percent last year.

Thus, understanding cultural traditions, preferences, and behaviors can help companies not only avoid embarrassing mistakes but also take advantage of cross-cultural opportunities.

The Impact of Marketing Strategy on Cultures

Whereas marketers worry about the impact of global cultures on their marketing strategies, others may worry about the impact of marketing strategies on global cultures. For example, social critics contend that large American multinationals, such as McDonald's, Coca-Cola, Starbucks, Nike, Google, Disney, and Facebook, aren't just globalizing their brands; they are Americanizing the world's cultures. Other elements of American culture have become pervasive worldwide. For instance, more people now study English in China than speak it in the United States. Of the 10 most watched TV shows in the world, 7 are American. If you assemble businesspeople from Brazil, Germany, and China, they'll likely transact in

English. And the thing that binds the world's teens together in a kind of global community, notes one observer, "is American culture—the music, the Hollywood fare, the electronic games, Google, Facebook, American consumer brands. The . . . rest of the world is becoming [evermore] like us—in ways good and bad."[22]

"Today, globalization often wears Mickey Mouse ears, eats Big Macs, drinks Coke or Pepsi, and does its computing with Windows," says Thomas Friedman in his book *The Lexus and the Olive Tree: Understanding Globalization*. "Some Chinese kids' first English word [is] Mickey," notes another writer.[23]

Critics worry that, under such "McDomination," countries around the globe are losing their individual cultural identities. Teens in Turkey watch MTV, connect with others globally through Facebook, and ask their parents for more Westernized clothes and other symbols of American pop culture and values. Grandmothers in small European villas no longer spend each morning visiting local meat, bread, and produce markets to gather the ingredients for dinner. Instead, they now shop at Walmart Supercenters. Women in Saudi Arabia see American films, question their societal roles, and shop at any of the country's growing number of Victoria's Secret boutiques. In China, most people never drank coffee before Starbucks entered the market. Now Chinese consumers rush to Starbucks stores "because it's a symbol of a new kind of lifestyle." » Similarly, in China, where McDonald's operates more than 80 restaurants in Beijing alone, nearly half of all children identify the chain as a domestic brand.

» **The impact of marketing strategy on culture: Nearly half of all children in China identify McDonald's as a domestic brand.**

Tomoko Kunihiro.

Such concerns have sometimes led to a backlash against American globalization. Well-known U.S. brands have become the targets of boycotts and protests in some international markets. As symbols of American capitalism, companies such as Coca-Cola, McDonald's, Nike, and KFC have been singled out by antiglobalization protestors in hot spots around the world, especially when anti-American sentiment peaks.

Despite such problems, defenders of globalization argue that concerns of Americanization and the potential damage to American brands are overblown. U.S. brands are doing very well internationally. In the most recent Millward Brown Optimor brand value survey of global consumer brands, 17 of the top 20 brands were American owned, including megabrands such as Apple, Google, IBM, McDonald's, Microsoft, Coca-Cola, GE, Amazon.com, and Walmart.[24] Many iconic American brands are soaring globally. For example, Chinese consumers appear to have an insatiable appetite for Apple iPhones and iPads. When Apple introduced its latest iPhone model in China last year, demand was so heavy that the company had to abandon sales in some Beijing stores to avert the threat of rioting by mobs of eager consumers. China is now Apple's second biggest market behind the United States. "It's mind-boggling that we can do this well," says Apple CEO Tim Cook.[25]

More fundamentally, the cultural exchange goes both ways: America gets as well as gives cultural influence. True, Hollywood dominates the global movie market, but British TV originated the programming that was Americanized into such hits as *The Office*, *American Idol*, and *Dancing with the Stars*. Although Chinese and Russian youth are donning NBA superstar jerseys, the increasing popularity of soccer in America has deep international roots.

Even American childhood has been increasingly influenced by European and Asian cultural imports. Most kids know all about imports such as Hello Kitty, the Bakugan Battle Brawler, or any of a host of Nintendo or Sega game characters. And J. K. Rowling's so-very-British Harry Potter books have shaped the thinking of a generation of American youngsters, not to mention the millions of American oldsters who fell under their spell as well. For the moment, English remains the dominant language of the Internet, and having Web access often means that third-world youth have greater exposure to American popular culture. Yet these same technologies let Eastern European students studying in the United States hear Webcast news and music from Poland, Romania, or Belarus.

Thus, globalization is a two-way street. If globalization has Mickey Mouse ears, it is also talking on a Samsung mobile phone, buying furniture at IKEA, driving a Toyota Camry, and watching a British-inspired show on a Panasonic plasma TV.

Deciding Whether to Go Global

Not all companies need to venture into international markets to survive. For example, most local businesses need to market well only in their local marketplaces. Operating domestically is easier and safer. Managers don't need to learn another country's language and laws. They don't have to deal with unstable currencies, face political and legal uncertainties, or redesign their products to suit different customer expectations. However, companies that operate in global industries, where their strategic positions in specific markets are affected strongly by their overall global positions, must compete on a regional or worldwide basis to succeed.

Any of several factors might draw a company into the international arena. For example, global competitors might attack the company's home market by offering better products or lower prices. The company might want to counterattack these competitors in their home markets to tie up their resources. The company's customers might be expanding abroad and require international servicing. Or, most likely, international markets might simply provide better opportunities for growth. For example, as we discovered in the story at the start of the chapter, Coca-Cola has emphasized international growth in recent years to offset stagnant or declining U.S. soft drink sales. Today, nearly 60 percent of Coca-Cola's sales come from outside the United States, and the company is making major pushes into 90 emerging markets, such as China, India, and the entire African continent.[26]

Before going abroad, the company must weigh several risks and answer many questions about its ability to operate globally. Can the company learn to understand the preferences and buyer behavior of consumers in other countries? Can it offer competitively attractive products? Will it be able to adapt to other countries' business cultures and deal effectively with foreign nationals? Do the company's managers have the necessary international experience? Has management considered the impact of regulations and the political environments of other countries?

Deciding Which Markets to Enter

Before going abroad, the company should try to define its international *marketing objectives and policies*. It should decide what *volume* of foreign sales it wants. Most companies start small when they go abroad. Some plan to stay small, seeing international sales as a small part of their business. Other companies have bigger plans, however, seeing international business as equal to or even more important than their domestic business.

The company also needs to choose in *how many* countries it wants to market. Companies must be careful not to spread themselves too thin or expand beyond their capabilities by operating in too many countries too soon. Next, the company needs to decide on the *types* of countries to enter. A country's attractiveness depends on the product, geographical factors, income and population, political climate, and other considerations. In recent years, many major new markets have emerged, offering both substantial opportunities and daunting challenges.

After listing possible international markets, the company must carefully evaluate each one. It must consider many factors. For example, Walmart's decision to enter Africa seems like a no-brainer: Taken as a whole, the African market is three times the size of China and is home to more than 1 billion people and 10 of the world's 20 fastest-growing economies. In fact, Walmart recently gained a toehold in Africa by acquiring a majority stake in South African retailer Massmart, which operates its Makro, Game, and other discount and warehouse stores mostly in South Africa but also in 13 other African countries.[27]

However, as Walmart considers expanding into African markets, it must ask some important questions. Can it compete effectively on a country-by-country basis with hundreds of local competitors? Will the various African governments be stable and supportive? Does Africa provide for the needed logistics technologies? Can Walmart master the varied and vastly different cultural and buying differences of African consumers?

Walmart's expansion in Africa will likely be a slow process, as it confronts many unfamiliar cultural, political, and logistical challenges. Along with the huge opportunities, many African countries rank among the world's most difficult places to do business. "You see a market like Nigeria [with a population of more than 150 million] and it feels like a big opportunity," says the chief executive of Walmart International. "But we've learned [that] we really need to think about it a city at a time as opposed to a country at a time."[28]

Possible global markets should be ranked on several factors, including market size, market growth, the cost of doing business, competitive advantage, and risk level. The goal is to determine the potential of each market, using indicators such as those shown in **>> Table 15.1**. Then the marketer must decide which markets offer the greatest long-run return on investment.

Author Comment
A company has many options for entering an international market, from simply exporting its products to working jointly with foreign companies to holding its own foreign-based operations.

Deciding How to Enter the Market

Once a company has decided to sell in a foreign country, it must determine the best mode of entry. Its choices are *exporting*, *joint venturing*, and *direct investment*. **>> Figure 15.2** shows three market entry strategies, along with the options each one offers. As the figure shows, each succeeding strategy involves more commitment and risk but also more control and potential profits.

Exporting

Exporting
Entering foreign markets by selling goods produced in the company's home country, often with little modification.

The simplest way to enter a foreign market is through **exporting**. The company may passively export its surpluses from time to time, or it may make an active commitment to expand exports to a particular market. In either case, the company produces

>> Table 15.1 Indicators of Market Potential

Demographic Characteristics	Sociocultural Factors
Education Population size and growth Population age composition	Consumer lifestyles, beliefs, and values Business norms and approaches Cultural and social norms Languages
Geographic Characteristics	**Political and Legal Factors**
Climate Country size Population density—urban, rural Transportation structure and market accessibility	National priorities Political stability Government attitudes toward global trade Government bureaucracy Monetary and trade regulations
Economic Factors	
GDP size and growth Income distribution Industrial infrastructure Natural resources Financial and human resources	

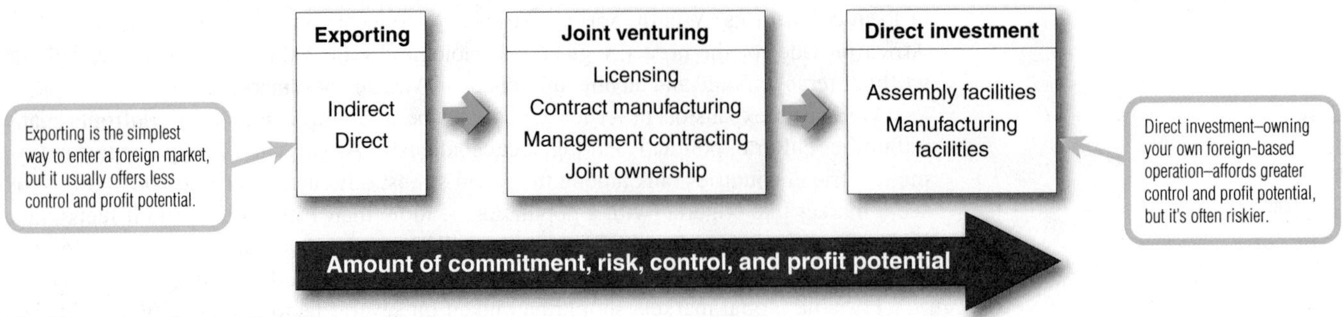

Exporting
Indirect
Direct
Joint venturing
Licensing
Contract manufacturing
Management contracting
Joint ownership
Direct investment
Assembly facilities
Manufacturing facilities
Exporting is the simplest way to enter a foreign market, but it usually offers less control and profit potential.
Direct investment–owning your own foreign-based operation–affords greater control and profit potential, but it's often riskier.
Amount of commitment, risk, control, and profit potential

Figure 15.2 Market Entry Strategies

all its goods in its home country. It may or may not modify them for the export market. Exporting involves the least change in the company's product lines, organization, investments, or mission.

Joint venturing
Entering foreign markets by joining with foreign companies to produce or market a product or service.

Licensing
Entering foreign markets through developing an agreement with a licensee in the foreign market.

Companies typically start with *indirect exporting*, working through independent international marketing intermediaries. Indirect exporting involves less investment because the firm does not require an overseas marketing organization or network. It also involves less risk. International marketing intermediaries bring know-how and services to the relationship, so the seller normally makes fewer mistakes. Sellers may eventually move into *direct exporting*, whereby they handle their own exports. The investment and risk are somewhat greater in this strategy, but so is the potential return.

Joint Venturing

A second method of entering a foreign market is by **joint venturing**—joining with foreign companies to produce or market products or services. Joint venturing differs from exporting in that the company joins with a host country partner to sell or market abroad. It differs from direct investment in that an association is formed with someone in the foreign country. There are four types of joint ventures: *licensing*, *contract manufacturing*, *management contracting*, and *joint ownership*.

Licensing

Licensing is a simple way for a manufacturer to enter international marketing. The company enters into an agreement with a licensee in the foreign market. For a fee or royalty payments, the licensee buys the right to use the company's manufacturing process, trademark, patent, trade secret, or other item of value. The company thus gains entry into a foreign market at little risk; at the same time, the licensee gains production expertise or a well-known product or name without having to start from scratch.

In Japan, Budweiser beer flows from Kirin breweries, and Mizkan produces Sunkist lemon juice, drinks, and dessert items. Coca-Cola markets internationally by licensing bottlers around the world and supplying them with the syrup needed to produce the product. Its global bottling partners range from the Coca-Cola Bottling Company of Saudi Arabia to Europe-based Coca-Cola Hellenic, which bottles and markets 136 Coca-Cola brands to 581 million people in 28 countries, from Italy and Greece to Nigeria and Russia.[29]

Licensing has potential disadvantages, however. The firm has less control over the licensee than it would over its own operations. Furthermore, if the licensee is very successful, the firm has given up these profits, and if and when the contract ends, it may find it has created a competitor.

Licensing: In Japan, Sunkist lemon juice is produced by Mizkan.

Contract Manufacturing

Contract manufacturing
A joint venture in which a company contracts with manufacturers in a foreign market to produce its product or provide its service.

Another option is **contract manufacturing**, in which the company makes agreements with manufacturers in the foreign market to produce its product or provide its service. Sears used this method in opening up department stores in Mexico and Spain, where it found qualified local manufacturers to produce many of the products it sells. The drawbacks of contract manufacturing are decreased control over the manufacturing process and loss of potential profits on manufacturing. The benefits are the chance to start faster, with less risk, and the later opportunity either to form a partnership with or buy out the local manufacturer.

Management Contracting

Management contracting
A joint venture in which the domestic firm supplies the management know-how to a foreign company that supplies the capital; the domestic firm exports management services rather than products.

Under **management contracting**, the domestic firm provides the management know-how to a foreign company that supplies the capital. In other words, the domestic firm exports management services rather than products. Hilton uses this arrangement in managing hotels around the world. For example, the hotel chain operates DoubleTree by Hilton hotels in countries ranging from the UK and Italy to Peru and Costa Rica, to China, Russia, and Tanzania. The properties are locally owned, but Hilton manages the hotels with its world-renowned hospitality expertise.[30]

Management contracting is a low-risk method of getting into a foreign market, and it yields income from the beginning. The arrangement is even more attractive if the contracting firm has an option to buy some share in the managed company later on. The arrangement is not sensible, however, if the company can put its scarce management talent to better uses or if it can make greater profits by undertaking the whole venture. Management contracting also prevents the company from setting up its own operations for a period of time.

Joint Ownership

Joint ownership
A cooperative venture in which a company creates a local business with investors in a foreign market, who share ownership and control.

Joint ownership ventures consist of one company joining forces with foreign investors to create a local business in which they share possession and control. A company may buy an interest in a local firm, or the two parties may form a new business venture. Joint ownership may be needed for economic or political reasons. For example, the firm may lack the financial, physical, or managerial resources to undertake the venture alone. Alternatively, a foreign government may require joint ownership as a condition for entry.

Often, companies form joint ownership ventures to merge their complementary strengths in developing a global marketing opportunity. For example, Chrysler's parent company, Fiat, recently formed a 50/50 joint venture with Chinese state-run Guangzhou Automobile Group (GAC) to produce Jeep vehicles in China. Jeep was one of the first Western auto brands sold in China, and the brand is well recognized and popular there. However, all of the Jeeps sold in China have been imported from the United States and subject to steep import tariffs, driving Jeep prices to sky-high levels. For example, before the joint venture, a top-of-the-line Jeep Grand Cherokee sold for as much as $205,000 in China, more than triple its U.S. price. Under the joint venture, once approved, Chrysler and GAC will partner to produce Jeeps in China, avoiding tariffs, reducing production costs, and allowing competitive Jeep prices in the world's largest automotive market.[31]

Joint ownership has certain drawbacks, however. The partners may disagree over investment, marketing, or other policies. Whereas many U.S. firms like to reinvest earnings for growth, local firms often prefer to take out these earnings; whereas U.S. firms emphasize the role of marketing, local investors may rely on selling.

Direct Investment

Direct investment
Entering a foreign market by developing foreign-based assembly or manufacturing facilities.

The biggest involvement in a foreign market comes through **direct investment**—the development of foreign-based assembly or manufacturing facilities. >> For example, Ford has made direct investments in several Asian countries, including India, China, and Thailand. It recently began building its second facility in India, a $1 billion state-of-the-art manufacturing and engineering plant that will produce 240,000 cars a year, helping to satisfy Ford's burgeoning demand in India and other Asian markets. Similarly, Honda and Toyota have made substantial direct manufacturing investments in North America. For example, more

» **Direct investment: Ford has made major direct investments in several countries, such as India, China, and Thailand, to help satisfy Ford's burgeoning demand in Asian markets.**

AFP/Getty Images.

than 87 percent of the Honda and Acura models sold in the United States are made in North America. "Our fundamental philosophy is to produce where we sell," says a Honda executive.[32]

If a company has gained experience in exporting and if the foreign market is large enough, foreign production facilities offer many advantages. The firm may have lower costs in the form of cheaper labor or raw materials, foreign government investment incentives, and freight savings. The firm may also improve its image in the host country because it creates jobs. Generally, a firm develops a deeper relationship with the government, customers, local suppliers, and distributors, allowing it to adapt its products to the local market better. Finally, the firm keeps full control over the investment and therefore can develop manufacturing and marketing policies that serve its long-term international objectives.

The main disadvantage of direct investment is that the firm faces many risks, such as restricted or devalued currencies, falling markets, or government changes. In some cases, a firm has no choice but to accept these risks if it wants to operate in the host country.

SPEED BUMP LINKING THE CONCEPTS

Slow down here and think about McDonald's global marketing issues.

- To what extent can McDonald's standardize for the Chinese market? What marketing strategy and program elements can be similar to those used in the United States and other parts of the Western world? Which ones must be adapted? Be specific.
- To what extent can McDonald's standardize its strategy, products, and programs for the Canadian market? What elements can be standardized and which must be adapted?
- To what extent are McDonald's "globalization" efforts contributing to "Americanization" of countries and cultures around the world? What are the positives and negatives of such cultural developments?

Author Comment
The major global marketing decision usually boils down to this: How much, if at all, should a company adapt its marketing strategy and programs to local markets? How might the answer differ for Boeing versus McDonald's?

Deciding on the Global Marketing Program

Companies that operate in one or more foreign markets must decide how much, if at all, to adapt their marketing strategies and programs to local conditions. At one extreme are global companies that use **standardized global marketing**, essentially using the same marketing strategy approaches and marketing mix worldwide. At the other extreme is **adapted global marketing**. In this case, the producer adjusts the marketing strategy and mix elements to each target market, resulting in more costs but hopefully producing a larger market share and return.

The question of whether to adapt or standardize the marketing strategy and program has been much debated over the years. On the one hand, some global marketers believe that technology is making the world a smaller place, and consumer needs around the world are becoming more similar. This paves the way for global brands and standardized global marketing. Global branding and standardization, in turn, result in greater brand power and reduced costs from economies of scale.

Standardized global marketing
An international marketing strategy that basically uses the same marketing strategy and mix in all of the company's international markets.

On the other hand, the marketing concept holds that marketing programs will be more effective engaging if tailored to the unique needs of each targeted customer group. If this

Adapted global marketing
An international marketing approach that adjusts the marketing strategy and mix elements to each international target market, which creates more costs but hopefully produces a larger market share and return.

concept applies within a country, it should apply even more across international markets. Despite global convergence, consumers in different countries still have widely varied cultural backgrounds. They still differ significantly in their needs and wants, spending power, product preferences, and shopping patterns. Because these differences are hard to change, most marketers today adapt their products, prices, channels, and promotions to fit consumer desires in each country.

However, global standardization is not an all-or-nothing proposition. It's a matter of degree. Most international marketers suggest that companies should "think globally but act locally"—that they should seek a balance between standardization and adaptation. Starbucks has found this balance internationally, leveraging its substantial global brand recognition but adapting its marketing and operations to specific markets. The company's overall brand strategy provides global strategic direction. Then regional or local units focus on adapting the strategy and brand to specific local markets such as India and China (see Marketing at Work 15.2). "The best brand organizations drive a single-minded brand purpose and then challenge and empower local marketers to develop the best activation mix to bring that to fruition in every market," says a global branding expert.[33]

Collectively, local brands still account for the overwhelming majority of consumers' purchases. "The vast majority of people still lead very local lives," says a global analyst. "By all means go global, but the first thing you have to do is win on the ground. You have to go local." Another analyst agrees: "You need to respect local culture and become part of it." A global brand must "engage with consumers in a way that feels local to them." Simon Clift, former chief marketing officer at global consumer-goods giant Unilever, put it this way: "We're trying to strike a balance between being mindlessly global and hopelessly local."[34]

McDonald's operates this way: It uses the same basic fast-food look, layout, and operating model in its restaurants around the world but adapts its menu and design to local tastes. For example, McDonald's France uses the power of its global brand and operating model but has redefined itself as a French company that adapts to the needs and preferences of French consumers:[35]

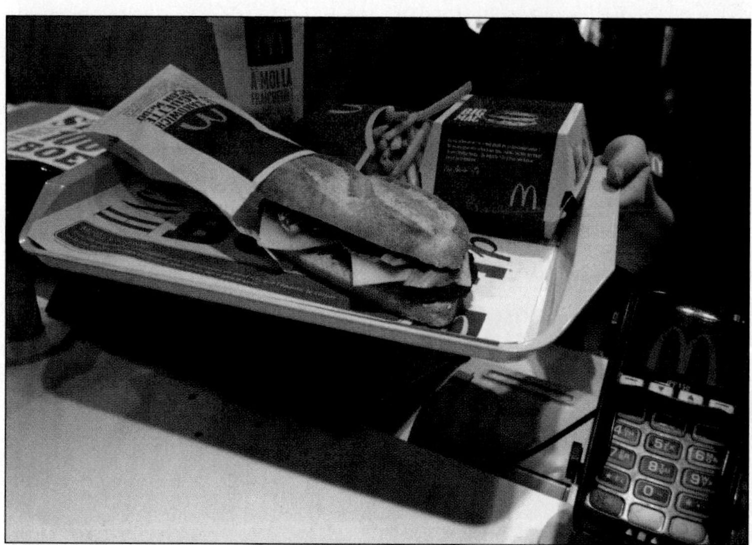

>> **Think globally, act locally: By leveraging the power of its global brand but constantly adapting to the needs and preferences of French consumers and their culture, McDonald's has turned France into its second-most-profitable world market.**

ERIC PIERMONT/AFP/Getty Images/Newscom.

"France—the land of haute cuisine, fine wine, and cheese—would be the last place you would expect to find a thriving [McDonald's]," opines one observer. Yet the fast-food giant has turned France into its second-most profitable world market. Although a McDonald's in Paris might at first seem a lot like one in Chicago, McDonald's has carefully adapted its French operations to the preferences of local customers. At the most basic level, although a majority of revenues still come from burgers and fries, McDonald's France has changed its menu to please the French palate. For example, it offers up burgers with French cheeses such as chevre, cantel, and bleu, topped off with whole-grain French mustard sauce. >> French consumers love baguettes, so McDonald's bakes them fresh in its restaurants and sells them in oh-so-French McBaguette sandwiches. And in response to the growing French trend for healthy eating, the menu in France includes reduced-salt french fries, fresh fruit, and "le Big Mac"—the McDonald's classic but with a whole-wheat-bun option.

But perhaps the biggest difference isn't in the food, but in the design of the restaurants themselves, which have been adapted to suit French lifestyles. For example, French meal times tend to be longer, with more food consumed per sitting. So McDonald's has refined its restaurant interiors to create a comfortable, welcoming environment where customers want to linger and perhaps order an additional coffee or dessert. McDonald's even provides tableside service. As a result, the average French McDonald's customer spends about four times what an American customer spends per visit.

MARKETING AT WORK 15.2

Starbucks in India: A Global Brand in a Local Market

Starbucks is now opening for business in India, with 12 stores currently open, 50 planned by the end of this year, and a bunch more to follow quickly. Given India's rapidly emerging economy and its huge population of well over 1.2 billion people, entering the Indian market seems like a no brainer for the global brand.

Opportunities abound for Starbucks in India. Long a country of tea drinkers, India is now in the midst of a coffee café explosion. The industry is growing by 20 percent a year, fueled by the nation's growing middle class and large youth population. India—especially the young adult segment—is ready for Starbucks. In a country that still largely disapproves of young adults, especially young women, socializing in bars or pubs, coffee shops provide ideal hangouts. "When you don't want to drink, when you just want to chill, you come here," says a 22-year-old female weeknight patron at a Coffee Bean & Tea Leaf outlet in New Delhi. It's worth paying 150 rupees (about $3) for a cup of coffee and time away from home with her friends.

If the coffee market is heating up in India, so is the Starbucks brand. Even though it's just now setting up shop there, thanks to Starbucks' global prowess, many Indians are already familiar with the brand. In fact, according to Anil Kumar Bhandari, president of India Coffee Trust, an industry trade organization, the growth of India's coffee market in the first place resulted in part from Starbucks' global success. "The growth didn't only come because [of local coffee shops. It] came because of the lifestyle that Starbucks started in the United States and other places." Says another young Indian consumer, "It has a brand. It has esteem." So, because of its global brand power, the café tables are already set for Starbucks as it enters India.

However, global brand power won't automatically translate into local brand success for Starbucks. India is very different from the United States, Canada, or Europe. To succeed in India's complex market environment, Starbucks must carefully adapt to the tastes of Indian consumers and the complexities of India's political, business, and social environments.

For example, doing business in India heavily favors insiders. By market capitalization, more than 70 percent of Indian business is family-controlled. Developing commercial relationships in India takes time and patience, and even then family ties can dominate. To make things even more challenging for outside firms, the Indian government is notoriously slow when it comes to making foreign investment decisions. For instance, in response to protests from local businesses, the Indian government recently put off a long-awaited decision to let foreign retailers own a 51 percent or greater stake in Indian retail operations. In such an uncertain political environment, foreign investment in India has declined in recent years and economic growth has slowed.

But Starbucks—the world's largest coffee chain with over 18,000 stores in 62 countries—is no stranger to the difficulties of entering new global markets. The company has studied India for years, learning all it can and patiently honing its entry strategy. To smooth the way, Starbucks forged a 50-50 joint venture with Tata Global Beverages, a division of India's largest business group. The Tata alliance eases the financial risks and gives Starbucks insider business and political status. It also helps the coffee-house giant to understand the needs of Indian consumers. According to John Culver, president of Starbucks China and Asia Pacific, even without government restrictions on foreign ownership, Starbucks would never have considered trying to go it alone in India. "We never considered 51 percent," he says. "When we looked at the opportunity to enter India, understanding the complexities of the market and the uniqueness that is India, we wanted to find a local business partner."

In entering India, Starbucks also faces a market that's percolating with well-established competitors. One local competitor—Café Coffee Day—dominates with more than 1,400 stores and a plan to open 200 more each year. Self-described as "India's favorite coffee shop, where the young and young at heart unwind," Café Coffee Day promises a world-class coffee experience at affordable prices. Several

>> Starbucks' global brand power won't automatically translate into local success in India. The brand must adapt to the tastes of Indian consumers and the complexities of India's political and business environments.

Hindustan Times.

foreign coffee chains have also invaded India, such as Italy's Lavazza and California-based Coffee Bean & Tea Leaf. Most competitors feature low prices, with small cappuccinos commonly selling for $1 or less.

But despite the growing competition, Starbucks has been welcomed in India, even by the leading local competitor. Given the huge size and rapid growth of the Indian coffee market, there appears to be plenty of room for all players. "There are a lot of foreign brands already available in India, and still it hasn't made any difference from a competition point of view," says Café Coffee Day's chief operating officer. And "when companies like Starbucks come in," he says, "the awareness levels go up tremendously [and] the overall market size grows." Adds another Café Coffee Day executive, "We will hopefully learn a few things from them." According to one analyst, at some point India can easily support 5,000 Starbucks, enough stores in India alone to increase Starbucks' worldwide count by nearly 30 percent.

Starbucks' strategy in India for adapting to local consumer preferences is still emerging, but many analysts expect that the company will apply the lessons it learned in China. When Starbucks entered China in 1998, given the strong Chinese tea-drinking culture, few observers expected success. But Starbucks quickly proved the doubters wrong; China will soon be Starbucks' largest market outside of the United States, with more than 500 stores now and 1,600 planned by the end of 2015.

Starbucks' success in China results from adapting its global brand strategy to the unique characteristics of Chinese consumers. Rather than forcing U.S. products on the Chinese, Starbucks developed new flavors—such as green-tea-flavored coffee drinks—that appeal to local tastes. Rather than pushing take-out orders, which account for most of its U.S. revenues, Starbucks promoted dine-in services—making its stores the perfect meeting place for Chinese professionals and their friends. And rather than just charging U.S.-style premium prices in China, Starbucks boosted prices even higher, positioning the brand as a status symbol for the rapidly growing Chinese middle and upper classes. Under this adapted strategy, Starbucks China is thriving.

For now, Indian consumers may not know which Starbucks size is bigger, grande or venti. And they might not know the exact difference between a Frappuccino and a Caffè Mocha. But all that will likely change soon as the Starbucks brand grows and prospers. Success will depend on how well Starbucks applies its global brand muscle to the unique tastes of Indian customers. According to Starbucks' president Culver, it's full steam ahead. "We're going to move as fast as possible in opening as many stores as we can, so long as we are successful and so long as we are embraced by the Indian consumers."

Sources: Melissa Allison, "Starbucks Welcomed in India, Tries to Convert Tea Drinkers," *Corpus Christi Caller Times,* February 4, 2013, www.caller.com/news/2013/feb/04/starbucks-welcomed-in-india-tries-to-convert-tea/; Vikas Bajaj, "After a Year of Delays, the First Starbucks Is to Open in Tea-Loving India This Fall," *New York Times*, January 31, 2012, p. B2; Erika Kinetz, "Starbucks India: Coffee Chain to Open First India Outpost with Tata Global Beverages," *Huffington Post,* January 30, 2012, www.huffingtonpost.com/2012/01/30/starbucks-india_n_1241553.html; Elliot Hannon, "Will Global Coffee Giant Starbucks Conquer India?" *Time*, January 31, 2012, http://world.time.com/2012/01/31/will-global-coffee-giant-starbucks-conquer-india/; Anita Chong Beattie, "Can Starbucks Make China Love Joe?" *Advertising Age,* November 5, 2012, pp. 20–21; and "Café Coffee Day Wants to Open 200 Cafes Every Year," *Mint*, January 30, 2013.

Product

Five strategies are used for adapting product and marketing communication strategies to a global market (see >> **Figure 15.3**).[36] We first discuss the three product strategies and then turn to the two communication strategies.

Straight product extension
Marketing a product in a foreign market without making any changes to the product.

Straight product extension means marketing a product in a foreign market without making any changes to the product. Top management tells its marketing people, "Take the product as is and find customers for it." The first step, however, should be to find out whether foreign consumers use that product and what form they prefer.

Straight extension has been successful in some cases and disastrous in others. Apple iPads, Gillette razors, Black & Decker tools, and even 7–11 Slurpees are all sold successfully in about the same form around the world. But when General Foods introduced its standard powdered JELL-O in the British market, it discovered that British consumers

>> **Figure 15.3** Five Global Product and Communications Strategies

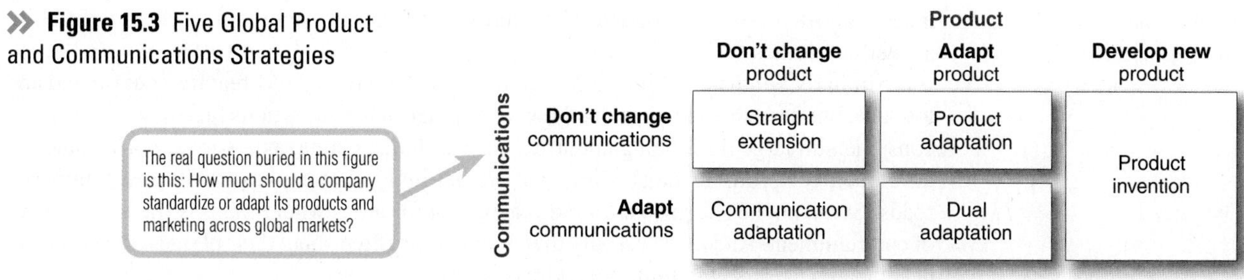

prefer a solid wafer or cake form. Likewise, Philips began to make a profit in Japan only after it reduced the size of its coffeemakers to fit into smaller Japanese kitchens and its shavers to fit smaller Japanese hands. And Panasonic's refrigerator sales in China surged 10-fold in a single year after it shaved the width by of its appliances by 15 percent to fit smaller Chinese kitchens.[37] Straight extension is tempting because it involves no additional product development costs, manufacturing changes, or new promotion. But it can be costly in the long run if products fail to satisfy consumers in specific global markets.

Product adaptation
Adapting a product to meet local conditions or wants in foreign markets.

Product adaptation involves changing the product to meet local requirements, conditions, or wants. For example, Kraft has adapted its popular Oreo cookie to the unique tastes of consumers all around the world, whether it's mango-and-orange flavored Oreos in the Asia Pacific region, green tea Oreos in China, a chocolate and peanut variety in Indonesia, or banana and dulce de leche in Argentina. Chinese Oreos are less sweet than the American standard; Oreos in India are less bitter.[38]

As another example, although the U.S. and European versions of the feisty little Fiat 500 might look a lot alike, Fiat has made stem-to-stern adaptations in the U.S. model to meet U.S. safety standards and American buyer expectations. To name just a few modifications, the U.S. Fiat 500 has a redesigned engine that offers the power demanded by U.S. consumers while simultaneously providing the better gas mileage and lower emissions required by the country's regulations. The gas tank is 40 percent larger to accommodate the longer driving distances that are typical in the United States, and there's lots more insulation in the U.S. car to keep it quiet enough for Americans. » Another big difference—the cupholders:[39]

> A silly matter to Europeans, but vital to Americans, the U.S. Fiat 500 has an enlarged pod of holders up front to fit U.S.-size drinks, instead of the small European holders, plus two additional holders at the rear of the floor console. The in-car beverage concept is so foreign to Europeans that the 500 design team didn't understand the need for more and bigger holders—until one engineer drew a cartoon of an American wearing one of those gimmick hats that hold two beer cans and have long tubes at straws. Then everybody said, "Ah, yes."

» **Product adaptation: The European and U.S. versions of the feisty little Fiat 500 look pretty much alike. But to meet the preferences of the U.S. buyers, Fiat adapted the car's interior from stem to stern, including an enlarged pod of bigger cupholders that are so important to Americans.**

PR NEWSWIRE.

Product invention
Creating new products or services for foreign markets.

Product invention consists of creating something new to meet the needs of consumers in a given country. As markets have gone global, companies ranging from appliance manufacturers and carmakers to candy and soft drink producers have developed products that meet the special purchasing needs of low-income consumers in developing economies. For example, Ford developed the economical, low-priced Figo model especially for entry-level consumers in India; GM created the inexpensive Baojun for China (the name means "treasured horse"). Chinese appliance producer Haier developed sturdier washing machines for rural users in emerging markets, where it found that lighter-duty machines often became clogged with mud when farmers used them to clean vegetables as well as clothes.[40]

Similarly, Finnish mobile phone maker Nokia has created full-featured but rugged and low-cost phones especially designed for the harsher living conditions faced by less-affluent consumers in large developing countries such as India, China, and Kenya. For instance, it developed dustproof keypads, which are crucial in dry, hot countries with many unpaved roads. Some phones have built-in radio antennas for areas where radio is the main source of entertainment. And after learning that poor people often share their phones, the company developed handsets with multiple address books.

Promotion

Companies can either adopt the same communication strategy they use in the home market or change it for each local market. Consider advertising messages. Some global companies use a standardized advertising theme around the world. For example, Chevrolet recently swapped out its previous, American-focused "Chevy Runs Deep" positioning and advertising theme with a more global "Find New Roads" theme. The new theme is one "that works in all markets," says a GM marketing executive. "The theme has meaning in mature markets like the U.S. as well as emerging markets like Russia and India, where the potential for continued growth is the greatest." The time is right for a more globally consistent Chevy brand message. Chevrolet sells cars in more the 140 countries and had over 20 global vehicle launches last year.[41]

Of course, even in highly standardized communications campaigns, some adjustments might be required for language and cultural differences. For example, in Western markets, fast-casual clothing retailer H&M runs fashion ads with models showing liberal amounts of bare skin. But in the Middle East, where attitudes toward public nudity are more conservative, the retailer runs the same ads digitally adapted to better cover its models.

Global companies often have difficulty crossing the language barrier, with results ranging from mild embarrassment to outright failure. Seemingly innocuous brand names and advertising phrases can take on unintended or hidden meanings when translated into other languages. For example, Interbrand of London, the firm that created household names such as Prozac and Acura, recently developed a brand name "hall of shame" list, which contained these and other foreign brand names you're never likely to see inside the local Kroger supermarket: Krapp toilet paper (Denmark), Plopp chocolate (Scandinavia), Crapsy Fruit cereal (France), Poo curry powder (Argentina), and Pschitt lemonade (France). Similarly, advertising themes often lose—or gain—something in the translation. In Chinese, the KFC slogan "finger-lickin' good" came out as "eat your fingers off." And Motorola's Hellomoto ringtone sounds like "Hello, Fatty" in India. Marketers must be watchful to avoid such mistakes.

Communication adaptation
A global communication strategy of fully adapting advertising messages to local markets.

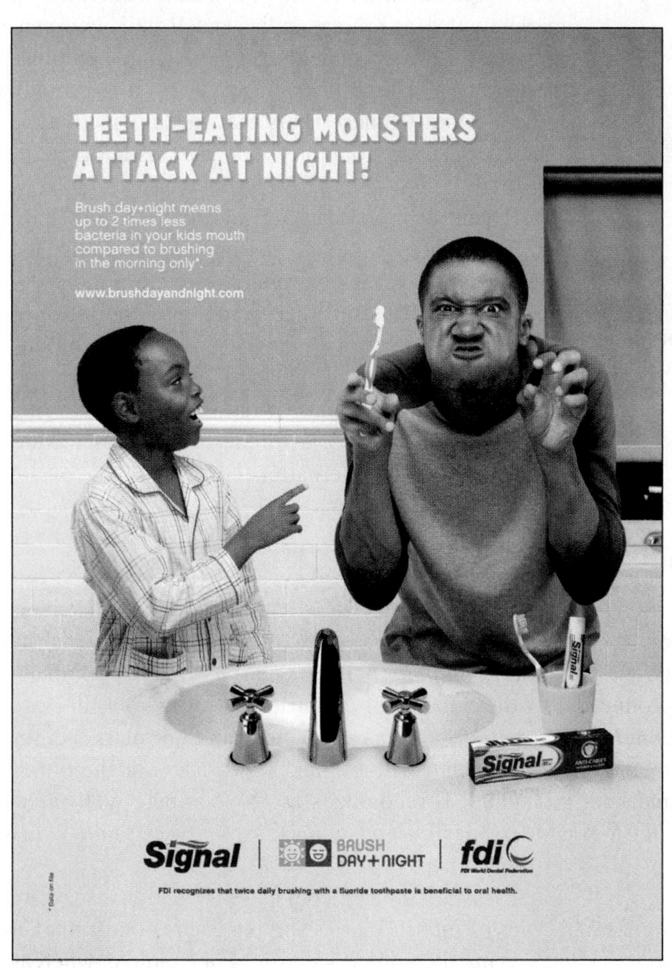

Adapting advertising messages: Whereas Western ads for Unilever toothpaste brands might emphasize whiter teeth, fresher breath, or greater sex appeal, its ads in Africa take a more educational approach emphasizing healthy teeth.

Unilever plc.

Other companies follow a strategy of **communication adaptation**, fully adapting their advertising messages to local markets. Consumer products marketer Unilever does this for many of its brands. For example, whereas ads for Unilever toothpaste brands in Western markets might emphasize anything from whiter teeth or fresher breath to greater sex appeal, ads in Africa take a more basic educational approach, emphasizing the importance of brushing twice a day. And Unilever adapts the positioning, formulation, and appeals for its Sunsilk Lively Clean & Fresh shampoo to serve the varying needs of consumers in different markets. Whereas its standard Western shampoo ads tend to show young women flirtatiously tossing their freshly-washed locks over their shoulders, Sunsilk's Lively Clean & Fresh ads in Malaysia show no hair at all. Instead, they feature modern young women wearing tudungs—traditional Muslim headscarves that completely cover the hair. To tap the large and growing Malaysian Islamic market, Unilever positions Lively Clean & Fresh directly to the "lifestyle of the tudung wearer," as a remedy for the problem of excess hair and scalp oil that wearing a tudung can cause.[42]

Media also need to be adapted internationally because media availability and regulations vary from country to country. TV advertising time is very limited in Europe, for instance, ranging from four hours a day in France to none in Scandinavian countries. Advertisers must buy time months in advance, and they have little control over airtimes. However, mobile phone ads are much more widely accepted in Europe and Asia than in the United States. Magazines also vary in effectiveness. For example, magazines are a major medium in Italy but a minor one in Austria. Newspapers are national in the United Kingdom but only local in Spain.[43]

Price

Companies also face many considerations in setting their international prices. For example, how might Makita price its tools globally? It could set a uniform price globally, but this amount would be too high of a price in poor countries and not high enough in rich ones. It could charge what consumers in each country would bear, but this strategy ignores differences in the actual costs from country to country. Finally, the company could use a standard markup of its costs everywhere, but this approach might price Makita out of the market in some countries where costs are high.

Regardless of how companies go about pricing their products, their foreign prices probably will be higher than their domestic prices for comparable products. An Apple iPad 3 that sells for $499 in the United States goes for $612 in the United Kingdom. Why? Apple faces a *price escalation* problem. It must add the cost of transportation, tariffs, importer margin, wholesaler margin, and retailer margin to its factory price. Depending on these added costs, a product may have to sell for two to five times as much in another country to make the same profit.

International pricing: Levi Strauss launched the Denizen brand, created for teens and young adults in emerging markets such as China, India, and Brazil who cannot afford Levi's-branded jeans.

Nelson Ching/Getty Images USA, Inc.

To overcome this problem when selling to less-affluent consumers in developing countries, many companies make simpler or smaller versions of their products that can be sold at lower prices. Others have introduced new, more affordable brands in emerging markets. For example, Levi launched the Denizen brand, created for teens and young adults in emerging markets such as China, India, and Brazil who cannot afford Levi's-branded jeans. The name combines the first four letters of *denim* with *zen*, a word with Japanese and Chinese roots that means "meditative state" or "escape from the hustle and bustle of everyday life."[44]

Recent economic and technological forces have had an impact on global pricing. For example, the Internet is making global price differences more obvious. When firms sell their wares over the Internet, customers can see how much products sell for in different countries. They can even order a given product directly from the company location or dealer offering the lowest price. This is forcing companies toward more standardized international pricing.

Distribution Channels

Whole-channel view
Designing international channels that take into account the entire global supply chain and marketing channel, forging an effective global value delivery network.

An international company must take a **whole-channel view** of the problem of distributing products to final consumers. **Figure 15.4** shows the two major links between the seller and the final buyer. The first link, *channels between nations*, moves company products from points of production to the borders of countries within which they are sold. The second link, *channels within nations*, moves products from their market entry points to the final consumers. The whole-channel view takes into account the entire global supply chain and marketing channel. It recognizes that to compete well internationally, the company must effectively design and manage an entire *global value delivery network*.

Channels of distribution within countries vary greatly from nation to nation. There are large differences in the numbers and types of intermediaries serving each country market and in the transportation infrastructure serving these intermediaries. For example, whereas large-scale retail chains dominate the U.S. scene, most of the retailing in other countries is done by small, independent retailers. In India or Indonesia, millions of retailers operate tiny shops or sell in open markets.

Even in world markets containing similar types of sellers, retailing practices can vary widely. For example, you'll find plenty of Walmarts, Carrefours, Tescos, and other retail

Distribution channels can vary dramatically around the world. For example, in the U.S., Coca-Cola distributes products through sophisticated retail channels. In less-developed countries, it delivers Coke using everything from push carts to delivery donkeys

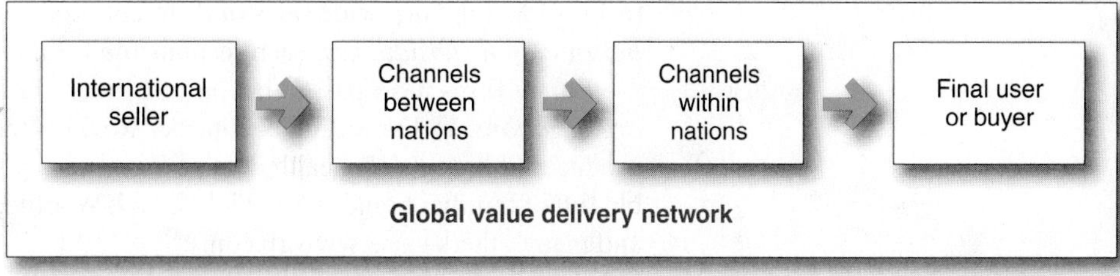

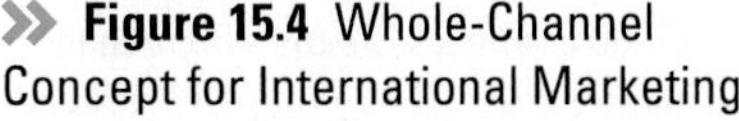

Figure 15.4 Whole-Channel Concept for International Marketing

superstores in major Chinese cities. But whereas consumer brands sold in such stores in Western markets rely largely on self-service, brands in China hire armies of uniformed in-store promoters—called "promoter girls" or "push girls"—to dispense samples and pitch their products person to person. In a Beijing Walmart, on any given weekend, you'll find 100 or more such promoters acquainting customers with products from Kraft, Unilever, P&G, Johnson & Johnson, and a slew of local competitors. "Chinese consumers know the brand name through media," says the director of a Chinese retail marketing service, "but they want to feel the product and get a detailed understanding before they make a purchase."[45]

Distribution channels vary from nation to nation. Whereas consumer brands sold Western superstores like Walmart or Target rely largely on self-service, these brands in China hire armies of uniformed in-store promoters to dispense samples and pitch their products in person.

Darcy Holdorf Photography.

Similarly, as we learned in the story about its ventures in Africa, Coca-Cola adapts its distribution methods to meet local challenges in global markets. For example, in Montevideo, Uruguay, where larger vehicles are challenged by traffic, parking, and pollution difficulties, Coca-Cola purchased 30 small, efficient, three-wheeled ZAP alternative transportation trucks. The little trucks average about one-fifth the fuel consumption and scoot around congested city streets with greater ease. In rural areas, Coca-Cola uses a manual delivery process. In China, an army of more than 10,000 Coca-Cola sales reps makes regular visits to small retailers, often on foot or bicycle. To reach the most isolated spots, the company even relies on teams of delivery donkeys. In Tanzania, 93 percent of Coca-Cola's products are manually delivered via pushcarts and bicycles.[46]

Author Comment

Many large companies, regardless of their "home country," now think of themselves as truly *global* organizations. They view the entire world as a single borderless market. For example, although headquartered in Chicago, Boeing is as comfortable selling planes to Lufthansa or Air China as to American Airlines.

Deciding on the Global Marketing Organization

Companies manage their international marketing activities in at least three different ways: Most companies first organize an export department, then create an international division, and finally become a global organization.

A firm normally gets into international marketing by simply shipping out its goods. If its international sales expand, the company will establish an *export department* with a sales manager and a few assistants. As sales increase, the export department can expand to include various marketing services so that it can actively go after business. If the firm moves into joint ventures or direct investment, the export department will no longer be adequate.

Many companies get involved in several international markets and ventures. A company may export to one country, license to another, have a joint ownership venture in a third, and own a subsidiary in a fourth. Sooner or later it will create *international divisions* or subsidiaries to handle all its international activity.

International divisions are organized in a variety of ways. An international division's corporate staff consists of marketing, manufacturing, research, finance, planning, and personnel specialists. It plans for and provides services to various operating units, which can be organized in one of three ways. They can be *geographical organizations*, with country managers who are responsible for salespeople, sales branches, distributors, and licensees in their respective countries. Or the operating units can be *world product groups*, each responsible for worldwide sales of different product groups. Finally, operating units can be *international subsidiaries*, each responsible for their own sales and profits.

Many firms have passed beyond the international division stage and are truly *global organizations*. For example, consider Reckitt Benckiser (RB), a $15.5-billion European producer of household, health, and personal care products and consumer goods with a stable full of familiar brands (Air Wick, Lysol, Woolite, Calgon, Mucinex, Clearasil, French's, and many others—see www.rb.com):[47]

European household, health, and consumer-goods producer Reckitt Benckiser has a truly global organization. "Most of our top managers . . . view themselves as global citizens rather than as citizens of any given nation."

Reckitt Benckiser plc.

RB operates in more than 60 countries. Its top 400 managers represent 53 different nationalities. The company is headquartered in the United Kingdom and its CEO is Indian. Its U.S. business is run by a Dutchman, its Russian business by an Italian, and its Australian business by a Brazilian. "Most of our top managers . . . view themselves as global citizens rather than as citizens of any given nation," says RB's chief executive officer.

RB recently relocated several of its operations to put key marketers in key countries within their regions. For example, it recently moved its Latin American headquarters from Miami to Sao Paulo, Brazil. The company has spent the past decade building a culture of global mobility because it thinks that's one of the best ways to generate new ideas and create global entrepreneurs. And it has paid off. Products launched in the past three years—all the result of global cross-fertilization—account for 35–40 percent of net revenue. Over the past few years, even during the economic downturn, the company has outperformed its rivals—P&G, Unilever, and Colgate—in growth.

Global organizations don't think of themselves as national marketers that sell abroad but as global marketers. The top corporate management and staff plan worldwide manufacturing facilities, marketing policies, financial flows, and logistical systems. The global operating units report directly to the chief executive or the executive committee of the organization, not to the head of an international division. Executives are trained in worldwide operations, not just domestic *or* international operations. Global companies recruit management from many countries, buy components and supplies where they cost the least, and invest where the expected returns are greatest.

Today, major companies must become more global if they hope to compete. As foreign companies successfully invade their domestic markets, companies must move more aggressively into foreign markets. They will have to change from companies that treat their international operations as secondary to companies that view the entire world as a single borderless market.

MyMarketingLab

Go to **mymktlab.com** to complete the problems marked with this icon .

END OF CHAPTER REVIEWING THE CONCEPTS

CHAPTER REVIEW AND KEY TERMS

Objectives Review

Companies today can no longer afford to pay attention only to their domestic market, regardless of its size. Many industries are global industries, and firms that operate globally achieve lower costs and higher brand awareness. At the same time, global marketing is risky because of variable exchange rates, unstable governments, tariffs and trade barriers, and several other factors. Given the potential gains and risks of international marketing, companies need a systematic way to make their global marketing decisions.

OBJECTIVE 1 Discuss how the international trade system and the economic, political-legal, and cultural environments affect a company's international marketing decisions. (pp 468–479)

A company must understand the *global marketing environment*, especially the international trade system. It should assess each foreign market's *economic*, *political-legal*, and *cultural characteristics*. The company can then decide whether it wants to go abroad and consider the potential risks and benefits. It must decide on the volume of international sales it wants, how many countries it wants to market in, and which specific markets it wants to enter. These decisions call for weighing the probable returns against the level of risk.

OBJECTIVE 2 Describe three key approaches to entering international markets. (pp 479–482)

The company must decide how to enter each chosen market—whether through *exporting*, *joint venturing*, or *direct investment*. Many companies start as exporters, move to joint ventures, and finally make a direct investment in foreign markets. In *exporting*, the company enters a foreign market by sending and selling products through international marketing intermediaries (indirect exporting) or the company's own department, branch, or sales representatives or agents (direct exporting). When establishing a *joint venture*, a company enters foreign markets by joining with foreign companies to produce or market a product or service. In *licensing*, the company enters a foreign market by contracting with a licensee in the foreign market and offering the right to use a manufacturing process, trademark, patent, trade secret, or other item of value for a fee or royalty.

OBJECTIVE 3 Explain how companies adapt their marketing strategies and mixes for international markets. (pp 482–489)

Companies must also decide how much their marketing strategies and their products, promotion, price, and channels should be adapted for each foreign market. At one extreme, global companies use *standardized global marketing* worldwide. Others use *adapted global marketing*, in which they adjust the marketing strategy and mix to each target market, bearing more costs but hoping for a larger market share and return. However, global standardization is not an all-or-nothing proposition. It's a matter of degree. Most international marketers suggest that companies should "think globally but act locally"—that they should seek a balance between globally standardized strategies and locally adapted marketing mix tactics.

OBJECTIVE 4 Identify the three major forms of international marketing organization. (pp 489–490)

The company must develop an effective organization for international marketing. Most firms start with an *export department* and graduate to an *international division*. A few become *global organizations*, with worldwide marketing planned and managed by the top officers of the company. Global organizations view the entire world as a single, borderless market.

Key Terms

Objective 1
Global firm (p 469)
Economic community (p 471)

Objective 2
Exporting (p 479)
Joint venturing (p 480)
Licensing (p 480)
Contract manufacturing (p 481)
Management contracting (p 481)
Joint ownership (p 481)
Direct investment (p 481)

Objective 3
Standardized global marketing (p 482)
Adapted global marketing (p 482)
Straight product extension (p 485)
Product adaptation (p 486)
Product invention (p 486)
Communication adaptation (p 487)
Whole-channel view (p 488)

DISCUSSION AND CRITICAL THINKING

Discussion Questions

15-1. Explain what is meant by the term *global firm* and list the major decisions involved in international marketing. (AACSB: Written and Oral Communication)

15-2. Discuss the four types of country industrial structures and the opportunities each offers to international marketers. (AACSB: Written and Oral Communication)

15-3. Discuss the three ways to enter foreign markets. Which is the best? (AACSB: Written and Oral Communication; Reflective Thinking)

15-4. Discuss the strategies used for adapting products to a global market. Which strategy is best? (AACSB: Written and Oral Communication; Reflective Thinking)

15-5. Discuss how companies manage their international marketing activities. (AACSB: Written and Oral Communication)

Critical Thinking Exercises

15-6. The United States restricts trade with several countries. Visit the U.S. Department of the Treasury at www.treasury.gov/resource-center/sanctions/Programs/Pages/Programs.aspx to learn more about economic and trade sanctions. Click on one of the programs to learn more about the sanctions. Are these tariff, quota, or embargo restrictions? To what extent do these trade restrictions allow U.S. businesses to export their products to the country or countries included? (AACSB: Written and Oral Communication; Information Technology; Reflective Thinking)

15-7. What is a *free trade zone*? Give an example of a free trade zone and research how successful it has been. (AACSB: Written and Oral Communication; Reflective Thinking)

15-8. One way to analyze the cultural differences among countries is to conduct a Hofestede analysis. Visit www.geert-hofstede.com to learn what this analysis considers. Develop a presentation explaining how three countries of your choice differ from the United States. (AACSB: Written and Oral Communication; Information Technology; Reflective Thinking)

MINICASES AND APPLICATIONS

Online, Mobile, and Social Media Marketing Pixels Instead of Pine

Swedish company IKEA releases a 300-plus-page catalog each year featuring its furniture in fashionably modern room settings. The 2013 catalog comes in 62 different versions for 43 countries. IKEA's photo shoots for the catalog take place in one of Europe's largest studios—94,000 square feet—which employs almost 300 photographers, interior designers, carpenters, and others involved in making each scene just perfect. The process is very labor-intensive and wasteful because rooms are built up and torn down and often thrown into a dumpster after the photo shoot. The catalog typically consumes 70 percent of the company's marketing budget each year. However, all that is being reduced thanks to technology. IKEA's catalog is going digital. Instead of a couch or bed or table or entire room, many items depicted in the catalogs are now merely pixels instead of pine. This year, 12 percent of the content online, in catalogs, and in brochures is not even real, and that proportion will increase to 25 percent next year. Using 3-D graphics to create the scenes, IKEA can cut costs and more easily manipulate imagery from one country to the next. Whereas Americans might prefer darker woods, a given living room can be shown with lighter woods for Japanese consumers. Don't expect to find any fake people or pets, however, because 3-D figures tend to look like ghosts.

15-9. Visit www.ikea.com and compare a catalog from one country to that of another. What differences do you notice? Can you discern that some photos are 3-D mock-ups instead of real rooms with furniture? (AACSB: Written and Oral Communication; Information Technology; Reflective Thinking)

Marketing Ethics India's Bitter Pill

India's Supreme Court delivered what might be the final nail in the coffin of pharmaceutical innovation in India by rejecting Novartis' attempt to win patent protection for a potentially life-saving drug. The ruling comes after more than six years of legal battles. Other multinational pharmaceutical companies have suffered setbacks related to patents as well. Bayer's patent for its expensive cancer drug was revoked after being challenged by an Indian generic drug manufacturer, and Bayer was even ordered to issue a license to the Indian company so it could copy Bayer's drug and sell it for one-thirtieth the price Bayer charged. Roche also had a patent revoked after challenges from local companies and health organizations. India reluctantly agreed to offer patent protection after joining the World Trade Organization in 1995, but it seems reluctant to grant or maintain patent protection to multinational pharmaceutical firms. India is a fast-growing market, with pharmaceuticals demand expected to reach almost $50 billion by 2020 from its current $11 billion. However, this market is dominated by low-cost Indian generic drug producers, and India's government seems bent on protecting that industry. The Supreme Court ruling was praised by public-health advocacy groups, such as Medicins Sans Frontieres (MSF), who see this as a way to get low-cost drugs in India and other developing nations as India is the largest supplier of low-cost HIV and other drugs to these nations. Novaritis' drug, Glivec, costs almost $2,000 per month compared with $200 per month for comparable generic versions in India, which didn't help the company's case. However, the company claims that 95 percent of 16,000 patients taking Glivec in India receive it free of charge through a company support program.

15-10. Debate both sides of this issue. Should pharmaceutical companies be granted patents in less-developed countries? (AACSB: Written and Oral Communication; Ethical Understanding and Reasoning)

15-11. Discuss another example of multinational companies having difficulty expanding into India. (AACSB: Written and Oral Communication; Reflective Thinking)

Marketing by the Numbers Alternative Attractive Markets

Colleges and universities in the United States offering graduate degrees enjoyed double-digit growth for nearly a decade, particularly from Chinese applicants. But that is changing. Applications from Chinese students declined 5 percent for the 2013–2014 academic year, dropping the overall graduate school application growth rate from foreign students to just 1 percent. This has schools that offer business, engineering, life sciences, and physical and earth sciences graduate degrees wondering how they will fill their classrooms. One bright spot is applications from Brazilians, which increased 24 percent because of a push by the Brazilian government to boost advanced degrees from U.S. schools. Brazil is currently the sixth largest economy in the world, but not enough of its citizens hold advanced degrees, which threatens the country's future growth. Many U.S. schools are wondering if this market is worthy of more marketing efforts to replace the lost Chinese applicants.

15-12. Develop a relevant demographic profile of Brazil to present to a graduate school director to inform him or her about this potential market of students. (AACSB: Written and Oral Communication; Information Technology; Reflective Thinking)

15-13. Is this an attractive market for U.S. graduate programs? Refer to Appendix 3: Marketing by the Numbers to develop a market potential estimation of this market. (AACSB: Written and Oral Communication; Analytical Thinking; Reflective Thinking)

Video Case The U.S. Film Industry

If you like movies, you've no doubt seen a foreign film at some point. But did you know that American films are some of the biggest and most anticipated foreign films in the world? In fact, foreign box office and DVD sales account for nearly 70 percent of all revenues of the U.S. film industry. With that much financial impact, foreign markets are playing a bigger and bigger role not only in the pricing, distribution, and promotion of U.S. films, but in developing the product itself.

This video illustrates the challenges faced by the U.S. film industry stemming from differences in the marketing environment in different international markets. The result is that this industry is now like any other export industry. The marketing mix must be adapted at an optimum level in order to meet the needs of global markets while still maintaining the benefits of standardization.

After viewing the video featuring the U.S. film industry, answer the following questions:

15-14. Which part of the marketing environment seems to be having the greatest impact on U.S. films abroad?

15-15. Which of the five strategies for adapting products and promotion for the global market is most relevant to the U.S. film industry?

15-16. Is the U.S. film industry now dependent upon foreign markets for success? Compare this to other U.S. exports.

Company Cases 15 IKEA / 5 Veterinary Pet Insurance

See Appendix 1 for cases appropriate for this chapter. **Case 15, IKEA: Making Life Better for the World's Many People**. IKEA manages to sell the same couch in 41 different countries by creating the perfect balance between standardization and adaptation. **Case 5, Veterinary Pet Insurance: Health Insurance for Our Furry—or Feathery—Friends**. Consumer decisions are influenced by numerous factors that go way beyond dollars and cents. Veterinary Pet Insurance recognizes the value consumers place on emotional bonds.

MyMarketingLab

Go to **mymktlab.com** for Auto-graded writing questions as well as the following Assisted-graded writing questions:

15-17. What factors do companies consider when deciding on possible global markets to enter? (AACSB: Written and Oral Communication; Reflective Thinking)

15-18. Visit www.ikea.com and compare a catalog from one country to that of another. Note the prices of some of the products. Convert some of the foreign prices to U.S. dollars and compare them to the prices in the U.S. catalog. Are the prices equivalent? Are they consistently higher or lower? (AACSB: Written and Oral Communication; Reflective Thinking)

15-19. Mymktlab Only—comprehensive writing assignment for this chapter.

16 Sustainable Marketing

Social Responsibility and Ethics

CHAPTER ROAD MAP

Objective Outline

Previewing the Concepts

In this final chapter, we'll examine the concepts of sustainable marketing, meeting the needs of consumers, businesses, and society—now and in the future—through socially and environmentally responsible marketing actions. We'll start by defining sustainable marketing and then look at some common criticisms of marketing as it impacts individual consumers, as well as public actions that promote sustainable marketing. Finally, we'll see how companies themselves can benefit from proactively pursuing sustainable marketing practices that bring value to not only individual customers but also society as a whole. Sustainable marketing actions are more than just the right thing to do; they're also good for business.

First, let's look at an example of sustainable marketing in action at Unilever, the world's third-largest consumer products company. For 14 years running, Unilever has been named sustainability leader in the food and beverage industry by the Dow Jones Sustainability Indexes. The company recently launched its Sustainable Living Plan, by which it intends to double its size by 2020 while at the same time reducing its impact on the planet and increasing the social benefits arising from its activities. That's an ambitious goal.

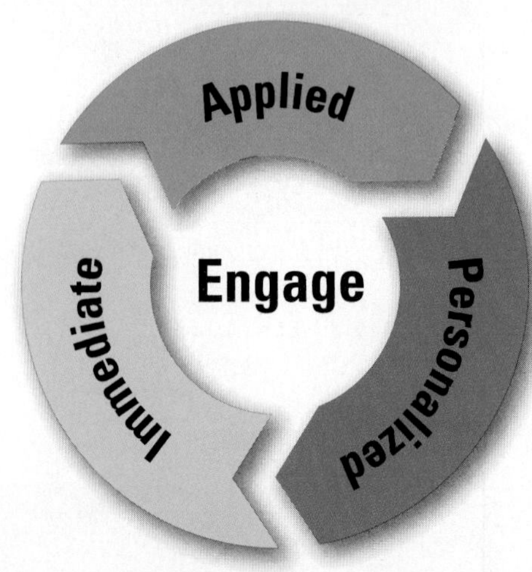

First Stop

Sustainability at Unilever: Creating a Better Future Every Day

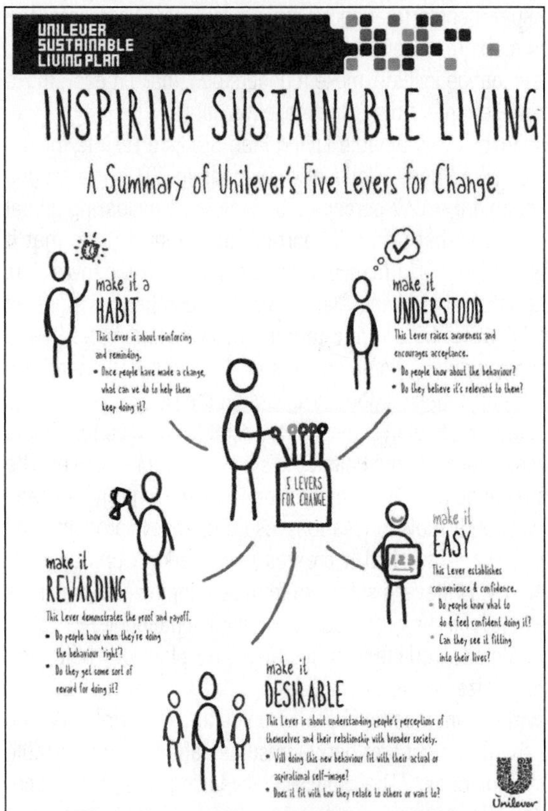

UNILEVER SUSTAINABLE LIVING PLAN
INSPIRING SUSTAINABLE LIVING
A Summary of Unilever's Five Levers for Change
make it a HABIT
This Lever is about reinforcing and reminding.
• Once people have made a change, what can we do to help them keep doing it?
make it UNDERSTOOD
This Lever raises awareness and encourages acceptance.
• Do people know about the behaviour?
• Do they believe it's relevant to them?
5 LEVERS FOR CHANGE
make it EASY
This Lever establishes convenience & confidence.
• Do people know what to do & feel confident doing it?
• Can they see it fitting into their lives?
make it REWARDING
This Lever demonstrates the proof and payoff.
• Do people know when they're doing the behaviour 'right'?
• Do they get some sort of reward for doing it?
make it DESIRABLE
This Lever is about understanding people's perceptions of themselves and their relationship with broader society.
• Will doing this new behaviour fit with their actual or aspirational self-image?
• Does it fit with how they relate to others or want to?
Unilever

» Under its Sustainable Living Plan, Unilever has identified "Five Levers for Change"—things it can do to inspire its more than 2 billion consumers around the world to adopt sustainable behaviors.

When Paul Polman took over as CEO of Unilever a few years ago, the foods, home, and personal care products company was a slumbering giant. Despite its stable of star-studded brands—including the likes of Dove, Axe, Noxema, Sunsilk, OMO, Hellmann's, Knorr, Lipton, and Ben & Jerry's—Unilever had experienced a decade of stagnant sales and profits. The company needed renewed energy and purpose. "To drag the world back to sanity, we need to know why we are here," said Polman.

To answer the "why are we here" question and find a more energizing mission, Polman looked beyond the usual corporate goals of growing sales, profits, and shareholder value. Instead, he asserted, growth results from accomplishing a broader social and environmental mission. Unilever exists "for consumers, not shareholders," he said. "If we are in sync with consumer needs and the environment in which we operate, and take responsibility for our [societal impact], then the shareholder will also be rewarded."

Evaluating and working on societal and environmental impact is nothing new at Unilever. Prior to Polman taking the reins, the company already had multiple programs in place to manage the impact of its products and operations. But the existing programs and results—while good—simply didn't go far enough for Polman. So in late 2010 Unilever launched its Sustainable Living Plan—an aggressive long-term plan that takes capitalism to the next level. Under the plan, the company has set out to "create a better future every day for people around the world: the people who work for us, those we do business with, the billions of people who use our products, and future generations whose quality of life depends on the way we protect the environment today." According to Polman, Unilever's long-run *commercial* success depends on how well it manages the *social* and *environmental* impact of its actions.

The Sustainable Living Plan sets out three major social and environmental objectives to be accomplished by 2020: "(1) To help more than one billion people take action to improve their health and well-being; (2) to halve the environmental footprint of the making and use of our products; and (3) to source 100 percent of our agricultural raw materials sustainably."

Under Unilever's Sustainable Living Plan, the consumer goods giant has set out to "create a better future every day for people around the world." Unilever's long-run *commercial* success depends on how well it manages the *social* and *environmental* impact of its actions.

The Sustainable Living Plan pulls together all of the work Unilever had already been doing and sets ambitious new sustainability goals. These goals span the entire value chain, from how the company sources raw materials to how consumers use and dispose of its products. "Our aim is to make our activities more sustainable and also encourage our customers, suppliers, and others to do the same," says the company.

On the "upstream supply side," more than half of Unilever's raw materials come from agriculture, so the company is helping suppliers develop sustainable farming practices that meet its own high expectations for environmental and social impact. Unilever assesses suppliers against two sets of standards. The first is the Unilever Supplier Code, which calls for socially responsible actions regarding human rights, labor practices, product safety, and care for the environment. Second, specifically for agricultural suppliers, the Unilever Sustainable Agriculture Code details Unilever's expectations for sustainable agriculture practices, so that it and its suppliers "can commit to the sustainability journey together."

But Unilever's Sustainable Living Plan goes far beyond simply creating more responsible supply and distribution chains. Approximately 68 percent of the total greenhouse gas footprint of Unilever's products, and 50 percent of the water footprint, occur during consumer use. So Unilever is also working with its consumers to improve the social and environmental impact of its products in use. Around 2 billion people in 190 markets worldwide use a Unilever product on any given day. Therefore, small everyday consumer actions can add up to a big difference. Unilever sums it up with this equation: "Unilever brands × small everyday actions × billions of consumers = big difference."

For example, almost one-third of households worldwide use Unilever laundry products to do their washing—approximately 125 billion washes every year. Therefore, under its Sustainable Living Plan, Unilever is both creating more eco-friendly laundry products and motivating consumers to improve their laundry habits.

Around the world, for instance, Unilever is encouraging consumers to wash clothes at lower temperatures and use the correct dosage of detergent. Unilever products such as OMO and Persil Small & Mighty concentrated laundry detergents use less packaging, making them cheaper and less polluting to transport. More important, they wash efficiently at lower temperatures and use less energy. Another Unilever product, Comfort One Rinse fabric conditioner, was created for hand washing clothes in developing and emerging markets where water is often in short supply. The innovative product requires only one bucket of water for rinsing rather than three, saving consumers time, effort, and 30 liters of water per wash.

Such energy and water savings don't show up on Unilever's income statement, but they will be extremely important to the people and the planet. Similarly, small changes in product nutrition and customer eating habits can have a surprisingly big impact on human health. "Ultimately," says the company, "we will only succeed if we inspire people around the world to take small, everyday actions that can add up to a big difference for the world." To meet this objective, Unilever has identified "Five Levers for Change"—things that its marketers can do to inspire people to adopt specific sustainable behaviors. The model helps marketers identify the barriers and triggers for change. The levers for change include: make it understood, make it easy, make it desirable, make it rewarding, and make it a habit.

Will Unilever's Sustainable Living Plan produce results for the company? So far, so good. Unilever's revenues in 2012 (the second year of the plan) grew 12.7 percent, a solid figure considering global market volatility. Perhaps more important, at the same time that it improves its top-line performance, Unilever is progressing toward its aggressive Sustainable Living Plan goals. The company is right on target with 54 of its 59 specific targets involving improved health and well-being, reducing its environmental footprint, and enhancing livelihoods. And it's making good progress on the other five.

The sustainability plan is not just the right thing to do for people and the environment, claims Polman, it's also right for Unilever. The quest for sustainability saves money by reducing energy use and minimizing waste. It fuels innovation, resulting in new products and new consumer benefits. And it creates new market opportunities: More than half of Unilever's sales are from developing countries, the very places that face the greatest sustainability challenges.

In all, Polman predicts, the sustainability plan will help Unilever double in size, while also creating a better future for billions of people without increasing the environmental footprint. "We do not believe there is a conflict between sustainability and profitable growth," he concludes. "The daily act of making and selling consumer goods drives economic and social progress. There are billions of people around the world who deserve the better quality of life that everyday products like soap, shampoo, and tea can provide. Sustainable living is not a pipedream. It can be done, and there is very little downside."[1]

Responsible marketers discover what consumers want and respond with market offerings that create value for buyers and capture value in return. The *marketing concept* is a philosophy of customer value and mutual gain. Its practice leads the economy by an invisible hand to satisfy the many and changing needs of millions of consumers.

Sustainable marketing
Socially and environmentally responsible marketing that meets the present needs of consumers and businesses while also preserving or enhancing the ability of future generations to meet their needs.

Not all marketers follow the marketing concept, however. In fact, some companies use questionable marketing practices that serve their own rather than consumers' interests. Moreover, even well-intentioned marketing actions that meet the current needs of some consumers may cause immediate or future harm to other consumers or the larger society. Responsible marketers must consider whether their actions are sustainable in the longer run.

This chapter examines sustainable marketing and the social and environmental effects of private marketing practices. First, we address the question: What is sustainable marketing and why is it important?

Author Comment
Marketers must think beyond immediate customer satisfaction and business performance toward strategies that preserve the world for future generations.

Sustainable Marketing

Sustainable marketing calls for socially and environmentally responsible actions that meet the present needs of consumers and businesses while also preserving or enhancing the ability of future generations to meet their needs. **Figure 16.1** compares the sustainable marketing concept with marketing concepts we studied in earlier chapters.

The *marketing concept* recognizes that organizations thrive from day to day by determining the current needs and wants of target customers and fulfilling those needs and wants more effectively and efficiently than competitors do. It focuses on meeting the company's

Figure 16.1 Sustainable Marketing

The marketing concept means meeting the current needs of both customers and the company. But that can sometimes mean compromising the future of both.

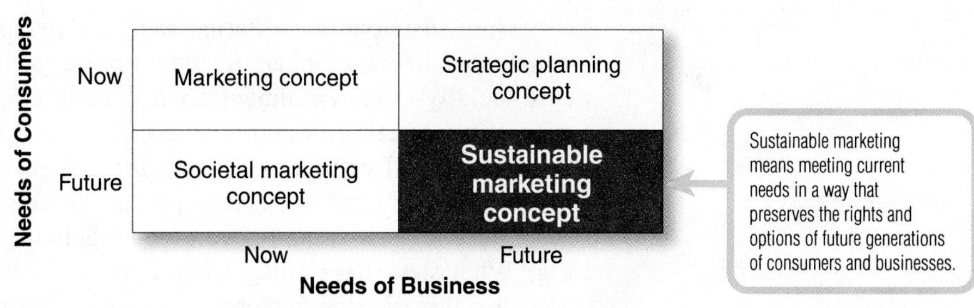

short-term sales, growth, and profit needs by engaging customers and giving customers what they want now. However, satisfying consumers' immediate needs and desires doesn't always serve the future best interests of either customers or the business.

For example, McDonald's early decisions to market tasty but fat- and salt-laden fast foods created immediate satisfaction for customers, as well as sales and profits for the company. However, critics assert that McDonald's and other fast-food chains contributed to a longer-term national obesity epidemic, damaging consumer health and burdening the national health system. In turn, many consumers began looking for healthier eating options, causing a slump in the sales and profits of the fast-food industry. Beyond issues of ethical behavior and social welfare, McDonald's was also criticized for the sizable environmental footprint of its vast global operations, everything from wasteful packaging and solid waste creation to inefficient energy use in its stores. Thus, McDonald's strategy was not sustainable in terms of either consumer or company benefit.

Whereas the *societal marketing concept* identified in Figure 16.1 considers the future welfare of consumers and the *strategic planning concept* considers future company needs, the *sustainable marketing concept* considers both. Sustainable marketing calls for socially and environmentally responsible actions that meet both the immediate and future needs of customers and the company.

For example, McDonald's has responded to these challenges in recent years with a more sustainable "Plan to Win" strategy of diversifying into salads, fruits, grilled chicken, low-fat milk, and other healthy fare. The company also launched a major multifaceted education campaign—called "it's what i eat and what i do . . . i'm lovin' it"—to help consumers better understand the keys to living balanced, active lifestyles. And recently, McDonald's began a "favorites under 400 calories" campaign in which 400-and-fewer-calorie items are featured in its advertising and on menu boards in its restaurant. The chain points out that 80 percent of its national menu is under 400 calories and that it wants to help customers feel better about the items they are choosing.[2]

Sustainable marketing: Under its "Plan to Win" strategy, McDonald's has created sustainable value for both customers and the company. Now, 80 percent of the chain's menu is under 400 calories, including this Egg White Delight McMuffin, which weighs in with 8 grams of whole grain against only 250 calories and 5 grams of fat.

The McDonald's "Plan to Win" strategy also addresses environmental issues. For example, it calls for food-supply sustainability, reduced and environmentally sustainable packaging, reuse and recycling, and more responsible store designs. McDonald's has even developed an environmental scorecard that rates its suppliers' performance in areas such as water use, energy use, and solid waste management.

McDonald's more sustainable strategy is benefiting the company as well as its customers. Since announcing its "Plan to Win" strategy, McDonald's sales have increased by almost 60 percent, and profits have more than tripled. Thus, McDonald's is well positioned for a sustainably profitable future.[3]

Truly sustainable marketing requires a smooth-functioning marketing system in which consumers, companies, public policy makers, and others work together to ensure socially and environmentally responsible marketing actions. Unfortunately, however, the marketing system doesn't always work smoothly. The following sections examine several sustainability questions: What are the most frequent social criticisms of marketing? What steps have private citizens taken to curb marketing ills? What steps have legislators and government agencies taken to promote sustainable marketing? What steps have enlightened companies taken to carry out socially responsible and ethical marketing that creates sustainable value for both individual customers and society as a whole?

Author Comment
In most ways, we all benefit greatly from marketing activities. However, like most other human endeavors, marketing has its flaws. Here we present both sides of some of the most common criticisms of marketing.

Social Criticisms of Marketing

Marketing receives much criticism. Some of this criticism is justified; much is not. Social critics claim that certain marketing practices hurt individual consumers, society as a whole, and other business firms.

Marketing's Impact on Individual Consumers

Consumers have many concerns about how well the American marketing system serves their interests. Surveys usually show that consumers hold mixed or even slightly unfavorable attitudes toward marketing practices. Consumer advocates, government agencies, and other critics have accused marketing of harming consumers through high prices, deceptive practices, high-pressure selling, shoddy or unsafe products, planned obsolescence, and poor service to disadvantaged consumers. Such questionable marketing practices are not sustainable in terms of long-term consumer or business welfare.

High Prices

Many critics charge that the American marketing system causes prices to be higher than they would be under more "sensible" systems. Such high prices are hard to swallow, especially when the economy is tight. Critics point to three factors—*high costs of distribution*, *high advertising and promotion costs*, and *excessive markups*.

High Costs of Distribution. A long-standing charge is that greedy marketing channel members mark up prices beyond the value of their services. Critics charge that there are too many intermediaries, that intermediaries are inefficient, or that they provide unnecessary or duplicate services. As a result, distribution costs too much, and consumers pay for these excessive costs in the form of higher prices.

How do resellers answer these charges? They argue that intermediaries do work that would otherwise have to be done by manufacturers or consumers. Markups reflect services that consumers themselves want—more convenience, larger stores and assortments, more service, longer store hours, return privileges, and others. In fact, they argue, retail competition is so intense that margins are actually quite low. If some resellers try to charge too much relative to the value they add, other resellers will step in with lower prices. Low-price stores such as Walmart, Costco, and other discounters pressure their competitors to operate efficiently and keep their prices down. In fact, in the wake of the recent recession, only the most efficient retailers have survived profitably.

High Advertising and Promotion Costs. Modern marketing is also accused of pushing up prices to finance heavy advertising and sales promotion. >> For example, a heavily promoted national brand sells for much more than a virtually identical non-branded or store-branded product. Differentiated products—cosmetics, detergents, toiletries—include promotion and packaging costs that can amount to 40 percent or more of the manufacturer's price to the retailer. Critics charge that much of this packaging and promotion adds only psychological, not functional, value to the product.

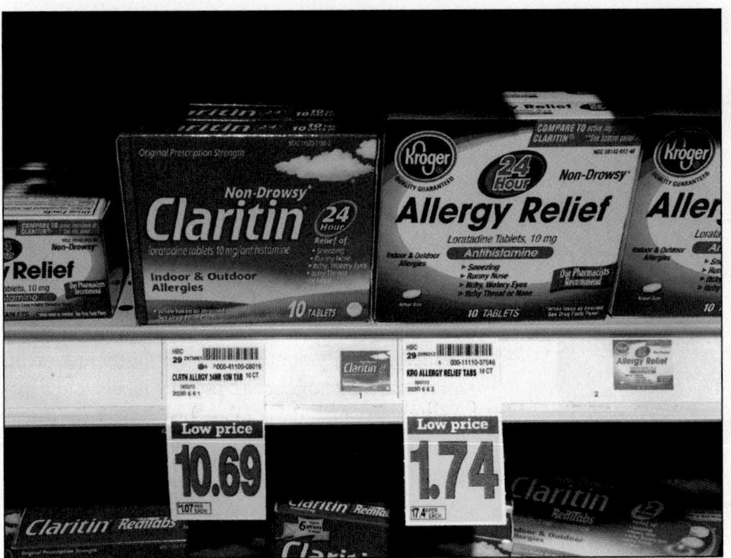

>> A heavily promoted national brand sells for much more than a virtually identical nonbranded or store-branded product. Critics charge that promotion adds only psychological value to the product rather than functional value.

Courtesy of Keri Miksza.

Marketers respond that although advertising adds to product costs, it also adds value by informing potential buyers of the availability and merits of a brand. Brand name products may cost more, but branding gives buyers assurances of consistent quality. Moreover, although consumers can usually buy functional versions of products at lower prices, they *want* and are willing to pay more for products that also provide psychological benefits—that make them feel wealthy, attractive, or special. In addition, heavy advertising and promotion may be necessary for a firm to match competitors' efforts; the business would lose "share of mind" if it did not match competitive spending.

At the same time, companies are cost conscious about promotion and try to spend their funds wisely. Today's more frugal consumers are demanding genuine value for the prices they pay. The continuing shift toward buying store brands and generics suggests that when it comes to value, consumers want action, not just talk.

Excessive Markups. Critics also charge that some companies mark up goods excessively. They point to the drug industry, where a pill costing five cents to make may cost the consumer $2 to buy. They point to the pricing tactics of funeral homes that prey on the confused emotions of bereaved relatives, and the high charges for auto repairs and other services.

Marketers respond that most businesses try to deal fairly with consumers because they want to build customer relationships and repeat business, and that most consumer abuses are unintentional. When shady marketers take advantage of consumers, they should be reported to Better Business Bureaus and state and federal agencies. Marketers also respond that consumers often don't understand the reasons for high markups. For example, pharmaceutical markups must cover the costs of purchasing, promoting, and distributing existing medicines, plus the high research and development (R&D) costs of formulating and testing new medicines. As pharmaceuticals company GlaxoSmithKline has stated in its ads, "Today's medicines finance tomorrow's miracles."

Deceptive Practices

Marketers are sometimes accused of deceptive practices that lead consumers to believe they will get more value than they actually do. Deceptive practices fall into three groups: pricing, promotion, and packaging. *Deceptive pricing* includes practices such as falsely advertising "factory" or "wholesale" prices or a large price reduction from a phony high retail list price. *Deceptive promotion* includes practices such as misrepresenting the product's features or performance or luring customers to the store for a bargain that is out of stock. *Deceptive packaging* includes exaggerating package contents through subtle design, using misleading labeling, or describing size in misleading terms.

Deceptive practices have led to legislation and other consumer protection actions. For example, in 1938 Congress enacted the Wheeler-Lea Act, which gave the Federal Trade Commission (FTC) power to regulate "unfair or deceptive acts or practices." The FTC has since published several guidelines listing deceptive practices. Despite regulations, however, some critics argue that deceptive claims are still common, even for well-known brands. For example, the FTC recently upheld charges that POM Wonderful made false and unsupported health claims for its pomegranate juice and supplements. Skechers recently paid $55 million to resolve allegations by the FTC and attorneys general in 44 states that it made false advertising claims that its rocker-bottom Shape-ups and other toning shoes would help customers tone muscles and lose weight.[4] And confections and candy

>> **Deceptive practices: Ferrero recently settled a class action suit claiming that ads for its popular, gooey-good Nutella chocolate hazelnut spread made deceptive claims that the product was "healthy" and "part of a balanced meal."**

REUTERS/Stefano Rellandini.

maker >> Ferrero recently paid out $3 million to settle a class action suit claiming that ads for its popular Nutella chocolate hazelnut spread made deceptive claims that the product was "healthy" and "part of a balanced meal."[5]

> It all began when a California mom filed a deceptive advertising claim after realizing that the Nutella she'd been feeding her 4-year-old daughter at breakfast was actually little short of the next best thing to a candy bar. While TV ads talked about Nutella's "simple, quality ingredients like hazelnuts, skim milk, and a hint of cocoa," product labels told a different story. Nutella is made primarily from sugar and palm oil. Each 2-tablespoon serving of the gooey-good spread contains 21 grams of sugar and 200 calories, with half of those calories coming from 11 grams of fat. Nutella ads never mentioned the sugar or fat. In addition to the $3-million deceptive advertising settlement, Ferrero has agreed to change its advertising and nutritional labels.

The toughest problem often is defining what is "deceptive." For instance, an advertiser's claim that its chewing gum will "rock your world" isn't intended to be taken literally. Instead, the advertiser might claim, it is "puffery"—innocent exaggeration for effect. However, others claim that puffery and alluring imagery can harm consumers in subtle ways. Think about the popular and long-running MasterCard Priceless commercials that once painted pictures of consumers fulfilling their priceless dreams despite the costs. The ads suggested that your credit card could make it happen. But critics charge that such imagery by credit card companies encouraged a spend-now-pay-later attitude that caused many consumers to *over*use their cards, contributing heavily to the nation's recent financial crisis.

Marketers argue that most companies avoid deceptive practices. Because such practices harm a company's business in the long run, they simply aren't sustainable. Profitable customer relationships are built on a foundation of value and trust. If consumers do not get what they expect, they will switch to more reliable products. In addition, consumers usually protect themselves from deception. Most consumers recognize a marketer's selling intent and are careful when they buy, sometimes even to the point of not believing completely true product claims.

High-Pressure Selling

Salespeople are sometimes accused of high-pressure selling that persuades people to buy goods they had no thought of buying. It is often said that insurance, real estate, and used cars are *sold*, not *bought*. Salespeople are trained to deliver smooth, canned talks to entice purchases. They sell hard because sales contests promise big prizes to those who sell the most. Similarly, TV infomercial pitchmen use "yell and sell" presentations that create a sense of consumer urgency that only those with the strongest willpower can resist.

But in most cases, marketers have little to gain from high-pressure selling. Although such tactics may work in one-time selling situations for short-term gain, most selling involves building long-term relationships with valued customers. High-pressure or deceptive selling can seriously damage such relationships. For example, imagine a P&G account manager trying to pressure a Walmart buyer or an IBM salesperson trying to browbeat an information technology manager at GE. It simply wouldn't work.

Shoddy, Harmful, or Unsafe Products

Another criticism concerns poor product quality or function. One complaint is that, too often, products and services are not made well or do not perform well. A second complaint concerns product safety. Product safety has been a problem for several reasons, including company indifference, increased product complexity, and poor quality control. A third complaint is that many products deliver little benefit, or may even be harmful.

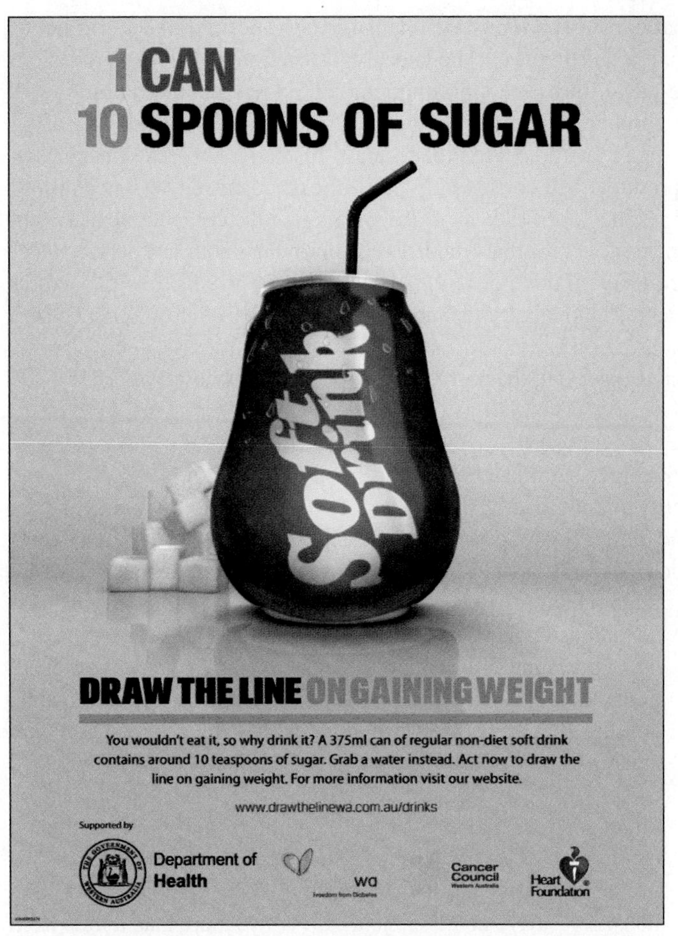

Harmful products: Is the soft drink industry being irresponsible by promoting overindulgence, or is it simply serving the wants of customers by offering products that ping consumer taste buds while letting consumers make their own consumption choices?

Department of Health Western Australia.

For example, think about the soft drink industry. Many critics blame the plentiful supply of sugar-laden, high-calorie soft drinks for the nation's rapidly growing obesity epidemic. Studies show that more than two-thirds of American adults are either obese or overweight. In addition, one-third of American children are obese. This national weight issue continues despite repeated medical studies showing that excess weight brings increased risks for heart disease, diabetes, and other maladies, even cancer.[6] The critics are quick to fault what they see as greedy beverage marketers cashing in on vulnerable consumers, turning us into a nation of Big Gulpers. New York City's mayor even tried to pass a ban on soft drinks 16 ounces and larger.

Is the soft drink industry being socially irresponsible by aggressively promoting overindulgence to ill-informed or unwary consumers? Or is it simply serving the wants of customers by offering products that ping consumer taste buds while letting consumers make their own consumption choices? Is it the industry's job to police public tastes? As in many matters of social responsibility, what's right and wrong may be a matter of opinion. Whereas some analysts criticize the industry, others suggest that responsibility lies with consumers. "Soft drinks have unfairly become the whipping boy of most anti-obesity campaigns," suggests one business reporter. "Maybe friends shouldn't give friends Big Gulps, but to my knowledge, no one's ever been forced to buy and drink one. There's an element of personal responsibility and control that [needs to be addressed]."[7]

Most manufacturers *want* to produce quality goods. After all, the way a company deals with product quality and safety problems can damage or help its reputation. Companies selling poor-quality or unsafe products risk damaging conflicts with consumer groups and regulators. Unsafe products can result in product liability suits and large awards for damages. More fundamentally, consumers who are unhappy with a firm's products may avoid future purchases and talk other consumers into doing the same. In today's social media and online review environment, word of poor quality can spread like wildfire. Thus, quality missteps are not consistent with sustainable marketing. Today's marketers know that good quality results in customer value and satisfaction, which in turn creates sustainable customer relationships.

Planned Obsolescence

Critics also have charged that some companies practice *planned obsolescence*, causing their products to become obsolete before they actually should need replacement. They accuse some producers of using materials and components that will break, wear, rust, or rot sooner than they should. And if the products themselves don't wear out fast enough, other companies are charged with *perceived obsolescence*—continually changing consumer concepts of acceptable styles to encourage more and earlier buying. An obvious example is constantly changing clothing fashions.

Still others are accused of introducing planned streams of new products that make older models obsolete, turning consumers into "serial replacers." Critics claim that this occurs in the consumer electronics industries. If you're like most people, you probably have a drawer full of yesterday's hottest technological gadgets—from mobile phones and cameras to iPods and flash drives—now reduced to the status of fossils. It seems that anything more than a year or two old is hopelessly out of date. For example, early iPods had non-removable batteries that failed in about 18 months, so that they had to be replaced. It wasn't until unhappy owners filed a class action suit that Apple started offering replacement batteries. Also, rapid new product launches—as many as three in one 18-month period—made older iPod models obsolete.[8]

Marketers respond that consumers *like* style changes; they get tired of the old goods and want a new look in fashion. Or they *want* the latest high-tech innovations, even if older models still work. No one has to buy a new product, and if too few people like it, it will simply fail. Finally, most companies do not design their products to break down earlier because they do not want to lose customers to other brands. Instead, they seek constant improvement to ensure that products will consistently meet or exceed customer expectations.

Much of the so-called planned obsolescence is the working of the competitive and technological forces in a free society—forces that lead to ever-improving goods and services. For example, if Apple produced a new iPhone or iPad that would last 10 years, few consumers would want it. Instead, buyers want the latest technological innovations. "Obsolescence isn't something companies are forcing on us," confirms one analyst. "It's progress, and it's something we pretty much demand. As usual, the market gives us exactly what we want."[9]

Poor Service to Disadvantaged Consumers

Finally, the American marketing system has been accused of poorly serving disadvantaged consumers. For example, critics claim that the urban poor often have to shop in smaller stores that carry inferior goods and charge higher prices. The presence of large national chain stores in low-income neighborhoods would help to keep prices down. However, the critics accuse major chain retailers of *redlining*, drawing a red line around disadvantaged neighborhoods and avoiding placing stores there.

For example, the nation's poor areas have 30 percent fewer supermarkets than affluent areas do. » As a result, many low-income consumers find themselves in *food deserts*, which are awash with small markets offering frozen pizzas, Cheetos, Moon Pies, and Cokes, but where fruits and vegetables or fresh fish and chicken are out of reach. Currently, some 23.5 million Americans—including 6.5 million children—live in low-income areas that lack stores selling affordable and nutritious foods. What's more, 2.3 million households have no access to a car but live more than a mile from a supermarket, forcing them to shop at convenience stores where expensive processed food is the only dietary choice. In turn, the lack of access to healthy, affordable fresh foods has a negative impact on the health of underserved consumers in these areas. Many national chains, such as Walmart, Walgreens, and SuperValu, have recently agreed to open or expand more stores that bring nutritious and fresh foods to underserved communities.[10]

» Underserved consumers: Because of the lack of supermarkets in low-income areas, many disadvantaged consumers find themselves in "food deserts," with little or no access to healthy, affordable fresh foods.

Clearly, better marketing systems must be built to service disadvantaged consumers. In fact, many marketers profitably target such consumers with legitimate goods and services that create real value. In cases in which marketers do not step in to fill the void, the government likely will. For example, the FTC has taken action against sellers that advertise false values, wrongfully deny services, or charge disadvantaged customers too much.

SPEED BUMP | LINKING THE CONCEPTS

Hit the brakes for a moment. Few marketers *want* to abuse or anger consumers—it's simply not good business. Still, some marketing abuses do occur.

- Think back over the past three months or so and list any instances in which you've suffered a marketing abuse such as those just discussed. Analyze your list: What kinds of companies were involved? Were the abuses intentional? What did the situations have in common?
- Pick one of the instances you listed and describe it in detail. How might you go about righting this wrong? Write out an action plan and then do something to remedy the abuse. If we all took such actions when wronged, there would be far fewer wrongs to right!

Marketing's Impact on Society as a Whole

The American marketing system has been accused of adding to several "evils" in American society at large, such as creating too much materialism, too few social goods, and a glut of cultural pollution.

False Wants and Too Much Materialism

Critics have charged that the marketing system urges too much interest in material possessions, and that America's love affair with worldly possessions is not sustainable. Too often, people are judged by what they *own* rather than by who they *are*. The critics do not view this interest in material things as a natural state of mind but rather as a matter of false wants created by marketing. Marketers, they claim, stimulate people's desires for goods and create materialistic models of the good life. Thus, marketers have created an endless cycle of mass consumption based on a distorted interpretation of the "American Dream."

In this view, marketing's purpose is to promote consumption, and the inevitable outcome of successful marketing is unsustainable *over*consumption. According to the critics, more is not always better. Some critics have taken their concerns straight to the public. >> For example, consumer activist Annie Leonard founded *The Story of Stuff* project with a 20-minute online video about the social and environmental consequences of America's love affair with stuff—"How our obsession with stuff is trashing the planet, our communities, and our health." The video has been viewed more than 11.7 million times online and in thousands of schools and community centers around the world.[11]

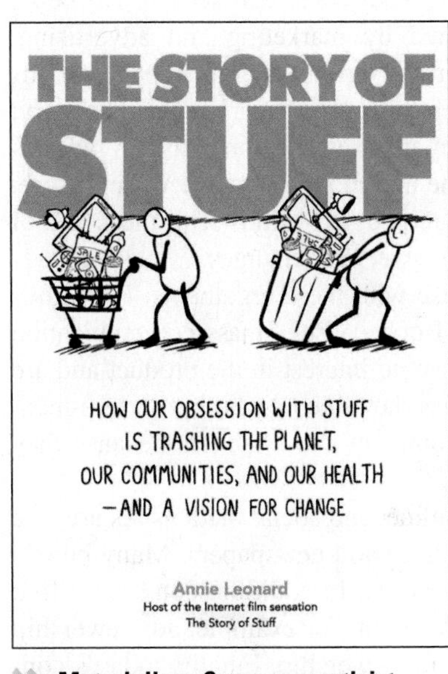

>> Materialism: Consumer activist Annie Leonard's "The Story of Stuff" video about the social and environmental consequences of America's love affair with stuff has been viewed more than 11.7 million times online and in thousands of schools and community centers around the world.

© dbimages/Alamy.

Marketers respond that such criticisms overstate the power of business to create needs. They claim people have strong defenses against advertising and other marketing tools. Marketers are most effective when they appeal to existing wants rather than when they attempt to create new ones. Furthermore, people seek information when making important purchases and often do not rely on single sources. Even minor purchases that may be affected by advertising messages lead to repeat purchases only if the product delivers the promised customer value. Finally, the high failure rate of new products shows that companies are not able to control demand.

On a deeper level, our wants and values are influenced not only by marketers but also by family, peer groups, religion, cultural background, and education. If Americans are highly materialistic, these values arose out of basic socialization processes that go much deeper than business and marketing could produce alone.

Moreover, consumption patterns and attitudes are also subject to larger forces, such as the economy. As discussed in Chapter 1, the recent Great Recession put a damper on materialism and conspicuous spending. Many observers predict a new age of more sensible consumption. As a result, instead of encouraging today's more sensible consumers to overspend their means, most marketers are working to help them find greater value with less.

Too Few Social Goods

Business has been accused of overselling private goods at the expense of public goods. As private goods increase, they require more public services that are usually not forthcoming. For example, an increase in automobile ownership (private good) requires more highways, traffic control, parking spaces, and police services (public goods). The overselling of private goods results in social costs. For cars, some of the social costs include traffic congestion, gasoline shortages, and air pollution. For example, American travelers lose, on average, 38 hours a year in traffic jams, costing the United States more than $100 billion a year—$818 per commuter. In the process, they waste 2.9 billion gallons of fuel and emit millions of tons of greenhouse gases.[12]

A way must be found to restore a balance between private and public goods. One option is to make producers bear the full social costs of their operations. For example, the government is requiring automobile manufacturers to build cars with more efficient engines and better pollution-control systems. Automakers will then raise their prices to cover the extra costs. If buyers find the price of some car models too high, however, these models will disappear. Demand will then move to those producers that can support the sum of the private and social costs.

» Balancing private and public goods: Raising the peak-load toll on the Bay Bridge between Oakland and San Francisco reduced traffic flow and cut the average wait time in half.

A second option is to make consumers pay the social costs. For example, many cities around the world are now charging congestion tolls in an effort to reduce traffic congestion. » To decrease rush hour traffic on the Bay Bridge between Oakland and San Francisco, California, the Metropolitan Transportation Commission charges a $6 toll during peak commute hours versus $4 at other times. The charge reduced the flow of drivers during peak hours, cutting the average 32-minute wait time some bridges approach in half.[13]

Cultural Pollution

Critics charge the marketing system with creating *cultural pollution*. They feel our senses are being constantly assaulted by marketing and advertising. Commercials interrupt serious programs; pages of ads obscure magazines; billboards mar beautiful scenery; spam fills our e-mailboxes; flashing display ads intrude on our online and mobile screens. What's more, the critics claim, these interruptions continually pollute people's minds with messages of materialism, sex, power, or status. Some critics call for sweeping changes.

Marketers answer the charges of commercial noise with these arguments: First, they hope that their ads primarily reach the target audience. But because of mass-communication channels, some ads are bound to reach people who have no interest in the product and are therefore bored or annoyed. People who buy magazines they like or who opt in to e-mail, social media, or mobile marketing programs rarely complain about the ads because they involve products and services of interest.

Second, because of ads, many television, radio, online, and social media sites are free to users. Ads also help keep down the costs of magazines and newspapers. Many people think viewing ads is a small price to pay for these benefits. In addition, consumers find many television commercials entertaining and seek them out; for example, ad viewership during the Super Bowl usually equals or exceeds game viewership. Finally, today's consumers have alternatives. For example, they can zip or zap TV commercials on recorded programs or avoid them altogether on many paid cable, satellite, and online channels. Thus, to hold consumer attention, advertisers are making their ads more entertaining and informative.

Marketing's Impact on Other Businesses

Critics also charge that a company's marketing practices can harm other companies and reduce competition. They identify three problems: acquisitions of competitors, marketing practices that create barriers to entry, and unfair competitive marketing practices.

Critics claim that firms are harmed and competition is reduced when companies expand by acquiring competitors rather than by developing their own new products. The large number of acquisitions and the rapid pace of industry consolidation over the past several decades have caused concern that vigorous young competitors will be absorbed, thereby reducing competition. In virtually every major industry—retailing, entertainment, financial services, utilities, transportation, automobiles, telecommunications, health care—the number of major competitors is shrinking.

Acquisition is a complex subject. In some cases, acquisitions can be good for society. The acquiring company may gain economies of scale that lead to lower costs and lower prices. In addition, a well-managed company may take over a poorly managed company and improve its efficiency. An industry that was not very competitive might become more competitive after the acquisition. But acquisitions can also be harmful, and therefore are closely regulated by the government.

Critics have also charged that marketing practices bar new companies from entering an industry. Large marketing companies can use patents and heavy promotion spending or tie up suppliers or dealers to keep out or drive out competitors. Those concerned with antitrust regulation recognize that some barriers are the natural result of the economic advantages of doing business on a large scale. Existing and new laws can challenge other barriers. For example, some critics have proposed a progressive tax on advertising spending to reduce the role of selling costs as a major barrier to entry.

Finally, some firms have, in fact, used unfair competitive marketing practices with the intention of hurting or destroying other firms. They may set their prices below costs, threaten to cut off business with suppliers, or discourage the buying of a competitor's products. Although various laws work to prevent such predatory competition, it is often difficult to prove that the intent or action was really predatory.

In recent years, Walmart has been accused of using predatory pricing in selected market areas to drive smaller, mom-and-pop retailers out of business. Walmart has become a lightning rod for protests by citizens in dozens of towns who worry that the megaretailer's unfair practices will choke out local businesses. However, whereas critics charge that Walmart's actions are predatory, others assert that its actions are just the healthy competition of a more-efficient company against less-efficient ones.

For instance, » when Walmart began a program to sell generic drugs at $4 a prescription, local pharmacists complained of predatory pricing. They charged that at those low prices, Walmart must be selling under cost to drive them out of business. But Walmart claimed that, given its substantial buying power and efficient operations, it could make a profit at those prices. The $4 pricing program, the retailer claimed, was not aimed at putting competitors out of business. Rather, it was simply a good competitive move that served customers better and brought more of them in the door. Moreover, Walmart's program drove down prescription prices at the pharmacies of other supermarkets and discount stores, such as Kroger and Target. Currently more than 300 prescription drugs are available for $4 at the various chains, and Walmart claims that the program has saved its customers more than $4.8 billion.[14]

» **Walmart prescription pricing: Is it predatory pricing or is it just good business?**

Associated Press.

Author Comment
Sustainable marketing isn't something that only businesses and governments can do. Through consumerism and environmentalism, consumers themselves can play an important role.

Consumer Actions to Promote Sustainable Marketing

Sustainable marketing calls for more responsible actions by both businesses and consumers. Because some people view businesses as the cause of many economic and social ills, grassroots movements have arisen from time to time to keep businesses in line. Two major movements have been *consumerism* and *environmentalism*.

Consumerism

Consumerism
An organized movement of citizens and government agencies designed to improve the rights and power of buyers in relation to sellers.

Consumerism is an organized movement of citizens and government agencies to improve the rights and power of buyers in relation to sellers. Traditional *sellers' rights* include the following:

- The right to introduce any product in any size and style, provided it is not hazardous to personal health or safety, or, if it is, to include proper warnings and controls
- The right to charge any price for the product, provided no discrimination exists among similar kinds of buyers
- The right to spend any amount to promote the product, provided it is not defined as unfair competition

- The right to use any product message, provided it is not misleading or dishonest in content or execution
- The right to use buying incentive programs, provided they are not unfair or misleading

Traditional *buyers' rights* include the following:

- The right not to buy a product that is offered for sale
- The right to expect the product to be safe
- The right to expect the product to perform as claimed

Comparing these rights, many believe that the balance of power lies on the seller's side. True, the buyer can refuse to buy. But critics feel that the buyer has too little information, education, and protection to make wise decisions when facing sophisticated sellers. Consumer advocates call for the following additional consumer rights:

- The right to be well informed about important aspects of the product
- The right to be protected against questionable products and marketing practices
- The right to influence products and marketing practices in ways that will improve "quality of life"
- The right to consume now in a way that will preserve the world for future generations of consumers

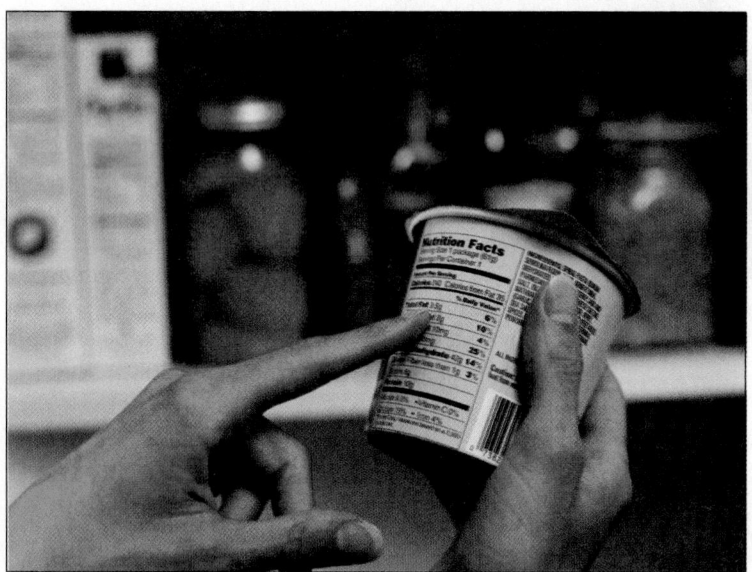

>> Consumer desire for more information led to packing labels with useful facts, from ingredients and nutrition facts to recycling and country of origin information.

Ryan McVay.

Each proposed right has led to more specific proposals by consumerists and consumer protection actions by the government. >> The right to be informed includes the right to know the true interest on a loan (truth in lending), the true cost per unit of a brand (unit pricing), the ingredients in a product (ingredient labeling), the nutritional value of foods (nutritional labeling), product freshness (open dating), and the true benefits of a product (truth in advertising). Proposals related to consumer protection include strengthening consumer rights in cases of business fraud and financial protection, requiring greater product safety, ensuring information privacy, and giving more power to government agencies. Proposals relating to quality of life include controlling the ingredients that go into certain products and packaging and reducing the level of advertising "noise." Proposals for preserving the world for future consumption include promoting the use of sustainable ingredients, recycling and reducing solid wastes, and managing energy consumption.

Sustainable marketing applies not only to businesses and governments but also to consumers. Consumers have not only the *right* but also the *responsibility* to protect themselves instead of leaving this function to the government or someone else. Consumers who believe they got a bad deal have several remedies available, including contacting the company or the media; contacting federal, state, or local agencies; and going to small-claims courts. Consumers should also make good consumption choices, rewarding companies that act responsibly while punishing those that don't. Ultimately, the move from irresponsible consumption to sustainable consumption is in the hands of consumers.

Environmentalism

Whereas consumerists consider whether the marketing system is efficiently serving consumer wants, environmentalists are concerned with marketing's effects on the environment

Environmentalism
An organized movement of concerned citizens, businesses, and government agencies designed to protect and improve people's current and future living environment.

and the environmental costs of serving consumer needs and wants. **Environmentalism** is an organized movement of concerned citizens, businesses, and government agencies designed to protect and improve people's current and future living environment.

Environmentalists are not against marketing and consumption; they simply want people and organizations to operate with more care for the environment. They call for doing away with what sustainability advocate and Unilever CEO Paul Polman calls "mindless consumption." According to Polman, "the road to well-being doesn't go via reduced consumption. It has to be done via more responsible consumption."[15] The marketing system's goal, environmentalists assert, should not be to maximize consumption, consumer choice, or consumer satisfaction but rather to maximize life quality. Life quality means not only the quantity and quality of consumer goods and services but also the quality of the environment, now and for future generations.

Environmentalism is concerned with damage to the ecosystem caused by global warming, resource depletion, toxic and solid wastes, litter, the availability of fresh water, and other problems. Other issues include the loss of recreational areas and the increase in health problems caused by bad air, polluted water, and chemically treated food.

Over the past several decades, such concerns have resulted in federal and state laws and regulations governing industrial commercial practices impacting the environment. Some companies have strongly resented and resisted such environmental regulations, claiming that they are too costly and have made their industries less competitive. These companies responded to consumer environmental concerns by doing only what was required to avert new regulations or keep environmentalists quiet.

Environmental sustainability
A management approach that involves developing strategies that both sustain the environment and produce profits for the company.

In recent years, however, most companies have accepted responsibility for doing no harm to the environment. They are shifting from protest to prevention and from regulation to responsibility. More and more companies are now adopting policies of **environmental sustainability**. Simply put, environmental sustainability is about generating profits while helping to save the planet. Today's enlightened companies are taking action not because someone is forcing them to or to reap short-run profits but because it's the right thing to do—because it's for their customers' well-being, the company's well-being, and the planet's environmental future. For example, fast-food chain Chipotle has successfully built its core mission around environmental sustainability (see Marketing at Work 16.1).

>> Figure 16.2 shows a grid that companies can use to gauge their progress toward environmental sustainability. It includes both internal and external *greening* activities that will pay off for the firm and environment in the short run, and *beyond greening* activities that will pay off in the longer term. At the most basic level, a company can practice *pollution prevention*. This involves more than pollution control—cleaning up waste after it has been created. Pollution prevention means eliminating or minimizing waste *before* it is created. Companies emphasizing prevention have responded with internal green marketing programs—designing and developing ecologically safer products, recyclable and biodegradable packaging, better pollution controls, and more energy-efficient operations.

For example, Nike makes shoes out of "environmentally preferred materials," recycles old sneakers, and educates young people about conservation, reuse, and recycling. Its revolutionary woven Flyknit shoes are lightweight, comfortable, and durable but produce 66 percent less material waste in production—the material wasted making each pair of Flyknits weighs only as much as a sheet of paper.

>> Figure 16.2 The Environmental Sustainability Portfolio

Source: Stuart L. Hart, "Innovation, Creative Destruction, and Sustainability," *Research Technology Management*, September–October 2005, pp. 21–27.

	Today: Greening	Tomorrow: Beyond Greening
Internal	**Pollution prevention** Eliminating or reducing waste before it is created	**New clean technology** Developing new sets of environmental skills and capabilities
External	**Product stewardship** Minimizing environmental impact throughout the entire product life cycle	**Sustainability vision** Creating a strategic framework for future sustainability

How does "environmental sustainability" relate to "marketing sustainability"? Environmental sustainability involves preserving the natural environment, whereas marketing sustainability is a broader concept that involves both the natural and social environments—pretty much everything in this chapter.

MARKETING AT WORK 16.1

Chipotle's Environmental Sustainability Mission: Food With Integrity

Envision this. You're sitting in a restaurant where the people—from the CEO on down to the kitchen crew—obsess over using only the finest ingredients. They come to work each morning inspired by all the "fresh produce and meats they have to marinate, rice they have to cook, and fresh herbs they have to chop," says the CEO. The restaurant prefers to use sustainable, naturally raised ingredients sourced from local family farms. This restaurant is on a mission not just to serve its customers good food but to change the way its entire industry produces food. This sounds like one of those high-falutin', gourmet specialty restaurants, right? Wrong. It's your neighborhood Chipotle Mexican Grill. That's right, it's a fast-food restaurant.

In an age when many fast-feeders seem to be finding ever-cheaper ingredients and centralizing much of their food preparation to cut costs and keep prices low, Chipotle is doing just the opposite. The chain's core sustainable mission is to serve "Food With Integrity." What does that mean? The company explains it this way:

> Chipotle is committed to finding the very best ingredients raised with respect for animals, the environment, and farmers. It means serving the very best sustainably raised food possible with an eye to great taste, great nutrition, and great value. It means that we support and sustain family farmers who respect the land and the animals in their care. It means that whenever possible we use meat from animals raised without the use of antibiotics or added hormones. And it means that we source organic and local produce when practical, and that we use dairy from cows raised without the use of synthetic hormones. In other words, "integrity" is kind of a funny word for "good."

When founder and CEO Steve Ells opened the first Chipotle in Denver in 1993, his primary goal was to make the best gourmet burrito around. However, as the chain grew, Ells found that he didn't like the way the ingredients Chipotle used were raised and processed. So in 2000, Chipotle began developing a supply chain with the goal of producing and using naturally raised, organic, hormone-free, non-genetically-modified ingredients. Pursuing this healthy-food mission was no easy task. As the fast-food industry increasingly moved toward low-cost, efficient food processing, factory farms were booming, whereas independent farms producing naturally raised and organic foods were in decline.

To obtain the ingredients it needed, Chipotle had to develop many new sources. To help that cause, the company founded the Chipotle Cultivate Foundation, which supports family farming and encourages sustainable farming methods. Such efforts have paid off. For example, when Chipotle first started serving naturally raised pork in 2000, there were only 60 to 70 farms producing meat for the Niman Ranch pork cooperative, an important Chipotle supplier. Now, there are over 700.

Sourcing such natural and organic ingredients not only serves Chipotle's sustainability mission, it results in one of the most nutritious, best-tasting fast-food burritos on the market— something the company can brag about to customers. "Typically, fast-food marketing is a game of trying to obscure the truth," says Chipotle's chief marketing officer. "The more people know about most fast-food companies, the less likely they'd want to be a customer." But Chipotle doesn't play that game. Instead, it commits fast-food heresy: Proudly telling customers what's really inside its burritos.

Chipotle chose the "Food With Integrity" slogan because it sends the right message in an appetizing way. "Saying that we don't buy dairy from cows that are given the hormone rBGH is not an appetizing message," says Ells. So the company is building its marketing campaign around the more positive message that food production should be healthier and more ethical. Chipotle communicates this positioning via an integrated mix of traditional and digital promotion venues, ranging from its Farm Team invitation-only loyalty program—by which customers earn rewards based not on frequent buying but on knowledge about food and how it is produced—to its Pasture Pandemonium smartphone app, where players try to get their pig across a pasture without getting trapped in pens or pricked by antibiotic needles.

Two years ago, Chipotle made a big splash during the broadcast for the Grammy Awards with its first-ever national television ad—a two-and-a-half-minute stop-motion animation film showing a family hog farm converting to an efficient, industrialized farm. Then, when the farmer realizes that it's not the right thing to do, he tears down his factory farm and reverts to raising hogs sustainably in open pastures. Willie Nelson provides the soundtrack with a cover of Coldplay's "The Scientist," giving the ad its name, "Back to the Start." Before it ever aired as a TV ad, the video played in 10,000 movie theaters and online, where it became a viral hit on YouTube. Viewers were urged to download the Willie Nelson tune via iTunes, with the proceeds going to the Chipotle Cultivate Foundation.

Companies with a socially responsible business model often struggle to grow and make profits. But Chipotle is proving that a company can do both. Last year, its 37,000 employees chopped, sliced, diced, and grilled their way to $2.7 billion in revenues and $278 million in profits at Chipotle's 1,410 restaurants in

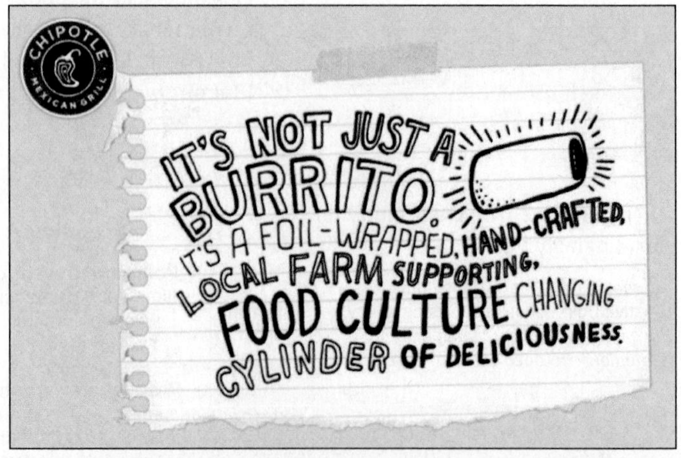

>> Fast-food chain Chipotle has successfully built its core mission around an environmental sustainability theme: "Food With Integrity."

41 states. And the chain is growing fast, opening a new restaurant almost every two days. In the past three years, Chipotle's stock price has tripled, suggesting that the company's investors are as pleased as its fast-growing corps of customers.

Founder and CEO Ells wants Chipotle to grow and make money. But ultimately, on a larger stage, he wants to change the way fast food is produced and sold—not just by Chipotle but by the entire industry. "We think the more people understand where their food comes from and the impact that has on independent family farmers [and] animal welfare, the more they're going to ask for better ingredients," says Ells. Whether customers stop by Chipotle's restaurants to support the cause, gobble down the tasty food, or both, it all suits Ells just fine. Chipotle's sustainability mission isn't an add-on, created just to position the company as "socially responsible." Doing good "is the company's ethos and ingrained in everything we do," says Chipotle's director of communications. "Chipotle is a very different kind of company where the deeper you dig into what's happening, the more there is to like and feel good about."

Sources: Based on information and quotes from Danielle Sacks, "Chipotle: For Exploding All the Rules of Fast Food," *Fast Company*, March 2012, pp. 125–126; John Trybus, "Chipotle's Chris Arnold and the Food With Integrity Approach to Corporate Social Responsibility," *The Social Strategist*, March 22, 2012, https://blogs.commons.georgetown.edu/socialimpact/2012/03/22/the-social-strategist-part-xvi-chipotle's-chris-arnold-and-the-food-with-integrity-approach-to-corporate-social-responsibility/; Emily Bryson York, "Chipotle Ups the Ante on Its Marketing," *Chicago Tribune*, September 30, 2011; Elizabeth Olson, "An Animated Ad with a Plot Line and a Moral," *New York Times*, February 10, 2012, p. B2; Ed Sealover, "Chipotle Rolls Out Expansion, Marketing Plans for 2013," *Denver Business Journal*, February 5, 2013; and information from www.chipotle.com and www.chipotle.com/en-US/fwi/fwi.aspx, accessed November 2013.

>> SC Johnson—maker of familiar household brands ranging from Windex, Pledge, Shout, and Scrubbing Bubbles to Ziploc, Off, and Raid—sells concentrated versions of all of its household cleaners in recyclable bottles, helping eliminate empty trigger bottles from entering landfills. The company currently obtains 100 percent of the electricity used at its largest global manufacturing facility from renewable sources. And by rating the environmental impact of product ingredients, it has cut millions of pounds of volatile organic compounds (VOCs) from its products. For example, by simple reformulating of its Windex glass cleaner, SC Johnson cut 1.8 million pounds of VOCs while giving the product 30 percent more cleaning power. SC Johnson boasts that since 1886, it has been "committed to working every day to do what's right for people, the planet, and generations to come."[16]

Honda of America boasts that its huge manufacturing plants now send almost no waste to landfills. For years, the auto giant has been on a search-and-destroy mission to eliminate waste. A majority of its North American plants now send no waste at all to landfills; the remaining few dump only small amounts of plastic and paper trash from their cafeterias. To ferret out sources of waste, Honda even sends teams of employees to comb through plant dumpsters and refuse piles. Such teams have initiated hundreds of waste-reduction and recycling efforts. Whether it's by reducing metal scrap in manufacturing processes or replacing cafeteria paper and plastic with washable dishware, during the past 10 years, Honda's garbage-picking employees have eliminated 4.4 billion pounds of potential landfill waste. Whereas the company sent 62.8 pounds of waste per car to landfills in 2001, it now sends only 1.8 pounds per car.[17]

At the next level, companies can practice *product stewardship*—minimizing not only pollution from production and product design but also all environmental impacts throughout the full product life cycle, while at the same time reducing costs. Many companies are adopting *design for environment (DFE)* and *cradle-to-cradle* practices. This involves thinking ahead to design products that are easier to recover, reuse, recycle, or safely return to nature after usage, thus becoming part of the ecological cycle. DFE and cradle-to-cradle practices not only help to sustain the environment, but they can also be highly profitable for the company.

For example, more than a decade ago, IBM started a business—IBM Global Asset Recovery Services—designed to reuse and recycle parts from returned mainframe computers and other equipment. Last year, IBM processed more than 37,900 metric tons of end-of-life products and product waste worldwide, stripping down old equipment to recover chips and valuable metals. The cumulative weight processed by IBM's remanufacturing and de-manufacturing operations would fill

>> Environmental sustainability: Among other sustainability efforts, SC Johnson obtains 100 percent of its electricity at its largest global manufacturing facility from renewable sources. Its products are "Now Made with Wind."

Image courtesy of SC Johnson.

4,480 rail cars stretching 49 miles. IBM Global Asset Recovery Services finds uses for more than 99 percent of what it takes in, sending less than 1 percent to landfills and incineration facilities. What started out as an environmental effort has now grown into a multibillion-dollar IBM business that profitably recycles electronic equipment at 22 sites worldwide.[18]

Today's *greening* activities focus on improving what companies already do to protect the environment. The *beyond greening* activities identified in Figure 16.2 look to the future. First, internally, companies can plan for *new clean technology*. Many organizations that have made good sustainability headway are still limited by existing technologies. To create fully sustainable strategies, they will need to develop innovative new technologies.

For example, by 2020, Coca-Cola has committed to reclaiming and recycling the equivalent of all the packaging it uses around the world. It has also pledged to dramatically reduce its overall environmental footprint. To accomplish these goals, the company invests heavily in new clean technologies that address a host of environmental issues, such as recycling, resource usage, and distribution:[19]

> First, to attack the solid waste problem caused by its plastic bottles, Coca-Cola invested heavily to build the world's largest state-of-the-art plastic-bottle-to-bottle recycling plant. As a more permanent solution, Coke is researching and testing new bottles made from aluminum, corn, or bioplastics. It has been steadily replacing its PET plastic bottles with PlantBottle packaging, which incorporates 30 percent plant-based materials. The company is also designing more eco-friendly distribution alternatives. Currently, some 10 million vending machines and refrigerated coolers gobble up energy and use potent greenhouse gases called hydrofluorocarbons (HFCs) to keep Cokes cold. To eliminate them, the company invested $40 million in research and recently began installing sleek new HFC-free coolers that use 30 to 40 percent less energy. Coca-Cola also aims to become "water neutral" by researching ways to help its bottlers add back all the fresh water they extract during the production of Coca-Cola beverages.

Finally, companies can develop a *sustainability vision*, which serves as a guide to the future. It shows how the company's products and services, processes, and policies must evolve and what new technologies must be developed to get there. This vision of sustainability provides a framework for pollution control, product stewardship, and new environmental technology for the company and others to follow.

Most companies today focus on the upper-left quadrant of the grid in Figure 16.2, investing most heavily in pollution prevention. Some forward-looking companies practice product stewardship and are developing new environmental technologies. However, emphasizing only one or two quadrants in the environmental sustainability grid can be shortsighted. Investing only in the left half of the grid puts a company in a good position today but leaves it vulnerable in the future. In contrast, a heavy emphasis on the right half suggests that a company has good environmental vision but lacks the skills needed to implement it. Thus, companies should work at developing all four dimensions of environmental sustainability.

Walmart, for example, is doing just that. Through its own environmental sustainability actions and its impact on the actions of suppliers, » Walmart has emerged in recent years as the world's super "eco-nanny":[20]

> When it comes to sustainability, perhaps no company in the world is doing more good these days than Walmart. That's right—big, bad Walmart. The giant retailer is now one of the world's biggest crusaders for the cause of saving the world for future generations. For starters, Walmart is rolling out new high-efficiency stores, each one saving more energy than the last. These stores use wind turbines to generate energy, high-output linear fluorescent lighting to reduce what energy stores do use, and native landscaping to cut down on watering and fertilizer. Store heating systems burn recovered cooking oil from the deli fryers and motor oil from the Tire and Lube Express centers. All organic waste, including produce, meats, and paper, is hauled off to a company that turns it into mulch for the garden.

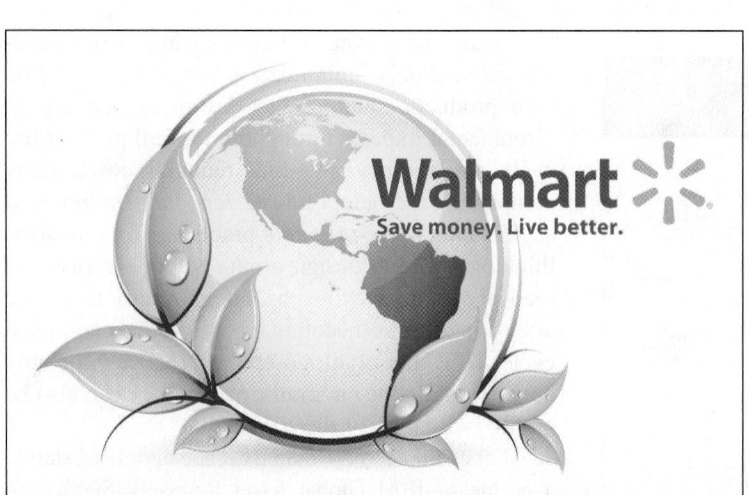

» For Walmart, sustainability is about more than just doing the right thing. Above all, it's strategy for sustainability makes good business sense—"driving out hidden costs, conserving our natural resources for future generations, and providing sustainable and affordable products for our customers so they can save money and live better."

AP Images/PRNewsFoto/Walmart; Bebay/iStockphoto.

Walmart is not only greening up its own operations but also laying down the eco-law to its vast network of 100,000 suppliers to get them to do the same. It recently announced plans to cut some 20 million metric tons of greenhouse gas emissions from its supply chain by the end of 2015—equivalent to removing more than 3.8 million cars from the road for a year. To get this done, Walmart is asking its huge corps of suppliers to examine the carbon life cycles of their products and rethink how they source, manufacture, package, and transport these goods. With its immense buying power, Walmart can humble even the mightiest supplier. When imposing its environmental demands on suppliers, Walmart has even more clout than government regulators. Whereas the EPA can only level nominal fines, Walmart can threaten a substantial chunk of a supplier's business.

For Walmart, leading the eco-charge is about more than just doing the right thing. Above all, it also makes good business sense. More efficient operations and less wasteful products are not only good for the environment but also save Walmart money. Lower costs, in turn, let Walmart do more of what it has always done best—save customers money.

Public Actions to Regulate Marketing

Citizen concerns about marketing practices will usually lead to public attention and legislative proposals. Many of the laws that affect marketing were identified in Chapter 3. The task is to translate these laws into a language that marketing executives understand as they make decisions about competitive relations, products, price, promotion, and distribution channels. >> **Figure 16.3** illustrates the major legal issues facing marketing management.

Author Comment
In the end, marketers themselves must take responsibility for sustainable marketing. That means operating in a responsible and ethical way to bring both immediate and future value to customers.

Business Actions toward Sustainable Marketing

At first, many companies opposed consumerism, environmentalism, and other elements of sustainable marketing. They thought the criticisms were either unfair or unimportant. But by now, most companies have grown to embrace sustainability principles as a way to create both immediate and future customer value and strengthen customer relationships.

Sustainable Marketing Principles

Under the sustainable marketing concept, a company's marketing should support the best long-run performance of the marketing system. It should be guided by five sustainable

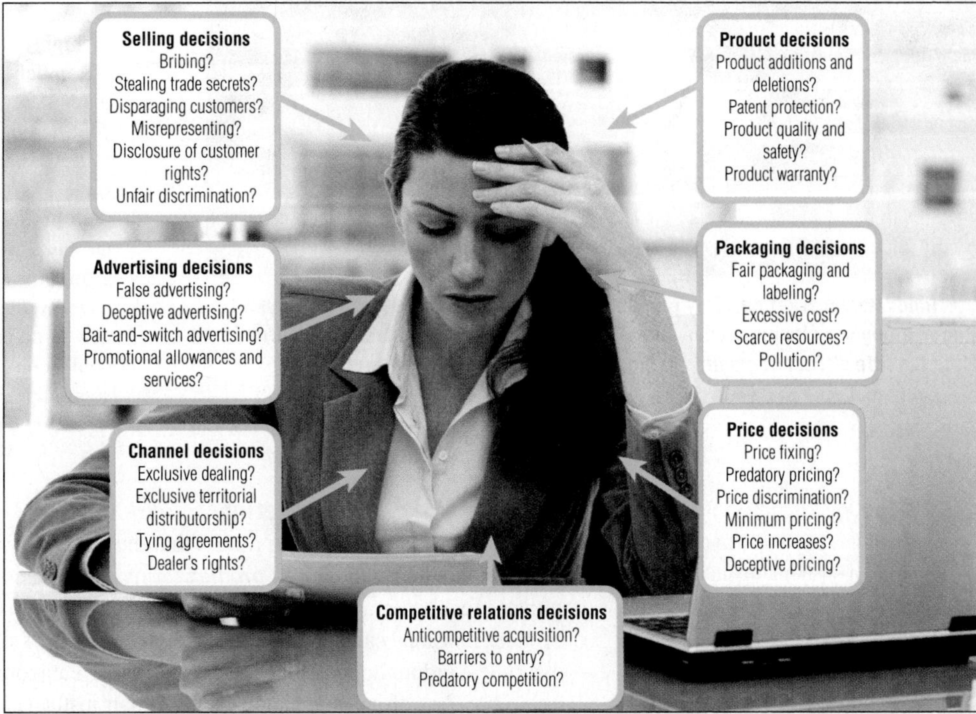

Selling decisions
Bribing?
Stealing trade secrets?
Disparaging customers?
Misrepresenting?
Disclosure of customer rights?
Unfair discrimination?
Product decisions
Product additions and deletions?
Patent protection?
Product quality and safety?
Product warranty?
Advertising decisions
False advertising?
Deceptive advertising?
Bait-and-switch advertising?
Promotional allowances and services?
Packaging decisions
Fair packaging and labeling?
Excessive cost?
Scarce resources?
Pollution?
Channel decisions
Exclusive dealing?
Exclusive territorial distributorship?
Tying agreements?
Dealer's rights?
Price decisions
Price fixing?
Predatory pricing?
Price discrimination?
Minimum pricing?
Price increases?
Deceptive pricing?
Competitive relations decisions
Anticompetitive acquisition?
Barriers to entry?
Predatory competition?

>> **Figure 16.3** Major Marketing Decision Areas That May Be Called into Question under the Law

Source: (photo) wavebreakmedia ltd/Shutterstock.com.

marketing principles: *consumer-oriented marketing*, *customer value marketing*, *innovative marketing*, *sense-of-mission marketing*, and *societal marketing*.

Consumer-Oriented Marketing

Consumer-oriented marketing
A principle of sustainable marketing holding that a company should view and organize its marketing activities from the consumer's point of view.

Consumer-oriented marketing means that the company should view and organize its marketing activities from the consumer's point of view. It should work hard to sense, serve, and satisfy the needs of a defined group of customers—both now and in the future. The good marketing companies that we've discussed throughout this text have had this in common: an all-consuming passion for delivering superior value to carefully chosen customers. Only by seeing the world through its customers' eyes can the company build sustainable and profitable customer relationships.

Customer Value Marketing

Customer value marketing
A principle of sustainable marketing holding that a company should put most of its resources into customer value–building marketing investments.

According to the principle of **customer value marketing**, the company should put most of its resources into customer value–building marketing investments. Many things marketers do—one-shot sales promotions, cosmetic product changes, direct-response advertising—may raise sales in the short run but add less *value* than would actual improvements in the product's quality, features, or convenience. Enlightened marketing calls for building long-run consumer loyalty and relationships by continually improving the value consumers receive from the firm's market offering. By creating value *for* consumers, the company can capture value *from* consumers in return.

Innovative Marketing

Innovative marketing
A principle of sustainable marketing that requires a company to seek real product and marketing improvements.

The principle of **innovative marketing** requires that the company continuously seek real product and marketing improvements. The company that overlooks new and better ways to do things will eventually lose customers to another company that has found a better way. Think back to the Nike story in Chapter 2:[21]

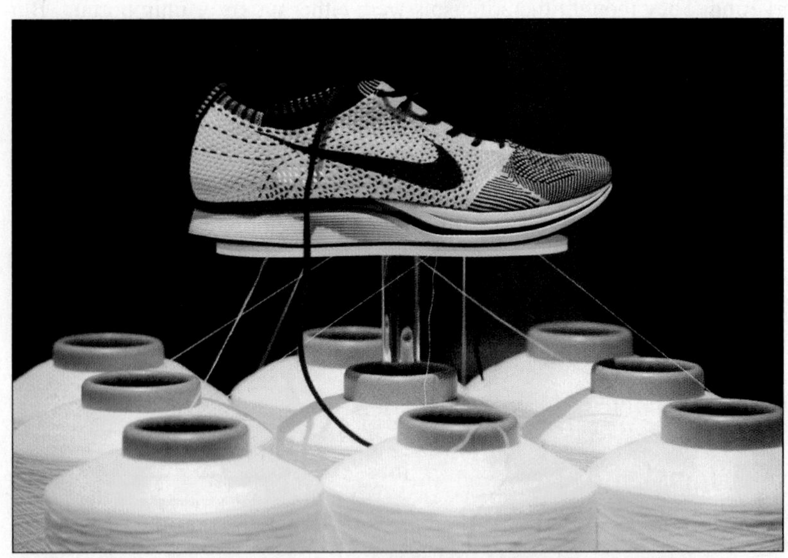

>> Innovative marketing: New products, such as the Nike FuelBand and Flyknit Racer, along with its innovative social media marketing efforts, recently earned Nike the title of *Fast Company*'s number one most innovative marketer.

Rodrigo Reyes Marin/AFLO/Newscom.

For nearly 50 years, through innovative marketing, Nike has built the ever-present swoosh into one of the world's best-known brand symbols. When sales languished in the late 1990s and new competitors made gains, Nike knew it had to reinvent itself via product and marketing innovation. "One of my fears is being this big, slow, constipated, bureaucratic company that's happy with its success," says Nike CEO Mark Parker. Instead, over the past few years, a hungry Nike has unleashed a number of highly successful new products. For example, the collaborative Apple Nike+ iPod sensor and the Nike FuelBand have created strong Nike brand communities. >> And with the new Nike Flyknit Racer, Nike has now reinvented the very way that shoes are manufactured. The featherweight Flyknit feels more like a sock with a sole. Woven not sewn, the Flyknit is super comfortable and durable, more affordable to make, and more environmentally friendly than traditional sneakers. Top off Nike's new products with a heavy investment in social media content and Nike remains the world's largest sports apparel company, an impressive 25 percent larger than closest rival adidas. Last year, *Fast Company* anointed Nike as the world's number one most innovative company.

Sense-of-Mission Marketing

Sense-of-mission marketing
A principle of sustainable marketing holding that a company should define its mission in broad social terms rather than narrow product terms.

Sense-of-mission marketing means that the company should define its mission in broad *social* terms rather than narrow *product* terms. When a company defines a social mission, employees feel better about their work and have a clearer sense of direction. Brands linked with broader missions can serve the best long-run interests of both the brand and consumers. For example, outdoor apparel and equipment maker Patagonia even goes so far as to urge customers to buy *less* of its merchandise. More than just sales and profits, Patagonia wants to "reimagine a world where we take only what nature can replace" (see Marketing at Work 16.2).

MARKETING AT WORK 16.2

Patagonia's "Conscious Consumption" Mission: Telling Consumers to Buy *Less*

Patagonia—the high-end outdoor clothing and gear company—was founded on a mission of using business to help save the planet. More than 40 years ago, mountain-climber entrepreneur Yvon Chouinard started the company with this enduring mission: "Build the best product, cause no unnecessary harm, use business to inspire and implement solutions to the environmental crisis." Now, Chouinard and Patagonia are taking that mission to new extremes. They're actually telling consumers "don't buy our products."

It started last year with a full-page *New York Times* ad on Black Friday, the day after Thanksgiving and heaviest shopping day of the year, showing Patagonia's best-selling R2 jacket and pronouncing "Don't Buy This Jacket." Patagonia backed the ad with messaging in its retail stores, at its Web site, and with additional ads at NYTimes.com. To top things off, Patagonia customers received a follow-up e-mail prior to Cyber Monday—the season's major online shopping day—reasserting the brand's buy less message. Here's part of what it said:

> Because Patagonia wants to be in business for a good long time—and leave a world inhabitable for our kids—we want to do the opposite of every other business today. We ask you to buy less and to reflect before you spend a dime on this jacket or anything else.
>
> The environmental cost of everything we make is astonishing. Consider the R2 Jacket shown, one of our best sellers. To make it required 135 liters of water, enough to meet the daily needs (three glasses a day) of 45 people. Its journey from its origin as 60% recycled polyester to our Reno warehouse generated nearly 20 pounds of carbon dioxide, 24 times the weight of the finished product. This jacket left behind, on its way to Reno, two-thirds its weight in waste. And this is a 60% recycled polyester jacket, knit and sewn to a high standard. But, as is true of all the things we can make and you can buy, this jacket comes with an environmental cost higher than its price.
>
> There is much to be done and plenty for us all to do. Don't buy what you don't need. Think twice before you buy anything. [Work with us] to reimagine a world where we take only what nature can replace.

A for-profit firm telling its customers to buy *less*? It sounds crazy. But that message is right on target with Patagonia's reason for being. Founder Chouinard contends that capitalism is on an unsustainable path. Today's companies and customers are wasting the world's resources by making and buying low-quality goods that they buy mindlessly and throw away too quickly. Instead, Chouinard and his company are calling for *conscious consumption,* asking customers to think before they buy and to stop consuming for consumption's sake.

Coming from Patagonia, a company that spends almost nothing on traditional advertising, the paradoxical "Don't Buy This Jacket" ad had tremendous impact. The Internet was soon ablaze with comments from online journalists, bloggers, and customers regarding the meaning and motivation behind Patagonia's message. Analysts speculated about whether the ad would help or harm sales—whether it would engage customers and build loyalty or be perceived as little more than a cheap marketing gimmick.

But to Patagonia, far from a marketing gimmick, the campaign expressed the brand's deeply held philosophy of sustainability. The purpose was to increase awareness of and participation in the Patagonia Common Threads Initiative, which urges customers to take a pledge to work together with the company to consume more responsibly. Common Threads rests on five Rs of joint action toward sustainability:

> *Reduce:* **WE** make useful gear that lasts a long time. **YOU** don't buy what you don't need.
>
> *Repair:* **WE** help you repair your Patagonia gear. **YOU** pledge to fix what's broken.
>
> *Reuse:* **WE** help find a home for Patagonia gear you no longer need. **YOU** sell or pass it on.

>> Sense-of-mission marketing: A for-profit company telling consumers to buy less sounds crazy. But it's right on target with Patagonia's conscious consumption mission.

Patagonia, Inc.

Recycle: **WE** take back your Patagonia gear that is worn out. **YOU** pledge to keep your stuff out of the landfill and incinerator.

Reimagine: **TOGETHER** we reimagine a world where we take only what nature can replace.

So Patagonia's conscious consumption solution seems pretty simple. Making, buying, repairing, and reusing higher-quality goods results in less consumption, which in turn uses fewer resources and lowers costs for everyone. "Have a Patagonia ski parka with a rip in the arm?" asks one reporter. "Don't throw it away and buy a new one. Send it back, and the company will sew it up. Is your tent beyond repair? Send it back, and Patagonia will recycle the material." Patagonia has always been committed to the idea of quality as a cure for overconsumption. To that end, it makes durable products with timeless designs, products that customers can keep and use for a long time.

So on that Black Friday weekend, while other companies were inundating customers with promotions that encouraged them to "buy, buy, buy," Patagonia stood on its founding principles. It said, "Hey, look: Only purchase what you need," explains Rob BonDurant, vice president of marketing and communications at Patagonia. "The message, 'Don't buy this jacket,' is obviously super counterintuitive to what a for-profit company would say, especially on a day like Black Friday, but honestly [it] is what we really were after, [communicating] this idea of evolving capitalism and conscious consumption that we wanted to effect."

Not just any company can pull off something like this—such a message can only work if it is real. Patagonia didn't just suddenly stick an ad in the *New York Times* on Black Friday. It had been sending—and living—this message for decades. Can other companies follow Patagonia's lead? "If it is [just] a marketing campaign, no," says BonDurant. "If it is a way they live their lives and do their business, absolutely. . . . The key to the whole effort [is]: Put your money where your mouth is," he says. "You can't just apply it to your messaging or to a particular window of time. It has to be done 24 hours a day, 365 days a year."

Pushing conscious consumption doesn't mean that Patagonia wants customers to stop buying its products. To the contrary, like other for-profit brands, Patagonia really does care about doing well on Black Friday and the rest of the holiday season. As a company that sells products mostly for cold-weather activities, Patagonia reaps a whopping 40 percent of its revenues during the final two months of the year. But to Patagonia, business is about more than making money. And according to BonDurant, the "Don't Buy This Jacket" campaign has more than paid for itself with the interest and involvement it created for the Common Threads Initiative. If the campaign also boosts sales, that's a nice bonus.

"It is not enough just to make good products anymore," says BonDurant. "There also has to be a message that people can buy into, that people feel they are a part of, that they can be solutions-based. That is what [Patagonia's "buy only what you need"] communication efforts are really all about."

Sources: Based on information from Katherine Ling, "Walking the Talk," *Marketing News*, March 15, 2012, p. 24; Brain Dumaine, "Built to Last," *Fortune*, August 13, 2012, p. 16; and www.patagonia.com/email/11/112811.htmland, www.patagonia.com/us/common-threads?src=112811_mt1, and www.patagonia.com/us/environmentalism, accessed November 2013.

As another example of sense-of-mission marketing, the PEDIGREE Brand makes good dog food, but that's not what the brand is really all about. Instead, six years ago, the brand came up with the manifesto, "We're for dogs." That statement is a perfect encapsulation of everything PEDIGREE stands for. "Everything that we do is because we love dogs," says a PEDIGREE marketer. "It's just so simple." This mission-focused positioning drives everything the brand does—internally and externally. One look at a PEDIGREE ad or a visit to the pedigree.com Web site confirms that the people behind the PEDIGREE Brand really do believe the "We're for dogs" mission. Associates are even encouraged to take their dogs to work. To further fulfill the "We're for dogs" brand promise, the company created the PEDIGREE Foundation, which, along with the PEDIGREE Adoption Drive campaign, has raised millions of dollars for helping "shelter dogs" find good homes. Sense-of-mission marketing has made PEDIGREE the world's number-one dog food brand.[22]

Some companies define their overall corporate missions in broad societal terms. For example, defined in narrow product terms, the mission of sports footwear and apparel maker PUMA might be "to sell sports shoes, clothing, and accessories." However, PUMA states its mission more broadly, as one of producing customer-satisfying products while also contributing to a sustainable future:[23]

> At PUMA, we believe that our position as the creative leader in sport lifestyles gives us the opportunity and the responsibility to contribute to a better world for the generations to come. A better world in our vision—PUMA Vision—would be safer, more peaceful, and more creative than the world we know today. We believe that by staying true to our values, inspiring the passion and talent of our people, working in sustainable, innovative ways, and doing our best to be Fair, Honest, Positive, and Creative, we will keep on making the products our customers love, and at the same time bring that vision of a better world a little closer every day. Through our programs of puma.safe (focusing on environmental and social issues),

puma.peace (supporting global peace) and puma.creative (supporting artists and creative organizations), we are providing real and practical expressions of this vision and building for ourselves and our stakeholders, among other things, a more sustainable future.

Under its PUMA Vision mission, the company has made substantial progress in developing more sustainable products, packaging, operations, and supply chains. It has also sponsored many innovative initiatives to carry forward its puma.peace and puma.creative missions. For example, it sponsored a series of "peace starts with me" videos aimed at "fostering a more peaceful world than the one we live in today." Although such efforts may not produce immediate sales, PUMA sees them as an important part of "who we are."

However, having a *double bottom line* of values and profits isn't easy. Over the years, companies such as Patagonia, Ben & Jerry's, The Body Shop, and Burt's Bees—all known and respected for putting "principles before profits"—have at times struggled with less-than-stellar financial returns. In recent years, however, a new generation of social entrepreneurs has emerged, well-trained business managers who know that to *do good*, they must first *do well* in terms of profitable business operations. Moreover, today, socially responsible business is no longer the sole province of small, socially conscious entrepreneurs. Many large, established companies and brands—from Walmart and Nike to Starbucks and PepsiCo—have adopted substantial social and environmental responsibility missions.

Societal Marketing

Societal marketing
A principle of sustainable marketing holding that a company should make marketing decisions by considering consumers' wants, the company's requirements, consumers' long-run interests, and society's long-run interests.

Deficient products
Products that have neither immediate appeal nor long-run benefits.

Pleasing products
Products that give high immediate satisfaction but may hurt consumers in the long run.

Salutary products
Products that have low immediate appeal but may benefit consumers in the long run.

Desirable products
Products that give both high immediate satisfaction and high long-run benefits.

Following the principle of **societal marketing**, a company makes marketing decisions by considering consumers' wants, the company's requirements, consumers' long-run interests, and society's long-run interests. Companies should be aware that neglecting consumer and societal long-run interests is a disservice to consumers and society. Alert companies view societal problems as opportunities.

Sustainable marketing calls for products that are not only pleasing but also beneficial. The difference is shown in >> **Figure 16.4**. Products can be classified according to their degree of immediate consumer satisfaction and long-run consumer benefit.

Deficient products, such as bad-tasting and ineffective medicine, have neither immediate appeal nor long-run benefits. **Pleasing products** give high immediate satisfaction but may hurt consumers in the long run. Examples include cigarettes and junk food. **Salutary products** have low immediate appeal but may benefit consumers in the long run, for instance, bicycle helmets or some insurance products. **Desirable products** give both high immediate satisfaction and high long-run benefits, such as a tasty *and* nutritious breakfast food.

Examples of desirable products abound. Philips AmbientLED light bulbs provide good lighting at the same time that they give long life and energy savings. Envirosax reusable shopping bags are stylish and affordable while also eliminating the need for less-eco-friendly disposable paper and plastic store bags. And Nau's durable, sustainable urban outdoor apparel fits the "modern mobile lifestyle." Nau clothing is environmentally sustainable—using only sustainable materials such as natural and renewable fibers produced in a sustainable manner and synthetic fibers that contain high recycled content. It's aesthetically sustainable—versatile and designed for lasting beauty.

>> **Figure 16.4** Societal Classification of Products

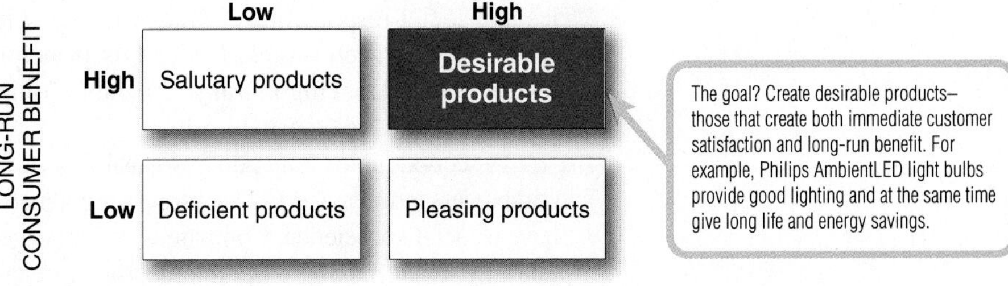
IMMEDIATE SATISFACTION
Low
High
LONG-RUN CONSUMER BENEFIT
High
Salutary products
Desirable products
Low
Deficient products
Pleasing products
The goal? Create desirable products–those that create both immediate customer satisfaction and long-run benefit. For example, Philips AmbientLED light bulbs provide good lighting and at the same time give long life and energy savings.

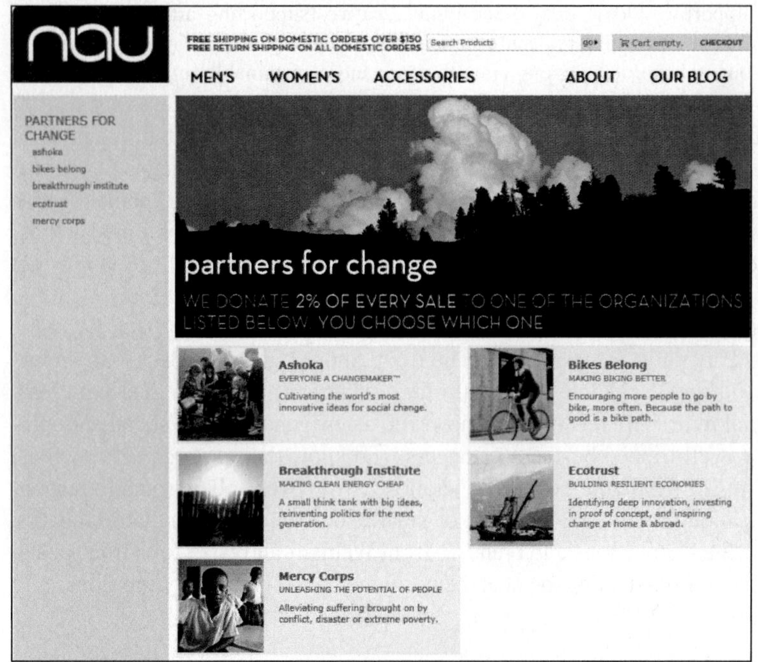

>> Desirable products: Nau's urban outdoor apparel products are environmentally, aesthetically, and socially sustainable. The company donates 2 percent of every sale to Partners for Change organizations chosen by customers.

Nau Holdings, LLC.

>>And Nau clothing is also socially sustainable—the company donates 2 percent of every sale to Partners for Change organizations and ensures that its factories adhere to its own strict code of conduct.[24]

Companies should try to turn all of their products into desirable products. The challenge posed by pleasing products is that they sell very well but may end up hurting the consumer. The product opportunity, therefore, is to add long-run benefits without reducing the product's pleasing qualities. The challenge posed by salutary products is to add some pleasing qualities so that they will become more desirable in consumers' minds.

For example, PepsiCo hired a team of "idealistic scientists," headed by a former director of the World Health Organization, to help the company create attractive new healthy product options while "making the bad stuff less bad." PepsiCo wants healthy products to be a $30-billion business for the company by 2020. The group of physicians, PhDs, and other health advocates, under the direction of PepsiCo's vice president for global health policy, looks for healthier ingredients that can go into multiple products as well as reductions of sugar, salt, and fat while maintaining the same flavor in its familiar products. For example, in 2011 Frito-Lay cut the salt in all of its potato chips by 25 percent. And, to help cut calories, it uses a zero-calorie sweetener, Pure Via, in its Tropicana Trop50 orange juice and Gatorade G2 brands.[25]

Marketing Ethics

Good ethics are a cornerstone of sustainable marketing. In the long run, unethical marketing harms customers and society as a whole. Further, it eventually damages a company's reputation and effectiveness, jeopardizing its very survival. Thus, the sustainable marketing goals of long-term consumer and business welfare can be achieved only through ethical marketing conduct.

Conscientious marketers face many moral dilemmas. The best thing to do is often unclear. Because not all managers have fine moral sensitivity, companies need to develop *corporate marketing ethics policies*—broad guidelines that everyone in the organization must follow. These policies should cover distributor relations, advertising standards, customer service, pricing, product development, and general ethical standards.

The finest guidelines cannot resolve all the difficult ethical situations the marketer faces. **>>Table 16.1** lists some difficult ethical issues marketers could face during their careers. If marketers choose immediate-sales-producing actions in all of these cases, their marketing behavior might well be described as immoral or even amoral. If they refuse to go along with *any* of the actions, they might be ineffective as marketing managers and unhappy because of the constant moral tension. Managers need a set of principles that will help them figure out the moral importance of each situation and decide how far they can go in good conscience.

But *what* principle should guide companies and marketing managers on issues of ethics and social responsibility? One philosophy is that the free market and the legal system should decide such issues. Under this principle, companies and their managers are not responsible for making moral judgments. Companies can in good conscience do whatever the market and legal systems allow.

A second philosophy puts responsibility not on the system but in the hands of individual companies and managers. This more enlightened philosophy suggests that a company should have a social conscience. Companies and managers should apply high standards of ethics and morality when making corporate decisions, regardless of "what the system allows." History provides an endless list of examples of company actions that were legal but highly irresponsible.

» Table 16.1 Some Morally Difficult Situations in Marketing

1. Your R&D department has slightly changed one of your company's products. It is not really "new and improved," but you know that putting this statement on the package and in advertising will increase sales. What would you do?
2. You have been asked to add a stripped-down model to your line that could be advertised to pull customers into the store. The product won't be very good, but salespeople will be able to switch buyers who come into the store up to higher-priced units. You are asked to give the green light for the stripped-down version. What would you do?
3. You are thinking of hiring a product manager who has just left a competitor's company. She would be more than happy to tell you all the competitor's plans for the coming year. What would you do?
4. One of your top dealers in an important territory recently has had family troubles, and his sales have slipped. It looks like it will take him a while to straighten out his family troubles. Meanwhile, you are losing many sales. Legally, on performance grounds, you can terminate the dealer's franchise and replace him. What would you do?
5. You have a chance to win a big account that will mean a lot to you and your company. The purchasing agent hints that a "gift" would influence the decision. Your assistant recommends sending a large-screen television to the buyer's home. What would you do?
6. You have heard that a competitor has a new product feature that will make a big difference in sales. The competitor will demonstrate the feature in a private dealer meeting at the annual trade show. You can easily send a snooper to this meeting to learn about the new feature. What would you do?
7. You have to choose between three advertising campaigns outlined by your agency. The first (a) is a soft-sell, honest, straight-information campaign. The second (b) uses sex-loaded emotional appeals and exaggerates the product's benefits. The third (c) involves a noisy, somewhat irritating commercial that is sure to gain audience attention. Pretests show that the campaigns are effective in the following order: c, b, and a. What would you do?
8. You are interviewing a capable female applicant for a job as salesperson. She is better qualified than the men who have been interviewed. Nevertheless, you know that in your industry some important customers prefer dealing with men, and you will lose some sales if you hire her. What would you do?

Each company and marketing manager must work out a philosophy of socially responsible and ethical behavior. Under the societal marketing concept, each manager must look beyond what is legal and allowed and develop standards based on personal integrity, corporate conscience, and long-run consumer welfare.

Dealing with issues of ethics and social responsibility in an open and forthright way helps to build and maintain strong customer relationships based on honesty and trust. For example, Graco—maker of strollers, car seats, and other children's products—relies heavily on parental trust to keep customers loyal. In January, 2010, after receiving seven reports of severe injuries to children's fingers caused by its strollers, Graco quickly recalled some 1.5 million units, making it the biggest stroller recall in history. But the company didn't stop with the official recall. Instead, it swiftly launched a proactive campaign to alert parents of the problem, answer their questions, and give them detailed advice on what steps to take. Graco went live and interactive with specific information on the Graco Blog, YouTube, Twitter, Facebook, and a dedicated Web page. For example, customers who messaged Graco's Twitter account received prompt responses from Graco's twitterers about whether their strollers were part of the recall plus useful, one-on-one information about how to order and install repair kits. Graco's swift and responsible actions drew praise from both public policy advocates and customers. "I will ALWAYS continue to use Graco products," tweeted one customer, "thanks to the way this was handled."[26]

As with environmentalism, the issue of ethics presents special challenges for international marketers. Business standards and practices vary a great deal from one country to the next. For example, bribes and kickbacks are illegal for U.S. firms, and various treaties against bribery and corruption have been signed and ratified by more than 60 countries. Yet these are still standard business practices in many countries. The World Bank estimates that bribes totaling more than $1 trillion per year are paid out worldwide. One study showed that the most flagrant bribe-paying firms were from Indonesia, Mexico, China, and Russia. Other countries where corruption is common include Somalia, Myanmar, and Haiti. The least corrupt were companies from Belgium, Switzerland, and the Netherlands.[27] The question arises as to whether a company must lower its ethical standards to compete effectively in countries with lower standards. The answer is no. Companies should make a commitment to a common set of shared standards worldwide.

Many industrial and professional associations have suggested codes of ethics, and many companies are now adopting their own codes. For example, the American Marketing Association, an international association of marketing managers and scholars, developed a code of ethics that calls on marketers to adopt the following ethical norms:[28]

- ***Do no harm.*** This means consciously avoiding harmful actions or omissions by embodying high ethical standards and adhering to all applicable laws and regulations in the choices we make.
- ***Foster trust in the marketing system.*** This means striving for good faith and fair dealing so as to contribute toward the efficacy of the exchange process as well as avoiding deception in product design, pricing, communication, and delivery or distribution.
- ***Embrace ethical values.*** This means building relationships and enhancing consumer confidence in the integrity of marketing by affirming these core values: honesty, responsibility, fairness, respect, transparency, and citizenship.

Companies are also developing programs to teach managers about important ethical issues and help them find the proper responses. They hold ethics workshops and seminars and create ethics committees. Furthermore, most major U.S. companies have appointed high-level ethics officers to champion ethical issues and help resolve ethics problems and concerns facing employees. And most companies have established their own codes of ethical conduct.

Google is a good example. >> Its official Google Code of Conduct is the mechanism by which the company puts its well-known "Don't be evil" motto into practice. The detailed code's core message is simple: Google employees (know inside as "Googlers") must earn users' faith and trust by holding themselves to the highest possible standards of ethical business conduct. The Google Code of Conduct is "about providing our users unbiased access to information, focusing on their needs, and giving them the best products and services that we can. But it's also about doing the right thing more generally—following the law, acting honorably, and treating each other with respect."

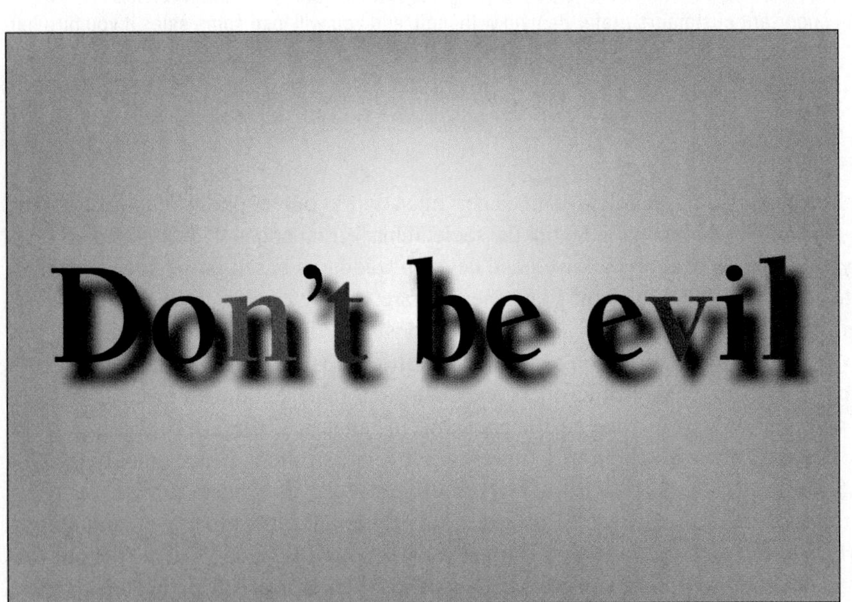

>> **Marketing ethics: Google's Code of Conduct is the mechanism by which the company puts it well-known "Don't be evil" motto into practice.**

Google requires all Googlers—from board members to the newest employee—to take personal responsibility for practicing both the spirit and letter of the code and encouraging other Googlers to do the same. It urges employees to report violations to their managers, to human resources representatives, or using an Ethics & Compliance hotline. "If you have a question or ever think that one of your fellow Googlers or the company as a whole may be falling short of our commitment, don't be silent," states the code. "We want—and need—to hear from you."[29]

Still, written codes and ethics programs do not ensure ethical behavior. Ethics and social responsibility require a total corporate commitment. They must be a component of the overall corporate culture. As the Google Code of Conduct concludes: "It's impossible to spell out every possible ethical scenario we might face. Instead, we rely on one another's good judgment to uphold a high standard of integrity for ourselves and our company. Remember . . . don't be evil. If you see something that isn't right, speak up!"

The Sustainable Company

At the foundation of marketing is the belief that companies that fulfill the needs and wants of customers will thrive. Companies that fail to meet customer needs or that intentionally or unintentionally harm customers, others in society, or future generations will decline.

Says one observer, "Sustainability is an emerging business megatrend, like electrification and mass production, that will profoundly affect companies' competitiveness and even their survival." Says another, "increasingly, companies and leaders will be assessed not only on immediate results but also on . . . the ultimate effects their actions have on societal wellbeing. This trend has been coming in small ways for years but now is surging. So pick up your recycled cup of fair-trade coffee, and get ready."[30]

Sustainable companies are those that create value for customers through socially, environmentally, and ethically responsible actions. Sustainable marketing goes beyond caring for the needs and wants of today's customers. It means having concern for tomorrow's customers in assuring the survival and success of the business, shareholders, employees, and the broader world in which they all live. It means pursuing the mission of a triple bottom line: "people, planet, profits."[31] Sustainable marketing provides the context in which companies can build profitable customer relationships by creating value *for* customers in order to capture value *from* customers in return—now and in the future.

MyMarketingLab

Go to **mymktlab.com** to complete the problems marked with this icon .

END OF CHAPTER REVIEWING THE CONCEPTS

CHAPTER REVIEW AND KEY TERMS

Objectives Review

In this chapter, we addressed many of the important *sustainable marketing* concepts related to marketing's sweeping impact on individual consumers, other businesses, and society as a whole. Sustainable marketing requires socially, environmentally, and ethically responsible actions that bring value to not only present-day consumers and businesses but also future generations and society as a whole. Sustainable companies are those that act responsibly to create value for customers in order to capture value from customers in return—now and in the future.

OBJECTIVE 1 Define *sustainable marketing* and discuss its importance. (pp 496–498)

Sustainable marketing calls for meeting the present needs of consumers and businesses while preserving or enhancing the ability of future generations to meet their needs. Whereas the marketing concept recognizes that companies thrive by fulfilling the day-to-day needs of customers, sustainable marketing calls for socially and environmentally responsible actions that meet both the immediate and future needs of customers and the company. Truly sustainable marketing requires a smooth-functioning marketing system in which consumers, companies, public policy makers, and others work together to ensure responsible marketing actions.

OBJECTIVE 2 Identify the major social criticisms of marketing. (pp 498–505)

Marketing's *impact on individual consumer welfare* has been criticized for its high prices, deceptive practices, high-pressure selling, shoddy or unsafe products, planned obsolescence, and poor service to disadvantaged consumers. Marketing's *impact on society* has been criticized for creating false wants and too much materialism, too few social goods, and cultural pollution. Critics have also denounced marketing's *impact on other businesses* for harming competitors and reducing competition through acquisitions, practices that create barriers to entry, and unfair competitive marketing practices. Some of these concerns are justified; some are not.

 **OBJECTIVE 3 Define *consumerism* and *environmentalism* and explain how they affect marketing strategies. (pp 505–511)**

Concerns about the marketing system have led to citizen action movements. *Consumerism* is an organized social movement intended to strengthen the rights and power of consumers relative to sellers. Alert marketers view it as an opportunity to serve consumers better by providing more consumer information, education, and protection. *Environmentalism* is an organized social movement seeking to minimize the harm done to the environment and quality of life by marketing practices. Most companies are now accepting responsibility for doing no environmental harm. They are adopting policies of *environmental sustainability*—developing strategies that both sustain the environment and produce profits for the company. Both consumerism and environmentalism are important components of sustainable marketing.

 **OBJECTIVE 4 Describe the principles of sustainable marketing. (pp 511–516)**

Many companies originally resisted these social movements and laws, but most now recognize a need for positive consumer information, education, and protection. Under the sustainable marketing concept, a company's marketing should support the best long-run performance of the marketing system. It should be guided by five sustainable marketing principles: *consumer-oriented marketing*, *customer value marketing*, *innovative marketing*, *sense-of-mission marketing*, and *societal marketing*.

 **OBJECTIVE 5 Explain the role of ethics in marketing. (pp 516–519)**

Increasingly, companies are responding to the need to provide company policies and guidelines to help their managers deal with questions of *marketing ethics*. Of course, even the best guidelines cannot resolve all the difficult ethical decisions that individuals and firms must make. But there are some principles from which marketers can choose. One principle states that the free market and the legal system should decide such issues. A second and more enlightened principle puts responsibility not on the system but in the hands of individual companies and managers. Each firm and marketing manager must work out a philosophy of socially responsible and ethical behavior. Under the sustainable marketing concept, managers must look beyond what is legal and allowable and develop standards based on personal integrity, corporate conscience, and long-term consumer welfare.

Key Terms

Objective 1
Sustainable marketing (p 496)

Objective 3
Consumerism (p 505)
Environmentalism (p 507)
Environmental sustainability (p 507)

Objective 4
Consumer-oriented marketing (p 512)
Customer value marketing (p 512)
Innovative marketing (p 512)
Sense-of-mission marketing (p 512)
Societal marketing (p 515)
Deficient products (p 515)
Pleasing products (p 515)
Salutary products (p 515)
Desirable products (p 515)

DISCUSSION AND CRITICAL THINKING

Discussion Questions

16-1. What is sustainable marketing? Explain how the sustainable marketing concept differs from the marketing concept and the societal marketing concept. (AACSB: Written and Oral Communication)

16-2. Discuss the types of harmful impact that marketing practices can have on competition and the associated problems. (AACSB: Written and Oral Communication)

 **16-3.** What is consumerism? What rights do consumers have, and why do some critics feel buyers need more protection? (AACSB: Written and Oral Communication)

16-4. What is environmental sustainability? How should companies gauge their progress toward achieving it? (AACSB: Written and Oral Communication)

Critical Thinking Exercises

16-5. Some cultures are more accepting than others of corrupt practices such as bribery. Corruption is not tolerated in the United States or by U.S. firms operating abroad. However, in some countries, it's the price of entry for many foreign firms. Visit www.transparency.org and look at the Corruption Perception Index (CPI) report. The CPI can range from 0 to 100, where a low index score means a country is perceived as highly corrupt and a higher score means highly ethical. Pick three countries that are rated as least corrupt and three that are highly corrupt and explain why you think they may be that way. (AACSB: Written and Oral Communication; Information Technology; Reflective Thinking)

16-6. Many consumers want to recycle, but rules vary among localities, making it difficult for consumers to know if something is recyclable. Voluntary "How2Recycle" labels are starting to appear on products to help consumers. Visit www.how2recycle.info/ to learn about these voluntary labels and the types of products that will be carrying them. Will these labels make it easier for consumers to recycle? (AACSB: Written and Oral Communication; Information Technology; Reflective Thinking)

16-7. Discuss an example of a company committing an unethical marketing practice. What was the violation? How was the unethical behavior dealt with? (AACSB: Written and Oral Communication; Reflective Thinking)

MINICASES AND APPLICATIONS

Online, Mobile, and Social Media Marketing Mobile Medical Apps

With the explosion of mobile devices and apps, it's not surprising that medical apps are taking off. There are apps to identify pills, track pregnancy, check for melanoma skin cancer, and even teach medical professionals how to read electrocardiograms. Some apps are replacing devices used by health-care professionals in hospitals and doctors' offices. There are more than 40,000 medical applications currently available, and the market is still in its infancy. The market's growth has caught the attention of the Food and Drug Administration (FDA), the agency regulating medical devices. So far, medical apps have been unregulated, but that is about to change. The FDA released guidelines requiring app developers to apply for FDA approval, which could take years. According to the Government Accountability Office, it takes the FDA six months to approve a device that is similar to an existing one and up to 20 months for new devices. According to another report, approval costs $24 million to $75 million. Not all apps would require FDA approval—only ones making medical claims. Although many developers think regulation is necessary to protect the public, most believe that the current process is too slow and a new regulatory framework is necessary.

16-8. Describe two examples of mobile apps for health-care providers. (AACSB: Written and Oral Communication; Information Technology)

16-9. Is regulatory approval of medical mobile apps necessary? Will the FDA's requirement for approval constrain innovation? Explain. (AACSB: Written and Oral Communication; Ethical Understanding and Reasoning; Reflective Thinking)

Marketing Ethics Right to Repair

Automobiles have become so complicated that mechanics need computers to diagnose problems. Independent car mechanics may have the computers, but they don't have the codes or tools necessary to diagnose and fix problems on newer-model cars. Those are reserved for car makers' dealerships. Some critics claim that creates an unfair advantage for auto dealerships over independent mechanics and auto-parts retailers and keeps repair prices higher for consumers. The Massachusetts Right to Repair Coalition put a stop to that by first getting a right to repair initiative on the November 2012 ballot, but it then got the state's legislature and governor to sign it into law before the vote even took place (voters did pass the law with an overwhelming 86 percent victory). In Massachusetts, car makers must make the diagnostic information available. On a national level, the Motor Vehicle Owner's Right to Repair Act was introduced in the House of Representatives in 2011, but it did not become federal law. Of course, automakers and dealerships opposed these initiatives. Opponents claim that right to repair initiatives will allow auto-parts makers access to manufacturers' proprietary information as well as endanger the safety of consumers resulting from possibly faulty repairs. Supporters of the initiatives say manufacturers are just looking to keep their unfair advantage and protect their repair business.

16-10. Are automobile manufacturers and their dealerships creating an unfair competitive advantage by not sharing information and special tools with independent mechanics? Write an argument supporting the automakers' actions.

(AACSB: Written and Oral Communication; Ethical Understanding and Reasoning; Reflective Thinking)

16-11. There is a similar initiative regarding owners' right to repair digital products. Discuss this initiative and its implications. (AACSB: Written and Oral Communication; Reflective Thinking)

Marketing by the Numbers The Cost of Sustainability

One element of sustainability is organic farming. But if you've priced organic foods, you know they are more expensive. Organic farming costs much more than conventional farming, and those costs are passed on to consumers. For example, a dozen conventionally farmed eggs costs consumers $1.50, whereas a dozen organic eggs costs $2.80. However, if prices get too high, consumers will not purchase the organic eggs. Suppose that the average fixed costs for conventionally farmed eggs are $1 million per year but they are twice that amount for organic eggs. Organic farmers' variable costs per dozen are twice as much as well, costing $1.80 per dozen. Refer to Appendix 3, Marketing by the Numbers, to answer the following questions.

16-12. Most large egg farmers sell eggs directly to retailers. What is the farmer's price per dozen to the retailer for conventional and organic eggs if the retailer's margin is 20 percent based on the retail price? (AACSB: Written and Oral Communication; Analytical Thinking)

16-13. How many dozen eggs does a conventional farmer need to sell to break even? How many does an organic farmer need to sell to break even? (AACSB: Written and Oral Communication; Analytical Thinking)

Video Case Life is good

Most companies these days are looking for ways to be more socially responsible in manufacturing and marketing the goods and services they produce. But only a few companies produce goods and services with the primary purpose of making the world a better place. Life is good is one of those companies. Most people are familiar with the cheerful logo of Life is good products. But few are aware of what the company does with its profits behind the scenes.

This video focuses on Life is good Playmakers, a nonprofit organization dedicated to helping children overcome life-threatening challenges. From the time Life is good started selling T-shirts in the early 1990s, its founders supported Playmakers. The relationship between the two organizations became progressively stronger, ultimately leading Life is good to make Playmakers an official branch of the company.

After viewing the video featuring Life is good, answer the following questions:

16-14. How many examples can you provide showing how Life is good defies the common social criticisms of marketing?

16-15. How does Life is good practice sustainable marketing principles?

16-16. With all its efforts to do *good*, can Life is good continue to do *well*? Explain.

Company Cases 16 Warby Parker / 4 Oracle

See Appendix 1 for cases appropriate for this chapter. **Case 16, Warby Parker: Eyewear with a Purpose.** Warby Parker makes high-quality, fashionable eyeglasses at a revolutionary price point—and distributes a free pair of glasses to a person in need for every pair purchased. **Case 4, Oracle: Getting a Grip on Big Data.** As technology allows for the gathering of more and more consumer data, Oracle is on the front line, helping companies harness Big Data as a means of forming stronger relationships with customers.

MyMarketingLab

Go to **mymktlab.com** for Auto-graded writing questions as well as the following Assisted-graded writing questions:

16-17. Critics claim that certain marketing practices hurt consumers. Discuss the bases for this claim and how marketers refute them. (AACSB: Written and Oral Communication)

16-18. Discuss the philosophies that might guide marketers facing ethical issues. (AACSB: Written and Oral Communication)

16-19. Mymktlab Only—comprehensive writing assignment for this chapter.

Appendix 1 **Company Cases**

Company Case 1

In-N-Out Burger: Customer Value the Old-Fashioned Way

In 1948, Harry and Esther Snyder opened the first In-N-Out Burger in Baldwin Park, California. It was a simple double drive-thru setup with the kitchen between two service lanes, a walk-up window, and outdoor seating. The menu consisted of burgers, shakes, soft drinks, and fries. This format was common for the time period. In fact, another burger joint that fit this same description opened up the very same year just 45 minutes away from the first In-N-Out Burger. It was called McDonald's. Today, McDonald's boasts over 34,000 stores worldwide that bring in more than $88 billion every year. In-N-Out has only 281 stores in five states, good for an estimated $625 million a year. Based on the outcomes, it would seem that McDonald's has emerged the clear victor.

But In-N-Out never wanted to be another McDonald's. And despite its smaller size—or perhaps because of it—In-N-Out's customers like the regional chain just the way it is. When it comes to customer satisfaction, In-N-Out beats McDonald's hands down. It regularly posts the highest customer satisfaction scores of any fast-food restaurant in its market areas. Compared to McDonald's customers, patrons of In-N-Out are *really* "lovin' it." Just about anyone who has been to an In-N-Out believes it's the best burger they've ever had. It comes as no surprise, then, that the average per-store sales for In-N-Out eclipse those of McDonald's and are double the industry average.

Breaking All the Rules

According to Stacy Perman, author of a definitive book on In-N-Out, the company has achieved unequivocal success by "breaking all the rules." By rules, Ms. Perman refers to the standard business practices for the fast-food industry and even retail in general. In-N-Out has maintained a tenacious focus on customer well-being, but it has done so by doing the unthinkable: not changing. The company's original philosophy is still in place today and best illustrates the basis for the company's rule breaking: "Give customers the freshest, highest quality foods you can buy and provide them with friendly service in a sparkling clean environment." The big burger giants might take exception to the idea that they aren't providing the same customer focus. But let's take a closer look at what these things mean to In-N-Out.

For starters, at In-N-Out, quality food means fresh food. Burgers are made from 100 percent pure beef—no additives, fillers, or preservatives. In-N-Out owns and operates its own patty-making commissaries, ensuring that every burger is fresh and never frozen. Vegetables are sliced and diced by hand in every restaurant. Fries are even made from whole potatoes. And, yes, milkshakes are made from real ice cream. In an industry that has progressively become more and more enamored with processing technologies such as cryogenically freezing foods and preparing all ingredients in off-site warehouses, In-N-Out is indeed an anomaly. In fact, you won't even find a freezer, heating lamp, or microwave oven in an In-N-Out restaurant. From the beginning, the company slogan has been "Quality you can taste." And customers are convinced that they can do just that.

In-N-Out hasn't changed its formula for freshness. But in another deviation from the norm, it also hasn't changed its menu. Unlike McDonald's or Wendy's, which introduce seemingly unending streams of new menu items, In-N-Out stays true to Harry Snyder's original mantra: "Keep it real simple. Do one thing and do it the best you can." This charge from the founder focuses on what the chain has always done well: making really good hamburgers, really good fries, and really good shakes—that's it. While others have focused on menu expansion in constant search of the next hit item to drive traffic, In-N-Out has tenaciously stuck to the basics. In fact, it took 60 years for the company to add 7up and Dr. Pepper to its menu.

Although the limited menu might seem restrictive, customers don't feel that way. In another demonstration of commitment to customers, In-N-Out employees will gladly make any of the menu items in a truly customized fashion. From the chain's earliest years, menu modifications became such a norm at In-N-Out that a "secret" menu emerged consisting of code words that aren't posted on regular menu boards. So customers in the know can order their burgers "animal style" (pickles, extra spread, grilled onions, and a mustard-fried patty). Whereas the "Double-Double" (double meat, double cheese) is on the menu, burgers can also be ordered in 3 × 3 or 4 × 4 configurations. Fries can also be order animal style (two slices of cheese, grilled onions, and spread), well done, or light. A Neapolitan shake is a mixture of chocolate, vanilla, and strawberry shakes. The list goes on and on. Knowledge of this secret menu is yet another thing that makes customers feel special.

It's not just In-N-Out's food that pleases customers. The chain also features well-trained employees who deliver unexpectedly friendly service. In-N-Out hires and retains outgoing, enthusiastic, and capable employees and treats them very well. It pays new part-time staff $10.50 an hour and gives them regular raises. Part-timers also receive paid vacations. General managers make over $100,000 a year plus bonuses and receive a full-benefit package that rivals anything in the corporate world. Managers who meet goals are sent on lavish trips with their spouses, often to Europe in first-class seats. For gala events, managers wear tuxedos. Executives believe that the men and women who run In-N-Out stores stand shoulder-to-shoulder with any blue-chip manager, and want them to feel that way. Managers are promoted from within. In fact, 80 percent of In-N-Out managers started at the very bottom. As a result, In-N-Out has one of the lowest turnover rates in an industry infamous for high turnover.

Happy, motivated employees help create loyal, satisfied customers. In fact, words like *loyal* and *satisfied* don't do justice to how customers feel about In-N-Out Burger. The restaurant chain has developed an unparalleled cult following. When a new In-N-Out first opens, the line of cars often stretches out a mile or more, and people stand in line for hours to get a burger, fries, and a shake. Fans have been known to camp overnight to be the first in line. When In-N-Out made its debut in Texas, one woman cried. "Pinch me, it just doesn't feel real," whimpered customer Danielle DeInnocentes, overcome with emotion as the reality of her newfound proximity to the burger chain set in.

Slow Growth Nurtures Fans

Some observers point out that it's probably more than just the food and the service that created In-N-Out's diehard customer base. Because of In-N-Out's slow-growth expansion strategy, you won't find one of the famous red-and-white stores with crisscrossed palm trees on every corner. By 1976, In-N-Out had grown to only 18 southern California stores, whereas McDonald's and Burger King had opened thousands of stores worldwide. It took In-N-Out 40 years to open its first non-California store in Las Vegas. And even as the company expands into Arizona, Utah, and Texas, it sticks tenaciously to its policy of not opening more than about 10 stores per year.

The lack of access to an In-N-Out in most states has created legions of cravers coast to coast. Fans have created countless Facebook pages, filled with posts by consumers begging the family-owned corporation to bring In-N-Out to their states. But In-N-Out's policy is driven by its commitment to quality. It will open a new store only when it has trained management and company-owned distribution centers in place.

The scarcity of In-N-Out stores only adds to its allure. Customers regularly go out of their way and drive long distances to get their fix. Having to drive a little further contributes to the feeling that going to In-N-Out is an event. Out-of-state visitors in the know often put an In-N-Out stop high on their list of things to do. Jeff Rose, a financial planner from Carbondale, Illinois, always stops at In-N-Out first when he visits Las Vegas to see his mother. "You have to pass it when you drive to her house," he says in his defense. "It's not like the time I paid an extra $40 in cab fare to visit an In-N-Out on the way to the San Diego airport."

Consistent with the other elements of its simple-yet-focused strategy, In-N-Out doesn't spend much on advertising—it doesn't have to. In fact, although the company doesn't release financial figures, some estimates place total promotional spending at less than 1 percent of revenues. McDonald's shells out 7 percent of its revenue on advertising. In-N-Out's small promotional budget is for local billboards and radio ads. But when it comes to really spreading the word, In-N-Out lets its customers do the heavy lifting. Customers truly are apostles for the brand. They proudly wear In-N-Out T-shirts and slap In-N-Out bumper stickers on their cars. Rabid regulars drag a constant stream of new devotees into restaurants, an act often referred to as "the conversion." They can't wait to pass along the secret menu codes and share the sublime pleasures of diving into a 4×4 animal style. "When you tell someone else what 'animal style' means," says an analyst, "you feel like you're passing on a secret handshake. People really get into the whole thing."

In-N-Out doesn't use paid endorsers, but word-of-mouth praise regularly flows from the mouths of A-list celebrities. When former *Tonight Show* host Conan O'Brien asked Tom Hanks what he recommended doing in Los Angeles, Hanks replied," One of the true great things about Los Angeles is In-N-Out Burger." Paris Hilton famously claimed she was on her way to In-N-Out when she was pulled over for a DUI. And paparazzi have snapped shots of scores of celebrities getting an In-N-Out fix, including Miley Cyrus, Selena Gomez, Christian Slater, and Nick Jonas. The fact that such celebrities aren't paid to pay homage to the brand underscores that In-N-Out is truly a hip place.

A Questionable Future?

Many analysts have questioned whether or not In-N-Out can sustain its unwavering 65-year run. For example, the company that had been run only by Harry, Esther, or one of their two sons for its first 58 years hit a barrier in 2006 when Esther Snyder passed away. The only direct descendant of the Snyder family at that time was 23-year-old Lynsi Martinez, who was not yet in a position to take over the company. That left In-N-Out in the hands of Mark Taylor, the former vice president of operations. But as directed by Esther Snyder's will, granddaughter Lynsi took over as In-N-Out's sixth president in 2010 before her 28th birthday. Often described as shy, Martinez has progressively gained ownership of the company and will have full control in 2017.

The changing of the executive guard has gone largely unnoticed by customers and fans, an indication that the In-N-Out legacy carries on. With long lines still snaking out the door of any location at lunchtime, demand seems as high as ever. "The more chains like McDonald's and Burger King change and expand, the more In-N-Out sticks to its guns," says the analyst. "In a way, it symbolizes the ideal American way of doing business: Treating people well, focusing on product quality, and being very successful." In-N-Out's customers couldn't agree more. When it comes to fast-food chains, delighted customers will tell you, "There's In-N-Out, and then there's everyone else."

Questions for Discussion

1. Describe In-N-Out in terms of the value it provides for customers.
2. Evaluate In-N-Out's performance relative to customer expectations. What is the outcome of this process?
3. Should In-N-Out adopt a high-growth strategy? Why or why not?
4. With so many customers thrilled by In-N-Out's "no-change" philosophy, why don't more burger chains follow suit?

Sources: Seth Lubove, "Youngest American Woman Billionaire Found with In-N-Out," *Bloomberg*, February 4, 2013, www.bloomberg.com/news/2013-02-04/youngest-american-woman-billionaire-found-with-in-n-out.html; Jay Weston, "In-N-Out Burger's 'Secret Menu' Revealed," *Huffington Post*, April 6, 2012, www.huffingtonpost.com/jay-weston/in-n-out-burgers-secret-menu_b_1407388.html; Meredith Land, "Inside The In-N-Out Burger Empire," *NBCDFW*, November 17, 2011, www.nbcdfw.com/the-scene/food-drink/Inside-the-In-N-Out-Burger-Empire-134008293.html; and www.in-n-out.com, accessed May 2013.

Company Case 2

Dyson: Solving Customer Problems in Ways They Never Imagined

From a head-on perspective, it has a sleek, stunning stainless steel design. With wings that extend downward at a 15-degree angle from its center, it appears ready for takeoff. The latest aeronautic design from Boeing? No. It's the most innovative sink faucet to hit the market in decades. Dyson—the company famous for vacuum cleaners, hand dryers, and fans unlike anything else on the market—is about to revolutionize the traditional sink faucet.

The Airblade Tap—a faucet that washes *and* dries hands with completely touch-free operation—is the latest in a line of revolutionary Dyson products that have reinvented their categories. In fact, Dyson was founded on a few very simple principles. First, every Dyson product must provide real consumer benefits that make life easier. Second, each product must take a totally unique approach to accomplishing common, everyday tasks. Finally, each Dyson product must infuse excitement into products that are so mundane, most people never think much about them.

The Man behind the Name

James Dyson was born and raised in the United Kingdom. After studying design at the Royal College of Art, he had initially planned to design and build geodesic structures for use as commercial space. But with no money to get his venture started, he took a job working for an acquaintance who handed him a blow torch and challenged him to create a prototype for an amphibious landing craft. With no welding experience, he figured things out on his own. Before long, the company was selling 200 boats a year based on his design.

That trial-and-error approach came naturally to Dyson, who applied it to create Dyson Inc.'s first product. In 1979, he had purchased what claimed was the most powerful vacuum cleaner on the market. He found it to be anything but. Instead, it seemed simply to move dirt around the room. This left Dyson wondering why no one had yet invented a decent vacuum cleaner. At that point, he remembered something he'd seen in an industrial sawmill—a cyclonic separator that removed dust from the air. Why wouldn't that approach work well in vacuum cleaners? "I thought no one was bothering to use technology in vacuum cleaners," said Dyson. Indeed, the core technology of vacuum motors at the time was more than 150 years old. "I saw a great opportunity to improve."

Dyson then did something that very few people would have the patience or the vision to do. He spent 15 years and made 5,127 vacuum prototypes—all based on a bag-less cyclonic separator—before he had the one that went to market. In his own words, "There were 5,126 failures. But I learned from each one. That's how I came up with a solution."

Dyson's all-new vacuum was far more than techno-gadgetry. Dyson had developed a completely new motor that ran at 110,000 revolutions per minute—three times faster than any other vacuum on the market. It provided tremendous suction that other brands simply couldn't match. The bag-less design was very effective at removing dirt and particles from the air, and the machine was much easier to clean out than vacuums requiring the messy process of changing bags. The vacuum also maneuvered more easily and could reach places other vacuums could not. Dyson's vacuum really worked.

With a finished product in hand, Dyson pitched it to all the appliance makers. None of them wanted it. So Dyson borrowed $900,000 and began manufacturing the vacuum himself. He then convinced a mail-order catalog to carry the Dyson instead of Hoover or Electrolux, "Because your catalog is boring." Dyson vacuums were soon picked up by other mail order catalogs, then by small appliance chains, and then by large department stores. By the late 1990s, Dyson's full line of vacuums were being distributed in multiple global markets. At that point, Dyson, the company that had quickly become known for vacuum cleaners, was already on to its next big thing.

The Dyson Method

During the development of Dyson's vacuums, a development model began to take shape. Take everyday products, focus on their shortcomings, and improve them to the point of reinvention.

"I like going for unglamorous products and making them a pleasure to use," Dyson told *Fortune* magazine. By taking this route, the company finds solutions to the problems it is trying to solve. At the same time, it sometimes finds solutions for other problems.

For example, the vacuum motor Dyson developed sucked air with unprecedented strength. But the flipside of vacuum suction is exhaust. Why couldn't such a motor blow air at wet hands so fast that the water would be pressed off in a squeegee-like manner, rather than the slow, evaporative approach employed by commercial hand dryers?

With that realization, Dyson created and launched the Airblade, a hand dryer that blows air through a .2-millimeter slot at 420 miles per hour. It dries hands in 12 seconds, rather than the more typical 40 seconds required by other hand dryers. It also uses cold air—a huge departure from the standard warm-air approach of existing commercial dryers. This not only reduced energy consumption by 75 percent—a major bonus for commercial enterprises that pay the electric bills—but customers were much more likely to use a product that worked fast and did the job right.

With very observable benefits, the Airblade was rapidly adopted by commercial customers. For example, as part of a comprehensive plan to improve its environmental impact, Los Angeles International Airport (LAX) was looking for a solution to the financial and environmental costs of manufacturing, distributing, and servicing the paper towel dispensers in more than 100 restrooms throughout its terminals. Switching to recycled paper towels helped, but only minimally. The energy used by conventional hand dryers made them an unattractive alternative. But when LAX management saw a demonstration of the Dyson Airblade, it was a no-brainer. With Airblades installed throughout its terminals, LAX was able to significantly reduce landfill waste as well as costs. The overwhelmingly positive feedback from travelers was icing on the cake.

Today's Airblades have evolved, guided by Dyson's customer-centric approach to developing products. With the first Airblade, it was apparent that all that high-powered air is noisy. So Dyson spent seven years and a staggering $42 million to develop the V4 motor, one of the smallest and quietest commercial motors available. The new Airblade is quieter and almost six pounds lighter than the original. But even more advanced is Dyson's new Blade V, a sleeker design that is 60 percent thinner than the Airblade, protruding only four inches from the wall.

Assessing Real Customer Needs

Although Dyson sees itself as a technology-driven company, it develops products with the end-user in mind. But rather than using traditional market research methods, Dyson takes a different approach. "Dyson avoids the kind of focus group techniques that are, frankly, completely averaging," says Adam Rostrom, group marketing director for Dyson. "Most companies start with the consumer and say, 'Hey Mr. or Mrs. X, what do you want from your toothbrush tomorrow or what do you want from your shampoo tomorrow?' The depressing reality is that often you won't get many inspiring answers."

Rather, Dyson's uses an approach it calls "interrogating products" to develop new products that produce real solutions to customer problems. After identifying the most obvious shortcomings for everyday products, it finds ways to improve them. It then tests prototypes with real consumers under heavy nondisclosure agreements. In this manner, Dyson can observe consumer reactions in the context of real people using products in their real lives.

This approach enables Dyson to develop revolutionary products like the Air Multiplier, a fan that moves large volumes of air around a room with no blades. In fact, the Air Multiplier looks nothing like a fan. By using technology similar to that found in turbochargers and jet engines, the Air Multiplier draws air in, amplifies it 18 times, and spits it back out in an uninterrupted stream that eliminates the buffeting and direct air pressure of conventional fans. Referring to the standard methods of assessing customer needs and wants, Rostrom explains, "If you . . . asked people what they wanted from their fan tomorrow, they wouldn't say 'get rid of the blades.' Our approach is about product breakthroughs rather than the approach of just running a focus group and testing a concept.

No-Nonsense Promotion

In yet another departure from conventional marketing, Dyson claims to shun one of the core concepts of marketing. "There is only one word that's banned in our company: brand," Mr. Dyson proclaimed at *Wired* magazine's *Disruption By Design* conference. What Dyson seems to mean is that the company is not about creating images and associations that do not originate with the quality and function of the product itself. "We're only as good as our latest product."

With its rigid focus on product quality and its innovative approaches to common problems, Dyson's approach to brand building centers on simply letting its products speak for themselves. Indeed, from the mid-1990s when it started promoting its bag-less vacuums, Dyson invested heavily in television advertising. But unlike most creative approaches, Dyson's ads are simple and straightforward, explaining to viewers immediately what the product is, what it does, and why they need one.

"It's a really rational subject matter that we work on, so we don't need to use white horses on beaches or anything like that," Rostrom says, referring to Dyson's no-nonsense approach to advertising. "We need only to explain the products. One thing we're careful to avoid is resorting to industry-standard ways of communicating—fluffy dogs and sleeping babies and so on. We don't want to blend in that way."

Today, Dyson complements traditional advertising with digital efforts. Like its TV advertising, such methods are simple, straightforward, and right to the point. For example, e-mail communications are used sparingly, targeted to existing customers, and timed for maximum impact. And beyond the media it buys, Dyson considers public relations as the promotional medium that carries most of the weight. From product reviews in the mainstream media to online reviews and tweets about its products, word of its Dyson's products gets around fast.

The Airblade Tap sink faucet, Dyson's most recent new product, is a microcosm of Dyson's marketing strategy. It took 125 engineers three years and 3,300 prototypes to develop the final product. The Airblade Tap provides clearly communicated solutions to everyday problems—solutions that make life easier. It solves those problems in ways that no other product has ever attempted, claiming to "reinvent the way we wash our hands." And it injects style into an otherwise boring product. Dyson sums it up this way: "Washing and drying your hands tends not to be a very pleasant experience. Water splashes, paper is wasted, and germs are passed along. The Tap is a totally different experience. You have your own sink, your own dryer." And at $1,500, it illustrates another element of the Dyson marketing mix—a high price point that communicates quality and benefits that are worth it.

If the Airblade Tap is a hit, it will serve to forward Dyson's goal of doubling its annual revenues of $1.5 billion "quite quickly." The company is not only continuing to demonstrate that it can come up with winning products again and again, it is expanding throughout the world at a rapid pace. Dyson products are sold in over 50 global markets, selling well in emerging economies as well as developed first-world nations. Dyson does well in both economic good times and recessionary periods. Dyson also sees another big move in its future—a chain of company stores (as many as 20,000 stores in the United States alone) carved in the image of Apple's beloved hangouts. From a single vacuum cleaner to what Dyson is today in less than 20 years—that's quite an evolution.

Questions for Discussion

1. Write a market-oriented mission statement for Dyson.
2. What are Dyson's goals and objectives?
3. Does Dyson have a business portfolio? Explain.
4. Discuss Dyson's marketing mix techniques and how they fit within the context of its business and marketing strategy.
5. Is Dyson a customer-centered company? Explain.

Sources: Omar Akhtar, "Three Questions for Design Genius Mr. Dyson," *Fortune*, February 5, 2013, www.tech.fortune.cnn.com/2013/02/05/3-questions-for-design-genius-Mr.-dyson/; Matt Warman, "Sir Mr. Dyson: Master of Invention Has the Wind Behind Him," *The Telegraph*, February 9, 2013, www.telegraph.co.uk/technology/news/9858568/Sir-Mr.-Dyson-master-of-invention-has-the-wind-behind-him.html; Jonathan Bacon, "Cleaning Up All over the World," *Marketing Week*, November 22, 2012, www.marketingweek.co.uk/trends/cleaning-up-all-over-the-world/4004751.article; Matthew Creamer, "Mr. Dyson: 'I Don't Believe in Brand'," *Advertising Age*, May 2, 2012, http://adage.com/print/234494; Kelsey Campbell-Dollaghan, "Dyson's Latest Coup: A $1,500 Sink Faucet That Dries Hands, Too," *Fastco Design*, February 5, 2013, www.fastcodesign.com/1671788/dyson-s-latest-coup-a-1500-sink-faucet-that-dries-hands-too; Burt Helm, "Dyson Marketing: So Simple, It's Brilliant," *The Marketing Robot*, April 16, 2012, www.themarketingrobot.com/dyson-marketing-so-simple-its-brilliant; Burt Helm, "How I Did It: Mr. Dyson," *Inc.*, February 28, 2012, www.inc.com/magazine/201203/burt-helm/how-i-did-it-Mr.-dyson.html; and information found at www.dyson.com, accessed June 2013.

Company Case 3

Xerox: Adapting to the Turbulent Marketing Environment

Xerox introduced the first plain-paper office copier more than 50 years ago. In the decades that followed, the company that invented photocopying flat-out dominated the industry it had created. The name Xerox became almost generic for copying (as in "I'll Xerox this for you"). Through the years, Xerox fought off round after round of rivals to stay atop the fiercely competitive copier industry. Through the late 1990s, Xerox's profits and stock price were soaring.

Then things went terribly wrong for Xerox. The legendary company's stock and fortunes took a stomach-churning dive. In only 18 months, Xerox lost some $38 billion in market value. Its stock price plunged from almost $70 in 1999 to under $5 by mid-2001. The once-dominant market leader found itself on the brink of bankruptcy. What happened? Blame it on change or—rather—on Xerox's failure to adapt to its rapidly changing marketing environment. The world was quickly going digital, but Xerox hadn't kept up.

In the new digital environment, Xerox customers no longer relied on the company's flagship products—standalone copiers—to share information and documents. Rather than pumping out and distributing stacks of black-and-white copies, they created digital documents and shared them electronically. Or they printed out multiple copies on their nearby networked printer. On a broader level, while Xerox was busy perfecting copy machines, customers were looking for more sophisticated "document management solutions." They wanted systems that would let them scan documents in Frankfurt, weave them into colorful, customized showpieces in San Francisco, and print them on demand in London—even altering for American spelling.

This left Xerox on the edge of financial disaster. "We didn't have any cash and few prospects for making any," says current Xerox CEO, Ursula Burns. "The one thing you wanted was good and strong leaders that were aligned and could get us through things and we didn't have that." Burns didn't realize it back then, but she would one day lead the company she began working for as a summer intern in 1981. In fact, Burns almost left the company in 2000, but her colleague and friend, Anne Mulcahy, became CEO and convinced her to stay. Burns was named a senior vice president and was then charged with cleaning house.

The Turnaround Begins

Task number one: Outsource Xerox's manufacturing. An often criticized and unpopular move, outsourcing was critical to Xerox's cost-saving efforts. Burns oversaw the process in a way that preserved quality while achieving the desired cost benefits. And she did so with the blessing of Xerox's employee union by convincing the union that it was either lose some jobs or have no jobs at all. With the restructuring of manufacturing, in only four years, Xerox's workforce dropped from 100,000 employees to 55,000. Although this and other efforts returned Xerox to profitability within a few years, the bigger question still remained: What business is Xerox really in?

To answer this question, Xerox renewed its focus on the customer. Xerox had always focused on copier hardware. But "we were being dragged by our customers into managing large, complex business processes for them," says Burns. Before developing new products, Xerox researchers held seemingly endless customer focus groups. Sophie Vandebroek, Xerox's chief technology officer, called this "dreaming with the customer." The goal, she argued, was "involving [Xerox] experts who know the technology with customers who know the pain points. . . . Ultimately innovation is about delighting the customer." In the process, Xerox discovered that understanding customers is just as important as understanding technology.

What Xerox learned is that customers didn't want just copiers; they wanted easier, faster, and less costly ways to share documents and information. As a result, the company had to rethink, redefine, and reinvent itself. Xerox underwent a remarkable transformation. It stopped defining itself as a "copier company." In fact, it even stopped making standalone copiers. Instead, Xerox began billing itself as the world's leading document-management technology and services enterprise. The company's newly minted mission was to help companies "be smarter about their documents."

This shift in emphasis created new customer relationships, as well as new competitors. Instead of selling copiers to equipment purchasing managers, Xerox found itself developing and selling document management systems to high-level information technology managers. Instead of competing head-on with copy machine competitors like Sharp, Canon, and Ricoh, Xerox was now squaring off against information technology companies like HP and IBM. Although it encountered many potholes along the way, the company once known as the iconic "copier company" became increasingly comfortable with its new identity as a document-management company.

Building New Strengths

Xerox's revenue, profits, and stock price began to show signs of recovery. But before it could declare it troubles over, yet another challenging environmental force arose—the Great Recession. The recession severely depressed Xerox's core printing and copying equipment and services business, and the company's sales and stock price tumbled once again. So in a major move to maintain its transition momentum, Xerox acquired Affiliated Computer Services (ACS), a $6.4 billion information technology (IT) services powerhouse with a foot in the door of seemingly every back office in the world. The expertise, capabilities, and established channels of ACS were just what Xerox needed to take its new business plan to fruition.

The synergy between Xerox, ACS, and other acquired companies has resulted in a broad portfolio of customer-focused products, software, and services that help the Xerox's customers manage documents and information. In fact, Xerox has introduced more than 130 innovative new products in the past four years. It now offers digital products and systems ranging from network printers and multifunction devices to color printing and publishing systems, digital presses, and "book factories." It also offers an impressive array of print management consulting and outsourcing services that help businesses develop online document archives, operate in-house print shops or mailrooms, analyze how employees can most efficiently share documents and knowledge, and build Internet-based processes for personalizing direct mail, invoices, and brochures.

These new products have allowed Xerox to supply solutions to clients, not just hardware. For example, Xerox has a new device for insurance company customers—a compact computer with scanning, printing, and Internet capabilities. Instead of relying on the U.S. Postal Service to transport hard copies of claims, these and related documents are scanned on-site, sorted, routed, and put immediately into a workflow system. This isn't just a fancy new gadget for the insurance companies. They are seeing real benefits. Error rates have plummeted along with processing times, and that means increases in revenues and customer satisfaction.

Dreaming Beyond Its Boundaries

Riding the combination of Xerox's former strengths and its new acquisitions, Burns and the Xerox team now have a utopian image of what lies ahead. They believe the tools and services they offer clients are getting smarter. "It's not just processing Medicaid payments," says Stephen Hoover, director of Xerox's research facilities. "It's using our social cognition research to add wellness support that helps people better manage conditions like diabetes." Hoover adds that the future may see a new generation of Xerox devices, such as those that can analyze real-time parking and traffic data for municipal customers, allowing them to help citizens locate parking spots or automatically ticket them when they are going too fast. Already, Xerox is market testing parking meters that are capable of calling 911 or taking photos when a button is pushed. Not all products such as these will hit the market, but Xerox now has a model that allows it to dream beyond its known boundaries.

In another example of smarter tools for clients, Xerox will soon rollout Ignite, a software and Web-based service that turns its copiers/scanners/printers already in service at schools around the world into paper-grading machines. Previous automated grading technologies (such as Scantron) worked only on multiple-choice responses filled out on special forms. But Ignite will grade work where answers are written in by students—even numeric math problems. The real revolutionary potential of Ignite, however, is not just in automated grading, but in taking the results and turning them into Web-accessible data that allow teachers to identify problem areas and make improvements to their techniques.

Throughout this corporate metamorphosis, Xerox isn't focused on trying to make better copiers. Rather, it is focused on improving any process that a business or government customer needs to perform and performing it more efficiently. Xerox's new machines have learned to read and understand the documents they scan, reducing complex tasks that once took weeks down to minutes or even seconds. From now on, Xerox wants to be a leading global document management and business-process technology and services provider.

With all the dazzling technologies emerging today, Burns acknowledges that the business services industry in which Xerox now operates is decidedly unsexy. But she also points out that "These are processes that companies need to run their businesses. They do it as a sideline; it's not their main thing." But running these seemingly mundane business processes is now Xerox's main thing. Xerox provides these basic document and IT services to customers so that customers can focus on what matters most—their real businesses.

Xerox's transition is still a work in progress. Over the last four years, the company's revenues are up 47 percent and profits have more than doubled. Its stock price, however, has struggled (it has yet to top $12), a sign that Xerox isn't doing as well as Wall Street thinks it should be. Part of the reason is that Xerox still relies to some extent on its copier and printer products for its success, even with its recent diversification strategy. And just as e-mail and desktop software killed photocopying, smartphones and tablets are killing inkjet and photo printers. But Xerox depends much less on such products than competitors such as Hewlett-Packard and Lexmark International do. Thus, experts predict, Xerox will rebound much more quickly than its rivals. Burns and crew are also confident that as Xerox continues its transition to solutions provider, the seeds it has planted over the past few years will soon bear fruit.

Xerox knows that change and renewal are ongoing and never-ending. "The one thing that's predictable about business is that it's fundamentally unpredictable," says the company's annual report. "Macroforces such as globalization, emerging technologies, and, most recently, depressed financial markets bring new challenges every day to businesses of all sizes." The message is clear. Even the most dominant companies can be vulnerable to the often turbulent and changing marketing environment. Companies that understand and adapt well to their environments can thrive. Those that don't risk their very survival.

Questions for Discussion

1. What microenvironmental factors have affected Xerox's performance since the late 1990s?
2. What macroenvironmental factors have affected Xerox's performance during that period?
3. By focusing on the business services industry, has Xerox pursued the best strategy? Why or why not?
4. What alternative strategy might Xerox have pursued following the first signs of declining revenues and profits?
5. Given Xerox's current situation, what recommendations would you make to Burns for the future of Xerox?

Sources: Quotes and other information from or based on Mia Lamar, "Xerox's Net Rises 10%, But Revenue Falls Short," *Wall Street Journal*, April 23, 2013, http://online.wsj.com/article/SB10001424127887324874204578440442381235524.html; Muneeza Iqbal, "The Makers: Xerox CEO Ursula Burns Tells Her Story," *Daily Finance*, February 27, 2013, www.dailyfinance.com/2013/02/25/ursula-burns-makers-pbs-xerox/; Ellen McGirt, "Fresh Copy: How Ursula Burns Reinvented Xerox," *Fast Company*, November 29, 2011, www.fastcompany.com/magazine/161/ursula-burns-xerox; Scott Gamm, "Xerox Works to Duplicate Copier Glory in Digital Services Model," *Forbes*, July 19, 2012, www.forbes.com/sites/scottgamm/2012/07/19/xerox-works-to-duplicate-copier-glory-in-digital-services-model/; Geoff Colvin, "Ursula Burns Launches Xerox into the Future," *Fortune*, May 3, 2010, p. 5; Matthew Daneman, "Xerox Stepping into Grading School Papers," *USA Today*, May 7, 2013, www.usatoday.com/story/tech/2013/05/07/xerox-school-grades/2140749/; and annual reports and other information at www.xerox.com, accessed May 2013.

Company Case 4

Oracle: Getting a Grip on Big Data

You may have heard the term "Big Data" and wondered just what it means. Consider this: every day, the people and systems of the world generate 2.5 quintillion bytes of new data (that's 2.5 billion gigabytes). Last year, that added up to about 1.8 zettabytes of information. A zettabyte is a trillion gigabytes. If you can't wrap your head around these numbers, let's just say that they are huge. If you were to put all that data on good old CD-ROMs, every person in the world would have 353 of them annually. If you stacked all 2.47 trillion CDs on top of one another, it would create a stack tall enough to go to the moon and back four times (and you thought you had storage problems). This is Big Data.

The amount of data that we humans and our beloved machines generate has been growing exponentially. Consider that if every word uttered by every human being who ever lived were written down and digitized, it would only equal two days' worth of the data that is being generated at today's rate. Of all the information that is stored today, 90 percent of it was created in the last two years alone. And of course, the data explosion isn't slowing down. By 2020, the amount of data generated every day will increase 20 times.

Just where does all that data come from? Consider that every Google search, Facebook status update, YouTube video, text message, and purchase transaction generates data. There are now 9 billion devices connected to the Internet; by the end of the decade, there will be 50 billion. Beyond just mobile devices and laptops, the number of smart machines that are talking to other smart machines is rapidly adding to the mass of connected devices. Utility meters, vending machines, appliances, automobiles, surgical devices, heavy industrial equipment, and even pets and shoes are now stuffed with technology that allows them to automatically collect consumption data and relay that information to the manufacturers, companies that own the systems that connect the machines, or any company that is willing to pay for such data.

Big Data: A Blessing and a Curse

This tsunami of data surging over corporations of all shapes and sizes is widely considered to be the most important issue in corporate strategy today. Ginni Rometty, CEO of IBM, recently predicted that Big Data will be the primary basis of competitive advantage in the future, calling it "the next natural resource." She thinks it will change how decisions are made, how value is created, and how value is delivered. Angela Ahrendts, CEO of Burberry, agrees. "Consumer data will be the biggest differentiator in the next two to three years. Whoever unlocks the reams of data and uses it strategically will win."

But harnessing and making sense of all this data is easier said than done. For decades, companies have made based on data they've gathered from their own transactions and stored in relational databases. When a company designs its own databases, the information is organized and structured. However, the flood of data from new sources, many of which are external, is much less structured and often incompatible with a given company's own data systems. For example, how do you store a photo, a sound bite, a video clip, or a Facebook status update in a way that it can be combined with other data and mined for useful insights?

Most companies are simply overwhelmed by Big Data. It's challenging enough to get up to speed with data as it exists today, much less prepare for the increases in tomorrow's data flows. Companies need guidance from experts who can do most of the heavy lifting in gathering and making sense of all that information. They desperately need help in gleaning Big Data insights that will put them ahead of the competition in making decisions that will win with consumers, vendors, and partners.

Oracle to the Rescue

That's where Oracle comes in. Oracle has specialized in computer hardware and software products since 1977. Now the third-largest software maker (behind Microsoft and IBM), Oracle builds database management, resource planning, customer relationship management, and supply chain management systems. All this expertise, plus the visionary leadership of founder and CEO Larry Ellison, has moved Oracle to the forefront of gathering, organizing, and analyzing Big Data. Oracle claims that it "offers the broadest and most integrated portfolio of products to help you acquire and organize these diverse data sources and analyze them alongside your existing data to find new insights and capitalize on hidden relationships."

Oracle's portfolio includes software, platform (the architecture that connects software to hardware), and hardware products. According to Bob Evans, Oracle's chief communications officer, "Oracle is the only tech company on Earth that has a full line at [each of these] levels." Oracle's portfolio of products is immense and includes database products that allow databases to collect, connect, integrate, and analyze. Its hardware systems include server products as well as Big Data appliances that are engineered to optimize all of Oracle's software products, as well as products from external sources.

With its completely integrated systems, Oracle can provide unique benefits to companies that other Big Data companies simply can't match. In the oil, gas, and mining industries, new machine-to-machine devices are being used to track exactly what's going into and coming out of each mine, reducing losses and maximizing profits. In the transportation industry, devices in shipping containers can monitor a shipment throughout its journey, keeping track of things like temperature, humidity, and even whether or not the container has been opened. And in the mobile services industry, virtual wallet services that let people pay for transactions with their phones are expanding rapidly and putting the capability in smartphones as well as traditional-feature phones. Oracle is at work in each of these situations, with expertise that lets clients gather and transmit data from enabled devices to systems that analyze the data in ways that provide better customer outcomes and maximize profits.

As an indication of Oracle's Big Data leadership and innovation, many of the products the company is now introducing to handle Big Data were designed well before terms such as "cloud computing" or even "Big Data" were being used. For example, the design of Oracle's Fusion applications—software suites designed to handle data management across corporate areas ranging from supply chain to human resources to customer relationship management—began in 2004. And Oracle began developing its most recent database product in 2007. Yet both of these products lines are optimized for the cloud, and both can be used on-site or over the Internet.

As another example of visionary development, Oracle's software-based enterprise applications have built-in social media capabilities. According to Abhay Parasnis, senior vice president of Oracle Public Cloud, "Oracle's social relationship management capabilities bring social into everything and can light up our core large object applications with social capabilities." No other company even attempted to do this, and it puts Oracle on the leading edge of pushing the industry to deliver the customer value benefits of social media.

Fighting for a Piece of the Pie

The recent developments in Big Data have sparked a frenzy of competitive activity. Massive competitors such as Microsoft, IBM, and Dell are all grabbing for a piece of the Big Data pie, and a deluge of start-ups such as Hadapt, Precog, and Platfora are joining the fray. Oracle threw fuel on the fire with the recent release of its Sparc T5 server series. Oracle CEO Larry Ellison framed the advantages of the Sparc line this way: "You can go faster, but only if you're willing to pay 80 percent less than what IBM charges."

Facing Oracle's new line of faster and cheaper products, Colin Parris, general manager for IBM's Power systems, quickly downplayed the advantages of faster machines. He suggested that the race for faster processors is a thing of the past. Instead, today's companies are much more concerned about reliability, security, and cost effectiveness. But considering how fast the Big Data world is moving, the speed advantage has real-world applications for executives who want to accelerate internal operations, make better decisions, and engage customers more intimately. When processes that formerly took weeks can be accomplished in just days, it provides competitive advantage in numerous ways.

Despite Oracle's apparent sizable lead in the race to dominate Big Data, the data giant faces challenges. For starters, many companies large and small are finding that they can fulfill their Big Data needs more efficiently by using cheap hardware and open-source software. For example, years ago when Google faced the problem of indexing the Internet for its search engine, it built a huge database system comprised of cheap hardware and internally developed software that got the job done. And Google isn't alone.

Additionally, in the past eight quarters, Oracle has missed its financial goals three times. That's hard for Wall Street to swallow. Although Big Data represents only a portion of Oracle's overall business, many analysts observe that many of the big innovations are happening at smaller, more nimble companies. Thus, many talented employees are jumping ship from the big developers, leaving the likes of Oracle with high turnover and less innovative minds.

So although Oracle has the expertise and products to tackle today's Big Data needs, it also has its work cut out for it. However, even as the young and nimble start-ups nip at Oracle's heals and the other big dogs fight for positions on the Big Data porch, there is little question that no other single company is better poised to help companies use Big Data to optimize marketing opportunities.

Questions for Discussion

1. Discuss ways that Oracle could provide clients with the ability to form better relationships with customers.
2. Discuss the similarities and differences between Big Data and the more traditional marketing research concepts found in Chapter 4.
3. Does competition from small start-ups really pose a big competitive threat to Oracle? Explain why or why not.
4. From a consumer point of view, what are some of the downsides to the developments in Big Data?
5. In the future, will consumers be more concerned about these downsides or less?

Sources: Andrew Gill, "IBM CEO Ginni Rometty Believes Big Data and Social Will Change Everything," *London Calling*, March 11, 2013, http://londoncalling.co/2013/03/ibm-ceo-ginni-rometty-believes-big-data-and-social-will-change-everything-how-about-other-ceos/; Bob Evans, "You Can Get a Chip Slower Than the New Sparc T5, You Just Have to Pay More," *Forbes*, April 2, 2013, www.forbes.com/sites/oracle/2013/04/02/big-data-performance-speed-cost/; "Billions of Reasons to Get Ready for Big Data," *Forbes*, December 12, 2013, www.forbes.com/sites/oracle/2012/12/13/billions-of-reasons-to-get-ready-for-big-data/; Bob Evans, "Larry Ellison Doesn't Get the Cloud," *Forbes*, October 9, 2012, www.forbes.com/sites/oracle/2013/04/02/big-data-performance-speed-cost/; Rolfe Winkler, "Oracle's Little Issue with Big Data," *Wall Street Journal*, April 9, 2012, http://online.wsj.com/article/SB10001424052702304587704577333823771344922.html; Ron Bodkin, "Cracks in the Oracle Empire," *Thinkbiganalytics*, March 25, 2013, http://thinkbiganalytics.com/big_data_affects_database_oracle/; and www.oracle.com/us/technologies/big-data/index.html, accessed May 2013.

Company Case 5

Veterinary Pet Insurance: Health Insurance for Our Furry—or Feathery—Friends

Health insurance for pets? Until recently, MetLife, Prudential, Northwestern Mutual, and most other large insurance companies haven't paid much attention to it. Instead, they've left the small piece of the insurance industry pie to more-focused niche companies. The largest of these peddlers of pet insurance (there are now 12 of them) is Veterinary Pet Insurance (VPI). And the business has become so lucrative that VPI was recently acquired by Nationwide, marking the first effort by large insurance companies to get into the business. VPI's mission is to "make the miracles of veterinary medicine affordable to all pet owners."

VPI was founded in 1980 by veterinarian Jack Stephens. He never intended to leave his practice, but his life took a dramatic turn when he visited a local grocery store and was identified by a client's daughter as "the man who killed Buffy." Stephens had euthanized the family dog two weeks earlier. He immediately began researching the possibility of creating medical pet insurance. "There is nothing more frustrating for a veterinarian than knowing that you can heal a sick patient, but the owner lacks the financial resources and instructs you to put the pet down," says Stephens. "I wanted to change that."

Pet insurance is a still-small but fast-growing segment of the insurance business. Insiders think the industry offers huge potential. Currently, 63 percent of all U.S. households own at least one pet. Collectively, Americans own some 78.2 million dogs, 86.4 million cats, and 8.3 million birds. And that doesn't include the hundreds of millions of pet fish, small animals, and reptiles. More than two-thirds have included their pets in holiday celebrations and one-third characterize their pet as a child. Some 42 percent of dogs now sleep in the same bed as their owners. Americans spend a whopping $55 billion a year on their pets, more than the gross domestic product of 121 countries in the world. They spend $14.3 billion of that on pet health care.

Unlike in Great Britain and Sweden, where almost half of all pets owners carry pet health insurance, relatively few pet owners in the United States now carry such coverage. However, according to recent studies, 41 percent of pet owners are at least somewhat worried they could not afford the medical bills for a sick cat or dog and nearly 75 percent are willing to go into debt to pay for veterinary care for their furry—or feathery—companions. And for many pet medical procedures, they'd have to! If not diagnosed quickly, even a mundane ear infection in a dog can result in $1,000 worth of medical treatment. Ten days of dialysis treatment can reach $12,000, and cancer treatment as much as $40,000. All of this adds up to a lot of potential growth for pet health insurers.

That's why Stephens started VPI. For a monthly fee ranging from $10 a month to $35 a month, VPI touts "plans for every pet and every budget." At the low end, plans cover accidents like broken bones and poisoning and carry a high deductible. The more expensive plans have a lower deductible and cover all types of diseases and conditions, even genetic issues. VPI plans help pay for office calls, prescriptions, treatments, lab fees, x-rays, surgery, and hospitalization.

Like its handful of competitors, VPI issues health insurance policies for dogs and cats. Unlike its competitors, VPI covers a menagerie of exotic pets as well. Among other critters, the Avian and Exotic Pet Plan covers birds, rabbits, ferrets, rats, guinea pigs, snakes, iguanas, chameleons, turtles, hedgehogs, and potbellied pigs. "There's such a vast array of pets," says a VPI executive, "and people love them. We have to respect that."

Unless you're a pet owner, you may not realize the kind of mischief pets can get into. A few years back, a VPI-insured dog got stuck in a refrigerator. While the dog chilled and waited for someone to rescue him, he took advantage of the opportunity and polished off an entire Thanksgiving ham. His owner finally found him, complete with a licked-clean ham bone and a mild case of hypothermia that needed to be treated. In honor of this pooch, VPI began giving an award each year—appropriately called the VPI Hambone Award—to the most unusual pet insurance claim.

The first recipient of the VPI Hambone Award was an English bulldog named Lulu, who swallowed 15 baby pacifiers, a bottle cap, and a piece of a basketball. Others include Harley, the pug who ate more than 100 rocks; Jojo, the boxer who lost a tooth when he bit the tire of a moving delivery truck; and Peanut, the dachshund-terrier mix who somehow buried himself after losing a fight with a skunk.

But perhaps Natasha, the Siberian Forest cat, presents the most harrowing survival story. Daryl Humdy of Oakland, California, arrived home just as his roommate was pulling his clothing out of the washing machine. Amongst the clothes was Natasha, shivering and crying. Apparently, while loading his laundry, the roommate went into the next room to grab more clothes, leaving the washing machine lid open. He returned, tossed in the clothes, shut the lid, and started the 35-minute cycle, detergent and all. How Natasha survived the entire wash-spin-rinse-spin process is anyone's guess. But after being treated for hypothermia and shock, Natasha was as good as new.

With stories like these happening every day, VPI is growing like a newborn puppy. VPI is by far the largest provider of pet insurance in the United States. Since its inception, VPI has issued more than 1 million policies, and it now serves more than 485,000 policyholders. Sales have grown rapidly, exceeding $200 million in policy premiums last year. That might not amount to much for the likes of MetLife, Prudential, or Northwestern Mutual, which rack up tens of billions of dollars in yearly revenues. But it's profitable business for small companies like VPI.

And there's room to grow. The cost of veterinary care has increased by an average of 6.8 percent over the past five years and will continue to increase in the future. More (and more expensive) procedures are being performed in specialties like cardiology, oncology, and ophthalmology. Even acupuncture, hospice, and writing prescriptions for medications like Prozac are part of a veterinarian's regular services. Yet currently, only about 3 percent of pet owners buy pet insurance.

As VPI pioneered the category of pet insurance in the United States, competitors took notice. Today, there are no less than 12 companies providing pet insurance to pet parents who want to protect the health and well-being of those they love. At one time, VPI held 95 percent of the pet insurance market. Experts now predict that within the next year, its share will be down to around 50 percent. But with the industry experiencing double-digit growth each year, it doesn't seem that VPIs revenue growth will slow down any time soon.

But VPI continues to pioneer new ways to provide for the well-being of beloved pets. For example, VPI has worked with major employers to have pet insurance added to the list of benefits employees can choose from. Today, one out of three *Fortune* 500 companies offers VPI as a voluntary employment benefit, making VPI policies available to an astounding 67 million people. Companies like Chipotle Mexican Grill, Deloitte LLP, T-Mobile, and Wells Fargo have found this to be a fantastic incentive to pet-loving employees when it comes to recruitment and retention. Some companies cover the entire premium. All of them provide at least a discount on the cost of VPI's premiums.

For those who go in with their eyes only partially opened, they may be in for some surprises when it comes to getting their claims paid. Like its competitors, VPI's policies carry limitations and exclusions, especially on the less expensive plans. Thus, there are plenty of cases where pet owners take their pets in for treatment of a disease or an accident, get sizable bills, and then find that their policies cover less than they were expecting. In some cases, they may find that the case isn't covered at all! For example, some policies don't cover genetic illnesses. Others may cover a lifelong illness only during the year it is diagnosed. And then there are maximum benefit limitations that, at times, don't come close to covering the bills.

In such situations, customers often come away disgruntled, having paid insurance premiums for months or even years, only to find that they still have to pay a hefty vet bill. But online forums are also replete with stories from pet owners, like those involving Lulu, JoJo, Peanut, and Natasha, who feel that the insurance definitely paid off. Consider this glowing recommendation:

> I am so impressed with VPI insurance. My Labrador, Jackson, has been dealing with severe allergies for years now and VPI insurance has taken care of all his needs. As he is only 4 yrs. old, when he recently herniated a disc in his back I really had no choice but to allow him to have surgery to correct the problem. If I didn't have VPI insurance it would have been an incredible financial burden. Not having to worry about the finances allowed me to concentrate on Jacksons' recovery. I am even more impressed that when renewal time came around, he was allowed to renew! I love VPI!

VPI can be a real comfort for policyholders. "I feel a lot better knowing that I have this coverage for my four-legged babies," says Carrie, another happy customer. VPI claims it will always "strive to make the miracles of modern medicine affordable." As more people become knowledgeable of VPI and share Carrie's point of view toward their pets, it's hard to think the pet insurance industry isn't just beginning to stretch its paws.

Questions for Discussion

1. Analyze the buyer decision process for a pet insurance customer.
2. Is the decision to buy pet insurance strictly an economic decision? Explain.
3. Explain how both positive and negative attitudes develop toward a brand like VPI. How might VPI change consumer attitudes toward the brand?
4. What explains the difference between pet insurance usage in the United States versus Great Britain or Sweden?
5. Will VPI continue to grow as it has in the past? Why or why not?

Sources: Herb Weisbaum, "Pet Insurance: A Good Deal? Or a Rip Off?" *NBC News*, www.nbcnews.com/id/43916934/ns/business-consumer_news/t/pet-insurance-good-deal-or-rip/#.UXAv7SvF2Vt, accessed April, 2013; "Pets Are Serious Business for Marketers," *Forbes*, April 15, 2013, www.forbes.com/sites/onmarketing/2013/04/15/pets-are-serious-business-for-marketers/; "Pet Business Trends 2013," www.embracepetinsurance.com/pet-industry/pet-trends/2013; "Fortune 500 Companies Expand Pet Health Insurance Offerings," http://press.petinsurance.com/pressroom/354.aspx, June 19, 2012; "Facebook Saves Canine's Life," http://press.petinsurance.com/pressroom/354.aspx, April 17, 2013; "Lab Breaks Leg But Bounces Back from Bicycle Attack," http://press.petinsurance.com/pressroom/377.aspx, February 27, 2013; "Kitten Gets Stuck in Washing Machine, Creating Near 'Cat'astrophe," http://press.petinsurance.com/pressroom/373.aspx, January 29, 2013; "Customer Reviews," www.petinsurance.com/pet-insurance-reviews.aspx, accessed April 2013; "All in the Family," *Marketing Management,* January/February 2008, p. 7; and information accessed at www.petinsurance.com, April 2013.

Company Case 6

Dove: Building Customer Relationships Everywhere, One Gender at a Time

When it comes to consumer packaged goods, Unilever is about as big as they come. One of the leading suppliers of food, home, and personal care products, Unilever products can be found in a whopping 7 out of 10 homes globally, are available in over 190 countries, and are used by more than 2 billion people on a daily basis. Having this kind of global scope is rare, and with revenues of more than $64 billion per year, you'd think that Unilever would be content to slow down a bit and tend to the businesses at hand. Instead, Unilever has set a goal to double its revenues by the year 2020.

How does Unilever do it? By continually creating and developing brands that form strong relationships with consumers in multiple consumer product market segments. If Unilever's portfolio of brands overlooks certain types of customers, then the company creates or acquires a new brand. This "house of brands" approach has made Unilever the proud owner of powerhouse brands such as Noxzema, Ragu, Axe, Ben & Jerry's, Slim-Fast, Hellmann's, Q-tips, Vaseline, Wish-Bone, and Dove, to name just a few.

Dove: Made for Women?

Take Dove, for example. Dove is the number-one brand of personal cleansing products in the United States, with a product portfolio that includes beauty bars, body washes, face care treatments, deodorants, body mists, hair care products, and styling aids. All by itself, the Dove brand pulls in over $2 billion a year for Unilever. But coming off its very successful long-term "Campaign for Real Beauty," Dove was starting to experience the stagnation that many mature brands face. Dove found that it was reaching the limits of expansion and the types of extensions it could support. After stumbling in its efforts to penetrate the hair care market, Unilever managers knew that Dove needed to discover a new way to grow.

Dove had always been an undeniably feminine brand. Everything about Dove's brand image—its name, logo, color palette, and communications—was created with women in mind. Although this laser-focused targeting had been a primary factor in the brand's decades-long success, ironically, it had become the brand's greatest limiting factor, especially given the rapid growth in the men's personal care products category. Could Dove sell its products to men? This question left Unilever managers conflicted. Success would provide the much-needed expansion for the brand. However, attempting to get men to perceive Dove as a manly brand risked damaging the brand's successful image among women. Additionally, Unilever already had a wildly successful men's personal care brand in Axe. However, with Dove, Unilever would be targeting men not interested in Axe's edgy—at times even risqué—and youthful image. Positioning Dove for men would require great care.

Breaking Out of the Box

Dove supported its decision to enter the men's care market with a comprehensive strategy and genuine consumer insight. Rather than simply releasing products designed for men under the standard Dove brand, Unilever created a brand within the brand—Dove Men+Care. This sub-brand provides a masculine foundation and much-needed separation from the core Dove brand. But just as important, Men+Care was extendable into virtually any type of men's personal care product. Dove also appealed to men through packaging design. With a base color of dark grey and a masculine palette of accent colors, the very appearance of Dove Men+Care products left no question as to the intended target customer.

Unilever's highly successful Axe personal care line targets single men age 24 and under who have an active interest in socializing and dating. So, by contrast, Dove Men+Care took aim at men age 25 to 54. Research revealed that men in this distinctive demographic were evolving. Typically married, they were taking on more household duties like cleaning and shopping than similarly aged men in prior decades. More than half of men in this category were buying their own personal care products, and most of the rest were influencing those purchases.

The first products in the Dove Men+Care portfolio were skin care items. The line included three body washes, two bar soaps, and a shower scrub, products strategically designed to complement each other. The idea was to appeal to "men who are comfortable in their own skin," but who were receptive to the proven moisturizing power of Dove products. Dove is one of the few personal care brands that most men had in their homes growing up. So there was an established level of brand recognition and brand knowledge.

Shortly after introducing the initial products, Dove added an antiperspirant to the Men+Care line. More recently, Dove Men+Care has become a more full-spectrum brand that includes facial care and hair care products. With its line of facial care products, Dove urges men to "Take better care of your face," whereas its hair care products promise, "3X stronger hair." These new product lines extend Dove's heritage in cleansing, moisturization, and providing the ultimate care.

The Dove Men+Care facial care products are designed to complement each other by helping men care for their skin in three easy steps: facial cleansing (cleanser that fights dryness), shaving (shaving gel that prevents irritation), and face care (post-shave balm sooths skin and a moisturizer that hydrates and protects). Dove's research revealed that 48 percent of men in the United States never use face wash and 46 percent never use a face moisturizer, even though most men admit they know they should. Rob Candelino, vice president of Unilever Skincare, explains the insight behind the facial care products and their positioning:

> Men today have a great deal to care about, from their families to their careers, but they don't always give their personal care the same level of attention. Neglecting to properly cleanse and moisturize their skin, or doing so but using harsh products like regular soap, all contribute to a man's face looking tired and feeling worn. New Dove Men+Care Face products seek to help men eliminate needless torture from their grooming routine and help put their best face forward when it matters most.

Unilever has taken great care to craft promotional messages consistent with the brand image of Dove Men+Care. The launch of its facial care products was accompanied by an ad showing the abuse a man's face takes. Snowballs, motor oil, pokes from a child, windburn from a roller coaster, and "deserved" slaps provided illustration for the tagline, "End the face torture." A series of follow-up ads showed real men describing their typical face care routine (soap, no moisturizer, stinging aftershave) followed by the results they experience ("It feels tight," "It doesn't feel good at all," and "Definitely stings").

Most recently, Dove has taken its advertising for Men+Care to a new level. According to Candelino, "We hear from 73 percent of men that they're falsely or inaccurately depicted in advertising." Specifically, says Candelino, the common depictions of men in advertising can be boiled down to three categories: guys obsessed with winning the affections of women, he-men who are into stereotypical manly activities such as body building or fast cars, and dads who are seen more as buffoons than respected parents. So Dove Men+Care launched a campaign to combat these caricatures as much as build its own brand. Called "Real Moments," the campaign promotes real-life fatherhood tales from father figures like Miami Heat star Dwyane Wade. Having just written a book entitled *A Father First: How My Life Became Bigger Than Basketball*, Wade was the perfect celebrity to give his endorsement. "When fans learn that playing 'Defense' for Dwyane Wade means teaching his sons how to guard a mini-hoop in his living room, instead of a fellow player during a professional game," says Candelino, "it hits home where men today place priority—caring for their family comes first."

An Instant Success

In a short period of time, Dove has accomplished a great deal. It successfully stepped outside the established boundaries of a brand created to target a specific market segment—women. In breaking beyond segment, the brand has become an authority on men's personal grooming. And Dove has done this without alienating its core segment of women.

Unilever's investment in Dove as a men's care brand seems to have paid off. Shortly after the new Dove Men+Care line debuted, SymphonyIRI put the new brand on its list of top 10 new products. In an annual study of most desirable brands, Dove ranked fourth among both women *and* men. Best of all for Unilever, Dove's previously flat overall sales rose 9.8 percent in Men+Care's first year on the market. It seems that Dove's stated objective for Dove Men+Care, to "allow men to better care for themselves so they can care for what matters most to them," is right on target.

Questions for Discussion

1. Using the full spectrum of segmentation variables, describe how Dove segments and targets the market for personal care products.
2. Which market targeting strategy is Dove following? Justify your answer.
3. Write a positioning statement for Dove Men+Care.
4. Can Dove and Dove Men+Care continue to succeed as side-by-side brands? Why or why not?

Sources: Based on information from John, Miziolek, "How Dove Reinvented Its Brand for Men," *Fast Company,* March, 14, 2012, www.fastcompany.com/1824772/how-dove-reinvented-its-brand-men; Jack Neff, "Dove Gives Guys a Break in Men+Care Push," *Advertising Age,* March 12, 2013, http://adage.com/print/240257/; "New NCAA Campaign Shares Real Moments Off-the-Court That Highlight How Men Care for What Matters," *Multivu,* March 13, 2013, www.multivu.com/mnr/60739-dove-men-care-real-moments; Ellen Byron, "Marketing Decoder—Dove Men+Care," *Wall Street Journal,* February 13, 2013, p. D2; Jacquelyn Smith, "The Best New Products," *Forbes,* March 29, 2011, www.forbes.com/sites/jacquelynsmith/2011/03/29/best-new-products/; and "Dove Men+Care Launches New Skin Care Range to Help Men Finally Care for Their Faces," *Reuters,* February 5, 2013.

Company Case 7

Zipcar: "It's Not about Cars—It's about Urban Life"

Imagine a world in which no one owns a car. Cars would still exist, but rather than owning cars, people would just share them. Sounds crazy, right? But Scott Griffith, CEO of Zipcar, the world's largest car-share company, paints a picture of just such an imaginary world. And he has nearly 800,000 passionate customers—or Zipsters, as they are called—who will back him up.

Zipcar specializes in renting out cars by the hour or day. Although this may sound like a minor variation on the established rental car agency business, car sharing—a concept pioneered by Zipcar—is an entirely different concept. As Griffith took the driver's seat of the young start-up company, he knew that if the company was going to achieve cruising speed, it needed to be far more than just another car service. Zipcar needed to be a well-positioned brand that appealed to a customer base with unfulfilled needs.

A Car Rental Company That Isn't about Cars

As Griffith considered what Zipcar had to offer, it was apparent that it couldn't be all things to all people. But the concept seemed particularly well suited to people who live or work in densely populated neighborhoods in cities such as New York City, Boston, Atlanta, San Francisco, and London. For these customers, owning a car (or a second or third car) is difficult, costly, and environmentally irresponsible. Interestingly, Zipcar doesn't see itself as a car-rental company. Instead, it's selling a lifestyle. "It's not about cars," says CEO Griffith, "it's about urban life. We're creating a lifestyle brand that happens to have a lot of cars."

Initially, the Zipcar brand was positioned exclusively round a value system. As an urban lifestyle brand, Zipcar focused on traits that city dwellers have in common. For starters, the lifestyle is rooted in environmental consciousness. At first, Zipcar focused on green-minded customers with promotional pitches such as "We ❤ Earth" and "Imagine a world with a million fewer cars on the road." Zipcar's vibrant green logo reflects this save-the-Earth philosophy. And Zipcar really does deliver on its environmental promises. Studies show that every shared Zipcar takes up to 20 cars off the road and cuts carbon emissions by up to 50 percent per user. On average, Zipsters travel 44 percent fewer miles than when they owned a car, leaving an average of 219 gallons of crude oil in the ground. Multiply all this out by 11,000 cars in Zipcar's fleet, and that's a pretty substantial impact on the environment.

But it wasn't long before Griffith realized that if Zipcar was going to grow, it needed to move beyond just being green. So the brand has broadened its positioning to include other urban lifestyle benefits—benefits that Zipcar appeals to on its site in response to the question, "Who exactly is the car-sharing type?" Zipcar provides these most common reasons for car-sharing:

- I don't want the hassle of owning a car.
- I want to save money.
- I take public transit, but need a car sometimes.
- Once in a while I need a second car.
- I need a big car for a big job.
- I want to impress my boss.

One of most important benefits Zipcar provides is convenience. Owning a car in a densely populated urban area can be a real hassle. Zipcar lets customers focus on driving, not on the complexities of car ownership. It gives them "Wheels when you want them," in four easy steps: "Join. Reserve. Unlock. Drive."

Fulfilling Consumer Needs

To join, you pay around $60 for an annual membership and receive your personal Zipcard, which unlocks any Zipcar vehicle located in urban areas around the world. Then, when you need a car, reserve one—minutes or months in advance—online, by phone, or using a smartphone app. You can choose the car you want, when and where you want it, and drive it for as little as $7.50 an hour, including gas, insurance, and free miles. When you're ready, walk to the car, hold your Zipcard to the windshield to unlock the doors, and you're good to go. When you're done, you drop the car off at the same parking spot—Zipcar worries about the maintenance and cleaning.

Zipcar not only eliminates the hassle of urban car ownership, it also saves money. By living with less, the average Zipster saves $600 a month on car payments, insurance, gas, maintenance, and other car ownership expenses. That's like getting a $10,000 a year raise after taxes. In an era when consumers have become more frugal, this is a big plus, especially for those looking to live more minimally.

Zipcar isn't for everyone—it doesn't try to be. Instead, it zeros in on a narrowly defined urban lifestyle positioning. For starters, Zipcar "pods" (a dozen or so vehicles located in a given neighborhood) are stocked from a portfolio of over 50 different models that trendy urbanites love. The vehicles are both hip and fuel efficient: Toyota Priuses, Honda CRVs, MINIs, Volvo S60s, BMW 328s, Toyota Tacomas, Toyota Siennas, Subaru Outbacks, and others. And Zipcar now has plug-in hybrids, fully electric vehicles, and full-size vans for big jobs. Each car has its own personality—a name and profile created by a Zipster. For example, Prius Ping "jogs in the morning; doesn't say much," whereas Civic Carlos "teaches yoga; loves to kayak." Such personal touches make it feel like you're borrowing the car from a friend, rather than being assigned whatever piece of metal happens to be available.

To further eliminate hassles and make Zipcar as convenient as possible, company promotional tactics are designed to appeal to city dwellers. The company's goal is for Zipsters to not have to walk more than seven minutes to get to one of its car pods—no easy task. "Even with today's highly targeted Web and mobile technologies, it's hard to target at that hyper-local level," says Griffith. "So our street teams do it block by block, zip code by zip code." Thus, in addition to local ads and transit advertising, Zipcar reps are beating the streets in true guerilla fashion.

With its eye sharply focused on maintaining the Zipcar image, the company is consistently developing new features that appeal to the tech-savvy urbanites. Recently, the company has shifted its focus a bit from being a Web-based business to being an overwhelmingly mobile concern. Soon, Zipcars will have in-car device holders for smartphones that will allow for easy plug-in and hands-free navigation. The interface between the cars and the users will allow playlists stored on the phone to be played through the car's audio system. Users will be provided with information specific to the vehicle they are in, a personalized deal recommendation service, and a real-time feedback loop where users can report on vehicle cleanliness, damage, and fuel levels.

Fostering Brand Community

Zipcar's orientation around the urban, environmentally conscious lifestyle fosters a tight-knit sense of customer community. Zipsters are as fanatically loyal as the hardcore fans of Harley-Davidson or Apple, brands that have been nurturing customer relationships for decades. Loyal Zipsters serve as neighborhood brand ambassadors; 30 percent of new members join up at the recommendation of existing customers. "When I meet another Zipcar member at a party or something, I feel like we have something in common," says one Brooklyn Zipster. "It's like we're both making intelligent choices about our lives." And just like Harley owners get together on weekends to ride, the Internet is littered with announcements for Zipster parties at bars, restaurants, and comedy clubs, among other places.

As Zipcar has taken off, it has broadened the appeal of its brand to include a different type of urban dweller—businesses and other organizations. Companies such as Google now encourage employees to be environmentally conscious by commuting via a company shuttle and then using Zipcars for both business and personal use during the day. Other companies are using Zipcar as an alternative to black sedans, long taxi rides, and congested parking lots. Government agencies are getting into the game as well. The city of Chicago recently partnered with Zipcar to provide a more efficient and sustainable transportation alternative for city agencies. And Washington, D.C., now saves more than $1 million a year using Zipcar. Fleet manager Ralph Burns says that he has departments lining up. "Agencies putting their budgets together for next year are calling me up and saying, 'Ralph, I've got 25 cars I want to get rid of!' "

How is Zipcar's strategy of positioning itself as an urban lifestyle brand working? By all accounts, the young car-sharing nicher has the pedal to the metal and its tires are smoking. In just the past 5 years, Zipcar's annual revenues have rocketed nearly five-fold, to more than $270 million. Zipcar has also reached the milestone of being profitable. And with 10 million people now within walking distance of a Zipcar, there's plenty of room to grow. As more cars are added, Zipcar's reach will only increase.

Zipcar's rapid growth has sounded alarms at the traditional car-rental giants. Enterprise, Hertz, Thrifty, and even U-Haul now have their own car-sharing operations. Avis also had one. But recently, Avis decided to shut down its own service and buy Zipcar for nearly $500 million. The Zipcar brand will now benefit from cost savings that the large-scale rental service enjoys.

As for the others, Zipcar has a big head start in terms of size and experience, cozy relationships in targeted neighborhoods, and an urban hipster cred that corporate giants like Hertz will have trouble matching. To Zipsters, Hertz rents cars, but Zipcar is a part of their hectic urban lives.

Questions for Discussion

1. Evaluate Zipcar based on benefit-based positioning.
2. Describe the beliefs and values associated with Zipcar's brand image.
3. Compare positioning based on benefits to positioning based on beliefs and values. Which is stronger?
4. Do you think the acquisition of Zipcar by Avis will be positive or negative for Zipcar?

Sources: Based on information from Mark Clothier, "Zipcar Soars after Profit Topped Analysts' Estimates," *Bloomberg.com*, November 9, 2012, www.bloomberg.com/news/2012-11-09/zipcar-soars-after-profit-topped-analysts-estimates.html; Darrell Etherington, "Zipcar CEO Details In-Car Assistant, Personalized Deals and Member Onboarding for Mobile App," *Techcrunch*, October 9, 2012, www.techcrunch.com/2012/10/09/zipcar-ceo-details-in-car-assistant-personalized-deals-and-member-onboarding-for-mobile-app/; Jerry Hirsch, "Zipcar CEO Talks about Car Sharing as Lifestyle Choice," *Seattle Times*, May 13, 2012, www.seattletimes.nwsource.com/html/businesstechnology/2018197748_inpersonzipcar14.html; Paul Keegan, "Zipcar: The Best New Idea in Business," *Fortune*, August 27, 2009, www.money.cnn.com/2009/08/26/news/companies/zipcar_car_rentals.fortune/; Stephanie Clifford, "How Fast Can This Thing Go, Anyway?" *Inc.*, March 1, 2008, www.inc.com/magazine/20080301/how-fast-can-this-thing-go-anyway.html; and www.zipcar.com, accessed May 2013.

Company Case 8

Google: New Product Innovation at the Speed of Light

Google is wildly innovative. It recently topped *Fast Company* magazine's list of the world's most innovative companies, and it regularly ranks among everyone else's top two or three most innovative. Google is also spectacularly successful. Despite formidable competition from giants such as Microsoft and Yahoo!, Google's share in its core business—online search—stands at a decisive 86 percent, more than five times the combined market shares of all other competitors combined. The company also dominates when it comes to paid search advertising, with 86 percent of that online ad segment. And that doesn't include paid search on mobile devices, where Google commands an even greater market share.

But Google has grown to become much more than just an Internet search and advertising company. Google's mission is "to organize the world's information and make it universally accessible and useful." In Google's view, information is a kind of natural resource—one to be mined, refined, and universally distributed. That idea unifies what would otherwise appear to be a widely diverse set of Google projects, such as mapping the world, searching the Internet on a smartphone screen, or even providing for the early detection of flu epidemics. If it has to do with harnessing and using information, Google's got it covered in some innovative way.

An Innovative Approach to Innovating

Perhaps more than anything else, Google knows how to innovate. At many companies, new product development is a cautious, step-by-step affair that might take a year or two to unfold. In contrast, Google's freewheeling new product development process moves at the speed of light. The nimble innovator implements major new services in less time than it takes competitors to refine and approve an initial idea. For example, a Google senior project manager describes the lightning-quick development of iGoogle, Google's customizable home page:

> It was clear to Google that there were two groups [of Google users]: people who loved the site's clean, classic look and people who wanted tons of information there—e-mail, news, local weather. [For those who wanted a fuller home page,] iGoogle started out with me and three engineers. I was 22, and I thought, "This is awesome." Six weeks later, we launched the first version. The happiness metrics were good, there was healthy growth, and [a few months later], we had [iGoogle fully operational with] a link on Google.com.

Such fast-paced innovation would boggle the minds of product developers at most other companies, but at Google it is standard operating procedure. "That's what we do," says Google's vice president for search products and user experience. "The hardest part about indoctrinating people into our culture is when engineers show me a prototype and I'm like, 'Great, let's go!' They'll say, 'Oh, no, it's not ready.' I tell them, 'The Googly thing is to launch it early on [as a beta product] and then to iterate, learning what the market wants—and making it great.'" Adds a Google engineering manager, "We set an operational tempo: When in doubt, do something. If you have two paths and you're not sure which is right, take the fastest path."

When it comes to new product development at Google, there are no two-year plans. The company's new product planning looks ahead only four to five months. Google would rather see projects fail quickly than see a carefully planned, long and drawn-out project fail.

Google's famously chaotic innovation process has unleashed a seemingly unending flurry of diverse products, most of which are market leaders in their categories. These include everything from an e-mail service (Gmail), a blog search engine (Google Blog Search), an online payment service (Google Checkout), and a photo-sharing service (Google Picasa) to a universal platform for mobile phone applications (Google Android), a faster-than-anything-else-out-there broadband network (Google Fiber), a cloud-friendly Internet browser (Chrome), projects for mapping and exploring the world (Google Maps and Google Earth), and even an early warning system for flu outbreaks in your area (Flu-Trends). Google claims that Flu-Trends has identified outbreaks two weeks before the U.S. Centers for Disease Control and Prevention.

Competing through Innovation

Not only is Google innovative, but it uses this core competency as a primary competitive weapon. Take some of its recent product introductions. First, there's Google Play. Even though it created the number-one smartphone operating system in the world—Android—Google still could not capture the purchases and activities of all those Android users when it came to apps and entertainment media. Nor could it come close to matching its operating-systems penetration in the tablet market. So Google combined and redesigned everything it had in that department and launched Google Play, an iTunes-like marketplace for apps, music, movies, and games. Although one reviewer claims that this launch "lacks the polish of Apple," he goes on to say that "there should be little doubt . . . about Google's determination to change that."

A second recent major product introduction is Google+, an all-purpose social network. With Google+, the search leader fired a shot right over the bow of Facebook. In response, Facebook founder and CEO Mark Zuckerberg put all Facebook employees on "lockdown" alert, working around the clock to copy the best features of Google+ and accelerate development of other Facebook features already being developed. In less than two years' time, Google+ has acquired over 500 million registered members, about half of those who now share their lives on Facebook, making it the second largest social networking site. Like Google Play, Google+ is a cutting-edge product. Such new products put Google in the dash for riches in completely new competitive arenas.

On a smaller scale, Google has added a feature to its mobile search app, Google Now, which has the industry buzzing. Clearly targeting Apple, Google Now features voice recognition that many observers think is even better than Apple's Siri. Based on a branch of artificial intelligence called deep learning, Google's voice recognition feature emulates the way the human brain recognizes patterns and engages in what we call thinking. Although it's extremely complicated and cutting-edge stuff, Google's experts still managed to crank out this feature in only nine months. And they aren't done. Google's experts are fast at work developing *image* recognition capabilities based on the same deep learning technology that will soon make searching images and even video more accurate and intuitive than ever.

Innovation without Borders

With Google's process and culture for innovation, even the sky doesn't seem to be the limit. No product illustrates that better that Google Glass, the wearable smart device that has the whole world talking. Worn like a pair of glasses, Google Glass has a tiny projection screen that hovers in front of the user's face that only the user can see. Voice recognition (the same as found in Google Now) and eye movement recognition provide instant response to the user's every desire and a truly hands-free experience. And that experience is oriented around having the entire virtual world more conveniently accessible than ever before. Still in the beta testing phase, it remains to be seen just what impact Google Glass will have. But based on reactions thus far, the impact will be nothing short of huge. After using Google Glass for only a few days, *Mashable's* editor-in-chief, Lance Ulanoff, dubbed it "the future." Says Ulanoff, "Google Glass could be the next big thing because it's a piece of powerful, yet elegant consumer technology that anyone can use with almost no training."

Google is open to new product ideas from just about any source. What ties it all together is the company's passion for helping people find and use information. Innovation is the responsibility of every Google employee. Google engineers are encouraged to spend 20 percent of their time developing their own "cool and wacky" new product ideas. And all new Google ideas are quickly tested in beta form by the ultimate judges—those who will use them. According to one observer, "Anytime you cram some 20,000 of the world's smartest people into one company, you can expect to grow a garden of unrelated ideas. Especially when you give some of those geniuses one workday a week—Google's famous '20 percent time'—to work on whatever projects fan their passions."

Such thinking sends Google beyond its own corporate boundaries in search of the next wave of big ideas. Recently, Google hosted what it called the "Solve For X" conference. The company invited about 50 of the smartest people in the world to tackle some of the world's biggest problems. The emphasis was on "radical." Just how radical were some of the ideas that emerged? How about turning contact lenses into computer monitors with heads-up displays packed full of data? Or how about solving the world's clean water problems through existing desalinization technologies? If that doesn't go far enough for you, how about using magnetic resonance imaging (MRI) technology to put images from the human mind onto a computer screen?

Just the fact that Google organized Solve For X indicates what type of innovator Google is. For Google, innovation is more than a process—it's part of the company's DNA. "Where does innovation happen at Google? It happens everywhere," says a Google research scientist.

If you talk to Googlers at various levels and departments, one powerful theme emerges: Whether they're designing search engines for the blind or preparing meals for their colleagues, these people feel that their work can change the world. The marvel of Google is its ability to continue to instill a sense of creative fearlessness and ambition in its employees. Prospective hires are often asked, "If you could change the world using Google's resources, what would you build?" But here, this isn't a goofy or even theoretical question: Google wants to know because thinking—and building—on that scale is what Google does. After all, this is the company that wants to make available online every page of every book ever published. Smaller-gauge ideas die of disinterest. When it comes to innovation, Google is different. But the difference isn't tangible. It's in the air—in the spirit of the place.

Questions for Discussion

1. Identify major similarities and differences between the new product development process at Google versus that found at most other companies.
2. Is Google's product development process customer centered? Team based? Systematic?
3. Considering the product life cycle, what challenges does Google face in managing its product portfolio?
4. Is there a limit to how big Google's product portfolio can grow? Explain.
5. Will Google be successful in markets where it does not dominate, such as social networks and app/entertainment stores? Why or why not?

Sources: Robert Hof, "Meet the Guy Who Helped Google Beat Apple's Siri," *Forbes*, May 1, 2013, www.forbes.com/sites/roberthof/2013/05/01/meet-the-guy-who-helped-google-beat-apples-siri/; "Covario Finds Q1 Global Paid Search Spending Grew 33 Percent over Last Year," March 28, 2013, www.marketwatch.com/story/covario-finds-q1-global-paid-search-spending-grew-33-percent-over-last-year-2013-03-28; www.karmasnack.com/about/search-engine-market-share/, accessed May, 2013; Matt Lynley, "Here Are the 17 Radical Ideas from Google's Top Genius Conference That Could Change the World," *Business Insider*, February 11, 2012, www.businessinsider.com/here-are-the-17-radical-ideas-from-googles-top-genius-conference-that-could-change-the-world-2012-2?op=1#ixzz21TPojmMs; Chuck Salter, "Google: The Faces and Voices of the World's Most Innovative Company," *Fast Company*, March 2008, pp. 74–88; "World's 50 Most Innovative Companies," *Fast Company*, March 2013, www.fastcompany.com/section/most-innovative-companies-2013; Lance Ulanoff, "This Is Why Google Glass Is the Future," *Mashable*, May 1, 2013, www.mashable.com/2013/04/30/google-glass-future/; and www.google.com, accessed November 2013.

Company Case 9

JCPenney: The Struggle to Find Optimum Price

JCPenney, the 110-year-old veteran retail chain, has been on a recent roller coaster ride. Years of stagnant and declining sales ushered in a new era—a new CEO, a new strategic plan, and a major price-based campaign to revamp JCPenney's image. When that failed, the retailer followed up with multiple revisions to the pricing campaign, changes to the overall strategic plan, and, finally, a return to the old CEO. But nothing so far has reversed JCPenney's declining sales nor slowed the flow of customers heading out the door. In fact, things are only getting worse for Penny's. Is there any hope for this failing icon of American retailing, or is it doomed to eventual extinction? Let's take a deeper look.

Fair and Square Pricing

As the new millennium debuted, things were looking pretty bright for JCPenney. Sales were at an all-time high of $32.5 billion and the company commanded a sizable share of the department store market. Then the market changed. Shoppers began spending less time at the mall and more time at discount stores like Walmart and Target, big-box general merchandise chains like Kohl's, and nimble specialty retailers like Bed, Bath, and Beyond and Sports Authority. JCPenney began steadily losing ground to these rivals. For a while, sales remained more or less stagnant. Then in 2005, they began to decline. Despite a brief flirtation with an all-time high stock price of $83 in 2007, by 2011 Penney's annual sales had bottomed out at $17 billion and its stock price plunged along with sales.

Desperate for a turnaround, JCPenney hired a new CEO, Ron Johnson, who had first cut his retailing teeth at Target and then worked wonders for a decade as head of retail operations at Apple. After taking time to analyze the company's situation, Johnson knew that the store needed to make dramatic changes. He announced a $1 billion, four-year transformation, one of the most sweeping retail makeovers in history, designed to radically reinvent the JCPenney customer experience. Penney's began making seismic changes across almost every aspect of its operations and marketing.

For starters, Johnson put the "department" back in department stores. Under the turnaround plan, each JCPenney store would be reorganized into a collection of 80 to 100 brand stores-within-a-store by 2015. The new stores would be a kind of "Main Street" of in-store brand shops spread along wider, less-cluttered aisles. Like Apple stores, Johnson wanted Penney's stores to be places where shoppers come to hang out. So each Penny's store would have a "Town Square" at its center, a large area featuring changing services and attractions, such as expert advice plus, say, free haircuts during back-to-school days or free hotdogs and ice cream in July.

Such operational changes were pretty revolutionary for JCPenney. But the lynchpin of Penney's revitalization was a new "Fair and Square" pricing strategy. As Penney's had fallen behind rivals in recent years, it had come to rely on deep and frequent discounts to drive sales. When Johnson arrived at JCPenney, the retailer was holding some 590 separate sales each year. Such sales were crushing margins and profits. Almost 75 percent of JCPenney's merchandise was being sold at discounts of 50 percent or more, and less than 1 percent was sold at full price.

JCPenney's new pricing ditched deep discounts and endless rounds of sales and coupons in favor of lower everyday prices. For starters, in an effort to put the "value" back into its price–value equation—to the benefit of both customers and the company—JCPenney cut its regular retail prices by about 40 percent across the board. It then installed a simpler, steadier, three-tiered pricing scheme: "Everyday" prices (red sales tags) featured regular lower prices on most merchandise throughout the store. "Month-long value" prices (white tags) applied to limited monthly themed sales events, such as "back-to-school" pricing in August. "Best prices" (blue tags) offered clearance prices on the first and third Fridays of every month.

All three sets of prices employed simplified tags and signage, with prices ending in "0," rather than ".99" or ".50," to suggest good value. And tags listed only one price, rather than making "previously priced at" comparisons. JCPenney made it clear that its "Fair and Square" pricing wasn't Walmart-like everyday low pricing. Penney's everyday prices were not as low as the biggest discounts it once offered. Instead, the goal was to offer fair, predictable prices for the value received. Penney's wanted to convey this message to consumers: Why play the "wait for the rock-bottom price" game when you can get good low prices every day on what you want, when you want it? Customers know the right price, Johnson reasoned, so why waste their time if the store can get to that price from the start?

A Bumpy Start

In early 2012, before any operational changes had begun, Penney's introduced the "Fair and Square" pricing campaign to the world. It ran ads showing shoppers screaming in frustration after missing out on limited-time sales events, arduously clipping coupons, or standing in long lines at night to be one of the few lucky customers to get "blowout" prices. "Enough. Is. Enough." concluded each ad in stark red letters. At Penney's Facebook page, consumers were greeted with more messages spoofing promotion-crazy retailers with pitches to "enjoy our biggest and best-ever crazy and exhausting and totally confusing sale."

The "Enough. Is. Enough." ad campaign announced that things would now be different at JCPenney. The chain set out to put an end to today's retail pricing insanity. Penney's halted coupons, doorbuster deals, and nonstop markdowns on artificially inflated prices. In their place, the chain launched its simplified everyday low pricing scheme with only occasional special promotions. Not only would the new pricing make life easier for promotion-weary customers, Penney's promised, it would also put much-needed money into the company's till.

"Fair and Square" pricing seemed to make sense, and the retail industry waited with anxious anticipation to see how JCPenney's promising transformation strategy would work out. The answer: Not well, at least not in the short run. In the year following implementation of the new strategy, deal-prone JCPenney regulars still looking for deep discounts reacted badly. Penny's sales plunged to the lowest levels in 25 years, threatening the chain's very survival. The critics piled on, asserting that Johnson should have changed pricing more gradually, allowing more time to implement the stores-within-a-store concept and to reorient core customers.

Within months, Johnson himself admitted that he'd underestimated how much JCPenney customers valued coupons and sales. As a result, by year's end, Penney's had eased up a bit and reversed some of its pricing changes. Although still moving ahead full steam with developing in-store brand shops, Penney's began once again offering regular sales. It even added back "suggested retail price" comparisons to some price tags. And everyday ads were urging customers to check out JCPenney's "unbelievably low prices every day" and to "Compare. Save. Smile."

Despite these reversals, however, Johnson and the chain remained "fully committed to great everyday value" pricing. Sales focused on only selected items important to driving sales during "key events and holidays"—for example, a 20-percent-off Valentine's Day jewelry sale. Penney's still relied on many fewer sales than in the old days—no more than 100 sales events per year versus the previous nearly 600 per year. And it retained the cleaner pricing look, with prices ending in full dollar digits rather than ".99" endings that suggested cheaper goods or discounts.

As a new year dawned, Johnson claimed to have learned from his mistakes, and remained optimistic. From the start, he predicted that transforming store layouts, merchandise, and in-store shopper experiences would take four years to complete. Besides, without a major change of direction, JCPenney seemed doomed to mounting losses and eventual failure. Johnson continued to hedge his bets for the future of the venerable old retail chain on finding the right balance of price and value. "We greatly look forward to year two of our transformation," said Johnson. "This is the year the new JCP will take form."

Turning around the Turnaround?

But when the year-end financials came out in February of 2013, revenues had dropped a whopping 25 percent to just $13 billion in just one year, a loss of more than $4 billion. Perhaps even worse, net profits fell 550 percent, a loss of a cool billion dollars. And JCPenney's stock price of less than $15 per share was less than half of what it had been when Johnson was hired. Having lost the support of customers, shareholders, and the board of directors, Ron Johnson stepped down as CEO after a brief two-year run.

Johnson's departure really didn't come as a surprise, but JCPenney's choice for a new CEO did. In an ironic move, Penney's reappointed former CEO Mike Ullman, the man who had immediately preceded Johnson. Within weeks, JCPenney ran an ad apologizing for the changes made under Johnson. "It's no secret. Recently, JCPenney changed," the ad's voice-over stated. "Some changes you liked and some you didn't, but what matters from mistakes is what we learn. We learned a very simple thing, to listen to you." The ad ended with the appeal, "Come back to JCPenney." The greater irony is that this apology ad was commissioned by Ron Johnson prior to his exit.

According to one retail analyst, "There is no question that an apology can help a brand recover from a setback. The key is, you then have to follow it up and live up to the apology." While Ullman has yet to make any major strategic announcements, a JCPenney circular that came out following the debut of the apology ad listed dozens and dozens of items on sale for Mother's Day. Also in the flyer was an online-only coupon offering shoppers 15 to 20 percent off. But even these sales provided no indication of new changes beyond Johnson's modifications to the strategic plan.

Moving forward, JCPenney now faces a serious pricing puzzle, one that's all too familiar to many retailers today: It can't live with sale prices, but neither can it live without them. The chain's previous diet of constant deals and deep discounts produced growing losses. But its attempts to wean customers off endless deals and move to everyday fair pricing produced even worse results. It is not yet clear what changes JCPenney will make. But one JCPenney executive put it bluntly: "I think that the consumer is ultimately going to decide that for us."

Questions for Discussion

1. Of the major pricing strategies, which one best describes JCPenney's "Fair and Square" pricing strategy?
2. Compare JCPenney's former traditional approach to pricing versus the "Fair and Square" pricing strategy. Discuss the advantages and disadvantages of each.
3. Discuss the role of product, place, and promotion in connection to "Fair and Square" pricing.
4. Did "Fair and Square" pricing fail for JCPenney? Explain your answer.
5. With Johnson out and Ullman in, what do you predict for JCPenney? What recommendations would you offer Ullman?

Sources: Quotes and other information found in Brad Tuttle, "JCPenney Reintroduces Fake Prices," *Time*, May 2, 2013, http://business.time.com/2013/05/02/jc-penney-reintroduces-fake-prices-and-lots-of-coupons-too-of-course/; Matt Townsend, "JCPenney Apologizes in Ad Developed under Former CEO," *Bloomberg*, May 1, 2013, www.bloomberg.com/news/2013-05-01/j-c-penney-apologizes-in-ad-developed-under-former-ceo.html; Natalie Zmuda, "JC Penney Reinvention Is Bold Bet, But Hardly Fail-Safe," *Advertising Age*, January 30, 2012, pp. 1, 22; Allison Miles, "Change Coming to Victoria's JC Penney Store," *McClatchy-Tribune Business News*, January 28, 2012; "JCPenney 'Enough Is Enough,'" *International Business Times*, February 1, 2012, accessed at www.ibtimes.com; Laura Heller, "Ron Johnson Out at JCPenney, Ending Its Year of Living Dangerously," *Forbes*, April 8, 2013, http://www.forbes.com/sites/lauraheller/2013/04/08/wow-ron-johnson-out-at-j-c-penney/; and Steve Denning, "JCPenney: Was Ron Johnson's Strategy Wrong?" *Forbes*, April 9, 2013, www.forbes.com/sites/stevedenning/2013/04/09/j-c-penney-was-ron-johnsons-strategy-wrong/.

Company Case 10

Corning: Feeding Innovation through the Supply Chain

Sometime around 1960, scientists at Corning made a significant advance while experimenting with ways to strengthen glass. Using a recently developed method that involved dipping glass in a hot potassium salt bath, they discovered that adding aluminum oxide to the glass before dipping produced a product with never-before-seen strength and durability. The scientists hurtled everything they could think of at this new super glass, including frozen chickens at high speeds, and even dropped it from the top of their nine-story building. They found that the new glass could withstand 100,000 pounds of pressure per square inch (normal glass can only handle about 7,000).

This super glass, Corning assumed, would surely be embraced by manufacturers of product ranging from eyeglasses to phone booths, prison windows, and automobile windshields. Corning named the glass Chemcor and put in on the market. But most potential customer companies did not deem the strength benefits of Chemcor worth the premium price mandated by its high cost of production. Making matters worse, when it did break, Chemcor had the potential to explode, leading the few companies that had placed orders to recall their products. When it realized that it had created an expensive upgrade nobody wanted, Corning shelved Chemcor in 1971.

Getting by with a Little Help from Suppliers . . .

When Amory Houghton, Sr., founded Corning in 1851, not even he could have foreseen the vast array of products his company would develop—products that would literally revolutionize the twenty-first century. Most people in the 1850s thought of glass as, well, just glass. But Corning thought differently. It went on to develop innovative products that would change the way people live, including light bulbs, television tubes, cookware, ceramic substrates, optical fiber, active-liquid crystal displays, and even missile nose cones. Corning achieved these feats because Houghton established research and development as the company's foundation.

From its origins, Corning has relied upon sound relationships with suppliers and customers to keep the innovation machine churning. On the supply side, producing the quantities of glass that pour off the Corning production lines requires massive amounts of sand (silicon dioxide). But because sand has such a high melting point, other chemicals—such as sodium oxide—are used to lower the melting point, making glass easier and cheaper to produce. Corning also relies on many elements and chemicals to give different types of glass their useful qualities. For example, Chemcor contains not only silicon dioxide, but also aluminum, magnesium, and sodium.

To keep the right kinds of chemicals and other raw materials flowing, price and quality are only baseline criteria at Corning. To maximize long-term success for itself and for its suppliers, Corning has also established a Supplier Code of

Conduct. The Code ensures that all supplier operations are conducted within the laws, customs, and cultural norms of the regions where Corning does business. It also ensures that they comply with the company's own corporate values. Corning invests considerable energy in selecting suppliers. The Code of Conduct includes specific criteria regarding ethics, labor, health and safety, and environmental concerns. On the surface, such criteria seem to have little to do with making glass. But Corning knows that such factors can ultimately affect the quality, price, and availability of the raw materials the company needs for making its products.

. . . and from the Supplied

Some of Corning's products are consumer products. For example, take Corningware. Corning scientist Don Stookey found that product by accident when a faulty temperature controller allowed a sample of photosensitive glass to reach 1,600 degrees rather than the intended 1,100 hundred degrees. He thought the result would be a blob of melted glass and a ruined furnace. On closer inspection, however, Stookey discovered that he had a milky white plate that was lighter than aluminum, harder than high-carbon steel, and far stronger than regular soda-lime glass. When he dropped it on the floor, instead of shattering, it bounced. When Corningware hit the market in 1959, it was a space-age wonder.

But most of Corning's products are supplied to manufacturers as components or raw materials in other products such as televisions and automobiles. That's where successful outcomes depend most on good supplier relationships. In this case, however, Corning is the supplier. Always on the lookout for ways to forge new relationships with manufacturing customers, Corning came up with an idea in 2005 when Motorola released the Razr V3, a mobile flip phone that featured a glass screen instead of the usual high-impact plastic. Maybe Chemcor—the super strong glass that Corning had shelved 1971—would make a good glass for mobile phones. The company quickly formed a team to explore the possibilities and code named the project Gorilla Glass. Its team's main goal was to reduce the thickness of the glass from its current 4 millimeters to something that could be used in a phone.

Within a few years, as the team was making progress on the thickness issue, Corning CEO Wendell Weeks received a phone call that would give Gorilla Glass its big chance. The call came from late Apple founder Steve Jobs. Jobs and Weeks had collaborated previously. In fact, Weeks had pitched to Jobs the idea of using laser-based microprojection technologies—something Corning scientists were toying with—to provide larger screens for increasingly smaller phones. Jobs said the idea was dumb and that he was working on something better—a device whose entire surface was a display. The world would soon know that product as the iPhone.

Jobs was relentless in getting the iPhone's design just right. A plastic face just wasn't good enough, he insisted. The iPhone would need a "silky, tough, smooth piece of glass." The problem was that no such glass product was commercially available. However, Jobs had heard about Corning's Gorilla Glass and thought it had potential. So he put in the call to Wendell Weeks.

Jobs explained that he needed a piece of smooth, clear glass that would resist scratches and breaking and act as a conductor for touchscreen technology. It also needed to be 1.3 millimeters thick. Weeks explained that Gorilla Glass might meet Jobs's needs but was nowhere near that thin. Undaunted, Jobs gave Weeks a seemingly impossible mandate—make millions of square feet of Gorilla Glass, make it ultrathin, and have it ready in six months, because the iPhone would be on store shelves in seven months.

The mandate posed many unknowns for Gorilla Glass. The product had never been mass produced, and it was unclear that a process could be developed to produce the quantity of glass that Apple needed. Weeks was also uncertain whether Gorilla Glass could be made so thin and still retain its strength. Even if these issues could be ironed out, how long would it take? So in responding to Jobs, Weeks did what any risk-taking CEO would do. He said, "yes." Then he formed a team to make it happen.

With such a tight deadline, Corning had no time to develop a new manufacturing process. Instead, the team adapted a process the company was already using—called fusion draw. This process could produce thinner glass while also speeding up the process. To maintain the desired toughness characteristics, the team tweaked the existing Gorilla Glass recipe. It changed the levels of several of the glass's seven individual components and added one new secret ingredient. But there was still one hitch. Corning only had one factory—in Harrodsburg, Kentucky—capable of producing glass by means of fusion draw. That plant's seven production lines were already going full blast to meet demand for sold-out LCD glass for TV panels. However, the factory was somehow able to squeeze Apple's initial Gorilla Glass order into one of its production lines. Incredibly, and ahead of schedule, Corning produced enough 1.3 millimeter Gorilla Glass to cover seven football fields.

The rest, as they say, is history. Every iPhone and iPad that Apple has ever sold features Gorilla Glass. Beyond that, the state-of-the-art Corning material is featured on more than 1 billion devices worldwide across 750 different products, including smartphones, tablets, notebooks, and TVs. In all, Corning supplies the glass for devices to 33 different companies. If you regularly touch or swipe a gadget, you have likely touched Gorilla Glass. In 2007, Corning sold $20 million worth of Gorilla Glass. Today, the product accounts for over $1 billion of the company's $8 billion total annual revenues.

But quantity doesn't begin to characterize the impact of Corning's relationships with manufacturers. In only a handful of years, a simple thing like a glass display has gone from a component to an aesthetic. When a user touches the outer layer of Gorilla Glass, the body closes the circuit between an electrode beneath the screen and the glass itself, transforming motion into data. It's a seamless partition that connects people's physical selves with the infinite digital world—so seamless, in fact, that most people have a hard time determining exactly where that partition exists.

The Ongoing Need for Good Supplier Relationships

The Corning Harrodsburg factory continues to churn out Gorilla Glass in five-square-foot panels. Robotic arms put the panels in wooden crates that are trucked to Louisville, Kentucky, and loaded onto a westbound train. When they reach the coast, they are loaded onto freighters and shipped off to a Corning facility in China, where they receive a finishing bath and are cut into gadget-sized rectangles.

But Corning's partnerships with customers like Apple are more important today than ever. For starters, Gorilla Glass isn't entirely unbreakable. Manufacturers round up broken devices that get returned and send them back to Corning, where a team tries to replicate activities that caused the breaks. The research provides vital information for developing new glass. If Corning learns how Gorilla Glass typically breaks, it can try to prevent those breaks in future products by altering the composition of the glass or tweaking the chemicals that strengthen it.

And Corning needs customer help in developing new versions of Gorilla Glass. New designs require ever-more-stringent specifications. Last year, Corning released Gorilla Glass 2—thinner and stronger than the original—in response to the demands of Apple, Samsung, Google, and others to allow them to make thinner devices. Gorilla Glass 3 is in development and promises to be 40 percent more scratch resistant than version 2.

Future designs will call for even more radical glass. That's why a new Corning product called Willow has been born out of Gorilla Glass. Willow is durable and light—a 100-micron-thick sheet of glass that bends and flexes like transparent paper. This is glass, not plastic. Corning is working with manufacturers for possible product platforms such as flexible smartphones, roll-up organic LED (OLED) displays, and even flexible solar cells.

It's these customer partnerships that have kept Corning on the cutting edge of innovation. Corning has had a successful partnership with Samsung in the television display industry dating back to the early days of television itself. That partnership continues today in the form of Samsung Corning Precision Materials, a joint venture that combines Samsung's display technology and Corning's glass expertise in the production of OLED displays—displays used by Samsung and sold to other companies. If partnerships like this are any indication, it doesn't take a looking glass to see that the future looks very bright for Corning.

Questions for Discussion

1. As completely as possible, sketch the value chain for Corning from raw materials to finished consumer goods.
2. Is Corning a producer, a consumer, or an intermediary? Explain.
3. Discuss Corning's channel management procedures. Do Apple and Samsung have similar procedures in place?
4. Identify all the reasons why Corning's partnerships are essential to its success.
5. With respect to marketing channels, what are some threats to Corning's future?

Sources: David Lidsky, "Corning: For Becoming the 800-Pound Gorilla of the Touch-Screen Business," *Fast Company*, February 11, 2013, www.fastcompany.com/most-innovative-companies/2013/corning; Bryan Gardiner, "Glass Works: How Corning Created the Ultrathin, Ultrastrong Material of the Future," *Wired*, September 24, 2012, www.wired.com/wiredscience/2012/09/ff-corning-gorilla-glass/all/; Charles Schelle, "Steve Jobs' Biographer Isaacson Shares Tales of Apple Founder's Genius," *Sarasota Patch*, January 16, 2013, sarasota.patch.com/articles/steve-jobs-biographer-isaacson-shares-tales-of-apple-founder-s-genius#photo-12987138; and information from www.corning.com/about_us/index.aspx, accessed November 2013.

Company Case 11

Dollar General: Today's Hottest Retailing Format

"Save time. Save money. Every day." Given today's economics, that sounds like a winning proposition. In fact, it's the slogan of discount retailer Dollar General—and it *is* a winning proposition. Dollar stores and other hard discounters are today's hottest retailing format, and Dollar General is the nation's leading dollar store.

Whereas the Walmarts, Costcos, and Targets of the world are big-box discounters, Dollar General and the other dollar stores are small-box discounters. They remain a relatively small threat to their bigger rivals. For example, the combined annual sales of all dollar stores amount to only about 15 percent of Walmart's annual sales. But they are one of the fastest-growing threats. Throughout the Great Recession, as the big-box discounters struggled, the dollar stores spurted, rapidly adding new stores, customers, and sales. In the post-recession economy, big-box stores have lumbered along at a lukewarm pace while the dollar stores have continued to thrive.

How is Dollar General doing it? A famous ad person once wrote, "A company can become incredibly successful if it can find a way to own a word. Not a complicated word. Not an invented one. The simple words are best, words taken right out of the dictionary." In this case, the word is "dollar." Not only have Dollar General and the others seized this critically differentiating word from Walmart and Target, they've also seized it from grocery stores, drug stores, and all other types of retailers that ever laid claim to low prices.

If you haven't been in a dollar store lately, you might be surprised at what you'll find. Back in the day, dollar stores sold mostly odd-lot assortments of novelties, factory overruns, closeouts, and outdated merchandise. Not anymore. "Dollar stores have come a long way, baby," says a retail analyst. "The Great Recession accelerated the iconic American chains' transformation from purveyors of kitschy $1 trinkets to discounters in a position to lure shoppers from the likes of supermarkets, drugstores, and Walmart stores." Dollar General now sells a carefully selected assortment of mostly brand-name items. Up to two-thirds of its sales come from groceries and household goods.

A Retail Concept Is Born

In the late 1800s, the Woolworth brothers invented the concept of five-and-dime stores. By the mid-1900s, it was apparent to J. L. Turner that although the original concept was a winner, inflation had watered it down to the point that the "five-and-dime" price point was no longer relevant. In 1955, Turner opened the first Dollar General store in Springfield, Kentucky. Following the lead of the Woolworth brothers, he priced no item in the store at more than one dollar. Word spread quickly, and the store was such a huge success that Turner and his son, Cal Turner Sr., quickly converted other stores they owned to Dollar Generals. Within a few years, they were operating 29 Dollar General stores generating $5 million a year in sales.

In turn, Cal Turner Jr. led Dollar General until 2002. By that time, the template was set and the momentum irreversible. Today, there are more than 10,000 Dollar General stores in 40 states. And today more than ever, Dollar General's cash registers are ringing. Last year, the company hit revenues of $16 billion. That's an average annual growth rate of 14 percent per year since the company went public in 1968. Even more significant, Dollar General's net profits have shot up to nearly 1 billion dollars today. In the next few years, Dollar General plans to grow to more than 12,000 stores (about the same as the number of McDonald's restaurants nationwide and more than 20 times the number of Target stores).

Saving Customers Money—and Time

Dollar General's "Save time. Save money. Every day." slogan isn't just for show. It's a carefully crafted statement of the store's value promise. In addition to low prices, the company emphasizes convenience and quality brands in its positioning statement: "Our goal is to provide our customers a better life. And we think our customers are best served when we keep it real and keep it simple. Dollar General stands for convenience, quality brands, and low prices. Dollar General's successful prototype makes shopping a truly hassle-free experience. We design small neighborhood stores with carefully edited merchandise assortments to make shopping simpler."

Saving money is clearly at the heart of Dollar General's positioning, demonstrating that the Turners were able to accomplish what the Woolworths could not. As the old five-and-dime format gave way to the dollar positioning, the Turners kept an eye on the marketing environment to ensure that their chain remained relevant. The result is that today's Dollar General is no longer a pure "dollar store" (about a quarter of its merchandise is priced at a dollar or less). Still, Dollar General has retained its positioning of having the lowest price point in retail.

Dollar General's prices on the brand-name products it carries are an estimated 20 percent lower than grocery store prices, 40 percent lower than drug stores, and roughly in line with those of the big-name discount stores. There are also plenty of savings to be had on dollar items and the increasing selection of Dollar General private-label merchandise. Finally, Dollar General gets a boost from customer perceptions of its dollar store format. The $1 price point not only draws customers in but also lets them shop a little more freely than they would elsewhere. Almost anything in the store can be had for less than $10.

When it comes to saving customers time, Dollar General's "hassle-free" and "keep it simple" model kicks in. Its carefully edited product assortment includes only about 10,000 core items (compared with 47,000 items in an average supermarket or 142,000 items in a Walmart supercenter), making things easier to find. But that doesn't mean that customers have to do without. As Dollar General points out, "We don't carry every brand and size, just the most popular ones." The focus is on life's simple necessities such as laundry detergent, toilet paper, soap, shampoo, and food items, with quality brands such as Gain, Clorox, Charmin, Dove, Pantene, Palmolive, Kraft, Betty Crocker, and Coca-Cola. Dollar General has even added brands such as Hanes underwear, L'Oréal cosmetics, and Rexall vitamins and herbal supplements.

Keeping it simple also means smaller stores—more than 25 Dollar General stores could fit inside the average Walmart supercenter. In addition, most stores are located in convenient strip malls, which usually allow customers to park right in front of a store. Once inside, customers encounter fewer aisles to navigate, fewer goods to consider, and smaller crowds to outwrangle than in big-box stores. All that adds up to a quick trip. The average Dollar General customer is in and out of the store in less than 10 minutes. Try that at a Walmart. And although Dollar General is experimenting with larger-format stores that carry produce, meat, and baked goods, those Super Dollar Generals are still much, much smaller and more manageable than a Walmart supercenter.

A Winning Combination

Keeping things simple for consumers also benefits the company's bottom line. Smaller stores are less expensive to operate, and locating them in smaller markets and less glamorous neighborhoods keeps real estate costs down as well. Dollar General's cost per square foot is as low as one-tenth that of supermarkets. By constructing its stores more cheaply, Dollar General is able to build more of them. In fact, Dollar General now has more stores in the United States than any other discounter.

Dollar General's product mix strategy also contributes to its financial performance. Although it carries a plentiful supply of top brands, it leans toward brands that are not market leaders. Furthermore, stores don't stock products in all sizes, just the ones that sell the best. Finally, Dollar General's merchandise buyers focus on getting the best deals possible at any given time. This opportunistic buying might mean that the chain stocks Heinz ketchup during one period and Hunts the next. Such practices contribute to lower costs and higher margins. And this unique approach to stocking its shelves gives Dollar General and its competitors another advantage over the big box stores—they actually have higher margins.

The post-recessionary trend toward more sensible consumer spending has given Dollar General and other dollar stores a real boost. Not only is Dollar General attracting more sales from existing customers, it's also attracting new higher-income customers. A recent survey showed that 65 percent of consumers with incomes under $50,000 had shopped at a dollar store in the past three months. However, 47 percent of households with incomes over $100,000 had done so as well. Although its core customers are still those who make less than $40,000 a year, Dollar General's fastest-growth segment is those earning more than $75,000 a year.

Put it all together, and things are sizzling right now at the nation's largest small-box discount retailer. Dollar General has the right value proposition for the times. But what will happen to Dollar General and its fellow dollar stores as economic conditions continue to improve? Will newly acquired customers abandon them and return to their previous shopping haunts?

Dollar General doesn't think so. Dollar stores seem to do as well in good times as in bad. The format had already been growing at a healthy rate before the Great Recession hit. And customers who switched over show no signs of relapsing into their old, free-spending ways. We "see signs of a new consumerism," says Dollar General's CEO, as people shift where they shop, switch to lower-cost brands, and stay generally more frugal. Company research shows that 95 percent of new customers plan to continue shopping at Dollar General even as the economy improves, the same percentage as old customers. Low prices and convenience, it seems, will not soon go out of style.

Questions for Discussion

1. Describe Dollar General according to the different types of retailers.
2. As a retail brand, assess the Dollar General strategy with respect to segmentation, targeting, differentiation, and positioning.
3. List all the reasons why Dollar General has been so successful over the past 40 years.
4. In competing against other brick-and-mortar retailers, will Dollar General succeed or fail in the long term? Support your answer.
5. Against online retailers, will Dollar General succeed or fail in the long term? Support your answer.

Sources: Christopher Matthews, "Will Dollar Stores Rule the Retail World?" *Time*, April 1, 2013, http://business.time.com/2013/04/01/will-dollar-stores-rule-the-retail-world/; Karen Talley and Melodie Warner, "Dollar General Profit Rises," *Wall Street Journal*, March 25, 2013, http://online.wsj.com/article/SB10001424127887323605404578382231185901840.html; Brad Thomas, "Dollar Stores Take on Wal-Mart, and Are Starting to Win," *Forbes*, April 16, 2012, www.forbes.com/sites/investor/2012/04/16/dollar-stores-take-on-wal-mart-and-are-starting-to-win/; Kelly Evans, "Dollar General Flexing Its Discount Muscle," *Wall Street Journal,* March 31, 2010, http://professional.wsj.com/article/SB10001424052702303601504575154192639081542.html?mg=reno64-wsj; and information from www.dollargeneral.com, accessed November 2013.

Company Case 12

The Super Bowl: More Than a Single Advertising Event—a Social-Media Frenzy

Every year around Super Bowl season, a debate heats up among advertising professionals and media pundits. At the core is the big question: Is Super Bowl Advertising worth the cost? Last year, major advertisers plunked down an average of $3.7 million per 30-second spot—that's $123,000 per second! And that's just for the airtime. Throw in ad production costs—which average $2 to $3 million per showcase commercial—and running even a single Super Bowl ad becomes a super-expensive proposition. Among other points, the naysayers assert that with costs so high, there is no reasonable hope for a decent return on the advertising investment.

But supporters of Super Bowl advertising have plenty of evidence on their side. For starters, the big game is always the most-watched television event of the year. Last year's Super Bowl drew more than 108 million viewers, making it the third-most-watched television event in history (following the 2012 and 2010 Super Bowl telecasts). In addition to sheer numbers of viewers, the Super Bowl stands alone as the TV program during which the ads draw as much or more viewership than the program itself. With that consideration, one recent study asserted that for consumer-packaged-goods firms, the return on investment (ROI) for one Super Bowl ad is equivalent to that of 250 regular TV ads.

Although there's no easy answer to the question of the value of the Super Bowl as an advertising venue, the debates of the past miss a key factor that has evolved over the last few years. These days, the Super Bowl is merely a gateway to something much bigger. Before the game begins and long after it's over, ad critics, media pundits, and consumers are previewing and reviewing, speculating, and rating the commercials. No longer do advertisers create an ad that will run for one 30-second time slot. They create a broader campaign that revolves around the Super Bowl ad, with strategies that include tactics for before, during, and after the game.

Before the Game

For many years, advertisers have recognized the potential for water cooler buzz about ads following the Super Bowl. As Internet video became prevalent, the focus turned to creating an ad with the potential to go viral. But in the past few of years, social media and mobile communications have changed the game once again. The previous rule of thumb was to build anticipation for ads by keeping them secret and unveiling them during the Super Bowl. But a few years ago, some advertisers decided to challenge this strategy by seeding information about their ads, releasing teaser ads, or even making the ad available for viewing online before the game—essentially starting the water cooler conversations early.

One of the most successful marketers to pioneer this strategy was Volkswagen, which had a stellar showing during the 2011 Super Bowl with its ad "The Force"—a 60-second spot featuring a pint-sized Darth Vader who surprises himself when he brings a Passat to life. After a heated internal debate over whether to release the spot early and ruin the surprise factor, Volkswagen decided to risk it. The decision paid off as "The Force" racked up more than 12 million views and became the most buzzed about commercial on Twitter before the kickoff of the Big Game. All that pregame buzz helped propel the ad to finish out the year as the most viral auto video, with over 63 million views. More important, Volkswagen reported its biggest increase in U.S. sales in nearly 40 years and was confident that its Super Bowl investment more than paid for itself.

Volkswagen's success fueled a pregame media frenzy for the 2012 Super Bowl, with 34 out of 54 advertisers posting their ads online in some form in the weeks leading up to the game. Referring to this trend, one media buyer said, "This is the first Super Bowl where social media has been an integral part of marketers' plans," suggesting that this is happening because marketers realize "you can get more bang for your buck." This year, almost all the ads that aired during the Super Bowl were viewable online in one form or another prior to the date of the big game. "So many people are launching commercials early to feed the beast," says a media analyst.

For Super Bowl XLVII, ad previews were available for ads from all different types of companies. Toyota's with "Wish Granted" starring Kaley Cuoco as a purple-clad genie gathered more than 11 million online views before the game, more than any other ad. Volkswagen came in at number two with over 6 million views for its ad and another 1.5 million views for the ad teaser.

But there's more than one way to measure ad success. Social media analytics company General Sentiment puts a dollar amount on this pregame ad screening. Its metric—called Impact Media Value—is a measure of consumer impact and awareness that identifies which Super Bowl advertisers are getting the most bang for their buck prior to the game. According to General Sentiment, numerous advertisers saw a powerful return on their investment in terms of both increased social media mentions and real revenue dollars generated before the game even aired. For example, after prereleasing its "Viva Young" ad online, Taco Bell saw its average daily media value increase from $322,109 to $768,418. Other top performers included Volkswagen, Mercedes-Benz, Sketchers, apparel brand Gildan, and first-time Super Bowl advertiser Wonderful Pistachios, with its remake of PSY's Gangnam Style video.

During the Game

In addition to pre-game festivities, companies are recognizing the potential to increase the effectiveness of their Super Bowl ads by engaging viewers during the game. The trend of "second screen viewing"—using a laptop or mobile device while watching TV—is exploding. One recent Nielsen survey revealed that 88 percent of tablet owners and 86 percent of smartphone owners had used their mobile devices while watching television in a 30-day period, numbers supported by social media activity during the 2013 Super Bowl. Across all social networks, game-related comments were three times higher than for the 2012 event. But more important, nearly 30 percent of the 20.9 million Super Bowl–related tweets sent during the game were about the ads. As a bonus, advertisers picked up thousands of new followers.

After the overwhelming success achieved from its animated "Polar Bowl" simulcast during the 2012 Super Bowl, Coca-Cola was more than ready to do battle in 2013. Nearly 40 executives from Coca-Cola and its advertising, social media, and PR agencies gathered at an office building in downtown Manhattan to manage the brand's second screen experience. "Mirage," an ad based on a desert race among showgirls, cowboys, a sheik, and some badlanders chasing a bottle of Coke, had been released online two weeks earlier. Consumers had been given the opportunity to vote for a team, determining which follow-up commercial would air right after the Super Bowl.

Coke's game-time activities included strategic retorts to Pepsi's digs at Coke. The team promoted photos being posted by previously identified Coke "super fans" who had been sent props from the filming of "Mirage." People live-streamed the game, called out plays, and tracked commercials as they aired. But the real activity began when "Mirage" aired. Coca-Cola listening teams for each of five social media platforms—Twitter, Facebook, Tumblr, Instagram, and YouTube—began executing routines they had practiced during five trial runs prior to the game. They gathered consumer comments into Google Docs while writers crafted responses and others pushed those responses back out through the social media outlets, complete with pre-packaged content.

All the while, voting for the microsite for the ad, CokeChase.com, experienced a massive spike in traffic from

33,000 visitors to over 1.3 million in a matter of minutes, making it difficult for team members to access their own site. Working through technical and other issues to ensure users could get through and vote paid off. As the polls closed, the showgirls were declared the winners. By then, the evidence of the campaign's success was evident. During the period of the game following the airing of "Mirage," the Coca-Cola brand experienced 8.2 million interactions and 910,000 votes, far exceeding their internal goals of 1.6 million interactions and 400,000 votes. "The interactions were really critical, in terms of seeing how much people really engaged with the content, so that's probably the thing I'm most pleasantly surprised with," said Pio Schunker, senior vice president of integrated marketing at Coca-Cola. "We struck out in a different direction, which was a risk, but it paid off."

The After Party

For Super Bowl advertisers, when the game is over, the advertising event is still in full swing. The traditional buzz factor results from the numerous "best and worst" lists generated by journalists and bloggers. And although "winners" and "losers" vary from list to list, it is clear that all ads that air on the Super Bowl achieve post-game buzz from all the online viewing and discussion.

Perhaps the greatest example of post-game buzz ever is Chrysler. The long-time number-three U.S. automaker kicked off its "Imported from Detroit" campaign during the 2011 Super Bowl with a two-minute epic featuring rapper Eminem and a resurgent Detroit as the back drop. For 2012, Chrysler produced the two-minute sequel, "It's Half-Time in America," a patriotic tribute to the soul of America starring Clint Eastwood. Both ads came out at the top of the heap in terms of pre-game buzz and post-game ratings, discussion, and views. The ads also served as anchors for a series of ads as part of an ongoing campaign. Sixteen months after the launch of the campaign, Chrysler won the Grand Effie—the top award granted at the advertising industry's Oscars. According to one jury member, "Imported from Detroit was the Grand Effie winner because they sold the product, the category, and the city."

But as the 2013 Super Bowl debuted, Chrysler revealed that it wasn't finished with its homage to rock-ribbed American values. Just prior to the second half of the game, the company aired "Whole Again," a two-minute tribute to the U.S. military and their loved ones narrated by Oprah Winfrey. In the form of a letter from the Jeep brand to the American people, Winfrey intoned, "Because when you're home, we're more than a family, we're a nation . . . that is whole again." If that wasn't enough to stand out as a tonic to the light-hearted, silly, and even confusing ads by other brands, Chrysler's ad during the second half topped off its Super Bowl patriotic three-peat. "Farmer," another two-minute epic, featured a voiceover of the tribute, "So God Made a Farmer," rendered by the late and legendary radio voice Paul Harvey. The spot served as a multimedia reminder of the role that perseverance and hard work played in making the United States a great nation. With more than 23 million views between the two ads in the few months following the Super Bowl, Chrysler showed for the third year in a row that it knows how to make ads that deliver long after they've stopped airing.

The efforts and successes by the most recent Super Bowl sponsors are far too numerous to mention here. And whether every tactic employed by every advertiser worked perfectly is not the point. The point is that now, more than ever, advertising during the Super Bowl isn't just about gaining huge exposure by running a single ad or group of ads in a television event with a huge audience. Instead, viewers watch, buzz, share, click, stream, and respond to Super Bowl ads before, during, and after the game. To get the most out of their investments, marketers must have a comprehensive program that takes advantage of the broad Super Bowl season.

Questions for Discussion

1. What factors have played the biggest role in changing the dynamics of Super Bowl advertising in recent years?
2. Discuss the concepts of reach, frequency, and impact as they relate to Super Bowl advertising. How does consideration and planning for these concepts differ between the Super Bowl and other television events?
3. When assessing return on investment, what objectives must Super Bowl advertisers consider?
4. Choose a brand that has not recently run a Super Bowl ad. Design an effective campaign with promotional tactics for before, during, and after the game.

Sources: Brian Steinberg, "Think the Super Bowl Is Over? Fox Starts Early Haggling for 2014," *Advertising Age*, February 5, 2013, http://adage.com/print/239620/; Michael Learmonth, "It's Official; Toyota Won the Super Bowl Pre-Game," *Advertising Age*, February 1, 2013, http://adage.com/print/239547/; Rae Annfera, "4 Reasons Why Pre-Game Content Is a Winning Super Bowl Strategy," *Fast Company*, accessed May, 2013, www.fastcocreate.com/1682308/; Gavin O'Malley, "Super Bowl Ads Gain 'Impact Value' before Game," January 31, 2013, www.mediapost.com/appyawards/article/192480/; Natalie Zmuda, "Watching the Super Bowl from Coca-Cola's War Room(s)," *Advertising Age,* February 4, 2013, http://adage.com/print/239582/; and Dale Buss, "Chrysler Scores Big—Twice—with Surprise Super Bowl Ads," *Forbes*, February 4, 2013, www.forbes.com/sites/dalebuss/2013/02/04/chrysler-scores-big-twice-with-surprise-super-bowl-ads/.

Company Case 13

Salesforce.com: Helping Companies Super-Charge the Selling Process

As online, mobile, and social media have proliferated, the nature of business-to-business (B-to-B) selling has changed. In fact, some have predicted the death of the professional salesperson, claiming that today's interactive technologies make it possible to sell products and services to the business customer with little to no human interaction.

But that perspective overlooks one very important characteristic of successful selling: The objective of making a sale and getting customers to purchase again and again is to build solid, enduring customer relationships. And to do that, salespeople are more important than ever. But these days, for salespeople to be effective at everything from prospecting to staying connected to customers between purchases, they must stay abreast of technologies that facilitate the management of customer relationships.

A New Era for Sales Support

Enter Salesforce.com. Marc Benioff started the online company in 1999 to compete in a crowded marketplace of companies that provide support to sales forces both large and small. At first glance, not much differentiated Salesforce.com's system. It seemed to be only one of many that enabled corporate sales representatives to gather and manage information about existing and prospective customers, leading to greater selling productivity.

But Salesforce.com's mission was nothing less than visionary. What made the company different was communicated in the Salesforce.com logo—the word "software" with a red circle around it and a line drawn through it. The company's call-in number was (and still is) "800-NOSOFTWARE." With Salesforce.com, Benioff was declaring the death of expensive packaged customer relationship management (CRM) software—the type peddled by then-industry leaders Siebel and SAP. With its stock symbol, "CRM," Benioff declared early on that Salesforce.com would be *the* force for helping business sales forces manage customer relationships.

Salesforce.com's products were subscription based and accessed through the Web. With nothing to install and no owned software, customers could get up and running quickly and inexpensively. Although that "cloud" model is standard practice for many companies today, it was a radical idea in 1999. But more than just introducing an innovative method for selling software, Benioff was establishing Salesforce.com as an innovative company that would consistently seek new ways to help companies achieve greater sales-force efficiency. Since its introduction, Salesforce.com has remained one step ahead of the competition by augmenting its products and services in ways that seem to foreshadow trends in business to business (B-to-B) selling.

During the last 10 years, the company has expanded from its core sales management services to a complete portfolio of Internet-based services that put every aspect of selling and sales management in the cloud. This includes Data.com (B-to-B sales and marketing account and contact data), Database .com (a cloud database), Site.com (cloud-based Internet content management), Desk.com (a social help desk for small business), Work.com (the leading sales performance management platform), and Sales Cloud (the world's number one sales app). A few years ago, Salesforce.com recognized that social media would play a huge role in B-to-B sales. To remain on the cutting edge, Salesforce.com acquired Radian6 (the social media monitoring firm used by more than half of *Fortune* 500 companies) and launched Chatter (a sort of Facebook for the business world).

The Salesforce.com product portfolio is carefully integrated so that each tool works with every other tool. And whereas each Salesforce.com product has broadened the company's offerings beyond sales-force support functions, each also facilitates the sales process. As Salesforce.com puts it, these tools allow companies to "supercharge their sales." Consider how Salesforce .com has helped the following companies achieve better-than-ever customer relationships through selling.

NBCUniversal

NBCUniversal (NBCU) is home to 20 popular media and entertainment brands, including NBC, CNBC, Bravo, Universal, and Telemundo. In the topsy-turvey media world, NBCUniversal has been challenged in recent years by the dramatic changes that have hit the industry, including the growing number of media outlets competing for viewer attention, the increased popularity of online media, and shifts in the nature and type of advertising. Because of NBCU's huge scope, it has perhaps been hit harder by the changes than any other media organization.

NBCU's media empire is so vast that it represents a combined total of more than 2 million ads every year. Managing that many ads across various channels for thousands of advertiser-customers was a daunting task. In fact, at one point, NBCU had more than 250 different portals for viewing information and interactions between the company and the advertisers who purchase its ad space. Managing that kind of interaction was fraught with lost opportunities for providing advertisers with the best way to reach the right customers with the right message.

Salesforce.com, however, has helped NBCU integrate its sales force across its customers. In fact, the portal for managing relationships is now simplified to only one view, allowing all sales reps in every NBCU property to see what all advertisers are doing across all properties. "As business moves into the 21st century, you need social collaboration tools to pull everything together," says Eric Johnson, vice president for sales-force effectiveness at NBCU. "Salesforce.com helps capture the collaboration that's happening across the company—to mobilize and grow the business." With the Salesforce.com portfolio of products, NBCU is able to distribute the right social information to account executives at the right time, dramatically improving customer relationships with advertisers. As a result, NBCU has seen big increases in cross-selling.

Salesforce.com tools enable sales reps to manage customer relationships better through more open internal collaboration as well. For example, when the NBCU product team comes up with new advertising and product placement opportunities, it uses Salesforce.com social tools to quickly provide the sales team with everything it needs to sell the new inventory. In this manner, sales reps are more connected than ever. And a better-equipped sales force is a happier sales force. "The collaboration with marketing in the first six months was meteoric," says Dan Sztorc, CNBC account executive. With Salesforce.com, he and his colleagues are continuously connected with each other and with the customers. "We're free to venture out and try different things and take some three-point shots."

NBCU gave all its account executives iPads equipped with a Salesforce.com app that allows them to access all of their Salesforce.com tools and other marketing and client information from any place, at any time. Just how successful has NBCU been with Salesforce.com's tools? "The first week we launched this application, we had a 300 percent return on investment," says Johnson. "Social collaboration, social networking—it's here to stay."

GE Capital

In the modern, more social world of business, GE Capital was beginning to realize the importance of building connections with its customers. "The power of the social enterprise in the B-to-B space is that you can really connect with your customers and bring them value in ways that everyday interactions don't typically allow," says Sigal Zarmi, chief information officer (CIO) of GE Capital. For this reason, GE Capital tapped into Salesforce.com's portfolio of tools.

One tactic that the company employed was building what it calls Access GE, a new collaborative community based on Salesforce.com's Force.com platform. After only five weeks of development, Access GE was launched, providing a thriving community where mid-market CEOs and CFOs could tap into the expertise of their peers as well as that of GE Capital employees. This allows executives at customer organizations to connect with GE and other customers based on similar needs and shared experiences, participating in discussions on topics of mutual interest.

As Access GE allows customers to receive better information more quickly, the power of Salesforce.com's social technologies is boosting collaboration among GE Capital's employees as well. The company's commercial sales team of more than 3,100 employees also connects on Chatter to share sales strategies, find internal experts, and uncover opportunities to cross-sell.

How does all this help to sell GE Capital's products and services? Access GE accelerates the time it takes for customers to get answers and information they seek in order to make purchase decisions. "We're connecting customers to GE Capital—and to each other—quickly, efficiently, and socially, building deeper relationships with important clients," explains Zarmi. "That's the power of the social network." All this has helped GE Capital better fulfill its mission to provide financing and expertise that helps its customers' capital go farther. With Salesforce.com's help, the company is also developing stronger and deeper connections to its customers, promoting greater employee engagement and collaboration, and achieving growth in ways that it had never before experienced.

Moving Forward with New Products

Based on the success of the customized social tool Access GE, Salesforce.com is expanding its product line. After all, Chatter is a one-to-many communication tool. With Access GE, Salesforce.com recognized the value that its clients could gain by having a many-to-many forum such as Access GE. For this reason, Salesforce.com has introduced Salesforce.com Communities as a branch of Chatter, providing an organized free-for-all for managers and client organizations to meet and collaborate online with each other as well as with company representatives.

Salesforce.com is quick to note that there are risks associated with giving customers an open forum. In addition to sharing valuable positive information, they can also air complaints and negative comments to thousands of customers at a time. But the innovative Salesforce.com has embraced that kind of risk from the beginning. With every new technology that it unveils, it focuses on the same trump card to convince reluctant users—productivity enhancements. With Chatter, customer users see an average of 12.5 percent gains in productivity over companies that do not use the B-to-B social network. And Salesforce.com expects that there will be similar productivity gains with Communities as well.

Salesforce.com has remained innovative from the start, keeping ahead of the trends and technologies that are shaping modern B-to-B interactions. In fact, it is so innovative that it has been number one on Forbes' list of Most Innovative Companies for the past two years in a row. Its tools are state-of-the-art, providing sales reps with a more accurate and timely infusion of customer information and insight into the sales process than ever before. And it doesn't appear to have any intentions of slowing down. Continuing to invest massive sums in developing and acquiring the technologies that keep it adapting in the ever-evolving marketing environment, Salesforce.com should continue to be a one-stop shop for any company with a sales force. As the company puts it, "With sales for the social enterprise, reps, managers, and execs have everything they need to win deals." Salesforce.com continues to deliver on its promise to supercharge sales.

Questions for Discussion

1. When Salesforce.com launched as an Internet-based service, how did that innovation help sales reps to interact better with customers?
2. Describe the differences that Salesforce.com has made for customers NBCU and GE Capital.
3. Consider the selling process. How might any of the Salesforce.com tools described in this case facilitate each step?
4. Looking forward, what products will Salesforce.com need to develop in order to remain on the cutting edge of supporting sales staff with information and collaboration?

Sources: Based on information from www.salesforce.com, accessed July, 2013. Also see Aaron Ricadela, "Salesforce Is a Cloud Computing King," *Businessweek*, February 14, 2013, www.businessweek.com/articles/2013-02-14/salesforce-is-a-cloud-computing-king; Victoria Barret, "Why Salesforce.com Ranks #1 on Forbes Most Innovative List," *Forbes*, September 12, 2013, www.forbes.com/sites/victoriabarret/2012/09/05/why-salesforce-com-ranks-1-on-forbes-most-innovative-list/; and Shel Israel, "Does Salesforce.com Own the Social Enterprise?" *Forbes*, March 20, 2012, www.forbes.com/sites/shelisrael/2012/03/20/does-salesforce-own-the-social-enterprise/.

Company Case 14

Pinterest: Revolutionizing the Web—Again

Ben Silbermann runs ragged. And it isn't because the 30-year-old husband is up before dawn every morning with his newborn son. It has a lot more to do with the fact that he is the founder and CEO of Pinterest, the latest "hottest Web site on the planet." In less than two years, Pinterest reached the milestone of 10 million unique monthly visitors—faster than any other Web site in history. At that time, it was driving more traffic than Google+, YouTube, and LinkedIn combined. One year later, it reached 50 million unique monthly visitors. Pinterest is growing so fast that trying to quantify its success with such a number seems pointless.

Rather, the impact of this brash young start-up can be observed in much more substantial ways. In fact, Pinterest seems to have accomplished the unlikely achievement of revolutionizing the Web—something that seems to happen every couple of years, rendering the event "likely." Like Amazon, Google, Facebook, and others before it, Pinterest has put businesses and other Web sites everywhere on notice that they'd better orient themselves around its platform or be left behind. And like the other Internet revolutionists before, Pinterest's impact has caused even the top dogs to stop and take notice. Indeed, Pinterest is changing Web design. It is also changing e-commerce. And it looks like Pinterest has solved one of the Internet's biggest problems.

The Discovery Problem

At first blush, Pinterest may sound like any other social media site, full of people sharing images and commenting on them. Silbermann's big idea for Pinterest came as he and college buddy Paul Sciarra struggled to make a business out of their first product, a shopping app called Tote. Although Tote failed to take off, it revealed a pent-up need among Internet users. Tote users didn't buy things (kind of a necessity for a shopping app). But they did e-mail themselves pictures of products to view later.

Silbermann—a lifetime collector of "stuff"—could identify with that. As a boy, he had a particular fascination with collecting bugs. "I really liked insects," he says. "All kinds: flies, grasshoppers, weevils." He spent his youth collecting, pinning, drying, tagging—creating his own private museum of natural history. So when Silbermann and Sciarra met Pinterest's third co-founder, Evan Sharp, the idea of a digital collection—of books, clothes, or even insects—as a powerful medium for self-expression began to take shape.

As the three began working on developing Pinterest, something about all-things-Internet bothered Silbermann. Despite the seemingly infinite possibilities for exploration, expression, and creation, he felt that the Internet was organized in a way that boxed people in. For starters, the nature of "search" in any online context may seem to promote discovery, but it actually stunts it. For example, Google depends on finely tuned queries in order to yield useful results. Try to find something when you're not quite sure what you want—say, "nice Father's Day gift" or even "very special Father's Day gift"—and Google isn't really much help. The bottom line is, if you try talking to Google like you would talk to a friend or a department store clerk, it won't know where to begin.

The belief that discovery is a problem on the Internet isn't original to Silbermann. In fact, it's an issue that many digital designers have struggled with since the launch of the Web, but no one has seemed to be able to solve. Take Amazon, for example. As successful as it is, Amazon's entire structure is set up like every other commerce site—a detailed system of menus and categories. To browse for something, users must function within this structure while at the same time being pulled in dozens of different directions by suggested items and competing products.

"You spend three hours buying a $20 toaster," says Barry Schwartz, psychology professor and author of *The Paradox of Choice*. "Amazon and Google pretty much stink at browsing," echoes Leland Rechis, director of product experience at Etsy. But Amazon and Google are not alone. The entire Internet is structured as a series of ever-more-specific menus, inconsistent with how the human mind works. The types of free-associative leaps that happen naturally as people walk through shopping malls, meander through a museum, or even drive down the street, are nearly impossible online.

As Silbermann and his co-founders worked to sketch out Pinterest, the three were intent on eliminating another limiting characteristic of online design. The social networks are all organized around "feeds"—lines of text or images organized by time. This setup makes it impossible to browse multiple images at once. The Pinterest team wanted to change this. "We were really excited about bringing something that wasn't immediate and real time, something that wasn't a chronological feed," says Sharp. They pictured a grid of images, rather than the directories, time stamps, and pagination so commonly imposed by the Web. The goal for Pinterest was to create an interface that would feel more like visiting a store or a museum.

As Pinterest took shape, there was no question in the minds of its creators that it was to be a social network at its core. As such, Silbermann's ability to look beyond the tunnel-vision of social media entrepreneurship set Pinterest apart from the pack in yet another way. Although the current social Web is frequented by millions, most of them are observers, not creators. Thus, they are only taking part of the experience on one level. Not everyone is a photographer, a filmmaker, or a broadcaster. "Most people don't have anything witty to say on Twitter or anything gripping to put on Facebook, but a lot of them are really interesting people," Silbermann says. "They have awesome taste in books or furniture or design, but there was no way to share that."

Something Completely Different

The Pinterest team's focus on solving some of the most limiting characteristics of the Internet yielded fruit. When Pinterest launched in March of 2010, it was widely hailed as one of the most visually stunning Internet sites ever. Silbermann, Sciarra, and Sharp worked through 50 working versions of the site, painstakingly tweaking column widths, layouts, and ways of presenting pictures to perfection. "From the beginning, we were aware that if we were going to get somebody to spend all this time putting together a collection, at the very least, the collection had to be beautiful," Silbermann says. Pinterest's grid is a key element of its design—interlocking images of fixed width and varying heights that rearranges itself every time a new image is pinned, meaning users rarely see the same home page twice.

Pinterest also bucked conventional online design in other ways. At a time when "gamification" was hot, Pinterest displayed no elements of competition. There is no leader board or any other means of identifying the most popular pinners. Pinterest also did away with page views—the predominate metric for illustrating growth and momentum. Rather, Pinterest's "infinite scroll" automatically loads more images as the user expands the browser or scrolls downward. With almost no time spent clicking or waiting for pages to load, this feature has proven addictive for many.

"When you open up Pinterest," Silbermann says, "you should feel like you've walked into a building full of stuff that only you are interested in. Everything should feel handpicked for you." As Pinterest debuted, it was obvious that Silbermann and his cohorts had succeeded. Pinterest page after Pinterest page have the feel of a collection designed by one to reflect their needs, ambitions, and desires. It's as if each person is saying, "Here are the beautiful things that make me who I am—or who I want to be." And there is no single theme to a pinboard. Pinterest is a place where young women plan their weddings, individuals create the ultimate wish list of food dishes, and couples assemble furniture sets for their new home. And departing from other social networks, every Pinterest home page is an ever-changing collage that is the sum of each user's choices.

Given that Pinterest's design has departed from Internet convention in so many ways, it's only natural that its growth dynamics would break from present trends. Most successful social services spread through early adopters on the nation's coasts, then break through to the masses. But Pinterest's growth has been scattered throughout the heartland, driven by such unlikely cohorts as the "bloggernacle" of tech-savvy young Mormons. Additionally, nearly 80 percent of Pinterest's users are women, most between the ages of 25 and 54—another demographic not normally associated with fast-growing social media sites.

Hope for Monetization

But perhaps the biggest splash that Pinterest has made in the Internet pool is its huge influence on consumer purchasing. Although many dot-coms have made a profit by selling online, the digital world in general still struggles with turning eyeballs into dollars. Even Facebook, although it turns a profit, prompts relatively few of its 1-billion-plus members to open their wallets.

But something about the combination of Pinterest's elegant design and smart social dynamics has users shopping like mad. According to e-commerce tracker RichRelevance, the average sale resulting from a Pinterest user following an image back to its source and then buying an item is $180. For Facebook users, it's only $80. And for Tweeters, it's only $70. Companies are already jumping on this opportunity. One of the primary ways brands are driving traffic to their own Pinterest or external site is by paying opinion leaders to pin an image of their product. For example, companies pay 31-year-old Satsuki Shibuya, a designer with more than a million followers, between $150 and $1,200 per image. And because of Pinterest's authentic feel, it's almost impossible to tell the difference between paid pins and unpaid pins—something that can't be said of other Web sites.

It's little wonder, then, that so many other social media sites have taken note of Pinterest. Numerous copycat sites (such as Fancy and Polyvore) have mimicked Pinterest's look and feel, right down to the font selections. The influence of Pinterest's design is also notable on sites such as Lady Gaga's social network LittleMonsters.com and the question-and-answer site Quora. Even Facebook's move to Timeline last year was notably Pinterest-like.

Despite all the ways that Pinterest has departed from the typical path of dot-com development, it has largely stayed the course in terms of making money. In other words, as of yet, Pinterest isn't generating any revenue, instead focusing on building its base and honing its site before it tries to do so. Still, Silbermann and friends are tossing lots of ideas around. For example, Pinterest could sell advertising, like so many other social media do. It could also adopt a referral fee model, retaining a percentage of the sale price of every item sold as the result of a pin. And there are other possibilities as well. Pinterest has had no trouble raising all the venture capital that it needs and has been valued at $2.5 billion, despite the fact that it is yet to earn a nickel. "There was never a doubt in our minds that we could make a s#*%load of money," says a former Pinterest employee. Apparently, investors feel the same way.

Questions for Discussion

1. Analyze the forces in the marketing environment that have contributed to Pinterest's explosion in popularity.
2. Why has Pinterest demonstrated such a high influence on consumers' decision to purchase products?
3. Discuss ways that companies can use Pinterest to build their own brands and generate sales.
4. What are some threats that Pinterest faces in the future? Give recommendations for dealing with those threats.

Sources: Based on information from Max Chafkin, "Can Ben Silbermann Turn Pinterest into the World's Greatest Shopfront?" *Fast Company*, October 2012, pp. 90–96+; Ekaterina Walter, "What the Pinterest Redesign Means for Brands," *Fast Company*, April 16, 2013, www.fastcompany.com/3008342/what-pinterest-redesign-means-brands; and J. J. Colao, "Why Is Pinterest a $2.5 Billion Company? An Early Investor Explains . . . ," *Forbes*, May 8, 2013, www.forbes.com/sites/jjcolao/2013/05/08/why-is-pinterest-a-2-5-billion-company-an-early-investor-explains/.

Company Case 15

IKEA: Making Life Better for the World's Many People

Walmart may be the biggest retailer in the world. But IKEA is the largest furniture retailer. Last year, more than 770 million shoppers flocked to the Scandinavian retailer's 338 huge stores in 41 countries, generating revenues of more than $36 billion. That's an average of over $106 million per store per year, about two-and-a-half times the average sales of a Walmart store. From Beijing to Moscow to Middletown, Ohio, customers pour into IKEA's stores for simple, practical furniture at affordable prices. IKEA is big and getting bigger—its sales have doubled during the past decade. But it's also practical and methodical, growing by only 20 or so superstores each year.

Even these big numbers don't begin to illustrate the impact that IKEA has had on consumers all over the world. Far more than just a big furniture chain, IKEA has achieved global growth and success by connecting with consumers of all nationalities and cultures. IKEA has excelled as a curator of people's lifestyles. Consumers around the world flock to IKEA to signal that they have arrived, that they both have good taste and recognize value. In fact, without IKEA, many people in the world would have little access to affordable, contemporary products for their homes. IKEA's mission is to "create a better everyday life for the many people." It accomplishes this seemingly impossible mission by striking just the right balance between global brand standardization and catering to the local cultural differences in markets around the world.

A Standardized Global Brand

In the 1940s, Ingvar Kamprad developed what became known as the "IKEA Concept." He was a native of Småland, Sweden, where the soil was poor and the people had a reputation for working hard, living frugally, and making the most of limited resources. The IKEA concept is founded on those characteristics—"offering a wide range of well-designed, functional home furnishing products at prices so low that as many people as possible will be able to afford them."

Some aspects of IKEA's products are consistent in all markets. For starters, its products are rooted in Swedish contemporary design. The classic, simple lines of IKEA design produce timeless products that few companies in any industry can match. For example, POANG—an upholstered chair based on a laminated, bentwood frame with only two front legs—was created in 1976 but remains one of the company's best-selling lines today. The same holds true for the BILLY bookcase. In fact, most of IKEA's best-selling products have been around for years. And that's how IKEA intends customers to enjoy them—for years.

Low price is a key common component of IKEA's products. The benchmark for every IKEA product is half the price of similar products from competitors. And with its relentless focus on cost-cutting, IKEA can keep the price of a product constant or even reduce it over time. Selling the same products in every market achieves scale that contributes to IKEA's low-cost structure. So does its "flat-pack" approach—designing furniture so that it can be packed and sold in pieces and assembled by customers at home.

IKEA stores around the world also share a standard design. For starters, they are huge. At an average size of 300,000 square feet, they are about 50 percent larger than the average Walmart Supercenter. These large stores let IKEA achieve another aspect of its global brand concept—a one-stop home shopping experience that includes furniture, appliances, and household goods for every room. Although such massive size may be overwhelming to some consumers, IKEA's stores are organized in three main sections. Its *showrooms* are set up in a series of rooms that not only show off each product, but also put the product in an actual room context, giving customers ideas for how they might use the product in their homes. The *marketplace* section contains the small items—everything from desk lamps to kitchen utensils—also organized by area of the home. The *warehouse* allows customers to pull their own furniture items in flat-pack boxes and cart them out. One main thoroughfare weaves its way clockwise through the store from one area to the next, a design that encourages customers to see the store in its entirety. Parents can drop their children in the Småland play area and the entire family can eat in the three-meal-a-day restaurant or the snack bar, making it easy to hang around and shop for hours.

Listening, Understanding, and Adapting

Although most of IKEA's standardized formula works in every market, the company has learned that one size does not fit all when it comes to global customers. So IKEA tweaks its marketing mix in different markets to better meet local consumer needs. The retailer seeks constant feedback from customers in stores, and it visits thousands more each year through in-home visits, observing how consumers live and asking about their dreams and challenges.

When the first U.S. IKEA store opened in Philadelphia in 1985, the beds that it carried were the same as those offered in its other world markets. But Americans weren't buying them, and sales suffered. As IKEA opened more U.S. stores, it worked to figure out the American style of sleeping. It learned that height, firmness, and maximum size are key bed characteristics sought by U.S. consumers. So, IKEA altered the composition of its mattresses and added king-size beds to the mix. Then, it altered the presentation and promotion of these products so the concept was clear. Not surprisingly, its sleep product lines really took off.

A more recent change that came about from listening to consumers in the United States and certain other markets is the offering of more services. Whereas picking, pulling, hauling, and assembling still works for most people, for others it was all just too much trouble. IKEA now offers flat-rate pricing on pulling orders and home delivery. It even maintains a list of contractors in each market that customers can call on to assemble the items in their homes.

Some markets have required more changes. As IKEA has expanded into Asia, for example, it has learned that customer needs vary substantially from those in Europe and the United States. Take China, for example. With some of the largest cities in the world, China has no shortage of customers. But most of China's 1.3 billion people don't buy home furnishings. So IKEA focuses instead on China's exploding middle class—"the many people" in growing urban populations who are more educated and fall into the 25-to-35 age range. For this reason, IKEA stores in China are located closer to city centers, rather than in the suburbs, and are located near a light-rail transportation line.

Some of the changes for IKEA China are based on the fundamental principle of stocking products that people in a given area will buy. In the United States, but not in China, mattresses are firmer. Whereas IKEA stores in China carry the same number of products as those in other parts of the world—most of them from the standard IKEA range—in China the company also stocks rice cookers and chopsticks. And when it stocked 250,000 placemats commemorating the year of the rooster, they sold out in weeks.

In massive city centers such as Beijing and Shanghai, home ownership among the middle class has gone from nearly zero to about 70 percent in the past 15 years. Because virtually all new homeowners have little sense for how to furnish and decorate a home, they are eager to learn from the West. However, not everything that works in more developed parts of the world works in China. For one thing, the average living space in China's crowded cities is much smaller than in Europe and the United States. An average Chinese family lives in a small apartment in a high-rise building, often with multigenerational family members. So in China, IKEA focuses on products geared toward saving space and organizing a household. And it helps consumers figure out how to live smart and organize in small living spaces.

Pricing in China is somewhat of a paradox. Chinese customers are attracted to IKEA's design and the comprehensive selection, so that's where IKEA puts its emphasis in terms of positioning. But at the same time, in emerging markets like China, low prices are the norm, and IKEA must cut prices drastically to remain competitive. When it first opened its doors in China more than a decade ago, IKEA found that it was more expensive than local low-priced firms. Competitors began selling copies of IKEA's designs at a fraction of the cost. Using its cost-cutting expertise, however, IKEA has brought prices in China down by more than 50 percent over the past 10 years. The classic Klippan sofa, for example, now costs only $160, a third of what it did a decade ago (the same sofa costs $470 in Sweden).

Another challenge in selling furniture in the world's most populated country is that there are significant differences across the country's many regions. For example, in some regions, apartments have smaller rooms. Thus, IKEA designs showrooms in those area to reflect the smaller size. Apartment buildings throughout China have balconies. But in northern China, balconies are widely used for food storage, whereas in southern China, they double as laundries. IKEA showrooms in these regions reflect such differences and regional needs.

The Chinese market features another unusual characteristic—gawkers. China's stores boast more traffic than IKEAs in any other part of the world (the Beijing store pulls in 28,000 customers on a Saturday—a strong week for a European store). But the majority of visitors are just hanging out and looking. Actually, many of them are there to enjoy the air conditioning, a cheap meal, and a place to relax in comfort. People often lounge for extended periods in showrooms as they would in their own living rooms. Some will even pull back the covers on an IKEA bed, take of their shoes, and hunker down for a good nap. Whereas this kind of behavior would get customers kicked out of IKEAs in any other market, management recognizes that with China's rapidly growing middle class, allowing such behavior is an investment in the future.

IKEA plans to expand its number of stores in China from 11 to 40 during the next seven years. But China is just an illustration of IKEA's strategy throughout the world. The company also plans to double its number of stores in the United States during the same period. And as IKEA continues to grow in existing markets, it is also eyeing new markets with vast, untapped potential. IKEA is currently laying the groundwork in India, where it plans 25 stores. Having doubled sales in the past decade, IKEA plans to double them again by 2020. And that's based on the same methodical growth of 20 to 25 new stores.

With its keen ability to understand the cultural differences of each market and to adapt its marketing mix accordingly, there doesn't seem to be much standing in IKEA's way.

Questions for Discussion

1. Does IKEA have a truly global strategy, or just a series of regional strategies? Explain.
2. Discuss IKEA's global strategy in terms of the five global product and communications strategies.
3. If IKEA can sell a sofa in China for $160, why doesn't it sell the product at that low price in all of its markets?
4. Can competitors easily duplicate IKEA's strategy? Why or why not?
5. Should IKEA expand more rapidly than 20 to 25 stores per year? Explain.

Sources: Based on information from www.ikea.com/ms/en_US/about_ikea/index.html, accessed August, 2013. Also see Anna Ringstrom, "IKEA Turns the Global Local for Asia Push," *Reuters*, March 6, 2013, www.reuters.com/article/2013/03/07/us-ikea-expansion-idUSBRE92606220130307; Walter Loeb, "IKEA Is a World-Wide Wonder," *Forbes*, December 5, 2012, www.forbes.com/sites/walterloeb/2012/12/05/ikea-is-a-world-wide-wonder/; Jenna Goudreau, "How IKEA Leveraged the Art of Listening to Global Dominance," *Forbes*, January 30, 2013, www.forbes.com/sites/jennagoudreau/2013/01/30/how-ikea-leveraged-the-art-of-listening-to-global-dominance/; Pan Kwan Yuk, "IKEA in China: Turning Gawkers into Consumers," *Financial Times*, April 4, 2013, http://blogs.ft.com/beyond-brics/2013/04/04/ikea-in-china-turning-gawkers-into-consumers/?Authorised=false#axzz2VAi2u6c8; and Jens Hansegard, "IKEA Taking China by Storm," *Wall Street Journal*, March 26, 2012, http://online.wsj.com/article/SB10001424052702304636404577293083481821536.html.

Company Case 16

Warby Parker: Eyewear with a Purpose

As young brothers in rural India, Toti and Omprakash Tewtia did everything together. They started a farming business together, and raised their families together. (Between the two of them, they have 15 children). Now grandfathers, the Tewtia brothers have three generations living in their home, kids running about, playing and laughing. It's a lively scene.

As they grew old together, their vision began to decline. When the highlight of your day is reading to your grandchildren, this is more than just an inconvenience. Story time would end in headaches, and then stopped altogether when the brothers couldn't see well enough to read.

Poor vision was taking a toll on their business as well. For years, they had cultivated the land in their village, but the last crop had been lost. How on earth could career farmers, who have been working the land since childhood have allowed this to happen? They couldn't see the insects that were ravaging their fields. Without proper glasses, their livelihood was put in jeopardy.

The Tewtia brothers live far away from an optical shop or an eye doctor. Although they had both been able to get reading glasses many years ago, they haven't been able to find new glasses as their prescription changed. All that changed when the folks from Warby Parker showed up. "We knew a good opportunity had come to us when we saw [them] drive into our village."

Now proudly sporting his new glasses, Toti looks in the mirror and sees a much younger man. "These glasses have taken me back to my young time!" Story time is again a nightly tradition for their grandkids. And with a healthy crop ready to harvest they're on top of their game.

The story of the Tewtia brothers is the story of cause-related marketing based on one-to-one giving—a hot concept that has really taken off in the past decade. It's also the story of Warby Parker—one of the hottest start-ups in the fashion industry.

Doing Well by Selling Cheap

It all started when four classmates at the University of Pennsylvania's Wharton School hatched a winning plan. One day, they realized that they were all complaining about how ridiculously expensive prescription eyeglasses are. "We each had [the same] experience: Walking to an optical shop, getting super excited about a pair of glasses, and walking out feeling like we got punched in the stomach," relates Neil Blumenthal, one of the four co-founders of Warby Parker. "We thought, there's got to be a better way here."

That's when the four business school students started doing some research to answer a simple question: Why are prescription eyeglasses so expensive? They discovered a few key reasons. For starters, although there are many eyeglass retailers, the majority of the industry is owned and controlled by one company. The Luxottica Group of Italy owns brands such as Oakley and Ray-Ban and retail chains such as LensCrafters, Pearle Vision, and Sunglass Hut. Luxottica's stranglehold on the eyeglass industry keeps prices high. The team also discovered that all those fancy fashion brands (e.g., Armani, Ralph Lauren, Gucci) emblazoned on eyewear frames don't actually make the glasses. The brands are licensed to manufacturers (most of them owned by Luxottica) and get a fat cut just for lending their brand names.

So Blumenthal and his buddies set out to create a business plan that would bypass the standard manufacturers and channels and reinvent how you buy eyewear. The core focus of their strategy was price, with style taking a close second. "The markups in this industry are insane," notes Blumenthal, pointing out that most glasses are sold for at least three times their wholesale price. To come in at a low price, Warby Parker developed its own line of fashionable frames in-house, contracted its own manufacturing, and opened up an online storefront to sell it all directly to customers. The price point: $95, including anti-glare polycarbonate lenses. That's one-third to one-sixth the price charged by major retailers. And Warby Parker sports some of the most fashionable designs around, all made from the same high-quality materials that the market leaders use.

Warby Parker opened its online shop in 2010. With almost no competitors selling glasses online, Warby Parker had a chance to really stand out. It made buying easy for customers with features such as virtual "try-ons," recommendations based on the shape of a customer's face, home try-ons of up to five frames, and free shipping for purchases and returns. After some public relations (PR) features in *GQ* and *Vogue*, the young start-up was inundated with purchases and requests for home try-ons. In fact, it had so many requests that it ran out of inventory and had a waitlist of 20,000 customers. Without the brickspace to welcome would-be customers, co-founder David Gilboa had an idea. "We said, well, the store's my apartment. Come on over." So Gilboa and his buddies were soon hosting people from all over Philadelphia, the company's home base. With glasses laid out on the dining room table, customers flowed in by the dozens, even hundreds. That experience really helped to solidify the company's ability to connect with customers and develop the type of customer service akin to customer service champs such as Amazon.com.

When Making a Profit Isn't Enough

Although the company's founders started with the objective of selling fashionable eyeglasses on the cheap, they quickly realized that they wanted to do more. They wanted to make a difference in people's lives on a more fundamental level. They found what they were seeking in a concept pioneered by do-gooder companies such as TOMS Shoes. For every pair of shoes TOMS sells, it donates a pair to a child in need, one who otherwise would not have access to shoes. The Warby Parker crew quickly went to work figuring out if they could do something similar with eyewear.

They learned that almost 1 billion people worldwide lack access to glasses. Without good vision, people like the Tewtia brothers are not able to work or learn to their full potential. With demand established, Warby Parker looked into feasibility of providing the supply. Although in business for only a short time, the company was not only breaking even at the $95 price point, it was making a nice margin. In fact, there was more than enough profits to cover the cost of donating a pair of glasses for every pair sold. By partnering with nonprofit organizations such as VisionSpring, Warby Parker could minimize the cost of finding people in need, determining their prescription, and distributing glasses to them.

What started as an afterthought quickly became Warby Parker's reason for doing business and one of its key selling points. The company calls it "buy a pair, give a pair" and has positioned the Warby Parker brand around the concept of doing good for others while getting really great products at prices much lower than customers might normally pay. "We believe that everyone has the right to see," the Warby Parker Web site states, adding that getting the correct glasses can add 20 percent to someone's income by increasing productivity and performance.

Warby Parker's one-for-one model is a bit different from the TOMS Shoes approach of taking its products out and delivering them to needy people in third-world countries. Instead, Warby Parker worked closely with VisionSpring to pioneer a new five-step plan:

1. Buy—Customers purchase a new pair of Warby Parker glasses.
2. Give—Warby Parker provides funding and/or glasses to nonprofit partners like VisionSpring.
3. Train—Warby Parker's nonprofit partners provide glasses and training to low-income entrepreneurs (especially women) in developing countries to start their own businesses selling glasses.
4. Sell—Local entrepreneurs sell affordable glasses, earning a livelihood and serving individuals in their communities who otherwise would not have access to glasses.
5. Buy—Individuals who previously couldn't afford glasses are able to purchase and wear the glasses they need to learn and work.

This model not only makes affordable glasses available to people who normally couldn't get them, it also provides jobs, creates businesses that stimulate local economies by continually providing a much-needed product, and empowers customers to make their own choices, avoiding the culture of dependence that accompanies most foreign assistance.

In little more than two years, Warby Parker has distributed more than 250,000 pairs of glasses throughout South America, South Asia, Africa, and even the United States. Warby Parker's model has touched the lives of people like Parmesh, a skilled carpenter in India whose business declined along with his eyesight. When VisionSpring rolled into his village, where there were no eye doctors, he signed up for a free eye exam and purchased a pair of glasses. Not only can he see better, but as he tells it, "I feel successful in these glasses. I think people respect me for the way I look in them." His business is once again booming.

Warby Parker's model is built around a snowball concept—helping one person has an impact on other people, who help even more people, and so on. Take the case of Juana, a 30-year-old mother who lives in Sololá, a mountainside village in Guatemala. From an early age, she was on her own and learned how to work hard and take care of herself. Recently, Juana received training from Community Enterprise Solutions, a nonprofit organization that helps distribute eyewear to people whose livelihoods have been compromised by poor vision. Now, in her tiny but well-organized and clean space, she offers free eye exams and sells eyeglasses, right alongside efficient wood stoves and water filters.

On the home front, Warby Parker is making it easier than ever for people of means to help others make a better life for themselves. The firm has recently started rolling out its own Warby Parker stores, third-place-style outlets that are designed for hanging out as much as they are for trying on and buying glasses. So not only can shoppers try out glasses online or at home, they can do so in person at a growing number of brick-and-mortar showrooms. Given the company's quick early success, it has no shortage of investors willing to provide the funds needed for expansion.

Plenty of companies now operate on a one-for-one business model—companies have applied this model to clothing (Polarbearicana), socks and footwear (ToeSox), water purification products (Bottle Bright), soap (Hand In Hand), and pet beds (AlphaPooch), to name just a few. But of all these do-good companies, Warby Parker is setting the bar very high. It not only gives a pair of glasses for every one purchased, its products are also cheaper—make that much cheaper—than competing goods, the opposite of most one-for-one operations. And Warby Parker's one-for-one model is setting a standard for not just giving products away, but for genuinely empowering people to help themselves while helping others to do the same. With all this and comfortable profits to boot, it isn't just rose-colored glasses that are making Warby Parker's future look bright.

Questions for Discussion

1. Discuss Warby Parker's business model in terms of the basic concept of sustainable marketing.
2. Give as many examples as you can for how Warby Parker defies the common social criticisms of marketing.
3. Of the five sustainable marketing principles, which one best describes Warby Parker's approach?
4. Analyze Warby Parker's business according to the Societal Classification of Products—desirable, salutary, pleasing, and deficient products.
5. Would Warby Parker be more or less financially successful if it were not so focused on social responsibility? Explain.

Sources: Extracts and case information based on information from www.warbyparker.com and www.shopwithmeaing.org/warby-parker-glasses-stylish-buy-one-give-one-eyewear/, accessed August, 2013. Also see Drake Baer, "Why Warby Parker Invited 20,000 Customers to Their Apartment," *Fast Company*, May 10, 2013, www.fastcompany.com/3009501/bottom-line/why-warby-parker-invited-20000-customers-to-their-apartment; Vanessa O'Connell, "Warby Parker Co-Founder Says Initial Vision Was All about Price," *Wall Street Journal*, July 18, 2012, http://online.wsj.com/article/SB10000872396390444097904577535111565440718.html; and Nina Strochlic, "Warby Parker Thrives by Giving Away Glasses Whenever It Sells a Pair," *The Daily Beast*, May 7, 2013, www.thedailybeast.com/articles/2013/05/07/warby-parker-thrives-by-giving-away-glasses-whenever-it-sells-a-pair.html.

Appendix 2 Marketing Plan

The Marketing Plan: An Introduction

As a marketer, you will need a good marketing plan to provide direction and focus for your brand, product, or company. With a detailed plan, any business will be better prepared to launch a new product or build sales for existing products. Nonprofit organizations also use marketing plans to guide their fundraising and outreach efforts. Even government agencies put together marketing plans for initiatives such as building public awareness of proper nutrition and stimulating area tourism.

The Purpose and Content of a Marketing Plan

Unlike a business plan, which offers a broad overview of the entire organization's mission, objectives, strategy, and resource allocation, a marketing plan has a more limited scope. It serves to document how the organization's strategic objectives will be achieved through specific marketing strategies and tactics, with the customer as the starting point. It is also linked to the plans of other departments within the organization. Suppose, for example, a marketing plan calls for selling 200,000 units annually. The production department must gear up to make that many units, the finance department must arrange funding to cover the expenses, the human resources department must be ready to hire and train staff, and so on. Without the appropriate level of organizational support and resources, no marketing plan can succeed.

Although the exact length and layout will vary from company to company, a marketing plan usually contains the sections described in Chapter 2. Smaller businesses may create shorter or less formal marketing plans, whereas corporations frequently require highly structured marketing plans. To guide implementation effectively, every part of the plan must be described in considerable detail. Sometimes a company will post its marketing plans on an intranet site, which allows managers and employees in different locations to consult specific sections and collaborate on additions or changes.

The Role of Research

Marketing plans are not created in a vacuum. To develop successful strategies and action programs, marketers need up-to-date information about the environment, the competition, and the market segments to be served. Often, analysis of internal data is the starting point for assessing the current marketing situation, supplemented by marketing intelligence and research investigating the overall market, the competition, key issues, and threats and opportunities. As the plan is put into effect, marketers use a variety of research techniques to measure progress toward objectives and identify areas for improvement if results fall short of projections.

Finally, marketing research helps marketers learn more about their customers' requirements, expectations, perceptions, and satisfaction levels. This deeper understanding provides a foundation for building competitive advantage through well-informed segmenting, targeting, differentiating, and positioning decisions. Thus, the marketing plan should outline what marketing research will be conducted and how the findings will be applied.

The Role of Relationships

The marketing plan shows how the company will establish and maintain profitable customer relationships. In the process, however, it also shapes a number of internal and external relationships. First, it affects how marketing personnel work with each other and with other departments to deliver value and satisfy customers. Second, it affects how the company works with suppliers, distributors, and strategic alliance partners to achieve the objectives listed in the plan. Third, it influences the company's dealings with other stakeholders, including government regulators, the media, and the community at large. All of these relationships are important to the organization's success, so they should be considered when a marketing plan is being developed.

From Marketing Plan to Marketing Action

Companies generally create yearly marketing plans, although some plans cover a longer period. Marketers start planning well in advance of the implementation date to allow time for marketing research, thorough analysis, management review, and coordination between departments. Then, after each action program begins, marketers monitor ongoing results, compare them with projections, analyze any differences, and take corrective steps as needed. Some marketers also prepare contingency plans for implementation if certain conditions emerge. Because of inevitable and sometimes unpredictable environmental changes, marketers must be ready to update and adapt marketing plans at any time.

For effective implementation and control, the marketing plan should define how progress toward objectives will be measured. Managers typically use budgets, schedules, and performance standards for monitoring and evaluating results. With budgets, they can compare planned expenditures with actual expenditures for a given week, month, or other period. Schedules allow management to see when tasks were supposed to be completed—and when they were actually completed. Performance standards track the outcomes of marketing programs to see whether the company is moving toward its objectives. Some examples of performance standards are market share, sales volume, product profitability, and customer satisfaction.

Sample Marketing Plan: Chill Beverage Company

Executive Summary

The Chill Beverage Company is preparing to launch a new line of vitamin-enhanced water called NutriWater. Although the bottled water market is maturing, the vitamin-enhanced water category is still growing. NutriWater will be positioned by the slogan "Expect more"—indicating that the brand offers more in the way of desirable product features and benefits at a competitive price. Chill Beverage is taking advantage of its existing experience and brand equity among its loyal current customer base of Millennials who consume its Chill Soda soft drink. NutriWater will target similar Millennials who are maturing and looking for an alternative to soft drinks and high-calorie sugared beverages.

The primary marketing objective is to achieve first-year U.S. sales of $30 million, roughly 2 percent of the enhanced water market. Based on this market share goal, the company expects to sell more than 17 million units the first year and break even in the final period of the year.

Current Marketing Situation

The Chill Beverage Company was founded in 2001 by an entrepreneur who had successfully built a company that primarily distributed niche and emerging products in the beverage industry. Its Chill Soda soft drink brand hit the market with six unique flavors in glass bottles. A few years later, the Chill Soda brand introduced an energy drink as well as a line of natural juice drinks. The company now markets dozens of Chill Soda flavors, many unique to the brand. Chill Beverage has grown its business every year since it was founded. In the most recent year, it achieved $185 million in revenue and net profits of $14.5 million. As part of its future growth strategy, Chill Beverage is currently preparing to enter a new beverage category with a line of vitamin-enhanced waters.

As a beverage category, bottled water experienced tremendous growth during the 1990s and 2000s. Currently, the average person in the United States consumes more than

28 gallons of bottled water every year, a number that has increased 20-fold in just 30 years. Bottled water consumption is second only to soft drink consumption, ahead of milk, beer, and coffee. Although bottled water growth has tapered off somewhat in recent years, it is still moderately strong at approximately 3 percent growth annually. Most other beverage categories have experienced declines. In the most recent year, 8.75 billion gallons of bottled water were sold in the United States with a value of more than $7.6 billion.

Competition is more intense now than ever as demand slows, industry consolidation continues, and new types of bottled water emerge. The U.S. market is dominated by three global corporations. With a portfolio of 12 brands (including Poland Spring, Nestlé Pure Life, and Arrowhead), Nestlé leads the market for "plain" bottled water. However, when all subcategories of bottled water are included (enhanced water, flavored water, and so on), Coca-Cola leads the U.S. market with a 22.9 percent share. Nestlé markets only plain waters but is number two at 21.5 percent of the total bottled water market. PepsiCo is third with 16.2 percent of the market. To demonstrate the strength of the vitamin-enhanced water segment, Coca-Cola's Vitaminwater has higher annual sales than any other bottled water brand.

To break into this market, dominated by huge global corporations and littered with dozens of other small players, Chill Beverage must carefully target specific segments with features and benefits valued by those segments.

Market Description

The bottled water market consists of many different types of water. Varieties of plain water include spring, purified, mineral, and distilled. Although these different types of water are sold as consumer products, they also serve as the core ingredient for other types of bottled waters, including enhanced water, flavored water, sparkling water, or any combination of those categories.

Although some consumers may not perceive much of a difference between brands, others are drawn to specific product features and benefits provided by different brands. For example, some consumers may perceive spring water as healthier than other types of water. Some may look for water that is optimized for hydration. Others seek additional nutritional benefits claimed by bottlers that enhance their brands with vitamins, minerals, herbs, and other additives. Still other consumers make selections based on flavor. The industry as a whole has positioned bottled water of all kinds as a low-calorie, healthy alternative to soft drinks, sports drinks, energy drinks, and other types of beverages.

Bottled water brands also distinguish themselves by size and type of container, multipacks, and refrigeration at point-of-sale. Chill Beverage's market for NutriWater consists of consumers of single-serving-sized bottled beverages who are looking for a healthy yet flavorful alternative. "Healthy" in this context means both low-calorie and enhanced nutritional content. This market includes traditional soft drink consumers who want to improve their health as well as non-soft drink consumers who want an option other than plain bottled water. Specific segments that Chill Beverage will target during the first year include athletes, the health conscious, the socially responsible, and Millennials who favor independent corporations. The Chill Soda brand has established a strong base of loyal customers, primarily among Millennials. This generational segment is becoming a prime target as it matures and seeks alternatives to full-calorie soft drinks. **>>Table A2.1** shows how NutriWater addresses the needs of targeted consumer segments.

Product Review

Chill Beverage's new line of vitamin-enhanced water—called NutriWater—offers the following features:

- Six new-age flavors including Peach Mango, Berry Pomegranate, Kiwi Dragonfruit, Mandarin Orange, Blueberry Grape, and Key Lime.
- Single-serving size, 20-ounce, PET recyclable bottles.
- Formulated for wellness, replenishment, and optimum energy.
- Full Recommended Daily Allowance (RDA) of essential vitamins and minerals (including electrolytes).

» Table A2.1 Segment Needs and Corresponding Features/Benefits of NutriWater

Targeted Segment	Customer Need	Corresponding Features/Benefits
Athletes	• Hydration and replenishment of essential minerals • Energy to maximize performance	• Electrolytes and carbohydrates • B vitamins, carbohydrates
Health conscious	• Maintain optimum weight • Optimize nutrition levels • Avoid harmful chemicals and additives • Desire to consume a tastier beverage than water	• Half the calories of fully sugared beverages • Higher levels of vitamins A, B, C, E, zinc, chromium, and folic acid than other products; vitamins unavailable in other products • All natural ingredients • Six new-age flavors
Socially conscious	• Support causes that help solve world's social problems	• 25 cent donation from each purchase to Vitamin Angels
Millennials	• Aversion to mass-media advertising technologically savvy • Counterculture attitude • Diet enhancement due to fast-paced lifestyle	• Less-invasive online and social networking promotional tactics • Small, privately held company • Full RDA levels of essential vitamins and minerals

- Higher vitamin concentration—vitamin levels are two to ten times higher than market-leading products, with more vitamins and minerals than any other brand.
- Additional vitamins—vitamins include A, E, and B2, as well as folic acid—none of which are contained in the market-leading products.
- All natural—no artificial flavors, colors, or preservatives.
- Sweetened with pure cane sugar and Stevia, a natural zero-calorie sweetener.
- Twenty-five cents from each purchase will be donated to Vitamin Angels, a nonprofit organization with a mission to prevent vitamin deficiency in at-risk children.

Competitive Review

As sales of bottled waters entered a strong growth phase in the 1990s, the category began to expand. In addition to the various types of plain water, new categories emerged. These included flavored waters—such as Aquafina's Flavorsplash—as well as enhanced waters. Enhanced waters emerged to bridge the gap between soft drinks and waters, appealing to people who knew they should drink more water and less soft drinks but still wanted flavor. Development of brands for this product variation has occurred primarily in startup and boutique beverage companies. In the 2000s, major beverage corporations acquired the most successful smaller brands, providing the bigger firms with a solid market position in this category and diversification in bottled waters in general. Currently, enhanced water sales account for approximately 18 percent of the total bottled water market.

The fragmentation of this category, combined with domination by the market leaders, has created a severely competitive environment. Although there is indirect competition posed by all types of bottled waters and even other types of beverages (soft drinks, energy drinks, juices, teas), this competitive analysis focuses on direct competition from enhanced water brands. For the purposes of this analysis, enhanced water is bottled water with additives that are intended to provide health and wellness benefits. The most common additives include vitamins, minerals (including electrolytes), and herbs. Most commonly, enhanced waters are sweetened, flavored, and colored. This definition distinguishes enhanced water from sports drinks that have the primary purpose of maximizing hydration by replenishing electrolytes.

Enhanced water brands are typically sweetened with a combination of some kind of sugar and a zero-calorie sweetener, resulting in about half the sugar content, carbohydrates, and calories of regular soft drinks and other sweetened beverages. The types of sweeteners used create a point of differentiation. Many brands, including the market leaders, sell both regular and zero-calorie varieties.

Pricing for this product is consistent across brands and varies by type of retail outlet, with convenience stores typically charging more than grocery stores. The price for a 20-ounce bottle ranges from $1.00 to $1.89, with some niche brands costing slightly more. Key competitors to Chill Beverage's NutriWater line include the following:

- ***Vitaminwater:*** Created in 2000 as a new product for Energy Brands' Glacéau, which was also the developer of Smartwater (distilled water with electrolytes). Coca-Cola purchased Energy Brands for $4.1 billion in 2007. Vitaminwater is sold in regular and zero-calorie versions. With 28 varieties, Vitaminwater offers more options than any brand on the market. Whereas Vitaminwater varieties are distinguished by flavor, they are named according to functional benefits such as Stur-D (healthy bones), Defense (strengthens immune system), Focus (mental clarity), and Restore (post work-out recovery). The brand's current slogan is "Hydration for every occasion—morning, noon, and night." Vitaminwater is vapor distilled, de-ionized, and/or filtered and is sweetened with crystalline fructose (corn syrup) and erythritol all-natural sweetener. Available in 20-ounce PET bottles and multipacks, Vitaminwater exceeds $830 million in annual sales and commands 61 percent of the enhanced waters market. More notably, it outsells all other bottled water brands, enhanced or otherwise, including Coca-Cola's own Dasani.
- ***SoBe Lifewater:*** PepsiCo bought SoBe in 2000. SoBe introduced Lifewater in 2008 with a hit Super Bowl ad as an answer to Coca-Cola's Vitaminwater. The Lifewater line includes 17 regular and zero-calorie varieties. Each bottle of Lifewater is designated by flavor and one of six different functional categories: Electrolytes, Lean Machine, B-Energy, C-Boost, Antioxidants, and Pure. Each variety is infused with a formulation of vitamins, minerals, and herbs designed to provide the claimed benefit. The most recent line—Pure—contains only water, a hint of flavor, and electrolytes. Sweetened with a combination of sugar and erythritol, Lifewater makes the claim to be "all natural." It contains no artificial flavors or colors. However, some analysts debate the "natural" designation for erythritol. Lifewater is sold in 20-ounce PET bottles and multipacks as well as one-liter PET bottles. With more than $269 million in annual revenues, Lifewater is the number two enhanced water brand, capturing 20 percent of the market.
- ***Propel Zero:*** Gatorade created Propel in 2000, just one year prior to PepsiCo's purchase of this leading sports drink marketer. Originally marketed and labeled as "fitness water," it is now available only as Propel Zero. Although the fitness water designation has been dropped, Propel Zero still leans toward that positioning with the label stating "REPLENISH + ENERGIZE + PROTECT." Propel Zero comes in seven flavors, each containing the same blend of B vitamins, vitamin C, vitamin E, antioxidants, and electrolytes. It is sweetened with sucralose. Propel Zero is available in a wider variety of sizes, with 16.9-, 20-, and 24-ounce PET bottles and multipacks. Propel Zero is also marketed in powder form to be added to bottled water. With $165 million in revenues, Propel Zero is the number three enhanced water brand with a 12 percent share of the enhanced waters market.
- ***RESCUE Water:*** The Arizona Beverage Company is best known as the number one producer of ready-to-drink bottled teas. However, it also bottles a variety of other beverages including smoothies, sports drinks, energy drinks, and juice blends. Its newest brand is RESCUE Water, introduced to the U.S. market in 2010. It sets itself apart from other enhanced waters with green tea extract added to a blend of vitamins and minerals. This provides a significant point of differentiation for those desiring green tea, but rules the brand out for the majority of customers who do not want it. It comes in five flavors, each with its own functional benefit. RESCUE Water touts other points of distinction as well, including branded Twinlab vitamins, all-natural ingredients, and a high-tech plastic bottle that resembles glass and maximizes freshness. Its Blueberry Coconut Hydrate variety contains real coconut water, an emerging alternative beverage category. Although RESCUE Water sales and market share figures are not yet known because of the product's newness, the Arizona Beverage Company is a multibillion dollar corporation with a long history of successful new product introductions.

» Table A2.2 Sample of Competitive Products

Competitor	Brand	Features
Coca-Cola	Vitaminwater	Regular and zero-calorie versions; 28 varieties; each flavor provides a different function based on blend of vitamins and minerals; vapor distilled, de-ionized, and/or filtered; sweetened with crystalline fructose and erythritol; 20-ounce single-serve or multi-pack.
PepsiCo	SoBe Lifewater	Regular and zero-calorie versions; 17 varieties; six different functional categories; vitamins, minerals, and herbs; Pure—mildly flavored, unsweetened water; sweetened with sugar and erythritol; "all natural"; 20-ounce single-serve and multi-packs as well as one-liter bottles.
PepsiCo	Propel Zero	Zero-calorie only; seven flavors; fitness positioning based on "Replenish + Energize + Protect"; B vitamins, vitamin C, vitamin E, antioxidants, and electrolytes; sweetened with sucralose; 16.9-ounce, 20-ounce, and 24-ounce PET bottles and multipacks; powdered packets.
Arizona Beverage	RESCUE Water	Full calorie only; five flavors, each with its own blend of vitamins and minerals; green tea extract (caffeine included); only brand with coconut water; Twinlab branded vitamins; high-tech plastic bottle.

- ***Niche brands:*** The market for enhanced waters includes at least four companies that market their wares on a small scale through independent retailers: Assure, Ex Aqua Vitamins, Ayala Herbal Water, and Skinny Water. Some brands feature exotic additives and/or artistic glass bottles.

Despite the strong competition, NutriWater believes it can create a relevant brand image and gain recognition among the targeted segments. The brand offers strong points of differentiation with higher and unique vitamin content, all-natural ingredients, and support for a relevant social cause. With other strategic assets, Chill Beverage is confident that it can establish a competitive advantage that will allow NutriWater to grow in the market. **»Table A2.2** shows a sample of competing products.

Channels and Logistics Review

The purchase of Vitaminwater by Coca-Cola left a huge hole in the independent distributor system. NutriWater will be distributed through an independent distributor to a network of retailers in the United States. This strategy will avoid some of the head-on competition for shelf space with the Coca-Cola and PepsiCo brands and will also directly target likely NutriWater customers. As with the rollout of the core Chill Soda brand, this strategy will focus on placing coolers in retail locations that will exclusively hold NutriWater. These retailers include:

- ***Grocery chains:*** Regional grocery chains such as HyVee in the Midwest, Wegman's in the east, and WinCo in the west.
- ***Health and natural food stores:*** Chains such as Whole Foods, as well as local health food co-ops.
- ***Fitness centers:*** National fitness center chains such as 24 Hour Fitness, Gold's Gym, and other regional chains.

As the brand gains acceptance, channels will expand into larger grocery chains, convenience stores, and unique locations relevant to the target customer segment.

Strengths, Weaknesses, Opportunities, and Threat Analysis

NutriWater has several powerful strengths on which to build, but its major weakness is lack of brand awareness and image. Major opportunities include a growing market and consumer trends targeted by NutriWater's product traits. Threats include barriers to entry posed by limited retail space, as well as image issues for the bottled water industry. **»Table A2.3** summarizes NutriWater's main strengths, weaknesses, opportunities, and threats.

» Table A2.3 NutriWater's Strengths, Weaknesses, Opportunities, and Threats

Strengths	Weaknesses
• Superior quality • Expertise in alternative beverage marketing • Social responsibility • Anti-establishment image	• Lack of brand awareness • Limited budget
Opportunities	**Threats**
• Growing market • Gap in the distribution network • Health trends • Anti-establishment image	• Limited shelf space • Image of enhanced waters • Environmental issues

Strengths

NutriWater can rely on the following important strengths:

1. ***Superior quality:*** NutriWater boasts the highest levels of added vitamins of any enhanced water, including full RDA levels of many vitamins. It is all natural with no artificial flavors, colors, or preservatives. It is sweetened with both pure cane sugar and the natural zero-calorie sweetener, Stevia.
2. ***Expertise in alternative beverage marketing:*** The Chill Soda brand went from nothing to a successful and rapidly growing soft drink brand with fiercely loyal customers in a matter of only one decade. This success was achieved by starting small and focusing on gaps in the marketplace.
3. ***Social responsibility:*** Every customer will have the added benefit of helping malnourished children throughout the world. Although the price of NutriWater is in line with other competitors, low promotional costs allow for the substantial charitable donation of 25 cents per bottle while maintaining profitability.
4. ***Anti-establishment image:*** The big brands have decent products and strong distribution relationships. But they also carry the image of the large, corporate establishments. Chill Beverage has achieved success with an underdog image while remaining privately held. Vitaminwater and SoBe were built on this same image, but both are now owned by major multinational corporations.

Weaknesses

1. ***Lack of brand awareness:*** As an entirely new brand, NutriWater will enter the market with limited or no brand awareness. The affiliation with Chill Soda will be kept at a minimum in order to prevent associations between NutriWater and soft drinks. This issue will be addressed through promotion and distribution strategies.
2. ***Limited budget:*** As a smaller company, Chill Beverage has much smaller funds available for promotional and research activities.

Opportunities

1. ***Growing market:*** Although growth in the overall market for bottled water has slowed to some extent, its current rate of growth in the 3 percent range is relatively strong among beverage categories. Of the top six beverage categories, soft drinks, beer, milk, and fruit drinks experienced declines. The growth for coffee was less than 1 percent. More important than the growth of bottled waters in general, the enhanced water category is experiencing growth in the high single and low double digits.

2. ***Gap in the distribution network:*** The market leaders distribute directly to retailers. This gives them an advantage in large national chains. However, no major enhanced water brands are currently being sold through independent distributors.
3. ***Health trends:*** Weight and nutrition continue to be issues for consumers in the United States. The country has the highest obesity rate for developed countries at 34 percent, with well over 60 percent of the population officially "overweight." Those numbers continue to rise. Additionally, Americans get 21 percent of their daily calories from beverages, a number that has tripled in the last three decades. Consumers still desire flavored beverages but look for lower calorie alternatives.
4. ***Anti-establishment image:*** Millennials (born between 1977 and 2000) maintain a higher aversion to mass marketing messages and global corporations than do Gen Xers and baby boomers.

Threats

1. ***Limited shelf space:*** Whereas competition is generally a threat for any type of product, competition in retail beverages is particularly high because of limited retail space. Carrying a new beverage product requires retailers to reduce shelf or cooler space already occupied by other brands.
2. ***Image of enhanced waters:*** The image of enhanced waters is currently in question as Coca-Cola recently fought a class-action lawsuit accusing it of violating Food and Drug Administration (FDA) regulations by promoting the health benefits of Vitaminwater. The lawsuit exposed the number one bottled water brand as basically sugar water with minimal nutritional value.
3. ***Environmental issues:*** Environmental groups continue to educate the public on the environmental costs of bottled water, including landfill waste, carbon emissions from production and transportation, and harmful effects of chemicals in plastics.

Objectives and Issues

Chill Beverage has set aggressive but achievable objectives for NutriWater for the first and second years of market entry.

First-Year Objectives

During the initial year on the market, Chill Beverage aims for NutriWater to achieve a 2 percent share of the enhanced water market, or approximately $30 million in sales, with break even achieved in the final period of the year. With an average retail price of $1.69, that equates with a sales goal of 17,751,480 bottles.

Second-Year Objectives

During the second year, Chill Beverage will unveil additional NutriWater flavors, including zero-calorie varieties. The second-year objective is to double sales from the first year, to $60 million.

Issues

In launching this new brand, the main issue is the ability to establish brand awareness and a meaningful brand image based on positioning that is relevant to target customer segments. Chill Beverage will invest in nontraditional means of promotion to accomplish these goals and to spark word-of-mouth sharing. Establishing distributor and retailer relationships will also be critical in order to make the product available and provide point-of-purchase communications. Brand awareness and knowledge will be measured in order to adjust marketing efforts as necessary.

Marketing Strategy

NutriWater's marketing strategy will involve developing a "more for the same" positioning based on extra benefits for the price. The brand will also establish channel differentiation, as it will be available in locations where major competing brands are not. The primary target segment is Millennials. This segment is comprised of tweens (ages 10 to 12), teens (13 to 18), and young adults (19 to 33). NutriWater will focus specifically on the young adult market. Subsets of this generational segment include athletes, the health conscious, and the socially responsible.

Positioning

NutriWater will be positioned on an "Expect more" value proposition. This will allow for differentiating the brand based on product features (expect more vitamin content and all natural ingredients), desirable benefits (expect greater nutritional benefits), and values (do more for a social cause). Marketing will focus on conveying that NutriWater is more than just a beverage: It gives customers much more for their money in a variety of ways.

Product Strategy

NutriWater will be sold with all the features described in the Product Review section. As awareness takes hold and retail availability increases, more varieties will be made available. A zero-calorie version will be added to the product line, providing a solid fit with the health benefits sought by consumers. Chill Beverage's considerable experience in brand-building will be applied as an integral part of the product strategy for NutriWater. All aspects of the marketing mix will be consistent with the brand.

Pricing

There is little price variation in the enhanced waters category, particularly among leading brands. For this reason, NutriWater will follow a competition-based pricing strategy. Given that NutriWater claims superior quality, it must be careful not to position itself as a lower-cost alternative. Manufacturers do not quote list prices on this type of beverage, and prices vary considerably based on type of retail outlet and whether or not the product is refrigerated. Regular prices for single 20-ounce bottles of competing products are as low as $1.00 in discount-retailer stores and as high as $1.89 in convenience stores. Because NutriWater will not be targeting discount retailers and convenience stores initially, this will allow Chill Beverage to set prices at the average to higher end of the range for similar products in the same outlets. For grocery chains, this should be approximately $1.49 per bottle, with that price rising to $1.89 at health food stores and fitness centers, where prices tend to be higher.

Distribution Strategy

Based on the information in the Channels and Logistics Review, NutriWater will employ a selective distribution strategy with well-known regional grocers, health and natural food stores, and fitness centers. This distribution strategy will be executed through a network of independent beverage distributors, as there are no other major brands of enhanced water following this strategy. Chill Beverage gained success for its core Chill Soda soft drink line using this method. It also placed coolers with the brand logo in truly unique venues such as skate, surf, and snowboarding shops; tattoo and piercing parlors; fashion stores; and music stores—places that would expose the brand to target customers. Then, the soft drink brand expanded by getting contracts with retailers such as Panera, Barnes & Noble, Target, and Starbucks. This same approach will be taken with NutriWater by starting small, then expanding into larger chains. NutriWater will not target all the same stores used originally by Chill Soda, as many of those outlets were unique to the positioning and target customer for the Chill Soda soft drink brand.

Marketing Communication Strategy

As with the core Chill Soda brand, the marketing communication strategy for NutriWater will not follow a strategy based on traditional mass-communication advertising. Initially, there will be no broadcast or print advertising. Promotional resources for NutriWater will focus on three areas:

- ***Online and mobile marketing:*** The typical target customer for NutriWater spends more time online than with traditional media channels. A core component for this strategy will be building Web and mobile brand sites and driving traffic to those sites by creating a presence on social networks, including Facebook, Google+, and Twitter. The Nutri-Water brand will also incorporate location-based services by Foursquare and Facebook to help drive traffic to retail locations. A mobile phone ad campaign will provide additional support to the online efforts.

- ***Trade promotions:*** Like the core Chill Soda brand, NutriWater's success will rely on relationships with retailers to create product availability. Primary incentives to retailers will include point-of-purchase displays, branded coolers, and volume incentives and contests. This push marketing strategy will combine with the other pull strategies.
- ***Event marketing:*** NutriWater will deploy teams in brand-labeled RVs to distribute product samples at events such as skiing and snowboarding competitions, golf tournaments, and concerts.

Marketing Research

To remain consistent with the online promotional approach, as well as using research methods that will effectively reach target customers, Chill Beverage will monitor online discussions via services such as Radian6. In this manner, the company will gauge customer perceptions of the brand, the products, and general satisfaction. For future development of the product and new distribution outlets, crowdsourcing methods will be utilized.

Action Programs

NutriWater will be introduced in February. The following are summaries of action programs that will be used during the first six months of the year to achieve the stated objectives.

January: Chill Beverage representatives will work with both independent distributors and retailers to educate them on the trade promotional campaign, incentives, and advantages for selling NutriWater. Representatives will also ensure that distributors and retailers are educated on product features and benefits as well as instructions for displaying point-of-purchase materials and coolers. The brand Web site and other sites such as Facebook will present teaser information about the product as well as availability dates and locations. Buzz will be enhanced by providing product samples to selected product reviewers, opinion leaders, influential bloggers, and celebrities.

February: On the date of availability, product coolers and point-of-purchase displays will be placed in retail locations. The full brand Web site and social network campaign will launch with full efforts on Facebook, Google+, and Twitter. This campaign will drive the "Expect more" slogan, as well as illustrate the ways that NutriWater delivers more than expected on product features, desirable benefits, and values by donating to Vitamin Angels and the social cause of battling vitamin deficiency in children.

March: To enhance the online and social marketing campaign, location-based services Foursquare and Facebook Places will be employed to drive traffic to retailers. Point-of-purchase displays and signage will be updated to support these efforts and to continue supporting retailers. The message of this campaign will focus on all aspects of "Expect more."

April: A mobile phone ad campaign will provide additional support, driving Web traffic to the brand Web site and social network sites, as well as driving traffic to retailers.

May: A trade sales contest will offer additional incentives and prizes to the distributors and retailers that sell the most NutriWater during a four-week period.

June: An event marketing campaign will mobilize a team of NutriWater representatives in NutriWater RVs to concerts and sports events. This will provide additional visibility for the brand as well as giving customers and potential customers the opportunity to sample products.

Budgets

Chill Beverage has set a first-year retail sales goal of $30 million with a projected average retail price of $1.69 per unit for a total of 17,751,480 units sold. With an average wholesale price of 85 cents per unit, this provides revenues of just over $15 million. Chill Beverage expects to break even during the final period of the first year. A break-even analysis assumes per-unit wholesale revenue of 85 cents per unit, a variable cost per unit of 14 cents, and estimated first-year fixed costs of $12,500,000. Based on these assumptions, the break-even calculation is:

$$\frac{\$12{,}500{,}000}{\$0.85/\text{unit} - \$0.14/\text{unit}} = 17{,}605{,}634$$

Controls

Chill Beverage is planning tight control measures to closely monitor product quality, brand awareness, brand image, and customer satisfaction. This will enable the company to react quickly in correcting any problems that may occur. Other early warning signals that will be monitored for signs of deviation from the plan include monthly sales (by segment and channel) and monthly expenses. Given the market's volatility, contingency plans are also in place to address fast-moving environmental changes such as shifting consumer preferences, new products, and new competition.

Sources: "Bottled Water Sales Continue to Sparkle," *Beverage Industry*, July 10, 2013, www.bevindustry.com/articles/86553-state-of-the-industry-bottled-water; "Jeffrey Klineman, "Restoring an Icon," *Beverage Spectrum Magazine,* December 2010, pp. 16–18; Ryan Underwood, "Jonesing for Soda," *Fast Company*, December 19, 2007, www.fastcompany.com; "New Playbook at Jones Soda," *Beverage Spectrum Magazine*, March 2008; Matt Casey, "Enhanced Options Divide a Category," *Beverage Spectrum Magazine*, December 2008, p. 74; and product and market information obtained from www.lifewater.com, www.vitaminwater.com, www.nestlewaters.com, www.drinkarizona.com, and www.jonessoda.com, August 2013.

Appendix 3 Marketing by the Numbers

Marketing managers are facing increased accountability for the financial implications of their actions. This appendix provides a basic introduction to measuring marketing financial performance. Such financial analysis guides marketers in making sound marketing decisions and in assessing the outcomes of those decisions.

The appendix is built around a hypothetical manufacturer of consumer electronics products—HD. The company is introducing a device that plays videos and television programming streamed over the Internet on multiple devices in a home, including high-definition televisions, tablets, and mobile phones. In this appendix, we will analyze the various decisions HD's marketing managers must make before and after the new product launch.

The appendix is organized into *three sections*. The *first section* introduces pricing, break-even, and margin analysis assessments that will guide the introduction of HD's new product. The *second section* discusses demand estimates, the marketing budget, and marketing performance measures. It begins with a discussion of estimating market potential and company sales. It then introduces the marketing budget, as illustrated through a *pro forma* profit-and-loss statement followed by the actual profit-and-loss statement. Next, we discuss marketing performance measures, with a focus on helping marketing managers to better defend their decisions from a financial perspective. In the *third section,* we analyze the financial implications of various marketing tactics.

Each of the three sections ends with a set of quantitative exercises that provide you with an opportunity to apply the concepts you learned to situations beyond HD.

Pricing, Break-Even, and Margin Analysis

Pricing Considerations

Determining price is one of the most important marketing mix decisions. The limiting factors are demand and costs. Demand factors, such as buyer-perceived value, set the price ceiling. The company's costs set the price floor. In between these two factors, marketers must consider competitors' prices and other factors such as reseller requirements, government regulations, and company objectives.

Most current competing Internet streaming products sell at retail prices between $100 and $500. We first consider HD's pricing decision from a cost perspective. Then, we consider consumer value, the competitive environment, and reseller requirements.

Determining Costs

Fixed costs
Costs that do not vary with production or sales level.

Variable costs
Costs that vary directly with the level of production.

Total costs
The sum of the fixed and variable costs for any given level of production.

Recall from Chapter 10 that there are different types of costs. **Fixed costs** do not vary with production or sales level and include costs such as rent, interest, depreciation, and clerical and management salaries. Regardless of the level of output, the company must pay these costs. Whereas total fixed costs remain constant as output increases, the fixed cost per unit (or average fixed cost) will decrease as output increases because the total fixed costs are spread across more units of output. **Variable costs** vary directly with the level of production and include costs related to the direct production of the product (such as costs of goods sold—COGS) and many of the marketing costs associated with selling it. Although these costs tend to be uniform for each unit produced, they are called variable because their total varies with the number of units produced. **Total costs** are the sum of the fixed and variable costs for any given level of production.

HD has invested $10 million in refurbishing an existing facility to manufacture the new video streaming product. Once production begins, the company estimates that it will incur fixed costs of $20 million per year. The variable cost to produce each device is estimated to be $125 and is expected to remain at that level for the output capacity of the facility.

Setting Price Based on Costs

Cost-plus pricing (or markup pricing)
A standard markup to the cost of the product.

HD starts with the cost-based approach to pricing discussed in Chapter 10. Recall that the simplest method, **cost-plus pricing** (or **markup pricing**), simply adds a standard markup to the cost of the product. To use this method, however, HD must specify expected unit sales so that total unit costs can be determined. Unit variable costs will remain constant regardless of the output, but *average unit fixed costs* will decrease as output increases.

To illustrate this method, suppose HD has fixed costs of $20 million, variable costs of $125 per unit, and expects unit sales of 1 million players. Thus, the cost per unit is given by:

$$\text{Unit cost} = \text{variable cost} + \frac{\text{fixed costs}}{\text{unit sales}} = \$125 + \frac{\$20{,}000{,}000}{1{,}000{,}000} = \$145$$

Relevant costs
Costs that will occur in the future and that will vary across the alternatives being considered.

Note that we do *not* include the initial investment of $10 million in the total fixed cost figure. It is not considered a fixed cost because it is not a *relevant* cost. **Relevant costs** are those that will occur in the future and that will vary across the alternatives being considered. HD's investment to refurbish the manufacturing facility was a one-time cost that will not reoccur in the future. Such past costs are *sunk costs* and should not be considered in future analyses.

Break-even price
The price at which total revenue equals total cost and profit is zero.

Also notice that if HD sells its product for $145, the price is equal to the total cost per unit. This is the **break-even price**—the price at which unit revenue (price) equals unit cost and profit is zero.

Suppose HD does not want to merely break even but rather wants to earn a 25% markup on sales. HD's markup price is:[1]

$$\text{Markup price} = \frac{\text{unit cost}}{(1 - \text{desired return on sales})} = \frac{\$145}{1 - 0.25} = \$193.33$$

This is the price at which HD would sell the product to resellers such as wholesalers or retailers to earn a 25% profit on sales.

Return on investment (ROI) pricing (or target-return pricing)
A cost-based pricing method that determines price based on a specified rate of return on investment.

Another approach HD could use is called **return on investment (ROI) pricing** (or **target-return pricing**). In this case, the company *would* consider the initial $10 million investment, but only to determine the dollar profit goal. Suppose the company wants a 30% return on its investment. The price necessary to satisfy this requirement can be determined by:

$$\text{ROI price} = \text{unit cost} + \frac{\text{ROI} \times \text{investment}}{\text{unit sales}} = \$145 + \frac{0.3 \times \$10{,}000{,}000}{1{,}000{,}000} = \$148$$

That is, if HD sells its product for $148, it will realize a 30% return on its initial investment of $10 million.

In these pricing calculations, unit cost is a function of the expected sales, which were estimated to be 1 million units. But what if actual sales were lower? Then the unit cost would be higher because the fixed costs would be spread over fewer units, and the realized percentage markup on sales or ROI would be lower. Alternatively, if sales are higher than the estimated 1 million units, unit cost would be lower than $145, so a lower price would produce the desired markup on sales or ROI. It's important to note that these cost-based pricing methods are *internally* focused and do not consider demand, competitors' prices, or reseller requirements. Because HD will be selling this product to consumers through wholesalers and retailers offering competing brands, the company must consider markup pricing from this perspective.

Setting Price Based on External Factors

Whereas costs determine the price floor, HD also must consider external factors when setting price. HD does not have the final say concerning the final price of its product to consumers—retailers do. So it must start with its suggested retail price and work back. In doing so, HD must consider the markups required by resellers that sell the product to consumers.

Markup
The difference between a company's selling price for a product and its cost to manufacture or purchase it.

In general, a dollar **markup** is the difference between a company's selling price for a product and its cost to manufacture or purchase it. For a retailer, then, the markup is the difference between the price it charges consumers and the cost the retailer must pay for the product. Thus, for any level of reseller:

$$\text{Dollar markup} = \text{selling price} - \text{cost}$$

Markups are usually expressed as a percentage, and there are two different ways to compute markups—on *cost* or on *selling price*:

$$\text{Markup percentage on cost} = \frac{\text{dollar markup}}{\text{cost}}$$

$$\text{Markup percentage on selling price} = \frac{\text{dollar markup}}{\text{selling price}}$$

To apply reseller margin analysis, HD must first set the suggested retail price and then work back to the price at which it must sell the product to a wholesaler. Suppose retailers expect a 30% margin and wholesalers want a 20% margin based on their respective selling prices. And suppose that HD sets a manufacturer's suggested retail price (MSRP) of $299.99 for its product.

HD selected the $299.99 MSRP because it is lower than most competitors' prices but is not so low that consumers might perceive it to be of poor quality. And the company's research shows that it is below the threshold at which more consumers are willing to purchase the product. By using buyers' perceptions of value and not the seller's cost to determine the MSRP, HD is using **value-based pricing**. For simplicity, we will use an MSRP of $300 in further analyses.

Value-based pricing
Offering just the right combination of quality and good service at a fair price.

To determine the price HD will charge wholesalers, we must first subtract the retailer's margin from the retail price to determine the retailer's cost ($300 – ($300 × 0.30) = $210). The retailer's cost is the wholesaler's price, so HD next subtracts the wholesaler's margin ($210 – ($210 × 0.20) = $168). Thus, the **markup chain**; representing the sequence of markups used by firms at each level in a channel for HD's new product is:

Markup chain
The sequence of markups used by firms at each level in a channel.

Suggested retail price:	$300
minus retail margin (30%):	– $ 90
Retailer's cost/wholesaler's price:	$210
minus wholesaler's margin (20%):	– $ 42
Wholesaler's cost/HD's price:	$168

By deducting the markups for each level in the markup chain, HD arrives at a price for the product to wholesalers of $168.

Break-Even and Margin Analysis

The previous analyses derived a value-based price of $168 for HD's product. Although this price is higher than the break-even price of $145 and covers costs, that price assumed a demand of 1 million units. But how many units and what level of dollar sales must HD achieve to break even at the $168 price? And what level of sales must be achieved to realize various profit goals? These questions can be answered through break-even and margin analysis.

Determining Break-Even Unit Volume and Dollar Sales

Break-even analysis
Analysis to determine the unit volume and dollar sales needed to be profitable given a particular price and cost structure.

Based on an understanding of costs, consumer value, the competitive environment, and reseller requirements, HD has decided to set its price to wholesalers at $168. At that price, what sales level will be needed for HD to break even or make a profit on its product? **Break-even analysis** determines the unit volume and dollar sales needed to be profitable given a particular price and cost structure. At the break-even point, total revenue equals total costs and profit is zero. Above this point, the company will make a profit; below it, the company will lose money. HD can calculate break-even volume using the following formula:

$$\text{Break-even volume} = \frac{\text{fixed costs}}{\text{price} - \text{unit variable cost}}$$

Unit contribution
The amount that each unit contributes to covering fixed costs—the difference between price and variable costs.

The denominator (price – unit variable cost) is called **unit contribution** (sometimes called contribution margin). It represents the amount that each unit contributes to covering fixed costs. Break-even volume represents the level of output at which all (variable and fixed) costs are covered. In HD's case, break-even unit volume is:

$$\text{Break-even volume} = \frac{\text{fixed cost}}{\text{price} - \text{variable cost}} = \frac{\$20{,}000{,}000}{\$168 - \$125} = 465{,}116.2 \text{ units}$$

Thus, at the given cost and pricing structure, HD will break even at 465,117 units.

To determine the break-even dollar sales, simply multiply unit break-even volume by the selling price:

$$\text{BE sales} = \text{BE}_{\text{vol}} \times \text{price} = 465{,}117 \times \$168 = \$78{,}139{,}656$$

Contribution margin
The unit contribution divided by the selling price.

Another way to calculate dollar break-even sales is to use the percentage contribution margin (hereafter referred to as **contribution margin**), which is the unit contribution divided by the selling price:

$$\text{Contribution margin} = \frac{\text{price} - \text{variable cost}}{\text{price}} = \frac{\$168 - \$125}{\$168} = 0.256 \text{ or } 25.6\%$$

Then,

$$\text{Break-even sales} = \frac{\text{fixed costs}}{\text{contribution margin}} = \frac{\$20{,}000{,}000}{0.256} = \$78{,}125{,}00$$

Note that the difference between the two break-even sales calculations is due to rounding.

Such break-even analysis helps HD by showing the unit volume needed to cover costs. If production capacity cannot attain this level of output, then the company should not launch this product. However, the unit break-even volume is well within HD's capacity. Of course, the bigger question concerns whether HD can sell this volume at the $168 price. We'll address that issue a little later.

Understanding contribution margin is useful in other types of analyses as well, particularly if unit prices and unit variable costs are unknown or if a company (say, a retailer) sells many products at different prices and knows the percentage of total sales variable costs represent. Whereas unit contribution is the difference between unit price and unit variable costs, total contribution is the difference between total sales and total variable costs. The overall contribution margin can be calculated by:

$$\text{Contribution margin} = \frac{\text{total sales} - \text{total variable costs}}{\text{total sales}}$$

Regardless of the actual level of sales, if the company knows what percentage of sales is represented by variable costs, it can calculate contribution margin. For example, HD's unit variable cost is \$125, or 74% of the selling price (\$125 ÷ \$168 = 0.74). That means for every \$1 of sales revenue for HD, \$0.74 represents variable costs, and the difference (\$0.26) represents contribution to fixed costs. But even if the company doesn't know its unit price and unit variable cost, it can calculate the contribution margin from total sales and total variable costs or from knowledge of the total cost structure. It can set total sales equal to 100% regardless of the actual absolute amount and determine the contribution margin:

$$\text{Contribution margin} = \frac{100\% - 74\%}{100\%} = \frac{1 - 0.74}{1} = 1 - 0.74 = 0.26 \text{ or } 26\%$$

Note that this matches the percentage calculated from the unit price and unit variable cost information. This alternative calculation will be very useful later when analyzing various marketing decisions.

Determining "Break Even" for Profit Goals

Although it is useful to know the break-even point, most companies are more interested in making a profit. Assume HD would like to realize a \$5 million profit in the first year. How many must it sell at the \$168 price to cover fixed costs and produce this profit? To determine this, HD can simply add the profit figure to fixed costs and again divide by the unit contribution to determine unit sales:

$$\text{Unit volume} = \frac{\text{fixed cost} + \text{profit goal}}{\text{price} - \text{variable cost}} = \frac{\$20{,}000{,}000 + \$5{,}000{,}000}{\$168 - \$125} = 581{,}395.3 \text{ units}$$

Thus, to earn a \$5 million profit, HD must sell 581,396 units. Multiply by price to determine dollar sales needed to achieve a \$5 million profit:

$$\text{Dollar sales} = 581{,}396 \text{ units} \times \$168 = \$97{,}674{,}528$$

Or use the contribution margin:

$$\text{Sales} = \frac{\text{fixed cost} + \text{profit goal}}{\text{contribution margin}} = \frac{\$20{,}000{,}000 + \$5{,}000{,}000}{0.256} = \$97{,}656{,}250$$

Again, note that the difference between the two break-even sales calculations is due to rounding.

As we saw previously, a profit goal can also be stated as a return on investment goal. For example, recall that HD wants a 30% return on its \$10 million investment. Thus, its absolute profit goal is \$3 million (\$10,000,000 × 0.30). This profit goal is treated the same way as in the previous example:[2]

$$\text{Unit volume} = \frac{\text{fixed cost} + \text{profit goal}}{\text{price} - \text{variable cost}} = \frac{\$20{,}000{,}000 + \$3{,}000{,}000}{\$168 - \$125} = 534{,}884 \text{ units}$$

$$\text{Dollar sales} = 534{,}884 \text{ units} \times \$168 = \$89{,}860{,}512$$

Or

$$\text{Dollar sales} = \frac{\text{fixed cost} + \text{profit goal}}{\text{contribution margin}} = \frac{\$20{,}000{,}000 + \$3{,}000{,}000}{0.256} = \$89{,}843{,}750$$

Finally, HD can express its profit goal as a percentage of sales, which we also saw in previous pricing analyses. Assume HD desires a 25% return on sales. To determine the unit and sales volume necessary to achieve this goal, the calculation is a little different from the previous two examples. In this case, we incorporate the profit goal into the unit contribution as an additional variable cost. Look at it this way: If 25% of each sale must go toward profits, that leaves only 75% of the selling price to cover fixed costs. Thus, the equation becomes:

$$\text{Unit volume} = \frac{\text{fixed cost}}{\text{price} - \text{variable cost} - (0.25 \times \text{price})} \text{ or } \frac{\text{fixed cost}}{(0.75 \times \text{price}) - \text{variable cost}}$$

So,

$$\text{Unit volume} = \frac{\$20{,}000{,}000}{(0.75 \times \$168) - \$125} = 20{,}000{,}000 \text{ units}$$

$$\text{Dollar sales necessary} = 20{,}000{,}000 \times \text{units} \times \$168 = \$3{,}360{,}000{,}000$$

Thus, HD would need more than $3 billion in sales to realize a 25% return on sales given its current price and cost structure! Could it possibly achieve this level of sales? The major point is this: Although break-even analysis can be useful in determining the level of sales needed to cover costs or to achieve a stated profit goal, it does not tell the company whether it is *possible* to achieve that level of sales at the specified price. To address this issue, HD needs to estimate demand for this product.

Before moving on, however, let's stop here and practice applying the concepts covered so far. Now that you have seen pricing and break-even concepts in action as they relate to HD's new product, here are several exercises for you to apply what you have learned in other contexts.

Marketing by the Numbers Exercise Set One

Now that you've studied pricing, break-even, and margin analysis as they relate to HD's new-product launch, use the following exercises to apply these concepts in other contexts.

1.1 Elkins, a manufacturer of ice makers, realizes a cost of $250 for every unit it produces. Its total fixed costs equal $5 million. If the company manufactures 500,000 units, compute the following:
a. unit cost
b. markup price if the company desires a 10% return on sales
c. ROI price if the company desires a 25% return on an investment of $1 million

1.2 A gift shop owner purchases items to sell in her store. She purchases a chair for $125 and sells it for $275. Determine the following:
a. dollar markup
b. markup percentage on cost
c. markup percentage on selling price

1.3 A consumer purchases a coffee maker from a retailer for $90. The retailer's markup is 30%, and the wholesaler's markup is 10%, both based on selling price. For what price does the manufacturer sell the product to the wholesaler?

1.4 A lawn mower manufacturer has a unit cost of $140 and wishes to achieve a margin of 30% based on selling price. If the manufacturer sells directly to a retailer who then adds a set margin of 40% based on selling price, determine the retail price charged to consumers.

1.5 Advanced Electronics manufactures DVDs and sells them directly to retailers who typically sell them for $20. Retailers take a 40% margin based on the retail selling price. Advanced's cost information is as follows:

DVD package and disc	$2.50/DVD
Royalties	$2.25/DVD
Advertising and promotion	$500,000
Overhead	$200,000

Calculate the following:

a. contribution per unit and contribution margin
b. break-even volume in DVD units and dollars
c. volume in DVD units and dollar sales necessary if Advanced's profit goal is 20% profit on sales
d. net profit if 5 million DVDs are sold

Demand Estimates, the Marketing Budget, and Marketing Performance Measures

Market Potential and Sales Estimates

HD has now calculated the sales needed to break even and to attain various profit goals on its new product. However, the company needs more information regarding demand in order to assess the feasibility of attaining the needed sales levels. This information is also needed for production and other decisions. For example, production schedules need to be developed and marketing tactics need to be planned.

Total market demand
The total volume that would be bought by a defined consumer group in a defined geographic area in a defined time period in a defined marketing environment under a defined level and mix of industry marketing effort.

Market potential
The upper limit of market demand.

The **total market demand** for a product or service is the total volume that would be bought by a defined consumer group in a defined geographic area in a defined time period in a defined marketing environment under a defined level and mix of industry marketing effort. Total market demand is not a fixed number but a function of the stated conditions. For example, next year's total market demand for this type of product will depend on how much other producers spend on marketing their brands. It also depends on many environmental factors, such as government regulations, economic conditions, and the level of consumer confidence in a given market. The upper limit of market demand is called **market potential**.

One general but practical method that HD might use for estimating total market demand uses three variables: (1) the number of prospective buyers, (2) the quantity purchased by an average buyer per year, and (3) the price of an average unit. Using these numbers, HD can estimate total market demand as follows:

$$Q = n \times q \times p$$

where

Q = total market demand
n = number of buyers in the market
q = quantity purchased by an average buyer per year
p = price of an average unit

Chain ratio method
Estimating market demand by multiplying a base number by a chain of adjusting percentages.

A variation of this approach is the **chain ratio method**. This method involves multiplying a base number by a chain of adjusting percentages. For example, HD's product is designed to stream high-definition video on high-definition televisions as well as play other video content streamed from the Internet to multiple devices in a home. Thus, consumers who do not own a high-definition television will not likely purchase this player. Additionally, only households with broadband Internet access will be able to use the product. Finally, not all HDTV-owning Internet households will be willing and able to purchase this product. HD can estimate U.S. demand using a chain of calculations like the following:

Total number of U.S. households
× The percentage of HDTV-owning U.S. households with broadband Internet access
× The percentage of these households willing and able to buy this device

The U.S. Census Bureau estimates that there are approximately 113 million households in the United States.[3] HD's research indicates that 60 percent of U.S. households own at least one HDTV and have broadband Internet access. Finally, the company's research also revealed that 30 percent of households possess the discretionary income needed and are willing to buy a product such as this. Then, the total number of households willing and able to purchase this product is:

$$113 \text{ million households} \times 0.60 \times 0.30 = 20.34 \text{ million households}$$

Households only need to purchase one device because it can stream content to other devices throughout the household. Assuming the average retail price across all brands is $350 for this product, the estimate of total market demand is as follows:

$$20.34 \text{ million households} \times 1 \text{ device per household} \times \$350 = \$7,119,000,000$$

This simple chain of calculations gives HD only a rough estimate of potential demand. However, more detailed chains involving additional segments and other qualifying factors would yield more accurate and refined estimates. Still, these are only *estimates* of market potential. They rely heavily on assumptions regarding adjusting percentages, average quantity, and average price. Thus, HD must make certain that its assumptions are reasonable and defendable. As can be seen, the overall market potential in dollar sales can vary widely given the average price used. For this reason, HD will use unit sales potential to determine its sales estimate for next year. Market potential in terms of units is 20.34 million (20.34 million households × 1 device per household).

Assuming that HD forecasts it will have a 3.66% market share in the first year after launching this product, then it can forecast unit sales at 20.34 million units × 0.0366 = 744,444 units. At a selling price of $168 per unit, this translates into sales of $125,066,592 (744,444 units × $168 per unit). For simplicity, further analyses will use forecasted sales of $125 million.

This unit volume estimate is well within HD's production capacity and exceeds not only the break-even estimate (465,117 units) calculated earlier, but also the volume necessary to realize a $5 million profit (581,396 units) or a 30% return on investment (534,884 units). However, this forecast falls well short of the volume necessary to realize a 25% return on sales (20 million units!) and may require that HD revise expectations.

To assess expected profits, we must now look at the budgeted expenses for launching this product. To do this, we will construct a pro forma profit-and-loss statement.

The Profit-and-Loss Statement and Marketing Budget

Pro forma (or **projected**) **profit-and-loss statement** (or **income statement** or **operating statement**)
A statement that shows projected revenues less budgeted expenses and estimates the projected net profit for an organization, product, or brand during a specific planning period, typically a year.

All marketing managers must account for the profit impact of their marketing strategies. A major tool for projecting such profit impact is a **pro forma** (or **projected**) **profit-and-loss statement** (also called an **income statement** or **operating statement**). A pro forma statement shows projected revenues less budgeted expenses and estimates the projected net profit for an organization, product, or brand during a specific planning period, typically a year. It includes direct product production costs, marketing expenses budgeted to attain a given sales forecast, and overhead expenses assigned to the organization or product. A profit-and-loss statement typically consists of several major components (see »**Table A3.1**):

- ***Net sales***—gross sales revenue minus returns and allowances (for example, trade, cash, quantity, and promotion allowances). HD's net sales for 2014 are estimated to be $125 million, as determined in the previous analysis.
- ***Cost of goods sold***—(sometimes called *cost of sales*)—the actual cost of the merchandise sold by a manufacturer or reseller. It includes the cost of inventory, purchases, and other costs associated with making the goods. HD's cost of goods sold is estimated to be 50% of net sales, or $62.5 million.
- ***Gross margin (or gross profit)***—the difference between net sales and cost of goods sold. HD's gross margin is estimated to be $62.5 million.
- ***Operating expenses***—the expenses incurred while doing business. These include all other expenses beyond the cost of goods sold that are necessary to conduct business.

» Table A3.1 Pro Forma Profit-and-Loss Statement for the 12-Month Period Ended December 31, 2014

			% of Sales
Net Sales		$125,000,000	100%
Cost of Goods Sold		62,500,000	50%
Gross Margin		$ 62,500,000	50%
Marketing Expenses			
Sales expenses	$17,500,000		
Promotion expenses	15,000,000		
Freight	12,500,000	45,000,000	36%
General and Administrative Expenses			
Managerial salaries and expenses	$2,000,000		
Indirect overhead	3,000,000	5,000,000	4%
Net Profit before Income Tax		$12,500,000	10%

Operating expenses can be presented in total or broken down in detail. Here, HD's estimated operating expenses include *marketing expenses* and *general and administrative expenses.*

Marketing expenses include sales expenses, promotion expenses, and distribution expenses. The new product will be sold through HD's sales force, so the company budgets $5 million for sales salaries. However, because sales representatives earn a 10% commission on sales, HD must also add a variable component to sales expenses of $12.5 million (10% of $125 million net sales), for a total budgeted sales expense of $17.5 million. HD sets its advertising and promotion to launch this product at $10 million. However, the company also budgets 4% of sales, or $5 million, for cooperative advertising allowances to retailers who promote HD's new product in their advertising. Thus, the total budgeted advertising and promotion expenses are $15 million ($10 million for advertising plus $5 million in co-op allowances). Finally, HD budgets 10% of net sales, or $12.5 million, for freight and delivery charges. In all, total marketing expenses are estimated to be $17.5 million + $15 million + $12.5 million = $45 million.

General and administrative expenses are estimated at $5 million, broken down into $2 million for managerial salaries and expenses for the marketing function and $3 million of indirect overhead allocated to this product by the corporate accountants (such as depreciation, interest, maintenance, and insurance). Total expenses for the year, then, are estimated to be $50 million ($45 million marketing expenses + $5 million in general and administrative expenses).

- ***Net profit before taxes***—profit earned after all costs are deducted. HD's estimated net profit before taxes is $12.5 million.

In all, as Table A3.1 shows, HD expects to earn a profit on its new product of $12.5 million in 2014. Also note that the percentage of sales that each component of the profit-and-loss statement represents is given in the right-hand column. These percentages are determined by dividing the cost figure by net sales (that is, marketing expenses represent 36% of net sales determined by $45 million ÷ $125 million). As can be seen, HD projects a net profit return on sales of 10% in the first year after launching this product.

Marketing Performance Measures

Now let's fast-forward a year. HD's product has been on the market for one year and management wants to assess its sales and profit performance. One way to assess this performance is to compute performance ratios derived from HD's **profit-and-loss statement** (or **income statement** or **operating statement**).

Profit-and-loss statement (or income statement or operating statement)
A statement that shows actual revenues less expenses and net profit for an organization, product, or brand during a specific planning period, typically a year.

Whereas the pro forma profit-and-loss statement shows *projected* financial performance, the statement given in **»Table A3.2** shows HD's *actual* financial performance based on actual sales, cost of goods sold, and expenses during the past year. By comparing the profit-and-loss statement from one period to the next, HD can gauge performance against goals, spot favorable or unfavorable trends, and take appropriate corrective action.

The profit-and-loss statement shows that HD lost $1 million rather than making the $12.5 million profit projected in the pro forma statement. Why? One obvious reason is that net sales fell $25 million short of estimated sales. Lower sales translated into lower variable costs associated with marketing the product. However, both fixed costs and the cost of goods sold as a percentage of sales exceeded expectations. Hence, the product's contribution margin was 21% rather than the estimated 26%. That is, variable costs represented 79% of sales (55% for cost of goods sold, 10% for sales commissions, 10% for freight, and 4% for co-op allowances). Recall that contribution margin can be calculated by subtracting that fraction from one (1 – 0.79 = 0.21). Total fixed costs were $22 million, $2 million more than estimated. Thus, the sales that HD needed to break even given this cost structure can be calculated as:

$$\text{Break-even sales} = \frac{\text{fixed costs}}{\text{contribution margin}} = \frac{\$22{,}000{,}000}{0.21} = \$104{,}761{,}905$$

If HD had achieved another $5 million in sales, it would have earned a profit.

Although HD's sales fell short of the forecasted sales, so did overall industry sales for this product. Overall industry sales were only $2.5 billion. That means that HD's **market share** was 4% ($100 million ÷ $2.5 billion = 0.04 = 4%), which was higher than forecasted. Thus, HD attained a higher-than-expected market share but the overall market sales were not as high as estimated.

Market share
Company sales divided by market sales.

» Table A3.2 Profit-and-Loss Statement for the 12-Month Period Ended December 31, 2014

			% of Sales
Net Sales		$100,000,000	100%
Cost of Goods Sold		55,000,000	55%
Gross Margin		$ 45,000,000	45%
Marketing Expenses			
Sales expenses	$15,000,000		
Promotion expenses	14,000,000		
Freight	10,000,000	39,000,000	39%
General and Administrative Expenses			
Managerial salaries and expenses	$2,000,000		
Indirect overhead	5,000,000	7,000,000	7%
Net Profit before Income Tax		($1,000,000)	(–1%)

Analytic Ratios

Operating ratios
The ratios of selected operating statement items to net sales.

The profit-and-loss statement provides the figures needed to compute some crucial **operating ratios**—the ratios of selected operating statement items to net sales. These ratios let marketers compare the firm's performance in one year to that in previous years (or with industry standards and competitors' performance in that year). The most commonly used operating ratios are the gross margin percentage, the net profit percentage, and the operating expense percentage. The inventory turnover rate and return on investment (ROI) are often used to measure managerial effectiveness and efficiency.

Gross margin percentage
The percentage of net sales remaining after cost of goods sold—calculated by dividing gross margin by net sales.

The **gross margin percentage** indicates the percentage of net sales remaining after cost of goods sold that can contribute to operating expenses and net profit before taxes. The higher this ratio, the more a firm has left to cover expenses and generate profit. HD's gross margin ratio was 45%:

$$\text{Gross margin percentage} = \frac{\text{gross margin}}{\text{net sales}} = \frac{\$45{,}000{,}000}{\$100{,}000{,}000} = 0.45 = 45\%$$

Note that this percentage is lower than estimated, and this ratio is seen easily in the percentage of sales column in Table A3.2. Stating items in the profit-and-loss statement as a percent of sales allows managers to quickly spot abnormal changes in costs over time. If there was previous history for this product and this ratio was declining, management should examine it more closely to determine why it has decreased (that is, because of a decrease in sales volume or price, an increase in costs, or a combination of these). In HD's case, net sales were $25 million lower than estimated, and cost of goods sold was higher than estimated (55% rather than the estimated 50%).

Net profit percentage
The percentage of each sales dollar going to profit—calculated by dividing net profits by net sales.

The **net profit percentage** shows the percentage of each sales dollar going to profit. It is calculated by dividing net profits by net sales:

$$\text{Net profit percentage} = \frac{\text{net profit}}{\text{net sales}} = \frac{-\$1{,}000{,}000}{\$100{,}000{,}000} = -0.01 = -1.0\%$$

This ratio is easily seen in the percent of sales column. HD's new product generated negative profits in the first year, not a good situation given that before the product launch net profits before taxes were estimated at more than $12 million. Later in this appendix, we will discuss further analyses the marketing manager should conduct to defend the product.

Operating expense percentage
The portion of net sales going to operating expenses—calculated by dividing total expenses by net sales.

The **operating expense percentage** indicates the portion of net sales going to operating expenses. Operating expenses include marketing and other expenses not directly related to marketing the product, such as indirect overhead assigned to this product. It is calculated by:

$$\text{Operating expense percentage} = \frac{\text{total expenses}}{\text{net sales}} = \frac{\$46{,}000{,}000}{\$100{,}000{,}000} = 0.46 = 46\%$$

This ratio can also be quickly determined from the percent of sales column in the profit-and-loss statement by adding the percentages for marketing expenses and general and administrative expenses (39% + 7%). Thus, 46 cents of every sales dollar went for operations. Although HD wants this ratio to be as low as possible, and 46% is not an alarming amount, it is of concern if it is increasing over time or if a loss is realized.

Inventory turnover rate (or stockturn rate)
The number of times an inventory turns over or is sold during a specified time period (often one year)—calculated based on costs, selling price, or units.

Another useful ratio is the **inventory turnover rate** (also called **stockturn rate** for resellers). The inventory turnover rate is the number of times an inventory turns over or is sold during a specified time period (often one year). This rate tells how quickly a business is moving inventory through the organization. Higher rates indicate that lower investments in inventory are made, thus freeing up funds for other investments. It may be computed on a cost, selling price, or unit basis. The formula based on cost is:

$$\text{Inventory turnover rate} = \frac{\text{cost of goods sold}}{\text{average inventory at cost}}$$

Assuming HD's beginning and ending inventories were $30 million and $20 million, respectively, the inventory turnover rate is:

$$\text{Inventory turnover rate} = \frac{\$55{,}000{,}000}{(\$30{,}000{,}000 + \$20{,}000{,}000)/2} = \frac{\$55{,}000{,}000}{\$25{,}000{,}000} = 2.2$$

That is, HD's inventory turned over 2.2 times in 2014. Normally, the higher the turnover rate, the higher the management efficiency and company profitability. However, this rate should be compared to industry averages, competitors' rates, and past performance to determine if HD is doing well. A competitor with similar sales but a higher inventory turnover rate will have fewer resources tied up in inventory, allowing it to invest in other areas of the business.

Return on investment (ROI)
A measure of managerial effectiveness and efficiency—net profit before taxes divided by total investment.

Companies frequently use **return on investment (ROI)** to measure managerial effectiveness and efficiency. For HD, ROI is the ratio of net profits to total investment required to manufacture the new product. This investment includes capital investments in land, buildings, and equipment (here, the initial $10 million to refurbish the manufacturing facility) plus inventory costs (HD's average inventory totaled $25 million), for a total of $35 million. Thus, HD's ROI for this product is:

$$\text{Return on investment} = \frac{\text{net profit before taxes}}{\text{investment}} = \frac{-\$1{,}000{,}000}{\$35{,}000{,}000} = -0.286 = -2.86\%$$

ROI is often used to compare alternatives, and a positive ROI is desired. The alternative with the highest ROI is preferred to other alternatives. HD needs to be concerned with the ROI realized. One obvious way HD can increase ROI is to increase net profit by reducing expenses. Another way is to reduce its investment, perhaps by investing less in inventory and turning it over more frequently.

Marketing Profitability Metrics

Given the previous financial results, you may be thinking that HD should drop this new product. But what arguments can marketers make for keeping or dropping this product? The obvious arguments for dropping the product are that first-year sales were well below expected levels and the product lost money, resulting in a negative return on investment.

So what would happen if HD did drop this product? Surprisingly, if the company drops the product, the profits for the total organization will decrease by $4 million! How can that be? Marketing managers need to look closely at the numbers in the profit-and-loss statement to determine the *net marketing contribution* for this product. In HD's case, the net marketing contribution for the product is $4 million, and if the company drops this product, that contribution will disappear as well. Let's look more closely at this concept to illustrate how marketing managers can better assess and defend their marketing strategies and programs.

Net Marketing Contribution

Net marketing contribution (NMC)
A measure of marketing profitability that includes only components of profitability controlled by marketing.

Net marketing contribution (NMC), along with other marketing metrics derived from it, measures *marketing* profitability. It includes only components of profitability that are controlled by marketing. Whereas the previous calculation of net profit before taxes from the profit-and-loss statement includes operating expenses not under marketing's control, NMC does not. Referring back to HD's profit-and-loss statement given in Table A3.2, we can calculate net marketing contribution for the product as:

$$\begin{aligned}\text{NMC} &= \text{net sales} - \text{cost of goods sold} - \text{marketing expenses} \\ &= \$100 \text{ million} - \$55 \text{ million} - \$41 \text{ million} = \$4 \text{ million}\end{aligned}$$

The marketing expenses include sales expenses ($15 million), promotion expenses ($14 million), freight expenses ($10 million), and the managerial salaries and expenses of the marketing function ($2 million), which total $41 million.

Thus, the product actually contributed $4 million to HD's profits. It was the $5 million of indirect overhead allocated to this product that caused the negative profit. Further, the amount allocated was $2 million more than estimated in the pro forma profit-and-loss statement. Indeed, if only the estimated amount had been allocated, the product would have earned a *profit* of $1 million rather than losing $1 million. If HD drops the product, the $5 million in fixed overhead expenses will not disappear—it will simply have to be allocated elsewhere. However, the $4 million in net marketing contribution *will* disappear.

Marketing Return on Sales and Investment

To get an even deeper understanding of the profit impact of marketing strategy, we'll now examine two measures of marketing efficiency—*marketing return on sales* (marketing ROS) and *marketing return on investment* (marketing ROI).[4]

Marketing return on sales (or marketing ROS)
The percent of net sales attributable to the net marketing contribution—calculated by dividing net marketing contribution by net sales.

Marketing return on sales (or **marketing ROS**) shows the percent of net sales attributable to the net marketing contribution. For our product, ROS is:

$$\text{Marketing ROS} = \frac{\text{net marketing contribution}}{\text{net sales}} = \frac{\$4{,}000{,}000}{\$100{,}000{,}000} = 0.04 = 4\%$$

Thus, out of every $100 of sales, the product returns $4 to HD's bottom line. A high marketing ROS is desirable. But to assess whether this is a good level of performance, HD must compare this figure to previous marketing ROS levels for the product, the ROSs of other products in the company's portfolio, and the ROSs of competing products.

Marketing return on investment (or marketing ROI)
A measure of the marketing productivity of a marketing investment—calculated by dividing net marketing contribution by marketing expenses.

Marketing return on investment (or **marketing ROI**) measures the marketing productivity of a marketing investment. In HD's case, the marketing investment is represented by $41 million of the total expenses. Thus, marketing ROI is:

$$\text{Marketing ROI} = \frac{\text{net marketing contribution}}{\text{marketing expenses}} = \frac{\$4{,}000{,}000}{\$41{,}000{,}000} = 0.0976 = 9.76\%$$

As with marketing ROS, a high value is desirable, but this figure should be compared with previous levels for the given product and with the marketing ROIs of competitors' products. Note from this equation that marketing ROI could be greater than 100%. This can be achieved by attaining a higher net marketing contribution and/or a lower total marketing expense.

In this section, we estimated market potential and sales, developed profit-and-loss statements, and examined financial measures of performance. In the next section, we discuss methods for analyzing the impact of various marketing tactics. However, before moving on to those analyses, here's another set of quantitative exercises to help you apply what you've learned to other situations.

Marketing by the Numbers Exercise Set Two

2.1 Determine the market potential for a product that has 20 million prospective buyers who purchase an average of 2 per year and price averages $50. How many units must a company sell if it desires a 10% share of this market?

2.2 Develop a profit-and-loss statement for the Westgate division of North Industries. This division manufactures light fixtures sold to consumers through home improvement and hardware stores. Cost of goods sold represents 40% of net sales. Marketing expenses include selling expenses, promotion expenses, and freight. Selling expenses include sales salaries totaling $3 million per year and sales commissions (5% of sales). The company spent $3 million on advertising last year, and freight costs were 10% of sales. Other costs include $2 million for managerial salaries and expenses for the marketing function and another $3 million for indirect overhead allocated to the division.

a. Develop the profit-and-loss statement if net sales were $20 million last year.
b. Develop the profit-and-loss statement if net sales were $40 million last year.
c. Calculate Westgate's break-even sales.

2.3 Using the profit-and-loss statement you developed in question 2.2b, and assuming that Westgate's beginning inventory was $11 million, ending inventory was $7 million, and total investment was $20 million including inventory, determine the following:

a. gross margin percentage
b. net profit percentage
c. operating expense percentage
d. inventory turnover rate
e. return on investment (ROI)
f. net marketing contribution
g. marketing return on sales (marketing ROS)
h. marketing return on investment (marketing ROI)
i. Is the Westgate division doing well? Explain your answer.

Financial Analysis of Marketing Tactics

Although the first-year profit performance for HD's new product was less than desired, management feels that this attractive market has excellent growth opportunities. Although the sales of HD's product were lower than initially projected, they were not unreasonable given the size of the current market. Thus, HD wants to explore new marketing tactics to help grow the market for this product and increase sales for the company.

For example, the company could increase advertising to promote more awareness of the new product and its category. It could add salespeople to secure greater product distribution. HD could decrease prices so that more consumers could afford its product. Finally, to expand the market, HD could introduce a lower-priced model in addition to the higher-priced original offering. Before pursuing any of these tactics, HD must analyze the financial implications of each.

Increase Advertising Expenditures

HD is considering boosting its advertising to make more people aware of the benefits of this device in general and of its own brand in particular. What if HD's marketers recommend increasing national advertising by 50% to $15 million (assume no change in the variable co-operative component of promotional expenditures)? This represents an increase in fixed costs of $5 million. What increase in sales will be needed to break even on this $5 million increase in fixed costs?

A quick way to answer this question is to divide the increase in fixed cost by the contribution margin, which we found in a previous analysis to be 21%:

$$\text{Increase in sales} = \frac{\text{increase in fixed cost}}{\text{contribution margin}} = \frac{\$5{,}000{,}000}{0.21} = \$23{,}809{,}524$$

Thus, a 50% increase in advertising expenditures must produce a sales increase of almost $24 million to just break even. That $24 million sales increase translates into an almost 1 percentage point increase in market share (1% of the $2.5 billion overall market equals $25 million). That is, to break even on the increased advertising expenditure, HD would have to increase its market share from 4% to 4.95% ($123,809,524 ÷ $2.5 billion = 0.0495 or 4.95% market share). All of this assumes that the total market will not grow, which might or might not be a reasonable assumption.

Increase Distribution Coverage

HD also wants to consider hiring more salespeople in order to call on new retailer accounts and increase distribution through more outlets. Even though HD sells directly to wholesalers, its sales representatives call on retail accounts to perform other functions in addition to selling, such as training retail salespeople. Currently, HD employs 60 sales reps who earn an average of $50,000 in salary plus 10% commission on sales. The product is currently sold to consumers through 1,875 retail outlets. Suppose HD wants to increase that number of outlets to 2,500, an increase of 625 retail outlets. How many additional salespeople will HD need, and what sales will be necessary to break even on the increased cost?

Workload method
An approach to determining sales force size based on the workload required and the time available for selling.

One method for determining what size sales force HD will need is the **workload method**. The workload method uses the following formula to determine the sales force size:

$$NS = \frac{NC \times FC \times LC}{TA}$$

where

NS = number of salespeople
NC = number of customers
FC = average frequency of customer calls per customer
LC = average length of customer call
TA = time an average salesperson has available for selling per year

HD's sales reps typically call on accounts an average of 20 times per year for about 2 hours per call. Although each sales rep works 2,000 hours per year (50 weeks per year × 40 hours per week), they spend about 15 hours per week on nonselling activities such as administrative duties and travel. Thus, the average annual available selling time per sales rep per year is 1,250 hours (50 weeks × 25 hours per week). We can now calculate how many sales reps HD will need to cover the anticipated 2,500 retail outlets:

$$NS = \frac{2{,}500 \times 20 \times 2}{1{,}250} = 80 \text{ salespeople}$$

Therefore, HD will need to hire 20 more salespeople. The cost to hire these reps will be $1 million (20 salespeople × $50,000 salary per sales person).

What increase in sales will be required to break even on this increase in fixed costs? The 10% commission is already accounted for in the contribution margin, so the contribution margin remains unchanged at 21%. Thus, the increase in sales needed to cover this increase in fixed costs can be calculated by:

$$\text{Increase in sales} = \frac{\text{increase in fixed cost}}{\text{contribution margin}} = \frac{\$1{,}000{,}000}{0.21} = \$4{,}761{,}905$$

That is, HD's sales must increase almost $5 million to break even on this tactic. So, how many new retail outlets will the company need to secure to achieve this sales increase? The average revenue generated per current outlet is $53,333 ($100 million in sales divided by 1,875 outlets). To achieve the nearly $5 million sales increase needed to break even, HD would need about 90 new outlets ($4,761,905 ÷ $53,333 = 89.3 outlets), or about 4.5 outlets per new rep. Given that current reps cover about 31 outlets apiece (1,875 outlets ÷ 60 reps), this seems very reasonable.

Decrease Price

HD is also considering lowering its price to increase sales revenue through increased volume. The company's research has shown that demand for most types of consumer electronics products is elastic—that is, the percentage increase in the quantity demanded is greater than the percentage decrease in price.

What increase in sales would be necessary to break even on a 10% decrease in price? That is, what increase in sales will be needed to maintain the total contribution that HD realized at the higher price? The current total contribution can be determined by multiplying the contribution margin by total sales:[5]

$$\begin{aligned}\text{Current total contribution} &= \text{contribution margin} \times \text{sales}\\ &= 0.21 \times \$100 \text{ million} = \$21\text{million}\end{aligned}$$

Price changes result in changes in unit contribution and contribution margin. Recall that the contribution margin of 21% was based on variable costs representing 79% of sales. Therefore, unit variable costs can be determined by multiplying the original price by this percentage: $168 × 0.79 = $132.72 per unit. If price is decreased by 10%, the new price is $151.20. However, variable costs do not change just because price decreased, so the contribution and contribution margin decrease as follows:

	Old	New (reduced 10%)
Price	$168	$151.20
– Unit variable cost	$132.72	$132.72
= Unit contribution	$35.28	$18.48
Contribution margin	$35.28/$168 = 0.21 or 21%	$18.48/$151.20 = 0.12 or 12%

So a 10% reduction in price results in a decrease in the contribution margin from 21% to 12%.[6] To determine the sales level needed to break even on this price reduction, we calculate the level of sales that must be attained at the new contribution margin to achieve the original total contribution of $21 million:

$$\text{New contribution margin} \times \text{new sales level} = \text{original total contribution}$$

So,

$$\text{New sales level} = \frac{\text{original contribution}}{\text{new contribution margin}} = \frac{\$21{,}000{,}000}{0.12} = \$175{,}000{,}000$$

Thus, sales must increase by $75 million ($175 million – $100 million) just to break even on a 10% price reduction. This means that HD must increase market share to 7% ($175 million ÷ $2.5 billion) to achieve the current level of profits (assuming no increase in the total market sales). The marketing manager must assess whether or not this is a reasonable goal.

Extend the Product Line

Cannibalization
The situation in which one product sold by a company takes a portion of its sales from other company products.

As a final option, HD is considering extending its product line by offering a lower-priced model. Of course, the new, lower-priced product would steal some sales from the higher-priced model. This is called **cannibalization**—the situation in which one product sold by a company takes a portion of its sales from other company products. If the new product has a lower contribution than the original product, the company's total contribution will decrease on the cannibalized sales. However, if the new product can generate enough new volume, it is worth considering.

To assess cannibalization, HD must look at the incremental contribution gained by having both products available. Recall in the previous analysis we determined that unit variable costs were $132.72 and unit contribution was just over $35. Assuming costs remain the same next year, HD can expect to realize a contribution per unit of approximately $35 for every unit of the original product sold.

Assume that the first model offered by HD is called HD1 and the new, lower-priced model is called HD2. HD2 will retail for $250, and resellers will take the same markup percentages on price as they do with the higher-priced model. Therefore, HD2's price to wholesalers will be $140 as follows:

Retail price:	$250
minus retail margin (30%):	–$ 75
Retailer's cost/wholesaler's price:	$175
minus wholesaler's margin (20%):	–$ 35
Wholesaler's cost/HD's price	$140

If HD2's variable costs are estimated to be $120, then its contribution per unit will equal $20 ($140 – $120 = $20). That means for every unit that HD2 cannibalizes from HD1, HD will *lose* $15 in contribution toward fixed costs and profit (that is, $\text{contribution}_{HD2} - \text{contribution}_{HD1} = \$20 - \$35 = -\$15$). You might conclude that HD should not pursue this tactic because it appears as though the company will be worse off if it introduces the lower-priced model. However, if HD2 captures enough *additional* sales, HD will be better off even though some HD1 sales are cannibalized. The company must examine what will happen to *total* contribution, which requires estimates of unit volume for both products.

Originally, HD estimated that next year's sales of HD1 would be 600,000 units. However, with the introduction of HD2, it now estimates that 200,000 of those sales will be cannibalized by the new model. If HD sells only 200,000 units of the new HD2 model (all cannibalized from HD1), the company would lose $3 million in total contribution (200,000 units × –$15 per cannibalized unit = –$3 million)—not a good outcome. However, HD estimates that HD2 will generate the 200,000 of cannibalized sales plus an *additional* 500,000 unit sales. Thus, the contribution on these additional HD2 units will be $10 million (i.e., 500,000 units × $20 per unit = $10 million). The net effect is that HD will gain $7 million in total contribution by introducing HD2.

The following table compares HD's total contribution with and without the introduction of HD2:

	HD1 Only	HD1 and HD2
HD1 contribution	600,000 units × $35 = $21,000,000	400,000 units × $35 = $14,000,000
HD2 contribution	0	700,000 units × $20 = $14,000,000
Total contribution	$21,000,000	$28,000,000

The difference in the total contribution is a net gain of $7 million ($28 million – $21 million). Based on this analysis, HD should introduce the HD2 model because it results in a positive incremental contribution. However, if fixed costs will increase by more than $7 million as a result of adding this model, then the net effect will be negative and HD should not pursue this tactic.

Now that you have seen these marketing tactic analysis concepts in action as they related to HD's new product, here are several exercises for you to apply what you have learned in this section in other contexts.

Marketing by the Numbers Exercise Set Three

3.1 Alliance, Inc. sells gas lamps to consumers through retail outlets. Total industry sales for Alliance's relevant market last year were $100 million, with Alliance's sales representing 5% of that total. Contribution margin is 25%. Alliance's sales force calls on retail outlets and each sales rep earns $50,000 per year plus 1% commission on all sales. Retailers receive a 40% margin on selling price and generate average revenue of $10,000 per outlet for Alliance.

a. The marketing manager has suggested increasing consumer advertising by $200,000. By how much would dollar sales need to increase to break even on this expenditure? What increase in overall market share does this represent?

b. Another suggestion is to hire two more sales representatives to gain new consumer retail accounts. How many new retail outlets would be necessary to break even on the increased cost of adding two sales reps?

c. A final suggestion is to make a 10% across-the-board price reduction. By how much would dollar sales need to increase to maintain Alliance's current contribution? (See endnote 6 to calculate the new contribution margin.)

d. Which suggestion do you think Alliance should implement? Explain your recommendation.

3.2 PepsiCo sells its soft drinks in approximately 400,000 retail establishments, such as supermarkets, discount stores, and convenience stores. Sales representatives call on each retail account weekly, which means each account is called on by a sales rep 52 times per year. The average length of a sales call is 75 minutes (or 1.25 hours).

An average salesperson works 2,000 hours per year (50 weeks per year × 40 hours per week), but each spends 10 hours a week on nonselling activities, such as administrative tasks and travel. How many salespeople does PepsiCo need?

3.3 Hair Zone manufactures a brand of hair-styling gel. It is considering adding a modified version of the product—a foam that provides stronger hold. Hair Zone's variable costs and prices to wholesalers are:

	Current Hair Gel	New Foam Product
Unit selling price	2.00	2.25
Unit variable costs	.85	1.25

Hair Zone expects to sell 1 million units of the new styling foam in the first year after introduction, but it expects that 60% of those sales will come from buyers who normally purchase Hair Zone's styling gel. Hair Zone estimates that it would sell 1.5 million units of the gel if it did not introduce the foam. If the fixed cost of launching the new foam will be $100,000 during the first year, should Hair Zone add the new product to its line? Why or why not?

Glossary

Adapted global marketing An international marketing approach that adjusts the marketing strategy and mix elements to each international target market, which creates more costs but hopefully produces a larger market share and return.

Administered VMS A vertical marketing system that coordinates successive stages of production and distribution through the size and power of one of the parties.

Adoption process The mental process through which an individual passes from first hearing about an innovation to final adoption.

Advertising Any paid form of nonpersonal presentation and promotion of ideas, goods, or services by an identified sponsor.

Advertising agency A marketing services firm that assists companies in planning, preparing, implementing, and evaluating all or portions of their advertising programs.

Advertising budget The dollars and other resources allocated to a product or a company advertising program.

Advertising media The vehicles through which advertising messages are delivered to their intended audiences.

Advertising objective A specific communication task to be accomplished with a specific target audience during a specific period of time.

Advertising strategy The strategy by which the company accomplishes its advertising objectives. It consists of two major elements: creating advertising messages and selecting advertising media.

Affordable method Setting the promotion budget at the level management thinks the company can afford.

Age and life-cycle segmentation Dividing a market into different age and life-cycle groups.

Agent A wholesaler who represents buyers or sellers on a relatively permanent basis, performs only a few functions, and does not take title to goods.

Allowance Promotional money paid by manufacturers to retailers in return for an agreement to feature the manufacturer's products in some way.

Approach The sales step in which a salesperson meets the customer for the first time.

Attitude A person's consistently favorable or unfavorable evaluations, feelings, and tendencies toward an object or idea.

Baby boomers The 78 million people born during the years following World War II and lasting until 1964.

Behavioral segmentation Dividing a market into segments based on consumer knowledge, attitudes, uses of a product, or responses to a product.

Behavioral targeting Using online consumer tracking data to target advertisements and marketing offers to specific consumers.

Belief A descriptive thought that a person holds about something.

Benefit segmentation Dividing the market into segments according to the different benefits that consumers seek from the product.

Blogs Online journals where people and companies post their thoughts and other content, usually related to narrowly defined topics.

Brand A name, term, sign, symbol, or design, or a combination of these, that identifies the products or services of one seller or group of sellers and differentiates them from those of competitors.

Brand content management Creating, inspiring, and sharing brand messages and conversations with and among consumers across a fluid mix of paid, owned, earned, and shared channels.

Brand equity The differential effect that knowing the brand name has on customer response to the product or its marketing.

Brand extension Extending an existing brand name to new product categories.

Branded community Web site A Web site that presents brand content that engages consumers and creates customer community around a brand.

Break-even pricing (target return pricing) Setting price to break even on the costs of making and marketing a product, or setting price to make a target return.

Broker A wholesaler who does not take title to goods and whose function is to bring buyers and sellers together and assist in negotiation.

Business analysis A review of the sales, costs, and profit projections for a new product to find out whether these factors satisfy the company's objectives.

Business buyer behavior The buying behavior of organizations that buy goods and services for use in the production of other products and services that are sold, rented, or supplied to others.

Business buying process The decision process by which business buyers determine which products and services their organizations need to purchase and then find, evaluate, and choose among alternative suppliers and brands.

Business portfolio The collection of businesses and products that make up the company.

Business promotions Sales promotion tools used to generate business leads, stimulate purchases, reward customers, and motivate salespeople.

Buying center All the individuals and units that play a role in the purchase decision-making process.

By-product pricing Setting a price for by-products in order to make the main product's price more competitive.

Captive-product pricing Setting a price for products that must be used along with a main product, such as blades for a razor and games for a video-game console.

Catalog marketing Direct marketing through print, video, or digital catalogs that are mailed to select customers, made available in stores, or presented online.

Category killer A giant specialty store that carries a very deep assortment of a particular line.

Causal research Marketing research to test hypotheses about cause-and-effect relationships.

Channel conflict Disagreements among marketing channel members on goals, roles, and rewards—who should do what and for what rewards.

Channel level A layer of intermediaries that performs some work in bringing the product and its ownership closer to the final buyer.

Closing The sales step in which a salesperson asks the customer for an order.

Co-branding The practice of using the established brand names of two different companies on the same product.

Cognitive dissonance Buyer discomfort caused by postpurchase conflict.

Commercialization Introducing a new product into the market.

Communication adaptation A global communication strategy of fully adapting advertising messages to local markets.

Competition-based pricing Setting prices based on competitors' strategies, prices, costs, and market offerings.

Competitive advantage An advantage over competitors gained by offering greater customer value, either by having lower prices or providing more benefits that justify higher prices.

Competitive marketing intelligence The systematic collection and analysis of publicly available information about consumers, competitors, and developments in the marketing environment.

Competitive-parity method Setting the promotion budget to match competitors' outlays.

Concentrated (niche) marketing A market-coverage strategy in which a firm goes after a large share of one or a few segments or niches.

Concept testing Testing new product concepts with a group of target consumers to find out if the concepts have strong consumer appeal.

Consumer buyer behavior The buying behavior of final consumers—individuals and households that buy goods and services for personal consumption.

Consumer market All the individuals and households that buy or acquire goods and services for personal consumption.

Consumer product A product bought by final consumers for personal consumption.

Consumer promotions Sales promotion tools used to boost short-term customer buying and engagement or enhance long-term customer relationships.

Consumer-generated marketing Brand exchanges created by consumers themselves—both invited and uninvited—by which consumers are playing an increasing role in shaping their own brand experiences and those of other consumers.

Consumer-oriented marketing A principle of sustainable marketing holding that a company should view and organize its marketing activities from the consumer's point of view.

Consumerism An organized movement of citizens and government agencies designed to improve the rights and power of buyers in relation to sellers.

Contract manufacturing A joint venture in which a company contracts with manufacturers in a foreign market to produce its product or provide its service.

Contractual VMS A vertical marketing system in which independent firms at different levels of production and distribution join together through contracts.

Convenience product A consumer product that customers usually buy frequently, immediately, and with minimal comparison and buying effort.

Convenience store A small store, located near a residential area, that is open long hours seven days a week and carries a limited line of high-turnover convenience goods.

Conventional distribution channel A channel consisting of one or more independent producers, wholesalers, and retailers, each a separate business seeking to maximize its own profits, perhaps even at the expense of profits for the system as a whole.

Corporate chains Two or more outlets that are commonly owned and controlled.

Corporate VMS A vertical marketing system that combines successive stages of production and distribution under single ownership—channel leadership is established through common ownership.

Cost-based pricing Setting prices based on the costs of producing, distributing, and selling the product plus a fair rate of return for effort and risk.

Cost-plus pricing (markup pricing) Adding a standard markup to the cost of the product.

Creative concept The compelling "big idea" that will bring an advertising message strategy to life in a distinctive and memorable way.

Cross-cultural marketing Including ethnic themes and cross-cultural perspectives within a brand's mainstream marketing, appealing to consumer similarities across subcultures rather than differences.

Crowdsourcing Inviting broad communities of people—customers, employees, independent scientists and researchers, and even the public at large—into the new product innovation process.

Cultural environment Institutions and other forces that affect society's basic values, perceptions, preferences, and behaviors.

Culture The set of basic values, perceptions, wants, and behaviors learned by a member of society from family and other important institutions.

Customer equity The total combined customer lifetime values of all of the company's customers.

Customer insights Fresh understandings of customers and the marketplace derived from marketing information that become the basis for creating customer value and relationships.

Customer lifetime value The value of the entire stream of purchases a customer makes over a lifetime of patronage.

Customer relationship management (CRM) Managing detailed information about individual customers and carefully managing customer touch points to maximize customer loyalty.

Customer relationship management The overall process of building and maintaining profitable customer relationships by delivering superior customer value and satisfaction.

Customer (or market) sales force structure A sales force organization in which salespeople specialize in selling only to certain customers or industries.

Customer satisfaction The extent to which a product's perceived performance matches a buyer's expectations.

Customer value marketing A principle of sustainable marketing holding that a company should put most of its resources into customer value–building marketing investments.

Customer value–based pricing Setting price based on buyers' perceptions of value rather than on the seller's cost.

Customer-centered new product development New product development that focuses on finding new ways to solve customer problems and create more customer-satisfying experiences.

Customer-engagement marketing Making the brand a meaningful part of consumers' conversations and lives by fostering direct and continuous customer involvement in shaping brand conversations, experiences, and community.

Customer-perceived value The customer's evaluation of the difference between all the benefits and all the costs of a marketing offer relative to those of competing offers.

Decline stage The PLC stage in which a product's sales fade away.

Deficient products Products that have neither immediate appeal nor long-run benefits.

Demand curve A curve that shows the number of units the market will buy in a given time period, at different prices that might be charged.

Demands Human wants that are backed by buying power.

Demographic segmentation Dividing the market into segments based on variables such as age, life-cycle stage, gender, income, occupation, education, religion, ethnicity, and generation.

Demography The study of human populations in terms of size, density, location, age, gender, race, occupation, and other statistics.

Department store A retail store that carries a wide variety of product lines, each operated as a separate department managed by specialist buyers or merchandisers.

Derived demand Business demand that ultimately comes from (derives from) the demand for consumer goods.

Descriptive research Marketing research to better describe marketing problems, situations, or markets, such as the market potential for a product or the demographics and attitudes of consumers.

Desirable products Products that give both high immediate satisfaction and high long-run benefits.

Differentiated (segmented) marketing A market-coverage strategy in which a firm decides to target several market segments and designs separate offers for each.

Differentiation Actually differentiating the market offering to create superior customer value.

Digital and social media marketing Using digital marketing tools such as Web sites, social media, mobile apps and ads, online video, e-mail, and blogs that engage consumers anywhere, anytime via their digital devices.

Direct and digital marketing Engaging directly with carefully targeted individual consumers and customer communities to both obtain an immediate response and build lasting customer relationships.

Direct investment Entering a foreign market by developing foreign-based assembly or manufacturing facilities.

Direct marketing channel A marketing channel that has no intermediary levels.

Direct-mail marketing Marketing that occurs by sending an offer, announcement, reminder, or other item directly to a person at a particular address.

Direct-response television (DRTV) marketing Direct marketing via television, including direct-response television advertising (or infomercials) and interactive television (iTV) advertising.

Discount A straight reduction in price on purchases during a stated period of time or in larger quantities.

Discount store A retail operation that sells standard merchandise at lower prices by accepting lower margins and selling at higher volume.

Disintermediation The cutting out of marketing channel intermediaries by product or service producers or the displacement of traditional resellers by radical new types of intermediaries.

Distribution center A large, highly automated warehouse designed to receive goods from various plants and suppliers, take orders, fill them efficiently, and deliver goods to customers as quickly as possible.

Diversification Company growth through starting up or acquiring businesses outside the company's current products and markets.

Dynamic pricing Adjusting prices continually to meet the characteristics and needs of individual customers and situations.

E-mail marketing Sending highly targeted, highly personalized, relationship-building marketing messages via e-mail.

E-procurement Purchasing through electronic connections between buyers and sellers—usually online.

Economic community A group of nations organized to work toward common goals in the regulation of international trade.

Economic environment Economic factors that affect consumer purchasing power and spending patterns.

Environmental sustainability A management approach that involves developing strategies that both sustain the environment and produce profits for the company.

Environmental sustainability Developing strategies and practices that create a world economy that the planet can support indefinitely.

Environmentalism An organized movement of concerned citizens, businesses, and government agencies designed to protect and improve people's current and future living environment.

Ethnographic research A form of observational research that involves sending trained observers to watch and interact with consumers in their "natural environments."

Event marketing (or event sponsorships) Creating a brand-marketing event or serving as a sole or participating sponsor of events created by others.

Exchange The act of obtaining a desired object from someone by offering something in return.

Exclusive distribution Giving a limited number of dealers the exclusive right to distribute the company's products in their territories.

Execution style The approach, style, tone, words, and format used for executing an advertising message.

Experimental research Gathering primary data by selecting matched groups of subjects, giving them different treatments, controlling related factors, and checking for differences in group responses.

Exploratory research Marketing research to gather preliminary information that will help define problems and suggest hypotheses.

Exporting Entering foreign markets by selling goods produced in the company's home country, often with little modification.

Factory outlet An off-price retailing operation that is owned and operated by a manufacturer and normally carries the manufacturer's surplus, discontinued, or irregular goods.

Fad A temporary period of unusually high sales driven by consumer enthusiasm and immediate product or brand popularity.

Fashion A currently accepted or popular style in a given field.

Fixed costs (overhead) Costs that do not vary with production or sales level.

Focus group interviewing Personal interviewing that involves inviting 6 to 10 people to gather for a few hours with a trained interviewer to talk about a product, service, or organization. The interviewer "focuses" the group discussion on important issues.

Follow-up The sales step in which a salesperson follows up after the sale to ensure customer satisfaction and repeat business.

Franchise A contractual association between a manufacturer, wholesaler, or service organization (a franchisor) and independent businesspeople (franchisees) who buy the right to own and operate one or more units in the franchise system.

Franchise organization A contractual vertical marketing system in which a channel member, called a franchisor, links several stages in the production-distribution process.

Gender segmentation Dividing a market into different segments based on gender.

Generation X The 49 million people born between 1965 and 1976 in the "birth dearth" following the baby boom.

Generation Z People born after 2000 (although many analysts include people born after 1995) who make up the kids, tweens, and teens markets.

Geographic segmentation Dividing a market into different geographical units, such as nations, states, regions, counties, cities, or even neighborhoods.

Global firm A firm that, by operating in more than one country, gains R&D, production, marketing, and financial advantages in its costs and reputation that are not available to purely domestic competitors.

Good-value pricing Offering just the right combination of quality and good service at a fair price.

Group Two or more people who interact to accomplish individual or mutual goals.

Growth stage The PLC stage in which a product's sales start climbing quickly.

Growth-share matrix A portfolio-planning method that evaluates a company's SBUs in terms of market growth rate and relative market share.

Handling objections The sales step in which a salesperson seeks out, clarifies, and overcomes any customer objections to buying.

Horizontal marketing system A channel arrangement in which two or more companies at one level join together to follow a new marketing opportunity.

Idea generation The systematic search for new product ideas.

Idea screening Screening new product ideas to spot good ones and drop poor ones as soon as possible.

Income segmentation Dividing a market into different income segments.

Independent off-price retailer An off-price retailer that is either independently owned and run or is a division of a larger retail corporation.

Indirect marketing channel A marketing channel containing one or more intermediary levels.

Individual marketing Tailoring products and marketing programs to the needs and preferences of individual customers.

Industrial product A product bought by individuals and organizations for further processing or for use in conducting a business.

Innovative marketing A principle of sustainable marketing that requires a company to seek real product and marketing improvements.

Inside sales force Salespeople who conduct business from their offices via telephone, online and social media interactions, or visits from prospective buyers.

Integrated logistics management The logistics concept that emphasizes teamwork—both inside the company and among all the marketing channel organizations—to maximize the performance of the entire distribution system.

Integrated marketing communications (IMC) Carefully integrating and coordinating the company's many communications channels to deliver a clear, consistent, and compelling message about the organization and its products.

Intensive distribution Stocking the product in as many outlets as possible.

Interactive marketing Training service employees in the fine art of interacting with customers to satisfy their needs.

Intermarket (cross-market) segmentation Forming segments of consumers who have similar needs and buying behaviors even though they are located in different countries.

Internal databases Electronic collections of consumer and market information obtained from data sources within the company network.

Internal marketing Orienting and motivating customer-contact employees and supporting service employees to work as a team to provide customer satisfaction.

Introduction stage The PLC stage in which a new product is first distributed and made available for purchase.

Joint ownership A cooperative venture in which a company creates a local business with investors in a foreign market, who share ownership and control.

Joint venturing Entering foreign markets by joining with foreign companies to produce or market a product or service.

Learning Changes in an individual's behavior arising from experience.

Licensing Entering foreign markets through developing an agreement with a licensee in the foreign market.

Lifestyle A person's pattern of living as expressed in his or her activities, interests, and opinions.

Line extension Extending an existing brand name to new forms, colors, sizes, ingredients, or flavors of an existing product category.

Local marketing Tailoring brands and marketing to the needs and wants of local customer segments—cities, neighborhoods, and even specific stores.

Macroenvironment The larger societal forces that affect the microenvironment—demographic, economic, natural, technological, political, and cultural forces.

Madison & Vine A term that has come to represent the merging of advertising and entertainment in an effort to break through the clutter and create new avenues for reaching customers with more engaging messages.

Management contracting A joint venture in which the domestic firm supplies the management know-how to a foreign company that supplies the capital; the domestic firm exports management services rather than products.

Manufacturers' and retailers' branches and offices Wholesaling by sellers or buyers themselves rather than through independent wholesalers.

Market The set of all actual and potential buyers of a product or service.

Market development Company growth by identifying and developing new market segments for current company products.

Market offerings Some combination of products, services, information, or experiences offered to a market to satisfy a need or want.

Market penetration Company growth by increasing sales of current products to current market segments without changing the product.

Market segment A group of consumers who respond in a similar way to a given set of marketing efforts.

Market segmentation Dividing a market into smaller segments of buyers with distinct needs, characteristics, or behaviors that might require separate marketing strategies or mixes.

Market targeting (targeting) Evaluating each market segment's attractiveness and selecting one or more segments to enter.

Market-penetration pricing Setting a low price for a new product in order to attract a large number of buyers and a large market share.

Market-skimming pricing (price skimming) Setting a high price for a new product to skim maximum revenues layer by layer from the segments willing to pay the high price; the company makes fewer but more profitable sales.

Marketing The process by which companies create value for customers and build strong customer relationships in order to capture value from customers in return.

Marketing channel (or distribution channel) A set of interdependent organizations that help make a product or service available for use or consumption by the consumer or business user.

Marketing channel design Designing effective marketing channels by analyzing customer needs, setting channel objectives, identifying major channel alternatives, and evaluating those alternatives.

Marketing channel management Selecting, managing, and motivating individual channel members and evaluating their performance over time.

Marketing concept A philosophy in which achieving organizational goals depends on knowing the needs and wants of target markets and delivering the desired satisfactions better than competitors do.

Marketing control Measuring and evaluating the results of marketing strategies and plans and taking corrective action to ensure that the objectives are achieved.

Marketing environment The actors and forces outside marketing that affect marketing management's ability to build and maintain successful relationships with target customers.

Marketing implementation Turning marketing strategies and plans into marketing actions to accomplish strategic marketing objectives.

Marketing information system (MIS) People and procedures dedicated to assessing information needs, developing the needed information, and helping decision makers to use the information to generate and validate actionable customer and market insights.

Marketing intermediaries Firms that help the company to promote, sell, and distribute its goods to final buyers.

Marketing logistics (or physical distribution) Planning, implementing, and controlling the physical flow of materials, final goods, and related information from points of origin to points of consumption to meet customer requirements at a profit.

Marketing management The art and science of choosing target markets and building profitable relationships with them.

Marketing mix The set of tactical marketing tools—product, price, place, and promotion—that the firm blends to produce the response it wants in the target market.

Marketing myopia The mistake of paying more attention to the specific products a company offers than to the benefits and experiences produced by these products.

Marketing research The systematic design, collection, analysis, and reporting of data relevant to a specific marketing situation facing an organization.

Marketing return on investment (or marketing ROI) The net return from a marketing investment divided by the costs of the marketing investment.

Marketing strategy The marketing logic by which the company hopes to create customer value and achieve profitable customer relationships.

Marketing strategy development Designing an initial marketing strategy for a new product based on the product concept.

Marketing Web site A Web site that interacts with consumers to move them closer to a direct purchase or other marketing outcome.

Maturity stage The PLC stage in which a product's sales growth slows or levels off.

Merchant wholesaler An independently owned wholesale business that takes title to the merchandise it handles.

Microenvironment The actors close to the company that affect its ability to serve its customers—the company, suppliers, marketing intermediaries, customer markets, competitors, and publics.

Micromarketing Tailoring products and marketing programs to the needs and wants of specific individuals and local customer segments; it includes *local marketing* and *individual marketing*.

Millennials (or Generation Y) The 83 million children of the baby boomers born between 1977 and 2000.

Mission statement A statement of the organization's purpose—what it wants to accomplish in the larger environment.

Mobile marketing Marketing messages, promotions, and other content delivered to on-the-go consumers through mobile phones, smartphones, tablets, and other mobile devices.

Modified rebuy A business buying situation in which the buyer wants to modify product specifications, prices, terms, or suppliers.

Motive (drive) A need that is sufficiently pressing to direct the person to seek satisfaction of the need.

Multichannel distribution system A distribution system in which a single firm sets up two or more marketing channels to reach one or more customer segments.

Multichannel marketing Marketing both through stores and other traditional offline channels and through digital, online, social media, and mobile channels.

Multimodal transportation Combining two or more modes of transportation.

Natural environment The physical environment and the natural resources that are needed as inputs by marketers or that are affected by marketing activities.

Needs States of felt deprivation.

New product A good, service, or idea that is perceived by some potential customers as new.

New product development The development of original products, product improvements, product modifications, and new brands through the firm's own product development efforts.

New task A business buying situation in which the buyer purchases a product or service for the first time.

Objective-and-task method Developing the promotion budget by (1) defining specific objectives, (2) determining the tasks that must be performed to achieve these objectives, and (3) estimating the costs of performing these tasks. The sum of these costs is the proposed promotion budget.

Observational research Gathering primary data by observing relevant people, actions, and situations.

Occasion segmentation Dividing the market into segments according to occasions when buyers get the idea to buy, actually make their purchase, or use the purchased item.

Off-price retailer A retailer that buys at less-than-regular wholesale prices and sells at less than retail.

Online advertising Advertising that appears while consumers are browsing online, including display ads, search-related ads, online classifieds, and other forms.

Online focus groups Gathering a small group of people online with a trained moderator to chat about a product, service, or organization and gain qualitative insights about consumer attitudes and behavior.

Online marketing Marketing via the Internet using company Web sites, online ads and promotions, e-mail, online video, and blogs.

Online marketing research Collecting primary data online through Internet surveys, online focus groups, Web-based experiments, or tracking consumers' online behavior.

Online social networks Online social communities—blogs, social networking Web sites, and other online communities—where people socialize or exchange information and opinions.

Opinion leader A person within a reference group who, because of special skills, knowledge, personality, or other characteristics, exerts social influence on others.

Optional-product pricing The pricing of optional or accessory products along with a main product.

Outside sales force (or field sales force) Salespeople who travel to call on customers in the field.

Packaging The activities of designing and producing the container or wrapper for a product.

Partner relationship management Working closely with partners in other company departments and outside the company to jointly bring greater value to customers.

Percentage-of-sales method Setting the promotion budget at a certain percentage of current or forecasted sales or as a percentage of the unit sales price.

Perception The process by which people select, organize, and interpret information to form a meaningful picture of the world.

Personal selling Personal customer interactions by the firm's sales force for the purpose of making sales and building customer relationships.

Personality The unique psychological characteristics that distinguish a person or group.

Pleasing products Products that give high immediate satisfaction but may hurt consumers in the long run.

Political environment Laws, government agencies, and pressure groups that influence and limit various organizations and individuals in a given society.

Portfolio analysis The process by which management evaluates the products and businesses that make up the company.

Positioning Arranging for a market offering to occupy a clear, distinctive, and desirable place relative to competing products in the minds of target consumers.

Positioning statement A statement that summarizes company or brand positioning using this form: To (target segment and need) our (brand) is (concept) that (point of difference).

Preapproach The sales step in which a salesperson learns as much as possible about a prospective customer before making a sales call.

Presentation The sales step in which a salesperson tells the "value story" to the buyer, showing how the company's offer solves the customer's problems.

Price The amount of money charged for a product or service, or the sum of the values that customers exchange for the benefits of having or using the product or service.

Price elasticity A measure of the sensitivity of demand to changes in price.

Primary data Information collected for the specific purpose at hand.

Product Anything that can be offered to a market for attention, acquisition, use, or consumption that might satisfy a want or need.

Product adaptation Adapting a product to meet local conditions or wants in foreign markets.

Product bundle pricing Combining several products and offering the bundle at a reduced price.

Product concept A detailed version of the new product idea stated in meaningful consumer terms.

Product concept The idea that consumers will favor products that offer the most quality, performance, and features; therefore, the organization should devote its energy to making continuous product improvements.

Product development Company growth by offering modified or new products to current market segments.

Product development Developing the product concept into a physical product to ensure that the product idea can be turned into a workable market offering.

Product invention Creating new products or services for foreign markets.

Product life cycle (PLC) The course of a product's sales and profits over its lifetime.

Product line A group of products that are closely related because they function in a similar manner, are sold to the same customer groups, are marketed through the same types of outlets, or fall within given price ranges.

Product line pricing Setting the price steps between various products in a product line based on cost differences between the products, customer evaluations of different features, and competitors' prices.

Product mix (or product portfolio) The set of all product lines and items that a particular seller offers for sale.

Product position The way a product is defined by consumers on important attributes—the place the product occupies in consumers' minds relative to competing products.

Product quality The characteristics of a product or service that bear on its ability to satisfy stated or implied customer needs.

Product sales force structure A sales force organization in which salespeople specialize in selling only a portion of the company's products or lines.

Product value analysis Carefully analyzing a product's or service's components to determine if they can be redesigned and made more effectively and efficiently to provide greater value.

Product/market expansion grid A portfolio-planning tool for identifying company growth opportunities through market penetration, market development, product development, or diversification.

Production concept The idea that consumers will favor products that are available and highly affordable; therefore, the organization should focus on improving production and distribution efficiency.

Promotion mix (or marketing communications mix) The specific blend of promotion tools that the company uses to engage consumers, persuasively communicate customer value, and build customer relationships.

Promotional pricing Temporarily pricing products below the list price, and sometimes even below cost, to increase short-run sales.

Prospecting The sales step in which a salesperson or company identifies qualified potential customers.

Psychographic segmentation Dividing a market into different segments based on social class, lifestyle, or personality characteristics.

Psychological pricing Pricing that considers the psychology of prices and not simply the economics; the price is used to say something about the product.

Public Any group that has an actual or potential interest in or impact on an organization's ability to achieve its objectives.

Public relations (PR) Building good relations with the company's various publics by obtaining favorable publicity, building up a good corporate image, and handling or heading off unfavorable rumors, stories, and events.

Pull strategy A promotion strategy that calls for spending a lot on consumer advertising and promotion to induce final consumers to buy the product, creating a demand vacuum that "pulls" the product through the channel.

Push strategy A promotion strategy that calls for using the sales force and trade promotion to push the product through channels. The producer promotes the product to channel members, which in turn promote it to final consumers.

Reference prices Prices that buyers carry in their minds and refer to when they look at a given product.

Retailer A business whose sales come *primarily* from retailing.

Retailing All the activities involved in selling goods or services directly to final consumers for their personal, nonbusiness use.

Return on advertising investment The net return on advertising investment divided by the costs of the advertising investment.

Sales force management Analyzing, planning, implementing, and controlling sales force activities.

Sales promotion Short-term incentives to encourage the purchase or sale of a product or a service.

Sales quota A standard that states the amount a salesperson should sell and how sales should be divided among the company's products.

Salesperson An individual who represents a company to customers by performing one or more of the following activities: prospecting, communicating, selling, servicing, information gathering, and relationship building.

Salutary products Products that have low immediate appeal but may benefit consumers in the long run.

Sample A segment of the population selected for marketing research to represent the population as a whole.

Secondary data Information that already exists somewhere, having been collected for another purpose.

Segmented pricing Selling a product or service at two or more prices, where the difference in prices is not based on differences in costs.

Selective distribution The use of more than one but fewer than all of the intermediaries that are willing to carry the company's products.

Selling concept The idea that consumers will not buy enough of the firm's products unless the firm undertakes a large-scale selling and promotion effort.

Selling process The steps that salespeople follow when selling, which include prospecting and qualifying, preapproach, approach, presentation and demonstration, handling objections, closing, and follow-up.

Sense-of-mission marketing A principle of sustainable marketing holding that a company should define its mission in broad social terms rather than narrow product terms.

Service An activity, benefit, or satisfaction offered for sale that is essentially intangible and does not result in the ownership of anything.

Service inseparability Services are produced and consumed at the same time and cannot be separated from their providers.

Service intangibility Services cannot be seen, tasted, felt, heard, or smelled before they are bought.

Service perishability Services cannot be stored for later sale or use.

Service profit chain The chain that links service firm profits with employee and customer satisfaction.

Service retailer A retailer whose product line is actually a service; examples include hotels, airlines, banks, colleges, and many others.

Service variability The quality of services may vary greatly depending on who provides them and when, where, and how they are provided.

Share of customer The portion of the customer's purchasing that a company gets in its product categories.

Shopper marketing Using in-store promotions and advertising to extend brand equity to "the last mile" and encourage favorable point-of-purchase decisions.

Shopping center A group of retail businesses built on a site that is planned, developed, owned, and managed as a unit.

Shopping product A consumer product that the customer, in the process of selecting and purchasing, usually compares on such attributes as suitability, quality, price, and style.

Showrooming The shopping practice of coming into retail store showrooms to check out merchandise and prices but instead buying from an online-only rival, sometimes while in the store.

Social class Relatively permanent and ordered divisions in a society whose members share similar values, interests, and behaviors.

Social marketing The use of commercial marketing concepts and tools in programs designed to influence individuals' behavior to improve their well-being and that of society.

Social media Independent and commercial online communities where people congregate, socialize, and exchange views and information.

Societal marketing A principle of sustainable marketing holding that a company should make marketing decisions by considering consumers' wants, the company's requirements, consumers' long-run interests, and society's long-run interests.

Societal marketing concept The idea that a company's marketing decisions should consider consumers' wants, the company's requirements, consumers' long-run interests, and society's long-run interests.

Spam Unsolicited, unwanted commercial e-mail messages.

Specialty product A consumer product with unique characteristics or brand identification for which a significant group of buyers is willing to make a special purchase effort.

Specialty store A retail store that carries a narrow product line with a deep assortment within that line.

Standardized global marketing An international marketing strategy that basically uses the same marketing strategy and mix in all of the company's international markets.

Store brand (or private brand) A brand created and owned by a reseller of a product or service.

Straight product extension Marketing a product in a foreign market without making any changes to the product.

Straight rebuy A business buying situation in which the buyer routinely reorders something without any modifications.

Strategic planning The process of developing and maintaining a strategic fit between the organization's goals and capabilities and its changing marketing opportunities.

Style A basic and distinctive mode of expression.

Subculture A group of people with shared value systems based on common life experiences and situations.

Supermarket A large, low-cost, low-margin, high-volume, self-service store that carries a wide variety of grocery and household products.

Superstore A store much larger than a regular supermarket that offers a large assortment of routinely purchased food products, nonfood items, and services.

Supplier development Systematic development of networks of supplier-partners to ensure an appropriate and dependable supply of products and materials for use in making products or reselling them to others.

Supply chain management Managing upstream and downstream value-added flows of materials, final goods, and related information among suppliers, the company, resellers, and final consumers.

Survey research Gathering primary data by asking people questions about their knowledge, attitudes, preferences, and buying behavior.

Sustainable marketing Socially and environmentally responsible marketing that meets the present needs of consumers and businesses while also preserving or enhancing the ability of future generations to meet their needs.

SWOT analysis An overall evaluation of the company's strengths (S), weaknesses (W), opportunities (O), and threats (T).

Systems selling (or solutions selling) Buying a packaged solution to a problem from a single seller, thus avoiding all the separate decisions involved in a complex buying situation.

Target costing Pricing that starts with an ideal selling price, then targets costs that will ensure that the price is met.

Target market A set of buyers sharing common needs or characteristics that the company decides to serve.

Team selling Using teams of people from sales, marketing, engineering, finance, technical support, and even upper management to service large, complex accounts.

Team-based new product development New product development in which various company departments work closely together, overlapping the steps in the product development process to save time and increase effectiveness.

Telemarketing Using the telephone to sell directly to customers.

Territorial sales force structure A sales force organization that assigns each salesperson to an exclusive geographic territory in which that salesperson sells the company's full line.

Test marketing The stage of new product development in which the product and its proposed marketing program are tested in realistic market settings.

Third-party logistics (3PL) provider An independent logistics provider that performs any or all of the functions required to get a client's product to market.

Total costs The sum of the fixed and variable costs for any given level of production.

Trade promotions Sales promotion tools used to persuade resellers to carry a brand, give it shelf space, and promote it in advertising.

Undifferentiated (mass) marketing A market-coverage strategy in which a firm decides to ignore market segment differences and go after the whole market with one offer.

Unsought product A consumer product that the consumer either does not know about or knows about but does not normally consider buying.

Value chain The series of internal departments that carry out value-creating activities to design, produce, market, deliver, and support a firm's products.

Value delivery network A network composed of the company, suppliers, distributors, and, ultimately, customers who partner with each other to improve the performance of the entire system in delivering customer value.

Value proposition The full positioning of a brand—the full mix of benefits on which it is positioned.

Value-added pricing Attaching value-added features and services to differentiate a company's offers and charging higher prices.

Variable costs Costs that vary directly with the level of production.

Vertical marketing system (VMS) A channel structure in which producers, wholesalers, and retailers act as a unified system. One channel member owns the others, has contracts with them, or has so much power that they all cooperate.

Viral marketing The digital version of word-of-mouth marketing: videos, ads, and other marketing content that is so infectious that customers will seek it out or pass it along to friends.

Wants The form human needs take as they are shaped by culture and individual personality.

Warehouse club An off-price retailer that sells a limited selection of brand name grocery items, appliances, clothing, and other goods at deep discounts to members who pay annual membership fees.

Whole-channel view Designing international channels that take into account the entire global supply chain and marketing channel, forging an effective global value delivery network.

Wholesaler A firm engaged *primarily* in wholesaling activities.

Wholesaling All the activities involved in selling goods and services to those buying for resale or business use.

Word-of-mouth influence The impact of the personal words and recommendations of trusted friends, associates, and other consumers on buying behavior.

References

Chapter 1

1. See Morten T. Hansen, Herminia Ibarra, and Urs Peyer, "The Best-Performing CEOs in the World," *Harvard Business Review,* January–February 2013, pp. 81–86; George Anders, "Inside Amazon's Idea Machine," *Forbes,* April 4, 2012, p. 1; Daniel Lyons, "The Customer Is Always Right," *Newsweek,* January 4, 2010, p. 85; George Anders, "Jeff Bezos's Top 10 Leadership Lessons," *Forbes*, April 4, 2012, www.forbes.com/sites/georgeanders/2012/04/04/bezos-tips/; Brad Stone and Jim Aley, "Amazon's Jeff Bezos Doesn't Care about Profit Margins," *Bloomberg Businessweek*, January 14, 2013, www.businessweek.com/articles/2013-01-08/amazons-jeff-bezos-doesnt-care-about-profit-margins; and annual reports and other information found at www.amazon.com and http://local.amazon.com/businesses, accessed November 2013.
2. See Keith O'Brien, "How McDonald's Came Back Bigger Than Ever," *New York Times,* May 4, 2012, www.nytimes.com/2012/05/06/magazine/how-mcdonalds-came-back-bigger-than-ever.html?pagewanted=all; Heather Kelly, "Facebook Mobile Users Surpass Desktop Users for First Time," *CNN Tech,* January 31, 2013, www.cnn.com/2013/01/30/tech/social-media/facebook-mobile-users; and "Global 500," *Fortune,* July 22, 2013, p. 134.
3. See Philip Kotler and Kevin Lane Keller, *Marketing Management,* 14th ed. (Upper Saddle River, NJ: Prentice Hall, 2012), p. 5.
4. The American Marketing Association offers the following definition: "Marketing is the activity, set of institutions, and processes for creating, communicating, delivering, and exchanging offerings that have value for customers, clients, partners, and society at large." See www.marketingpower.com/_layouts/Dictionary.aspx?dLetter=M, accessed November 2013.
5. See "50 Years of Helping Customers Save Money and Live Better," Walmart Annual Report, www.walmartstores.com/sites/annual-report/2012/WalMart_AR.pdf, March 2013, p. 5; Dan Sewell, "Kroger CEO Often Roams Aisles, Wielding Carte Blanche," *Journal Gazette* (Fort Wayne, IN), November 15, 2010, www.journalgazette.net/article/20101115/BIZ/311159958/-1/BIZ09; Christine Birkner, "10 Minutes with Ashlee Yingling," *Marketing News,* May 31, 2013, pp. 24–28; and "McDonald's Listening Tour," accessed at www.aboutmcdonalds.com, July 2013.
6. See www.michigan.org and www.adcouncil.org/default.aspx?id=602, accessed September 2013; and "Childhood Obesity—Let's Move," Ad Council, www.adcouncil.org/Our-Work/Current-Work/Health/Childhood-Obesity-Prevention, accessed November 2013.
7. See Theodore Levitt's classic article, "Marketing Myopia," *Harvard Business Review*, July–August 1960, pp. 45–56. For more recent discussions, see Lance A. Bettencourt, "Debunking Myths about Customer Needs," *Marketing Management*, January/February 2009, pp. 46–51; N. Craig Smith, Minette E. Drumright, and Mary C. Gentile, "The New Marketing Myopia," *Journal of Public Policy & Marketing*, Spring 2010, pp. 4–11; and Roberto Friedmann, "What Business Are You In?" *Marketing Management,* Summer 2011, pp. 18–23.
8. See J. J. McCorvey, "Bird of Play," *Fast Company,* December 2012/January 2013, pp. 100–107+; and www.angrybirds.com, accessed November 2013.
9. "Henry Ford, Faster Horses, and Market Research," *Research Arts,* January 25, 2011, www.researcharts.com/2011/01/henry-ford-faster-horses-and-market-research/.
10. See Michael E. Porter and Mark R. Kramer, "Creating Shared Value," *Harvard Business Review*, January–February 2011, pp. 63–77; Vivian Gee, "Creating Shared Value," *Huffington Post,* January 29, 2012, www.huffingtonpost.com/vivian-gee/creating-shared-value_1_b_1240228.html; and "Shared Value," www.fsg.org, accessed October 2013.
11. Michael Krauss, "Evolution of an Academic: Kotler on Marketing 3.0," *Marketing News*, January 30, 2011, p. 12.
12. Based on information from www.responsibility.ups.com/Sustainability and www.responsibility.ups.com/community, accessed November 2013.
13. Based on information from www.weber.com, accessed May 2013.
14. See "JetBlue Airways Awarded Eighth Consecutive Customer Satisfaction J.D. Power and Associates Honor," June 13, 2012, http://blog.jetblue.com/index.php/2012/06/13/jetblue-airways-awarded-eighth-consecutive-customer-satisfaction-j-d-power-and-associates-honor/; Kelly Liyakasa, "Customer Experience Is Critical in Net Promoter Benchmarks," *CRM Magazine*, June 2012, www.destinationcrm.com/Articles/Columns-Departments/Insight/Customer-Experience-Is-Critical-in-Net--Promoter-Benchmarks-82569.aspx; and http://experience.jetblue.com/, www.jetblue.com/about/; and http://blog.jetblue.com, accessed November 2013.
15. Ron Ruggless, "Panera Loyalty Program Approaches 10M Members," *Nation's Restaurant News*, March 8, 2012, http://nrn.com/article/panera-loyalty-program-approaches-10m-members; and http://mypanera.panerabread.com/, accessed November 2013.
16. For more information, see www.apple.com/usergroups/ and www.webernation.com, accessed November 2013.
17. Based on information from Noreen O'Leary, "Hertz Learns Value of Sharing in Purchase Cycle," *Adweek*, May 30, 2012; "Hertz Fans Share It Up! on Facebook," *PRNewswire*, April 11, 2012, www.prnewswire.com/news-releases/hertz-fans-share-it-up-on-facebook-146987185.html; "The Top 10 Social Media Success Stories of 2012 & What We Can Learn from Them," *Social Media Strategies Summit Blog,* November 28, 2012, http://socialmediastrategiessummit.com/blog/the-top-10-social-media-success-stories-of-2012-what-we-can-learn-from-them; and www.Hertz.com, accessed November 2013.
18. Gordon Wyner, "Getting Engaged," Marketing Management, Fall 2012, pp. 4–10. For more discussion on customer engagement, see Don E. Schultz, "Social Media's Slippery Slope," *Marketing Management,* February 2013, pp. 20–21.
19. See mystarbucksidea.force.com, accessed November 2013.
20. "2013 USA Today Facebook Super Bowl Ad Meter," http://admeter.usatoday.com/, accessed May 2013; Christopher Heine, "Frito-Lay Likes the Data from Doritos' 'Crash the Super Bowl,'" *Adweek*, February 7, 2013, www.adweek.com/news/technology/frito-lay-likes-data-doritos-crash-super-bowl-147127"; and www.crashthesuperbowl.com, accessed May 2013.
21. See Gavin O'Malley, "Entries Pour in for Heinz Ketchup Commercial Contest," August 13, 2007, http://publications.mediapost.com; and www.youtube.com/watch?v=JGY-ubAJSyI, accessed November 2013.

22. "Stew Leonard's," *Hoover's Company Records*, July 15, 2012, www.hoovers.com; and www.stew-leonards.com/html/about.cfm, accessed November 2013.
23. Graham Brown, "MobileYouth Key Statistics," March 28, 2008, www.mobileyouth.org/?s=MobileYouth+Key+Statistics. For interesting discussions of customer lifetime value, see Norman W. Marshall, "Commitment, Loyalty, and Customer Lifetime Value: Investigating the Relationships among Key Determinants," *Journal of Business & Economics Research,* August 2010, pp. 67–85; and Christian Gronroos and Pekka Helle, "Return on Relationships: Conceptual Understanding and Measurement of Mutual Gains from Relational Business Engagements," *Journal of Business & Industrial Marketing,* Vol. 27, No. 5, 2012, pp. 344–359.
24. Based on quotes and information from Brad Stone, "What's in the Box? Instant Gratification," *Bloomberg Businessweek*, November 29–December 5, 2010, pp. 39–40; JP Mangalindan, "Amazon's Prime and Punishment," *CNNMoney,* February 21, 2012, http://tech.fortune.cnn.com/2012/02/21/prime-and-punishment/; Marcus Wohlsen, "Why Amazon Prime Could Soon Cost You Next to Nothing," *Wired,* March 13, 2013, www.wired.com/business/2013/03/amazon-prime-could-soon-cost-next-to-nothing; and www.amazon.com/gp/prime/ref=footer_prime, accessed November 2013.
25. For more discussions on customer equity, see Roland T. Rust, Valerie A. Zeithaml, and Katherine N. Lemon, *Driving Customer Equity* (New York: Free Press, 2000); Rust, Lemon, and Zeithaml, "Return on Marketing: Using Customer Equity to Focus Marketing Strategy," *Journal of Marketing*, January 2004, pp. 109–127; Dominique M. Hanssens, Daniel Thorpe, and Carl Finkbeiner, "Marketing When Customer Equity Matters," *Harvard Business Review*, May 2008, pp. 117–124; Christian Gronroos and Pekka Helle, "Return on Relationships: Conceptual Understanding and Measurement of Mutual Gains from Relational Business Engagements," *Journal of Business & Industrial Marketing,* Vol. 27, No. 5, 2012, pp. 344–359; and Peter C. Verhoef and Katherine N. Lemon, "Successful Customer Value Management: Key Lessons and Emerging Trends," *European Management Journal,* February 2013, p. 1.
26. This example is adapted from information found in Rust, Lemon, and Zeithaml, "Where Should the Next Marketing Dollar Go?" *Marketing Management*, September–October 2001, pp. 24–28; with information from Dan Slater, "She Drives a Cadillac," *Fast Company,* February 2012, pp. 26–28; and Jeff Bennett and Joeseph B. White, "New Cadillac, Old Dilemma," *Wall Street Journal,* March 27, 2013, p. B1.
27. Based on Werner Reinartz and V. Kumar, "The Mismanagement of Customer Loyalty," *Harvard Business Review*, July 2002, pp. 86–94. Also see Stanley F. Slater, Jakki J. Mohr, and Sanjit Sengupta, "Know Your Customer," *Marketing Management,* February 2009, pp. 37–44; and Crina O. Tarasi, et al., "Balancing Risk and Return in a Customer Portfolio," *Journal of Marketing,* May 2011, pp. 1–17.
28. See "It Keeps Growing and Growing," *Harvard Business Review,* October 2012, pp. 32–33; and Stuart Feil, "Mobile on the Cusp (Again)," *Adweek,* February 11, 2013, pp. M1–M3+.
29. Mobile facts from "Voice: One Screen to Rule Them All," *Adweek,* February 13, 2013, www.adweek.com/print/147137; and "Social Networking Eats Up 3+ Hours Per Day for the Average American User," *MarketingCharts,* January 9, 2013, www.marketingcharts.com/wp/interactive/social-networking-eats-up-3-hours-per-day-for-the-average-american-user-26049/.
30. For these and other examples, see "The State of Online Branded Communities," *Comblu,* November 2012, p. 17, http://comblu.com/thoughtleadership/the-state-of-online-branded-communities-2012.
31. See Stuart Feil, "How to Win Friends and Influence People," *Adweek,* September 12, 2013, pp. S1–S7; and Joe Mandese, "Carat Projects Digital at One-Fifth of All Ad Spend, Beginning to Dominate Key Markets," *MediaPost News,* March 20, 2013, www.mediapost.com/publications/article/196238/carat-projects-digital-at-one-fifth-of-all-ad-spen.html#axzz2PsYL9uFf.
32. Christopher Heine, "Brands Favor Social Shares over Likes: Chatter Is the Key," *Adweek,* April 1, 2013, www.adweek.com/print/148256.
33. See Feil, "How to Win Friends and Influence People," pp. S1–S7; and www.youtube.com/watch?v=4P6Qwppw-3U, accessed November 2013.
34. Michael Applebaum, "Mobile Magnetism," *Adweek,* June 25, 2012, pp. S1–S9; and Nelson, "Voice: One Screen to Rule Them All."
35. See Applebaum, "Mobile Magnetism," p. S7; and Brian Quintion, "2012 PRO Award Winner: Catapult Action Biased Marketing for Mars Petcare," *Chief Marketer,* August 3, 2012, www.chiefmarketer.com/agencies/2012-pro-award-winner-catapult-action-biased-marketing-for-mars-petcare-03082012. PEDIGREE® is a registered trademark of Mars, Incorporated. The trademark is used with permission. Mars, Incorporated is not associated with Pearson Education, Inc. The image of the PEDIGREE® Advertisement is printed with permission of Mars, Incorporated.
36. See John Gerzema, "How U.S. Consumers Are Steering the Spend Shift," *Advertising Age*, October 11, 2010, p. 26; and Gregg Fairbrothers and Catalina Gorla, "The Decline and Rise of Thrift," *Forbes*, April 23, 2012, www.forbes.com/sites/greggfairbrothers/2012/04/23/the-decline-and-rise-of-thrift/.
37. See Matt Townsend, "Why Target's Cheap-Chic Glamour Is Fading," *Bloomberg Businessweek,* September 26, 2012, pp. 30–31; and "Our Mission," http://sites.target.com/site/en/company/page.jsp?contentId=WCMP04-031699, accessed August 2013.
38. See Natalie Zmuda, "St. Jude's Goes from Humble Beginnings to Media Ubiquity," *Advertising Age,* February 14, 2011, p. 37; and various pages at www.stjude.org, accessed November 2013.
39. "The Top Advertisers in the US," www.adbrands.net/us/index.html, accessed March 2013; and "Annual 2013: Marketing," *Advertising Age,* December 31, 2012, p. 16. For more on social marketing, see Philip Kotler and Nancy R. Lee, *Social Marketing: Influencing Behaviors for Good*, 3rd ed. (Thousand Oaks, CA: Sage Publications, 2008).
40. www.aboutmcdonalds.com/mcd and www.nikeinc.com, accessed May 2013.
41. Quotes and information found at www.patagonia.com/web/us/-contribution/patagonia.go?assetid=2329, accessed November 2013.

Chapter 2

1. Based on information from Austin Carr, "Nike: The No. 1 Most Innovative Company of 2013," *Fast Company*, March 2013, pp. 89–93+; Mary Lisbeth D'Amico, "Report Sends Nike and Adidas to Head of Digital Marketing Class," *Clickz*, September 25, 2012, www.clickz.com/clickz/news/2208172/report-sends-nike-and-adidas-to-head-of-digital-marketing-class; Brian Morrissey, "Nike Plus Starts to Open Up to Web," *Adweek,* July 20–July 27, 2009, p. 8; Sebastian Joseph, "Nike Takes Social Media In-House," *Marketing Week*, January 3, 2013, www.marketingweek.co.uk/sectors/sport/nike-takes-social-media-in-house/4005240.article; and http://nikeplus.nike.com/plus/, accessed November 2013.
2. The NASA mission statement is from www.nasa.gov/about/highlights/what_does_nasa_do.html, accessed November 2013.
3. For more discussion of mission statements and examples, both good and bad, see Jack and Suzy Welch, "State Your Business; Too Many Mission Statements Are Loaded with Fatheaded Jargon. Play It Straight," *BusinessWeek*, January 14, 2008, p. 80; Piet Levy, "Mission vs. Vision," *Marketing News,* February 28, 2011, p. 10; Setayesh Sattari et al., "How Readable Are Mission Statements? An

Exploratory Study," *Corporate Communications*," 2011, p. 4; and www.missionstatements.com/fortune_500_mission_statements .html, accessed November 2013.

4. Based on information from "Buffalo Wild Wings," a 22SQUARED case study, September 5, 2012, accessed at www.22squared.com/our-work/case-studies/; and www.buffalowildwings.com/about/, accessed July 2013. Buffalo Wild Wings® is a registered trademark of Buffalo Wild Wings, Inc.
5. Information about Heinz and its mission from www.heinz.com/our-company/about-heinz/mission-and-values.aspx and www .heinz.com, accessed November 2013.
6. The following discussion is based in part on information found at www.bcg.com/documents/file13904.pdf, accessed November 2013.
7. Lisa Richwine, "Disney Earnings Beat Despite Shaky Economy," *Reuters.com*, February 8, 2012, www.reuters.com/article/2012/02/08/us-disney-idUSTRE8161TE20120208; and http://corporate.disney .go.com/investors/annual_reports.html, accessed July 2013.
8. H. Igor Ansoff, "Strategies for Diversification," *Harvard Business Review*, September–October 1957, pp. 113–124.
9. Facts in this and the following paragraphs are based on information found in Tess Steins, "Starbucks Details Plans for Energy Drink, International Expansion," *Wall Street Journal*, March 21, 2012, http://online.wsj.com/article/SB10001424052702304636 404577295673557464182.html; David A. Kaplan, "Strong Coffee," *Fortune*, December 12, 2011, pp. 101–115; Jon Carter, "Starbucks: For Infusing a Steady Stream of New Ideas to Revise Its Business," *Fast Company*, March 2012, pp. 112+; "Starbucks CEO Howard Schultz Opens Annual Meeting of Shareholders," *Wireless News,* March 25, 2013; and www.starbucks.com, accessed November 2013.
10. See Michael E. Porter, *Competitive Advantage: Creating and Sustaining Superior Performance* (New York: Free Press, 1985); and Michael E. Porter, "What Is Strategy?" *Harvard Business Review*, November–December 1996, pp. 61–78. Also see "The Value Chain," www.quickmba.com/strategy/value-chain, accessed July 2013; and Philip Kotler and Kevin Lane Keller, *Marketing Management*, 14th ed. (Upper Saddle River, NJ: Prentice Hall, 2012), pp. 34–35 and pp. 203–204.
11. Nirmalya Kumar, "The CEO's Marketing Manifesto," *Marketing Management*, November–December 2008, pp. 24–29; and Tom French and others, "We're All Marketers Now," McKinsey Quarterly, July 2011, www.mckinseyquarterly.com/Were_all_marketers_now_2834.
12. See www.gapinc.com/content/gapinc/html/aboutus/ourbrands/gap .html, accessed June 2013.
13. See http://nikeinc.com/pages/about-nike-inc, accessed November 2013.
14. "100 Leading National Advertisers," *Advertising Age*, June 25, 2012, p. 14.
15. The four Ps classification was first suggested by E. Jerome McCarthy, *Basic Marketing: A Managerial Approach* (Homewood, IL: Irwin, 1960). For the four Cs, other proposed classifications, and more discussion, see Robert Lauterborn, "New Marketing Litany: 4P's Passé C-Words Take Over," *Advertising Age*, October 1, 1990, p. 26; Phillip Kotler, "Alphabet Soup," *Marketing Management*, March–April 2006, p. 51; Nirmalya Kumer, "The CEO's Marketing Manifesto," *Marketing Management*, November/December 2008, pp. 24–29; Richard Ettenson and others, "Rethinking the 4 Ps," *Harvard Business Review,* January–February 2013, p. 26; and Roy McClean, "Marketing 101—4 C's versus the 4 P's of Marketing," www.customfitfocus.com/marketing-1.htm, accessed November 2013.
16. For more discussion of the chief marketing officer position, see Philip Kotler and Kevin Lane Keller, *Marketing Management*, 14th ed. (Upper Saddle River, NJ: Prentice Hall, 2012), p. 17; Natalie Zmuda, "When CMOs Learn to Love Data, They'll Be VIPs," *Advertising Age*, February 13, 2012, p. 2; "Customer Service: Make Room for a New Face on Your Team: The Rise of the Chief Customer Officer," *INC.,* April 2012, pp. 102+; and George S. Day and Robert Malcolm, "The CMO and the Future of Marketing," *Marketing Management,* Spring 2012, pp. 34–44.
17. Paul Albright, "Metrics Must Show Impact of Marketing on Revenue," *DM News,* December 1, 2011, p. 15; "Study Finds Marketers Don't Practice ROI They Preach," *Advertising Age*, March 11, 2012, http://adage.com/article/233243/; and "Accountability Remains Senior Marketers' Top Concern," *Marketing Charts,* March 7, 2013, www.marketingcharts.com/wp/topics/branding/accountability-remains-senior-marketers-top-concern-27565/.
18. For more on marketing dashboards and financial measures of marketing performance, see "We Believe Research Should Lead to Action," *Marketing News*, November 15, 2009, p. 30; Ofer Mintz and Imran S. Currim, "What Drives Managerial Use of Marketing Financial Metrics and Does Metric Use Affect Performance of Marketing-Mix Activities?" *Journal of Marketing,* March 2013, pp. 17–40; and http://marketingnpv.com/dashboard-platform, accessed November 2013.
19. For a full discussion of this model and details on customer-centered measures of return on marketing investment, see Roland T. Rust, Katherine N. Lemon, and Valerie A. Zeithaml, "Return on Marketing: Using Customer Equity to Focus Marketing Strategy," *Journal of Marketing*, January 2004, pp. 109–127; Roland T. Rust, Katherine N. Lemon, and Das Narayandas, *Customer Equity Management* (Upper Saddle River, NJ: Prentice Hall, 2005); Roland T. Rust, "Seeking Higher ROI? Base Strategy on Customer Equity," *Advertising Age,* September 10, 2007, pp. 26–27; Andreas Persson and Lynette Ryals, "Customer Assets and Customer Equity: Management and Measurement Issues," *Marketing Theory,* December 2010, pp. 417–436; and Kirsten Korosec, "'Tomāto, Tomäto'? Not Exactly," *Marketing News*, January 13, 2012, p. 8.
20. "Marketing Strategy: Diageo CMO: 'Workers Must Be Able to Count,'" *Marketing Week*, June 3, 2010, p. 5. Also see Art Weinstein and Shane Smith, "Game Plan: How Can Marketers Face the Challenge of Managing Customer Metrics?" *Marketing Management,* Fall 2012, pp. 24–32; and Francis Yu, "Why Is It So Hard to Prove ROI When Data and Metrics Are So Abundant?" *Advertising Age,* October 15, 2012, p. 27.

Chapter 3

1. Based on information from Ashley Vance, "Microsoft Sees a New Image of Itself in Windows 8," *Business Week*, October 29, 2012, pp. 41–42: Rolfe Winkler, "Microsoft's Marriage Made in Dell," *Wall Street Journal*, February 6, 2013, p. C14; Spencer Jakab, "Microsoft Holds More Than Meets the Eye," *Wall Street Journal*, January 23, 2013, p. C1; Rolfe Winkler, "Microsoft's Same Old New Problem," *Wall Street Journal*, January 25, 2013, p. C10; Ashlee Vance and Dina Bass, "Microsoft's Office 2013 Is Software for the Cloud," *Bloomberg Businessweek,* January 29, 2013, www.businessweek.com/articles/2013-01-29/microsofts-old-software-comes-with-a-new-image; Haydn Shaughnessy, "Here's How Microsoft Plans on Expanding Its Device and OS Business," *Forbes*, April 25, 2013, www.forbes.com/sites/haydnshaughnessy/2013/04/25/heres-how-microsoft-plans-on-expanding-its-device-and-os-business/?ss=strategies-solutions; Ritsuko Ando and Bill Rigby, "Microsoft Swallows Nokia's Phone Business for $7.2 Billion," September 3, 2013, www.reuters.com/article/2013/09/03/us-microsoft-nokia-idUSBRE98202V20130903;

and annual reports and other information from www.microsoft.com/investor/default.aspx, accessed November 2013.

2. Information from www.ikea.com, accessed November 2013.
3. Information from Robert J. Benes, Abbie Jarman, and Ashley Williams, "2007 NRA Sets Records," www.chefmagazine.com, accessed September 2007; and www.thecoca-colacompany.com/dynamic/press_center/ and www.cokesolutions.com, accessed November 2013.
4. See www.lifeisgood.com/#!/playmakers/, accessed November 2013.
5. World POPClock, U.S. Census Bureau, at www.census.gov/popclock/, accessed May 2013. This Web site provides continuously updated projections of the U.S. and world populations.
6. U.S. Census Bureau projections and POPClock Projection, at www.census.gov/main/www/popclock.html, accessed July 2013.
7. See Wayne Friedman, "Ad Dollars Shift as Boomers Age," *Media Daily News,* July 5, 2012, www.mediapost.com/publications/article/178187/#axzz2S9pYRPYV; and "The 50+ Demo Is Soaring," *AARP,* http://advertise.aarp.org/insights/, accessed November 2013.
8. See "Keeping Up with the Baby Boomers," *MarketWatch,* March 20,2012, www.marketwatch.com/story/keeping-up-with-the-baby-boomers-2012-03-20.
9. See www.eldertreks.com, accessed November 2013.
10. For more discussion, see Bernadette Turner, "Generation X. . . . Let's GO!" *New Pittsburgh Courier,* March 2–March 8, 2011, p. A11; Piet Levy, "Segmentation by Generation," *Marketing News*, May 15, 2011, pp. 20–23; and Leonard Klie, "Gen X: Stuck in the Middle," *Customer Relationship Management,* February 2012, pp. 24–29.
11. Julie Jargon, "DQ Dips into Humor," *Wall Street Journal,* May 26, 2011, p. B6; and "Dairy Queen and Subway Top Lists of Most Effective QSR Advertising," *Quick Serve Leader*, http://quickserveleader.com/article/dairy-queen-and-subway-top-lists-most-effective-qsr-advertising, accessed March 2013.
12. Piet Levy, "Segmentation by Generation," p. 23. Also see Sarah Mahoney, "Struggling, Gen Y Redefines Wants, Needs," *Marketing Daily,* March 5, 2012, www.mediapost.com/publications/article/169424/struggling-gen-y-redefines-wants-needs.html?print; and Greg Petro, "Millennial Engagement and Loyalty—Make Them Part of the Process," *Forbes,* March 21, 2013, www.forbes.com/sites/gregpetro/2013/03/21/millennial-engagement-and-loyalty-make-them-part-of-the-process/.
13. See Dale Buss, "Hamsterbranding: Kia and Chevy Know How to Score with Millennials," *BrandChannel,* July 30, 2012, www.brandchannel.com/home/post/2012/07/30/Kia-Hamsters-Millennials-073012.aspx; Kurt Earnst, "Kia Bares Its 2014 Soul, Offering a Better Ride," *Christian Science Monitor,* March 28, 2013, www.csmonitor.com/Business/In-Gear/2013/0328/Kia-bares-its-2014-Soul-offering-a-better-ride Kia Motors America; and www.youtube.com/watch?v=o0B5vuAYk94 and www.kia.com/us/#/soul/videos, accessed November 2013.
14. See Heather Chaet, "The Tween Machine," *Adweek,* June 25, 2012, www.adweek.com/print/141357.
15. The first quote is from Cynthia Boris, "Generation Z: If They're Awake, They're Online," *Marketing Pilgrim,* March 20, 2013, www.marketingpilgrim.com/2013/03/generation-z-if-theyre-awake-theyre-online.html. For the second quote and an excellent overall summary of Generation Z and its brand implications, see "Gen Z: Digital in Their DNA," *JWT*, April 2012, www.jwtintelligence.com/wp-content/uploads/2012/04/F_INTERNAL_Gen_Z_0418122.pdf.
16. See "GenZ: Digital in Their DNA"; and Shannon Bryant, "'Generation Z' Children More Tech-Savvy; Prefer Gadgets, Not Toys," *Marketing Forecast,* April 3, 2013, www.marketingforecast.com/archives/23277.
17. Robert Klara, "It's Not Easy Being Tween," *Adweek,* June 27, 2012, www.adweek.com/print/141378.
18. See "Netflix 'Just for Kids' Now on iPad," October 1, 2012, http://blog.netflix.com/2012/10/netflix-just-for-kids-now-on-ipad.html; and http://movies.netflix.com/Kids, accessed November 2013.
19. Heather Chaet, "The Tween Machine," *Adweek,* June 25, 2012, www.adweek.com/print/141357.
20. U.S. Census Bureau, "Households by Type: 2000 and 2010," Table 2, *Households and Families 2010*, April 2012, www.census.gov/prod/cen2010/briefs/c2010br-14.pdf; and "Modern Families," *Adweek,* August 20, 2012, pp. 14–15.
21. U.S. Census Bureau, "Facts for Features," March 2013, www.census.gov/newsroom/releases/archives/facts_for_features_special_editions/cb13-ff04.html; and U.S. Census Bureau, "America's Families and Living Arrangements: 2012," Table FG1, www.census.gov/hhes/families/data/cps2012.html, accessed July 2013.
22. See Marissa Miley and Ann Mack, "The New Female Consumer: The Rise of the Real Mom," *Advertising Age,* November 16, 2009, p. A1; and Christine Birkner, "Mom's the Word," *Marketing News,* May 15, 2011, p. 8.
23. U.S. Census Bureau, "Geographical Mobility/Migration," www.census.gov/population/www/socdemo/migrate.html, accessed September 2013.
24. See U.S. Census Bureau, "Metropolitan and Micropolitan Statistical Areas," www.census.gov/population/metro/, accessed June 2013; and "The 536 Micropolitan Statistical Areas of the United States of America," *Wikipedia,* http://en.wikipedia.org/wiki/List_of_Micropolitan_Statistical_Areas, accessed June 2013.
25. Mary C. Noonan and Jennifer L. Glass, "The Hard Truth about Telecommuting," *Monthly Labor Review*, June 2012, www.bls.gov/opub/mlr/2012/06/art3full.pdf.
26. See "About WebEx," www.webex.com/about-webex/index.html, accessed November 2013; "What Is Cloud Computing?" www.salesforce.com/cloudcomputing, accessed November 2013; and www.regus.com and http://grindspaces.com, accessed November 2013.
27. U.S. Census Bureau, "Educational Attainment," www.census.gov/hhes/socdemo/education/, accessed July 2013.
28. *S*ee U.S. Census Bureau, "The 2012 Statistical Abstract: Education," Tables 229 and 276, www.census.gov/compendia/statab/cats/education.html; and U.S. Department of Labor, "Employment Projections: 2010–2020 Summary," February 1, 2012, www.bls.gov/ooh/.
29. See U.S. Census Bureau, "U.S. Population Projections," www.census.gov/population/projections/, accessed June 2013; U.S. Census Bureau, "America's Foreign Born in the Last 50 Years," www.census.gov/how/infographics/foreign_born.html, accessed June 2013; and U.S. Census Bureau, "2012 National Population Projections," www.census.gov/population/projections/data/national/2012.html, accessed June 2013.
30. "New Initiative Aims to 'Imagine a Future' for One Million Black Girls over the Next Three Years," press release, July 2012, www.myblackisbeautiful.com/press/imagine_a_future_release.php; "Procter & Gamble's My Black Is Beautiful Honored with City of Cincinnati Proclamation," *PR Newswire,* May 21, 2010; and information from www.myblackisbeautiful.com, accessed November 2013.
31. "America's LGBT 2012 Buying Power Projected at $790 Billion," *Echelon Magazine*, March 27, 2012, www.echelonmagazine.com/index.php?id=2597&title=America%60s_LGBT_2012_Buying_Power_Projected_at_$790_Billion.
32. See Brandon Miller, "And the Winner Is . . ." *Out Traveler*, Winter 2008, pp. 64–65; Tanya Irwin, "American Airlines, GayCities Partner for Promo," *Marketing Daily,* January 15, 2012, www.mediapost.com/publications/article/165789/american-airlines-gaycities-partner-for-promo.html; Leanne Italie, "Gay-Themed Ads Are

Becoming More Mainstream," *Huffington Post,* March 6, 2013, www.huffingtonpost.com/2013/03/06/gay-themed-ads-mainstream-_n_2821745.html; and www.aa.com/rainbow, accessed November 2013.

33. Witeck-Combs Communications, "America's Disability Market at a Glance," http://www.witeck.com/wp/files/Americas-Disability-Market-at-a-Glance-FINAL-5-25-2006.pdf; and U.S. Census Bureau, "Nearly 1 in 5 People Have a Disability in the U.S., Census Bureau Reports," press release, July 25, 2012, www.census.gov/newsroom/releases/archives/miscellaneous/cb12-134.html.
34. Based on information from "50 Most Innovative Companies: Azul—For Converting Bus Riders into Frequent Fliers," www.fastcompany.com/most-innovative-companies/2011/profile/azul.php; "Azul CEO Neeleman on Brazil, U.S. Airline Industry," *Bloomberg Businessweek,* December 14, 2012, www.businessweek.com/videos/2012-12-14/azul-ceo-neeleman-on-brazil-u-dot-s-dot-airline-industry; and www.voeazul.com.br/, accessed November 2013.
35. See U.S. Census Bureau, "Income, Poverty, and Health Insurance Coverage in the United States: 2011," Table 2, September 2012, www.census.gov/hhes/www/hlthins/data/incpovhlth.
36. See "Warm Weather Puts Chill on Brands' Winters," *Advertising Age,* February 19, 2012, http://adage.com/print/232824; Alex Taylor III, "Toyota's Comeback Kid," *Fortune,* February 27, 2012, pp. 72–79; and Rick Newman, "Toyota's Back in the Fast Lane," *US News,* February 6, 2013, www.usnews.com/news/blogs/rick-newman/2013/02/06/toyotas-back-in-the-fast-lane.
37. The 2030 Water Resources Group, www.2030wrg.org, accessed June 2013; and "The World's Water," *Pacific Institute,* www.worldwater.org/data.html, accessed July 2013.
38. Information from www.timberland.com and http://earthkeepers.timberland.com/?camp=S:G:SPC:timberland_earthkeepers:TBL#/howweact, accessed June 2013.
39. See Maid Napolitano, "RFID Surges Ahead," *Materials Handling,* April 2012, pp. S48–S50; Walter Loeb, "Macy's Wins with Technology," *Forbes,* July 10, 2013, www.forbes.com/sites/walterloeb/2012/07/10/macys-wins-with-technology/; and "Burberry Introduces Smart Personalization for Shoppers," *Integer,* March 25, 2013, http://shopperculture.integer.com/2013/03/burberry-introduces-smart-personalization-for-shoppers.html.
40. See "A $1 Billion Project to Remake the Disney World Experience, Using RFID," www.fastcodesign.com/1671616/a-1-billion-project-to-remake-the-disney-world-experience-using-rfid#1; and Brooks Barnes, "At Disney Parks, a Bracelet Meant to Build Loyalty (and Sales), *New York Times,* January 7, 2013, p. B1.
41. See "Warby Parker—Stylish Buy One Give One Eyewear Helps Restore Vision and Hope," *Shop with Meaning,* http://shopwithmeaning.org/warby-parker-glasses-stylish-buy-one-give-one-eyewear/, accessed June 2013; and "Warby Parker: Do Good," www.warbyparker.com/do-good/#home, accessed November 2013.
42. John Biggs, "Three Things Warby Parker Did to Launch a Successful Lifestyle Brand," *TechCrunch,* May 7, 2013, http://techcrunch.com/2013/05/07/the-three-things-warby-parker-did-to-launch-a-successful-lifestyle-brand/.
43. See "The Growth of Cause Marketing," www.causemarketingforum.com/site/c.bkLUKcOTLkK4E/b.6452355/apps/s/content.asp?ct=8965443, accessed July 2013.
44. See "10 Crucial Consumer Trends for 2010," *Trendwatching.com,* http://trendwatching.com/trends/pdf/trendwatching%202009-12%2010trends.pdf; and "The F-Factor," *Trendwatching.com,* May 2011, http://trendwatching.com/trends/pdf/trendwatching%202009-12%2010trends.pdf.
45. Sherry Turkle, "The Flight from Conversation," *New York Times,* April 21, 2013, www.nytimes.com/2012/04/22/opinion/sunday/the-flight-from-conversation.html?pagewanted=all&_r=2&.
46. "The F-Factor," *Trendingwatching.com*, p. 1.
47. See Stuart Elliott, "This Column Was 100% Made in America," *New York Times,* February 15, 2012; Jeff Bennett and Suzanne Vranica, "Chrysler Dealers Defend 'Halftime in America' Ad," *Wall Street Journal,* February 9, 2012, http://online.wsj.com/article/SB10001424052970204136404577211391719237160.html; and Brent Snavely, "Chrysler Keeps 'Imported from Detroit' Tagline," *USA Today,* April 24, 2013, www.usatoday.com/story/money/cars/2013/04/24/chrysler-imported-from-detroit/2110611/.
48. www.lohas.com, accessed November 2013.
49. See www.tomsofmaine.com/home, accessed November 2013.
50. "U.S. Organic Market Surpasses $31 Billion in 2011," *What's New in Organic*, July 2012, www.ota.com/pics/documents/WhatsNews-54c.pdf.
51. The Pew Forum on Religion & Public Life, "Nones on the Rise," www.pewforum.org/Unaffiliated/nones-on-the-rise.aspx, October 9, 2012.
52. For more discussion, see Diana Butler Bass, "The End of Church," *Huffington Post*, February 18, 2012, www.huffingtonpost.com/diana-butler-bass/the-end-of-church_b_1284954.html.
53. Paula Forbes, "Taco Bell Ad: Thank You for Suing Us," January 28, 2011, *Eater,* http://eater.com/archives/2011/01/28/taco-bell-ad-thanks-firm-for-law-suit.php; "Law Firm Voluntarily Withdraws Class-Action Lawsuit against Taco Bell," April 19, 2011, http://money.msn.com/business-news/article.aspx?feed=BW&date=20110419&id=13327023; Bruce Horovitz, "Taco Bell Comes Out of Its Shell to Ring in New Menu," *USA Today,* February 20, 2012, www.usatoday.com/money/industries/food/story/2012-02-20/taco-bell/53157494/1; and www.tacobell.com/nutrition/food-facts/BeefQuality, accessed July 2013.

Chapter 4

1. Based on information found in Natalie Zmuda, "Pepsi Tackles Identity Crisis after Fielding Biggest Consumer-Research Push in Decades," *Advertising Age*, May 7, 2012, pp. 1, 14; Martinne Geller, "Pepsi Pushing People to 'Live for Now,'" *Reuters,* April 30, 2012, www.reuters.com/article/2012/04/30/us-pepsi-idUSBRE83T0EP20120430; Natalie Zmuda, "Pepsi Debuts First Global Campaign," *Advertising Age*, April 30, 2012, http://adage.com/article/print/234379; Jen Chaney, "Beyoncé, Now Brought to You by Pepsi," *Washington Post*, December 10, 2012; Ravi Balakrishnan, "Is the 'Right Here Right Now' Campaign a Game Changer for Pepsi?" *The Economic Times (Online),* February 6, 2012, http://articles.economictimes.indiatimes.com/2013-02-06/news/36949962_1_homi-battiwalla-pepsico-india-surjo-dutt; and Natalie Zmuda, "Pepsi Puts the Public in Super Bowl Spot," *Advertising Age,* January 7, 2013, p. 10.
2. Sheilynn McCale, "Apple Has Sold 300M iPods, Currently Holds 78 Percent of the Music Player Market," *The New Web,* October 4, 2011, http://thenextweb.com/apple/2011/10/04/apple-has-sold-300m--ipods-currently-holds-78-of-the-music-player-market/; "iPod Still Has 70% of the MP3 Player Market," *MacTech,* July 24, 2012, http://www.mactech.com/2012/07/24/ipod-still-has-70-mp3-player-market; and "Apple iPhone 5 and Stunning New iPods Set Stage for Strongest December Quarter Ever," *Forbes,* September 12, 2012, www.forbes.com.
3. Helen Leggatt, "IBM: Marketers Suffering from Data Overload," *BizReport,* October 12, 2011, http://www.bizreport.com/2011/10/ibm-marketers-suffering-data-overload.html#; Carey Toane, "Listening: The New Metric," *Strategy*, September 2009, p. 45; and Margarita Tartakovsky, "Overcoming Information Overload," *PsychCentral,* January 21, 2013, http://psychcentral.com/blog/archives/2013/01/21/overcoming-information-overload/.

4. Piet Levy, "A Day with Stan Sthanunathan," *Marketing News,* February 28, 2011, pp. 11+.
5. See www.walmartstores.com/Suppliers/248.aspx and http://retaillinkblog.com/what-is-walmarts-retail-link-system/3, accessed November 2013.
6. See James Aldridge, "USAA Posts $2 Billion in Net Income in 2011," *San Antonio Business Journal,* March 12, 2012; Scott Horstein, "Use Care with That Database," *Sales & Marketing Management*, May 2006, p. 22; Jean McGregor, "Customer Service Champs: USAA's Battle Plan," *Bloomberg BusinessWeek,* March 1, 2010, pp. 40–43; James Aldridge, "USAA Ranks High in Customer Satisfaction for Insurance, Banking," *Business Journal,* January 3, 2013, www.bizjournals.com/sanantonio/news/2013/01/03/usaa-ranks-high-in-customer.html; and www.usaa.com, accessed November 2013.
7. Based on information from Adam Ostrow, "Inside the Gatorade's Social Media Command Center," June 6, 2010, accessed at http://mashable.com/2010/06/15/gatorade-sical-media-mission-control/; Valery Bauerlein, "Gatorade's 'Mission': Using Social Media to Boost Sales," *Wall Street Journal Asia*, September 15, 2010, p. 8; and Natalie Zmuda, "Gatorade: We're Necessary Performance Gear," *Advertising Age*, January 2, 2012.
8. Example based on information from Michal Lev-Ram, "Samsung's Road to Mobile Domination," *Fortune,* February 4, 2013, pp. 99–101; Jason Gilbert, "Samsung Mocks iPhone 5, Apple Fanboys Again in New Galaxy S3 Commercial," *Huffington Post,* September 1, 2012, www.huffingtonpost.com/2012/09/20/samsung-mocks-iphone-5-commercial_n_1898443.html; and Suzanne Vranica, "Tweets Spawn Ad Campaigns," *Wall Street Journal,* October 22, 2012, p. B5.
9. Irena Slutsky, "'Chief Listeners Use Technology to Track, Sort Company Mentioned," *Advertising Age*, August 30, 2010, http://adage.com/digital/article?article_id=145618; also see Tina Sharkey, "Who Is Your Chief Listening Officer?" *Forbes,* March 3, 2012, www.forbes.com/sites/tinasharkey/2012/03/13/who-is-your-chief-listening-officer/.
10. Adam Lashinsky, "The Secrets Apple Keeps," *Fortune,* February 6, 2012, pp. 85–94.
11. George Chidi, "Confessions of a Corporate Spy," *Inc.*, February 2013, pp. 72–77.
12. See http://biz.yahoo.com/ic/101/101316.html, accessed July 2013; and Josh Kohn-Lindquist, "A Monstrous SWOT: Big Growth at a Cheaper Price," *The Motley Fool,* November 15, 2012, http://beta.fool.com/joryko/2012/11/15/monster-swot/16557/.
13. For more on research firms that supply marketing information, see Jack Honomichl, "2012 Honomichl Top 50," special section, *Marketing News*, June 2012. Other information from www.nielsen.com/us/en/measurement/retail-measurement.html and http://thefuturescompany.com/what-we-do/us-yankelovich-monitor, accessed September 2013.
14. See www.symphonyiri.com/?TabId=159&productid=83, accessed November 2013.
15. See Jennifer Reingold, "Can P&G Make Money in Places Where People Earn $2 a Day?" *Fortune*, January 17, 2011, pp. 86–91; and C. K. Prahalad, "Bottom of the Pyramid as a Source of Breakthrough Innovations," *Journal of Product Innovation Management*, January 2012, pp. 6–12.
16. For more discussion of online ethnography, see Pradeep K. Tyagi, "Webnography: A New Tool to Conduct Marketing Research," *Journal of American Academy of Business*, March 2010, pp. 262–268; Robert V. Kozinets, "Netnography: The Marketer's Secret Weapon," March 2010, accessed at http://info.netbase.com/rs/netbase/images/Netnography_WP; and http://en.wikipedia.org/wiki/Online_ethnography, accessed December 2013.
17. Example adapted from information found in "My Dinner with Lexus," *Automotive News,* November 29, 2010, www.autonews.com/apps/pbcs.dll/article?AID=/20101129/RETAIL03/311299949/1292; and "An Evening with Lexus," YouTube video, www.youtube.com/watch?v=LweS8EScADY, accessed December 2013.
18. See "Pew Internet: Health," *Pew Internet,* February 1, 2013, http://pewinternet.org/Commentary/2011/November/Pew-Internet-Health.aspx; and "Internet World Stats," accessed February 2013, www.internetworldstats.com/stats.htm.
19. For more information, see www.focusvision.com and www.youtube.com/watch?v=PG8RZl2dvNY, accessed November 2013.
20. Derek Kreindler, "Lexus Soliciting Customer Feedback with Lexus Advisory Board," August 24, 2010, *Automotive News*, www.autoguide.com/auto-news/2010/08/lexus-soliciting-customer-feedback-with-lexus-advisory-board.html; "20,000 Customers Sign up for the Lexus Advisory Board," August 30, 2010, accessed at www.4wheelsnews.com/20000-customers-signed-up-for-the-lexus-advisory-board/; and www.lexusadvisoryboard.com, accessed November 2013.
21. For more discussion of online behavioral and social tracking and targeting, see Amit Avner, "How Social Targeting Can Lead to Discovery," *Adotas*, February 7, 2012, www.adotas.com/2012/02/how-social-targeting-can-lead-to-discovery/; Edward Wyatt and Tanzina Vega, "Conflict over How Open 'Do Not Track' Talks Will Be," *New York Times*, March 30, 2012, p. B3; Thomas Claburn, "Microsoft Finds People Want More Privacy Control," *Informationweek–Online,* January 24, 2013, www.informationweek.com/windows/security/microsoft-finds-people-want-more-privacy/240146932; and Lisa M. Thomas, "We Know Where You've Been: Emerging Rules in Online Behavioral Advertising," *Computer and Internet Lawyer*, February 2013, pp. 16–19.
22. Based on information from "Time Warner Opens NYC Neuromarketing Lab," *Neuromarketing,* January 26, 2012, www.neurosciencemarketing.com/blog/articles/new-labs.htm; Amy Chozick, "These Lab Specimens Watch 3-D Television," *New York Times,* January 25, 2012, p. B3; and Sam Thielman, "Time Warner's Media Lab Knows What You Like to Watch," *Adweek,* February 4, 2013, http://www.adweek.com/news/technology/time-warner-s-media-lab-knows-what-you-watch-147045. Also see www.timewarnermedialab.com.
23. Jessica Tsai, "Are You Smarter Than a Neuromarketer?" *Customer Relationship Management*, January 2010, pp. 19–20.
24. See "NeuroFocus Received Gran Ogilvy Award from the Advertising Research Foundation," *PRNewswire,* April 2, 2009, accessed at www.neurofocus.com/news/ogilvy_neurofocus.htm; and Adam L. Penenberg, "NeuroFocus Uses Neuromarketing to Hack Your Brain," *Fast Company*, August 8, 2011, www.fastcompany.com/magazine/158/neuromarketing-intel-paypal.
25. Allison Schiff, "Macy's CMO Shares Loyalty Insights at NRF Big Show," *Direct Marketing News*, January 16, 2012, www.dmnews.com/macys-cmo-shares-loyalty-insights-at-nrf-big-show/article/223344/; and Alex Palmer, "Macy's Transformation," *Direct Marketing News*, April 1, 2012, www.dmnews.com/macys-transformation/article/233631/3/.
26. "1-800-Flowers.com Customer Connection Blooms with SAS Business Analytics," www.sas.com/success/1800flowers.html, accessed September 2013.
27. See www.pensketruckleasing.com/leasing/precision/precision_features.html, accessed November 2013.
28. Based on information in Ann Zimmerman, "Small Business; Do the Research," *Wall Street Journal*, May 9, 2005, p. R3; with additional information and insights from John Tozzi, "Market Research on the Cheap," *BusinessWeek*, January 9, 2008, www.businessweek.com/smallbiz/content/jan2008/sb2008019_352779.htm; "Understanding

the Basics of Small Business Market Research," *All Business,* http://www.allbusiness.com/marketing/market-research/2587-1.html#axzz2K8T92eOR, accessed February 2013; and www.bibbentuckers.com, accessed September 2013.

29. For some good advice on conducting market research in a small business, search "conducting market research," at www.sba.gov or see "Researching Your Market," *Entrepreneur*, www.entrepreneur.com/article/43024-1, accessed November 2013.
30. See "Top 25 Global Market Research Organizations," *Marketing News*, August 31, 2012, pp. 16+; and www.nielsen.com/us/en/about-us.html and www.nielsen.com/global/en.html?worldWideSelected=true, accessed November 2013.
31. For these and other examples, see "From Tactical to Personal: Synovate's Tips for Conducting Marketing Research in Emerging Markets," *Marketing News,* April 30, 2011, pp. 20–22. Internet stats are from http://data.worldbank.org/indicator/IT.NET.USER.P2, accessed July 2013.
32. Subhash C. Jain, *International Marketing Management*, 3rd ed. (Boston: PWS-Kent, 1990), p. 338. For more discussion on international marketing research issues and solutions, see Warren J. Keegan and Mark C. Green, *Global Marketing*, 6th ed. (Upper Saddle River, NJ: Prentice Hall, 2011), pp. 170–201.
33. See Andrew Roberts, "In Some Stores, All Eyes Are on You," *Bloomberg Businessweek*, December 10, pp. 32–33; and Emma K. McDonald, Hugh N. Wilson, and Unut Konus, "Better Customer Insight—In Real Time," *Harvard Business Review,* September 2012, pp. 102–107.
34. Tina Sharkey, "Who Is Your Chief Listening Officer?" *Forbes,* March 13, 2012, www.forbes.com/sites/tinasharkey/2012/03/13/who-is-your-chief-listening-officer/.
35. Juan Martinez, "Marketing Marauders or Consumer Counselors?" *CRM Magazine,* January 2011, accessed at www.destinationcrm.com. Also see Laure McKay, "Eye on Customers: Are Consumers Comfortable with or Creeped out by Online Data Collection Tactics?" *CRM Magazine,* January 2011, accessed at www.destinationcrm.com; Ki Mae Heussner, "Whose Life Is It, Anyway?" *Adweek,* January 16, 2012, pp. 22–26; and Ted Gotsch, "'Do Not Track' Privacy Effort Can Mislead Public, Experts Say," *Cybersecurity Policy Report*, November 5, 2012.
36. Thomas Clayburn, "Microsoft Finds People Want More Privacy Control," *Informationweek–Online,* January 24, 2013, www.informationweek.com/windows/security/microsoft-finds-people-want-more-privacy/240146932.
37. "ICC/ESOMAR International Code of Marketing and Social Research Practice," www.esomar.org/index.php/codes-guidelines.html, accessed July 2013. Also see "Respondent Bill of Rights," www.mra-net.org/ga/billofrights.cfm, accessed December 2013.
38. "FTC Complaint Charges Deceptive Advertising by POM Wonderful," September 27, 2010, http://www.ftc.gov/opa/2010/09/pom.shtm; Chris MacDonald, "Fruit Juice Ads and Sour Grapes," *Canadian Business*, July 16, 2012, p. 17; and Ashley Post, "FTC Issues Final Ruling against POM Wonderful," *Inside Counsel. Break News*, January 17, 2013.
39. Information at www.casro.org/codeofstandards.cfm#intro, accessed December 2013.

Chapter 5

1. Based on information found in Tom Foster, "The GoPro Army," *Inc.,* January 26, 2012, www.inc.com/magazine/201202/the-gopro-army.html; Tom Foster, "How GoPro Measures Social Engagement," *Inc.,* January 26, 2012, www.inc.com/magazine/201202/the-bare-truth-gopro-social--engagement.html; Peter Burrows, "GoPro's Incredible Small, Durable Camcorder," *Bloomberg Businessweek,* June 30, 2011, www.businessweek.com/magazine/gopros-incredible-small--durable-camcorder-07012011.html; Casey Newton, "GoPro Positioned to Grab Big Slice of Global Market," *San Francisco Chronicle,* May 6, 2011, p. D1; Peter Burrows, "GoPro Widens the View of Its Customer Base," *Bloomberg Businessweek,* October 23, 2012, pp. 43–44; Tim Peterson, "GoPro Boosts Sales via Snap and Share," *Adweek,* January, 2013, pp. 12–13; and www.GoPro.com and http://-gopro.com/about-us/, accessed September 2013.
2. Consumer expenditure figures from https://www.cia.gov/library/publications/the-world-factbook/geos/us.html. Population figures from the World POPClock, U.S. Census Bureau, www.census.gov/main/www/popclock.html, accessed March 2013. This Web site provides continuously updated projections of U.S. and world populations.
3. For these and other statistics, see Jeff Koyen, "The Truth about Hispanic Consumers," special advertising section, *Adweek,* March 12, 2012, pp. H1–H8; *Advertising Age Hispanic Fact Pack,* July 23, 2012, pp. 38–39; and U.S. Census Bureau, "U.S. Population Projections," http://www.census.gov/population/projections/data/national/2012/summarytables.html, accessed August 2013.
4. Laurie Sullivan, "Google Puts Resources behind U.S. Hispanic Market," *Online Media Daily,* January 27, 2012, accessed at www.mediapost.com/publications/article/143763/; "Hispanics More Active on Social Media Than Other Ethnicities," *eMarketer,* March 2, 2012, www.emarketer.com/Articles/Print.aspx?R=1008877; and "Google Hispanic Marketing Forum 2012: Case Studies," www.thinkwithgoogle.com/insights/library/videos/google-hispanic-2012-case-studies/, accessed March 2013.
5. "Nestlé's New Construye El Mejor Nido ('Create the Best Nest') Program Supports Hispanic Heritage Month," *PRNewswire*, September 29, 2011; Elena del Valle, "Nestlé Targets U.S. Spanish Speakers with New Efforts," *Hispanic Marketing and Public Relations*, November 9, 2011, www.hispanicmpr.com/2011/11/09/nestle-targets-u-s-spanish-speakers-with-new-efforts/; and www.elmejornido.com/, accessed September 2013.
6. See Nisa Islam Muhammad, "Black America's Buying Power Estimated to Reach $1.1 Trillion by 2015," *Final Call*, October 5, 2012, www.finalcall.com/artman/publish/Business_amp_Money_12/article_9251.shtml; information from "Reaching Black Consumers", www.reachingblackconsumers.com, accessed March 2013; and U.S. Census Bureau, "U.S. Population Projections," www.census.gov/population/projections/data/national/2012/summarytables.html, accessed August 2013.
7. "Ford Debuts African-American Campaign for 2013 Escape with Humorous Creative," *Target Market News*, June 6, 2012, http://targetmarketnews.com/storyid06071201.htm; "UniWorld Group: Multi-Cultural Marketing: The Work," www.ford.com/benew/, accessed July 2013.
8. See Sam Fahmy, "Despite Recession, Hispanic and Asian Buying Power Expected to Surge in U.S." November 4, 2010, accessed at www.terry.uga.edu/news/releases/2010/minority-buying-power-report.html; Neda Ulaby, "Corporate America Takes on Multilingual PR," NPR, May 5, 2011, www.npr.org/2011/05/05/135985502/-corporate-america-take-on-multilingual-pr; and U.S. Census Bureau, "U.S. Population Projections," www.census.gov/population/projections/data/national/2012/summarytables.html, accessed August 2013.
9. See Michael Applebaum, "Winning Campaigns," *AdWeek*, September 30, 2011, www.adweek.com/sa-article/winning-campaigns-135366; Intertrend, "I'm Connected," www.intertrend.com/#project?project_id=180162245350985, and https://apps.facebook.com/imconnected/, accessed July 2013.

10. Eleftheria Parpis, "Goodbye Color Codes," *Adweek,* September 27, 2010, pp. 24–25; "Ethnic Marketing: McDonald's Is Lovin' It," *Bloomberg BusinessWeek,* July 18, 2010, pp. 22–23; Stuart Elliott, "Mosaic Marketing Takes a Fresh Look at Changing Society," *New York Times,* July 18, 2011, p. B3; "Ethnic Advertising: One Message or Many?," *The Economist*, December 31, 2011; and Alex Frias, "5 Tips to Refresh Your Multicultural Marketing Strategy in 2013," *Forbes,* February 8, 2013, www.forbes.com/sites/theyec/2013/02/08/5-tips-to-refresh-your-multicultural-marketing-strategy-in-2013/.
11. Adam Bluestein, "Make Money in 2013 (and Beyond)," *Inc.,* December 2012/January 2013, pp. 58–65, here p. 64.
12. Based on information from Julie Liesse, "The Big Idea," *Advertising Age,* November 28, 2011, pp. C4–C6; and "Philips's 'Wake up the Town," www.ketchum.com/philips's-"wake-town," accessed July 2013.
13. Eve Tahmincioglu, "Majority of Dads Say They Do the Grocery Shopping," *Life Inc.,* June 15, 2012, http://lifeinc.today.com/_news/2012/06/15/12238737-majority-of-dads-say-they-do-the-grocery-shopping?lite; Samantha Murphy, "Stereotype Debunked: Women Buy More Technology Than Men," http://mashable.com/2012/01/09/women-and-technology/, January 9, 2012; and Chris Slocumb, "Women Outspend Men 3 to 2 on Technology Purchases," ClarityQuest, January 3, 2013, http://www.clarityqst.com/women-outspend-men-3-to-2-on-technology-purchases/.
14. See Laura A. Flurry, "Children's Influence in Family Decision Making: Examining the Impact of the Changing American Family," *Journal of Business Research,* April 2007, pp. 322–330; "Tween Years Prove to Be Rewarding for Toymakers," *USA Today,* December 22, 2010, p. 1B; and Michael R. Solomon, *Consumer Behavior,* 9th ed. (Upper Saddle River, NJ: Pearson Publishing, 2011), pp. 435–439.
15. Information on Acxiom's Personicx segmentation system accessed at www.acxiom.com/Ideas-and-Innovation/Self-Assessment-Tools/, November 2013.
16. For these and other examples and quotes, see www.carhartt.com, accessed September 2013.
17. See Stuart Elliott, "Penney's New Approach Takes Target-Like Tack," *New York Times,* January 25, 2012; and Laura Heller, "Mission Accomplished: J.C.Penney Was the Most Interesting Retailer of 2012," *Forbes,* February 8, 2013, www.forbes.com/sites/lauraheller/2013/02/08/mission-accomplished-jcpenney-was-the-most-interesting-retailer-of-2012/.
18. REI information from www.rei.com/aboutrei/about_rei.html and other pages at the www.rei.com site, accessed September 2013.
19. See www.thebenjamin.com/DreamDog.aspx, www.dogtv.com, and www.neuticles.com/faq.php; accessed September 2013.
20. See Jennifer Aaker, "Dimensions of Measuring Brand Personality," *Journal of Marketing Research*, August 1997, pp. 347–356; and Kevin Lane Keller, *Strategic Brand Management*, 3rd ed. (Upper Saddle River, New Jersey, 2008), pp. 66–67. For more on brand personality, see Lucia Malär, Harley Kromer, Wayne D. Hoyer, and Bettina Nyffenegger, "Emotional Brand Attachment and Brand Personality: The Relative Importance of the Actual and the Ideal Self," *Journal of Marketing,* July 2011, pp. 35–52; and Jack Neff, "Just How Well-Defined Is Your Brand's Ideal?" *Advertising Age,* January 16, 2012, p. 4.
21. See www.skullcandy.com, www.skullcandy.com/blog, and http://investors.skullcandy.com/index.cfm, accessed September 2013.
22. See Abraham H. Maslow, "A Theory of Human Motivation," *Psychological Review*, 50 (1943), pp. 370–396. Also see Maslow, *Motivation and Personality*, 3rd ed. (New York: HarperCollins Publishers, 1987); and Michael R. Solomon, *Consumer Behavior,* 9th ed. (Upper Saddle River, NJ: Prentice Hall, 2011), pp. 135–136.
23. Ellen Moore, "Letter to My Colleague: We Can Do Better," *Adweek,* December 22, 2010, www.adweek.com/news/advertising-branding/letter-my-colleagues-we-can-do-better-104084.
24. For more reading, see Lawrence R. Samuel, *Freud on Madison Avenue: Motivation Research and Subliminal Advertising in America* (Philadelphia: University of Pennsylvania Press, 2010); Charles R. Acland, *Swift Viewing: The Popular Life of Subliminal Influence* (Duke University Press, 2011); and Christopher Shea, "The History of Subliminal Ads," *Wall Street Journal*, February 15, 2012, http://blogs.wsj.com/ideas-market/2012/02/15/the-history-of-subliminal-ads/.
25. Example based on information found in John Berman, "Shrek Boosts Vidalia Onion Sales," June 29, 2010, http://abcnews.go.com/WN/shrek-boosts-vidalia-onion-sales/story?id=11047273; and "Vidalia Onion Committee Cinches Triple Crown of National Marketing Awards," October 20, 2011, www.vidaliaonion.org/news/vidalia_onion_committee_cinches_triple_crown_of_national_marketing_awards. Vidalia® is a registered certification mark of Georgia Department of Agriculture.
26. See Leon Festinger, *A Theory of Cognitive Dissonance* (Stanford, CA: Stanford University Press, 1957); Cynthia Crossen, "'Cognitive Dissonance' Became a Milestone in the 1950s Psychology," *Wall Street Journal*, December 12, 2006, p. B1; and Anupam Bawa and Purva Kansal, "Cognitive Dissonance and the Marketing of Services: Some Issues," *Journal of Services Research*, October 2008–March 2009, p. 31.
27. The following discussion draws from the work of Everett M. Rogers. See his *Diffusion of Innovations*, 5th ed. (New York: Free Press, 2003).
28. Nick Bunkley, "Hyundai, Using a Safety Net, Wins Market Share," *New York Times,* February 5, 2009; and Noreen O'Leary, "Chevy Launches 'Love It or Return It' Promo," *Adweek,* July 10, 2012, www.adweek.com/news/advertising-branding/chevy-launches-love-it-or-return-it-promo-141772.
29. Based on Rogers, *Diffusion of Innovation*, p. 281. For more discussion, see http://en.wikipedia.org/Everett_Rogers, accessed November 2013.
30. "High Definition Is the New Normal," *Nielsen Wire*, October 17, 2012, http://blog.nielsen.com/nielsenwire/media_entertainment/high-definition-is-the-new-normal/.
31. See www.omnexus.com/sf/dow/?id=plastics, accessed March 2010; and http://plastics.dow.com/, accessed September 2013.
32. This classic categorization was first introduced in Patrick J. Robinson, Charles W. Faris, and Yoram Wind, *Industrial Buying Behavior and Creative Marketing* (Boston: Allyn & Bacon, 1967). Also see James C. Anderson, James A. Narus, and Das Narayandas, *Business Market Management*, 3rd ed. (Upper Saddle River, NJ: Prentice Hall, 2009), Chapter 3; and Philip Kotler and Kevin Lane Keller, *Marketing Management*, 14th ed. (Upper Saddle River, NJ: Prentice Hall, 2012), Chapter 7.
33. Based on information from "Six Flags Entertainment Corporation: Improving Business Efficiency with Enterprise Asset Management," July 12, 2012, http://www-01.ibm.com/software/success/cssdb.nsf/CS/LWIS-8W5Q84?OpenDocument&Site=default&cty=en_us; and www-01.ibm.com/software/tivoli/products/maximo-asset-mgmt/, accessed November 2013.
34. Based on information from "USG Print Campaign," *Communications Arts,* June 6, 2012, www.commarts.com/exhibit/usg-corporation-print.html; "BtoB's Best—Integrated Campaign:

USG Corp.," October 8, 2012, www.btobonline.com/article/20121008/ADVERTISING02/310089984/btobs-best-integrated-campaign-less-than-200-000-usg-corp; and www.usg.com/company/about-usg.html and www.weighthasbeenlifted.com, accessed September 2013.

35. Robinson, Faris, and Wind, *Industrial Buying Behavior,* p. 14. Also see Kotler and Keller, *Marketing Management,* pp. 197–203.
36. See https://homedepotlink.homedepot.com/en-us/Pages/default.aspx, accessed May 2013.
37. For this and other examples, see "10 Great Web Sites," *BtoB Online*, September 13, 2010. Other information from www.shawfloors.com/About-Shaw/Retailer-Support, accessed November 2013.

Chapter 6

1. Based on information from Peter Himler, "Liquid Gold," *Forbes,* January 7, 2013, www.forbes.com/sites/peterhimler/2013/01/07/liquid-gold/; "P&G's Detergents (Tide, Ariel) More Valuable Than Gillette Razors," *Trefis,* June 10, 2010, www.trefis.com/stock/pg/articles/16380/pgs-detergents-tide-ariel-more-valuable-than-gillette-razors/2010-06-10; Dan Monk, "Procter & Gamble Washing out Rivals with Tide Pods, Analyst Says," *Business Courier,* September 7, 2012, www.bizjournals.com/cincinnati/print-edition/2012/09/07/procter-gamble-washing-out-rivals.html?page=all; and www.pg.com/en_US/investors/financial_reporting/annual_reports.shtml, and www.pg.com/en_US/brands/index.shtml, accessed July 2013.
2. See "Domino's Pizza Continues Bringing Mobile Ordering to the Masses with New Android App and Free Smartphone Offer," *Sacramento Bee,* February 27, 2012; and https://order.dominos.com/en/pages/content/content.jsp?page=apps&so=hpnf&panelnumber=3&panelname=apps, accessed September 2013.
3. See Joan Voight, "Marriott Chain Adds Some Local Flavor," *Adweek,* January 7, 2013, p. 9; "Renaissance Hotels Launches New Navigator Program to Help Guests Discover 'Hidden Gems' of Various Cities around the World," January 13, 2011, http://news.marriott.com/2011/01/renaissance-hotels-launches-new-navigator-program-to-help-guests-discover-hidden-gems-of-various-cit.html; and http://renaissance-hotels.marriott.com/r-navigator; accessed September 2013.
4. Keenan Mayo, "Amazon Eyes the Kids' Tablet Market," *Bloomberg Businessweek*, December 12, 2012, p. 34; and www.amazon.com/gp/feature.html?ie=UTF8&docId=1000863021, accessed September 2013.
5. Joel Stein, "The Men's 'Skin Care' Product Boom," *Time,* October 30, 2010, www.time.com/time/magazine/article/0,9171,2025576,00.html; Kristen Vinakmens, "Beauty Forecast 2013, *Cosmetics,* January/February 2013, p. 56; and www.menaji.com, accessed September 2013.
6. Noreen O'Leary, "Talk to Her," *Adweek,* February 27, 2012, www.adweek.com/news/advertising-branding/talk-her-138529; Andrew Adam Newman, "Axe Adds Fragrance for Women to Its Lineup," *New York Times*, January 8, 2012; and www.axeanarchy.axe.us/, accessed September 2013.
7. Example from Richard Baker, "Retail Trends—Luxury Marketing: The End of a Mega-Trend," *Retail*, June/July 2009, pp. 8–12.
8. See www.vfc.com/brands, accessed October 2013.
9. Trek example based on information from www.trekbikes.com/us/en/, accessed March 2013.
10. See Lisa Jennings, "CKE: Advertising, Turkey Burgers Drive Sales," *Restaurant News,* April 12, 2013, http://nrn.com/latest-headlines/cke-advertising-turkey-burgers-drive-sales; and Meaghan Murphy, "Nina Agdal Follows Kate Upton as Carl's Jr. Spokesmodel, Lands Super Bowl Commercial," *Fox News,* February 1, 2013, www.foxnews.com/entertainment/2013/02/01/nina-agdal-follows-kate-upton-as-carl-jr-spokesmodel-lands-super-bowl/.
11. See www.patagonia.com/us/ambassadors, accessed September 2013.
12. For more on the PRIZM Lifestyle Segmentation System, see www.MyBestSegments.com, accessed September 2013.
13. See www.starbucksfs.com and http://starbucksocs.com/, accessed November 2013.
14. "See Coca-Cola Launches Global Music Effort to Connect with Teens," *Advertising Age*, March 3, 2011, accessed at http://adage.com/print/149204; "Coca-Cola's London 2012 Game Plan: WooTeens through Music, Parents through Sustainability," *BrandChannel,* September 29, 2011, http://brandchannel.com/home/post/2011/09/29/Coca-Cola-London-2012-Move-to-the-Beat.aspx; Mark Miller, "Coca-Cola Music Strategy Strengthened by $10M Spotify Stake," *Brand Channel,* November 15, 2012, www.brandchannel.com/home/post/2012/11/15/Spotify-Coca-Cola-Stake-111512.aspx; David Moth, "Coca-Cola Reveals Lessons Learned from Its London Olympics Marketing," February 6, 2013, http://econsultancy.com/us/blog/62023-coca-cola-reveals-lessons-learned-from-its-london-olympics-marketing; and www.coca-cola.com/music, accessed July 2013.
15. See Michael Porter, *Competitive Advantage* (New York: Free Press, 1985), pp. 4–8, 234–236. For more recent discussions, see Kenneth Sawka and Bill Fiora, "The Four Analytical Techniques Every Analyst Must Know: 2. Porter's Five Forces Analysis," *Competitive Intelligence Magazine*, May–June 2003, p. 57; and Philip Kotler and Kevin Lane Keller, *Marketing Management*, 14th ed. (Upper Saddle River, NJ: Prentice Hall, 2012), p. 232.
16. Example adapted from Philip Kotler and Kevin Lane Keller, *Marketing Management*, 14th ed., p. 233. Also see Brad van Auken, "Leveraging the Brand: Hallmark Case Study," January 11, 2008, www.brandstrategyinsider.com; "Hallmark Breaks out of Special-Occasion Mold," *Advertising Age,* July 6, 2011, www.adage.com/print/228558; and www.hallmark.com, accessed September 2013.
17. Janet H. Cho, "American Greetings' CEO and Family Members Want to Buy the Company for $581 million," *Cleveland Plain Dealer,* September 26, 2012.
18. Store information found at www.walmartstores.com, www.wholefoodsmarket.com, and www.kroger.com, accessed September 2013.
19. Based on information from "America's Fastest-Growing Retailer," *Inc.*, September 1, 2010; David Moin, "Modcloth's M.O.," *Women's Wear Daily*, June 15, 2011; Jordan Speer, "Get Feedback. It Closes the Loop," *Apparel,* November 2011, p. 2; Kim-mai Cutler, "Tapping into Shifting Buyer Habits, ModCloth Launches and iPad App," *Tech Crunch,* February 7, 2013, http://techcrunch.com/2013/02/07/modcloth-ipa/; and www.modcloth.com, accessed September 2013.
20. See Cotton Timberlake, "With Stores Nationwide, Macy's Goes Local," *Bloomberg BusinessWeek,* October 4–10, 2010, pp. 21–22; Robert Klara, "For the New Macy's, All Marketing Is Local," *Adweek,* June 7, 2010, pp. 25–26; "Macy's Launches Millennial Strategy," *MRketplace,* March 22, 2012, www.mrketplace.com/30516/macys-launches-millennial-strategy/#; and Zacks Equity Research, "Macy's January Sales Soar," *Yahoo!Finance,* February 8, 2013, http://finance.yahoo.com/news/macys-january-sales-soar-180843732.html. For other localization examples, see Philip Kotler and Kevin Lane Keller, *Marketing Management*, 14th ed. (Upper Saddle River, NJ: Prentice Hall, 2012), pp. 234–235.

21. Based on information found in Samantha Murphy, "SoLoMo Revolution Picks up Where Hyperlocal Search Left Off," *Mashable*, January 12, 2012, http://mashable.com/2012/01/12/solomo-hyperlocal-search/; "Localeze/15miles Fifth Annual comScore Local Search Usage Study Reveals SoLoMo Revolution Has Taken Over," *Business Wire*, February 29, 2012; and Joe Ruiz, "What Is SoMoLo and Why Is It Important to Marketers?" *Business2Community*, February 1, 2013, www.business2community.com/marketing/what-is-somolo-and-why-is-it-important-to-marketers-0395281.
22. Based on information found in Gwendolyn Bounds, "The Rise of Holiday Me-tailers," *Wall Street Journal*, December 8, 2010, p. D1; Abbey Klaassen, "Harley-Davidson Breaks Consumer-Created Work from Victors & Spoils," *Advertising Age*, February 14, 2012, http://adage.com/print?article_id=148873; and www.harley-davidson.com/en_US/Content/Pages/H-D1_Customization/h-d1_customization.html, accessed September 2013.
23. Julie Jargon, "McDonald's under Pressure to Fire Ronald," *Wall Street Journal*, May 18, 2011; Stephanie Strom, "McDonald's Trims *Its* Happy Meal," *New York Times*, July 26, 2011; "McDonald's Introduces New Automatic Offerings of Fruit in Every Happy Meal," *PRNewswire*, January 20, 2012; and "Judge Dismisses Happy Meal Lawsuit," *Advertising Age*, April 4, 2012, http://adage.com/print/233946.
24. "Marketing to Kids: Toy Sellers' Bonanza or Parental Danger Zone?" Knowledge@Wharton, December 5, 2012, http://knowledge.wharton.upenn.edu/article.cfm?articleid=3127. Examples based on information from www.barbie.com/activities/fun_games/#whats-hot and www.nick.com/club/, accessed July 2013.
25. See "IC3 2011 Internet Crime Report Released," May 10, 2012, www.ic3.gov/media/default.aspx.
26. SUV sales data furnished by www.WardsAuto.com, accessed March 2013. Price data from www.edmunds.com, accessed March 2013.
27. See "Zappos Family Core Values," http://about.zappos.com/our-unique-culture/zappos-core-values; and http://about.zappos.com/, accessed September 2013.
28. Quote from "Singapore Airlines: Company Information," www.singaporeair.com, accessed September 2013.
29. Based on information from Kotler and Keller, *Marketing Management*, 14th ed., p. 336; and www.heartsonfire.com/Learn-About-Our-Diamonds.aspx, accessed March 2013.
30. See Bobby J. Calder and Steven J. Reagan, "Brand Design," in Dawn Iacobucci, ed., *Kellogg on Marketing* (New York: John Wiley & Sons, 2001), p. 61. For more discussion, see Kotler and Keller, *Marketing Management*, 14th ed., Chapter 10.

Chapter 7

1. See Anthony Kosner, "Mobile First: How ESPN Delivers to the Best Available Screen," *Forbes*, January 30, 2012, www.forbes.com/sites/anthonykosner/2012/01/30/mobile-first-how-espn-delivers-to-the-best-available-screen/2/; Nick Summers, "Big, Bigger, Biggest," *Newsweek*, January 23, 2012, p. 4; Kenneth R. Gosselin, "ESPN in the Zone," *McClatchy-Tribune Business News*, January 20, 2013; and information from http://mediakit.espn.go.com/home.aspx, http://espnmediazone.com/us/about-espn/, and www.espn.com accessed October 2013.
2. Based on information found at www.starbucks.com/about-us/our-heritage, accessed March 2013.
3. See "Kaiser Permanente: Health Isn't an Industry. It's a Cause." www.c-e.com/work/clients/Kaiser-Permanente.html, accessed March 2013.
4. See www.neworleansonline.com, www.michigan.org, and www.thebrandusa.com, accessed October 2013.
5. For more on social marketing, see Alan R. Andreasen, *Social Marketing in the 21st Century* (Thousand Oaks, CA: Sage Publications, 2006); Philip Kotler and Nancy Lee, *Social Marketing: Influencing Behaviors for Good*, 4th ed. (Thousand Oaks, CA: Sage Publications, 2011); and www.adcouncil.com and www.social-marketing.org, accessed October 2013.
6. Quotes and definitions from Philip Kotler, *Kotler on Marketing* (New York: Free Press, 1999), p. 17; and www.asq.org/glossary/q.html, accessed October 2013.
7. Based on information from "Nest Labs Introduces the World's First Learning Thermostat," October 25, 2011, www.nest.com/press/nest-labs-introduces-worlds-first-learning-thermostat/; Katie Fehrenbacher, "'Hundreds of Thousands' of Nest Learning Thermostats Sold," *GigaOM*, September 4, 2012, http://gigaom.com/2012/09/04/hundreds-of-thousands-of-nest-learning-thermostats-sold/; and www.nest.com/living-with-nest/, accessed October 2013.
8. Andy Goldsmith, "Coke vs. Pepsi: The Taste They Don't Want You to Know About," *The 60-Second Marketer*, www.60secondmarketer.com/60SecondArticles/Branding/cokevs.pepsitast.html, accessed September 2011. Also see, Hans Villarica, "This Is Why You Fall in Love with Brands," *The Atlantic*, April 13, 2012, www.theatlantic.com/business/archive/2012/04/this-is-why-you-fall-in-love-with-brands/255448/.
9. See http://cutieskids.com/what-is-a-cutie/, accessed October 2013.
10. See Christine Birkner, "Packaging: Thinking outside of the Box," *Marketing News*, March 30, 2011, pp. 12–15; "FMI—Supermarket Facts," www.fmi.org/facts_figs/?fuseaction=superfact, accessed May 2013; and "Our Retail Divisions," http://news.walmart.com/news-archive/2005/01/07/our-retail-divisions, accessed May 2013.
11. See Collin Dunn, "Packaging Design at Its Worst," *Treehugger.com*, July 6, 2009, www.treehugger.com/galleries/2009/07/packaging-design-at-its-worst.php; "The Sustainable and Green Packaging Market: 2011–2021," *PR Newswire*, December 1, 2011; and "The Gallery of Wrap Rage," www.amazon.com/Packaging-Videos-Green/b?ie=UTF8&node=1234279011, accessed May 2013.
12. Based on information from "PUMA Clever Little Bag," www.idsa.org/puma-clever-little-bag, accessed March 2012; and www.puma.com/cleverlittlebag, accessed October 2013.
13. Natalie Zmuda, "What Went into the Updated Pepsi Logo," *Advertising Age*, October 27, 2008, p. 6; "New Pepsi Logo Kicks off Campaign," *McClatchy-Tribune Business News*, January 15, 2010; and "Pepsi Logo—Design and History," February 4, 2011, www.logodesignsense.com/blog/pepsi-logo-design/.
14. See "Leggo Your Logo," *Adweek*, December 6, 2010, p. 12; "New Gap Logo a Neural Failure," October 10, 2010, www.newscientist.com/blogs/shortsharpscience/2010/10/-normal-0-false-false-2.html; "Marketer in the News," *Marketing*, February 9, 2011, p. 8; Robert Klara, "New American Airlines Logo Triggers Ire and a Sense of Déjà vu," *Adweek*, January 18, 2013, www.adweek.com/print/146659; and www.designboom.com/design/futurebrand-american-airlines-rebrand/, accessed June 2013.
15. Based on information from "Company Values," www.llbean.com/customerService/aboutLLBean/company_values.html; www.llbean.com/customerService/aboutLLBean/company_history.html?nav=s1-ln; and other pages at www.llbean.com, accessed October 2013.

16. See the AT&T Support Web site, www.att.com/esupport/, accessed April 2013, and "BMW Adapts Apple Genius Model in Its Dealerships," *Advertising Age,* February 10, 2013, www.adage.com/print/239683.
17. Based on an example from Philip Kotler and Kevin Lane Keller, *Marketing Management,* 14th ed. (Upper Saddle River, NJ: Prentice Hall, 2012), p. 341, with additional information from http://en.wikipedia.org/wiki/BMW and www.bmwusa.com/standard/content/byo/default.aspx, accessed September 2013.
18. Information on Campbell Soup Company's product mix from http://investor.campbellsoupcompany.com/phoenix.zhtml?c=88650&p=irol-reportsannual, accessed June 2013.
19. See "Table 1.2.5 Gross Domestic Product by Major Type of Product," U.S. Bureau of Economic Analysis, January 27, 2012, www.bea.gov/national/nipaweb/TableView.asp?SelectedTable=19&Freq=Qtr&FirstYear=2009&LastYear=2011; and "List of Countries by GDP Sector Composition," http://en.wikipedia.org/wiki/List_of_countries_by_GDP_sector_composition, accessed April 2013.
20. Based on information from Leonard Berry and Neeli-Bendapudi, "Clueing in Customers," *Harvard Business Review*, February 2003, pp. 100–106; Jeff Hansel, "Mayo Hits the Blogosphere," *McClatchy-Tribune Business News*, January 22, 2009; "Mayo Clinic Model of Care," www.mayo.edu/pmts/mc4200-mc4299/mc4270.pdf, accessed August 2013; and www.mayoclinic.org, accessed September 2013.
21. See James L. Heskett, W. Earl Sasser, Jr., and Leonard A. Schlesinger, *The Service Profit Chain: How Leading Companies Link Profit and Growth to Loyalty, Satisfaction, and Value* (New York: Free Press, 1997); and Heskett, Sasser, and Schlesinger, *The Value Profit Chain: Treat Employees Like Customers and Customers Like Employees* (New York: Free Press, 2003). Also see John Marshall and Dave Mayer, "Activate a Brand Internally," *Marketing Management,* Winter 2012, pp. 37–44.
22. David Rohde, "The Anti-Walmart: The Secret Sauce of Wegmans Is People," *The Atlantic,* March 23, 2012, www.theatlantic.com/business/archive/2012/03/the-anti-walmart-the-secret-sauce-of-wegmans-is-people/254994/. Also see Carmine Gallo, "How Wegmans, Apple Store, and Ritz-Carlton Win Loyal Customers," *Forbes,* December 11, 2012, www.forbes.com/sites/carminegallo/2012/12/11/how-wegmans-apple-store-and-the-ritz-carlton-wins-loyal-customers/.
23. See annual reports and information accessed at http://phx.corporate-ir.net/phoenix.zhtml?c=132215&p=irol-irhome, October 2013.
24. See "United States: Prescription Drugs," www.statehealthfacts.org/profileind.jsp?sub=66&rgn=1&cat=5, accessed April 2013; and "Postal Facts," http://about.usps.com/who-we-are/postal-facts/welcome.htm, accessed June 2013.
25. See Terry Maxon, "Horrible Flight? Airlines' Apology Experts Will Make It up to You," *McClatchy-Tribune News Service*, August 24, 2010; and Katie Morell, "Lessons from Southwest Airlines' Stellar Customer Service," *ehotelier.com,* August 29, 2012, http://ehotelier.com/hospitality-news/item.php?id=23931_0_11_0M_C.
26. Adapted from Sarah Kessler, "The Future of the Hotel Industry and Social Media," *Mashable!*, October 19 2010, http://mashable.com/2010/10/18/hotel-industry-social-media/; and Jeff Williams, "Marriott's SM Team Gets It," *HD Leader,* September 14, 2010, http://hdleader.com/2010/09/14/marriotts-sm-team-gets-it/. Also see https://twitter.com/MarriottIntl, accessed August 2013.
27. For more discussion on the trade-offs between service productivity and service quality, see Roland T. Rust and Ming-Hui Huang, "Optimizing Service Productivity," *Journal of Marketing,* March 2012, pp. 47–66.
28. See "McAtlas Shrugged," *Foreign Policy*, May–June 2001, pp. 26–37; and Kotler and Keller, *Marketing Management*, 14th ed., p. 256.
29. Quotes from Jack Trout, "'Branding' Simplified," *Forbes*, April 19, 2007, www.forbes.com; and a presentation by Jason Kilar at the Kenan-Flagler Business School, University of North Carolina at Chapel Hill, Fall 2009.
30. For more on Young & Rubicam's BrandAsset Valuator, see W. Ronald Lane, Karen Whitehill King, and Tom Reichert, *Kleppner's Advertising Procedure*, 18th ed. (Upper Saddle River, NJ: Pearson Prentice Hall, 2011), pp. 83–84; "Brand Asset Valuator," *ValueBasedManagement.net*, www.valuebasedmanagement.net/methods_brand_asset_valuator.html, accessed June 2013; and http://bavconsulting.com, accessed June 2013.
31. See Millward Brown Optimor, "BrandZ Top 100 Most Valuable Global Brands 2012," www.millwardbrown.com/brandz/2012/Documents/2012_BrandZ_Top100_Chart.pdf.
32. See Scott Davis, *Brand Asset Management*, 2nd ed. (San Francisco: Jossey-Bass, 2002). For more on brand positioning, see Kotler and Keller, *Marketing Management*, 14th ed., Chapter 10.
33. See "For P&G, Success Lies in More Than Merely a Dryer Diaper," *Advertising Age*, October 15, 2007, p. 20; Jack Neff, "Stengel Discusses Transition at P&G," *Advertising Age*, July 21, 2008, p. 17; Jack Neff, "Just How Well-Defined Is Your Brand's Ideal?" *Advertising Age,* January 16, 2012, p. 4; and www.pampers.com, accessed June 2013.
34. See www.saatchi.com/the_lovemarks_company and www.lovemarks.com, accessed September 2013; and Aaron Ahuvia Rajeev and Richard P. Bagozzi, "Brand Love," *Journal of Marketing,* March 2012, pp. 1–16.
35. Susan Wong, "Foods OK, But Some Can't Stomach More Ad Increases," *Brandweek*, January 5, 2009, p. 7; and "Store-Brand Taste-Off," *Consumer Reports*, October 2012, p. 16.
36. See Trefis, "Private Label Surge Threatens Polo Ralph Lauren," *The Street*, July 8, 2010, www.thestreet.com/story/10801997/private-label-surge-threatens-polo-ralph-lauren.html; "Private Label Market Share Sets a New Record," *Store Brands Decisions,* June 28, 2011, www.storebrandsdecisions.com/news/2011/06/28/private-label-market-share-sets-a-new-record-; and "The Private World of Private Label Food Brands," *Food Processing*, August 3, 2012, www.foodprocessing.com/articles/2012/private-world-of-private-label.html.
37. See information from Ely Portillo, "In Weak Economy, Store Brands Prosper," *McClatchy-Tribune News Service,* March 18, 2011; "Top 35 Breakout: Who Sells the Most Private Label? *Private Label Buyer*, April 16, 2012, www.privatelabelbuyer.com/articles/86615--top-35-breakout---who-sells-the-most-private-label; http://news.walmart.com/media-library/, accessed April 2013; and www.wholefoodsmarket.com/products/365-everyday-value.php, accessed April 2013.
38. Pat Reynolds, "Shoppers Believe Private Label = National Brands in Different Packaging," *Packaging World,* February 26, 2013, www.packworld.com/venue/private-label/shoppers-believe-private-label-national-brands-different-packaging.
39. Hannah Karp, "Store Brands Step up Their Game, and Prices," *Wall Street Journal*, January 31, 2012, www.wsj.com; and "Weekly Watch: Billion-Dollar Brands," *Advertising Age,* October 29, 2012, p. 18.
40. "Top 125 Global Licensors Account for Billions in Retail Sales," *PR Newswire*, May 11, 2012, www.prnewswire.com/news-releases/top-125-global-licensors-account-for-billions-in-retail-sales-151108985.html; Jenna Goudreau, "Disney Princess Tops List of the 20 Best-Selling Entertainment Products," *Forbes,* September 17, 2012,

www.forbes.com/sites/jennagoudreau/2012/09/17/disney-princess-tops-list-of-the-20-best-selling-entertainment-products/; and www.licensingexpo.com, accessed June 2013.

41. For this and other examples, see "Tim Hortons and Cold Stone: Co-Branding Strategies," *BusinessWeek*, July 10, 2009, www.businessweek.com/smallbiz/content/jul2009/sb20090710_574574.htm; Dan Beem, "The Case for Co-Branding," *Forbes*, March 16, 2010, accessed at www.forbes.com; and www.timhortons.com/ca/en/about/investing.html, accessed November 2013.
42. Quote from www.apple.com/ipod/nike/, accessed June 2013.
43. See "The Brand That Launched 1000 Ships," *Bloomberg Businessweek*, October 3–October 9, 2011, p. 30; and www.fritolay.com/our-snacks/doritos.html, accessed June 2013.
44. For interesting lists of good and bad brand extension candidates, see Christina Austin, "See the 10 Worst Brand Extensions Currently on the Market," *Business Insider*, February 9, 2013, www.businessinsider.com/the-10-worst-brand-extensions-2013-2?op=1; and Brad Tuttle, "Why Some Brand Extensions Are Brilliant and Others Are Just Awkward," *Time*, February 7, 2013, http://business.time.com/2013/02/07/why-some-brand-extensions-are-brilliant-and-others-are-just-awkward/.
45. Paul Hochman, "Ford's Big Reveal," *Fast Company*, April 2010, pp. 90–95.
46. "Global Marketers 2012," *Advertising Age*, December 10, 2012, pp. 16–18.
47. Stephen Cole, "Value of the Brand," *CA Magazine*, May 2005, pp. 39–40. Also see "The Power of Customer Service," *Fortune*, December 3, 2012, www.timeincnewsgroupcustompub.com/sections/121203_Disney.pdf.

Chapter 8

1. Brian X. Chen, "Samsung Emerges as a Potent Rival to Apple's Cool," *New York Times*, February 11, 2013, p. B1; Chris Foresman, "Apple Owns U.S. Smartphone Market while Samsung Dominates Worldwide," *ARS Technica*, August 9, 2012, http://arstechnica.com/apple/2012/08/apple-owns-us-smartphone-market-while-samsung-dominates-worldwide/; Laurie Burkitt, "Samsung Courts Consumers, Marketers," *Forbes*, June 7, 2010, p. 27; "Best Global Brands 2012: Samsung," *Interbrand*, www.interbrand.com/en/best-global-brands/2012/Samsung; "Samsung Garners the Most 2012 International Design Excellence Awards," July 1, 2012, www.samsung.com/us/news/20208; Max Chafkin, "Samsung: For Elevating Imitation to an Art Form," *Fast Company*, March 2013, p. 108; and information from www.sony.com and www.samsung.com, accessed October 2013.
2. "Apple Reports Record Results: 47.8 Million iPhones Sold; 22.9 Million iPads Sold," January 23, 2013, www.apple.com/pr/library/2013/01/23Apple-Reports-Record-Results.html.
3. Marsha Lindsey, "8 Ways to Ensure Your New-Product Launch Succeeds," *Fast Company*, April 3, 2012, www.fastcompany.com/1829483/8-ways-ensure-your-new-product-launch-succeeds.
4. See Paul Sloane, "Source of Innovative Ideas," *Yahoo! Voices*, June 16, 2010, http://voices.yahoo.com/sources-innovative-ideas-6185898.html; and "R&D Spending Returns to Pre-ecession Levels, Finds Booz & Company Global Innovation 1000 Study," October 10, 2012, www.booz.com/global/home/press/display/51296501.
5. Based on information from "Hack Week @ Twitter," January 25, 2012, blog.twitter.com/2012/01/hack-week-twitter.html; "Twitter's 'Hack Week,' 7 Days for New Ideas," *Mashable*, January 26, 2012, http://mashable.com/2012/01/26/twitter-hack-week/; "Hack Week: Efficiency Edition," April 26, 2012, http://blog.twitter.com/2012/04/hack-week-efficiency-edition.html; and "Twitter's 'Hack Week,' 7 Days for New Ideas," *Mashable* video, www.youtube.com/watch?v=8dZZqDOu80o, accessed October 2013.
6. Based on information from Matthew Kronsberg, "How Lego's Great Adventure in Geek-Sourcing Snapped into Place and Boosted the Brand," *Fast Company*, February 2, 2012, www.fastcompany.com/1812959/lego-cuusoo-minecraft-lord-of-rings-hayabusa; "LEGO Minecraft Micro World Details Unveiled, Available for Pre-Order," February 16, 2012, http://aboutus.lego.com/en-us/news-room/2012/february/lego-minecraft-micro-world/; Yann Cramer, "LEGO Minecraft: A Lesson in Crowdsourcing," *Innovation Excellence*, December 27, 2012, www.innovationexcellence.com/blog/2012/12/27/lego-minecraft-a-lesson-in-crowdsourcing/; and http://lego.cuusoo.com/, accessed October 2013.
7. See Andrew Abbott, "Announcing the PayPal Mobile App Challenge Winners!" February 8, 2011, http://topcoder.com/home/x/2011/02/08/announcing-the-paypal-mobile-app-challenges-winners/; and www.topcoder.com and https://www.x.com, accessed June 2013.
8. Guido Jouret, "Inside Cisco's Search for the Next Big Idea," *Harvard Business Review*, September 2009, pp. 43–45; Geoff Livingston, "Real Challenges to Crowdsourcing for Social Good," *Mashable*, October 12, 2010, http://mashable.com/2010/10/12/social-good-crowdsourcing; and www.cisco.com/web/solutions/iprize/index.html, accessed August 2013.
9. See George S. Day, "Is It Real? Can We Win? Is It Worth Doing?" *Harvard Business Review*, December 2007, pp. 110–120.
10. This example is based on Tesla Motors and information obtained from www.teslamotors.com, accessed April 2013. Also see, Jim Motavalli, "Why the Tesla Model X Is a Home Run," *Forbes*, February 13, 2012, www.forbes.com/sites/eco-nomics/2012/02/13/why-the-tesla-model-x-is-a-home-run/; and Ryan Bradley, "Full Charge Ahead," *Fortune*, February 4, 2013, pp. 10–13.
11. Information from www.patagonia.com/us/ambassadors and http://weartest.newbalance.com, accessed May 2013.
12. Susan Berfield, "Baristas, Patrons Steaming over Starbucks VIA," *Bloomberg BusinessWeek*, November 13, 2009; and Jodi Westbury, "Starbucks VIA—A Success to Build On," www.jodiwestbury.com/2011/01/28/starbucks-via-a-success-to-build-on/, accessed January 28, 2011; and "Starbucks Exceeds Goals with More Than 100 Million Starbucks K-Pacs Packs Shipped," *Business Wire*, January 27, 2012.
13. Based on information from "How Post Pulled off a Six-Month Cereal Launch," *Advertising Age*, February 10, 2013, p. 12.
14. For information on BehaviorScan Rx, see www.symphonyiri.com/?TabId=159&productid=75, accessed May 2013.
15. See Jack Neff, "P&G Reinvents Laundry with $150 Million Tide Pods Launch," *Advertising Age*, April 26, 2011, www.adage.com/print/227208/; and Sheila Shayon, "Microsoft Unleashes Global Marketing Blitz for Windows 8, New Devices," *BrandChannel*, October 25, 2012, www.brandchannel.com/home/post/2012/10/25/Microsoft-Global-Windows-8-Launch-102512.aspx.
16. Beth Snyder Bulik, "Microsoft Spends $1B on Operating System Launch, But Are Ads Windows-Washing?" *Advertising Age*, October 29, 2012, p. 10; and Mary Jo Foley, "Microsoft to Open Its Holiday Pop-Up Retail Stores on October 26," *ZDNet*, October 2, 2012, www.zdnet.com/microsoft-to-open-its-holiday-pop-up-retail-stores-on-october-26-7000005113/.
17. See Robert G. Cooper, "Formula for Success," *Marketing Management*, March–April 2006, pp. 19–23; Christoph Fuchs and Martin Schreier, "Customer Empowerment in New Product Development," *Product Innovation Management*, January 2011, pp. 17–32; and Robert Safien, "The Lessons of Innovation," *Fast Company*, March 2012, p. 18.

18. This Samsung example is based on information from Chen, "Samsung Emerges as a Potent Rival to Apple's Cool," p. B1.
19. Based on information from Peter Burrows, "Google's Bid to Be Everything to Everyone," *Bloomberg Businessweek,* February 20–February 26, 2012, pp. 37–38; Chuck Salter, "Google: The Faces and Voices of the World's Most Innovative Company," *Fast Company,* March 2008, pp. 74–88; David Pogue, "Geniuses at Play, on the Job," *New York Times,* February 26, 2009, p. B1; "World's 50 Most Innovative Companies," *Fast Company,* March 2013, pp. 100–102; and www.google.com and www.googlelabs.com, accessed September 2013.
20. This definition is based on one found in Bryan Lilly and Tammy R. Nelson, "Fads: Segmenting the Fad-Buyer Market," *Journal of Consumer Marketing*, Vol. 20, No. 3, 2003, pp. 252–265.
21. See Katya Kazakina and Robert Johnson, "A Fad's Father Seeks a Sequel," *New York Times*, May 30, 2004, www.nytimes.com; John Schwartz, "The Joy of Silly," *New York Times*, January 20, 2008, p. 5; and www.crazyfads.com, accessed October 2013.
22. Based on information from Stuart Elliott, "3M Says, 'Go Ahead, Make Something of It,'" *New York Times,* January 28, 2013, www.nytimes.com/2013/01/28/business/mutfund/3m-says-go-ahead-make-something-of-it.html?pagewanted=2&tntemail0=y&_r=3&emc=tnt; and "Post-it Brand. Go Ahead," www.youtube.com/watch?v=sWDplhUfvU4, accessed October 2013.
23. Stephanie Clifford, "Go Digitally, Directly to Jail? Classic Toys Learn New Clicks," *New York Times,* February 25, 2012; and http://mattelapptivity.com/app-toys-games/hot-wheels/, accessed July 2013.
24. Elaine Wong, "Kellogg Makes Special K a Way of Life," *Adweek*, June 7, 2010, p. 18; and www.kellogg.com and www.specialk.com, accessed October 2013.
25. For a more comprehensive discussion of marketing strategies over the course of the PLC, see Philip Kotler and Kevin Lane Keller, *Marketing Management*, 14th ed. (Upper Saddle River, NJ: Prentice Hall, 2012), pp. 310–317.
26. See Nick Bunkley, "Toyota Still Not Off the Hook," *Automotive News,* December 31, 2012, p. 3.
27. Based on information found in Celia Hatton, "KFC's Finger-Lickin' Success in China," CBS News, March 6, 2011, www.cbsnews.com/2100-3445_162-20039783.html; Maggie Starvish, "KFC's Explosive Growth in China," *HBS Working Knowledge,* June 17, 2011, http://hbswk.hbs.edu/cgi-bin/print/6704.html; David E. Bell and Mary L. Shelman, "KFC's Radical Approach to China," *Harvard Business Review,* November 2011, pp. 137–142; and www.yum.com/brands/china.asp, accessed October 2013.
28. Information from www.db.com, accessed November 2013.
29. Information from www.interpublic.com and www.mccann.com, accessed November 2013.
30. See "Global Powers of Retailing 2012," www.deloitte.com; "Walmart Corporate International," http://walmartstores.com/AboutUs/246.aspx, accessed October 2013; and information from www.carrefour.com, accessed October 2013.

Chapter 9

1. Quotes, extracts, and other information based on Glenn Llopis, "Why Trader Joe's Stands out from All the Rest in the Grocery Business," *Forbes,* September 5, 2011, www.forbes.com/sites/glennllopis/2011/09/05/why-trader-joes-stands-out-from-all-the-rest-in-the-grocery-business/; Shan Li, "Trader Joe's Tries to Keep Quirky Vibe as It Expands Quickly," *Los Angeles Times*, October 26, 2011; Alicia Wallace, "Crowded Boulder Grocery Field Awaits Trader Joe's," *McClatchy-Tribune Business News,* January 30, 2012; Anna Sowa, "Trader Joe's: Why the Hype?" *McClatchy-Tribune Business News,* March 27, 2008; Beth Kowitt, "Inside the Secret World of Trader Joe's," *Fortune*, August 23, 2010, pp. 86–96; "SN's Top 75 Retailers & Wholesalers 2013," *Supermarket News,* http://supermarketnews.com/top-75-retailers-wholesalers-2013; Emma Sapong, "Trader Joe's Has Them Wowed," *McClatchy-Tribune Business News,* February 17, 2013; and www.traderjoes.com, accessed October 2013.
2. For more on the importance of sound pricing strategy, see Thomas T. Nagle, John Hogan, and Joseph Zale, *The Strategy and Tactics of Pricing: A Guide to Growing More Profitably*, 5th ed. (Upper Saddle River, NJ: Prentice Hall, 2011), Chapter 1.
3. Based on information from Anne Marie Chaker, "For a Steinway, I Did It My Way," *Wall Street Journal*, May 22, 2008, www.wsj.com; Brett Arends, "Steinway & Sons: A Grand Investment?" *SmartMoney,* March 20, 2012, www.smartmoney.com/invest/stocks/steinway--sons-a-grand-investment-1332195987741/; and www.steinway.com/steinway and www.steinway.com/steinway/quotes.shtml, accessed October 2013.
4. See Christine Birkner, "Marketing in 2012: The End of the Middle?" *Marketing News,* January 31, 2012, pp. 22–23. Also see Marianne Wilson, "Report: Consumers Still Frugal: Shopping Less Channels," *Chain Store Age,* February 25, 2013, http://chainstoreage.com/article/report-consumers-still-frugal-shopping-less-channels.
5. Based on information from http://aldi.us/us/html/company/about_aldi_ENU_HTML.htm; http://aldi.us/us/html/company/17541_17551_ENU_HTML.htm; and www.aldiuscareers.com/OurVision.aspx, accessed October 2013.
6. See Maria Puente, "Theaters Turn up the Luxury," *USA Today*, March 12, 2010, p. 1A; "Expansion Ahead for iPic Entertainment: Two New Visionary Movie Theater Escapes Announced for Boca Raton and Hallandale, Florida," *Business Wire,* February 16, 2012; and information from http://dinein.amctheatres.com, accessed October 2013.
7. Based on information from "Pharmaca Integrative Pharmacy," *Retail Merchandiser*, May/June 2010, p. 30; Rachel Brown, "Pharmaca Marries Mainstream," *WWD,* May 11, 2007, p. 10; Amanda Gaines and Lisa Marshall, "Transform Your Store," *Natural Foods Merchandiser*, January 2012, pp. 23+; and www.pharmaca.com, accessed October 2013.
8. See Stan Schroeder, "Vertu's Luxury Android Smartphone Costs $10,000, *Mashable,* February 12, 2013, http://mashable.com/2013/02/12/vertu-ti/; and www.vertu.com, accessed October 2013.
9. Based on information found in Joseph Weber, "Over a Buck for Dinner? Outrageous," *BusinessWeek*, March 9, 2009, p. 57; and Tom Mulier and Matthew Boyle, "Dollar Dinners from ConAgra's Threatened by Costs," *Bloomberg Businessweek,* August 19, 2010, www.businessweek.com.
10. For more information, see Annie Gasparro, "Whole Foods Aims to Alter 'Price Perception' as It Expands," *Wall Street Journal,* February 15, 2012; Ben Fox Rubin, "Whole Foods' Profit Rises 33%," *Wall Street Journal,* February 8, 2012; Annie Gasparro, "More Affordable Groceries Are Costing Whole Foods," *Wall Street Journal,* February 14, 2013, http://online.wsj.com/article/SB10001424127887324616604578302780625291880.html; and www.wholefoodsmarket.com, accessed September 2013.
11. Based on information found in Jens Hansegard, "IKEA Taking China by Storm," *Wall Street Journal,* March 26, 2012, http://online.wsj.com/article/SB10001424052702304636404577293083481821536.html; Mei Fong, "IKEA Hits Home in China; The Swedish Design Giant, Unlike Other Retailers, Slashes Prices for

the Chinese," *Wall Street Journal*, March 3, 2006, p. B1; Anna Ringstrom, "One Size Doesn't Fit All: IKEA Goes Local for China, India," *The Globe and Mail*, March 7, 2013, www.theglobeandmail.com/article9444097/; and www.ikea.com/ms/en_US/about_ikea/facts_and_figures/index.html, accessed July 2013.

12. Donna Tam, "16GB Kindle Fire HD Costs Amazon $207 to Make," *CNET News*, November 5, 2012, http://news.cnet.com/8301-1023_3-57545487-93/.
13. See http://www.dollarshaveclub.com/, accessed July 2013.
14. Example based on information from Duane Stanford, "Coke Engineers Its Orange Juice—With an Algorithm," *Bloomberg Businessweek*, January 31, 2013, http://www.businessweek.com/articles/2013-01-31/coke-engineers-its-orange-juice-with-an-algorithm#p2.
15. For this and other examples, see Peter Coy, "Why the Price Is Rarely Right," *Bloomberg Businessweek*, February 1 & 8, 2010, pp. 77–78.
16. See Anthony Allred, E. K. Valentin, and Goutam Chakraborty, "Pricing Risky Services: Preference and Quality Considerations," *Journal of Product and Brand Management*, Vol. 19, No. 1, 2010, p. 54, Kenneth C. Manning and David E. Sprott, "Price Endings, Left-Digit Effects, and Choice," *Journal of Consumer Research*, August 2009, pp. 328–336; and Martin Lindstrom, "The Psychology behind the Sweet Spots of Pricing," *Fast Company*, March 27, 2012, www.fastcompany.com/1826172/psychology-behind-sweet-spots-pricing.
17. See Peter Weedfald, "Address Price-Roaming Rather Instead of Worrying about Showrooming," *Dealerscope*, January 2013, www.dealerscope.com/article/address-price-roaming-instead-worrying-showrooming/1; and Dana Mattioli, "Holiday Price War Rages in Real Time," *Wall Street Journal*, November 24, 2012, p. A1.
18. See Justin D. Martin, "Dynamic Pricing: Internet Retailers Are Treating Us Like Foreign Tourists in Egypt," *Christian Science Monitor*, January 7, 2011; Patrick Rishe, "Dynamic Pricing: The Future of Ticket Pricing in Sports," *Forbes*, January 6, 2012, www.forbes.com/sites/prishe/2012/01/06/dynamic-pricing-the-future-of-ticket-pricing-in-sports/; and Mike Southon, "Time to Ensure the Price Is Right," *Financial Times*, January 21, 2012, p. 30.
19. For more on showrooming, see Ann Zimmerman, "Can Retailers Halt 'Showrooming'?" *Wall Street Journal*, April 11, 2012, p. B1; Bob Ankosko, "Retailers Embrace Showrooming," *Dealerscope*, January 2013, www.dealerscope.com/article/mobile-shopping-seen-opportunity-engage-customers/1; and "Consumers Visit Retailers, Then Go Online for Cheaper Sources," *Adweek*, March 14, 2013, www.adweek.com/print/147777.
20. Matthew Boyle, "Unilever: Taking on the World, One Stall at a Time," *Bloomberg Businessweek*, January 7, 2013, pp. 18–20.
21. Information from Maureen Morrison, "Seattle's Best Launches First Major Ad Campaign," *Advertising Age*, January 10, 2011, www.adage.com/print/148118; "Starbuck's Kid Brother Grows up Fast," *Bloomberg Businessweek*, April 25–May 1, 2011, pp. 26–27; "Seattle's Best Coffee: Forget the Flowers, Poems, and Chocolate," *Marketing Weekly News*, February 25, 2012, p. 585; and www.seattlesbest.com and www.starbucks.com, accessed July 2013.
22. For discussions of these issues, see Dhruv Grewel and Larry D. Compeau, "Pricing and Public Policy: A Research Agenda and Overview of the Special Issue," *Journal of Public Policy and Marketing*, Spring 1999, pp. 3–10; Walter L. Baker, Michael V. Marn, and Craig C. Zawada, *The Price Advantage* (Hoboken, New Jersey: John Wiley & Sons, 2010), Appendix 2; and Thomas T. Nagle, John E. Hogan, and Joseph Zale, *The Strategy and Tactics of Pricing*, 5th ed. (Upper Saddle River, NJ: Prentice Hall, 2011).
23. See Lucian Constantin, "Update: EU Fines CRT Makers $1.92B for Price-Fixing," *Computerworld*, December 5, 2012, www.computerworld.com/s/article/9234343/.
24. Based on information found in Lynn Leary, "Publishers and Booksellers See a 'Predatory' Amazon," *NPR Books*, January 23, 2012, www.npr.org/2012/01/23/145468105; and Allison Frankel, "Bookstores Accuse Amazon (not Apple!) and Publishers of E-Books Cartel," Thompson Reuters, February 20, 2013, http://newsandinsight.thomsonreuters.com/New_York/News/2013/02_-_February/Bookstores_accuse_Amazon_%28not_Apple!%29_and_publishers_of_e-books_cartel/.
25. "FTC Guides against Deceptive Pricing," www.ftc.gov/bcp/guides/decptprc.htm, accessed October 2013.

Chapter 10

1. Based on information from Greg Satell, "What Neflix's 'House of Cards' Means for the Future of TV," *Forbes*, March 4, 2013, www.forbes.com/sites/gregsatell/2013/03/04/what-netflixs-house-of-cards-means-for-the-future-of-tv/; Greg Bensinger, "Netflix Posts Surprise Profit," *Wall Street Journal*, January 23, 2013, http://online.wsj.com/article/SB10001424127887324039504578260182003808560.html; Stu Woo, "Under Fire, Netflix Rewinds DVD Plan," *Wall Street Journal*, October 11, 2011, p. A1; Ronald Grover and Cliff Edwards, "Can Netflix Find Its Future by Abandoning Its Past?" *Bloomberg Businessweek*, September 26–October 2, 2011, pp. 29–30; Stu Woo and Ian Sherr, "Netflix Recovers Subscribers," *Wall Street Journal*, January 26, 2012, p. B1; Dan Mitchell, "Why Netflix Can't Keep Winning," *Fortune*, January 22, 2013, http://tech.fortune.cnn.com/2013/01/22/why-netflix-cant-keep-winning/; and www.netflix.com, accessed November 2013.
2. See Bert Helm, "At KFC, a Battle among the Chicken-Hearted," *Bloomberg Businessweek*," August 16–August 29, 2010, p. 19; and Diane Brady, "YUM's Big Game of Chicken," *Bloomberg Businessweek*, March 29, 2012, pp. 64–69.
3. "The Kroger Co. Fact Book," http://ir.kroger.com/phoenix.zhtml?c=106409&p=irol-reportsAnnual, accessed November 2013.
4. See "Fashion Forward; Inditex," *The Economist*, March 24, 2012, pp. 63–64; Suza Hansen, "How Zara Grew into the World's Largest Fashion Retailer," *New York Times*, November 9, 2012; and information from the Inditex Press Dossier, www.inditex.com/en/press/information/press_kit, accessed November 2013.
5. Franchising facts from www.azfranchises.com/franchisefacts.htm, accessed May 2013. Also see "2013 Franchise Business Economic Outlook," December 17, 2012, www.franchise.org/Franchise-News-Detail.aspx?id=58916.
6. See Martinne Geller and Jessica Wohl, "Analysis: Walmart's Price Push Tests Manufacturers' Prowess," *Reuters*, March 6, 2012; and Qingyi Huang, Vincent R. Nijs, Karsten Hansen, and Eric T. Anderson, "Wal-Mart's Impact on Supplier Profits," *Harvard Business Review*, April 2012, pp. 131–144.
7. See "General Mills: Joint Ventures," www.generalmills.com/en/Company/Businesses/International/Joint_ventures.aspx, accessed November 2013.
8. For more discussion, see Miguel Bustillo, "Best Buy Forced to Rethink Big Box," *Wall Street Journal*, March 30, 2012, p. B1; and Jack D. Hidary, "5 Ways to Save Best Buy from Extinction," *CNNMoney*, January 3, 2013, http://tech.fortune.cnn.com/2013/01/03/5-ways-to-save-best-buy-from-extinction/.
9. Julie Bosman, "The Bookstore's Last Stand," *New York Times*, January 28, 2012; and Jeffrey Trachtenberg, "Corporate News: Barnes & Noble, Nook Struggle—Revenue at Chain's Consumer

Stores Fell 10.9% over the Holiday Selling Season," *Wall Street Journal*, January 4, 2013, p. B2.
10. Information from www.marykay.com/en-US/About-Mary-Kay/Pages/CountrySelector.aspx, accessed November 2013.
11. See "Logistics Costs Remain High in China: Report," *WantChina Times.com*, February 16, 2013, www.wantchinatimes.com/news-subclass-cnt.aspx?id=20130216000007&cid=1102.
12. Based on information from Julie Jargon, "Asia Delivers for McDonald's," *Wall Street Journal*, December 13, 2011, http://online.wsj.com/article/SB10001424052970204397704577074982151549316.html; "Feel Like a Burger? Dial M for McDonald's Japan," *Asia Pulse*, January 23, 2012; and McDonald's annual reports, www.aboutmcdonalds.com/mcd/investors/annual_reports.html, accessed August 2013.
13. Mark Ritson, "Why Retailers Call the Shots," *Marketing*, February 18, 2009, p. 24; Kim Bhasin, "Costco Kicks Out Coke and Replaces It with Pepsi in Food Courts," *Business Insider,* February 15, 2013, www.businessinsider.com/costco-hot-dog-combo-coke-pepsi-2013-2; and www.costco.com/diapers.html, accessed November 2013.
14. See Patrick Burnson, "23rd Annual State of Logistics Report: Slow and Steady," www.logisticsmgmt.com/images/site/LM1207_CovStateofLogistics_Rail.pdf, accessed November 2013.
15. William B. Cassidy, "Walmart Squeezes Costs from Supply Chain," *Journal of Commerce,* January 5, 2010; and "Walmart to Save $150 Million Thanks to Sustainability Programs," *Triple Pundit,* October 16, 2012, www.triplepundit.com/2012/10/walmart-save-150-million-sustainability-programs/.
16. Andy Brack, "Piggly Wiggly Center Offers Info-Packed Field Trip," *Charleston Currents*, January 4, 2010, www.charlestoncurrents.com/issue/10_issues/10.0104.html; and information from http://en.wikipedia.org/wiki/Piggly_wiggly and http://walmartstores.com, accessed August 2013.
17. Bill Mongrelluzzo, "Supply Chain Expert Sees Profits in Sustainability," *Journal of Commerce*, March 11, 2010, www.joc.com/logistics-economy/sustainability-can-lead-profits-says-expert. SC Johnson example from "SC Johnson Reduces Greenhouse Gasses by the Truckload," CRS Press Release, www.csrwire.com/press_releases/22882-SC-Johnson-Reduces-Greenhouse-Gases-by-the-Truckload. Also see "SC Johnson Named Recipient of 2012 SmartWay Excellence Award by the United States Environmental Protection Agency," *PRNewswire,* October 12, 2012.
18. See Ted LaBorde, "Home Depot Opens New Record Limited Distribution Center in Westfield," *masslive.com*, December 14, 2010, www.masslive.com/news/index.ssf/2010/12/home_depot_opens_new_rapid_dep.html; "Home Depot Distribution Efficiencies Improve In-Stock Positions," *Retailed Info Systems News*, November 21, 2011, http://risnews.edgl.com/retail-best-practices/Home-Depot-Distribution-Efficiencies-Improve-In-Stock-Positions76905; and www.homedepot.com, accessed November 2013.
19. See Evan West, "These Robots Play Fetch," Fast Company, July–August 2007, pp. 49–50; "Rise of the Orange Machines," *Bloomberg Businessweek*, November 15–November 21, 2010, p. 47; Julianne Pepitone, "Amazon Buys Army of Robots," *CNNMoney*, March 20, 2012, http://money.cnn.com/2012/03/20/technology/amazon-kiva-robots/index.htm; and www.kivasystems.com, accessed November 2013.
20. See Maida Napolitano, "RFID Surges Ahead," *Logistics Management,* April 2012, pp. 47–49; and "Research and Markets: Global RFID Market Forecast to 2014," *Business Wire*, April 2012.
21. Michael Margreta, Chester Ford, and M. Adhi Dipo, "U.S. Freight on the Move: Highlights from the 2007 Commodity Flow Survey Preliminary Data," September 30, 2009, www.bts.gov/publications/special_reports_and_issue_briefs/special_report/2009_09_30/html/entire.html; Bureau of Transportation Statistics, "Pocket Guide to Transportation 2012," January 2012, http://apps.bts.gov/publications/pocket_guide_to_transportation/2012/; and American Trucking Association, www.trucking.org, accessed November 2013.
22. See Walmart's supplier requirements at http://corporate.walmart.com/suppliers, accessed November 2013.
23. For this and other UPS examples and information, see "Toshiba Laptop Repair," accessed at http://pressroom.ups.com/Video/Toshiba+Laptop+Repair, May 2013; and www.thenewlogistics.com and www.ups.com/content/us/en/about/facts/worldwide.html, accessed July 2013.
24. David Biederman, "3PL Slowdown Goes Global," *Journal of Commerce*, February 8, 2010, www.joc.com/logistics-economy/3pl-slowdown-goes-global; Patrick Burnson, "Top 50 3PLs: Getting the Balance Right," *Supply Chain Management Review*, July/August 2011, p. 4; and Evan Armstrong, "2011/2012 Annual Review & Outlook: 3PLs Weathering the Storm," *Journal of Commerce*, January 6,2012, www.joc.com/logistics-economy/3pls-weathering-storm.

Chapter 11

1. Based on information from Farhad Manjoo, "Dot Convert," *Fast Company*, December 2012/January 2013, pp. 113–116+; Emily Jane Fox, "Walmart: The $200 Billion Grocer," *CNNMoney,* January 31, 2013, http://money.cnn.com/2013/01/31/news/companies/walmart-grocery/index.html; John Huey, "Wal-Mart: Will It Take over the World?" *Fortune*, January 30, 1998, pp. 52–61; Michael Barbano and Stuart Elliott, "Clinging to Its Roots, Wal-Mart Steps Back from an Edgy, New Image," *New York Times,* December 10, 2006, www.nytimes.com/2006/12/10/business/worldbusiness/10iht-walmart.3845671.html; Geoff Colvin, "Wal-Mart's Makeover," *Fortune,* December 26, 2011, pp. 50–55; "Global 500: The World's Largest Corporations." *Fortune*, July 22, 2013, pp. 133+; and information found at http://corporate.walmart.com/our-story/heritage/sam-walton and www.walmartstores.com, accessed November 2013.
2. See "Shopper Decisions Made In-Store by OgilvyAction," www.wpp.com/wpp/marketing/consumerinsights/shopper-decisions-made-instore.htm, accessed May 2013; and "Winning in the Last Mile," www.memacogilvy.com/WhatWeDo/WhatWeDo_en_gb.aspx?DisciplineId=w3JirMc8Wk0=, accessed May 2013. Retail sales statistics from "Monthly and Annual Retail Trade," U.S. Census Bureau, www.census.gov/retail/, accessed May 2013.
3. Jack Neff, "P&G Pushes Design in Brand-Building Strategy," April 12, 2010, http://adage.com/print?article_id=143211; and "The Zero Moment of Truth: A New Marketing Strategy," *Google Inside Adwords,* July 6, 2011, http://adwords.blogspot.com/2011/07/zero-moment-of-truth-new-marketing.html.
4. For more on digital aspects of shopper marketing, see Ellen Byron, "In-Store Sales Begin at Home," *Wall Street Journal,* April 25, 2011, www.wsj.com; Ann Zimmerman, "Can Retailers Halt 'Showrooming'?" *Wall Street Journal,* April 11, 2012, p. B1; "Consumers Visit Retailers, Then Go Online for Cheaper Sources," *Adweek,* March 14, 2013, www.adweek.com/print/147777; Lori Johnson, "Google and the Zero Moment of Truth," *Branding Personality,* March 6, 2013, www.brandingpersonality.com/google-and-the-zero-moment-of-truth/; and "ZMOT," *Amazon Digital Services*, www.zeromomentoftruth.com/, accessed November 2013.

5. See Annie Gasparro and Timothy W. Martin, "What's Wrong with America's Supermarkets?" *Wall Street Journal*, July 13, 2012, p. B1; Symphony IRI Group, "Channel Migration: Charting a Course on the Voyage of for Value," August 2012, www.pbaa.net/attach/Supplemental-%20T_T-August-2012_Channel-Migration-1.pdf; and Jennifer Haderspeck, "Competing for Consumer Share," *Beverage Industry*, January 2013, pp. 38, 40.
6. Timothy W. Martin, "May I Help You?" *Wall Street Journal*, April 22, 2009, http://online.wsj.com/article/SB124025177889535871.html; "The Top 10 Companies by Revenue," *Inc.*, August 22, 2011, www.inc.com/ss/2011-inc-5000-top-10-companies-revenue; "The American Customer Satisfaction Index," www.theacsi.org/index.php?option=com_content&view=article&id=12&Itemid=110, accessed November 2013; and www.publix.com, accessed November 2013.
7. Based on information from Stephanie Strom, "7-Eleven Shifts Focus to Healthier Food Options," *New York Times*, December 24, 2012, www.nytimes.com/2012/12/25/business/7-eleven-stores-focus-on-healthier-food-options.html?partner=rss&emc=rss; Vanessa Wong, "In Convenience Stores: More Food, Fewer Cigarettes," *Bloomberg Businessweek*, January 17, 2013, www.businessweek.com/articles/2013-01-17/in-convenience-stores-more-food-fewer-cigarettes; and http://corp.7-eleven.com, accessed November 2013.
8. Karen Brune Mathis, "Wal-Mart Supercenters Top Count of Southeast Regional Retailers," *Jacksonville Daily Record*, October 19, 2012, www.jaxdailyrecord.com/showstory.php?Story_id=537805; "Walmart Reinforces Financial Priorities," October 10, 2012, http://news.walmart.com/news-archive/2012/10/10/walmart-reinforces-financial-priorities-growth-leverage-returns-company-lowers-fiscal-2014-capital-plan-from-current-year; and "Supermarket Facts," www.fmi.org/facts_figs/?fuseaction=superfact, accessed July 2013.
9. See John Jannarone, "Will Dollar General Be Leading Retailers into Battle?" *Wall Street Journal*, June 6, 2011, p. C10; Gary Stern, "Are All Dollar Stores Alike? Not If They Want to Win," *Investor's Business Daily*, September 6, 2011; and "Dollar General to Open 635 New Stores and Create More Than 6,000 New Jobs in 2013," January 23, 2013, http://newscenter.dollargeneral.com/article_display.cfm?article_id=1848.
10. Based on information from "Retail Quick Facts: 10 Things about Costco You Probably Don't Know," *RetailSails*, April 27, 2011, http://retailsails.com/2011/04/27/retail-quick-facts-10-things-about-costco-you-probably-dont-know/; Matthew Boyle, "Why Costco Is So Addictive," *Fortune*, October 25, 2006, pp. 126–132; "2012 Top 100 Retailers," *NRF Stores*, July 2012, www.stores.org/2012/Top-100-Retailers#.UTfu8RkrO2x; Kim Bhasin, "Costco Kicks Out Coke and Replaces It with Pepsi in Food Courts," *Business Insider*, February 15, 2013, www.businessinsider.com/costco-hot-dog-combo-coke-pepsi-2013-2; and www.costco.com and http://shop.costco.com/Membership/Welcome/Amazing-Facts.aspx, accessed November 2013.
11. Company information from "Subway—38,000 and Still Growing," *Chain Store Guide*, November 6, 2012, http://newsroom.chainstoreguide.com/2012/11/subway-38000-and-still-growing/; and www.aboutmcdonalds.com/mcd and www.subway.com/subwayroot/About_Us/default.aspx, accessed July 2013.
12. Based on information from Maureen Morrison, "Fast-Casual Burger Joints Snag a Seat at the Table," *Advertising Age*, September 26, 2011, http://adage.com/print/230005/; Karen Weise, "Behind Five Guys' Beloved Burgers," *Bloomberg Businessweek*, August 11, 2011, www.businessweek.com/printer/magazine/behind-five-guys-beloved-burgers-08112011.html; Monte Burke, "Five Guys Burgers: America's Fastest Growing Restaurant Chain," *Forbes*, August 6, 2012; and www.aboutmcdonalds.com/mcd and www.fiveguys.com, accessed November 2013.
13. Based on information from "How Do You See This Experiential Retailing Trend Working Its Way across Retail?" *Integrated Retailing*, www.integratedretailing.com/?cat=12, accessed May 2013; and www.llbean.com, www.llbean.com/llb/shop/1000001692?nav=ftlink, and www.llbean.com/llb/shop/1000001704?page=campus-lander#, accessed November 2013.
14. Ibid.
15. See Yelena Moroz Alpert, "How Color Affects Your Spending," *Real Simple*, March 2013, p. 148; Sandy Smith, "Scents and Sellability," *Stores*, July 2009, www.stores.org/stores-magazine-july-2009/scents-and-sellability; "The Smell of Success," *Marketing Management*, Fall 2012, pp. 36–44; James Archer, "Let Them Sniff, Customers Will Buy More," *Inc.*, January 23, 2013, www.inc.com/james-archer/let-them-sniff-customers-will-buy-more.html; and www.scentair.com, accessed November 2013.
16. See "Retail Social Media Top 10," *Retail Customer Experience*, January 10, 2013, www.retailcustomerexperience.com/blog/9655/Retail-Social-Media-Top-10-Infographic; and various social media sites for Walmart and Sprouts, accessed July 2013.
17. For definitions of these and other types of shopping centers, see "Dictionary," *American Marketing Association*, www.marketingpower.com/_layouts/Dictionary.aspx, accessed November 2013.
18. Courtenay Edelhart, "Malls Can't Take Customers for Granted as New Outdoor Centers Pop Up," *McClatchy-Tribune Business News*, January 16, 2010; Eric Schwartzberg, "Lifestyle Centers Draw Retailers, Shoppers," *The Oxford Press*, November 21, 2011, www.oxfordpress.com/news/oxford-news/lifestyle-centers-draw--retailers-shoppers--1287539.html; and "It's the End of the Mall as We Know It," *Real Estate Weekly*, February 22, 2013, www.rew-online.com/2013/02/22/its-the-end-of-the-mall-as-we-know-it/.
19. See H. Lee Murphy, "Life Ebbs Out of Many Lifestyle Centers," *National Real Estate Investor*, May 1, 2011, p. 31; Jon Chavez, "Major Retail Expansion Called Unlikely," *McClatchy-Tribune Business News*, March 18, 2012; and Robbie Moore, "The Death of the American Mall and the Rebirth of Public Space," *The International*, February 26, 2013, www.theinternational.org/articles/354-the-death-of-the-american-mall-and-the-re.
20. See David Kaplan, "A Permanent Trend of Pop-Up Shops," *McClatchy-Tribune Business News*, December 21, 2011; Carolyn King, "Target Brings Jason Wu to Canada," *Wall Street Journal*, February 23, 2012; Judith Lamont, "Tuning in to Customers: Optimizing the Online Experience," *KM World*, February 2012, pp. 8–9; and Burt Helm, "Gilt Groupe's Kevin Ryan: What Works, and Doesn't Work, in Flash Sales," *Inc.com*, February 20, 2013, www.inc.com/burt-helm/gilt-groupe-kevin-ryan-flash-sales.html.
21. See www.rpminc.com/consumer.asp, accessed October 2013.
22. Thad Rueter, "E-Retail Spending to Increase to 62% by 2016," *Internet Retailer*, February 27, 2012, www.internetretailer.com/2012/02/27/e-retail-spending-increase-45-2016; and U.S. Census Bureau News, "Quarterly Retail E-Commerce Sales, 4th Quarter 2013," February 15, 2013, www.census.gov/retail/mrts/www/data/pdf/ec_current.pdf.
23. See Ann Zimmerman, "Can Retailers Halt 'Showrooming'?" *Wall Street Journal*, April 11, 2012, p. B1; "Data Points: Spending It," *Adweek*, April 16, 2012, pp. 24–25; and "Consumers Visit Retailers, Then Go Online for Cheaper Sources," *Adweek*, March 14, 2013, www.adweek.com/print/147777.

24. "Top 500 Guide," *Internet Retailer*, www.internetretailer.com/top500/list/, accessed July 2013.
25. Adam Blair, "Williams-Sonoma Invests $75M in Fast-Growing, Profitable E-Commerce," *RIS,* March 22, 2011, http://risnews.edgl.com/retail-best-practices/Williams-Sonoma-Invests-$75M-in-Fast-Growing,-Profitable-E-Commerce71523; J. A. Graham, "Williams-Sonoma—Well Done But Not Over-Cooked," *Foolish Blogging Network*, February 6, 2013, http://beta.fool.com/lekitkat/2013/02/06/williams-sonoma-well-done-over-cooked/22873/; and Paul Demery, "The Web Accounts for Three-Quarters of Williams-Sonoma Growth in 2012," March 27, 2013, www.internetretailer.com/2013/03/27/web-accounts-three-quarters-williams-sonomas-growth.
26. See "Eastern Mountain Sports Blazes New Trails with VeriFone iPad Retailing Solution," January 12, 2012, www.verifone.com/2012/eastern-mountain-sports-blazes-new-trails-with-verifone-ipad-retailing-solution.aspx.
27. See "Walmart Labs: Social," www.walmartlabs.com/social/, accessed May 2013; Mark J. Miller, "Walmart and Apple Test Mobile Self-Checkouts," *Brand Channel,* September 5, 2012, www.brandchannel.com/home/?tag=/%40WalmartLabs; and "Our Strategy: Winning in Global E-Commerce," *Walmart 2012 Annual Report*, www.walmartstores.com/sites/annual-report/2012/WalMart_AR.pdf, March 2013, pp. 12–13.
28. "Kohl's Opens Eight New Stores Creating Approximately 1,000 Jobs," *Business Wire,* March 8, 2012; and www.kohlsgreenscene.com, accessed November 2013.
29. See www.staples.com/sbd/cre/marketing/easy-on-the-planet/recycling-and-eco-services.html, accessed November 2013.
30. See http://news.walmart.com/walmart-facts/corporate-financial-fact-sheet, accessed July 2013.
31. See "Global Powers of Retailing 2013," *Deloitte*, January 2013, accessed at www.deloitte.com/view/en_CH/ch/industries/consumer_business/a21917cfaa74c310VgnVCM2000003356f70aRCRD.htm.
32. Grainger facts and other information are from the "Grainger: Beyond the Box Fact Book", accessed at http://invest.grainger.com/phoenix.zhtml?c=76754&p=irol-irFactBook and www.grainger.com, accessed November 2013.
33. "Top 500 Guide," *Internet Retailer*, www.internetretailer.com/top500/list/, accessed July 2013; and www.grainger.com, accessed November 2013.
34. Information from "About Us," www.mckesson.com; and "Supply Management Online," www.mckesson.com/en_us/McKesson.com/For+Pharmacies/Retail+National+Chains/Ordering+and+Inventory+Management/Supply+Management+Online.html, accessed May 2013.
35. Facts from www.supervalu.com, accessed November 2013.

Chapter 12

1. Based on information from "The Cow Campaign: A Brief History," www.chick-fil-a.com/Cows/Campaign-History, accessed July 2013; "Company Fact Sheet," www.chick-fil-a.com/Company/Highlights-Fact-Sheets, accessed July 2013; Thomas Pardee, "Armed with a Beloved Product and a Strong Commitment to Customer Service, Fast Feeder Continues to Grow," *Advertising Age,* October 18, 2010, http://adage.com/print/146491/; Emily Bryson York, "Game of Chicken against Leader Pays Off for Chick-fil-A, Popeyes," *Advertising Age,* May 3, 2010, http://adage.com/print/143642/; Brian Morrissey, "Chick-fil-A's Strategy: Give Your Fans Something to Do," *AdWeek*, October 3, 2009, www.adweek.com/print/106477; and information from various other pages and press releases at www.chick-fil-a.com and www.chick-fil-a.com/Pressroom/Press-Releases, accessed November 2013.
2. For other definitions, see www.marketingpower.com/_layouts/-Dictionary.aspx, accessed November 2013.
3. Joe Mandese, "Carat Projects Digital at One-Fifth of All Ad Spend, Beginning to Dominate Key Markets," *Online Media Daily,* March 20, 2013, www.mediapost.com/publications/article/196238/; and "ZenithOptimedia Forecasts 4.1% Growth in Global Adspend in 2013," December 3, 2012, www.zenithoptimedia.com/zenith/zenithoptimedia-forecasts-4-1-growth-in-global-adspend-in-2013.
4. Chris Anderson, "The 'Angry Birds in Space' Video Marketing Campaign," *The Video Marketer,* March 22, 2012, http://blog.wooshii.com/the-angry-birds-in-space-video-marketing-campaign/; and "Samsung, Wieden & Kennedy Rule Ad Age's 2013 Viral Video Awards," *Advertising Age,* April 16, 2013, http://adage.com/print/240900/. McDonald's and Our Food. Your Questions. are trademarks licensed from McDonald's Corporation. McDonald's et Nos aliments. Vos questions. sont des marques de commerce utilisées en vertu d'une licence de McDonald's Corporation.
5. This example is based on information from Stuart Elliott, "Ad for Method Celebrates the Madness," *New York Times,* March 12, 2012, p. B1; and "Method Brings 'Clean Happy' Campaign to TV," *Business Wire,* March 4, 2013, www.businesswire.com/news/home/20130304005445/en/Method-Brings-%E2%80%9CClean-Happy%E2%80%9D-Campaign-TV.
6. "Annual 2013: Marketers," *Advertising Age,* December 31, 2012, p. 9.
7. See Jon Lafayette, "4A's Conference: Agencies Urged to Embrace New Technologies," *Broadcasting & Cable,* March 8, 2011, www.broadcastingcable.com/article/464951-4A_s_Conference_Agencies_Urged_To_Embrace_New_Technologies.php; David Gelles, "Advertisers Rush to Master Fresh Set of Skills," *Financial Times,* March 7, 2012, www.ft.com/intl/cms/s/0/8383bbae-5e20-11e1-b1e9-00144feabdc0.html#axzz1xUrmM3KK; and Steve McKee, "Integrated Marketing: If you Knew It, You'd Do It," *Bloomberg Businessweek,* May 10,2012, www.businessweek.com/articles/2012-05-10/integrated-marketing-if-you-knew-it-youd-do-it#p2.
8. See "Thrill of the Chase: Coca-Cola Invites Fans to Shape Storyline of Big Game Ad," *Coca-Cola Journey,* January 25, 2013, www.coca-colacompany.com/stories/thrill-of-the-chase-coca-cola-invites-fans-to-shape-storyline-of-big-game-ad; Dale Buss, "Super Bowl Ad Watch: Crowdsourcing Peaks with Coke's 'Mirage' Campaign, *BrandChannel,* January 22, 2013, www.brandchannel.com/home/post/2013/01/22/SuperBowl-Coke-012213.aspx; and Natalie Zmuda, "Watching the Super Bowl from Coca-Cola's War Room(s)," *Advertising Age,* February 4, 2013, http://adage.com/print/239582/.
9. See "Super Bowl Just Shy of TV Record," *ESPN.com*, February 4, 2013, http://espn.go.com/nfl/playoffs/2012/story/_/id/8913211/; Michael Cieply and Brooks Barnes, "Academy Award Show Raises Ratings and Hackles," *NYTimes.com,* February 25, 2013, www.nytimes.com/2013/02/26/movies/awardsseason/higher-ratings-and-controversy-for-seth-macfarlane-at-oscars.html; "Ratings: *NCIS* Draws Second-Largest Audience Ever," *TVLine.com,* January 16, 2013, http://tvline.com/2013/01/16/ratings-ncis-second-largest-audience-ever; and James Richie, "P&G Plans to Save Money with Bigger Ads," *Business Courier,* February 22, 2013, www.bizjournals.com/cincinnati/blog/2013/02/pg-plans-to-save-money-with-bigger-ads.html.
10. See discussions at Mike Ishmael, "The Cost of a Sales Call," October 22, 2012, http://4dsales.com/the-cost-of-a-sales-call/; Jeff Green, "The New Willy Loman Survives by Staying Home," *Bloomberg Businessweek,* January 14–January 20, 2013, pp. 16–17;

and "What Is the Real Cost of a B2B Sales Call?" accessed at www.marketing-playbook.com/sales-marketing-strategy/what-is-the-real-cost-of-a-b2b-sales-call, October 2013.

11. Jack Neff, "Unilever Ad Spending Hits New Heights," *Advertising Age*, January 23, 2013, http://adage.com/print/239348/.
12. "Global Ad Spend Grows 3.2% in 2012," April 11, 2013, www.nielsen.com/us/en/newswire/2013/global-ad-spend-grows-3.2-percent-in-2012.html; "Kantar Media Reports U.S. Advertising Expenditures Increased 3 Percent in 2012," March 11, 2013, http://kantarmediana.com/intelligence/press/us-advertising-expenditures-increased-3-percent-2012; and "Advertisers," *Advertising Age: Annual 2013,* December 31, 2012, pp. 9, 13.
13. See Alexandra Bruell, "Government Agencies Gird for Cuts Due to Sequestration," *Advertising Age*, March 4, 2013, http://adage.com/print/240132/; and "CDC Anti-Smoking Campaign Launched," March 29, 2013, www.wjla.com/articles/2013/03/cdc-anti-smoking-campaign-launched-86867.html.
14. "Walmart Gets Boost from Local-Price-Comparison Ads," *Advertising Age,* June 25, 2013, www.adage.com/print/242755.
15. "Take the Bing It On Challenge," September 6, 2012, www.bing.com/blogs/site_blogs/b/search/archive/2012/09/06/challenge-announce.aspx; and "Take the Bing It On Challenge at a Microsoft Store Near You," May 10, 2013, www.bing.com/blogs/site_blogs/b/search/archive/2013/05/10/take-the-bing-it-on-challenge-at-a-microsoft-store-near-you.aspx.
16. For this and other examples of comparative advertising, see "Kraft, Sara Lee Call Truce in Weiner War," *Chicago Tribune,* September 8, 2011; "What Marketers Can Learn from the Great Weiner War," *Advertising Age,* August 17, 2011, http://adage.com/print/229299/; and Gabriel Beltrone, "Creatives Discuss How to Be Provocative and Effective," *Adweek,* May 8, 2012, www.adweek.com/print/140140.
17. For more on setting promotion budgets, see W. Ronald Lane, Karen Whitehill King, and J. Thomas Russell, *Kleppner's Advertising Procedure*, 18th ed. (Upper Saddle River, NJ: Prentice Hall, 2011), Chapter 6.
18. See Jean Halliday, "Thinking Big Takes Audi from Obscure to Awesome," *Advertising Age*, February 2, 2009, accessed at http://adage.com/print?article_id=134234; and Chad Thomas and Andreas Cremer, "Audi Feels a Need for Speed in the U.S.," *Bloomberg BusinessWeek*, November 22, 2010, p 1; Tito F. Hermoso, "Watch Out for Audi," *BusinessWorld,* June 15, 2011, p. 1; and Carey Vanderborg, "Audi Looks to Top BMW and Mercedes in 2013 with A3 Sedan," *International Business Times,* March 13, 12013, www.ibtimes.com/audi-looks-top-bmw-mercedes-2013-a3-sedan-photo-1123549#.
19. "Forget the Bundle, Consumers Have an Appetite for Choice," *Videomind,* December 16, 2011, http://videomind.ooyala.com/blog/forget-bundle-consumers-have-appetite-choice; and "Number of Magazine Titles," www.magazine.org/ASME/EDITORIAL_TRENDS/1093.aspx, accessed July 2012.
20. "Results of 4A's 2011 Television Production Cost Survey," January 22, 2013, www.aaaa.org/news/bulletins/pages/tvprod_01222013.aspx; Brian Steinberg, "TV Ad Prices," *Advertising Age*, October 21, 2012, http://adage.com/printl/237874/; and Lisa de Moraes, "Super Bowl Commercial Prices Spike as Execs Weigh If It's Better to Release Ads Early Online," *Washington Post*, February 2, 2013, www.washingtonpost.com/blogs/tv-column/post/super-bowl-commercial-prices-spike-as-execs-weigh-if-its-better-to-release-ads-early-online/2013/02/01/27535c8c-6bfc-11e2-bd36-c0fe61a205f6_blog.html.
21. "Advertising in the U.S.: Synovate Global Survey Shows Internet, Innovation and Online Privacy a Must," December 3, 2009, accessed at www.synovate.com/news/article/2009/12/advertising-in-the-us-synovate-global-survey-shows-internet-innovation-and-online-privacy-a-must.html; and "Disconnect: Marketers Say TV Ads More Effective in General, Yet Traditional Spots 'Dissatisfy,'" *TVexchanger.com*, February 16, 2012, www.tvexchanger.com/interactive-tv-news/disconnect-marketers-say-tv-ads-more-effective-in-general-yet-traditional-spots-dissatisfy/.
22. Jared Sternberg, "The DVR Ate My Ad—A Lot More People Fast-Forward through TV Commercials Than You Think," *The Sternberg Report*, April 5, 2011, http://thestarryeye.typepad.com/sternberg/2011/04/the-dvr-ate-my-ad-a-lot-more-people-fast-forward-through-commercials-than-you-think.html; Brian Stelter, "On Sundays, the DVR Runneth Over," *New York Times*, April 20, 2012, p. C1; and David Goetzl, "TV Spending Nears $80 Billion, DVR Penetration Chasing 50%," *Media Post,* April 22, 2013, www.mediapost.com/publications/article/198659/#axzz2TrrvRBkB.
23. Abe Sauer, "Announcing the 2013 Brandcameo Product Placement Award Winners," *BrandChannel*, February 25, 2013, www.brandchannel.com/home/post/Brandchannel-9th-Brandcameo-Product-Placement-Awards-022513.aspx.
24. Andrew Hampp, "Web Series Shows a Bit of Quality Can Help Sell 'Crap,'" *Advertising* Age, January 11, 2010, p. 10; "Ford Introduces All-New Fusion with Groundbreaking Transmedia Campaign," *Marketing Weekly News*, July 14, 2012, p. 277; Beecher Tuttle, "IKEA's Hit Web Show: An Entertaining Ad," *Wall Street Journal*, September 7, 2012, http://online.wsj.com/article/SB10000872396390444358404577609932125128046.html.
25. For facts and more examples, see Bruce Horovitz, Laura Petrecca, and Gary Strauss, "Super Bowl AdMeter Winner: Score One for the Doritos Baby," *USA Today*, February 7, 2012; Laura Petrecca, "Doritos AdMeter Winners Each Receive a $1 Million Bonus," *USA Today*, February 8, 2012; "2013 USA Today Facebook Super Bowl Ad Meter," http://admeter.usatoday.com/, accessed May 2013; Christopher Heine, "Frito-Lay Likes the Data from Doritos' 'Crash the Super Bowl,'" *Adweek*, February 7, 2013, www.adweek.com/news/technology/frito-lay-likes-data-doritos-crash-super-bowl-147127; and www.crashthesuperbowl.com, accessed June 2013.
26. Quotes and other information from Lauren Drell, "User Generated Content: Lessons from 4 Killer Ad Campaigns," *American Express Open Forum,* January 28, 2013, https://www.openforum.com/articles/lessons-from-4-killer-ugc-campaigns/; and http://thesweatlife.lululemon.com/, accessed October 2013.
27. Michael Bourne, "Sailing the 14 Social C's," *Mullen*, February 12, 2012, www.mullen.com/sailing-the-14-social-cs.
28. Antony Young, "Get Beyond the 30-Second Ad: In a World of Many Platforms, It's a Must," *Advertising Age,* April 12, 2013, http://adage.com/article/cmo-strategy/30-ad-a/240857/; and "The Weather Channel's Innovative Mobile Advertising," April 4, 2013, http://talkingnewmedia.blogspot.com/2013/04/the-weather-channels-innovative-mobile.html.
29. Brian Steinberg, "Viewer-Engagement Rankings Signal Change for TV Industry," *Advertising Age*, May 10, 2010, p. 12. For more on measuring engagement, see Kirby Thornton, "Neilsen Engages Twitter for TV Insights," *Media Is Power,* March 21, 2013, http://www.mediaispower.com/nielsen-engages-twitter-for-tv-insights/#sthash.yOJpbk51.ggCAZYJ5.dpbs; and "New Data Correlates Social Engagement with Traditional Radio Ratings," *PR Newswire,* April 10, 2013, www.prnewswire.com/news-releases/202264391.html.
30. Tavis Coburn, "Mayhem on Madison Avenue," *Fast Company,* January 2011, pp. 110–115.

31. Joe Tripoti, "Coca-Cola Marketing Shifts from Impressions to Expressions," April 27, 2011, http://blogs.hbr.org/cs/2011/04/coca-colas_marketing_shift_fro.html; and Devon Glenn, "Coca-Cola on Social Content: 'Expressions Are More Valuable than Impressions,'" *Social Times,* September 11, 2012, http://socialtimes.com/coca-cola-on-social-content-expressions-are-more-valuable-than-impressions_b104547. Also see Paul Dunay, "Engagement Advertising: The Future of Brand Advertising?" *Forbes,* March 12, 2013, www.forbes.com/sites/gyro/2013/03/12/engagement-advertising-the-future-of-brand-advertising/.
32. See "Nielsen: Most Tablet/Smartphone Users Watch TV at Same Time," *Electronista*, April 5, 2012, www.electronista.com/articles/12/04/05/simultaneous.use.prevalent.in.us.market/.
33. *Forbes* and *Bloomberg Businessweek* cost and circulation data found online at http://bloombergmedia.com/pdfs/bbw_rates.pdf and www.forbesmedia.com, accessed November 2013.
34. For these and other examples, see Christopher Heine, "Lexus Nabs 100K Video Views on Facebook—in 10 Minutes," *Adweek,* January 23, 2013, www.adweek.com/news/technology/print/146726; and Matt McGee, "Oreo, Audi, and Walgreens Newsjack Super Bowl 'Blackout Bowl,'" *Marketing Land,* February 3, 2013, http://marketingland.com/oreo-audi-walgreens-market-quickly-during-super-bowl-blackout-32407.
35. Information on advertising agency revenues from "Agency Report," *Advertising Age,* April 29, 2013, pp. 32–46.
36. Based on Glen Broom and Bey-Ling Sha, *Cutlip & Center's Effective Public Relations*, 11th ed. (Upper Saddle River, NJ: Prentice Hall, 2013), Chapter 1.
37. Information from "The Heart Truth: Making Healthy Hearts Fashionable," Ogilvy Public Relations Worldwide, www.ogilvypr.com/en/case-study/heart-truth?page=0; and www.goredforwomen.org; www.nhlbi.nih.gov/educational/hearttruth/, and www.nhlbi.nih.gov/educational/hearttruth/about/index.htm, accessed November 2013.
38. See Geoffrey Fowler and Ben Worthen, "Buzz Powers iPad Launch," *Wall Street Journal*, April 2, 2010; "Apple iPad Sales Top 2 Million since Launch," *Tribune-Review* (Pittsburgh), June 2, 2010; "PR Pros Must Be Apple's iPad as a True Game-Changer," *PRweek*, May 2010, p. 23; Yukari Iwatani Kane, "Apple's iPad 2 Chalks up Strong Sales in Weekend Debut," *Wall Street Journal*, March 14, 2011, http://online.wsj.com/article/SB10001424052748704027504576198832667732862.html; and "Apple Launches New iPad," March 7, 2012, www.apple.com/pr/library/2012/03/07Apple-Launches-New-iPad.html.
39. Sarah Skerik, "An Emerging PR Trend: Content PR Strategy and Tactics," *PR Newswire,* January 15, 2013, http://blog.prnewswire.com/2013/01/15/an-emerging-pr-trend-content-pr-strategy-tactics/.
40. Example based on information from Julie Liesse, "The Big Idea," *Advertising Age,* November 28, 2011, pp. C4–C6; and www.wrangler.com/store/WRG_STORE_US/en_US/style/92nb0bt.html, accessed November 2013.

Chapter 13

1. Portions based on information found in Jesi Hempel, "IBM's All-Star Salesman," *Fortune*, September 26, 2008, http://money.cnn.com/2008/09/23/technology/hempel_IBM.fortune/index.htm; and www.03.ibm.com/employment/jobs/softwaresales/ and www-03.ibm.com/ibm/history/ibm100/us/en/icons/ibmsales/, accessed November 2013.
2. See Philip Kotler, Neil Rackham, and Suj Krishnaswamy, "Ending the War between Sales and Marketing," *Harvard Business Review*, July–August 2006, pp. 68–78; Elizabeth A. Sullivan, "The Ties That Bind," *Marketing News*, May 15, 2010; Allan Mayer, "Improving the Relationships between Sales and Marketing," *OneAccord,* May 30, 2012, www.oneaccordpartners.com/blog/bid/132539/; and Philip Kotler and Kevin Lane Keller, *Marketing Management,* 14th ed. (Upper Saddle River, NJ: Prentice Hall, 2012), p. 554.
3. See Henry Canaday, "How One Enterprise Sales Force Works with Channels Partners to Maintain and Build Sales," *Selling Power,* May 13, 2013, www.sellingpower.com/enterprise-sales/.
4. "Selling Power 500: The Largest Sales Force in America," *Selling Power,* September 2012, pp. 34, 40.
5. See discussions in Mike Ishmael, "The Cost of a Sales Call," October 22, 2012, http://4dsales.com/the-cost-of-a-sales-call/; Jeff Green, "The New Willy Loman Survives by Staying Home," *Bloomberg Businessweek,* January 14–January 20, pp. 16–17; and "What Is the Real Cost of a B2B Sales Call?" www.marketing-playbook.com/sales-marketing-strategy/what-is-the-real-cost-of-a-b2b-sales-call, accessed April 2013.
6. Green, "The New Willy Loman Survives by Staying Home," pp. 16–17.
7. Quote and facts from Jim Domanski, "Special Report: The 2012 B@B Tele-Sales Trend Report," www.salesopedia.com/downloads/2012%20B2B%20Tele-Sales%20Trend%20Special%20Reportl.pdf, accessed July 2013.
8. See "Case Study: Climax Portable Machine Tools," www.selltis.com/productCaseStudiesClimaxPortableMachineTools.aspx; and www.climaxportable.com, accessed November 2013.
9. "Customer Business Development," www.experiencepg.com/jobs/customer-business-development-sales.aspx, accessed November 2013.
10. Scott Fuhr, "Good Hiring Makes Good Cents," *Selling Power,* July/August/September 2012, pp. 20–21.
11. For this and more information and discussion, see www.gallupaustralia.com.au/consulting/118729/sales-force-effectiveness.aspx, accessed July 2012; Lynette Ryals and Iain Davies, "Do You Really Know Who Your Best Salespeople Are?" *Harvard Business Review*, December 2010, pp. 34–35; "The 10 Skills of Super' Salespeople," www.businesspartnerships.ca/articles/the_10_skills_of_super_salespeople.phtml, accessed July 2012; and "Profile of a Super Seller," *Selling Power,* October/November/December 2012, pp. 12–13.
12. Barbara Hendricks, "Strengths-Based Selling," February 8, 2011, www.gallup.com/press/146246/Strengths-Based-Selling.aspx.
13. Corporate Visions, Inc., "ADP Case Study," http://corporatevisions.com/v5/documents/secure_downloads/CVI_caseStudy_ADP.pdf, accessed June 2013; and Henry Canaday, "Higher Expectations," *Selling Power,* November/December 2011, pp. 50–51.
14. Based on information found in Sara Donnelly, "Staying in the Game," *Pharmaceutical Executive*, May 2008, pp. 158–159; Bayer Healthcare Pharmaceuticals, Inc., "Improving Sales Force Effectiveness: Bayer's Experiment with New Technology," 2008, www.icmrindia.org/casestudies/catalogue/Marketing/MKTG200.htm; Tanya Lewis, "Concentric," *Medical Marketing and Media*, July 2008, p. 59; www.hydraframe.com/mobile/project_repracе.htm, accessed July 2012; Andrew Tolve, "Pharma Sales: How Simulation Can Help Reps Sell," *Eye for Pharma,* March 28, 2012, http://social.eyeforpharma.com/sales/pharma-sales-how-simulation-can-help-reps-sell; and Dario Priolo, "Nine Trends in Sales Force Effectiveness and Learning and Development for 2013," *The Richardson Sales Excellence Review,* December 19, 2012, http://blogs.richardson.com/2012/12/19/nine-trends-in-sales-force-effectiveness-and-learning-development-for-2013/.

15. For this and more discussion, see Joseph Kornak, "07 Compensation Survey: What's It All Worth?" *Sales & Marketing Management*, May 2007, pp. 28–39; William L. Cron and Thomas E. DeCarlo, *Dalrymple's Sales Management*, 10th ed. (New York: John Wiley & Sons Inc., 2009), p. 303; Ken Sundheim, "How Sales Professionals Are Paid," *Salesopedia*, www.salesopedia.com/compensation-compensationdesign, accessed July 2013; and Alexander Group, "2013 Sales Compensation Trends Survey Results," January 4, 2013, www.alexandergroup.com/resources/survey-findings.
16. See Paul Vinogradov, "Are Your Sales People Getting Enough Quality Sales Time?" *Alexander Group*, May 7, 2013, www.alexandergroup.com/blog/are-your-sales-people-getting-enough-quality-sales-time/.
17. Lain Chroust Ehmann, "Sales Up!" *Selling Power*, January/February 2011, p. 40. Also see Scott Gillum, "The Disappearing Sales Process," *Forbes*, January 7, 2013, www.forbes.com/sites/gyro/2013/01/07/the-disappearing-sales-process/; and Matt Dixon and Steve Richard, "Solution Selling Is Dead: Why 2013 Is the Year of B2B Insight Selling," *Openview*, http://labs.openviewpartners.com/solution-selling-is-dead-2013-year-of-b2b-insight-selling/.
18. Brent Adamson, Matthew Dixon, and Nicholas Toman, "The End of Solution Sales," *Harvard Business Review*, July–August 2012, pp. 61–68.
19. Barbara Giamanco and Kent Gregoire, "Tweet Me, Friend Me, Make Me Buy," *Harvard Business Review*, July–August 2012, pp. 88–94.
20. Giamanco and Gregoire, "Tweet Me, Friend Me, Make Me Buy," p. 90.
21. Based on information from Elizabeth A. Sullivan, "B-to-B Marketers: One-to-One Marketing," *Marketing News*, May 15, 2009, pp. 11–13. Also see Henry Canaday, "A Socially Salable World," *Selling Power*, April/May/June 2012, pp. 46–50; and Green, "The New Willy Loman Survives by Staying Home," pp. 16–17. For more on Makino's social networking efforts, see www.facebook.com/MakinoMachine, www.youtube.com/user/MakinoMachineTools, and http://twitter.com/#!/makinomachine, accessed November 2013.
22. Example based on information from James C. Anderson, Nirmalya Kumar, and James A. Narus, "Become a Value Merchant," *Sales & Marketing Management*, May 6, 2008, pp. 20–23; and "Business Market Value Merchants," *Marketing Management*, March/April 2008, pp. 31+. For more discussion and examples, see Heather Baldwin, "Deeper Value Delivery," *Selling Power*, September/October 2010, p. 16; and Thomas P. Reilly, "Value-Added Selling Is Smart," *Selling Power*, June 27, 2012, www.sellingpower.com/content/article.php?a=8917.
23. Kantar Retail, *Making Connections: Trade Promotion Integration across the Marketing Landscape* (Wilton, CT: Kantar Retail, July 2012), p. 5.
24. "High Level of Promotions Pushes Down Grocery Spend," *Retail Week*, September 13, 2011.
25. Kantar Retail, *Making Connections: Trade Promotion Integration Across the Marketing Landscape*, p. 6.
26. "Kroger Doubles Fuel Discount Opportunities for Summer," May 25,2012, www.csnews.com/top-story-kroger_doubles_fuel_discount_opportunities_for_summer-61195.html; and www.kroger.com/fuel/Pages/A1.aspx, accessed June 2013.
27. NCH Marketing Services, "NCH Annual Topline U.S. CPG Coupon Facts Report for Year-End 2012," January 2013, www2.nchmarketing.com/ResourceCenter/assets/0/22/28/76/226/457/735949da63a14f209014dd04c27f1472.pdf.
28. See NCH Marketing Services, "NCH Annual Topline U.S. CPG Coupon Facts Report for Year-End 2012"; "Mobile Spurs Digital Coupon User Growth," *eMarketer*, January 31, 2013, www.emarketer.com/Article/Mobile-Spurs-Digital-Coupon-User-Growth/1009639; and Laurie Sullivan, "Digital Coupons Impact New Product Awareness, Brand Recall," *Online Media Daily*, May 9, 2013, www.mediapost.com/publications/article/199931/#axzz2TNtmqZwq.
29. Based on information from "Walgreens Brings Mobile Couponing and Exclusive Offers to Smartphone Users Beginning Black Friday," November 17, 2011, http://news.walgreens.com/article_display.cfm?article_id=5504; Kunar Patel, "At Walgreens, a Mobile Check-In Acts Like a Circular," *Advertising Age*, February 8, 2012, http://adage.com/print/232584/; and www.walgreens.com/topic/apps/learn_about_mobile_browser_app.jsp, accessed June 2013.
30. See www.happymeal.com/en_US/, accessed July 2013.
31. See "2011 Estimate of Promotional Products Distributor Sales," www.ppai.org/inside-ppai/research/Documents/2011%20SalesVolume%20Sheet.pdf, accessed July 2012.
32. Based on information found in Patrick Hanlon, "Face Slams: Event Marketing Takes Off," *Forbes*, May 9, 2012, www.forbes.com/sites/patrickhanlon/2012/05/09/face-slams-event-marketing-takes-off/; and www.redbull.com/en/events and www.redbull.com/cs/Satellite/en_INT/RedBull/HolyShit/011242745950125, accessed June 2013. The referenced wing suit flying video can be found at http://player.vimeo.com/video/31481531?autoplay=1.
33. Kantar Retail, *Making Connections: Trade Promotion Integration across the Marketing Landscape*, p. 10.
34. See "2012 CES Attendee Audit Summary Results," www.cesweb.org/cesweb/media/CESWeb/Documents/Exhibitor/2012_CES_Audit.pdf, accessed May 2013; "Bauma 2013 Records Highest Ever Attendance," *Construction Week*, April 22, 2013, www.constructionweekonline.com/article-22027-bauma-2013-records-highest-ever-attendance/#.UZPTULXYdyI; and "Bauma 2013 Equipment Show Sees Record Attendance of 530,000," *CMBOL*, April 23, 2013, www.cmbol.com/news/detail/2013/04/2013042314194724.shtm.

Chapter 14

1. Based on information from Josh Constine, "Facebook Will Launch Content-Specific News Feeds, Bigger Photos, and Ads," *Techcrunch*, March 5, 2013, http://techcrunch.com/2013/03/05/facebook-news-feeds-launch/; Emmanuel Maiberg, "The Top 25 Facebook Games of May 2013," May 1, 2013, www.insidesocialgames.com/2013/05/01/the-top-25-facebook-games-of-may-2013/; "Facebook's Sales Chief: Madison Avenue Doesn't Understand Us Yet," *Advertising Age*, April 29, 2011, www.adage.com/print/227314/; Ingrid Lunden, "Spotify: The Music Service that Facebook Could Have Been, Wanted to Be, or Might Be One Day?" *Techcrunch*, December 6, 2012, http://techcrunch.com/2012/12/06/spotify-the-music-service-that-facebook-could-have-been-wanted-to-be-or-might-be-one-day/; Jim Edwards, "How Facebook Will Reach $12 Billion in Revenue," *Business Insider*, December 18, 2012, www.businessinsider.com/facebooks-annual-revenues-by-year-2012-12; Ashlee Vance, "Facebook: The Making of 1 Billion Users," *Businessweek*, October 4, 2012, www.businessweek.com/articles/2012-10-04/facebook-the-making-of-1-billion-users#p5; and information from www.facebook.com, accessed November 2013.
2. ComBlu, "The State of Online Branded Communities," http://comblu.com/downloads/ComBlu_StateOfOnlineCommunities_2012.pdf,

November 2012, p. 17; and www.mountaindew.com, accessed November 2013.

3. For these and other direct marketing statistics in this section, see Direct Marketing Association, *The DMA 2013 Statistical Fact Book*, 35th ed., April 2013; Direct Marketing Association, *The Power of Direct Marketing: 2011–2012 Edition*, August 2011; "DMA Releases New 'Power of Direct' Report," October 2, 2011, www.the-dma.org/cgi/dispannouncements?article=1590; and a wealth of other information at www.the-dma.org, accessed November 2013.
4. Mark Walsh, "Online Ad Spending Up 15% to $37 Billion in 2012," *Online Media Daily*, April 16, 2013, www.mediapost.com/publications/article/198161/#axzz2UF0vT3rk; Thad Rueter, "E-retail Spending to Increase 62% by 2016," *Internet Retailer*, February 27, 2012, www.internetretailer.com/2012/02/27/e-retail-spending-increase-45-2016; Sucharita Mulpuru, "US Online Retail Forecast, 2012 to 2017," March 13, 2013, www.forrester.com/US+Online+Retail+Forecast+2012+To+2017/fulltext/-/E-RES93281?objectid=RES93281; and Joe Mandewse, "Initial 2013 Broadcast Spending Reflects Tough Comps with 2012," *Media Daily News*, March 25, 2013, www.mediapost.com/publications/article/196533/#axzz2UF0vT3rk.
5. See Christopher Heine, "Ads in Real Time, All the Time," *Adweek*, February 18, 2013, p. 9.
6. See "Household Internet Usage In and Outside the Home," U.S. Census Bureau, www.census.gov/compendia/statab/2012/tables/12s1155.pdf, accessed July 2013; "How People Spend Their Time Online," February 2, 2012, www.go-gulf.com/blog/online-time; "Global Mobile Statistics 2013," *MobiThinking*, March 2013, http://mobithinking.com/mobile-marketing-tools/latest-mobile-stats/a#smartphonepenetration; and www.internetworldstats.com/stats.htm, accessed July 2013.
7. See Natash Lomas, "Forrester: U.S. Online Retail Sales to Rise to $370BN by 2017 (10% CAGR) as Ecommerce Motors on with Help from Tablets and Phones," *TechCrunch*, March 13, 2013, http://techcrunch.com/2013/03/13/forrester-2012-2017-ecommerce-forecast/; "Monthly and Annual Retail Trade," U.S. Census Bureau, www.census.gov/retail, accessed July 2013; and "At the #NRF13: Web-Influenced Purchases Drive Retail Sales," *Review Trackers*, January 15, 2013, www.reviewtrackers.com/nrf13-web-influenced-purchases-drive-retail-sales-both-online-offline.
8. See "Internet Retailer: Top 500 Guide," www.internetretailer.com/top500/list, accessed November 2013.
9. See "How Staples Generates More than $10 Billion in Online Sales," March 7, 2012, http://electronicbankingoptions.com/2012/03/07/how-staples-generates-more-than-10-billion-in-online-sales/; and Staples data from annual reports and other information found at www.staples.com, accessed November 2013.
10. See ComBlu, "The State of Online Branded Communities," http://comblu.com/downloads/ComBlu_StateOfOnlineCommunities_2012.pdf, November 2012, p. 19; and www.espn.com, accessed November 2013.
11. Regina Antony, "How Marketers Allocate Their Digital Marketing Budgets," *SlideShare*, March 21, 2013, www.slideshare.net/reginaantony/gartner-digital-marketing-spend-2013-report.
12. See "IAC Internet Advertising Competition: Best Rich Media Online Ad," www.iacaward.org/iac/winners_detail.asp?yr=all&award_level=best&medium=Rich%20media%20Online%20Ad; and "Gatorade—Prime Rich Media Takeover," http://www.iacaward.org/iac/winner.asp?eid=10379, both accessed July 2013.
13. *IAB Internet Advertising Revenue Report, 2012 Full Year Results*, April 2013, www.iab.net/media/file/IAB_Internet_Advertising_Revenue_Report_FY_2012_rev.pdf; and Google annual reports, http://investor.google.com/proxy.html, accessed November 2013.
14. See "Internet 2011 in Numbers," *Pingdom*, January 17, 2012, http://royal.pingdom.com/2012/01/17/internet-2011-in-numbers; Ken Magill, "Email Remains ROI King; Net Marketing Set to Overtake DM, Says DMA," *The Magill Report*, October 4, 2011, www.magillreport.com/Email-Remains-ROI-King-Net-Marketing-Set-to-Overtake-DM/; "Marketing Sherpa Benchmark Report: 2013 Email Marketing," *Marketing Sherpa*, www.marketingsherpa.com/data/public/reports/benchmark-reports/EXCERPT-BMR-2013-Email-Marketing.pdf, p. 14, accessed July 2013; Arthur Middleton Hughes, "Why Email Marketing Is King," *Harvard Business Review*, August 21, 2012, http://blogs.hbr.org/cs/2012/08/why_email_marketing_is_king.html; and Juliette Kopecky, "An Investigation into the ROI of Direct Mail vs. Email Marketing," *Hubspot*, January 10, 2013, http://blog.hubspot.com/blog/tabid/6307/bid/34032/An-Investigation-Into-the-ROI-of-Direct-Mail-vs-Email-Marketing-DATA.aspx.
15. See Elizabeth A. Sullivan, "Targeting to the Extreme," *Marketing News*, June 15, 2010, pp. 17–19; and Dianna Dilworth, "NHL Scores Goal with Single Game Ticket Sales to Far-Flung Loyal Hockey Fans," *Direct Marketing*, July 1, 2012, www.dmnews.com/article/246912/#. For more examples of outstanding e-mail marketing campaigns, see "Marketing Sherpa Email Awards 2013," *Marketing Sherpa*, www.meclabs.com/training/misc/emailsummit/sherpa/Email_Awards_2013.pdf.
16. Jeff Goldman, "Spam Down, Phishing Up in March 2013," *eSecurity Planet*, April 23, 2013, www.esecurityplanet.com/network-security/spam-down-phishing-up-in-march-2013.html.
17. Linda Moses, "Online Video Ads Have Higher Impact Than TV Ads," *Adweek*, May 1, 2013, www.adweek.com/print/148982.
18. For these and other examples, see "Samsung, Wieden & Kennedy Rule Ad Age's 2013 Viral Video Awards," *Advertising Age*, April 16, 2013, http://adage.com/article/240900/.
19. Laura Heller, "'Ship My Pants': Kmart's Unexpected Viral Hit," *Forbes*, April 15, 2013, www.forbes.com/sites/lauraheller/2013/04/15/ship-my-pants-kmarts-unexpected-viral-hit/.
20. Michael Learmonth, "Fresh Numbers: Honda Won Super Bowl Before It Even Began," *Advertising Age*, February 6, 2012, http://adage.com/print/232543/.
21. David Gelles, "The Public Image: Volkswagen's 'The Force' Campaign," *Financial Times*, February 22, 2011, p. 14; and Troy Dreier, "The Force Was Strong with This One," *Streaming Media Magazine*, April/May 2011, pp. 66–68. Also see Thales Teixeira, "The New Science of Viral Ads," *Harvard Business Review*, March 2012, pp. 25–28.
22. "State of the Blogging World in 2012," *New Media Expo Blog*, July 25, 2012, www.blogworld.com/2012/07/25/state-of-the-blogging-world-in-2012.
23. See http://en.community.dell.com/dell-blogs/default.aspx and www.youtube.com/user/DellVlog, accessed November 2013.
24. "Marketers Up the Ante on Social Media Sponsorships," *eMarketer*, July 13, 2012, www.emarketer.com/Articles/Print.aspx?R=1009188.
25. Based on information found in Keith O'Brien, "How McDonald's Came Back Bigger Than Ever," *New York Times*, May 6, 2012, p. MM44.
26. Stuart Feil, "How to Win Friends and Influence People," *Adweek*, September 10, 2013, pp. S1–S2.

27. "Facebook Statistics," www.socialbakers.com/facebook-statistics/, accessed May 2013; Mark Hachman, "Facebook Used by Half of the World's Internet Users, Save Asia," *PC Magazine*, February 2, 2012, www.pcmag.com/article2/0,2817,2399732,00.asp; "List of Countries by Population," http://en.wikipedia.org/wiki/List_of_countries_by_population, accessed October 2013; and www.youtube.com/yt/press/statistics.html, accessed November 2013.
28. For these and other examples, see www.yub.com, www.kaboodle.com, www.gofishn.com, www.dogster.com, www.farmersonly.com, www.myTransponder.com, and www.cafemom.com, all accessed November 2013.
29. "Happy Birthday to Nike+," *Run247*, May 23, 2011, www.run247.com/articles/article-1337-happy-birthday-to-nike%2B.html; "Nike Shows Us How to Adapt to a Digital Era," *AD60*, February 27, 2012, www.ad60.com/2012/02/27/nike-shows-adapt-digital-era/; and www.nikeplus.nike.com, accessed November 2013.
30. Karl Greenberg, "Volvo Uses Twitter Chat for Digital Focus Groups," *Marketing Daily*, May 29, 2013, www.mediapost.com/publications/article/201309/#axzz2UsMXTPXB.
31. Based on information found at Tim Nudd, "Online Test Just Wants to Make You Happy," *Adweek*, March 18, 2013, www.adweek.com/adfreak/oreo-wraps-cookie-vs-creme-campaign-dozens-goofy-videos-148017; and Lisa Lacy, "Oreo to Fans: Cookie or Crème?" *ClickZ*, February 7, 2013, www.clickz.com/clickz/news/2241725/oreo-to-fans-cookie-or-creme.
32. See "The State of Online Branded Communities," *Comblu*, November 2012, p. 17, http://comblu.com/thoughtleadership/the-state-of-online-branded-communities-2012; and http://pinterest.com/wholefoods/, accessed November 2013.
33. Example and quotes from Kashmir Hill, "#McDStories: When a Hashtag Becomes a Bashtag," *Forbes*, January 24, 2012, www.forbes.com/sites/kashmirhill/2012/01/24/mcdstories-when-a-hashtag-becomes-a-bashtag/; Gabriel Beltrone, "Brand #Fail," *Adweek*, May 15, 2012, www.adweek.com/news/advertising-branding/brand-fail-140368; Michael Bourne, "Sailing of 14 Social Cs," *Mullen Advertising*, February, 13, 2012, www.mullen.com/sailing-the-14-social-cs/; and "#Bashtag: Avoiding User Outcry in Social Media," *WordStream*, March 8, 2013, www.wordstream.com/blog/ws/2013/03/07/bashtag-avoiding-social-media-backlash.
34. Melissa Allison, "Re-Creating the Coffee Klatch Online," *Raleigh News & Observer*," May 6, 2013, p. 1D; and www.facebook.com/Starbucks and https://twitter.com/Starbucks, accessed July 2013.
35. Facts in this paragraph are from "USA Smartphone Penetration Level Reaches 57 Percent," *Cellular News*, April 5, 2013, www.cellular-news.com/story/59386.php; Nielsenwire, "State of the Appnation—A Year of Change and Growth in U.S. Smartphones," May 16, 2012, www.nielsen.com/us/en/reports/2012/state-of-the-media-the-social-media-report-2012.html; CTIA.org, accessed May 2013; and "The Mobile Movement," www.thinkwithgoogle.com/insights/emea/library/studies/the-mobile-movement, accessed May 2013.
36. Jonathan Nelson, "Voice: One Screen to Rule Them All," *Adweek*, February 13, 2013, p. 15; Stephen Willard, "Study: People Check Their Cell Phones Every Six Minutes, 150 Times a Day," *Elite Daily*, February 11, 2013, http://elitedaily.com/news/world/study-people-check-cell-phones-minutes-150-times-day/; and John Fetto, "Americans Spend 58 Minutes a Day on Their Smartphones," *Experian*, May 28, 2013, www.experian.com/blogs/marketing-forward/2013/05/28/americans-spend-58-minutes-a-day-on-their-smartphones/.
37. "IAB Internet Advertising Revenue Report," April 2013, www.iab.net/media/file/IAB_Internet_Advertising_Revenue_Report_FY_2012_rev.pdf; and "The Mobile Movement," accessed at www.thinkwithgoogle.com/insights/emea/library/studies/the-mobile-movement, May 2013.
38. See Lauren Johnson, "McDonald's Beefs Up Advertising Strategy with Mobile Game," *Mobile Marketer*, March 28, 2013, www.mobilemarketer.com/cms/news/advertising/12447.html; and Rimma Kats, "McDonald's Beefs up Mobile Efforts via Targeted Campaign," *Mobile Marketing*, August 16, 2013, www.mobilemarketer.com/cms/news/advertising/13553.html.
39. Adapted from Giselle Tsirulnik, "Most Impressive Mobile Advertising Campaigns in 2010," December 29, 2010, www.mobilemarketer.com/cms/news/advertising/8617.html.
40. "Location, Location, Location," *Adweek*, February 13, 2012, pp. M9–M11. For the Macy's and other examples, see Michael Applebaum, "Mobile Magnetism," *Adweek*, June 24, 2012, p. S7.
41. See DMA, *The Power of Direct Marketing, 2011–2012 Edition*; "It's Never Been Easier to Send Direct Mail," *PRNewswire*, June 8, 2011.
42. Julie Liesse, "When Times Are Hard, Mail Works," *Advertising Age*, March 30, 2009, p. 14; Paul Vogel, "Marketers Are Rediscovering the Value of Mail," *Deliver Magazine*, January 11, 2011, www.delivermagazine.com/2011/01/marketers-are-rediscovering-the-value-of-mail/; and "The Resurrection of Direct Mail in 2012," *PRWeb*, www.prweb.com/releases/Direct-mail/Resurection/prweb9301877.htm, accessed July 2012.
43. Bruce Britt, "Marketing Leaders Discuss the Resurgence of Direct Mail," *Deliver Magazine*, January 18, 2011, www.delivermagazine.com/2011/01/marketing-leaders-discuss-resurgence-of-direct-mail/.
44. See "Catalog Spree Survey Shows 89.8 Percent of Shoppers Prefer Digital Catalogs," April 19, 2012, http://catalogspree.com/catalog-spree-survey-shows-89-8-percent-of-shoppers-prefer-digital-catalogs; and www.landsend.com/mobile/index.html and http://catalogspree.com/, accessed November 2013.
45. Jeffrey Ball, "Power Shift: In Digital Era, Marketers Still Prefer a Paper Trail," *Wall Street Journal*, October 16, 2009, p. A3; Jennifer Valentino-DeVries, "With Catalogs, Opt-Out Policies Vary," *Wall Street Journal*, April 13, 2011, p. B7; Lois Geller, "Why Are Printed Catalogs Still Around?" *Forbes*, October 10, 2012, www.forbes.com/sites/loisgeller/2012/10/16/why-are-printed-catalogs-still-around/; and *The DMA 2012 Statistical Fact Book*.
46. Ball, "Power Shift: In Digital Era, Marketers Still Prefer a Paper Trail"; "Report: Catalogs Increasingly Drive Online Sales," RetailCustomerExperience.com, March 17, 2010, www.retailcustomerexperience.com/article/21521/Report-Catalogs-increasingly-drive-online-sales; and "Catalogs Drive Online Sales, Says MarketReach Research," February 19, 2013, www.dma.org.uk/news/catalogues-drive-online-sales-says-marketreach-research.
47. DMA, *The Power of Direct Marketing, 2011–2012 Edition.*
48. Melissa Hoffmann, "Report: Telecommunications Advances Affecting Do Not Call Registry," *Direct Marketing News*, December 30, 2011, www.dmnews.com/report-telecommunications-advances-affecting-do-not-call-registry/article/221264/; Jim Handy, "Does the 'Do Not Call' List Even Work?" *Forbes*, February 27, 2013, www.forbes.com/sites/jimhandy/2013/02/27/does-the-do-not-call-list-even-work/; and www.donotcall.gov, accessed July 2013.
49. See Rachel Brown, "Perry, Fischer, Lavigne Tapped for Proactiv," *WWD*, January 13, 2010, p. 3; Rahul Parikh, "Proactiv's Celebrity Shell Game," Salon.com, February 28, 2011, www

.salon.com/2011/02/28/proactiv_celebrity_sham; "Three Proactiv Social Media Campaigns Named Finalists for PR News' Social Media Icon Awards," *PRNewswire,* April 17, 2013; and www.proactiv.com, accessed November 2013.

50. Mercedes Cardona, "Hampton's PajamaJeans Go Viral with DRTV Campaign," *Direct Marketing News*, December 2011, p. 17; and http://ec2-54-245-244-125.us-west-2.compute.amazonaws.com/ad/7IOT/pajama-jeans, November July 2013.
51. Stephanie Rosenbloom, "The New Touch-Face of Vending Machines," *New York Times*, May 25, 2010, accessed at www.nytimes.com/2010/05/26/business/26vending.html; "Automating Retail Success," www.businessweek.com/adsections/2011/pdf/111114_Verizon3.pdf; accessed July 2012; and "The Kiosk and Self-Service Top Five," *Kiosk Marketplace,* April 17, 2013, www.kioskmarketplace.com/article/211559/.
52. "Best Buy: Consumer Electronics Retailing on the Go," www.zoomsystems.com/our-partners/partner-portfolio/; and www.zoomsystems.com/about-us/company-overview/, accessed April 2013.
53. See Internet Crime Complaint Center, www.ic3.gov, accessed November 2013.
54. See Molly Bernhart Walker, "America's Less Concerned about Internet Security," *FierceGovernmentIT*, May 10, 2012, www.fiercegovernmentit.com/story/americans-less-concerned-about-internet-security/2012-05-10.
55. See Susan Dominus, "Underage on Facebook," *MSN Living*, March 15, 2012; http://living.msn.com/family-parenting/underage-on-facebook-5; Josh Wolford "Facebook Still Has a Big Problem with Underage Users, and They Know It," *WebProNews*, January 24, 2013, www.webpronews.com/facebook-still-has-a-big-problem-with-underage-users-and-they-know-it-2013-01.
56. Hadley Malcolm, "Millennials Don't Worry about Online Privacy," *USA Today,* April 21, 2013.
57. Based on information from Michael Bush, "My Life, Seen through the Eyes of Marketers," *Advertising Age,* April 26, 2010, http://adage.com/print/143479.
58. See "Facebook to Make Targeted Ads More Transparent for Users," *Advertising Age,* February 4, 2013, http://adage.com/article/239564/; and www.aboutads.info/, accessed November 2013.
59. See Wendy Davis, "Rockefeller Urges FTC to Move Faster on COPPA Rules," *Daily Online Examiner*, May 19, 2011, www.mediapost.com/publications/?fa=Articles.showArticle&art_aid=150867; and http://epic.org/privacy/kids/ and http://business.ftc.gov/privacy-and-security/children%E2%80%99s-privacy, accessed October 2013.
60. Information on TRUSTe at www.truste.com, accessed November 2013.
61. Information on the DMA Privacy Promise at www.the-dma.org/cgi/dispissue?article=129 and www.dmaconsumers.org/privacy.html, accessed November 2013.

Chapter 15

1. Based on information from Monica Mark, "Coca-Cola and Nestlé Target New Markets in Africa," *The Guardian*, May 4, 2012, www.guardian.co.uk/world/2012/may/04/coca-cola-nestle-markets-africa; Duane Stanford, "Africa: Coke's Last Frontier," *Bloomberg Businessweek,* November 1, 2010, pp. 54–61; Annaleigh Vallie, "Coke Turns 125 and Has Much Life Ahead," *Business Day,* May 16, 2011, www.businessday.co.za/articles/Content.aspx?id_142848; "Coca-Cola Makes Big Bets on Africa's Future," *Trefis*, May 25, 2012, www.trefis.com/stock/ko/articles/123022/coca-cola-makes-big-bets-on-africas-future/2012-05-25; "Deloitte on Africa," Deloitte, www.deloitte.com/assets/Dcom-SouthAfrica/Local%20Assets/Documents/rise_and_rise.pdf, accessed July 2013; and Coca-Cola annual reports and other information from www.thecoca-colacompany.com, accessed November 2013.
2. Data from "Fortune 500," *Fortune*, May 2013, http://money.cnn.com/magazines/fortune/fortune500/; Christopher Stolarski, "The FDI Effect," Marquette University Research and Scholarship 2011, www.marquette.edu/research/documents/discover-2011-FDI-effect.pdf; and "List of Countries by GDP: List by the CIA World Factbook," Wikipedia, http://en.wikipedia.org/wiki/List_of_countries_by_GDP_(nominal), accessed November 2013.
3. "Trade to Remain Subdued in 2013 after Sluggish Growth in 2012 as European Economies Continue to Struggle," WTO Press Release, April 10, 2013, www.wto.org/english/news_e/pres13_e/pr688_e.htm.
4. Information from www.michelin.com/corporate, www.jnj.com, and www.caterpillar.com, accessed November 2013.
5. See www.otisworldwide.com/d1-about.html and UTC Annual Report 2012, http://2012ar.utc.com/assets/pdfs/UTCAR12_Full_Report.pdf, accessed July 2013.
6. Rob Schmitz, "Trade Spat between China and EU Threatens Exports of Solar Panels, Wine," *Marketplace,* June 6, 2013, www.marketplace.org/topics/world/trade-spat-between-china-and-eu-threatens-exports-solar-panels-wine.
7. See Dexter Roberts and Michael Wei, "China's New Protectionism" *Bloomberg Businessweek,* October 27, 2011, www.businessweek.com/magazine/chinas-new-protectionism-10272011.html; and Arun Sudhaman, "Walmart Brings in PR Counsel in China," *The Holmes Report,* April 24, 2012, www.holmesreport.com/news-info/11755/WalMart-Brings-In-PR-Counsel-In-China.aspx.
8. "What Is the WTO?" www.wto.org/english/thewto_e/whatis_e/what_we_do_e.htm, accessed November 2013.
9. "Mexico Confident as WTO Leadership Race Wraps Up," *Economic Times*, May 6, 2013, http://economictimes.indiatimes.com/news/international-business/mexico-confident-as-wto-leadership-race-wraps-up/articleshow/19918085.cms; *WTO Annual Report 2012*, www.wto.org/english/res_e/publications_e/anrep12_e.htm, accessed May 2013; and World Trade Organization, "10 Benefits of the WTO Trading System," www.wto.org/english/thewto_e/whatis_e/10ben_e/10b00_e.htm, accessed November 2013.
10. "The EU at a Glance," http://europa.eu/about-eu/index_en.htm; and "EU Statistics and Opinion Polls," http://europa.eu/documentation/statistics-polls/index_en.htm; accessed November 2013.
11. "Economic and Monetary Affairs," http://europa.eu/pol/emu/index_en.htm, accessed October 2013; Dan O'Brien, "Risk of Euro Break-Up Now Higher Than Ever Before," *The Irish Times*, April 5, 2013, www.irishtimes.com/business/economy/europe/risk-of-euro-break-up-now-higher-than-ever-before-1.1349443; and "European Union: The Euro," http://europa.eu/about-eu/basic-information/money/euro/, accessed November 2013.
12. CIA, *The World Factbook*, https://www.cia.gov/library/publications/the-world-factbook, accessed November 2013.
13. Statistics and other information from CIA, *The World Factbook*; and Office of the United States Trade Representative, "Joint Statement from 2012 NAFTA Commission Meeting," April 2012, www.ustr.gov/about-us/press-office/press-releases/2012/april/joint-statement-2012-nafta-commission-meeting.

14. See "Explainer: What Is UNASUR?" www.as-coa.org/articles/explainer-what-unasur, accessed November 2013; and http://en.wikipedia.org/wiki/Union_of_South_American_Nations, accessed November 2013.
15. Example based on information found in Bruce Einhorn, "Alan Mulally's Asian Sales Call," *Bloomberg BusinessWeek*, April 12, 2010, pp. 41–43; "Ford, Volkswagen Eye Up North India to Set Up New Facilities," *Businessline*, December 8, 2010, p. 1; and "Ford to Tag New Figo 2012 Less by INR 16,000," *Crazy About Cars,* March 9, 2012, www.carzy.co.in/blog/car-news/ford-tag-figo-2012-inr-16000.html/.
16. See "2012 Investment Climate Statement—Russia," U.S. Bureau of Economic and Business Affairs, May 2013, www.state.gov/e/eb/rls/othr/ics/2012/191223.htm; and "Welcome to the U.S. Commercial Service in Russia," http://export.gov/russia/, accessed November 2013.
17. Laurent Belsie, "What Will Venezuela Do with Its Oil?" *Christian Science Monitor,* March 6, 2013, www.csmonitor.com/Environment/2013/0307/What-will-Venezuela-do-with-its-oil-Top-five-energy-challenges-after-Chavez/Oil-bartering; and International Reciprocal Trade Association, www.irta.com/modern-trade-a-barter.html, accessed November 2013.
18. For these and other examples, see Emma Hall, "Do You Know Your Rites? BBDO Does," *Advertising Age*, May 21, 2007, p. 22.
19. Jamie Bryan, "The Mintz Dynasty," *Fast Company*, April 2006, pp. 56–61; Viji Sundaram, "Offensive Durga Display Dropped," *India-West*, February 2006, p. A1; and Emily Bryson York and Rupal Parekh, "Burger King's MO: Offend, Earn Media, Apologize, Repeat," *Advertising Age*, July 8, 2009, accessed at http://adage.com/print?article_id=137801.
20. For these and other examples, see Bill Chappell, "Bill Gates' Handshake with South Korea's Park Sparks Debate," *NPR*, April 23, 2013, www.npr.org/blogs/thetwo-way/2013/04/23/178650537/bill-gates-handshake-with-south-koreas-park-sparks-debate; "Managing Quality Across the (Global) Organization, Its Stakeholders, Suppliers, and Customers," Chartered Quality Institute, www.thecqi.org/Knowledge-Hub/Knowledge-portal/Corporate-strategy/Managing-quality-globally, accessed October 2013.
21. Quotes and other information found in David Pierson, "Beijing Loves IKEA—but Not for Shopping," *Los Angeles Times,* August 25, 2009, http://articles.latimes.com/2009/aug/25/business/fi-china-ikea25; Michael Wei, "In IKEA's China Stores, Loitering Is Encouraged," *Bloomberg Businessweek,* November 1, 2010, pp. 22–23; Jens Hansegard, "Ikea Taking China by Storm," *Wall Street Journal,* March 2012, http://online.wsj.com/article/SB10001424052702304636404577293083481821536.html; and Pan Kwan Yuk, "IKEA in China: Turning Gawkers into Customers," *BeyondBrics*, April 4, 2013, http://blogs.ft.com/beyond-brics/2013/04/04/ikea-in-china-turning-gawkers-into-consumers/?#axzz2SobYFh98.
22. Andres Martinez, "The Next American Century," *Time*, March 22, 2010, p. 1.
23. Thomas L. Friedman, *The Lexus and the Olive Tree: Understanding Globalization* (New York: Anchor Books, 2000); and Michael Wei and Margaret Conley, "Global Brands: Some Chinese Kids' First Word: Mickey," *Bloomberg Businessweek,* June 19, 2011, pp. 24–25.
24. "BrandZ Top 100 Most Valuable Global Brands 2013," Millward Brown Optimor, www.millwardbrown.com/brandz/2013/Top100/Docs/2013_BrandZ_Top100_Chart.pdf, accessed November 2013.
25. See Kim-Mai Cutler, "Apple's Chinese iPhone Sales 'Mind-Boggling,' Bring China Revenues to $7.9 Billion," *Tech Crunch,* April 24, 2012, http://techcrunch.com/2012/04/24/apples-iphone-sales-in-china-are-up-by-fivefold-from-a-year-ago/; Nick Wingfield, "Apple Profit Rises on Higher iPhone and iPad Sales," *New York Times,* April 24, 2012, p. B1; and Chuck Jones, "Apple's iPhone Share Continues to Increase in Urban China," *Forbes,* February 26, 2013, www.forbes.com/sites/chuckjones/2013/02/26/apples-iphone-share-continues-to-increase-in-urban-china.
26. William J. Holstein, "How Coca-Cola Manages 90 Emerging Markets," *Strategy+Business*, November 7, 2011, www.strategy-business.com/article/00093?gko=f3ca6; "2012 Annual Report," accessed at www.coca-colacompany.com/investors/annual-other-reports; and other financial and review data from www.coca-colacompany.com/our-company/, accessed November 2013.
27. See Lucas Kawa, "The 20 Fastest Growing Economies in the World," *Business Insider,* October 24, 1012, www.businessinsider.com/worlds-fastest-economies-2012-10?op=1; and Janice Kew, "Walmart Brand Favored in Massmart's Africa Drive," *Bloomberg,* April 16, 2013, www.bloomberg.com/news/2013-04-15/wal-mart-brand-favored-in-massmart-s-africa-growth-drive.html.
28. Barney Jopson and Andrew England, "Walmart to Apply 'Sweat and Muscle' to Africa," *Financial Times,* June 5, 2011, p. 18; Emma Hall, "Marketers, Agencies Eye Booming Africa for Expansion," *Advertising Age,* June 13, 2011, p. 28; and Addis Ababa, "Walmart Focused on Existing Africa Markets," *Reuters,* May 10, 2012, www.reuters.com/article/idUSBRE8490L120120510.
29. See www.coca-colahellenic.com/aboutus/, accessed November 2013.
30. See http://en.wikipedia.org/wiki/Doubletree, accessed November 2013.
31. Mike Ramsey and Christina Rogers, "Chrysler's Jeep Faces Uphill Climb in China," *Wall Street Journal,* May 10, 2013, p. B4.
32. "Ford India Lays Foundation Store for Sanand Plant," March 22, 2012, www.drivingford.in/tag/ford-india-plant/; Alan Ohnsman, "Major Auto Production at Toyota, Honda Boosts U.S. Economy," July 17, 2012, www.autonews.com; and Aradhana Aravindan, "Ford Looks to Ride Emerging Market mini-SUV Boom in India," *Reuters*, June 17, 2013, www.reuters.com/article/idUSBRE95G0RJ20130617.
33. Marc de Swaan Arons, "There Is Absolutely a Need for One Single Global Vision," *Marketing News,* September 30, 2011, p. 30.
34. Quotes from Andrew McMains, "To Compete Globally, Brands Must Adapt," *Adweek*, September 25, 2008, www.adweek.com; Pankaj Ghemawat, "Regional Strategies for Global Leadership," *Harvard Business Review*, December 2005, pp. 97–108; Eric Pfanner, "The Myth of the Global Brand," *New York Times*, January 11, 2009, www.nytimes.com; and de Swaan Arons, "There Is Absolutely a Need for One Single Global Vision," p. 30. Also see Pankej Ghemawat, "Finding Your Strategy in the New Landscape," *Harvard Business Review*, March 2010, pp. 54–60.
35. Based on information from Lucy Fancourt, Bredesen Lewis, and Nicholas Majka, "Born in the USA, Made in France: How McDonald's Succeeds in the Land of Michelin Stars," Knowledge@Wharton, January 3, 2012, http://knowledge.wharton.upenn.edu/article.cfm?articleid=2906; and Richard Vines and Caroline Connan, "McDonald's Wins over French Chef with McBaguette Sandwich," *Bloomberg*, January 15, 2013, www.bloomberg.com/news/2013-01-15/mcdonald-s-wins-over-french-chef-with-mcbaguette-sandwich.html.
36. See Warren J. Keegan and Mark C. Green, *Global Marketing*, 7th ed. (Upper Saddle River, NJ: Prentice Hall, 2013), pp. 303–308.

37. Toshiro Wakayama, Junjiro Shintaku, and Tomofumi Amano, "What Panasonic Learned in China," *Harvard Business Review,* December 2012, pp. 109–113.
38. For these and other examples, see Bruce Einhorn, "There's More to Oreo Than Black and White," *Bloomberg Businessweek,* May 3, 2012, www.businessweek.com/articles/2012-05-03/theres-more-to-oreo-than-black-and-white.
39. James R. Healey, "Fiat 500: Little Car Shoulders Huge Responsibility in U.S.; Retro Cutie Had to Be Redone from Inside Out for Sale Here," *USA Today*, June 1, 2011, p. B1; and "New 2012 Fiat 500 Named 'Best Car' in Travel + Leisure Annual Design Awards Issue," *PRNewswire,* February 15, 2012.
40. See "Easier Said Than Done," *The Economist*, April 15, 2010, www.economist.com/node/15879299; and Normandy Madden, "In China, Multinationals Forgo Adaptation for New-Brand Creation," *Advertising Age,* January 17, 2011, p. 10.
41. Jeffrey N. Ross, "Chevrolet Will 'Find New Roads' as Brand Grows Globally: Aligns around the World behind Singular Vision," January 8, 2013, http://media.gm.com/media/us/en/gm/news.detail.html/content/Pages/news/us/en/2013/Jan/0107-find-new-roads.html.
42. Emma Hall, "Marketers, Agencies Eye Booming Africa for Expansion," *Advertising Age,* June 13, 2011, p. 28; and Liz Gooch, "The Biggest Thing since China: Global Companies Awake to the Muslim Consumer, and Marketers Follow Suit," *International Herald Tribune,* August 12, 2010, p. 1.
43. See George E. Belch and Michael A. Belch, *Advertising and Promotion: An Integrated Marketing Communications Perspective*, 8th ed. (New York: McGraw-Hill, 2011), Chapter 20; Shintero Okazaki and Charles R. Taylor, "What Is SMS Advertising and Why Do Multinationals Adopt It?" *Journal of Business Research*, January 2008, pp. 4–12; and Warren J. Keegan and Mark C. Green, *Global Marketing*, 7th ed. (Upper Saddle River, NJ: Prentice Hall, 2013), pp. 398–400.
44. For these and other examples, see Normandy Madden, "In China, Multinationals Forgo Adaptation for New-Brand Creation," *Advertising Age,* January 17, 2011, p. 10; Cristina Drafta, "Levi Strauss Targets Asia with Denizen," *EverythingPR,* May 16, 2011, www.pamil-visions.net/denizen/228239/; and www.levistrauss.com/brands/denizen, accessed October 2013.
45. Anita Chang Beattie, "Catching the Eye of a Chinese Shopper," *Advertising Age,* December 10, 2013, pp. 20–21.
46. See "Coca-Cola Rolls Out New Distribution Model with ZAP," ZAP, January 23, 2008, www.zapworld.com/zap-coca-cola-truck; Jane Nelson, Eriko Ishikawa, and Alexis Geaneotes, "Developing Inclusive Business Models: A Review of Coca-Cola's Manual Distribution Centers in Ethiopia and Tanzania," Harvard Kennedy School, 2009, www.hks.harvard.edu/m-rcbg/CSRI/publications/other_10_MDC_report.pdf; and "How Coca-Cola's Distribution System Works," *Colalife,* December 19, 2010, www.colalife.org/2010/12/19/how-coca-colas-distribution-system-works. For some interesting photos of Coca-Cola distribution methods in third-world and emerging markets, see www.flickr.com/photos/73509998@N00/sets/72157594299144032, accessed October 2013.
47. Based on information found in Bart Becht, "Building a Company without Borders," *Harvard Business Review*, April 2010, pp. 103–106; "From Cincy to Singapore: Why P&G, Others Are Moving Key HQs," *Advertising Age,* June 10, 2012, http://adage.com/print/235288; G. A. Chester, "3 Things to Love about Reckett Benckiser," *Daily Finance,* June 19, 2013, http://www.dailyfinance.com/2013/06/19/3-things-to-love-about-reckitt-benckiser/; and www.rb.com/Investors-media/Investor-information, accessed November 2013.

Chapter 16

1. Quotes and other information from or adapted from Andrew Saunders, "Paul Polman of Unilever," *Management Today*, March 2011, pp. 42–47; Adi Ignatius, "Captain Planet," *Harvard Business Review,* June 2012, pp. 2–8; and www.unileverusa.com/Images/USLP-Progress-Report-2012-FI_tcm23-352007.pdf and other reports and documents found at www.unileverusa.com/sustainable-living/, accessed November 2013.
2. "McDonald's Launches Marketing for 'Favorites under 400 Calories' Platform," *Advertising Age*, July 24, 2012, http://adage.com/print/236291/. See also www.mcdonalds.com/us/en/food/meal_bundles/favoritesunder400.html, accessed October 2013.
3. McDonald's financial information and other facts from www.aboutmcdonalds.com/mcd/investors.html and www.aboutmcdonalds.com/mcd, accessed November 2013.
4. Brent Kendall, "Skechers Settles with FTC over Deceptive-Advertising of Toning Shoes," *Wall Street Journal*, May 17, 2012, p. B3; and "Challenging Deceptive Advertising and Marketing," www.ftc.gov/os/highlights/2013/topics/deceptiveAdvertising.shtml, accessed November 2013.
5. Based on information from Ted Burnham, "Nutella Maker May Settle Deceptive Ad Lawsuit for $3 Million," *NPR*, April 26, 2012, http://www.npr.org/blogs/thesalt/2012/04/26/151454929/nutella-maker-may-settle-deceptive-ad-lawsuit-for-3-million; and https://nutellaclassactionsettlement.com/, accessed July 2013.
6. See Ian Cooper, "Obesity in America: What about the 66%?" Examiner.com, June 1, 2012; and "Overweight and Obesity," Centers for Disease Control and Prevention, "Overweight and Obesity," www.cdc.gov/obesity/data/index.html and www.obesityinamerica.org, accessed July 2013.
7. Elena Ferretti, "Soft Drinks Are the Whipping Boy of Anti-Obesity Campaigns," *Fox News*, June 1, 2012, www.foxnews.com/leisure/2012/06/01/soda-ban/. Also see Stephanie Strom, "In Ads, Coke Confronts Soda's Link to Obesity," *New York Times*, January 14, 2013.
8. See "Law Targets Obsolete Products," April 22, 2013, *The Connexion,* www.connexionfrance.com/Planned-obsolescence-obsolete-products-iPod-washing-machine-printers-14655-view-article.html.
9. Rob Walker, "Replacement Therapy," *Atlantic Monthly*, September 2011, p. 38.
10. See Karen Auge, "Planting Seed in Food Deserts: Neighborhood Gardens, Produce in Corner Stores," *Denver Post*, April 18, 2010, p. 1; Spence Cooper, "National Food Chains Join First Lady to Reach 'Food Deserts,'" *Friends Eat*, July 25, 2011, http://blog.friendseat.com/michelle-obama-program-reaches-food-deserts; and U.S. Department of Agriculture, "Creating Access to Healthy, Affordable Food," http://apps.ams.usda.gov/fooddeserts, accessed July 2013.
11. See "The Story of Stuff," www.storyofstuff.com, accessed November 2013.
12. See Texas Transportation Institute, "As Traffic Jams Worsen, Commuters Allowing Extra Time for Urgent Trips," February 5, 2013, http://mobility.tamu.edu/ums/media-information/press-release/.
13. See Michael Cabanatuan, "Tolls Thin Traffic in Bay Bridge Carpool Lanes," *San Francisco Chronicle*, November 7, 2011, www.sfgate.com/news/article/Tolls-thin-traffic-in-Bay-Bridge-carpool-lanes-2323670.php#photo-1829296; and http://bata.mtc.ca.gov/bridges/sf-oak-bay.htm, accessed November 2013.
14. See Martin Sipkoff, "Four-Dollar Pricing Considered Boom or Bust," *Drug Topics*, August 2008, p. 4S; and Sarah Bruyn Jones, "Economic Survival Guide: Drug Discounts Common Now," *McClatchy-Tribune Business News*, February 23, 2009; "Walmart Launches National Advertising Campaign to Show 'The Real

Walmart,' " May 4, 2013, http://news.walmart.com/news-archive/2013/05/04/walmart-launches-national-advertising-campaign-to-show-the-real-walmart; and www.walmart.com/cp/PI-4-Prescriptions/1078664, accessed November 2013.

15. See Philip Kotler, "Reinventing Marketing to Manage the Environmental Imperative," *Journal of Marketing*, July 2011, pp. 132–135; and Kai Ryssdal, "Unilever CEO: For Sustainable Business, Go against 'Mindless Consumption,' " *Marketplace,* June 11, 2013, www.marketplace.org/topics/sustainability/consumed/unilever-ceo-paul-polman-sustainble-business.
16. See Matt Townsend, "Is Nike's Flyknit the Swoosh of the Future?" *Bloomberg Businessweek,* March 19, 2012, pp. 31–32; and "SC Johnson Integrity," www.scjohnson.com/en/commitment/overview.aspx, accessed November 2013.
17. Based on information in Drew Winter, "Honda Workers Eliminate Landfill Waste," *WardsAuto,* August 1, 2011, http://wardsauto.com/news-amp-analysis/honda-workers-eliminate-landfill-waste; and Jim Motavalli, "Automakers Work to Achieve Zero-Waste Goals," *New York Times,* March 1, 2013, http://wheels.blogs.nytimes.com/2013/03/01/automakers-work-to-achieve-zero-waste-goals/.
18. See Alan S. Brown, "The Many Shades of Green," *Mechanical Engineering*, January 2009, http://memagazine.asme.org/Articles/2009/January/Many_Shades_Green.cfm; and www-03.ibm.com/financing/us/recovery/large/disposal.html and www.ibm.com/ibm/environment/products/recycling.shtml, accessed November 2013.
19. Based on information from Simon Houpt, "Beyond the Bottle: Coke Trumpets Its Green Initiatives," *The Globe and Mail (Toronto)*, January 13, 2011; Marc Gunther, "Coca-Cola's Green Crusader," *Fortune,* April 28, 2008, p. 150; "Coca-Cola to Install 1,800 CO_2 Coolers in North America," April 30, 2009, www.r744.com/articles/2009-04-30-coca-cola-to-install-1800-co2-coolers-in-north-america.php; "Position Statement on Climate Protection," January 1, 2012, www.coca-colacompany.com/stories/position-statement-on-climate-protection; and www.coca-colacompany.com/our-company/plantbottle, accessed July 2013.
20. Based on information from "Walmart," *Fast Company*, March 2010, p. 66; "Walmart Eliminates More Than 80 Percent of Its Waste in California That Would Otherwise Go to Landfills," March 17, 2011, http://walmartstores.com/pressroom/news/10553.aspx; Jack Neff, "Why Walmart Has More Green Clout Than Anyone," *Advertising Age,* October 15, 2007, p. 1; Denise Lee Yohn, "A Big, Green, Reluctant Hug for Retailing's 800-lb. Gorilla," *Brandweek,* May 5, 2008, p. 61; Edward Humes, *Force of Nature: The Unlikely Story of Walmart's Green Revolution* (New York: HarperCollins, 2011); Jack Neff, "For Walmart, Sustainability Is Slow Going," *Advertising Age,* April 23, 2012, p. 6; and "Sustainability," http://walmartstores.com/sustainability/, accessed November 2013.
21. Quote from Austin Carr, "Nike: The No. 1 Most Innovative Company of 2013," *Fast Company*, March 2013, www.fastcompany.com/most-innovative-companies/2013/nike.
22. Information from Eleftheria Parpis, "Must Love Dogs," *Adweek*, February 18, 2008, accessed at www.adweek.com; and www.pedigree.com and www.mars.com/global/global-brands/pedigree.aspx, accessed July 2013. PEDIGREE® is a registered trademark of Mars, Incorporated.
23. Based on information found at http://about.puma.com/sustainability/, accessed October 2013.
24. Information from www.nau.com, accessed November 2013.
25. Nanette Byrnes, "Pepsi Brings in the Health Police," *Bloomberg Businessweek*, January 25, 2010, pp. 50–51; Mike Esterl, "You Put What in This Chip?" *Wall Street Journal*, March 24, 2011, p. D1; and www.pepsico.com/Purpose/Human-Sustainability/Our-Products.html, accessed November 2013.
26. Example based on information from Kelly Voelker, "Social Media's Role in Issue Management," *SlideShare,* April 7, 2010, www.slideshare.net/socialmediaorg/blogwell-cincinnatti-social-media-case-study-graco-presented-by-kelly-voelker; and David Grant, "Moms a-Twitter over Graco's Stroller Recall Response," *Christian Science Monitor,* January 10, 2010, www.csmonitor.com/Business/2010/0121/Moms-a-Twitter-over-Graco-s-stroller-recall-response.
27. See Transparency International, "Bribe Payers Index 2011," http://bpi.transparency.org/bpi2011, and "Global Corruption Barometer 2010/2011," http://gcb.transparency.org/gcb201011. Also see Michael Montgomery, "The Cost of Corruption," American RadioWorks, http://americanradioworks.publicradio.org/features/corruption/, accessed August 2012.
28. See www.marketingpower.com/AboutAMA/Pages/Statement%20of%20Ethics.aspx, accessed November 2013.
29. See http://investor.google.com/corporate/code-of-conduct.html#toc-VIII, accessed November 2013.
30. David A. Lubin and Daniel C. Esty, "The Sustainability Imperative," *Harvard Business Review*, May 2010, pp. 41–50; and Roasbeth Moss Kanter, "It's Time to Take Full Responsibility," *Harvard Business Review*, October 2010, p. 42.
31. "Why Companies Can No Longer Afford to Ignore Their Social Responsibilities," *Time*, May 28, 2012, http://business.time.com/2012/05/28/why-companies-can-no-longer-afford-to-ignore-their-social-responsibilities/.

Appendix 3

1. This is derived by rearranging the following equation and solving for price: Percentage markup = (price − cost) ÷ price.
2. Again, using the basic profit equation, we set profit equal to ROI × I: ROI × I = (P × Q) − TFC − (Q × UVC). Solving for Q gives Q = (TFC + (ROI × I)) ÷ (P − UVC).
3. U.S. Census Bureau, www.census.gov/prod/1/pop/p25-1129.pdf, accessed October 26, 2009.
4. See Roger J. Best, *Market-Based Management,* 4th ed. (Upper Saddle River, NJ: Prentice Hall, 2005).
5. Total contribution can also be determined from the unit contribution and unit volume: Total contribution = unit contribution × unit sales. Total units sold in 2014 were 595,238 units, which can be determined by dividing total sales by price per unit ($100 million ÷ $168). Total contribution = $35.28 contribution per unit × 595,238 units = $20,999,996.64 (difference due to rounding).
6. Recall that the contribution margin of 21% was based on variable costs representing 79% of sales. Therefore, if we do not know price, we can set it equal to $1.00. If price equals $1.00, 79 cents represents variable costs and 21 cents represents unit contribution. If price is decreased by 10%, the new price is $0.90. However, variable costs do not change just because price decreased, so the unit contribution and contribution margin decrease as follows:

	Old	**New (reduced 10 percent)**
Price	$1.00	$0.90
− Unit variable cost	$0.79	$0.79
= Unit contribution	$0.21	$0.11
Contribution margin	$0.21/$1.00 = 0.21 or 21%	$0.11/$0.90 = 0.12 or 12%

Indexes

Name, Company, Brand, and Organization

N

Subject Index

C

T

U

V

W

Z